THE PHILOSOPHY OF
BRAND BLANSHARD

THE LIBRARY OF LIVING PHILOSOPHERS

Paul Arthur Schilpp, Editor

Already Published:

THE PHILOSOPHY OF JOHN DEWEY (1939)*
THE PHILOSOPHY OF GEORGE SANTAYANA (1940)
THE PHILOSOPHY OF ALFRED NORTH WHITEHEAD (1941)*
THE PHILOSOPHY OF G. E. MOORE (1942)
THE PHILOSOPHY OF BERTRAND RUSSELL (1944)*
THE PHILOSOPHY OF ERNST CASSIRER (1949)
ALBERT EINSTEIN: PHILOSOPHER-SCIENTIST (1949)
THE PHILOSOPHY OF SARVEPALLI RADHAKRISHNAN (1952)*
THE PHILOSOPHY OF KARL JASPERS (1957)
THE PHILOSOPHY OF C. D. BROAD (1959)
THE PHILOSOPHY OF RUDOLF CARNAP (1963)
THE PHILOSOPHY OF MARTIN BUBER (1967)
THE PHILOSOPHY OF C. I. LEWIS (1968)
THE PHILOSOPHY OF KARL POPPER (1974)
THE PHILOSOPHY OF BRAND BLANSHARD (1980)
THE PHILOSOPHY OF JEAN-PAUL SARTRE (1981)

In Preparation:

THE PHILOSOPHY OF GEORG HENRIK von WRIGHT
THE PHILOSOPHY OF GABRIEL MARCEL
THE PHILOSOPHY OF W . V. QUINE

*Available only from University Microfilms International.

Brand Blanshard

THE LIBRARY OF LIVING PHILOSOPHERS
VOLUME XV

THE PHILOSOPHY OF
BRAND BLANSHARD

EDITED BY
PAUL ARTHUR SCHILPP
NORTHWESTERN UNIVERSITY &
SOUTHERN ILLINOIS UNIVERSITY

LA SALLE, ILLINOIS • OPEN COURT • ESTABLISHED 1887

THE PHILOSOPHY OF BRAND BLANSHARD

FIRST EDITION

Library of Congress Cataloging in Publication Data

The Philosophy of Brand Blanshard.
  (The Library of living philosophers ; v. 15)
  "Bibliography of the writings of Brand Blanshard
to 1980, compiled by John Howie": p.
  Includes index.
  1. Blanshard, Brand, 1892-   —Addresses, essays,
lectures. I. Blanshard, Brand, 1892-   II. Schilpp,
Paul Arthur, 1897-   III. Series: Library of living
philosophers ; v. 15.
B945.B564P46   191   79-20754

ISBN 0-87548-349-6

The Library of Living Philosophers is published under the sponsorship of Southern Illinois University—Carbondale.

GENERAL INTRODUCTION*
TO
"THE LIBRARY OF LIVING PHILOSOPHERS"

According to the late F. C. S. Schiller, the greatest obstacle to fruitful discussion in philosophy is "the curious etiquette which apparently taboos the asking of questions about a philosopher's meaning while he is alive." The "interminable controversies which fill the histories of philosophy," he goes on to say, "could have been ended at once by asking the living philosophers a few searching questions."

The confident optimism of this last remark undoubtedly goes too far. Living thinkers have often been asked "a few searching questions," but their answers have not stopped "interminable controversies" about their real meaning. It is nonetheless true that there would be far greater clarity of understanding than is now often the case if more such searching questions had been directed to great thinkers while they were still alive.

This, at any rate, is the basic thought behind the present undertaking. The volumes of *The Library of Living Philosophers* can in no sense take the place of the major writings of great and original thinkers. Students who would know the philosophies of such men as John Dewey, George Santayana, Alfred North Whitehead, G. E. Moore, Bertrand Russell, Ernst Cassirer, Karl Jaspers, Rudolf Carnap, Martin Buber, et al., will still need to read the writings of these men. There is no substitute for first-hand contact with the original thought of the philosopher himself. Least of all does this *Library* pretend to be such a substitute. The *Library* in fact will spare neither effort nor expense in offering to the student the best possible guide to the published writings of a given thinker. We shall attempt to meet this aim by providing at the end of each volume in our series as nearly complete a bibliography of the published work of the philosopher in question as possible. Nor should one overlook the fact that essays in each volume cannot but finally lead to this

*This General Introduction, setting forth the underlying conception of this *Library*, is purposely reprinted in each volume (with only very minor changes).

same goal. The interpretative and critical discussions of the various phases of a great thinker's work and, most of all, the reply of the thinker himself, are bound to lead the reader to the works of the philosopher himself.

At the same time, there is no denying that different experts find different ideas in the writings of the same philosopher. This is as true of the appreciative interpreter and grateful disciple as it is of the critical opponent. Nor can it be denied that such differences of reading and of interpretation on the part of other experts often leave the neophyte aghast before the whole maze of widely varying and even opposing interpretations. Who is right and whose interpretation shall he accept? When the doctors disagree among themselves, what is the poor student to do? If, in desperation, he decides that all of the interpreters are probably wrong and that the only thing for him to do is to go back to the original writings of the philosopher himself and then make his own decision—uninfluenced (as if this were possible) by the interpretation of anyone else—the result is not that he has actually come to the meaning of the original philosopher himself, but rather that he has set up one more interpretation, which may differ to a greater or lesser degree from the interpretations already existing. It is clear that in this direction lies chaos, just the kind of chaos which Schiller has so graphically and inimitably described.[1]

It is curious that until now no way of escaping this difficulty has been seriously considered. It has not occurred to students of philosophy that one effective way of meeting the problem at least partially is to put these varying interpretations and critiques before the philosopher while he is still alive and to ask him to act at one and the same time as both defendant and judge. If the world's great living philosophers can be induced to cooperate in an enterprise whereby their own work can, at least to some extent, be saved from becoming merely "desiccated lecture-fodder," which on the one hand "provides innocuous sustenance for ruminant professors," and on the other hand gives an opportunity to such ruminants and their understudies to "speculate safely, endlessly, and fruitlessly, about what a philosopher must have meant" (Schiller), they will have taken a long step toward making their intentions more clearly comprehensible.

With this in mind, *The Library of Living Philosophers* expects to publish at more or less regular intervals a volume on each of the greater among the world's living philosophers. In each case it will be the purpose of the editor of the *Library* to bring together in the volume the interpretations and criticisms of a wide range of that particular thinker's scholarly contemporaries, each of whom will be given a free hand to discuss the specific phase of the thinker's work that has been assigned to him. All contributed essays will finally be submitted to the philosopher with whose work and thought they are concerned, for his careful perusal and reply. And, although it would be expecting too much to imagine that the philosopher's reply will be able to stop all differences of interpretation and of critique, this should at least serve the purpose of stopping certain of the grosser and more general kinds of misinterpretation. If no further gain than this were to come from the present and projected volumes of this *Library*, it would seem to be fully justified.

In carrying out this principal purpose of the *Library*, the editor announces that (as far as is humanly possible) each volume will contain the following elements:

First, an intellectual autobiography of the thinker whenever this can be secured; in any case an authoritative and authorized biography;

Second, a series of expository and critical articles written by the leading exponents and opponents of the philosopher's thought;

Third, the reply to the critics and commentators by the philosopher himself; and

Fourth, a bibliography of writings of the philosopher to provide a ready instrument to give access to his writings and thought.

The editor has deemed it desirable to secure the services of an Advisory Board of philosophers to aid him in the selection of the subjects of future volumes. The names of the seven prominent American philosophers who have consented to serve appear on the next page. To each of them the editor expresses his sincere gratitude.

Future volumes in this series will appear in as rapid succession as is feasible in view of the scholarly nature of this *Library*. The next volume in this series will probably be devoted to the philosophy of Jean-Paul Sartre.

Through the generosity of the Edward C. Hegeler Foundation, the publication of many of the volumes of this *Library* was made possible. For the support of future volumes, additional funds are still needed. The *Library* would be grateful, therefore, for additional gifts and donations. Moreover, since November 6th, 1947, any gifts or donations made to The Library of Living Philosophers, Inc., are deductible by the donors in arriving at their taxable net income in conformity with the Internal Revenue Code of the Treasury Department of the United States of America.

DEPARTMENT OF PHILOSOPHY
NORTHWESTERN UNIVERSITY AND
SOUTHERN ILLINOIS UNIVERSITY

P.A.S.
Editor

1. In his essay "Must Philosophers Disagree?" in the volume of the same title (London: Macmillan, 1934), from which the above quotations were taken.

ADVISORY BOARD

ACKNOWLEDGMENTS

The editor hereby gratefully acknowledges his obligation and sincere gratitude to all the publishers of Professor Blanshard's books and publications, most specifically to George Allen & Unwin, Ltd., for their kind and uniform courtesy in permitting us to quote—sometimes at some length—from Professor Blanshard's writings.

PAUL A. SCHILPP

*Deceased.

TABLE OF CONTENTS

PREFACE

It certainly is high time that a volume in this series should be devoted to the work and thought of a philosophical rationalist. And Professor Brand Blanshard is perhaps the most distinguished living proponent of that great tradition. Like Bradley, Bosanquet, and Royce before him, Blanshard is an ardent idealist, but he is not a disciple of any one of them. His rationalism is decisively his own; he is a truly original thinker, as anyone who has read him carefully and open-mindedly will attest.

The dominance of analytic philosophy during the last few decades in the English-speaking philosophical world is markedly lessening; and in no small measure this has been the result of Blanshard's own incisive criticisms of analytic philosophy in his *Reason and Analysis* and other writings.

It is because of the ever-growing awareness of rationalistic philosophy as an alternative to analytic philosophy that the present work is extraordinarily timely, coming to terms as it does with every aspect of Blanshard's rationalistic philosophy.

Blanshard's remarkable intellectual autobiography brings to life many of the foremost philosophers of the early part of this century, both in the United States and abroad. And Blanshard's replies to his critics are notable for his meticulous and careful reading of the essays and his lucid and reasonable replies to each of the contributors.

Readers familiar with previous volumes in this series are advised of a rather radical change in the structure of this one. In all preceding volumes the philosopher's "Replies" appeared as section III, between the contributed essays and the Bibliography. In the present case Professor Blanshard preferred to have his reply to each contributor appear immediately following the contributed essay itself. This makes it easier for the reader, who need not search for the philosopher's reply to an essay.

It may be self-evident that these volumes could not have come into being without the co-operation of each and all of the thirty contributors. But such self-evidence is no reason for omitting the editor's appreciation to these scholars for their very valuable contributions. After all, Professor Blanshard would have had nothing to which to reply had it not been for the contributed papers. My thanks to each of them. Two of them, Professor A. C. Ewing and Professor George F. Thomas, unfortunately did not live to see their contributions in print.

It only remains for me to express my sincere appreciation to those persons who have been most helpful in the preparation of this work and without whose invaluable efforts the appearance of these volumes would have suffered additional great delays. Foremost among them is Roberta W. Yerkes (Mrs. Brand Blanshard), for many years an editor at the Yale University Press, who performed yeoman service at a time when the editor himself was temporarily more or less incapacitated. It is quite impossible to do justice to such invaluable help. Next I must mention Dr. Hans Rudnick, of Southern Illinois University's English Department, who came to the editor's aid in a similar fashion when S.I.U.'s administration was perceptive and kind enough to appoint him as Assistant to the Editor. They have my most heartfelt appreciation and gratitude.

Professor Blanshard himself gave unstintingly of his time and energy and never ceased to be cooperative and helpful. For all of his patience and help I owe him a greater debt than I can express or repay.

Our publisher, Open Court Publishing Company of La Salle, Illinois, is continuing its never failing support of this, a major publishing project of no mean proportions. Our gratitude is especially due to its President, Mr. M. Blouke Carus, and its Vice President, Mr. Howard R. Webber, as well as to Mr. Thomas G. Anderson.

Finally, I wish to express my sincere gratitude to the administration of Southern Illinois University, particularly to President Warren W. Brandt, Academic Vice-President Frank E. Horton, and Dr. Michael R. Dingerson, Associate Dean of the Graduate School and Director of Research Development and Administration. The administration has supported this project with the greatest of generosity and consideration, and without its help it would have been very difficult to complete the editing of this volume.

DEPARTMENT OF PHILOSOPHY   PAUL ARTHUR SCHILPP
SOUTHERN ILLINOIS UNIVERSITY
CARBONDALE, ILLINOIS
OCTOBER 1978

WORKS BY BRAND BLANSHARD
FREQUENTLY CITED,
WITH SHORT TITLES

Books

NT   *The Nature of Thought.* 2 vols. London: George Allen & Unwin, 1939; New York: Macmillan Co., 1940; present distributor, New York: Humanities Press.

PAE   *Philosophy in American Education: Its Tasks and Opportunities.* By Brand Blanshard, C. J. Ducasse, C. W. Hendel, A. E. Murphy, and M. C. Otto. New York and London: Harper & Brothers, 1945.

Style   *On Philosophical Style.* Manchester, England: University of Manchester Press, 1954. Midland Book edition: Bloomington and London: Indiana University Press, 1967.

RG   *Reason and Goodness.* London: George Allen & Unwin; New York: Macmillan Co., 1961; present distributor, New York: Humanities Press.

RA   *Reason and Analysis.* La Salle, Ill.: Open Court Publishing Co.; London: George Allen & Unwin, 1962. Open Court paperback, 1973.

RB   *Reason and Belief.* London: George Allen & Unwin, 1974; New Haven: Yale University Press, 1975.

Uses   *The Uses of a Liberal Education and Other Talks to Students.* Edited by Eugene Freeman. La Salle, Ill.: Open Court Publishing Co., 1973.

Shorter Pieces

"NM"   "The Nature of Mind." *Journal of Philosophy* 38 (April 10, 1941): 207–16.

"P of A"   "The Philosophy of Analysis." *Proceedings of the British Academy* 38 (1952): 39–69.

"IE" "The Impasse in Ethics—and a Way Out." Berkeley and Los Angeles: University of California Press, 1955. University of California Publications in Philosophy, 28: 93–112.

PI *Philosophical Interrogations.* Edited by Sydney and Beatrice Rome. New York: Holt, Rinehart & Winston, 1964. (Blanshard's interrogation of John Wild on "Ethics," 123–25. "Interrogation of Brand Blanshard," conducted by Louis O. Mink, 201–57.)

"IR" "Internal Relations and Their Importance to Philosophy." *Review of Metaphysics* 21 (December 1967): 227–36.

THE PHILOSOPHY OF
BRAND BLANSHARD

PART ONE

AUTOBIOGRAPHY
OF BRAND BLANSHARD

Autobiography

Wordsworth was able to write: "The thought of our past years in me doth breed / Perpetual benediction." The thought of mine does not. I have felt an inner resistance to dwelling on my childhood and youth, for though there was much happiness in them, there were also years of anxiety, deprivation, and strain. I have no memory of my mother, who died before I was a year old, and I last saw my father when I was nine. My brother and I were brought up by a grandmother on an income of about four hundred and fifty dollars a year.

I was born in the tiny town of Fredericksburg, Ohio, on August 27 (Hegel's birthday) in 1892. A few years ago I was spending a week at the

I

WORDSWORTH was able to write, "The thought of our past years in me doth breed/Perpetual benediction." The thought of mine does not. I have long felt an inner resistance to dwelling on my childhood and youth, for though there was much happiness in them, they were also years of anxiety, deprivation, and strain. I have no memory of my mother, who died before I was a year old, and last saw my father when I was nine. My brother Paul and I were brought up by a grandmother on an income of about $450 a year.

I was born in the tiny town of Fredericksburg, Ohio, on August 27 (Hegel's birthday) in 1892. A few years ago I was spending a week at the College of Wooster in Ohio, and was told that Fredericksburg was seven miles away. It was only a name to me, but when I expressed a curiosity to see it, a kind friend volunteered to drive me there. Knowing that my father, between periods of study at Oberlin Seminary, had been the minister of a Congregational church in the town, I asked at the corner grocery where the church was. It had been torn down long ago. Was there anyone whose memory of the town would go back more than seventy years? Well, there was a very old lady who lived a short way up the street; she might have memories as remote as that. I sought her out and told her my name. She almost embraced me. Yes, she had known my father, a pale, earnest young man, whom she thought I resembled; and she remembered the pink-cheeked, merry young woman who was my mother. In fact, they had lived next door, and she still remembered the excitement in that house when my mother, to her own bewildered astonishment, gave birth to twin sons. Such events were less well managed in those days than now, and she suffered severely. Two weeks later she wrote a long letter to her sister, which I have in my possession, describing her experiences with a frankness rare in Victorian days, and recounting the excited flurry of trying to find a double baby carriage and to lay in a double supply of swaddling clothes. She attempted some description of the new arrivals. One of them had a fine head and was obviously promising; the other and unexpected one had a small head and big ears, and was obviously less promising. This meant me.

Our father and mother were both Canadians by birth, who became American citizens. Their own fathers had been immigrants to Canada, my father's father coming from Yorkshire, and my mother's from northern Ireland. A few generations back in my father's line was a French Huguenot who had brought to England the good French name of Blanchard. He seems to have wanted to retain something of the French pronunciation, so he spelled his name in English with an "s," and when, some years ago, I visited the little village in Yorkshire where the family had lived, I found a row of Blanshard headstones in the cemetery, all of them with the "s" spelling. This spelling has been a nuisance. It pointlessly disguises the old French name, and since the "c" form is almost universal, the variant is continually misspelled, and people cannot find me in the telephone book.

Grandfather Shem Blanshard came from Yorkshire to Ontario about 1860. Though he had no more than a secondary education, he was a Methodist minister, and for the many remaining years of his life he followed the practice of his time among Methodist preachers and moved to a new parish every three years. He married Orminda Adams, of a farming family near Toronto. This family was a branch of the Adams family of Massachusetts; Orminda, who was our grandmother, was able to recall what the connection was, but it has disappeared from my memory. Shem and Orminda Blanshard must have led a bleak and straitened life, for the winters around Georgian Bay, where a number of their parishes lay, were long and severe, the conditions of living primitive, and money and books in short supply. They would no sooner become at home in a community than they had to pull up stakes, move to a new one, and begin all over again. They had two children, a son Francis, who was our father, and a daughter who died in infancy. I was told that grandfather Shem, a stocky man with a large square beard, used to dandle his grandsons on his knee and sing to them, but he died before I could form any memory of him.

Our mother, Emily Coulter Blanshard, was one of twelve children. Her father had a farm in what is now a prosperous part of the city of Toronto. Neither of her parents had had much schooling, but since she was the ablest of the twelve, they contrived to send her to the Hamilton Ladies College, where she was valedictorian of her class and won a Governor-General's gold medal for proficiency in her studies. From such reports as I have been able to glean about her, she was strong and active physically, had a sunny and sociable disposition, and was full of gaiety and humor. It is certain that if she had lived the lot of her two infants would have been very different. But she was the victim of a tragedy that intrudes into my thought on the problem of evil. In the summer of 1893 she went to her parents' farm near Toronto to see her family and show them her two sons. She had occasion to go down cellar one evening, carrying a lamp in her hand. Perhaps she caught her foot in her long dress; at any rate she stumbled and fell downstairs. The kerosene from the lamp spilled out on her dress and her hair, setting them both on fire. She ran screaming upstairs again, but before the blaze could be put out she was so badly burned that she died the next morning.

Our father hurried up from Fredericksburg by the slow trains of the day to attend the funeral and collect his sons, aged eleven months. He never really recovered from this blow. His future, which had seemed full of promise, changed to gray overnight. He had long been frail-looking, and shortly after his loss he was warned that his lungs were touched by consumption, a much dreaded disease in those times. He went back to Oberlin Seminary, taking his parents with him, finished his degree, and accepted the pastorate of a small Congregational church in Grand Rapids, Michigan. His salary was minute, and he did a good deal of work that would not now be undertaken by the minister; I still have some of the cards that he printed on a little press of his own for distribution at the church door. His father Shem had died in Oberlin, and the care of his children now devolved on his mother. He worked hard—probably much too hard, for the consumption grew worse, and he was advised to take a vacation in the dry climate of a western state. He did go west for a short time, and came back feeling better. But the disease was creeping steadily on.

He decided to move to a less exacting charge, which he found in the little farming community of Edinburg, in northern Ohio, and he moved his family there about 1899. He was a good preacher, I think, though my memory of his presence in the pulpit is very dim. He was skillful with carpentering tools; I recall that he once made for Paul and me a pair of admirably effective crossbows (of course there had to be two if either was given anything). On Sunday morning he would preach at Edinburg, and in the afternoon at Atwater, a few miles away; we used to walk out along the dusty Atwater road to meet his buggy and be driven home by him behind his skittish little mare. He would occasionally give one of us the reins, but the horse could instantly tell the difference and would begin to run home at a precipitate pace, so that our father would have to take over again.

He was a kind and considerate father and son, and I cannot remember that he ever lost his temper or did an unreasonable thing. He could indeed be firm with his sons, and I recall being abruptly banished from the table when I used what seemed to him offensive language. But throughout the years that my brother and I can recollect, the clouds of his loss and his illness were hanging over him, and my memory of him carries the impression of a fixed resignation which he tried to conceal. His coughing grew worse, and in 1902 he set out again for the West. There is etched in my memory the look on his pale, grim face, with its sandy Van Dyke beard, as he stood on the station platform at Rootstown, Ohio, waiting for the train. We did not see him again. He was pastor for a short time of the First Congregational Church of Helena, Montana, but finding the climate there too severe, he went south to Albuquerque, New Mexico, where he lived in a tent and started making pieces of furniture for sale. Letters regularly came from him, making the best of his bleak and lonely life. The letters ceased on March 28, 1904, when he was found dead in his tent.

I am clearer about my father's character than about his mind. There seems to have been something of the saint about him, which was perhaps intensified by the religious atmosphere of a Victorian nonconformist parsonage. I hope that his genes have passed on to me a little of his quiet, firm, and equable self-command. On the intellectual side, Oberlin was a revelation to him, with such figures on its staff—liberal for their time—as G. H. Fairchild, James Brand, E. I. Bosworth, and Henry Churchill King. Two of his admirations he registered in the names of his sons. During his youth, Henry Ward Beecher was in his palmy period in Plymouth Church, Brooklyn, and I recall on my father's shelves a complete red-bound set of Beecher's *Plymouth Pulpit Sermons*. He had apparently selected in advance the name of his son: it would be Paul Beecher Blanshard. When a supernumerary son appeared, there was a flurry of search for a further name, which must be parallel with the first. "Percy" seemed like a balance for "Paul," and for "Beecher" he found a balance in the name of his local hero, James Brand. So the extra son became "Percy Brand Blanshard." By the time I reached my army days I had had enough of "Percy," and quietly dropped it.

The views of Strauss and Renan and the great controversy over Darwinism were then stirring the waters at Oberlin, and my father was no doubt affected by them. My impression is that by the end of his life, influenced perhaps by reflection on the meaningless loss of a wife whom he needed so desperately and the imminent wiping out of his own life, so much needed by his sons, he was moving beyond the orbit of his father's Methodism and his own earlier beliefs. He would probably have called himself a liberal in both theology and politics. Among his papers I found typewritten lectures on a number of men he much admired, among them his contemporaries Anthony Ashley Cooper, who became Lord Shaftesbury, and W. E. Gladstone. There were also letters indicating that he was thinking of leaving the ministry for a life in business.

For two years before our father's death, his sons had been in the charge of his mother, Orminda Blanshard. We had to move out of the modest Edinburg parsonage where we had been living, and when the fateful telegram arrived, we were renting rooms in the house of a local farmer. For the next dozen years our grandmother was the head of the house for my brother and me. It was fortunate for us that we had her care, and it was perhaps fortunate for her that she had someone to care for and to give her lonely life some point and interest. Her earlier years had not been easy. When she married Shem, who was much older than she, she had been a beautiful but frail young woman with the tubercular tendency that ran in her family. She was not prepared for the role of minister's wife to which she was suddenly called. She found herself expected not only to cook and to preside at her husband's table, but also to teach Sunday school classes, visit the members of the parish, and perhaps organize the women in groups for community service. She had no background for such work, apparently realized it early, and retreated into herself. Her husband did not know how to give her the advice and encouragement she needed, and she gradually became something of a recluse. During the years when I knew her, she seldom went out to a meal or entertained a guest; meeting people was a strain, and a knock at the door brought a tightening around the heart. I am sure this attitude had its effect on me. I have never been able to throw off self-consciousness or a sense of tension in meeting other persons, or to feel quite at ease with them, though I do not think they know it; I have developed a protective habit of glib talk that conceals it fairly well. My grandmother, after losing a three-year-old daughter, had adopted a girl of about the same age who, it was hoped, would be a companion for her, but as the child grew up relations with her foster mother became strained, and neither enjoyed being with the other.

This was largely the result of my grandmother's very puritanical standards. She disapproved on religious grounds of dancing, theatergoing, smoking, drinking, playing on the Sabbath, swearing, novel-reading of most kinds, and anything but the most seemly and carefully regulated intimations of an interest in sex. She saw to it that her grandsons went regularly to church and Sunday school, and was troubled when they showed interest in dubious books, infidel ideas, or girls. She kept a firm hand on us, and violations of her stringent code were dealt with scathingly, at times in telling Biblical language. It sounds like a grim life for two growing boys. We did not find it so. Underneath her severity we knew there was a devoted affection, which would make any sacrifice for us. Her son had been the joy and pride of her life; in his two boys she had all that was left of him; and if either of us came down, as we persisted in doing, with measles, scarlatina, mumps, or poison ivy, her concern was touching. After our mother's death, there had been some talk of separating us, the Blanshard side of the family taking one of us and the Coulter side the other. Our grandmother would have none of this, and we have always been grateful to her for it; as long as we were together, straitened circumstances mattered little. How she managed the family exchequer I do not know. Her only income was a small annuity from the "superannuation fund" of the Methodist church in Canada. On this she fed us, clothed us, housed us, and in some measure educated us.

Though we began our schooling in Grand Rapids, my first definite memories of schooldays come from Edinburg, where the two-story wooden schoolhouse stood near the center of the village. Paul and I, at the age of about nine, were appointed janitors of the school; we tramped over on winter mornings to start a fire in the potbellied stove and stayed after school to sweep the floors. When a class was convened, it met at the front of the room, while the rest of the pupils remained at their desks and studied, dreamed, or threw paper wads as the spirit moved them. I must have been a fairly satisfactory pupil, for I won a prize in the form of an anthology of English literature, in which I later found to my dismay that both Dryden and Keats had been overlooked. Most of the pupils were the sons and daughters of local farmers, who had no intention of further schooling. To the boys, the most exciting part of the year was the football season. The game was played in those days without the complete protective armor of the present-day gladiators, and broken arms and legs were common. The principal himself, who was apparently allowed to play on the team, became a local hero by breaking his leg and appearing in class for many weeks in a cast. Even I, who was too light and small for the game, managed to snap off a front tooth in some scrub encounter, and it took me many years to get a proper denture to replace it.

Edinburg was a township of rolling farm country, where in a few minutes one could be in open fields or maple woods. I gained much from living there, not in the way of book learning but in acquaintance with nature and with the processes of extracting a living from it. I helped with the horse and cow that my father briefly kept, chopped wood for the stove, raked leaves in the fall and shoveled snow in the winter, carried buckets of sap at maple syrup time, explored the woods for violets and jack-in-the-pulpits, climbed trees and visited swimming holes, and learned something about the look of birds' eggs, toads, and garden snakes. There was, of course, no movie theater or television in those days, and only an occasional entertainment in the town hall, which was visited by circuit-riding hypnotists and conjurors. We learned to make our own hockey sticks, bows and arrows. There was so little traffic that we could play baseball in the main road, although the village had an occasional interruption when a "horseless carriage" came noisily and dustily by, frightening all the horses and drawing the astonished and not very friendly scrutiny of the burghers.

It was a healthy life, and Paul and I flourished under it. Our food was of the simplest, but with milk at four cents a quart, and bread, eggs, cornmeal, and vegetables cheap, we fared pretty well. I cannot remember that we were ever bored. The days were full of work and play, and in the evenings we studied our lessons under the kerosene lamps or perhaps read G. A. Henty or the *Youth's Companion,* both popular in those days. Our grandmother managed to get a little melodeon with pedals, on which I learned to play simple hymns, but apart from that, music had no part in our lives. Our grandmother gave us each a Bible, which we prized and occasionally read. Perhaps as a result of this I won a Sunday school prize in the form of a book, but the donors were so certain it would be won by a girl that I was presented with *Mildred in Roselands*. I was too disappointed to read it.

In the course of his pastorate in Grand Rapids, my father had made a visit with his family to northern Michigan. My grandmother suffered severely from hay fever, as did I, and he rightly thought that a few weeks on the shore of Lake Michigan would give us relief. He rented a cottage at Bay View, a mile north of Petoskey on Little Traverse Bay. Bay View was a very unusual sort of town. It was founded as a religious summer resort, and consisted of several hundred cottages built on terraces overlooking the great lake. It developed into a middle western Chautauqua, with an admirable program of lectures, concerts, plays, and summer courses of study. Our grandmother fell in love with the place and took us back there each summer from Edinburg. She found a small cottage at the farthest bounds of the town which she could buy for $175, and settled in with her charges for three or four months annually. For some years this little house, unlined within and built of rough pine boards, was our real home. There was running water in it, but no bathroom, and cooking was done in a wood-burning stove with wood we could now chop for ourselves. By the time we were nine or ten, Paul and I were fairly adept at doing simple jobs of painting and carpentry, and under our grandmother's direction we planted young maples about the house, carried water from a spring to keep them alive, and put in a vegetable garden.

The migration to Bay View was an inspiration on her part; it gave her some independence, and to her grandsons it was a godsend. It meant much for us physically. We were only a few minutes away from the primeval forest on one side and Lake Michigan on the other, where we managed to secure a scow and go fishing for perch and sunfish. A golf course opened up across the road from our house, and we happily caddied for the not very numerous players. We worked as dishwashers for two dollars a week at the Howard House, a local hotel, and this brought with it the privilege of playing at off hours on its tennis court. We had many a joyous game of shinny with sticks we cut in the woods.

Bay View meant even more to us on the intellectual side. We secured jobs as ticket takers and bell ringers for the Chautauqua season, which enabled us to hear a great variety of preachers, lecturers, and singers. We listened attentively to President King of Oberlin, the Quaker Elbert Russell of Earlham, the somewhat histrionic Methodist bishops Hughes and Berry, and Frank W. Gunsaulus and John Balcom Shaw of Chicago. We heard Ben Greet in his Shakespearean repertoire, and I was particularly attracted by the performance of one young actress who played Rosalind in *As You Like It*. Nearly half a century later I saw her play again in London, where, as Dame Sybil Thorndike, she was one of the lights of the British stage. We heard David Bispham and Ernestine Schumann-Heink sing. We heard William Jennings Bryan deliver his famous lecture on "The Prince of Peace," in which he proved the existence of God by pointing to the marvel of a watermelon coming through so small a stem. I recall that for this lecture I was late and had to sit at the back of a large auditorium; I wondered whether I could hear him. As soon as he began, all doubts disappeared. His powerful voice and practiced enunciation made every syllable distinct.

As I listened to these many speakers, an interest began to awaken in their techniques. I used to take notes on their addresses, observing how well or ill organized they were, how they began and ended, how much they appealed to reason and how much to feeling, and how effectively voice and gesture were used in their presentation. This was the beginning of a lasting interest first in spoken, and then in written, style. With saw and hammer I made a speaker's stand, set it up in a clump of birch trees, and proceeded to read and speechify to the breezes, with the trees rustling their applause. I began to hear what I read, and to note the cadences of the writers who had an ear for rhythm. A little later I found in a high school library a collection of speeches by great orators, which I sampled admiringly. At the same time I was beginning to take an interest in poetry and kept on hand a copy of *Paradise Lost*. It dawned on me that there is a music of speech, of which all the great poets and orators had command. The speeches that attracted me most as I read them were the simpler and more dramatic ones, like those of Wendell Phillips; of those I heard, I particularly liked Bishop Hughes because he could tear a passion to tatters with such abandon. But I recognized that there were levels of intellectual force far beyond the powers of such men. In my early teens I somehow contracted an admiration for Edmund Burke that has stayed with me through the years, and it thrilled me to have the chance, in a high school English class, to study and analyze the great speech that should have prevented the American Revolution, the speech *On Conciliation with America*. I feel some satisfaction in the accident that I write these notes in the little New Hampshire town of Franklin, which produced the one American in history who ranks with Burke and the other immortals of the spoken word, Daniel Webster.

In Bay View Paul and I got the concession for a newsstand, which a local carpenter built to our juvenile specifications. We ordered newspapers from the chief cities from which the summer resorters came, sold them at a nickel a copy, and made two or three cents on each sale. We also had delivery routes which took us on foot to all parts of the town. I have always been glad that I had the experience of earning money by this kind of minute piecework. Those who live exclusively on salaries often fail to realize the equivalent in work of a nickel, a dime, or a dollar. As a result of my early experience I have always borne this equivalence at the back of my mind; and while it may have made me overcautious in money matters, it has also given me some business sense and respect for men of business. After those days of bit by bit earning, my later times have all seemed easy; I have generally felt overpaid.

For some years in our middle teens the firm of "Blanshard Bros." was in the writing as well as the selling end of the newspaper business; we reported the Bay View news for the Petoskey *Daily Resorter*. We had to produce a column or two of news every day, which we went about collecting like bees after honey, writing it up at night or in the early morning, and taking our product personally to the editorial office in Petoskey. This too was a valuable practice, though on rainy days when nothing happened it could be grueling. Since we were writing for print, we were forced to pay regard to conciseness and clearness of statement, and since we had no typewriter, we had to produce copy that could go to the printer in handwritten form. It was an enlightening adventure for us, however painful for editor, printer, and readers.

The trip from Ohio to northern Michigan was a long one, involving train travel to Cleveland, a trip by steamer across Lake Erie to Detroit, and a long, slow journey by train up the Michigan lower peninsula to Bay View. My grandmother dreaded this, and when we were ready for the ninth grade, she decided to move to Petoskey rather than return to Ohio. We remained in Bay View until the cold weather set in, walking the mile and a half to school daily, then moved into rooms in Petoskey. Football was a leading interest at the high school, and again the principal achieved some glory with his pupils by breaking a leg in the game. With the new school came an improvement in teaching. I began the study of Latin and algebra, without doing very well in either. The high school had a debating team of which I was a member, but here my reading of speeches did me an odd disservice. Some of these—Cicero's and Chatham's, for example—had made free use of invective, and in an interschool debate I thought I would try this too; so I showered my unfortunate opponent with sarcasms, carefully thought up in advance. It was a disgraceful exhibition, and the nice young woman who was our coach almost wept with mortification.

During our two winters in northern Michigan we learned to ski and skate. Our inlet of Lake Michigan froze several feet thick, and we were told that horse races had at times been held on the ice. Our grandmother began to long for an escape from this intense cold, and, being footloose, she decided to take us to a town where there would be a really good school. Some young acquaintances among the resorters at Bay View told us favorable tales about the Detroit Central High School, and in the fall of 1908 the three of us, with purses slightly fattened by summer earnings, packed our bags and set out for

Detroit. After some search we found rooms not far from the school. Our grandmother, from long experience, had learned how to face new scenes and strange faces without being daunted. She found a Methodist church to attend, but I cannot remember that any friends ever came to our apartment, or that she visited anyone else; her life was increasingly concentrated on her grandsons, and, apart from them, she must have been very lonely.

But to Paul and me Detroit was a new and absorbing world. The high school was large and competently staffed. There were modern, well-lighted classrooms, laboratories for the science courses, coaches for the various sports, and flourishing student societies. For the first time we had some men teachers, a point of importance to boys like us. Also for the first time I was able to take courses in physics, chemistry, and German, all well taught. I became genuinely interested in my studies, and perhaps too anxious to do well in them; at any rate I rather prided myself on being able to keep at them until I almost fell from my chair in fatigue. I can now see, as I look back, that I suffered from both physical undernourishment and nervous overstrain.

At Detroit the interest in public speaking that had begun at Bay View found a congenial outlet in the House of Representatives, a student body organized on the Congressional model, in which I was the "gentleman from Arizona." Week by week we argued problems of American political policy; I still have the elaborate brief of a speech I made against the Monroe Doctrine. It is a pity, I think, that this sort of debating, once much cultivated in our high schools and colleges, has gone out of fashion, for it not only stimulates interest in public affairs but provides an admirable discipline in the organization of thought. I threw myself into it with enthusiasm, and in the annual contest in public speaking won a gold medal provided by a philanthropic brewer of the city. I began to think of following my father's vocation as a minister, and took long walks on Sunday mornings to downtown Detroit to hear Dr. John H. Boyd at the First Presbyterian Church. Boyd was a graduate of Princeton, which made me want to go there too, and with a wild hope I even took the Princeton entrance examinations. But this was a blind alley, for the cost of tuition was far beyond my range.

I tried unsuccessfully for the position of catcher on the Central High School baseball team; my arm was too weak for a line throw to second base. Though I was now having to wear glasses, I found that I could wear them with surprisingly little danger or difficulty inside a catcher's mask. The time was one of much enthusiasm for baseball in Detroit, for the immortal Ty Cobb was carrying his team to one American League pennant after another; and Paul and I would steal away of a Saturday afternoon to watch him from the ten-cent bleachers, established, not very ethically, on roof tops adjoining Navin Field. Am I wrong, I wonder, in thinking that the game lost some of its excitement when it substituted its present emphasis on power hitting for Cobb's type of strategic batting and adventurous baserunning?

As the two profitable years in Detroit drew to an end, the question arose, not whether we should go to college, but where. It was settled for us by two facts: the low tuition at the state university and our grandmother's mobility. We could attend the University of Michigan at Ann Arbor, if I remember rightly, for forty dollars a year, which brought it within our range. And since we had no fixed winter home, we were as free to live in a university town as anywhere else. So in the fall of 1910 we moved into rooms in Ann Arbor.

Ann Arbor

The University of Michigan was not then the mammoth institution it has since become; there were about five thousand students. But it had already reached a position of high respect among the state universities under the leadership of James Burrill Angell, who had been an ambassador to China and who was the father of President Angell of Yale. It had many scholars and teachers of standing: Kelsey in Latin, D'Ooge in Greek, Adams and Taylor in economics, Cooley in sociology, Pillsbury in psychology, Wenley, Parker, and R. W. Sellars in philosophy. Unfortunately in the student mind these were all overshadowed by "Hurry-Up" Yost, the football coach who year after year had turned out teams of myrmidons that rode through all opposition like human tanks. Fraternities and sororities were well established and had many attractive houses near the campus, but my brother and I were not interested in them nor they in us.

One sunny afternoon in the fall of 1910 I went as a timorous newcomer into a large hall where freshman advisers were sitting at scattered tables. I knew fairly well what courses I wanted to elect, but was uncertain as to the choice between Greek and mathematics. It happened that the adviser assigned me was that excellent scholar, Campbell Bonner, chairman of the department of Greek. He no doubt tried to advise me impartially, but I ended by taking Greek. I have sometimes wondered what would have happened if I had made the other choice. It would have closed Oxford to me and altered the course of my life incalculably.

Much of my work during the next three years was devoted to Greek and Latin literature. Was it worthwhile? In view of what those studies opened up to me practically, I cannot regret them; but on the intellectual side it must be admitted that they were not very rewarding. I did reach the point where I could, with difficulty and a dictionary, plod through the *Apology* of Plato or the *Alcestis* of Euripides. But I question whether the result was commensurate with the time and effort expended. No doubt it would all have been valuable if I had gone into Greek professionally or into research in Greek philosophy. But I did neither. From the few works I read so laboriously I gained little idea of the sweep and grace of the Greek mind—less, I suspect, than if I had devoted the same time to reading a wide range of classics in translation, or reading them in Greek with a translation before me, which was of course discouraged. I have found that if I read a paragraph first in English and then, with its meaning in mind, read it in the original, I learn a good deal of the language and lose less of the author's sense than if I puzzle it out word by word, with incessant breaks in the thread of thought through reference to the dictionary. Could not this method be more used? At any rate, my Greek is now a fading memory of impatient and forced labor; what I had of it is gone. For this I have only myself to blame. Still, I suspect there was something wrong about the theory that governed language study in those days—possibly also in later days. Students were permitted or encouraged to take a variety of languages. But there is not much point in acquiring a smattering of several languages, only to abandon them before one can use any of them with ease or profit; a language should be a key to unlock the treasures of a particular culture and cannot do that so long as one stands outside the door fumbling with the lock. In university study a language should be carried through to proficiency or not begun at all.

The delight of my sophomore year was the beginning of work in philosophy. My appetite for the subject had long been growing. People take to philosophy by very different routes—some through Zeno's puzzles, some through the shock of a friend's death, some through doubts about right and wrong. My route was perhaps the commonest one—through the hope of certainty in religion. I could hardly accept my grandmother's fundamentalist views, but neither did I simply reject them; religion seemed to me a tangled mass of high aspirations, mystical gropings, and questionable dogmas, and I longed to sort them out. The first piece of philosophical writing that I seemed to understand was not of a religious kind, however; it was an article in the *Cosmopolitan Magazine,* which someone, perhaps my father, had left about, "The Breadth of Herbert Spencer's Teaching." The pride I felt in having understood it, indeed the very look of that old magazine, are with me still. A little later I picked up Mark Hopkins' *Evidences of Christianity* and one or two books by Borden Bowne, which left me with the impression that philosophical inquiry was no danger to religious belief, that, on the contrary, philosophy was the formidable and trusty Excalibur which was in the end the true defense of religion, and I wanted to be an Arthur who could wield that sword. When I began formal work in philosophy, the thought was at the back of my mind that I should probably follow my father's star into theology and that I should find philosophy the most useful of tools.

The introductory course at Michigan was taught by Robert Mark Wenley, a Scotsman trained under Edward Caird at Glasgow and a popular figure on the campus. He had succeeded John Dewey as department head at Michigan, a somewhat unequal exchange, though quite possibly one that increased local interest in the subject, since Wenley was a skillful and eloquent lecturer. He was not an original or systematic philosopher; his gift was for philosophico-literary criticism which, in his lectures, was offered with a grace and facility of language unusual then at Michigan, and, in his writing, with Carlylese verbal fireworks that sometimes distracted too much of one's attention. When I first knew him he was already a campus character, with a reputation for doing unpredictable things. During a lecture he was quite capable, if the class's attention wandered, of dropping a book on the floor with a loud report, or if he spied an unfortunate student in the back row deep in the *Michigan Daily*, of stamping down from the platform, leaning over the youngster's shoulder and demanding what it was that he found more interesting than the wisdom emanating from the rostrum. His classes were large, and in some of them he had no assistance with the reading of papers. His way of dealing with these was characteristic. He would take perhaps a hundred long term essays to his attic study in the morning and emerge in the evening with the entire lot read, graded, and briefly commented on. He could catch the gist and quality of an essay with extreme rapidity, though he refused to be bothered with details. In my junior year he appointed me a reader in his introductory course. I was not ready for such responsibility, but Wenley's budget was limited, he had a Scotsman's economy, and he saw that for thirty dollars a month he had a reader who was at least literate and was starry-eyed about his subject. Wenley did not set a philosophic pattern that I was tempted to follow, but he was very kind to me and I owe him much.

I saw less of the other members of the department. Alfred Lloyd, who was shortly to become dean of the Graduate School, was Wenley's second in command. He had a splendid dome of a head, with a wisdom and benignity that went with it; but there was a baffling obscurity in his speech and writing that limited his audience. The reverse was true of DeWitt Parker, who had recently come from Harvard; Parker was a model of lucid and orderly exposition, and was rapidly gaining a large following for his lectures in aesthetics. Charles Vibbert was chiefly notable for his knowledge of France and its philosophy; he had married a French wife, and the two returned wistfully to Paris at every opportunity. The other senior member of the department was Roy Sellars. I do not think he has ever had the recognition he deserved. He was a pioneer in naturalism, in critical realism, in humanistic religion, and in philosophic socialism. Perhaps he wrote too much too soon; at any rate in his early writing he permitted himself a certain looseness of expression that did not help him with the impatient analysts of a later day. His brilliant son Wilfrid, whom I knew in Ann Arbor as a boy, was later to become a valued colleague at Yale. Among my student friends at Michigan was a pale and lame young man who was also to be a colleague at Yale, the psychologist Clark Hull.

In the long Ann Arbor winters it was important to keep fit, and I took regular workouts in the university gymnasium. But I soon recognized that competitive athletics in a place like Michigan was not for me. I tried to run the half mile, but found myself surrounded by human antelopes who left me nowhere. In baseball the best I could do was play on my class team. Still, baseball was interesting in those days at Michigan, even from a distance. The baseball coach was a vigorous young man named Branch Rickey, who was later to become an outstanding figure in the professional game; and in the class just behind me there appeared a boy from Akron, Ohio, whom Rickey quickly recognized as a genius with a ball and bat. He pitched for the freshman engineers, and I seem to remember that in an abbreviated game against our team (I was perhaps fortunately on the sidelines that day) he struck out twenty of twenty-one batters he faced. A few years later Rickey brought him to St. Louis, where George Sisler made a record that rocketed him into baseball's Hall of Fame.

If competitive athletics was beyond me, competitive speaking was not. By this time I was clear that speeches were not essays, and I had worked hard on a style suitable to the spoken word. In my sophomore year I entered the lists in a "peace oratorical contest" that had been organized on a large scale, and in this series I won the university, state, interstate, and national contests. The next year I competed for the $100 university prize in public speaking, won it, and represented the university in the contest of the "Northern Oratorical League." I entered this last contest sleepless and overtrained, and lost my touch. I came out third.

At the beginning of my junior year I tried another kind of competition. In those days all applicants for a Rhodes scholarship were required to take the Oxford "responsions," that is, the entrance examinations in Greek, Latin, and elementary mathematics required of applicants in England. I took these examinations and passed. The candidates had to prepare a statement of interests and intentions, present their academic record along with letters from their instructors, and appear for an interview before a state committee. My teachers must have outdone themselves on my behalf, and Professor Wenley weighed in with a letter that I am sure counted for much. I doubt whether I should have stood a chance if the conditions now governing such appointments had been in force. In those days the Greek requirement excluded the great majority of possible candidates. However that may be, the committee gave me the appointment. I knew it was a turning point in my life. I was so overwhelmed and intoxicated by the prospect suddenly opened to me that when I got home to our rooms on Willard Street I literally pulled the knob off the door in my eagerness to tell the news.

Exhilarating as my prospect now was, it contained one sad feature; my brother and I would have to part. We were not identical twins; we did not look alike; and our tastes and interests were at some points markedly different. Paul showed more enterprise and courage than I did where independent action was required; in recent summers he had left Bay View and gone on the road alone as a book salesman. But for nearly twenty years we had been inseparable, getting the same grades in school, playing the same games, and pursuing much the same studies. The position of either of us alone in those years would have been forlorn. Together, each of us had someone to play with, to talk to, to confide in, to lay plans with, a comrade with whom to face the world. Strange to say, I cannot remember that we ever quarreled. Having been everything to each other, we suddenly took divergent paths and did not see each other for four years. When I returned, Paul was married and launched on a career, or rather a variety of careers, that were far afield from mine. He went on to complete his course at Michigan with a Phi Beta Kappa, entered the Harvard Divinity School on a scholarship, and in spite of much self-searching briefly entered the ministry. Then in succession he became a labor organizer, a lecturer in the colleges for the League for Industrial Democracy, an economic adviser to the State Department in the Caribbean, commissioner of investigation in LaGuardia's cabinet in New York City, and in his later years the author of a series of critical books on the Roman Catholic church that have made his writings known to far more readers than are ever likely to look at mine.

About the first of October 1913, I set out for Boston, from which the Cunarder *Franconia* was to take a party of Rhodes scholars to England. My first impression of the East was not happy, for, having to change trains at Albany, I was robbed of most of my summer earnings while waiting in the station. Boston partly made up for this, for I was able to visit, with due reverence, some of the cradles of American national life.

Oxford

I cannot remember much of the voyage to Liverpool. I do remember the train ride to Oxford, the little locomotive—so unlike the black mammoths that I had seen puffing in and out of Cleveland—and the neatly hedged green fields that made England look like a great garden. As the train approached Oxford, I looked eagerly out of the windows; there, sure enough, were its spires and towers in the misty distance, and my heart began to beat faster. At the station I took a horse-drawn hansom cab, and asked the driver to take me to Merton College.

I despair of putting in words what Oxford meant to me. It surely meant far more than to some who were better prepared to take it in stride and to be blasé about it. To a youth straight from the Middle West it was overwhelming. For one thing, the mere antiquity that surrounded me was like nothing I had known. At my college of Merton was a library in which some of the books were still chained to their places so that they could not be run off with by the skittish young monks of the 1300s. The ghost of Duns Scotus (d. 1308) was alleged to walk there, appearing only from the ankles up, since he refused to recognize a newfangled floor put in five or six centuries ago. The University of Michigan was to me a venerable institution, since it went back to 1834. When I had my first dinner in Merton, I sat down in a dining hall where scholars were eating and arguing two centuries before Columbus.

I have always belonged to Carlyle's sect of hero-worshipers, and to such a person Oxford is like Mecca to a Moslem. The walls are covered with the portraits of authors, bishops, and statesmen who once sat on the benches on which their faces now look down; the quadrangles are alive with memories; the very air is misty with them. If I brought to Oxford little else, I brought at least a passionate admiration for great literature and those who created it. There was a new kind of excitement for me in taking "Addison's Walk" at Magdalen, in knowing that from that window across the High Street Shelley had dropped his pamphlets on the heads of passers-by, that Dr. Johnson had left his boots outside a certain door at Pembroke, that in this room at Lincoln Wesley had prayed and wrestled with his sins, that from another room not far away Newman had looked out for the last time at the "snapdragons of Trinity." Remote figures became strangely real. It was a former warden of my college, William Harvey, who had discovered the circulation of the blood. I found out with delight that my own room was probably the one occupied fifty years before by George Saintsbury. And all these were a bare beginning. Hobbes and Locke, Gibbon and Froude, Gladstone and Asquith, Morris and Arnold and Swinburne and Hopkins and Auden and Eliot all spent part of their youth in Oxford and left a part of themselves there. And here was I in the midst of them, translated by some sort of miracle from my newsstand in Bay View.

Even in its theory of education, Oxford was unlike anything I had known. The American theory was, roughly, that human knowledge consisted of parts that could be mastered piece by piece. So we took five three-hour courses, making fifteen credits, per semester, and when we had completed 8 x 15 units, or 120, we were granted our degree. The English theory was that the aim of education was not so much knowledge as the eliciting of one's powers, so the student was given great freedom of experimentation along the way, but had to pass a week of taxing examinations at the end. These examinations would not be directed to finding holes in his knowledge; he would be asked to answer perhaps three of a dozen questions, but his answers must be essays in which the facts were penetrated and interpreted by his own thought. The instruction was designed to further this sort of achievement. The student met with his tutor once a week to read him an essay, which was subjected to careful criticism and discussion, so that his powers of analysis, argument, and expression were under continual stimulus, and his particular strengths and weaknesses prescribed for. Certain courses of lectures were usually recommended to him by his tutor, but no record was kept of his attendance. Such a system permits a tailoring of education to individual needs, though it is expensive of tutorial time and in our own monster universities would be prohibitively so.

I was fortunate in both my college and my tutor. Though Merton was small—about 140 students—it was the oldest and one of the best endowed of the Oxford colleges and had an able staff of fellows. Sir Walter Raleigh—the professor, not the pirate—held the Merton chair of English Literature and occasionally attended our undergraduate literary society, the Bodley, and read us a paper. Heathcote Garrod, later to become professor of poetry at Oxford, Norton Professor at Harvard, and editor of the *Oxford Book of Latin Verse,* was the tutor in Greek. I saw little of Garrod as an undergraduate, but came later to admire his books greatly for their discerning criticism and their exquisite style. The tutor in Latin was W. H. Fyfe, who was also Principal of the "Postmasters," as the holders of Merton scholarships were called, and who became head of Queen's University, Canada. At first I expected to see a good deal of the classical scholars, since my intention was to take "Greats," the famous old honors school of ancient literature, history, and philosophy. But it soon became apparent that if I pursued this course I should be spending most of my time on the languages, in which I was less well prepared than my English contemporaries, and this I was reluctant to do. After I had produced a few essays for my tutor, I applied, with his support, for permission to enroll for the graduate degree of B.Sc., where I could work entirely in philosophy and the degree would depend upon a thesis.

This tutor, who was to mean much to me, was not my own choice. One of the few Oxford dons of whom I had any knowledge was F. C. S. Schiller of Corpus Christi College, who was the leading English pragmatist, and I had at first been inclined to seek admittance to Corpus for work with him. Professor Wenley would not hear of this, and told me that I ought to apply to Merton and to work with Joachim if possible. I complied. I did in the end take some of my writing to Schiller, who gave me valued criticism, but I have never been attracted by pragmatism, and work with Schiller might have involved unfortunate tensions. I have always been grateful for Wenley's advice.

Harold Henry Joachim, when I first knew him, was forty-five years old. He was a slender man with a mat of curly reddish hair, thick-lensed glasses, a diffident manner, and a gentle, almost deferential way of speaking. His wife, who was also his cousin, was the daughter of the distinguished violinist Joseph Joachim, and he was a violinist of some attainments himself. I soon found that reading an essay to Joachim was a chastening experience. He was never severe in the ordinary sense, but I came to understand that if his comment on an essay was "very interesting, Mr. Blanshard," he was expressing delicate disapproval. Any inexactitude, any overstatement, any taking of refuge behind a metaphor, was visibly a pain to him; and I recall how, when I once let myself go with something to the effect that Locke had drawn near to the precipice of skepticism, and looking over, had shudderingly drawn back, Joachim settled further into his chair with a kind of low moan. His scholarship, and the implicit demands it made upon his students, were humbling.

His first requirement of me as a freshman was that I read Descartes's *Meditations,* and he kindly intimated that if I had any trouble with the Latin I could read it in French instead. He used to lecture on the *Nicomachean Ethics,* and the rumor, apocryphal but suggestive, was current in the college that if you began any sentence in the Greek text, Joachim could finish it for you. His lectures were orderly, lucid, and precise, but quite without spontaneity, since he read them word for word. Furthermore, he read them in a voice so gentle that it was not always easy to follow. Curiously enough, he used this relative inaudibility as a means of keeping order in the class, though inadvertently, for he was wholly without guile. "Gentlemen," he would say, in beginning a course of lectures, "my voice is not very strong, and if anyone finds difficulty in hearing, will he please shuffle his feet, and I will understand the signal." During the lecture, some restless barbarian, not too allured by the problems of immediacy in the perceptual judgment, would shift in his chair. Joachim would look up sympathetically through his thick glasses, turn back the page with a "Thank you," and read the last sentences over again. It was an excellent prescription for wrapping an audience in silence.

Academic Oxford is in session for less than half the year—three terms of eight weeks each. This implies that much if not most of the work must be done in the vacations. It also means that the terms are crowded with activities, not academic only, but athletic, literary, and convivial. One traditional Oxford activity is that of the undergraduate discussion societies, which are numberless. The most famous of them is the Oxford Union. It is modeled on the House of Commons, and has in fact been the training ground for much of Britain's political leadership during the past century. It is conducted—at least it was in my day—with some ceremony; the officers of the society all wore full dress—tailcoats and white ties; and the president, whose function was that of the Speaker of the Commons, directed its affairs with a firm parliamentary hand. The Union had so much standing that it could secure without difficulty the leading members of Parliament as visitors and participants in its debates. I recall that when Lloyd George was chancellor of the Exchequer I heard him in a debate on one of his own proposed reforms, speaking fourth on the program. The little "Welsh wizard" was of course an advanced liberal, and he was addressing an undergraduate audience whose fathers were for the most part intensely hostile conservatives; but he carried the house by storm with his humor, adroitness, and eloquence.

Many of the undergraduates were already exhibiting qualities for which they were to be known in later years. I remember particularly Harold Laski of New College, standing very erect, with his round head of neatly brushed hair parted in the middle, and pouring out the flood of effortless rhetoric that later was to enthrall so many audiences on both sides of the Atlantic. C. E. M. Joad of Balliol, the future philosopher, was so much of a wag that he had some trouble in getting himself taken seriously. This was far from true of Jan Hofmeyer, Rhodes scholar from South Africa, a young genius who, to the great loss of the liberal cause in his country, was to die prematurely. It must be admitted that the Joad type of speaking was more popular in the union than that of Laski or Hofmeyer. It was the style represented at its best by Philip Guedalla, who had been president of the Union just before my time, a style that depended more for its effect on wit and clever epigram than on force of argument. I spoke occasionally in the Union and once introduced a bill there, but I was not ready or witty enough to feel at home in this style of discussion.

I took a more active part in other and smaller societies. These generally met in some member's room, where a fire burned brightly in the grate, and the members sat on anything available, which often meant the floor, and listened to a paper which, on its conclusion, they proceeded to take to pieces. I was impressed by their skill in this dismemberment. British students were in some ways less resourceful than American; they had not (at least fifty years ago) had to make their own way in the world; they had not worked with their hands; they had lived a sheltered, though not a pampered, life. But they seemed to me more at home among ideas, and better able to dissect and discuss them, than we Americans were. Much of this skill was due, no doubt, to the exacting discipline of their "public," i.e. private, schools. Boys who had been through Eton, Harrow, or Winchester had already received a training, narrow in range but thorough, which made most Americans of the same age seem awkward and fumbling. But their interests and their nimbleness were due more largely perhaps to their families than to their schools. Most of them came in those days from homes which, if they were not aristocratic, at least had books lying around and where the paterfamilias would express himself forcibly at breakfast about the *Times* "leader" of the morning. They came by their public interests through domestic contagion. It was a quickening experience for an American to exchange ideas with them.

I made lasting and valuable friendships with some of these students. One of them, Carl Shrewsbury, was a distant cousin of mine, whose home in Lincolnshire was always open to me when I had time to go. Another was Kuruvila Zachariah, a charming Indian from Madras, who took a first class in history and became a professor, I think also vice-chancellor, of the University of Calcutta. In the spring vacation of my second year I went on a reading party to Swanage in Dorset with two other students. One was an Englishman of Anglo-German parentage, Karl Culpin, who was soon, like my cousin Shrewsbury and many of the best men of their generation, to be killed in the war. The other member of the trio was an American on whom I shall pause for a while, since he lived to play an important part in the literary life of Britain, T. S. Eliot.

Eliot

In 1914, when I first knew Eliot, he was a handsome man of twenty-six, four years my senior, who had already had a rich academic experience. He had studied ancient and modern languages at Harvard, had been a favorite student of Bertrand Russell's in symbolic logic when Russell was at Harvard for his Lowell Lectures, had studied philosophy under Royce and Santayana, had dabbled in Sanskrit and Oriental philosophy, had spent a year in Paris listening to Bergson and perfecting his French, and had now come to Merton to complete a Harvard thesis on the philosophy of Bradley under the direction of my own tutor, Joachim. Though slender of build, Eliot was sturdy physically, and entered at once into the Merton rowing program; I recall a race between two "fours" in which Eliot stroked the winning boat; I was in the losing one. In our vacation at Swanage Culpin, Eliot and I lived and had our meals together, and had many walks and talks along the seaside. But Eliot never wore his heart on his sleeve and I do not think that the other students felt they knew him well. Not that he was at all unfriendly, but he had something of the attitude toward his fellowmen that Royce ascribes to Hegel, a genuine interest in observing and recording them, together with an emotional aloofness from them. Although he had already written "Prufrock" and other pieces, I cannot recall that he ever read or mentioned them to us, and except for an occasional remark ("What a lazy mind Emerson had!") he gave no indication of the depth of his interest in literature. He was apparently committed to philosophy. Strangely enough, he spent most of the day with *Principia Mathematica* propped up before him on the dining table. Not that he felt any affinity for Russell's philosophy, or attached much philosophical importance to mathematical logic; but he had discovered that he had a facility for manipulating its symbols, and he said later that it gave him a curious sense of power to do so. His interest centered in Bradley, and since he and I were both studying Bradley with Joachim, we had some common ground.

Eliot completed the thesis on Bradley and sent it back to Harvard, where it was read and approved by Royce. But instead of returning to take his oral examination, he remained in England, took positions successively in a secondary school and a bank, and married an English girl. When he did finally revisit America, he had shifted permanently to literature, and he never did take the Harvard degree. Several decades later, when he had become a luminary in the world of letters, a devotee dug the thesis out of the Harvard library and with his permission published it. I read it then for the first time. It brought back memories of Swanage and aroused a train of reflection: if Eliot had remained in philosophy, would he have achieved anything like the position that he actually achieved in literature? I can only think not; he surely made the right decision. He later said of this one philosophical work of his that he could no longer understand it; and one does need to read Bradley to understand Eliot's exposition of him rather than the other way about. Able as he was, Eliot was haunted in his philosophy by the same obscurity that is often complained of in his poetry, and obscurity in philosophy is perhaps less readily condoned. Furthermore, he was committed to the Bradleyan type of metaphysics, and after the First World War the tide of philosophy set in a very different direction. Eliot could not, with all his gifts, have stemmed that tide, and like others of similar bent would no doubt have felt himself isolated.

I saw a little of him in later days in London and in St. Andrews, where he came to receive an honorary degree. By that time he had traveled an immense distance in a new direction of his own, followed by general acclaim. His career, as I look back at it, shows an extraordinary independence and integrity. It was difficult for an American to break into English letters, above all into its inner circles; the tradition that Americans are shrewd businessmen and engineers but frontiersmen in the humanities dies hard. Nevertheless Eliot won the Order of Merit, a recognition that Britain reserves for its own and its best. He did this not only by the originality of his verse but also by sheer solidity of scholarship. Many readers must have wondered whether there was not some tinsel about the glittering bits of linguistic learning with which he embellished some of his poems. When once I was sitting next to E. R. Dodds, the Regius Professor of Greek at Oxford, I asked him whether he had any opinion on this point so far as Eliot's Greek was concerned. He said that he had no doubt of Eliot here; that he had himself sat in a small advanced seminar with him under J. A. Stewart on the *Enneads* of Plotinus, a peculiarly knotty text, and that Eliot was quite able to hold his own. It may be added that he rode to eminence not on a currently popular wave of thought, but against the tide. He was an avowed royalist, classicist, and Anglo-Catholic when all these positions were in disfavor. Where he and his time were well matched was in his exposure of the wasteland of the twenties, with its hollow men and their thousand lost golf balls, and its hollow women measuring out their lives with coffee spoons.

Somewhere in middle life he became dissatisfied with this negative attitude and underwent a kind of religious conversion. He would have liked to hold up a way of life that would be as positive and magnetic as the wasteland had been repellent, and in his later poems and plays he did this so far as he could. I do not find these productions very satisfying, partly because of the difficulty of being sure what they mean, partly because high Anglicanism, even when supported by classicism and royalism, is hardly an adequate prescription for the ills that beset us. Still, having known something of the ability and thought that went into his work, and his loyalty to the truth as he saw it, I cannot dismiss lightly anything he said. His views on politics and religion were not mine, but he was a great man, and, I would add, a genuinely good man. I have always been grateful for having known him.

Bradley

Whether Eliot ever met Bradley, whom he had come to Oxford to study, I do not know. The chances are that he did not. Bradley had by then become a recluse, living in his rooms in Fellows' Quad at Merton, but seldom seen by anyone. He was, I think, the last holder of a life fellowship at Merton, which enabled him to live in the college as long as he wished, without teaching obligations. He never lectured, never took pupils, never attended philosophical meetings, and seldom discussed philosophy with anyone, even at Oxford; indeed most of the philosophers there had never seen him. Like Spinoza, he lived alone and thought. This isolation was not wholly a matter of preference. Bradley's health was precarious; he was nervous and high-strung; if he went out to dinner, people were prone to involve him in philosophical discussion, which upset his digestion; so he found it more prudent to dine alone on "two ducks' eggs and rice pudding," as Garrod told me. He did not enjoy contact with undergraduates, and was inclined to flee in termtime to France. To be sure, he did once take some pupils briefly for his colleague William Wallace, who was off on vacation and asked his help; but when Wallace returned and inquired how he had got on with them, Bradley replied that he could not understand them. He had a reputation, probably based on the severe manner of his controversial writing, of being something of a bear.

Happily I did not find him so. In my last year at Oxford I felt that it would be sad to leave without seeing a man who was so close at hand and to whom I owed so much, and I wrote him a letter saying that there were certain points in his *Logic* that I should like to discuss with him. He replied in a pleasant note and fixed a time. There was no suggestion of a bear in the figure who opened the door for me.

He was a courtly, square-set, Victorian gentleman of military erectness, rather formally dressed. With his well-trimmed grey beard, he was said to look like George Meredith. He talked very much as he wrote. When I asked him a question, he would look out of the window for a moment in silence, and then give his answer in a rounded paragraph of neat, crisp sentences. He kindly suggested my coming again, and I went back for another long talk with him. Most of what he said is now lost with the years, but a few tags remain. He talked about James and Dewey, with both of whom he had been in controversy, and evidently thought Dewey the more formidable philosopher of the two (though in the debate between James and Bradley in the pages of *Mind* I came to think James had the better of the argument). He made the certainly true remark that Bosanquet had lost some deserved recognition because of his unfortunate style. He had been revising his *Logic,* whose first edition had been selling at fantastic prices, and said that if he had known I was about he might have called me in to help with it. I knew how absurd that was, but it was the sort of remark that, absurd or not, sticks like a burr in a young man's memory.

There are readers of the present day who may feel that the veneration I felt for Bradley was itself a little absurd. I make no apologies for it. Bradley was easily first not only in Oxford philosophy but among all the British philosophers of his time. The dons were in awe of him. His achievement, like Eliot's in literature, was the more notable because at the beginning he had been swimming against the stream. British philosophy is traditionally empiricist in its leaning, and this empiricism had been fortified by the persuasive *Logic* of John Stuart Mill. To be sure, empiricism had been criticized ably—I think unanswerably—by Thomas Hill Green in his massive introductions to Locke, Berkeley, and Hume; but Green had died young, with most of his work unpublished, and when it did reach print, his manner made heavy going for his readers. (Incidentally, though Green had died in the 1880s, his widow, the sister of John Addington Symonds, was one of the great ladies of Oxford in my early days there.) It was Bradley who picked up Green's sword, which he wielded with incomparable address. He had learned from Green and Hegel that experience is more than a chaos of sensations, and that thinking is not a mere drifting along a line of associations; that experience is on the contrary shot through with necessary connections and that thought at its best is a movement under rational constraint. He had given some augury of his powers and his position in the *Ethical Studies* of 1876, but it was the *Principles of Logic* of 1883 that first revealed the full extent of those powers.

Joachim sent me off with this book on an early vacation, and asked me on my return whether I did not find it "exciting." There are not many books on logic about which that would be the most natural question to ask, but Bradley's *Logic* is exciting. Like Hegel's *Phenomenology,* it was a voyage of discovery on the part of a mind that was finding itself, but it has an exhilaration that Hegel has not, because it is also the creation of an artist in words. Logic takes wings when Bradley writes it. Partly, this results from his delight in his developing thought, partly—it must be admitted—from a less laudable delight in scoring off the imbeciles who blunder into his path. As he winds his dialectical way from a psychological beginning to a metaphysical culmination, he is forever stopping along the road to pour rhetorical fusillades at some unfortunate Bain, Mill, or Lewes, or even to give eloquent voice to misgivings about Hegel himself. One of these misgivings is so memorably put that it has reappeared in *The Oxford Book of English Prose,* the only passage, I should guess, that has ever found its way from a book of logic into an anthology of great literature.

No doubt Bradley's strong appeal to me had something to do with the religious root that sustained much idealist thinking. Green and the Cairds were profoundly religious men, and Bradley had been brought up in a household belonging to the evangelical "Clapham" sect. Though he turned later with some bitterness against Christian belief and even Christian ethics, he said in the preface to his *Appearance* that for some men philosophy was a means of experiencing Deity, and that probably no one who did not feel this had ever greatly cared for metaphysics. Here, as in much else, he was sealed of the tribe of Spinoza. The work of analysis was important for him, and he had spent much of his life at it; but without an ulterior interest that was essentially religious, such brainwork could not have supported itself; it would have been for him a vine cut at the root. As Eliot pointed out in comparing him with Bergson, there was a strong touch of mysticism in Bradley, showing itself not only in his curious interest in subrational immediate experience, but also in his adumbrations of a superrational Absolute. Bradley regarded philosophy as the intellectual means of adjusting oneself to the universe, of trying to see things steadily and whole; and for him such a search was both speculative and religious. He would have considered as visionless and molelike the preoccupation of some contemporary analysts with making distinctions within distinctions for their own sake, without any view to their wider bearings on the world and man's place in it.

Bradley, who died in 1924, lived to see the coming of a new type of logic. It was introduced to the philosophical world by Russell, who for a time was a follower of Bradley and who was a distant relative of Joachim's. Unfortunately, neither Bradley nor Joachim ever made much of the new logic. Bradley avowed that he could not follow it, and this was no doubt true; mathematics was either so difficult or so repellent to him that he had trouble—so it was reported—in passing his Oxford entrance examinations in arithmetic. This left him at a great disadvantage when he came to cross swords with Russell. But it is easy to make too much of this deficiency, as logicians of broad gauge, such as Clarence Lewis and Russell himself, would admit. Valuable as symbolic logic undoubtedly is, the ultimate concepts of logic and the theory of knowledge can be stated without it; and it would be a needless loss if students of philosophy were to turn away from thinkers like Bradley and McTaggart because they wrote entirely in English.

Though Bradley never appeared in public, he took his duties to the college seriously, and attended fellows' meetings faithfully. In his later years he was by far the most distinguished figure in the college, and his presence was sometimes intimidating to the younger fellows. Their relations with him were not eased by his increasing deafness; I was told that when a motion was made, he would on occasion rise from his place, go round the table, cup his ear intently above its proposer, then resume his place and present a formidable series of crisp arguments why it should be rejected. His critical powers did not always have a constructive result. I was told, I think by an Oxford teacher of aesthetics, that A. C. Bradley, the distinguished author of *Shakespearean Tragedy,* wrote a book on aesthetics and took it to his elder brother for advice. The advice was pointed, as always: "Burn it, Andrew, burn it"; and the book did not see the light. To be sure, Bradley's critical powers were exercised on no one more unsparingly than on himself.

Writing seems to have become more difficult for him with the years. Garrod told me that if the fellows commissioned him to do so simple a task as to redraft the library rules, it cost him a struggle, since he insisted on complete clarity and no unnecessary word. Perhaps the one philosopher in Oxford who was not in awe of him was Schiller, who lived just over the wall from him in Corpus, and, like Bradley, was a gifted writer. The exchanges between these two make an amusing study in invective. Schiller loved nothing better than to shoot arrows, artfully sharpened, over the wall in Bradley's direction. Bradley would ignore them for a time like an old lion pestered by gnats, then rouse himself and reply with a shattering roar. It was, after all, a rather unedifying spectacle, reminding one of the vendetta between Housman and the German Latinists.

Beneath his bristling surface, Bradley had much of the romantic in him. His rare little book, *Aphorisms,* makes it clear that he had a warm heart and knew what it was to be in love. Many persons have wondered who the mysterious 'E-H-' was to whom *Appearance and Reality* was dedicated. She was in fact a French woman, married to an American engineer who seems not to have minded the attachment to his wife of an eminent foreign philosopher. She could not follow the difficult dialectics of the book that had been laid at her feet, and asked Bradley to explain it to her. He did so in a carefully written précis of its argument. This she duly read, and then, according to report, having no further use for it, burned it. How Oxford students would have liked to get their hands on that little sketch! Many years later, at Bradley's funeral, there appeared an unknown lady, dressed and veiled in black, who disappeared as quietly as she had come. It was E-H-, arrived from France for a last salute to a friend whose affection, if not his greatness, she could understand.

Oxford Dons

Though the influence of Bradley was strong throughout my days at Oxford, it was modified by that of others, of whom I remember particularly Webb and Rashdall. C. C. J. Webb was for a time my tutor. I had had to fix on a subject for my thesis, and with thoughts of a career in the church still floating in my mind, I decided to attempt a subject that was fascinating, even though beyond me. It was the influence upon each other of the idea of man and the idea of God since Augustine. Joachim realized that he was not the adviser for this sort of enterprise, and sent me to Webb at Magdalen. In getting underway with the thesis, I wrote several long essays for Webb and he gave me the benefit of patient and acute criticism; I could not have had a more competent adviser. He later became a Gifford lecturer and the first holder of a new chair at Oxford in the philosophy of religion. Unfortunately my work with him was cut short by the war, and when I returned after a four years' absence, my interest had changed its direction. But I have always thought of him gratefully, and was touched, when in 1953 I gave a lecture at the British Academy, to see his friendly face in the front row. Though about ninety years old, he had come up from his home in Aylesbury to greet a pupil of nearly forty years before.

Another of the teachers whom I listened to with profit was Hastings Rashdall, who lectured on "Idealism and Its Critics" to large audiences in the New College dining hall. I well remember his ruddy face and his black-gowned stocky figure as he laid down the law to us on chilly mornings while a big fire blazed on the hearth and students' pens raced across their notebooks. He was particularly popular with students preparing for examinations, for he had a way of laying out the case in numbered arguments that was a very present help in time of trouble. He had no use for Bradley's absolutism, which, with due deference, he attacked in print; his own idealism was rather of the Berkeleian variety, and he used it much as Berkeley did for a sturdy defense of theism. Shortly after I heard him, he left Oxford to become canon of Hereford and later dean of Carlisle. Both in the church and in the philosophic community he has been less honored than he deserves. He was one of the best minds in the Church of England, but his orthodoxy was suspect to heads of the hierarchy; he did not believe, for example, in an omnipotent Deity. And his ethics was so closely bound up with his religion and his metaphysics as to raise the eyebrows of later Oxford moralists. Furthermore, he scattered his energies widely, like a scholar of the Renaissance, producing three works, all masterly, in three different fields, so that most of those who read him probably knew him on one side only. His *History of the Mediaeval Universities*, in three volumes, is the standard work in its field; his Bampton Lectures on *The Atonement* raised the level of British theology; and his two-volume *Theory of Good and Evil,* whose position is essentially the same as Moore's in *Principia Ethica,* is wider in its range than Moore's, and richer in its practical wisdom, though admittedly less acute. For many years I used it in a seminar at Swarthmore, along with a printed syllabus of my own, with what I thought were happy results.

Rashdall was not free from the little infirmities that are at once amusing and endearing to the colleagues of a distinguished man. He was a dogmatic mind, confident in the demonstrative character of his own case. A. D. Lindsay told me that he had been a member of a small group that met regularly for discussion in Rashdall's rooms, with Rashdall himself in the chair. In opening each meeting, the chairman would summarize the results of the previous discussion, and the members gradually learned that the upshot of each discussion was the chairman's own conclusion. The orderliness of mind so appreciated by the students generated some legends about him. Rashdall was married late to a lady much younger than himself. Someone reported seeing the two of them emerging on the Cowley Road from a walk across the fields, and Rashdall's patient voice could be heard saying, "Now thirteenthly, my dear. . . ." It is sad to think that as a philosopher he is now little read, for his books are full of solid and profitable thought.

There were other philosophers of note then lecturing in Oxford. During my first year, Cook Wilson was still the Wykeham Professor of Logic, delivering some of the lectures published in *Statement and Inference;* but Joachim presumably did not think me ready for him, and as he died shortly afterward, I missed him altogether. I heard A. L. Smith, Master of Balliol, and Walter Moberly, afterward Principal of the University of Birmingham, on political philosophy, H. J. Paton, later Whyte's Professor but then a young don in military uniform, on aesthetics, and E. F. Carritt on the philosophy of history.

Of J. A. Smith, the Waynflete Professor of Metaphysics, I saw a good deal, for I attended assiduously the weekly conferences he held in his rooms at Magdalen. I can still see him clearly in memory, looking at me benignly through gold-rimmed spectacles, his snow-white hair parted in the middle. Unfortunately he is an example of how quickly reputations can fade. Few remember him now, but for a time early in the century he was the most respected philosophy don in Oxford. Though he was a Crocean, not a Bradleian, idealist, he was a great friend of Joachim's, and I have a prized photograph of the two of them, in characteristic attitudes, on a walk along the Isis. Smith was an excellent Greek scholar and one of the editors of the Oxford *Aristotle.* Indeed he had a remarkable gift for languages generally; finding himself ill one weekend in Rome, but curious as to what Croce was saying, he read an Italian grammar on Sunday and was reading Croce by the end of the week. He was so resourceful a mind that we students used to think up especially difficult problems to put to him at his conferences; I cannot recall that we ever caught him out. When he came to America, he was a guest for a few days at our house in Swarthmore (which happened to be the house where Benjamin West was born); it was a delight to have him sit in at one of my seminars and deal with the questions of my students as once he had dealt with my own. He had been one of the brilliant young Scots who went to Balliol to work with Caird and Jowett. Now he was old and tired; he did not know what to make of America; when he asked for something to read and I said I had some of Scott's novels about, his pleasure was touching. As Oxford's premier professor of philosophy, he made the opening address at the World Congress of Philosophy convened at Oxford in 1929, but it was not an impressive performance, and many perhaps wondered how he had reached the eminence he obviously held. The fact was, I think, that though he was a man of outstanding abilities he did not know how to organize them fruitfully; he needed a wife to see that he cashed his paychecks instead of using them as bookmarks, and that he gave himself time for writing. He published virtually nothing, with the result that when he died the riches of his thought and learning vanished completely.

Philosophers were not the only people I listened to in Oxford. Bernard Shaw appeared there and administered some of his verbal shocks to a packed audience in the Examination Schools. Gilbert Chesterton rolled in and treated us to an evening of his fireworks of wit and paradox. His friend Hilaire Belloc came also and gave an address of which I can remember nothing except the tremendous booming voice in which it was delivered. In this respect, however, Belloc was outdone by Canon Scott Holland, who introduced John R. Mott one evening in the Balliol dining hall. Holland had for many years been a canon in that cave of the winds, St. Paul's, where it is difficult for anyone to make himself heard; and his voice, as he called the meeting to order, came like a crack of thunder out of a clear sky. I heard Baron von Hügel, the Catholic scholar, talking about mysticism. I heard C. W. C. Oman, professor of modern history, who had many years before been secretary of the Oxford Society for Psychical Research and who told us how he had investigated the accompaniment of two young women on the road to Summertown by a troop of eighteenth-century ghosts; the problem was never solved to his satisfaction. Being myself the secretary of one or two undergraduate societies, I had the business of securing papers for them. I recall approaching G. D. H. Cole with some diffidence for a paper, and was pleased to get an instant acceptance; Cole turned out essays, reviews, detective novels, and treatises on political science in an incessant stream, and to address a student society was almost a relaxation for him.

Among the persons I heard in Oxford or London were three of the most remarkable women of the time. Annie Besant, leader of the theosophical movement, was in England on a visit from her Indian headquarters, and after hearing her I could understand something of her strange hold on her followers. Emmeline Pankhurst, the women's suffrage leader, proved to be far from the firebrand she was sometimes reputed to be; when I heard her, she was a model of dignity, grace, and sense. And no one who heard Maude Royden in those days was likely to agree with Dr. Johnson in his estimate of women preachers.

Still with the possibility of the ministry in my head, I used to go about on London vacations sampling incumbents of the city pulpits. R. J. Campbell of the City Temple was a favorite; but during the war he dismayed his admirers by suddenly recanting the New Theology of which he was a leader, urging the destruction of his books, and going over to the Church of England. I had a talk with him once in his City Temple study, in which he gave me wise and kind advice. Dean Inge was one of my favorites. He had been invited by Asquith to the Deanery of St. Paul's from a professorship at Cambridge in the deliberate attempt to keep St. Paul's one of the literary centers of Britain. It has been served by a long series of distinguished minds reaching from the scholar John Colet and the poet John Donne to the historian R. W. Church; among its philosophers have been H. L. Mansel, whose position was close to Kierkegaard's but far more lucidly stated; W. R. Inge himself, a neoplatonist and an authority on Plotinus; and W. R. Matthews. I have twenty of Dean Inge's books on my shelves. Bernard Shaw once remarked of him that if one wanted the best prose in England, one would find it in St. Paul's.

Germany

I was resolved to see something of France and Germany as well as England, so in the Christmas vacation of 1913 I set out for the country that I thought would mean most to me philosophically, Germany. The Rhodes stipend was £300 a year, which in those days enabled one to live comfortably in England, and, with due economy, to travel on the continent. I headed for Dresden, where I went to ten operas in rapid succession, sat with the appropriate rapture before the Sistine Madonna, and sipped cocoa with whipped cream in restaurants. I was impressed by what music meant to even humble people in Dresden. Workingmen would come early and climb to the gallery of the opera house with a score in one hand and a package of blood sausages in the other; they would follow the music eagerly with the score open on their knees, hissing angrily at any unnecessary noise. After a few weeks of Dresden I went on to Berlin, where I hoped to hear Friedrich Paulsen lecture, for I greatly admired his *Introduction to Philosophy*. But when I inquired at the porter's office of the main university building where Paulsen was lecturing, the sad reply was, "Ach, er ist tot, er ist tot."

The next summer I went back to Germany, taking the idyllic boat trip up the Rhine past Cologne to Heidelberg. I stayed three weeks in that charming old town, working at German and philosophy, walking along the Philosophenweg, where Hegel had walked a century before, and seeing a little of the university life that was just closing down for the summer. Hearing that a Mensur, or student's duel, was scheduled for a certain time, and that the public was excluded, I climbed on the roof of an outhouse and watched the performance through a window. It was not a very exciting affair, the antagonists beating away at each other's masked heads in ritualistic fashion until one of them drew blood. I do not know whether this sort of thing still goes on; I hope not. More memorable was the chance to hear one of the last lectures of the noted historian of philosophy, Wilhelm Windelband. I went to the hall at the appointed time, forgetting that German lectures began a quarter of an hour late, but was well rewarded when the great old scholar, then stooped, lame, and sallow faced, came limping down the aisle to the rostrum. He sat in a chair, and lectured with fluency and animation. I also managed a visit to Leipzig to hear Wilhelm Wundt, who was a striking contrast to Windelband. Though he was eighty-one years old, he was tall, erect, and vigorous, and gave his lecture with ease and effectiveness to the stamping applause of his students. Wundt's learning and productiveness, reminding one of Lotze's, would be hard to parallel among present-day philosophers. I heard that an American student of his in psychology, James McKeen Cattell, gave him a typewriter in gratitude for help received, whereupon Wundt's river of production swelled to a Mississippi flood.

In early July of 1914 I left Heidelberg for Göttingen. The university there was not in session, and I stayed quietly in a pension and worked away at the language. As July wore on, the reports in the German newspapers became more and more ominous. The Austrian Archduke Franz Ferdinand had been assassinated at Sarajevo on June 28. In consequence Austria was making threatening demands on Serbia, and Russia was in turn making threatening gestures against Austria. The position of Britain was in doubt. Excitement in Germany ran high, since it was clear that if Russia moved openly against Austria Germany would come to Austria's support. The German newspapers reflected the popular fear and contempt of the Russians; the Czar was believed to have malevolent designs against Germany; Russian spies were supposed to be everywhere and to be making for the borders. "*Unser Kaiser*" was a great, wise, and fearless man who would know what to do. What was one to believe? It was hard to resist the nearly unanimous sentiment of the Germans that they were threatened by conspiring enemies, but I knew on August 4 when Britain came into the war that I had not been getting the full story. Many attempts have been made to document a case against Britain and in favor of Germany, and documentary study is of course important. But public sentiment is also important. I had seen enough of England to know that it did not expect a war, that it was unprepared for it, that it hated and dreaded the war. I had seen enough of Germany to feel its intense nationalism, its strange misunderstanding of "perfidious Albion," its admiration of the military type, and its readiness to march anywhere at the call of its impulsive and not very intelligent Kaiser. I suppose Oxford had done its work on me. At any rate, I felt sure that when such men as Asquith and Grey were charged with aggression against legions who were already slashing their way through neutral Belgium, the picture was out of focus.

Passports in those days were regarded as unnecessary, and the war caught me in Germany without one. At Hanover I was issued a temporary passport by the American consul, Mr. Michelson, son of the famous scientist of the Michelson-Morley experiment. But it was nearly a month before I was able to get out of Germany by way of a refugee train going from Berlin via Hanover to Rotterdam. That month in Göttingen was anxious and unpleasant. My accent was English enough to arouse questions, and after Britain entered the war, the banks would not exchange British money. It was an immense relief to get back to England again, where the issues of the war could be freely discussed, and where John Morley and Bertrand Russell were publicly opposing it. I felt sorry for the young Englishmen I saw drilling with broomsticks in London squares, and wondered how they could stand up to the disciplined phalanxes on the other side.

My English friends at Oxford had signed up for military service; most of them gained commissions; and since, when they went into action in the early days of the war, they were wearing their Sam Browne belts, with leather straps aslant over their shoulders, they made easy marks for German sharpshooters and were cut down in sickening numbers. H. J. Paton later remarked to me that if there had been a certain poverty in British philosophy in the last half-century it was largely due to Britain's loss in war of the best men of two generations.

I went back to Oxford, but it was not the same. Most of the students had vanished into the armed services. Cook Wilson, the logician, was organizing and drilling a bicycle corps, though the value of such an outfit in modern war was not very clear. Classes consisted largely of foreigners and the physically unfit. Undergraduate activities faded away. I competed for the Newdigate prize in poetry only to learn that it had been suspended till peace returned. America was not to enter the war for another two-and-a-half years, but the American students were increasingly embarrassed to be seen cycling through the streets to the tennis courts in white flannels. The American Club met on Saturday nights, and our well-liked ambassador, Walter Hines Page, came down from London to address us and answer our anxious questions. I was in doubt what to do. It was possible to go on at Oxford, but no longer in good heart, nor did I want to go home and act as if the war did not exist.

Mesopotamia

I ended by signing up with the British Army Y.M.C.A. This involved a sharp break with everything I had been and done, for it soon turned out that I was to be sent to India. My good friend Oliver Carmichael signed up at the same time. Carmichael was a congenial traveling companion with whom I had gone down the Rhine a year earlier, and though I saw little of him in later years, I followed with pleasure his notable career as chancellor of Vanderbilt University, president of the University of Alabama, and head of the Carnegie Foundation. In August 1915 we embarked on the P. & O. steamer *Kaiser-i-Hind* for Bombay. It was a three-week voyage. My chief reading en route was Mill's *Political Economy,* a useful book for a long voyage, though the rolling of the top-heavy ship sometimes left me with no stomach for this or anything else. Through the Mediterranean the ship mounted a gun on the stern in case submarines appeared; fortunately none did. We went through Suez and found the Red Sea in August an oven; we slept and sweated on deck, pitying the stokers down below. The Indian Ocean stays in my memory for a wonderful night in which the sea turned white from a vast mass of microorganisms floating on the surface under a bright moon and a starlit sky.

We awoke one morning to find ourselves anchored off Bombay. At once I had a sense of being in another world. At first it was superficial only; the waving palms, the minarets and onion-domed mosques, the sacred cows wandering in the streets, the dark faces under white turbans, all seemed like something out of the *Arabian Nights.* But even when I had grown familiar with these scenes and made many Indian friends, the sense of the remoteness of India never left me. At nearly every point Indian culture and the Indian consciousness are different from those of the West—sometimes for the better, sometimes for the worse, but always different. Indians feel differently about women, about art and architecture and music, about animals and their use for food, about work, manual and intellectual, about social classes, about political privileges and responsibilities, indeed about virtually everything except the multiplication table. Indian religion, from the cruelties of Kali-worship to the noble serenity of Buddha, is strange to Western minds, and the tension between Hindu and Moslem is unintelligible to any of us except perhaps the extremer sectarians of Ulster. I came to feel that even philosophy, ideally the same the world over, meant something different to the Indian mind, to which Western analysis often seems like the chopping of straw, while Indian philosophy seems to the Westerner like a blend of dialectic with mysticism. There are thinkers like Radhakrishnan—whom I came to know in Oxford, though not as well as I could wish—who have managed to bridge the gulf, but they are very rare indeed.

My first stay in India lasted only a week. Carmichael and I were sent up into the hills to Poona to get our land legs again; then we were interviewed in

Bombay by E. C. Carter, general secretary of the Indian Y.M.C.A. and later
to hold the same office in France. Carter sent Carmichael to East Africa and
me to Mesopotamia. So I set out on another week of traveling, first by a
coastal steamer to Karachi, then by a troopship carrying Australian soldiers
up the Persian Gulf. I slept on deck with the troops. We were landed at Basra,
seventy-five miles up the Shatt-el-Arab, the great river that carries the united
Tigris and Euphrates to the sea. Basra was a base camp for the British Ex-
peditionary Force that was trying to break the hold of Turkey, then a German ally, on the region now called Iraq, which formed a natural pathway for
the Germans to India.

With an assistant, I was put in charge of the Y.M.C.A. activities in this
base camp, our job being to do anything that civilians could to keep up the
morale of the troops. We had an old Pathé moving-picture machine that was
operated by turning a crank, and used to give shows with a screen made of a
bedsheet hung between palm trees. The film invariably broke, and had to be
rapidly mended to the groans of the audience sitting on the ground. We ran a
canteen where tea, coffee, and cakes baked by local Arabs could be bought
for a penny or two by way of supplementing the rations. In a modest reading
room in a tent a few books and magazines were on display. We organized occasional shows in which volunteers put on assorted acts. We visited hospital
wards with sweets and cigarettes—much in demand and not then frowned
on—and wrote letters and cards for men who could not manage it themselves.
Sometimes we held religious services at which, with no great confidence or
effect, I sermonized. We had a phonograph with a supply of popular records.
Once I was entertaining a contingent of Indian lascars with this phonograph.
During a number of Western records the Indians chattered away without
attention to the music. Then I put on a Hindustani song; immediately the
chatter stopped and they were all attention. I remarked to a friend on this example of our appreciating only the music that we are familiar with. On that
he put me right. "You didn't know that the records you were playing were
obscene?"

Generally we wore khaki shirts and shorts, sufficiently different from the
soldiers' to be fairly easily distinguished. Once this difference got me into
trouble. On a Sunday evening at Basra, I hired an Arab boatman to take me
across the Shatt-el-Arab, a half mile or so wide, so that I could speak to a
meeting of enlisted men at a camp some distance from the river on the other
side. The meeting over, I started walking back across the dark plain to the
river. A pair of headlights coming toward me proved to be a car carrying a
British captain and some Sikh soldiers. It passed me and halted, and soon I
was halted myself by a couple of turbaned Sikhs coming after me with
bayonets fixed. They escorted me back to the camp and put me in the
guardhouse. The captain thought he had picked up a spy or other suspicious
character. By chance the corporal in charge of the guardhouse that night was

an American adventurer from New Orleans whom I had met before; he was able, to the captain's disgust, to identify me as the harmless creature from Basra that I claimed to be.

After four months at Basra—September 1915 to January 1916—I was moved a hundred miles up the Tigris to Amara for four months of the same kind of work. Amara was roughly a hundred miles south of Kut-el-Amara, a black name in British military history. In the early days of the campaign, the British general, Sir Charles Townsend, a dashing figure much admired by his men, had led a rapid advance up the river, taking the Turks by surprise through his sheer audacity. He had taken Amara, so I was told, by mere bluff, steaming into the middle of the town in a flatboat accompanied by a group of his officers, and demanding instant surrender as the condition of sparing the town from destruction. The Turkish commander, assuming that Townsend would not take such a risk without a large force behind him, did surrender. Townsend swept on to Ctesiphon, not far below his goal of Baghdad. But there nemesis caught up with him. The Turks forced him back to Kut-el-Amara, and, surrounding him there, cut off his retreat down the Tigris, and held him and his troops beleaguered till they were eating rats to stay alive. The British troops to the south of him were making desperate efforts to relieve him and to force a passage up the river with supplies. I got up the river far enough to see the flash of the relieving force's guns, and came back to Amara on a flatboat whose deck was covered with dead and wounded. Alongside us was a scow full of Turkish prisoners.

All efforts to relieve Townsend failed, and on April 29, 1916, he surrendered. In the wards at Amara I saw some of the costs of his audacity. There were more wounded than could be properly cared for, and some of the sights and sounds of those days were burnt into my memory; unconscious men with the flies swarming in the corners of their eyes, a sergeant wounded in the head, with his hands tied so that he could not tear off the bandages in his delirium, the shriek in the night of some young man who suddenly realized that life was over for him. I was never wounded or sick myself during those months, or even in genuine danger. But I saw enough of the seamy side of war to hate it and to detest all glorification of it. I am not a pacifist. When a Hitler turns himself loose on the world, I am not clear that there is any acceptable alternative to halting him by force. But as a rationalist, I do not think that there is any sort of dispute that honest men would find beyond adjudication by reason, and I look with distrust both on the cynics who call war inevitable and on the philosophers who intone that "reason is and must be the slave of the passions."

Life in Mesopotamia in the fall and winter of 1915–16 was naturally grim, but I had been warned to take certain precautions that proved useful.

The water I drank was purple with potassium permanganate, and I never swam in the river, as the Indian soldiers could do without ill results. In the fall I slept on the roof of a mud-brick house, first shaking from my blanket the brown film of dust that came in from the desert. In winter I lived in a hut sided with reed matting, which was comfortable enough, though it was not comfortable to be nipped in the mouth at night by some wandering rat. The surrounding Arabs were not so much politically hostile—they were no friends of the Turks—as unscrupulous and covetous; they were adept at slipping a hand under the side of a tent at night and vanishing into the desert with a soldier's gun. This became so common that when a thief was caught at Amara, the commander there had a scaffold built across the river in full view of the town, where the culprit was hanged as a warning to all. The attitude of the Arabs, natural enough perhaps, made any wandering alone imprudent, and though Ur of the Chaldees, the birthplace of Abraham, was not many miles from Basra, I was never able to visit it.

India

In the late spring of 1916 I went back to India. The student secretary of the Y.M.C.A. in Bombay was an Englishman who wanted war-connected service; he took my place in Mesopotamia, and I took his in Bombay. In June I was given charge of a hostel in the Girgaum district of the city, housing some fifty young men, most of them students at the university. Here again my assignment was to make myself useful in as many ways as I could, this time to students rather than to soldiers. These students were a very diverse group. They came from all over India; among them were Muslims, Christians, and Hindus of various castes; they spoke Gujarati, Marathi, Tamil, and Telugu, and though they could all manage some Hindi, English was the language of their instruction and interchange. For the most part, they were students at Wilson College, a nearby branch of the university, and the head of that college, Dr. Mackichan, was the chairman of my board of trustees.

This new post was more congenial than the one in Mesopotamia. I was again mixing with college students, and did some tutoring in logic and English literature. Being an American rather than an Englishman gave me a certain advantage with the students. I was not a member of the British hierarchy that governed them, so I was less formidable, and they could talk with me more freely. They were kind and cooperative friends whom I remember gratefully, particularly an Indian Christian named Fletcher, who was my assistant secretary. I had to keep the accounts of the hostel, see that the rooms were kept in repair, arrange for lectures and discussion groups, and meet occasionally with the trustees to give a report and receive advice. I was supposed also to keep an eye on the students' health, which, in the Bombay climate, required exercise. I organized and played on a cricket team, though I had never played the game before, and no doubt made a sorry sight to a decent cricketer. I think my trustees and students regarded my work as successful, but on looking back, I can see that I was not made to be an administrator, and that to be truly good in such an office demands more boldness, confidence, and ease with others than I have ever been able to acquire.

Life in Bombay was of course far less primitive than life on the Tigris. Indeed it seemed to me luxurious. I had an apartment of my own in the hostel, where I was able to sleep under a mosquito net and an electric fan. I had $125 a month to cover expenses, which, at the miserable wages of Indian labor in those days, supported a cook and an orderly and covered my own food and clothes. For a Westerner the monsoon season in July and August was debilitating; the combination of heat and moisture, which makes books moulder away, does it also to human beings; and malaria-bearing mosquitoes were then a constant danger. Once I returned from a business trip to Calcutta to find with horror that a young man in my hostel had just died of what was believed to be the plague. He was not one of my students but a student's guest, who had contracted the disease elsewhere. After frantically taking medical advice, I kept the hostel open without ill results.

My work in Mesopotamia had been under the direction of the Y.M.C.A. of India, which saw an opportunity to use me in raising much-needed funds for the continuation of this work. So I was sent on speaking trips to various parts of India, and since work with the troops was regarded as a national service, the Y.M.C.A. found it easy to get government officials to take the chair at its meetings. Our meeting in Calcutta was presided over by Lord Ronaldshay, governor of Bengal; in the United Provinces by the governor, Lord Meston; and in Simla by Lord Chelmsford, the viceroy. At this last meeting I had as a fellow speaker a British general from Mesopotamia who said that in passing the Garden of Eden he had hitched his boat to the tree of knowledge of good and evil. But Chelmsford was grim and tense; he was himself a British military officer, and things had not been going well in the campaign on the Tigris.

On these trips I had many memorable glimpses into the past and present life of this fascinating subcontinent. At Simla I climbed the small mountain sacred to the monkey god Hanuman, which has a temple dedicated to him on its summit. On the way down I had a genuine fright when a number of large monkeys accompanied me on both sides of the path, chattering angrily; I pretended a nonchalance that I was far from feeling, and they dropped back after a time. I saw the old forts of the moguls at Agra, and the Taj Mahal, which, in spite of all its exploitation on picture cards, is surely the most beautiful memorial ever erected by one human being to the memory of another. In the hills above Bombay I saw a kind of cathedral, not built, but carved out of solid rock, and nearby some enormous caves, with ribbed ceilings, made many centuries ago by Buddhist monks, but now inhabited by thousands of bats which filled the air with a whirring mass at a stranger's approach. South India I never saw except for a brief trip to Bangalore.

The guest room in my hostel at Bombay was occupied for some months by the distinguished Greek scholar of the University of Manchester, James Hope Moulton. Moulton was making a study of Zoroastrianism, the religion of the large and prosperous colony of Parsees in Bombay. Though some forty years my senior, he was a delightful companion. It seemed strange to me that he could combine with his sophisticated New Testament scholarship an almost fundamentalist religious belief; but when intelligence and an affectionate disposition are permeated, as they were in his case, by Christian humility and piety, the product, though it would disdain aiming at any such end, is likely to have much charm. Moulton made fun of my interest in logic, but he helped me to see that the thinking or scholarship that refuses to give any account of itself in terms of the enrichment of human life is a pretty expensive luxury. He had just lost his son in the war, and before I left Bombay it was my melancholy task to write his own obituary. On his way home Moulton's ship was torpedoed in the Mediterranean, and after gallant work at the oars of a lifeboat he succumbed on reaching land.

To my permanent loss, I was too busy with administrative work to have much time for Indian philosophy, religion, art, or politics; and, at least on the political side, India has changed so much in the last quarter century that impressions drawn from before that time are of doubtful relevance now. Still, the basic problems of India are perennial ones. The greatest of them is growing more serious daily—too many people. The problem is complicated by the fact that the bulk of the people are not concentrated in cities, as in our own country, but scattered in thousands of villages, and are therefore harder to reach with help or instruction. India was swept by a surge of hope when she was given her freedom after the war, and her experiment in democracy, the most massive ever made, deserves the sympathy and aid of democrats everywhere. But even fifty years ago the sheer inertia of that vast mass of hundreds of millions of people aroused despair, and the Indian population is growing by the equivalent of the total population of Australia every year. Great advances have been made in health, but the tragic fact is that every fall in the mortality rate makes this major problem more serious. And overpopulation affects morale. In spite of the contrast often drawn between the "spirituality" of India and the "materialism" of the West, I felt in the moral atmosphere a resignation that was almost depression, a sense of the hopelessness of individual effort and the unimportance of the individual life. It was rooted, I think, in the powerlessness of any one person among these teeming and multiplying millions. Is not the same feeling beginning to appear in America?

The faiths of India did not seem to me to help. They are religions of resignation rather than of aspiration. The caste system received a religious blessing from Hinduism, and hence is far more difficult to uproot than if it were a merely social or economic stratification. Even Buddhism is a religion of pessimism, considering life as chiefly suffering, from which the best hope of escape is through the extinction of personal life in Nirvana. The doctrine of Maya, that all the scenes and events of ordinary life are illusion, tends rather toward a retreat into quietism than toward an effort to make things better. Indian mysticism, like much of the mysticism of the West, is a means of escape from a hard and painful present. What seems to me more needed in India is a gospel of battle with the present. The "commercial" West could certainly do with more of the contemplative spirit of the East, but even in the interest of better contemplation, India needs the science and expertise of the West.

Working with university students aroused my interest in the Indian educational system. It was a British creation, following lines laid down by Macaulay in 1835. There were to be three educational summits, one at each apex of the Indian triangle, in the form of three great universities at Calcutta, Bombay, and Madras, and from these summits streams of enlightenment were to flow down to the common people. The plan did not work out quite as anticipated. University students were more interested in securing positions in the governing hierarchy than in returning to their villages and opening schools, and the gulf between the educated few and the illiterate many remained as broad as ever. How much this has changed after the achievement of independence I do not know. But the success of the new democracy seems to turn, as in other countries, on the diffusion of education, and here India's problem is unique. To find subsidies, schools, and teachers for its thousands of scattered villages presents a difficult task even to the highest statesmanship.

In education and in other areas, India's attitude toward Britain was and remains ambivalent. Though "colonialism" was not, in the early 1900s, the dirty word it has since become, there was much resentment against the white and alien masters. This was wholly natural; the British position in India was an anomaly approaching absurdity. Here was a subcontinent of more than three hundred million people whose supreme decisions were made for them by emissaries from an island on the other side of the world—an island, the Indians would add, whose inhabitants were still painting themselves with woad when India had already produced the religion of Buddha, the morality of the *Baghavad Gita,* and the philosophic system of Sankara. All India looked forward to the day when the yoke would be thrown off. Mr. Attlee's government showed rare statesmanship in anticipating the day by removing the yoke voluntarily. His task was eased by the genius of Gandhi, who in his curious love-hate relation with the British was typical of much Indian feeling. The large-minded withdrawal won the respect and, strangely enough, the loyalty of India. It remained by choice within the Commonwealth; it adopted the British type of parliamentary government; its courts took over British conceptions of justice; English remained the chief language of its universities; and it still sends many of its most promising youths, as it did in Nehru's day, to Britain for education. Britain extracted many dubious fortunes from India, but in the minds of more Indians than would probably say so, the imports of British ideas went far toward balancing the exports of Indian wealth.

India is a fascinating place for the reflective visitor. Cut off by the Himalayas and wide seas from any intimacy with other peoples, it has developed a culture that is unique. And since, until modern times, communication among its own provinces was difficult, it developed a heterogeneous set of cultures and languages within itself. In spite of the heroic efforts of Gandhi to keep the country together, it broke in two almost as soon as it gained independence, and strains between the two countries are still intense. One great difficulty, even for the India that remains, is the lack of a common language; and shortly after independence, a determined attack on this problem was made through legislation. There were two candidates for the position of common language, Hindustani and English. Seldom has a government faced an issue that presented alternatives of such consequence. The Indian government hesitated; either choice would impose on millions of people a language that was unfamiliar. The decision was for Hindustani; under the circumstances it would have been unrealistic to expect anything else. But it is tempting to speculate on what might have been. Suppose that English, already the common language of the universities, had become the standard language of the subcontinent. Not only would the future science and scholarship of India have been open to the West, but the language now most widely current in the world, with its rich freight of science, philosophy, and literature, would have been opened to the common man in India. East and West would, in many senses, have spoken each other's language. There would of course have been losses; India would have been further removed from her own past, though much of that past, embalmed in Sanskrit, has already become remote. I do not question that plurality of cultures is a good thing for mankind. But plurality of languages is an almost unmitigated curse, raising barriers at every point against understanding and sympathy. Any retreat for nationalistic reasons from community of language seems to me self-defeating. The attempt of the Irish nationalists to reinstate Gaelic as the common tongue was a move toward isolation from the modern world; and much as I admire the achievements of Israel, I can only think that its return to ancient Hebrew as its common tongue will entail more loss than gain.

The future of India is heavily veiled. Democracy on its scale and with its ratio of literacy has never before been attempted, and when poverty is so widespread, and so many feel that they have nothing to lose, the appeal to political extremism is bound to be strong. The revolutions proposed by extremists are of course always "liberations," though they usually end in dictatorships. Since India, rendered insecure by the attitude of China and Pakistan, is in need of friends, she has been clasping the proffered hand of Russia. It seems to me possible that, driven to desperation by her problems, she will take the Communist direction, and if she does, I do not think it would be incumbent on us to charge her with a self-evident mistake. "All forms of government are relative in their value," and it may be that at this point of her history, democracy of the Western type is not the best suited to her needs. For her poverty-stricken millions, a small increase in security may mean more than freedom of thought and speech, and a return to some imperial Asoka might produce more unity than a common parliament. The trouble is, of course, that the Asoka kind of dictatorship is not the most probable kind.

Return from the East

My stay in India ended in June 1917. The United States had entered the war two months before, and I was ready to go home. My Indian students, among whom I had many friends, gave me a set of books, with their names inscribed in them, and the volumes still have a proud place on my shelves. The Mediterranean route home had been closed by submarines, so I set out on the long voyage around Ceylon, across the Indian Ocean to Singapore, thence to China and Japan and across the Pacific. I traveled in the British India steamer *Malta* as far as Hong Kong, then, surmising correctly that this might be my last chance to see something of the Far East, made a long inland journey that took me to Canton, Shanghai, Peking, Mukden, and Seoul, and then in Japan to Kobe, Osaka, Tokyo, and Yokohama. In China I felt half way home, as measured not in miles but in moral atmosphere. China, like India, was poor, but the poverty seemed to be lightened by more of humor, hope, and energy; perhaps the sunny practicality of Confucius had something to do with it, in contrast to the resignation of the Indian religions. In any case I felt, after only a week or two in China, somewhat as Russell and Dewey did, who made longer visits a few years later and came back with much praise and affection for the Chinese. At Canton I saw the rows of brick cells where medieval aspirants to government posts went through their terrific examinations. At Shanghai I attended a Chinese opera with eager interest, though with only the dimmest idea of what was going on. At Peking, still a

Y.M.C.A. secretary and with the central building of the Association as my base, I went about in a rickshaw gaping at the imperial palace and the other standard sights of that ancient city. Then, wanting to get off the beaten path, and traveling for economy's sake with crowds of peasants, I went north as far as Mukden, down through Korea, and then by boat across the straits to Japan.

I had only a week or so in Japan, and my memories of that beautiful country are too blurred to be worth recording. I had no passage arranged across the Pacific, but was fortunate enough to find room on a Dutch steamer that touched at Yokohama on its way from the East Indies to San Francisco. The three-week voyage was broken only at Honolulu, where there was time for a visit to the beach at Waikiki.

During the three-week voyage from Japan to San Francisco I was reading Sidgwick's *Methods of Ethics;* I had picked up in a Bombay bookstore a secondhand copy which had written in it the name of the Walter Raleigh whom I had admired at Oxford and who had spent some time in India in his youth. Though I cannot accept the hedonistic conclusions of Sidgwick's book, I am inclined to agree with Broad that it is the finest work on ethics in English.

When I reached San Francisco, I had too little money left to pay my way to Michigan, which was my own fault entirely. Working as I did for expenses and thinking that the Y.M.C.A. had paid me more than I needed, I had sent back to it from Singapore what I calculated to be the excess, and now it looked as if I might be stranded. A kindly uncle lived in Los Angeles and I went there in search of him, but he was out of town. I then appealed to the Southern Pacific for classification as a missionary. The railroad gallantly acceded, and by eking out its missionary fare with a tightened belt, I reached Bay View as the summer was ending in 1917. My grandmother was still there and my brother came up from Florida to greet me.

I went to a recruiting officer in Petoskey to find where I stood about military service. Though I was physically in good shape, I was told that my near-sightedness without glasses would qualify me only for some form of limited service. Such service was essentially what I had been doing in Mesopotamia, and I decided that if I could not do anything more useful, I would register for the draft, await my call, and get in as much professional training as I could in the meantime. Persistence might have got me into some form of service. But my two years in the East had left no doubt that such interest and competence as I had were in philosophy, and I was panting to get back to it. The draft call did finally come, and I had a year of service in the U. S. Army, chiefly in France, but the call was long enough deferred to allow me an invaluable year at Columbia.

I had returned from the East with an empty purse. But under an insurance policy of my father's, each of his sons had been left $500, and though our grandmother as our guardian might have drawn on this, she had characteristically refused to touch a penny of it, so that my share had grown over the years to $900. This might be stretched far enough by supplementary earnings, I thought, to cover a year of study. But where? In 1917 the leading American philosopher was undoubtedly John Dewey; Royce had died the year before, and James in 1910. Dewey was then at Columbia, so in September of 1917 I set out for New York. Looking around for work, I found a law student, Charles W. McClumpha, who had been struck by polio a year or two earlier, and was ready to pay the rent of a roommate in return for wheeling him to classes and helping him with daily exercises. I became this roommate. McClumpha went on to a successful career as an attorney in Paris, and though our paths have seldom crossed in later years, we have remained firm friends.

Dewey

I looked forward with some excitement to seeing and hearing John Dewey. Those who worked with him will not be surprised to learn that the first impression fell short of expectations. Dewey ambled into the classroom in a relaxed and absent-minded way, sat down in a chair, looked out the window, and began talking in something like a drawl. As he talked, he kept crumpling the single sheet of notepaper he held in his hand. There was little form in his lecturing—no feeling for an audience, no reaching for effect, nothing arresting or quotable; he thought aloud for an hour, and that was the lecture. It was only after the hour was over and the student read his notes that he realized how free from wandering and how argumentatively firm the lecture had been. My first disappointment in Dewey was the more natural because my pattern of philosophizing had been set by Bradley, and there could hardly have been a greater contrast than between Bradley's nervous incisiveness and Dewey's way of plodding fumblingly along, whether in speech or writing.

Nevertheless I came to admire Dewey cordially. He seems to me the most original thinker America has produced. One of his books is called *The Influence of Darwin on Philosophy,* and someone has remarked that this describes Dewey himself. He biologized philosophy. He held that the judgment, the most elementary act of thought, was the adoption of a "plan of action" aimed at surmounting some block to the behavior of the organism; he called his theory "instrumentalism" because he conceived of thought as an *instrument* of organic adjustment. Thought for its own sake, thought of the Platonic type that is purely theoretic and contemplative, he regarded as at best a luxury and at worst a disease in which thinking runs wild, conforming to Santayana's description of the fanatic as one "who redoubles his effort when he has forgotten his aim." This theory of thought as essentially practical Dewey developed into a system of magisterial sweep. The theory appeared in his educational work as a defense of learning by doing, in his ethics as a doctrine of growth as the end, in his philosophy of religion through an interpretation of faith as dedication to long-range ends, in the history of philosophy as a devaluation of the Greek philosophical tradition.

There is a wealth of wise obiter dicta in his writings in all these fields, particularly when he touches on the psychology of thinking. But his thought in all of them has a common root in his pragmatic theory of thought, and that theory I have never been able to accept. Dewey is probably right that thinking originated in the race under the pressure of practical need; man needed to think in order to get food, to keep warm, and to guard himself against enemies; necessity was the mother of invention. Dewey holds that what thought was originally it still is, a device for the prudent ordering of behavior. But the fact that it was, and still is, used for practical purposes should not blind us to the fact that it has an end of its own. That end is knowing. The practical and theoretical ends are quite distinct and easily distinguishable. Columbus's judgment that the earth was round was an instrument to his end of sailing round it; true. But his judgment was not merely that; it was meant as a statement of fact. Its cognitive meaning and its practical intention were not the same, and the truth of the judgment was wholly different from its utility. The judgment worked, to be sure, but it worked because it was already true; it did not become true only when it worked. It is the essence of pragmatism to confuse meaning with intention, and truth with utility or with verification in practice. This criticism seems to be simple and straightforward, and I do not think that any of the three leaders of the pragmatic movement—James, Schiller, and Dewey—ever met it satisfactorily.

Dewey came nearest to doing so, and his defense was ingenious. I remember a meeting of his course in Types of Logical Theory in which this criticism was raised by one of the students, perhaps Irwin Edman, who was a respectful though critical listener. Dewey was stressing the practical aspect of thinking, and though I cannot, after more than half a century, remember the words of the exchange, I well remember its gist. Student: "Do you really think, Mr. Dewey, that when Kant sat down to reflect about the categories, his thought could be called a plan of *action*? Surely Kant himself would say that his interest was purely theoretic. And aren't we bound to accept his own report of what he was doing?" Dewey: "I have often thought that metaphysical thinking is like athletics. The football player may say that his interest is simply and solely in getting the ball beyond that stripe at the end of the field. But this can't be right. If it were, he would get up some dark night and put it there. No, his interest lies in getting it there against competent opposition and in accordance with the rules of the game. Well, Kant was playing a game in which he too was trying to outplay his rivals, but in accordance with the rules of the logical game, by being more subtle, more thorough, more consistent, than any of them. He too was playing for success in the one game in which he was a master, the game of reflective analysis." I was not convinced. But there is enough force in the analogy to make one pause; and it illustrates Dewey's readiness and resourcefulness when students tried to pin him against a wall.

Not that he was ever disingenuous, or played merely for victory himself. He was notoriously objective and gently impersonal in controversy, and his love of truth was transparent. Nevertheless pragmatism is a dangerous creed. If it rests, as I think it does, on a misreading of our aim in thinking, it is bound to use arguments in all sincerity that to nonbelievers must seem irrelevant, and to ascribe motives to others that they will want to disavow. It was the unhappy lot of Schiller, I fear, to be virtually frozen out of Oxford by the reluctance of the other dons to cross swords with him. It seemed to follow from his personalistic pragmatism that, in any controversy, that side was proved right which actually prevailed, i.e. succeeded in getting itself accepted, and that psychological victory was to be a warrant of truth. Philosophers were reluctant to enter the lists with an opponent who so conceived the rules. No such resistance was ever shown, so far as I know, to controversy with James or Dewey, though James did mystify his colleagues in *The Will to Believe* by holding that we had a moral right to believe what we were logically not entitled to believe.

I gave some agitated thought in those days to how one could argue with a pragmatist at all. If two persons are to argue profitably, there must be some common ground to meet on; there must be at least an implicit agreement as to what relevance and truth are to mean. If the two parties differ on so fundamental an issue as the nature of truth, every consideration offered by one of them as true may be rejected by the other as false, and to insist on its truth will be a begging of the question. Indeed the two parties will not be discussing the same issue. If one party says that truth is coherence, he will be saying that this assertion coheres, and the other, in denying it, will only be asserting that it does not work. And no proposition offered in support of either interpretation will bear the same meaning for both. I concluded, and still believe, that the only way to carry conviction in such a debate is to show one's opponent that his profession does not correspond to his practice; for example, though he thinks he means "working" by "truth," he is implicitly assuming it to be something else. This can be shown, I think, to a candid supporter of either James or Dewey. I suspect that neither of them meant, in saying "truth is working," merely that this proposition works; and when they came to the judgment of the past, their contention that its truth lay in its future consequences was in obvious conflict with what they commonly meant.

In the course of my year at Columbia, a middle-aged visitor used to appear at times in Dewey's seminars. He was Albert C. Barnes, the Philadelphia chemist who had discovered argyrol and, through its manufacture and sale, had amassed a substantial fortune. As a result of reading Dewey's *Democracy and Education,* Barnes had become a devotee of its author. His main interest outside his business was in art; and the walls of his house in Philadelphia were covered with Manets and Monets, Matisses and Picassos. How sound he was as a critic I do not know, but he had an almost uncanny prescience of what artists would be in demand ten or twenty years later. He had in mind the founding of a museum or institute of art, in which visitors would be instructed in art appreciation, and he turned to Dewey as a master of education for advice. Dewey encouraged him to write, and the two learned much from each other, as was attested by Barnes's dedication of his book *The Art in Painting* to Dewey and Dewey's dedication of his *Art as Experience* to Barnes.

While attending a course of Dewey's in social philosophy, Barnes suggested that this philosophy might profit by a closer look at fact. He brought to Dewey's attention that there was a large Polish community in Philadelphia which was proving curiously resistant to "Americanization," retaining the mores, the ideas, and the language it had brought from abroad, and forming a sort of cyst in the body politic. Would Dewey care to investigate this on the spot? Yes, very much, Dewey replied; could he bring some of his graduate students with him? Barnes agreed, and proceeded to buy a house for the group on Richmond Street in the middle of the Polish district. Dewey selected as his collaborators Irwin Edman, Frances Bradshaw (who was to become my wife), Anzia Yezierska, later known for her perceptive novels, my brother Paul, who was now also a student at Columbia, and me. As soon as the academic year was over, Dewey and his little flock settled into the house on Richmond Street and began their investigation.

We divided the field. Dewey was to investigate the politics of the community. Miss Bradshaw was to inquire into its education and to supervise household affairs; Miss Yezierska and Edward Ryglewicz (a member of the local community) were to serve as interpreters; I was to study religious attitudes; Edman's assignment has fallen from my memory; and my brother's services were soon dispensed with by Mr. Barnes because of the suspicion that Paul knew too much non-Deweyan economics and sociology to have an open mind. We spent the summer in our researches, and two small books emerged. Dewey's inquiries into Polish politics soon embroiled him in the tangled politics of Poland itself. It was wartime; Russia had gone Communist and the Russian army had collapsed; Poland was in German hands; and the four million Poles in the United States were being rallied to the cause of an independent Poland by Paderewski. Dewey was suspicious of the kind of regime Paderewski was supporting for Poland, and he devoted his report chiefly to an analysis of the character and prospects of the contending Polish factions and to the recommendation of an American policy regarding them. His report was printed by Mr. Barnes and sent to the State Department for study, but how much influence it had, if any, I never learned. The only other report that reached print was my own. Before I completed it, my call came for military service, and I had to write much of it in England in 1919 after returning to civilian life, and from notes and memories now grown cold. I sent the manuscript to Mr. Barnes, who published it as *The Church and the Polish Immigrant*, a book in paper covers. It is not a good book; I had no opportunity to proofread it; and so far as I know, it has not had the slightest influence anywhere.

That summer in Philadelphia meant much, however, to the little band of collaborators. We came to know Dewey better, and to see something of his way of working. He was the most persistently thoughtful person I have known. Thinking had become a habit and a way of life with him, and he paid so little attention to what was going on around him that he could continue his thinking under almost any conditions. His assistant Max Eastman wrote of him: "As a logician Dewey is at his best with one child climbing up his pants leg and another fishing in his inkwell." "By taking an apartment at the corner of Broadway and Fifty-sixth Street, a fourth-floor apartment fronting on both streets, he managed to surround himself with enough noise so that he could get some thinking done."[1] I have seen him, obviously lost in thought, come out of his office door into the middle of the old Butler Library in Philosophy Hall, suddenly look round him, wake up to where he was, and beat a sheepish retreat into his office again.

He was the most unpretentious of men, and was embarrassed to be regarded as a celebrity. In some ways he was all his life a Vermont farmer, endowed with a reflective mind of outsized proportions. Indeed for a time he did have a small farm on Long Island where he kept chickens and raised vegetables, selling his products to the neighbors; and the story is well known of how, as he rose to speak at a woman's club, a wealthy member exclaimed, "Why that looks exactly like our egg-man!" I recall that a Philadelphia minister, who had heard that the eminent philosopher was in his neighborhood, called at our house one afternoon to pay his respects, only to be met by an unlikely bucolic figure in shirt sleeves and suspenders who admitted to the name of Dewey, and during the conversation fell gently asleep in his rocking chair. Dewey was a democrat and without vanity. Mr. Barnes, a bluff and blustery person, with whom he got on splendidly, said that he could talk with Dewey as he would with a barkeep. Dewey was quite ready to call on us for criticism of what he was writing, and since he was reflecting continuously, he poured out articles and books with ease and in a steady stream. When we heard his battered typewriter clattering away of an evening, we could predict that at breakfast there would be another article for the *New Republic* for us to read and criticize.

As a talker Dewey was neither shy nor aggressive. He was ready to talk if he had something to say, but he did not care to make talk, and disliked having to rise to an occasion. In that year 1917–18 the executive officer of the philosophy department, John Coss, arranged a student-faculty exchange of ideas on the teaching of philosophy, which we graduate students attended with eager interest. To wind up the evening's discussion, Coss said something about our good fortune in having with us America's leading authority on the philosophy of education, and called on Professor John Dewey. There was a pause and a hush of expectancy. Dewey remarked that in teaching logic he thought it was a good thing to begin with the study of fallacies—and stopped. The remark was pointed and pertinent, but was that all we were to have? Dewey was not disposed to say more, and when he felt that way, he was not to be moved from the outside. This was not indifference or aloofness; it was of a piece with his curious inability to play up to an audience or an occasion, to act any part not dictated by the state of his thought at the moment. It was bound up with his special kind of integrity, which would not go an inch out of its way to make itself seem important or impressive. Anything in the way of fireworks was to Dewey impossible.

I have wondered at times how it was that in a country where popularity so commonly turns on the freakish, the glamorous, and the theatrical, a homespun philosopher who disdained these things should have achieved so great a name and influence. He had none of the charm of William James; his speech was not moving nor his presence impressive; his prose was without grace or flow or sparkle. Nevertheless he was at the time of his death by far the most influential American philosopher. How is it to be explained? Partly, no doubt, by the astonishing range and volume of his writing. Partly, again, by a technical competence that, despite a certain looseness of language, impressed his peers and sent his name percolating down to thousands who never read a page of his. But many philosophers have been highly productive and highly respected without achieving more than a fraction of Dewey's influence. The ground of this influence was suggested when the University of Paris, in conferring a degree upon him in 1930, called him "the most profound and complete expression of American genius." That must have made him wince, and if it is a little grandiloquent, let us say that his success was born of the happy conjunction of the man with his time. Americans in Dewey's lifetime still had the frontier in their blood; they were prone to action rather than reflection, and were suspicious of anyone who by preference sat in a corner and reflected on the universe. Here was a philosopher who told them they were right in this, that even a philosophy should get results, and that if it failed to prove itself in practice it might better be dispensed with. Education was in trouble, for the tradition that centered in the little red schoolhouse was beginning to wear thin. Dewey produced, as if on demand, an educational philosophy that blended democracy, education, and practice in one stimulating brew. He was a democrat, a liberal, and a sympathizer with labor when the challenge to the great corporations was getting under way. He was a humanist in religion when Darwinism and its aftermath had shaken the creeds. As an educational leader, he was called into council by the awakening countries such as Turkey, Japan, and China, when they needed advice on educational reform. Dewey's powers were great, but they were enhanced in effect by his happy fortune of living in the right age and place.

Montague and Others

Though Dewey was the brightest gem in Columbia's diadem of philosophers, he was not the only one, nor indeed the one from whom I learned most about teaching. That debt I owe to Montague. He had the gift of penetrating through to the essentials of any philosophic position and stating them with a succinctness, lucidity, and order that awoke in his hearers a somewhat euphoric sense of mastery. With a strong visual imagination, he always wanted a blackboard for his lectures, for he could put almost anything in diagrams. His lectures were modeled, I suspect, on those of his teacher Palmer at Harvard, which he says "were incomparably the most finished, both as to content and to form, of all that I have ever heard. . . ."[2] Montague's were never finished in the sense of being elaborately prepared, for if he knew beforehand the general line of his argument, he could always clothe it impromptu in a felicitous verbal dress. About forty years ago, when I was secretary of the Eastern Division of the Philosophical Association, I had arranged for the annual meeting a symposium on the philosophy of religion in which Whitehead was to be the chief participant. On the day before the symposium I received the discouraging word that Whitehead was ill and could not come. I asked Montague whether he would be willing on the spur of the moment to take Whitehead's place. He accepted readily, and gave the most effective address of the symposium.

This ability to mobilize his thoughts and words on call was not without its penalties. It tempted him to give to peripheral enthusiasms more time than he could afford. He confessed to having had for more than twenty-five years the delight of the circle-squarer in odd mathematical puzzles, with results "not enough as yet to justify the hours filched from philosophy"; and for so good a chess player, a game at the Faculty Club was always a temptation hard to resist. That he succeeded in finishing several books was largely due to his devoted colleague at Barnard, Helen Parkhurst, who gathered together his scattered papers and prodded him into rounding them out into books. And excellent books they were. The most useful of them, *The Ways of Knowing*, was modeled to some extent on Sidgwick's *Methods of Ethics* and provides excellent examples of his power to order and elucidate his themes. Many of my own classes in the theory of knowledge have read this book to their profit.

Montague lived long enough to see the coming of a new brand of philosophy which attempted to settle traditional problems by analyzing the meanings of words. He disbelieved, deplored, and detested it. He was a philosopher of old-fashioned, generous proportions who dealt by preference with such problems as the nature of truth, the relation of body to mind and of mechanism to teleology, the character of the good life, the existence of God, and the chances of surviving death. The only one of these of which he thought he had an original solution was the mind-body problem, and he has left a remarkable account of a kind of mystic vision in which this solution presented itself. It has often been supposed that if the energy passing across the synapses of the brain gives rise to consciousness some of this energy must be lost out of the physical world and the law of conservation therefore violated. Montague held that it is not lost, but converted into potential energy, and that this potential energy provided the stuff of the mental. Was the mind then *in* the brain? Yes, but it existed in a fourth spatial dimension of its own, a dimension in which many intensive differences could be found at the same point. Montague attempted over and over again to explain this theory to others, but he admitted that he had never made a convert to it, and though I repeatedly tried to understand it, I never could. This failure to make himself understood was an enduring grief to Montague, though he took it with his usual humor and freedom from resentment. It was the more puzzling to everyone because his standards of clarity were unusually high.

Montague used to say that there were two great virtues, courage and sympathy. He exemplified both. Though his academic life gave few occasions for courage of the physical kind, his intellectual courage was constantly in evidence. It was shown in his singular combination of unpopular views, for example his conjunction of materialism with the beliefs in a limited Deity and the probability—though a low one—of the soul's surviving death. He gave an omnibus course at Columbia with a title that was something like "Socialism, Anarchism, Feminism, and Christianity," and came out with original and surprising views on all these topics. He also had the courage to change his mind publicly; he admitted that the New Realism, which with a group of colleagues he had launched in 1906, had proved itself untenable by its inability to deal with error, and that the socialism of his earlier years had been exposed as utopian by the Russian and other experiments with it. Though his inner light occasionally misled him, Montague had an almost Cartesian confidence in it. And his insight did combine, in a persuasive way, common sense, intellectual clearness, and a large and quiet sanity, so that his statement of a case was often pardonably taken as the voice of reason itself. There must be many of his students, now professors of philosophy, in whose teaching a discerning ear could catch the accents of Montague's voice. I should like to think they might be caught in mine.

The ethical end for Montague was the fulfillment of human capacity, not for this man or that, but for all men. Courage is necessary if such fulfillment is to be secured for oneself, sympathy if it is to be secured for others. Montague's own sympathy for those who were in pain or trouble was acute. Much as he approved of Christian ethics for its altruism, he could not accept its asceticism; he saw no virtue in poverty or self-denial as such. And he was haunted by the thought of the suffering in the world. "Pessimists as yet have hardly scratched the surface of life's woe. I venture to believe that, should one ever come with the ability to give us in his writing a vivid first-hand sense of even a tithe of those agonies actually existing at a single moment, his words would burn our eyes blind, and melt the foulest hearts with pity." To say with traditional theism that these were a necessary means to man's education and happiness, or, in Royce's version, that when seen by the eye of the Absolute they were not really evil, seemed to him a culpable trifling with human misery. He was ready to repudiate "any God who ever lived in heaven if with omnipotence to draw upon he had ordained . . . the puzzled mounting wretchedness of a single dog lost on the streets of a city." I recall that once a question arose in his class as to the Christian Science dismissal of evil as illusion. Montague's comment was that an "illusory" pain may be as painful as a real one, and that in any case to conceive pain as an illusion does not get rid of evil, since illusion is itself evil. If there is a good answer to this criticism, I do not know what it is. Montague illustrated well the paradoxes of the rational man; such a man will be passionately dispassionate, but will know that to be rational one must have passionate sympathies, loves, and hates. In my private gallery, his picture has a secure place as one of the most lovable persons I have known.

F. J. E. Woodbridge was in those days dean of the Columbia Graduate School, and I saw less of him than of Montague. His lectures on the history of philosophy must have been prepared largely on the train as he came to his busy office of a morning. They were memorable lectures nevertheless, full of zest, humane insights, and inimitable chuckles. Woodbridge had a vivid imagination and seemed almost as much at home with Socrates in the Athenian agora as with his friends on 116th Street. His great hero was Aristotle; "I owe to Aristotle my conception of metaphysics and the love if it." "He has said everything that I have ever said or shall ever say."[3] Once in later years when he and I had been examining together at Bard College on the Hudson and we were returning to New York on the train, he suddenly said, "Blanshard, do you suppose Aristotle ever really existed?" This from an Aristotelian scholar? I was dumb. But it only meant that Woodbridge had been brooding again about his favorite philosopher and doubted whether the vast and varied corpus of his work could have been produced by any single mind. Perhaps "Aristotle" was a factory or a school.

Woodbridge's course on the history of philosophy was naturally popular, and it remained so when it was taken over by his friend and pupil, J. H. Randall. What distinguished this course, apart from the lectures, was an elaborate syllabus composed of questions on all the major figures and schools of philosophy. As a student I found this so valuable that when I became a teacher I often prepared syllabi of weekly readings and questions for my own courses. To construct such a syllabus is itself a valuable exercise, compelling one to isolate and formulate the essentials in a complex problem or system of thought, and helping the student likewise in his analysis. This suggestion regarding method, together with the impression of a powerful personality, were the main things I took away from my contact with Woodbridge. I knew nothing at the time of the extreme realism that he was to develop a little later in *The Realm of Mind,* and when I did come to know it, I was not convinced by it. And unhappily, readers who know Woodbridge only in his writing get a very faint image of what he was as a person.

Columbia gave me my first chance to teach. In the second semester of my year there, I taught an introductory class in philosophy and a senior seminar on Bradley. I had an extraordinary stroke of luck in the personnel of this little seminar. There were only four members, but three of the four went on to become professors of philosophy at Columbia: John Randall, James Gutmann, and Horace Friess, all of whom were to remain my valued friends for more than fifty years. Among the graduate students were other friends who also were to achieve much: Irwin Edman, then a brilliant youngster who astonished us by his encylopedic memory and his gift for expression; Seelye Bixler, later professor of theology at Harvard and president of Colby; Herbert Schneider, the historian of American thought; Sterling Lamprecht, professor at Illinois and Amherst; and Frances Bradshaw, who was to mean to me most of all.

I had spent six years in university work without a degree to show for it. At the end of the year at Columbia I received an M.A. by reason of taking the preliminary examinations for the doctorate and submitting a thesis on Hume's theory of judgment. About the same time Michigan generously gave me my B.A. degree, though I had left at the end of my junior year, and added to it a Phi Beta Kappa which must have been due to the friendly representation of Professor Wenley.

France

As the investigation in Philadelphia was drawing to a close, my call came from the army. I went first to Camp Greene in North Carolina, and about two months later to Camp Mills, near New York. I was attached as a first sergeant to Base Hospital 123, which was about to go overseas. Frances Bradshaw, who had become an instructor in philosophy at Hollins College, Virginia, came up to say good-bye. We had attended Columbia classes together, had gone to Philadelphia together, and in the course of that adventure had become engaged. The good-bye at Camp Mills was too much for us, and with a common impulse we dashed off to Yonkers, where Frances had a friend and former pastor, who married us. This hastily improvised event was the beginning of forty-eight years of devoted and happy companionship. The threads of our lives were so closely intertwined during most of the years that followed that I can hardly disentangle them, and from now on I shall be telling two stories in one, though the best in both—the long passages of quiet happiness—do not translate well into print.

Frances had been a brilliant student at Smith College, where her widowed mother was a professor of English literature, and she took an M.A. in philosophy at the same time I did. The Deweyan pragmatism was more attractive to her than it was to me, and I am afraid I tempted her away from it without converting her to anything else. Some years later she took her doctorate at Columbia with a dissertation on aesthetics which was published as *The Retreat from Likeness in the Theory of Painting.* It may suggest to the reader something of her quality and my good fortune if I add that she was the author of two other admirable books, one a study of *The Portraits of Wordsworth,* the other a biography of *Frank Aydelotte of Swarthmore,* that she was for fifteen years a dean of Swarthmore College, outranking her husband in the academic hierarchy, that she was honored with a doctorate of laws from her alma mater, and that when she came in later years to New Haven she was soon made president of the League of Women Voters and a member of the mayor's commission to draw up a new charter for the city.

The wedding and the good-bye came virtually together, and it was ten interminable months before I saw her again. Our unit crossed to Liverpool on a transport, was shipped by night train to a camp near Winchester, and almost immediately afterward crossed the Channel to le Havre. A few days later, we were sent on to a camp at Mars-sur-Alliers, a few miles from Nevers, where we took over a hospital already full of sick and wounded, with many prisoners in like condition soon to be added. But I saw little of the patients. As sergeant major of the outfit, it was my job to handle the routine paper work of the unit.

There are dreary passages in every life, of which one tends to forget the details just because they are so gray that there is no point or pleasure in recalling them. The France of that winter was a France of leaden skies overhead and a sea of mud underfoot, of cold barracks and long mess lines, and, so far as my own work was concerned, of the making of incessant reports and the interminable filling out of forms. It was drudgery, and drudgery of an unheroic kind. The nearest I came to combat was with a drunken sergeant of my own unit, who went berserk with a poker in the barracks. If I came through with health intact myself, it was due very largely to luck. I had inherited my father's respiratory weakness, and should probably have gone out like a light if the 1918 flu, which cost us many men at Camp Greene, had happened to touch me, or if any one of a large number of contingencies had happened in Mesopotamia, or at Mars-sur-Alliers, or after an operation at Toulouse. As I look back I can see that though I have had some minor reverses, my good fortune has been extraordinary at all the main crossroads of my journey.

My luck stayed with me, even in that sea of mud. The war was over, and the American high command foresaw the danger of disintegrating morale among the hundreds of thousands of men waiting in France for available ships to take them home. With true imagination it thought up, among other devices, a university to which qualified men could be transferred from their units to pursue studies of their choice during the period of waiting. To be sure, a university needs a faculty as well as a student body, but this obstacle was quickly surmounted; there were plenty of scholars in the army, as one could find from their service records. Suddenly an order came through detaching me from my unit and assigning me to the new University of Beaune as an instructor in philosophy.

Only Americans could have conceived and constructed such an institution as this. The barracks of an old encampment were taken over and transformed. There suddenly appeared a library, numerous classrooms, a faculty of all degrees of qualification, a respectable list of university departments, an inviting variety of courses, and a large student body. John Erskine of Columbia was placed at its head, and I recall with amusement the tall figure of Erskine in uniform trying to communicate to rows of uniforms before him the delights that lay in store for them in the exquisite cadences of Walter Pater's style. Erskine seemed to bring it off, though perhaps the military discipline of his audience had something to do with it. My own assignment was the history of philosophy. When I inquired into the library holdings in this field, I found that none had yet arrived. The enterprise of spinning the history of philosophy, spiderlike, from my own entrails was barely averted by the discovery of a copy in French of Weber's *History of Philosophy,* and with this precious aid I started lecturing.

It was an institution where academic credits or strict assessments of performance were not practicable, so a carefree spirit reigned. Much as students appreciated the chance to do some reading and thinking, what they wanted above all was to forget the cursed war and get home, and they kept disappearing without warning when notice came that their transports were waiting at Cherbourg or le Havre. Something of the same spirit reigned in the faculty. It was all a bit of a lark, a way of profitably marking time; the world would little note nor long remember what they said or did there. I was happy to be among academic people again, and was fortunate in my department head, Ralph Tyler Flewelling. He was, I think, a chaplain in the army, and was in course of moving into philosophy from the ministry. I know little of his philosophical work, but he was a wise and considerate colleague. I never saw him after leaving Beaune, but twenty-five years later a letter came from him out of the blue. He was head of the school of philosophy at the University of Southern California, and he was asking me to join his department again as a visiting professor. Remembering the days at Beaune, I should greatly have enjoyed doing so, but the invitation came on the eve of my going to Yale, and I had to say No. Among other friends at Beaune was Walter Agard, then a corporal, later Wisconsin's eminent classicist.

The university wound down as the students trooped homeward. I did not want to go home; I wanted to return to Oxford if possible for the last year of my scholarship. The Rhodes trustees had a rule, however, that no holder could retain his scholarship if he married. I now learned with delight that the trustees had suspended their rule for scholars married during the war. I wrote to Frances that I would secure my discharge in England if she would join me there, and we had a honeymoon, ten months delayed, in the Isle of Wight.

Oxford Again

Then Oxford again. We settled down in "digs" in Marston Street, off the Iffley Road, and I went vicariously through a second introduction to that bewitching place. Frances entered the university herself as a noncollegiate student, and had an excellent tutor, Mrs. J. L. Stocks. She also gained some free tuition, for it was then considered improper for a woman student to visit the rooms of a male tutor alone, and she served as the chaperon at a friend's tutorials. The knowledge she acquired of Oxford manners and customs was an immense advantage to her when, many years later, she wrote her biography of Frank Aydelotte, the Rhodes scholar president of Swarthmore.

I went back to Oxford with whetted interests, and with purposes more sharply defined. The four years of absence had made it plain that my field was philosophy, not religion. To Professor Webb's disappointment, I abandoned my thesis on the idea of God and cast about for a new subject. My former tutor, Harold Joachim, now Wykeham Professor of Logic, was lecturing on judgment; the challenging ideas of Dewey were still tumbling about in my head; and the two facts united to push me toward an analysis of Dewey's theory of judgment. I gained little help on this subject from Joachim or anyone else, for pragmatism was not a popular philosophy at Oxford, and

Dewey was almost unread. At the end of the year, two formidable examiners, Sir David Ross and H. W. B. Joseph, were named to read my thesis and examine me orally. They could have given me a bad time, but I gained the impression that they agreed on the whole with my estimate of the Deweyan theory, which pointed to many difficulties in it. Both were to become my valued and helpful friends.

Joseph

It may be well to say something of these and other Oxford dons who helped to shape my thought, though in doing so I shall telescope impressions drawn from this final year as a student and from a later year (1929–30) when I revisited Oxford on a Guggenheim fellowship. Of all these men, it was Joseph who meant most to me. I owed much to conversation with him for help with *The Nature of Thought,* and later to his writings for help with *Reason and Goodness* and *Reason and Analysis.* When I was at work on the first of these three, I read and reread his Herbert Spencer Lecture on evolution, and I was convinced by it that one cannot explain growth or development, still less conscious and purposive process, by any mechanistic laws. He helped me to the view that mind at all its levels is irreducibly teleological. When at one point I was struggling with the problem of how a universal was related to the individuals that fall under it, I asked Joseph if he would take a walk with me round the Port Meadow and discuss the problem. On this walk he passed on to me an idea that first came perhaps from Cook Wilson of how the universal could be conceived as a potentiality of which the individuals are the realization; the idea seemed to me illuminating and I used it freely in my book. On its completion I sent him a copy. It was characteristic of him that he should not only have read the two volumes through, but also have sent me an immense and searching commentary on it, written out in his minute script.

I listened intently to his lectures on ethical theory, later published as *Some Problems in Ethics.* In these lectures he gave his formal answer to Prichard's deontology, while Prichard sat immediately in front of him in the New College dining hall, taking it all in, no doubt with much silent wrestling. Joseph's insistence that the right depends on the good, and that an act derives its rightness from its contributoriness to a form of life which is itself the ethical end, is not far, I think, from the view I tried to present in *Reason and Goodness.* The debt to Joseph of *Reason and Analysis* is also considerable, though some of it is to writings that have not yet seen the light. Sometime in the 1930s Joseph gave a course of lectures on "Internal Relations" in which he subjected the logical theories of Russell and Wittgenstein to what I suspect is the most searching criticism they have received. After his death these lectures were in the possession of one of his executors, to whom I wrote, asking if I might see them. He kindly lent them to me: I read them and thought them masterly. They strengthened my growing conviction that Russellian logic would not do.

Joseph has not been appreciated at his true worth. I had a high respect for Joachim, as did Joseph himself, who wrote a generous account of his friend and colleague for the British Academy; but in the light of later developments I can only think it would have been better if, when the Wykeham chair of logic became vacant at the death of Cook Wilson, Joseph rather than Joachim had been named as his successor. Joachim's interest was in the philosophical interpretation of judgment, which he handled in illuminating fashion, but he had little interest in or regard for the new ideas on logic that were beginning to swirl about Cambridge; and when they blew up into a storm that threatened Oxford also, he did not know how to deal with them. Joseph did. He gave some notion of what he could do in two articles in *Mind* in 1932–33, entitled "A Defence of Free-Thinking in Logistics," which were ostensibly a criticism of a new book on logic by Miss Stebbing, but were really directed beyond her at her teacher, Bertrand Russell. Miss Stebbing replied somewhat scornfully, which brought Joseph back into the fray. I thought, and still think, that the result was a pretty complete rout for the Cambridge logicians. But the tide by then had risen to such proportions that there was no stopping it. If Joseph had had the freedom of a professorial chair and had directed his attention seriously upon either the first or the second Wittgenstein, British philosophy would not have been carried so far off course.

Joseph was a unique and fascinating personality. He was short of stature, but broad-shouldered and remarkably strong. He had a whim of bicycling on his birthday as many miles as there had been years in his life, and it was reported that on his sixty-ninth birthday, when his long trip fell short of the requisite number, he cycled up and down the Banbury Road till it was completed. He was a tireless walker, a teacher who carried a prodigious load of weekly hours, and the workhorse of the New College fellowship in all that pertained to the welfare of the college, including personal attention to its lofty roofs and gutters. After his retirement, he became a councillor of the city of Oxford and chairman of its committee on education, where he showed the same exactitude and vigilance of mind that had made him so valuable a member on university committees.

The convolutions of Joseph's thought and style were the subject of both despair and pleasantry among his students. There was current a limerick about him:

A New College tutor named Joseph
Says nobody knows if he knows if
He knows if he knows,
Which accounts, I suppose,
For the mental confusion of Joseph.

"He wrote, as he spoke, with ease, but his readers have none," said his colleague A. H. Smith.[4] His writing ran to long sentences, with intricately related clauses and subclauses, and I recall that at his lectures there were ripples of laughter among the students over the impossibility of transporting into their notebooks the leaves or branches of these verbal banyan trees. It was an overcomplicated style for lectures, but not necessarily bad for careful readers, for it reflected Joseph's subtle and complex thought with great fidelity. It reminded one at times of the involutions of the later Henry James, but it was the product, as was James's style also, not of carelessness or haste but of a deliberate art that had become so habitual as to be second nature; he not only wrote in it but thought and spoke in it. As an undergraduate Joseph had won the Arnold prize for English prose, and when I gave him Wilder's *The Woman of Andros,* he commented with special pleasure and discernment on its style. He has been charged with being obscure, but he is seldom that; it is rather that with an eye for subtle distinctions and connections he combines an ideal of extreme compression in statement, so that it is difficult to follow him except by close attention, and to skim him is impossible. He is never mechanical or perfunctory. His best book, his *Introduction to Logic,* has passages of genuine though austere beauty, and the illustrations that he gives of syllogism and other forms of reasoning are often delightful in themselves.

In his kindness, Joseph was unsparing of himself; in intellectual matters he was unsparing of both himself and others. Some of his students regarded him as a terror, for he could take to pieces a careless essay in a way that exposed remorselessly the nakedness of the land. But for those who could bear it, this intellectual severity provided a priceless discipline. And when he gave full and annotating attention to a manuscript or a book, as he often did, his criticism was invaluable. Certainly the commentary he gave me on my own first book, at once minute and massive, was the best I ever received. He could perform such service the more readily because his mind worked with extreme rapidity. The process of brooding and groping that most philosophers know too well seemed unnecessary for him; his sharp intelligence would penetrate at a stroke to the essence of the matter. "It seemed, indeed,"—I quote Warden Smith again—"that with almost inconceivable rapidity his thought became fixed in a precise linguistic form, and that in consequence he was able to compose his philosophical work with a combination of speed and precision which I am sure must be rare in the history of philosophical writing."[5]

Ross and Prichard

The other of my two examiners at Oxford, Sir David Ross, I knew less well, though I listened to his lectures on Kant's ethics, and read his own ethical works with keen interest. My impression of him was the same as that reported by A. K. Stout: "He is not only an Aristotelian scholar, but he also has an Aristotelian frame of mind—moderate, critical, balanced, thorough, and, above all, judicious. He values and possesses what Aristotle called 'practical wisdom' no less than speculative ability." This practical wisdom led to a continual demand for his services as an administrator—as provost of Oriel, vice-chancellor of the university, president of the Classical Association, president of the British Academy, and chairman of the Royal Commission on the Press. He seems to have had the enviable power of turning instantly and serenely from one type of activity to a wholly different one. A former student of Ross's told me that when he called on him at Oriel he found him in his study, deep in writing his Gifford Lectures. The visitor was warmly welcomed; the points he raised were dealt with quickly and courteously; but as he left the room he could hear Ross's pen racing across the paper again before he reached the door. Preoccupied with administrative work and with editing the Oxford translation of Aristotle, Ross did not publish a work of his own thought until he was past fifty. Then came two books on ethics admirably argued and lucidly written, which presented the strongest case yet made for a new type of ethical theory against the ideal utilitarianism of Moore and Rashdall. Ross was economical of both time and words, but he could talk brilliantly. I recall a conversation in the Oriel common room in which he and Percy Simpson differed on whether A. E. Housman had been justified in his disdainful references to religion; the talk lingers in my memory as among the best I have ever heard.

Though Ross was by far the most effective expositor of the deontological ethics, he freely owned that the main ideas of that ethics had come from his friend and colleague Harold Prichard. To Prichard too I owe much, though rather for the stimulus of walks and talks with him than for appropriable ideas. So far as I recall, our discussions were always on one or other of two topics, sense perception and duty. There comes back to me a protracted argument that we had in the rain before a pillar box at the corner of Woodstock and Banbury roads on the question whether, in perceiving that object, we were mistaking a patch of red color for a pillar box, Prichard holding (erroneously, I still think) that we were. What he will be chiefly remembered for is the theory of obligation which he first broached in a startling essay of 1912 entitled "Does Moral Philosophy Rest on a Mistake?" The major ethical tradition of the West, he pointed out, had followed the Greeks in holding that the ground of duty was the goodness of the foreseeable consequences of an act. This thesis he denied, adducing many cases in which it was our duty to act in one way, though a calculation of consequences would clearly prompt another. Duty often has no grounds at all, he maintained; we see something to be our duty self-evidently, and not as an inference from anything else. In Prichard's lectures on ethics, which I attended, he argued vigorously for this position, though I was never persuaded of it. Prichard, Ross, and Carritt, who took roughly the same view in ethics, admitted that the self-evident prima facie duty to repay a debt, for example, might be outweighed by a competing obligation to produce good consequences, as when one defers payment of a debt in order to secure the medication necessary to save a life; and it seemed to me that as a ground for this stronger obligation there must be some common character of which there was more in one case than in the other. Prichard held that there was none; one could see that one course was more obligatory than the other, but this was an ultimate insight for which no reason could be given. This I found unsatisfactory. Prichard was known to be at work on a substantial book on ethics; E. F. Carritt, who much admired him, predicted that when it came out it would rank with Sidgwick's *Methods of Ethics*. But Prichard never finished it, and in the slender volume that Ross edited after his death there was disappointingly little that was new. Ross was right, nevertheless, in saying that "in him we had one of the very finest philosophical minds of the whole generation to which he belonged."[6]

It is of course this side of him that is most important, but there were other sides also that impressed me. He was one of the few Oxford philosophers who were at home in mathematics, most of them having come into philosophy through the door of Greek and Latin classics. Prichard came into the subject with a first class in Mathematical Moderations behind him, though he never went on from this, so far as I know, to an interest in mathematical logic. Again, he achieved what he did against odds that for a time seemed forbidding, for having been physically strong and a fine tennis player in his youth, he was felled by a paralytic stroke in early manhood. From this he seems to have made a complete recovery. His lectures were marked not only by the acuteness of their argument but also, and to the amusement of his audience, by his unself-conscious bodily contortions; he wrestled with his reading stand as well as with his opponents until one wondered whether he and it would end on the floor together. Nor can I forget the pleasant times I had at the Prichards' house at No. 6 Linton Road. Mrs. Prichard had herself taken a first in Greats at Oxford, and there seemed to be no dull moments in the talk that went on around their hospitable fireside. As I look back on the pains taken by Joseph, Joachim, Prichard, and Carritt (of whom more shortly) to ease the path as well as lighten the darkness of a rather raw young alien, I feel sure there was some connection between the exacting ethical ideals that all of them taught and their extraordinarily generous personal lives. Their sense of duty was as exacting in practice as their logical sense was vigilant in their thinking.

Of the other Oxford dons I saw less. I heard A. D. Lindsay lecture on political theory, but did not come to know him till 1929, when his wife, who was a Quaker, discovered that Frances and I were members of the Society of Friends, and asked us in occasionally for luncheon. Lindsay came to

Swarthmore in the thirties as a Cooper Foundation lecturer, and later to Yale, where I met him still again. He was a delightful guest, an incomparable raconteur of Scottish stories, and blessed with a most retentive memory. Once in the course of a dinner party at Swarthmore, I differed with him about his indeterminism. Some ten years later, I found myself at his side at another dinner party in New Haven, and without any prompting from me, he began where we had left off: "No, Blanshard, you can't hold that view on determinism, for . . ." He was not, I thought, a particularly effective lecturer, but he became something of an educational statesman, first as Master of Balliol and, under his later title of Lord Lindsay of Birker, as founder and first head of the University of Keele.

I attended Price's course on perception, and thought him the best lecturer on philosophy I had heard. He was lecturing in those days in Balliol hall, fixing his gaze on the remote right-hand corner of the ceiling and seldom looking at his auditors. The lectures were so lucid, fluent, and perfectly organized that it seemed as if he must be reading them, but I could find nothing in the spot on the ceiling to support this hypothesis. To my regret, I saw little of Gilbert Ryle. But during the many years beginning about 1935 that I was American treasurer of the Mind Association, I had occasional correspondence with him; and once in the fifties I read a paper critical of his conception of philosophy to the dons' philosophical club. I sent it to Ryle in advance, and he read a paper in reply. I recall that Hampshire was in the chair and that Austin took part in the discussion, but even the gist of that discussion has now vanished from memory. My relations were closer over the years with the British secretary of *Mind*, John Mabbott, an excellent administrator as well as philosopher, who became president of St. John's. Of the just-mentioned John Austin I saw something on both sides of the sea, and although I thought his attempt to solve philosophical questions by appeal to the uses of words was on the whole a blind alley, I could only agree with the general opinion as to his extraordinary ability.

Two Murrays

Though I had little contact with scholars outside the field of philosophy, two stand out in memory, both with the name of Murray. In my undergraduate days Sir James A. H. Murray, the editor of the great *Oxford Dictionary*, was living with his daughters in north Oxford, and to students they were a hospitable household. I was occasionally invited there for lunch or tea, and was fascinated to hear Murray discuss the far-ranging problems of his immense work, involving correspondence with eminent scholars and humble word-hobbyists the world over, who supplied some 1,500,000 illustrations of English word usage. When I ventured once to ask Murray when he expected to finish the work, which he began in 1879, he answered that he would never see the end of it, since there was one great hurdle left to surmount, the letter *S*. C. E. M. Joad must have been enjoying the Murrays' hospitality at about the same time I did, but fortunately our visits did not coincide. I say "fortunately" because, as Joad admitted later, he was engaged in playing on this household what he called "practical jokes," and they were of a kind of which I should have been sorry to be suspected. One of them was to upset a large bottle of mucilage over Sir James's worktable, gumming together masses of the invaluable slips of paper with which he was working; another was to carry Brussells sprouts in his pocket from the luncheon table up to the nursery and secrete them inside a child's rocking horse, producing a stench whose source it was almost impossible to locate.

I am tempted to a further word about this extraordinary man. Joad was a clever and ready speaker, long a favorite on the "brains trust program" of the British Broadcasting Corporation, an effective teacher at Birkbeck College, London, and a voluminous writer of philosophical books. One of these was a vigorous onslaught on logical positivism, which did not increase his popularity with the younger generation of philosophers. His books are crotchety, prejudiced, and egotistic, but he had an eye for issues that were intellectually and humanly important, and he wrote about them with a gusto that makes him almost always interesting. In some respects he served the public well; he was an enthusiastic proponent of good music, social reform, and the preservation of the English countryside. His detestations were frank and numerous, and they included Americans; he performed the remarkable feat of producing, without visiting America, a book called *The Babbitt Warren,* which was divided into three sections called "Truth," "Beauty," and "Goodness," each proving with documentation that Americans had no idea of what the term meant. Joad presided once when I lectured at Birkbeck College, but he courteously kept this animus under cover, partly perhaps because I was dealing with emotivism in ethics, on which my position was close to his. His penchant for what he insisted on calling practical jokes at last recoiled on him with a vengeance. In going from London to his home in the country, it amused him, by changing cars and other devices, to outwit the Great Western Railroad and pay no fares. Suspicion was aroused, detectives were set to watch him, and the game ended in a magistrate's court and a stiff fine. In England much is tolerated in public figures, but this sort of thing is not, and it put an end abruptly to Joad's public career. In his later years the attitude of scornful contempt for religion that he had maintained through most of his life was exchanged for one of remorseful faith, but the change came too late to have much effect on the public image of him.

The other of the two Murrays I met at Oxford was Gilbert Murray, Regius Professor of Greek and translator of Euripides. He had a tennis court on his grounds on Boar's Hill and I used to be called in to take part in doubles matches, which he preferred to singles by reason of his advancing years. He used to play boldly at the net with his glasses on, and once, narrowly missing that venerated head with a hard drive, I felt that I had also narrowly missed an unvenerated place in history. He had served, as Price and Broad did later, as president of the British Society for Psychical Research; and when guests were present in his living room, he used often to play a game designed to test his powers of reading other minds. He would be sent out of the room and out of earshot; the guests remaining in the room would agree upon some scene from history or literature which they would try to transmit to him in silence; he would then return and, without aid from words or gestures, try to make out what it was. He kept records of several hundred of these experiments, with their results, and these records were summarized and appraised for the Society by Mrs. Henry Sidgwick and Mrs. A. W. Verrall of Cambridge. They were very rigorous critics, but they held—on good grounds, I think—that the measure of his success was inexplicable by any theory but that of telepathy. To my regret, I never had a chance to take part in one of these sessions.

I did have enough contact with Murray and his writings, however, to come to think of him as not only a great man but that rare type of great man whose distinction lies in his reasonableness. I was told that he was considered, and nearly appointed, as ambassador to the United States, where he would have been a very popular envoy. There was no question, of course, of his scholarship; his academic brilliance was such that he succeeded Sir Richard Jebb as professor of Greek at Glasgow within about a year of taking his B.A. But what impressed people was less his scholarship than the temper of his mind. A colleague who knew him well said: "I doubt if Murray ever acted, except on the spur of the moment—and such moments occur to every man—without first asking himself if what he proposed to do were just and considerate. This is the teaching of Greek moralists and indeed of Greek literature in general; *audi alteram partem* is characteristic of all their best writers, and is what enabled them to create Greek drama and science and philosophy. Murray was like them in this, that his appeal was always to reason and humanity."[7] In my own thought, reasonableness has come to seem the greatest of human virtues, and I suppose it is this priceless quality in Murray that has made him a hero of mine.

Harvard

A student who takes the degree of bachelor of letters or bachelor of science at Oxford is not in the best position to secure an American post, for these degrees are given without the "first," "second," and other classes that indicate the quality of his work. The D. Phil. in its present form did not exist when I went to Oxford, and when it did come into existence, the standard set for it was such as to discourage candidates. One of the earliest candidates, so I was told by a don, was a man who afterward filled with distinction one of the most coveted philosophic chairs in Scotland. He submitted as his thesis a book that helped in securing this chair, a book now generally recognized as a work of remarkable ability. It was submitted for the degree and rejected by the examiners, Joseph and Prichard, who, in answer to the question what *would* pass their scrutiny, instanced their own books as works that would not measure up. Fortunately the standard has since been lowered, at least out of the stratosphere. For more reasons than one, I felt the need of an American doctorate and, learning that R. F. A. Hoernlé, the friend and interpreter of Bosanquet, was executive officer of the department at Harvard, I wrote to him about admission there. He replied most helpfully; indeed I was given a Sears scholarship for the following year, 1920–21. We returned to America joyfully in the summer, found a small flat in Cambridge on Howland Street, and settled down to a year of grimly hard work.

Apart from the scholarship, we had little or no money, and Frances set out to find work in Boston. After a week or two of trudging Boston streets and getting polite rebuffs from Boston offices, she received the offer of an instructorship in English at Wellesley, which she happily accepted. I used to see her off on the subway at Harvard Square early in the morning, her apple cheeks contrasting vividly with the gray faces of workingmen going resignedly to their jobs. My own schedule was one that would probably not be permitted today. Everything necessary for the degree somehow had to get done in one year, including the qualifying examinations, the language examinations, the topical examinations, the writing of the dissertation, and the departmental examination on it. We could allow ourselves but a very stinted ration of amusements, and I managed to come through physically only in virtue of a workout in the Harvard gymnasium every afternoon. The thesis was due on the first of May. On that day I typed the last page, and with a sense of weary triumph left it late in the evening at Professor Hocking's door on Quincy Street.

The director assigned for my thesis was C. I. Lewis, then a young man known only for his work in symbolic logic. He was a kindly and considerate counselor, who was ready, nevertheless, if sharp things needed to be said, to say them. They were soon needed in my case. Since my intention to write on the nature of judgment at Oxford had been sidetracked into a discussion of pragmatism, I decided to return to the subject and try to deal with it comprehensively. I sat in the Widener Library and thought and wrote for some two months; then I took the result to Lewis for his criticism. He said it was respectable work in the German manner, plodding and minute, but that it was leading nowhere. He was right, and I hastily changed the ground plan of my thesis. Still, it has always been hard for me to write to a plan. I can seldom tell in advance where I am going to come out; I sit down and follow the lead of a developing course of thought, and when I have gone on as long as I can afford to, I turn off the tap. Then I break the matter up into chapters and sections. This is the way my books have been written. It makes for continuity of argument, but it also makes for undue length. I usually exceed any limit set me for an article or book. I brought down *The Nature of Thought* to 1,132 pages only by omitting substantial blocks from the text, and in order to keep *Reason and Analysis* to a single volume, my patient publisher had to overcrowd its pages.

The Harvard of 1920 was not the Harvard of 1900. According to President Tucker of Dartmouth, the philosophy department of that earlier time, with James, Royce, Palmer, Santayana, and Münsterberg, was not only the best philosophy department in the country but the best department the country had had, of any kind. By 1920 this great group had disintegrated. James had died in 1910; Münsterberg and Royce died during the war, both broken by it; Santayana had emigrated in 1912 from a country in which he always felt himself an alien. Only Palmer was still about, a wisp of a man, still to be seen at times marching imperiously out into the hateful traffic of Harvard Square and bringing it to a halt. All later Harvard departments of philosophy have had to suffer comparison with this galaxy of stars, always and rather unfairly to their disadvantage. But by any standard except this impossible one, the department of 1920 was a distinguished group.

Its most eminent member was William Ernest Hocking, who occupied the spacious Alford chair of Natural Religion, Moral Philosophy, and Civil Polity. Hocking had come to Harvard from Iowa as an undergraduate at the advanced age of twenty-six, bringing with him two interests that were struggling for dominance, one in religion, the other in science. He had been brought up, he said, by a father who was "sternly pious" in a home where "naturalism in any form was not a matter of debate; it was simply a pathetic blindness. . . ." At about fifteen, he had stumbled on a copy of Herbert Spencer's *First Principles,* and as he wrote later, "Thoroughly against my will, and with a sense of unmeasured inner tragedy, Spencer convinced me."[8] But he had heard that there were philosophers who had gone beyond even Spencer, and he came to Harvard in search of them. He found them. In particular he found Royce, whose fusion of religion with logic in a metaphysical idealism solved his conflict far more satisfactorily than did Spencer's bleak agnosticism.

Hocking's most important book, *The Meaning of God in Human Experience,* was an attempt to elaborate a metaphysic that would do justice to religion. Mysticism played a much larger part in his system than it did in Royce's, though the book presented not so much a philosophical system as a set of ruminations on religion, scattering acute psychological insights along the way. I attended his class in metaphysics, of which Charles Hartshorne, still I think an undergraduate, was also a member. Hocking gave us a sense of large resources under easy control. Once at the beginning of a two-hour session he opened his briefcase to take out his notes and found that he had failed to bring them along. It seemed to make no difference; the lecture proceeded as if nothing had happened. The impression of power that he gave was due in part to his physical fitness and strength; he was a square-set man with a fine head, a florid face, and a body that enabled him to heave stones and beams into place in building his New Hampshire farmhouse. As was appropriate in an Alford professor, he had an extraordinary range of interests and talents. He was a skillful portrait painter; he had been an engineer, a teacher of mathematics, and a high school principal, and with his wife founded the Shady Hill School in Cambridge; he was a student of non-Christian religions, and after going round the world on the Laymen's Foreign Mission Inquiry, wrote a book proposing an eclectic world faith; he went to the troubled Near East and wrote another book on the Arab-Israeli problem; as a philosophical psychologist he wrote still another illuminating book on *Human Nature and Its Remaking;* he gave the Gifford Lectures in Glasgow and the Hibbert Lectures in Oxford; at the age of eighty-five, he gave the presidential address to the American Metaphysical Society. He was a man loaded with honors, and justly so.

His later years were clouded by two disappointments. Try as he would, he could not mould his Gifford Lectures into shape for publication. "I shan't regret the delay," he wrote me August 31, 1958, "if it means that I can do more perfectly what I then intended to do. It was 1939 when I got through, and our heads were immersed in the preludes to Britain's war, gas masks for every person including visitors (I still have mine). . . ." Unfortunately when the war was over and he could sit down again to what he had written, he found that a new world had emerged to which so many adjustments had to be made that the whole work required rethinking. Even philosophy had changed so radically that he found adjustment to it difficult. There lay his second disappointment. He looked with incredulous eyes on a new race of philosophers confidently solving by appeals to the usage of words problems to which he had devoted years of reflection. Philosophy had moved away from him; it had become an enterprise in which his kind of speculation seemed to have no part. It was as if, overnight and by some strange fall of the dice, his position of leadership in the philosophic community had been exchanged for that of a rather dimly remembered outsider. He accepted the change gallantly, but was also bewildered by it. I gather that his book on *The Meaning of God* continues to be read in theological schools for its study of mysticism, but students of philosophy, even those who go back to James and Peirce and Royce, seldom take the further step to Hocking. They are losers thereby.

In addition to Hocking's class on metaphysics, I attended Perry's seminar on epistemology. I made a bad start with Perry by taking as the subject of my first paper the realism of E. B. Holt and treating it as an impossible view.

Holt and Perry were collaborators in *The New Realism,* and Perry took my attack, I fear, as the expression of a typically smug idealist disdain for the petty pinpricks of American realists. The fact is that I had, and have, great respect for Perry's work, which like Hocking's is now too little known. This fading interest is natural enough as regards some of Perry's books, for example *Present Philosophical Tendencies* and *The Present Conflict of Ideals,* as well as his reflections on the Second World War, since they were written specifically for his own time; but it is not justified regarding his *General Theory of Value,* in which he offers a fuller account of the field than any of the "emotivists" who were shortly to follow him. Of all his books, the one most likely to endure is his life of William James, which is one of the best biographies this country has produced.

Perry was a less impressive figure than Hocking—a slight, swarthy man with coal black hair and dark eyes. But his intelligence and his pen were incessantly active, and since he was able to turn everything to account in the way of publication, his productivity was enormous. What he will be remembered for in philosophy, apart from his theory of value, is no doubt his realism. The best part of this realism was not its positive but its negative part, its exposure of idealist errors; and the names Perry gave to these have become part of the philosophy student's equipment—the arguments from the egocentric predicament, from initial predication, and from exclusive particularity. They did not dispose of Berkeley, but they did dispose, and decisively, of some of Berkeley's favorite arguments. Indeed Perry was an uncomfortable gadfly to idealism at a time when it needed gadflies. I remember attending an Ingersoll Lecture, delivered by an eminent theologian from the Divinity School, and dealing, as Ingersoll Lectures always do, with immortality. The lecturer began by waving aside the scientific approach of psychical research as mistaken in principle, and then went on to the standard line that God existed and was benevolent, and that a benevolent Deity would not create beings like ourselves, only to let them be blotted out. Hocking and Perry were both there, and as they emerged afterward into the hall, I saw Perry moor himself alongside Hocking as the little *Monitor* did alongside the *Merrimac,* and looking up indignantly, say, "Is this really the best you idealists can do on immortality?" I did not catch the reply. But the question was typical of Perry, and was surely in order. "God's in his heaven/All's right with the world" is a pleasant enough song on the lips of a peasant girl, but is less impressive when offered as a premise by a philosopher.

Hocking, Perry, and Lewis were the only members of the Harvard department with whom I had regular contact, and one of these, Lewis, I saw only for occasional advice. Hoernlé had gone, and Whitehead's arrival was still three years away. The pressure of work was such that I had to keep classes to a minimum. I had to forego many studies that I should have dearly liked to pursue—with Woods in Oriental philosophy, Sheffer in logic, Demos in Plato, and McDougall in psychology, to say nothing of the feast of courses that Harvard offered in nonphilosophical fare. As the strenuous year drew to a close, other concerns arose that could not so readily be neglected. I had to find a post. In the spring M. Carey Thomas, Bryn Mawr's rather formidable president, descended on the Harvard Yard in search of young recruits. Her philosophers, Theodore and Grace de Laguna, were about to go on sabbatical leave, and she needed replacements. Frances and I were invited to Bryn Mawr for consultation, but before the time to go, there came an offer of an assistant professorship from my alma mater, Michigan, which we agreed was not to be turned down. That summer we spent partly in New York, where I taught a course at Columbia in the philosophy of religion, and partly in Northampton, where Frances's mother was a professor at Smith College.

University of Michigan

In the eight years I had been away from Ann Arbor it had not greatly changed. Marion Leroy Burton, who had been Frances's president at Smith College, was now the dynamic head of the university, and in his brief period there he laid the groundwork for a large expansion. Burton was not an educational philosopher, but he had one gift in abundance, the power of speech; I have known only one college head who rivaled him in this respect, George E. Vincent of Minnesota. Burton built a great auditorium partly in order that he might speak to his students en masse, and at an opening session of the university he would hold five thousand of them spellbound for a solid hour and a quarter. He once went before a committee of the state legislature and asked for the unprecedented sum of nine million dollars for his university. He got it, and I heard a member of the committee say that if he had asked for nineteen million they would probably have succumbed. Burton had been president of Smith when Calvin Coolidge was mayor of Northampton, and when Coolidge ran for president of the United States, he asked his old friend to place his name in nomination; Burton did so with great effect.

That first year of teaching at Ann Arbor was probably the hardest I have ever faced. I had thirteen hours of classes in four different courses, and with great numbers of papers to read; being already weary when it began, I almost cracked under the strain. Even when for a period I went on half time, I was still teaching six classes a week, of about thirty students each, with all their papers to read myself. As I look back over forty years of teaching, it is this task of paper-reading that stands out as the most monumental burden. Nor do I see any satisfactory way of avoiding it. Students in philosophy should be made to write, and write often; it is an indispensable means to precision of thought. And what they write should be read carefully, with plenty of comment and criticism. That puts a heavy cross on the shoulders of the instructor.

The writing of half-formed minds is not profitable reading, and the worse the paper, the more attention it requires. Furthermore, to criticize pointedly, one needs a fresh head, for a weary and reluctant mind cannot keep its attention fixed.

Sitting at my desk at night, with a green eyeshade on, and a mountainous pile of papers at my elbow, I have thought up desperate expedients to lighten the labor. Once, finding that I was making the same criticism repeatedly, I had a set of twenty often-needed remarks made into rubber stamps, which hung on revolving racks on my desk. I would reach out for the appropriate one and apply it firmly: "Cloudy," "Elephantiasis," "This could be left out and not missed," "One more for the awkward squad," "Yes and No; disentanglement needed," "What precisely is the bearing of this?" or a mere inarticulate cry of pain, "Oh, Oh, Oh!" There were handy exclamations of pleasure too: "Well thought out," "Excellent," "Very much to the point." Later I tried another scheme, printing on an 8 1/2 x 11 green sheet forty comments in forty squares or boxes, half of them dealing with substance and half with form; a space was left at the bottom for a written comment on the paper as a whole. For each paper I checked the boxes containing the relevant remarks. This device had an advantage I had not anticipated. The students would study not only the comments checked but all the others too, and try deliberately to avoid getting pilloried in any of the boxes. These devices helped a little, if only by their novelty, to lighten the weary load.

My salary as assistant professor was $2,600 a year and supplementations of it were not unwelcome. Ann Arbor was only an hour by rail from Detroit, and for one semester I traveled to the city weekly to teach an adult extension class in logic. These adults were eager enough, but the class met on Friday night, and I came reluctantly to the conclusion that logic was not a subject for tired and sleepy adults at the end of a week's work. Once I was called in to Detroit by a group of social workers to have a debate on the Johnson Immigration Bill with a young Lutheran preacher, known as a sympathizer with labor who had made trouble for Henry Ford. The young man was Reinhold Niebuhr.

The most productive of my contacts with Detroit was with Henry G. Stevens, a philanthropic bachelor of large means who had become interested in improving the level of social work in the city. He wanted to find someone who would produce for him a digest of those results of recent psychology that would be of use in social work, and who could perhaps put them in book form. He consulted his friend Wenley about it, and Wenley suggested me. For two years I devoted half my time to studies along this line, and to conferences with Stevens and his associates in Detroit. Nothing much came of this, for we discovered books and pamphlets that already did the work well enough; but the inquiry was to have momentous results for me. It made clear that the psychology and philosophy I knew had been moving along divergent lines, particularly in their account of thought processes. Thought, for the philosopher, was an activity that was, or might be, under rational control; at its best it could develop the topic engaging it by moving along a path of necessary connection. Psychology assumed, on the contrary, that thought was governed exclusively by association, or perhaps by neural connections which were ultimately of a mechanical kind. It was out of my attempt to bridge this gap that the train of reflection started which issued many years later in *The Nature of Thought*.

After two years in an apartment, Frances and I bought a modest house of our own. In our first year there, we had as our guest for both semesters a visiting professor at the university who became a lifetime friend, Edgar Carritt, fellow of University College, Oxford. We had had our own difficulties in adjusting ourselves to England; we now had the amusing experience of watching a thoroughgoing Oxonian who had never been out of Europe adjust himself to the American Midwest. He was a good sportsman about it, but he was in for many surprises. I remember his dismay when, on going to the lecture room for his first lecture on aesthetics, he found that, through some confusion, the room was occupied by a course in the psychology of advertising, whose existence as a university subject no Oxonian had ever surmised. I remember too his delight at the eager attention given his lectures by his students in ethics, followed by his incredulous disillusionment when he came to read their papers; he started by failing all the early papers he read, supposing them to be isolated cases of illiteracy, only to find that he must reread and try to upgrade them if he was to avoid flunking most of the class. Happily, this was not the whole story. "The level of lecture classes," he wrote later, "was certainly lower than at Oxford, but a post-graduate class, which I also took, was quite equal to ours."[9] Carritt enabled me to look with foreign and freshly appraising eyes at much that I had scarcely thought about in our American educational system, for example the difficulty of getting objective judgments without external examiners, the variation of standards from course to course, the implicit snobbery of the fraternity system, the oddity of great institutions of learning being represented by semiprofessional football teams. But Carritt was equally ready to see the pluses of American university life: the availability of higher education at low cost to any student of ability and energy, the easy relations between students and faculty, and between men and women, the freedom from self-consciousness and class-consciousness, the genuine democracy, and—most attractive of all—the ingenuous middle western combination of friendliness and moral idealism.

Carritt was some fifteen years my senior, and a veteran philosophy don; indeed he was one of the leaders, with Ross and Prichard, of the new intuitional ethics. I saw him daily, walked with him through the Ann Arbor countryside, and played tennis with him until the snow forced us into the gymnasium for regular rounds of handball. He was sturdy of body; in his youth he had been stroke oar of his college boat, and he believed in keeping physically fit; in Ann Arbor he used to run round the block before breakfast, and if on our walks he came to a river, it was his delight to strip and plunge into it. He was for me a new type of man. Comfort, clothes, and money meant little to him; beauty in art and nature meant much; and duty meant most of all. His sense of duty, without ever being obtrusive or censorious, was always in control, so that victory in the little daily struggles with a torpid flesh and a reluctant will seemed to have become effortless through being habitual. He did not think that philosophy had much practical effect, but his ethics certainly did in his own case. There was an athletic, no-nonsense rigor and stoicism about his character that was a tonic to weaker brethren. He gave much thought to political theory, which led to his becoming a socialist on moral grounds. At Oxford he lectured on "Dialectical Materialism" at a time when Marx was so little known there that the Waynflete professor asked him why he had given his lectures so queer a title, which no one had ever heard of. He never accepted communism, but it was a tragedy that nearly disrupted his family that his wife and his five sons did. One of them became an editor of *The Daily Worker,* a second was killed while serving with an ambulance corps in Spain, and a third, a greatly gifted boy who shared their opinions, died of tuberculosis contracted in war service.

Carritt was far in advance of me philosophically, particularly in ethics and aesthetics, and my constant exchange with him did much to open my eyes and sharpen my thought. He did not, I think, influence my writing. One would expect that a man of such sensitive aesthetic perception would be an artist in expression, but he was not, and I suspect that his aesthetic studies may themselves have stood in his way. Holding that in a perfect work of art there were no excrescences and that everything must contribute to the whole, he complained to me of the "nimiety," the too-muchness, of such excellent writers as A. E. Taylor, and tried to strip his own writing bare of all but essentials. The result was that it was compressed at times to the point of being elliptical and almost crabbed. A more significant result, however, was that the series of small books he published are all as full of substance as a nut is of meat; his *Theory of Morals* probably says more about ethics than any other book of its size in English. I owed so much to Carritt, though less in the way of ideas than in the way of discipline and temper, that, when, fifteen years after his return to England, I published *The Nature of Thought,* I dedicated it to him jointly with my tutor Harold Joachim. Until he died in 1964 at the age of eighty-eight, I continued to receive delightful letters from him, and we always sought out him and his wife when we went back to England. I know that he was disappointed when, in the controversy between Prichard and him on the one side and Joseph on the other over the ground of rightness in ethics, I came out on Joseph's side, but he was not a man to whose friendship that would make any difference.

Swarthmore

We were prepared to spend the rest of our lives in Ann Arbor, and should have been happy to do so. But in the spring of 1925 there came an inquiry that we could not ignore from Frank Aydelotte, the president of Swarthmore College. I had met Aydelotte in England in 1920 when he was attending a dinner in London, given, if I remember rightly, by the Pilgrim Trust. H. A. L. Fisher was toastmaster, and among the speakers were Arthur Balfour and the American ambassador, John W. Davis. For some reason the organizers wanted an undergraduate too on the program, and summoned me from Oxford. I went quakingly and spoke my piece, which Aydelotte must have liked, for here he was, considering me for his college. Frances and I went to Swarthmore for the Easter weekend and were looked over by many appraising but friendly eyes. We did some looking and listening of our own. The campus was a mass of flower and blossom. Swarthmore was a Quaker college and we attended service on Sunday in the Friends' Meeting House. Jesse Holmes of the philosophy department spoke. His Easter message was in substance that we should be wise to make the most of this life while we could, since we should be a long time dead. This was a new sort of Easter sermon, and I reflected that if it was found acceptable by Swarthmore Friends, free thought and speech were in vogue among them. Aydelotte offered me an associate professorship, and bade us go home and think it over. We did, and found that we wanted very much to go. Wenley protested that I was making a mistake, that my future lay in a university, not in a small college. With sorrow, for I was deeply indebted to Wenley, I took a different view and we accepted the Swarthmore offer.

The acceptance was not as rash as it might seem. I knew enough about Aydelotte to expect the unexpected from any institution that he headed. Something must be said at once about this remarkable man in whose educational adventures I was to be involved for the next fourteen years. He was an unprepossessing figure, with an odd-shaped head almost as bald as an egg, with very large ears, and a right arm so lame that he shook hands with his left hand. He hailed from the little town of Sullivan, Indiana, where he had had a rather inadequate schooling, and from Indiana University where he had been "all-Indiana end" on the football team. While teaching high school and coaching football in Louisville, he heard that a set of scholarships at Oxford had just been established by the will of Cecil Rhodes, and though he was near the upper age limit for candidates, he applied and was appointed. If ever an appointment justified itself, his did. The somewhat rough young diamond landed in Brasenose, the college of Walter Pater, pursued English literature under the direction of Walter Raleigh, and came away an enthusiastic and almost intoxicated Oxonian. He thought the Oxford-Cambridge tutorial method enormously superior to the German lecture method, which American universities had been widely adopting, and resolved that if he ever had the opportunity, he would try to adapt it to American use.

With his appointment in 1921 as head of a modest college of five hundred students, and with a Board of Managers that gave him a free hand, his opportunity came. He was a man of tremendous energy, "a steam-engine in trousers," and in his nineteen years at Swarthmore he remade the college. At the same time, as American secretary to the Rhodes Trust, he transformed the system of selecting Rhodes scholars, doing so much for Anglo-American relations by the way that he was summoned across the ocean by the Queen and invested with the order of knighthood. He gaily shook hands with her with his left hand.

Aydelotte was an educational statesman whose originality lay in synthesizing Oxford with the Midwest. He was a product of midwestern democracy and thoroughly believed in it; everyone should have the privilege of going as fast and far as his abilities made possible. On the other hand, such democracy held dangers, the chief of which was that of making the good the enemy of the best. People may be equal in their rights, but they are not equal in their powers or their ambition, and the attempt to educate everyone is only too likely to end by educating no one; the standard will be set by the many, and it will be a standard far below the level of the gifted few. In Oxford, as Aydelotte had known it, the better men were not held back in this way by the many; they were given a large freedom to order their own work; they were encouraged to advance at their own pace; and if they were really better than others, this was not hidden, but clearly recognized in the rankings with which they took their degrees. Aydelotte did not see why the British stress on quality should not be combined with the American stress on quantity. His aim, to use the title of one of his books, was at "breaking the educational lockstep" by which the abler students were forced to march in step with the less able, or as *Time* reported when it placed his face on its cover, "he would reprieve democracy from mediocrity." This was of course too large an end for anyone to achieve singlehanded. What Aydelotte did was to make educators more keenly aware of the conflict in the American ideal and to try to solve it for his own educational microcosm.

The plan was simple enough. At the end of their second year, students were allowed to apply for admission to "honors study." If admitted, their final two years followed an entirely different pattern from their first two. They would elect to work in three fields, say philosophy, politics, and economics. But instead of attending twelve to fifteen classes a week, they would meet with their instructors in two weekly seminars of three to six members. These seminars, which lasted three hours and sometimes four, usually met in the instructors' own living rooms, with refreshments served after the first two hours or so. Short papers were read, with the group as a whole acting as critics, but most of the time was devoted to discussion in which students and instructors joined in hunting down a conclusion on the issue under review. This method was not equally applicable to all subjects, but for philosophy it was ideal. Philosophy, as Plato said, *is* a dialogue, with another or with oneself; and it is hard to conceive a better method of teaching it than the one devised by Socrates, in which the student is encouraged to try his hand at some baffling philosophic problem, to follow his first suggestion through until he runs into unacceptable consequences, to begin again more carefully, and thus gradually to learn the reflective method of attack on problems generally. Aydelotte probably adopted the seminar method rather than that of individual tutorials because the latter would be so expensive, but some of those who used it came to think it really preferable. Certainly when I started working with Joachim, the interval between him and myself was so great that in conversing with him alone I was frozen into almost inarticulate self-consciousness. A student at Swarthmore did not feel this way. If he faltered, there were always others to carry the ball till he got his wind again and could come back into the fray at his own time. I felt that I gained more satisfactory results with this method than with any other I have ever used. In seminars of a dozen or more, the individual feeling of engagement may be low; in a class of twenty-five to thirty, it falls still lower; in the large lecture classes, all one can do is to provide the best model one can of attack on philosophic problems, in the hope that some students will be incited to follow it. But in discussion in a small group, all must be engaged, and if the instructor has three hours for it every week, he acquires an intimate sense of the powers and shortcomings of each member. The method did much to change the attitude of the students from one of passive reception to one of active engagement, which in philosophy is all-important. The results gradually made themselves apparent. Swarthmore passed in the course of a few student generations from academic mediocrity to the highest proportion in the nation of seniors who went on to graduate school.

The twenty years Frances and I spent at Swarthmore were hard-working and happy years. We were both involved to the full. Frances's abilities were soon discovered; she was made assistant, then associate, and finally regular dean of women; and since she was not only a social but an academic dean, supervising women's admissions and counseling them on their work, her days were crowded. For many years I had eight o'clock classes on every day of the week except Sunday. Our popular chow dog would escort me to my eight o'clock class, then return and conduct Frances to her office at nine. We lived in five different houses, most of them on the campus itself, and since the faculty was a small and fairly compact community, we lived in a circle of friends.

Aydelotte, as the American secretary for the Rhodes scholarships, was in a good position to note the Americans of exceptional promise that came out of Oxford, and over the years he added many of them to his own staff. I was particularly happy about his additions to the philosophy department. When I came to Swarthmore, it had consisted of one man in his sixties, Jesse Holmes, an energetic social idealist who was the pillar of the Friends' Meeting and who had run repeatedly for governor of Pennsylvania on the socialist ticket, but whose academic training had been in chemistry rather than philosophy. When a young man is brought into a department with an older man whom it is evident that he will soon supplant, the position is likely to generate sparks, but I had nothing but magnanimity from Jesse Holmes. How judicious Aydelotte was in building up the department is shown by the fact that all the young men he chose went on, after varying lengths of service, to more distinguished posts. Two of them were Rhodes scholars: John Nason, who was to succeed Aydelotte as president of the college, and George Thomas, who was to become chairman of the department of religion at Princeton. Two others were brought from Yale, both of whom went on to presidencies in the Philosophical Association: Richard Brandt, now at Michigan, and Maurice Mandelbaum, now at Johns Hopkins. My own place was taken when I left by Roderick Firth, now Alford Professor at Harvard. Monroe Beardsley, who has distinguished himself in aesthetics, went from Yale to Swarthmore shortly after I made my move in the opposite direction.

Early in the Swarthmore period we joined the Society of Friends, and I have retained my membership ever since. Anyone who lives among Friends must be impressed by certain things about them—their sense of the importance of the inward life, a charity that is keenly alive to human needs and takes steps without ostentation to satisfy them, a preference for living simply, even when means are present to live otherwise, gentleness and the avoidance of violence, and a stress on practical goodness rather than adherence to a creed. This last trait of the Quakers made membership possible for me. There were many articles of belief prescribed by the churches that I could not accept, whereas among the Friends the only prescription seemed to be the belief in an inner light, and even of that no one interpretation was insisted on. I was happy and at home among the Quakers. Unfortunately, tension arose in the Society before and during the Second World War. Friends are traditionally pacifist; that is the attitude for which they are most generally known. In the face of Hitler, pacifism was impossible for me; I said so; indeed I fear I became something of a thorn in the flesh of the Society; and on moving away from Swarthmore during the war, I ceased to be active as a member. I shall have a little more to say about this when I come to my religious opinions.

Two Philosophical Clubs

In the course of the Swarthmore years I became a member of two philosophical groups that were to mean much to me. One of them, the Fullerton Club, I had some part in founding. On an autumn day of 1925, in Aydelotte's study, I asked Edgar Singer of the University of Pennsylvania whether the many philosophers in the Philadelphia area ever met to discuss their common problems. He said they did not. We agreed that this was a pity, and started forthwith to get in touch with department chairmen in the area, who welcomed our proposal to form a club. For a year or two the new society met at the University of Pennsylvania. Theodore de Laguna was its second president; I was the first; Singer, who was *facile princeps* among us, steadfastly declined the honor. After experimenting with various meeting places, the club settled on the Deanery at Bryn Mawr as the most convenient center. The Fullerton Club still flourishes after nearly half a century, and with a greatly increased membership. Its name, which has been a subject of wonder at times, was a suggestion of my own, supported by Singer. George Stuart Fullerton had been a teacher of philosophy at Pennsylvania who died in the year I came to Swarthmore; I greatly admired his work, particularly his *System of Metaphysics;* and though I never met him, his memory was still green in Singer's mind and mine. Over the years I read many papers to the club, the first of them an attempted dismemberment of Watsonian behaviorism. Singer, a kind of behaviorist himself, seems to have held his fire with his usual urbanity.

Singer was a puzzling figure to me, and I am sure to many others. Quiet of manner and unprepossessing of appearance, he was nevertheless the head of the table in any company where he appeared. He had the air and manner of a patrician, and spoke as one having behind his words a rich experience and a mellow culture. Students from many fields used to attend his lectures, not so much perhaps because of any strong interest in philosophy as because they enjoyed the spell he wove about them as a lecturer. I recently met an eminent scholar in English literature who was a colleague of Singer's, and who vividly recalled after some fifty years how Singer had taken a group of guests out to his porch one summer evening and for two hours held them enthralled by an account, perfectly ordered and finely phrased, of the development of his thought. He was a gifted linguist who studded his writing with glowing bits from Latin, French, German, and Italian literature. All this was the more surprising when one learned that he had come into philosophy from engineering and had devoted much time to mathematics.

Impressive as Singer's attainments were, however, he had little influence outside the circle in which his remarkable personality could make itself felt. Why was this? Largely, I think, because he suffered from the weakness of his strength. He had such distaste for the commonplace that he overdid his avoidance of it and committed himself to a way of writing that was precious and self-conscious; an example of what I mean may be found in the Adams and Montague volumes of *Contemporary American Philosophy* of 1930. Singer was asked for an article which "should embody its author's philosophical creed, together with the circumstances in his life history which influenced him in reaching it."[10] His article, which he entitled *"Confessio Philosophi,"* is a profoundly reflective essay, but I doubt whether Sherlock Holmes himself could have deduced from it where or when Singer lived, where he had gone to school or college, what teachers had influenced him, or even what were his leading beliefs. Too often in his later years—could it have been under the influence of Santayana?—he substituted semipoetic musing for straightforward statement and argument, leaving his reader bewildered. I think of him as a remarkable mind whose insights were too often muffled rather than communicated by his highly individual style.

More important to me than the Fullerton Club was another, to which I was admitted about 1932. I doubt if it had a name, but it was sometimes called the New York Philosophy Club. A small group, with a normal attendance of twelve or fifteen, it met once a month in the Faculty Club at Columbia. It had a fixed ritual, which a restless member would sometimes try to change, but never successfully. First there was a tea about 4:30, then at 5:00 a paper of some length and substance, then a discussion of the paper, and finally an excellent dinner at which the talk continued. The host for the dinner was also chairman of the meeting, his chief obligation being the enforcement of a rule which, so far as I know, was peculiar to this society: when the paper concluded, the time remaining was divided by the number of guests present, with a little extra time granted to the reader for a reply; all members were expected to give their views about the paper and to keep them within the allotted time. The requirement to speak presented no difficulty, for everyone had his own views; the only difficulty was to keep the more articulate members within limits, and that proved at times an impossible task.

I gained more from this club than from any other I have belonged to, and for some forty years I attended its meetings regularly. It gave me a chance to meet and talk with many of the men I most respected in American philosophy. The Columbia philosophers always supplied its nucleus, which, when I joined, included Dewey, Woodbridge, Montague, Bush, and Schneider, with Nagel, Edman, Randall, Friess, Kristeller, Gutmann, Hofstadter, and Morgenbesser coming in over the years. There were several representatives of Union Seminary: Reinhold Niebuhr, Eugene Lyman,

William Adams Brown, Paul Tillich. From New York University there was
Sidney Hook, and from City College Morris Cohen and Harry Overstreet.
From Yale came Wilmon Sheldon, Charles Bakewell, Wilbur Urban, and
Filmer Northrop. Charles Hendel and Theodore Greene, both then of
Princeton, both later of Yale, were also members, and Walter Stace soon
followed. From farther afield, and hence appearing less regularly, were
Ducasse of Brown, Singer of Pennsylvania, and Lovejoy of Johns Hopkins.

Occasionally the club would catch European visitors on the wing, and
have papers from them—such visitors as Russell, Moore, Ewing, and Price.
Some of the members were vivid characters and famous names. Reinhold
Niebuhr was always arresting when he talked on politics, though I never
found him equally convincing on theology. With Morris Cohen's rationalism
I recognized that I had much in common, and I was flattered when he told me
that he would like to have me succeed him at City College. I naturally gave
this careful thought, though the conclusion was not what he generously
wished. At our meetings, Cohen was an acute and formidable critic whose
presence was enough to make any knowing reader apprehensive. But I came to
feel that our best critic—indeed probably the best philosophical critic that
this country has produced—was Arthur Lovejoy. When Lovejoy set his mind
to the examination of pragmatism, or Carnapian linguisticism, or, as in *The
Revolt Against Dualism,* the current forms of monism, the damage was
irreparable.

Some of our meetings were especially memorable. At a meeting in the
thirties Dewey, recently returned from Mexico, described the experiences of
his committee in investigating the case of Trotsky versus Stalin, and made
clear his high regard for Trotsky's resourcefulness and intelligence in dealing
with the committee's questions. At another meeting Robert Oppenheimer
defended some of the speculations of the newer physics against its philosophic
critics. At a meeting in the forties Paul Tillich undertook to expound his
views on the Absolute and "the ground of being." It happened that G. E.
Moore was in the group that evening, and everyone looked forward with
great interest to what Moore would say. When his time came, there was an
ominous pause, and then Moore broke out, "I am sorry to say that there is
not a single sentence in Professor Tillich's paper, not a single sentence, that I
have been able to understand. Would Professor Tillich give me just one
proposition that he thinks I *might* be able to understand?" Tillich, as I recall,
was too dumbfounded to reply. It was the most direct confrontation I have
known between German speculation and British analysis.

G. E. Moore

The name of G. E. Moore is charged with memories for me, for he and his
wife Dorothy were guests in our house for six months during the war. We saw

him first in rather odd circumstances in the spring of 1920, when Frances and I were on a visit to Cambridge. We were riding our bicycles one day when we met a man pushing a perambulator with a baby in it down the middle of the dusty road. He was bare-headed, with a wealth of grey hair flying in the wind, and with a look of intense preoccupation on his face. "I would wager that that man was G. E. Moore," I said to my wife when we next got off our cycles. I had never met him and had no idea what he looked like, but there seemed to be in the preoccupied figure something I had felt in his books. We met him a few days later at his house, and sure enough— In the end I came to know him well through walks and talks in the Swarthmore woods and in the Vermont countryside, where we had a summer house at Peacham; and whenever we later returned to England, we made 86 Chesterton Road, Cambridge, a place of pilgrimage. Moore and his wife came to us in 1942 after he had taught for a semester each at Smith, Princeton, Mills College, and Columbia. He had retired from his Cambridge chair, and I think they both felt it more patriotic to go abroad than to continue consuming rations in hard-pressed England.

Moore's standing as a philosopher has grown since his death, for he is regarded as one of the founding fathers of the analytic philosophy which has spread through the English-speaking world. He was a remarkable mind, and to have been able for six months to see him daily and raise countless questions with him was an immense if somewhat astringent stimulus. I will try to set down, for what they are worth, my impressions of him. The major ones were three—of his strenuousness, of his honesty, and of his extraordinary clearness.

First as to his strenuousness. He did not like to have philosophical questions raised casually or in passing; if he was to discuss them at all, he must discuss them in full dress; he must give his whole mind to them, and try to think and speak with the utmost precision. He used to reproach himself with laziness, but if this ever did show itself, it was rather in a reluctance to begin the hard labor of thinking than in any laxness of effort once it was begun. He was notoriously unable in any course of lectures to cover the proposed ground, for under his intense scrutiny the initial problems would break into subproblems, and these again into sub-subproblems, which must all be somehow dealt with if the major problem was to be solved. In the course on perception that he gave, with variations, in all four of the American colleges where he lectured, he would produce a matchbox early in the discussion—usually an easy thing to do, since he loved his pipe—and begin reflecting on whether the gray patch he saw or the rough surface he felt belonged to the physical matchbox or was a contribution of his own mind; and the last lecture would find him struggling with the problem still. It was much the same in ethics. He would ask what one really meant by calling an experience good, only to find that a dismaying series of ambiguities and obscurities had to be cleared up before an answer could be ventured. Indeed to these two problems—the status of sense-data and the meaning of good—Moore gave much of his philosophical life, and one may take it as evidence both of the difficulty of philosophical problems and of the intensity of his self-questioning that after sixty years of reflection he was uncertain of the answer to either.

It was part of Moore's strenuousness to be vehement and emotionally involved. No one who knew him would name serenity as his leading characteristic. He had such a passion for getting things right that if a student or colleague showed himself indifferent to important distinctions or unable to make them—a "stupe," to use a word of his—he could grow very impatient. In his time at Swarthmore he used to hold a weekly conference hour when students could come and put to him questions that were troubling them. One evening when the weather was bad, only one student turned up, a student of physics who wanted to discuss the relation of body and mind. Moore thought it would be well to make the issue specific, so he took as a starting point the relation of the sensation of blue to the change in ocular nerve and brain which presumably caused it. The student replied that this was no problem, since he *meant* by his sensation of blue this physical change. I could feel Moore's blood pressure rising. He explained that however these things were related, they surely could not be the same; one did not *mean* by "my experience of blue" the same thing as by "a motion of particles in my nerves or brain." The student insisted that he did mean exactly this. Moore was too indignant to go on; he did not conceive it as part of his duty to suffer fools gladly; and after a period of ominous silence I led him away. In these matters he was no respecter of persons, and a perverse or careless colleague was as likely as a student to stir the grapes of wrath. I did not always agree with Moore myself, and I must at times have taxed his patience severely, but I came to recognize in the veins standing out on his flushed forehead the sign that a storm was brewing and that it would be prudent to proceed cautiously.

Moore's honesty was a natural appendage of his strenuousness in the pursuit of truth. No philosopher likes to admit that he has been loose or confused or self-contradictory; but if Moore was sometimes harsh to others, he was merciless to himself. He was ready to exclaim, as McTaggart did when error was brought home to him, "I am a worm and no man." Susan Stebbing, in a paper on "Moore's Influence," says: "At a symposium of the Aristotelian Society, on 'Internal Relations,' the two symposiasts based their remarks on Moore's well-known paper on that subject. Moore expressed genuine surprise that they should do so. He expressed himself as unable to understand what he could *possibly* have meant by the views he had previously stated, and was quite convinced that they were wrong."[11] Most students would regard *Principia Ethica* as the best of his books, but he told me that he thought this place belonged to his little book on *Ethics* in the Home University Library, presumably because he considered it most free from mistakes. He tried to be honest not only about his errors but about the degrees to which he felt drawn to one view or to another. He wrote in 1942, and repeated to me in discussion, that he felt equally drawn to the new emotivist view that "X is good" is an expression of feeling and to his old view that it is a judgment ascribing a character. When I saw him some eight years later in Cambridge, I asked him whether he still felt equally drawn to the two positions. He answered emphatically no; he was now much more inclined to think his earlier view the right one. When I saw him for the last time in 1955, I put the question again. He had now forgotten that he had ever felt equally drawn in the two directions, and was more emphatic still that the earlier judgment was the sounder. It was evident at this interview that his powers were failing. Still he would not claim to see where he did not see; the reluctant answer "I don't know" came more frequently than before.

It is worth recording that Moore's honesty extended to his expressed opinions about other people and their work. Many teachers of philosophy will probably have felt as a thorn in the flesh the conflicting claims of truthfulness and kindness in dealing with their students. One must write a comment on a given paper; one may set down either the bleak negative that expresses accurately one's intellectual assessment and will leave the student desolated, or a less damning but also less accurate one that will leave him with some hope or encouragement. Moore had felt the difficulty; he once remarked that his teacher Sidgwick had seemed rather cold to his students, and interested too exclusively in their intellectual abilities, a judgment, incidentally, from which many would have dissented. I do not know how Moore himself tempered the wind to shorn lambs, but he felt no call to do this to other philosophers, and with his exacting standards of precision and clarity, he was very frugal of praise for them. Most philosophers, past and present, seemed to him culpably loose and obscure; the only one, so far as I recall, who was exempted from such criticism was Wittgenstein; and even he was not really exempt, for in Moore's copy of the *Philosophical Investigations,* which I own, he put more than five hundred question marks in the margins. His attitude toward Wittgenstein, his readiness while professor to attend the younger man's lectures and try to learn from him, has often been remarked on as striking evidence of humility. I am not sure it was that. Moore's was not so much an humble as a remarkably objective mind, and when he was convinced that another, Wittgenstein or Frank Ramsey for example, was abler than he was, he thought it the part of good sense to learn from him what he could.

The two qualities I have mentioned, strenuousness and honesty, were closely linked with a third, an insistence on clarity. There are philosophers who hold that clarity and profundity are hardly compatible with each other, and that when a philosopher dives into the Heideggerian depths of being and nonbeing, thought and its expression are bound to be murky. Moore would not agree. He would probably have said, with George Saintsbury, that all things end in bafflement, but that one ought not to be baffled too soon. He thought that most obscurity was needless, and that in any case it was the philosopher's business to dispel it. His chief concern was with clear and exact analysis, not with the extension of knowledge or the elaboration of a system. He was not a scholar's philosopher, though he had been a classical student; he would not claim a detailed knowledge of the history of philosophy; nor was he, I suspect, much interested in it. What he did want was to see things clearly for himself. Such a mind needs little in the way of scholarly apparatus. When I heard that he was coming to our house in a tiny Vermont village, I was naturally anxious as to whether we could supply what he needed in the way of workroom, desk, and books. I found that he needed nothing. He was quite content to sit in a rocking chair with a pipe in his mouth and a tablet on his knee. His philosophizing was a process of clearing his own thoughts, and that could be done from within.

Moore's presence was the most powerful antidote to muddle that I have known. His example raised the level of clarity in the philosophic community as respects both thought and writing. One of the commonest sources of confusion, he suggested, lay in failing to make clear what question precisely one was asking. Take the ancient problem of freedom. To some persons this problem means whether they can do what they please; to others it is whether, assuming that they can do what they please, their choice itself has a cause; to others, it is whether the action under review is subject to external restraint; to others it is whether they are robots, whose behavior is determined mechanically; to others it is whether their conduct is predictable; to others, finally, it is whether they are fated to a certain future regardless of their own wills. These are very different questions, and anyone who supposes that in answering one of them he is answering the others is bound to be confused. Moore was convinced, and surely with justice, that many philosophic questions, once they are precisely stated, virtually solve themselves. Another source of confusion lay in thinking too abstractly and so failing to put ideas to the test of common sense. It sounds impressive to say that one disbelieves in the reality of time, but does this mean that one has really taken no time in saying so, and hence has not said it at all? That is much less persuasive. Philosophers have set down their conviction that space is unreal; would they be equally ready to say that they set nothing down, since if space is unreal there is really no paper to set it down on? Moore's ever-present matchbox was an important aid to epistemological clarity; and when he was challenged to prove the existence of an external world, he amused and amazed the British Academy by holding up a hand and saying in effect, "I know I have a hand; I know that it is part of the external world; so there must be such a world. We are all more certain of these things than of any of the considerations produced by philosophers to disprove them." The argument was almost too simple to believe, but it was powerful nevertheless.

Moore achieved his clearness, then, partly because he defined his problems so sharply, partly because in illustration and analysis he clung to what was homely and familiar. But he was clear in expression as well as in thought. In his case, this was a notable achievement, for his thought was often anything but simple, and he would not buy clarity by leaving out needed qualifications. This resulted at times, as in his reply to critics in the Moore volume of this Library, in sentences of Brobdingnagian size, with qualifications within qualifications, all explicitly set out. The argument is clear for all that. Not that it is easy reading. One has to attend carefully, even strenuously, but if one fails to follow, it is not because of any obscurity in either thought or statement, but because of the complexity of the argument itself. Moore detested pedantry, pretentiousness, and the jargon of the philosophical marketplace, which he suspected of being a cover for flabbiness of thought. It is worth remarking that he almost never resorted to symbolic expression in setting out his ideas, and when he did, as in the essay on "Internal Relations," the formulas did not greatly help. Like his contemporaries at the other three corners of Trinity's Great Quad of clarity, McTaggart, Russell, and Broad, he could state subtle and complex arguments in straightforward English, without resort to big words or verbal coinages. In this respect he has provided a model to those philosophers who suppose that technical mastery must be shown by technicality of style.

There are two respects in which I think Moore's passion for clarity led him astray. He is needlessly wordy through repetition. He was inclined to demur when I made this criticism of him, and the defect, if defect it is, is a pardonable one, since it is incurred in the interest of clearness. But while clearness is the chief virtue of philosophic writing, it is not the only one; and if the reader will sample a few pages of what Moore considered his best written work, the *Ethics,* I think he will see what I mean. A great many words could be left out without sacrificing clarity, and with advantage to the reader's patience. Again, in trying to avoid imprecision, Moore sometimes so belabored the trivial that a mountain gave birth to a mouse. A perhaps disputable case in point is his fifty-page essay on the theory of descriptions in the Russell volume of this Library. Of that essay Russell remarked: "I admire, as always, his patience in tracking down ambiguities and differences of possible interpretation. . . . It seems my worst mistake was to suppose that, if Scott was the author of *Waverley,* he must have *written Waverley,* whereas Homer (or whoever was the author of the *Iliad*) probably never wrote the *Iliad* down. I acknowledge this error with equanimity."[12] Russell once remarked to me that a tendency to occupy himself with verbal distinctions grew on Moore with the years; and one suspects that the preoccupation with technical detail that showed itself among his analytic successors was greater than Moore himself would have approved. This is not the kind of fault to which speculative philosophy, with all its other faults, was prone. A. E. Taylor noted that all philosophers of the first rank have been marked by "a massive common sense," by which he meant an ability to judge the truth or importance of a particular suggestion through seeing its place in a wide and reflectively ordered experience. This is not the common sense to which Moore took his appeal, but it is something from which the analytic movement would have profited.

I have been commenting on Moore's intellectual traits, which, in a man of his philosophic distinction, are the most important ones. But he had other traits of interest. For example, he liked German music. At our house in Vermont he would sit down at the piano and sing Schubert lustily to his own spirited accompaniment. He liked novels in which character was clearly portrayed. On a series of evenings in our living room he read us, with obvious enjoyment and with dramatic effect, the whole of Jane Austen's *Sense and Sensibility* and George Gissing's *The Odd Women*. He showed the same vigilant eye for inconsistencies of portrayal as for inconsistencies of theory, and if Miss Austen said something of Elinor Dashwood on page 236 that did not comport with what she had said on page 57, Moore would catch and tut-tut the discrepancy. He had an intelligent layman's interest in science, and since he and his wife were fond of reading to each other, they had even covered Darwin's *Origin of Species* in this manner. He reported that Russell had once urged him to take a course in calculus with Whitehead; Moore did not follow the advice, though he did read a good deal of Russell's own writing on the philosophy of mathematics. He had what, to my envious ignorance, seemed an impressive knowledge of botany, and on our walks together I seldom caught him out with a tree or flower that he could not identify. He took a mild interest in current events, but spent little time over newspapers or magazines; and he was so suspicious of inaccuracies in the reporting of war news that he tended to confine himself to official communiqués.

We often discussed ethics, but seldom morals. I once reminded him of some of the considerations that had made Ross hold to the rightness of certain actions that produced less than the greatest good. Moore's reply was simply, "It still seems to me self-evident that it is our duty to make the world as much better as we can." He was a master in ethical theory, but he did not conceive himself as specially qualified to pass opinions on politics or social issues, and he did not take the interest or part in them that was taken by Sidgwick, Russell, and Dewey. Nor did I feel in him that imaginative concern for other persons in which the ethical convictions of Prichard and Joseph were so attractively reflected. I did think I noted, however, a strong strain of puritanism in his attitudes on morals. About religion he never talked of his own accord. I once pressed him to tell me something about his religious views. His answer was, "I see no good reason to believe that there is a God; do you?" That was all. When asked to address the weekly college chapel on any subject of his choice, he declined on the ground that for such an occasion he could not think of anything to say.

As a conversationalist, Moore was apt to be disappointing. His talk did not run, as Russell's often did, to clever witticism or sparkling repartee. He had little interest in small talk and none in gossip; and he did not have the social sense that would invent something to say to keep the ice from forming. He was capable of smoking his pipe through a party in abstracted and contented silence. Further he lacked the curiosity about the quirks and oddities of the human nature around him that makes for lively and amusing commentary. This was the more regrettable because he had been in intimate contact with some of the most remarkable persons of his time. He had been, for example, the guiding philosopher of the Bloomsbury group, whose members had included Maynard Keynes, Lytton Strachey, Leonard and Virginia Woolf, E. M. Forster, and Roger Fry. I tried to tempt him at times into reminiscence about these people. "You knew Lytton Strachey, didn't you? What was he like?" "Yes, I knew him; he used to come to my rooms and ask me to play and sing Schubert to him." But even at that promising cue the interchange would sag, and would not be resumed except under the direct questioning that I was reluctant to press. A question about whether Keynes was right on probability or intrinsic value might have started something; to Moore theories seemed to be more interesting than persons.

My debt to Moore, particularly in ethics, is great, and I should be more worth reading if it were greater. I did not manage to see eye to eye with him altogether; my search for metaphysical system was more sanguine than he thought sensible; and much as I respected his characteristically Cambridge specialism, I admired still more the temper and range of his teacher Henry Sidgwick. But for combined sharpness, precision, and lucidity, Moore stands alone. And no one could talk with him day by day without gaining a new idea of what intellectual integrity meant.

Russell

During Moore's period at Swarthmore, Russell and his wife were living not many miles away in a fine stone house at Malvern, bought for him by my former employer, A. C. Barnes. One day a note came from Lady Russell inviting the Moores and ourselves to tea. Moore declined, on the ground that he was indisposed, which was true, I think, in more senses than one; the two men, whose names are so often joined, and who owed so much to each other, were not temperamentally congenial. But Dorothy Moore accepted, and Frances and I drove her to the house, which was in the neighborhood of Bryn Mawr. I recall only two things about this visit. Russell was in a jovial mood, and taking me into his study, pointed to an old silhouette on the wall. It was the likeness of a philosopher, he said; could I tell who it was? I have a fair eye for philosophic physiognomies, but this had me baffled. "That," said Russell, "is my godfather, John Stuart Mill." It was the strange and unlikely truth. Russell was born in 1872; Mill died in 1873; Russell's parents, the Amberleys, had been devoted admirers of Mill; and though none of them had any clear religious beliefs, Mill had consented to serve as godfather and had sent the infant an inscribed silver cup. The other fragment of memory from that visit is a remark of Russell's about James. He had evidently been engaged on the chapter on James for his *History of Western Philosophy,* and had been rereading the essay on "The Will to Believe." "Isn't it immoral!" he exclaimed.

I did not know Russell nearly as well as I did Moore, but I read far more of him, partly because there was so much more of him to read; between forty and fifty of his volumes are on my shelves. He came to Ann Arbor in the early twenties to lecture on the structure of the atom, and kept his audience amused with such comparisons as that between the behavior of electrons in passing from orbit to orbit and the behavior of fleas in hopping unseen from one place to another. With a few other young philosophers, I took him to a basement café in the Michigan Union and plied him with food and questions. I asked what ground he had for believing in Occam's razor. He replied that it was incapable of proof but that we could not help believing it, and that experience appeared to confirm it. I sent him a copy of *The Nature of Thought* in 1942, and though it contained a sharp criticism of his *Analysis of Mind,* he wrote me a pleasant letter about it, reminding me that Joachim, to whom the book was dedicated, was a relative of his who had drawn up for him, when he was eighteen, a list of readings, including the *Logics* of Bradley and Bosanquet; "they started me on philosophy," he said. In October 1968 I went to McMaster University in Canada to give an address at the opening of the Russell Collection to the public. This collection of Russell's books and manuscripts, which had been acquired earlier that year, will undoubtedly be a Mecca for students of his work. He must have had a larger volume of correspondence than any other philosopher in history, including Voltaire, for the collection contains more than 120,000 letters, with "a few thousand" temporarily reserved; and more than 4,500 correspondents are listed by name. His library also was acquired by McMaster, including Wittgenstein's library, which Russell bought from him in 1919. I was happy that I could add one small item to the collection myself. Moore had written part of his essay on

Russell's theory of description in our house in Peacham, Vermont, and had left the manuscript with me. I sent it to the Russell Collection.

Russell was as ready as Moore to change his views with changing evidence. He started with Hegelian idealism; from this he shifted to one of the most extreme realisms on record; and toward the end of his life he shifted back to a Berkeleian position regarding all that is immediately experienced. It will be recalled that according to Montague the chief difficulty with the New Realism was that it could not deal with error. Russell boldly met this difficulty, not by withdrawing from realism but by defiantly becoming more realistic still; he was prepared to regard all the strange shapes seen as one walks round a table and all the bats' heads seen by the alcoholic as members of an independent physical order. This position was examined by Lovejoy in *The Revolt Against Dualism,* and when he finished, not much was left of it. Russell, alive to the force of such criticism, beat a slow retreat. By 1948, when *Human Knowledge: Its Scope and Limits* appeared, he was writing, "if percepts are 'mental,' as I should contend, then spatial relations which are ingredients of percepts are also mental."[13] Indeed the space and time of common life with all their contents were now regarded as mind-dependent, and the problem of the theory of knowledge was to find some way of correlating items in the realm of sense with the events in the realm of physics that gave rise to them. Our "real" world, the plain man's world of tables and chairs, of green grass and blue skies, is a panorama in the minds of its beholders. In comparison, the physical world was a ghostly affair that lay at the end of a precarious inference, and matter had resolved itself into "a wave of probability undulating in nothingness."

Moore was the very type of a Cambridge specialist; Russell was a Renaissance universalist. Russell wrote on every branch of philosophy except aesthetics. When I asked him once why he had not written on that too, he replied, "because I don't know anything about it," though he added characteristically, "that is not a very good excuse, for my friends tell me that it has not deterred me from writing on other subjects." He has been charged with turning out potboilers which were loosely and hastily thrown together, and no doubt in the vast volume of his writing one does find a wide variation in quality. His *History of Western Philosophy* is not the place to go for accurate philosophic reportage; his views on religion seem to me too unsympathetic and negative; and his later anti-Americanism, which led him to range an American president alongside Hitler, embarrassed many of his admirers. But even in second-grade Russell there are the trenchancy and force of a remarkable mind. If one does not get Aristotle quite as he was from the *History,* one gets at least the enlightening impression that one great logician formed of another. The defects of Christianity pointed out in *Why I Am Not a Christian* are real defects, even if the virtues are too largely ignored. And though Russell's indictment of American policy was too much like a prosecutor's brief, what he loved above all—rationality—and what he hated above all—cruelty—were surely the right things, whether he found them in the right places or not.

How many philosophers, one wonders, have succeeded in being readable through thousands of pages? Russell's success is the more striking because he was in one sense not a stylist at all. He did, to be sure, fall under the influence for a time of his literary brother-in-law, Logan Pearsall Smith, whose gods were Flaubert and Walter Pater; and he showed what he could do in the rhetorical vein when he wrote *A Free Man's Worship,* "a work," he said later, "of which I do not now think well." Until he was twenty-one, he wanted to write like John Stuart Mill. But he came to think that, for him at least, imitation involved insincerity, and that the true ideal was one derived from mathematics; "I wished to say everything in the smallest number of words in which it could be said clearly."[14] The result is a style dominated by simple declarative sentences, and so nicely adjusted to his way of thinking that he could write without revision. He had another mode of economizing his energies in writing, namely a strategic use of the subconscious. When he had to write an article, or essay, he would give intense attention long beforehand to defining the issues he wanted to deal with and summoning up such relevant knowledge as he had. He would then commit the matter to his subconscious until two weeks or so before the article was due, when he usually found that he could write it straight off with very little effort. What led him to rely on this method, he said, was his experience in preparing his Lowell Lectures on *Our Knowledge of the External World.* The lectures were to be given in Boston at the beginning of 1914. He struggled with the problem through most of the preceding year, only to reach the end of the year in frustration and despair. Since the time was short, he arranged to dictate to a stenographer what straggling ideas might come. "Next morning, as she came in at the door," he recalled, "I suddenly saw exactly what I had to say, and proceeded to dictate the whole book without a moment's hesitation."[15] When I was writing the chapter on "The Subconscious in Invention" for *The Nature of Thought,* I found many instances of such use of the subliminal mind, but I doubt if there is any philosopher for whom it has proved such a cornucopia as for Russell.

What I admire most about Russell, however, is not his writing but his rationalism. Not rationalism in the technical sense, for he abandoned that when his pupil Wittgenstein convinced him on a walking trip in Norway that mathematics was only a vast tautology. By rationalism here I mean the rational temper, the habitual appeal to reason as the only ultimate arbiter of men's differences of view. Russell was involved almost continuously in political and moral controversy; he lost his Trinity fellowship and went to jail over the First World War; he was refused the right to teach in New York because of his views on marriage and morals; he was bitterly attacked for his opinions on Hiroshima and Vietnam. But he was always ready to present reasons for his beliefs, and to reconsider them if these reasons could be shown unsound. Most persons are much worse in theory than in practice, but Russell's practice was sometimes better than his theory. From middle life on, he was prey to the unfortunate doctrine, which for a while even Moore found seductive, that moral judgments are only expressions of feeling or desire, and, as incapable of truth or falsity, cannot be made out by evidence. But neither in controversy nor in practice did he behave as if he took this seriously. He never ceased to argue on moral issues, to assume that where men differed there was an objective truth to be found, or to believe that the highest human goodness lay in acting rationally. He acted himself like an eighteenth-century rationalist, and the man whom he regarded as "the noblest and most lovable of the great philosophers"[16] was that archrationalist Spinoza. It can hardly be doubted that in the annals of practical rationalism Russell will rank high.

European Interludes

I cannot think that in saying so much about philosophers I admire I am wandering from autobiography, for all admiration is self-disclosure. But to return to the years at Swarthmore. It was there that I spent the central part of my life, the years from thirty-three to fifty-three. The teaching load was too heavy to admit of much writing in termtime; that had to be done in vacations or on leave; and the summer vacations were abbreviated at their beginning by weariness, and at their end by hay fever. Fortunately in 1929 a Guggenheim fellowship gave me a free year. Frances and I went to Paris, and after a short stay took the long trip overland to Vienna, where we spent the summer. We worked in the mornings and got away most afternoons either for walks in the city parks and the surrounding hills, or else for tennis on the banks of the Danube, where mis-hit balls would often go into the river and get free transport to Budapest and the Black Sea. The old Vienna had not wholly disappeared; the air was still full of music; and I decided that if I had any kind of musical sense, here was the place to nurture it. So I went round to the leading cellist of the Vienna municipal orchestra, Rudolf Mayr, and asked if he would help me buy a cello and start me on it. He kindly did both. I thought and still think that with its rich and mellow tone the cello is the finest of all instruments. I worked industriously at it for many months, brought it home with me to America, and for many years would occasionally get it out and make lovely wistful sounds on it. But I had aimed too high. A cello is a musician's instrument, and it calls for undivided devotion. I came slowly to the conclusion that I had neither the time nor the talent to be a musician.

But I have continued to speculate at times on the place of music among the arts. Music is often held to have no relation to poetry. "Like most poets," wrote Andrew Lang, "I myself detest the sister art, and don't know anything about it."[17] Even of Swinburne, who is in a sense the most musical of poets, his friend Edmund Gosse remarked that he "did not recognise the difference between one tune and another," though adding that "he took a cerebral interest in music."[18] But perhaps this "cerebral interest" should be looked at more closely. Music is the most abstract of the arts, whose materials are only sounds and intervals of time, and the curious affinity has often been noted between music and mathematics; indeed Leibniz suggested that music is the pleasure one experiences when counting without being aware that one is counting. If this is oversimple, it remains true that there is something very primitive in the satisfaction of a regular beat, something that goes back perhaps to the beating of the heart. I suppose a sufficiently learned historian of music could trace a continuous line of advance running from the tom-tom to Bach, the developing mind being able to hold a more and more complex pattern of sound within the control of the recurrent beat. If music is looked at in this somewhat Leibnizian way, it is surely not alien to poetry. Indeed music, poetry, oratory, and "numerous" prose are all exhibitions of such variety in unity, of holding a complex pattern of sound within a simple pattern of time. Everyone feels satisfaction in the exercise of this power. But where I fall in the long line between the tom-tom and Bach I do not know. I think I am a little beyond the tom-tom, for I detest the popular music of today, much of which, with its deafening blare and its pitiless pounding drumbeat, seems like a flight back to the jungle. I gather that such flights are themselves recurrent affairs, for a predecessor at Yale, Charles A. Bennett, was already complaining in his own day of a "Subway Suite, orchestrated for two klaxons, three files, one siren, two tom-toms, and five cats."

After the summer in Vienna, Frances returned to her post as dean at Swarthmore, to rejoin me in the following spring. I grimly holed up in England, determined to make headway with the manuscript of *The Nature of Thought*. The first four hundred pages of it were written that year, partly in Oxford and partly at the British Museum. At Oxford I had rooms in the same house with Sarvepalli Radhakrishnan, to whom another volume in this Library is devoted, though we were both so busy that we saw far less of each other than I at least should have wished. He lived, I fear, on a philosophic island at Oxford, for the philosophers there were already in retreat from idealism and were beyond the eloquence even of Radhakrishnan. Still less were they likely to be moved by the mysticism so often pervasive of Indian thought.

At the beginning of September 1930 the seventh World Congress of Philosophy met at Oxford, and I reported it for the *Journal of Philosophy* (October 23, 1930). It was exhilarating to see and hear distinguished figures that I had known only in print. The great old Samuel Alexander was there from Manchester, flourishing his ear trumpet. Oddly enough no one from either Oxford or Cambridge read a paper. Brunschvicg, Bouglé, and Parodi were there from France; Aliotta, Enriques, and Ruggiero from Italy; Driesch and Müller-Freienfels from Germany; Lutoslawski, Tatarkiewicz, and Kotarbinski from Poland; Lunacharsky from Russia; Lossky from Prague. The veteran who aroused most general interest was undoubtedly Benedetto Croce, the Neopolitan idealist, who had an influential following at Oxford. (He was an unusual-looking man, with large irregular features, and he went about with a lovely daughter; irreverent youth described the pair as "Beauty and the Beast.")

The congress proved to be a watershed between the old philosophy and the new. A shadow of the shape of things to come was discernible in a paper by Moritz Schlick of Vienna. He announced that the first person in modern times to see the function of philosophy "with absolute clearness" was Ludwig Wittgenstein, who had seen that science is the only knowledge worthy of the name, and that the true work of philosophy lies in discovering the meaning of scientific propositions and how they are to be made out. As a result of this discovery "we are witnessing the beginning of a new era of philosophy." "Metaphysical tendencies will be entirely abandoned, simply because there is no such thing as metaphysics, the apparent descriptions of it being just nonsensical phrases." To most members of the congress this conception of philosophy seemed thoroughly unconvincing, and to me it still seems so after forty years. But we should certainly have been shaken if we had realized how nearly Schlick's prediction of the death of metaphysics was to be fulfilled.

Though I made good progress with my book in this year of freedom, it was eight years more before I could call it done. We came back to England in 1938, and I rounded it out that fall in the Museum library. By this time it had swollen to an immense mass of manuscript, and I wondered whether any publisher would take it. Allen & Unwin, publishers of Ruskin and Bertrand Russell, had an office that I had often passed in Museum Street, and desperation makes one bold. I put the manuscript into a suitcase which it filled to capacity, and one rainy afternoon lugged it round to Allen & Unwin's door. The young man who received it gave me a wan smile of sympathy, took my address, and said the company would let me know if they were interested. It was clear what he thought the answer would be. But not long afterward came a note saying that on the recommendation of their reader, Dr. J. E. Turner of Liverpool, the company was accepting it for publication. The next autumn it appeared in the Muirhead Library of Philosophy in two volumes. During its preparation for the press, I received much help from Dr. Turner and made the acquaintance of my publisher, Sir Stanley Unwin, who with his firm has befriended me ever since.

Unfortunately *The Nature of Thought* appeared at the worst possible time. The winds of philosophic fashion were already veering in new directions; the book was tagged by hasty reviewers as another product of the idealist mill; and that tag was becoming a brand of Cain. Furthermore, World War II broke out when the book was in press, and people's minds were naturally engrossed with other issues. Shortly after its publication, the great blitz fell on London. One of Hitler's bombs found Allen & Unwin's warehouse and destroyed more than a million volumes at one stroke. Among them was half the edition of *The Nature of Thought*.

Happily the publication of the book had some fruit of a more pleasant kind. Someone on the nominating committee of the Philosophical Association, Edgar Brightman perhaps, must have seen the book and liked it, for at the meeting of the Eastern Division in 1941, I was elected president for 1942. Because the meetings for that and the following year were suspended by reason of restrictions on war travel, I held office for two annual terms. Nevertheless, since both meetings at which my presidential address might have been given were canceled, I never gave one at all. So far as I know, I am the only president in association history to hold that forlorn distinction.

A Commission on Philosophy

In 1943 the Board of Officers of the Philosophical Association undertook a review of the place of philosophy in American education. They appointed a commission to report on "the function of philosophy in liberal education and in the development of a free and reflective life in the community." The Board called for nominations to this commission from the membership generally, and from the names so submitted selected a group of five to make the study. They were Arthur Murphy, chairman; Charles Hendel, secretary; Curt Ducasse, Max C. Otto, and myself. Funds were supplied by the Rockefeller Foundation. The commission set out to gather facts, opinions, and advice from philosophers in every part of the country. It organized and participated in two-day conferences in Chicago, Berkeley, Los Angeles, New Orleans, Baltimore, New York, and Boston. When these conferences were over, the commissioners held a further series of conferences of their own to gather the sense of the hundreds of letters that had come in, to thrash out differences of opinion, to divide responsibilities in drafting the report, and finally to criticize each other's contributions.

I enjoyed the months of service on this commission. They might have been debilitating if the members had been prickly toward each other, for we had to travel thousands of miles in each other's company, crossing the continent twice by train. One member in fact did not take these long trips with us. Max Otto seems to have felt, as the one pragmatist in the group, that his conception of philosophy and its function was so different from that of the rest of us that his presence would be an apple of discord; so, though he was personally well liked, he worked in comparative independence. The four who did make the circuit together formed a congenial group. Arthur Murphy, stoutish, pink-cheeked, jolly and cherubic, had an irrepressible sense of humor, and when he and Ducasse, his former colleague at Brown, fell to exchanging banter with each other, I wished that a recorder had been on hand. Murphy had a rare gift of extempore speech, and when called on for his views on a philosophical matter, could pour out his thought in a sequence of elaborate but well knit sentences that were impressive both at the time and in review. Ducasse was of a different type. A lean, fastidiously dressed aesthetician, French by birth and with the accent that no Frenchman loses, however long his exile, Ducasse was one of the most distinguished of American philosophers. He had come into philosophy late, after a strange and varied career in business in Mexico and California, about which he used to regale us with romantic stories. With Charles Hendel, efficient and hard-working secretary of the commission, and at that time chairman of the department at Yale, I formed a friendship that was continued for many years at New Haven.

The report of the commission was published by Harper in 1945 as a three-hundred-page book called *Philosophy in American Education*. It had a respectful though somewhat tepid reception by the press and the profession. Its main effect, I think, was to give reflective assurance to teachers of philosophy that they were engaged in something important. As I look back on our correspondence and our conferences, two demands for aid from philosophy stand out, one of them coming from the academic community, the other from the wider public.

The first was a demand for aid in integration, by which was meant in those days the integration not of races but of ideas. There was a sense at our conferences that liberal education was not doing for its students what it ought to do, and that philosophy was in a unique position to give it the aid it needed. The volume of human knowledge was expanding at a bewildering speed; indeed, it was exploding in all directions. The universities were attempting to keep abreast of this expanding knowledge and purvey it to their students. The result was to spread out before the students a vast indigestible surfeit of courses; even small colleges were now offering as many subjects as were formerly offered by large universities. The problem had been made more acute for the student by the elective system, which suggested that of the varied fare before him one subject was about as nutritious as another, and that he was free to combine them as he wished. He was suffering in consequence from malnutrition amid plenty. The only way that occurred to him of unifying his studies was specialization—losing himself among his chemical test tubes or burrowing into some historical period; he thus avoided becoming a smatterer by becoming a mole. And such burrowing persisted in later life. One of our conferees said that when he fell into conversation with a new colleague at the faculty club, the stranger, a historian, introduced himself with the remark, "I am the Andrew Jackson period." Robert Hutchins of Chicago, whom we interviewed in his office, with the roar of Chicago in our ears, complained that American college graduates shared almost no common ground except the world series and the weather.

Many thought that in this situation philosophy had much to offer, and the commission agreed. Philosophy is in a peculiar position among the liberal disciplines. It has no subject matter of its own; the stuff for its reflection is supplied by art, religion, and the sciences, of which it is the natural extension. If they form the central part of the spectrum of knowledge, philosophy is its infrared and ultraviolet ends; logically it begins before they do and goes on when their work is done. It raises two types of question about these other disciplines. First, how are their fundamental terms to be defined—terms such as cause, fact, person, right, value—and how are their fundamental assumptions, the possibility of perceptual knowledge, for example, or the law of causality, to be made out? And secondly, when the results of their inquiries are in, how are they to be put together into a consistent whole? For the answer to this question, reflective men have always turned to philosophy; indeed its greatest traditional problems—the relation of body and mind, the place of value in a world of fact, the place of freedom in a world of law, the relation of mechanism to purpose, of science to religion—are precisely attempts to put fragmented human knowledge into an intelligible whole. The instrument of this synthesis is reflection. Philosophy, of course, has no monopoly of that instrument. But it is the discipline that cultivates it most assiduously; and only by its cultivated use can the scattered islands be linked and the intellectual traveler enabled to pass without losing his way from the realm of physics to the realm of mind and from anthropology to ethics. What happens to specialism, even in able hands, when unleavened by philosophy, may be seen on all sides in our increasingly specialized world. In psychology it may be seen in a crude behaviorism, in anthropology in the glib conclusion that among "patterns of culture" there is no real better or worse, in religion in the teaching that revelation is a realm sealed off from rational support or attack. Philosophy is the most effective protection against such provincialism. It refuses to recognize fences or frontiers. It brings all assumptions and all conclusions within the range of a common reason. The kind of reflection that it stands for is therefore an increasingly valuable component in any liberal education.

On the value of philosophy in education, the commission not only were agreed but could fairly be called a set of evangelists. To the other demand constantly made in their conferences, they had to give a more qualified answer. Many of the conferees had noted with concern the decline of religious belief. What concerned them was not merely the loss of faith but the loss of the moral commitments that had accompanied the lost faith. They complained in language that still has a familiar ring that youth seemed to have nothing left to believe in; and their apprehension was fortified by the disturbing impression that youth in the Fascist and Communist countries showed a more unified and zealous commitment to their own tarnished ideals than democratic youth did to their purer ones. Should not philosophers show a more active concern about this defection from longstanding beliefs and ideals?

Here we had to reduce our claims for philosophy. For as soon as it accepts a brief for anything except the devotion to reason itself, it abdicates its title to special respect. Philosophy is either nonpartisan or not strictly philosophy at all. This does not mean that philosophers as such should not have strong convictions, but only that the convictions should *issue from* their inquiry, not precede it. Philosophy as such cannot commit itself to Christianity, or peace, or freedom, or democracy. Its one commitment is to being as rational as possible. If thinking rationally entails the acceptance of certain religious beliefs, if acting rationally entails the espousing of certain ideals, philosophy may embrace these—not otherwise. Philosophers have often and effectively used their powers of reasoning in the support of beliefs adopted on nonrational grounds; Macaulay accused Burke of doing it habitually, and Russell held that even the massive philosophy of Aquinas reduced itself for the most part to special pleading for what was accepted on faith. Christian philosophy, or democratic philosophy, or "positive thinking," however productive of happy results, is always dangerous because none of these puts first things first. The business of the philosopher, as of the scientist, is not to make out a client's case, but to see things as they are.

Current causes and parties are looking in the wrong quarter, then, if they retain philosophy as an attorney for the defense. Does it follow that philosophy has no gospel of its own to put forward? The commission (or at least one member of it) did not think so. Philosophy is the persistent attempt to understand the nature of things by the exercise of reason, and it has its own injunction, namely, loyalty to reason in thought and practice. There are those who would reject such an imperative as one-sided, as exalting intellect at the expense of the nonrational parts of our nature, as sicklying over man's intuitions and all his full-blooded impulses with the pale cast of thought. The objection is natural but ill-founded. The only intuition with any authority is itself a form of reason, and the intellect which the greater philosophers have believed in is not only a player with concepts but also a moulder of impulse, feeling, and desire.

I must say something about this later, for if there is anything in my philosophy that I should hope might last, it is the quite unoriginal but none the less important thesis that the rational life is at once the worthiest of lives and the most valuable. I am convinced that this sets an ideal more unexceptionable than any of the rivals that are being offered us in such profusion, an ideal free of the defects from which (as I have argued elsewhere) even Christianity suffers. If it is objected that the ideal calls for a self-discipline too exacting to have much chance at present against more colorful and dramatic gospels, I can only agree. But the immediate invitingness of an ideal to the average man is no test of its validity.

The work of the commission was still in progress when on Christmas eve of 1943 I had a telephone call from Washington. The Armed Forces Institute, under the direction of Col. Francis Spaulding, had been charged with the duty of enabling soldiers, so far as possible, to continue their education while in service. What was envisaged was a variety of courses, each with its appropriate book or books, which must be intelligible enough to allow a man in service, with a certain amount of free time, to read and understand them on his own. In some fields, including philosophy, it had been concluded that the right books did not exist and that new ones must be written. I was informed by the telephone call that four men had been selected to collaborate in the writing of an introduction to philosophy for the forces: Hocking of Harvard, Hendel of Yale, Randall of Columbia, and I. We were to have the book completed by March 1, about two months away. Our work was to be coordinated by Chancellor W. P. Tolley of Syracuse. In the end two books were produced, and in not much more than the allotted time. We all thought that the text should be accompanied by a book of selections from the greater philosophers, and this was edited at Syracuse by Professors Piper and Hoople. The four authors of the textbook divided the work before them into five parts. Hocking wrote the first and the last, dealing chiefly with metaphysics, I wrote the second, on ethics, Hendel the third, on politics, and Randall the fourth, on religion. The book, of about five hundred pages, was published by Macmillan with the title *Preface to Philosophy*. How widely it was used in the army I do not know. But our sedulous attempt at simplicity and clarity did make the book a usable one for beginners, and it was adopted in a number of colleges after it had done its work in the army. The position taken in my section on ethics is closer to Moore's than it would be if I were writing it now, but there is not much in it that I should feel called upon to change.

Yale

It was probably my association with Charles Hendel on both the commission and the *Preface to Philosophy* that led to my invitation to Yale in the fall of 1944. Frances and I had to take careful stock of present and future, for acceptance would mean the resignation of two posts; as a dean at Swarthmore she was more deeply implicated in the life of the college than I. Happily we fully agreed about the wisdom of a change. For nearly twenty years she had been carrying a heavy burden of administrative duties, besides responsibility for a mother who, at the height of a career as professor of English literature at Smith College, had been reduced to seventeen years of helplessness and speechlessness by a paralytic stroke. Frances was ready for relief and I was ready for a change. The college granted me leave for the spring semester of 1945, during which I went to New Haven, explored the housing situation, and bought a house. The war was still on; Yale, departing from old tradition, was holding summer sessions; and I began my teaching there in the summer of 1945. Charles Hendel was away in Shrivenham, England, on a teaching assignment in the services, and I was asked to take on his duties as department chairman.

I began work at Yale with some trepidation. It was one thing to teach philosophy in a small Quaker college; it was another to teach it in a great university with a graduate school of high standards. Besides, Yale had a reputation for social sophistication and "white-shoeism" not calculated to put a Quaker at ease. Happily my apprehensions on this score proved groundless. From the beginning I found the Yale community congenial, friendly, unassuming, hard-working, and devoted in its manifold fields to the life of the mind. The transition was made easier for me by one fact that soon became apparent: the university was not a set of graduate schools with an anemic undergraduate appendage dangling below, but a distinguished college of the liberal arts with a graduate school added above. It was Yale College that formed the vigorous heart of the University. The most distinguished teachers had their affiliations there rather than in the graduate school, and great stress had been traditionally placed on undergraduate teaching. Indeed I doubt whether there was any college in the country where the standards of teaching were so consistently high. Charles Hendel, who was an efficient chairman, and William C. DeVane, an admirable humanist dean, were both committed to maintaining these standards.

I was at Yale for the sixteen years from 1945 until my retirement in 1961. For seven of these years I was department chairman without a reduction of the regular load of teaching. Oddly enough, my experience at Swarthmore, which was wholly with undergraduates, prepared me better for my work in the graduate school than for my work in Yale College. It was not difficult to adapt the seminar methods I had been using to the needs of graduate students; but Yale required one form of teaching that I had not previously used at all, namely lecturing to large undergraduate classes. I have never regarded lecturing as a good way to teach philosophy, because it cannot assure that active dialogue of the mind with itself or with another in which philosophizing consists. But American universities have found no effective alternative to it where instruction must be offered to hundreds of students at once. I was regularly asked to give introductory courses at Yale, with classes numbering up to four, five, or even seven hundred students.

I concluded that if lecturing to such numbers had to be done it should be made as much of an art as possible, and I set myself to learn its techniques. Many teachers are bored by having to repeat their courses; I never was. The more familiar I became with the subject matter of a course, the more free I was to attend to matters of form, and it was only when I was giving an introductory course for about the fortieth time that I had it approximately where I wanted it—and then it was time to retire. I could never extemporize a lecture; I am not good at thinking on my feet; and I could not have managed the method my quick-witted colleague Paul Weiss adopted of resolving the lecture into a process of give-and-take between floor and rostrum. What I gradually found that I could do, if I had thought the lecture carefully through, was to leave its phrasing to the occasion, and for the last ten years or so I dispensed with any kind of notes. The effect of this practice on students is out of all proportion to its difficulty or real deserts. It sweeps away the gossamer veil between speaker and hearers that notes always create, with their suggestion that such food for thought as the lecturer is dispensing is old stuff that he has long kept in his larder. And if the more freely given lecture really comes off, it communicates the idea that there is something exhilarating about thinking a problem through, and something worth emulating in the clean statement of a case. No doubt philosophers have much to knit their brows and wring their hands about, and, following the practice of a certain eminent philosopher, it became the fashion among some of his admirers to make these into a public rite. It is better, I think, that the process should be completed before it reaches the rostrum. Students are not likely to find blood, sweat, and tears attractive before they have some notion what may be gained by them.

My administrative work at Yale limited the range of my courses. My seminars in the graduate school were confined in later years to the theory of knowledge, metaphysics, and ethics. Many years earlier at Ann Arbor I had given a course in types of logical theory, and for a time at Yale I divided a year's seminar in logic with Frederic Fitch; but with the coming into dominance of symbolic logic, in which I was not greatly interested, I moved away from this field. I once offered a seminar in the logic of Hegel, but decided not to do so again. It was embarrassingly hard to be sure of Hegel's meaning; indeed at the end of the course I was not quite sure that any single step in his long procession through the categories really followed from the preceding step. My most frequent offerings in the graduate school were two courses running through the year, one in selected problems in epistemology and metaphysics, the other in types of ethical theory. For each of these courses I worked out a detailed syllabus, circulating each week a bibliography and questions for self-examination. No doubt there were students who found this too schoolmasterish for their taste, but there were more, I thought, who were grateful for it.

The experience of graduate teaching forced several conclusions upon me. One was that too much seminar time is wasted by the reading aloud of student papers. It is true that their presentation for criticism may be valuable, and in my Swarthmore seminars, where the groups were small, the papers short, and the periods three or four hours long, it was standard practice. But my Yale seminars were much larger; papers by graduate students needed more time; the period was limited to two hours; and I soon found that a single rambling essay could spoil a seminar. My usual practice was to require papers but to read them outside the seminar, comment on them in writing, and see the student, if he wished, for personal conference. Secondly, seminar discussion needs firm guidance. To allow it to develop into a "bull session" is neglect of duty on the part of the instructor. The argument should be kept to the main issues, and if possible followed through to a conclusion. Students who are excessively vocal require the sort of curbing—not always easy—that leaves them their self-respect, and the reticent must be brought into the discussion, by direct questioning if need be. Thirdly, the discussion will be more alive if the teacher frankly avows his own position. He is more than the chairman of a meeting, he is the senior scholar present, to whose views the students are most ready to listen, and against whose wits they are eager to try their own. At any rate, when we were discussing an important issue—determinism, causality, utilitarianism—I tried not only to keep the discussion to the track of the relevant considerations pro and con but to show how these considerations carried one on to a certain conclusion. A seminar at its best should be a joint effort to solve one problem, philosophy embodied in a public act. The kind of direction most helpful here is one that combines a clear conviction with a readiness to explore every objection that can be adduced against the conviction. In short, the conduct of a seminar is a narrow lane hedged with thorny personal sensitivities and intersected by numberless inviting paths that lead into bogs. I have often wound up a session with a sad sense of defeat, and seldom or never with a sense of full success. But I felt again at Yale, as I had at Swarthmore, that to sit week after week in a circle of youth bent on the pursuit of a common reason was one of the most satisfying lots that the world had to offer. I was a lucky and happy man.

Yale Colleagues

I was fortunate too in my colleagues. Though the Yale department increased in number fourfold or fivefold in the years following the war, it was still small when I came; Charles Hendel had been brought in to build it up. Its three senior men, Bakewell, Sheldon, and Urban, had all recently retired but were still on the scene, and gave me a friendly welcome.

Charles Bakewell was a distinguished figure as he walked about the campus, handsome and impeccably dressed, with piercing dark eyes looking out from a strong face under a crown of snow-white hair. After many years of teaching, he had gone to Washington as Congressman-at-large from Connecticut. Philosophically this was not a very helpful diversion. Bakewell had been a brilliant and promising pupil of James and Royce (he had been with James on his last walking expedition in California); he was a Greek scholar and had early edited a well-known *Source Book in Greek Philosophy;* he had been a favorite of Thomas Davidson, and had inherited Davidson's celebrated camp at Glenmore. But the scholarly book on Socrates that was to be the chief work of his life somehow postponed itself until, with continued distractions and increasing years, he found that he could not complete it; and he seemed to me a disappointed man.

The case was very different with Wilmon Sheldon. Though he had not been a prolific writer during his long years of teaching at Dartmouth and Yale, retirement gave him the freedom that he needed, and the pent-up reflections of a lifetime came pouring out in a stream of books. Sheldon was a speculative philosopher built on old and generous lines. He took no stock in analytic and positivist theories and cheerfully went his own way. Until he was past ninety, one saw him swinging along New Haven streets to his office at Silliman College, always with a benignant greeting for any friend he met. Sheldon was a remarkable character. His naturally affectionate disposition was reinforced by a deep religiousness; he had managed to convince himself that love and reason were two sides of a single coin; and one of his last books, entitled *Agapology,* was a work in praise of love. He was welcome in any philosophic gathering for his eirenic temper as well as for his shrewdness of mind. A connoisseur of food and drink (though he insisted he was merely a gourmand, not a gourmet), he was also a lover of long walks, exhausting to anyone else, and a keen botanist, who professed to be more proud of a species of grass, discovered by him and named for him, than of any of his philosophic achievements. Sheldon holds a bright place in my memory.

Of Wilbur Urban I saw less, though he wanted me to succeed him at Dartmouth and I did succeed him—after a brief interval filled by Cassirer—at Yale. His big book on *Language and Reality* has not received the attention it deserves, in spite of its raising many of the questions canvassed later by the linguistic philosophers. Urban's life was in his thought; he confessed that for him *Metaphysik allein macht selig.* In his youth he had gone to Germany and worked with Eucken and Liebmann at Jena, and with Wundt at Leipzig. Germany became his spiritual home. Somewhat lonely by natural tendency, he was made more lonely by his German affinities, for he did not, I think, approve of our entrance into either of the great wars against Germany. Incidentally, Urban once told me that when he began his teaching at Trinity College after his strenuous years in Germany, he was threatened with a nervous breakdown; his physician warned him against evening work, saying that he would do well to cultivate some mindless relaxation such as looking at moving pictures. Urban followed this advice, and like Wittgenstein, with whom he could have had little else in common, developed a fondness for movies; Frances and I discovered, not quite too late, that he enjoyed being asked by his friends to see movies with them. Urban and Sheldon were very unlike, but it was interesting and puzzling to me that both of them could maintain a serene religious faith in the face of difficulties that seemed to me profoundly perturbing.

My colleagues in the Yale department were all busy and hard worked, and we saw less of each other than we should have liked. They were a remarkable group. Northrop in law and the philosophy of science; Hendel, Brumbaugh, and Calhoun in the history of philosophy; Weiss in metaphysics; Margenau in the philosophy of science; Fitch and Anderson in logic; Hempel and Pap in logical empiricism; John Smith in the philosophy of religion; Greene in aesthetics; Wells in the philosophy of language; and, at the end my period there, Hanson in the philosophy of science and Wilfrid Sellars in the theory of knowledge—they were a brilliant group; and behind them was an echelon of outstanding younger men. Their positions were very diverse. Indeed this diversity gave the department of the fifties its special strength; its deliberately adopted policy was to secure the ablest representatives of the leading schools of thought. The result was that for a time the Yale department was ranked No. 1 in the country by the committee of the Carnegie Foundation that undertakes that invidious business. Some American departments seem to have abjured this policy with a view to inculcating only the "right" philosophy, or "modern" or "analytic" or "exact" philosophy. And it is true that the disunity of philosophers as compared with scientists is something of a scandal. But it is a scandal with which philosophers have had to live for many centuries, and it will not be scotched by the proclamation of some new school that it has discovered the one true method. The strongest departments will continue to be those that, with ability and dedication on the part of their members, admit diversity of position and encourage their students to adopt those methods and conclusions that commend themselves after they have heard the divergent views presented as forcibly as may be.

It is tempting to produce a gallery of sketches of my colleagues at Yale, most of whom are still happily in the land of the living, but it would be impertinent to make them sit for portraits to my inadequate pen. Perhaps, however, I may say a little about two of them who are no longer alive.

Arthur Pap was the sharpest mind we had at Yale in my time. He was crotchety, wayward, angular, passionate, but he had an intellect like a razor blade. He was destined to live among storms, either outward or inward. He was one of the Jews who had fled from German Switzerland before the threat of a Hitler invasion and had found a tortuous escape route through France, Spain, and Portugal. He reached New York at nineteen. Young Pap was a fine pianist who had dreams of a concert career. He entered the Juilliard School and practiced eight hours a day. But he also managed to attend Columbia University where, after a struggle, philosophy displaced music in his affections. He brought with him from Europe an aggressive Hegelianism, and went to Yale for an M.A. under Cassirer, but in the course of writing a Columbia dissertation on "The A Priori in Physical Theory," he did a right-about-face and came out an equally aggressive positivist. After brief and not notably placid ventures in teaching at four universities, he was appointed to an assistant professorship at Yale. Less than four years later, at a casual checkup on his health, it was discovered that he was suffering from a form of nephritis for which there was no known cure. A few months later, in 1959, working continuously to the end, he died, at the age of thirty-eight, leaving a wife and four small children behind him.

It is hard to predict what Pap would have done if he had lived. His mind was constantly and almost feverishly in motion, and though he was tenacious of his opinions, he could relinquish or revise them; he not only moved from Hegelianism to positivism, but rapidly outgrew some of the central notions of positivism, for example that all a priori statements are analytic and say nothing about reality. He produced in his short life five books on philosophy of high technical virtuosity and scores of articles and reviews. It seems hardly possible that he should have maintained this pace while teaching a full schedule of graduate and undergraduate courses, but if he had lived and not burned himself out he would have become, I think, one of the leading figures in the philosophical world. He would have become so not through skill in presentation, for he was a hasty writer with no great interest in form, and not by range of knowledge, for his interests were limited, but by the fierce intensity and keenness of his analytic vision.

A very different colleague whom I also remember affectionately was Theodore Greene. Our acquaintance was of long standing, for during an emergency at Swarthmore I induced him to commute from Princeton for a semester and take my honors seminars; and when *The Nature of Thought* appeared, he reviewed it discerningly for the *Journal of Philosophy*. Greene was a tall and powerful figure, but had been crippled by some disease that affected the sockets of his hips, so that he could walk only with canes or crutches. For all that, he was the most mobile of philosophers. He had been born—of missionary parents, I think—in Constantinople. Before I knew him he had been a Y.M.C.A. secretary in Mesopotamia and a teacher for two years in India, though his periods in both countries were a little later than mine and we did not meet. He took his doctorate in Edinburgh, Scotland; and later life found him teaching not only in Yale and Princeton but in California, Texas, Georgia, Mississippi, Maine, the Middle East, and Hong Kong. Greene's interests were concentrated in the humanities, particularly in aesthetics, ethics, and religion. He was brought to Yale in 1946, and in bringing him, President Seymour had him in mind, I think, as a prospective head for one of the Yale colleges. At any rate, a year later he became master of Silliman.

Greene was an excellent talker and a superlative teacher, and was especially effective in lecturing to introductory courses. For some reason not clear to me, he was less effective in graduate seminars, perhaps because he was impatient of the logical and analytic techniques that were coming into fashion. He had no use for emotivist theories of morals, and in aesthetics he held firmly to cognitive values in art and to objective standards of criticism. These were not very popular views, and his most ambitious book, *The Arts and the Art of Criticism,* was mercilessly reviewed. Still he was happy with his Yale students and colleagues. Naturally enough, he was in widespread demand as a lecturer and baccalaureate speaker. His wife, however, was not in good health, and, to the department's surprise and regret, after nine years at Yale he accepted an invitation from Scripps College, California. Some unfortunate disagreement developed with the administration there, and Greene resigned, to start on a pilgrimage that took him round the world and back at the end to New Haven. For a term or two he taught at the American University at Beirut, but it was a time of turmoil in the Arab countries, and, threatened with a nervous breakdown, he moved on, and taught for a time at Yale-in-China, Hong Kong. But the smoggy atmosphere there proving too much for his health, he soon moved on again. For brief periods he stayed in Honolulu, hoping, though in vain, that departments of an analytic cast would be interested in his kind of philosophizing. Returning to America, he taught briefly at the University of Mississippi, at Agnes Scott College, Atlanta, and at Bowdoin College, Maine, where on a lecture visit I found him and his wife happily ensconced on the top floor of the skyscraper that Bowdoin has run up out of the Maine woods. He was very popular there, so much so that the students virtually insisted that the college confer on him an honorary doctorate, which it did. But I found him hungry also to return to New Haven. In 1968 he came, buying a house from me on Lawrence Street, and in the summer of 1969 he and his wife moved in with pleasant anticipations of renewing old friendships. About the first of August they drove to the Maine coast to spend the month in a house offered to them by a Silliman colleague. One night a fire was reported as having been observed from the sea, and it proved to be the house where they were staying. A fire company was sent to the spot, but the house was beyond saving, and the bodies of Ted and Betty Greene were found among the ashes. No one knows what happened, and presumably no one will ever know. On inspection of his will, it was discovered that he had left his New Haven house, in gratitude, to Bowdoin.

St. Andrews

One day, in going through my office mail in the old Linsly-Chittenden Hall, I came upon an airmail letter from Scotland. It bore the name of E. P. Dickie, a name that at the time meant nothing to me but is now that of a dear friend. He was professor of divinity at St. Andrews University, and his letter was an invitation to deliver the Gifford Lectures at St. Andrews in 1952 and 1953. It was a totally unexpected bolt from a clear sky, which both delighted and overwhelmed me. Could I live up to such an appointment? The lectureship had been held by only six Americans, whose names put me in my place: James, Royce, Dewey, Hocking, Perry, and Niebuhr. The lectures dealt mainly with religion, and I was no theologian. I turned to Lord Gifford's will to see more precisely what was required.

This will was a remarkable document. It had been drawn up in 1885, and was a model of academic statesmanship, fixing in clear but liberal terms the territory he wished his lecturers to explore. Their two fields were to be religion and ethics. As for prior religious commitments, the lecturers, he said, should not be required to "subscribe any declaration of belief or to make any promise of any kind, they may be of any denomination whatever, or of no denomination at all (and many earnest and high-minded men prefer to belong to no ecclesiastical denomination); they may be of any religion or way of thinking, or as is sometimes said, they may be of no religion, or they may be so-called sceptics or agnostics or free-thinkers, provided only that the 'patrons' [i.e. the electors] will use diligence to secure that they be able, reverent men, true thinkers, sincere lovers of and earnest inquirers after truth." Then came the most surprising specification of all, considering that it was laid down by a religious man of the Victorian era. "I wish the lecturers to treat their subject as a strictly natural science . . . without reference to or reliance upon any supposed special exceptional or so-called miraculous revelation. I wish it considered just as astronomy or chemistry is."

That took a weight off my mind, as it has, I am sure, from many other lecturers, and it gave the electors a range of choice that has enabled them over the years to secure men as diverse as James Ward and Dean Inge, Arthur Balfour and A. S. Eddington, Edward Caird and Werner Heisenberg. Perhaps the appointments that came nearest to straining Lord Gifford's rules were those of Brunner and Barth, not of course because they were unbelievers but because they believed so much; both were unqualified revelationists. Barth began his lectures by admitting the oddity of his lecturing on a "natural theology" whose validity he denied. But he thought that to establish that invalidity would at least be relevant to the terms of the will. And I dare say that the generous Lord Gifford would have agreed.

The Gifford appointment normally calls for twenty lectures, ten each in two successive years. Since I should need the time between the two series to prepare for the second of them, I asked the authorities at Yale whether they would let me go for a year and a half, and they consented. We fixed our passage on the *Queen Mary* for an early day in January 1952. When the day came, I was still struggling under a pile of examination papers, and the registrar needed my report before I left for Scotland. I shall not forget that nightmare of a day, with both of us immersed in the infinite details of preparation for a long absence from home—passports, luggage, arrangements about the house, keys, tickets, good-byes—and to top it all, the pile of unfinished papers. Frances was a tower of strength on these occasions. We took an evening train for New York and there in the Grand Central Station I finished my papers and mailed my report just in time to arrive at the pier by taxi a few minutes before the midnight sailing time, and disappear through a hole in the great black cliff of the *Queen Mary*.

We spent a total of ten months in St. Andrews, and became very fond of the town and its friendly people. It is a little town of gray stone, battered by the winds and waves of the North Sea, but it is heavily charged with history. It has been celebrated by the first of its Gifford lecturers, Andrew Lang, in a poem which pairs it with Oxford in the poet's memory and which could serve as part of my own autobiography:

St. Andrews by the northern sea.
A haunted town it is to me!
A little city worn and gray,
The gray North Ocean girds it round,
And o'er the rocks, and up the bay,
The long sea-rollers surge and sound. [From "Almae Matres"]

St. Andrews University was founded in 1411, but it was already a bishopric five centuries before that. There in the town kirk John Knox preached his first sermon in public, and it is a wry measure of the effectiveness of his preaching that it led his hearers to strip their Catholic cathedral, which was one of the largest in Europe. It now stands, a majestic ruin, at the convergence of the town's main avenues. Besides its university, St. Andrews is famous for another institution, the Royal and Ancient Golf Club, which may be said without fear of contradiction to be the capital of the golfing universe. For some months we had an apartment that overlooked the course, or quartet of courses, that belong to this ancient club, and when the weather permitted, as it did at most times of the year, we would go out on the least difficult of them and play a few exhilarating holes on the springy turf, with two sounds constantly in our ears, the roar of the North Sea in the offing and the twittering of skylarks overhead.

My closest friend at St. Andrews was T. M. Knox, professor of moral philosophy, who became principal just before I arrived, and is now Sir Malcolm Knox. A man of diverse talents and remarkable force of character, he has had three separate careers and succeeded in all of them; he has been a businessman in Africa, a Greats don in Oxford, and the administrative head of a university—all this in addition to serving as Gifford lecturer, translating Hegel's aesthetics, and founding the *Philosophical Quarterly*. I owe him much, and dedicated *Reason and Goodness* to him. He agreed with the critical part of the book but, alas, was disappointed with the constructive part; he thought I had gone too far in compromising with ethical naturalism.

He and his wife Dorothy were living in those days in an apartment on the Scores, a road on the seafront, and it was their hospitable habit in termtime to hold an open house on Sunday evenings. Frances and I turned up there regularly to listen to the excellent talk, to hear anecdotes of our elders and betters in St. Andrews history—Chalmers and Ferrier, Stout and Taylor, Burnet and Bosanquet, Wisdom and Broad—to have our spines tingled with the ghost stories with which St. Andrews's history is rife, and to exchange ideas with colleagues on philosophy, politics, and religion. One of the most interesting members of this group was W. L. Lorimer, an eminent classicist and Fellow of the British Academy, who was full of eloquent likes and dislikes, including a passionate Scottish nationalism and an equally intense aversion for the Roman church. Another was John Coates, who one evening told of an experience so unusual that it has embedded itself in my memory. He was serving during the war on the northwest frontier of India, and once when lying on the ground, gun in hand, he idly dug his toes into the earth. Finding a slight depression, he turned and explored it a little further. He found in it a cache of coins, which appeared, strangely enough, to be Greek. He sent the collection to the numismatic department of the British Museum, and sure enough, they turned out to be genuine coins of Alexander the Great, which had presumably lain there undisturbed for more than two thousand years.

Some, of which the British Museum had duplicates, were sent to other institutions, and Mr. Coates later stumbled on part of his treasure a second time in the museum at Calcutta.

My lectures were given every Thursday, except during the spring holidays, between early February and early May in the United College of St. Salvator and St. Leonard, at six in the afternoon. I wondered whether at the end of a series of twenty lectures I should have any auditors left, an apprehension not lightened by learning that the eminent James Ward had ended his lectures talking to a minute remnant in Stout's study. But the attendance at most of the lectures was better than I had any right to expect, and the lecture room was made almost gay by the scarlet gowns of the undergraduates scattered through the audience.

The first ten lectures were devoted to "Reason and Its Critics." The critics to whom I paid most attention were, first, those theologians who held that revelation could override the findings of reason, and next those philosophical critics who held that necessary statements could provide no light about the nature of things. In the latter part of this series, in which I undertook a reply to those linguistic analysts who would reduce rational necessities to conventions or linguistic rules, I think I had my audience with me; the Scots are notoriously less ready than the Sassenachs, as their southern neighbors are sometimes called, to abandon metaphysics. The earlier part of the series had somewhat rougher going. A syllabus sketching the argument of the lectures had been distributed in advance, and some who received a copy were not inclined to take such heresies passively. A professor from a neighboring institution proposed to come and reply to me publicly, but was dissuaded by a third party. The Catholic students' society invited Father Corbishley of Campion Hall, Oxford, to come and defend the faith. I went to hear his address, and found him a fair adversary, embarrassed at having to answer me without having read or heard my lectures. A red-gowned undergraduate spied me in the audience, and suggested that I be called on in turn for a reply. This had not been part of the program, but I did make a brief reply and was listened to courteously. A little later a Barthian theologian took me to task in the Edinburgh *Scotsman* for saying that Barth was an antirationalist. His argument was a remarkable one. Reason had to conform itself to the law of noncontradiction; Barth had shown that the world was one in which this law was transcended; hence to adjust one's thinking to the contradictoriness of things was the most rational thing to do. I replied that if this was rationalism it was certainly a new and very odd kind. I was comforted, when I met Paul Tillich shortly afterward, to learn that he was on my side.

The second series dealt with "Reason and Goodness" and stated the argument that was developed in extended form in my book of that title. When I finished the double series and looked back at what I had written, I was not at all satisfied with it, and instead of publishing it as it stood, I set out to remould it into more acceptable form. Before I had finished this, an invitation came from the American Philosophical Association to give the Carus Lectures. This meant another large-scale undertaking, and it put me in a quandary from which I escaped only through the kindness of St. Andrews. Much of the matter in the first series dealt rather with the theory of knowledge than with the appropriate fields of theology and ethics, and I asked the authorities there whether they would have any objection if I took this matter out and made it the nucleus of the Carus volume, while so rewriting the Gifford volume as to deal with theology exclusively. They agreed. This greatly eased my work for the Carus Lectures, but it deferred the completion of the second Gifford volume beyond all expectation or perhaps excuse. That volume has now been published, though such parts of it as come under review in this book were seen by the critics only in typescript. What I have been slowly working out is a trilogy on reason which supplements *The Nature of Thought. Reason and Analysis* defends my conception of reason in the light of contemporary analytic theories; *Reason and Goodness* applies the conception to ethics and politics; *Reason and Belief* applies it to the chief forms of Christian theology.

English Interludes

During the long interlude between the close of the first series in May 1952 and the beginning of the second in February 1953 we stayed in England. It was a fruitful time for both of us. At the suggestion of her friend Helen Darbishire, the Wordsworth scholar, Frances did most of the research and writing for *The Portraits of Wordsworth,* while I kept inching along on my second series. We spent a pleasant summer in Cambridge, where Alfred Ewing allowed us to occupy his house while he was away in the Lake Country, and where I was able to renew my discussions with Moore. Our good fortune continued into the autumn. We heard that Sir Richard Livingstone, the classical scholar, was going on a visit to America and was seeking to rent his house in Oxford for almost precisely the period for which we needed one. For some months we had a commodious residence, two servants, and rather more than all the comforts of home. On the way back to Scotland we stopped over with Dorothy Emmet, professor of philosophy in Manchester, who had invited me to give the Adamson Lecture there. I took for my subject "Philosophical Style." This lecture, which first appeared in the *Yale Review,* was published as a tiny book by the Manchester University Press in England and by the Indiana University Press in this country. It is the nearest thing to a popular success that I have written.

In 1951 I had been made a corresponding (i.e. foreign) member of the British Academy. The next year, while still in St. Andrews, I was twice asked to put this membership to use. The first invitation was to give the Hertz Lecture, one of the two or three annual philosophical lectures that are presented to the Academy; I had to steal away to London between St. Andrews engagements in March in order to give it. The audiences at these lectures are not composed of specialists but of interested members of the general public, and I chose the large subject of "The Philosophy of Analysis." I found five theses to be commonly urged by the analytic philosophers of the day. These were: (1) that the meaning of a statement of fact lies in what would verify it in sense perception; (2) that necessary statements report our own meanings only, and say nothing about nature; (3) that no empirical facts are related necessarily to any others; (4) that moral "judgments" are neither true nor false; (5) that the business of philosophy is the clarification of terms. These theses seemed to me false without exception, and I stated the case against them as concisely as I could. I still think this case a sound one, though it is argued much more briefly than in *Reason and Analysis*. The address was printed by the Academy in its *Proceedings* for 1952, and in separate form as a pamphlet.

The other request from the Academy came shortly after this lecture. The year 1952 marked the Academy's fiftieth anniversary, and a formal banquet was planned for its members on June 6 at the Goldsmiths' Hall in London. Would I come and speak for the Academy's foreign Fellows? I accepted, though with trepidation. This was not reduced by a glance at the toast-list as I entered the hall; and when I sat down on that epicurean occasion I had little interest in the sumptuous food, for I had glanced at the high table. Ranged along it were the Duke of Wellington, the President of the Royal Academy, a former Chancellor of the Exchequer, and the Vice Chancellor of Oxford, all among the speakers. In so paralyzing a situation, I had known that there would be no safety for me in leaving anything to inspiration, so my speech, such as it was, was filed in my memory and my pocket. The subject was "The British Scholar." I had done so much criticizing of recent British thought that I was grateful for the chance to acknowledge my great debt to British teachers. Perhaps I may be allowed to quote from the yellowing notes of that speech a foreigner's impressions of the British scholar. I said:

> The dominant impression is one that at first statement may be a little nettling; it is that of the splendid amateur. Let me try to explain. My own subject, and the only one of which I can speak with any knowledge, is philosophy. Think what a different sort of being the British philosopher has been from, let us say, his Teutonic counterpart. Nearly every German philosopher of consequence has been a university professor. Go down the line of them—Kant, Hegel, Schelling, Fichte, Lotze, Dilthey, Wundt, Windelband, even Nietzsche; all were holders of academic chairs. In the great tradition of British philosophy very few have been professors. Bacon, Hobbes, Locke, Berkeley, Hume, Mill, Spencer, Bradley never owned a chair among them.

Nor is the story wholly different in other fields. Take history. Ranke, Mommsen, Harnack, Döllinger, Curtius, Niebuhr, Treitschke, Troeltsch—all professors again. On the other hand, Gibbon was a private gentleman of some means, Hume was a librarian and secretary to an embassy, Grote was a banker, Macaulay was a member of the Commons, Creighton and J. R. Green were clergymen, Carlyle was a free-lance journalist; Froude was, to be sure, a university professor, but only between the ages of seventy-four and seventy-six. Or take criticism. Johnson, Hazlitt, Coleridge, De Quincey, Lamb never taught, and though Arnold held for a term a chair of poetry, who ever heard of *Professor* Arnold?

Now it is not such facts, arresting as they are, that are important; it is what they symbolize about British scholarship. The amateur spirit is subtly and significantly different from the professional or professorial spirit. For one thing, it has zest. There is a wind among its willows, a fresh wind that blows where it lists, and so has the gusto of freedom. Take a page of Kant at random, and then take a page from either of his contemporaries across the Channel, Berkeley or Hume, and you will feel the difference I have in mind. The German was probably the greater thinker, but what a struggle he makes of it; *hic labor, hic opus est;* he is dutifully and wearily rolling his big stones uphill. Where a man's treasure is, you feel his heart should be also, while this seems like mere day labor. But you have no trouble in knowing where Hume's or Berkeley's heart is; it is there beating palpably through the words with a vitality that is infectious. They too are capable of hard work, but they remind you of one of the happiest of all facts, that work may be play, that work is what you do because you have to, and play the same thing done because you want to.

There is one of the prime marks of the amateur spirit: it has the gusto of delight in activity freely chosen. . . .

This spirit of the amateur scholar has stolen over into the ranks of the professionals. To take living examples would bring me too near home, but can one imagine scholars more unweighted with pedantic trappings than the Cambridge man who started the school of English literature at Oxford, or the Oxford man who started the school of English literature at Cambridge? For the scholar, said Walter Raleigh, "among dead authors there is no dead man"; "The first and last secret of a good style," said Quiller-Couch, "consists in thinking with the heart as well as with the head." These scholars practiced what they preached. . . . Who ever carried a greater weight of learning than that unregenerate old Tory Victorian, George Saintsbury? Who ever carried such a weight with more of the temper of a schoolboy on holiday? [*ULE,* 282–84]

The months in Scotland were not given over wholly to the two lecture series. Along with each of them I conducted a seminar for St. Andrews students, the first in the theory of knowledge, the second in ethics. And there were lecture trips to Edinburgh, where we stayed with Norman Kemp Smith, whom I had met many years before in the Wenleys' house in Ann Arbor; to Glasgow, where my host was C. A. Campbell, my distinguished successor as Gifford lecturer at St. Andrews; and to Belfast as the guest of Professor MacBeath. We managed, too, to see something of the Scottish highlands, and to visit the island of Skye. What clings in memory from this island is the strange slate-like peaks of the Coolin Hills, which stand out like the stark mountains of the moon, and the unaccustomed noises—the day-long skirl of bagpipes at a piping contest in Portree, and the call of multitudinous lambs for their mothers that waked us in the dawn at Sligachan.

When the St. Andrews duties were finished, we set out for Dublin, where the Mind Association was commemorating the two hundredth anniversary of the death of Berkeley. Between sessions we seized the chance of seeing a play at the historic Abbey Theatre and drank a full draught of Irish humor.

Salzburg

The rest of that summer of 1953 was memorable. I had agreed to serve as a faculty member in the Seminar for American Studies in Salzburg. For a few days it looked as if this service might not be rendered. On the way across the Irish Sea from Dublin, we noticed that one side of my face was growing redder and bigger than the other, and soon realized that I was in the grip of erysipelas, from which I had suffered before. Our plans were so firmly laid for the trip through England, across the Channel, and down through Europe, that we carried them through, though as soon as we reached Salzburg I went into a hospital. Fortunately the excellent physicians there had just the right antibiotics, and I was out and about in a few days.

The Salzburg seminar had grown out of an idea that occurred to some Harvard scholars after the Second World War. In Europe there was a new interest in American culture, but few European scholars had the means to cross the sea and learn about it themselves. The aim of the seminar was to bring America to them. Several dozen younger scholars are still selected year by year from all over Europe to attend the Salzburg conferences, with most of their expenses paid. The instruction is in English, which is increasingly the second language of European students. The instructors are American professors, lawyers, men of letters, and artists, and between them they cover all the important aspects of American life. Since British and American philosophies have been so closely related in recent decades, I was permitted at the seminars to talk about both. My students were a mature and varied group from many countries. One of them, Mihailo Marković, now professor of philosophy at Belgrade, has become one of the leading philosophers of Jugoslavia, and another, Maria Luisa Stringa, has become professor of philosophy at the University of Florence, and a well-known interpreter of American thought.

These were days when McCarthyism was at its height in the United States, and the young Europeans were all concerned about it. They arranged an evening meeting in which they could express their disillusionment and dismay. I had forgotten what happened until, in writing this, I turned up a report written for a Heidelberg journal by Gert Kalow, a journalist in attendance. Since it overrates my own small part, I will leave it in what Gibbon calls "the decent obscurity of a learned language."

> Die Amerikaner nehmen die schwersten Attacken gelassen hin. Bis sich einer der Lehrer erhob (Professor Blanshard) und einen Aufsatz verlas, den er zu diesem Problem in der New York Times veröffentlicht hatte. Die Europäer verstummten. Hier war alles, was sie ausgesprochen hatten, an Schärfe und Klarheit, aber auch an Besonnenheit übertroffen. Phänomen der ungeheuer wachen amerikanischen Selbstkritik. Das Resultat war: Vertrauen. "Man kann mit den Amerikanern reden."[19]

I may add that for writing the very letter so well received by the young Europeans I was bitterly attacked by Messrs. Buckley and Bozell in their defense of Mr. McCarthy.

Life in Salzburg, where students and teachers dressed informally, where meals were simple and democracy prevailed, was in striking contrast to the surroundings. Our headquarters were in the Schloss Leopoldskron, a former palace of the princely bishops who ruled this region in the eighteenth century. It was a great baroque structure full of mirrors, intricate carving, and splendidly parqueted floors, and appropriately supplemented by a lake with swans. The most celebrated citizen of the old town was Mozart, whose carefully preserved birthplace remains a Mecca for music lovers. We were too busy to hear much of the music with which the town overflows, or even to see much more of the countryside than the snow-capped mountains in the distance. Frances was absorbed in tutoring students who needed help with their English, and I with my lectures on James, Dewey, and contemporary schools. I still occasionally wear with pleasure the peasant jacket with horn buttons and green lapels that I bought at Salzburg, and smoke the pipe with its curved stem and covered bowl that is smoked by burghers of the town.

Later Years at Yale

It was good to see New Haven again at the end of that summer of 1953, after an absence of a year and a half, and to resume the C major of life at Yale. While we were abroad, I had received a letter from the new president of Yale, Whitney Griswold, proposing that on my return I become master of one of the Yale colleges. We had carefully considered the opportunity (such a post is for two persons rather than one) and had declined. For my own part, I had no doubt that my business was with philosophy, not with administration.

One marked change did occur, however, in our way of life. We had been for many years in the habit of spending the summer in the house in Peacham, Vermont, that we had bought in the early thirties. With the prospect of two successive summers abroad, we sold it in 1951. We did so with regret, for Peacham had a congenial colony of colleagues which, at one time or another, included Herbert Schneider, John Randall, James Gutmann and Horace Friess of Columbia, Sterling Lamprecht of Amherst, Arthur Todd of Northwestern, Ernest Bogart of Illinois, and Howard Mumford Jones, Crane Brinton, and Edwin Kemble of Harvard.

Sometimes when we were unable to be there we rented the house for the summer. The most memorable of our tenants was the president of the Carnegie Endowment for International Peace, who had been a leading figure at the foundation of the United Nations in San Francisco. He had been coming to Peacham for several summers with his wife, and they were both well liked in the village. His name was Alger Hiss. He was living in our house in the summer of 1949 when the storm broke over his head in a trial for treason, with a hung jury its result. This trial and his conviction of perjury at a second trial early next year disturbed me deeply. Though I did not know him intimately, I had seen enough of him to be at first confident, as were the other people in the village, that this was another case of McCarthyite persecution. Among those who had worked and played with him on the village tennis court, who had seen him in the local church and talked with him of an evening in their homes, there was not only a sense that he was unusually able but also a feeling (I distinctly remember this) that he was an unusually transparent character. When he was charged with secretly passing classified documents to Russian spies, and then with systematically lying about his extensive connections with a Communist underworld, it was rather as if a friend next door, who had always been the best of neighbors, were suddenly proclaimed to be really Jack the Ripper. The charges were incredible. But as the evidence at the two trials unrolled, the first confidence of the village faltered. What about those "pumpkin papers" that Chambers produced in evidence? Did not the experts testify that they could have been typed only on Hiss's Woodstock typewriter? The hypothesis that he was a Mr. Hyde as well as a Dr. Jekyll seemed to be the only one that covered the facts. Nevertheless to his friends it was also a hypothesis revoltingly out of accord with all they had known of him. That is the feeble position in which many, including myself, are still bogged down in this tragic case. I have no blame for the twenty out of twenty-four jurors who felt it necessary, on the evidence before them, to bring in a verdict of guilty. I cannot believe, either, that the man I knew was what Prosecutor Murphy insisted on describing as a blend of Benedict Arnold and Judas Iscariot. Something in this famous case has yet to come out.

One of the advantages, if advantage it is, of being at a large university as opposed to a college is that it gives one a higher rostrum from which one's voice may be more widely heard. After coming to Yale I had many more invitations to give lectures or series of lectures. I once checked the American colleges at which I had lectured and was able to name 115; the number must now be nearer 140. Many of these lectures were addressed to general student audiences and dealt with topics of current interest, such as "Conformity,"

"The Life of the Spirit in a Machine Age," "In Defense of the Humanities," "The Difficulties of Being Reasonable," "Sanity in Thought and Art," "The Test of a University," "The Uses of a Liberal Education." The lecture was usually followed by a discussion period, which I much enjoyed; and if I had a whole day at a college, I often found it possible to throw in an extra lecture or two, or hold a seminar. Sometimes when I expressed a willingness to do this, I was given a real workout; I have delivered as many as four lectures in a day, and seven in two days. This was less arduous than it seems, for I commonly read my lectures. They were less deadly, I hope, than this sounds, for they were written to speak, rather than to be read, and the difference is great. I have been quite shameless about repeating addresses. If a lecture has not been published, and has not been given before within a hundred miles of the spot, it will be none the worse for its repetition, and may well be better.

Presenting a series of lectures, particularly if there is a stipulation that they be printed, as with the Gifford and Carus lectures, is of course a more difficult matter. In the Carus series only three lectures are usually given, for they are planned for presentation at one of the divisional meetings of the Philosophical Association, which never last for more than three days. But the first Carus Lectures set a standard that makes their successors feel they are falling short unless they produce a formidable volume. The two first series were Dewey's *Experience and Nature* and Lovejoy's *Revolt Against Dualism,* classics both. My own *Reason and Analysis* at least kept up the avoirdupois. In 1948 I was invited to give the William Belden Nobel series at Harvard, along with a weekly seminar in ethics at the Harvard Divinity School. I devoted the four lectures to "Present-Day Leaders in Ethical Thought," with particular attention to Westermarck, Moore, Ross, and Brunner. For purposes of publication, these lectures were incorporated with my Giffords by permission of the Harvard Board of Preachers. I have given various other series: the Nielsen Lectures at Smith College; the Otis Lectures at Wheaton College, Massachusetts; two Matchette series, one at Wesleyan University and one at Brooklyn College; and other series at Notre Dame, the College of Wooster, the University of Utah, and the University of Southern California.

Three Societies

Through most of my years at Yale I was a member of three societies so stimulating that I tried to attend their meetings regularly. One was a little group of New Haven residents called the Social Science Club, which has managed to exist for a hundred years from its own inner momentum, without officers or a constitution. It is composed about half-and-half of Yale academics and New Haven professional men, and meets monthly for a dinner and a paper by one of its members. It does a professor good to belong to such a group. If he is stuffy, pompous, or pedantic, the group will feel it, and subtly let him know that they feel it. Men of the world can provide him some gauge of his intelligibility and the importance of what he is doing. When I say "intelligibility," I do not mean that a philosopher is bound to make himself clear to everyone. Still, philosophy does not generally, like mathematical physics, presuppose technical information and skill; it starts from everyday experience and its reasoning can be followed by intelligent laymen. If a philosopher finds that an exposition of his subject to a group of lawyers, doctors, and clergymen leaves them groping in a fog, he may well consider whether he is exuding some of the fog himself. Similarly, of the importance of issues. It is true that "practical men" are not the arbiters of philosophical importance, for this does not lie, as James and Dewey intended, in the difference a theory makes in practice; the decision whether the law of contradiction states an ontological fact or merely a linguistic rule makes no practical difference at all, but is one of the most important theoretical questions that can be raised. Nevertheless some of the inquiries that currently engross the minds of philosophers, scientists, and scholars have little significance, theoretical or practical; and if they had to be defended before a jury of men of the world, they would be exposed as the busywork they really are. However this may be, I suspect that my philosophy is less irresponsible for having had occasionally to run the gauntlet of criticism from other professions.

The second of the three societies just mentioned is the American Philosophical Society, the ancient society in Philadelphia founded by Benjamin Franklin. I have been attending its meetings with profit for nearly a quarter century. The term "philosophical" in its name is a misnomer; of its several hundred members, only about half a dozen at present are philosophers by profession. Most of the members are "natural philosophers" in Franklin's sense, that is, inquirers into nature, or natural scientists. Though the discussions have often been beyond my competence, it has been a pleasure to sit in at the papers and discussions of these scientists, not only because their programs are organized with care and skill but also because the participants include many of the best minds in their fields. Furthermore these men of science seem on the whole a happy group. As eminently successful in their own fields, it is natural enough that they should be. But there is rather more to it than that. Science is, or tries to be, objective, impersonal, and rational; it takes one out of oneself in a way that literature and art do not. "Men of science . . . ," Bertrand Russell has remarked, "are far less often temperamentally unhappy than artists are, and in the main the men who do great work in science are happy men, whose happiness is derived primarily from their work."[20] That is my impression also. Is it merely an accident, for example, that of the six American men who have received Nobel prizes for literature five were temporary or confirmed alcoholics? That is not a record of great happiness, and one would expect it to remain long unmatched by our Nobel prizemen in science.

The third of my three societies is the American Theological Society. It is a group of eighty or ninety members, chiefly teachers of theology and religion. Beginning as exclusively Protestant, it now includes Catholics and Jews. In such a group I am something of a whited sepulcher, for I am far more skeptical of religious dogma than my fellow members probably take me to be. Once, however, I found myself in an odd way to the right of the membership rather than to the left. This was when it fell to my lot to give the presidential address to the Society in 1956. I spoke on "The Ethics of Belief," and took so stringent a view as to what intellectual morality required as to make most of my good colleagues appear libertines; to their dismay, I rapped even their beloved William James over the knuckles for the permissiveness of his "will to believe."

In a group of theologians, this sort of note strikes home with perturbing sharpness. Theologians are generally men of high ethical sensitiveness, but they are drawn by this very sensitiveness in opposite directions. If they are members of some Christian church, loyalty demands subscription to its creed. On the other hand, theology intends to be a science; science is the unconditional pursuit of one goal, namely truth, and for its devotee any deflection from this goal is itself infidelity. From some form of infidelity the honest theologian can thus hardly hope to escape. If he follows his reason where it leads, he will strain and probably break the creed of his sect, and thus be unfaithful to his religious professions. If he adheres to his sectarian creed in the face of the provincialism that reason almost certainly discloses in it, he is unfaithful to truth itself. Hence theologians today are suffering from a divided mind; and though this is an ancient malady among them, the advance of science in a world prevailingly secular already has made it widespread and acute. There is among them a wistful tentativeness, a groping self-critical uncertainty, that would be foreign to any corresponding body of natural scientists. Hence my own feelings when I am among them are ambivalent. Morally sensitive and self-critical as they are, they have been through some dark passages of the mind that scientists have no occasion to enter and have developed sympathies that scientists seldom feel. They possess a kind of inward richness that gives them, to me at least, a special attractiveness as persons and friends. At the same time their built-in brakes against following the argument over precipices, their double loyalties to a religion and a reason that are more often than not inharmonious, give me a sense of blunted powers and anxious evasions, and I begin to long for the crisper air of philosophy and science.

Retirement

Yale professors retire at sixty-eight, and at the end of the academic year 1960–61 I gave my last lecture, met my last seminar, and cleared my desk for the last time. Charles Hendel had retired two years before, and I had once more been called in to act as chairman. That part of my duties I was not reluctant to lay down. And when I walked out the door, I did not return. Ex-chairmen who haunt their old places like ghosts after their heirs have taken over are nuisances.

In the years that followed, the department went through a period of *Sturm und Drang;* it divided with some bitterness about the promotion of a younger member, and it had to face the strange student revolution of 1968 to 1970. I am grateful that my work was done before the breaking of these storms. How I should have handled them I do not know, but I am sure I should have been in difficulty. The appeal to violence on the part of noisy minorities is to me inconsistent with the spirit and principles of an institution of learning, and I could not approve of the way in which great universities capitulated to their demands. I am no authoritarian, but neither do I think that a university is or should be a democracy. If research, reflection, breadth of learning, and length of experience do not give the faculty a better judgment than the students, it is not clear what is the point of an education at all. When I recall how callow I was as an undergraduate, how easily I was taken in by pedagogical tinsel, and how little experience I had against which to appraise what the university offered me, the readiness of some faculty members to give to students' voices a weight equal to their own, even in the planning of a curriculum or the selection of a president, seems to me an abjuring of respon-sibility. If I had continued in office, I should probably have had to say such things, and been denounced as a result. I might have added what I still think, that youth is overpraised and overrated in this country in comparison with maturity. This is not merely the conservatism of age, though perhaps I was born old; for I felt this way even in youth. Granted that there is some cant in Browning's talk about "the last of life for which the first was made," my own history has been one of "fallings away, vanishings" of many prejudices, fears, provincialisms, and ill-judged ambitions that burdened my younger years. I should not want to be governed by people like "myself when young," and though a generation brought up on television and instant news from everywhere is certainly more knowing than we were, I am not sure that it is very much wiser.

I had enjoyed teaching more than administration, but I had no great desire to continue this either, in spite of many opportunities to do so. The year after my retirement we spent at the newly created Center for Advanced Studies at Wesleyan University, where the conditions for study and writing were excellent and where the presence of such colleagues as George Boas, Seelye Bixler, and (for a short time) Lord Snow was an added stimulus. In the year following, I did return to teaching for one term. I gave a series of weekly lectures on the philosophy of religion at the University of Minnesota, accom-panying them with a weekly seminar in the same field. It was my first experience of teaching in one of the new and gigantic modern "pluriversities" which are destined to have an increasing part in American education. The lectures dealt with the tensions between faith and reason, and they were followed by discussion periods in a separate place, which were well attended and sometimes very spirited. They were made more so by a small group of conservative Lutherans who stoutly maintained against me the literal inerrancy of Scripture. From these discussions I carried away the impression that the difference between the fundamentalist and the liberal is not necessarily in intellectual acuteness; some of these Lutherans were very acute indeed. Perhaps the difference lies rather in the extent to which thinking on these matters is kept in a special compartment or is subjected to free criticism by one's knowledge as a whole. Whether the naturalist or the supernaturalist view of the world is accepted should be determined, I think, by one's sense of overall probability, based on thousands of particular probabilities.

For some years in the sixties I was a member of the Executive Committee of the Fédération Internationale des Sociétés de Philosophie. A meeting of this committee was held in Israel in April 1965, conjointly with a conference on the philosophy of history arranged by the University of Jerusalem. Frances and I extended this trip into a four-month visit to Europe and the Middle East. The most memorable part of it was a week in Israel and two or three weeks in Greece. What impressed us most about Israel was the contrast between the barrenness of its rocky and sandy soil and the extraordinary vigor of the new civilization that it has managed to build on this soil. Without offering any comment on the tortured conflict between Arabs and Israelis, one may at least remark on the tragic loss involved in this conflict for the Middle East as a whole. If what Israel has made of its barren countryside could be taken by its neighbors as a pilot experiment rather than as a threat, the advantage to the entire Levant would be incalculable.

After a week in Jerusalem, we paid a five-day visit by sea to Rhodes, Crete, Delos, Mykonos, and Patmos. At the cave on Patmos where Saint John is alleged to have written *Revelation,* the Greek Orthodox priest in attendance pointed to three convergent lines in the rock overhead as the place where it had opened for the revelation to occur. In this kind of religion I admit that I could not take much interest. It was otherwise when we reached Athens. The old and broken building that stands out on its hill above the city is to me the most moving sight in the world, the exquisite symbol of the most astonishing burst of civilization that man has known. But for many travelers to the Acropolis it is more even than that. In the course of our visit to it, I picked up at a nearby bookstall Ernest Renan's essay *Prière sur l'Acropole* and found that in spite of its fervid rhetoric I could subscribe to nearly all of it. It is true that the men who built the Parthenon, like the man who wrote *Revelation,* were devotees of mythology, for the goddess Athena no more existed than the four horsemen of the Apocalypse. But Athena was a goddess of reason, and there is no such figure in Biblical mythology. For rationalists her house is the temple of what she stood for. The great structure of white marble, standing in sharp outline against the blue Greek sky, and perfect in its grace and balance, was for me the symbol of reason itself, and of the clarity and order it seeks to bring into man's understanding of his world. Socrates and Plato must often have lifted their eyes to it as they walked the Athenian streets and pursued those discussions which were themselves exercises in the religion of their temple. It still stands on its hill above the noisy city, a reminder to the generations that come and go below it that there once was a people who caught a vision of what the life of reason might be, though the pursuit of their ideal ended, like this magnificent symbol of it, in ruin. With Renan and so many others, drawn from all the countries of the earth, who have come to see it and to feast their minds on what it meant and may still mean, I felt some of my pettinesses and provincialisms slipping away. Here was my true church. I did not need to travel farther in search of it.

The trip to the Middle East, rich as it was in new experience, was marred by illness. We both came down with influenza, Frances's case being more severe than mine. By the time of our return we thought her recovery was complete, but I suspect her heart had been affected in a way that neither she nor her doctors realized. She went about her work much as usual during the year that followed, though often feeling vaguely unwell. But on December 9, 1966, came the heaviest blow of my life. She was struck by a heart attack about nine in the evening, and died in the hospital a few hours later. The attack was appallingly sudden, and I was totally unprepared for it. We had worked together so intimately and so long that, without her, my world fell apart.

One thing I could do. She had been engaged for some years on a biography of Frank Aydelotte, with whom she had worked as dean while he was president of Swarthmore, and she had completed it except for two chapters. I made it my first business during the year that followed to write these chapters and prepare the book for the press. It has now appeared, and carries a memoir of her as a preface. The two and a half years that followed her death were for me years of loneliness, failing health, and failing motives. I was not made to live alone.

In 1969 I married again. Roberta Yerkes Blanshard would not wish me to say much about her here, and I must content myself with a fact or two. She is the daughter of my former neighbor and colleague, the psychobiologist Robert M. Yerkes; she is a loyal alumna of Bryn Mawr College; she was for many years an editor at the Yale University Press. I owe her an access of great happiness, as well, perhaps, as my being about at all to write this history of myself and my opinions.

Some Personal Details

Before turning to the second of these histories, I should like for a special reason to go on a little longer with the first. When I am reading the biographies of others, I enjoy the sort of details that, trivial perhaps in themselves, reveal the subject's temper and quality—his hobbies, his health, his tastes in literature and the arts, his likes and dislikes—and my readers may also have some interest in such details. So I add a few of them for what they may be worth.

Physically I am totally unremarkable, being somewhere near the median in every respect. My height is 5 feet 8 1/2 inches, and my weight 150 pounds. My activity in sports has been limited from an early age by the necessity for wearing glasses, and as a student I was too light to be an athlete. But I enjoyed baseball, played tennis for my college at Oxford, and still play a zealous though incompetent game of golf. In youth I suffered much from hay fever, and was highly susceptible to colds and influenza, but thanks to the impressive advance of allergic medicine, my health in these respects has improved with age. If I have achieved anything, it has been by dint of regular habits, the husbanding of a limited supply of energy, and inching steadily along. Throughout my middle years I was a poor sleeper, but I found that if one was able to ignore bad nights, the consequences to one's work were not too serious. I may have been influenced more than I knew by the Puritan ethic and its gospel of work. Though I detest most things connected with war, I find myself reading with admiration the accounts of military men who had a gift for getting things done—Caesar, Marlborough, Wellington.

I have few hobbies or avocations. In a very small way I am a printer, with a printing press in the cellar on which for many years I have printed my own stationery, experimenting with a variety of types. I am fond of all the appurtenances of a well-kept office, and take a childish pleasure in the IBM electric space-adjusting typewriter, and in a needlessly ample supply of fountain pens, picked up in all conditions and serviced by myself. These gadgets avail less than they should, for I am a poor correspondent, and have never been able to work out a satisfactory method of dealing with the flood of letters, solicitations for aid, offprints from colleagues, and requests for recommendations that submerge one's desk; I generally have a bad conscience for neglecting either them or my work. Academic people cannot afford secretaries, and attempts to compose by dictation to a machine have, in my case, been failures. Even attempts to compose on the typewriter have not been very successful. Most of my writing has been done in longhand, revised in the same way, and then typed by myself.

My chief avocation has been reading and I have slowly collected a library of four or five thousand volumes which is a constant solace and delight. It contains very little fiction, not because I am uninterested in fiction but because, being a somewhat slow reader, I find it too expensive of time. I am very fond of poetry, which I delight in reading aloud. My tastes run to the older masters and the Victorians, and I must confess that I have found little I cared for in the poetry of recent years. In my library there are many shelves of biography, which include of course the great biographies—Boswell's *Johnson,* Lockhart's *Scott,* Trevelyan's *Macaulay,* Froude's *Carlyle,* and some others that rank high with me, such as Perry's *William James.* I am fond too of reading history—not so much the philosophic historians as those who can tell a story, notably Macaulay and Froude. Gibbon has a special place; there is something enthralling in the serene eighteenth-century rationality with which he unrolls his majestic panorama.

In literary criticism as in history, it is not the philosophers that I am drawn to—they are often pedantic—but the minds with authentic likes and dislikes which come through in vivid expression—Hazlitt, Raleigh, Saintsbury, Strachey, F. L. Lucas. These names at once betray my partiality for style, for those writers who have a gift not only for communicating ideas but for bathing them as they issue in the colors of their own individual temperaments.

This is a dangerous taste for a philosopher, particularly if he allows it to affect his own writing. For the business of the philosopher is with the argument exclusively, and there is something in Bradley's lament that "to converse with shadows, he must become himself a shade." If he lets himself go in his writing, as Nietzsche did, and becomes a prophet, he loses caste as a philosopher, and rightly; even if he loiters along the way to savor his phrases, as Santayana inclines to do, he sets up a tension in the reader's mind between the prime intellectual interest and one that is aesthetic and diversionary. Carlyle said of Mill that he was "sawdust to the masthead," which is the inevitable charge against the philosopher if he sticks to his last and refuses to "think with his blood." Carlyle did think with his blood; he became a prophet, and on the issues of his day he often wrote claptrap. The philosophers whose thought is a white light, with themselves and their desires kept resolutely out (one thinks here of Sidgwick), are commonly regarded as dull.

Is the philosopher then condemned to sawdust or claptrap? Not quite, I think. It is true that he is writing "the literature of knowledge," not "the literature of power," and is committed by the nature of his enterprise to dealing severely with anything wayward, emotional, or decorative; he must often follow Quiller-Couch's advice, "Murder your darlings." But the mere communication of ideas from mind to mind with a minimum of friction is itself an art that calls for literary craftsmanship—timely example, a judicious compression here and expansion there, a disposition of matter that bears in mind both logical order and psychological ease, and all the resources of verbal exactitude, a cultivated ear, and the courtesy that finds its natural expression in clearness.

I do not know how to rate myself on the intellectual side, but if the standard were set by the other members of the Library of Living Philosophers, I should not rank high. Nor am I a scholar. Scholarship requires time, and the time of an American college teacher is too largely preempted to allow the necessary freedom. I loved reading, but such freedom as I had I devoted rather to thinking and writing than to the sort of reading that "maketh a full man." Here my needs and habits differ from those of many of my colleagues. Some of them were social philosophers, doing their best thinking in company; the active exchange of ideas with other minds is a necessity for them. That has not been my own case. Of course I have profited greatly from discussions with colleagues, but I am inhibited in company and work best alone. I hardly understand the complaint I sometimes hear that, owing to "isolation," a person has lacked the stimulus necessary to produce. If I have any gift at all in philosophy, I suppose it is that of retiring into a corner with a problem and thinking about it in a fairly patient and orderly way. At least that is how my books have been written. They have been spun out of my vitals, spider-fashion, chiefly in academic vacations. None of them, except some early chapters of my first book, has been submitted to other philosophers before going to the publisher.

Among my interests has been a not very active one in psychical research. The a priori dismissal of inquiries in this field by American scientists and philosophers is not, I think, to their credit. My friend C. J. Ducasse, who wrote extensively on the subject and pursued researches of his own, was a respected exception. In 1955, at his invitation, I gave the Graham Lecture at Brown University on "Proof in Psychical Research." I have attended some séances, at which things happened that were inexplicable to me, but I have had no significant experiences of my own; as regards everything supernormal I am normal to a disgusting degree; I have never had so much as a telepathic experience, though with a twin brother one would suppose the conditions fairly propitious. I cannot go as far as Ducasse or Broad in accepting the claims of psychical research, but I think the experiments of Gilbert Murray and others have established the fact of telepathy pretty conclusively. And this is of philosophic importance, for it suggests not only that the traditional account of our knowledge of other minds has been too narrow, but also that mind is less dependent on body than has been supposed. And it drives one further nail into the coffin of behaviorism.

The Rational Temper

"Rationalism" has been with me more than the name of a favored theory; it stands for the way of life I most admire. I do not conceive of reason as exhausted in exercises in logic and mathematics. It is the organ of choice among values, and therefore the ultimate compass of practical life also. Life in accordance with it might well have the primary place among our admirations. In America the scale of popular estimation has gone so far awry that eccentricity and waywardness are advantages rather than defects. Actors and actresses called "stars," who behave like tantrum-riddled children; stupid but noisy prizefighters, egotistic chess players, a theater in which a rational man would be a quaint and exotic figure; exploitation on the screen of aggression, revenge, and violence, with public applause; art that disowns meaning and prides itself on formlessness, best sellers in which every character is selfish or sinister or mentally sick—the whole popular hierarchy of interests and admirations seems crazily askew. One recalls Lowes Dickinson's comment that modern literature is one vast hospital. In this bedlam of plaudits for the moronic and the perverse, the voice of mere reasonableness is a scarcely audible whisper.

Yet our hope lies in that whisper. Even those philosophers who, like Russell, hold that values are outside the province of reason find themselves appealing to reason and pleading for more rationality when they discuss political issues or international affairs. If the problems that now confront and divide Americans—problems of race, sex, crime, the environment, overpopulation—cannot be solved by rational methods, they cannot be solved at all. Only disciplined and reasonable minds can deal with them adequately, and then only with the support of a public that can recognize reasonableness when they see it. Yet reasonableness is a virtue that lacks public appeal. It is recognized as a virtue, but it remains to most men the dullest of the virtues. It quickens no pulses, as courage does, even wrongheaded courage. Is there any chance of its achieving the place it deserves in general recognition?

Probably not. The old Adam in man, the passions that make him behave irrationally, such as anger, cupidity, and fear, are far older in the race and more firmly embedded in human nature than the reflectiveness that might control them. But such control is a matter of degree, and it is helped or retarded as the image of the reasonable man rises or falls in the general estimation. Adam Smith shrewdly remarked that "the great secret of education is to direct vanity to proper objects," and if he is right, what is important here is that people should come to pin their self-respect to being reasonable. This relocation of pride does not seem an impossible dream.

I can bear witness that a change in this respect is at least possible. Though I have always been a hero-worshiper, my heroes have changed with the years. I admired Nietzsche once; I do not now; egotism and willfulness have no place in a rational mind. I once admired Luther; I now prefer Erasmus. In my youth I listened admiringly to the ill-instructed eloquence of William Jennings Bryan; it seems strange now that he should ever have led the party of which Woodrow Wilson was a member. I have come to prefer the Jeffersons of the world to the Jacksons, the Benjamin Franklins to the Patrick Henrys, the

Turgots to the Dantons, the Asquiths to the Lloyd Georges. In literature I have experienced the common swing from the romantic to the classic. "In all things," said Dostoievsky, "I go to the uttermost extreme; my life long, I have never been acquainted with moderation." From such a man I turn with relief to someone like Henry James. In philosophy I find myself crossing battle lines in pursuit of my admirations. Fortunately the rational temper is not confined to rationalists. Locke and Hume, Mill and Sidgwick are not of my speculative camp, but they exhibit the spirit in which I think philosophy should be pursued. "The love of truth," said Locke, "is the principal part of human perfection in this world, and the seedplot of all other virtues." That is a sweeping and indeed astonishing statement to make. But is it not true?

II

A Budding Rationalism

I must try now to sketch the growth of my views in philosophy. Some nodes of this reflective development have been noted in the account of my contacts with teachers and colleagues, to whom I owe much more, of course, than I can explicitly recall. On the other hand, I do not believe that my thought is a set of echoes merely. Indeed it has sometimes seemed that I was born a rationalist, in the sense that no other way of thinking has ever had much appeal to me and no efforts on the part of teachers to wean me away from it have had much effect. Is it possible to trace the beginnings in conscious reflection of this position I have held for so many years? I think it is.

In undergraduate days at Michigan I made the acquaintance of Spinoza, who is a dangerously seductive thinker to set before reflective youth. It is not merely that he is a romantic figure in the contrast between the poverty of his outward life in an Amsterdam garret and the magnificent sweep of his thought; it is also that his view of the world as an intelligible whole, set as a puzzle for unravelment by human reason, is as simple in its conception as it is impressive in its development. I remember doing a callow paper for Alfred Lloyd in Spinoza's manner, complete with axioms and postulates, and attempting to prove—I do not remember what. When, a year or two later, I began to work with Joachim, I read his scholarly *Ethics of Spinoza,* and

Bradley richly fertilized my budding rationalism with his own neo-Spinozism. It was the position of all these men that there is a *conatus* or drive in human nature that demands for its satisfaction an understanding of the world, a vision of the whole, in which the nature and place of each thing is to be understood only by seeing its place in an all-inclusive order. Philosophy is the systematic attempt at the apprehension of that order.

So much is the common knowledge of all students of Spinoza. But one may know something without making it one's own in any vital way. The meaning of this sort of rationalism did not fully come home to me until I began grubbing about in my own psychological processes. I have mentioned that in my first years of teaching at Michigan I was asked by Henry Stevens, a Detroit philanthropist, to make a study of such results of recent psychology as might be of value to social workers. In the course of these researches, I soon discovered that between the account of the thought process implicit in the philosophers I had been studying and the accounts of the same thing by psychologists there was an enormous gap. The rationalists assumed that thought was, or might be, rationally guided, that at its best it moved under the constraint of the logical connections in its subject matter. To the psychologists, this was mere metaphysical speculation. They liked to think of themselves as empirical scientists; and necessities, either in thought or in nature, were beyond the range of their inspection. Most of them seemed to be associationists, who explained the passage from one thought to another by such factors as the recency, frequency, and vividness of past association. On a lower level of complacent myopia were the behaviorists, led by John B. Watson, who announced that he could not find consciousness in his test tubes, and hence there was no such thing. No help was to be gained from that quarter. Dewey's useful *How We Think,* which had appeared in 1910, was a work of much more sophistication but it overstressed the control of thinking by practical needs and ends. None of these writers seemed to take seriously the contention of Spinoza and Bradley that thought had an end of its own, namely rational insight or understanding, and that this end could direct and control the process. Had the rationalists misconceived the nature of thought?

My answer to this question took two volumes and many years. I set myself to examine my own thinking carefully, to observe what set it in motion, and to note how, and if possible why, it moved as it did from one point to another. Much in Dewey's account I could gratefully accept. Reflective thought first arose, he conjectured, because man found himself in a "block-situation" in which the resort to ideas was the only means of escape. Primitive man, for example, was chased by a bear and came to a river. If he could form the thought of pushing himself out on a log, it might well make the difference between life and death; necessity was the mother of invention. Thought was a biological instrument of adjustment and survival; that is why

Dewey called his theory "instrumentalism"; the value of thinking lay in its utility, and because of this utility it was selected for survival.

So far Dewey made admirable sense. But he went much further; he said that what thinking was in the beginning it remains today; in its very essence it was a practical device and an instrument of change. Here I could not follow. It seemed to me perfectly clear that in thinking about history or geometry my interest might be in knowing, not in doing, and that seeing something clearly with "the eye of the mind" was obviously different from getting something done. Dewey, I thought, confounded the theoretical end with the practical. These are easily distinguishable in present thought, and they are really different from the beginning, even though in primitive thought the practical motive may completely dominate over the cognitive. The primitive man who scans the riverbank with the thought that he could get to safety if he could find a log and push himself out on it is making, whether explicitly or not, a hypothetical judgment. That judgment may have immense utility. But its truth and its utility are not the same thing; the judgment might still have been true if not acted upon at all. And I was convinced that from the very beginning, however overlaid and dominated it may be by urgent practical demands, thought has a special end of its own. What it wants is to *know*. It is in essence a pursuit of truth.

But the impulse to know seems itself to have many ends, not just one—indeed to have as many ends as there are questions it may answer. What kind of tree is that? Who commanded the Franks at Tours? What is the age of the earth? Which is farther west, the Pacific or the Caribbean mouth of the Panama Canal? The impulse to know seems to be directed in each of these questions to the ascertainment of an isolated fact, and there are countless such facts, to any one of which it might be directed. Thought is like the beam of a flashlight, which may focus on any spot of the world around us, to the exclusion of the rest. But this statement needs to be qualified. The isolation is never complete. In answering any of these questions, we are placing the supposedly isolated fact in a context of relations. To say what kind of tree that is is to classify it, to identify it as one kind of tree among others. Who commanded at Tours? Unless the interest is merely in a name tag, the answer, Charles Martel, identifies a figure through manifold activities and relations that he sustained with others. To grasp the age of the earth *is* to grasp the relations in time of its beginning to preceding events and to the events of its subsequent history. To answer the question about the Panama Canal is to grasp not only the relations of the two outlets to their respective oceans, but their relations to each other, which are the more instructive for offering a shock to expectation.

These examples, taken at random, suggest that to answer any question we have to fall back on relations. Now the relations that thought seeks to uncover are of many kinds. In the examples just taken, the questions are What? Who? When? and Where? and the answers involve classification, identification, time, and space. But of all the questions that inquiry can raise, the one most interesting to the philosopher is Why? It is the only question in whose answer the theoretic impulse can find full satisfaction. When an answer is given that reports an "isolated" fact, the practical interest that brought theory into play may be satisfied, but there is always more for theory to do: it can always ask *why* this fact should be as it is. That tree is a beech. Yes, but why is it so classified? Because it has thin, smooth, gray bark and glossy, oval leaves. For the casual inquirer, that is enough and perhaps more than enough. But for the persistent theorist it is only the beginning. *Why* should beech bark be thin or smooth or gray? *Why* should the leaves be glossy or oval? And when the answers to these questions have been found by reference to further facts about cellular structure or behavior, the same question can be repeated, *Why* are these facts as they are? It looks like a process without end. Could one not go on asking Why? indefinitely?

It was clear that I had to find out whether there was any kind of insight in which thought could come to rest. In raising the question Why? we are endeavoring to understand. But what does understanding anything mean? We understand it when we see how it is to be explained. But what does explanation mean? In general it means placing some fact not now understood in a context of relations that renders it intelligible. But the relations that link what is to be explained with the context that explains it may again be of various kinds. You see a man climbing a tree, and you wonder why he is doing it. Then on a branch above him you see a cat, and the explanation is clear enough; he is trying to rescue that cat. You are here explaining through a special kind of relation, the relation of means and end. Or your watch has stopped. Why? You recall that you forgot to wind it last night. That is also explanation, but it explains through a causal relation. Or you are crossing a square field by a diagonal path that runs from corner to corner. The path cuts the field into two triangles. Are these equal? Yes, but why do you say so with such confidence? Because the Why? asks for, and is answered by, a peculiarly certain kind of insight. If the sides of the field are equal, and its corners are really right angles, and the path across it is straight, one can see that the triangles are equal because they *have* to be; they could not possibly be otherwise. The explanation is logical because it moves through necessary or logical relations. Furthermore, the warrant for this insight does not lie in its own self-evidence merely. It has behind it the entire geometrical system with which it is bound up, for this system itself would have to be abandoned unless this explanation were accepted.

These three are the most familiar types of explanation. Which is the most satisfactory? Only the last of them answers the question Why? in so decisive a form that it cannot be raised again. When one shows that something is necessarily true, or that it follows necessarily from something already accepted, it is pointless to ask why it should hold, for one has the answer already; one has seen why it holds in the clearest manner possible. To grasp something as necessarily true is to see that it could not be otherwise, and when one has seen that, one has reached the *ne plus ultra* of explanation. In regard to either of the other forms, the question *can* be asked again. That it can about causal explanation was made clear by Hume. He showed that we do not normally see why a cause produces its effect, why the nail goes in when the hammer strikes it. We have always found that it regularly does, but to know that it regularly does is not to see *why* it does. Causal explanation never gives full understanding. Neither does teleological explanation. Here the question Why? can be raised twice over; one may ask why the chosen means should subserve the end, and why the end should be thought desirable. The first is a causal question, to which the remarks just made apply again. The second raises the thorny problem how a judgment of value is to be validated. That is too large an issue to embark on here. But by way of indicating what I should say if called upon, I may suggest two conclusions I have elsewhere argued for, first that value judgments are really judgments and not exclamations or imperatives merely, and second, that their validation is not wholly unlike the process of rational or logical explanation.

Reason as an Immanent Control

Enough has now been said to make clear why, in my early reflections in Detroit, I concluded that the psychological accounts of thought then current would not do. The behaviorists quite obviously, and the associationists only a little less obviously, treated man as if he were an animal without being a rational animal. And the fact is that man *is* rational, even if only occasionally and brokenly so. By that I mean, in this context, that he can genuinely reason, that he can follow a line of necessity in his thinking. When he raises and answers the question whether the diagonal of a square divides it into two equal triangles, it is absurd to say that he is merely making a conditioned bodily reflex or that his mind is governed by association merely. He concludes as he does because, given the premises he starts with, his thought has been governed by logical necessity in reaching its conclusion.

One must be careful how one puts the point, for the easiest way to put it is one that belies the significance of man's rationality at the outset. Suppose I am engaged in a process of logical reasoning. I am deducing what follows from a preposition in Euclid, or completing a syllogism from two given premises, or constructing a series beginning with the number 1 in which each succeeding number is three times its predecessor. Let us take the last of these. In constructing such a series, one begins, "1, 3, 9 . . ."; very well, what is the next number? You say "27." Good; why did that particular number leap into your thought? The natural answer is, "Because I saw that the rule of the series required it." But it is important to see that that cannot be correct. For the question is why this number appeared in your thought, while in order to see that the rule of the series requires it you must have the number in thought already. What made you think of it cannot include your thinking of it; that would be arguing in a circle. So far as I could see, there was only one way out, and that was to say that you think "27" not because you *see* that the rule of the series required it, but because the rule *does* require it. Is this a trivial difference? On the contrary, it is a metaphysical watershed. For if you are to avoid confusion here, you must say that what carries you along to the conclusion is not your own mind merely, but the object before your mind, the structure of what you are thinking of, the logical relations that obtain in your subject matter. You are under the constraint of an order that you did not make. To the extent that you succeed in thinking rationally, your reasoning is under the control of a reason, in the sense of a framework of necessary relations, that is independent of you. You think as you do because it is not merely you that guides the thinking; you have surrendered yourself to an external and logical order along whose lines you find yourself carried.

I realized that two very different conceptions of man were at stake in this interpretation. Man can be conceived in terms of where he has come from or where he is going, of what he has been or what he may be. Many psychologists, in their impatience to make their study "scientific," construe him in terms of what he has been; they insist on his physiological and biological roots, and try to understand his thought process as a modification of the behavior of rats and pigeons. Such studies are not irrelevant, for man is in fact an animal. But in one respect he has emerged from the level on which all other animals live; he can think conceptually. That is, he can not only think of things in their absence but can fix his attention on their characters in abstraction and grasp the connections of these characters with others. This power has carried him up the slope of evolution at an accelerating pace, and he is living on a level that no other animal has reached, the level of law. He has found that in the infinitely various and changing scene about him, the qualities of things are interrelated in patterns that are themselves changeless. So he is living in two worlds at once. In one of them, where his forebears have lived, he is a creature of momentary sensations and fluctuating impulses. In the other, through his grasp of law, he can in some measure both understand the present and predict the future. As Plato saw, he is in process of escape from a realm of flux into a timeless realm of essences, of mastering nature and his own human nature through understanding it.

There are also varieties and levels in this understanding itself. At its best and clearest it takes the logical form we have described, in which the presence of necessity leaves no alternative explanation possible. But necessity is of diverse types. When we ask why a composer wrote an A natural rather than an A sharp, or why Tennyson wrote "Now sleeps the crimson petal, now the white" rather than "the yellow petal," it would seem strange to speak of logical necessity. But some sort of necessity is plainly at work. The artist is trying to create an aesthetic whole, and this imposes its own requirements; once he has committed himself to it, he is not free to choose his notes or words by whim. Similarly there are moral necessities. The judgment that intense joy is intrinsically more worth having than intense pain does not have a merely contingent truth; it is necessary, whether one winces at "logically necessary" or not. Furthermore, there are degrees of necessity; or if that is too paradoxical a notion, degrees of approximation to necessity. Why is that child crying? Suppose the answer is given, "Because he has just broken his favorite toy." Is that really unintelligible—as little intelligible, say, as that sensations of red are produced by wavelengths of about seven ten-thousandths of a millimeter? Surely not. It is not as cleanly and abstractly intelligible as an algebraic proof, granted; but neither is it a chance conjunction; it is something between the two, and nearer, I should say, to necessity than to conjunction. Why is Jones so oddly aggressive? or why so indifferent to the other sex? If a psychoanalyst answers in the first case by bringing to light an inferiority complex, and in the second an Oedipus complex, does he have no more insight than if he had depended solely on Mill's methods? To say so is to do less than justice to the sort of understanding we have, fragmentary as it is, of the workings of human nature. If this falls short of our understanding of the Pythagorean theorem, it is certainly a great deal more than zero.

In the light of these distinctions, let us look for a moment at the commonsense world. What sort of scene does it present? It is a hurly-burly and a hodgepodge. Rocks and trees, animals and persons, continents and stars, are scattered about in space and time in a way that suggests no plan, system, or pattern. To be sure, everything in the world is related to everything else by relations of identity and difference, and all things seem to be in a single space and time. But these are such abstract and gossamer linkages as to provide no richness of understanding. Try to carry through any of the common types of explanation so as to make it comprehensive, and it always breaks down. You can explain a man's action in climbing a tree by saying that it is a means to getting the cat, but try to explain the cat or the man in that way, as an economical means to a desirable end, and you are invariably defeated, if only by the problem of evil. You can explain the stopping of your watch by the lack of tension in its spring, and that by your failure to wind it, and that in turn by your forgetting to do so; but even if you succeed in isolating a causal thread, you inevitably lose it in infinity. Furthermore, millions of different events are occurring at this moment, and simultaneous events cannot be (in the ordinary sense) causes or effects of each other. And if you turn to logical explanation, how little even that explains! Many philosophers of the present day are convinced that every existing thing and event is logically unconnected with any other and could disappear from the world without necessarily affecting anything else.

Such a rubbish-heap view of the world I cannot accept. It is inconsistent with the postulate on which my rationalism proceeds. Let me try to explain. Philosophy, as I conceive it, is a persistent attempt to satisfy the theoretical impulse; such satisfaction is achieved only when the question Why? has been finally answered; and that answer in turn is achieved only with the grasp of necessity. But granting that thought is thus seeking necessity and can be fully satisfied with nothing less, how do we know that the world will supply it? The fact is that the hunger for understanding no more guarantees an intelligible world than a hunger for caviar ensures all we want of it. May we not at any time stumble upon a thing or event that is so unconnected with anything around it as to be unintelligible—not only beyond our grasp at the moment, but essentially and forever inexplicable? The existence of such an element can hardly be denied a priori. On the other hand no hopelessly opaque surd seems yet to have appeared. One is reminded of Einstein's remark, "The most incomprehensible fact of the universe is that it is comprehensible." And it would be gratuitous defeatism to launch the enterprise of understanding the world with the assumption that it cannot succeed. In raising the question Why? it is surely reasonable to assume that there is an answer to be found, whether in fact we find it or not. To quote Einstein again, "Certain it is that a conviction, akin to religious feeling, of the rationality or intelligibility of the world lies behind all scientific work of a high order."[21] There need be nothing dogmatic about such a connection. I take it not as a fact or a conclusion, but as a postulate merely, demanded by the inquiry and progressively confirmed as the inquiry proceeds, but incapable of a final confirmation until the long process reaches its term. But unless at every step of the inquiry one can assume that intelligibility lies ahead, there would be no point in going on. The ultimate intelligibility of things is thus the working postulate of a rationalist philosophy.

My reflection so far had left me with two large and independent ideas: the idea of thought as a movement toward an end of its own, and the idea of the world as a rational or intelligible whole. The first of these was the main theme of the first volume of *The Nature of Thought*, while the second, with its implications, was the concern of the second volume. I began with psychology. I thought I saw with increasing clearness as the study proceeded that any psychology that is to deal adequately with cognition must issue in epistemology and metaphysics. I could learn nothing about the nature or movement of thought from the naive dogmatism of the behaviorists. I learned a little more from Titchener's *Psychology of the Thought Processes*, though not as much as I hoped. Though Titchener was in advance of the behaviorists, his innocence of philosophy entangled him with a low-grade philosophy, a sensationism which made any plausible account of the grasp of relations impossible. Far more profitable was Sir William Mitchell's *Structure and Growth of the Mind*, a book that brought philosophy to bear on psychology with illuminating results. Mitchell's understanding of the mind had been fertilized by Hegel, Green, and Bradley. It was evident that I should have to make two studies, one of the growth of the theoretic impulse, the other of that structure of the world which it was seeking to uncover. Perhaps I should say something of how my thought developed in each of these areas.

Mind as Purposive

It was clear to me from the outset that the movement of thought is teleological. Indeed I was inclined to think that purposive endeavor was the earmark of mind generally. This was the view I urged in a symposium on "The Nature of Mind" with E. A. Singer and C. I. Lewis at the Philosophical Association meeting of 1940. I had been confirmed in it by a study of L. T. Hobhouse's admirable books on mind in evolution, particularly his *Development and Purpose*. Hobhouse did not treat the advance of mind with the metaphysical massiveness of Hegel, but he was closer to scientific fact; and he saw clearly how inadequate was the mechanical type of causation to genuinely mental processes. So did McDougall, whose theory of instinct is now old-fashioned, but who had far more insight into mental operations than many of his successors. Both Hobhouse and McDougall believed they had caught the presence of mind far down in the evolutionary scale, as low as the solitary wasp or the yucca moth, perhaps even as low as the earthworm. But such inference from behavior is analogical, and more precarious as the analogy weakens. The basis of all such argument and the only conclusive evidence that a mental process is purposive is one's own direct awareness.

Consider how plain this evidence is. Suppose a man sets himself to write a limerick. Is it not clear that the metrical scheme to be filled out will exercise its influence not only on his acceptance of a given suggestion but on what suggestions will present themselves? He will reach out—fumblingly perhaps and with awkward results, but never merely at random—after phrases and ideas that complete the pattern with which he starts. Or suppose he must replace a tire on his car. His purpose, here as before, will suggest the means to its realization, which will not now be a line of iambic tetrameter, but perhaps a tire iron to remove the hubcap and a wrench to loosen the nuts. Or he wants to buy a birthday present for Susan. It is not very likely that this purpose would call up either a limerick line or a tire iron. What he wants is something that will please Susan, be obtainable, and fall within his means, and this will appoint the range over which his ideas play—a box of chocolates, a scarf, earrings, a wristwatch. It is sometimes supposed that thought is as haphazard in reaching its ends as nature is alleged to be in improving the species; that it produces a mere litter of ideas, one of which by happy accident may prove viable. But conscious purpose does not act in so hit-or-miss a way. The end not only selects among the means that are offered; it largely controls those offerings themselves. It reaches down into the subconscious levels to invite some and to snub others. At its best it dominates completely the course of its own fulfillment.

Once the observer has seen how heavily charged with purpose mind is, at least at its human level, he is less prone to the illusion that it can be explained by leveling down. He may often understand the lower in terms of the higher; he can never wholly understand the higher in terms of the lower. What mind is like can be understood only from within, by starting from one's own conscious processes and then, if one wishes, extrapolating from them. I could see that my own consciousness was end-dominated, and I thought I could see the sort of end toward which one strand within it, namely reflective thought, was directed. This end was not explicitly present in my thinking, indeed it required insistent questioning to bring it to light. But an end may be immanently operative in one's thought without ever having been explicitly recognized or defined. The rules of logic are at work in one's mind long before one has sat in a logic class or heard of the syllogism; as Locke put it, God did not make man merely two-legged and leave it to Aristotle to make him rational; one may recognize that thought has gone off the rails when one commits an undistributed middle or an illicit major without knowing the name of the fallacy or the rule that is being violated. There is of course much in this working of an implicit ideal that we do not understand. How can an ideal be present and at work without our being aware of it? Does it make sense to say that a bird acts purposively in building its nest, even though it never thinks explicitly of its goal at all? Such questions are not easy to answer. But animal behavior seems to be continuous with processes in ourselves that we can see to be end-directed, and neither in the individual nor in the race should we deny ourselves the light that may be thrown upon a process by considering ends that lie far ahead.

Thought in Perception

If thought is an evolving purposive process directed toward understanding, and understanding lies in a grasp of relations, there should be evidence of the working of this purpose below the reflective level. In the first six chapters of *The Nature of Thought* I gave some account of this evidence. It was already present in the simplest act of perception. For perception is judgment. It is not mere sensation; it is the attaching of meaning to something sensed, a noting of its significance. Sensing red or hearing a sharp sound is not perception; it becomes perception when the color signalizes the presence of a red ball, or the sound is recognized as the barking of a dog. A child touches a flame and is burnt. The next time he sees the flame, he sees it differently, for because of his past experience he now reads it as something dangerous. Perception links a subject with a predicate. It marks the entry of the mind into the world of relations. It is the first short, stumbling step in the adventure of thought in understanding its world.

The relations apprehended in early perception are miscellaneous, vaguely apprehended, and enlightening only in low degree. I gave much attention to the patterns we find in the commonsense world of things, and it became clear to me that our grouping of qualities into things was determined less by the demands of necessity or intelligibility than by such relative accidents as joint appearance and practical convenience. The redness and roundness of a ball, for example, may regularly come together and move together; either may serve as the sign of the other or of the ball; and they are ascribed to the same thing. But their relation is mere togetherness, and of all relations "and" is the least enlightening. A spoon is taken as one thing, not because its qualities are linked by necessary connections, but because to take them as one thing serves a useful purpose when we are dealing with food. The things about us seem so fixed and unquestionable and their lines of demarcation so natural, that the suggestion comes as something of a shock that in dividing them as we do we have not been carving nature at the joints but consulting our own convenience. Is a cubic foot of the mid-Pacific or a cubic mile of sky a *thing*? It is just as real as a table or a chair, but we should never think of taking it as a thing because this would serve no useful purpose. Shrink our body to the size of an ant's or elongate it to the height of Everest, and would even tables and chairs remain things to us any longer? To be sure, not all the relations used in breaking the world into things are of this arbitrary kind, for the canons of logic and arithmetic and the forms of space and time are also at work in the process. But these alone would not account for the present grouping of qualities, for they would admit millions of groupings other than those we know.

Many writers considered it absurd to take a perception as a judgment, and more so to call it an inference. For Dewey, thought meant reflective thought, which came into operation only when normal responses were blocked and a means had to be found to get around the block; where there was no such obstacle, there was no problem and no thought. You were not thinking, for example, when you recognized without question the man walking ahead of you on the street as your friend John. There was one very significant fact, however, that made this view impossible for me, namely the fact that perception can err. One may tap the man on the shoulder, and find when he turns around that he is not John, but a total stranger. Now it is only thought that can be mistaken. A sensation, a physical response, cannot intelligibly be called untrue. Judgment is the simplest act of thought that is capable of truth or falsity; that indeed is its definition; and to concede its presence in perception is unavoidable if perception is to yield either knowledge or error. There was of course nothing new in this account; it was echoing Mill and Spencer.

The inevitable objection to making perception a form of judgment was that this overintellectualized it. And it is true that in perceiving a car or a tree we do not need, and do not employ, the explicitness and definition of full-dress judgment. The ideal supplement to sense is used implicitly. This called for a fuller account. What was the nature of perceptual meaning? What were its functions? Did it have any distinguishable structure? I devoted to these points about a hundred pages of my book. Some theorists, I found, were inclined to reduce perceptual meaning to a "motor set," that is, a physical state of readiness to react; others to a state of the brain; others still to a set of ideas subconsciously entertained. I examined these theories and found none of them satisfactory. The best I could offer instead was a theory of perceptual meaning as consisting of dispositions. I admitted the difficulty of saying what these dispositions were. Still, it was fairly easy to see how they behaved. If they were not fully conscious ideas, at least they acted as if they were; they acted like allies of the dominant conscious interest, massing themselves in support of it and ready to spring into visibility on call. An object lying in the road will be interpreted differently by the dog who sniffs it, the motorist who avoids it, and the man who is retracing his steps in frantic search for his wallet. And the same man will attach varying meanings to the "same" object as his interest shifts. A stone in his path will be interpreted in one way when he stubs his toe on it, in another when he pauses over it as a geological curiosity, and in a third when he seizes on it as a missile to fend off an attack.

The study of perceptual meaning seemed curiously neglected. At the time I was dealing with it, about 1930, there was much discussion of sense-data and much also about explicit reasoning, but the very existence of what I called "the inferential element in perception" was widely denied. I thought it not only existed but had an interesting and complex organization that could be studied with profit. The presence and organization of an implicit meaning-mass explain why the mechanic, even when inarticulate, may gather at once what is wrong with an ailing machine; why some persons, with no better eyes than others, are very much better observers; why a keen observer in one field may be blind in another; why a poor memory may coexist with an excellent judgment; and why our "intuitions" about others should so often be correct, even when we fumble in assigning the grounds for them. Intelligence may vary greatly within the perceptual level. One mind may show a much greater-than-average power to transfer a meaning-mass from one subject to another through the implicit grasp of an identity between them. Animal intelligence is wholly, or almost wholly, of the perceptual type, but it shows immense variations, from that of Fabre's wasps (perhaps even from that of Jennings's amoebae) to that of Yerkes's apes. And these variations appear to be entirely a matter of the acquisition, flexibility, and range of perceptual meaning.

The leap from animal thought to human comes with the achievement of free ideas, when meanings are no longer tied to what is given in sense, but can be used at will for reference to what is absent and remote. Such ideas we all employ constantly. But what exactly is in one's mind when one uses such an idea? The differences among philosophers and psychologists when they try to answer this question are so extreme as to be almost ludicrous; and the diversity enlarged my own task. For my usual way of dealing with a difficult issue is to compare the alternative theories about it, reaching my goal by elimination, and arguing that a certain conclusion must hold because nothing else will do. And in the search for an acceptable theory of ideas, I was faced with something like chaos. The British empiricists and such psychologists as Titchener identified the idea with an image. For the Bertrand Russell of *The Analysis of Mind*, it was sometimes an image, sometimes a set of words, which might mean its object either by resembling it or by producing similar effects. For Ogden and Richards in *The Meaning of Meaning,* it was "a modification of the nervous system" similar to what has been caused by its object in the past. For the behaviorists it was a movement of the organs of speech. For the pragmatists it was a "plan of action." For the extreme realists it was a mental act of awareness, its content or object being in every case independent of the act. For the critical realists it was the awareness of a timeless essence that might or might not belong to anything existent. I set myself to analyze and weigh all these theories, and to use them as stepping-stones to a theory of my own.

It is nearly always easier to see what is not true than what is. As I look back at my criticisms of these theories of the idea, they still seem to me cogent, more so perhaps than my effort at construction. The theory that the thought of something is an image or copy of it is an enticing one, which dies hard. After a long run among empiricists and commonsense philosophers, it was revived by Wittgenstein, who had almost certainly never read Green on the British empiricists, if indeed he had read the empiricists themselves; his form of the copy theory I tried to deal with in a later book. I devoted a chapter in *The Nature of Thought* to Russell's form of the theory, but do not know whether my criticism of the various image theories was ever taken seriously.

Behaviorism

My strictures on behaviorism did have some hearing. Behaviorism is a doctrine to which I have returned again and again. As early as 1928 I wrote an article in the *Philosophical Review* on "Behaviorism and the Theory of Knowledge," taking for special attention the views of E. B. Holt. Holt was an able but crotchety thinker whose philosophy began with an extreme realism and ended in an extreme materialism. He seems to have been convinced by his teacher James, and his colleague Perry, that nothing is dependent on awareness of it, that everything we sense or think about has an independent being of its own—not only tables and chairs but the secondary qualities, the pink rats of the alcoholic, and even the square root of minus one. He went on to conceive awareness, not as a mental act, but as purely physical, a way of reacting on the part of the organism. In my article I pointed out some of the difficulties of this theory, and was surprised and pleased to receive a letter (June 30, 1928) from President Angell of Yale, formerly professor of psychology at Chicago, expressing hearty agreement with my criticism. He added: "Philosophically (and psychologically too, for that matter—in many respects) the positions of my old pupil Watson are simply ridiculous and, like the post-French revolutionary mechanistic rationalizing, will die a natural death at no remote date." I fear that materialism, in its theoretical simplicity, answers to a desire more deeply rooted in human nature than Angell suspected. It is an odd monster of a theory, hydra-headed and phoenixlike, whose assailants no sooner cut off one of its heads than it grows another; indeed it keeps resurrecting itself, when all its heads have been amputated, again and again. Watson's special form of it is the reembodiment of Hobbes's suggestion of long ago, "Ratio, now, is but *oratio*."

It was Watson whom I took for examination when treating the behaviorist theory of thought. His theory was a pleasant one to deal with because it was so simple and so free from philosophic sophistication; he held philosophy in hearty contempt. "Thought is the action of language mechanisms"; "thinking with us is sub-vocal talking." All that was really needed to refute such a theory was to show that thought and speech were independent variables, that speech sometimes varied while thought remained the same, and that thought sometimes varied while speech remained the same. To illustrate the first point: a German and a Frenchman may surely think the same thought and yet express it in different words; on Watson's theory, they *could* not be thinking the same thing, for the words *were* the thought. As to the other point: using an example of James's, I have sometimes written on a blackboard the French words, *Pas de lieu Rhône que nous,* and asked a student to read it. He says, "Paddle your own canoe," and it comes home to him with a slight shock that he has been repeating the words of a familiar proverb. Now if saying the words is all there is to having the thought, there should be no difference between reciting them without their meaning and with it; but there plainly is a difference; that explains the slight shock when one realizes what one has been doing.

When Watson's identification of thought with speech was criticized, he fell back on its identification with "covert" bodily processes, such as changes in the brain. He was hardly to be dislodged from this retreat by incursions into cerebral physiology; it was better to raise at once the ultimate question, Can *any* conscious process—perception, memory, inference, desire—be identified with a physical process, that is, in the end, with matter in motion? Of course if a person insists that this is what he means by such terms, he must be granted the last word. But if he admits the possibility that he may be mistaken, he may reconsider; and how anyone after such reconsideration can continue to say that what he really means by his toothache or by his image of Abraham Lincoln is a movement of physical particles in his brain, I do not understand. The pain or the image may be as intimately connected *causally* with the brain event as he wishes, but to say that is not to identify the two but to admit their difference, since cause and effect are two, not one. Furthermore, Watson's argument that since there is no such thing as consciousness people who use "mental" terms must mean by them nervous changes can be effectively met historically. How could a savage who complained of a toothache have meant by it a change in a dental nerve when he had no notion that nerves existed? Or consider Aristotle, who had much to say about thought. Did he really mean by it a process in the brain? The uncooperative philosopher has left it on record that the function of the brain is to lubricate the eyes, and that pure intellection, or logical reasoning, has no bodily correlate at all. Since, then, he could hardly have meant by thought a change in the brain, and there was no consciousness for him to mean, he must have been talking about nothing. The conclusion is less than convincing.

The controversy with the behaviorist must no doubt be settled, like that with the pragmatist, by the success of one party or the other in showing to his opponent the inconsistency between his professions and his practice. The pragmatist does not mean by the truth of a historical judgment, for example, its having desirable consequences now; surely that must be evident when he looks candidly at his own meaning. Similarly when the behaviorist talks about his image of Lincoln—clear, or dim, or mistaken—he cannot intelligibly mean that these characters belong to the scurrying of electronic currents along nerve filaments in his head. There are no two things in the world more obviously different from each other than a pain and a motion of physical particles; and I can only confess that there is something mysterious to me in the state of mind of anyone who can think them the same.

Nevertheless this position is still held by persons of scientific standing. It is taught in substance by B. F. Skinner, with whom I have had some interesting exchanges. In 1964, Professor Skinner and some younger colleagues of similar views presented a series of papers at the American Philosophical Society in Philadelphia. It happened to be the four-hundredth anniversary of the birth of Shakespeare, and the society had arranged that at the beginning of the session some of the great monologues from the Shakespearean plays should be read to the members by actors of distinction. When the time came for discussing the papers, I asked Mr. Skinner if, in his opinion, what is commonly meant by Shakespeare's mind—for example his ideas, desires, and purposes—made any difference to what he put down on paper. Mr. Skinner answered no; the only factors that could have affected his behavior were physical ones. The audience consisted chiefly of scientists, but I thought I heard something like a gasp. Shakespeare's *ideas* made no difference in his writing of *Hamlet*? His *body* wrote Othello, without assistance from his thought or his designs? I was not yet prepared to accept this. Professor Boring, who was in the chair, asked me after the meeting whether I would be willing to write a criticism of the papers for publication in the *Proceedings*. I was happy to do so, and in February 1965 the criticism was printed under the title "Critical Reflections on Behaviorism." Mr. Skinner and I were invited by the program committee of the American Psychological Association to debate "the problem of consciousness" at a meeting of the association in Chicago in September 1965, and our speeches were published in the *Journal of Phenomenology* in March 1967. I returned to the subject still again in a lecture on "The Limits of Naturalism" given at the University of New York at Brockport, and since then printed more than once.

Pragmatism

When I came to deal in my book with the pragmatic theory of thought, I was able to use some of the argumentation of my Oxford and Harvard theses. Incidentally, the four outstanding exponents of this position all called it by different names; Peirce's theory was "pragmaticism," James's, "pragmatism," Dewey's, "instrumentalism," and Schiller's, "humanism." Of these versions, Dewey's instrumentalism was the most original and the most responsibly argued. I never read much of Peirce, undoubtedly to my loss; probably I was put off by reading the essay sometimes taken as the earliest manifesto of pragmatism, "How to Make Our Ideas Clear." His own thought in this essay, though fairly clear, is far from convincing; the grounds for this opinion are given in *Reason and Analysis*. James, though better reading than Peirce or Dewey, never thought his theory rigorously through; he is capable, for example, of reckoning among the factors determining the truth of a belief the consequences (in the sense of implications) that are entailed by the belief, the consequences (in the sense of advantages to the believer) that may follow from holding it, and the consequences (in the sense of effects) of the fact referred to by it—all as if they were equally relevant. I admire James greatly; he seems to me one of the most attractive figures personally in the history of philosophy. But his philosophizing lacked precision and thoroughness, and it fared badly at the hands of such critics as Moore, Russell, Taylor, and McTaggart. As for Schiller, the last of this distinguished quartet, his humanism frankly abandoned hope of thinking impersonally or achieving objective results. "In reality our knowing is driven and guided at every step by our subjective interests and preferences, our desires, our needs, and our ends."[22] This view, I think, discredits itself, along with philosophy generally. If it is true, it too must have been arrived at through "subjective interests and preferences." And in that case, why believe it?

The root error of pragmatism, it seemed to me, was a confusion about the end or aim of thought. Thought aims at knowing, not at doing. The confusion is probably implicit in James's dedication of his *Pragmatism* to John Stuart Mill, "whom my fancy likes to picture as our leader, were he alive to-day." James perhaps assumed that if Mill appealed to consequences in determining the rightness of an act he would do likewise in determining the truth of a belief. I do not think it likely that Mill would have accepted the parallel. The pursuit of truth is the attempt to adjust thought to fact; the pursuit of goodness is the attempt to adjust fact to thought, in the sense of moulding it to our intentions. Thought seeks to reflect the world, morality to make it better. No doubt the two kinds of pursuit do generally support each other; the man who knows is in a better position to do right, and the moral man will recognize knowledge as one of his goods. But the two ends are not the same, nor therefore the two pursuits. There is much knowledge that has little or no effect on practice, and much devoted pursuit of human betterness that brings little or no illumination of mind. Thought and action are not to be confounded.

Realism

When I came to realistic theories of knowledge, I discovered a curious reluctance to accept ideas at all. This stemmed from the distinction between act and object, which was made by Brentano and was used with much effect by Moore in his "Refutation of Idealism." Moore argued that even in the experience of colors and sounds one could distinguish between the act of awareness and the sense-datum one was aware of, and that while the act was clearly mental this raised no presumption that the object also was mental. A like distinction was made in the realm of ideas, and the content of the idea distinguished from the act of thinking it. This distinction seemed less plausible at the higher level than at the lower, but I took the line of denying it on both levels. I could not find the alleged "acts" of awareness. Moore admitted that when he attempted to catch them introspectively he found them "transparent"; they had no character of their own and had to be distinguished from each other by reference to their objects. This view had the odd consequence that psychology was largely reduced to a description of the indescribable. I was fortified in my skepticism by learning that Russell, after accepting Moore's distinction as clear and philosophically important, had himself abandoned mental acts as unnecessary and unverifiable. For such acts I substituted mental events. The appearance and disappearance, sometimes voluntary, sometimes involuntary, of sensory, imaginal, and conceptual content seemed to me to cover the ground.

Perhaps I should note, in passing, that I have never been able to accept the realist view that the objects of direct experience are independent of consciousness. Indeed everything we sense or feel seems to me to exist only in consciousness. In this view I am again fortified by recalling the outcome of Russell's struggles with this problem. Though a leader of the extreme realists in early life, he had arrived by 1948 at a position close to Berkeley's about the objects of direct awareness. All of them, he concluded, even perceptual space and time, were mind-dependent. This did not mean, of course, that he was a convert to idealism, for the whole world of physics, which provided the causes of perception, remained outside the circle of experience. Though I have been inclined throughout to be a Berkeleian about objects of perception, some of the main arguments by which Berkeley supported his position, notably the *esse et percipi* argument which he thought so powerful, struck me as unconvincing; and it was puzzling to find a thinker as critical as Bradley urging that because we never in fact find qualities existing except in relation to a perceiver, therefore they cannot so exist. Nevertheless the facts of illusion and color blindness show that some sensed qualities cannot reasonably be taken as anything but subjective; and when we reflect on how the experience of them arises, and how similar this is to the generation of normal experiences, we can only conclude that if either is subjective both are. This is not the place to argue the matter; suffice it to say that the case for the mind-dependence of all immediately experienced qualities seems to me extremely strong.

Realists face a dilemma. If they take what is apprehended in perception or thought as existing independently, they reify illusions; if they take it as a representative in consciousness of the object, they are dualists, and must show cause why they should not be skeptics. The critical realists believed they had escaped between the horns of this dilemma by their resort to essences. An essence, according to Santayana, is a universal, that is, a quality or relation that may be realized or not in some existent thing, but in either case has its being in a timeless world of subsistence. For example, we perceive or think of the apple before us; its redness and roundness are qualities that in themselves never began and will never cease to be; some event in the history of our organism makes us engage them at a certain time. We take them on animal faith as belonging to an existent apple, and if good fortune is with us we are right, though of this we can never be quite certain. This was an intriguing theory, which was carefully worked out by Santayana and expounded at length in his inimitable style.

My main doubt about the essence rested on its strange implications regarding the relations of body and mind. Santayana's essences were "vestal virgins," suffering no violation from the world of matter, and bearing no issue in it. When we see or think of anything, "This descent or incarnation of essences cannot be their own doing, since all essences are inert and non-existent." Nor is it our own doing: "A world of accidents, arbitrary and treacherous, first lends to the eternal a temporal existence and a place in the flux."[23] Santayana went so far as to hold that no essence appearing in consciousness made any difference to what appeared there next.

These consequences of the theory did not seem to me tenable, nor therefore the theory itself. Did what Santayana thought make no difference to what he put on paper? This is a curious conclusion considering what he did put down. If he sees an apple as red, is this because the organism "lends to the eternal a temporal existence and a place in the flux"? This is a fine phrase, but its scientific translation would seem to be that the nervous change in eye and brain gives rise to the red sensum, producing its hue as truly as its existence. And if Santayana writes as persuasively as he does and follows at least some of his arguments so cogently to their conclusion, is this to be set down as accident? He modestly insists that it is. "The mind cannot pursue the roots of things into the darkness . . . it must be satisfied with noting their passing aspect, which is but an essence; and it must follow the chase, carried by its own galloping substance, to see what aspect they may wear next."[24] In the "dark engine" of the brain, no necessity is at work. Thus the life of reason is a life in which reason takes no part. Santayana sits at his desk and unfolds the splendid volume of his thought in orderly procession, but he never reaches a conclusion because the evidence requires it, never is led from any thought to the next by any thread of necessity in what is before him. It is only that the changing substance of his body, galloping along unguided, takes him past a row of billboards, which have been idling there from eternity, and that on recollecting their sequence at the end of the mad gallop he finds that, by some sort of miracle, they make continuous sense.

All this I disbelieved. It was not the way my own mind worked, nor could I believe it of Santayana's. At bottom the trouble lay in his incongruous combination of Plato and Democritus, of eternal and changeless essences with a thoroughgoing materialism as to the nature and operations of mind. It was incredible that the two worlds should lie side by side in this way, with no interaction at any point. To be sure, one need not deny the being of either realm. We did not invent the multiplication table; we discovered it; and it does in some sense belong to a world without end and without beginning. Nor is the world of physics an invention. I think my excellent tutor, Joachim, really doubted whether its entities existed, though if, by assuming their existence, one can make atomic bombs, the evidence is fairly compelling. But how are the realms related, the eternal and the temporal, the realms of permanence and of change? No philosopher yet has had an adequate answer to that question. But I thought that such idealists as Hegel and Green had dealt with it more realistically than Santayana. They had at least admitted what A. E. Taylor called "the initiative of the eternal" in directing human consciousness and action. I could not swallow Santayana's epiphenomenalism. That the universals appearing in consciousness do make a difference to the course of thought, that they exercise some constraint on what we say and do, seemed to me so plain a fact that anyone who denied it must accept a crushing burden of proof.

A Theory of the Idea

Having made the circuit of these theories of the idea, I had now to try my own hand. I had learned much from the tour. By accepting and rejecting elements from all the theories, I had set myself a conundrum. "What sort of thing must that be which refers to an object, yet is not the object; which calls words and images in aid, yet is itself neither word nor copy; which changes with bodily changes, but is more than any bodily change; which is always a means to an end, though not always to an end that is practical?" (*NT*, 1:473.)

That was the riddle I had to solve. And the more I thought about it, the clearer it seemed that the only relation that would answer to all the demands at once was the relation between purpose and fulfillment. Having quoted the riddle, let me quote also my solution to it.

> Thought in its essence is an attempt to attain, in the sense of achieving identity with, a special end of its own. The relation between idea and object must be conceived teleologically, as the relation of that which is partially realized to the same thing more fully realized. When we say that an idea is *of* an object, we are saying that the idea is a purpose which the object alone would fulfil, that it is a potentiality which this object alone would actualize, a content informed by an impulse to become this object. Its nature is hence not fully intelligible except in the light of what it seeks to become. Mind, in taking thought, attempts to pass beyond its present experience to what it would be but is not yet, and so far as it has the thought of this end, it already *is* the end *in posse*. The idea is thus both identical with its object and different from it. It is identical in the sense in which anything that truly develops is identical with what it becomes. It is different in the sense in which any purpose partially realized is different from the same purpose realized wholly. [*NT*, 1:473]

Universals

What specially commended this theory was the way it seemed to solve the problem of general ideas. Traditional logic approached the problem with an easy confidence. The concept *man,* for example, was assigned two meanings, one of which was a reference to the individuals to whom the name "man" would unhesitatingly be applied—white, black, brown, red, yellow men, old men and children yet unborn, men with arms and legs, and basket cases without either, male and female, philosophers and idiots, Neanderthals and Einsteins—can any set of characters possessed in common by all these individuals be isolated and clearly conceived? I could find no such concept in my own mind. And as I climbed higher on the tree of Porphyry from man to animal, and then to living being, and then again to mere being, I was less and less able to form the necessary abstraction. The concept *animal* gave little trouble in practice, and there should be correspondingly little difficulty in isolating what was common to Aristotle and an amoeba. In fact there is great difficulty.

Nor is it classes of individuals only that offer difficulty, for the same problem arises with classes of qualities. It is easy enough to think of the class of colors, but what precisely is color as such, color that is of no color but is identical in all colors? Attempts have been made to abstract and define this essence, but the definitions are sought-out and difficult, while the concept is used with no sense of difficulty at all.

Now suppose these concepts to be reinterpreted. Suppose the concept of man is taken as an incipient purpose or intention which would find its fulfillment only in the range of men; suppose the concept of color is not some figment abstracted from the range of colors, but the kind of thought which, if developed and specified, would realize itself in the experienced range of colors; does not that answer more nearly than the traditional view to the content that is actually present when we think these concepts? It seemed to me that it did. And while I can hardly believe that the theory, as I somewhat feebly developed it, will stand up under rigorous investigation, I still think that something like it may be true. If a general idea is not an effort to realize in some degree within experience a range of individuals in which it could recognize itself as fulfilled, at least it is something curiously like this.

My attack on the traditional notion of the general idea required me to rethink my view of universals. According to traditional logic, as just noted, we can isolate from the swarm of qualities belonging to an individual man or animal a nucleus called "manness" or "animality," and we can say that these nuclei exist independently of being thought. Not believing that these nuclei could be clearly conceived, I did not believe that such vague entities existed in nature either. I recognized that on the reality of universals I had to part com-

pany with such venerated masters as Plato and Hegel. Did it follow that I was
a nominalist? Not at all. I was moving toward a world of universals rather
than a world of particulars. I recognized three types of universal. First there
were universals like animality whose embodiments were individuals; these,
which I called *generic* universals, existed in thought only. Second, there were
universals like color, which I called *qualitative* universals; these were embodied, for example, in the various specific colors; and they too, as distinct
from their embodiments, were mental conveniences rather than natural existents. But now what of these specific colors themselves? Were they universals or particulars? A given apple has a determinate shade of red, together
with a determinate shape, weight, and taste. It was clear that each of these
specific qualities might appear elsewhere, and if so, they were genuine universals. They must be so considered even though, as already wholly determinate,
they had no species falling under them, and even though they were presented
in sense. They alone of the three types of universal seemed to me actual existents. I called them *specific* universals.

So classing them gave rise to another problem. Had I not drifted irresponsibly into a world where no place was left for particulars? I sat at my desk and
looked at the rows of shapes and colors on my bookshelves. These were all
universals. I heard the cheep of a bird outside; that too I was calling a set of
universals. Where in my world did I meet with anything *except* universals?
Most philosophers of the past had thought it obvious enough that there were
both universals and particulars; man had tried to get on with particulars only;
but I seemed to be climbing toward a lonely and somewhat absurd peak from
which nothing but universals could be descried.

I asked myself what a particular was. It was of course something in which
a universal was particularized. Yes, but what was it exactly that served to
particularize a universal, for example the redness of this apple? My friend and
teacher Montague gave what seemed to me a sensible answer: it was presentation or occurrence at a point in space or time. What I mean by *this* red shade
is the shade that now presents itself to the left of that orange and to the right
of that plate. What particularizes so far is a set of spatial relations. But what
of these relations themselves; are *they* universals or particulars? It was
obvious that "to the left of" and "to the right of" were relations that could
occur elsewhere, and hence must be universals. But a strange consequence
followed. If what particularizes universals is itself universal, does not any
given particular resolve itself away into universals? Particulars seemed to
have vanished.

I took my problem to Montague in person. Sometime in the thirties I
spent a weekend with him on his farm in the Catskills, and we wrestled with
the problem together. His candor, lucidity, and courtesy made him a delightful partner in discussion. He agreed that what particularized the shade of red

was its relations to what was around it, and he agreed that these relations were themselves universals. "Then does not your particular," I asked, "resolve itself into a set of universals?" "If so," he answered, "it is because we have left it incompletely specified. All we need is to complete the process. Keep on widening the circle of relations until you have included everything else in space. Surely then we should have achieved what was completely and uniquely particular." "I agree," I said, "if that space is itself unique. But is it? A plurality of spaces seems at least possible; indeed dream space is not in waking space nor continuous with it. And one could say the same of times." "Very well," said Montague; "I will reply by widening my specifications again. This shade will achieve particularity when, and only when, its relations are specified not only to all else in its own space and time, but to all else in all other spaces and times." But with this, it seemed to me that the difference between us had vanished. What he was saying, in effect, was that complete particularity could be attained only when the relation of a given content was specified to everything else in the universe. The universe or the absolute is unrepeatable by definition; indeed it is itself the only particular or individual. That was a startling conclusion, but there was nothing novel in it. If I was not mistaken, it was the common property of Spinoza and Hegel, of Bosanquet and Royce.

There are existentialist philosophers who would refuse to take the first step on this road. The color of the apple does fall in a certain point in a field of relations, they would admit, but what makes it particular is not its relations but its *existence*. The existence of something is not a quality or a set of relations; it is not a content or character of any kind. It may be indicated without any expressed judgment by simply pointing. Now we remark in passing that this appeal to pointing is a false step. For to point at something is as truly a specifying of it by indicating its place among others as a spoken judgment is. Nevertheless I do not dismiss the existentialist protest as wholly without force. It does have some force, though what this amounts to is very difficult to see. If the contention is that an existent color is more intense, or steady, or obtrusive, or uncontrollable than a merely imagined one and these supply the meaning of "existence," the case has been given up, for these are all characters again. On the other hand, if a particular is regarded as a compound of two constituents, a universal and something called existence, which is not characterizable in any way, thought has reached a blind alley. It is asserting the reality of something so elusive that the very question, "What are you asserting to be real?" is unanswerable, for no *what* is being asserted at all. We are told that existence is the most important constituent that a particular can have, but that in asserting it we are not asserting any content of any kind—in which case our "judgment" can only be meaningless. This is the sort of paradox that makes some existentialists rub their hands in glee, since it opens the door to elements that thought is helpless to deal with. I will only say for the present that while I am not wholly satisfied with my own view of particularity, I am still less satisfied with this kind of theory, if one can call it a theory at all.

Thought as a Drive Toward System

My thought, so far, had been concerned exclusively with ideas. To be sure, in studying them I was also studying judgment, since I held that ideas normally appear only in judgment. But I was impatient to move on to the analysis of reflective thinking. In this movement there was no sharp break. The growth of thought is a continuous one from perception, in which an inferential element is already at work, into full-blown inference. Thought at all its levels I took as the product of a single drive toward understanding. It is an attempt to construct on the ground of experience a world that, as intelligible, will satisfy the intellect. Not of course that this is its sole service, for human nature has other ends, moral, aesthetic, and practical, to which thought is an indispensable means. But its own distinctive drive is toward understanding, and the nature of its end becomes clearer as thought rises in the scale. That understanding involves interconnection within a system is plain enough in advanced cases, such as explanation in geometry or in grasping the structure of constitutional government with its various checks and balances. But, standing on these high levels and looking back, we can also see that the same ideal has been at work throughout the ascent. The child who observes that the dog barks and the cat meows is launched on a course that, carried through, will take him to science and philosophy; he is already feeling after grounds for the barking and meowing in the animal species that exhibit them. If he goes on to observe that the dog wags its tail when pleased and the cat when displeased, the ground is now being singled out with a degree more of discernment. But intellect from first to last is one continuous search for connections that will make more intelligible what experience presses upon us in disorderly profusion.

Our commonsense world is itself an attempt at system, however vaguely the lines of connection within it are drawn. It is a system that has been slowly elaborated by the race, though it may be quickly taken over by the individual. It provides the permanent standing ground for every leap of reflection. A problem is a felt need to assimilate something foreign into the system of this familiar world. The simile that seemed most natural to me was that of a continent with an island offshore which must be somehow connected to the mainland, for the occasion of reflection is always the appearance in the offing of something that presents a challenge to assimilation by our established system of thought. "What an odd piece of flint this! Could it be an Indian arrowhead?" "Oh dear, what can the matter be, Johnny's so long at the fair."

"Why should the tides rise and fall as they do?" Different as these problems are, they show the same general pattern in their nature and their solution. When the flint, by its shape and its surface, gives signs of human working, it can be filed away in a definite place in our intellectual cabinet as a human artifact. If the forsaken damsel recalls that Johnny had business to attend to at Banbury Cross on his way home from the fair, she can perhaps reconcile her disturbed mind to his absence. And when the tides are seen as cases of the pull of sun and moon, instances of the same laws as govern the fall of the rain, their strange behavior is domesticated in the world of familiar things.

The Movement of Reflection

My study of the movement of reflection in the second volume of *The Nature of Thought* has had little notice or influence. This is not surprising, since there were plenty of other books, easily obtainable, that covered similar ground: Dewey's *How We Think,* Dimnet's *Art of Thinking,* Graham Wallas's *Art of Thought,* and others. My own book was large and expensive, and its study of the thought process was embedded in a philosophical context that to many students would seem forbidding. But on going back to it again after more than thirty years, I do think it has something to say that in most of the other writers was left almost untouched. These writers had dealt effectively with the topics of my earlier chapters, "How Reflection Starts," "Specifying the Problem," and "Observation," but they had not dealt adequately with that leap of invention which is after all the main segment of the process. It was at this point that my old battle with the psychologists came to a head. Here even the account of reasoning given by James seemed inadequate. The generally accepted view was that a man sat down with some problem, for example the purpose of that projecting pole on the prow of the ferryboat, and allowed a ragtag and bobtail of similars to parade across the reviewing ground of his attention until, with luck, one of them would give him the clue he needed.

Competent thinking bears little resemblance to this hit-or-miss process. The mistake is fundamental, for it amounts to a misconception of the nature of thought and to some extent also the nature of mind. Mind is a set of strivings; thought is a striving after wider understanding; and a wider understanding is the assimilation by one's intellectual world of something that challenges it from without, the appropriation of a foreign element by a system already present. When that system is simple and abstract, the leap of inference may be instant, with none of that Micawberish waiting for something to turn up which is so conspicuous in the traditional account. When one is given the arc of a semicircle and asked to complete it, one certainly does not wait for a variety of lines, straight and curved, to saunter across the theater of one's mind until by happy chance a curve of the right degree presents itself. No one thinks that way; the curve extends itself into a circle by one quick confident leap. So again when a competent mind adds a list of numbers or solves an equation; there need be nothing experimental or groping about it.

The movement of thought is not in principle different when one turns from such abstract to more concrete types of thinking. Here I was helped by Bosanquet's book, probably little read now, *Implication and Linear Inference*. He showed by many examples that systems which lack the formal necessity of logic or mathematics may still exercise firm control over their own development and use. An electrician is called in to find why the kitchen lights fail to go on. He does not rummage through a set of alternatives suggested by similarity to the present situation; he knows that before any fixture in a good electric circuit is overheated a fuse will be blown out; so a blown fuse is the first thing he looks for. You find that the price of a coat of Harris tweed is far higher in this country than in England; why? An economist would not indulge in mere surmises as to the explanation; he would ask at once whether there is a tariff on wool, for he knows that when in a system of free trade there is a wide disparity of prices, goods flow to where the prices are higher until these are equalized, and that if they are not so equalized, the flow must be impeded by some artificial barrier. A dramatist has reached the last act of his play; how shall he complete it? Of course the end is not as rigidly dictated as it is in solving an equation, but neither is the artist free to follow any impulse that may arise, and the more completely he is in command of the structure he is creating (or the structure is in command of him), the more the range of his alternatives is narrowed.

My study of the movement of inference confirmed the suspicion with which I began my researches in Detroit. A descriptive psychology of the thought process is bound to be superficial. To understand that process, one must get inside it; and to get inside it is to realize that it is the pursuit of a special end. It is a psychological process directed toward a logical goal, and hence under some degree of constraint by that goal. The psychologist who cannot share the goal or feel its operation in thinking will miss the essence of the process; indeed a science of thought in the ordinary sense is an illusion or an imposture, like a science of art or of goodness. Mind on its intellectual side is a restless and inchoate system of ideas informed in its advance by the implicit ideal of a more perfect order in which its search can find fulfillment. The system that would satisfy the intellect is not a scientific fact, in the sense of a fact in nature that can be observed and reported on. Yet its influence over the movement of thought is like the pull of the moon on the tides. A man who has not felt its power can only gape at thought vacuously, as Peter Bell did at the primrose. And for the sort of scientist who, in serene inconsistency with his activity of the moment, denies all teleological behavior, the thinker must remain a man of inscrutable mystery.

No doubt the rationalist would be going too far if he maintained that in his groping reflection of the moment he could trace the operation of the ultimate end of thought, in the sense of a system all-comprehensive and perfectly ordered. In our actual thinking it is always some minor system that we find at work—that of number when we are engrossed in arithmetic, or idealized space when we work in geometry, or the appropriate aesthetic whole if we are bent on composing in poetry or music. Furthermore, these wholes may never at any point in the process be formulated explicitly. How they exert control without ever putting in an appearance was a point of much interest to me. Fortunately I was writing at a time when the guidance of conscious processes by the subconscious or the unconscious had been made familiar by Freud; and though I was never a disciple of Freud's, I was inclined to agree with McDougall that he had thrown more light on the working of the mind than any other psychologist since Aristotle. I was impressed and puzzled by finding how much of the thought process, including the leap of invention itself, could apparently go on below the level of explicit awareness.

So I gave myself for a time to a study of the subconscious in invention, and wrote a chapter on it for the book. In my casual reading I had run across dramatic cases in which a scientist had made a discovery or a man of letters had produced a poem without conscious effort, apparently as a result of processes that had gone on below the level of his awareness. Freud's attention had been chiefly given to the ways in which reason was distorted by such processes. My own interest was, on the contrary, in the way in which they could hold the train of thought on its track or even carry it to its goal. I found many instances of creative thinking of this kind in the most diverse fields. The word "creative" is one that I hesitate to use because so much nonsense has accumulated about it; even university teachers sometimes assume that the writing of incoherent fiction or formless verse is "creative" while the bringing to light of the "double helix" in genetics is not creation but mere discovery. But from the point of view of the seeking mind, discovery and invention are equally creative and follow the same track. Through comparing notes about their work that had been left by such writers as Stevenson and Henry James, by poets like Shelley and Coleridge, by musicians like Brahms and Beethoven, and by scientists like Gauss and Poincaré, I thought I found a more or less uniform pattern by which subconsciousness had been successfully employed. Many illuminating cases have been added to the public record since this study was made, and not least the account by Bertrand Russell, already referred to, of the way he poured out his own cornucopia of thought and writing. Perhaps our population of books, as of people, has reached the point of diminishing returns, but assuming that production is still desirable, I think young workers in the field of philosophy might profit greatly from mastering the now well-known techniques for enlisting the aid of their secondary selves.

The part of *The Nature of Thought* that has aroused most interest and criticism is the last part, in which I defend coherence as both the test and the nature of truth, contend that truth is a matter of degree, and go on to consider various theories of necessity: the empiricist, the formalist, and what I called the theory of concrete necessity. On most of the topics there discussed, my views have not greatly changed, though on some of them the criticisms of colleagues have led to second thoughts. I am still inclined to say that we must test truth by coherence, but I am less confident than I was that coherence exhausts the meaning of truth. Similarly, though I think the doctrine of internal relations applies over a great range of terms and propositions, that range, I now think, is more restricted than I once believed. I am more keenly aware than before of the paradox of holding at once to specific universals, such as the number three or a definite shade of red, supposed to be identical in various contexts, and also to a doctrine of internal relations, since this doctrine, if held without qualification, would make such identities impossible. But since it is in this area that I expect my critics in this book to be most active, it is perhaps best to leave further reflections on it for my reply.

The Changing Climate of Philosophy

It has already been remarked that *The Nature of Thought,* my first book of any significance, appeared under the worst of conditions. The Second World War had just broken out; the attention of Britons was engrossed elsewhere; and when the book appeared in the United States a year later, Americans too were becoming involved. The philosophical climate was hardly more favorable than the political. Here the change was due mainly to Wittgenstein. I think it was Gilbert Ryle who remarked that for most philosophers it would be enough to spark one revolution in philosophy, but that Wittgenstein had been responsible for two. He has been the chief philosophical innovator of this century in Britain and America. This is in itself a curious and surprising fact. The British tradition in philosophy, whether in its empirical or its idealist strain, has been marked by humanistic interest, logical lucidity, and literary grace, as is testified by such names as Bacon, Hobbes, Locke, Berkeley, Hume, Mill, the Cairds, Bradley, Taylor, and McTaggart. Philosophy in their hands became at times technical, but it never wholly lost touch with the common man; an intelligent and thoughtful reader, even though unversed in philosophy, could pick up their books, open a chapter at random, and recognize that their authors were saying something intelligible about a problem he could see to be important. Wittgenstein changed all this. An Austrian engineer, trained in mathematics, his *Tractatus* is one of the most cryptic of philosophical works, a series of numbered paragraphs, many of them consisting of single sentences, whose meaning and bearing are obscure. His only other important book, *Philosophical Investigations,* is more conventional in form, but disorderly, repetitious, and involved.

There are many who regard Wittgenstein as a genius and many who regard him as a philosophical disaster. It is possible for a man to be both of these at once. He had a remarkable gift for focusing all his powers on some technical problem like the relations between a sentence, a proposition, and a fact, and coming up with a solution that owed little or nothing to any philosopher who had ever written about the problem before. Sometimes the solution was really novel; sometimes, as in his picture theory of the correspondence of sentence and fact, it illustrated Santayana's remark that those who are ignorant of the past are doomed to repeat it. But whether they were novel or naive, his conclusions were offered to the world with breathtaking confidence; one was given to understand that the main problems of philosophy were now definitively solved. The fact that the definitive solutions announced in his first book were largely retracted in his second had singularly little effect on the enthusiasm of his followers, who received the linguistic theories of his later days with the same eager reverence they had shown toward the earlier ones.

I do not profess to understand all this. Many things must have contributed to the vogue of Wittgenstein, including the disillusionment with prevailing thought after the First World War, the new importance of science (he made philosophy the logic of science), the appearance of Russell's logic, with its attendant philosophy of logical atomism, the shift of interest shown by Moore from precarious speculation about sweeping problems to the exact discussion of smaller and more sharply defined ones. Whatever the causes that ushered in the Wittgensteinian era, it was a very different era from any that had gone before.

In some ways it marked an advance. It was an era of analysis, in which philosophers were trying to dissect their thought into its ultimate components, arriving first at atomic propositions, and then pressing on to their simple predicates and their curiously elusive subjects. It was an era in which the wings of metaphysics were clipped clean off by the insistence that one was gabbling meaninglessly if one referred to anything that could not be given in sense. John Wisdom could write articles that ran on like Dickens serials through many issues of *Mind,* on such subjects as logical constructions, which were the analytic substitute for inference to the unverifiable, and our knowledge of other minds, which on positivist principles was an unauthorized intruder. Such explorations, though often a strain on patience, were not wholly unprofitable. At many points they gave an implied and merited rebuke to a speculative philosophy that had become "too much at ease in Zion." Writers like the Cairds and the early Taylor were all too likely to solve particular problems by asking what solution would fit into the system they were constructing, and adopting it because it did so. Writers like Bosanquet and even Bradley would write about the concrete universal or internal relations in a sweeping way that proved unconvincing when applied to particular cases. Here a model was provided by Moore, who wielded his razor on these concepts with great effect.

Indeed it was salutary though sometimes paralyzing to the philosopher of those days to realize as he wrote that he would be held accountable by acute and unsparing critics for every loosely used word. Nor was it any longer possible to cover the weakness of an argument under the mantle of solemnity and sonority. McTaggart had confessed to an inveterate suspicion of "the kind of philosophy that emanates from the west of Scotland"; the analysts shared this suspicion; and solemn references to "him in whom we live and move and have our being" were heard with more impatience than reverence. An argument must stand on its own feet, and not allow itself to be carried across crevices and over objections by a following wind of even exalted emotion.

As there were obvious gains in the new temper of philosophy, so also there were losses. One was a loss of perspective. When Royce or Ward or Bradley dwelt at length on a technical point, one could be sure that it was a point of importance, whose implications ran far beyond itself. The minute philosophers of the Wittgensteinian era were capable of fixing their eyes on some patch in their front yard without once lifting them to the fence, let alone to the hills. And analysis for its own sake, unbridled by theory, easily runs wild. It started, indeed, a centrifugal movement in philosophy, a movement toward pluralism in which the scattered members of the philosophic community each cultivated his plot with small concern either for the wider bearing of his labor or for the traditional ends of the philosopher's quest. The professional journals became philosophic drugstores, in which no inference could be made from the article offered on one counter to what would appear on the next. The common interest that had held philosophers together thinned almost to the vanishing point. I felt this keenly in watching the slow disintegration of the New York Philosophy Club, which had meant so much to me. I recalled a time when Dewey, Cohen, Lovejoy, Woodbridge, Singer, Niebuhr, and Montague, far apart as they were, could meet on common ground, where each found the others' theses and criticisms intelligible. Now the member working in deontic logic or linguistics would be merely mystifying to the specialist in Plato, and the theologian would feel like a pilgrim and a stranger. Members more often invoked the privilege of silence when the time came to make comments, or stayed away when papers were announced that fell outside their own fields. The new specialism was issuing in a new provincialism.

Unfortunately it brought with it also a loss of tolerance. I do not think the older speculative philosophers had been notably wanting in this. They were indeed taken aback by the mathematical philosophy of Russell, the onslaughts on their vagueness by Moore, and the uncompromising realism of Alexander, but they listened respectfully to the insurgents and were sometimes persuaded by them. The Wittgensteinians were less charitable. They wanted it clear that a revolution had occurred and that the ancien régime was out. Their interest in the history of philosophy before 1922 declined, and they turned instead to the evidence provided in each other's papers of new advances against the dark. The logicians and moralists of the preceding generation became suddenly old-fashioned, for Joachim and Joseph were not adepts at mathematical logic, and Ross and Prichard espoused the somewhat quaint view that moral "judgments" were judgments and even objectively true. There were philosophers of great ability who remained anti-Jacobins in the revolution—A. C. Ewing, H. J. Paton, C. A. Campbell, Sir Malcolm Knox, Geoffrey Mure, Errol Harris, among others—but they became increasingly dim voices crying in the wilderness. As chairs became vacant, first in British, then in American universities, they were filled by analysts, until in Britain at least the new thought dominated the field completely and the channel that divided British and continental thought became an "unplumbed, salt, estranging sea."

In America, where British epidemics manage eventually, if slowly, to arrive, the symptoms were less dismaying, partly because the body affected was so vast, partly because the ablest exponent of the new way of thinking in this country, Rudolf Carnap, enveloped his case in a hard integument of Teutonic symbols. Britain had Ayer and Ryle, both skillful masters of the language; America had no one comparable with them. But apart from this pair, the revolutions in the two countries were similar in being carried out chiefly by literary *sansculottes*. Along with the moral fervor and the religious undertones of the Cairds and Taylor, the Jacobins threw out their grace, and ambled through the pages of the journals in a manner pedestrian enough to avert any suspicion of skyey influences or humanistic taste. Philosophy became undiluted prose.

I respected the new theories for their clearness and precision, particularly when stated by Ayer, though I was not convinced by them. Those of us who were skeptical about them dealt with them as best we could at the time, but the waves of change came so fast that we had no sooner braced ourselves to meet one of them than we were engulfed by another. Ewing's articles on "Meaninglessness" and "The Linguistic Theory of A Priori Propositions" offered resistance of an effective and to me decisive kind, but the current was so strong that to oppose it, even with refutations, was—to use a figure of James's—like trying to stop the Mississippi by driving stakes in it; old man river just kept rolling along. Ayer's *Language, Truth and Logic* came out in 1936. It was an astonishing tour de force by an Oxonian in his twenties, which challenged the prevailing metaphysics and ethics of Oxford in a way that could not be ignored. Since it was a challenge also to my own ways of thinking, I felt that I must say something about it, and I devoted a chapter to it in *The Nature of Thought* three years later. I returned to the subject in a Hertz Lecture on "The Philosophy of Analysis," given at the British Academy in 1953, and again, for the first time in adequate detail, in the Carus Lectures of 1959, published two years later in expanded form as *Reason and Analysis.*

Logical Empiricism

The philosophers of analysis differed widely among themselves, and never formed a school. But the group that in the thirties and forties was the spearhead of the movement, the positivists or, as they preferred to be called, the logical empiricists, did have a set of doctrines that members held in common and that were clearly of philosophic importance.

The first of these they regarded as their main weapon against metaphysics, the verifiability theory of meaning. It was in essence a return to Hume. No statement of fact was meaningful or, therefore, a statement at all, unless it referred to, and might be verified by, something that could be given in sense. The theory seemed at first glance neither novel nor very alarming. But some younger philosophers, groping about in metaphysical mists, heard in it the welcome horn of a rescue party. They learned with relief that since one could not settle the questions of God, freedom, and immortality by appeals to sense, such old bones of metaphysical contention were literally nonsense and could now be thrown out, along with homoiousian versus homoousian and supra- versus infralapsarianism. If one failed to discern any figures at the bottom of the Heideggerian well, it was perhaps after all not because one was blind, but because there was nothing there to see. Philosophy might now hope to gain something of the clarity and respectability of science.

In some measure I could share this welcoming attitude. I had no great turn for abstraction, and felt more at home with the simple idealism of Berkeley, for example, than with the austere and magisterial Hegel, where the line between profundity and nonsense was so much harder to draw. Was I, after all, an analyst myself? Certainly not if Wittgenstein was to be my guru; Hegel seemed luminous beside him. Ayer was different; he was saying something I could follow, something that was clean-cut and surprisingly persuasive. But at a second or third reading, it was less so. The verifiability theory of meaning, which was the head and front of positivism, disintegrated in my hands when I began to examine it. It said that a statement about fact was meaningful only if it could be verified in sense; but not even in theory could a universal proposition of this kind be verified in sense; so it was not meaningful itself. The positivists presently became aware of this paradox, and substituted for the proposition a rule which they declared it prudent to follow in the making of statements. But how could it be followed prudently unless the original statement was significant and true? So a process of reformulation began. In *Reason and Analysis* I distinguished seven different stages in the development of the verifiability principle and plodded down the line, considering the credibility of each. None of them proved acceptable. If this was the gleaming sword that was to put an end to speculative philosophy, that philosophy could consider itself reprieved.

The positivists' second principle they considered scarcely less effective than the first as a weapon against metaphysics. Traditional speculation about the world from Plato to Whitehead had been based on deductive reasoning. McTaggart, for example, in the extended argument of *The Nature of Existence* only twice found it necessary to appeal to perception, once to show that something existed, and again to show that what existed was more than one; all else was a priori reasoning. Now if the reasoning used in speculation was of this a priori kind, it merited careful study. The new empiricists fixed their sharp eyes on the process and came up with some startling conclusions. All a priori or necessary reasoning, they said, had a threefold character; it was analytic, linguistic, and conventional. By "analytic" they sometimes meant what Kant meant by the term, that the meaning of the predicate was contained in that of the subject, but they preferred to put it differently: an analytic statement was one whose contradictory was self-contradictory; to take a well-worn example, "Bachelors are unmarried men." In virtue of the meanings we attach to "bachelor" and "unmarried men" we can see that to affirm the first of someone and to deny the second would be to contradict oneself. This holds because of our uses of words; we use "bachelor" and "unmarried man" in the same way; if we did not—if we used "bachelor" to refer to planets or porpoises—the statement would obviously not be necessary. And since the necessity thus turns on the use of words, it is a linguistic necessity. Now definition is always arbitrary in the sense that we could define our words otherwise. Our actual definitions are thus conventions. Carnap put the matter uncompromisingly when he asserted that even the propositions of logic were conventions.

I could find little in all this but confusion and error. I could see that "Bachelors are unmarried men" was an analytic statement, though it was a carefully contrived one; who but Noah Webster and his colleagues ever said things of this kind? But there seemed to me plenty of necessary statements that were not analytic; I took "Whatever is red is extended" as an example to pull about. Being extended is not the same as being red, nor is it a part of this, though it is entailed by it; and if the nonextension of something entails its not being red, this follows through a denial of the consequent, not through the exposure of a self-contradiction in the subject. And I could make no sense of linguistic necessities. It is not words, in the sense of sounds or squiggles, that necessitates, but the nature of what is designated by those words. The word "triangle" necessitates nothing and could be replaced without change of implication by *drei-eck;* what necessitates is the geometrical figure which these words single out. And once one has reached the figure, one finds nothing arbitary in what that figure entails. It is confusion to suppose that because the names one attaches to an object and its attributes are arbitrary, the attributes one assigns to it are themselves arbitrary. Verbal definition is being confounded with real definition. Verbal definition reports the way in which a word is used, and is the business of the lexicographer. Real definition reports the attributes of an object, and is reached by analysis of that object or reflection upon it. And if I start with a conceived triangle, it is absurd to say that I am at liberty to assign to it what attributes I choose. Its nature prescribes some attributes with a necessity as absolute as that with which it excludes others.

The third position of the logical empiricists I found as paradoxical as the first two. It was again a position of major importance and one that, if true, would undermine the rationalist view of the world. If necessary reasoning merely reported how we used words, its use to report the nature of things was futile. Rationalists had traditionally supposed that in tracing the lines of necessity, whether about space or time or number or substance, they were learning something about the bony structure of the world. The new empiricists thought differently. They did not, to be sure, follow the steps of older empiricists like Mill and try to explain the necessities away into empirical generalizations. They frankly admitted that the necessities were genuine. But they denied their significance for our knowledge of the world. If the very laws of logic were merely statements of how we used, or proposed to use, words, what right had we to take them as revelatory of the real? None. The third position of the logical empiricists thus involved the reconceiving of logic. It was a convenience in the ordering of thought, not a clue to the nature of things.

Here was an issue of real concern to me. If this were true, it broke the back of my rationalism. What was more important, Plato and Aquinas, Descartes and Spinoza, Leibniz, Bradley, and McTaggart were all revealed as laboring under a gigantic and somewhat naive illusion. Bradley, for example, had rested the constructive part of his *Appearance* on the certainty of the law of contradiction. He was sure of one thing above all: what was real was not self-contradictory. Even this modest starting point was now taken away. The show of logical rigor with which speculative reasoning had been conducted in the past was mere window dressing, for such rigor signified nothing in this sort of enterprise; indeed, since there was no guarantee that the lines in the web of nature corresponded to the lines of thought, such rigor might distort the picture more than the ramblings of incoherence. Here the new empiricists reluctantly joined hands with their natural foes, existentialists, in a common revolt against rationalism.

I noted a curious fact, however, about this new philosophy of logic. Though logic applied only to our meanings and said nothing about a reality beyond, the logic used in supporting this position was never supposed to apply to the speaker's meanings only; it was taken without question to be objective, decisive, and universally binding. What the positivist was saying was: logic is only subjectively valid—except the logic I am now using in arguing my case; that logic you must accept, since it is valid objectively. And this was incoherent, for the logic assumed to be objectively valid was the same logic that was said to hold of our meanings only. Indeed the very suggestion that there might be alternatives to necessary statements was incoherent, for what necessity means is that such alternatives are excluded. And if they are excluded, what could one mean by saying that nature might be at odds with logic? One would be saying something that by the positivist's own standard was therefore meaningless. A skepticism so fundamental as to involve distrust of logic cannot even state its case.

I have sometimes spoken of my rationalism as a faith. And a faith it is, in the sense that one cannot prove it. Any attempt to demonstrate that logic holds of the nature of things must appeal at every step to the objective validity of the logic that is under scrutiny, and hence can only beg that question. Nevertheless the rationalist's appeal to faith is very far from that of religion, with which it has sometimes been equated. There is nothing obviously necessary in an appeal to the existence of the Jewish or Christian God or the Hindu Brama; such faith may be either taken or left without disaster to the intellectual edifice in which one lives. But the faith of the rationalist, at least in its essentials, is a faith that is natural and even unavoidable. That the world is a place that we can learn about by rational thought is a position which, though incapable of proof, is so central to all experience that without it we could not take one step of reflection or perception. Such a faith is not a leap beyond the evidence, but the acceptance of an imperative imposed by the nature of thought itself.

Analysts were by no means all positivists, and as the carefully constructed fabric of positivism showed signs of coming apart, there was a certain scurrying among the analysts to escape identification with the lost cause. Before long it was hard to find anyone who was willing to admit to the name of positivist. Nevertheless it was the positivists who were the true pioneers of the analytic movement. One or other of the three positions that have been mentioned, or some modification of them, continued to be held by large numbers of analysts.

Emotivist Ethics

As for the fourth position, it was of a different kind. It followed, indeed, from the other positivist theses, but it was arrived at independently by many philosophers who had little sympathy with those theses. It was advanced, for example, by a vigorous critic of the analytic movement, Winston Barnes, who in a paper on "Ethics without Propositions" urged the view that moral judgments were not, strictly speaking, judgments or cognitions at all, but expressions of favoring or hostile attitudes on the part of the speaker. Analytic philosophers soon recognized, however, that this was a position to which they were committed by the positivist theory of knowledge. For how were judgments of right and wrong to be classified? They were obviously not necessary statements; stealing or the taking of human life is not always wrong. Nor were they factual statements in the sense that they could be verified in perception, for rightness and wrongness could not be sensed. Since they were thus neither a priori nor empirical, and these two covered the ground of cognitive statements, they could not be cognitive at all. They did not express knowledge; they were not true or false; what they expressed must therefore be emotions, or perhaps commands or entreaties. This conclusion was soon being embraced by analysts of all types. It received an extended defense in Charles Stevenson's *Ethics and Language,* and was persuasive enough, as we have seen, to raise self-questioning in the mind of G. E. Moore.

Moore was living in my house during one period of this self-questioning, and I had the advantage of discussing the issue with him. One important ground of his doubt about the emotivists I could not in the end accept. At the crucial point where statements of intrinsic goodness were involved, he held that we were not only ascribing a character to an object, but ascribing a character so strangely unlike any other that we could say almost nothing about it. It was not "natural" or "descriptive" in the sense of being a constituent of its object like roundness or weight; it could not be analyzed, for it was completely simple; and hence it could not be defined either, since we could not single out in it a genus or differentia. It was this nonnatural, simple quality that Moore thought we were ascribing to something whenever we judged it to be intrinsically good, whether it was the taste of an ice-cream cone, the sense of duty, or the experience of a Schubert song. I searched for this quality in my own thought, and for a time I must have believed that I had succeeded, for in the volume *Preface to Philosophy* what I offered in the way of ethics was substantially Moore's "ideal utilitarianism." But in the end I could not accept his alternative to emotivism, for this simple nonnatural quality eluded me.

Relativist Ethics

I never wavered, however, in thinking that Moore and traditional philosophy were right on the main issue. Moral judgment is really judgment. There is such a thing as moral assertion, moral opinion, moral belief. Why can one say this so confidently? Ultimately, I suppose, because of a direct awareness of one's intention in judging morally. But there is much supporting evidence. Moral convictions may contradict each other, as emotions cannot. In 1972 the Supreme Court considered the question whether the death penalty should be regarded as "cruel and unusual punishment." The court, which divided five to four, thought it was showing a genuine difference of opinion on this obviously moral issue; the minority opinion contradicted that of the majority. On emotivist assumptions, such a contradiction would be impossible, for an emotion of repugnance cannot *contradict* an emotion of attraction. Again, it seemed to me plain enough that on moral matters we sometimes make mistakes; that we could sometimes defend our views by argument; that we could see some experiences to be really better, in the sense of intrinsically more valuable, than others, and some cultures to be really higher than others. All this the new ethics ruled out as illusion.

It was natural that I should feel strongly about this development. It challenged a great deal more than an abstract theory; it shocked accepted convictions, ideals, and standards all along the line, and if true, destroyed the possibility of a genuinely rational ethics. Some distinguished moralists, for example Ross and Paton, could not disguise their sense of outrage, and spoke out in wrath. I too felt outraged. It seemed to me that some of the advocates of the new doctrine discussed it with an insensitivity to its implications which suggested that they were either playing an intellectual game or were strangely obtuse to human values. But I recognized that moral indignation is not argument, and that the issue must be settled, as the emotivists claimed, by analysis. I tried to meet the theory on its own ground. When Sir Malcolm Knox invited me to contribute to the new *Philosophical Quarterly,* I sent him an article on "The New Subjectivism in Ethics," which listed some of the paradoxes in the emotivist position. One of these paradoxes, to which I have still not heard a clear answer, was that on the new principles it would be unintelligible to say that there had been anything good or evil in the past. A statement applying either adjective to a past event could express only a present feeling, not a characteristic of the past event itself. There was no escape in saying that contemporaries of the event had felt approval or repugnance, for that was not a value statement at all, but a statement of fact.

It seemed to me fair controversy to point out also that the advocates of the theory found it impossible to practice it. Russell was an example. No one insisted more courageously or eloquently on the need for rationality in conduct; and during the Vietnam War Russell was all for trying President Johnson before a court of intellectuals who would presumably judge the case by rational standards. How Russell could reconcile such action with a declaration that rational standards in ethics were impossible I did not understand. Neither, I think, did Russell. He admitted dissatisfaction with his theory, but could find no error in his analysis. There were other supporters of emotivism whose practice was similarly at variance with their theory and in advance of it. Some distinguished positivists were refugees from Nazi terror, and were courageously outspoken in their denunciation of it. When their students pointed out that on their principles ethical judgments were merely expressions of feeling and there was no rational way of choosing between Nazi feelings and their own, they found it hard to give an adequate answer.

This discussion of my differences with the early analysts has led into ethics and gives me an opportunity to say something about my ethical views. As an undergraduate I never took a course in ethics. But in the thirty-six years of my teaching at Swarthmore and Yale, I had to teach the subject nearly every year. The basis of many of my Swarthmore seminars was Rashdall's *Theory of Good and Evil*, on which I prepared a printed syllabus, with the bibliographies that formed a regular part of my syllabi. This work was a fortunate choice. Rashdall dedicated it to two of his teachers, Green and Sidgwick; and it combines something of the massive philosophic judgment of the first with the acuteness of the second. It appeared at about the same time as Moore's *Principia Ethica*, which was the pioneer work of purely intellectual analysis in ethics and was far more influential. But Rashdall is full of sober sense, shrewd criticism of historic moralists, judicious illustration, and, not least, moral seriousness. The same could be said of Paulsen's *System of Ethics*, which I also used from time to time in introductory classes. I recall the just remark of John Findlay about a current work of linguistic analysis, that it read as if its author had never had a moral experience. Of course I do not believe in reducing ethics to preaching, but neither do I believe in reducing it to logic-chopping; and the virtue of writers like Rashdall and Paulsen is that while alive to the importance of both, they surrender to neither.

These philosophers were objectivists in ethics. This strengthened my arm, for during the years of my teaching relativism was having its heyday.

Sumner's *Folkways* had started a vogue among sociologists with its doctrine that "the mores can make anything right." This was followed by works of similar tendency by Franz Boas, who was still at Columbia during my days there, by Westermarck, Malinowski, Ruth Benedict, Margaret Mead, and many more. It was thought a mark of sophistication among students to say that morals were only relative, that there was hardly a moral rule accepted by one culture that was not rejected in others, and that to claim for any practice that it was *the* right one, or even that it was better than some rival, was dogmatism. In the First World War, and still more in the Second, many students were shipped as soldiers to far places, where they could see for themselves how different were the mores of Paris or Papua from what they had known in Gopher Prairie. A belief in objective standards in ethics seemed old-fashioned and provincial. The facts of moral diversity brought to light by the social scientists had disposed of such claims once for all.

This I disbelieved. Even the reports of diversity rested, I thought, on a confusion of means and ends. I followed Sidgwick in thinking that moral rules were means gradually adopted by a group because they led to desirable results; its members would obviously profit if a respect for truth, persons, and property could be made to prevail. Now the rules adopted by different societies did vary dramatically, as the sociologists said. The nineteenth-century Chinese paid homage to their fathers, while the nineteenth-century Fijians, when their fathers showed signs of senility, put them to death. Spaniards believed in monogamy, Moslems in polygamy, Tibetans in polyandry. But if moral practices are really means to ends, it does not follow that because practices differ the ends men are seeking to attain by them differ likewise. Closer study of the Fijians revealed that they were not as indifferent to their elders' welfare as their apparently unfeeling custom suggested; indeed, holding the belief that one carried into the next world the complement of powers with which one left the present world, they considered that the despatching of parents before they lost their powers was a far-seeing service to them. Again, diverse marriage customs may in different circumstances contribute to the same human ends. Where the numbers of the sexes are equal, the general happiness may be best promoted by monogamy; where men outnumber women as a result of female infanticide or other causes, this happiness may be better attained by polyandry; and where the reverse is the case, or women are economically helpless, polygamy may supply the best means to the same result.

Far more significant than this diversity of practice, interesting as it is, would be the discovery that the diverse practices were directed toward identical ends. And I believe that this latter is substantially true, though it is not the sort of thesis that readily lends itself to observation or statistics. Sane men everywhere want to be happy. Though the love of knowledge may, as Housman said, be the faintest of human passions, it is universally present; who would not choose, if the choice were open to him, to understand the world about him rather than be ignorant of it? All men seem to prefer pleasure to intense pain; some degree of order, beauty, and comfort to disorder, filth, and misery; health of mind and body to disease, security to fear and anxiety, friendship to general hatred by their kind. It is not very likely that what makes life worth living to a Russian would be without interest to a Chinese or an American. I will begin to believe that the intrinsic goods of life differ from culture to culture when I hear that in the United Nations a Russian has risen to plead for a new treaty on the ground that it will increase the ignorance or unhappiness of his people, or that a Chinese has begged for aid in promoting cholera or idiocy in his homeland. If such a development seems absurd, it is because the major ends that men are seeking, like the major ends they seek to avoid, are the same the world over. Indeed that is why discussion in the United Nations is possible at all. Discussion about means is feasible when the question is what means will best promote a common end, but there is no ground for decision if the ends and standards themselves differ. Fortunately, men are more deeply unified by their community of ends than they are divided by the diversity of means. What is important morally is not these differing means, which are plastic to change, but the intrinsic goods that set their dominant and lasting aims.

The fulfillment of men's capacities for these overriding goods and the enjoyment that attends such fulfillments are sought alike by men everywhere. And if so, cultural relativism is false. Men have a common standard because their ultimate ends are held in common. That standard lies in the production of the greatest intrinsic good, taking into account all those who are influenced by the action. In a given situation there is as a rule only one such action that would produce the greatest good, and it is this action that is right. On such a view it seems absurd to argue that when people, or peoples, have different views as to what this action is, they are somehow all correct; what follows is merely that they think themselves correct. But so long as their ultimate ends are the same, the American can argue with the Papuan that his headhunting is wrong, because it destroys for others the possibilities that give value to life and which he can see on reflection to be of the same value in others' lives as in his own. The Japanese can argue with the American that he should cultivate his sense of beauty, since there are delights in the experience of flower and garden that he is missing and would welcome if only he knew what they were. In such cases one is not appealing to a standard unique to a particular culture, but to goods that are seen to be valuable as such, and therefore everywhere, if they are seen at all. The recognition of such goods is what having an objective standard means.

Intrinsic Goodness

In the constructive part of *Reason and Goodness,* I set myself to examine the idea of intrinsic goodness. I examined in perhaps wearisome detail the theories of Westermarck and the emotivists, of Dewey, Perry, Moore, and others. The theory I came out with was not a preconceived one, but a genuine result of this comparative study. The theory may be briefly put as follows. Goodness or value exists only in the realm of experience. And when an experience is intrinsically good, it will always be found to have two characteristics. In the first place, it will be the fulfillment of some impulse or drive of human nature. It could not, I thought, be an accident that all the great intrinsic goods answered to the central needs of that nature, the goods of food and drink, of sex and love, of knowledge, friendship, and beauty. If man had no capacity or interest for such things, would they have any value for him? I could only answer No. What man finds good is, as Aristotle saw, appointed by his nature; if he were a dolphin, a chimpanzee, or an archangel, the experiences of which he was capable and therefore the goods that he could recognize would vary widely from ours. The same is true within limits among men themselves. The man who is color-blind will not find as much value in painting, or the tone-deaf man in music, or the moron in the principles of logic, as other men do; and the genius in these areas will find a great deal more. So far, the intrinsic values of an experience will be the function of its fulfilling character, of its realizing some capacity and urge of human nature.

Is this the only condition of intrinsic goodness? It seemed to me clear that there was another, the element in which Mill and Sidgwick had found the sole condition, namely pleasure. They were mistaken in making it the sole condition; and Mill in effect admitted this in saying that he would rather be a discontented Socrates than a contented pig; it was the magnificent intellectual and moral fulfillment of Socrates' life, not an overplus of pleasure, that tipped the scale for Socrates. But though not a sufficient condition, the hedonic element, which I preferred to call satisfaction, was still a necessary condition of intrinsic value. If Socrates had derived no satisfaction from his restlessly active mind, if Michelangelo took as little pleasure as he sometimes perversely alleged in wielding his brush and chisel, if the athlete felt no more thrill in competition and victory than a prisoner on a stone-pile, would their experiences have had the sort of value that would make men prize them and seek them out? To this question I thought Mill's answer the right one—an answer that may have derived from his own experience of nervous collapse at twenty when he found that his power of enjoyment, even in his own extraordinary achievements, had suddenly vanished. Life, when he could take no pleasure in it, was vapid and drained of value.

I knew what Moore and Ross would say to this theory. They would say that my two conditions, fulfillment and satisfaction, might really be conditions of goodness, but did not, either singly or jointly, *constitute* goodness; one must not confuse "good-making characteristics" with goodness itself. But this meant a return to the notion of goodness as a nonnatural quality, and I had searched for this in vain. Moore and Ross seem to have felt that, without this unique quality, goodness would lose its mandatory power over natural desire; it was perhaps a relic of Kant's two-world view of the ethical imperative as standing outside and above human impulses with an absolute authority over them. That there was indeed a nonempirical element in human nature was plain enough to me as a rationalist, but I did not think that Moore was drawing the line at the right place. Reason operated in the good life, not, as Kant would have it, by laying down an abstract exceptionless rule, nor, as Moore would have it, by disclosing a nonnatural quality lying like a gem amid the dross, but rather by so ordering and harmonizing impulses as to give them their largest fulfillment.

Was it true that this office of reason fell short of the dignity and authority of the old moral law? Emotionally it did. Conscience had been associated so long and so intimately with "the voice of God" that it had accumulated a religious aura, and was invested with awe and reverence. I could not help thinking that Kant's moral law and Moore's nonnatural quality were both in part by-products of this traditional attitude called into existence to provide appropriate objects for it. Moore's inward struggle between emotivism and objectivism grew out of this tradition. He was so keenly aware that moral judgments were steeped in emotion that he could find plausibility in the suggestion that they expressed emotions merely. But that they were judgments claiming objective truth had a still greater plausibility, and the only way he saw of giving them a content worthy of moral emotion was to make them ascriptive of a nonnatural character. The emotion was then appropriate to the character, and the character justified the emotion. Moore felt unable to drop either one without disloyalty to moral experience as he knew it.

Since I was convinced that Moore was right as to the truth and falsity of moral judgments, but wrong as to what was asserted, I had to find a new content for the judgment of intrinsic good. Here the naturalism of Aristotle gave a helpful clue. Aristotle's insight that the great goods of human nature lay in the fulfillment of its needs would have seemed to Moore an interesting observation but one that, introduced into ethics proper, would be a "naturalistic fallacy," since it would confuse a natural condition of goodness with the nonnatural goodness itself. My own fresh step was to deny that this was a confusion, to find in the fulfillment of human nature and the satisfaction that accompanied it the very essence of goodness.

Where did this leave those attitudes of awe and reverence traditionally associated with the moral law? Were they not left hanging in the air to wither away through the lack of an appropriate object? There was some point in this charge. I did think that the religious aura with which conscience had been invested was an alien importation, and that when the suggestions were removed of an anthropomorphic Deity hovering over our choices, pleased or angered by them, and rewarding or punishing us accordingly, the traditional moral feeling was bound to lose something of its emotional coloring. But I could not see that genuine moral seriousness needed to rest upon illusions. When the illusions were gone, moral choices still remained the most important of all choices; on them it depended whether a life was to reach its end or to be thrown away; and the standing hierarchy of values not only remained standing, but remained with a starker clearness now that rational criticism had stripped away the old theological barnacles. Morality does not lose its importance when its roots are traced into the subsoil of nature and human nature. I was breaking with supernaturalism in theology, and I found myself ready to break also with the ethical supernaturalism of Kant and the nonnaturalism of Moore. The moral law was not an irruption from a nonnatural order. It was a dictate of the reason I had studied in *The Nature of Thought*, which I had there found moulding perception and which I now found moulding desire and choice, into greater fullness and coherence.

The book in which I developed these views, *Reason and Goodness*, has had little effect, and such attention as it received has been largely unfavorable. From C. A. Campbell in the *Philosophical Quarterly* and from Errol Harris in the *Yale Review* it did receive heartening appreciation and understanding, not without helpful criticism. But the reviewer in *Ethics*, a specialist in ancient philosophy, spent more space in setting me right about Epicurus than I had spent in misrepresenting him, and held that anyone so ignorant of Aristotle should hold his peace about him. The reviewer in *Mind*, a specialist in Hume, suggested that I was degenerating into a *raconteur*, and had got one of Hume's doctrines quite wrong. The writer in the *Philosophical Review* sniffed immorality in both the teaching and its author. I was bewildered by the wildly differing estimates of the same book, as I was again a year later when *Reason and Analysis* appeared. If these books were as ill argued and ill written as some of the reviewers intimated, other reviewers must have been blind. Opinions are of course suspect when one's own books are concerned, but it may be worth confessing that the more reviews I have read of others' books as well as my own, the more puzzled I have become as to the standards prevailing in current philosophy. When in the twenties and thirties one saw a review in *Mind* by C. D. Broad or A. E. Taylor, one expected, and usually found, a judgment that was detailed, rounded, and impartial. It is perhaps unreasonable to expect such standards to maintain themselves. At any rate, reviewing of this kind has become rare. The member of one school, asked to review a book from another, whets his knife in the opening sentences, and lays about him remorselessly; did not the author, after all, have a chance to know the truth and did he not prefer instead to live in the old night? Out upon him! Just as Whitehead dismissed Hegel's metaphysics because Hegel knew little mathematics, so the analysts dismiss Whitehead's metaphysics because he did not know linguistic analysis, and the disciple of Wittgenstein II dismisses the disciple of Wittgenstein I because he was reared on the old testament, and has not received the new dispensation. This is parochialism. The genuinely philosophic critic does not assume that reason is wholly different as it works in one's own mind and another's, and that the shaft of light that it brings us falls from heaven on one school only.

Early Religious Impressions

It was the Gifford lectureship that gave me the stimulus to set my ethical thought in order. It gave me a like opportunity in religion; for the two subjects that form the province of the lectures are moral philosophy and natural theology. The Gifford committees of the Scottish universities have shown no disposition, however, to confine their invitations to specialists in these fields. They have felt at liberty to invite men whose work lay far from either of them, like Eddington, Jeans, and Heisenberg. The question they have asked is whether the quality of a man's performance in his own area, whatever it may be, justifies the expectation that he will have something significant to say on morals or religion. Poorly as my own previous work would compare with the work of men like these, it was evidently by similar reasoning that an invitation came my way, for I had done nothing of note in either field. In ethics I had such background as belongs to a college teacher of the subject, but in religion I did not have even that slender basis to stand on. It is time to say something of the equipment I did bring to my religious studies.

I was at least a son and grandson of the manse. Though in effect I lost my father when I was nine, I had sat with a small son's admiration under his preaching, absorbing his attitude even when failing to follow his thought. In reading later some of the men who formed his mind, such as Edward Increase Bosworth and Henry Churchill King, I can see that the religious atmosphere he lived in would today be called stuffy. King, to be sure, had worked at the Harvard Divinity School, where he thought the professors dangerously liberal; and in a brief period of study at Göttingen he had made contact with a mind of true distinction, Rudolf Hermann Lotze. But the religious problems of the Oberlin of that day, and presumably of my father, were not the radical ones; they were the intermediate ones that present themselves to minds too secure or too timid to delve around the roots: granting the truth of all the main Christian doctrines, how shall we interpret Darwin, Lyell, and Robertson Smith so as to retain the substance of the faith? Accepting New Testament ethics as obviously inspired, how shall we apply it to American social life? Oberlin under Fairchild and King had escaped from the somewhat hysterical evangelism of President Finney, but it retained the reputation of being religiously safe, though susceptible at times to liberal rufflings of its waters.

The religious tone of my early years was set by the Methodism of my Canadian grandfather, tempered by the Congregationalism of his Oberlin-educated son. My grandfather disappeared from the scene when I was about three; my father, a few years later, left his family for the West in his hopeful though also hopeless search for health. My grandmother, to whose charge my brother and I were then committed, was stamped with the seal of her husband rather than her son, and that meant the nonconformity of Yorkshire about the middle of the last century. These Wesleyans took religion with tremendous seriousness. One's eternal prospects were at stake, both in one's belief and in one's conduct; and conduct was so bound up with belief that to allow the invasion of doubt was itself a breach of morality. The emphasis was not so much on the creed, though this was important enough to my grandfather, I gathered, to make him think that the scheme of salvation should be somewhere sketched in every sermon; the great stress was on religious experience. And this experience ought to be profoundly emotional. One's status among the saved was best ensured by a definite and dated conversion, preferably cataclysmic, which was understood to be a supernatural visitation, and which ran through the emotional gamut from a pit of despair to the ecstatic heights of assured salvation. I never had this experience. But the atmosphere in which I lived led me to take religious experience as the best of religious evidences; and the mysticism of such poets as Whittier and Wordsworth, when I came to read them, seemed to lend confirmation to this view.

It is a view more likely to persuade adolescence than any later period of life. But being of an introspective turn of mind, when I emerged from adolescence I began a study of these religious states which was progressively disillusioning. In James's *Varieties,* in Leuba's and Starbuck's studies of mysticism, I found naturalistic explanations which, while not quite excluding a transcendental element (such exclusion is in principle impossible), suggested plausible alternatives. James's way of dealing with the phenomena of sudden conversion was an example in point. He showed that while a man continued in his normal way of life, a set of sympathies with a quite different way of life could form themselves subconsciously into a coherent and competing whole, until at an auspicious moment some sudden nudge—"A fancy from a flower-bell, someone's death / A chorus-ending from Euripides"— would in a moment bring the submerged self into dominance, as if an iceberg had turned turtle. I was interested enough in religious questions to join the Wesley Society in my first year at Oxford, but when I read to the society a paper on "The Subconscious Self in Religious Experience" some members shook their heads over me. They thought, and perhaps rightly, that they saw more clearly than I did the end of such reflections.

Mysticism

For a critical mind, the evidential value attached to religious experience is likely to depend on the attitude taken toward mysticism, for that is the most intense of religious experiences and, if its claim is well grounded, the most revealing. This claim, to which I have given much attention, has proved curiously baffling to philosophers. Many have refused to take it seriously. They would admit the intensity and exaltation of the experience, but decline to admit that it is cognitive. Others have conceded its claim to knowledge, but have held that this knowledge cannot be assessed by reason, since the mystic has entered a realm where thought cannot follow; his insight can be reached only by an intuition that has left reasoning and the rules of logic behind. Most philosophers have found such intuition an unpalatable morsel. I recall the shock that was given to the Philosophical Association when one of its keenest and clearest heads, Walter Stace of Princeton, devoted his presidential address to an uncompromising defense of mystical insight. I asked him some time later whether he thought the mystic could meaningfully claim to have transcended the law of contradiction itself. He answered Yes; the true mystic might well see, in a way not open to the rest of us, that the two sides of a contradiction were both true. When philosophers I respect hold this language, I hardly know what to say. An apprehension of truth that is also an apprehension of its falsity seems to me an apprehension of nothing, and therefore not an apprehension at all. *What* is it that is being said? The mystic answers that the question is unfair, that if the insight is not one that uses concepts it cannot be reported in words, which are names for concepts. But if this is true, should not the mystic, when he descends from his mount of vision, content himself with smiling, or at most trying to convey his technique to others in order that they may repeat his experience? It is idle to try to state what he has seen if, as he has expressly told us, it is unreportable.

But this is just what mystics do. They argue the unarguable and describe the indescribable with lyric abandon. And considering the diversity of their times and cultures, their reports of what they have seen have a surprising degree of unity. For the most part, they report that the world is one, and that diversity is an illusion; that it is good, and evil an illusion; that it is eternal, and time an illusion. It is hard, of course, to attach definite meaning to these statements. Does the statement that diversity is an illusion mean, for example, that the words "diversity" and "illusion" are not really diverse, but the same; and if so, what becomes of the assertion? Evil, we learn, is an illusion;

but then illusion is itself an evil; and if so, one is retaining evil in the very act of dismissing it. Is the statement that time is unreal to be taken as implying that since one has taken time in making the statement, one has not really made it at all? The mystic replies that his statements are not to be taken literally; they are merely "thrown out at the truth," as Arnold might say; they are approximations to it, intimations that show us the direction in which to look for it.

The trouble with this is that different mystical experiences, which seem to be equally authentic, indicate that we should look for truth in opposite directions. Sufi mystics, who are Mohammedans, see God as one. But Saint Theresa, a Christian mystic and a well accredited one, has left it on record that she had risen to a vision of how God could be three. Most mystics have held reality to be good, but it should not be forgotten that there are demonic or satanic mystics who have been vouchsafed glimpses into the leering malignance that, for them, surrounds and besets humanity. Emerson says that if one rises to a high enough point of view one can see that man must be immortal; and Tennyson had a mystic experience in which he saw that death was "an almost laughable impossibility." But Tennyson's contemporary, John Addington Symonds, had more than one mystical "apprehension of a coming dissolution, the grim conviction that this state was the last state of the conscious self . . . ."[25] These "insights" bring with them an overwhelming sense of truth; that is, the same overwhelming certainty attaches itself to positions which, expressed with as much approximation to truth as is practicable, are inconsistent with each other. And for the philosopher who has not had such experiences and for whom his own halting reason is the only tool at hand, that almost settles the matter. If the validity of mystical experience must be purchased at the price of the law of contradiction, then such experience, however induced—whether by drugs, by yoga exercises, by evangelistic appeals, by poetry, by drums and dances, by contemplation of one's navel or the word OM, or by fasting and meditation—cannot be accepted by a rationalist. There is nothing arbitrary in this stress on consistency, as we have seen in discussing positivism. "Nature has said it." No one ever tries to break logic, as McTaggart remarked, but what logic breaks him.

This does not mean that I deny all value to mystical experience. Hocking and Rufus Jones have shown that its moral and practical value may be considerable. And at a time when empiricism is in the saddle, with its doctrine that all knowledge of the world springs from sense perception and must return to it as the final test, the tradition that there are other forms of knowledge must be kept alive. There are philosophers who regard any claim to nonempirical knowledge as itself essentially mystical. In that case I too am a mystic. Judgments of right and wrong, of beauty, of consistency, of the meanings of terms, are not to be tested by sense. And as the more steadfast rationalists, like Spinoza and Hegel, rise toward that vision of the whole which forms their admitted end, they are bound to reach levels that seem to those panting behind them to be up somewhere in the clouds. But the harmony that they are seeking is not an abstraction in which the details are lost; if it were, what would be harmonized? And a harmony that was not at least a consistency exclusive of contradiction would not be a harmony in which intellect could rest. The mysticism of the true rationalist is not a repudiation of logic, nor a flight into the night where all cows are black. He is convinced that to leave the law of contradiction behind is to leap out of intelligibility into gibberish. Hence the choice between mysticism and logic is for him no choice at all.

I suspect that most mystics have confused certainty and certitude. Certainty is the sort of assurance Descartes was seeking, the sort that belongs to conceptual clearness and distinctness; it belongs, for example, to the apprehension that two and two are four, or that two straight lines cannot enclose a space. Certitude is the emotion of conviction. It may reach a high intensity when the conceptual content is minimal or blurred, as when the drunken patriot swears with conviction about his country's always being right, or about his country, right or wrong; or when the infatuated lover swears to the incomparable beauty of his lady's shell-like ear. The two kinds of assurance are different in the extreme, but nothing is easier than to confound them. It would not be difficult, in these days of "drug-culture," to make a case against mystic *Schwärmerei* as a degenerate rather than an advanced form of experience. But instead of taking it at its lowest, let us look at it for a moment from a point near its highest.

Wordsworth's "Tintern Abbey" is a fine example of nature mysticism.

> . . . I have felt
> A presence that disturbs me with the joy
> Of elevated thoughts; a sense sublime
> Of something far more deeply interfused,
> Whose dwelling is the light of setting suns
> And the round ocean and the living air . . . .

Two accounts may be given of what happened to Wordsworth on this famous visit to the Wye valley. The first, and the one he apparently accepted, is that he had an immediate experience of a mind or spirit other than his own, which was immanent in nature. The other account cannot be put so simply. From early years he had lived with nature, which was his constant source of refreshment and delight. Now it is well known that every perception of a natural object carries with it a freight of meaning drawn from past experience. The meaning, for example, with which one perceives an apple may vary greatly, from that of the young child through that of the ordinary man, up to that of the botanist or apple-fancier, or again to that of Newton who, according to legend, apperceived in a falling apple the law that held the planets in their orbits.

But perceptual meaning is not cognitive only; it may also be emotive. Sights and sounds, even tastes and smells, that have been associated with vivid feelings of joy or pain carry the echoes of these feelings with them, sometimes in force and volume, when they present themselves again. For Wordsworth the perception of a river, a valley, or a mountain was charged with past delights. When he looked at the ruin in the valley, in its setting of peaceful beauty, man and occasion seem to have been right for each other. The scene was a key that unlocked the floodgates of his feeling—feelings stored up over the years; what he saw was invested for him with "a light that never was on sea or land." This was not the light of understanding, in any ordinary sense, and it would seem absurd to try to turn it into propositions. It was meaning or significance if one wishes, but emotive significance. Its volume was so great and its uprush so effortless as to seem, not a creation of the poet's own, but a communication from an indwelling spirit of nature. Of this there could be doubt; but that the experience was of great significance there could be none; the quality of the feeling was all the evidence needed. But if one takes the experience as a disclosure of what was there in nature, is one not passing too readily from emotive to cognitive meaning, and mistaking certitude for certainty? The step is easy and tempting. But it is a dubious shortcut to a conclusion so large and speculative that only a critical reason could arrive at it responsibly.

The Influence of the Manse

Such reflections were doing their work before I read my paper at Oxford on the subconscious in religion; and they extended to other religious experiences. They shook my Protestant confidence in what it was that religious experience established. But they did not, at least for the time, deflect my interest in following my father's footsteps into some kind of religious career. That interest awoke in me early. Many a preacher's son seems to have been alienated from the faith by having had to sit under his father's sermons. This was far from true of me. I acquired an early interest in sermons which is with me still. In Bay View, I kept notes of the sermons I heard. In Detroit I trudged downtown Sunday by Sunday to hear the sermons of John H. Boyd. In London I made it a point to visit churches where I had heard there were preachers of note, and thus listened to R. J. Campbell, Archdeacon Wilberforce, Dean Inge, Campbell Morgan, Fort Newton, Maude Royden, John H. Jowett. What is more, I bought and read sermons. I still have on my shelves the three volumes of F. W. Robertson, the eight volumes of Newman's *Parochial and Plain Sermons*, three or four volumes of the remarkable prose poetry of James Martineau, and many another volume by Dean Church, Dean Inge, and John Caird (all favorites for their style); by Canons Liddon, Mozley, and Scott Holland; by Phillips Brooks, Charles E. Jefferson, H. E. Fosdick, Charles Reynolds Brown. If I had kept away from philosophy, I might have followed in my father's wake and become a more or less successful popular preacher in some suburban pulpit. But philosophy has a way of tearing at one's creed until it is too threadbare for pulpit use.

My early interest in sermons had a fresh stimulus and outlet when I went to Swarthmore. There was a Friends' Meeting House in the middle of the campus. The chairman of my department, Jesse Holmes, was the leading spirit of the Friends' community and the nearest approach to a minister that the meeting had; and he was eager that I, as his prospective successor, should also take an interest in the society. Frances and I had no difficulty in doing so. We both took part freely in the vocal ministry of the meeting during our twenty years at the college. Indeed, I served for some years as chairman of the meeting's "committee on ministry and counsel."

To some persons all this may seem strange and a little hypocritical. Have you not admitted that your creed was crumbling? How then could you belong to a religious society at all, let alone perform some of the functions of the ministry? These questions are quite in order. The answer lies in the character of the Society of Friends. The society has been accepted, with some hesitation, by the American Council of Churches, but it is not a church at all in the sense of having clearly defined articles of belief. Its nearest approach to a creed is its doctrine of an "inner light," but the interpretation of this light is largely left to the members themselves, and varies as one passes from conservative to liberal branches of the society. Fortunately for me, the Swarthmore Meeting belonged to the most liberal branch, and never brought pressure on me regarding any belief. I have no doubt that some members were pained by the absence from my testimony of convictions they held essential. My ministry, if one could so call it, was always ethical rather than theological. There is surely room for such a ministry. The moral life is a matter of infinite difficulty, and of infinite possibilities for idealism, discernment, and criticism; one who confines himself to it need never want for issues. To the distress of some, but with the valued sympathy of many, I treated the society as in the main an ethical society, a group eager to explore the meaning of the good life and to make their own lives, on the moral side, more sensitive and more rational.

But is not a morality amputated from religion an anomalous thing, without any objective base or any adequate motive for practice? I can only reject the implications of that question. The ends to which the good life is directed are certain great intrinsic goods, whose value is not a deduction from any set of theological or metaphysical beliefs, but to sane men is self-evident.

If anyone denies this value, no arguments are likely to convince him. Many persons of course believe that religion and morality are welded together indissolubly, so that if religious belief were to go, morality would go with it; "now that the Devil is dead," said Mr. Punch, "we may all do what we please." But Mr. Punch was mistaken, and if he did do what he suggests, he would merely be acting irrationally. Even if theology were to vanish, the values that make men act as they do would still remain, and would retain their relative order. That happiness is better than misery and knowledge than ignorance are things that one accepts because they are obviously true; they do not rest on anything so tenuous as a theological belief, speculative in its nature and acceptable in fact to only a fraction of mankind.

No doubt religious beliefs have made an enormous difference in men's conduct, particularly the belief that certain Biblical injunctions are divine mandates, and that infinite rewards and punishments will be meted out in another life. But such beliefs have done much to confuse the moral scene. For one thing, they have muddied men's motives. Selfish desires for a reward or for an escape from pain have been exalted to a place they do not deserve, and moral priorities thus inverted. Sincerity has been compromised, for it is idle to pretend that speculative theological doctrines are more certain than the moral insights supposed to depend on them. This pretension to certainty seemed more indefensible the more I thought about it. Granted that the Saint Francises and the Loyolas of the world did much good on the strength of their confident belief that they had received their marching orders from above, it is equally true that Torquemada and his inquisitors did much evil on the strength of the apparently divine command, "Thou shalt not suffer a witch to live." What impressed me was that as soon as these theological considerations were thrown into the scale, it was tipped decisively, but tipped by factors that could outweigh any human goods or evils. Actual human suffering could be pushed aside as of small account by doctrines supposed to be of infinite weight.

My first expression of this view was not happily received. In 1944 I was invited by an interdenominational group, led by the public-spirited Rabbi Finkelstein, to contribute to a symposium on Science, Philosophy, and Religion. I accepted, and wrote a paper on "Theology and the Value of the Individual." I devoted it largely to this thesis of the danger involved in throwing into the moral scale theological considerations of supposedly infinite weight when human goods were at issue; and I took as examples the official attitudes of the Catholic church on birth control, abortion, and the choice between mother and child when such choice is medically necessary. My paper, though written by invitation, was refused a place in the symposium, presumably through Catholic objection on the program committee. It is only fair to add that such a rejection would be less likely now, and that many thoughtful Catholics are themselves concerned at the overriding of moral certainties by theological uncertainties. The conservative would reply that Christian dogmas are by no means "theological uncertainties," since they are guaranteed by revelation. I devoted much of my Gifford Lectures to a study of that position, as developed by both Catholic and Protestant thinkers. The question comes back to an ethics of belief. I held that no-one, acting on a theological mandate, has a right to make others suffer unless he is certain of that mandate; and the question then becomes, Has he a right to such "certainty"? The supernaturalist maintains that he does, whether reason supports it or not. I tried to show, on the contrary, that the indulgence of a "will to believe" when not under constraint by the evidence is defensible on neither moral nor rational grounds.

Pacifism

My reflections thus ran afoul of some widely accepted theological traditions. Since liberal Friends make little of such traditions, however, this did not disturb my position among them. At one point, however, tension did develop. Friends are traditionally pacifist. This does not mean that all of them are; many of their young men served in the armed forces, and during the war uniforms were to be seen surprisingly often in the meetings. Still, the Friends' testimony against war has been their best-known and most distinctive attitude in matters of public policy; and it was unhappily on this issue that my unity with them failed.

What I had seen of the First World War had, to be sure, left me with a cordial hatred of the whole brutal and brutalizing business, so that I had much sympathy with the Quaker feeling about war. But I do not think that a rigid rule can be laid down here, any more than for the other contingencies of life; and the thirties were a trying decade for anyone with pacifist leanings. I was an enthusiastic supporter, for example, of the League of Nations; I thought that the main mission of the League was to maintain peace; and I viewed with mounting concern the League's failure to accomplish its mission. To succeed it had to do more than mobilize world opinion. The League did mobilize and deliver that opinion, only to find it rejected with derision by one brigand state after another. If a man goes berserk in a civilized community, it is the business of the people's representatives to do something about him, to restrain him by force if that is the only way. If a state launches itself upon a career of conquest at the expense of its neighbors, it seemed to me the business of the League to take any action necessary, even to the use of joint force, to halt the outlaw. The alternative was a return to international anarchy.

When Japan launched its invasion of Manchuria in 1931, there was no doubt that its act was aggression, with no shred of justification in international law. I thought that the other powers should take immediate joint action, with all the force required to halt the aggressor. Most Friends demurred to this view, on the ground of the general opposition to violence and of the expenditure of life involved. I thought that the alternative was an expenditure of lives ten times as great through restoring international anarchy. This gloomy prophecy, which called indeed for no great foresight, turned out to be true. Mussolini, seeing that world opinion could be flouted with impunity, went into Ethiopia; and Hitler, with two examples of successful aggression before him, went into the Ruhr, while the League wrung its hands in discredited impotence. It was a bitter defeat for those who had hoped they were on the threshold of international government.

At the outset of the war, the Friends and the Swarthmore student body were so strongly opposed to American intervention that many put the British and Nazi causes very much on a level. A Nazi-Fascist propagandist was invited to debate with me in the Swarthmore Meeting House; and though I thought I stated my case acceptably, the vote of the audience was exactly even for the two sides. The Friends listened to me throughout these years with their usual tolerance, in the belief that I was at least trying to follow my inner light, however dim; they even printed in the Friends' journals some sharply critical articles of mine on pacifism. But I was no doubt an embarrassment to them. When I moved to New Haven as the war was ending in 1945, I pondered whether to continue in the local meeting the activities I had maintained at Swarthmore. I decided not to do so. This was less on the ground of any disaffection, however, than of a consideration of the community's needs and my own. Yale students were presented week by week in Battell Chapel with the best preachers in the country, and the need of my minor ministry was not apparent. But I think affectionately of the Friends, of whom I have been a member now for nearly fifty years.

Liberalism versus Neo-orthodoxy

Toward the end of my Swarthmore days I was invited by the Harvard Divinity School to give the Dudleian Lecture there, and I spoke on the Quaker concept of an inner light. A few years later I returned to Cambridge to give a course of Noble Lectures. In preparing this course I became interested for the first time in the theological ethics of Kierkegaard, Barth, and Brunner; and in the Gifford Lectures of 1952–53 I continued and enlarged my study of these theories.

The problem in both these series was how far to carry my liberalism. By liberalism I mean the attempt to adjust religious belief to developing thought in philosophy and science. The American who preceded me among the Gifford lecturers, Reinhold Niebuhr, exemplified a tendency the opposite of mine; he said that he found himself, as the years went on, leaning further to the left in politics and further to the right in theology. I had first met this brilliant man when he was a Lutheran pastor in Detroit, and met him again from time to time in the New York Philosophy Club. Since we agreed on the war, I think he used some material of mine in his journal *Christianity and Crisis*. I always found him impressive when he was discussing politics, though less so when he was discussing theology. As a theologian, he stood in a distinguished line of conservative thinkers that extended from Luther through Kierkegaard to Brunner and Barth. Their type of theology had a renaissance in the first half of the present century and, as already noted, three of the leaders of this renaissance—Brunner and Barth as well as Niebuhr himself—had served as Gifford lecturers; Brunner indeed immediately preceded me at St. Andrews. At a time when the trend was to take both ethics and theology out of the province of reason, it seemed to me that an examination of the place of reason in these fields was very much in order. *Reason and Goodness* was devoted to this problem in ethics, *Reason and Belief* to the parallel problem in religion.

Of the twenty lectures, I gave only two or three to the neo-orthodox theologians. But I was dissatisfied when I later read what I had written about them, and greatly altered and expanded it in rewriting. My study of this theology had begun with Kierkegaard, had gone on from him to Brunner and Barth, and ended by a study of the forefather of them all, Martin Luther himself. Kierkegaard both puzzled and repelled me. This strange figure was for a time so completely forgotten that even biographical dictionaries did not record him. He was resurrected in the thirties by some devoted translators, notably Walter Lowrie and David Swenson, and not many years later he had become required reading in colleges and universities throughout the country. I made a study of his most important philosophical work, *Concluding Unscientific Postscript* (an oddly named book, since, though rightly described as "unscientific," it was a "postscript" of about a quarter of a million words, with a curious inability to conclude, in either sense of the term). In this work, Kierkegaard swings back and forth between the disparagement of reason and his pride in using it, forgetting that if the disparagement is sound, his argumentation is not, and that if his philosophizing is valid, his attack on reason is not. And the character of the man—his exploitation of his love affair, his coldness to his mother and his brother the bishop, his adjurations to love from a heart simmering with hatreds, his comparisons of himself with Christ, his continual self-preoccupation—seemed to me remote from the sainthood conferred upon him by himself and many of his followers. I hope that in my criticism of this twisted genius, who provides so ill a model of either thought or conduct, I have done something to break the spell he has exercised over so many for so long.

The negative attitude I developed toward this succession of thinkers was surprising and rather painful to me. Though I had known little about them, I had heard them spoken of with such respect that I approached them with high expectations. My experience with Luther was like my experience with Kierkegaard. The man was a genius unquestionably, with enormous energy, massive Biblical learning, and of course indomitable courage, but his theology seemed to me a riot of irrationality and even cruelty. I came to wonder whether Froude was not right in thinking that it would have been better for mankind if Erasmus rather than Luther had presided over the Reformation. Luther taught that God would punish men excruciatingly and eternally for doing what he himself had made them do, and that unless men accepted this as compatible with divine justice and goodness, they would arouse further wrath from on high. Theology in these terms is a horror, and ethics nonsense.

Luther and his successors indeed saw this with varying degrees of clearness, and tried to soften its impact with the doctrine that God is "wholly other." According to Brunner, there is complete discontinuity between divine and human ethics, and according to Barth, a similar discontinuity between divine and human reason. As it happened, I had met this doctrine before. Something very like it had been urged by a thinker I admired, H. L. Mansel, the formidable dean of St. Paul's in the middle of the last century, who had stated the case with a logical force beyond the capacity of these theologians. Unhappily for his influence, his book, *The Limits of Religious Thought*, was reviewed and demolished by Mill in his *Examination of Hamilton*. My own examination of Mansel's successors could claim no such result. But it became clear as I proceeded that the appeal to the double standard of reason and revelation must end in logical schizophrenia, and I tried to work this out with regard to each of my theologians. I held that there is only one standard of truth, namely the standard implicitly at work in any attempt to think at all. The rationalist element in my philosophy, already present in *The Nature of Thought*, was reinforced rather than weakened by this skirmish with conservative theologians.

Critique of Catholicism

My study of reason in theology did not confine itself to Protestantism; indeed the St. Andrews lectures began with a critique of the relation between reason and belief in Catholicism. The Catholic view is more generous to reason than the Protestant. No theologian has ever brought as massive an intelligence as that of Saint Thomas to the defense of the faith, and the church insists that even when dogma is unintelligible it is not because the dogma is beyond reason as such, but only because our own reason is as yet too feeble to comprehend it. Still the Catholic appeals to revelation over a wider area of belief than does the Protestant, if only because the Catholic Bible, described officially as "inspired in all its parts," is greater by seven books than the Protestant Bible. My criticism of the Catholic view was based on the ground of inconsistencies both in the received content of revelation and between this content and the accepted conclusions of science.

In May 1972, my brother and I were invited to participate in a "dialogue" between Catholics and Humanists in New York City, and though I do not fit very well into a Humanist pigeonhole, I attended as a member of the Humanist group. I presented a paper that criticized the Catholic position on the ground of the inconsistencies just mentioned. The line of reply astonished me. The presence of the inconsistencies was not denied; the answer was that the horse I was flogging was now disowned and dead. Popes and councils had indeed required of the faithful an acceptance of certain dogmas, and these requirements were still there on the Catholic books. But the popes and councils had exceeded their authority; they were philosophically and scientifically somewhat inept, and were certainly not representative of the new Catholicism. Instead of the church's being monolithic, as I had supposed, it was in fact a plurality of often conflicting schools of thought which were now, in spite of an unhappy tradition, at liberty to follow the argument where it led. This calm defiance of authority in the most authoritarian of the Christian churches took my breath away. If the Catholics I met at this session are typical of the new Catholicism, then the church of Vatican I, and indeed of Vatican II, is fast disintegrating, and my criticism would apply only to the traditional element within it. But the insurgents have not as yet captured the crest of Vatican Hill, and until they do, the critic of Catholic theology can only assume that what the church stands for is what its popes and councils say it does.

Reflections on Religion

My thought on religion is still in process of growth. My views on any subject seem to advance only by negations; I try one theory after another and reach a stable view only after zigzagging my way along between alternative theories till I arrive at one that survives the criticisms made of the others. What I cannot believe, I know far more clearly than what I ought to believe.

Religion as I conceive it is the attitude of the whole man—including his thought, his feelings, and the commitments of his will—toward what he takes to be ultimately true and good. But his conception of what is thus true and good varies with his level of civilization and his personal level of reflectiveness. For millenniums man's reflection took the form of myth, in which what was imaginatively satisfying was not sharply distinguished from what was true. Only relatively late, when a Socratic keenness came on the scene, were the demands of intellect and imagination clearly separated, and intelligence enabled to play freely and critically on the ultimate nature of things. It reached something like that freedom in the three great thinkers of Greece. It never reached it in Palestine. And through an unhappy twist of fortune, the church fathers made the use of such freedom a sin. That left them, however, a certain limited range. From the rich litter of Old Testament history, myth, and poetry, from the fragments of Jesus' teaching as reported in the Gospels, and from Saint Paul's strange theology of salvation by imputed goodness, the church fathers constructed an edifice of dogma in which the Western mind was to live for more than a thousand years. It was an edifice constructed not from facts of nature or experience but, as the fathers supposed, from the more solid bricks and stones of revelation; and its architects, working without the aid of science, critical history, or free reason, threw up towers and pinnacles of anthropomorphic theory about the Deity and his intentions, and about the origin and destiny of man. The Catholic and Protestant theories examined in *Reason and Belief* were integral parts of this ancient structure. Most secular philosophers believe that the imposing edifice is now a wreck, of historical interest only, with the winds of science whistling through its bare ruined choirs and slowly reducing the great fabric to rubble. Modern thought is disinclined to take it seriously. There I disagree. I do take it seriously, even where I do not accept it. I was raised in it, and I wanted to know, if only for my own satisfaction, whether it could still make a habitable home. Furthermore, any structure of faith to which millions of people have looked over many centuries for their philosophy and moral guidance, as well as for solace and hope, can hardly be mere delusion. What is humanly so important deserves the attention of humane minds.

My examination did not find the structure to be one that I could live in myself with comfort. But I do not like treatments of religion that are merely negative. Religion in the past may have been, as Freud suggests, very largely an illusion, but it is not that in essence, unless human life in general is based upon illusion. In a sense, no doubt, it is. Man's thought about the ultimate, as Feuerbach contended, has been generally a projection of his own image upon the face of the infinite, and as his conception of his own nature changed, the explicit object of his religion changed with it. He has not yet graduated from anthropomorphism, though the speculative pioneers who are leading his advance have nearly won freedom from it. In moving beyond anthropomorphism, however, they are not moving beyond religion. To say this would be to confine religion to one stretch of the human journey, without seeing how permanent and inescapable an attitude it is. Religion does not cease to be religion when one view of the ultimate is replaced by another; it only ceases to be that kind or stage of religion. What could be more arbitrary than for a fundamentalist to deny religion to Spinoza because the conception of the ultimate held by that "God-intoxicated" man was more thoroughly moulded by reflection than his own? The ultimate is there; it is what it is; and in the end there can be only one true religion, the religion that sees things as they are. But there are infinitely many degrees of approach to this, and so long as new conceptions are offered sincerely and self-critically, they are to be welcomed, not anathematized.

I have never felt at ease in speculation about "ultimate reality." My powers are better suited for flights at a middle level where one is less likely to lose one's bearings. But in a philosophy like mine, metaphysics and religion alike converge upon an Absolute, that is, upon the universe as the ultimate and inclusive system of all things. My ideas on this remote consummation of thought are tentative, as they no doubt should be, but they have been much affected by the conclusions I reached about goodness in my reflections on ethics.

What is meant by saying that the Absolute is good? It probably means one of three things. (1) It might mean that the universe is intrinsically good in the sense that a human experience is good. Such intrinsic goodness, which I took to be the main concept of ethics, consisted, I thought, in the fulfillment and satisfaction of impulse on the part of a conscious being. Could goodness in this sense be attributed to the universe as a whole? That the whole embraced or included it went without saying. But to ascribe goodness to the whole of things in the sense in which it applied to one's own experience would be to say that the universe had urges or impulses or unrealized desires. These assertions might be true, but was there any compelling reason to believe them? I did not see that there was. In spite of my general sympathy with idealism, I saw no way of proving that the universe was mental in the sense of being a field of consciousness. I did think, and I still do, that everything of which we are immediately aware exists only in consciousness, and that we reach the world of matter only at the end of an inference. But what was the status of matter? What was the place in the world of the objects of modern physics, the realm of protons and electrons, of wavicles and quasars? That matter too belongs in the realm of mind has been accepted not only by some speculative philosophers but also by some competent scientists, for example Eddington; and I thought this might be true, though the traditional idealist ways of proving it seemed unsatisfactory. But to say that the universe had impulses, yearnings, or unsatisfied desires seemed more like myth or poetic fancy than responsible philosophizing.

(2) The assertion that ultimate reality was good might mean, secondly, that the world was *morally* good. Now to say that a man is morally good means that he has a bent of will that inclines him to do what he believes to be right. To say the same thing of the universe is presumably to ascribe to it a

like tendency. But does this make sense? Can we say that the universe faces choices, that it sees and generally does the better, though perhaps occasionally the worse, that though tempted as we are it wants to do its duty to all concerned and normally strives to do so? This is so plainly a projection on the face of the infinite of our own human condition that it seems almost superfluous to point out that the universe has no "others" and hence no duties in the familiar human and social sense.

(3) But to call ultimate reality good may have a third meaning. It may mean that, in the light of the amount and distribution of intrinsic goods and evils in the world, it can be called good on the whole. This may mean either (a) that the amount of good is greater than that of evil, or (b) that what appears to us as evil would not be evil at all if it were seen in the context of the whole.

Neither view seems tenable. (a) How can we speak with any confidence of the comparative amounts of good and evil in the universe? It would be difficult to make the necessary estimate even regarding our own small planet. We know, for example, that the amount of pain in biological history has been immense, but we know far too little to be able to calculate its amount or know how that amount compares with the amount of good. Still less can we compare these amounts in the universe at large. The proportion borne by the part of the universe we know to the part we do not know is far less than that of the known to the unknown parts of the earth's history. It is not that the questions raised here are unintelligible questions, but that any answers to them would be guesses, not firm conclusions. (b) The goodness of the world is sometimes arrived at, not by weighing goods and evils against each other, but by attempting to see them in the perspective of the whole. It is argued that what appears to us evil would then lose this appearance and be seen as a necessary component in a world from which evil had disappeared. This again is ambiguous. (i) If it suggests that in such a view all that now seems evil will be seen as a necessary *means* to good, it flies in the face of such evidence as we have. For all we can see, the death of an infant or an animal in extreme pain often produces no equivalent good, either in the short run or in the long, and if anyone contends that it does, he is relying on faith, not on evidence. And it is with evidence that we are concerned. (ii) Sometimes evil is dealt with, not as a means to good, but as a component in an organic whole in which, when seen in context, it loses its character as evil. But this view is self-defeating. It threatens to subvert our moral standards altogether. If our sense of value is so unreliable that the agony we take as a very paradigm of evil may not be really evil, but good, there seems to be no reason why we should take anything as really evil. And if we can take nothing as really evil, neither can we take anything as really good. But in that case the problem itself is illusory, for it arose from our conviction of a genuine difference between good and evil. If there is no real difference, there is no real problem.

Considerations such as these led me to an unconventional religious position. It was not an idealist view, if that implied, as Norman Kemp Smith believed, that "spiritual values have a determining voice in the ordering of the Universe";[26] for, as just explained, I saw no ground for calling the universe good in any accepted sense of that term. Goodness was confined, for all we knew, to conscious life on earth, for that alone provided the conditions under which values could arise. Moral perfection was for me an ideal, not, as with Royce and many other idealists, an already realized fact. If the term "God" implied such perfection, then God was not an existent being but a projected one, who would come to exist only if the moral ideal were realized by striving human beings. One could hardly identify God with the process of coming to be, for he remained an object of reverence, and one does not reverence the fact of evolution. Nevertheless he exists in the sense that he is the immanent end which is realizing or incarnating itself in the process of advance. In this sense, then, I could accept the idealist thesis that "spiritual values have a determining voice in the ordering of the Universe"; for if such values are not attributable to the Absolute, neither are they impotent by-products of matter, as Santayana supposed. Immanent ends, in a way imperfectly understood, exercise some control over the process of their coming to be; purpose makes a difference in human behavior and, through that behavior, in the world.

It may be said that to use the term "God" for the ideal end of human endeavor rather than for an existent and perfect being is to take an unwarranted liberty with established usage. I agree. Though the practice is common enough, it seemed to me semantically and ethically dubious to adopt the terms of religious persons, but use them in deceptively different ways. If "God" means an existent being, all-powerful, all-wise, and all-good, who made and governs the world for ends that are in our sense good, I do not see how a philosopher can consistently believe in such a being. On the other hand, if anyone says that because I am unable to accept this being I am therefore repudiating religion, I must demur. The term "religion" is a very broad one, and there is no call to tie it to an irrational and moribund theology. If one looks at the activity it so broadly designates, in East and West, in the primitive past and the more critical present, one is not taking an undue liberty with the term in defining it as man's attempt to adjust himself to ultimate reality. Religion so conceived will last as long as man does.

In attempting to adjust my own thought to reality, I have had to abandon both the traditional concept of God as distinct from the world and the anthropomorphic concept of his goodness. Of course I still believe in the authority of the moral law, not now as a divine command, but as a rationally based ideal. Indeed I believe it is something more; it is an active force in the moulding of human nature toward fuller realization. I know that religion as here conceived may not seem to be religion at all to traditional Catholics or Protestants. But at least it leaves religion with meaning and importance; it keeps reverence alive, even while redirecting it; it leaves morality with all the authority it ever really had; and it makes religion not only a live option but an unavoidable one.

Brand Blanshard

Works Cited in Autobiography

[1] Max Eastman, *Heroes I Have Known* (New York: Simon & Schuster, 1942), 293, 308.
[2] W. P. Montague, "Confessions of an Animistic Materialist," in *Contemporary American Philosophy*, ed. G. P. Adams and W. P. Montague, 2 vols. (London: Allen & Unwin; New York: Macmillan Co., 1930), 2:137.
[3] F. J. E. Woodbridge in *Contemporary American Philosophy*, 2:434, 433.
[4] A. H. Smith, "Horace William Brindley Joseph," *Proceedings of the British Academy* 31 (1945):380.
[5] [A. H. Smith], "H. W. B. Joseph, 1867–1943. An Address Delivered in Chapel by the Subwarden of New College 20 November 1943" (Oxford: Oxford University Press, n.d.), 10.
[6] W. D. Ross, "Prefatory Note" in H. A. Prichard, *Moral Obligation* (Oxford: Clarendon Press, 1949).
[7] J. A. K. Thomson, "Gilbert Murray," *Proceedings of the British Academy* 43 (1957):257.
[8] W. E. Hocking in *Contemporary American Philosophy*, 1:386, 387.
[9] E. F. Carritt, *Fifty Years a Don* (privately printed, 1960), 44–45.
[10] *Contemporary American Philosophy*, 2:289 n.
[11] Susan Stebbing, "Moore's Influence," in *The Philosophy of G. E. Moore*, Library of Living Philosophers, vol. 4 (La Salle, Ill.: Open Court, 1942), 532
[12] *The Philosophy of Bertrand Russell*, Library of Living Philosophers, vol. 5 (1944), 690.
[13] Bertrand Russell, *Human Knowledge: Its Scope and Limits* (New York: Simon & Schuster, 1948), 201–2.
[14] Bertrand Russell, "How I Write," *Portraits from Memory, and Other Essays* (New York: Simon & Schuster, 1956), 212, 210.
[15] Ibid., 211–12.
[16] Bertrand Russell, *A History of Western Philosophy* (New York: Simon & Schuster, 1945), 569.
[17] Andrew Lang, *Essays in Little* (London: Henry & Co., 1891), 42.
[18] Edmund Gosse, *Portraits and Sketches* (New York: Charles Scribner's Sons, 1912), 29.
[19] Gert Kalow, "Ein Sommersemester in Salzburg," *Ruperto-Carola*, Dec. 1953. "The Americans take even the most severe attacks quite calmly. Till one of the teachers arose (Professor Blanshard) and read an article on this problem which he had published in the *New York Times*. The Europeans were speechless. Everything they had expressed was here surpassed not only in acuteness and clarity but also in discretion. Here was the phenomenon of the immensely awake American self-critique. The result was trust. 'One can talk with the Americans.' "
[20] Bertrand Russell, *The Conquest of Happiness* (New York: Horace Liveright, 1930), 217.
[21] Albert Einstein, *Ideas and Opinions* (New York: Crown Publishers, 1954), 262. I owe notice of these passages to Professor Schilpp.
[22] F. C. S. Schiller, *Humanism* (London and New York: Macmillan & Co., 1903), 10.
[23] George Santayana, *The Realm of Matter* (London: Constable, 1930), 84.
[24] Ibid., 103–4.
[25] J. A Symonds, as quoted in Horatio Brown, *John Addington Symonds: A Biography* (London, 1895), 1:30.
[26] N. K. Smith, *Prolegomena to an Idealist Theory of Knowledge* (London: Macmillan & Co., 1924), 1.

PART TWO

DESCRIPTIVE AND CRITICAL ESSAYS ON THE PHILOSOPHY OF BRAND BLANSHARD, WITH REPLIES

EDITOR'S NOTE: *Readers familiar with previous volumes in this series are advised of a rather radical change in the structure of this one. In all preceding volumes the philosopher's "Replies" appeared as section III, between the contributed essays and the Bibliography. In the present case Professor Blanshard preferred to have his reply to each contributor appear immediately following the contributed essay itself. This makes it easier for the reader, who need not search for the philosopher's reply to an essay.*

I   THE OFFICE OF PHILOSOPHY

1 BLANSHARD'S CONCEPTION OF THE NATURE AND FUNCTION OF PHILOSOPHY
Sterling M. McMurrin

HEINRICH Gomperz once said of Fichte that he philosophized with his fist on the table. I suspect that a fist-on-the-table commitment to philosophy has characterized idealists generally. Certainly this is true of Brand Blanshard. In Blanshard's work there is no suggestion of indifference, triviality, or pedantry. Philosophy for him is not an academic game or an exercise in intellectual virtuosity. Nor is it the servant of theology, science, or practical affairs. It is, rather, the completion of science, indeed of all knowing, as a striving to apprehend the nature of things. In principle the very meaning of philosophy, which issues from the nature of thought itself, guarantees its integrity and autonomy. Blanshard belongs to the disappearing race of scholar-philosophers whose large perspective and wisdom are grounded in their extensive learning and experience and whose vocation is a life-and-death concern for the things that matter most. It is quite impossible to read his work without feeling the impact of the high purpose with which it is vested.

It is doubtful that any philosopher has defined philosophy or described its function more intently than Brand Blanshard, or by both direct and indirect discussion given its meaning a more thorough treatment in his work. Certainly none has been a more determined and dedicated advocate of the pursuit of philosophy as he conceived it. Blanshard would be the first to point out that his conception of philosophy is neither original nor new, indeed that it has pervaded philosophy from the beginning and entered his thought as part and parcel of the rationalism and idealism of which he is a most distinguished representative. He is an advocate and defender of the great tradition that philosophy is the attempt of reason upon the world.

Although it has other motivations as well, philosophy for Blanshard is basically committed to the discovery and disclosure of truth. There is in human nature a basic drive to know, an urge to understand. Philosophy follows from the very nature of man. Its failures prove simply that it is difficult to be reasonable, especially in those matters of ultimate concern in both thought and practice which command the attention of philosophers. "In any genuine philosophic mind the love of truth is a steady gravitational pull which operates to correct all defections from it, even when the sun that exerts the pull is clouded over. The true philosopher is a man with an intellectual conscience . . ." (*Reason and Analysis* [*RA*], 98). The failures of philosophers are their own; they do not follow from any failure of the world to conform to the structure of reason. Among the current causes of failure is the conception that philosophy consists essentially of the "sharpening of the tools of thought" rather than the use of them in the pursuit of the ultimate problems.

It is somewhat unsettling that the chief controversy now engaged in by philosophy is the question of its own nature, its technical function, and its meaning in the culture. This question is not new; in diverse and subtle ways it has intruded into philosophical discussion since its beginnings. But the radical nature of contemporary positivism, analysis, and existentialism, and the uncommon talent which has supported their attack upon the traditional format of philosophy, have made it an acute issue in current thought, an issue that has adversely affected the status of philosophy in intellectual life and has injured its effectiveness in practical affairs. It is the basic question of whether philosophy can lay claim to substantive knowledge or is an activity only. It is fortunate that a philosopher of Brand Blanshard's stature should commit so much of his attention and energy to this matter.

The meaning of philosophy is not simply a special problem to which Blanshard has given incidental or occasional attention. It is not one which he has treated casually. In a sense the entire corpus of his philosophical writing is both an argument supporting and advocating his conception of philosophy and a critique of opponents of that conception. The strength of his position lies in part in the fact that his conception of philosophy follows from the method and substance of his own thought. Blanshard's well-known analysis of the nature of thought from the psychology of perception to logical inference, and his contributions to epistemological theory and the concept of truth, are essentially a study of the process and structure of rationality. His metaphysics is concerned primarily with the intelligible structure of the world, its capacity to be an object of knowledge by virtue of the internal relations which define necessary causal connections. In his ethics and aesthetics he is predisposed by a concern for the role of reason in the determination of the good and artistic. In religion he insists firmly that belief should be underwritten by reasonableness.

Most philosophers are probably inclined to define philosophy ideally by a model more or less patterned after their own method of philosophizing. As a rationalist who insists on the primacy of reason, Blanshard is not unique in this respect. In *The Logical Syntax of Language*, for instance, Carnap defined philosophy exclusively in terms of logical syntax, as the analysis of the logical syntax of the language of science (Part V, "Philosophy and Syntax"). Later, in his *Introduction to Semantics,* after his involvement with American pragmatism, he included semantics and "perhaps" pragmatics in the meaning of philosophy. "The field of theoretical philosophy is no longer restricted to syntax but is regarded as comprehending the whole analysis of language, including syntax and semantics and perhaps also pragmatics."[1] Many of the present generation of graduate students have been tutored to believe that philosophy is simply the doing of the kind of thing that was done by Wittgenstein, who clearly conceived of philosophy in terms of his own presuppositions and method. Or, consider an example of a philosopher with a more speculative bent. Stephen C. Pepper, whose substantive philosophy has consisted especially of his "world hypotheses," defines philosophy as essentially at its "heart" the construction of world hypotheses.[2] This identification of philosophy with one's own way of going about it is perhaps more or less inevitable and may be the most useful access to philosophy's function. After all, philosophy does not exist in the abstract. It is real only in the process and substance of actual philosophic thought.

It is doubtful that any advocate of rationalism has been more thoroughgoing or more consistent than Blanshard. None has stated its case as clearly or as persuasively. His work is such an impressive culmination of the rationalist tradition that it seems fair to question whether anything in principle remains to be added. It is also doubtful that any rationalist has been more sophisticated in his knowledge of the pitfalls of rationalism, more hopeful of a reconciliation of the claims of rationalism and empiricism, or more competent to engage in frontal attack the critiques leveled against rationalism by empiricism and positivism. As a critical rationalism, generated out of the controversy on the merits of rationalistic method and idealistic metaphysics, Blanshard's philosophy incorporates within itself its own defenses of its methodology and main tenets. It is a defense that is essentially an offense against its critics. In a very real and dramatic way, Blanshard goes forth in virtually every chapter and every essay to engage the enemy on his own ground.

For a committed rationalist to define philosophy in terms of reason seems obvious enough, but it inevitably opens up a multitude of problems, both practical and theoretical: all the problems which the concept of rationalism suggests in an era dominated by empirical method and by the naturalistic and positivistic temper. It invites risks not only of technical error but also of ambiguity, excessive generality, or the pedantic narrowness that so often plagues the writing of professional philosophers. But Blanshard is anything but pedantic, and though he opens Pandora's box, to keep reason on the philosophic throne he undertakes to dispose of those troubles with uncommon patience, persistence, thoroughness, and technical skill.

Although he is a rationalist through and through, and an ardent defender of the logical ground of rationalism, it is not simply reason in a narrow methodological sense that Blanshard champions as the central meaning of philosophy. Rather it is reason in the large: reason as reflective thought, reasonableness as an attitude of mind, respect for knowledge and evidence, and in matters having practical implications, reason as sanity, common sense, and wisdom. Reason as rationalism is a source of knowledge for Blanshard, and it is the test of knowledge; but reason as rationality is a larger and in a sense a practical ideal. It is this large ideal of rationality that is the hallmark of philosophy. Where it is found, an argument may be totally unacceptable because untrue, but it may be judged, nevertheless, as genuine philosophy.

This is the picture gained from a reading and assessment of Blanshard's total work and also clearly exhibited in some of his shorter pieces—a defense of reason as a spacious and open meaning of rationality. It seems to me that there can be no argument with him here, with either this broad conception of philosophy or his insistence that philosophizing should in fact at least conform to that conception. And I fully concur in his commitment to both philosophy's intrinsic worth and its value as a social force. Indeed, nowhere can be found a statement that more effectively sets forth the meaning of philosophy in terms of rationality and the practical wisdom which it engenders, or that more clearly exhibits the theoretic failures and practical dangers of irrationality.

But there is a difficulty in treating Blanshard's position on philosophy, a difficulty that lies in the fact that while his writings are interlaced, indeed inspired, with his vigorous attack on irrationality and his advocacy of rationality, he is quite naturally and more or less constantly involved in the technical defense of his own rationalism and in the attack on its philosophic enemies. I am enthusiastic about his insistence upon rationality and reasonableness and agree with much of his carefully worked critique of the opposing schools. But I am still unable to concur with essential technical facets of his rationalism or its associated metaphysical idealism. I cannot accept the tie of logic with metaphysics which yields the world view of the idealist. This, of course, would be quite immaterial to the point of Blanshard's conception of philosophy if it were not for the fact that he has inclinations to identify the attack of reason upon the world with his own kind of attack, his own brand of rationalism, which on his terms implies an idealistic metaphysics. To treat his conception of philosophy is to move between rationality in the large and rationalism as a technical method, and the reader is not always sure when these fully coincide, or just where he is between the two. For the ultimate vindication of rationality and reasonableness is found by Blanshard in the technical claims of rationalism and the idealistic metaphysics which, he argues, follows from it, or in a sense is necessarily presupposed by it. For him to consider his own rationalism, which indeed he shares with other eminent philosophers of his tradition, as the correct or proper model of rationality goes without saying. But this raises the question, in spite of occasional disclaimers, of whether he considers such nonrationalists as pragmatists or existentialists to be legitimate occupants or illicit poachers upon philosophic territory that is underwritten by the metaphysics of the authentic reasoners, the rationalists. I confess that this is a question that gives me much concern, which I have been unable fully to set at rest by a study of his work.

Blanshard holds that both reason as the source of knowledge and rationality as a practical ideal have in this century been the objects of the most "massive and sustained" attack that they have suffered in the past two thousand years. He finds, I believe quite correctly, that in the present century several revolutionary social forces have contributed to irrationalism: two great wars, the reign of dictators, the advance of technology, the secularization of life, the cold war between East and West (*RA*, 27). As a result there has come a decline of reasonableness and of trust in reason in both theoretical and practical matters. Even the remarkable successes of science have been accompanied by the loss of reliance upon reason in issues pertaining to values.

The attack upon reason, of course, has reached all departments of the culture—philosophy, theology, psychology, sociology, politics, and the several branches of the arts—producing a loss of sanity in society generally. While in philosophy reason is replaced with convention, perception, or a reliance upon practical consequences, in theology it yields to dogmatic revelation, in psychology to instinct, in sociology to feeling and desire, in politics to class and national demands, and in art to taste without principle. There is in all of these an opposition to authentic reason, which is the reliable method of apprehending the true, beautiful, and good because it grounds its pronouncements on "canons of necessary and universal validity."

Blanshard is convinced that the most insidious growth of irrationalism has been within the camp of philosophy itself. Accordingly, his entire work virtually takes the form of a grand criticism of the philosophic opponents of rationalism. Naturalism in its most extreme behavioristic form, instrumentalism, positivism, linguistic analysis, and existentialism have been "derogatory of reason in its traditional use." For Blanshard, because they undermine its integrity as "an attempt on the nature of things by reason," they are in a sense at odds with the authentic purpose of philosophy (*RA*, 36).

Professor Blanshard has full respect for the strength of his opposition, a respect which is not the least source of the strength of his own argument. "I suspect," he says,

> that the dominance of the analytic philosophy would shrink the horizons of both theory and conduct, and make life a bleaker and drearier business. But I cannot, like some of my colleagues, take this philosophy lightly. It seems

to me significant, formidably advocated, and in some respects highly plausible. The only proper way to deal with it is to approach it with the respect due to its extremely able proponents, and with the assumption that they may be right. [*RA*, 98–99]

It is not the intent of this paper to analyze or criticize Blanshard's attack on the enemies of rationalism and metaphysics, but simply to indicate its bearing on his own conception of the nature and function of philosophy. His refusal to capitulate to analysis indicates the intensity of his commitment to the fundamental value of substantive philosophy and exhibits the fist-on-the-table determination and stubbornness of the idealist who has brought the essentials of the old rationalism and idealism, intact but with new armor, into the era and arena of the new thought.

Blanshard has entered fully into the controversies over the theoretic possibility of metaphysics and the cognitive status of value judgments as well as the implied question of the relation of philosophy to science. His concern is at least threefold: First, to contest the argument of those logical and linguistic analysts who relegate philosophy to the status of an activity only, thereby depriving it of any substantive element of its own and subordinating it to a questionable service to science or common discourse. The very meaning of philosophy for him requires that philosophy have something of its own to say, not simply that it pass judgment on the statements of others or even that it serve as a synopsis or synthesis of the propositions of science. There must be something which can be regarded as philosophical knowledge—knowledge that is genuinely substantive, knowledge that is relevant to the questions which most deeply and ultimately concern us. Second, to defend the possibility of metaphysics, not because nonmetaphysical statements may not otherwise be available to philosophy, but because the entire task of making sense of experience, the whole enterprise of reason, including science itself, is lost if there is no possibility of reason coming to grips with reality. Here is the heart of Blanshard's philosophic interest. And third, to defend the cognitive character of at least some normative judgments, both ethical and aesthetic, against the emotive and pragmatic treatments of value sentences. For Blanshard ethics requires the possibility in principle of genuine knowledge in affirmation of end values. He refuses to reduce the knowledge function of value judgments to hypothetical status and instrumental purposes. Unless these three interrelated defenses are successful, Blanshard would insist, philosophy as a concern for the large questions which have traditionally defined it is clearly an impossibility.

In insisting upon reason and reasonableness as the hallmarks of philosophy, Blanshard has set a proper imprint upon it. Whatever else it may be, genuinely philosophical discussion must be rational. Two difficulties, however, plague this position. To let the matter rest with reason is far too general and unrestrictive. Certainly Blanshard does not mean that discourse is philosophical simply because it is rational, for it could be both rational and trivial. Triviality has no place in his conception of philosophy, even though he holds that in principle philosophy can deal with anything at all. Where the line on philosophy, which need not be sharp, is drawn is not entirely clear. But at least it apparently should distinguish issues which are basic in character and which incline toward the ultimate in importance.

There is, moreover, the even more important problem of the line between philosophy and science and the relationship which obtains between them. In rejecting the radical empirical, positivistic, and analytical distinctions between philosophy and science, Blanshard seems to be left without a clear separation of the two. In a sense, of course, he probably wants no sharp separation, if indeed he wants any basic distinction at all. For in principle the pursuit of knowledge is a unity, and the difference between science and philosophy appears therefore mainly as one of degree. He conceives both as concerned with factual matters, as having genuine factual meaning. They are both cognitive, substantive enterprises; both seek understanding through explanation; and for both logical coherence is the test of truth. The possibility in principle of confirming or infirming sentences in metaphysics is for Blanshard no different essentially from confirming or infirming the propositions of science. Philosophy for him would seem in principle to be a more complete, more adequate system of knowledge, while science in its current form—dependent as it is upon empirical method and therefore under multiple strictures—is at best partial and incomplete. Where empirical science must settle for probabilities, philosophy, as rationalistic metaphysics, respecting science but at least partially free from its restrictions, can move toward the more complete, more total, more certain. In its search for explanatory laws, science is inevitably caught in the consideration of efficient cause. Its end product therefore is not concerned with the concretely real in its internal relatedness to the totality of reality. It is concerned, rather, with universals taken in abstraction from the totality by a method that apprehends its objects only in their external relations. It therefore yields a partial and to that extent distorted view of reality.

Here, of course, is the crux of Blanshard's whole treatment of the nature of philosophy, his theory of internal relations as the basic description of reality. Needless to say, he admits the speculative character of this position, but he argues that without it the whole enterprise of knowledge must yield to a basic skepticism. He insists that science as we know it would be impossible on any other ground. In its basic character the world of reality is an absolute system where in its essential being everything is an integral part of a context and cannot be properly perceived in abstraction from that context. In opposition to the basic principle of Humean cause, causal relationships are themselves necessary, making the world of reality the kind of thing that conforms and responds to the necessitarian character of reason. And it responds fully only to reason. This large and ultimate ontological assumption is the foundation of the whole matter. Without it, Blanshard's defense of the *philosophia perennis* would lose its strength. For his advocacy of rationality and reasonableness as large qualities which should be cultivated by the philosophic mind is grounded squarely upon his defenses of rationalistic method that are in turn tied to his idealistic metaphysical speculations. It is this which makes him distrustful of the "reason" of the nonrationalist. "After all," he says, "philosophy is an attempt to think logically about the world; and unless the logic that governs our thinking answers to the way in which the world is put together, why attempt by any effort of thought to trace the lines of the world order?" (*RA*, 251).

In objective idealism of the type advocated by Blanshard the relation of metaphysics to value philosophy is more than intimate—it is a matter of identity. In a sense, values are facts, metaphysical facts. And since metaphysical knowledge is a possibility, the cognitive apprehension of values is a possibility. The common distinction between fact and value is basically obliterated, as is that between science and metaphysics. To save metaphysics is to save the cognitive property of normative judgments. This is what Blanshard proposes to do; indeed he insists he has done it, and that in doing so he has justified the doctrine that philosophy is a rational/cognitive attempt upon reality where reality includes values.

It is of interest that pragmatism at this point is the diametric opposite of idealism but that it nevertheless yields a somewhat similar result—the elimination of the bifurcation of fact and value. For where in idealism values are elements in the intricate, interrelated, coherent system of facts, in pragmatism, in both its popular and technical formulations, factual propositions are in a sense valuations—a position most obvious in Schiller but not absent in either James or Dewey. It is especially in logical empiricism that the distinction between fact and value has been made rigorous and the total impossibility of assigning cognitive value to normative judgments argued. Blanshard will have nothing of the fact-value bifurcation set up by the positivists and some other empiricists, nor will he settle for the inversions of pragmatism or its relegation of the cognitive properties of value sentences to hypothetical or instrumental status. His aim is genuine, reliable knowledge of end values as the foundation of moral philosophy and aesthetics. For Blanshard "moral judgments are an expression of reason" (*Reason and Goodness* [*RG*], 91) but they are nevertheless assertions of genuine *oughts*, not simply disguised assertions of what is. They are statements setting forth the objective properties of acts, not simply subjective reports of feelings regarding those acts. The practical end of reason applied to moral issues is freedom, which is rational responsibility in the choice of value alternatives.

I appreciate the great importance of the claim to value knowledge which Blanshard and others have so earnestly made, and I do not discount the strength of their arguments, but I am not persuaded that the case has been or can be made except on the instrumental grounds in principle defined by pragmatism. That the positivistic position has required continual criticism and revision does not invalidate its basic claim that value judgments are in principle different from factual statements. Further, there is the question of whether Blanshard has adequately weighed the large element of rationality and, indeed, cognition, that can figure in both morals and art even when the possibility of knowledge of end values is denied. Instrumentalist ethics, for instance, which is in principle compatible with the positivistic treatment of value judgments, allows a large field for the play of reason as well as for the role of knowledge in determining ends even though a knowledge of "intrinsic" values is held to be impossible. Nor are knowledge and reason irrelevant to the search for the good life even under an emotive interpretation of value judgments.

It is a matter of more than passing interest that both Dewey and Blanshard have sought the same philosophic end, the justification of a science of values, by routes which are directly opposed. Certainly Dewey was committed, as is Blanshard, to the supreme importance of bringing intelligence, reason, and knowledge into the arena of moral judgment. A science of values, though limited by its instrumentalist character, was the end product of his philosophy. Dewey would not admit that Blanshard has achieved his goal of establishing cognition of end values. Blanshard would no doubt agree that Dewey reached his goal, but would hold that its instrumentalist character renders it unsatisfactory because instrumentalism is intrinsically a partial and incomplete system. It is the difference between a metaphysician who insists on continuing the search for the summum bonum and the principles of right conduct and a social psychologist who is convinced that morality is the practical resolution of conflicts occasioned by interest and desire.

Consistent with his general attitude toward linguistic analysis, Blanshard is intensely critical of those for whom ethics is essentially a dealing with such normative terms as "good" and "right." He deplores the attitude that "meta-ethics has no ethical implications and may be discussed in a logical vacuum, antiseptic to moral commitments" (*RG,* 263). Nevertheless, he holds that the linguistic analysts have laid the foundations for a revolt against the emotivism in ethics that regarded moral judgments as nothing more than expressions of emotions and was a total denial of the possibility of a reasonable approach to moral values. Indeed, he holds that in a somewhat disguised manner the linguists themselves have been searching, though unsuccessfully, for a place for reason in moral philosophy.

It is perhaps fair to suggest that Blanshard would rank the major schools in the following descending order if called upon to appraise their philosophical merit: idealism, realism, positivism, linguistic analysis, and last, existentialism. It is obvious that he should have high respect for realism, which in general shares the philosophical aims of idealism, goes through many of the same philosophical motions as idealism, and indeed often shares its technical doctrine with some forms of idealism. Notwithstanding that it is the chief enemy, positivism ranks high because of its rationality and technical thoroughness; and linguistic analysis avoids complete condemnation because even it is a search for meaningfulness. But Blanshard does not hesitate to exhibit his distaste for existentialism as a philosophy, whether religious or secular. Indeed, his attitude toward it may be more aptly described as contempt. The grounds for this opposition appear to be its phenomenological method as well as its nonrational and irrational results. At times in its enthusiasm for immediacy and subjectivity existentialism steps over the threshold of Blanshard's concept of philosophic respectability. Yet although he may have judged existentialism by its more extreme instances, I doubt that he would be willing to say that it is not philosophical. For he clearly holds that even the irrationalist employs in his philosophical argument the very processes of reason whose products he deplores. However much he is committed to rationalism and idealism, Blanshard holds that "In philosophy there is no orthodoxy and hence properly no heresy. . . ."[3] Immediately upon this, in the same sentence, comes the warning that "any view that presents itself with a respectable show of reason has a claim to consideration." Elsewhere, in a reference to two unacceptable theses of Marx, Blanshard explicitly states that "they are speculative flights which must be demonstrated, if at all, by the sort of dialectic which is none the less philosophy because it is bad philosophy."[4]

I rather think that however bad his dialectic, Marx is more acceptable to Blanshard as a philosopher than is Kierkegaard or Heidegger, for he at least had a healthy respect for reason and reasonableness and went through the motions of reasoning. But I hope I am correct in holding that Blanshard would not rule out the existentialists entirely, for it seems to me that even with his strong commitment to rationalism he would agree that in their subjectivism the existentialists have identified and elucidated important facets of experience and reality. I refer especially to the fact of creative freedom, which may be more effectively encountered, though not explained, by the methods of existentialism than through the avenues of typical rational discourse.

Blanshard will hear nothing of the crucial existentialist contention that traditional rationalism sacrifices the individual for the universal. The individual, he insists, is well treated in general propositions. "All men are mortal" is about me, for if I do not die, it is false, and if it is true, I will not survive. But quite apart from the existential status of general propositions, such a logical handling of the issue, somewhat reminiscent of Epicurus' treatment of the fear of death, is not likely to convince those whose philosophy is so consciously directed away from the abstract and toward the uniqueness and freedom of the individual. On his own ground, Blanshard may reject this use of "abstract."

It is entirely understandable that Blanshard should have more respect for logical positivism as an enemy than he has for existentialism. For whatever the error of its assumptions or conclusions, in its technique of analysis, positivism is built on a rational base. And however much it is committed to Humean empirical principles, it is heavy-laden with logic and does not have the nonrational flavor of existentialism, with its dependence on subjective depth psychology and its proliferation of oracular pronouncements. Nevertheless, it may be hoped that in the future Blanshard will have an opportunity to give further attention to the grounds of existentialism, for though prompted no doubt more by large-scale social failures than by failures in scientific or speculative theory, existentialism appears to be a persistent protest in philosophy.

Brand Blanshard's work exhibits a fine artistic sensibility, and the problems of aesthetics are not the least of his interests. Any reference to art and aesthetics opens up again the issue of reason. He is as opposed to irrationality in art as in morals or metaphysics, and his polemic against it, as in his Riecker Lecture, *On Sanity in Thought and Art,*[5] has the same vigor that infuses his attack upon Kierkegaardian religious thought. The objects of artistic apprehension have status in the structure of reality and they are not to be excluded, therefore, from the domain of knowledge and reason. Art is an analogue of morals, and aesthetics an analogue of ethics, and in principle the same arguments which establish the cognitive character of moral judgments argue for cognition in art. It appears that Blanshard means to say that statements such as "Killing is evil" or "Michelangelo's Sistine ceiling is sublime" are true or false in principle in the same way that "This key is made of iron" is true or false.

I am not persuaded by his argument at this point, though I may be pushing the matter further than he intends. But it does seem to me that his position that art can be rational or irrational makes eminently good sense, just as I would agree that moral judgments or actions can be rational or irrational. I am attracted to his introduction of the concept of "sanity," especially in relation to art as in his Riecker Lecture. He applies to art a principle borrowed from the ethics of Hobhouse, that "The aim of thought was at breadth and harmony of judgment; the aim of practice was at breadth and harmony in the realization of impulse. Fanaticism, arbitrariness, self-will, asceticism, the repression of any impulse or any man except in the interest of fuller expression on the whole, was ruled out as unreasonable" (*On Sanity,*4). Here Blanshard quotes from Bosanquet's Gifford Lectures: "We adhere to Plato's conclusion that objects of our likings possess as much satisfactoriness—which we identify with value—as they possess of reality and trueness." This, says Blanshard, "was just Bradley's principle of breadth and harmony again," which was applied by Hobhouse to ethics. It is "a measure of goodness and beauty as well as truth" (6). This idealistic doctrine which ties truth, goodness, and beauty together Blanshard is at pains to preserve and reassert. He laments the disappearance from painting of objective meaning as "something aesthetically irrelevant" and holds that "Poetry, no more than art or theology, can surrender itself to meaninglessness without capitulating at the same time to charlatans." (22).

I am enthusiastic about Blanshard's insistence that art as well as morals and religion should be both sane and reasonable, that there is sanity among values as well as among beliefs. And it seems to me that it makes eminently good sense to say that art, morals, and religion should not be divorced from knowledge, but that knowledge and reason are essential to them. Moreover, I believe that we can make sense when we talk of meaning in art as in morals and religion and science. But I fail to see that the meaning which is central to art or to morals is the same cognitive meaning that one claims in metaphysics or theology and which we usually agree is found in science. I find that I can go all the way with Blanshard up to that point. But I am afraid that that is the crucial point of his whole philosophy. Perhaps, nevertheless, he would agree that even if he were wrong in his apparent basic claim that fact sentences are not in principle different from value judgments, this would not necessarily mean that reason, knowledge, and sanity are not appropriate to art and morals. But possibly I misunderstand him, as there seems to be a shift in his terminology as he moves from science to morals to art. Possibly sanity in art is not intended to be equated with knowledge in science. And perhaps the intelligibility that characterizes the whole interrelated system of reality, its amenability to reason, is intended by Blanshard as an umbrella concept that covers more than one kind of meaning—cognitive and others.

At this writing Blanshard's promised volume *Reason and Belief* is still unpublished. It is not possible, therefore, to explore in detail the ramifications of his philosophy of religion. Occasional essays, however, no doubt provide the key to his view; as might be expected, it is again an insistence upon the primacy of reason and the importance of knowledge. These writings exhibit the same commitment to reason that characterizes his philosophy generally. Arguing against the currents of empiricism and positivism, Blanshard refuses to abandon the possibility of a rational theology; and in vigorous objection to recent and current irrationalism in religion, he insists upon a reasonable ground for religious belief. The subjectivity and passion which much contemporary religion substitutes for objective grounds of intellectual assent are the objects of his most intense philosophical polemic. He will have nothing of the Kierkegaardian decision of the will that is divorced from even the pretense of cognition and reason. Such subjectivity prostitutes the very idea of truth by replacing objective truth with personal commitment and replacing "conformity of statement to fact" with intensity of passion.

Blanshard turns a deaf ear to the claim that paradox, contradiction, and the unintelligible are properly at the heart of religion. If religion is to be more than a travesty of both thought and experience it must demand the resolution of paradox and contradiction. He has a healthy contempt for Kierkegaard's assertion, so popular with recent religious irrationalists, that faith is achieved only through a "crucifixion of the understanding" (*RB*, 241). "Reason may be a poor thing," says Blanshard, in a passage that I applaud, "but it is the best we have, and the theology that discards it may live to rue its recklessness" (*On Sanity,* 13).

Blanshard's insistence on a rational ground for faith is not an argument for an extreme intellectualization of religion. To reduce religion to a set of theological beliefs would be as damaging a distortion as to make of it entirely a subjective matter of enthusiasm, decision, and action. His argument is rather that a reasonable theology and a rationally determined set of values are essential to religion if its subjectivity is to be contained and if it is not to be reduced to a pure, meaningless immediacy. "Without religious thought," he holds, "religious feeling would be without form and void, and religious commitment would be to nothing."[6] With this I fully concur. Without a serious attempt at a reasonable theology, religion can become an undisciplined passion that is morally irresponsible as well as intellectually vacuous.

Since the rise of German idealism in the last century and its close involvement with the philosophy of religion and scholarly work in the history of religion, there has developed a discernible tendency for idealists as a group to appear, at least, to assume a kind of philosophic proprietorship over matters pertaining to religion. Being among those who regard religion as compatible with several styles of metaphysics—as much at home, for instance, with realism as with idealism—I find it refreshing that Blanshard apparently does not press this claim. His own idealistic metaphysics is entirely compatible with the more sophisticated developments in natural theology, and considering his strong commitment to that metaphysics, he no doubt regards it as the best ground for theology. But his main concern would seem to be that religion be rational, not that the metaphysical ground for theology be idealistic.

Blanshard's commitment to the worth of philosophy is well exhibited in his conception of the place of philosophy in education. His views on this matter are found in several places, and were explicitly expressed when he served as a member of the Commission on the Function of Philosophy in Liberal Education, established in 1943 by the American Philosophical Association to examine the state of academic philosophy and determine its appropriate role in the postwar world. His essays in the volume issued by the Commission, *Philosophy in American Education: Its Tasks and Opportunities,* report and interpret the opinions of numerous persons in academic philosophy, but I believe they reveal his own position.

His view of the place of philosophical studies in the curriculum is entirely consonant with his conception of the nature of philosophy. Education has two fundamental goals: the cultivation of a disciplined power to think and a disciplined sense of values. The sciences are conducive to the first goal but not the second. The humanities, with philosophy at the center, are concerned with both.

Blanshard regards the debate on the nature of philosophy—whether it is properly a contemplative and rational attempt to interpret and understand the world and discriminate authentic values, or is essentially analytical, an activity without substance—as fundamental to the whole philosophy of education. Given satisfactory conditions of administration, curriculum planning, and teaching personnel, academic philosophy, whether conceived in terms of separate courses or as the basic ingredient of other subjects, may be expected to function as an integrative agent in overcoming the segmentation of knowledge and confusion of learning that characterize much college and university education. This task, he rightly insists, is beyond the powers of history, literature, or the sciences. Despite its internal diversities, philosophy should serve as a general agent of unification in education by revealing the basic grounds of human experience and by cultivating in both thought and behavior the common human convictions that are the key to overcoming the insularity which characterizes the typical mind. Finally, philosophy should satisfy the large demand made upon education for a reasoned ground for belief and moral decision and action—provided, of course, it is a substantive discipline.

Blanshard grants that these are ideal commitments of academic philosophy, commitments whose fulfillment is commonly made impossible by numerous subtle factors, not the least of which is the weakness in philosophers themselves—their capacity for demolition as against construction, their frequent disunity, their characteristic individualism and lack of teamwork, and their all too common indifference to the world's problems. No doubt today he would find less indifference among philosophers, and possibly more teamwork. His study insists, nevertheless, that the negative facets of philosophy do not outweigh its constructive powers, that there is a fundamental unity which fails to meet the eye, and that the very power of philosophy to effect change depends upon its character of detachment. The practical strength that ideally resides in philosophic detachment should be even more evident now than at the time of the work of Blanshard and his colleagues on the Commission. What he advocated is not the detachment of indifference, which would destroy the practical relevance of philosophy, but the detachment of objectivity, which is essential to its true nature as a genuine rational endeavor. Only on this ground can academic philosophy become an effective agent of social change.

In the forties when the Commission submitted its report, Blanshard had great hope that philosophy could transform education and thereby deeply affect the quality of life. The demand on philosophy was both great and urgent, yet despite its weaknesses and failures it should have been equal to the task. But since then philosophy in American colleges and universities has moved even farther away from his conception of its proper nature and function, and the educational scene has been greatly complicated. Philosophy seems less qualified now to be an agent of unification in the educational process, which is even more segmented, confused, and lacking in a ground for meaning. If this predicament of philosophy in today's education grieves Brand Blanshard, there are many who share his disappointment and concern.

On the more general question of the impact of philosophy on practical affairs, Blanshard holds that the truth lies somewhere between Hegel on the one side and Marx and Freud on the other. The causal impact of philosophic ideas on large social movements is clearly exemplified by Locke and the American Revolution, Rousseau and the French Revolution, or Marx and the rise of communism. Generalizations on the full nature and extent of philosophic influence are questionable, since ideas are not unalloyed elements of the social complex and their impact varies on different minds. But Blanshard is confident that while Hegel is correct that ideas are not simply symptoms of nonideational underlying causes, Marx and Freud are wrong in their claim that reason is in bondage to economic or psychological forces. He insists that intellectual insight can be an "independent factor" in affecting the social process. Marx and Freud underestimate the influence of reason, but Hegel overstates it.

I agree fully with Blanshard's mediating position, which argues for the real power of reason but does not hold it to be *the* controlling force in social affairs. "Human nature," he says,

> is a set of desires, of which the impulse to know is one. This drive has its own distinct aim, namely the vision of the world as it is. It is a fundamental drive because all the other and more "practical" drives depend upon it, in the

sense that all of them require adjustment to what the cognitive drive discloses as the real world. What we know, or think we know, provides the setting, the environment, the conditions, of what we do.[7]

Nevertheless, insists Blanshard, philosophy as such is an inquiry directed to an intellectual end. As citizen, a philosopher may pursue the improvement of society, but as philosopher he pursues knowledge and understanding. Here is the detachment of philosophy. The philosopher's influence on affairs comes as a by-product of his reasonableness, his reflections on the ends of life, his clarifying analysis of rights, or his critical examination of social ideals. The impact of philosophy on society is not due, as some pragmatists hold, to the fact that theories are plans for action, and certainly is not accounted for by the other extreme view, "the unprincipled indulgence of curiosity." Philosophy should not be condemned when it is socially futile, but it deserves no credit as indulgence in "unrestricted theoretical laissez faire," an indulgence which Blanshard obviously detects in some of today's academic exercises. "Since," he says,

> philosophy is the attempt to understand the fundamental nature of man and his world, any inquiry is intellectually justified in the degree to which it promises to further such understanding. An inquiry may be both exceedingly technical and without practical utility—for example, an inquiry into the nature of implication—and yet throw a flood of light on the ideal of understanding and the structure of the world; if so, it is important. But when an inquiry promises neither utility nor illumination, it becomes—to use a dangerously popular phrase—an academic question.[8]

I am quite in agreement with Blanshard in his views on the social function of philosophy. They are a timely warning against the rather widespread current tendency to identify philosophy with social action, a tendency which has contributed a fair share to our present academic confusion. Nevertheless, although it is not the purpose of this paper to examine Blanshard's theory of thought, it is appropriate here to raise the question whether thought, and thereby philosophy, technically enjoy the large degree of autonomy in relation to practical issues which Blanshard ascribes to them. While agreeing with his basic objection to Dewey's treatment of theories as plans of action, a view which seems to me to be based on only one facet of the matter, I believe that Blanshard separates thought too clearly from the practical circumstances in which it may originate and be nourished, and that, accordingly, he runs the risk of divorcing philosophy too sharply from the processes of social change. A full history of philosophy, if one were possible, would surely exhibit not only a large impact of philosophic ideas on the social process but a marked involvement of the origin and development of these ideas with practical conditions. Blanshard will agree that philosophy and philosophers are part and parcel of the total historical process, not above it. But there is the question whether his own theory of thought adequately provides for this involvement of ideas with affairs.

It seems appropriate in closing to comment briefly on Blanshard's interest in "philosophical style," an interest not unrelated to his concern for reason and reasonableness in philosophy. However difficult philosophy may be, he insists, it is in principle communicable, as some philosophers have clearly shown, and those who desire to escape the charge that they are purveyors of the meaningless should make a serious effort to be understood. Blanshard does not argue for the preoccupation with style that produces literary flourish at the price of "sterility of thought," but for the cultivation of style that makes the communication of ideas both possible and effective.

In his delightful essay *On Philosophical Style,* a piece which deserves wide reading, he has analyzed the literary problems peculiar to philosophy, considering both the nature of the subject and the legitimate expectations of readers as well as the temperament appropriate to philosophers. There is no justification, he insists, for the barbarisms which some philosophical writers inflict upon their victimized readers—outlandish terminology, interminable and hopelessly involved sentences, abstruse declamations, and argument unsupported by concrete example—all done without the grace of either plain sense or the rhythm which any respectable literature should display. These qualities not only characterize great writing; they are exhibited even in the talk of peasants. "The problem of style," says Blanshard, "is not a problem of words and sentences merely, but of being the right kind of mind." (*Style,* 69).

How the philosopher, whose vocation is a concern for the truth of fundamental concepts and whose very character must be judged by his objectivity, is to steer a course free from prejudice and passion and yet express fully his humanness, his commitment to truth, and his enthusiasm for the importance of his own ideas is here the burden of Blanshard's interest. The objectivity of authentic philosophy, unlike that of science, cannot be cultivated in an atmosphere free from the forces which stir men's souls, for philosophy engages ideas that embody the hopes and fears of mankind.

Blanshard supports his insistence that philosophy can be written with meaning and grace by a roster of those who have been successful: Plato, Locke, Berkeley, Bradley, James, and Russell, to mention only a few. Berkeley, especially, proved that philosophy can be written clearly, simply, and gracefully. But against these there stands a formidable array of those who wrote badly, sometimes so badly that understanding even by their peers is almost out of the question: Kant, Hegel, T. H. Green, Dewey, and Heidegger.

To the first list I would add the name of Blanshard himself. Few philosophers approach him in clarity of explanation and felicity of expression. He is an admirable example of a writer who, to mention his own canons, cultivates style without sacrificing substance, and expounds concretely by example without losing the strength of his abstractions; whose words and sentences have a rhythm which not only brings artistry to his work but contributes to his unusual capacity to communicate and be understood. More than that, his writing abounds with subtle and sophisticated humor that often makes the reading a pure delight. For example: "There are philosophers, or pseudo-philosophers, to understand whom would be a reflection on the reader's own wit" (*Style,* 28). The only criticism I would offer of his treatise on style is that here he failed to treat adequately, except by his own example, the quality of humor that would appear to be an essential ingredient of style and that is such an obvious factor in the enrichment of his own writing.

Perhaps I should conclude these comments by asserting again my sincere admiration for Brand Blanshard's work and my enthusiastic agreement with his determination to preserve the substantive content of philosophy and his concern for the decline of reasonableness and the rise of irrationalism. That he has built on foundations laid especially by the German idealists of the last century and their British successors is obvious and is frequently acknowledged by him. But though his philosophy is constructed on ground cleared or partially cleared by others, he has enjoyed the use of more sophisticated tools and been confronted by more formidable critics, and has as a consequence brought rationalism and idealism to a more refined and more acceptable state. I believe, moreover, that his pen has been and is a powerful influence in the crusade to stem the tide of irrationalism and destroy the "cult of unintelligibility." I cannot accept his technical rationalism with its coherence concept of truth, for I think it fails to do justice to the experiential bases of knowledge. And I cannot accept his real world of the absolute interconnectedness of all things and all events, for I think in its necessitarian character it fails to provide for the world's contingencies and freedoms. But I must say that I wish Blanshard could clearly and finally prove his position, for then we could look for certainties in place of our probabilities and perhaps could find meanings in a world that appears so meaningless.

Blanshard is not the first to come to the defense of philosophy; even Plato found it necessary to mount an attack against its detractors. Nor will he be the last. But certainly he must be counted among the most thoughtful, most eloquent, and most courageous. The closing passage of *The Nature of Thought* (1939) is a fitting expression of his faith in the eventual victory of the life of reason, written in a moment of sadness in the knowledge of reason's decline and threatened defeat.

We conclude this book at a time when the recognition of [a common standard of judgment and obligation], set by a common intelligence, and adequate as a court of appeal to the settlement of even national differences, is receding into the distance. The philosopher's way of protesting is perhaps too qualified and muffled to be heard; certainly it is when the drift toward chaos once gains momentum. But the writer would like to think that the insistent and reiterated emphasis, maintained throughout this work, on the membership of minds in one intelligible order may serve, however minutely, to confirm the belief in a common reason, and the hope and faith that in the end it will prevail. [*NT*, 2:520]

His Riecker Lecture of 1962 closes with a courageous prophecy that indeed enjoys some support from the recent resurgence of metaphysics.

The main tradition in philosophy is one that runs down from Plato through Hegel to Whitehead, a tradition that has stood for system and sweep of vision—and it will come back. The main tradition in ethics is one that has run from Aristotle through Spinoza to Butler and Green and Bradley; it too will come back. There is a great tradition in criticism that has run from Longinus through Goethe to Arnold and, at his best, Eliot; surely that will revive. These traditions are not really dead; they are only sleeping. This shrill shout of mine is an attempt to wake them up. [*On Sanity*, 23]

STERLING M. MCMURRIN

DEPARTMENT OF PHILOSOPHY
THE GRADUATE SCHOOL
UNIVERSITY OF UTAH

NOTES

[1]Rudolf Carnap, *Introduction to Semantics* (Cambridge: Harvard University Press, 1942), 246.
[2]Stephen C. Pepper, "The Search for Comprehension, or World Hypotheses," in *The Nature of Philosophical Inquiry*, ed. Joseph Bobik (Notre Dame, Ind.: Notre Dame University Press, 1970).
[3]"Current Issues in Education," *The Monist* 52, no. 1 (January 1968): 26.
[4]"Can the Philosopher Influence Social Change?" *Journal of Philosophy* 51, no. 24 (November 25, 1954): 743.
[5]*On Sanity in Thought and Art* (Tucson: University of Arizona Press, 1962).
[6]From an unpublished paper, "Kierkegaard on Religious Knowledge," presented to the Personalist Discussion Group at the meeting of the American Philosophical Association, Boston, December 1966.
[7]"Can the Philosopher Influence Social Change?" 746.
[8]Ibid., 751.

INTRODUCTION TO THE REPLIES
BY
BRAND BLANSHARD

M ANY, indeed most, of my critics do not confine themselves to any one aspect of my philosophy, and with such an array of sharpshooters aiming at so limited a target, I expected to be perforated pretty frequently in the same spot; there was bound, I thought, to be much repetition. So I proposed at first to order my reply by reference to topics and arguments, which would enable me to deal with several critics at once. This proved impracticable. The critics took lines of their own, and there was much less repetition than I expected. It seemed impossible to do justice to such various and individual writers without a separate reply to each.

May I add at once that the comparative length of my replies is not to be taken as any indication whatever of the relative merit I attach to the papers. Some writers have contented themselves for the most part with restating my theories from their own point of view; some have concentrated on a single small area of my work; some have challenged me at dozens of points in ways that I could not ignore. Probably none of my critics will feel that he has been done full justice, and no doubt he will be right. Whether a critic agrees with me or not, whether or not in the light of his criticism I have had to change my view—and occasionally I have been left no alternative—I am deeply grateful to those who have taken many hours from their own work to give to mine. What a philosopher wants is not necessarily to be agreed with; he knows that this is at best an only partly attainable goal; what he wants is that his thought should be seriously reckoned with by his peers. All my critics have done me this honor; and considering that they must have been nearly as astonished as I was to find myself in this gallery at all, I am the more grateful for the pains they have taken, even in wielding their scalpels at my expense. I am the wiser for each of their examinations, and my system, if it can be called such, is certainly more worth taking seriously because they have forced me to rethink it at so many points.

1. REPLY TO STERLING M. MCMURRIN

Blanshard's Conception of the Nature and Function of Philosophy

Mr. McMurrin has written an essay on the nature and function of philosophy as I conceive them. He describes me as "a defender of the great tradition that philosophy is the attempt of reason upon the world." That I am. I am regarded, I think, as a traditionalist in philosophy, and this is probably true in at least three senses. First, there can be very little in what I have said that has not been said before. Secondly, I am out of step with most forms of current philosophy. When one eminent contemporary writes that philosophy is the logical syntax of language, or another that it is the clarification of the language of science, I can only say that this is very remote from what I seem to be doing when I philosophize. Philosophy seems to me something far more massive, engrossing, and significant than this. Thirdly, my general aim in philosophizing has been that of many minds in the past. Unless I have misread them, I stand in the tradition of Plato, Descartes, Spinoza, Green, and Bradley. Just as there are philosophers whose way of thinking is especially congenial to me, so there are others from whom I recognize a deep divergence of end and method—most members, for example, of the existentialist and pragmatic schools. In the pages that follow I shall confine myself for the most part to meeting Mr. McMurrin's main question and trying to make clearer my conception of what the business of philosophy is.

Philosophy, broadly conceived, is a persistent raising of the question Why? It may be objected that this is a description that does not define, that the same is done in many other disciplines also—in the formal and natural sciences, in religion, indeed in the making of countless everyday decisions. Philosophy so conceived would infiltrate every department of life. Well, so it does, and so it should. Philosophy is not a special subject like geology or history; it is rather a special kind of activity. Taken at its loftiest, it is the attempt to understand the world. But the world is inexhaustible in its extent and its variety, and the work of understanding can proceed only by the solution of numberless more specific problems that lie along the way. Philosophy, as I conceive of it, is a continual effort, made by individual minds but sustained by a congenital and racial drive, to render its world intelligible.

A Racial Drive

Philosophy, then, is both an individual and a racial drive. Where is the evidence for such a drive? In the first instance in the mere awareness of what we are about when we are thinking. Thinking is done in many interests. One may think with one's head under the hood of one's car in the attempt to get it running again; one may think to checkmate an opponent in chess, to pass an examination, to find one's correct income tax, to reach New York by five o'clock. The pragmatist is thus quite right that thinking is an instrument employed for many ends. But in all these cases, however practical is the interest that drives our thinking, we can distinguish this practical interest from another which, however weak, is definitely there, and sharply distinct. In trying to do something, we are also trying to learn something. We want to know what is amiss with our motor; we want to know what our situation would be if our opponent moved his knight; to answer our examination question we must know the value of pi; to complete our income tax we must know what "depreciation" means; to reach Grand Central by five o'clock we must know something about the schedules of train, bus, and plane. To know the facts is one thing; to use this knowledge in the service of a practical end is quite another. And when I speak of a theoretical or cognitive drive, I am speaking of the interest in knowing as distinct from the thousand other interests and purposes with which that knowledge is bound up and which it serves. Impulses are to be distinguished by their ends, and the immediate end of the cognitive impulse is knowledge. It is never practice. The knowledge that by moving his knight your opponent could at the next move capture your queen's bishop is important to your strategy; but that itself is not a knowledge of anything practical; it would remain true in precisely the same sense, whatever use it may be put to. Knowing is not acting, though it may be essential to acting successfully. We could analyze the other cases in the same way.

This interest in knowing shows itself almost from the start of our conscious life. The foundation of all later knowledge lies in the primitive grasp of identity and difference. To identify the warm milk bottle as something distinct from the red ball is to take a tentative step toward knowledge of the world. Knowledge always involves relations, for its immediate object is truth, and the simplest truth involves the relation of two components expressed as *that* S is P. When the field of consciousness, natively a mere blur, begins to break up into things and qualities, they prove to be related to each other in many patterns—some of them categorical like space and time, some of them matters of association like that of the candle and the burn or the bottle and the milk. The ways in which the commonsense world of perceptual objects emerges from the aboriginal mist have been discussed in the early chapters of *The Nature of Thought.*

No one would call common sense a branch or a stage of philosophy if he were thinking of philosophy as an academic subject. Nevertheless the commonsense world in which the plain man lives is a construction that rests on philosophical insights. Every perception is an implicit inference (*Nature of Thought,* chap. 2), and every color or shape that is seen is in a sense a question propounded to the interpreting mind. Not of course that the datum is an explicit question or its interpretation an explicit answer. But when the child takes one shape before him as a bottle, another as a ball, and still another as a cat, he is in effect meeting a series of challenges with a series of intellectual constructions; it was in this sense that John Stuart Mill said that the drawing of inferences was the main business of life. Within a few years the child is living in a world of trees and houses, mountains and clouds, men and women, all of them known through perceptual inference.

Furthermore, there are no islands in his world. The things and persons that tenant it are related by space, time, causation, degree, means-end, and many other relations. Not all these relations contribute equally to his understanding of the world. That the chair is to the left of the table and that one lamp goes on before another seem to be mere matters of fact, the grasp of which explains nothing. This is not strictly true. To grasp anything in its context contributes to understanding its place in the whole of things. But it must be agreed that some relations are more helpful in the work of understanding than others, three of them in particular.

These three are causality, means-end, and entailment, each of which dominates a large field of its own. In the natural sciences, causation dominates. To understand the rainbow, or the smallpox, or a nuclear explosion, one must grasp the causal law connecting the event with its antecedents. In explaining human behavior, the most useful relation is that of means and end. Why did Smith withdraw his balance at the bank, or Jones snub his friend in the street, or Robinson decide to move to Sacramento? We say that we understand these actions when we learn the purposes with which these men behaved as they did. Again, in the formal sciences of logic and mathematics, understanding means as a rule the grasp of entailment. If you ask why the diagonal of a square should divide it into equal parts, or why in a hypothetical syllogism you can reason validly from affirming the antecedent but not the consequent, the answer would consist in a demonstration from accepted premises.

Philosophy an Activity, Not a Subject

We can now see why philosophy is not a subject like physics which marks off a certain area of the world—matter in motion—or astronomy which marks off another—the relations of celestial bodies—and studies the laws that govern it. It is true that these sciences are permeated by philosophy, for they contain a great deal of reflective thought directed to the special end of understanding; that is what philosophizing means, and Newton rightly thought of himself as a "natural philosopher." Such an interest may penetrate and dominate any field of study; someone has said that philosophy is the study of everything else philosophically. This does not, of course, *reduce* the other disciplines to philosophy. Much of botany and biology consists of classification; much history is a narration of events in temporal order; and much psychology is a description of mental processes or even of the physical responses of rats and pigeons. But biology in the hands of Darwin became a gushing well of philosophy; Gibbon, though not on the whole perhaps a philosophical historian, certainly became one when in his fifteenth chapter he undertook to explain the expansion of Christianity; and Freud's explanation of religion is so charged with philosophy that the line between his psychology and his philosophy is beyond drawing.

The proposals, then, so commonly made in philosophy textbooks to mark off the respective areas of philosophy, the sciences, and the humanities are bound, I think, to fail. Indeed, I am not sure that the ideal university would have any department of philosophy at all, not because philosophy would be unrepresented in it but because philosophy would so permeate all its disciplines that a special department would hardly be needed. Press the question Why? as you work in any physics laboratory, and you are bound to ask how the things we see are related to the "wheeling systems" of the atomic realm. Press the same question in anthropology and you are bound to ask whether there are any moral standards by which Greek or Christian civilization can be ranked above that of Borneo. Press it in a study of *Hamlet* and you soon find yourself asking what are the conditions that would most fully satisfy our aesthetic demands. These are philosophic questions. Every study so far as it is an attempt to understand is philosophy. Or, to put it otherwise, the drive to know, to understand, to explain or render things intelligible is a trunk with many branches running out through all the arts and all the sciences. It does not exhaust them, for there is much in all of them that contributes little to its special interest. But that interest should be felt everywhere.

Critical and Speculative Philosophy

The advance of intelligence from perception to the level of organized common sense, from there to science, and from there again to philosophy is one unbroken movement. Why then has philosophy been separated from the sciences and given a province of its own? Chiefly, I answer, as a matter of convenience. Broad's gift for lucid classifying has lent currency to another view. He divides philosophy into two kinds, critical and speculative. Critical philosophy again has two functions. First, it takes the key words of science and defines them with precision. Scientists feel no especial fuzziness when they speak of a place or a date, or a substance, or a cause, or a motion. They find that they can get on with the ordinary meaning of these terms, which commonly raise no question; and if ultimate exactitude is not necessary for their immediate purpose, it seems good policy to let sleeping dogs lie. But of course all these terms are notoriously troublesome when one tries to assign them exact meanings, and the scientist is only too happy to let the philosopher do the worrying about them.

Similarly, there are assumptions generally made by scientists and laymen alike, for example, that all events have causes, that the same kinds of causes produce the same kinds of effects, that we can gain through perception a reliable knowledge of nature. By accepting these propositions as true, a scientist can move to what interests him, the particular inquiry in hand, whereas if he were to delay over them till he had grounded them beyond doubt, he might be halted indefinitely. So he hands these over also, with a feeling of good riddance, to the philosopher. But of course both the meaning of his central terms and the truth of his major assumptions lie directly in his path, for he must have some answer to these questions if he is to reach full clarity and certainty even in his special inquiries. Critical philosophy is not therefore a discipline distinct from science; it is a part of science in the sense of a natural continuation or development of it. But since it is a matter of pure theory, to which observation and experiment are mostly irrelevant, the working scientist turns it over to those with a taste for such pure theory.

Speculative philosophy has a more obvious claim to being a separate province than critical philosophy. For speculative philosophy is an attempt to review the different kinds of human experience and the conclusions of the various sciences and to correlate the results into a consistent whole. No one science, of course, is qualified to do this, and it is natural enough that the work of synthesis should be turned over to a group of minds with a marked breadth of interest and knowledge. But the attempt at synthesis is not dependent on such a group. It would be attempted by individual scientists in any case, for a scientist is normally a man and not a mole. He cannot carry on his work without occasionally looking over the fence into other fields, and noting that in places the fences are down. The study of volition and sensation belongs to psychology, but who could study either without taking into account the apparent interaction of bodily and conscious states, and then he is facing the metaphysical problem of matter and mind. If he is a behaviorist, he finds that he must acknowledge the facts of consciousness or become ridiculous. Anyone who thinks about human conduct and its struggles after the ideal is bound at some point to raise the question whether the nature that produced him is indifferent to these values, and then he is in metaphysics again, struggling with theism and thinking the thoughts of Job after him. A man as a scientist can and must specialize. But a scientist remains a man, and every department he works in somewhere impinges on every other. And if to understand is to place things in a context that makes them intelligible, then for the man of strong theoretic impulse his own area of study becomes only one of the "colored counties" that make the map of the world, and he will see it as part of a single country of the mind that stretches on every side to the horizon.

The Career of Knowledge

This upward thrust of the impulse to know has so far been described only as it occurs in the individual mind. But it is as old as the history of the race, and indeed much older. It is at work in the instinctive curiosity shown at many levels in the mind of the animal. Apes are brimming with curiosity about the insects on each other's backs, the ticking of watches, and the reflections in mirrors, and when stimulated by the desire for food, can fit rods together and build towers of boxes in a way that obviously calls for some modest powers of reasoning. Instinctive curiosity goes much further down in the animal mind, though as the argument from analogy grows feebler it is harder to be sure of its presence. Biologists have been confronted with fascinating problems by the behavior of von Frisch's bees, which not only showed the familiar discrimination between types of pollen but were able to communicate to their fellows the direction and distance of desirable gardens by means of appropriate dances. It is not easy to interpret such communication without attributing to the bees a grasp of directions and distances which at this level seems incredible.

What emerges from this sketch is that philosophy, far from being the foible of this or that eccentric web-spinner, is the product of a deeply rooted social urge. The career of knowledge began millions of years ago with the first act of discrimination of this from that. As perception improved, both the this and the that became complex things, whose presented characters were merely a core surrounded by a mass of characters that clung to it from past association, that mass of half-conscious expectations which psychologists used to call an apperception mass. Thus the commonsense world of things came into being. And as thought slowly liberated itself from its ties to the sensibly given, and achieved more freedom in directing its attention, the characters and relations of things were abstracted and made the object of explicit thought. Thus science was born. It cut across the world of things, connecting character with character. The law of gravitation, for example, though it applies to particular things, connects them through the abstractions of mass and distance. Some of these connections such as means-end, causation, and entailment were seen to be especially illuminating in their explanatory power, showing that the linked objects were not isolated monads but parts of an extended webwork of necessity. This process of understanding through contexts is advancing at an accelerating speed.

We have described it as an intellectual drive. It is actually much more. Impulse and feeling, desire and will, have objects, and, as intelligence grows, these objects are transformed. In *Reason and Goodness* I have tried to show how thought operates within desire, so that an ambition directed at first at selfish and sensual goods is redirected to intrinsically greater goods more justly distributed. In *Reason and Belief* I have tried to show how religious impulse and feeling first created their objects of fear and worship, developed these by a theology which was diverted from its rational course by the idea of a superrational revelation, and are slowly freeing themselves from mythology into a religion and a morality that are rationally guided. Indeed philosophy, considered in perspective as the thrust of intelligence to understand its world, is the chief transforming power of human nature and its history.

This is likely to be confirmed in ways now beyond anticipation as history advances. Take the exploration, at once scientific and philosophical, of the relation between body and mind. Decade by decade, in the work of Sherrington, Penfield, Adrian, the geneticists, and others, the physical conditions governing memory, intelligence, and sanity generally have been brought more clearly to light. It must still be admitted, as it was with all frankness by Sherrington, that on the central question of *how* brain tissue gives rise, if indeed it does, to consciousness or the converse question *how* consciousness affects currents in neural fibers, as it seems to do, we are as much in the dark as ever. But much progress has been made in pinpointing the cerebral changes that are correlated with specific changes in consciousness. It is difficult to set any limit to the improvements in human nature that knowledge of this kind may make possible. If we know that certain kinds of intelligence, for example, depend on the permeability of the synapses in a certain portion of the brain, and that this in turn depends on certain electrochemical resistance to the passage across them of nerve currents, it is quite conceivable that by controlling this resistance intelligence could be enlarged. Added length of life has already been achieved, and as the science of gerontology advances there is no reason why the process of aging should not be retarded and perhaps halted. As religious and other objections to the control of the quality and quantity of future humanity are laid to rest, the increasing knowledge of genes and their connection with the qualities and defects of human nature should raise the level of health, ability, and character. Even if man's mind is more completely dependent on his body than he likes to think, a full knowledge of that body would give him a power now undreamed of to remould this mind itself. Unfortunately his powers of destruction are growing even faster than his self-knowledge or self-control, and there is some ground for Einstein's remark that if the third world war is fought with nuclear weapons the fourth will be fought with bows and arrows.

If I have said a good deal on the nature and function of philosophy, it is because Mr. McMurrin devoted a long paper to it, wondered if he had caught correctly the drift of my own account, and thought that the relation of philosophy to science in that account was in need of clarification. He has caught my meaning very well, and what I have been saying is not a correction of his report of it but rather an attempt to put it in wider perspective. My thought on the nature of philosophy does not stand alone but is part of a larger theory that involves incursions or raids into psychology and biology.

Rationalism

Mr. McMurrin puts to me some definite questions. Would a rationalist, as extreme as he rightly takes me to be, recognize an existentialist as a philosopher at all? Yes, I answer, so far as the existentialist attempts a reflective support of his case; and in spite of his suspicions of reason he commonly does. Kierkegaard, for example, argued elaborately that Hegel's rationalism, the chief alternative to his view, moved entirely in a world of concepts which nowhere touched the existent, and that liberal theology was only an attempt, as impious as it was futile, to capture Deity in a rickety crate of logic. So far as Kierkegaard attempts to make out his case by argument, however unconvincingly, he is a philosopher. But when he claims an immediate ineffable contact with an existent which is neither describable nor assertible with enough definiteness to be rationally defended, he seems to me a mystic rather than a philosopher; and when, as in the Abraham and Isaac case, he assigns to Deity an ethic and a logic in flat contradiction with our own, he seems to have become a prophet, and a somewhat mad one. A philosopher is, for me, a person who is at least trying to think rationally. Minds equally devoted to reason may disagree profoundly, for being reasonable is one of the hardest things in the world. But so far as a man renounces reason as his means of knowing and depends for his insight on intuition, or mystic vision, or revelation from beyond nature, he may be rising to very exalted levels but he is not engaged in what I call philosophy.

Mr. McMurrin wonders what precisely I mean by "reason." It is a large and difficult question, and I have been criticized for using the term too narrowly. Mr. Warnock in his article on "Reason" in the *Encyclopedia of Philosophy* quotes my definition, "the faculty and function of grasping necessary connections," and points out that this seems "excessively restrictive." So it is. But Mr. Warnock also shows that the term has varying senses any one of which may be appropriate when used in a special context. To this kind of variation in use I plead guilty. The definition quoted above is from *Reason and Analysis,* where it was appropriate to the issue between rationalist and empiricist which I was discussing. But when I came to the issue between rationalism and religion in *Reason and Belief,* I saw that it would be absurd to cling to this definition, since it is not reason in this sense with which revealed religion has been chiefly in conflict. The "reason" that revelationists, both Catholic and Protestant, have been attacking as inadequate in religion is not reason in this narrow sense but man's natural powers of cognition generally; and to meet their charge I redefined the term in this sense.

Again in *Reason and Goodness* I take the view that reason is involved both in inferring the consequences of a given decision and in weighing the intrinsic values involved against each other. But the inference is causal, not demonstrative; and the insight that knowledge is better than ignorance is also not demonstrative, though it does seem to me necessary. Thus the meaning I attach to "reason" does vary, as I think it must if the live issues in these different fields are to be fairly faced. I tried to make plain in what sense I was using the term in these different contexts, though I may well have failed to make it plain enough.

Mr. McMurrin raises other questions which I hope to return to. In particular he gently chides me for my attitude toward pragmatism, whose theory of the judgment he thinks I have rejected too uncompromisingly. Since another essay has been devoted specially to my critique of pragmatism, it seems better to reserve comment till I come to this essay. In view of Mr. McMurrin's sharp difference with me at this point, I find it very reassuring that he has found so much to agree with both in the substance and the spirit of what I have to say.

II ETHICS

2 BLANSHARD'S VIEW OF GOOD
Alfred C. Ewing

T HE article will naturally be concerned mainly with Blanshard's *Reason and Goodness (RG)*. In the preface he says that this book, like his *Reason and Analysis* and his then unpublished *Reason and Belief,* is "concerned with the vindication of reason against recent philosophical attacks," and I myself think that his chief service in philosophy consists in having provided an excellent defence of a moderate rationalism against an extreme empiricism at a time when the whole tendency of thought is in the opposite direction, at least in the English-speaking world. In the field of ethics, as elsewhere, however, "a rationalist theory" may mean different things. (1) It may mean a theory which seeks to base ethics on formal proofs. Blanshard is certainly not a rationalist in this sense. (2) It may mean what is now commonly called a cognitive account of ethics, provided the account allows a place to a priori reasoning while claiming objective validity for it. In this sense Blanshard is a rationalist, although, as we shall see, he goes very far, I think too far, in his concessions to empirical naturalism and does not leave it clear to my mind just where the a priori elements come. But I am very glad to say that he has no mercy for the theories which maintain that no ethical pronouncement has any more claim to be *objectively* true than any other.

(3) It may mean a theory which in determining particular duties emphasizes reason rather than feeling. In this sense Blanshard may be described as a rationalist on the whole, though he insists on the importance and indeed necessity of feeling. At least he is in this respect a rationalist insofar as any reasonable philosopher can be, while criticizing those who, like Saint Francis and defenders of "situation-ethics" today, make love the sole criterion of what is right. Reason is needed both to determine what is really best for the person loved and to secure justice, it being impossible to love all men impartially, unless indeed we secure a verbal victory for the advocates of love by defining it in such a way that, unless it leads to right action, we do not call it "true love." At the same time Blanshard insists that, if we relied solely

on reason and left no place for feeling, we should have left no value in life. Feeling is needed to supply the content of value judgments and some motive to do right. I do not wish to challenge him here, nor in regard to his admirable and moving picture of what a fully rational man would be like (*RG*, chap. 15). To ignore feeling would of course not be at all rational.

Nor do I intend to dwell on Blanshard's criticisms of those theories which deny the objectivity of ethics. The only important criticism I have to make of him here is the negative one that he does not deal with a middle-of-the-way theory which maintains that what we call moral judgments are really non-cognitive in character, but yet admits that there is among them an objective distinction between right and wrong in a sense which cannot be reduced merely to a difference in the actual attitudes of people. Such a view is one toward which many philosophers, originally influenced more by the arguments for an emotive view, are tending, though I do not think it can be consistently maintained without admitting at some point a cognitive claim, even if moral judgments are primarily practical and not cognitive.[1] With Blanshard's criticisms of thoroughgoing subjectivism, emotivism, and imperativism I am very much in sympathy and certainly do not wish to oppose him here, whether I should want to state all the objections precisely in his way or not.

Where I shall join issue with him is over his definition of good. While rejecting subjectivism unequivocally, he does not maintain the same hostile attitude to naturalism, but himself adopts a view which he calls naturalistic, though whether it is appropriately called so might still be considered a matter for question. He prefaces the statement of his own views by a criticism of three other views, Moore's, Perry's and my own (chap. 10). I agree with his criticisms of the first two, but must say something in defence of my own type of view. It should be noted that Blanshard's criticisms are directed against the form of my view expressed in *The Definition of Good*.[2] The amended view which I put forward in *Second Thoughts in Moral Philosophy* came out too late for him to consider it in writing his own book. But both my books have in common the adoption of an indefinable ought as the primary concept in ethics in place of an indefinable good and the definition of good as what ought to be the object of a proattitude. (The situation was complicated by the facts that there plainly are at least two different senses of "ought" involved, a strictly moral and a nonmoral; and, in *The Definition of Good,* I made the nonmoral one the most fundamental concept under the term "fitting."[3] I came later to think this term misleading, and in *Second Thoughts* put forward a view which made the moral sense of "ought" central. I do not wish to discuss the difference between my two views here, since it is not covered by Blanshard's argument.) The chief motive for my rejection of the view of good as an indefinable quality was my inability to form any idea of this alleged indefinable quality, a motive which was also decisive with Blanshard. It then occurred to me that, if we defined good as what ought to be the object of a proattitude, this would cover all the senses of good relevant to ethics and value theory, subsidiary senses being distinguished by differences in the proattitude involved as well as by the distinction between the two senses of ought. I made "ought" and not "good" the fundamental term in the definition, because it seemed to me that I had a clear idea of what was meant by ought as distinct from any factual concept, but no idea of anything in the concept of good which could not be reduced to this definition.

Blanshard's chief objection to my view is that, if we ought to favour an object, this can only be because the object is good, thus involving me in a vicious circle (*RG*, 284). To this objection I had already replied by saying that the ground why we ought to adopt a proattitude toward something lay in its concrete factual characteristics; but this seemed to Blanshard to be going back on my objections to naturalism. I should, however, insist on a distinction here. To say that certain natural characteristics provide the reason why something is (ought to be) favoured is very different from saying that its goodness is just its possession of these qualities. I accept the former type of view but reject the latter. To take Blanshard's own definition, I do not see any objection to saying that characteristics such as satisfying and fulfilling should provide a ground for holding something to be good; but it does not seem that to say that it is good is the same as to say that it has these qualities. It is true that this distinction should, as Blanshard says,[4] have debarred me from bringing forward as a general objection to naturalism that it provides no ground for obligation, as I did in *The Definition of Good*. Here I shall quote from my *Second Thoughts in Moral Philosophy*:

> The mistake of naturalism as such is not that it supposes normative propositions to follow from factual but that it reduces normative propositions to factual. I certainly held and still hold it one objection among others against most naturalist definitions of good that the particular property to which they claim to reduce good is not one that could possibly constitute an adequate reason or at least not the sole reason why we ought to do something. For instance, we cannot say that the reason why we morally ought to do things is that most people approve of them. But this is not an objection to all naturalist theories, at least not to one which defines "good" by giving a list of the properties which can make something intrinsically good. There remains however the objection that we cannot identify a normative proposition with any list of factual ones. [*Second Thoughts*, 99]

Blanshard's theory obviously is one of the theories to which these words apply, at least insofar as it can rightly be called "naturalist," but more of that later. I think that at any rate I can escape the charge of a vicious circle.

The tendency one has to think Blanshard's criticism cogent may be explained as follows. The definition of good as what ought to be the object of a proattitude is elastic in the sense that it covers a number of different subordinate meanings according to the meaning of ought and the particular proattitude in question. Now the applicability of some of these may depend on the applicability of another, and I do think that something can be such that it ought to be (in the moral sense of "ought") an object of the proattitude of seeking to pursue it for its own sake only if it ought to be (in the nonmoral sense of "ought," which I now hold is the sense in which it reduces to what is reasonable) an object of the proattitude of welcoming for its own sake on the part of the person who experienced it. It would not be one's duty to seek to produce for its own sake a state of mind or experience for others, or even reasonable to pursue it for oneself, if it were not an experience or state which it would be reasonable to welcome for its own sake if attained. So, even on my own view, I am already presupposing that something is good in one sense if I say that I ought to pursue it. It cannot be intrinsically good in the sense in which the intrinsic goodness or otherwise of something is most commonly discussed by philosophers without also being intrinsically good in another sense generically similar but specifically different.

Blanshard also makes it an objection to my view that one could pronounce the death of a child from starvation in China and the similar death of one's own child as equally evil without committing oneself to the view that one ought to or that it would be fitting to feel as much distress about one as about the other. My answer is that in *The Definition of Good* I erred insofar as I gave my account mainly in terms of feeling.[5] One can pronounce the starvation of one's own child and a Chinese child as equally bad in the sense that, other things being equal, equal efforts ought to be made to prevent them, though of course the fact that the child is one's own makes other things not equal. There is no reason to conclude that one ought to be equally miserable about them.

Blanshard regards his own definition of ethical terms as naturalistic, but not quite in the usual sense of the term, as we shall see later. And he thinks his definition is not exposed to the stock objection against naturalism derived from Moore, to the effect that we can agree that something conforms to any proposed naturalistic definition and yet meaningfully doubt whether it is good. For "take any experience you wish that at once fulfills a drive of human nature and brings pleasure or happiness with it, ask about this experience whether it is intrinsically worth having, and we suggest that you have the answer already" (*RG*, 320). But it seems to me that the proposition that such an experience is good is clearly synthetic. Many philosophers have disagreed with such a view in that they quite consciously and deliberately maintained that all that mattered was the quantity of pleasure (satisfaction), thus ruling out altogether the notion that fulfillment was a relevant additional qualification. Pleasure has more generally been deemed an intrinsic good, but we have not to go so far as ascetics to find this denied. Ross came to the conclusion that pleasure was not intrinsically good except in the sense of being an actual object of desire, which is very different from any sense in which he elsewhere used the term "intrinsically good." That what satisfies and fulfills is good seems to me rather an illuminating generalization from what we find good in particular instances than a proposition directly self-evident, still less analytic in character. Further, there seems to me good ground for denying its unrestricted truth, even if, as is the case with me, one disagrees with both Ross and the pure hedonists. For it seems to me that by no means all experiences which satisfy and fulfill are intrinsically good, as Blanshard's view would commit one to maintain. Suppose a man thinks himself wronged by somebody else and inflicts a malicious injury on him just because he wants to give him pain. There is no doubt that a great number have got some degree of satisfaction in that way, even if, as the moralists remind us, it was not as great or lasting as the man expected beforehand and had unwelcome consequences for himself in the long run. It was also the fulfillment of a drive which, as history and psychology show, is fairly fundamental in human nature, though with highly civilized people rarely shown in its cruder forms, the desire for revenge. Should it not then be intrinsically good on Blanshard's definition of good? It is not merely that its consequences are bad. This can be brought out by considering the case of a witch who falsely believed that to roast a waxen image of her enemy in front of a slow fire would cause him great pain, and carried on the process of roasting. In this case the action would cause no suffering to the person against whom it was directed, at least unless he knew about it. Yet, it would still be a great evil that anybody should be in such a state of mind as the witch; and the more she enjoyed it the greater the evil. It would be a great evil even if she died the next minute and there was no time for her state of mind then to have evil effects in the future on her character. Again, very many people have held that it was intrinsically evil to indulge in certain kinds of sexual behaviour, though there was no doubt that for certain people this behaviour gave satisfaction and fulfilled, at least partially, a basic drive, the sex instinct. I do not myself see any contradiction in taking this view.

I therefore do not think that Blanshard's definition escapes the best-known argument against naturalism. There is indeed the possibility which Blanshard suggests that a reader who doubts whether the qualities which he specifies do and do alone make something good is suffering from a confusion, so that he is not clear what he does really mean by "good."

> It may show simply that his meaning is so indefinite that any crystallization of it into words would strike him as failing to equate with what he had in mind. If this is the case, his rejection of our proposed meaning has no significance, for he would reject any other definite suggestion with equal promptitude. A definition of good is not to be dismissed merely because it fails to comport with a mental cloud. [RG, 320]

I certainly should not claim to be free of the philosophical vice of confusion, but I am confident that I am not suffering from it to such an extent, and I do not think Blanshard would accuse me of so great a degree of confusion as that. It certainly seems to me that I have in mind a clear definition of good and that I mean by good something which cannot be equated with any list of factual properties. I want to be able to express myself on the question whether what satisfies and fulfills is good without asserting either a tautology or a formal contradiction, and I cannot do so in the language which Blanshard provides. What he does is to abandon in despair the attempt at a definition of good in the sense in which "definition" has usually been understood and fall back on saying what classes of things are good.

> Indeed there is something absurd in the notion that the most tortured problems of speculation can be cleared up by catching the meaning with which plain men use common words. The fact is that plain men use these words as one would expect them to—effectively enough for their purposes, but most loosely and uncritically for the philosopher's purpose; and the more fundamental the term, the more vaguely they use it.
>
> The words "hammer," "nail," "cup" and "saucer" they use with some exactness. The words "life," "feeling," "thought" and "good" they use with such a wealth of woolly meanings that the attempt to extract any precise and common significance is misguided effort. [RG, 290–91]

This may be expressed by saying that he has given up the attempt to find a definition of the intention of "good" and so substituted a definition in terms of the extension. To confuse the two is a fallacy already pointed out by Plato, but I do not think that with Blanshard it is a case of confusion. It is rather a case of a reasoned change of approach. He has however left a question unanswered, namely what account can be given of the intensional meaning, and it seems to me a much more vital question than he thinks. For if there is not something in common between the intensional senses in which different people use "good," how can they discuss with any profit what things are good? It should be noted that, when the question of what things are good is raised in the sense in which he discusses it, "good" means "intrinsically good"; this is already a philosophical rather than a commonsense term, and as such, unless it stands for a simple discernible quality or relation, it should be capable of definition. I should also claim, though of course Blanshard would not agree with this, that I have shown it capable *ambulando* by giving a definition "such as ought to be the object of a proattitude," which covered all important senses of good and by adding the words "for its own sake" could be narrowed down to cover the sense I have just mentioned, "intrinsically good."

Let us now consider Blanshard's view as to what is intrinsically good not as a definition of goodness but as an answer to the question what kinds of things are good or what qualities make them good. His answer is that what are good are experiences which fulfill and satisfy. Whether there is anything intrinsically good which does not come under this heading might well be doubted, but the terms require further explanation, as does "fulfillment." This concept is used by Blanshard as a qualification to exclude the view that all satisfactions (or pleasures) equal in amount are equal in value (intrinsically). It involves the notion that parts of our nature are higher, more worthy of fulfillment than others. The difficulty seems to me to lie in explaining what is meant by fulfillment without already presupposing a value term and so introducing a vicious circle in one's account of the good. Especially for this reason I should like to have found more said about the criteria for deciding which fulfillments were of greater value. There is an obvious and relevant distinction where you find a man delighted with a very silly theory of his and another deriving apparently much less satisfaction from a theory that really advanced our insight greatly, perhaps just because he realized its imperfections and limitations, or where you find an analogous situation in art, or a man thoroughly satisfied that he has led a highly virtuous life because he has done nothing for which he could be sent to prison compared to a really good man who is still much beset by the consciousness of his moral imperfections. It is plain that in all these fields fulfillment may be greater where satisfaction is less. We should be very often prepared to value higher the less pleasant state of mind because in it the capacities of humanity were fulfilled more fully. Here the criteria are imminent in the activity; you will find them discussed in ethics, aesthetics, and epistemology.

It is plain that there is a reasonable sense in which we can say that fulfillment is greater if it is really successful than if it is only thought so by the agent. But when it is a question of comparing two whole fields of activity and deciding that one brings greater fulfillment than another, we need a different statement of criteria. On this turns the well-known distinction between higher and lower kinds of pleasurable activity which was recognized by Mill but, because he was not prepared to drop pure hedonism, expressed in a self-contradictory way. Are the desires, the satisfaction of which brings greater fulfillment, those which are more essential? Not necessarily. There is no desire the fulfillment of which is more essential than that for food and drink. Without its fulfillment, at least in some considerable degree, none of our other desires could be fulfilled, because we should not survive to fulfill them; but this does not make their fulfillment intrinsically more valuable than the fulfillment of the desire to write good books on philosophy, without which fulfillment most people can live very happily. Another criterion appears when Blanshard refers to the Aristotelian view that the good life for us consists in doing what man and man alone can do. Unfortunately, many of the things that man alone can do are by no means particularly good, and a further explanation is required. There is a suggestion that the high value attributed to understanding is connected with the fact that understanding is a necessary condition of the characteristically human life. It is also suggested that a wide understanding of the connection of things fulfills our nature more fully than a knowledge of unconnected facts. Similarly, I might add, a man's nature on the intellectual side is fulfilled more by a study which helps one toward understanding things, at least in the sense of bringing phenomena into a coherent system, than in, say, playing chess, great as may be the opportunities for the display of intellect given by that game. At the same time, Blanshard wisely insists that we cannot lay down a hierarchical table of activities specifying the order of their values irrespective of person and context. A man will fulfill himself better as a good farmer than as a bad philosopher, and it is desirable that even a good philosopher should have some variety in his life by often realizing himself in a nonphilosophical way (I think intrinsically desirable and not merely instrumentally).

But what about fulfillments which are not good but evil? Till near his death Hitler seems to have been highly successful in fulfilling his nature. He had a strongly developed disposition to hate the Jews and others and so bring evil upon them. His acts fulfill this disposition thoroughly and he thereby probably got great satisfaction. But his fulfillment and satisfaction were evil and not good. We should further note that if an evil act fulfills a man's nature, it seems much worse and not better than if it were due to passion or an occasional impulse that took a man by surprise and led him to do something which was incongruous with his character. One might try to meet this objection by the reply that the evil of such acts lay in their effects on other men. Hitler's acts certainly led to the effective prevention of Jews from satisfying and fulfilling themselves. But this, in itself, would make them only instrumentally bad, and it is surely plain that Hitler's state of mind was also intrinsically evil. Yet, when discussing the question whether moral virtue is intrinsically good, Blanshard defines an intrinsic good as one which is "the fulfilment and satisfaction of impulse-desire," apparently for the agent (*RG*, 333). Satisfaction he had maintained to be a necessary condition of intrinsic goodness, and so by parity of evil wickedness could only be intrinsically evil if the wicked man disliked it for its own sake, which would seem to make him less and not more wicked.

The quality of intrinsic goodness which has been most fervently emphasized is moral virtue. Blanshard does not share in giving it this strong emphasis, at least insofar as it means dutifulness, but he does admit it to have intrinsic value as well as extrinsic, though he thinks the latter much more important in this case. Now virtue in general or, if the two are to be distinguished, the quality of dutifulness, is nothing apart from its manifestation in particular acts and states of mind. But behaviour and state of mind that especially exemplify moral good commonly involve sacrifice, which brings suffering or at least considerable loss of satisfaction. No doubt there is also some element of satisfaction present in the thought that one has done right; for if the agent had not cared a cent whether he did his duty or not, he would certainly have not done it if confronted with any serious temptation. But satisfaction seems to be much less prominent in our moral evaluations than it should be according to Blanshard's account. It must be present or at least have been present in some degree or the moral act would not have been performed at all, but it is not a factor in making the state of mind or act admirable or morally good. And other things being equal, commonly the more prominent we think the element of satisfaction to have been in the agent's mind the less we should praise his action. How would Blanshard fit this into his theory? The highest moral qualities seem to be shown more by going against than by going in accord with what most satisfies. Would he say that more than adequate compensation for the sacrifice is provided by the degree in which men fulfill themselves by performing such acts, though the sacrifice may just consist in the nonfulfillment of a large part of the agent's nature? Similarly, the highest forms of love are displayed in cases involving sacrifice, and though here, if it is real love, the agent must feel a real satisfaction in helping the object of his love, the situation may well be one in which as far as his feelings are concerned suffering is the predominant factor, e.g. when tending a parent, spouse, or child who is hopelessly ill. Yet I should say the display of such love has great intrinsic value even if the situation as a whole is evil rather than good. Does Blanshard's account do justice to the values that consist in a triumph over evil conditions which cannot remove the evil but makes wonderfully the best of it?

On the other hand, with intellectual and aesthetic goods satisfaction seems to me essential in a more direct way. I am inclined to think with Blanshard that the experience of these would be valueless if there were no satisfaction, but I am also inclined to think that this is only a limiting case which is hardly possible. Certainly a man possessed of much intellectual insight might be so worried or depressed that he derived next to no enjoyment from it for a time, but if he grasped a new connection intelligently while he was in that condition he must have attended to it to some extent, and I doubt whether the grasping of it could yield no satisfaction at all, though the amount might be very much reduced by his unhappy condition. But I am inclined to think that it is the intrinsic character of the content of experiences that gives them value rather than the fact that they satisfy.

As regards fulfillment, that is evidently regarded by Blanshard as also a necessary condition of intrinsic goodness, but since he repudiates the idea that this means that no experience is intrinsically good unless it is the object of a preexisting desire, the objection might be raised that the introduction of "fulfillment" is merely a verbal point, since it amounts to saying that I cannot be satisfied by anything unless I have the capacity to be satisfied by it. But this would be unfair. The point of introducing the notion of fulfillment has already been seen to be Blanshard's way of distinguishing the quality of different pleasures, a most important distinction. I should prefer to make the point by distinguishing between the intensity and the width or depth of satisfactions. There are some satisfactions which seem, so to speak, to affect a greater part of the man and affect it more deeply than others which may be superficially keener. A man not too sensitive to poetry might still realize this about a poem, though he actually got more enjoyment quantitatively from his dinner. It does seem to me that a tautology is being uttered, if it is said that there can be no satisfaction without fulfillment; but it by no means follows that the degree of satisfaction must be in exact proportion to the degree of fulfillment, and for this reason I think that Blanshard's introduction of the notion of fulfillment is relevant and important. And I might agree to saying that the criterion of the intrinsic goodness of something lay in its satisfying and fulfilling without committing myself to saying that this is either the basic reason which makes it good or identical with its goodness.

Blanshard regards his theory as taking a middle course concerning naturalism.

> The non-natural quality of goodness, even fittingness as a non-natural character, both of which have proved so hard for naturalists to detect, are no longer required. Whether an object does in fact fulfil and satisfy is something that can be determined without going outside nature as we conceive it. But then on the other hand we do not conceive human nature as naturalists commonly do. It is so thoroughly teleological that it cannot be understood apart from what it is seeking to become. What is good, then, in the sense of what would wholly fulfil and satisfy, is not to be determined by an empirical study of what men actually like, desire or approve. That is evidence, to be sure; whatever does in fact fulfil and satisfy is good so far; but human desires, and therefore human good, run immeasurably beyond this. No such good is ever final. [*RG*, 316]

This puzzles me. If what is good is not determined by an empirical study of what actually fulfills and satisfies men now, how is it determined? Not by a miraculous precognition of the future? My perplexity is by no means diminished when I find that in a passage which criticizes my own view he seems to be denying naturalism altogether:

> Goodness comes only when in the object there is something that answers to favour, something "such as" to require and deserve it. And you cannot fill that blank called "such as" with neutral natural qualities, with round holes or coastal inlets or physical frequencies;[6] you cannot even fill it with St. Francises or with the giving of all one has to feed the poor, if these are con-

sidered solely as natural events. As such, they are mere facts, none of them better than any other. If saintliness and generosity are such as to merit favouring, it must be because there is something in them that goes beyond their "factual characteristics" and equally goes beyond a mere blank cheque on our favour. What is this? I think we must answer, a goodness that they have already. [*RG*, 286]

Yet is it not a mere natural event that something satisfies and fulfills a man? I do not see why not, unless value-terms conceived as nonnatural be already presupposed in the notions of fulfilling or of satisfying, which does not seem to be Blanshard's intention. This raises a further question. He did not intend his ethics to be wholly empirical. If not, how precisely does the a priori element come in? The good is certainly conceived by him not so much as what actually fulfills and satisfies as what would fulfill and satisfy in the long run. But how do we know what would satisfy and fulfill in the long run? It is no doubt to a large extent a matter of empirical generalizations. For example, having tasted whisky a few times, I know it has altogether failed to give me satisfaction (in fact I dislike the taste), and, as I have good inductive evidence that that kind of drink gives me displeasure, I should be foolish to try it again. Somebody else having sampled it more freely might come to the conclusion that he had better not sample it again because it interfered with the fulfillment of his higher nature, though in the first instance it was very satisfying. My decision was the fruit of a purely empirical generalization, but a decision which brings in a reference to the distinction between higher and lower capacities is rather a different position. It seems to involve an a priori judgment as to what is higher and lower. Is it an a priori judgment, for instance, that intellectual insight into the answer to a philosophical problem is a higher satisfaction than, say, an enjoyable taste? Many philosophers who make such a judgment would say it was. Would Blanshard? Or would he say that it was merely a matter of experience? Would he say that philosophical insight was just found empirically to fulfill a greater part of our nature than eating a sweet? Again, is a priori thought involved in passing from what has satisfied in the past to what will satisfy in the future? He insists that, as we develop, the things which give satisfaction or dissatisfaction change drastically in quality. Can we in advance of experience foresee at all what will satisfy us as we develop from what has satisfied us in the past? Or are any such predictions merely based on the experience of others who have found as they grew up for example, that mere schoolboy adventure stories palled? Is there on the other hand any a priori element analogous to that present when we see a priori how a series in mathematics unfolds itself from its earlier terms?

There is one field of thought where Blanshard is prepared to admit the a priori in strong opposition to the general philosophical opinion of the day, and here I agree with him. This is the field of causation, and his views here may well have a significance for his ethical theories. When he has discussed the matter he has maintained what I have called the entailment theory of causation. According to this view, there is a logical and not merely a factual connection between cause and effect which we cannot indeed usually see for ourselves but must postulate to account for our success in inductive arguments and for the frequent occurrence of regularities in the natural world which would otherwise amount to the most fantastic of coincidences. It further seems to us in the psychological sphere at least that we can sometimes see such an a priori connection. Blanshard thinks that one thing we can see a priori is that certain experiences which give us pleasure or distress must likewise give pleasure or distress to everybody who should have such an experience. We must indeed be careful what we are saying here: the sight of a particular scene in the Lake District gave me great pleasure last Sunday, but it by no means follows that it would have given everybody pleasure. Many people would not have appreciated it at all, but in that case it must have been that their experience was different from mine. Again I might not have enjoyed it myself if I had been in a depressed mood, but then that would have been because I could not or did not attend to it sufficiently. I either did not notice the combination of lakes and hills or it did not make the same picture to me as it did in my happier mood. And similarly with the person uninterested in scenery or the—aesthetically often gifted—judge of the eighteenth century who might have looked on such scenery as bleak and horrid in character. As psychology shows, there are very different ways of looking at the same thing, and what we know a priori, if anything, is that the same experience which we had would give equal happiness to other people, not that looking at the same physical object would. The experiences of two people looking at the same thing may well be quite different in character, and if they are not having the same experience, there is no reason to be surprised if one enjoys and the other dislikes it. It is the experience, not the physical things or sounds called beautiful, which has intrinsic value or the reverse. There is no absurdity in a tone-deaf man not enjoying Beethoven's music. But it does seem that the same experience qualitatively must give pleasure or the reverse to everyone who has it. Take the most painful experience you can recall, and ask whether you can conceive the possibility of anybody whatever liking it. This is not contradicted by the masochist, unless it could be proved that his experience was really the same as other people's. He may have a different sensibility and not have felt the pain as we should, or he may have felt the pain and its unpleasantness had been outweighed by other factors in his total state of mind, sexual pleasure, satisfaction with his fortitude, a tender emotion connected with enduring pain for one he loved, a sort of religious ecstasy, etc. But it does seem to me evident that with markedly pleasant and painful experiences we can see a priori that nobody could have had the same experience as a whole and not experienced satisfaction in the one case and in the other its reverse. Now if we can see a priori that a particular experience must satisfy or dissatisfy and fulfill or the reverse, we must, on Blanshard's view, at least be able to see a priori that it must be good or bad. Its goodness or badness will follow a priori from its other characteristics as the nonnaturalist like Moore maintains, though there will be a difference in the view of what constitutes goodness.

The entailment theory of causation is relevant to Blanshard's ethics also in another respect. I raised earlier the difficulty that conduct such as Hitler indulged in presumably fulfilled his nature and gave him much satisfaction and yet was evil in character. I mentioned the possible reply that such conduct thwarted the fulfillment of others, but said it might be objected that this made it only instrumentally and not intrinsically evil. But if we can see that such dispositions tend by their inherent nature a priori and not merely *per accidens* to the thwarting, ruin, and misery of others, it seems we can regard them as intrinsically and not merely instrumentally evil. We might add a priori arguments like Spinoza's to show that they also tended to the ruin of the person who had them, or at least against his ultimate satisfaction and fulfillment in a better fashion so that injustice was intrinsically, as Plato put it, a disease in the soul. Its own intrinsic evil could not then really be separated from the evil effects entailed by it. I should much like to have a more precise account of where the a priori element in Blanshard's ethics lies and how it differs from ordinary naturalism.

It remains to consider Blanshard's notion of right and duty (in view of what he says [*RB,* 322], I shall not describe him as giving definitions, though he comes very near to doing so). He is, primarily at least, a utilitarian in that he starts his discussion by laying it down that "an action is right if, and only if, it tends to bring into being as much experience that is at once satisfying and fulfilling as any alternative action" (321). This is for him to say that it is the act or one of the acts which will tend to produce the greatest good in the situation. The point of introducing the word "tend" is to cover the case where a man does what he could reasonably expect from the evidence before him to produce the greatest good or as much good as any alternative action in his power, but where owing to some unfavorable concatenation of circumstances which he could not be expected to foresee his act does not do this. Such an account however still requires Blanshard to deal with the cases produced by deontologists of actions which would strike almost any moral man as right and obligatory, because they are definitely required by a well-established moral rule, but yet seem to be less liable to produce good than harm. Blanshard's answer to these hard cases is to say that what we ought to consider is not the value of the consequences of the particular act we propose to do but of the consequences of the practice it exemplifies. I may well do more good than harm by breaking a promise, but the institution of promise-keeping is so important that except in extreme cases I ought to keep the promise nonetheless. Thus, in an article on "Morality and Politics," he says:

> One can see on reflection that respect for property is bound up with one pattern of life, and stealing with another; and that one cannot fairly tear either out of that pattern and consider it out of the context. If stealing is right, so is deception, which is normally a part of it; so is the destruction of confidence; so is the disregard of other people's feelings, hopes and desires. These further practices are in principle bound up with it, and one cannot justify stealing without committing oneself to these too. What one must ask, therefore, is whether one is prepared to accept, not the single act, but the pattern of action, the network of practice, to which this act belongs. . . . Respect for what others have is right because it is an integral part of a form of life that, as a whole, is good; stealing is wrong because the way of life implied in it would be a human disaster. And the plain man would feel, instinctively but soundly, that stealing a pen and taking the weapon of a dangerous criminal, though both could be called theft, belong to wholly different patterns of living.[7]

He goes on immediately after the passage just quoted to give what comes at any rate as near to a definition of right as his book ever does give and says: "That act—or more precisely, the network of practices involved in it—is right which would produce the greatest good." Difficulties certainly arise here. Suppose act A in this case would do the greatest good, but it belongs to a network of practices which do harm. It would do harm to drop the practice of administering penicillin for infections in favour of the medical practices for infections that immediately preceded its discovery, but does it follow that it would be the duty of a doctor to give penicillin to a patient who was known to be allergic to it, so that it would make him worse than he was before? Yet, there are doubtless many cases of possible acts which would, taken in themselves, do more good than harm, but which we ought not to do because if generally done the results would be disastrous. An example would be my evading taxes on the ground that I should miss the money very appreciably, while the few pounds one man paid would not make any appreciable difference to the welfare of society. It is thus not easy to distinguish between the cases where the argument from universalization is good and where it is bad, and there has certainly been too much said about this question for Blanshard to deal with it so cursorily.

I am inclined to think that the cases where we are justified in saying that it is wrong to do so and so, though its effects are good rather than bad, on the ground that if everybody acted in the way proposed the results would be bad, are cases where the action could be said to be *unfair,* because the person who did it was benefiting from the observance of a rule by others while not playing his part in observing it himself. A utilitarian might then perhaps bring this under his scheme by saying that such intrinsically unfair acts are bad in themselves and you must include under the evil produced not only the effects of an act but any intrinsic evil belonging to the act itself. Blanshard would have to admit that such acts could be intrinsically evil, since there is certainly a widespread and natural aversion, though of course not as widespread as we should like, to acting unfairly, and this is not merely something which people dislike for its effects but which gives them a bad conscience in itself.

In the above I have dwelt on views of Blanshard with which I disagree or about which I am at least very doubtful and ignored the very large part of his book with which I agree. I certainly am in substantial agreement with his criticisms of other philosophers and especially value *Reason and Goodness* as a refutation of emotivism and subjectivism and a balanced account of the place of reason in life which can be set against the irrationalist tendency that today pervades so much of philosophy as well as popular thought.

ALFRED C. EWING

CAMBRIDGE UNIVERSITY
ENGLAND

NOTES

[1]Cf. my *Second Thoughts in Moral Philosophy* (London: Routledge & Kegan Paul; New York: Macmillan Co., 1959).

[2]*The Definition of Good* (New York: Macmillan Co.; London: Routledge, 1947).

[3]I, however, did not commit myself to the view that ought in its moral sense is to be analyzed in terms of fittingness (cf. *RG*, 282), but only put this forward as a somewhat dubious suggestion (*The Definition of Good*, 168).

[4]*RG*, 285. Cf. *The Definition of Good*, 56.

[5]Cf. my *Second Thoughts*, 88.

[6]These examples, thus quoted out of their context, will seem very odd, but they were introduced by Blanshard to make the point that the term "fitting" commonly is applied in a non-evaluative sense and requires some further qualifications to make it a value term, as I did in *The Definition of Good*.

[7]In *Ethics and Society*, ed. R.T. De George (Garden City, N.Y.: Doubleday, Anchor Books, 1966; London: Macmillan Co., 1968), 12–13. The passage is in accord with the views expressed in *RG*.

2. Reply to A. C. Ewing

Blanshard's View of Good

Alfred Ewing died on May 14, 1973. Happily and with characteristic promptness, he had sent in his essay before illness overtook him. He had been my close friend for many years. He reviewed my *Nature of Thought* for *Mind* more than thirty years ago, and from that time on we remained in touch with each other through talk and correspondence. I usually sought him out on my visits to England, and he usually spent some time with me when he came to the United States. We were drawn together by many things, among which was a common skepticism regarding some of the newer fashions in philosophy; and it is suggestive of one strong opinion of his which I shared that he should have entitled one of his last books *Non-linguistic Philosophy*. I owe much to his long row of admirable volumes. Like some other adherents of the more traditional styles of philosophizing, he was without the honor that he deserved in his own country, though his incisive critical essays, quietly written but stored with argumentative dynamite, must have taken effect upon such positivists and post-positivists as read him. Ewing had so sure a sense for the logical weaknesses of an opponent's position that I was always relieved when I found him on my side in a controversy, and apprehensive when he was disposed to be critical. Ethics was one of the subjects on which we differed, and in his essay in this volume his rapier is pointed, as if by some magnetic attraction, at the most vulnerable points in my ethical armor.

Intrinsic Goodness

His special concern is my conception of intrinsic goodness. In view of the centrality of this conception, perhaps I may be allowed to digress for a moment and say how I arrived at it. One day in 1916 or 1917 I dropped into a bookshop in Bombay and there found a secondhand copy of Sidgwick's *Methods of Ethics;* it carried the name of its previous owner, Sir Walter Raleigh, then Merton Professor of English Literature at Oxford, who was a fellow of my own college. I made the treatise my special reading on a long trip by boat across the Pacific in 1917. Sidgwick fascinated me by his combination of precision, lucidity, and literary ease on the one hand with humanity and common sense on the other, and ever since he has remained one of my models. His thesis that the objective rightness of an action depends on the character of its consequences seemed to me then, and still seems, cogently argued. What I could not accept was his hedonism, which he shared with one of his own heroes, John Stuart Mill. The weakness of this view came out clearly, I thought, in Mill's famous essay. He raised the curious but crucial question whether he would rather be Socrates and unhappy or the most blissfully happy of well-fed pigs, and admitted with characteristic candor that he would rather be Socrates, though this was quite inconsistent with his teaching that pleasure or happiness was the only component that made an experience intrinsically good. If he would rather be an unhappy Socrates, that must mean that there was something other than happiness that made the experience of Socrates more worth while than the most exquisite experiences of the sty. What was this component? Mill suggested that it was the superior *quality* of Socrates' pleasure, but that this was something different from pleasure itself was made clear by the fact that it added nothing to the quantity of pleasure experienced. In the intrinsic goodness of the Socratic experience, then, something other than pleasure was clearly involved.

What could this element be? Plainly it had something to do with Socrates' splendidly developed mind. To be sure, no one of sense would deny the pig a mind with sensations, feelings, and appetites; but its world was a miserably meager one compared with the magnificent ranges of which the philosopher's mind was free. What completely overbalanced the happiness of the sty was the experience of that developed, reflective mind; and I could not understand why Mill and Sidgwick should not have plainly said so. I began to ask whether this simple bit of analysis would not apply to other cases of intrinsic value; and after trying out imaginatively a large number of such cases, I concluded that my interpretation of Mill's choice would hold of intrinsic goods generally. Every experience that was valued in and for itself had two sides. The hedonists were right in saying that it must have a positive rather than a negative affective tone; it must carry some flush of pleasure with it or, as I preferred to call it, satisfaction. But it must also be fulfilling: it must fulfill in its degree some urge or drive of human nature. In Socrates the most obvious fulfillment was intellectual, the realization of the powers of a large intelligence. But the fulfillment might be of drives or urges of different kinds—aesthetic, for example, or athletic, or sympathetic, or power-seeking.

But suppose one grants that every experience that is intrinsically good does contain the factors of being fulfilling and satisfying; are we to say that these constitute its goodness, or that they are merely characteristics from which its goodness may be inferred? To the layman this may seem an insignificant question. But it did not seem so to three of my former teachers, Rashdall, Moore, and Ross. They all thought it intelligible to ask of any experience that had these characters whether it was also good, a question that would have been meaningless if goodness consisted of these characters. And for years I was so much under their influence as to hold also that goodness was a distinct "nonnatural" quality, that is, one that a psychologist would never note along with pleasure, sensation, ideas, and so on, in drawing up an inventory of mental content. The more I fixed my attention, however, on this abstract nonnatural goodness that all goods had in common—the experiences of music, a serene conscience, a good dinner, a victory at tennis—the more ghostly and elusive it seemed. I could find no clear content in it apart from the good-making characteristics themselves. So I concluded that the goodness of all intrinsically good experiences reduced to these two factors in alliance, their being fulfilling of human nature and their carrying with them that tone of pleasure or happiness that was the normal by-product of such fulfillment.

Ewing agreed both with the rejection of hedonism and with my inability to find any content in Moore's nonnatural goodness. But it seemed to him clear that there was more in the notion of goodness than the two characters I had found in it, and more indeed than any list of such characters could provide. In short he could not accept my "naturalism." In his excellent book, *The Definition of Good,* he arrived at a new and in some ways very attractive view: what is good, he said, is what we ought to favor. Considering *ought* a much clearer notion than *good,* and one that could not be reduced to naturalistic terms, he proposed to make it the primary term of his ethics. In *Reason and Goodness* I criticized this view on the ground that if we knew we ought to favor something we must already know it to be good, and that his definition thus presupposed the good it sought to define. Ewing replied to this criticism in his book *Second Thoughts on Moral Philosophy* and again more briefly in the essay before us. His arguments have not removed my uneasiness with his definition, though I prefer not to reopen the argument here. I do not think our definitions are as far apart as they may seem. Ewing agrees that if we are to understand what "good" means in a particular case, we must know those qualities of the object in virtue of which we favor it, though these qualities are not the goodness; I am inclined to say they are. But I do not hold this with complete confidence, and if one is going to break with naturalism, Ewing's view seems to me a highly plausible alternative.

To come now to his criticisms, there is one that I may best deal with at once. He says that I have given up the attempt to find an intension for the word "good" and fallen back on the extension. I see no ground for this in my work except perhaps an expression of despair over the woolliness and ambiguity of common speech when abstractions of large importance are being used. Such terms as "life," "mind," "self," "religion," "good," are used in very various senses, and of some of these terms there is no definition that would command general assent. I admitted that my own definition of "good" would not at once be welcomed by the plain man as what best formulated his meaning. I did say, however, that if he rejected it at first, he would probably come round to it at the last. But I was certainly attempting to bring a common meaning to light, and I was far from substituting a list of good things or "goods" for their intension or essence. The extraction of that meaning has proved a perplexing task for the most acute of philosophers, but at least I was venturing on the attempt.

Motives and Fulfillments

But Ewing has other and far more formidable criticisms. He points out that Hitler (who is becoming a classic in ethical discussions) realized or fulfilled his malice against the Jews in wholesale and murderous fashion, and no doubt took much satisfaction in doing so, but that it would be outrageous to call this kind of action good. I agree, of course. As moralists we first should be clear, however, what question we are answering. I assume that it is whether a certain course of action was right or wrong, and here my answer would be the same as that of all other sane men. The rightness of an action turns upon its consequences, not to the agent alone, but to everyone affected by it, and on this theory Hitler's action was hideously and monstrously wrong. Whatever self-realization or satisfaction he may have found in it, the intrinsic evils he produced outweighed beyond calculation any goods he may have achieved for himself or others. His actions snuffed out the lives of millions, and if evil consists of frustration and misery as goodness does of fulfillment and satisfaction, he must be judged as most people would judge him, as one of the worst of all moral disasters.

Ewing has no quarrel with me here. But he would differ seriously at the next step of reflection. Would not intrinsic evil have attached to Hitler's motive even if no action had emerged from it? The moral quality of an action, its goodness or badness, is quite distinct from its rightness or wrongness, and Ewing follows Ross in making its moral goodness depend upon the motive. A good motive normally tends to a right action, and a bad motive to a wrong one. But the correlation does not always hold. A man with the most generous of motives may try to save his friend from an approaching car, but owing to bodily awkwardness trip him up and throw him under its wheels. Technically the act was wrong because it probably led to worse results than would mere inaction, but no one would say that the agent was morally bad, for his intentions were of the highest. A thug may shoot at a policeman, miss him, and put out of action instead a fellow thug on the other side. The action may benefit the community, but whatever the result, we should ordinarily say that the malice which meant to kill a policeman was evil. Ewing presses this home against me. If anything in the world is intrinsically good, he would say, it is the sense of duty; if anything is intrinsically bad, it is the malice that would deliberately harm another. He takes the case of a "witch" who, in accordance with primitive belief, thinks she can work harm on someone she hates by making a model of him and sticking pins in it. She does no harm to her enemy; but does not her motive make her as morally bad as if she did? She fulfills her hatred in some degree and takes satisfaction in it. Her state of mind should therefore on my theory be good. But it is undeniably bad. Even if she had done nothing at all but sit and stew in her hatred, this would still have been bad, for hatred is an evil state of mind.

I adduced this objection to my theory in *Reason and Goodness,* but do not think my answer to it was adequate. The question is how a mere motive can be good or evil before it realizes itself in action. My answer was that motive and action were so generally associated with good or evil consequences that this latter good or evil reflected itself back on the motives which, though in strictness only instrumentally good or evil, came to be thought of as intrinsically so. But the plain man does not think a good motive is good only as a means; he regards it as good in itself; and in this I now think he is right. Nor does it seem difficult to reconcile this more acceptable view with my theory.

A motive is more than a mere predecessor of an action; it is incipient action itself. The woman who sits and thinks of the harm she would like to inflict on her enemy is reacting to him whether that reaction reaches the overt stage or not. "But what if it never reaches the overt stage?" I may be asked. "It will then produce no evil consequences to others, and as for the agent, since it is a partial realization of his capacity for malice, it should be regarded as good." One might appeal in answer to the considerations offered by Plato and Spinoza about the way malice destroys the health of the soul. But there are considerations nearer to hand. I have argued in my book on ethics that actions should be stifled, even if fulfilling and satisfying to the agent, when they produce an overbalancing frustration and pain in others. A malicious motive is an incipient action of just this kind; its entertainment, still more its cultivation, tends to produce the action appropriate to it, and such action is best inhibited by being cut off at the source.

"Still," it may be insisted, "such action is not an inevitable sequel of the motive, and you have even admitted that the worst motives at times produce effects that are desirable. So you cannot say that the evil of the effects inheres necessarily or intrinsically in the motive." But here Ewing himself supplies the answer. He writes: "if we can see that such dispositions tend by their inherent nature a priori and not merely *per accidens* to the thwarting, ruin, and misery of others, it seems we can regard them as intrinsically and not merely instrumentally evil." And I hold that we *can* see a priori that benevolent motives *tend* to produce good results and malicious motives evil ones. This will be denied automatically by those who are committed to the dogma that all a priori propositions are logico-mathematical tautologies; but that dogma has been refuted long ago. And if the tendency to produce evil can be seen to inhere in a motive necessarily, we have the right to call it intrinsically evil.

Satisfaction and Fulfillment

Ewing finds further difficulty with my account of the relation of the two components that make anything intrinsically good. There is no correlation, he says, between fulfillment and satisfaction; one may go high while the other is low. An astrologer, for example, may devise a very silly theory and regard it with great glee, while a sober astronomer, more alert to the difficulties, may find much less satisfaction in a theory that contains far more truth. Michelangelo may take less satisfaction in the Sistine ceiling than a modern dauber does with his "masterpieces" in running paint; and it is notorious that a saint may be less complacent about his goodness than the man whose test of goodness lies in keeping out of jail. Now there is some misunderstanding in this objection. I have never argued that the graphs of fulfillment and pleasure ran parallel to each other; indeed in my discussion of the matter I expressly cited instances to the contrary. Michelangelo's melancholy disposition and the dauber's habitual euphoria may defeat one's natural expectations about pleasure and quality of work. What I did hold is that both components are necessary to intrinsic value, that fulfillment without any trace of satisfaction in it is dry as ashes; and the feelings of an idiot, all "sound and fury signifying nothing," are vacuous. It is true nevertheless that in the normal scholar or artist or athlete increasing achievement does bring increasing enjoyment. Occasional exceptions do not wholly destroy that rule.

Again, Ewing is discontented with my conception of fulfillment. So am I. But he accepts part of my defense when he agrees that within some of the leading drives of our nature we can recognize immanent ends toward which the drives are directed. An advance toward these ends is what an increase in fulfillment means. My *Nature of Thought* is a study of how one of these drives, the theoretic impulse, fulfills itself as it achieves a wider scope and more perfect integration of knowledge. If two men read their daily newspapers and one of them registers all the facts reported there while the other in addition grasps their interconnections, there is no doubt that, so far, the second is on a higher level of fulfillment on the cognitive side. The end of the theoretic impulse is the understanding of the world, and a mind fulfills itself more completely as it approximates this end. The moral impulse also has its distinctive end whose fulfillment may be measured in similar fashion. I should say that there is likewise an aesthetic impulse, though with differing modes of fulfillment in the various arts. In all these inner demands we can see what advance or fulfillment means, seldom perhaps with the clarity that we should wish, but, as Aristotle would say, with such clarity as the subject matter admits of.

These are only three of the many drives of human nature; indeed I have described that nature as a quiverful of arrows of desire. Such impulses are purposive; the appearance of desire marks the fixation of a proximate goal. Some of them are more groping and their ends less clearly defined than the three just mentioned, but some of them are even more definitely directed and their fulfillment therefore more easy to measure. There is a drive for bodily prowess, for example, which finds its commonest expression through sports; and the football field, the baseball diamond, the wrestler's mat, the tennis court, and the basketball floor provide measures that are in constant use. Students disagree as to the nature and number of instincts; some avoid the name altogether; but there can be no rational doubt that congenital urges or drives exist, and I see no objection to speaking of the maternal or the gregarious or the sexual instinct, or of the one that heads the list for Hobbes and Hocking, the instinct for power. These instincts or impulses exist in different degrees of strength and of advancement in different persons. To measure their fulfillment independently of each other is often impossible, for they may grow together like mutually supporting vines; how much did the intellectual interest and the desire for power contribute to each other in such careers as those of Richelieu and Metternich? In my writing on ethics, I have given the intellectual interest a much higher place than is given it by most moralists because in an increasingly complex society its development is necessary to forecast the consequences of alternative lines of action and, through its balancing of those consequences, to keep conduct on a moral course. Our impulses are often wayward and too often at war with each other. I have held consistently that it is only reason that can serve as the arbiter and guide.

Measuring degrees of fulfillment against each other is easy or difficult according to circumstances. It is relatively easy between two levels of fulfillment of the same drive. It is more difficult when a variety of drives contribute to the states of mind to be compared. It is more difficult still when the states of mind compared belong to quite different kinds of drive. It is most difficult of all when one is called on to compare different types of drive in different minds. Two boys of equal promise are competing for a scholarship, the one to work in music, the other in linguistics; which should be appointed? No judge could be competent in such a case unless he had gone a fair distance into each kind of competing activity and could therefore sympathize with each ambition and estimate its achievement. In such cases behavioristic tests will probably fail utterly and exact degrees of measurement will certainly be impossible. But two points should be noted. Unless values are commensurable, morality itself is rendered meaningless; moral problems always involve choice between values. Secondly, those of my critics who offer ethical views face the same difficulties. Ewing would go with me in saying that one should review the values involved in each alternative; he would then ask in the light of this review which *obligation* is the strongest. But I do not see how he could answer this latter question without knowing which course would produce the largest good; and then his difficulties resolve themselves into mine.

He intimates that in choices of this kind I fall back on the view that some activities of our nature are higher than others, but that I have given no clear account of this difference. I am not sure that I am more guilty here than my critic. He has no hesitation in placing the intellectual achievement of the accomplished philosopher above that of the accomplished chess player, and I note with pleasure his added comment: ". . . Blanshard wisely insists that we cannot lay down a hierarchical table of activities specifying the order of their values irrespective of person and context." William James said somewhere that our graduate schools were full of the bald-headed and bald-hearted who were the ruins of excellent farmers. James would probably have been an indifferent farmer, and the farmer would cut an unenviable figure in the chair of William James. The dispute as to whether one activity *as such* is higher than another is a pretty unprofitable one, for the question in practice is always between *degrees* of fulfillment of the impulses compared.

The A Priori and the Empirical in Ethics

Ewing is unclear, again, as to the parts played in my ethics by a priori and empirical knowledge. Probably categorical answers without any attempt to elaborate these answers would be the most appropriate reply. The discovery that some activities are pleasant and others not is clearly empirical; and Ewing's inference that since he found whisky distasteful at his first few exposures to it he would continue to find it so is also empirical, though, since our tastes notoriously change, it is highly fallible. The discovery that one is responsive to music and a dunce at algebra is again empirical. The judgment that one pain or pleasure is more intense than another is empirical. The judgment that intense pleasure is intrinsically more worth having than intense pain is, I think, a priori. Similarly the judgment that one state of mind fulfills more completely than another a certain drive of our nature is at least sometimes a priori, though I am not sure that it always is. For example, the insight that an ordered understanding of a group of facts is nearer to the theoretic ideal than the mere knowledge of the scattered items severally seems to me an a priori insight, while the judgment of a mile runner that he has run better today than yesterday seems chiefly empirical. Also empirical is the judgment that objects the experience of which I find fulfilling will be found so by others, though the judgment that a qualitatively identical experience would be found so by others is, I think, a priori. What about the determination of the ends of our impulses? This is done, I think, by a projection into possibility of the line of our past advance. In *The Nature of Thought* I reviewed the kinds of answer to the question Why? which would bring an inquiry to rest; and found the most unquestionable answer to lie in the necessitation by the context of the point one had failed to understand. I then extrapolated from this partial fulfillment of my intellectual interest to what would fulfill it generally and wholly. This inference was, I am inclined to think, a priori, rather than empirical, although I am less disposed than most philosophers to draw a sharp line between the two, and should not be disturbed to find that both kinds of inference had been involved. Finally, what of the appraisal of states of mind belonging to two very different kinds of activity, one in philosophy, let us say, and the other in music? Regarding this I feel confident that there is at least an objective truth to be found; my reading of Plato this evening will or will not be intrinsically more worth while than my listening to sonatas by Mozart, however difficult the decision and however elusive its grounds may be. Emotivism is here bankrupt.

How is the decision made? Rashdall and Moore, Ross and Ewing would agree that the decision is made by an act of intuition. Is this intuition itself empirical, like the perception that one leaf is larger than another, or is it a priori and, if true at all, necessarily true? I think it is the latter, like the judgment that extreme happiness is intrinsically more desirable than extreme misery. This does not mean, of course, that such judgments are infallible. Mathematics is an a priori science, but ask any student whether it is possible to make mistakes in it.

Naturalism

After all these explanations Ewing would, I am sure, return to a question that he would regard as not satisfactorily answered: Is a purely naturalistic ethics possible? If such an ethics is required to move wholly on the empirical level, it is evident that my answer must be No. But naturalism in ethics commonly means what Moore meant by it, an account in which no terms are used that fall outside the province of natural science; and since his meaning of "good" did clearly fall outside this province, he considered himself a nonnaturalist. Though Ewing rejects this concept of goodness, he insists that Moore was right that ethics cannot do without nonnaturalistic terms. He thinks that, more or less unconsciously, I have taken the same position, that my notion of the intrinsic goodness of an experience assumes a quality quite other than fulfillment and the satisfaction that supervenes upon it. And I admit that I find most naturalistic moralists quite unsatisfactory. Sidgwick, who was the ablest of them, could not in the end rest content with hedonism and introduced a notion of goodness whose content was not exhausted by pleasure.

On a question on which Sidgwick and Moore both wavered, one had better not be dogmatic. And whether fulfillment and satisfaction define goodness or are merely "good-making characteristics" is not a world-shaking question in any case. But I can only say that I still incline to the view developed in *Reason and Goodness* that to call an experience intrinsically good *is* to say that it is fulfilling and satisfying. That implies that I deny the imputation of "the naturalistic fallacy" and should not accept Moore's probable criticism that he could meaningfully ask of an experience known to be thus fulfilling and satisfying whether it was good or not, since in knowing these characteristics of it he would be already knowing its goodness. I grant that the *definiendum* and the *definiens* do not at first present themselves as at all equivalent; they come to seem so only as the result of patient analysis. Furthermore, I think that the word "good" has an aura of emotional and associative meaning that is not exhausted in the terms in which I have defined it and that this may account for the apparent nonnaturalism. The term carries a penumbra drawn from a great variety of likings, from its associations with moral goodness, and, for many, with religious devotion. The word thus has a mixed volume of emotive meaning. But to say that it has no meaning except this seems plainly false. When we say that an experience is good, we mean to say something true. Emotivism has to deny this. On my definition, I do not have to deny it; I can keep the emotive meaning and also keep it in its place.

In *Reason and Belief* I have argued against a two-world theory, a world of nature with another and supernatural world erected on top of it and from time to time breaking into it with Lutheran breaches of natural law and Kierkegaardian irruptions of an irrational morality. The nonnaturalisms of Moore and Ewing are of course extremely different from this sort of supernaturalism. But for anyone who is trying to understand the world, the more seamless it is the better, and even this sort of nonnaturalism introduces a discontinuity that makes understanding harder. The world is in any case far from seamless; between body and mind, for example, there is a gap that no intelligence has successfully crossed. And Occam's ruthless razor would have us cut off all nonnatural superveniences unless they are absolutely necessary. *Is* the notion of a nonnatural goodness or oughtness thus necessary? If the only way to keep the objectivity of moral judgment were to accept it, I should do so, since it seems to me so clear that moral judgments do possess objective truth. But objectivity is not at risk in the naturalism here outlined. And the theory ties ethics to evolution and human nature in what seems to me an illuminating way. It naturalizes human goodness without, I hope, degrading it.

3 UNDERSTANDING AND FORGIVENESS
Elizabeth L. Beardsley

I

IN recent years, philosophers interested in the implications of determinism for ethics have devoted themselves chiefly to examining the concept of moral responsibility and those moral judgments which presuppose it. The examination has been fruitful, and portions of Blanshard's work are pertinent to it. But a closely related, and in some respects even more fundamental, issue has been overlooked. Blanshard's work provides a particularly good opportunity to consider this related issue, which (as I formulate it) concerns the implications of intelligibilism for ethics.

I regard determinism, in Blanshard's philosophy, as fundamentally a manifestation of a general philosophic outlook which I shall call "intelligibilism" (if a noted philosophical stylist can put up with so barbarous a neologism). He might prefer "rationalism," but the latter term is best reserved, I think, for a specific epistemological thesis: that "a priori reason [can] grasp substantial truths about the world."[1] Of course Blanshard is a rationalist, but he is also a proponent of the thesis that *every entity can (in principle) be understood.* This thesis is what I call "intelligibilism."

The concept *understand* has been construed in various ways. Blanshard's concept is best explicated by his statement that an entity is understood when it has been "apprehended as part of a system which is taken to render it necessary."[2]

Blanshard has not addressed himself directly to the issue of the implications of intelligibilism for ethics, but the issue has evidently engaged his attention from time to time. A particularly interesting passage occurs in an early chapter of *Reason and Goodness* (*RG*), "Stoicism and the Supremacy of Reason." Here Blanshard has been describing—with characteristic eloquence—the role of reason in achieving equanimity. He continues:

> In this attempt to deal with the ills of the world by understanding them there is a difficulty which has always given trouble to those who have tried to

retain optimism along with a thoroughgoing rationalism. If evil things lose their evil when placed in a broad explanatory context, are not good things bound to lose their goodness when treated in the same way? . . . The argument, if valid at all, lets loose a sort of tidal wave whose final work, as Spinoza saw, is not to turn apparent evil into good, but to engulf all good and evil in a limitless grey sea. [*RG,* 49]

The main thrust of this passage is to argue that *if* to understand something (to place it in "a broad explanatory context") invalidates negative appraisals of it, positive appraisals fare no better. This is an important application of a general principle that I shall call "moral parallelism." Nonphilosophers sometimes ignore moral parallelism[3] and sometimes proclaim it with an air of discovery.[4] Philosophers, with somewhat greater logical sophistication, are more often careful to state that nonnormative considerations which invalidate negative moral judgments also invalidate those which are positive.[5]

According to Blanshard, *if* understanding something cuts away its disvalue, we have here a two-edged sword which cuts away its value as well. But *do* evil things lose their evil when they are understood? The question is left open in the passage cited. But Blanshard appears to hold that, for at least one subclass of moral judgments, understanding does produce a "loss of evil." This view emerges most clearly in the discussion in which Blanshard cites (*RG,* 44, 445), with evident respect, the proverb *"Tout comprendre, c'est tout pardonner."* This principle, though I too respect it, I shall disrespectfully dub "C–P." Blanshard appears to take the forgiving of an act based on an understanding of certain of its features as a paradigm of an evil thing's loss of evil.

And I think we must agree that if understanding can be shown to invalidate any moral judgment, it will be the moral judgment that is somehow withdrawn in forgiveness.

As I understand it, the connection between Blanshard's intelligibilism and his defense of determinism[6] can be formulated in the following way. Intelligibilism is a thesis about entities in general, determinism a thesis about events; so that determinism, being in this respect the narrower thesis, does not entail intelligibilism. Nor does the reverse entailment hold, since the determinist asserts that events (including human actions) have causes, whereas the intelligibilist can allow for other kinds of explanation or understanding (if there are other kinds). Yet it is evident that the intelligibilism of *The Nature of Thought* provides a favorable philosophic soil for Blanshard's "Case for Determinism."

If, however, we restrict both theses to actions, their connection becomes more intimate. The action-determinist holds that all actions have causes; the action-intelligibilist holds that all actions can (in principle) be understood.

The first thesis entails the second, though the second (since it is at least logically possible that reasons are not causes) does not entail the first.

An inquiry into the implications of intelligibilism for ethics needs to be cast into a manageable form. Here it is helpful[7] to consider whether the thesis that certain moral judgments are invalidated by intelligibilism can be defended by an argument comparable to that used by so-called "hard determinists" to defend the thesis that certain moral judgments are invalidated by determinism.[8] I shall return to this question in the final section of this essay.

II

An account of C–P is evidently needed, and I shall now propose one. I hope thereby to make a contribution to the neglected project of analyzing a principle more often invoked than examined.

Expressions of the form "to f is to g" may be used with either descriptive or normative force, or—as I think C–P is typically used—with elements of both. I interpret C–P as making, in its descriptive aspect, the following assertion: (D) that when Y believes that X's performance of act A had a certain feature F, Y tends to forgive X for A. And I interpret C–P as making, in its normative aspect, the following claim: (N) that the possession of F by X's performance of A constitutes a good reason for forgiving X for A. C–P is thus, on my view, a hybrid thesis, making both a descriptive assertion (D) and a normative claim (N). The examination of (D) belongs to psychology; but the examination of (N) belongs to moral philosophy. Accordingly, I shall in this section of my essay inquire whether there is a feature of an agent's performance of an act that can be considered a good reason for forgiving the agent for that act. For this task an analysis of the concept of *forgive* (*pardonner*) is required.

What is needed is not a complete phenomenological account of the complex moral attitude of forgiveness, but something more limited in scope. I shall assume that an attitude cannot be characterized without referring to the judgments on which it is founded, and that *moral* attitudes are founded on *moral* judgments.[9] In identifying such judgments it is immensely helpful, I think, to examine what it is to perform the illocutionary act of expressing the attitude in question.[10]

In expressing forgiveness (E–F) of an agent X for his act A, a speaker S makes the following representations:

(1) that X did A;

(2) that A was wrong;

(3) that A was in some respect an offense against S;[11]

(4) that (2) and (3) are good reasons for S to feel resentment toward X for A;[12]

(5) that because of another consideration, S does not feel resentment toward X for A.

These five representations are the constitutive conditions for the illocutionary act of expressing forgiveness of X for A. I shall assume that the "other consideration" mentioned in (5) of E–F is the possession by X's performance of A of the "feature F" claimed (in N of C–P) as a good reason for forgiving X for A.

The kinds of moral judgment that may appear on first consideration to provide good reasons for forgiving X for A can be readily specified: (1) justification of A (judgments that A was not wrong); (2) exculpation of X (judgments that X was not blameworthy for A), and (3) positive moral appraisal of A (judgments that A was morally good).[13] On closer examination, however, the claims of these kinds of judgment to provide good reasons for forgiving X for A can be seen to vary greatly in strength, as I shall try to show.

(1) Justification can be ruled out immediately on logical grounds. Its logical deficiency for the purpose at hand emerges clearly if we consider a remark expressing forgiveness and citing the justification of A as the speaker's reason for forgiving:

(J1) "Because I now see that A was not really wrong, I forgive X for A."

If my analysis of E–F is acceptable, J1 is incoherent, since its first clause contradicts one of the representations made in its second clause. The appropriate sequel to "A was not really wrong" is "There is nothing to forgive in what X did."

(2) We must now consider whether exculpatory considerations provide good reasons for forgiving X for A. Here I shall assume that there are two major grounds for exculpation: the claim that A was unavoidable for X ("X couldn't help doing A"), and the claim that A was not done by X with the intention of doing A ("X didn't mean to do A"). Let us consider two remarks expressing forgiveness on the ground that X is not blameworthy for A:

(J2) "Because I now see that X really couldn't have avoided A, I forgive X for A."

(J3) "Because I now see that X didn't mean to do A, I forgive X for A."

Neither J2 nor J3 is incoherent, if my analysis of E–F is sound, for E–F is silent concerning X's ability to have avoided A and concerning X's intention in doing A.

As far as the representations made directly by E–F are concerned, that is. But we should not overlook the possibility that an analysis of one of those representations might reveal something at odds with an exculpatory judgment. If, for example, (2) in E–F (the judgment that A is wrong) must itself be analyzed in terms of a claim that X could have avoided A or that X intended to do A, then exculpation will be indirectly inconsistent with E–F, and cannot provide a good reason for forgiving X for A.

I believe that exculpation should probably be ruled out. And though I shall not here present the analysis of moral condemnation that would be required to support my view, a few additional reflections may be in order.

First, one should note the difficulty (impossibility?) of finding act-terms sufficiently neutral with respect to avoidability and intention to enable us to say that it is the *same* act that is both excused and forgiven. As the appropriate sequel to "A was not really wrong" is "X did nothing that calls for forgiveness," so the appropriate sequel to "X could not have avoided A" or "X did not mean to do A" may be "A is not what X did."[14]

Second, we must be alert to the possible significance of considerations of *degree*. A circumstance which lowers the agent's degree of culpability might be a good reason for lowering the degree of the victim's resentment, though not for withdrawing it altogether. This line of thought can be applied very clearly to exculpations (deculpations?) of the sort set forth in J5, where we can easily see that even if X did not intend to do A, he may still have been reckless or negligent.[15]

But considerations of degree may also be important in connection with exculpations of the other sort. We tend to think of acts as simply avoidable or unavoidable, instead of seeking to determine how difficult it would have been for *this* agent to have avoided *this* act.[16] I shall return to this matter in section III.

(3) Finally, we must ask whether positive moral appraisal of A (the judgment that A was morally good) provides a good reason for forgiving X for A. I accept here the concept of moral goodness delineated by Ross, who held that the moral goodness of an act depends on the moral goodness of the desire from which the act springs. Ross attributed moral goodness to three human desires, of which two were the desire to do one's duty and the desire to produce some pleasure, or avoid some pain, for another being. We may consider two remarks expressing forgiveness on the ground that X acted from a morally good desire:

(J4) "Because I now see that X really was trying to do what he thought was right, I forgive X for A."

(J5) "Because I now see that X really wanted to be helpful, I forgive X for A."

These remarks do not state explicitly that the desire specified is morally good. We are entitled to assume, however, that it is because of their moral goodness that a conscientious desire (in J4) and a benevolent desire (in J5) are claimed as good reasons for forgiving X for A.

J4 and J5 are free from the direct logical inconsistency I charged against J1, and also from the indirect logical inconsistencies which J2 and J3 could, I think, be shown to exhibit. E–F, as here analyzed, makes no representation concerning the desire from which X did A. The representations that E–F does make should, of course, be carefully analyzed to ascertain what they in turn represent. Ross's invaluable insight that "Moral goodness is quite distinct from and independent of rightness, which . . . belongs to acts *not* in virtue of the motives they proceed from, but in virtue of the nature of what is done"[17] would, if reflected consistently in moral discourse, be immensely clarifying. But as moral language now functions, the locution "A was wrong" suggests that A was done from a desire which, if not morally bad, was at best morally neutral. The thought of this imputed desire causes resentment, and is felt to be a good reason for resentment. It would be too much to claim that the illocutionary act of condemning an act as wrong actually *represents* that its agent acted from a morally bad or morally neutral desire. But it is unrealistic to deny that a negative suggestion concerning the agent's desire is conveyed. Perhaps the best way to describe this situation is to say that the judgment that an act was wrong carries with it a rebuttable presumption that the act was not morally good. Judgments such as J4 and J5 rebut this presumption, and thus remove the reason for resenting X for A. But the absence of a reason for resentment is a good reason for withdrawing resentment. That is to say, for forgiving.

III

With respect to the question what moral judgments are good reasons for forgiving an agent for an act, I have argued for a positive thesis, that favorable moral appraisal is a good reason, and for two negative theses, that justification is not a good reason, and that, while exculpation has too many problematic features to be easily assessed, it is probably not a good reason for forgiveness. I believe that my positive thesis is in harmony with certain aspects of Blanshard's treatment of C–P. I base this opinion primarily on his discussion, in the concluding chapter of *Reason and Goodness,* of the appropriate moral attitude to be taken by someone (call him "Smith") who has been hurt by a false statement made by Jones. Blanshard, in their discussion, seems to say that Jones's motive is more fundamental in determining the appropriate attitude for Smith than Jones's intention or the wrongness of his act, important as these considerations are (*RG,* 444–45).

But Blanshard then goes on to consider the appropriate attitude for Smith to take, should it turn out that Jones's act was morally evil, stemming, e.g. from malice. This is an important question. Blanshard does not use the same terms as the present essay, but what he says adds valuable points to our discussion. The passage should be quoted:

> Malice in others, particularly if they pose as our friends, is of course deplorable. Still as a rule it is far more damaging to the malicious person

than to his victims; and as a reflective man contemplates it steadily, he sees that most of his resentment against it is a waste of his own substance. Malice is the symptom of moral disease, the sign of a maimed and disfigured spirit. It always has its causes in frustration, inadequacy, self-misjudgment, and the like. To the master of serenity, like Marcus Aurelius, it has seemed a more appropriate object of compassion than of anger. . . . [*RG*, 445]

Magnanimity radiates from these words, yet several philosophical questions need to be asked.

What Blanshard says here serves to extend my account of E–F and C–P. He is considering whether, and if so on what grounds, forgiveness is justified in the case of an agent who has acted from a morally bad motive. His answer is that the forgiveness *is* justified, and his reasons (set forth obliquely) merit serious consideration. He does not—being a convinced consequentialist in ethics—appeal to a general "duty of forgiveness." But we may discern in the Blanshard passage three lines of thought which purport to show that there are good reasons for Smith to forgive Jones.

1. First, there appears to be a claim that the roots (causes) of Jones's malice are found in circumstances that exculpate him for having become a malicious person. Presumably further investigation into Jones's life would show that this is true, but we do not need to investigate Jones's particular case, since we already know that malice *always* "has its causes in frustration, inadequacy, self-misjudgment, and the like."

The claim that malice always has certain kinds of cause is one that I cannot assess: taken literally, it is doubtless overstated, though to take a rhetorical turn of phrase so literally would be pedantic. The normative claim here seems to be that malice, having been caused by the factors specified, is excusable, i.e. that a person is not culpable for having "permitted" himself to become malicious. This appears to be exculpation on the ground of unavoidability. The *difficulty* of avoiding the growth of malice, rather than the *impossibility* of doing so might be better cited here as ground for exculpation. In any case, exculpation is not forgiveness, nor does Blanshard say directly that it is. What he does suggest, translated into the language of my account, is that it is not enough, in considering what moral attitude should be taken toward X, for A to ascertain X's motive (his morally good or bad desire); we go on to ask what produced that desire. If X is not culpable for having a malicious desire (perhaps because he has developed nonculpably into a malicious person), then resentment toward X for A is not justified, and he should be forgiven for A. I believe that the reminder that we can look behind the motive (not for another motive, of course, but for causes) is both helpful and unhelpful. Helpful, in that having a morally bad desire, or even a morally bad trait, may be judged excusable when it is considered as the product of a process. Unhelpful, in that a desire or trait can also be considered in itself, rather than as a product. Considered in this way, desires and traits have moral value or disvalue in themselves, as Ross so clearly showed. Thus favorable (or unfavorable) moral appraisal can serve as a fundamental reason for forgiving or resenting X for A. Other moral questions *can* be asked about desires and traits, but in determining whether forgiveness of X for A is justified, these other questions *need* not be asked. They belong to a different moral inquiry.

2. Second, Blanshard claims that resentment would be "wasteful" for Smith. I take this to be, in part at least, a justification of adopting the attitude of forgiveness rather than resentment, on the ground that the former would have less disutility. If this interpretation is incorrect, the term "wasteful" calls for explanation. And if Blanshard does wish to appeal to utility here, I can only register a respectful dissent. Backward-looking moral attitudes like resentment, forgiveness, and remorse seem to me to pose insurmountable problems for utilitarianism. But this is too complex an issue to be treated here.[18]

3. The third argument used to justify Smith's forgiveness of Jones for acting maliciously is that since a malicious person damages himself more than he damages others, compassion toward him is more appropriate than resentment. I believe that an important moral truth has been expressed here. Whether or not a malicious person harms himself more than he harms others, he is surely a fit object for compassion. And whether or not he consciously *feels* harmed by his own malice, he has missed a great good in missing that blessedness which, as Spinoza so wisely said, is not the reward of virtue but is virtue itself.[19] If the malicious person is not remorseful, but content or even joyful in his malice, he has missed blessedness by so much the more.

The claim that a malicious person is a fit object of compassion seems to me eminently justified, but one may question whether compassion is not compatible with some measure of moral resentment. In any case, compassion is not forgiveness, which is a moral attitude founded on certain moral judgments. Compassionateness is a virtue, but compassion is nevertheless not a moral attitude.

Blanshard's arguments to justify forgiving X for A even where A was a morally bad act (stemming from a morally bad desire) seem to me unsuccessful. But if his reasons are not acceptable, can better reasons be found? For example, even though Blanshard cannot consistently appeal to a "duty of forgiveness," should such an appeal be made?

I believe that there is no "duty of forgiveness," not even a prima facie duty. Forgiveness is a response which is, or is not, deserved, an attitude the adoption of which in a given case has (or lacks) a good reason. There is, however, a duty to ascertain whether that good reason is present in any given case. There is a duty to seek diligently for the truth concerning any feature of X's performance of A which, if present, would justify forgiving X for A.

But there is no assurance that this feature (a morally good motive) is actually present. I am reminded here of a sardonic passage from a recent film review: "Good people cherish the belief that to know all is to forgive all; it is an article of liberal faith that at the very point at which you know enough about a man to have contempt for him, you know too much to have contempt for him."[20] Whether or not this is "liberal faith," it is moral superstition.[21]

Although there is no "duty of forgiveness," a capacity for forgiveness (a disposition to forgive when forgiveness is justified) is a moral virtue. Is a capacity for resentment (a disposition to resent X's doing of A when resentment is justified) equally a moral virtue?

An adequate answer to this question cannot be given in brief compass, but I shall suggest the general direction of my own thinking. I believe that though resentment is sometimes justified, as forgiveness sometimes is, a capacity for resentment is not a moral virtue. A capacity for moral indignation is a desirable trait, and when it is a question of moral indignation on behalf of another, the capacity for adopting this attitude is a moral virtue. But resentment is moral indignation on behalf of oneself. A capacity for resentment is a desirable trait. We admire those who "stand up for their rights," and to refuse to become indignant on one's own behalf would be to fail to treat humanity in one's own person in the same way as humanity in the person of another. Therefore, to repress resentment is wrong. But capacity for justified resentment is linked to self-love, whereas capacity for justified forgiveness is linked to concern for others, and for the principle of fairness. It is this difference that makes the latter a moral virtue, while the former is merely a desirable trait.

If the capacity for forgiveness is a moral virtue, while the capacity for resentment is not, what has happened to moral parallelism? Very briefly, I should say that we have found a level at which the principle does not hold. If human desires may be morally neutral (as is true of self-regarding desires as such), then human characteristics cannot all be classified as virtues or vices. I have not said nearly enough to deal adequately with these difficult questions; but I hope I have said enough to provide material for comment by Blanshard, whose defense of moral parallelism, in the passage quoted in section I, is so very perceptive and forceful.

IV

We must now turn to *understand,* the second key concept in C–P. If my treatment of C–P and my analysis of E–F are acceptable, then what must be understood, when anyone justifiably forgives X for A, is the nature of X's motive in doing A. Can we say that in understanding X's motive in doing A we have apprehended anything "as part of a system," or placed anything in "a broad explanatory context"? We have explained why X did A, by giving X's *reason* (motive, desire). This is not causal explanation as such, but it is a conceptually legitimate answer to the question "Why did X's doing of A happen?" A, or the doing of A by X, has certainly been placed in an explanatory context, and perhaps there is no conclusive objection to saying that the explanandum has been apprehended as part of a system.

But an objection might be raised on the ground that when Y gains insight into X's motive for doing A, Y's understanding of the motive itself does not fit the "system" formula. Hampshire has argued, convincingly as I think, that in the case of knowing one's own reasons for believing, intending, or acting one does not "*need* inductive, experimental argument in order to be assured justifiably that so-and-so is the reason. . . ."[22] If he is right, to understand an action is not necessarily to apprehend it as part of a "system." And what is true of understanding one's own actions may also be true of understanding the actions of others. Even if my accounts of C–P and E–F need to be revised at some points, as they undoubtedly do, it would appear that the understanding required for justifiable forgiveness must somehow be concerned with acquiring a sense of how the situation looked to X himself when he did A, a sense of what *he* believed, what *he* desired. Such a sense seems rather different from apprehending as part of a "system." Not all moral judgments require this empathic knowledge for their justification, as Ewing and others have made very clear;[23] but the moral questions posed by the justification of forgiveness surely do.

Perhaps the empathic identification with another person needed to understand him in the sense required can be gained only in a close personal relationship. If this were true, it would not follow that "Forgiving . . . is always an eminently personal . . . affair in which *what* was done is forgiven for the sake of *who* did it."[24] Considerations justifying forgiveness have nothing whatever to do with "who did it." To deny this is to deny that forgiveness is a moral attitude.

We return, finally, to the question: What are the implications of intelligibilism for ethics?

The answer, if what I have argued in this essay is correct, is that intelligibilism invalidates no subclass of moral judgments. If any moral judgments were jeopardized by intelligibilism, it would be those which form the basis of the attitude of moral resentment. But I have found no warrant for saying that all acts whose reasons are understood (or understandable) are justifiably to be forgiven. I have maintained that forgiveness is justified by the *nature* of an agent's reason for what he did, not by the consideration that he *had* a reason, or that the reason can be known. But if even C–P cannot give us a paradigm of how an evil thing can "lose" its evil by being understood, the prospect of showing a general connection between intelligibilism and other moral judgments is poor. And as far as other (nonmoral) normative judgments are concerned, intelligibilism is even less threatening. There is no "tidal wave," and no "limitless grey sea."

It cannot even be claimed that the case for "hard intelligibilism" (the view that all moral judgments of a certain kind are invalidated by intelligibilism) is as strong as the case for hard determinism (the view that all judgments of praise and blame are invalidated by determinism). Hard determinism is sometimes defended by an argument of the following general sort:

> [Hard determinists] contend that the same reasoning which leads us to withhold praise and blame from agents whose acts were committed involuntarily will, when combined with the thesis of determinism, lead on inexorably to the conclusion that no one ever deserves praise or blame for anything. They are haunted by the knowledge that many of the causal antecedents of acts have not been investigated by [soft determinists]; and most particularly they are haunted by the knowledge that not all of the causal antecedents of voluntary acts are voluntary acts. Thus they come to believe that no distinction between "voluntary" and "involuntary" acts that a determinist can consistently make can sustain the moral weight that it must bear if we are to judge men praiseworthy or blameworthy. How, they ask, could we ever be justified in blaming or praising someone for a voluntary act and not an involuntary one, when we know full well that even the voluntary act can be traced back to causes—environmental or hereditary—belonging to a world the agent never made?[25]

Vital to the above argument is the assumption that the cause-effect relation is such that we can "trace back" causes in a sequence, arriving eventually at factors beyond an agent's control. But reasons, qua reasons, are conceptually very different. We cannot trace back a reason for a reason, and therefore there is a crucial asymmetry between hard determinism and hard intelligibilism. The enterprise of proving hard intelligibilism does not seem to be a very promising one.

ELIZABETH L. BEARDSLEY

DEPARTMENT OF PHILOSOPHY
TEMPLE UNIVERSITY

NOTES

[1]Bernard Williams, "Rationalism," in *The Encyclopedia of Philosophy,* ed. Paul Edwards (New York: Macmillan Co., and Free Press, 1967), 7:69.

[2]*The Nature of Thought,* 2:27. In this paper I shall set aside any questions raised by the reference to necessity.

[3]This charge against psychoanalytic theorists is effectively made by G. Gorer, "Psychoanalysis and the World," in *Psychoanalysis Observed,* ed. C. Rycroft (New York: Coward-McCann, 1967), 32.

[4]See B. F. Skinner, *Beyond Freedom and Dignity* (New York: Alfred A. Knopf, 1971), 44 ff.

[5]See, e.g. the influential essay by John Hospers, "What Means This Freedom?" in *Determinism and Freedom in the Age of Modern Science*, ed. S. Hook (New York: New York University Press, 1958), 137.

[6]Blanshard, "The Case for Determinism," in *Determinism and Freedom*.

[7]I am greatly indebted to my colleague M. C. Beardsley for discussing this formulation with me.

[8]Blanshard's own support of "soft determinism" is expressed, without using this term, in "The Case for Determinism," 25.

[9]See W. P. Alston, "Moral Attitudes and Moral Judgments," *Nous* 2 (1968):1–23; and E. L. Beardsley, "Moral Disapproval and Moral Indignation," *Philosophy and Phenomenological Research* 31 (1970):161–76.

[10]This illocutionary act belongs to what J. L. Austin called the class of "behabitives" (see *How to Do Things with Words*, Lecture 12). I shall not here question the assumption that behabitives are a special kind of illocutionary act, although I have come to doubt this. In reflecting on this issue, I have profited from conversations with Mary Van Houten.

[11]The expression "offense against S" is intended to be neutral with respect to the issue between consequentialism and deontologism in ethics.

[12]I am indebted to Joseph Butler's classic discussions of resentment and forgiveness in *Fifteen Sermons* (1726), sermons 8 and 9.

[13]This concept of moral goodness employed throughout this paper is that of W. D. Ross, set forth in *The Right and the Good* (Oxford: Clarendon Press, 1930), chap. 7.

[14]Austin pointed out that "breaking a cup" can refer to either a voluntary or an involuntary act; but he does not seem to have noted that the same point applies to "dropping a tea tray," the example so central to his distinction between justification and excuse. See p. 124 and p. 139 in "A Plea for Excuses," in *Philosophical Papers of J. L. Austin*, eds. J. O. Urmson and G. J. Warnock (London: Oxford University Press, 1961).

[15]For degrees of culpability (moral as well as legal) the most illuminating ranking is that of the *Model Penal Code* of the American Law Institute (Philadelphia: 1962), 25 ff.

[16]See Alvin Goldman's discussion of "costs" in *A Theory of Action* (Englewood Cliffs, N.J.: Prentice-Hall, 1970), chap. 7.

[17]Ross, *Right and the Good*, 156.

[18]See E. L. Beardsley, "A Plea for Deserts," *American Philosophical Quarterly* 6 (1969):33–42.

[19]*Ethics*, pt. V. prop. 42.

[20]Barbara Harrison, in *Ms* (Aug. 1972), 15.

[21]Blanshard's discussion of the possibility of malice (*RG*, 340 ff.) is very different in tone and level.

[22]Stuart Hampshire, *Freedom of Mind* (Princeton: Princeton University Press, 1971), 7. (Lindley Lecture, copyright 1967 by the Department of Philosophy, University of Kansas.)

[23]A. C. Ewing, *The Definition of Good* (New York: Macmillan Co.; London: Routledge, 1947), chap. 4.

[24]Hannah Arendt, *The Human Condition* (Chicago: University of Chicago Press, 1958), 241.

[25]E. L. Beardsley, "Determinism and Moral Perspectives," *Philosophy and Phenomenological Research* 21 (1960):3–4.

3. Reply to Elizabeth L. Beardsley
Understanding and Forgiveness

I well remember Elizabeth Lane Beardsley as she sat in my logic class at Swarthmore some forty years ago. She was so much the ablest student in the class as to make the instructor uneasy if he ventured to disagree with her about the validity of Fapesmo or Datisi; and he felt the old uneasiness rising again as he read her essay for this volume on "Understanding and Forgiveness." Unfortunately I have had very little to say in my books about forgiveness, and Mrs. Beardsley has read very shrewdly and fairly between the lines to extract a doctrine worth criticizing. Her task would have been greatly eased if her eye had fallen on a paper of mine on "Retribution Revisited," published, with critical comments from others, in *Philosophical Perspectives on Punishment* (Charles C Thomas Co., 1968). My views on retribution and forgiveness are more fully stated there than anywhere else, and Mrs. Beardsley would have had a broader target to shoot at.

This no doubt would be asking for trouble, and I have enough on my hands in answering her present carefully reasoned paper. Probably the best way to begin from the reader's point of view is to give the sense of her argument as I understand it.

The main issue between Mrs. Beardsley and me is whether determinism in my form is consistent with forgiveness; I hold that it is; she apparently thinks that it is not. My determinism takes the form of maintaining that every event is connected causally with every other, either directly or indirectly. I hold, furthermore, that though we can seldom see a necessary connection between cause and effect, such connections are always present, and the grasp of them would render all events intelligible. The implication is that we live in an intelligible world. Mrs. Beardsley, rightly though ruefully putting clearness above euphony, describes my system as "intelligibilism."

"Intelligibilism" and Forgiveness

What now are the implications of intelligibilism for forgiveness? Let us take an example. And let us make it a concrete one; I shrink from using symbols anywhere, but particularly in dealing with moral cases. Jones was in Macy's store yesterday, and was seen to take a pair of children's shoes from the counter, stick them into his pocket, and saunter out. On the face of it this was theft, and we resent it. Would understanding the causes that led Jones to act as he did justify us in forgiving him? To simplify the discussion, Mrs. Beardsley conceives forgiveness as the dropping of an attitude of resentment. Such an attitude is normally based on the judgment that Jones has done something wrong. Hence the dropping of our resentment in such cases will depend on a change in our moral judgment about the act. I have maintained that one who comes to understand the act thoroughly will probably change his moral appraisal of it, with a corresponding change in his attitude. Mrs. Beardsley proceeds to list the aspects of the act regarding which an altered judgment might affect our resentment.

First, we may be simply mistaken about the act's being wrong. It turns out that Jones had already paid the attendant for the shoes, and was now merely picking up his legitimate purchase. In such a case our resentment would presumably vanish at once. There is nothing left to resent. Forgiveness with nothing to forgive is logically absurd. To my surprise, Mrs. Beardsley regards this case as irrelevant to the issue. We have not really forgiven a wrong action, she points out, for no such action occurred. I agree that this is technically correct. But is it irrelevant to the thesis I was maintaining? I was maintaining that the fuller understanding of a given case might reveal to us that it was not what it appeared to be, but something morally so different that a revised attitude toward it was called for. To say that a change of known character in an act makes it a different object for us seems to me clear. But to insist that the argument is irrelevant because we are now dealing with a different act seems to deny that we can talk of an act's changing at all; with the new character the old act has vanished and been replaced by something else without itself becoming new. This, as Kant pointed out, would deny the possibility of change, which demands that the "it" that changes should remain the same "it" throughout the process. To go into the metaphysics of this issue would take us pretty far afield. Perhaps my thesis would be more acceptable if restated slightly. With increasing understanding of an act, we may see that it is not what it seemed to be. Our understanding may reveal in it a character that changes the appropriateness of the attitude we formerly took toward it. Logical difficulties could again be raised with this, but it seems to me to describe fairly accurately a common moral experience.

Mrs. Beardsley turns next to "exculpations," that is, judgments that the agent was not to blame for what he did. First, what he did may have been unavoidable. Jones turns out on investigation to have been allowed to leave a hospital where he is under treatment for persisting kleptomania. When apprehended he confesses at once that he had no need of the shoes, but found the temptation to take them irresistible, and begs to be put under surveillance again. Here our resentment may be redirected against the hospital that allowed him out, but if we are convinced that the hapless agent is telling the truth, our resentment against himself would certainly diminish or disappear. That is, an understanding of the act in the light of its antecedents that makes us more ready to forgive it.

Another way of exculpating Jones cited by Mrs. Beardsley is to show that his intention in doing the act was not what it appeared to be. It looked like deliberate theft. But "deliberate theft" may cover a multitude of sins. Under questioning Jones reveals a disturbed and disturbing history. He is a black child of the ghetto, who has been taught at home that the white race are systematic oppressors and exploiters of his people; his own experiences of them have been chiefly of insult and contempt, real or imagined; he is without a job; he has a wife and child depending on him; and to make the pile complete, his child has no shoes. He is ignorant of the agencies that American society has provided for those in desperate circumstances. Anything he does at the expense of a white institution he considers fair revenge for what has been done to him and his people in the past. His dominant intention now is to help his child, and what others call theft he would dismiss as "getting even." Would an understanding of the complex of ideas and intentions out of which his act has issued have any effect on our resentment?

I think it would and should. I do not think it should cancel our resentment altogether; for we cannot concede to anyone the right to divide society into brutes and their victims, and to plunder the majority at will. But with our new understanding of the moving factors in the case, our first unqualified verdict would be softened, and so accordingly would our degree of resentment. The intention with which an act is done is a morally important part of it, and we could hardly feel toward Jones the sort of resentment we should feel toward a millionaire playboy who did "the same thing."

Mrs. Beardsley writes: "I believe that exculpation should probably be ruled out" as grounds justifying forgiveness. I confess that I do not see why. In one of several explanatory notes, she suggests that the reasons are in part of a kind just considered.

> First, one should note the difficulty (impossibility?) of finding act-terms sufficiently neutral with respect to avoidability and intention to enable us to say that it is the *same* act that is both excused and forgiven. As the appropriate sequel to "A was not really wrong" is "X did nothing that calls for forgiveness," so the appropriate sequel to "X could not have avoided A" or "X did not mean to do A" may be "A is not what X did."

In reading this passage I could not help wondering whether Mrs. Beardsley had been reading John Austin and taking him too seriously. Austin writes in his "A Plea for Excuses" (*Philosophical Papers*, 149):[1] "For we can generally split up what might be named as one action in several distinct ways, into different *stretches* or *phases* or *stages*. . . . we can dismantle the machinery of

the act, and describe (and excuse) separately the intelligence, the appreciation, the planning, the decision, the execution and so forth." I suppose it
might be maintained (though I am not sure it would by Mrs. Beardsley) that
if we excuse Jones's action, we are strictly excusing only a stretch or stage of
it which constituted its intention. If Mr. Austin meant to imply this, it seems
to me an example of how the cult of ordinary language can misreport ordinary meaning. The plain man would surely say that he was excusing Jones
for what he did—period. He would no doubt admit that it was in virtue of his
new understanding of Jones's intention that he dropped his resentment
against him, but he would not think of the intention as a separate act, or
stretch, or stage in a string of such things, but as part and parcel of an act that
was first resented as a whole and then as a whole condoned.

Determinism and Forgiveness

Mrs. Beardsley goes on to raise an important and disturbing question for
any naturalistic moralist who believes that the present life of the mind has
grown continuously out of a material world from which both thought and
conscience were absent. In that case are not all our acts unavoidable in the
sense that they are dependent on physical conditions given which they could
not have been different? And if thus inevitable, are they not, one and all, excusable? But if everything is excusable and equally so, is there any remaining
reason for calling anything right or wrong? Is not this the final and absurd
meaning of *tout comprendre c'est tout pardonner*?

Though Mrs. Beardsley does not put the case as baldly as this, many
critics would. It is true that I am an evolutionary naturalist (though in an essay on "The Limits of Naturalism" in *Contemporary American Philosophy* I
have tried to state some needed qualifications). How does such a cosmology
bear on our present issue? It would certainly not imply, as I think Mrs.
Beardsley would agree, that right and wrong, good and evil, would be can-
celled by such a heritage. The "dragons of the prime / That tare each other
in their slime" no doubt suffered horribly, and to deny that their suffering
was an evil merely because it was caused would be perverse. But if the intrinsic goods and evils of those days were genuine goods and evils though fully
conditioned, we can say no less of the goods and evils of today. And since the
objective rightness and wrongness of actions depend, in my view, on their
productivity of good and evil, right and wrong would remain under determinism very much what they are.

But the matter is not as simple as that. We seem to have been led by im-
peccable argument into intolerable paradox. Wrong still exists; but as inevitable, it is condonable; and if condonable, it would appear to be not wrong
after all.

If suffering is evil, then the wrongdoing that produces that suffering will certainly be resented, whether caused or not. But here the free-willist and the determinist arrive at a fork in the road. According to the free-willist, the future was open; Jones might have acted otherwise; and he should presumably be punished according to the degree of his guilt, measured roughly by the clearness of his knowledge that he was doing wrong. This punishment is retributive, and it is imposed because, with the possibility of avoiding wrong open to him, the agent declined it. Such punishment is out of court for the determinist. He may abhor the act both in itself and for the evil it produces, but if he metes out punishment for it, his eye will be on the future rather than the past. It is not merely that a man's degree of guilt is beyond ascertaining; it is that the guilt itself in the indeterminist's sense is a myth, and punishment for it is the piling of one evil upon another. On the other hand, the determinist's attitude toward the wrongdoer would, or should, be one of comprehensive charity; "there but for the grace of God go I." He will forgive the wrongdoer with the compassion of one who knows that with the inner and outer forces working upon him at the moment of decision, he could have done no other. But he will not spare his hand against him either. If a man can be made by certain forces to do wrong, he can be made by other forces to do right; and the aim of the determinist will be so to arrange the forces, inward and outward, that govern decisions as to deter from wrong and promote the right. Such forgiveness does not wipe out the difference between right and wrong. But it does make forgiveness on a large scale rational, and it keeps that forgiveness within lines that are theoretically clear.

I am anxious to speak plainly on this important and delicate issue, and it may be well to summarize. Mrs. Beardsley follows Ross in placing the distinctively moral quality of the action in its motive; if the act is done from the sense of duty, it exhibits moral goodness, even if it is stupid and disastrous; if it is done from malice, it is wicked, even though it should turn out by accident to be beneficial. And it is upon this motive that the propriety of forgiveness turns. In all this I agree. The point on which we differ is whether forgiveness can ever be extended to the evil motive itself, to genuine malice. Mrs. Beardsley would say No. And if all she means by forgiveness is the dropping of resentment, I can still agree. Since malice is evil in itself and evil in its fruits, it is clearly to be treated as an enemy. But forgiveness, as I conceive it, goes beyond the mere dropping of resentment. It is an attitude more feasible to the "intelligibilist" than to others. He sees, or thinks he sees, that malice too is among the inevitables. Hateful as it is, it is not a mere wanton election of evil for evil's sake. It springs from a background, no doubt inexhaustible, of mistreatment, misunderstanding, and perhaps ill-assorted genes, given which compassion will recognize that it too was inescapable. That seems to me to call for the forgiving of the agent, even while for society's sake we justly shackle and imprison him. So I do recognize, as Mrs. Beardsley rightly charges, a duty of forgiveness.

Moral Parallelism

In the course of her essay, Mrs. Beardsley raises several other issues which, while not quite central to the argument, are well worth attention. One concerns what she calls "moral parallelism." Philosophers have often tried to explain evil away, only to find that their argument, by a parallel application, would equally well explain goodness away. Rationalists in particular are liable to an illicit optimism, and Mrs. Beardsley suspects that I too have fallen prey to it. Now the rationalist's argument may take two very different forms which in my own mind have very different consequences.

(1) There is the argument used by such idealists as Bradley and Royce, which involved the doctrine of internal relations. This doctrine would make the nature of a term depend on its relations, so that you do not understand what it really is until you see it in its relations to the world as a whole. Is an earthworm what it is to another earthworm, what it is to the bird that eats it, what it is to the child who wonders at it, what it is to Darwin, who wrote masterly books about it, or what it would be to some understanding as much superior to Darwin's as Darwin's is to the earthworm's? If one starts on this line of speculation, one is bound to end up with this last answer. But that implies that nothing is really what it seems to be; for as the circle of relations widens, the "it" at the center changes too until it ceases to be recognizable as the same thing. So Royce would say that evil, seen in its place in the whole of things, could not possibly remain the evil that we know; it would be transformed, and transformed away. Now the trouble with this argument is that it is double-edged: it seems to explain away goodness as easily as it does evil. So we end with a universe in which good and evil have equally evaporated and we are lost in "a limitless grey sea."

I have to admit that I once found the argument of Royce and Bradley tempting. In *The Nature of Thought* I developed a doctrine of internal relations that pointed in the same direction, though I did not develop it on its ethical side. But my mind has not stood quite motionless for forty years. It is clearer to me now than it was then that a completely unrestricted doctrine of internal relations will not do. Bradley bravely tries to carry it through, but he ends in self-contradiction. He holds, for example, that everything, as now known to us, is unreal. But if so, the law of contradiction by which we test the reality of anything is itself unreal and unreliable, which means that all thought, including his own philosophy, is defeated at the outset. The doctrine of extreme and unqualified internality must therefore be modified. The world is not "a limitless grey sea." There are things in it that do not wholly lose their character and validity even in an absolute. The law of contradiction is one; the distinction between good and evil is another. This is not the place to develop the revisions that the doctrine requires. Suffice it to say that if I ever did hold the view that, seen in their full contexts, extreme happiness is no better intrinsically than extreme misery, I abandoned it long ago. So if I am charged with the moral parallelism that rests on this sort of base, I plead not guilty.

(2) But the argument may take a different form. I do hold, soundly or not, that things in the universe are interrelated, both causally and logically, and that to understand anything means to see it in its relations. This applies to human choice or decision as much as to anything else. To understand Jones's decision to take the shoes means to see it as the inevitable product of the influences working on his mind and body at the time. Now, as I have already explained, such an understanding does not destroy good or evil. The love of Saint Francis does not lose its goodness, nor does the sadism of Jack the Ripper lose its evil, when seen as having causes; the one remains lovable, the other hateful. My intelligibilism does not imply that malice somehow "loses its evil." But even intense evil may be dealt with rationally. And I hold that the rational way of dealing with it is to understand its causes and root them out, not to inflict further evil on those whom nature and society have made evil already. On neither interpretation of the "moral parallelism" argument, therefore, do I hold that we can make evil "lose its evil" by understanding it.

Again, Mrs. Beardsley thinks that when we gain insight into the-motives that govern an action of ourselves or another, such understanding does not fit easily into my theory that understanding or explanation is always through system. She quotes Stuart Hampshire to the effect that in knowing one's own reasons for acting one does not need the apparatus of inductive, experimental argument. This is true. But I do not think that our finding these reasons introspectively or intuitively is an argument against the view that to understand an act we must travel beyond itself. And the further we can travel relevantly, the fuller our explanation. As Sir Francis Galton pointed out, actions that at the moment of performance seem perfectly spontaneous and "free"—the decision to call Smith on the telephone, to buy a book from a bookseller's window, to invite someone to become one's bride—may be seen on retrospection to stand at the meeting point of a broad field of forces converging perhaps subconsciously upon the same decision. This seems to me a case of understanding through system, even though the system may be a small one. And when a psychoanalyst undertakes to discover why a patient has an irrational fear of birds, or an irresistible tendency to keep washing his hands, the explanation may be found to have ramifying roots that go many years deep.

Despite her acutely argued criticism of some of my ethical positions and a familiarity with the relevant literature obviously larger than mine, I hope

Mrs. Beardsley will not object to my thinking that our positions in ethics have far more in common than at variance with each other.

1. J. L. Austin, "A Plea for Excuses," *Philosophical Papers* (Oxford: Clarendon Press, 1961), 149.

4   THE IMPASSE IN ETHICS AND BLANSHARD'S WAY OUT
Oliver A. Johnson

BLANSHARD entitled his Howison Lecture, which he delivered at the University of California, Berkeley, in 1954, "The Impasse in Ethics— and a Way Out" ("IE").[1] The title is an understatement, for in the lecture he threads his way through a total of three impasses which have, in his mind, thrown blocks in the way of twentieth-century moral philosophers who have sought a firm foundation for ethical theory. To understand the nature of these impasses it is necessary to appreciate the situation in moral philosophy at the beginning of the century, which Blanshard describes as one of almost universal agreement. In Germany, France, Britain, and America the accepted doctrine was ideal utilitarianism or teleological ethics, characterized by Blanshard as the view that one should "always so act as to produce the largest amount of intrinsic goodness, goodness being a simple nonnatural quality that belonged self-evidently to experiences of various kinds" ("IE," 94). The history of ethics in our century has been punctuated by attacks on this position coming from philosophers of three quite divergent persuasions: (1) the deontologists, (2) the emotivists, and (3) the naturalists. In his lecture Blanshard argues that these waves of attack have proved the ideal utilitarian theory, as held at the beginning of the century, untenable; but he believes nevertheless that, with suitable modifications, it can be rehabilitated and formulated in a way that is capable of meeting the objections of its detractors. This he attempts to do in the course of his lecture, examining each impasse created by the successive attackers in order.

In my essay I shall follow Blanshard as he picks his way through the three roadblocks of contemporary ethical theory. Before I begin on this expedition, however, I should make a few preliminary remarks. It seems to me that Blanshard has identified the most serious issues that have arisen in recent ethical theory—if one limits his attention to Anglo-American philosophy, as, in the body of his lecture, Blanshard actually does. How a German or French philosopher would view the history of ethics during this period offers an interesting speculation but one which I shall not pursue. Turning to the impasses that have been created by the three attacks on the teleological tradition, although I agree with Blanshard regarding their importance, I think that the range of their significance is quite broad. The deontologists raise an issue that is basically intramural among moral philosophers. Although they disagree with teleologists over how our moral actions are to be justified, the alternative they offer has little effect on other realms of philosophy, intellectual disciplines outside of philosophy, or practical life. The naturalists, however, broaden the scope of the controversy, by raising the issue of the relationship between moral judgments and the empirical generalizations of natural science. The emotivists, finally, by their attack on the possibility of meaning in ethics, attempt to destroy the rational foundations underlying the moral life of man. As for Blanshard's responses to these varied attacks, I should perhaps say at the outset that I find myself in general agreement with the conclusions he reaches. To the extent that I shall differ with him, my criticisms will be directed to the arguments he advances to reach those conclusions. Once again, I think his line of reasoning is essentially sound but in certain instances I find it incomplete. I should like, therefore, in this essay to try to fill in what I believe to be the most serious of the gaps he has left. Since my main disagreement with him arises over his discussion of naturalism (although this involves also a problem arising out of his remarks on deontology), I shall concentrate most of my attention on that portion of his lecture. On the many points at which I agree with him, I shall, correspondingly, have little to say.

These preliminaries finished, let us turn to the three impasses Blanshard finds in twentieth-century ethics, beginning with that created by the deontologists.

I

To the conscientious person, who wishes to do his duty but finds himself in a situation in which he is faced by an array of conflicting moral claims and in his bewilderment turns to the ethicist for counsel, the ideal utilitarian offers simple advice: You ought to do the act that will maximize the good. As Blanshard points out, most of the leading ethicists in the West at the turn of the century would agree that such advice was correct. Their perhaps too complacent unanimity was rudely shattered by H. A. Prichard in 1912, who in his now famous article "Does Moral Philosophy Rest on a Mistake?" flatly rejected not only the utilitarian method for determining our duties but the results to which employment of that method led. According to Prichard, an individual trying to decide what he ought to do in a complex moral situation should not, as the utilitarians recommend, concentrate his attention on an evaluation of the consequences that would be produced by the various alternative acts he might perform; rather, he should contemplate the situation in which he finds himself, allowing his capacities for moral thinking to reveal directly to him the act that he ought to do. In Prichard's words, ". . . if we do doubt whether there is really an obligation to originate A in a situation B, the remedy lies not in any process of general thinking, but in getting face to face with a particular instance of the situation B, and then directly appreciating the obligation to originate A in that situation."[2] Or, as Prichard's follower W. D. Ross later put it, when we have a moral decision to make, we always find ourselves faced with a number of competing claims or prima facie duties, each exerting moral pressure on us. Our task is to weigh these conflicting claims directly and then perform the act that will fulfill the most pressing of them. In so acting we shall have done our duty.[3]

If one goes about reaching his practical moral decisions in the way recommended by the deontologists, he finds, Prichard and Ross both maintain, that certain types of action exert a heavier moral pressure on him than do others. For example, all other things being equal, one has a stronger obligation to perform an act benefiting a person to whom he has made a promise than one benefiting someone to whom he has made no promise. Consequently, even though one might produce better results by breaking his promise to the first person to confer a benefit on the second, he can still recognize that he ought to keep his promise, for this duty overrides his obligation to produce good. Because that is true, the utilitarians' advice "Always maximize the good" must be mistaken.[4]

Blanshard believes that utilitarianism can successfully meet the challenge of the deontologists, but only if it broadens the concept of value well beyond the limits that most utilitarians have drawn. To illustrate and defend his conception of a viable utilitarianism, he meets the deontologists on their own strongest ground by presenting a moral situation that seems incapable of resolution in utilitarian terms. Consider, he suggests, the following moral predicament: A judge, in a city racked with hoodlumism, is presiding at the trial of a man accused of a particularly brutal crime. The man has a criminal record, is suspected of being a ringleader of the hoodlums, and seems, on the basis of strong circumstantial evidence, to be guilty. The judge is convinced that if he convicts the man the effects will be very beneficial for law and order in the city. But the judge also has personal eyewitness evidence, which he alone possesses, that the man is innocent of the crime. What verdict should he render? A utilitarian would presumably advise "Convict"; the good consequences to be gained by such a decision will justify it. A deontologist would presumably advise "Acquit"; the prima facie duty of justice outweighs that of producing good results. Even if the world should be made a worse place by such a decision, our moral insight tells us that this is what the judge ought to do.

As a utilitarian Blanshard finds himself caught in a dilemma over this case. On the one side, he agrees with the deontologists that the judge ought to acquit; on the other, he finds it "incredible" ("IE," 97) that anyone can have a duty to act in a way that would make the world worse. He breaks the impasse by attacking the second horn of the dilemma. "I agree that the judge should acquit the innocent man; I cannot agree that in so doing he would be making the world worse" (ibid.). To support this stand he must offer convincing reasons why an action whose consequences appear less good than those of a contrary action has, appearances to the contrary, nevertheless the better results. He does so by arguing that the moral consequences of the alternative actions open to the judge are much more far-reaching and fundamental than would at first appear. What we must weigh in the balance is not simply the values lost or gained to a city in which a spate of hoodlumism is either curbed or goes unchecked but, more broadly, those of a community in which a guardian of its human rights either protects or abrogates one of the most basic of these—the right to justice before the law. Now, Blanshard argues, justice is not an intellectual abstraction but a fundamental element in a way of life among men that is intrinsically good. For the judge to reach an unjust verdict, therefore, would contribute to a diminution of communal values far more serious, because more basic and far-reaching, than any temporary unpleasantness that might flow from his upholding of justice. As Blanshard sums the matter up:

> It is important, we should all agree, that a crime wave should be discouraged. But it is far more important to maintain those relations of honor, truthfulness, and justice which touch our lives at a thousand points and make a society like ours possible. If these things may be repudiated in their own peculiar shrine, then, to put it crudely, anything goes. The foundations of our communal life have caved in. ["IE," 98]

I think that Blanshard's decision about the judge's duty, whether adequately justified by his argument or not, is correct. That the judge ought to have acquitted the defendant is a verdict that can be based not only on an appeal to moral intuition, as Blanshard apparently does, but much more convincingly, I believe, on the use of logical argument. That the judge would, by his decision to acquit, make a greater contribution to value than by a decision to convict is a much harder case to make. To pursue the argument in detail would require more space than I have, but I do think that Blanshard has grasped the essential point. A human community in which a just way of life is realized embodies a value of inestimable worth. For a judge, whose chief function is to preserve and protect this way of life, to tamper with it on behalf of realizing temporary goods is an ephemeral gain at most and surely not sufficient to justify the dangers it poses of irrevocable later losses. So on grounds of utility I would concur with Blanshard's advice to the judge.

But a problem still remains. Even if we agree that the judge would promote better consequences on the whole by acquitting than he would by convicting, can we therefore conclude, as Blanshard and the utilitarians do, that this fact provides a moral justification for his action if he acquits? To explain the difficulty I find at this stage of the argument, let me return to a final point that Blanshard makes against the deontologists ("IE," 98–99). Starting from the view, held by Ross, that we ought to choose a community in which the material goods of life are distributed justly in preference to one in which they are distributed unjustly, even though the total amount of happiness in each community is the same, Blanshard then goes on to ask: Why ought we to do so? To such a question, he points out, the deontologists have no answer to give. They can offer no *reason* why a just community ought to be preferred to an unjust community. They simply apprehend this to be true directly; for them it is a case of moral intuition. Blanshard is not satisfied with this. Rather, he believes we can and ought to provide some reason for our choice. What the reason should be is obvious to him: A just community is intrinsically better than an unjust community. Because it is better it ought to be chosen.

Blanshard is, I think, right in his view that our moral choices and decisions need to be supported by reasons. He is right also in his claim that the utilitarian theory does offer such supporting reasons in a way in which the deontological theory does not. Nevertheless, one can question whether the reasons that utilitarians give are fully satisfactory. The adequacy of such reasons can be challenged on two quite different grounds: (1) A question can be raised about the nature and sufficiency of their own support, and (2) the thesis that they are successful in performing the function of supporting our moral choices can be denied. Let us look further into both of these points.

(1) Blanshard believes that a just community is better than an unjust one. Furthermore, its goodness must be intrinsic rather than instrumental; otherwise it would not have been possible for him to make an appeal to the value of justice in his answer to the deontologists' attack on traditional utilitarianism embodied in the case of the judge. A state of justice, Blanshard thus maintains, is intrinsically good. But what reason can he offer in support of this judgment? Here we must be careful that we do not derail ourselves. For it would be tempting to answer that the reason why a state of justice is good is that it distributes rewards and punishments to individuals on the basis of merit. The first difficulty that such a reason presents to the utilitarian is that it cancels his advantage against the deontologist. For the latter could argue in an analogous way by maintaining that we ought to act justly and that the reason why we ought to do so is that, if we do, we shall be distributing rewards and punishments to individuals on the basis of merit. In such an

argument both utilitarian and deontologist are appealing equally to a description of the state of affairs that we use the term "justice" to denote, in the first case to justify our calling the state of affairs intrinsically good and in the second to justify our claim that we have a duty to promote it. So neither gains an advantage against the other. The second difficulty—and it also affects both utilitarian and deontologist—is that the appeal is in neither case convincing. For the goodness of a just state of affairs, described as one in which rewards and punishments are distributed to individuals on the basis of merit, no more follows from its description than does its badness. Likewise, a duty to promote such a state of affairs no more follows from its description than a duty to promote its opposite. Knowledge of the meaning of justice does not imply knowledge either of its intrinsic goodness or of any duty we may have to promote it. The kind of reason we must seek, if it is to provide the support we need to conclude either that justice is good or that it ought to be promoted, must be one that is capable of underwriting our claim to know these things. To the truth of such claims a description of the nature of justice is so far logically irrelevant.

The crucial question, then, that the utilitarian must answer is: What reasons can he give for believing that a just state of affairs is intrinsically good? How does he know this to be true? Faced with the parallel question "How do you know that justice ought to be promoted?" a deontologist has a ready reply: "I need no reasons; I know it because it is self-evident to me." Of course, Blanshard can offer a similar answer. "I need no reasons either; I know that justice is intrinsically good because this is self-evident to me." I am inclined to believe that he would in fact respond in this vein. From the way in which he concludes his critique of the deontologists ("IE," 99) one is left with the strong impression that this is indeed the line he would take. If so, his utilitarianism rests epistemologically, like both the utilitarianism of Rashdall and Moore and the deontology of Prichard and Ross, on an appeal to moral intuition.[5] If this be so, then it is subject to the same kind of epistemological attack to which all of these other writers have been subjected. But in the case of Blanshard the situation is complicated by the conclusions he reaches regarding the third impasse in ethics, that provoked by the naturalists (which I shall consider later in detail). If, as he contends in that argument, the concept of good can be defined in naturalistic terms, then he would have to agree, by implication, that, if justice is intrinsically good, a state of justice must fulfill the naturalistic conditions contained in his definition of good. Can he show this to be true? Unfortunately, he does not discuss the issue, except very briefly at the end of his lecture in a passage that is difficult to interpret because, although he apparently wishes to maintain that justice is intrinsically good, the argument he offers establishes only that it is instrumentally good (cf. "IE," 111–12). There remains, therefore, some discrepancy between his answer to the deontologists and his naturalistic conception of value.

(2) The second criticism of the adequacy of the reasons utilitarians offer in support of our moral choices comes from Prichard. According to the utilitarian theory, the judge ought to acquit the defendant because his doing so will promote better consequences than would result from his convicting him. The judge's obligation to act is, thus, based on or supported by the goodness to be gained by his action. Now Prichard directly denies the possibility of such a relationship. In a much discussed sentence in his article "Does Moral Philosophy Rest on a Mistake?" he writes: "An 'ought,' if it is to be derived at all, can only be derived from another 'ought.' "[6] The crucial word in this declaration is "derived." What does Prichard mean by it? The first point to be made is that he is not speaking descriptively, for, if he were, he would clearly be in error. Many moral philosophers have "derived" "oughts" from things other than "oughts." For example, in his analysis of the case of the judge, Blanshard argues that the reason why the judge ought to acquit is that to do so would be to act justly, and justice is intrinsically good. Thus he "derives" the "ought" of the judge's obligation from the intrinsic goodness of justice. To this obvious fact Prichard would reply that the quotation marks cannot be removed from around "derives," for any such attempted "derivation" must of necessity be unsuccessful. For when he claims that an "ought" can be derived only from another "ought," he is speaking not of what philosophers have in fact said they have done but rather of what they can legitimately accomplish. His point is normative, not descriptive.

The reason why it is illegitimate to derive an "ought" from anything else than another "ought" is that it is logically impossible to do so. If one attempts such a "derivation" he finds himself committing a non sequitur. To return to Blanshard's illustration, the utilitarian line of reasoning can be formalized as follows:

The judge, by acquitting the defendant, will be promoting justice.
Justice is intrinsically good. Therefore:
The judge ought to acquit.

That this attempted deduction is formally invalid is obvious, for it introduces the concept "ought" in its conclusion without having made any provision for it in the premises. And the same objection could be offered to any argument that attempted to "deduce" a moral obligation from premises that did not contain the concept of moral obligation.

In response to Prichard's critique a utilitarian could point out that the reason why the conclusion does not follow from the premises is that the argument is incomplete. What is required is the addition of another premise, which consists of the utilitarian theory itself, formulated as a theory of moral obligation.

The judge, by acquitting the defendant, will be promoting justice.
Justice is intrinsically good.
One ought always to maximize the good. Therefore:
The judge ought to acquit.
The argument, as now formulated, is logically valid. Furthermore, it satisfies Prichard's stipulation that an "ought," if it is to be derived at all, must be derived only from another "ought." The only question remaining is whether it is also cogent. Can the reasons given in the premises establish that the conclusion is true? They can only if they themselves are true. But here the utilitarian finds himself the object of the deontologists' original attack. If the deontologists are correct, the utilitarian premise added to the second argument—i.e. One ought always to maximize the good—is false. For they claim to know, on the grounds of intuitive self-evidence, that, at least sometimes, one ought not to maximize the good. If this is true, one cannot employ an argument whose premises are concerned with intrinsic goodness, even in Blanshard's expanded sense in which a state of justice is seen to be good in itself, and succeed in drawing conclusions about what we ought to do. If the concept of duty is essential to moral philosophy, no teleological ethics can ever prove adequate. Whether an answer can be found to this argument within the limits of a viable utilitarianism remains to be seen. Blanshard does himself offer an answer, in his discussion of the third impasse in contemporary ethics. Because I believe this to be the most serious problem facing his or any other utilitarian type of ethical theory, I shall review his answer in considerable detail when I reach the third impasse. In the meantime, another roadblock—that created by the emotivists—needs to be cleared away.

II

Had I been writing this essay thirty years ago I would almost surely have devoted much more attention to the emotive theory of ethics than to that of the deontologists. For the impasse created by the emotivists struck the philosophical world with an impact that made the dispute between utilitarians and deontologists seem little more than a tempest in a teacup. But time changes things, including philosophical perspectives. Today one must still take very seriously the objections that Prichard raised against the tradition over a half-century ago; the emotive theory, on the other hand, holds interest only for the historian of ethics. Why this change in fortune? A general answer is easy to give: The deontological theory offers an interpretation of the moral life not only supportable by strong arguments but resilient in the face of attack; the emotive theory, on the contrary, is incapable of holding its own once it comes under sustained and systematic critical scrutiny. That the emotive theory should not have had a long philosophical life could have been predicted at the outset; that its demise should have been so abrupt, however, is due to the energetic, penetrating, and devastating counterattack mounted against it early on by a relatively small number of ethicists, among whom Blanshard was a prominent figure.[7] The part he played in hastening the end of emotivism is, I think, of considerably greater significance than he himself has recognized (cf. "IE," 103).

At this late date it is hard to say much that is new about the emotive theory. The ground has been so well covered and the theory itself so completely demolished that anything I could add in the way of critical comment would almost surely be redundant. So I shall limit myself to a few remarks, setting the career of emotivism in its historical perspective as I view it a generation later.

I shall begin with Blanshard—viewing the emotive theory as being centrally concerned with the question of meaning. The notion of emotive meaning, as it occurs in the central thesis of the theory that ethical utterances have emotive meaning only, is quite odd. One is inclined to say, indeed, that it is not a concept of *meaning* at all, but rather a misleading phrase whose significance lies not in describing a special type of meaning that ethical utterances possess but in denying that such utterances have any meaning, even while conferring the title on them. For emotive "meaning" must be contrasted sharply with cognitive meaning, which an utterance possesses only if it is possible that it be true or false. Because ethical utterances can be neither, hence cannot convey any information about the world—and, specifically, about good and bad, right and wrong—such utterances, despite the deceptively cognitive form they assume, must be devoid of cognitive meaning. The essential message of the emotive theory, thus, is not constructive—to confer some special sense of meaning on ethical utterances—but destructive—to deny them the one kind of meaning that really counts.

To evaluate the emotivists' contention that ethical utterances have no cognitive meaning, it is necessary to have some conception of the meaning of "meaning." On what grounds can anyone say that a proposition either possesses or lacks meaning? To pursue this issue in detail, besides being too great an undertaking for this essay, is actually not essential for our purposes. All that we need do is to draw a distinction between two conceptions of meaning, which I shall call, respectively, (1) the descriptive and (2) the normative analysis of meaning. According to the descriptive analysis, meaning must be construed in relation to the speakers who use a language rather than in relation to the words they utter. The correct way to phrase a question about meaning is not to ask, "What does that statement mean?" but rather "What does he mean by that statement?" Speech is a human activity employed to accomplish human ends. People use language to convey meanings they wish to express. According to the descriptive analysis, to understand the meaning of a word or proposition, we must determine what its users intend by it, for that is what gives it its meaning. From this analysis it follows that, if people ordinarily employ certain propositions to express meanings they wish to convey, these propositions cannot be meaningless. The normative analysis, on the other hand, holds that the question of whether a term or proposition is meaningful turns on its satisfaction of some standard or criterion of meaning. If it fulfills the criterion, it is meaningful; if it fails to do so, it is meaningless. On this analysis, it is possible for people to use certain propositions regularly, believing them to be meaningful, when in fact they are meaningless.

In his critique of the emotive theory, Blanshard begins by assuming a descriptive analysis of the nature of meaning and asks: If we examine the meanings that people give to the normative utterances they employ, do we find that they characteristically avoid using such utterances as carriers of cognitive meaning, limiting their use instead to the expression of emotion? Or do they, on the contrary, mean to use these utterances to make statements that they believe to be true, hence cognitively meaningful? The answer, Blanshard believes, is apparent. When, in 1945, the people of the world discovered what had been going on at Auschwitz, Buchenwald, and Belsen and judged that such mass murder of innocent human beings was evil, they did mean to agree in asserting something true. However much emotion some may have felt at the time they expressed their opinion, their judgment of evil was a judgment, not an outburst of feeling. In holding the contrary, the emotivists are, in Blanshard's opinion, embracing a view that is not just mistaken but "absurd" ("IE," 103). In this judgment I fully concur. If one accepts a descriptive analysis of meaning, then the emotive theory of ethics must be dismissed as offering a grotesque parody of what people in general mean by their ethical utterances.

To some extent the emotivists have recognized that their theory is incompatible with a descriptive analysis of meaning in ethics (although, as Blanshard points out ["IE," 102], they have usually been far from clear about the way in which they intend "meaning" to be understood when they claim that ethical utterances possess nothing but emotive "meaning"). When pressed they usually shift their stand from a descriptive to a normative analysis of meaning. The reason why ethical utterances lack cognitive meaning, they argue, is not that people never use them to try to state true propositions—they do—but rather because, whatever people may in fact try to do, they cannot succeed in using them in this way. For the utterances do not satisfy the criterion essential to qualify them as cognitively meaningful propositions.

Its appeal to a normative analysis of meaning to support its case reveals the most significant theoretical feature of the emotive theory of ethics—that it is not, like most other ethical theories, an independent analysis based on an examination of its ostensible subject matter but rather a conclusion derived from a general position in philosophy. I think it is fair to say that no serious thinker would ever have embraced the emotive theory if his interest had been simply to provide an interpretation of the moral life of man. The emotivists were, in fact, driven to their ethical theory. Almost without exception they were logical positivists. As such they accepted a general theory of meaning which demanded that ethical utterances be judged cognitively meaningless. It is quite apparent from their writings that, having decided that ethics must be banned from the realm of cognitive meaning, they merely shopped around until they came upon the notion of emotive "meaning" and concluded that it offered the most plausible means for explaining away these troublesome "pseudopropositions."

To demolish the emotive theory, therefore, it is not sufficient simply to establish that it totally misconstrues the meaning that we normally give to our ethical utterances. For the heart of the matter lies elsewhere, in the epistemology of logical positivism and in particular in its criterion of cognitive meaning, the verification principle, from which the emotive theory of ethics is a derivation. This most critics of the emotive theory have recognized. From the beginning they have devoted much attention to the verification principle, with the well-known result of its total destruction as a normative criterion of meaning. Blanshard has had a share in this effort and in his book *Reason and Analysis* sums up the case against the verification principle as it had been built up by critics of positivism over a quarter of a century.[8] I do not need to repeat his account here but should only add, from a historical perspective, that it was the unanswerable attacks launched against the verification principle by Blanshard and others that were primarily responsible for the collapse of logical positivism. And once the normative principle of meaning on which the emotive theory of ethics rested had been demolished, and the theory had to support itself by an appeal to a descriptive analysis of meaning, it was soon seen to be, as Blanshard says, absurd, and has quickly faded, along with its parent, into well-deserved oblivion.

The impasse in ethics generated by logical positivism and its emotive theory has long since been broken. Although most of us can still remember the consternation the positivists created in philosophical circles a generation ago, it is hard, when one views the movement historically, to avoid a certain amount of bemusement regarding the entire episode. Indeed, I should suggest that, if one were to read the writings of the positivists today and to review dispassionately the controversies of that past era, he might find himself in sympathy with the conclusion that I have reached; namely, that logical positivism in its essence was not really a philosophical but a *religious* movement. The most striking feature of the main polemical writings of the positivists—books like Carnap's *Philosophy and Logical Syntax,* Ayer's *Language, Truth and Logic,* Reichenbach's *The Rise of Scientific Philosophy*—is that these are the works not of analysts but of enthusiasts. They had a cause—to save philosophy from its sins—and a dogma—the verification principle. Even after their dogma had been discredited they still clung to it, performing mental acrobatics well worthy of Jesuits in their attempts to salvage it from destruction. Even in internal polemics, their endless factional disputes over such issues as the proper formulation of the verification principle and the precise limits of cognitive meaning, they exhibit the same kinds of convolution in support of dogma that are characteristic of much of Scholastic argumentation in the Middle Ages. On the other hand, their writings are singularly lacking in philosophical qualities, particularly such characteristics as dispassionate objectivity, emotively neutral terminology, the imaginative appreciation of alternative points of view, and the pursuit of truth for its own sake. Nevertheless, as a religious movement logical positivism was bound to end in failure. Not only was it addressed to an inappropriate constituency, professional philosophers, but it lacked the ceremonial and charismatic trappings without which no religion can long flourish.[9]

III

The third impasse in contemporary ethics, that created by the naturalists, is different in an important respect from the other two. Whereas both the deontologists and the emotivists, in their quite different ways, rejected the utilitarian or teleological tradition, the naturalists did not. As Blanshard points out, many of the most eminent figures in the history of ethics from Plato to Mill combined naturalism with utilitarianism (cf. "IE," 106). The theory that the naturalists opposed was the quite specific form of utilitarianism that dominated ethical theory at the beginning of our century and received its best-known expression in the *Principia Ethica* of G. E. Moore. Their quarrel with Moore centered on a single issue, the question of the definability of "good." Whereas he claimed that "good" is undefinable, the naturalists demurred and proceeded to offer a number of definitions of it.

In the controversy surrounding this impasse Blanshard comes down on the side of the naturalists and against Moore. What he attempts to do is to offer a definition of "good," then show not only that his interpretation of what "good" means gives a more satisfactory account of the nature of that concept than does the Moorian view but also that it provides a theoretical basis in terms of which all the main issues of ethics can be successfully resolved.[10] In this final section I shall review each of these theses, the first two briefly and the last at greater length. I should say at the outset that I agree with Blanshard on almost all of his conclusions as well as most of his arguments. However, at one point I believe that he fails to make the case that he wishes to establish. That case can, I think, be made, and I shall conclude by offering some suggestions about the way in which it must be done.

To begin, Blanshard rejects Moore's view that "good" is a simple, non-natural, indefinable quality. As he writes:

> ... when moralists began to think about Moore's analysis, many of them had to report doubt whether they had ever known such a quality and indeed whether there was any such quality to know. It was a philosophic will-o'-the-wisp that dissolved when one tried to lay hold of it. . . . Now if, when an analysis of a common meaning is offered, many or most qualified persons can find nothing in their thought that answers to the analysis, the criticism is inevitable that the analysis has failed to catch what is really meant.
> With this criticism I agree. . . . Like many others, I find it hard to verify this nonnatural quality of goodness. ["IE," 106]

To comprehend the meaning of "good," Blanshard contends, one must begin, not as Moore did with an intuition of a simple quality, but rather with an understanding of the nature of man as a being evolved from simpler animal species but with abilities and potentialities far exceeding those of his evolutionary forebears. ". . . I think that goods and bads," he writes, "are more firmly rooted in human nature than the ideal utilitarians would admit" ("IE," 106). Using human nature as the basis for his conclusions, he goes on to argue that the good for man consists in two components—satisfaction and fulfillment (cf. "IE," 108 ff.). The first expresses his recognition of the element of truth in hedonism; unless a person gains satisfaction from an experience, that experience has no value. "Enjoyment is not all there is to goodness; at this date there is no need to stop over that. But it is so essential to any experience we call good that if it vanishes, the value vanishes with it" ("IE," 109). The other component of goodness, fulfillment, takes us beyond hedonism. It encompasses the value we realize when we fully meet the demands of our nature—for food and drink, play, friends, things of beauty, and enlightenment. In a passage in *Reason and Goodness* Blanshard sums up his conception of value as follows:

> The kind of consideration on which we are embarking is so different from our earlier analyses that it may be well to set down briefly and at once the view of goodness that will gradually emerge from it. We shall hold that only experiences are directly or immediately good. When they are good intrinsically, they perform a double function: they fulfil an impulse, drive or need, and in so doing they give satisfaction or pleasure. Both components, fulfilment and satisfaction, are necessary, and they vary independently of each other. But both are always partial in the sense that they apply to a limited set of needs; and they are always provisional or incomplete, so that goodness is a matter of degree. It is to be measured against an ideal good, which is the kind of life which would fulfil and satisfy wholly. [*RG*, 293]

The critic of Blanshard's ethics might well take issue with such a conception of goodness, arguing either that satisfaction and fulfillment do not encompass all the values to be found in human life, or, alternatively, that experiences which are fulfilling and satisfying need not always be good. Although some questions about the theory might be raised on these grounds—particularly, I believe, by the observation that the fulfillment of an evil impulse, with its resultant satisfaction, may well be considered to be an experience that is not intrinsically good[11]—nevertheless I doubt that such reservations would affect the integrity of the position in any serious way. On the whole, Blanshard's account of the nature of goodness, modified, perhaps, in certain minor details, seems to me to offer one of the most defensible statements of an ethical ideal to be found in the literature.

If, with Blanshard, we accept the view that satisfaction and fulfillment are intrinsically good, we may next ask the question: What is the relationship between the goodness of an experience and its satisfying and fulfilling characteristics? Are they the same or are they different? When Blanshard states that satisfaction and fulfillment are intrinsically good, he might mean that an experience which is satisfying and fulfilling is, because it possesses these characteristics, also an intrinsically good experience. On such an interpretation the goodness of the experience is an added quality that it acquires by possessing the characteristics of satisfaction and fulfillment. They are not the same as good but a necessary condition of its existence. This is the interpretation on which Moore would insist. The other interpretation is to deny any distinction in meaning between satisfaction and fulfillment on the one hand and goodness on the other. To say either that an experience is satisfying and fulfilling or that it is intrinsically good is to convey in different words the identically same meaning. This is Blanshard's interpretation. "To say of an experience that it is intrinsically good means, then, two things: first, that it satisfies; and second, that it fulfils. . . . To fulfil and satisfy what nature prompts is not only good; it is what goodness means" ("IE," 110). By *defining* goodness, Blanshard thus allies himself with the naturalists. He also makes himself liable to an objection first stated by Moore a half-century before he wrote the words I have just quoted; he commits, in Moore's famous phrase, the "naturalistic fallacy."

That Blanshard does not take the "naturalistic fallacy" too seriously is indicated by the fact that he fails even to mention it in his Howison Lecture.[12] In attempting to arbitrate between Moore and Blanshard on this point, I find myself of divided mind. On the one hand, the "naturalistic fallacy" has been abundantly demonstrated by writers since Moore not to be the fallacy he believed it to be. To go over again at this late date the well-worn arguments would be gratuitous. Nevertheless, a problem remains at the very heart of ethical theory, a problem that I think Moore was attempting, however unsuccessfully, to articulate in his "naturalistic fallacy" argument. Ironically, his own intuitive utilitarianism is no more able to cope with this problem than the naturalistic utilitarian theories of his opponents. Since the difficulty remains—and, I think, plagues Blanshard's moral philosophy—I shall consider it at some length here.

Any ethical theory, if it is to provide a full explanation of its subject matter, must address itself to two different but related questions: What is the good life for man? and How ought we, as moral beings, to act? One of the perennial problems of ethics, revealed in the twentieth century by the impasse created by the deontologists, concerns the relationship between the answers that one gives to these two questions. According to the dominant teleological tradition, the first is the important question; once one has answered it he is ready to hand an answer to the second. If, as a utilitarian would hold, the moral injunction "One ought always to maximize the good" gives a full account of man's moral obligations, then it follows that, once we have discovered what the good is, we always know, without need for any further argument, how we ought to act. But, as Prichard has emphasized, the utilitarians' reasoning on this issue lacks cogency. In their argument they attempt to derive our moral obligations from a conception of the nature of goodness; in this, however, they cannot succeed, for an "ought" can be derived only from another "ought."

Since Blanshard is a utilitarian, he attempts to resolve the issue of the relationship between our duties and the good in utilitarian terms. In doing so, he makes himself liable to the logical strictures that Prichard raised against the tradition. At the very end of his Howison Lecture he faces this issue and in a paragraph offers not one, but two, views regarding the relationship between goodness and duty. A question might be raised as to whether the two views he offers are consistent with each other, but I shall not concern myself with that; I shall concentrate on what I believe to be the more important point of whether either theory offers a viable account of the nature of man's moral obligations and, particularly, of the basis on which these rest.

After completing his definition of good in terms of satisfaction and fulfillment, Blanshard concludes his lecture by changing the subject from goodness to duty. The transition he makes is abrupt. He writes: "I have been speaking about goodness; but in thus conceiving goodness we are also defining the nature of duty" ("IE," 110). This statement about duty and its relationship to goodness, if I understand it correctly, can be elaborated as follows: To say, as Blanshard does, that a conception of goodness provides a definition of duty is to imply that the two concepts, goodness and duty, are identical in meaning. Since he has already argued that goodness is a characteristic of human experiences, and specifically that it is identical to experiences that are satisfying and fulfilling, it would have to follow for him that a moral obligation is identical to an experience that is satisfying and fulfilling. Now I find this impossible to accept. It may be very difficult to determine just what a moral obligation is but I am quite sure that Blanshard would agree with me that it is *not* the same thing as a satisfying and fulfilling experience. When, after talking of our experiences and their satisfying, fulfilling qualities, we then raise the question of how we ought as moral beings to act, it seems as clear to me as anything could be that we are changing the subject.

That Blanshard would, despite his definition of duty that I have just quoted, admit such a distinction in meaning is indicated by the fact that, immediately following the definition, he goes on to present an argument in which he appears to deduce our duties from his view of goodness.

> To the man who declines to recognize duty we offer not some dubious authority or a threat about the future, but a simple question or two. "Do you want health, understanding, friendship?" "Yes, of course; they are what make life worth while." "If it is good that you should have them, is there any ground for denying that it is good for others to have them?" "No." "Do you agree that course X is a necessary means if these things that make life worth living are to be achieved?" "Yes, so it appears." "Then you cannot reject course X without repudiating your own reason and the central demands of your own nature." ["IE," 111]

This quotation reveals a small but important shift in Blanshard's position. If duty means the same as goodness, it is not necessary to appeal to the goodness of the ends we all desire to justify the conclusion that we have an obligation to act in a certain way. That Blanshard does offer such an argument makes it clear that he recognizes a distinction in meaning between the two. Nevertheless, he just as clearly believes that the two concepts are so closely related that the appeal to such ends can supply a good reason in support of the conclusion he draws about what we ought to do. Is he right in this view? In what sense, if any, does the conclusion he reaches in his little dialogue follow from the questions and answers that he uses to lead up to it?

To answer these questions, I suggest that Blanshard's conclusion is not the only one that might be drawn from what has been said before. That his conclusion does not follow from the premises in any logically tight way is clear from the fact that one could, without self-contradiction, accept all of the dialogue up to the conclusion and then reject it. To make this point a bit more specific, let us suppose that Blanshard is addressing his questions to a naturalistic utilitarian, who is also an egoist. Could such a respondent not, in complete logical consistency, reply to Blanshard's final statement in the following vein: "I agree that I must follow course X in order to produce health, understanding, and friendship for others but I find that following course X will not produce anything that my nature demands for me; on the contrary, doing so will cause me considerable inconvenience and discomfort. Since I am concerned only about things that make my own life worth living, I recognize no obligation to pursue them on behalf of others. Furthermore, I see no grounds in your dialogue to support your allegation that my refusal to recognize the obligation you confront me with involves me in repudiating my own reason. On the contrary, I find my position not only rational but consistent with the responses I gave to your earlier questions."

I should like to make several comments about the words I have just put into the mouth of my hypothetical egoist. First, his egoism is a repudiation of morality. By refusing to recognize any obligation to promote the goods of others, he is, in effect, denying that his conduct is subject to moral constraint. Rather, he is implying that he is morally at liberty to follow the bent of his own needs and desires without consideration for the interests of anyone else.[13]

Secondly, Blanshard's dialogue does allow the kind of egoistic rejoinder that I have suggested. That this is true results in part from the fact that he makes a debatable transition in the course of his argument. If, as he contends, everyone desires certain ends, such as health, understanding, and friendship, then any individual's refusal to follow a course of action necessary for him to realize these ends would be a repudiation of both his reason and the central demands of his nature. With this we can agree. We can agree also that, if these ends are good for any individual, they are good for all. But here our agreement with Blanshard ends. For from these arguments it follows only that no individual can refuse to pursue such ends *for himself* without repudiating his own reason and nature. It does not follow that to refuse to pursue them on behalf of people other than himself involves him in a similar repudiation. Therefore, if I am correct in my view that when we talk of moral obligation we are referring to what each individual owes to his fellows, we must conclude that Blanshard offers no grounds in his dialogue for morally condemning the self-interested stance of the egoist.

But it is possible that Blanshard would disagree with me regarding the necessarily social nature of our moral obligations, holding rather that we have duties to ourselves as much as we have to others. In *Reason and Goodness,* at least, he appears to go even further by implying that our moral obligations might well have no connection with the interests of anyone other than ourselves. "Moral obligation *is* . . . the claim upon us of ends appointed by our own nature" (*RG,* 333). This definition has implications that I find unacceptable. Since an egoist might in all truthfulness say that his nature is such that the only claims that it presses upon him are those that concern his own welfare, could he not conclude, consistently with Blanshard's definition, that, in his single-minded pursuit of such personal ends, he is fulfilling his whole duty as a moral being? I cannot agree with such a conclusion, for, as I have already said, I believe that egoism is the repudiation rather than the fulfillment of the claims of morality. What Blanshard fails to do, both in his dialogue and in his definition of moral obligation, is to make a vital distinction—between the prudential "ought," which has no moral content, and the moral "ought," the "ought" of moral obligation. Instead, in the dialogue he begins his argument by appealing to the former and then shifts ground in order to reach a conclusion about the latter.

Even though the argument of his dialogue does not, in my judgment, establish the immorality of a policy of totally self-interested action, I am quite sure that Blanshard would agree with me that egoism is incompatible with morality. If so, we might ask, could his dialogue be revised to avoid the shift he makes in it and thus gain the cogency it lacks? Before we could agree to this possibility, we must recognize another, somewhat different problem that plagues his argument. It concerns the relationship between the premises as a whole (exemplified in the series of questions and answers) and the final conclusion that he reaches. As I have already noted, that conclusion does not follow logically from the premises. Every assertion made in the premises could be true and the conclusion nevertheless false. Since it may not be apparent why I say this, perhaps I should clarify my point here. The problem turns on Blanshard's purpose, which may be obscured by the dialogue form in which he casts the argument. What we must remember is that he is attempting to demonstrate to a doubter that he has duties. His method of doing so is to establish that certain ends are intrinsically good and then to conclude that our duty as moral beings is to promote these goods. But the difficulty lies right at this point: How does it follow from the fact that something is good that we have a duty to promote it? Surely the connection is not a logical one for there is no logical contradiction in the proposition "X is intrinsically good yet no one has any duty to promote it." Since Blanshard is clearly convinced that we can derive conclusions about our duties from premises about the intrinsic goodness of certain experiences, he must be relying on a different kind of connection between premises and conclusion than that of logical entailment. What kind of connection could this be?

The answer we must give reveals the methodology on which, I think, Blanshard often relies in his Howison Lecture to support his ethical conclusions. The thesis that we ought to promote those ends that are intrinsically good is, for him, intuitively self-evident. Although we may deny such a duty without logical contradiction, we cannot, if we are honest, clear-thinking, and morally sincere, persist in such a denial. The moral insight that all of us possess forbids our doing so.

I must confess that I have always found the appeal to intuition in ethics more persuasive than have most contemporary moral philosophers. Nevertheless, it does have serious weaknesses. Since these have been so thoroughly aired in the literature, I shall not take the time to review them here. My own view is that for a philosopher to appeal to intuition to support his conclusions about our moral obligations is to adopt a methodology that he cannot justify, not only because of its own weaknesses but also because he has available to him a far stronger means for accomplishing the same result.

This judgment leads me to my final comment about the egoistic rejoinder to Blanshard's dialogue that I offered earlier. Although he does not substantiate his claim, Blanshard is, I think, right in his conclusion that anyone who refuses to recognize duties to others is repudiating his own reason. That Blanshard would have made a stronger case for his view had he devoted more attention to the problem than the one paragraph that appears at the end of his Howison Lecture is, in fact, attested by his discussion of moral obligation in *Reason and Goodness*, which occupies most of a chapter. Here he carries the argument significantly beyond his earlier brief remarks. In a passage which has a clear resemblance to the dialogue that I have been criticizing but which emphasizes much more strongly a point of great theoretical importance, he writes:

> A right act, then, is one that tends to bring into being at least as much in the way of satisfying and fulfilling experience as would any available alternative. But experience for whom? For me, or you, or some third party? We can only answer that from the point of view of value, this query is irrelevant. We are often called upon, of course, to choose between producing goods for ourselves and goods for others, but the choice is in principle the same as in choosing between goods of our own. If what makes anything good is the fulfilment and satisfaction of impulse-desire, and a given experience of my neighbour's performs this office as well as one of my own, it is as good as my own, and in the reckoning of rights and duties must count as equal to it. Goodness is no respecter of persons. . . . [*RG*, 322]

In this passage Blanshard is, I think, moving along the right track toward finding a reason that can provide a logically rigorous justification of the reality of duty. The argument on which he embarks, if pursued, is capable of establishing that anyone who, like the egoist, fails to recognize moral obligations to others is acting irrationally, in the strictest, logical meaning of that term. However, to illuminate the full force of the argument it is necessary to elaborate it more fully than Blanshard has done. To conclude this essay I should like to offer some suggestions regarding the implications that can be drawn from the quotation I have taken from *Reason and Goodness* and show that these do in fact lead to the conclusion that, to be rational, we must recognize our moral obligations to our fellows. I should like to think that Blanshard would find these remarks congenial to his own way of thinking.

The crux of the issue lies in Blanshard's statement "Goodness is no respecter of persons." If we agree that satisfaction is good, then it does not matter, as far as value is concerned, who is satisfied. My satisfaction is as good as your equal satisfaction, and vice versa. One cannot, therefore, legitimately appeal to the satisfaction that his action will produce as a reason for pursuing his own ends in preference to those of others, for exactly the same reason can be offered to justify a contrary course of action. Self-preferring action thus is arbitrary and hence irrational. To this argument, however, an egoist might object, asserting that he has a reason for preferentially promoting his own satisfactions; he enjoys them and he doesn't enjoy those of others. Is this a good reason? It could be replied that his enjoyment of them does not distinguish his satisfactions from those of others, for they equally enjoy their own satisfactions. But in rejoinder the egoist might counter: "Good; let them pursue their satisfactions and I shall pursue mine." But such a response will not yet do. For it could be pointed out that other people expect the egoist to make a contribution to their interests; they are not willing to be left free to provide for themselves on the condition that he be allowed to pursue his own ends in complete disregard of theirs. Is their expectation reasonable? Does each member of a community have a right to have his good promoted by all of the others? I think that the only way in which the egoist can consistently deny such a right, and thus absolve himself of any obligation to his fellows, is to repudiate the right as being one that he himself possesses. Or, to put the point somewhat differently, to be consistent the egoist must fulfill the conditions that he laid down earlier about seeking his own satisfactions and allowing others to seek theirs. Specifically, he must release his fellows from the obligation to perform any acts on his behalf. For immediately he makes a claim on anyone else, he must grant others the right to make equal claims on himself. That is to say, he must recognize a moral obligation to them. Now it is impossible for any individual to satisfy the conditions laid down in the egoist's conception of social life. No one can live in a human community without making use of other people to serve his own ends. No individual is or can be an island. As long as he is part of a community he must depend on his fellows and they in turn on him. As he makes claims on them, so too he has obligations to them. To assert his claims (as he must do) and at the same time to deny his obligations (as the egoist recommends) is to be irrational. And it is its essential irrationality that destroys the egoist's denial of morality and confirms the reality of our duties to others.

The three impasses that Blanshard finds in contemporary ethical theory have, I think, been generally broken down. Nor would it be too much to say that he has had a large hand in the dismantling process. As a result ethics can truly be said to have advanced in the twentieth century. To conclude that all problems have been resolved, however, would be unduly optimistic. As I have just indicated, Blanshard must still reckon with a fourth impasse, one not just of the twentieth century but of the entire history of ethics—the problem of the justification of moral obligation. Although he has made a promising initial assault on this impasse, many stones still remain to be removed from the path.

OLIVER A. JOHNSON

DEPARTMENT OF PHILOSOPHY
UNIVERSITY OF CALIFORNIA, RIVERSIDE

NOTES

[1]Brand Blanshard, "The Impasse in Ethics—and a Way Out," in *University of California Publications in Philosophy,* vol. 28, no. 2 (Berkeley and Los Angeles: University of California Press, 1955), 93–112. Referred to henceforth as "IE."

[2]H. A. Prichard, "Does Moral Philosophy Rest on a Mistake?" *Mind,* n.s., 21 (1912): 37.

[3]Cf. W. D. Ross, *The Right and the Good* (Oxford: At the Clarendon Press, 1930), chap. 2.

[4]The deontologists do not deny that we have a prima facie duty to promote good consequences; they claim only that we have other prima facie duties as well, which cannot be reduced to that duty but can override it. Logically, their position is not the contrary but the contradictory of teleological ethics.

[5]On several occasions in "IE" (cf. pp. 96–97, 99, 103, 111), as well as in other writings, Blanshard appeals to moral insight, the moral beliefs of the ordinary man, what we "see" to be true, etc., in support of his ethical views. I shall return to his use of intuition in resolving a particular theoretical issue later.

[6]Prichard, "Does Moral Philosophy Rest on a Mistake?" 24. The point is not original with Prichard, however, for it can be found in even fuller form in a famous passage in Hume's *Treatise,* bk. III, pt. I, sec. 1.

[7]Cf. particularly his articles, "The New Subjectivism in Ethics," *Philosophy and Phenomenological Research* 9 (1948–49): 504–11, and "Subjectivism in Ethics—A Criticism," *Philosophical Quarterly* 1 (1950–51): 127–39.

[8]*Reason and Analysis,* chap. 5. In this book he writes: "We come now to a difficulty that has dogged the verifiability criterion from the beginning and in all its forms. It makes a statement about what is, and what is not, meaningful. Is this itself meaningful? No statement is meaningful, it tells us, which cannot be verified in sense perception. Little by little the suspicion grew and was confirmed that such a criterion was doomed to die by self strangulation" (239).

[9]I should make it clear that the interpretation of logical positivism I have just given is my own. I do not know to what extent, if any, Blanshard would agree with me.

[10]Although Blanshard places himself in the naturalists' camp, in his major work on ethics, *Reason and Goodness,* he points out that his naturalism differs from that of most others of the naturalistic persuasion. As he puts it, "Whether an object does in fact fulfil and satisfy is something that can be determined without going outside nature as we conceive it. But then on the other hand we do not conceive human nature as naturalists commonly do. It is so thoroughly teleological that it cannot be understood apart from what it is seeking to become" (*RG,* 316).

[11]Blanshard discusses this objection very briefly; cf. "IE," 110. I think he needs to consider the matter further, for the problem has implications for other areas of his ethical theory.

[12]However, in *Reason and Goodness* he discusses it at some length, offering reasons why he does not find Moore's views on goodness convincing. Cf. *RG,* 268 ff. and 319 ff.

[13]To the counterargument that an individual might pursue both health and understanding without acknowledging any duties to his fellows but that he could not gain friendship without recognizing the moral claims of others, the obvious reply is that, if an egoist were to cultivate other people to gain their friendship and thus to reap its rewards, we should hardly describe his action as being morally motivated but should rather credit him with the morally dubious ability of being able to use his "friends" for his own ends.

4. Reply to Oliver A. Johnson

The Impasse in Ethics and Blanshard's Way Out

Mr. Johnson has chosen for his attention my Howison Lecture on "The Impasse in Ethics—and a Way Out."[1] He reminds me rightly that I have dealt in that paper not with one impasse only but with three, and he has important remarks to make about my handling of each of them. I have found his essay pleasant reading, partly by reason of its clear and orderly presentation, partly because of the evidence it gives, even where it differs from my ethical position, of a full and sympathetic understanding of it. The three crises discussed are the confrontation between the utilitarians and the deontologists, the threat of emotivism, and the rift in the utilitarian camp between the "ideal utilitarians" and the naturalists. These are all issues that were more urgent in 1954, when the Howison Lecture was given, than they are in the minds of present-day moralists, but as Mr. Johnson has no difficulty in showing, they remain of great ethical importance. I shall take his comments on them in order.

Teleology versus Deontology

My position in ethics is teleological. I prefer this term to "utilitarian" because the latter suggests that the end is usefulness, and usefulness is never a good in itself. It is an instrumental good, like that of furniture or a good weapon or a good tool. A teleological ethics, as the name implies, holds that conduct should be directed to an end, but an end that is good in itself and not merely as a means to something else. Teleological moralists have generally identified this end with the greatest good on the whole, that is, the greatest net surplus of good over evil if one takes into account all the goods and evils produced in those affected by it. Moore in his later life preferred to put it in this way: it is self-evident that we ought to make the world as much better as we can. This is my own view also, though I have had to differ with Moore as to whether good can be analyzed and defined. I think that in one form or another this teleological view has been the dominant one in Western ethical thought.

Its main challenge has come from intuitionism, another name that covers a wide variety of theories. One very influential though often unrecognized form of it was the ethics of Christianity, which estimated the rightness or wrongness of conduct rather by its motive than by its effects, and has received its most persuasive formal statement from James Martineau. A more rigorously rational form of intuitionism was offered by Kant in his categorical imperative. But to my mind the most convincing form of rationalist intuitionism yet developed is that of the deontologists of a generation ago, whose first manifesto was Prichard's article "Has Moral Philosophy Been Based on a Mistake?" and whose best presentation is in Sir David Ross's books, *The Right and the Good* and *The Foundations of Ethics*. The case of the deontologists, as they called themselves, was in the main simple and effective. It admitted that the teleologists' rule about producing the greatest good was valid for most conduct, but that in some cases it broke down and was therefore an unreliable guide. You borrow some money from a rich friend, promising to return it on a certain day. You know that he has forgotten all about the transaction and that a local charity could use the money to great advantage. Should you repay it nevertheless? Of course you should, said the deontologists, even though greater good might well be produced by giving it to charity. Or a friend of yours who has lent you $5,000 dies after getting a promise from you that you will use the amount in erecting a monument to him in the local cemetery. The promise is verbal; no one knows about it; no one will blame you if you do not carry it out; and you are sure that a new car would do you a great deal more good than a stone would do for him. What should you do? Without one moment of hesitation, say the deontologists, and without any shilly-shallying about whose advantage would be served, you should put up that stone. The repayment of debts and the keeping of promises are not duties that rest on nice calculations of advantage; all conscientious men regard them as self-evident obligations. This does not mean that they are absolute; Ross's intuitionism is made far more plausible by his frank recognition of the importance of consequences. If using your dead friend's money for an operation on his son was the only way of saving the son's life, Ross would no doubt relent. But even so he would deny that the judgment rested on comparing goods. Putting up the monument might produce no good at all. Nevertheless your promise has a claim on you in virtue of being a promise, and what you are weighing is the strength of that moral claim against the moral claim of the advantage to the son.

Teleologists are in difficulty when such cases are adduced, and Ross is surely close to our actual way of thinking about them. If I may indulge in a stray bit of reminiscence, I remember putting a part of Ross's case to Moore over luncheon one day, and Moore's slow and earnest reply: "It still seems to me self-evident that I should make the world as much better as I can." That remains my own conviction. It is also Mr. Johnson's. Where then does he differ from me? His difficulty is a relatively technical one: while agreeing with my teleological conclusion, he doubts the validity of my argument for it.

Utilitarianism and Justice

It will be well, then, to look at the argument used in the paper of mine with which Mr. Johnson is chiefly concerned. By way of testing the teleologists' case, I looked round for the strongest sort of exception that their critics threw at them. I conceived the case (whether borrowed or contrived I do not now remember) of a magistrate who had to pass judgment in unusual circumstances. He is in a town where peace and order are threatened by a gang of thugs convinced that they can defy the law with impunity. One of them comes before the judge charged with a serious crime. The circumstantial evidence against him is overwhelming, but the judge and the judge alone knows one crucial fact, for he happens to have seen the man out fishing in a distant stream at the very time when the crime was committed. What should he do? He reflects that in the interest of the greater good this man should be behind bars; his conviction would increase the local security; it would tend to discourage the rising hoodlumism; and since the judge alone knows the crucial fact, he could maintain the credit of his court by merely keeping silence. Should he not convict? To this there would be a virtually unanimous chorus of "noes" from decent ordinary citizens, including Mr. Johnson and myself. But in joining in this chorus, are we not deserting the principle of the greater good for that very different principle, *Fiat justitia, ruat caelum?*

To this my reply was that a wider notion of consequences than that traditionally accepted by utilitarians must be recognized. Among the consequences must be included not only those following causally from this particular act but also those that were logically implied by this kind of act. The court is an essential part of a system of government much larger than itself, upon whose effective functioning depends the community's welfare. The deliberate conviction of an innocent man by an official specially charged with finding and acting on evidence would be a serious breach in that system. And the breach would not be single but manifold. Besides a judge's malfeasance in office, it involves gross injustice to the man charged, a betrayal of public confidence, and a deliberate lie to the community. Again, if these forms of wrongdoing are to be condoned in this instance, they must in consistency be condoned wherever it suits the mind of a public servant to gain what he conceives as the public's advantage by committing similar breaches of trust and truth. The true consequence of the judge's giving a judgment against the evidence is thus a weakening of the entire system of trust and confidence upon which the security and happiness of the community depends. And this is a consequence much worse than the release of a man, however much of a scoundrel he may otherwise be, who is innocent of the charge against him.

In the conclusion of the line of argument here given in compressed form, Mr. Johnson is still with me. Where does he part company? He thinks the argument falls short in at least two respects.

(1) He says that in order to make out my case I accept justice as an intrinsic good, and if I do that, I lose my advantage over the deontologists. For if I make justice a state of affairs whose intrinsic goodness is self-evident, I am taking essentially the stand of Ross himself.

Now I suspect some misunderstanding here. (a) Ross did not take the state of justice to be intrinsically good, though he sometimes wrote in a way that made this interpretation natural. At one point, for example, he raised the intriguing question: Suppose one could create either of two communities, both containing equal amounts of good, but in one of which the goods are distributed justly, and in the other unjustly; which community should one choose? Ross of course answers that he would choose the just community. It was protested that he had no reason for the choice because he had expressly disclaimed that in justice as a state of affairs there was any goodness at all. As in the telling of truth and the keeping of promises, we should adhere to them in practice not because of the goodness either of themselves or of their consequences, but for no *reason* whatever. One should choose the just community, though even with its justice it contained no greater good. This seemed to me a strange position, but so far as I know, Ross never withdrew from it to the position that justice is intrinsically good.

(b) Nor do I hold myself that justice is thus good, though I have evidently expressed myself ambiguously about it. If I had committed myself to it, Mr. Johnson could easily have replied with an argument that he is kind enough not to use. For I have said that intrinsic goodness lies only in experience, and the set of arrangements in which justice consists can hardly be called an experience. But if I do not concede that justice is intrinsically good, am I not in the same position as Ross, of being unable to offer any reason why it should be preferred? No, I think not. (i) Hume, Mill, and Sidgwick all rested the duty of justice on its consequences; I too can point to these consequences; and in the broadened sense of consequence I have above referred to, I can add many more. (ii) Either of these appeals to consequences may be supplemented by a different kind of consideration. In my latest book (*Reason and Belief*) I have argued that there is an ethics of belief according to which it is self-evidently right, even in matters religious, to follow the evidence where it leads. Now justice, which has been called the most intellectual of the virtues, does involve, I think, the acceptance of certain self-evident truths. Examples are: One man's good, other things equal, should be regarded as of the same intrinsic importance as the like good of anyone else; or in the distribution of respect and of goods, it is more fitting that merit should be rewarded than that wickedness should. These statements fulfill Sidgwick's well-known requirements for axiomatic truths. It seems to me therefore right and reasonable for intelligent persons to recognize them and act on them. And in doing so, according to my ethics, they are producing further intrinsic good, which lies partly in the fulfillment of their own impulse for understanding and partly in increasing the likelihood of similar practice in others. This is not a position open, as I see it, to the deontologists. But it is both open to, and required by, my own way of thinking in ethics. It is not offered as a major consideration, but it is worth mention, for a scrupulous regard for justice may raise the intellectual tone of a community. When it comes to offering reasons for justice in conduct, it therefore seems to me that, on the whole and despite Mr. Johnson's doubts, my ethics is in a better position than Ross's.

(2) Mr. Johnson has a further doubt about the utilitarian case for justice, this time suggested by Prichard. "An 'ought,' if it is to be derived at all," says Prichard, "can only be derived from another 'ought.' " Here the teleologist is alleged to be in a dilemma. For if, in his argument for acting justly, he argues with no "ought" in his premises, as he commonly does, his argument seems invalid. And if he does use an "ought" he begs the question. This will be clearer in illustration. (I alter Mr. Johnson's examples to conform to a correction just made about the intrinsic good of justice in my own theory.) Suppose one argues:

The judge, by acquitting the defendant, will be promoting justice.

Justice is a means of maximizing good.

Therefore the judge ought to acquit.

This, says Mr. Johnson, is formally invalid because an "ought" is introduced into the conclusion without appearing in the premises. This of course is true. Nevertheless the reasoning seems to me sound, since it is essentially a synthetic necessary insight and in such an insight it is perfectly legitimate to introduce something new in the predicate. From the realization that course A is a means of maximizing the good, one passes directly to the conclusion, "Then I ought to do A." For the teleologist, this is the nerve of his position. And since the argument is really sound, it admits of statement in correct syllogistic form:

All acts that maximize the good ought to be done.

This act of justice maximizes the good.

Therefore this act should be done.

Mr. Johnson objects that an argument of this kind offers as its major premise the very proposition that the deontologist is concerned to deny. True again. But the teleologist can hardly be expected to abandon the appeal to a proposition which he regards as self-evident and which is apparently beyond proof in any other way because an opponent does not accept it. Sooner or later in ethics the appeal to intuition is unavoidable, though it must be remembered that an intuition may itself be a form of reason. If we have an opponent who rejects our intuition as not self-evident, our right course is not to abandon our principle but to show to our opponent, if we can, that his alleged exceptions to the principle are not really exceptions at all. That is the line we have taken.

Emotivism

I shall say little about Mr. Johnson's discussion of emotivism because I so fully agree with it. He is inclined to wonder, as he looks back, that so implausible a theory should have gained such popularity and I can only share this wonder. In part the reception of emotivism was due, I suppose, to its having been required by the new epistemology of positivism, whose verification principle found no place for judgments of value. In some small part it may have resulted from disillusionment with the ethics of Moore. Moore, though never a positivist, was a pioneer and idol of the analytic philosophers, and when they looked for his indefinable, nonnatural concept of good and failed to find it, the temptation was great to say that there was no cognitive meaning present at all. However that may be, Mr. Johnson thinks that emotivism has now had its day and may be forgotten. I am somewhat less sanguine than he. As I have tried to show in *Reason and Goodness,* the interest in reducing moral approval to an emotion or an attitude has a long past in philosophy, and I suspect that, in new or resurrected forms, it will have a long future.

As for its appearance in the thirties and forties, there were two aspects that I confess surprised me. One was that it flourished in such close association in place and time with the ordinary language philosophy; for if there is anything clear, it is that the ordinary man, using his ordinary language, means to say something true when he calls war evil or the enfranchisement of women right. The other cause for surprise was finding that some of the most effective spokesmen for the emotive theory were persons who had been forced out of their homeland by the accursed Hitler. They must have regarded him as the very incarnation of evil, but their adoption of the emotive theory cut the ground from under their own feet. They became mere plaintive protesters with no more case against the Nazis than the Nazis had against them. The whole moral debate became frivolous.

Mr. Johnson is inclined in retrospect to view the upsurge of positivism and emotivism as a kind of religious movement, the product of enthusiasm rather than of objective analysis. The movement did, I think, have a pretty strong coloring of this kind. Many of the positivists were scientists turned philosophers, who looked upon themselves as the young knights who had come to save philosophy from itself by introducing into it the scientific method. Not all of them were well equipped for this task. Wittgenstein, for example, had a very fragmentary knowledge of the history of philosophy together with a boundless confidence in his ability to reform it, which he proceeded to do, not once but twice. The dragon that the young Saint Georges set out to slay was of course metaphysics, the great enemy, ensconced in clouds of speculative obscurity. I do not think their evangelical fervor for clarity was wholly misguided. Much of the metaphysics and theology of the generation that preceded them had been tiresomely pretentious and obscure, and some housecleaning was in order. But like other enthusiasts, they outdid themselves in their zeal. I doubt whether those who set out with their pailful of disinfectants to purify the "house of intellect" from metaphysics were a great and obvious improvement over the Josephs and the Prichards, the McTaggarts and the Whiteheads who preceded them. Was it not Whitehead who said that if man cannot live by bread alone, neither can he live by disinfectants?

"Ought" and "Good"

In the third part of Mr. Johnson's essay he inquires into the relation of duty and goodness, the ought and the good. He puts accurately what it is that I take to make anything good, but he thinks my language suggests two quite different notions of how duty and goodness are related. He quotes a sentence from "The Impasse in Ethics" which runs as follows: "I have been speaking about goodness; but in thus conceiving goodness we are also defining the nature of duty." He reads this as saying "that the two concepts, goodness and duty, are identical in meaning." Of course to say that is nonsense, as he does not fail to point out, though in kindlier terms. What I meant to suggest was that with a clear conception of goodness we had all that was necessary for the future conception of duty, for goodness is that which duty tries to produce. I was saying that, as between those who take duty and those who take goodness as the prime conception of ethics, I was taking my stand with the latter. Once you know the possibilities in the way of good in a certain situation, you can go on to derive your duty. Your duty is to choose the most promising of them and the means most likely to produce it.

Mr. Johnson thinks that in this same essay I describe my theory in terms that suggest egoism. I can only plead in extenuation that one cannot say all that needs to be said in one lecture. At any rate I feel sure that Mr. Johnson, who knows my other writings on ethics, would not classify me as an egoist. It must be admitted, however, that anyone who takes self-realization or self-fulfillment as the end is very likely to be so classified. He is bound to concern himself with what will realize or fulfill a *self*, taking it for granted that he will be read as talking not about his own self but any and all selves. Thus it was a shock to me to read in so discerning a writer as Broad that T. H. Green was an egoist, and it is something of a shock to learn that my own expressions were capable of a like interpretation. But Mr. Johnson is no doubt correct that I should have made it clearer how one passes from the proposition that one ought to pursue the fulfillment and satisfaction of one's own nature to the very different proposition that one should promote the like good in others. How is one to deal with an egoist who insists that though he feels the pull of his own prospective good, he feels none at all toward the good of others? "Why should I put myself out for a good I am never going to realize?"

Now you cannot refute an egoist if his egoism is a Kierkegaardian commitment. You cannot deny or disprove an act of will. But as soon as he puts into a proposition the belief on which he is evidently proceeding, I think he is lost. This proposition is that an experience in another mind, even when qualitatively identical with a good experience of his own, is not to be regarded as good. And this is merely irrational. If being fulfilling and satisfying is what defines goodness, one cannot confer the name on one experience and deny it to the same kind of experience in another mind. The egoist may try to include in his definition of goodness its presence in one mind only, his own. But that is as arbitrary as to say that two and two are four only when this presents itself to one's own mind but not when it presents itself to another. The intrinsic goodness of an experience is no more a function of time, place, or person where it appears than is the truth of a proposition. To prize one's own happiness and be indifferent to another's is a clear case of irrationality.

But why should I be rational? If to this question one wants a rational answer, one has the answer already; one's nature supplies it even in asking the question; the craving for rationality is part of being human. Why should one believe that two and two are four rather than seven? I suppose because it is true, and the interest of one's knowing nature is in truth, not in falsity. Why in truth? Because truth reveals reality, and it is only by fulfilling this cognitive interest that we can live in a real world rather than in one of illusion and insanity. A person may choose, if he wishes, to live in an insane world, and to object that he cannot do so consistently will presumably not interest him, for consistency is part of the baggage he now wants to get rid of. To me this seems mere suicide. The craving for truth is part of my nature, and in a sense the most important part, for only as it is fulfilled am I able to see with any clearness the ends of the other needs and hungers of my nature. I hold with all deliberateness that to be moral is to be rational, and to be rational is to be moral. Thus egoism is the living of a lie.

Mr. Johnson concludes his essay by saying that though I have dealt more or less successfully with three impasses in ethics, there remains a fourth where I have been less successful. That fourth is the problem how to justify moral obligation. What he means by this, I suspect, is that while a naturalistic definition of goodness such as I have given is plausible, a definition of "ought" in such terms is much less plausible. Nevertheless I have attempted to give such a definition in *Reason and Goodness*. It is very probably inadequate, but as Mr. Johnson did not develop his criticism of it, no reply seems here to be called for.

I prize greatly not only the amount of agreement Mr. Johnson has shown with my general position in ethics, but also what he says about the influence that my writing has had in the phasing out of the three positions I was attacking in 1954. The praise I think is overgenerous. Indeed it gives rise to a fifth ethical problem that has at times troubled me: Is it moral to take satisfaction in praise that one believes to overshoot the truth?

1. Brand Blanshard, "The Impasse in Ethics—and a Way Out," Howison Lecture, 1954. University of California Publications in Philosophy, vol. 28, no. 2 (Berkeley and Los Angeles: University of California Press, 1955), 93–112.

5 BLANSHARD ON "INTRINSIC GOODNESS"
John Howie

FOR Blanshard "intrinsic goodness" is an object of pursuit and consists in what is valued and sought for its own sake. As long as something is considered a means to something else of value, it is not appropriately called intrinsically good. It must be sought for its own sake if it is to be considered intrinsically good.

What is sought for its own sake? Blanshard answers that only some type of experience can be sought. Superficially, a person may suppose that what he seeks is some object. But in fact no one seeks some object per se. Rather, what one seeks is the experience of that object. To claim that goodness lies in the object alone is to introduce into one's experience of value a distinctness of parts obtained only by abstraction. Blanshard rejects the view of Inge, Urban, and Nicolai Hartmann that values are independent of man's experience of them, and that values somehow stand over against us as eternal essences that are there whether man shares them or not. In the enjoyment of a painting, for example, one cannot simply distinguish within the experience the enjoyment from that which is enjoyed. The value or goodness is the-painting-enjoyed. The painting and the appreciation of it are so blended that it is false to insist that the value lies in the one or the other considered in isolation. The blending is a part of the inherent nature of value itself. Moreover, one cannot know what another person finds good merely by knowing in the abstract that the person is enjoying something, without any notion that what satisfies him is a painting. It is the painting and the appreciation in union that constitute the goodness.

What sort of experience is intrinsically good? Blanshard replies that an experience is intrinsically good whenever it fulfills an impulse, drive, or need, and in so doing brings satisfaction or pleasure. The satisfaction and the fulfillment are both necessary for intrinsic good. If an experience is merely satisfying or pleasing, without also being fulfilling, it is not intrinsically good, or it is somehow only deficiently good. If an experience is merely fulfilling without also being satisfying, it is not intrinsically good.

The fulfillment and the satisfaction may vary in an independent way. The fulfillment may be more nearly complete, and the satisfaction or attending pleasure may be relatively minimal. Moreover, the fulfillment and satisfaction are always partial and provisional. The fulfillment and satisfaction are only partial because they apply to a limited set of needs. Although the satisfaction meets an essential need or needs, it does not meet all of man's essential needs. The fulfillment and satisfaction are only provisional since they are to be measured against an ideal good, a wholly satisfying and fulfilling life. As an ethical end "the good" is the most comprehensive possible fulfillment and satisfaction of the impulse-desires of all men. The sort of impulse-desires whose satisfaction is the good are the self-amending kind, those connected with thought and experience rather than de facto desires.

As Blanshard acknowledges, his view presupposes a certain view of human consciousness, impulse, desire, satisfaction, and fulfillment. It is important to have in mind these underlying aspects of his view. It will repay us to note at least briefly these features.

For Blanshard consciousness is goal-seeking from its inception. Goal-directed behavior is not something acquired as such through either learning or experience. In all its activities consciousness is goal-directed. At a most elementary level, instinct, employing a preformed structure of the organism, is a felt tendency toward a certain course of behavior. Impulse, by contrast, is a felt tendency operating without the guidance of such a structure. The absence of this structure means that the guidance the impulse has is not physiologically determined. Desire is a felt tendency toward a course of behavior with a consciousness of the end (or goal) that would satisfy the desire.

Consciousness of an end or goal in carrying out a course of behavior alters that behavior at every stage in its execution. No mechanical performance can duplicate the human pursuit of an end. Such pursuit and achievement differs from mechanical process and accomplishment because the human being is aware of each sequential step as a stage necessary for the attainment of the end. This consciousness of steps as leading to a goal means that, should conditions so require, an alteration in the process is possible. Such an alteration might mean that a desire could attain its end in more than one way. Without the awareness of the end no such variation would be possible. Desire, then, because it always includes an awareness of the end, is amenable to a wide variety of means for its satisfaction. This is not to say that the end will vary. Rather, it is to say that the manner and means for the attainment of satisfaction may vary over a wide range in view of different conditions one may confront.

Moreover, human desire, unlike that of animals, is not chained to sense experience. A human being can desire something before he has it, as he has it, afterward, and even when it is not. His desire is not restricted to whatever is present to sense experience.

Our major goods as human beings answer to the essential kinds of impulse-desire. What are the essential kinds? Choosing not to discuss the various kinds of impulse-desires, Blanshard restricts himself to a consideration of two basic impulse-desires of human nature: the theoretic impulse and the aesthetic impulse. "Goodness," Blanshard says in summary, "is satisfactoriness, which consists jointly in the fulfilment of impulse-desire by the content it demands and the attendant satisfaction" (*Reason and Goodness* [*RG*], 302).[1]

What is fulfillment? And what is satisfaction? "Fulfilment," Blanshard explains, "is achieving the end that our impulse is seeking; satisfaction is the feeling that attends this fulfilment" (*RG*, 309). Fulfillment varies for the different ends our impulse-desires may have. And the standards of goodness for the fulfillment of each different impulse-desire will also vary. The good called knowledge, for example, is its fulfilling of the theoretic impulse. The theoretic impulse has within it a purpose whose aim of understanding things can be recognized once its aim is achieved (304).

By understanding Blanshard means knowing not alone that a fact is so but why it is so. To understand a theorem in Euclidean geometry, for example, is to grasp how other statements lead one to the theorem. To understand the War of 1812 is to know not only the facts about the battles and incidents on the high seas but also the underlying conditions that made these battles and events happen as they did. To understand something fully is to grasp all of the implications to which the theorem or statement commits us.[2]

Although the purpose of an impulse may be only retrospectively recognized, it is operative throughout the process. The good called beauty, for example, is roughly speaking whatever meaningfully fulfills the aesthetic impulse—namely, harmony and proportion.[3] What fulfills the theoretic impulse is different from what fulfills the aesthetic impulse. Accordingly, one should not expect that the same standards would apply to both.

In appraising Blanshard's ethical perspective it is worthwhile to underscore both its points of strength and its weaknesses or inadequacies. In large measure the strength of his view is a compound of his telling criticisms of naturalistic approaches (including the behavioristic), emotivism (Carnap and Ayer), and deontological emphases (especially those of W. D. Ross).

A point of strength is his recognition in a fresh and clear-eyed way of the inadequacies of a naturalistic view of consciousness.[4] These inadequacies, as he sees them, all cluster around the commonsense position that a naturalistic view of consciousness cannot hold to its meaning consistently.

Consider the failings of the naturalistic view. For naturalism headaches and toothaches are merely motions of the molecules of one's brain. But, Blanshard has us ask, why should one consider this set of motions in itself objectionable when one cannot distinguish it from a hundred thousand other motions? The reason that this set of motions is objectionable is precisely because it is painful. Its painfulness (which is, after all, a conscious experience) is what makes it objectionable. But in denying this conscious experience the naturalist is denying the very thing whose existence makes an explanation of the situation possible. Moreover, to the extent that the naturalist takes medicine to remove the pain, his very action belies his theory.

Think further. Are the traits that one assigns to mental events and those he assigns to physical events the same? Does a pain or a memory have a mass, velocity, or direction as any physical change would have? Certainly not. Why then does the naturalist refuse to distinguish between the physical event and the mental event?

Moreover, are the relations that obtain between physical events and mental events the same? As Hume succinctly put it, "A moral reflection cannot be placed on the right or on the left hand of a passion; nor can a smell or sound be either of a circular or a square figure" (*Treatise,* pt. IV, sec. 5). Sensations, ideas, feelings, volitions—the contents of mind—plainly do not have the same relations as physical events.

At the heart of the naturalist view of consciousness is the notion that a conscious event can be identified with a change in the brain. But how can the two be the same? Consider carefully. What is meant by a conscious experience is certainly different from what is meant by a change in the brain. The nervous impulses that are the correlates of the radically different sensations of hearing and seeing are the same in structure and movement. But if the sensations are radically different while the nervous changes are apparently alike, then what one means by sensations must be distinct from what he means by physical changes. The attempt to identify the physical change with the mental event always involves a tacit admission that the two cannot be identified. Indeed, how would one "know" that a brain change was "a sensation of touch" unless he already had definite knowledge of the touch sensation beforehand? How would one know that a particular brain change was a sensation of sight unless he already had definite knowledge of the sight sensation beforehand? The correlation of the one with the other presupposes a knowledge of the sensation so correlated in each case.

It would certainly be in the spirit of Blanshard's criticisms to indicate that mind performs certain functions that brain cannot perform. Thus, for example, mind observes itself while no known movement of matter in motion can perform that function. Again, mind spans the past as well as the present and may, on occasion, accurately anticipate the future. Memory cannot be explained by traces in the brain (whether chemical or electrical) left by past experiences because the traces are present traces. The reference of a present trace to a past event cannot be accomplished by a present motion in the brain. The present trace of a past event is known to be something other than a mere present impression by a mind which can appropriately locate it in the past. In all these respects mind functions in ways and manners inconceivable for brain.

For Blanshard the failures of naturalism are most apparent when one considers meaning. What after all is communicated? Surely, it is meanings. But meanings are not mere series of sounds or certain movements of the vocal cords. A meaning is something that can be supported by evidence. It is something distinct from a series of sounds or movements. The naturalist, then, in the final analysis, finds himself in the strange predicament of being unable to comply with his theory and successfully communicate it. In order to explain the meaning of his theory he must, in effect, abandon his theory. A theory which can offer no adequate basis for meaning at least is seen to be a meaningless theory. The naturalistic view of consciousness is shown to be untenable.

Another strength of Blanshard's view is his recognition of the pivotal issue between his own view and early positivism or emotivism. The decisive issue as he conceives it is the objectivity of moral judgments. Are moral judgments true or false independently of one's thought and feeling? Does the "fact" or state of things reported in one's moral judgment depend for its being what it is, or for its being at all, on my happening to think or to feel about it? May a moral judgment be objective in the same way as a factual judgment? In contrast to the emotivists (e.g. Carnap, and Ayer at least in his early writings), Blanshard affirms:

> a moral judgment is as objective as a judgment in science. For of any proposed action it is either true or not that it will have certain consequences in the way of experience; and of these consequences it is either true or not that they will be as good, in the sense defined, as any alternative consequences. If it is, the action is right, objectively and impersonally right, and it would still be right whatever the speaker or his culture or even mankind as a whole happened to think about it.[5]

By thus insisting on the objectivity of moral judgment Blanshard takes his stand against what he calls "the new subjectivism" of Carnap and Ayer.[6]

Carnap held that a moral judgment was neither a statement of fact nor a statement of necessity. It was not a statement of fact because it could not be verified by any appeal to sensory experience. It was not a statement of necessity because it was not intended to be universally applicable. Therefore the moral judgment is not an assertion at all, and accordingly, what it expresses is neither true nor false. Carnap held that the moral judgment was an imperative. By this he apparently meant that it expressed a demand, command, or at least, request, that someone do something. Blanshard admits that such a view does capture the meaning of some ethical statements and some ethical judgments. But he objects that it does not, even then, express the full meaning of those judgments. A moral judgment may often be expressed to elicit an action of a certain sort. But a moral judgment may perform other functions as well. It may be expressed to indicate the moral quality of some action or attitude. In such instances there may be no attempt to evoke an action from one's hearers. A moral judgment about a hypothetical situation or a past or future action or attitude would perform this function. If the United States were to use hydrogen bombs against the North Vietnamese, it would be wrong. A hypothetical statement of this sort involves no entreaty or command; it expresses a comment on the moral quality of a hypothetical action. Similarly, if one says, "Senate radicals did wrong in impeaching President Andrew Johnson," it is clear that no action is being requested. Rather, the person is simply saying that a past action is morally wrong. To say, as Carnap must, according to his theory, that such a statement says nothing is therefore untrue. Statements of this sort are intended to refer to some moral quality or characteristic of the action at the time it occurred, or, in the hypothetical case, at the time the action would have occurred had the stipulated condition prevailed. To say that moral judgments only express imperatives is to overlook their objective reference to the past or to hypothetical situations.

In distinction from Carnap's view, Ayer's position is that a moral judgment is an expression of approving or disapproving, a favorable or unfavorable feeling. Since it is an expression of feeling or an attempt to elicit feeling, it cannot be either true or false. One cannot speak of its effectiveness in accomplishing its end, but its effectiveness must be seen in relation to a subjective state or states, whether it be that of the speaker or hearer or both. In any case the moral judgment has no objective referent.

What is wrong with this new subjectivism? Repeatedly, Blanshard has carefully indicated the inadequacies of this ethical perspective.[7] His criticisms indicate the implausible implications of the theory. It cannot, he protests, offer a credible account of moral judgments upon the past, the present, or the future. Suppose one says, "The Salem witch trials were great wrongs." To say that these trials were wrong is to say that they were wrong when they actually occurred. Surely this is the plain meaning of such a statement. And yet the new subjectivism denies it. It holds that when one makes such a statement he is only expressing a feeling now present to him, or a feeling he hopes to evoke in his hearers. The meaning of the statement is governed entirely by its reference to one's own feeling, or feelings that one hopes to arouse. It has no reference to anything other than a subjective state. But surely this is a distortion, if not indeed a perversion, of what is plainly meant.

What about a moral judgment upon the present? A student may say, "It is wrong that little children are being burned by napalm in Vietnam." If one makes such a statement it is clear that he means to characterize the actual burning of children, to say that it is wrong even now as it is occurring. But the new subjectivism will not allow this. It insists that all one is doing in making such a statement is expressing his feeling about the burning of Vietnamese children. The word "wrong" expresses no quality or characteristic of the situation but only one's feeling about it. But suppose that one did not know about the use of napalm and consequently did not make the statement about its being wrong to burn children. Would he then be willing to say that nothing wrong had occurred? Surely he would not. But he must be willing to say this if he adopts the viewpoint under examination. If one is not willing to say that nothing wrong is occurring, then he is saying that the burning of children (once he learns of it) is wrong when and as it occurred, regardless of whether anyone took up a certain attitude toward it or expressed his feelings about it.

Take the third sort of situation. Suppose an individual to assert: "If the United States employs germ warfare, it will be doing something wicked." Is the person simply expressing his horror about an event which, when it does come, has no moral character at all? For the new subjectivism this is the case. Surely what the individual means is that the use of germ warfare will be hideously wrong if and when it is done. The ethical perspective under examination misconstrues the meaning of moral judgments about the past, the present, and the future.

Moreover, it misconceives the relationship between feeling and moral judgment. It insists that moral judgments always vary directly with the feelings that one is seeking to evoke or express. This, Blanshard notes, is plainly false.

It may be admitted that feeling usually accompanies a moral judgment in an intimate way. When we say, for example, that "The Mai Lai killings were atrociously wrong," we usually feel some revulsion toward that situation. Likewise, when we say the self-sacrifice and service of Albert Schweitzer is right or good, we feel some attraction for it. But although feeling may ordinarily accompany moral judgment, it certainly does not accompany it without exception. One may very well make a moral judgment without the presence of feeling. Moreover, moral judgments do sometimes vary with the intensity of the emotion felt. Approval may vary from admiration to reverence. Disapproval may vary from mild dislike to virtually uncontrollable anger. One's moral judgment often corresponds to the variance in these feelings of approval and disapproval. But this again is not always the case. One's feelings may outrun his moral judgment, or his feelings may be disparately mild compared to his moral judgment. There is, then, no direct interdependence between the feelings one undergoes and the moral judgments he makes. The new subjectivism which asserts there is such a direct relationship is therefore in error.

For this perspective, moreover, feelings are never morally appropriate. The appropriateness of a feeling is governed by something other than the psychic state of the experient. For this new subjectivism no attitude or feeling is any more appropriate than any other. How can a feeling of attraction be more appropriate than a feeling of revulsion if there is nothing "good" or "bad," "right" or "wrong," independent of the person undergoing the feeling? Goodness or badness is a moral complexion bestowed by the feelings and not having reference to anything objectively independent of those psychic states.

Consider an application of the method of concomitant variation. If the new subjectivism is true, then will any variation in feeling involve a corresponding variation of badness and goodness? If there is no feeling present, is the moral judgment then meaningless? If there is a virtually overwhelming feeling of attraction, does this really mean that goodness is unmistakable? If there is an overwhelming feeling of revulsion, does this mean that badness is present to a corresponding extent? If the new subjectivism is true, then the individual is required to answer all of these questions affirmatively. Surely, common sense would suggest a negative answer.

But, as Blanshard explains, there is more. The new subjectivism makes mistakes about value impossible. How can an error about good or bad, right or wrong, occur? The distinction between what is subjectively right and what is objectively right is impossible.

Usually moralists have taken pains to distinguish between what is subjectively right and what is objectively right. The objectively right, they have often said, is that act which in the given situation in view of all the circumstances would be the best act to do. One's notion of duty is grounded in such an objectively right act. One's duty is to discover and execute this objectively right act. But what happens if this distinction between what is objectively right and what is subjectively right is abolished? It makes it impossible for one to be mistaken about what is right. If something is subjectively right, then it is right in the only sense in which one can speak. It is therefore impossible for an individual to be mistaken. But, doesn't such a view run counter to the content of our experience? Haven't we found and done actions that we thought were right ones, but sometime later discovered we were mistaken? The act may have been subjectively right; it was not objectively right. The distinction, however worn by age, seems still required to account for our experience.

The distinction is certainly not an unimportant one. A little reflection will lay the matter bare. Suppose for a moment that there is no distinction between the objectively right and the subjectively right. Would not the abolition of this distinction destroy the motive for self-improvement? Would it not remove the ground for self-criticism? Why search and seek further if our present feeling of approval is right? If present feeling is the final arbiter, there is no motive for further search. It will not do to reply to this criticism that by further thought one could discover an action that would satisfy one's feelings more completely than the present one and that this is the action one should seek. What is meant by such an assertion? It means either that there is some action that would objectively satisfy more of one's feelings (and thus contradicts the theory) or else that, if at the time I don't feel it is better, it isn't better, and hence there is no motive to seek it. With the departure of this difference in feeling goes the motive for self-improvement. This new subjectivism seems to place a premium on a myopic complacency.

Does not this theory also destroy the ground for self-criticism? On this theory there is no obligation to feel about any act in any particular way, since there is nothing in any act that would make it more suitable than any other. What have we left as a basis for self-criticism? Only one group of feelings or a feeling-complex which can be compared to other feelings. But we cannot even compare such feelings as to their goodness or badness on this theory. What would be the basis for the comparison? Certainly not anything outside the feeling, because the theory will not allow it. But neither can the standard for comparison be something within the feeling. On this theory the present feeling constitutes the rightness or wrongness of the action undertaken. If one now feels differently about some action that he executed in the past, his present feeling governs the rightness or wrongness of the action. For this view it does not matter that at the time of the deed one may have felt approval whereas now one feels disapproval. The present feeling determines the rightness or wrongness. It is difficult to see how on this view right and wrong, good and bad, are anything other than the playthings of our passing whims and fancies.

Take the matter a step further. What is the bearing of this new subjectivism upon the international problems we confront? The assumption underlying the character of the United Nations is that there is a right and a wrong in the conduct of nations. The assumption is that people as a people have certain "rights,"[8] regardless of how one may feel about them. In signing the Charter nations were recognizing these rights and not merely expressing a collective or corporate feeling. Were the Nazis wrong in killing hundreds of thousands of Jews? Did the United States do wrong to defoliate vast sections of Vietnam? On this theory it would be meaningless to call either of these two actions wrong. If the nation felt approval for what it did, then it was right with the same justification that could be supplied for the disapproval of the Jews or North Vietnamese. On this view there can be no appeal to discussion, evidence, and argument. No nation can be shown to be wrong. International courts, if they are so brazen as to claim to decide cases morally, are simply misguided. There are no common principles by which a court could pronounce on the matter. In summary, then, the new subjectivism cannot account for the objective reference which common sense appropriately ascribes to moral judgments.

Blanshard is also essentially correct in rejecting the major tenet of the deontologists.[9] The inadequacy of deontological ethics he discovers primarily in its explanation for one's sense of obligation to do the right. He admits that the deontologists are correct in their insistence that, for example, one's duty to keep promises is not a result merely of the consequences. Further, the deontologists are essentially correct in saying that duty is not invariably based on a goodness that is subsequent to the act, but that sometimes duty is based on the character of the act itself.

What he objects to is the further step the deontologists take. For example, W. D. Ross holds that it is our duty to keep our promises even though no good at all results either for the individual or for the community by our doing so. Promise-keeping, repaying debts, and telling the truth are obligations that have a self-evident necessity. Between the rightness of doing these deeds and goodness, of whatever sort, there is no general relation.

It is this general deontological claim that must be rejected. Blanshard invites us to consider the matter carefully. The deontologists are asking us to bring one state of affairs into being that is admittedly worse than another state of affairs. They are insisting that we have an obligation to bring the worse rather than the better state of affairs into being. This obligation, the deontologists tell us, has nothing to do with either the character of the action or the state of things resulting from the action. Such an obligation appears as less than rational.

If the position of W. D. Ross is taken as typical of the deontological approach, other criticisms may be offered. Ross appears not to be consistent in his view. Generally, he holds that motives and consequences of an action are the only things that have intrinsic goodness. However, when he comes to justice, he insists that justice is an intrinsic good regardless of consequences or motives. The goodness of justice is the set of arrangements in which the virtuous men are happy and the wicked unhappy. Why should *this* set of arrangements be different from all others? Why should not the conditions under which debts are repaid or promises kept also have intrinsic worth? Ross gives us no basis for holding that whereas justice is a set of arrangements that is self-evidently good, these other arrangements are obviously worthless. Is Ross consistent in applying his own approach? Blanshard thinks not.

Moreover, Ross holds that to ask for a reason why an action is our duty is meaningless. It may be acknowledged that if one knows that it is his duty to repay a debt, it is pointless to ask why. Or, if one knows it is his duty to tell the truth, it is idle to ask why. Or, if he knows it is his duty to keep his promise, it is superfluous to ask why. But of course these are not the crucial tests. There are other situations in which a person, unsure of what is his duty, might ask for guidance concerning it. In such a situation he may want to know why the paying of the debt, the truth-telling, or the promise-keeping is obligatory. Suppose that the repaying of a debt brings considerable pain and hardship upon someone. A person might be reluctant to bring about such hardship, particularly if it fell upon someone other than the debtor. Now, there clearly is a basis for *not* paying the debt. Is there a reason why one ought to pay the debt anyhow? Cases of this sort put the deontologist in a bad light for he can give no reason. But doesn't it seem irrational, after all, to say that a person ought to do something even though to his best knowledge it produces pain and hardship unbalanced by good of any sort? At any rate the giving of a reason why is certainly not an impertinence and is actually required for rational action.

Blanshard does not question that the obligatoriness of a kind of action may be considered rational. A kind of action may itself be intrinsically good. If it is, then the individual is obligated to execute such an action. The duty to undertake such an action cannot be based on the moral neutrality of the action. To ground the right in such a fashion makes it the subject of whim and caprice.

Another problem with the deontological approach is that, on such a view, right actions have no single underlying principle. There is no common ground for calling some actions (rather than others) obligatory. Some actions are obligatory because they have the character of promise-keeping, debt-paying, or truth-telling, while other actions are right because they produce the greatest good. But do not all ethical disputes rest on the assumption that there is a common character to things or deeds that makes them right? Such an assumption seems to underlie the focus that is required for an actual conflict of belief. Suppose one individual to assert that it is wrong for United States soldiers to be participating in the Vietnam war and another person to say that it is right. Both viewpoints assume that there is some characteristic or characteristics that make such participation objectively right or wrong. Such an assumption is the basis for the conflict of belief. Without it they are simply making assertions about two entirely different matters.

The deontologists are in error in supposing that the general ethical principle—so act as to produce the greatest good—admits of exceptions. Blanshard holds that the exceptions often mentioned by the deontologists are not actually exceptions to the principle, if it be properly conceived.

Consider then one stock case often brought forward—that of punishment. The deontologists hold that in this instance the rule of the greatest good does not hold. Let us suppose that a judge in time of great social tension and stress is convinced that the conviction of an innocent man will keep order in the community. The residents are assumed not to know of the innocence of the man; the judge alone knows of his innocence. The deontologists would say that action in accord with the greatest good requires the judge to convict the innocent man. But they are surely mistaken. For the judge to convict him is not to act for the greatest good, because the verdict rendered (in order to serve the principle of the greatest good) must be such that it does not undercut the judicial system as a whole. If the judge convicts an innocent man, such an outrageous act might bring discredit upon the whole judicial system. If this were the case, it would certainly not be true that the judge who convicted the innocent man acted in terms of the greatest good. If the court bases its judgment on insufficient evidence, or renders a judgment opposed to the evidence, then it has betrayed the reason underlying its own institution. And the greatest good cannot be so served.

The deontologists, then, Blanshard argues, are mistaken in supposing that the rightness of an action may ever be opposed to the goodness produced by the action. The principle of the greatest good is still the maxim by which right actions are to be guided. Cases adduced to undermine this principle when properly described and understood actually support the principle.

Blanshard refers approvingly to Sidgwick's argument that the right depends upon the good. Although (as we have already seen) he defines good in a much more inclusive way, he does hold that Sidgwick's argument is fundamentally sound. What Sidgwick shows is that the major types of virtue are connected in an essential (rather than accidental) way with goodness. This connection suggests that we call actions right because of their conduciveness to good. The argument, then, is a genetic one. It attempts to show a nonaccidental connection between right and good based on how the connection came to be. The genesis of the connection between right and good, if essential, will serve as a warrant for holding that the right depends upon the good.

The advantages of Blanshard's view, then, in summary, are to be found in his insistence (in opposition to the emotivists and others) that value must be objective, his affirmation (in contrast to naturalistic and behavioristic views) that mind is essentially teleological, and his acknowledgment, in preference to the deontological approach, that right depends upon good. All of these emphases tend to make Blanshard's perspective a very attractive one.

But his view suffers from some defects and inadequacies which we should not overlook. First, there are two ambiguities inherent in his conception of intrinsic goodness. He has said that an experience is intrinsically good if it both satisfies and fulfills. What is ambiguous is his notion of satisfaction, and the relationship said to obtain between satisfaction and fulfillment.

Consider the ambiguity in his notion of satisfaction. Sometimes it means a pleasurable occurrence (RG, 317), and sometimes it is used as a synonym for happiness.[10] Again, sometimes satisfaction refers to the feeling tone of an experience, or "satisfactoriness" (302, 313). Now, there is little doubt that such terms as "pleasure" and "happiness" are notoriously difficult to distinguish. One can appreciate the problem Blanshard confronts. Although a precise distinction may be difficult to make, some distinction does seem to be required. Can I undergo a pleasurable experience without it being conducive to happiness? To this question, it would seem, one must answer "Yes." Such an affirmation means, in the final analysis, that pleasure and happiness are not identical. It does not tell one how to distinguish between them in any precise way, but it does indicate that a distinction is necessary.

The second ambiguity is found in the way Blanshard conceives the relationship between the two components of intrinsic goodness: satisfaction and fulfillment. For him both satisfaction and fulfillment are necessary for intrinsic good. His main point seems to be that intrinsic good simply could not be, apart from both satisfaction and fulfillment. Moreover, as we noted, fulfillment and satisfaction are always partial and provisional. They must be measured against an ideal good, namely, a life which would fulfill and satisfy wholly. But, on the one hand, Blanshard says that fulfillment and satisfaction may *vary independently of each other* (*RG,* 293), and, on the other, he holds that *satisfaction is dependent upon fulfillment* (301). How can the two essential components of intrinsic goodness vary independently of each other if one of the components depends upon the other? Thus, for example, in referring to the aim of the "theoretic impulse" he says that it seeks "something which, because of its special character, fulfils the aim of the cognitive impulse, and *which because of this fulfilment, satisfies*" (ibid.; my italics). What is the nature of this dependence? How can it be conceived so that the two components can still be said to vary independently? If it is conceived as a causal dependence, as the above statement might suggest, then the two components cannot vary independently of each other.

But, perhaps Blanshard means that, although there is no causal dependence of satisfaction upon fulfillment, the satisfaction is never found apart from the fulfillment. He states that "goodness is satisfactoriness, which consists jointly in the fulfilment of impulse-desire by the content it demands and the attendant satisfaction" (*RG,* 302). If this be so, then the fulfillment would seem to be more basic to intrinsic goodness than satisfaction. The content required for satisfaction would seem to be more basic than the feeling-tone that attends satisfaction. This understanding of the matter only heightens the difficulty of conceiving how fulfillment and satisfaction can vary independently of each other.

Another inadequacy of Blanshard's view is his failure to discuss the various "drives" or "impulse-desires" of human nature. He mentions only two such drives: the theoretic and aesthetic impulses. While acknowledging that there may be other such conative drives, he declines explaining them, chiefly, it would seem, on the ground that their ends are not entirely independent of each other. Although it should be admitted that such discrimination is not easy, it must be insisted that without a specification of these drives the notion of fulfillment is almost vacuous. The fact that the ends which would fulfill these impulse-desires are not entirely independent of each other seems to underscore the need for a specification of these drives rather than to serve as a ground for the failure to discuss them.

Our own list of these basic drives need make no pretense to completeness. It will suffice to explain briefly some of the more generally recognized ones and to show how these may give content to the notion of fulfillment. Consider first what W. E. Hocking has called the "will to power." Although Hocking is in error in making it the central aim of man, it is certainly an important drive. A person who is attempting to achieve a given objective and meets a difficulty or obstacle will ordinarily desire to overcome that difficulty or obstacle. Generally, he will not be content to relinquish the attainment of his objective.

What he experiences upon overcoming the obstruction is elation. The sense of elation seems to vary, in part at least, with the amount of exertion required to overcome the resistance impeding the achievement. Ordinarily, a person feels more elation or a stronger sense of elation when he has overcome a more complex network of obstacles. Conversely, when what he intends to achieve requires overcoming fewer obstacles or less obstructive things, he experiences less elation or a weaker sense of elation.

Adventure for its own sake may fill many an empty niche. Man climbs the Himalayas not because he has to but just because they are there. He breaks records for the exultation that comes from breaking them. He pits himself against the weather and sea in Kon-tiki exploits to prove to himself that he can endure and triumph. Any obstacle which stands as a challenge can yield fulfillment in its overcoming.

Moreover, this drive for mastery, or desire to overcome obstacles, is present and experienced even when the objective is not attained or achieved. It is felt as effort expended for overcoming restrictions. It is what Charles Arthur Campbell calls "effort of will,"[11] seen not in its relation to a resistant set of human desires but in relation to obstacles or difficulties impeding or preventing the attainment of an end proposed by the self.

Although the case cannot here be argued, this desire for mastery or "will to power" does not appear to be reducible to a form of anger or aggressiveness. Nor does it appear to be something learned wholly apart from an already present potentiality for that sort of action.

It may be, of course, that the general aim to overcome resistance is informed by the content resulting from the exercise of the theoretic impulse. But this need not mean that the desire for mastery is any less basic to human nature. It is not claimed that any of these drives are fully developed in isolation from the others. Fulfillment, then, would seem to mean, in part at least, the satisfaction of one's desire for mastery.

Two other drives are often mentioned.[12] The first of these has been called "succor-sympathy." It is the normal person's desire to relieve another person's distress or suffering. It is usually experienced as an urge or prompting to alleviate or remove the suffering or distress. It is sometimes felt in relation to other living creatures as well as to other human beings.

The human being seems to have some awareness of the aim of this drive apart from learning. It may be (as Blanshard suggests with regard to the theoretic impulse) that he comes to know the aim of this drive only by relieving suffering and distress. But some awareness of the aim is necessary for its initial expressions. In any case, what one does acquire through learning is a knowledge of appropriate modes of expressing this succor-sympathy.

This drive, again, is infused and guided by the theoretic impulse. Without knowledge and understanding this drive may express itself in the relief of one's own emotional tension rather than the easing of another's distress. It cannot operate effectively apart from the content that fulfills the theoretic impulse. Fulfillment means, then, in part at least, the satisfaction of one's succor-sympathy drive.

Another basic drive is "awe-respect." A person ordinarily experiences, in the presence of another who is superior to him in some way, a feeling of respect or deference. This feeling is not solely a by-product of envy or fear; it arises whether or not one desires the same skills or achievements for himself, and would hardly be present if it were an offshoot of envy. Moreover, it may arise when a sense of fear would be wholly irrelevant to the situation. This suggests that it is not some aftereffect or concomitant of fear.

Careful inspection of our experience also shows that fear and respect differ. Obedience from fear and obedience from respect are two entirely different matters. Often there are differences in the actual deeds done. But invariably anyone who has obeyed from these two different motives knows that it feels different to act from respect and to act from fear. The drive for respect, then, it would seem, cannot be reduced to fear.

It is a part of fulfillment that one's "awe-respect" drive be satisfied. It includes, as we have seen, meeting the demands of one's drive for mastery and succor-sympathy as well as those of the theoretic and aesthetic impulses.

As soon as we acknowledge more than one impulse-desire, a cluster of problems comes to the forefront. For example, if one admits that there is an aesthetic impulse and a theoretic impulse, the problem of how to resolve a conflict between the satisfaction of these two comes into being. The fact that Blanshard insists upon the autonomy of the standards of goodness for the various impulse-desires does not help the matter (*RG*, 303–4). He holds that the good called knowledge is not to be judged by the same standards as the good called beauty for the plausible reason that what fulfills and satisfies these two impulse-desires is different (understanding, for the theoretic impulse; harmony and proportion for the aesthetic impulse) (ibid.). But if the standards are so different, one may ask, how is one to judge which of these impulse-desires to satisfy? How can one reach a decision in cases where the fulfilling of each of these desires is mutually exclusive? If the standards are so different, what is the common measure by which one can assess their comparative merit? It does not seem that Blanshard can satisfactorily answer these questions.

What would be required to answer such questions? Perhaps nothing less than a theory of human nature. To date he has not formulated such a theory, although hints as to the direction he might take have been given in chapters 11 and 13 of his *Reason and Goodness* and, earlier, in *The Nature of Thought*. If his insistence upon different standards for the various impulse-desires is taken seriously, it would seem that his theory of human nature would need to place these impulse-desires in a hierarchy. Such a hierarchy might eliminate the problem of resolving conflicts. However, it would give birth to the troublesome issue of justifying the preference of fulfillment of one impulse-desire over another. How Blanshard might resolve this issue it is difficult to see.

JOHN HOWIE

DEPARTMENT OF PHILOSOPHY
SOUTHERN ILLINOIS UNIVERSITY—CARBONDALE

NOTES

[1] The 1966 second impression as corrected is used throughout.

[2] For view of understanding see vol. 2 of *The Nature of Thought* (*NT*), esp. chaps. 18, 26, and 32.

[3] See Blanshard, *On Sanity in Thought and Art* (Tucson: University of Arizona Press, 1962). Blanshard does not hold a narrow view of art as that which employs the common media—paint, stone, and sound. Rather, he insists, "Anything is art that is an attempt at effective expression of what we think and feel" ("Life as Art," *Swarthmore College Bulletin* 45, no. 3 [November 1947]: 6). In this baccalaureate address Blanshard suggests that what would satisfy and fulfill the aesthetic impulse would be characterized, minimally at least, by spontaneity, craftsmanship, and the economy of means to end.

[4] For almost fifty years Blanshard has been unsparing in his criticisms of behaviorism and, indeed, all naturalistic views of consciousness. See his "Behaviorism and the Theory of Knowledge," *Philosophical Review* 37 (July 1928): 328–52; *The Nature of Thought*, vol. 1, chap. 9; "Critical Reflections on Behaviorism," *Proceedings of the American Philosophical Society* 109, no. 1 (February 1965): 22–28; "The Problem of Consciousness—A Debate" [with B. F. Skinner], *Philosophy and Phenomenological Research* 27, no. 3 (March 1967): 317–37; "The

Limits of Naturalism," in *Mind, Science and History,* eds. H. E. Kiefer and M. K. Munitz (Albany: State University of New York Press, 1970), 3–33.

[5]Blanshard, "The Objectivity of Moral Judgment," *Revue internationale de philosophie* 70 (1964): 378.

[6]See Blanshard, "The New Subjectivism in Ethics," *Philosophy and Phenomenological Research* 9, no. 3 (1948–49): 504–11.

[7]See Blanshard, "The Impasse in Ethics—and a Way Out," *University of California Publications in Philosophy* 28, no. 2 (1955): 3–24; "Subjectivism in Ethics—A Criticism," *Philosophical Quarterly* (St. Andrews) 1, no. 2 (January 1951): 127–39.

[8]For Blanshard a "right" is simply a duty considered from the opposite end. To decide, then, whether one has a right, for example, to pursue happiness is to ascertain whether other persons have a duty to allow me to seek happiness. Right and duty stand in reciprocal relationships. Blanshard's view also means that there are no "inalienable rights" of individuals or nations. Since nations, like individuals, have duties, nations also have rights. But neither the rights nor the duties are "inalienable" or "absolute." See Blanshard's discussion in his "Part II, Personal Ethics," in *Preface to Philosophy: Textbook* by W. E. Hocking, B. Blanshard, C. W. Hendel, J. H. Randall, Jr. (New York: Macmillan Co. [1946], 1960), 179–80.

[9]See Blanshard, "The Impasse in Ethics," and *RG,* chap. 6.

[10]Blanshard, "The Objectivity of Moral Judgment," 378.

[11]C. A. Campbell, *In Defence of Free Will* (London: George Allen & Unwin, 1967), 77.

[12]We are following the treatment of "psychic needs" as given by Peter A. Bertocci in his *Introduction to the Philosophy of Religion* (Englewood Cliffs, N.J.: Prentice-Hall, 1956), 211–12, 214.

5. REPLY TO JOHN HOWIE
Blanshard on "Intrinsic Goodness"

I am in debt to Mr. Howie for his heroic labor in ferreting out my *obiter scripta* of many years, sometimes hidden away in little-known journals, and ordering them into the respectable bibliography that appears at the end of this volume. And as I read the first two-thirds of his essay, which defends the substance of my ethical theory against its contemporary critics, it began to look as if my pleasant but brief reply would reduce itself to thanks and nothing else. But toward the end of his essay Mr. Howie confesses dissatisfaction with my ethical theory at several points, and this gives me at least the chance to try to remove his misgivings.

Mr. Howie notes that by calling an experience intrinsically good, I mean that it combines the two characters of fulfilling some urge or drive of our nature and of giving the satisfaction that such fulfillment normally entails. Sometimes, he points out, I am content to describe this satisfaction or positive affective tone as pleasure; sometimes I describe it as happiness. Mr. Howie thinks that this leaves a certain ambiguity in my account; for pleasure and happiness are not the same. A man may, for example, undergo a pleasurable experience without its contributing to his happiness.

I agree that it is useful to differentiate these two terms. We should not be using "happiness" very felicitously if we applied it to the experience of a bowl of mushroom soup, and we should not be using "pleasure" in a very discriminating way if we spoke of the pleasure of having numerous friends or of an outstanding success in life. Yet the two experiences are both forms of positive feeling tone, and they are so continuous with each other that there are many cases where either term could be used with equal propriety. In general, pleasure is more transient and more definitely focused; happiness is more enduring and more diffused. Both attend the fulfillment of impulses or desires, but pleasure attends the short-range impulses like hunger, thirst, sex, or the desire to win a game; happiness comes with the fulfillment of long-range desires like those for success or for a harmonious family life. Mr.

Howie indeed thinks that a pleasure may not add to one's happiness. True; the happiness of an embittered and frustrated man may not be increased by a good dinner, for there is no happiness to add to; but his unhappiness may be in some degree alleviated by it, which comes to very much the same thing. Pleasure and happiness may both be described in the words by which Sidgwick defined pleasure; it is "the kind of feeling which . . . when we experience it, we apprehend as desirable or preferable." With these glosses, I do not think my usage is seriously misleading.

Satisfaction and Fulfillment

Mr. Howie next points to what looks like a flat inconsistency in my account of intrinsic goodness. As a rule, I make satisfaction dependent on fulfillment; but I also say that the two components vary independently of each other. Now if there exists in fact the causal relation I allege in the first statement, the independent variation alleged in the second cannot hold.

The objection would be unanswerable if I *defined* satisfaction or pleasure as the effect of fulfillment. Normally it *is* the attendant on fulfillment of impulse, is dependent on it, and varies with the degree of fulfillment. But the rule is not a hard-and-fast one, for there is always another factor at work in the production of such mental states, namely the condition of the nervous system. If that system is functioning badly, the normal sequence of mental changes may be affected profoundly. For example, long-standing desires may be fulfilled without the happiness that normally attends them; in *Reason and Goodness* (p. 53) I cited in illustration the well-known case of Mill. He had reached the height of his intellectual powers and was fulfilling them with notable success when suddenly all satisfaction in them vanished, and for some months he ceased to care whether he lived or died. Apparently he had inflicted serious injury on his nervous system by persistently overstraining it. So fulfillment by itself does not guarantee pleasure or happiness. Nor is such satisfaction invariably the sign of fulfillment. A state of the nervous system may be produced, either by nature or by artifice, that gives intense pleasure without any basis in the fulfillment of normal impulse or desire. The congenital idiot may live in a state of constant euphoria, and the addict of opium or heroin may experience spells of ecstasy while his normal powers are disintegrating. I recognize, therefore, that my generalization about the connection of fulfillment with pleasure is not exceptionless. It is not a scientific law. Still, it holds in the main; it remains the rule, even though the rule has its exceptions. So it is fair enough, I think, to say that pleasure is normally the by-product of fulfillment and to admit that in abnormal cases the two may vary independently of each other.

Mr. Howie wonders whether I regard these two components of intrinsic goodness as of equal importance, or one of them as the more essential. I make pleasure attendant upon fulfillment, but not fulfillment dependent upon pleasure. Is fulfillment, then, the more important of the two? The answer is Yes. I am nearer to being a self-realizationist than to being a hedonist. It is the expansion and growth of the self that is the condition of pleasure and happiness, not the other way about, though of course I admit that pleasure may be a stimulus and bait as well as a by-product.

The Range of Impulses

Again, Mr. Howie objects that if one is to base the good life on the fulfillment of the impulses, urges, and drives of human nature, these drives should be classified or at least listed, and some account provided of their relations to each other. It would have been desirable, I agree, to have a fuller catalogue of these drives, a fuller account of the course of each, and a fuller report on their interactions. Mr. Howie says I have confined myself to two such drives, the theoretic impulse and the aesthetic. I would say that I have done even worse. I have given an account of only one, the theoretic impulse, which was studied in *The Nature of Thought*. The aesthetic impulse I have touched upon only casually and superficially.

My apology for this limitation is threefold. First, in my only book on ethics such a classification of human impulse was unnecessary to my purpose. I was concerned with the rightness and goodness of conduct, and though these concepts could not be made clear without reference to the conative side of human nature, an exhaustive study of human drives was not needed for this limited purpose. Secondly, the science to which one would naturally turn for aid in such an inquiry, psychology, was in a state of chaos. Hocking, who, like his predecessors Royce and James, was a psychologist as well as a philosopher, recognized one overmastering drive, the seeking of power; but Thorndike recognized over two hundred instinctive drives, and other psychologists produced lists of intermediate but greatly varying length. The psychologist I found most helpful was McDougall, whose *Social Psychology* still seems to me a very valuable book, though in its many editions it too offered differing lists of human drives. I not unnaturally hesitated to rush in where so many able investigators found it impossible to agree. Thirdly, the various impulse-desires must be distinguished by their ends, and the normal pursuit of any of these ends may become entangled almost inextricably with the pursuit of others. This had already come out clearly in my study of the theoretical impulse, which has one of the most clearly defined of all ends, yet is used so continually to further ends other than its own that we are often left uncertain which end is dominant. The paths of development of the noncognitive impulses would often be harder to trace than that of the theoretic impulse itself, since their ends not only are mutually supporting but sometimes blend into a complete fusion. Mr. Howie himself is inclined to take seriously Hocking's suggestion of power as the overall end; but he finds it difficult to say whether the love of adventure and the love of mastery are to be absorbed into it or to remain separate but contributory drives. I would not suggest that the sort of problems raised here are insoluble. But they require great insight into human nature, great subtlety of discrimination, and a great deal of paper and time. I cannot claim the necessary supply of any of these.

Conflict of Impulses

Mr. Howie's final difficulty is how, on my theory, a competition between two types of fulfillment is to be settled. If one has to compare two levels of fulfillment within the same drive, the theoretical, for example, the problem is usually easy enough. To recognize a daisy, to grasp how malaria is transmitted, and to understand the quantum theory are on very different levels of intellectual development. Comparison becomes harder when it involves fulfillments within different drives. A man like Charles Ives or Wallace Stevens may be strongly attracted by two widely differing ends, on the one hand power and success in the business world, on the other the composition of music or poetry. It is interesting to note that both these men solved the problem in the same way, by a compromise in which their energy in business provided enough resources to enable them to pursue the rival vocation as an avocation. Of course so convenient a way out is not always available. Then what? It is not the sort of problem that one man can confidently solve for another. When a man finds that he has two remarkable abilities which support two equally strong propensities, the practical difficulty of deciding between them may lead to a Hamlet-like paralysis or to a dilettantish and unproductive seesaw. The difficulty, I would point out, is not so much with the theory as with its practical application. What the doubter must do in principle is clear enough: he should contemplate (1) the two pursuits and the probability of reaching success in each; (2) the by-products in the way of value produced by each; (3) the values bestowed on others by his pursuit of each. One or two refinements apart, he must then compare the total values on each side and elect the larger total. The comparison is more difficult on my theory than it is on those of Sidgwick, Moore, or Rashdall, for what they had to compare was the always commensurable amounts of a single quality. Comparative fulfillments are obviously harder to appraise, for in such appraisal one must take into account the strength and ability displayed in differing propensities. The writers just mentioned all thought that when the totals of value on each side were weighed against each other, it was intuition that made the decision. The appeal to intuition often marks, I know, a breakdown of the analysis. But the fact of intuition seems to me undeniable, and if there is any logician or moralist who has been able to escape the appeal to it, I do not know who he is. If we can choose between different works of art by intuition, or between two degrees of moral goodness, or two amounts of happiness, I do not know why we should not be able to compare in the same way two amounts of intrinsic value defined in my own way.

I have pointed out that before Mr. Howie comes to his criticism of my theory, he offers a vigorous defense of it against some contemporary critics with whom he differs as sharply as I do. With full appreciation for this, I should perhaps add that at some points my understanding of these critics is somewhat different from his. For example, he conceives naturalism in a way that I have myself conceived it at times, as the view that the world is exhaustively composed of matter in motion. But it should be admitted that there are many scientists like the eminent contributor to this volume, Henry Margenau, who would unhesitatingly call themselves naturalists but would reject behaviorism as the "clever-silly" doctrine which is all that Broad (or I) can see in it. Again, though I am encouraged to find Mr. Howie standing with me unequivocally against the emotivists, might they not justly demur at one attribution of doctrine to them? Mr. Howie reads them as saying of such a statement as "The Salem witch trials were great wrongs," that "It has no reference to anything other than a subjective state." They would reply, I think, that such a statement certainly referred to the trials, for these formed the subject thought about; what the statement did not do was to ascribe to the subject any moral attribute, for there were no such things. The subject has an objective reference, but not the predicate. Further, in dealing with the deontologists Mr. Howie states Sir David Ross's position in a way that could mislead the unwary. ". . . W. D. Ross holds that it is our duty to keep our promises even though no good at all results either for the individual or for the community by our doing so." Now Ross does hold that it is a prima facie duty to keep a promise, and he adheres to this even in some cases in which the greater good would seem to lie in breaking the promise. But he does not say, "Keep your promises though the heavens fall." He would admit that in some cases where keeping the promise entailed great misery or the breaking of it some great good, it may be our clear duty to break the promise. His case is much the more persuasive for this agreement with the utilitarian that consequences are important; what he denies is that they are all-important. Once more, Mr. Howie supports me as against Ross in the explanation of why a judge should not condemn an innocent man. But this is one of the hardest cases for the teleological moralist to deal with. The difficulty is pressed home by Oliver Johnson in this volume, and Mr. Howie would, I think, be interested both in his essay and in my reply.

I am grateful for Mr. Howie's sympathetic support on some issues where my views have had little notice, for example, my criticism of emotivism, my insistence on the objectivity of moral judgment, and my claim that such objectivity is indispensable if international bodies like the United Nations are to have a rational basis. Mr. Howie has, I suspect, read more of my work than any other living person. I am encouraged by the realization that he has not only survived such an ordeal but apparently flourished under it.

6 REASON, FEELING, AND WORLD VIEW
W. T. Jones

I N *Reason and Goodness* Blanshard seeks to ascertain "the position of reason . . . in ethics" (*RG,* 13). In this paper I am not going to argue that Blanshard's account of the relation between reason and feeling is incorrect. Rather, I am going to put forward the view that his account of this relationship is relative to a particular world view. Further, since the various accounts of this relationship which he criticizes are also world-view relative, but relative to different world views, I consider the disagreement between Blanshard and his opponents regarding the places of reason and feeling in ethics as nonterminable—nonterminability being a characteristic feature of many philosophical disagreements.[1]

I do not expect to convince Blanshard, and, indeed, I shall not argue, or attempt to prove, my case. Rather, I shall simply present it. First I shall give what seems to me to be a persuasive example of the way in which philosophical theories reflect and are limited by world views, and the example I shall offer is Blanshard's ethical theory as it is set out in *Reason and Goodness.* I hope that philosophical readers, including Blanshard, will not be too impatient with this section of the paper, on the grounds that it is not proper philosophy but merely a crude sort of anthropology. However inadequate and inconclusive this particular case may be thought to be, the assumptions underlying it are common to a large body of social scientists, and they raise questions that philosophers ought to face.

In the second section of the paper I discuss some of these questions. After trying to anticipate the reply that I think Blanshard would make to this relativization of his ethical theory and, by implication, of philosophical theory generally, I shall offer some counterconsiderations. Naturally, since, as I hold, theories are world-view relative, these counterconsiderations will take a form appropriate to a particular world view—in this case, mine. This is why I believe I shall not be able to convince Blanshard.

But why, I may be asked, if I anticipate that the disagreement between Blanshard and myself is nonterminable, do I bother to write this paper at all? Well, first, I do not think questions lose interest for being, or for being thought to be, nonterminable; indeed, in some respects they thereby gain interest. And, second, if I cannot convince Blanshard, I may yet be able to persuade others. And those who are thus persuaded will be led to a conception of what it is to "do" philosophy that departs markedly from currently received opinion.

I

Before I try to expose the world view underlying both the method of argument employed in, and the conclusions reached in, *Reason and Goodness,* I must say what I mean by a world view, and introduce an apparatus for comparing one world view with another.

By a world view, then, I mean a configuration of structural elements, both cognitive and attitudinal, in terms of which such extensive regions of an individual's experience are organized that we can say these sets fashion this individual's world.[2] The cognitive and attitudinal elements that constitute a world view thus do not differ in kind, but only in scope, from those ordinary muscular and perceptual sets that also selectively organize the experimental field but that range over much more limited regions of the field. Any physical habit is a simple example of such a muscular set—for instance, the habit of adjusting the muscles in our arm to make the effort needed to pick up a tennis racquet. Xenophobia is an example of a set that functions in a similar way but that structures a larger domain of experience. An attitude of hostility to foreigners causes aspects of the experiential field to stand out prominently that are passed over unnoticed by those whose attitude toward foreigners is open and friendly. Because the world of the xenophobe and the world of the xenophile differ, they are likely to argue inconclusively about, say, the trustworthiness of foreigners. Each regards his bias not as a bias but as an empirical hypothesis. Each can point to evidence which, in his judgment, verifies his hypothesis but which the other rejects as inadequate, for each attends selectively to aspects of the experiential field that support his bias.

Sets that organize not merely this or that region of a man's experience but very extensive ranges of his experience constitute, collectively, what I call his world view.[3] Before I describe, for illustrative purposes, three such sets, we need the notion of what I call a "dimension." A dimension is an array of dispositional sets rank-ordered from a set that P (e.g. that all foreigners are untrustworthy) to a set that non-P (e.g. that no foreigner is untrustworthy). Thus a dimension consists of a number of points, each of which may be the locus of the dispositional set of some individual. The closer together the loci of any two individuals are, the more likely it is that they will be able to reach agreement on specific empirical questions (e.g. the character of some particular foreigner). The farther apart their loci are, the more likely it is that they will disagree about the trustworthiness of this foreigner. Further, other things being equal, midrange loci are likely to be weakly charged and so relatively flexible; polar loci, in contrast, are likely to be highly charged and rigid. Accordingly, bipolar sets, i.e. sets that are not only far apart but also highly charged, are likely to generate nonterminable disagreements.

The dimensions I am now going to define may be thought of as forming a matrix within which the world views of various individuals can be located. Obviously, the larger the number of dimensions used, the greater the precision with which similarities and differences between world views can be specified. However, since my purpose here is not to give an exhaustive description of Blanshard's world view, but merely to illustrate the case for world-view relativism by reference to Blanshard's ethical theory, it will be enough to use a simple matrix of three dimensions. I call the dimensions in this matrix (1) static/dynamic, (2) immediacy/mediation, (3) continuity/discreteness.[4]

(1) The first of the dimensions in this matrix, the *static/dynamic* dimension, is an array of biases (dispositions) ranging from a preference for the unchanging to a contrasting preference for the changing. In economics, in psychology, in sociology, this difference in perspective, or in outlook on the world, is reflected, for instance, in the contrasting preferences for equilibrium and disequilibrium models. Historians are divided by the same difference in bias—for instance, between those interested in studying revolutionary periods and those who prefer to concentrate on periods in which change is so slow as to be virtually imperceptible. In painting this same difference—here one might want to speak of a difference in "style"—occurs. As an example, think of two paintings of the same subject, say, the Adoration of the Kings. For Dürer, all is calm, poised, and at rest; for Rubens, all is tumult, excitement, and movement. Or think of the contrast between a Mondrian and a Kandinsky.

(2) I call the second dimension in this matrix *immediacy/mediation*. This is the difference between what is lived through, what is directly experienced, and what is experienced from outside, from a distance. This dimension can also be described in terms of the notion of participant-observation. Some people are more participants than observers; some are more observers than participants. Some people prefer natural, informal social and business relationships; they like "simple" people. Others enjoy protocol, distance, "good manners," and, generally, sophisticated types. This difference in bias also turns up in educational theory and educational practice: Some people prefer the lecture system, in which the teacher stands behind a lectern,

separated by physical as well as psychological space from his students. Others prefer an approximation to sensitivity training rather than formal education. And, as a final example, think of the difference between the "feeling heart" that the romanticists believed should guide men's actions and the long-range, enlightened self-interest that the Age of Reason advocated.

(3) *Continuity/discreteness,* the last dimension in this matrix, is a contrast between (i) an emphasis on interrelatedness, on contextuality, and on degree-differences and (ii) an emphasis on sharp distinctions, on ideal types, and on encapsulated atomistic entities. Wordsworth's feeling that "we murder to dissect" is an example of continuity bias. Logical analysis seems to be murder because it divides up, and classifies, a world that continuity bias perceives as a living whole. In contrast, there is Butler's aphorism, "Everything is itself and not another thing." Butler's vision of the universe was radically different from Wordsworth's; his universe is not an organic whole but simply a collection of items. Accordingly, logical analysis ("dissection") is an entirely proper procedure; the only problem, from this perspective, is to make sure that the distinctions we draw correspond to those that exist in rerum natura.

In painting the same difference in vision occurs. Think of Rembrandt's perception of objects, where everything merges into everything else, and Van Eyck's, where each object in the picture space is sharply and clearly distinguished from every other object. Whether the objects are near or far away—in a distant field seen through a window—each is encapsulated, complete in itself.

I have introduced these three dimensions with nonphilosophical examples in order to indicate the great variety of cultural products—poetry, painting, the social sciences—which these sets structure. But, at least on this view of world views, philosophical theories are marked by the same structural features. Philosophers with strong dynamic bias, for instance, experience change as so prominent a feature of the world that for them the central metaphysical problem is to explain the appearance of permanence. Philosophers with a strong static bias have exactly the opposite problem: how to explain the appearance of change. Thus two philosophers—e.g. Heraclitus and Parmenides—may develop diametrically opposed theories as a result of differences in dispositional set that cause one of them systematically to focus on features of experience that the other systematically ignores or minimizes. In a word, a philosopher's world view gives his theory a characteristic shape, or structure, that distinguishes it from philosophical theories based on differing world views. This is the general thesis that I shall now illustrate by reference to Blanshard's ethical theory.

I shall begin by calling attention to a metaphor that recurs frequently in *Reason and Goodness.* In every philosophical theory there is at least one

representative, or modal, metaphor—in Descartes it is laying the foundations
and finding the right path, in Hume it is billiard balls on a billiard table, in
Hegel it is the bud that develops into a blossom and then into fruit—that displays the underlying configuration of biases that is worked out and rational-
ized in the theory itself. In *Reason and Goodness* one of these modal
metaphors is that of a pendulum that swings back and forth in decreasing
arcs until it comes to rest at the stabilized midpoint between the two extremes
of its path. Among many references that might be cited are "the pendulum
movement we are tracing" (*RG,* 90), "the swings of the dialectical pendulum" (103), and "the pendulum began to swing back again" (139). Indeed,
Blanshard views "the entire moral history of the west" (68) as a movement
back and forth between a too arid rationalism on the one hand and a too
passionate feeling on the other hand (for instance, 79). As with a pendulum,
however, this history is perceived by Blanshard not merely as a recurrent
passage from one extreme to the other but as a movement to a stable
equilibrium. The opposition between reason and feeling has progressively
narrowed in the course of time; "there has been a more or less steady advance, in which the suggestions of one school have been corrected and
supplemented by the suggestions of another" (72), so that reason and feeling
are gradually brought "into some sort of harmony"(41).

Though Blanshard sometimes uses the term "dialectical" to characterize
this movement (for instance, *RG,* 72, 79), he is quite aware that his model is
not Hegelian.[5] In Hegel's view the extreme positions are in continuous
dynamic opposition: every phase is *aufgehoben* in the successive phase, and
all is carried forward ceaselessly, without rest. Blanshard, in contrast, reads
the same history as a movement toward a midpoint in which fluctuations are
gradually reduced and a static equilibrium is achieved.

Further, this pendulum metaphor, which dominates Blanshard's survey of
the history of ethical theory, also underlies the chapters in which he expounds
what he takes to be the correct view of the relation between reason and feeling. The philosophical issue is "What are the roles of intelligence and of the
non-rational parts of our nature in achieving the good life?" (*RG,* 29).
Blanshard's answer is that achievement of the good life "requires us to take a
middle course" (315). Since "*The* good is what would be satisfactory in the
end" (302), and since the exclusion of either reason or feeling from life
"makes the other sterile" (70), some sort of "mixture" is necessary.[6] Until
the right mixture is achieved, "tension" is inevitable, and tension, it is taken
for granted, is bad. The operational words throughout are "balance and
sanity" (36), the stable equilibrium that results from the right mixture of
reason and feeling in life.

Thus the same metaphor underlies both philosophical analysis, which
aims at discovering the "right" mixture, and historical description, which

aims at reporting what has actually occurred. And this metaphor reveals a rather strong static bias—not as strong, certainly, as Descartes', but nevertheless in marked contrast to the dynamic bias implicit in Hegel's metaphor of the living plant, each of whose successive stages is merely an unstable passage from past to future. As a result of the different configuration of bias that is revealed in this metaphor, Hegel read very differently both the history of ethical theory and the "right" relation between reason and feeling.

Another metaphor that appears almost as frequently in *Reason and Goodness* as the pendulum metaphor is the metaphor of judicial review. Thus, for instance, emotivism is criticized because "It allows no objective court of appeal to which ethical disputes may be carried" (*RG,* 234). Again, writing of "the appeal to an accepted taboo," Blanshard points out that "Such an appeal can provide at best only a provisional justification which must be reviewed by a superior court before it can be granted real legitimacy" (260).[7] It is suggestive that the court envisaged in this metaphor is appellate—that is, at several removes from the immediate issue. Being more removed, it is presumably more impartial, more objective. Reason and feeling are, as it were, plaintiff and defendant before the bar. It is the judge's task to reconcile their excessive claims by assigning each what is rightfully due it. Note how this judicial metaphor and the pendulum metaphor come together: justice is the striking of a balance between claims, and this balance, when it has been formulated by the final appellate court, is definitive: the case is settled.[8]

Thus in Blanshard's world view strong mediation bias is coupled with static bias: In the first place, truth is the point of stable equilibrium, the point where the pendulum finally comes to rest. In the second place, this point of balance is found only by distancing oneself so that one can, neutrally and from outside, weigh the claims of those who are involved and so render an impartial and objective verdict, which they, precisely because they *are* involved, cannot achieve.[9]

This brings us to the third dimension in our illustrative matrix—continuity/discreteness. There can hardly be doubt about Blanshard's locus on this dimension. Strong continuity bias is evident in his emphasis on system and in his rejection of what he calls "loose ends" (*RG,* 431) and "mere togetherness" (344). For instance, "The theoretic impulse has as its end a system whose parts are necessarily and intelligibly interconnected . . ." (343). Also: ". . . relations there always are. For to understand a point *is* to see its relations with something else . . ." (430). In a word, so far as a point is "merely" a point, i.e. disconnected from everything else, it is unintelligible. Let the point expand as much as one likes, if we were ever to reach a limiting bound such that we found ourselves dealing with an encapsulated entity, we would again be confronted with the unintelligible; the "theoretic impulse"

would be frustrated. Accordingly, the world cannot consist in sheerly jux-
taposed, discrete entities, however extensive. It must be one, a continuous
whole. Or, as this vision of the universe is expressed in a revealing metaphor:

> . . . we have picked up a few pebbles only on the shore, and . . . a limitless sea
> stretches before us; we cannot surmise what a full exploration would reveal;
> but we know that, whatever it was, it would be continuous with what we now
> know. . . . [*RG*, 306]

The pebbles are mere facts, hardly intelligible ("our little knowledge")
because, and so far as, they are fragmentary and cut off from the context (the
sea) in which they actually exist.

Here, then, is a philosophical theory that reflects a pretheoretical vision of
the world. The coherence theory of truth and the doctrine of internal relations
do not prove—as, officially, they are supposed to do—that the vision is
veridical. Rather, the vision renders the theory and the doctrine convincing—to those who share the vision. To those who do not share it (Hume and
Russell, for example) the theory and the doctrine, so far from being convincing, are not even remotely plausible. Think, for instance, of what Hume
would make of Blanshard's assertion that though "we cannot surmise what a
full exploration" of the sea "would reveal, . . . we know that, whatever it was,
it would be continuous. . . ." Given Blanshard's continuity bias, this is an
eminently rational and logical conclusion. Given Hume's discreteness bias,
given, that is, his vision of things as "loose and separate," it is a wholly
irrational leap of faith: there is no reason to suppose that the next pebble we
chance on will be like the last one. From Hume's vision of reality the principle of induction cannot be defended; from Blanshard's, it cannot be challenged. Each is led to his conclusion by considerations that to him are
irrefutable but to his opponent worthless. How can this be? I suggest that
though philosophers think of themselves as reaching their conclusions by a
series of logical steps, each of which is contemplated neutrally and weighed
objectively, their conclusions are contained from the start in their different
pretheoretical visions of the world.

This is one example of how a difference in world view generates nonterminable disagreements. Others will come to light if we now consider some
features of Blanshard's theory that result from the association, in his world
view, of continuity bias with static bias and mediation bias. Philosophers with
the more usual static/mediation/discrete configuration will of course share
Blanshard's conception of reason as an impartial judge weighing the issues
impartially from the outside. To them, as to Blanshard, adoption of this
stance is self-evidently the necessary condition for reaching the truth. But
philosophers in whose world view mediation bias is associated with discreteness bias, instead of with continuity bias, are likely to be hostile to the
notion of system, which Blanshard finds so congenial. Since these

philosophers envisage the universe, not as a limitless sea, but as a very large collection of pebbles, they are quite content to gather pebbles one by one, for each pebble is itself and not another thing; each is complete in itself. Hence these philosophers do not experience that nisus to the whole and to completeness that is so prominent a feature of Blanshard's theory. Hence, again, these philosophers (Kant, for instance) are likely to be less sympathetic to feeling than is Blanshard. For feeling is integrative and synthetic, and philosophers with strong discreteness bias handle problems not by synthesis but by analysis. In contrast, for Blanshard the elementary datum—the terminus of the analytical method—is only the starting point. His notion of explanation is to expand from this datum to the whole, and since this expansion can never be carried out completely and in detail, feeling has an important role: confined as we are to the shore, we can yet have a sense of the limitlessness and unity of the sea.

Or consider Blanshard's advocacy of balance. Philosophers whose loci fall within the static/mediate/discrete region of this matrix are likely to share Blanshard's admiration for the midpoint. Like Blanshard, they will talk about "balance and sanity." But since, within this general region of the matrix, many specific differences in locus occur, these advocates of the mean may differ widely about where the mean is. What occurs is, as it were, a kind of perspectival foreshortening. Since each philosopher weighs the relative importance of reason and feeling in the light of his own configuration of biases, each philosopher locates the point of balance nearer his own position. Given this particular world view, words like "balance," "mean," and "middle course" are honorific terms by which philosophers reaffirm the rightness of a position they have adopted on other grounds. They do not call the position correct because they have ascertained it to be at the midpoint; they dignify it as at the midpoint because they feel it to be correct.

But given a different world view—given, for instance, dynamic bias and immediacy bias—"balance," "mean," and "middle course" are pejorative terms. Thus for Kierkegaard those pendulum swings that, in Blanshard's view, gradually bring us to a stabilized truth are "mere approximations." For Nietzsche "reasonableness," so far from being an ideal, is a figment of little minds.

To Blanshard, naturally, such assertions are "unreasonable"—so unreasonable that he rules Kierkegaard and Nietzsche out of order and out of court. Speaking more in sadness than in anger, as befits a man of reason, he contrasts them with Sidgwick, a model of "fairness and good sense." Unfortunately most readers find Sidgwick "irredeemably dull," while Nietzsche and Kierkegaard, "who speak in tones of prophesy, . . . are listened to with a respect they ill deserve" (*RG*, 91).

This evaluation is interesting because it reveals how immediacy bias looks from the perspective of mediation bias. Blanshard appears to believe—so strong is his mediation bias—that if he can only convince Kierkegaard and Nietzsche that they are prophets, they will admit the error of their ways and reform. But to continue the legal metaphor—a metaphor that would not be congenial to Kierkegaard and Nietzsche—the facts are not at issue: Nietzsche and Kierkegaard do not deny being prophets; they glory in being prophets. Blanshard cannot eject them from court on grounds of their unreasonableness; they reject the jurisdiction of the tribunal before which he has brought his case. Whereas he is making a reasoned case for reason and a balanced case for balance before the court of balance and sanity, they are making a passionate plea for passion and an extreme demand for extremes before the throne of passion and of feeling.

This, then, is the case of world-view relativism that I undertook to set out. It is illustrative only, not complete, but perhaps enough has been said to show what is meant by world-view relativism, and it is time therefore to turn to some of the philosophical issues it generates.

II

If I am correct about Blanshard's world view, he will not find my case persuasive. But he should not find it wholly ridiculous, for, though he does not talk about world views in so many words,[10] a good deal of *Reason and Goodness* is actually concerned with what I call world views. Indeed, the historical sketch to which the first six chapters are devoted presupposes a typology of personality that is discussed in some detail in chapters 2, 3, and 15. Here Blanshard distinguishes two types of personality—men of reason and men of feeling—and traces the history of ethical theory back to these differences in personality; men of reason tend to develop a type of ethical theory that is clearly distinguishable from the type developed by men of feeling. The dialectical movement that he finds to characterize the history of moral theory is traced back to the fact that men of reason and men of feeling appear alternatively on the philosophical scene.

I have simply replaced the complex and unanalyzed notions of reason and feeling with a set of dimensions along which the sorts of personality differences Blanshard is talking about may be scaled a bit more precisely. Thus instead of treating the history of moral theory as a simple alternation between men of reason (Marcus Aurelius, Epictetus, Samuel Clarke) and men of feeling (Saint Francis, Shaftesbury, Hutcheson), our matrix provides the possibility of differentiating men of reason from each other in terms of differing loci on these three dimensions, and so for men of feeling. As an example, consider Blanshard's discussion of Hume. Hume may indeed be an antirationalist in the sense that he "sides with the 'sentimentalists' " on the question of who is "judge and master" (*RG*, 87). But Hume shares the static/mediate/discrete configuration with that paradigmatic rationalist, Descartes. He makes the characteristically rationalistic assumption that the mediate stance, which weighs competing claims from outside, is correct. Indeed, he differs from the typical rationalist only in that he believes that the number of cases is severely restricted in which evidence will be sufficient to render a verdict either way. The judicial metaphor is entirely congenial to Hume's thought; he simply believes that, as a matter of fact, most cases are "not proven."

Hence, though (as I think) the matrix I have introduced permits a somewhat more refined description than does Blanshard's dyadic typology, I do not see that my approach differs in any fundamental way from his. Moreover, Blanshard would surely agree that he himself is a man of reason and that his theory has features characteristic of theories developed by other men of reason. Where, then, do he and I differ?

We differ, I think, because Blanshard will claim that it is, and must be, possible to rise above one's biases, to transcend the limitations of one's world view. It is, he would say, precisely men of reason who can do this, and this is what renders them superior to men of feeling. The first step toward freeing ourselves from the limitations of our world view is to bring these biases up to the level of conscious awareness. This is why he has conjoined a history of moral theory with logical analysis. Because the history of moral theory reveals the influence of bias in the past, students of this history can guard themselves against such influences in the future. Of course, Blanshard would add, no one can achieve absolute impartiality and objectivity. But impartiality and objectivity are in principle possible; they are "valid ideals" to aim at. Finally, he would insist that cases like the one I have just presented are irrelevant to the question whether it is possible in principle to transcend the perspectival limitations of our world view. This is a philosophical question, not a question in empirical science, and it cannot be settled by appeal to the sort of evidence obtained in learning theory, in cognitive psychology, or in cultural anthropology. For anything that psychology or anthropology might attempt to bring forward as evidence in support of the thesis that no one can transcend the limitations of his world view must be exempted from this limitation. Otherwise what is put forward is irrelevant to the question; it is not *evidence* one way or the other.

This, in broad outline, is the sort of reply I think Blanshard would make. To summarize: Blanshard will hold not only that I have not proved his theory to be world-view relative, but also that I cannot prove it to be. I can't prove it, for the very good reason that the view I have put forward undermines the essence of proof. Hence world-view relativism is self-stultifying, inchoate, and incoherent.

I agree that I haven't proved it—but then I have not tried to; I have only presented a case that I hope may be persuasive, though not to those whose world view differs markedly from the world view underlying this view of world views. I also agree that I can't prove it, but that is because, as I shall suggest later on (335 ff.), proof is a feature of, and so relative to, a different world view. And I agree, finally, that these admissions are stultifying—but not *self*-stultifying; they are stultifying only from the perspective of that other world view. To explicate these differences in perspective I shall now examine in more detail the arguments against world-view relativism that I have attributed to Blanshard, and then introduce counterconsiderations.

Subjectivism, according to Blanshard, "implies that no statement of right or good is ever true" (*RG,* 220), "that no two persons ever use the word 'right' or 'good' in the same sense" (221), that "no two of us ever agree in ethical belief" (222), and also that we never disagree (224). Again, it follows from the theory that "no one ever makes a mistake on a moral question" (226). Further, though we all believe "that we can correct, and continue to correct, mistaken notions in morals," that is, that "progress is possible," subjectivism "implies that such judgments are without objective meaning" (227). Next, the theory implies "that one can never give relevant *reasons* for or against an ethical judgment" (228). And finally, the theory "allows no objective court of appeal to which ethical disputes may be carried" (234). Without what T.S. Eliot called a "permanent standard," Blanshard argues, "There is no real guilt, no real innocence. This seems to me ethical anarchy" (236).[11]

These arguments were of course directed, not against world-view relativism, but against the particular form of subjectivism that Blanshard calls emotivism. I shall not raise the question here whether emotivism is actually committed, as Blanshard claims, to a subjectivism so extreme that the theory implies that "no one of us ever uses [the word 'right' or 'good'] in the same sense twice" (*RG,* 221). But certainly world-view relativism is not, for a world view is usually shared by large numbers of people.[12] Argument, discourse, and moral progress are thus not excluded by world-view relativism but are made possible by the communality of beliefs and attitudes that define a particular system (or "ethos," or "form of life"). To put this in terms of our matrix: the closer together within a matrix the loci of two individuals lie, the more likely it is that disagreements between these individuals will be terminable. Within any region of the matrix rationality—if this be defined broadly as the capacity to find relevant arguments, to accept common rules of evidence, to agree on an "objective court of appeal"—is attainable. Further, the bounds of a region are by no means sharply defined. The various configurations are merely statistical averages, and there is always a good deal of variation from one individual to another. Those who are far apart on one dimension may be quite close together on others.

Some of what I have said in the last paragraph Blanshard will probably find congenial—for instance, that rationality and intelligibility arise within a system, for this fits in with his insistence that "understanding a point" consists in discovering the context of relations in which this point stands. But he will certainly not find congenial what I have said about there being a plurality of such systems. Indeed, given his world view, the notion of a plurality of systems is self-contradictory: If we think through rigorously what is meant by system we see, according to Blanshard, that "in the end" there can be but one, infinite, all-inclusive system. For however large a finite system may be in practice (large enough, in practice, to permit extensive areas of agreement), if it is finite, we sooner or later come to the limits of that system, and when this happens intelligibility ends.

Obviously, the phrase "sooner or later" isn't to be taken literally; there may never be a time at which we actually reach the bounds of the system. But that fact is irrelevant, Blanshard would hold. If the system within which we are operating has bounds, then this system is unintelligible. And this unintelligibility infects, as it were, all of the agreements that may have been reached within the system, rendering them all unintelligible.[13] The agreements—for instance, the agreement that so-and-so is innocent and so-and-so guilty—may, as a matter of fact, still stand in the sense that nobody ever challenges them. But the finitude of the system within which the arguments by which guilt and innocence were thought to have been established shows that all of these arguments are logically "irrelevant," because they are "ultimately" unintelligible. Hence, though the sentences handed down by the court may never be challenged, there is nevertheless "no real guilt, no real innocence."

Thus it looks as if the disagreement between Blanshard and world-view relativism may turn on the question whether or not there must, as Blanshard contends, "in the end" be one all-inclusive system. This, I think, is the way Blanshard himself might formulate the disagreement. At one point, arguing against Hare, he says that Hare's position is that "when we come to a conflict between two conflicting ways of life, . . . the choice between them [is] a matter, not of rational judgment, but of a non-rational decision or act of will . . ." (*RG*, 254). Blanshard then repeats the arguments with which we are now familiar—that in this event "the ultimately differing parties . . . are not really differing in opinion or belief," because the arguments they adduce are not relevant—and ends by saying, "These things I cannot accept" (255).

The following comments seem in order:

(I) To me Blanshard at this point is making exactly the sort of "irrational commitment" which he condemns "imperativism" for making. Now, from the perspective of world-view relativism, such a commitment is entirely appropriate: Indeed, when a disagreement across systems occurs the parties to the dispute can only hope to agree to differ, unless nonrational forms of persuasion move one or the other from the belief-value system to which he is committed (see below, p. 336). But is not such a stance inappropriate for a professed rationalist, who maintains that all stances must be rationally defensible? To some readers Blanshard's adoption of an "irrational" stance at this point might even constitute a persuasive case of world-view relativism.

Doubtless Blanshard will reply that a commitment to rationalism is unique in that, precisely because it is a commitment to rationalism, it is not irrational. But the conclusion I draw—which, naturally, conforms to my view of world views—is that the whole rationalist program, as Blanshard conceives it, is relative to *his* world view. At one point Blanshard comes close to saying this himself. Arguing that "Meta-ethics cannot be pursued responsibly in divorce from ethics" (*RG*, 264), he points out that "To adopt certain meanings for 'right' and 'good' as the valid ones is also to elect a way of life" (263). I suggest that the word "rational," as much as the words "right" and "good," has a variety of possible meanings, each of which reflects a particular "way of life"—a phrase which seems to me about equivalent to what I mean by a world view.

(II) Since Blanshard agrees that in actual practice we deal only with finite, or limited, systems, let us ask what it means to say that nonetheless there "must be" one all-inclusive system. That is, what do such phrases as "in the end," "really," and "ultimately" mean? How do these phrases, and such similar ones as "in principle" and "in theory," function in the sentences that contain them? Here are some examples from *Reason and Goodness*:

> (a) "[Goodness] is to be measured against an ideal good, which is the kind of life which would fulfil and satisfy wholly" (293).
> (b) "*The* good is what would be satisfactory in the end" (302).
> (c) ". . . movement toward an end" (304).
> (d) ". . . the ideal of reason . . . has presented itself as a system in which nothing is merely an accident, but is connected intelligibly with everything else by necessary relations" (305).
> (e) "*The* good . . . is the most comprehensive possible fulfilment and satisfaction of impulse-desire. . . .* That there is and must be such a good, supreme over all others, we can see . . ." (311).
> (f) "No such good is ever final" (316).
> (g) "*The* good is nothing short of what would fulfil and satisfy wholly" (343).
> (h) "No actual good is absolute, if that means one in which we should be contented to rest permanently" (*RG*, 307).

Elsewhere[14] I have distinguished what I call designative (or informational) discourse from what I call expressive discourse. I regard this as a degree-difference: expressive discourse always contains at least some information; informational discourse is always at least marginally expressive. But

I call discourse "expressive" if it functions primarily to express feeling, i.e. to communicate an attitude, and if it does this in ways likely to evoke a similar attitude in the reader. Further, discourse which the author intends to function in a purely informational way may, in point of fact, be functioning primarily in an expressive way. This is true, I think, of large parts of philosophical discourse. While the philosophical author believes himself to be conveying information about reality he is, in large measure, conveying attitudes generated by his world view.

As a simple, nonphilosophical, example of the difference between informational and expressive discourse, contrast "I am ready to die" and "Out, out, brief candle!" The latter does indeed convey information, and much of the same information as that conveyed by the former, but, unlike the former, it also strongly expresses an attitude toward this information and does so in a form likely to evoke a similar attitude in us.

With this contrast in mind, let us turn back to the sentences I have cited from *Reason and Goodness*. I suggest that, despite their grammatical form, these sentences are primarily expressive rather than informational, and that what they express is tension between what I shall call a demand for closure and a demand for completeness—both of which are generated within Blanshard's world view. Static bias leads Blanshard to want to find a permanent rest for intellect in its quest for truth and a final court of appeals for will in its quest for goodness. This is the demand for closure. Now, when static bias is associated, as it usually is, with discreteness bias, neither the truth nor the good looks so problematic as they look when, as in Blanshard's case, static bias is associated with continuity bias. Discreteness bias makes one content with finite truths, for each encapsulated proposition is complete in itself. One man may well know more truths than another man, but not more truth—for discreteness bias the notion of degrees of truth is not only unnecessary but absurd. The drive of static bias to closure is thus easily satisfied.

Continuity bias alters the perspective radically. Since for continuity bias no encapsulated proposition is complete, closure is defeated. Hence there is a drive for completeness. Now when, as usually happens, continuity bias is associated with dynamic bias, it is possible to enter into, and enjoy, a never-ending process of truth seeking; it is experienced as a high adventure. Here again, as with static/discreteness, no strain occurs. But strain does occur when continuity bias is associated with static bias—a never-ending process is not an adventure but a frustration.

Strain also occurs at another point in a configuration like Blanshard's. Mediation bias calls for adopting an observer stance in the pursuit of truth, but continuity bias demands a more intimate relationship between knower and known. Very strong continuity bias—stronger than Blanshard's—

probably results in some form of mysticism, of which there are faint, but only faint, echoes in *Reason and Goodness,* for instance in the metaphor of the sea (*RG,* 306), already discussed in another connection.

Now I think that a part of what is being expressed in the sentences before us is some of this strain. Note for instance the interesting shifts in tense between present— —(d), (e)— —and conditional— —(a), (b), (g). The present satisfies the demand for closure by suggesting that closure is achieved. The conditional expresses the demand for completeness. The tense shifts occur as one or the other of these demands comes into focus.

Or consider (f) and (h). The demand for closure that Blanshard himself experiences makes him sensitive to our all too human tendency to dogmatism, i.e. readiness to close, even if what we close on is only finite. His demand for completeness makes him emphasize the importance of resisting this temptation. Hence these sentences express a kind of double injunction, an appeal and a warning: "Don't despair of reaching the truth, but don't allow yourself ever to fall into the trap of believing you have reached it!" Thus he writes that, so far from being discouraged by the "illimitable demand" generated by the demand for completeness, we should rather take pride in it. He reminds us that the discontent we experience in the face of incompleteness has been called, "and perhaps with justice, 'divine discontent' " (*RG,* 307). Indeed, "The command to continue the search is . . . addressed by human nature to itself . . ." (331).

That this is eloquent writing I think will be admitted, even by those who may not themselves be moved by it. And my point is precisely that it *is* eloquent; it expresses a particular complex attitude toward rationality, and it expresses it in a way that tends to evoke a similar attitude in many readers. This particular complex attitude, with its particular weighting of appeal and warning, differs discernibly from the attitude of a Descartes, with his very strong static/mediate/discrete configuration, and also from the attitude of a Hegel, with strong dynamic and continuous bias and a midrange locus on the immediacy/mediation dimension. This is why I suggest that "to adopt a certain meaning" for a term like "rationality," as much as to adopt one for "right" and for "good," is "to elect a way of life."

III

Judging by Blanshard's arguments against emotivism, I think it likely that at this point he will want to confront me with a dilemma. Consider my discourse about the relativity to world view of Blanshard's discourse about rationality and systemic all-inclusiveness: Is my discourse relative to my world view, as I say that his discourse is relative to his world view? If I claim that it is not, I must show why my discourse is immune to the relativity I attribute to his, and any argument that allows mine to escape relativity would apply to his as well. On the other hand, if I admit that my discourse about Blanshard's discourse is relative to my world view, what reasons can I give for expecting him, or anyone else, to accept what I say about his discourse? It will be seen that this is an application of the basic argument that any theory asserting the subjectivism of theory is "incoherent" because it contradicts itself.

We may agree that a theory that exempts itself from an assertion of universal relativism is self-contradictory. But, in the first place, it is worth noting that not all philosophers are as disturbed by contradiction as Blanshard is. Nietzsche, for instance, reveled in contradiction. For him it was a game, the point of which was never to settle anywhere long enough to be caught out. Thus he declares flatly that everything is interpretation, not text; and then, before a lumbering critic manages to formulate the classic objection, Nietzsche states it for him: "Let us admit that this, too, would be only an interpretation—and you will be eager enough to make this objection! Well, all the better!"[15] At this point a rationalist may exclaim crossly that he cannot take seriously anyone who reasons in such a fashion. But this attitude would not disturb Nietzsche, who did not take rationalists seriously. Nietzsche would not object, I suppose, if such a critic were simply to walk away from Nietzsche's game, saying that he didn't want to play any longer, but it is different if the critic insists on Nietzsche's game being played according to the critic's rules, on the grounds these are *the* rules for game playing.

However, it is not the first, but the second, horn of Blanshard's dilemma on which world-view relativism is impaled—though of course impalement inflicts a mortal wound only within the context of a particular world view. The view of world views that I have put forward is self-referential. If I understand Blanshard's criticism of relativism, it may be rephrased by saying that relativism absolutizes itself and thereby becomes incoherent. This may be true of emotivism, the version of relativism examined in *Reason and Goodness*. But world-view relativism relativizes relativism, and relativizes it to a particular world view.[16] An absolutized relativism argues for relativism and seeks to prove it. A relativized relativism eschews attempts to prove relativism, for it views argument and proof as relative to a particular world view; they are a part of the "way of life" for which rationalists opt. This is why I have described myself as putting forward suggestions and counterconsiderations and as looking for a persuasive case.

It seems that there are two main types of strategy that can be used in presenting persuasive cases. One of these may be called shock treatment. This is the strategy used by Kierkegaard and Nietzsche, and it consists in trying to jolt the reader out of one world view and into another. It presupposes that change in world view is a form of conversion, on the Pauline model. It may be said, indeed, that God presented an exceptionally persuasive case to Saul on the road to Damascus. The other main strategy, the strategy used, for instance, by Wittgenstein, adopts a gradualistic and suggestive therapy. It consists in selecting the case closest to the one at issue that one believes will be read favorably, i.e. in the light one wants it read, and then bringing forward the similarities between this case and the one at issue.[17]

Both of these strategies presuppose that world-view differences are fundamental. They do not deny that an individual can on occasion be moved from one world view to another; the point of the two strategies is precisely so to move him. But because they take world-view differences seriously, it is the problem of how to effect such a move that is in focus for them. These strategies of course acknowledge that argument and proof have a role; their role is to promote agreements within systems, i.e. within world views. But for thinkers whose world view emphasizes world-view differences, this activity is not particularly important or interesting; it is not in focus.

In contrast, the strategy of argument and proof presupposes that world-view differences are not fundamental. It does not deny, of course, that there are differences in world view, but it holds that these can be transcended without much difficulty and by the method of argument and proof. Thinkers whose world view minimizes world-view differences do not deny that something like conversion on occasion occurs, but this phenomenon, so far from being of importance, is not in focus for them. They associate it with psychological abnormality and so regard it as outside the bounds of logic and philosophy.[18]

My way of saying what I have just said was designed to call attention to, rather than to disguise, the fact that it presupposes the point at issue. It presupposes, that is, that world-view differences are fundamental. For instance, I wrote above that "Thinkers whose world view minimizes world-view differences do not deny. . . ." But this description of the position of these thinkers would be quite unacceptable to them: From their point of view their minimization of world-view differences does not simply reflect a world view—naturally! Well, then, let them describe their position in their own language. It will turn out that this description also presupposes the point at issue, this time by minimizing world-view differences.

The limitation to which I am calling attention isn't, from my point of view, a special feature of a particular world view—though it is easier to notice the limitation from the perspective of a world view that takes world views seriously, for this is one of the aspects of experience that comes into focus for such a world view. But every strategy—the strategy of argument and proof as much as the strategies of shock treatment and suggestive therapy—presupposes what, for the other, is the point at issue. For the point at issue is precisely the vision of the world that underlies the whole way of life of which this strategy is a part.

And now I have to add that this way of describing the point at issue also assumes the point at issue. For instance, the fact that I find this limitation acceptable, and that Blanshard does not, fits in, of course, with my world view. And of course I think that the reason I find it acceptable is that it does fit in with mine, and that the reason he does not is that it does not fit in with his. But Blanshard would not accept this account of why he does not find the account I have given acceptable. From his point of view (of course, he would reject the limitation conveyed in this phrase), it must be possible, at least ideally, to strike a balance between estimates that exaggerate the difference world views make and estimates that underestimate the difference they make. And while he would allow that one can never actually achieve the absolute zero point of complete neutrality and equilibrium in which one's judgment exactly formulates the amount of difference a world view "really" makes, there is nothing in principle to prevent. . . . And I will reply. . . . But let us not climb on board this particular merry-go-round again.

IV

Finally I return to the question of transcendence in order to try to narrow—not, I fear, dissolve—my difference with Blanshard. After all, one would like to be in alliance, not in nonterminable disagreement, with a philosopher one so much admires and respects, above all a philosopher to whom one's own formative years owe so much.

First, then, I shall distinguish the question whether men can move, or be moved, from one world view to another from the question whether men can free themselves from world views altogether. As regards the first question, my answer is yes. Men on occasion move, or are moved, from one world view to another. How readily an individual moves depends on the rigidity of his configuration, and this (in my language) is a function of how far out on the various dimensions his loci are and how strongly charged these loci are. Weakly charged, midrange loci are readily modifiable; here the strategy of argument and proof is particularly appropriate. Highly charged, polar loci are movable, if at all, by such strategies as shock treatment and suggestive therapy. I think that some of what I have just written is probably translatable into language that Blanshard would find acceptable.

It is the second question that is likely to become nonterminable. For my part, I think that men can probably learn to discount their biases to some extent (this is different from merely shifting from one set of biases to another). I also think that coming to self-awareness is an important element in this learning. Further, I think it desirable to learn to discount bias as much as one

can. To this extent I am a rationalist like Blanshard: I think that what I am
calling "discounting" is an important part of what Blanshard calls "being
reasonable." So far, then, I think what I am saying may be translatable into
language Blanshard would find acceptable.

But now I would add that the judgment that discounting is desirable is a
reflection of a particular world view—one that involves strong mediation
bias. Hence (i) we don't free ourselves from this bias by adopting a discounting
stance toward it; we reinforce it. And (ii) it cannot be proved that those
with strong immediacy bias are "wrong" in refusing to adopt a discounting
stance.

Can this be translated into language that Blanshard would find acceptable? I doubt it, but let me begin by calling attention to the fact that
Blanshard and I agree—at least, I think we agree—on two points. We agree
that one can discount one's world view to some extent, and we agree that one
can never reach a perfect balance between over- and under-discounting. Of
course, we probably differ about the extent to which discounting is possible; I
suspect Blanshard tends, in particular cases, to be more optimistic than I am.
However, if we differ only over the degree of discounting that is possible, we
are not in fundamental disagreement. Again, though Blanshard agrees that a
perfect balance is impossible, he would want to add that aiming at such a
balance—where, if we *could* reach it, objectivity and truth *would* be attained—is a "valid ideal." And this is not a phrase I particularly like. But
what does our disagreement about this phrase amount to? Would Blanshard
perhaps be willing to say that in calling balance a "valid ideal" he is seeking
to describe the attitude he recommends us to adopt in the face of the agreed-
on inability to achieve a perfect balance? If he accepts this description of how
"valid ideal" is functioning in the sentences in which it occurs, then we differ
less in respect to the attitude we believe it appropriate to adopt than in respect
to the appropriate language in which to describe the appropriate attitude. If
that is how we differ, then the difference between us has been narrowed.

But would Blanshard want to say that there can be only one phrase that is
"really" appropriate and that it is either true or false that "valid ideal" is this
phrase? Or would he permit me to say that one's choice of one phrase rather
than another as appropriate reflects one's world view? I fear he may feel that
in this last move I have thrown away everything that is important.

Let me therefore try once more. It will be seen that my strategy for
narrowing our disagreement has been to translate seemingly substantive
questions into linguistic questions. In its most general form this consists in
suggesting that the central question of *Reason and Goodness* is not to ascertain the "positions" of reason and feeling in ethics, but rather to discuss the
roles in human life of the language of reason and the language of feeling.
Would Blanshard agree? Might we then not also agree that there are elements

in experience for which, and there are circumstances in which, the language of feeling is more appropriate than the language of reason? If so, then, once again, our disagreement has been narrowed, for though I might assign a larger role to the language of feeling than Blanshard does, we would now be differing only in detail, not fundamentally. Or would Blanshard hold that the language of reason has an absolute priority—at least in principle? I can agree, providing, of course, the phrases "absolute priority" and "in principle" are understood to be in the language of feeling, not in the language of reason. Would Blanshard accept this? If not, we are back where we started. Though at one moment it may look as if our views are converging, at another we are as far apart as ever. Blanshard's replies and my counterconsiderations have simply been passing each other, each circling within its own world view—or so it seems to me. This, of course, is what I have all along thought would be the case, and it is what Blanshard "cannot accept." Naturally, I hold that the difference between accepting and being unable to accept a disagreement as nonterminable is a difference in feeling and so nonterminable by reason. Blanshard will disagree. And what about this disagreement about whether that disagreement is terminable by reason? Is it terminable by reason? I think not.

Is there anything more to be said at this point? No; it would seem there is not.

W. T. JONES

DIVISION OF THE HUMANITIES AND SOCIAL SCIENCES
CALIFORNIA INSTITUTE OF TECHNOLOGY

NOTES

[1] For a general statement of the thesis that differences in world view cause nonterminable disagreements in philosophy, see W.T. Jones, "Philosophical Disagreements and World Views," in *Proceedings and Addresses of the American Philosophical Association* 43 (1969–70). The present paper is in effect a case study illustrative of this thesis.

[2] For the epistemological underpinning of this view of world views, see W.T. Jones, *The Sciences and the Humanities* (Berkeley and Los Angeles: University of California Press, 1965), where world-view sets are deep structures in the backgrounds by which foregrounds are interpreted.

[3] It is possible to talk about the world view of a group or a society if and to the extent that similar configurations of sets characterize substantial numbers of the individual members of that group or society. In this paper, however, I shall be concentrating on differences in the world views of individual philosophers, not of whole societies.

[4] A preliminary description of a seven-dimensional matrix was given in W.T. Jones, *The Romantic Syndrome* (The Hague: Martinus Nijhoff, 1961). A revised version is contained in "World Views: Their Nature and Their Function," in *Current Anthropology* 13 (February 1972). Since the present paper is intended as a continuation of "Philosophical Disagreements and World Views" (note 1, above), I have used the same three-dimensional matrix that I introduced there.

⁵Compare for instance, ". . . if our dialectic were Hegelian . . ." (*RG*, 81).

⁶Blanshard uses this word in connection with his discussion of duty: "Are we to say, then, that dutifulness . . . is an extrinsic, not an intrinsic, good? No. . . . The truth would seem to be that it is a mixture of the two" (*RG*, 333). Here again the underlying notion is that extremes are bad because they are in disequilibrium.

⁷Some language that might initially suggest a military metaphor—"attack," "defense"—actually fits into the judicial-review pattern, since Blanshard couples attack and defense with "vindication" (for instance, *RG*, 13). Clearly, it is of legal attack and defense that he is thinking.

⁸And who is the impartial judge, or arbiter, of these claims? Reason. Some may think it a little odd for an advocate of impartiality to allow reason to adjudicate a case to which it is a party. Will not reason always decide in favor of itself—that is, in favor of impartiality, balance, and "reasonableness"?

⁹Numerous other passages reveal a preference for distancing, for taking oneself outside of events, in contrast to participating in them as they occur. Think, for instance, of the recommendations to "look over our own shoulder, so to speak" (*RG*, 435), and to keep "oneself in check" (439). There is also the praise of "*aequanimitas,* evenness of spirit, stability . . . imperturbability . . ." (442) and of "serenity" (445), all of which reflects mediation bias.

¹⁰As a matter of fact the term "world view" does turn up, but only in the analytical table of contents (*RG*, 17).

¹¹These arguments repeat, and elaborate on, "the paradoxes of subjectivism," discussed in an earlier chapter (*RG*, 136–38). The common thread running through all of them is that relativism makes argument and discourse—makes rationality—impossible.

¹²See note 3, above.

¹³Compare *RG*, 254, where Blanshard argues that theories that allow for the justification of moral imperatives by reference to a "wider system" break down if it turns out that the wider system rests "in turn on a non-rational commitment, [for] then all the commitments that depend on it are similarly in the end indefensible." This irrationalism "at the last step . . . calls the whole advance into question."

¹⁴See *The Sciences and the Humanities*, 243–61, for an application of this approach to discourse about the summum bonum and about freedom of the will.

¹⁵Friedrich Nietzsche, *Beyond Good and Evil*, trans. Marianne Cowan (Chicago: Henry Regnery, 1955), 26.

¹⁶The account I have given of discourse about an "all-inclusive" system is quite different from positivistic reductionism. In the first place, I don't say that expressive discourse is "meaningless." In the second place, I think that discourse denying the existence of an all-inclusive system is just as expressive as is discourse affirming it; the former simply expresses a different world view, or "way of life," from the latter.

¹⁷To me, the case I presented in the first section of this paper conforms more to the Wittgensteinian model than to the Nietzschean, but Blanshard, on reading that he has a static/mediate/continuous world view, may well suspect me of attempting the strategy of shock treatment.

¹⁸Blanshard says he "cannot accept" the view that there are nonterminable disagreements because, if there were any such disagreements, one "could only say, 'Take it or leave it' " (*RG*, 255). But from the point of view of a theory that takes world-view differences as fundamental and so "accepts" them, a nonterminable disagreement, so far from being a hopeless dead-end, is only the point at which to begin the strategies of shock treatment and suggestive therapy.

6. Reply to W. T. Jones

Reason, Feeling, and World View

Mr. Jones has written a paper unlike any other in this book. The other writers have selected certain theories of mine for scrutiny and questioning. Mr. Jones attempts something more fundamental. He thinks that my very conception of philosophy, in common with that of most other philosophers, is gravely mistaken. Accordingly he first sketches the new conception of philosophy which he believes should replace the old, and then undertakes to show how my moral philosophy confirms the new conception, though intermittently and unwittingly, even while explicitly rejecting it. This is a novel and interesting mode of attack, the more so because Mr. Jones states his case clearly, has thought it out in detail, and is even able to predict with impressive prescience what line my reply will take, giving his rejoinder in advance. This is an exciting challenge.

A New Relativism

What Mr. Jones offers us is a new kind of relativism. He thinks that a philosophy is not a set of insights into the nature of things, a set of impartial reasonings and objective judgments, but rather a by-product of our peculiar mental constitution. He holds that when a philosopher believes himself to be following the configurations of the world his thought is actually controlled by his own mental set. Such a set is an attitude, partly cognitive, though largely emotional, which determines the objects or concepts on which the thinker bends his attention, and the way he uses evidence about them. Xenophobia is a simple example. Some people react to those of another race or nation with fixed hostility; others treat them with indifference; others still with a special liking. Now a philosophy is a more comprehensive set of this kind. "Sets that organize not merely this or that region of a man's experience but very extensive ranges of his experience constitute, collectively, what I call his world view." With regard to crucial objects and issues, the sets of philosophers will be found to differ widely; indeed Mr. Jones, who certainly knows his history of philosophy, says they cover virtually all the points on the spectrum of attitudes. Such a spectrum he calls a dimension. He selects three of these dimensions as of especial importance for philosophy.

The first of them is the spectrum of attitudes that range from the love of the static to the love of the dynamic, from the preference for the enduring and changeless at one extreme to that for process, movement, change, on the other. In this dimension Parmenides lies at one end of the spectrum and Heraclitus at the other. For Parmenides the unchanging was the only reality, and the problem was how change got into the world at all; for Heraclitus flux or change was the one reality, and the problem was to find anything permanent. The second spectrum is called the continuity-discreteness dimension. Some minds are so made as to fasten their interest upon the interrelatedness of things and to regard the differences as merely matters of degree; others are so constituted as to look for "encapsulated atomistic entities" with an emphasis on the sharp distinctions between them. Wordsworth, with his mystical feeling of the oneness of things and his conviction that "we murder to dissect," lies at one extreme; the logical atomists of the present day lie at the other. The third dimension is that of immediacy-mediation. This represents the difference between those who prefer to "live through" an experience and sink themselves in it and those who prefer to contemplate it from the outside; it is the difference between the participant and the observer. I think Mr. Jones would recognize Bergson as a mind of the first type and Russell as an example of the second.

Any given philosopher will have an attitude that fixes his place on each of these three dimensions, and on others that for brevity's sake Mr. Jones omits. The synthesis of these attitudes is all-important, for it constitutes his world view, and this world view determines the issues he chooses for attention, the evidence he is willing to take into account, and the conclusions to which he commits himself. He is probably serenely content in the belief that he accepts a world of substances rather than events because an invincible logic has driven him to it. That is also the belief of his opponent. Each maximizes the importance of the evidence that leads in his direction, and minimizes or overlooks the evidence that points the other way. Mr. Jones is quite frank in calling such sets biases; they are essentially a matter of likings, of temperamental affinities or aversions; the "reasons" so readily offered on both sides are not the actual movers of belief; they only paper over the underlying congenialities and antipathies that are the actual springs of conviction. Mr. Jones's conception of philosophy is a little like the conception of religion held by Santayana, who said that anyone who took its dogmas as serious candidates for truth was beyond the range of profitable discussion. To put it baldly, philosophy is not the product of an impersonal reason; it is a reflection of the dominant biases in the mind of the thinker himself.

Of course this holds of me and my rationalism. Mr. Jones is able to assign my place on each of the three dimensions; my biases are for the static as opposed to the dynamic, for continuity as opposed to discreteness, and for mediation as opposed to the immediate. A representative of this static-continuity-mediation world view will insist on the objective truth or falsity of propositions, and on testing them by their coherence within a system. He will make much of logical connections and logical reasoning, and will try to suppress any bias that might lead him off the logical course. His stress will be on rationality, for to abandon rationality in favor of anything dictated by impulse, feeling, or desire is to abandon the quest of truth. Mr. Jones has noted my low regard for Kierkegaard and Nietzsche because of their own low regard for consistency and reasonableness. But a regard for consistency and reasonableness is itself a mental set, and "For Nietzsche 'reasonableness,' so far from being an ideal, is a figment of little minds." The difference, then, between the irrationalist and the man who reveres rationality is what Mr. Jones would describe as a "non-terminable disagreement." "Rational" designates a psychological peculiarity of preference, but it is not more worthy of veneration and no more likely to be true than the propensity for irrationalism.

The Dilemma of Relativism

Mr. Jones has anticipated the natural first criticism of this theory. It is confronted by an obvious dilemma. Is it offered as a philosophy itself, that is, as a way of thinking that can claim truth as opposed to traditional conceptions now seen to be false? If so, then it is admitting the thesis that it is chiefly concerned to deny, namely that by taking thought we *can* apprehend what is objectively true, and the philosophy is self-refuting. On the other hand, is the new view offered with no claim to truth, but merely as the expression of the author's own interests and preferences? In that case why should we accept it rather than any one of a hundred other products of bias which are today offered in the marketplace? Mr. Jones's reply, as I understand it, is to reject the first horn, and with qualifications to accept the second. Let us examine both the rejection and the acceptance.

Mr. Jones of course sees that if he offers as objectively true a philosophy maintaining that no philosophy is objectively true, he contradicts himself. But why not contradict oneself? He has granted Kierkegaard and Nietzsche that privilege if they prefer it. If he forgoes it himself, it must be because he has a preference for thinking consistently. Why should he prefer this? He is precluded from giving an answer by his position that the basic conceptions of philosophy are not determined by reasons; preferences are his ultimates, and to give reasons for them would be inconsistency again. Once more, why does he consider that to save his position he must escape from the dilemma confronting him? It is because he sees that if he fails to escape he will be involved in inconsistency. Throughout the presentation of his case, Mr. Jones is writing with the same respect for logic as is shown by philosophers traditionally. Why? That there is nothing further in this respect than a non-rational preference I find it hard to believe. I suspect that despite his sincere disavowals Mr. Jones does have a reason for preferring consistency, and that this is the same reason the rest of us would give, namely that unless our thought is consistent it cannot be true.

There is something odd in arguing with a philosopher as to whether he means to say what is true. I will not stop to argue that being true means being objectively true; all truth is objective truth; "true for me" means only that I think something true, not that it is in fact true. Mr. Jones insists that he is not reporting nor meaning to report truth about the world, but is drawing a picture of the world that is congenial to him. But when he tells us this, is he still only drawing a congenial picture? If he says Yes, we are not communicating with each other, for what I am demurring to is certainly not his, or anyone else's, entertaining himself with congenial visions. If he says No, then he is presumably telling us what he takes to be the truth about his own attitude; and in that case he has left his vision behind and is attempting, like other philosophers, to report things as they are. And what is he doing when he *denies* that traditional philosophers have been right in their conception of philosophy? It sounds as if he meant that their conception of what they were doing did not correspond with the facts of the case, and we are back to objective truth. Hence, neither when Mr. Jones asserts nor when he denies is he doing or trying to do what other philosophers suppose to be their exclusive business, namely judging about the nature of things.

If this is the case, what is there for a critic to do? I certainly do not want to impose inhibitions on Mr. Jones's dreaming dreams or seeing congenial visions; he has, as I happen to know, a delightful disposition, and I do not know why he should not indulge it in so harmless and satisfying a way. But when he says that philosophy *consists* of the large-scale indulgence of such visions, that our cognitive apprehension of the way things are is rooted in precognitive attitudes, that the attempt at being logical is itself the expression of a nonrational preference for this sort of arrangement, I can only shake my head. Among the controls of thought this seems to me to leave out what is most important and distinctive.

There is no precognitive orientation which in different minds sets different goals for thought. Thought from the beginning is a distinctive activity with a goal of its own. That is the apprehension of its object, the adjustment of its ideas to the world. The process is at work in the simplest perception, which is in fact already judgment. The child, having been treated to a taste of sugar, tries for itself what looks like the same thing, only to be repelled by a taste of salt. The distinction between appearance and reality is already getting lodgment in his mind. To think is to try to lay hold through judgment of things as they are. It is not an attempt to synthesize rainbows into a glorious igloo for the spirit; it is not a spree of prejudice in which nonrational likes and dislikes can have a field day of their own. To the framework of logic in which thought tries to move there is no legitimate alternative. "Thinking," as Bradley says, "is the attempt to satisfy a special impulse, and the attempt implies an assumption about reality. You may avoid the assumption so far as you decline to think, but, if you sit down to the game, there is only one way of playing" (*Appearance and Reality,* 153).[1] That way is dictated by the norms that are immanent in the activity of thought. The laws of identity and contradiction, the fact that two and two make four and not seven, the fact that from a given proposition or pair of propositions some things follow and others do not—these are not matters of preference that we can dispense with if we find them uncongenial. We can, to be sure, hold inconsistent beliefs, add incorrectly, and draw fallacious conclusions. But we can also see that in thus violating the norms set for us by reason we are also sacrificing our chance for truth and thus betraying the purpose of thinking at all.

The reader will remember that Mr. Jones was confronting a dilemma: either his philosophy of philosophy is offered as objectively true or it is not. He rejects the first horn as inconsistent with his general conception of philosophy. We noted this bias of his in favor of consistency, and argued that it was not a bias at all, but the immanent demand of thought itself. Indeed, although Mr. Jones avows that he is rejecting the first horn—the offering of his theory as truth—we have contended that this rejection is intellectually impossible. For if in offering it he is engaged in thought at all, he must be trying to discover something true about the world, since that is what thinking is, not a process of dreaming dreams or seeing visions or following psychological compulsions.

Let us turn now to the second horn, which Mr. Jones elects: he is offering us a philosophy proposed not as objectively true, but rather as the view of things most congenial to his own preferences and biases. To this the philosopher's first reaction is likely to be: "In that case I have no criticism to offer." For the business of criticism in philosophy is to say how true or false a theory is, and if nothing is offered as truth, criticism is impertinence. But the impression remains irresistible that what Mr. Jones is offering us is not autobiography merely nor merely what he *prefers* to think other philosophers may be doing. He is surely offering us his conviction about what philosophers are really doing, whatever they may suppose themselves to be doing. In his presidential address to the Pacific Division in 1970 he made that clear; he presented his theory as a hypothesis to account for the extreme differences encountered among philosophers, and in *The Romantic Syndrome* he provides a well-peopled gallery of artists and scientists, historians and theologians, as well as philosophers, whose views he believes to have been determined in the same manner.

A hypothesis of this kind may be very enlightening, as I think Mr. Jones's theory is in many cases. We are all affected by bias, even those who struggle hardest to free themselves from it, and for many persons Mr. Jones's pages must make self-revealing reading. But the struggle avails nothing if bias is built in and universal and there is no standard of truth, attainable independently of bias, by which departures into error may be judged. And I am not sure that when Mr. Jones has finished he has left us anything at all in the way of a standard of truth or an area of certainty from which aberrations may be measured. The impression I gain from his essay is that our "precognitive" dispositions are all-pervading, determining both the objects we attend to and the kinds of connection we recognize between them. And if that interpretation is correct, it leads straight to skepticism. Mr. Jones is not a solipsist, or if he is he is a gratifyingly inconsistent and jolly one. He surely believes that there is a world of some kind standing over against us, a world we did not make and which is waiting to engulf us in its good time. This world must have a character of its own. Any given event in it is either governed by causation or not; an ink bottle is a substance in Aristotle's sense, or in Locke's sense, or in McTaggart's sense, or in some other sense, or not at all; space is made up of unextended points or not, time of indivisible instants or not. If thought, adhering to its immanent logical norms, can trace the lines of any configuration in its world or truly grasp any fact, it has some path of access into the universe outside it. On the other hand, if what it attends to in the way of objects and relations, and what it accepts as valid in the way of reasoning, is determined by inner "preferences," "likings," "biases," "dispositions," then knowledge becomes an accident, and an accident sufficiently improbable to make skepticism one's natural philosophy. It might be replied that while skepticism would be natural if one considered only the extremes on Mr. Jones's axes of preference, the probability of genuine knowledge increases when one considers that near the middle on each axis there is a cluster of coincident preferences. This would follow, however, only if centrality on the axis meant the closer reflection in thought of the nature of things. But I find nothing to indicate that this is the case. And if thought at all points is determined not by the character of the object but by pressures from within, those preferences that fall in the middle are no more likely to represent truth than those at the extremes.

It may be said: "Why not be a skeptic?" Everyone who has studied, as Mr. Jones has done so widely, the history of philosophy must have had this position almost forced upon him by the apparently insuperable differences among philosophers of the highest ability. But the answer is that general skepticism is a simple impossibility. The man who knows that he knows nothing knows at least that, and if he says he doubts that he knows, he is claiming to know that he doubts. Whether Mr. Jones would hold that bias enters in even to such kinds of knowledge as this I do not know, but I suspect he would. And then we are back in the old dilemma; if he knows anything, he has escaped, so far, from bias; if he makes no claim to knowledge, there is nothing to refute.

Kinds of Bias

As for the explanatory value of the biases themselves, I must confess that while I think them often illuminating in history and various forms of art, I do not find them equally valuable in philosophy. A "mother-fixation," the hatred of a father, the love of a woman, may be enormously powerful deflectors of thought and conduct. But fixation on anything so abstract as the static, or continuity, or mediation is not, I should have thought, the sort of passion that would pull any philosopher bent on truth very far out of his orbit. This is the clearer when we consider that every one of Mr. Jones's axes is such that it is impossible to stress one of the terminal pair of ideas without attention to its opposite. When Plato sought for the identities that formed his ideas, he had to single them out from the flux in which they lay; Russell, who is cited as an example of discreteness-domination, devoted long and careful study to the nature of continuity; Bergson, who is a prime example of an immediacy orientation, finds himself forced by this very preoccupation to give special attention to the "frozen" intuitions of the world of space. If philosophers, dealing with problems of ultimate complexity, find themselves stressing one element rather than others, there seem to me to be simpler explanations than that of a precognitive disposition in its favor. They may be recognizing that this element has not received the notice it deserved, or they may be making an impartial attempt to interpret the limited evidence available, or they may be trying to keep within the limits of their own intellectual skill. This does not deny that sheer irrational prejudice may be at work even in philosophical minds. Mr. Jones writes of Kierkegaard: "Whereas Kant set up the distinction [between *Erlebnis* and *Erfahrung*] in order to give 'due consideration' to both claimants, Kierkegaard set it up only in order to knock down and trample on one of them. Instead of starting from a stance of impartiality, Kierkegaard started from a subjective commitment to subjective truth that wholly rejects objective truth as worthless" (Presidential Address, Pacific Division, American Philosophical Association, 1970).[2] We agree that here antirational prejudice is clearly visible. At the same time it should be remembered that Kierkegaard, like Nietzsche, spent much of his life teetering on the ragged edge of sanity.

This suggests that I find important truth in Mr. Jones's position: bias is an almost universally present factor in our thinking. But whereas Mr. Jones takes it as inevitable, I take it as a danger to be avoided. My book on *Reason and Goodness* ends in a burst of laudation for the man who knows his biases and makes the allowances needed to cancel them. Mr. Jones finds evidence, however, in my writing on ethics that I agree with his theory more than I realize. In my discussion of the swing of the pendulum in ethical history between the stress on feeling and the stress on reason as the essence of moral judgment, he finds a "dyadic typology" that is significantly parallel to his own. And this parallel would indeed be significant if it brought to light a certain conclusion. If all the philosophers who made feeling the guide of life or the essential factor in moral judgment had been found to be committed to this view by native temperament, and all those who took reason as the guide were found to be similarly committed to rationality, the case would indeed provide evidence for Mr. Jones's thesis. But that was not my argument, nor did I reach any such conclusion. I did not attempt to correlate philosophers' theories with their temperaments, and do not think I could have succeeded if I had. Those who have stood for the supremacy of feeling in moral "judgment" have often been far from romantic or emotional in their own personal predilections; think of Hume, Westermarck, Russell, and Ayer. And I doubt whether among those who stressed the place of reason in morals, from Marcus Aurelius to Sidgwick, there could be traced any common lack of emotional warmth.

Mr. Jones also thinks that some of my own ethical positions express nonrational commitments rather than rational judgments. He cites as a case in point my criticism of Professor Hare's *The Language of Morals*. Hare argues that a moral judgment, which he regards as essentially an imperative, can be supported by reason, though only up to a certain point. One can defend a particular action by showing that it coheres with a way of life as a whole, which would be breached and weakened if one failed to take such action. But if this way of life as a whole is challenged, he thinks our power of rational defense is at an end; all we can do is to make an unreasoned commitment of the will. I commended Hare for holding, as against the emotivists, that an act can be thus rationally defended by showing its implication with a way of life. But I insisted that this advance was largely nullified by his admission that the way of life itself rested on a nonrational commitment; for then all its included practices fell under the same nonrational shadow. On this Mr. Jones comments: "To me Blanshard at this point is making exactly the sort of 'irrational commitment' which he condemns 'imperativism' for making." It is true that I did not stop to develop the case against such "irrational commitment," since I thought I had done that sufficiently in the preceding chapter on emotivism, to which I referred. But I should have thought the whole trend of the book would have guarded me against an imputation of such a commitment. The main position of that work is that the objective rightness of an action turns on the comparative amounts of intrinsic good produced. If a man supports a proposed law, for example, as an integral part of the system of free enterprise, and his opponent happens to be a communist, the argument will probably soon move to the comparative value of the two systems as a whole. Would this issue, on my view, have to be settled by a non-rational commitment? Emphatically not. Its settlement would depend on a consideration of the comparative contribution of the two systems in the way of intrinsic values to mankind. The calculation of those values may be as difficult as you please, but the practical difficulty of the calculation does not affect the truth of the principle. The bringing to light of these goods and evils and their weighing against each other are not to be accomplished by (of all things) some sort of nonrational commitment; they require the most intense and instructed thinking that any moralist or economist can bring to bear.

Blanshardian Biases

It is not, however, in regard to particular doctrines only that bias has entered into my moral philosophy; my ways of thinking in ethics generally and indeed my whole philosophy represent the convergence of a set of biases. Among philosophies, mine can be pretty accurately pinpointed by the places it occupies on Mr. Jones's three principal axes, those of static-dynamic, of continuity-discreteness, and of immediacy-mediation. If you ask where I stand as a philosopher, Mr. Jones is prepared to answer with a three-dimensional graph in which it appears that my philosophy is a combination of the static, the continuous, and the mediational.

A philosopher should be grateful for this sort of pigeonholing, for whether he agrees with it or not, it indicates where an able colleague who has studied him, and probably many others who have not, believe him to stand. And a classification so confidently made is not unlikely to aid in one's self-understanding. It has certainly aided in mine.

But when I study the grounds on which the classification is made, my own confidence in it declines. The chief ground for considering me a static seems to be my use of the metaphor of a pendulum. I point out that in the history of ethics there has been a swing back and forth between rationalist and emotivist types of theory. The swings do not necessarily show a shortening of the arc between its extremes; indeed I point out that in recent years—in the controversy between deontologists and emotivists—the two sides seem farther apart than ever. What I do say is that a study of the historical controversy sharpens the issue for us, that there is a truth to be found about the rightful places of reason and feeling in moral judgment, that this truth will pretty certainly lie between the two extremes, and that this truth is to be discovered by

rigorous analysis. I do not say that the truth lies where the historical pendulum comes to rest, if it ever does; men may agree on the wrong view. The
"rest" in virtue of which I should be classified as a "static" is not the de facto
rest of a historic pendulum, but the rest of a stable insight into objective truth.
What my being a static therefore amounts to is my conviction that there is a
permanent ethical truth to which, by continued reflection, we can approximate. But far from placing me at a particular point on an axis, this
merely groups me with the majority of all philosophers. For surely most of
them have believed, when they have asked what makes an action right, that
the question has an answer, that there is some stable truth about it to be discovered.

Indeed I suspect that Mr. Jones could have produced even stronger
evidence to prove that I am a "dynamic" than what he adduces for my being
a "static." For I hold that the moral life is a constant struggle toward an end
that will never in fact be realized. I have described a human personality as essentially a set of impulse-desires that keep us always in motion toward
fulfillments that are never complete but are merely plateaus preparatory to a
further ascent. Indeed, the truth about me is that I am a pilgrim carrying a
banner with the strange device "Excelsior" on a road that winds up hill all the
way on stepping-stones of my dead selves, and I do not know why Mr. Jones
instead of branding me as a static should not pin on my bosom the red badge
of courage for obtruding upon my fellowman, in season and out, my exhor-
tations to build more stately mansions for their souls. Could he not find
grounds for at least nominating me to a wistful candidacy for the rank of
"dynamic"?

Again, on the axis of mediation-immediacy, I am placed well out toward
the mediation end. That is probably where I belong. But the evidence adduced
for placing me there seems about as slender as the evidence of the pendulum
metaphor; it is my use of "the metaphor of judicial review." In discussing the
claims of reason and feeling to be the rightful determinants of moral judgment, I have said that we must do our best, as a good judge does, to see all
aspects of the case and give them their just due. But if this makes me a
mediationist, I am again lost in the crowd. Many philosophers would say that
philosophy is practically identical with mediation in this sense. It is the
attempt in considering mind and body, for example, or determinism and free
will, or the nature of truth, to take all the evidence into account and give as
objective a judgment as possible. There have been few philosophers in history
who would not have accepted that as at least one of their principal functions.
Philosophers of all schools are continually introducing references to "the
ideal spectator," or using the special terms of courts of law: "judicial impartiality," "prejudiced testimony," "the burden of proof," "special pleading"
(of which Russell says that Aquinas's whole philosophy was an example), and

many others. If the conspicuous use of the notion of a judge makes one a mediationist, then Kierkegaard is more a mediationist than I am; consider the play he makes with the character of Judge William. And any line of reasoning which lands Kierkegaard and me in the same neighborhood should make a judicial review of its procedure.

Once more, Mr. Jones has no doubt where my place is on the continuity-discreteness axis; it is very near the continuity end. He is right in this. I do hold that every thing and every event is bound up causally and logically with every other. But to say that this is an example of continuity *bias,* in my use of that term, is justified only if it is shown that I have been deflected by prejudice from the path of valid argument. Mr. Jones quotes from me a remark favoring continuity in the sense just used, and adds: "Given Blanshard's continuity bias, this is an eminently rational and logical conclusion. Given Hume's discreteness bias, given, that is, his vision of things as 'loose and separate,' it is a wholly irrational leap of faith. . . ." But I have argued in detail for the kind of continuity to which I subscribe; and shown, as I thought clearly, that Hume's discreteness theory cannot stand. Why it should be supposed without an examination of these arguments that my conclusion is a "leap of faith" rather than a valid conclusion from the evidence I do not know. In short, I accept my election to the apostles of the continuum, but I claim the right to be among them from having been admitted through their front door. The only way to convince me that I crept in through the back door of prejudice is to show me where I went off the straight and narrow path.

Depth of Root in Bias

I gather that the infection of bias from which all philosophers suffer is contracted extremely early, and operates powerfully and continuously. If this is true, a static philosopher should remain a static philosopher to the end, and a mediationist should show an unswerving adherence to the mediationist line. How then account for philosophers who change their minds, perhaps repeatedly? John Wild, if I remember rightly, began as a Berkeleian, shifted in middle life to neo-Thomism, then became a Platonist, and ended as a Husserlian type of existentialist. Does this mean that he had an unusually fully equipped quiver of biases from the beginning which took turns in breaking loose, or that a bias may exist in latent form through most of a lifetime before something touches it off, or what? Where on one's graph is one to place Bertrand Russell? He began as a Hegelian, which means a bias toward continuity; he became a logical atomist, which means a bias toward the extremest form of discreteness. Again, he moved from idealism to the farthest bounds of realism, and finally came back to idealism for all that was immediately experienced combined with realism for the world of physics. In ethics he began with Moore's ideal utilitarianism with its stress on the objectivity of moral judgment, but owing, he says, to some considerations adduced by Santayana, he became an emotivist. I am inclined to interpret these changes as the movements of an extraordinarily honest mind in trying to adjust its thought to new arguments and fresh evidence. I do not see how they can be accounted for if Russell was dominated from the beginning by any single set of biases.

"From the beginning." One of my troubles with Mr. Jones's theory is that I am not clear what this phrase means for him. He speaks of the biases as "precognitive," but what exactly does this signify? A bias must have some object if it is to be for or against anything, and before cognition has begun, there are no objects at all. If a bias has no object, it is not a bias; if it has an object, it is not precognitive. And if the bias has as its object some philosophic abstraction like continuity or discreteness, precognitive biases become all the more mysterious.

Mr. Jones asks whether the commitment to reason itself is not just another precognitive commitment. I answer No, on the grounds just stated. What may exist and sometimes does is a very high inborn capacity for grasping necessary relations, which, if stimulated early, may show itself in surprising intellectual achievements; and these in turn tend to confirm and intensify the interest in rationality. But it would be absurd to say that the cognitive interest itself is a nonrational one. The theoretical impulse is from the very earliest perceptual judgment the attempt to grasp things in relation, and this is the essence of what I call rationality. A "bias for rationality" is strictly meaningless, for a bias is something that deflects one from rationality, not something that propels one toward it. To have a bias for being rational is like suffering from a bias for truth, or like a poet's bias for beauty.

Here we come to what I am afraid is the "nonterminable disagreement" between Mr. Jones and me. Indeed if the cognitive impulse is just another wind blowing from the cavern of the self, and all its concepts are merely pennons veering with the breezes from within, what could the changing signals tell us about the world outside? Nothing. Philosophy is surely futile. Philosophers have tried to think objectively because they thought that by so doing they were gaining light about the world; they believed that if they tried hard enough they could repress the biases that would dim or discolor that light. Mr. Jones tells us not only that the love of truth is a bias, but even that the repression of distorting biases is expressive of another bias. To me that means that philosophy's occupation is gone. The only path to truth is objective thinking, and if such thinking is impossible, the whole enterprise is vain.

Here is the ultimate disagreement between Mr. Jones and me. At the end of his paper he makes a friendly effort to narrow the difference. May not that difference be merely a linguistic one? When I talk about being rational as the condition of gaining truth, and objectivity of thinking as the condition of being rational, may I not be using the language of feeling, and not, as I profess, the language of assertion? "Would Blanshard accept this?" Mr. Jones asks. Alas the reply must be, Absolutely not. That is asking me to admit that when Socrates proved to the slave boy that there was a priori knowledge, that when Descartes declared that he could not doubt that he doubted, when Mill gave his historic argument for liberty of thought and speech, when Huxley exposed the inconsistency of biology and Genesis, they were all driven by nonrational preferences of their own. If that is "true," to use a word that has now lost its meaning, why not give up philosophy for shuffleboard or chess? It is only if our thought at some point can somewhere engage the nature that lies around us, can lay hold of some strand within the webwork of the world, or, as I incline to put it, place itself under the guidance of a reason that presses itself upon us, that philosophy can have any hope of seeing things as they are. And we cannot see things as they are if our thoughts are puppets pulled by invisible strings.

Mr. Jones has made it clear that this is the answer he expected from me. And I think I can predict his rejoinder. His very predicting with such success what I should say is the best of evidence of his thesis. My prejudice for reason is unbudgeable and complete.

1. F. H. Bradley, *Appearance and Reality*, 2d rev. ed. (London: Swan Sonnenschein; New York: Macmillan Co., 1908), 153.
2. W. T. Jones, "Philosophical Disagreements and World Views," Presidential address, Pacific Division, American Philosophical Association, March 27, 1970. *Proceedings of the American Philosophical Association* 43 (1969–70): 36.

7   BRAND BLANSHARD'S THEORY OF ETHICS
Henry Margenau

THIS article, written to honor the philosopher whose insistence on reason impressed and guided me early in my efforts as a physicist and who later became a revered colleague and friend, is intended to deal with the motivations for ethical conduct: concern with what is right and with what is good. It makes explicit reference chiefly to Blanshard's two major publications on ethics: "The Impasse in Ethics—and a Way Out" ("IE"),[1] and *Reason and Goodness* (*RG*). What I hope to achieve, rather selfishly, is to show forth a large measure of fundamental agreement between Brand Blanshard's ethical rationalism and my own systematic analysis of the ethical process—the relation between the genesis of norms, values, and ethical goals—in *Ethics and Science*.[2]

My discourse, and the application of the following analysis to Blanshard's work, will be clarified if I state at once two peripheral points which I have not encountered in his writings but on which I have strong views that may possibly depart from his. The first is that there is a difference between ethics and jurisprudence; that there may be circumstances in which the two conflict. The second affirms the occurrence of human actions so unique that neither the laws of jurisprudence nor those of ethics suffice to provide guidance. Of these I shall speak later. Of the former, the distinction between ethics and law, brief mention will be made at once, for it enters in an example discussed intriguingly in the beginning of "The Impasse in Ethics."

A doctor dashing through a red traffic light on his way to a dying patient breaks a law but performs an ethical act. Instances in which one obeys a law but sins in other ways are too common to be specified. Perhaps a little of the failure to distinguish between ethics and law is evident in Blanshard's example ("IE," 96) involving the judge who is to pronounce judgment on a renowned murderer. The murderer is a menace to society and should, for the good of the community, be removed from it. All witnesses testify to his guilt;

but the judge, by strange coincidence, knows the accused to be innocent in this instance, for he has seen him at a distant place at the time of the murder. Justice demands that the defendant be acquitted, the good of society that he be sentenced. If ethics and law are disentangled in this hypothetical example no problem arises. For legally, the judge would have to disqualify himself, act as a witness, and offer his testimony against that of the other witnesses. The verdict would then be based upon the total evidence at hand, and no ethical considerations would enter.

However, if there were no laws rooted in statutes and precedents, and the decision were to be based only on the judge's ethical principles, Blanshard's disposal of the case would be convincing. He holds that a conviction, though superficially seeming to promote the *good* of the community while defying *justice*, on closer analysis does violence to both justice and the good.

> It would involve at once the breaking of multiple engagements, the telling to the public of an untruth, and the doing of grave injustice. Now the keeping of engagements, the telling of truth, and the doing of justice are essential parts of the community's plan of life. To violate them officially is to do far more than to injure a particular person; it is to challenge and disrupt this plan of life as a whole. . . . it would bring down the house in which we are living about our ears. ["IE," 98]

In other words, violating justice also violates the good of society. Deontology and utilitarianism are somehow related, right is an aspect of good, and a distinction between them is largely artificial.

With Blanshard's and the reader's forbearance I should like to illuminate this rarely acknowledged affinity between the right and the good, the retroactive source of obligation and the forward-looking goal of benefaction, and to show that in a full and systematic theory of ethics each is a major and indispensable component. Indeed one is useless without the other. What I am about to present in this context is a résumé of a more extensive story which has fallen on deaf ears among philosophers. The reason is probably that I drew an uncomfortably close parallel between ethics and science, which in our present milieu is hazardous and perhaps offensive. On this occasion I shall mend my ways.

The literature on ethics from Socrates to this day presents overwhelming evidence of the futility of starting an analysis of the subject with attempts to define such fluid terms as value, virtue, justice, and the good. For their meaning is entirely dependent, not upon the circumstances surrounding an action (for I do not believe in the so-called relativity of ethical norms), but upon the sociohistorical and the epistemological context in which they are used. I therefore wish to focus attention upon the sociohistorical genesis and the epistemological coherence of actual, working ethical systems, to present their structure, and point incidentally to the places within that structure where the good, the just, etc. are lodged. Questions as to whether goodness is a natural or a nonnatural quality, whether value and justice are universal seem to me entirely misguided unless the larger framework in which these terms arise is given. The confusion attending the use of the adjective "good" is further muddied by its purely linguistic ambiguity: a good heart, understood physiologically, is something entirely different from its ethical implication. Noting here that "good," when applied to objects, designates something entirely different from its quality in human actions, let me henceforth in this article confine its meaning to human actions.

The framework in question, the sociohistorical as well as epistemological context of all ethical systems, will now be sketched. Ethics is a normative discipline; its function is to exhort or forbid, and the language of this function is the imperative. The natural linguistic mood of all other disciplines is the indicative. The ethical imperatives may be blunt (the Hebrew "Thou shalt"), moderate (Buddha's recommendations "leading to satisfaction"), or sugar-coated ("Blessed are those who"); they seem to stand at the temporal beginning of every historical system of ethics that has survived. And as we shall see, they are also the epistemological starting point. The origins of these ethical imperatives need not concern us here; attention is given to them in my *Ethics and Science*. We merely note that they are as obscure, as varied, as mysterious as every creative human act, such as the formulation of a successful postulate in logic, mathematics, or exact natural science. I regard the emergence of imperatives as the first phase of an ethical system. They may be relatively complete or incomplete, covering much or little of human behavior. They never can cover all of it.

The imperatives when accepted and practiced by a group of men, a nation, or a culture engender a typical mode of behavior. In a certain sense this mode is entailed by the imperatives; but entailment in ethics differs from logical entailment: it is not instantaneous nor unambiguously inferential; the mode evolves in time through living, through adherence to the imperatives by a group of people. The evolution is essentially a collective one. A single person living by a unique set of precepts may present an example of heroism or criminality but not necessarily of ethics.

We speak of the mode of behavior consequent upon acceptance of a set of imperatives or commandments as embodying the *values* of the group. However, the looseness of the word "value" forces us to introduce an important distinction at this point. Since the commandments are postulational, and cannot be proved to be in any sense compulsory, true, or objective, the values they generate carry none but conventional obligation. They imply an "is" but not an "ought." Elsewhere I have called them *de facto* values or *est* values in order to distinguish them from normative or *esto* values. One of the central questions of ethics is: What is the distinction between est and esto values? And how do the former attain the status of the latter?

These questions, which arise in every normative discipline, are akin to the question of empirical truth in the factual domain. A postulate, a hypothesis, a theory has consequences which may or may not be in accord with observable fact. In the former case we speak of the theory as true, in the latter as false. (This statement is only roughly true; but this is not the place to elaborate.) De facto values correspond to untested consequences of a theory; esto values to confirmed consequences. Confirmation of factual theories is reasonably well understood and relatively simple because the consequences of a theory can be tested against *nature*. In ethics, no such protocol for reference exists.

There are, to be sure, many advocates of the view that human nature supplies this reference. There are passages in "The Impasse in Ethics," especially near the end of the essay, which suggest that Blanshard is among them. I shall return to this point below, requesting the reader here to reserve judgment upon it. If the factual values, like health, happiness, freedom, honesty, agree with human nature, they undergo promotion to *norms* and acquire the power of discrimination between right and wrong. To take this view would be to establish a very close parallelism between ethics and science. I am prevented from accepting it because of the difficulties I encounter in defining human nature with sufficient precision to make this endeavor work. Rather than belabor the point, let me note one crucial difference between nature and human nature: there is what earlier philosophers have called uniformity of nature; uniformity of human nature has never been assumed. Nature presents inviolable laws; human nature does not.

There are, however, human ideals, human goals, describing what man wants, not what he is. They are by no means the same for all men, and this is the cause of much confusion in ethics. As a matter of fact, however, every society practicing a discernible ethical code has made its choice of goals, and on examination it comes as a strange surprise that the agreement in their selection is overwhelming. I have used the plural, goals, thus denying that a single principle, like happiness, survival, or freedom can ever serve as a satisfactory goal. To name a few additional goals (I called them primary values in *Ethics and Science*), I cite Stoic imperturbability, imitation of ethical models like the life of Christ, the peace that passes understanding, and the Buddhist's nirvana.

But if there is a multiplicity of moral goals and if they are not prescribed by human nature, how are they selected and what are their warrants for being properly chosen?

There may be no a priori warrants which present knowledge can reveal. The fact is that certain imperatives historically, through the genesis of sets of values, have in some measure attained chosen goals. They have proved themselves in a pragmatic historical sense successful, that is to say, imperatives and goals were found to be consistent. The consistency at issue here is not a purely logical one: it emerges primarily as harmony between initial commandments and ethical ends, established through the process of communal living. Such consistency is not assured; Hitler's ethics failed because its imperatives violated even the minimal goal of all systems of ethics, which is survival of the group practicing it.

The question of the *logical* connection between imperatives and goals, i.e. the systematic start and end of the system, is not easy to answer. Sometimes an imperative does imply a goal or vice versa. "Thou shalt not kill" vaguely implies survival, or perhaps the other way around. Yet the implication is hardly cogent in a syllogistic sense, for a society may perish from causes other than murder. In other instances the logical connection is even more questionable; the imperative of honesty cannot be shown to lead always to happinesss, individual or collective. Thus, when claiming that the consistency of commandments and goals evolves through living, a process having temporal duration, we are stating its major character but not excluding logical entailment.

The preceding account forces us to an admission which is unpleasant to some minds: the beginning and the end of the ethical enterprise, imperatives and goals, are subject to arbitrary choice, or to use a more polite phrase, are postulational. Our system is open-ended. People can disagree in their obedience to imperatives and in their choice of goals; all that history can show is whether or to what extent the two phases are consistent, whether one leads to the other. Is this enough to bestow significance upon a system?

Two things must here be said. First, such potential multiplicity exists in all fields of human endeavor, the explanatory as well as the normative. Explanatory hypotheses, scientific postulates, are freely chosen. In order to fit observed phenomena, other postulational devices called rules of correspondence must be introduced. Here, too, we find arbitrary elements at both ends of the conceptual scheme. Alternate sets of hypothetical premises, with different rules of correspondence, can explain the same given phenomenon. Hence there is nothing singular about the situation in ethics.

The second point relates to an astonishing observation. In all extant systems of ethics one finds remarkable agreement with respect to the choice of imperatives and goals. The latter are rarely documented explicitly or distinctly named (exceptions are Christian love—agape or charity—and the Eastern nirvana); they appear mostly in elaborate discourses on the theory of ethics and are taken to be mutually exclusive—hence hedonism, utilitarianism, deontology—when as a matter of fact the goals of these artificially disparate schools are entirely compatible and complementary. No system of ethics is built upon the sole goal of pleasure or happiness; it is a coherent set of goals or ends that counts.

I now conclude the systematic exposition and turn to its adequacy for an understanding of Blanshard's ethics. Imperatives, through communal living, generate values. But these are de facto values, devoid of normative claims, imposing no obligation. Beyond them stand ethical goals (also called primary values). If the de facto (est) values create the state of affairs envisioned in the goals, they are validated, become normative (esto) values, and impose obligation. The "is" of the former has become an "ought."

As to the openness of this "metaethics," there seems to be no obvious rational way of avoiding it. The human race has been uncomfortable with it and has closed the open ends by coupling ethics with religion, claiming imperatives and goals to be divinely inspired. This, I believe, is the only way in which the open-endedness can be avoided.

Blanshard's eloquent argument concerning the intricate involvement of the right and the good, of justice and benevolence, resolves itself in the following simple manner. Given a valid (i.e. validated in the manner outlined above) system of ethics, then obedience to the imperatives is *duty*, is right, and, if the imperatives include the golden rule, it is justice. *Goodness*, on the other hand, is conformity with or an approach to the goals. Since a valid system assures us of consistency between imperatives and goals, a right or just action is also a good action. This merely echoes Blanshard's conviction that Plato, Aristotle, Aquinas, Hobbes, Spinoza, Hegel, Green, and Mill "all held that the goodness of anything was so bound up with the fulfilling of needs or desires that such fulfillment entered into, and supplied in whole or part the very meaning of, goodness" ("IE," 106). I have here merely tried to make this statement more explicit.

In his customary and distinguished rational vein our philosopher indicts and condemns emotivism as an ethical theory. Here I can do nothing but applaud; for I should find it difficult to be as kind in my rejection of this most inadequate view. In the first place, I know of no living human code which takes emotivism seriously; emotivism provides no basis even for that measure of objectivity which in fact exists among moral practices. Furthermore I wince at the phrase, a *feeling* of approval; for if approval is not a judgment my understanding of psychology is all wrong. And judgment differs from instinctual feelings or irrational reflexes by being based on deliberation, i.e. on reasoning.

Earlier in this essay I raised serious doubts about the suitability of "human nature" to furnish ethical goals and hence, in view of our identification of the good with conformity to goals, to define the good. This seems to contradict Blanshard's statement: Goodness "consists in the satisfaction and fulfilment of human nature" ("IE," 112).

I believe we are encountering here first a question of semantics which can be eliminated easily. For I have taken the term "human nature" very literally, using it as the counterpart of ordinary nature. It then signifies what man is, not what he wishes or aspires to be. And it seems clear that man's actual present attributes, individually or statistically, are not the ingredients of goodness. What Blanshard means ought to be termed *ideal* human nature, which is a vast extrapolation upon the characteristics of man's observed behavior and then becomes precisely identical with our goals.

However, any reference to ideal nature or goals poses a problem of substance as well as language. For there is no unanimity among men, nor among writers on ethics, as to what these goals are or how they are to be selected. We have claimed that they are implicitly present in every functioning ethical system and ascribed their origin to postulational choice. This claim needs elaboration.

If ethics were a more formal discipline its theorists might be expected to set forth a list of imperatives and of primary values or goals. In actual fact this is done very informally, more often in religious writings than in treatises on ethics. Three such goals, called inalienable rights, are listed in the American Declaration of Independence: life, liberty, and the pursuit of happiness, and it is claimed that their divine bestowal is a self-evident truth. The logic here is spurious, but the clear statement is one of the best attempts at listing ethical goals in any language. The list is hardly sufficient, to be sure, but its presence in one of the most successfully provocative documents is significant. What actually happens in the evolution of ethical ideals is this. There is in every society a vague understanding of *some* goals, perhaps the three just mentioned. The best individuals, in the eyes of their fellowmen, are those who achieve them while adhering to the commandments the society has adopted. (Life, liberty, and happiness attained by stealing or lying will not count!) These best men have the most audible voice in affirming, judging, and adding to the established goals until finally a well rounded, more or less complete set emerges. I do not believe that any set can ever be said to be a final one: the symbolic approach to a final set of primary values resembles our search for truth, which is likewise never fully within our grasp. Judgments as to goals can be conforming or corrective, but the process of evolution is usually slow, very much slower than the corresponding movement in special explanatory disciplines like the sciences. It is saddening to reflect that the many crises which trouble our times are occasioned by the slowness of the ethical evolution in comparison with so-called scientific progress.

From all this it follows that there can be no *static* objectivity within a given system of ethics. The possibility of evolution, of changes in imperatives and goals, and hence in the intermediate area of values (both est and esto!) is always present. Blanshard's ideal human nature may change in the flux of human circumstances just as nature changes in the ordinary process of evolution. In other words, I do not believe that absolute good is within our grasp.

Having cast doubt upon objectivity of goals in the sense of temporal stability, I hasten to affirm their intersubjectivity. Ethics is a collective concern; in it only the experience of a group counts. An individual may occasionally attain some ethical goals while violating some commandments. His experience counts as little toward or against the validity of an ethical system as does the throw of a single die toward the law concerning the probability of its occurrence. From this point of view, then, what is called relativistic or relational ethics, which allows a change of norms with circumstances, must be rejected. Ethics, justice, and duty are interpersonal.

But objectivity is limited in a further sense. Blanshard, in discrediting emotivism, raises the question of an international ethic, affirming, it seems, the possibility of it. From the scheme here outlined it follows that the conditions for its emergence are these: Agreement must exist with respect to the choice of both imperatives and goals. Since these are not preordained or logically derivable, such agreement cannot be assumed. Even valid ethical systems, i.e. systems in which commandments match the goals, may conceivably disagree at both ends. Frankly, I feel uneasy about this contingency, and I tend to disregard it for the following reasons.

First of all, historical observation shows an unexpected, almost unreasonable measure of actual agreement between commandments as well as conceptions of ideal human nature among nations. Although one cannot prove it, there seems to be a convergence upon some sort of unique limit vaguely visible at the end of the diverse ethical roads. Perhaps there is a unique ideal human nature, which is beyond our present grasp. To discuss it further, however, would involve us in all the difficulties that engulf the biologist who wishes to specify the end of natural evolution, and more.

The second reason for my belief in the possibility of international ethical adjudication is this. The search for truth, too, is in principle subject to similar ambiguities. As previously mentioned, phenomena in the external world can sometimes be "explained" by different theories, i.e. by conceptual systems with different initial postulates and different rules of correspondence. This has in fact happened quite frequently in the history of science. But in the end one or more of the competing theories have always been abandoned because they failed to satisfy certain ideal, metaphysical guiding principles or they violated the phenomena upon closer inspection. The distinction of truth descended upon only one. Why this should be so is a logical mystery expressible only as intellectual awe at the very possibility of our understanding the world. For me, this feeling is transformed to hope in connection with the uniqueness of man's ethical enterprise. In this sense, therefore, I agree with Blanshard in entertaining the possibility of intercultural ethics.

In concluding this essay it seems permissible to ask, and try to answer, a question raised at the beginning, a question perhaps not wholly germane to the problems here under consideration, although related to them. Must ethics, both in the forms criticized by Blanshard and those affirmed by him (and in this exposition), be regarded as man's ultimate concern? There are several reasons why the answer might be negative.

The first has to do with a unique feature of ethics. Since it rests upon man-made laws which can be broken, it must reckon with the contingencies of their infraction. But if its imperatives included, or were coupled with, provisions for dealing with their violation, it would be like jurisprudence and surrender much of the spirit of personal involvement; it would surrender its philosophic depth in favor of the shallowness of law. Thus, strictly speaking, such virtues as forgiveness, mercy, charity, and compassion cannot be strictly parts of our ethical imperatives, which imply *duty* and seek the *good*. These facts point to a transethical domain which deals with infractions of the ethical code.

The other reason lies in the circumstance that ethics is a collective enterprise based on the past experiences of our race and incapable of foreseeing future conditions. Nor could it possibly accommodate in its commandments and goals all the singular and unexpected life situations that have occurred in the past: the incompleteness of ethics, its incompetence to regulate *all* human contingencies become evident in what is called ethical conflicts, and they re-quire resolution by other than ethical norms. Socrates' suicide is a case in point, or even better, Seneca's self-inflicted death. His country's ethical im-peratives forbade killing (even oneself, though this was challenged by Seneca himself who urged: *Quid erubescitis, patet exitus!*) and lying. His choice was between condoning Nero's matricide, lying, or committing suicide, and he chose the latter. He violated traditional ethics. He acted on maxims that transcend ordinary ethics; he made a very personal decision which no code prescribed; he sought what, in "The Pursuit of Significance"[3] and in another context I have called personal significance or personal dedication. I do not like these phrases but cannot find a better one. The point is that such decisions are not governed by any rules, processes, or strategies known to common sense or science or ethics. I refer here to singular acts of dedication, of personal sacrifice, of altruism which reason or morals can neither justify nor condemn, of the choice of ideals far beyond ordinary human reach.

The occurrence of unique, transethical situations is inevitable; but this is also true about transgression of the ordinary ethical norms. Absolute com-pliance with moral imperatives is impossible for man, and remorse is an in-escapable human emotion. This fact is symbolized in Western literature by one of the profoundest allegories of all scriptures, the story of man's fall, the doctrine of original sin.

In an individual life our natural incompetence before the moral law has two effects, one which determines our attitude toward others and one toward ourselves. The former instills the attitudes of charity, forbearance, and forgiveness, which bear little relation to duty and the striving for good. To be sure, the argument has been made that the forgiving of sin makes for happiness on the part of the sinner, but its force is canceled by the equally prevalent argument that punishment of criminals is good for society as a whole. The point we wish to make is that forgiveness and absolution of sin are virtues beyond ethics.

The second effect turns reflection upon ourselves, creates the tendency to cleanse one's soul from guilt, the craving for redemption; it produces the liberating effect of the confession, of the "Pater peccavi." All these are agonizing indications of man's cosmic frustration, his fear of moral insignificance.

To surmount it, he has found aid in the ideas of personal atonement, divine grace, and redemption. Our discourse here takes on distinctly religious overtones, but it is hard to see how they can be avoided; for moral frustration is one of the natural roots of religion, the miracle of the lawfulness of nature being the other. The history of this theme is long and universal, yet it is current today. Luther's contribution to it caused the Reformation. His formula that "he who is unjust is just" carries it to an extreme, but it recurs in the writings of many contemporary existentialists, e.g. in Tillich's "courage to accept oneself as accepted in spite of being unacceptable."[4] The religious doctrine of divine grace sums up what is essential in man's reflections upon his moral inadequacy.

Thus, it seems to me, there is a kind of significance that goes beyond ethics. It comes to us through personal dedication in the form of responses to the challenge of moral despair, through acts of dedication to ideals beyond the call of duty, through heroism, high adventure, supreme sacrifice which no ethical code demands.

HENRY MARGENAU

DEPARTMENT OF PHYSICS
YALE UNIVERSITY

NOTES

[1]"The Impasse in Ethics—and a Way Out," *University of California Publications in Philosophy* 28, no. 2 (1955):96.
[2]H. Margenau, *Ethics and Science* (Princeton: Van Nostrand Reinhold, 1964).
[3]H. Margenau, "The Pursuit of Significance," in *Main Currents in Modern Thought* 23 (January 1967):65.
[4]Paul Tillich, *The Courage to Be* (New Haven: Yale University Press, 1952), 164.

7. REPLY TO HENRY MARGENAU
Blanshard's Theory of Ethics

Mr. Margenau writes from a point of view different from that of any other of my critics. He writes as a physicist of eminence who seeks to introduce into ethics some of the rigor of method that is generally admitted to have been achieved in the physical sciences. If his position is to be fully understood, his present paper should be read in connection with his volume on *Ethics and Science*[1] in which the parallel between science as it is actually pursued and ethics as he thinks it ought to be pursued is developed in detail. I will not attempt to follow him through the steps of scientific method, but since his main criticism is that I do not adhere to the pattern of ethical inquiry which that method suggests, it would be well to begin with a statement, however brief, of what he takes that pattern to be.

He holds that the data with which ethics start are the set of commands or imperatives that people actually obey. They vary from group to group. They may be the taboo-ridden maxims of a primitive society; they may be the Ten Commandments; they may be a set of copy-book headings inscribed in popular memory and habits: "Don't steal," "Don't lie," "Don't pick needless quarrels with other people." The habits that conform to such commands carry what Mr. Margenau calls the de facto values of the group. The only obligation they impose is conventional; that is, their only sanction is the disapproval of the group if they are violated.

Most of us accept and try to conform to such demands without giving much thought to the reasons for doing so. But occasionally obedience demands of us a sharp personal sacrifice; the poor man who sees a rich man drop his wallet may have a strong temptation to pocket it and forget, if he can, the injunction not to steal. He may go on and raise the question why he should not steal if the advantage to himself would be great and the loss to the rich man small. He wants to know how the injunction against stealing is to be validated.

Ethics and Scientific Method

It is at this point that Mr. Margenau's respect for scientific method makes its most distinctive contribution to his ethics. In both physics and ethics we start with what we take to be given facts, but find that in order to explain and confirm we must build bridges, sometimes hard to construct, between them and the ultimate "certainties" with which we want to connect them. A boy throws a ball straight up into the air, and notices that it slows down at the top of its flight, then begins to move slowly downward again, and finally falls with increasing speed to the ground. Why does it behave this way? He may turn the question aside with a "Well, it always does," but of course for the physicist that is no answer. Why does it *always* behave in this way? The answer consists, Mr. Margenau says, in showing that this behavior *must* be what it is if we accept certain remote and highly abstract postulates which are necessary to the life of science: the law of causality, the law of gravitation, and Galileo's law of the accelerating velocity of falling bodies. If the behavior of the ball can be deductively connected with these postulates, it is as fully explained as science can explain it. Why are these abstractions called postulates rather than axioms? Because axioms are supposed to be self-evident, and none of these propositions is self-evident. Indeed the day of axioms is over; even the axioms of Euclid are now all regarded as postulates. And what exactly is a postulate? It is a proposition that, while neither self-evident nor empirically provable, is confirmed without exception by the course of our experience. Since it is unprovable, it is not to be taken as final; experience *may* overturn it; alternatives that were at first thought impossible may be proposed and successfully applied, as Riemann's alternative to the postulate of parallels proved to be applicable in Einsteinian physics. But for the present the accepted postulates hold the ground, and any observed behavior that can be shown to follow from them is regarded as fully explained.

To return now to ethics. Just as the rule about the behavior of the ball is validated through being connected with an ultimate postulate, so the rule about treating one's neighbor kindly or not stealing his property is validated by being connected with a "primary value." Primary values are those that in a given society are taken as ultimate. Sometimes they are received as laid down by God himself or his earthly representative, as the commandment of universal love is received among Christians, or the endeavor to achieve Nirvana is among Buddhists. Philosophers of influence have proclaimed the supremacy of many primary values; one long line of thinkers from Aristippus to Sidgwick has given the palm to happiness; some of the evolutionists have given it to mere survival; Aristotle and Spinoza found the greatest of all goods in understanding. Now suppose a devoted Christian is considering whether to contribute to a hospital or to buy himself a case of liquor; his ultimate question would be which conforms more fully with the Christian principle of love. Suppose a surgeon decides that the amputation of a patient's leg is surgically "indicated"; how can he defend a procedure that will involve his patient in much pain and inconvenience? Probably by saying that the infliction of the pain on his patient was the necessary means to his long-run happiness. If the surgeon is reasonably sure of this connection, he normally proceeds with a clear conscience.

We must fix our eye for a moment on these primary or ultimate values. Is it possible, as many philosophers have thought, to reduce them to a single summum bonum? Mr. Margenau believes this to be as impossible as it would be to reduce all the postulates of science to one by deducing from it all the others. The thing cannot be done. Similarly the values men have accepted as primary not only differ from each other; they are often contradictory of each other. Self-realization and self-sacrifice cannot both be taken consistently as ends; nor can understanding and pleasure, nor power and love. How does a group determine its end? Mr. Margenau would say that the selection is arbitrary, in the sense that none of the primary values is self-evidencing or necessary and that to the end selected there are always alternatives; indeed the selection may be largely accidental. The rise of an outstanding prophet or moralist or the needs of a time may exalt one value over others "by selecting from the qualities exhibited by collective human behavior a special one, or a set of them (e.g., power over others, personal happiness, collective happiness, love, self-fulfillment, or the peace that passeth understanding) using it consistently thereafter as its principle of validation" (*Ethics and Science,* 173). Of course these primary values cannot themselves be validated, for they are the source of all validation. And they are not related to the imperatives of common life as the postulates of science are related to observed events; the imperatives may tend to produce the primary values, but the relation is not as a rule a necessary one.

A Question of Direction

I must apologize to Mr. Margenau for this very inadequate sketch of a parallel between ethics and science that in his own statement of it calls for a volume. But even a brief sketch may report accurately the general drift of a theory, and this general drift is all that I have space here to discuss. And I do have doubts about it. For one thing, the movement of thought between postulates and observed facts on the one side and the movement between primary values and observed practices on the other, instead of running parallel with each other, run in opposite directions. The movement in science is downward and deductive from postulates to the observations that verify them. When astronomers wanted a crucial test as between Einstein's and Newton's laws of gravitation, they deduced the location of a certain star as seen during an eclipse of the sun; on Einstein's theory it should appear in one place, on Newton's in another; and the observed position bore out the theory of Einstein. On Galileo's theory of falling bodies, all of them fell with equal acceleration toward the earth. The only satisfactory way of verifying this theory was through observed events; and when a vacuum was produced and a metal ball and a feather allowed to drop in it, they validated Galileo's theory by reaching the floor together. Now the movement between observed ethical practices and the primary values that validate them is in precisely the opposite direction. We do not start with these primary values and move down by deduction to particular practices; we start with particular practices and validate them by finding whether they contribute causally to the achievement of the primary values. This difference in direction seems to me clearly involved in Mr. Margenau's account, but it surely forms a large exception to the parallelism he seeks to find between scientific and ethical methods.

The Authority of Common Sense

Mr. Margenau believes, rightly I think, that the study of ethics may most profitably begin at the commonsense level and with the rules people actually obey. What I find especially interesting in Mr. Margenau's account of these rules is the degree of authority he attributes to them. "Since the commandments are postulational, and cannot be proved to be in any sense compulsory, true or objective, the values they generate carry none but conventional obligation. They imply an 'is' but not an 'ought'." I cannot think that this description applies to the commonsense imperatives that we actually follow. These are not mere conventions. The members of the community feel that a far greater weight of authority lies behind them than the approval or disapproval of their neighbors. Nor are these rules regarded as hypotheses in need of confirmation. The classic survey of the morality of common sense is, I suppose, that of Sidgwick in Book III of *The Methods of Ethics*. He points out that this morality is chiefly based on axioms or imperatives ("Don't lie," "Don't steal," etc.), which are commonly taken either as self-evident or divinely enjoined. Either kind of validation would put them beyond the range of mere convention and give them something like absolute authority. Even when these grounds for accepting the imperatives are washed away, as they largely have been, the rules retain a hold on men's sense of obligation that is singularly strong.

Why should they do so? Sidgwick's answer is, I think, the right one: When we begin to reflect on them, we see that conformity to them is bound up with the welfare of the community and disregard of them with its injury. This sense of the consequences of rules of practice is not explicitly in mind when we act, though it may quickly become so on reflection. The original adoption of these social practices is lost in the mists of prehistory, but there is no reason to doubt that it sprang from the experience of group suffering as the result of one practice and group advantage as the result of another. Nor is there anything fanciful in supposing that connections grasped by primitive man are grasped at times of doubt or debate by modern man and provide a powerful, even if normally subconscious, sanction for his behavior. The imperatives of common sense are neither *is's* as opposed to *oughts,* nor arbitrary choices, nor conventions; they are already oughts, firmly felt and strongly validated, though with a validation that seldom needs to be dragged to light.

Primary Values

Though Mr. Margenau wisely begins with the morality of common life, he soon turns to the all-important primary values through which in the end all imperatives must be made good. Since his ethics as a whole depends upon them, it will be well to examine briefly his main theses about them. His account of them turns largely on his conviction, already noted, that they correspond in character to the postulates of science. In line with this parallelism, he offers the following description of them: (1) they are arbitrary in the sense of being hypotheses, ventures of thought, experiments in living; (2) they are independent of each other, though they tend to be complementary of each other; (3) they are incapable of proof. Let us look at these contentions in order.

(1) That the primary values are arbitrary and that there is no clear way of separating the sheep from the goats among them is suggested by the wealth of such goods that Mr. Margenau enumerates and is apparently ready to take seriously. Self-realization, self-sacrifice, happiness, love, knowledge, nirvana, beauty, power, survival, health, wealth, and the peace that passeth understanding are all mentioned. What are the sources from which this hospitable list is drawn? Apparently they are the somewhat random suggestions of history. Various groups of people, in varying times and places, have actually adopted these ends as the goals of their lives. Any goal that has been thus adopted is thereby nominated for inclusion. Is there any ground for selecting between them or for thinning the list? Mr. Margenau wants to give the same answer here as he would if asked about the list of postulates in science. If so asked, he would begin by throwing out self-evidence as discredited. He would say that the only basis for choice among scientific postulates is their success or unsuccess in yielding propositions that can be verified in experience. Can this basis be similarly used in choosing among primary goods? Obviously not. For in counting them as primary goods, we have recognized them as ultimate, and therefore not to be validated by any ulterior consequences. And these two are

the only two modes of validation of primary goods that Mr. Margenau discusses. We are thus left with a plethora of goals dictated by capricious human preference and with no means of deciding between them. Consistently with this position, Mr. Margenau's ethical system apparently has no summum bonum of its own. The only candidates to which he gives critical consideration are hedonism and the categorical imperative of Kant, both of which he rejects.

Now ethical pluralism is not an ethical system at all. If it is to become so, some account must be given of how a rational man is to choose among the ends of life. The nearest approach to such a ground of choice that is offered seems to be this: if some group selects a goal and lives in such a way as to realize it, their end and their way of life have been thereby vindicated. Suppose one group chooses the goal of Christian love, achieving it only intermittently, and another group chooses the goal of being continuously "high" on drugs and achieves it with complete success; is this second way of life more fully vindicated than the first? I am sure Mr. Margenau would say No, but I am not at all clear how, as a moralist, he would support this judgment. Or suppose that my aim is to accumulate the largest collection of stamps in the world, that your aim is to become the most accomplished physicist in the world, and that both of us succeed. Which life is more worth living? Again I find no principle in Mr. Margenau's ethics that could assure either of us that he had chosen the better part.

At some points in his book Mr. Margenau does indeed suggest a quite different mode of validation even for primary values. Usually in listing such values he mentions kinds of good that can exist only in consciousness, such as happiness, love, and knowledge. But he insists on making ethics a purely empirical science, and conscious states like these are not what the empirical scientist usually means by observable facts. So Mr. Margenau at certain points abandons the view that they stand at the end of the line, and adopts observable behavior as the test of the presence of values. He describes values as "mere stepping stones toward observed behavior," and suggests that commands will be fulfilled or reach their end only when they "lead to a specific selection of qualities in observed behavior" (*Ethics and Science,* 170). Now Mr. Margenau well knows my views on the kind of naturalism that identifies conscious with material states or changes. Any attempt to identify ethical ends with observable behavior or to appraise them by it seems to me irresponsible. Love and happiness and knowledge are not pieces of observed or observable behavior, however closely they may be associated with such behavior causally or otherwise, and if the ultimate test of conduct is bodily movement, we are not being offered an ethics at all. Values exist in consciousness and only there; so much so that if consciousness were to cease at this moment on the planet, nothing of the slightest value would remain, to the best of our knowledge, in the universe. But Mr. Margenau discusses states of consciousness so freely that I do him the honor of assuming him incapable of taking materialism seriously.

(2) If the analogy holds between the postulates of science and the primary values of ethics, these values are independent of each other. But the relations among the many ultimate values that Mr. Margenau names are left almost wholly undiscussed. It is pointed out that if one attempts to realize several of them together they should be consistent with each other, but that is about all. And it seems to me that in a pluralistic ethics of this sort the interrelations of the values need to be carefully dealt with. Wealth and health, for example, are not primary values at all, but conditions that make those values possible. So, I think, is life or survival; life as such is not desirable, as distinct from the states of mind it supports, a truth that becomes painfully clear in cases of wracking and incurable disease or degenerative senility. Nirvana, if it means the absorption of the individual into a universal consciousness, is hardly an end that lends itself to empirical study. Self-realization and self-sacrifice, power and peace, knowledge and happiness, are goods that generally stand in each other's way, but may occasionally promote each other. Are these values suitable to some natures and cut off from others? If achieved, are they equally satisfying and fulfilling? To what extent are some of them necessary to others? In an ethics lacking a summum bonum, these questions call for exploration.

(3) More important perhaps is the question whether any of the claims to goodness can be proved. Holding again to the parallel with scientific postulates, which admit of confirmation but not of proof, Mr. Margenau maintains that one cannot *prove* the goodness of any of the primary values. He admits that if self-evidence could be appealed to, the case would be different. And I think that to rule out self-evidence in this field because it has been found inapplicable to some of the postulates of science is to carry the reaction against it too far. At some points of thought everyone does and must employ self-evidence. Whenever Mr. Margenau derives an implication from one of his postulates, he is admitting the validity of self-evidence—the self-evidence with which one proposition follows from another. Now every normal person would agree that pleasure is something worth having, whether it is the only thing worth having or not. If he were asked to prove this, he would probably reply first that the demand seemed rather silly, and then on a little reflection admit that he could not possibly prove it if this meant deducing it from something clearer or more certain or more general than itself; and about this he would surely be right. But does it follow that such propositions as "pleasure is good" or "the experience of a delicious dessert is intrinsically more desirable than the experience of a tooth extraction without anesthetics" are empirical propositions that are only probably true? The conclusion seems to me contrary to fact. We are not saying merely, "I happen to prefer

pleasure to extreme pain, though other people may not"; we are saying that anyone of sane mind, contemplating precisely these experiences, would judge as we do, just as they would judge that four is greater than three. The relation of "intrinsically better than" is not a relation between tastes of ours which may vary, nor is it merely a relation of uniform accompaniment, but a relation which, so long as the two terms remain what they are, *could* not be otherwise. It is a necessary relation, intuitively seen.

Mr. Margenau rejects this. It can be refuted, he thinks, by pointing to "instances which *contradict* happiness and pleasure as human aims, with the reminder that a truth, if self-evident, cannot be violated. But there have been men who preferred to *suffer* for a noble purpose. Throughout the ages one encounters groups which practiced self-denial, self-mortification as a method to attain ethical perfection" (*Ethics and Science,* 201–2). But (a) this is an *ignoratio elenchi.* You do not prove that happiness is not a good in itself by showing that it is prudent to dispense with it occasionally for the sake of a greater happiness. You do not prove that pain is not an intrinsic evil by showing that it is sometimes wise for a person to visit his dentist. The question at issue regarding happiness is whether it is intrinsically, not whether it is instrumentally, good. (b) Nor can one refute the contention that happiness is intrinsically and necessarily good by citing instances of persons who appeared to prefer pain, any more than one refutes $7+5=12$ by citing children or bank cashiers who made mistakes in addition. There may have been persons who preferred the exquisite experience of being burnt at the stake to the experience of a continued and happy life, though I have not heard of them; the martyrs are irrelevant here, since they believed that their suffering was the means to some great reward. But even if they elected the fire for its own sake, we should surely take that not as evidence that being burnt alive was an end devoutly to be wished, but as evidence of an unsound mind. They would not be successfully *contradicting* the proposition that happiness is better than misery; they would not be *seeing* that the pain was better, any more than the man who believes himself to be Napoleon shows that he *knows* himself to be. He is merely exhibiting a mental twist. (c) Part of Mr. Margenau's difficulty in rejecting the self-evident goodness of happiness, a doctrine on which moralists as acute and as different as Sidgwick, Ross, and Moore can agree, is that it involves the acceptance of synthetic a priori truths, and that there are no such things. He finds it "difficult to argue" with persons who accept such truths, for "they are unimpressed by the universal catastrophe which has swept away all self-evident synthetic truths from logic, mathematics, and natural science" (ibid., 201). I confess to being one of these anachronisms. I do not think that a priori synthetic truths have been banished either from natural science or from ethics. This is not the place to renew an old controversy; I can only say that I have stated the case for the synthetic a priori in

Reason and Analysis, and will stick to it until Mr. Margenau or some other connoisseur of these matters shows me the error of my ways.

There is much else in Mr. Margenau's ethical theory that is interesting and challenging, but I have perhaps spent more space already than is permissible in examining it and must turn abruptly to the strictures he offers from this base upon my own ethical theory.

Needs and Goods

His main criticism is that in selecting certain goals from the profusion that history offers I employ too loose a criterion, namely conformity to human nature. He interprets my position as follows: "If the factual values, like health, happiness, freedom, honesty agree with human nature, they undergo promotion to *norms* and acquire the power of discrimination between right and wrong . . . . I am prevented from accepting [this view] because of the difficulties I encounter in defining human nature with sufficient precision to make this endeavor work." Now if I had said that we consider things good merely because they "agree with human nature," the criticism would be more than justified. But I said a great deal more. I never contented myself with "agreement with human nature"; I connected specific goods with specific drives or impulses, which is a different and far more definite undertaking.

(1) What I did was to correlate the main intrinsic goods with the recognized major needs of human nature. Those major needs are for food, drink, companionship, enlightenment, sex, social approval, and various other things on which psychologists are less agreed. These needs issue in demands or drives which require fulfillment. It seemed to me incredible that the correspondence between the characteristic fulfillments of these drives and the intrinsic goods of life should be a matter of chance, though many moralists have passed it by unnoticed. One can take a list of the fundamental urges of human nature drawn up by a "dynamic psychologist" and then a list of intrinsic goods drawn up independently by moralists, and find a degree of correspondence between them that could mean only one thing, that the values are rooted in the needs.

(2) Mr. Margenau expresses astonishment that "In all extant systems of ethics one finds remarkable agreement with respect to the choice of imperatives and goals." On his own theory of the "arbitrariness" of these imperatives and goals, this agreement is indeed astonishing, and one that urgently calls for explanation. On my own theory that explanation is provided. Human beings show similar values, immediate and remote, because human nature is in the main alike "from China to Peru." It does, to be sure, evolve, and Mr. Margenau has made it a difficulty for my theory that human nature changes. Far from being a difficulty, however, it is a corroboration of my theory. For according to that theory, the development of an impulse or its

entanglement with others would involve similar changes in the purity or the richness of the values required to fulfill it; and this is precisely what we find. The curiosity shown by the chimpanzee, though strong and various, has become something very different in the theoretical interest of an Aristotle, which is presumably a growth from that primitive root. The relation of pithecanthropus to his mate has certainly suffered alteration when it reappears after some millions of years in the love of Romeo for Juliet. I do not think that Mr. Margenau's theory, scientifically oriented as it is, explains these correlations as satisfactorily as my own rather simple hypothesis.

(3) There is one sense, however, in which the sweeping phrase "agrees with human nature" may be accepted, and I think it adds even further credibility to my theory. This theory marks out the limits within which values seem to occur. It does so in two ways. (a) It limits values to experience. There are those who say that whatever exists has value, that a chunk of ice on some frozen satellite of Saturn is intrinsically good. I can attach no meaning to such a statement. Unless this bit of matter is contemplated and found desirable or the reverse by some consciousness of which we know nothing, there is no place where the goodness could reside. My theory is thus a subjective one in that it makes value relative to consciousness. Would it be correct to say further that it is relative to human consciousness? No, for consciousness extends downward in the evolutional scale far below the emergence of humanity; animals have their instinctive drives which have their own humble fulfillments no less truly, though less abundantly, than ourselves. (b) My theory marks the upper and lower limits within which all the values known to us occur. A rose, for example, is an object in whose attractive color and fragrance we take much satisfaction; it therefore has value for us. A bee creeps into its center, busies itself there for a time, and flies off with a cargo of pollen. Has the bee too found the rose attractive? Probably. But what its experiences are like, whether the color and fragrance of the flower enter into the experience of the insect visitor, we do not know. It is only goods that are more or less like our own, such as our dog's delight in companionship, that we can in some degree understand; human satisfactions are the base from which we must project subhuman satisfactions. Again, it is possible that there are superhuman intelligences who can catch "the music of the spheres" as the stars move in their courses; and there is a passage somewhere in Newman that suggests that when we feel a sudden exaltation of spirit it may be because our guardian angel has brushed us with his wing. But these are plays of the imagination rather than hypotheses to be taken seriously; so far as our knowledge goes, all the good and bad in the universe are concentrated in human beings and their animal cousins. That is exactly what our view of the nature of value would lead us to expect. The eternal values of Dean Inge's mystical neo-Platonism are the by-products of religious hope, rather than the

results of careful analysis. The limits of the spectrum of values are appointed by conscious responsiveness.

An International Ethics

Mr. Margenau raises in his paper the important question whether there is or can be an international ethics, and reflects on the comparative availability of his theory and my own as a basis for such an ethics. He sees that, on the face of it, his theory would provide a precarious foundation. If such an ethics is to be achieved, "Agreement must exist with respect to the choice of both imperatives and goals. Since these are not preordained or logically derivable, such agreement can not be assumed." Still Mr. Margenau hopes that this common ethics will emerge. He offers two grounds for his hope. First there is the fact, already noted, of "an unexpected, almost unreasonable measure of actual agreement" in imperatives and ideals. We have just seen that though this is indeed "almost unreasonable" on Mr. Margenau's theory, it is what would be expected on the theory here defended.

The second ground for Mr. Margenau's hope lies in the analogy between the pursuit of goodness and the pursuit of truth. In the long pursuit of scientific truth we can observe a slow convergence toward a single system of belief. Often there will appear competing theories both apparently explaining the same facts with equal adequacy. But in the long run one of them will prove inconsistent with the body of accepted truth or with new data and will be dismissed, so that little by little a system is achieved which, because of its comprehensiveness and consistency, is accepted as true. Why this system should give us truth is for Mr. Margenau "a logical mystery expressible only as intellectual awe at the very possibility of our understanding the world." His awe at this possibility I fully share.

What puzzles me is his halting his speculation where he does. He believes that science is gradually constructing a system which, as it becomes more inclusive and its parts more closely interrelated, is approximating truth. How is this possible unless the world which our thought reveals is itself a system of this kind? Mr. Margenau moves within one step of the sort of rationalism I defend and then draws back from it as too daring a plunge into metaphysics for a physicist to take. I have not hesitated to take that plunge myself, though in the form of a postulate only. I commend to Mr. Margenau this addition to his set of postulates: the world to which the system of science is approximating is itself a logical system. He would not commit himself thereby to this thesis as an established one, but he would be accepting the assumption almost forced on us by his own account of the progress of science.

To return from this brief digression, Mr. Margenau thinks that the analogy between the pursuit of truth and that of goodness confirms the hope for an international ethics. Does this analogy hold? His own account of the two pursuits does not encourage us on the point. For though he does not contend, as I do, that truth lies in the approximation of our own system of thought to the system that constitutes the world, he does believe that there is a world of objective fact against which we can check our hypotheses, trimming and moulding them into an increasing correspondence. Now if men find themselves in closer agreement on objective fact, it is surely because this world of fact is there, and is the same for all. When the physicist of Moscow and the physicist of New Haven study the uranium atom, they inevitably tend to agree, for regarding the uranium atom, truth is one. Is the case similar in the pursuit of the good? Unfortunately not. There is no physical order against which our discrepant moral judgments can be checked, nor is there, for Mr. Margenau, a rational method of choice whose general use would guarantee convergence of ideals. On the contrary, he says that both the imperatives and the ultimate ends of ethics are arbitrary, and the only way to validate an imperative is to see whether it leads in fact to its arbitrary end. And he admits that under such conditions the agreement upon ideals is not something to be expected. Thus the analogy on which Mr. Margenau grounds much of his hope for an international ethics seems on examination to melt away.

In my own alternative theory the hope is more firmly based. If I believe in an international ethics, it is because my ethical theory is based on the constitution of the human mind, and because there is good reason for believing that the human mind is essentially the same in the Andaman Islands as in the Hebrides. I do not mean that we find identity in marriage customs or modes of dress; I mean that the central drives of human nature, the demands for food, drink, sex, companionship, adjustment to the world through knowledge, for example, are the same everywhere. That means that the basic goods of life are also the same everywhere. And the recognition of mutual rights depends on this identity of ends. The United Nations has a committee on human rights which proceeds on the assumption that if the people of a given country want life, liberty, and the pursuit of happiness for themselves, it is their duty to grant the conditions of these goods to others. The argument is simple and its force all but universally conceded, though at times action lags behind belief. I agree with Mr. Margenau that law has an ethical base, and above all international law, which almost resolves itself into ethics, since as yet there is no world government to give it sanctions. The ethical ground of such law was mapped convincingly by T. H. Green in his *Prolegomena to Ethics* and *Principles of Political Obligation*. Green held that in human minds everywhere there was a common reason at work which shaped human impulses to a joint and rational end, and that all claims of a man or a nation against another are based on the assumption that granting the claim would promote the common good. This is the only adequate ground I know for international rights and duties.

Transethical Ethics

One further point. At the end of his paper, Mr. Margenau takes the position that there are some problems of ethics that defy an ethical solution and can be dealt with only on a transethical level, presumably that of religion. The need for such a higher level is made clear, he thinks, by three considerations. First, ethics can lay down rules of conduct, but it cannot legislate for infractions of them. "If its imperatives included, or were coupled with, provisions for dealing with their violation, it would be like jurisprudence and surrender much of the spirit of personal involvement; it would surrender its philosophic depth in favor of the shallowness of law. Thus, strictly speaking, such virtues as forgiveness, mercy, charity, and compassion cannot be strictly parts of our ethical imperatives, which imply *duty* and seek the *good*. These facts point to a transethical domain which deals with infractions of the ethical code." This way of thinking puzzles me. If ethics deals with our duty to produce the good in our relations with others, why should it separate out our duties to wrongdoers as falling beyond its province? In another essay in this volume, the problem of forgiveness is dealt with as a straightforward ethical problem, though of course a difficult one. It is hard to see that mercy, charity, and compassion are in a different case. Indeed the problem of punishment, with its question how far these attitudes should be indulged or inhibited in our treatment of offenders, is a standard problem for moralists; Rashdall, for example, devotes a weighty chapter to "Punishment and Forgiveness." A moralist who believes that he should always try to produce the greatest good will take this as his governing principle in dealing with offenders, and if he finds that no two offenders should be dealt with in quite the same way, that is nothing against the principle. To appeal to some transethical authority for guidance is likely, I suspect, to do more harm than good.

In a second type of case Mr. Margenau's attitude may command more sympathy. It is the case where the problem is unique and therefore not specifically provided for by any of the moral rules one knows. Mr. Margenau cites as instances Socrates and Seneca, who committed suicide rather than obey a command of their rulers that they thought wrong. "The point is that such decisions are not governed by any rules, processes or strategies known to common sense or science or ethics. I refer here to singular acts of dedication, of personal sacrifice, of altruism which reason or morals can neither justify nor condemn, of the choice of ideals far beyond ordinary human reach."

In essence, the question Mr. Margenau is here raising is another question of traditional ethics: Can a man do more than his duty? Are there genuine acts of supererogation? Are there acts which it would be right to do but not wrong to omit? When on Scott's antarctic expedition Captain Oates saw that with his frozen feet he was delaying the company's attempt to reach their home base, he deliberately slipped out into the arctic night and did not return. While Schweitzer was still a young theologian full of scholarly promise, he broke it all off, studied medicine, and went to the African jungle as a medical missionary. These are acts of which we ordinarily think and speak as "beyond the call of duty." And of course Mr. Margenau is right that they require a heroism and sacrifice which it would be utterly unreasonable to impose on the plain man as a duty. And yet to say that a man can go beyond his duty is to commit oneself to the paradox that one can do what is more right than the right, and that it is sometimes right to content oneself with less than the greatest good. For moralists of my own stripe this paradox is galling, because it renders suspect the general rule of duty: Always so act as to produce what is, to the best of your knowledge, the greatest good. Of course this rule is terribly hard to live by, but I do not see my way to giving it up. And I should be very reluctant to give it up to the notion that if one is noble enough one may try to produce more than the greatest good, for that is absurd. It is better, I think, to hold to the demanding rule, to admit that one cannot exceed it, and then to add that people's duties vary extremely with both outer and inner circumstances. Few persons are ever placed in the desperate external circumstances of Captain Oates. Not everyone is built like Albert Schweitzer; there are few who could have done what he did, few indeed who would so much as think of it. One's duties are limited by one's nature. Socrates and Seneca were men of quite exceptional sensitiveness and reflectiveness, whose duties, for that very reason, differed from those of ordinary men. They would no doubt have said that they were only doing their duty, and it is perhaps best to let that stand. It may be added that some supersaints and heroes in living up to the impossible dream were in fact doing not more than right but less. If Socrates had bowed to the will of his jurors and taken the ship for Delos, his tale would have had a less dramatic impact on history, but is it quite clear that he would have chosen the lesser good? Who knows? But I for one should be prepared to say that *if* the verdict of historical consequence could be unrolled and were found to weigh against his choice of death, we should have to say that even a fastidious conscience backed by the supremest heroism may err like common men.

The third path that conducts Mr. Margenau beyond the bounds of the ethical is the inevitability of moral frustration. We are all sinners and unhappily we all know that we shall continue to be. "This fact," says Mr. Margenau, "is symbolized in Western literature by one of the profoundest allegories of all scriptures, the story of man's fall, the doctrine of original sin." Reflection on this continuing moral failure "creates the tendency to cleanse one's soul from guilt, the craving for redemption; it produces the liberating effect of the confession of the 'Pater peccavi.' All these are agonizing indications of man's cosmic frustration, his fear of moral insignificance." And in all of them "there is a kind of significance that goes beyond ethics." These ideas of man's universal guilt and his need for absolution through atonement are of course fundamental ideas in Western religion. And in certain traditions of that religion, particularly the tradition that runs from Luther through Kierkegaard to Brunner and Barth, the notion that religion has an authority superseding even that of rational ethics has claimed a Biblical and divine sanction. This claim I can only deny. I have given my own reasons in detail in a book published after Mr. Margenau's essay was written, and I shall have to return to the issue in comment on Mr. Irish's essay. It will be enough at present to say that I hold ethics to be an autonomous science and never at any point derivative in its authority from theology. If theological teaching comes into conflict with the insights of a rational ethics, as in my judgment it clearly does in the doctrine of original sin, in Kierkegaard's hymn to Abraham, and in the teaching that one man can expiate the sins of another, morality has the right of way. A superrational morality is an infrarational morality.

If I have written at such length on the views of my friend and colleague Henry Margenau, it has been partly because I thought that so courageous an incursion into ethics by an eminent scientist as his *Ethics and Science* deserved more consideration than it had received. My comment would have been less negative if I had not had to consider his book as the formidable revolving turret from which his fire on my own position was directed. He will, I trust, forgive me if I have been overdogmatic or oversummary. If he were writing about my physics rather than I about his ethics, I wince to think of the slaughter that would ensue.

1. Henry Margenau, *Ethics and Science* (Princeton, N.J.: Van Nostrand, 1964).

III POLITICAL THEORY

8 BLANSHARD'S POLITICAL PHILOSOPHY
Richard T. De George

IN 1937 Brand Blanshard argued that there is "no fixed connection at all" between rationalism and reaction on the one hand, and between empiricism and liberalism on the other. The article was entitled "Metaphysics and Social Attitudes."[1] In it Blanshard succinctly and in the urbane style for which he has become well known, showed by way of concrete illustration how there were many clear and obvious counterexamples to any sort of simple generalization one might wish to make about the alleged necessary connection between a philosopher's metaphysical position and his political or social attitudes.

What of the connection between one's social and political attitudes and one's ethics? Is there any necessary link between the two? On this Blanshard is less clear. He has maintained that conformity to an ethics of consequences "would make a large difference in our political theory and practice"[2] and that adherence to such ethical views as relativism or emotivism would lead to anarchy in politics.[3] The argument seems to go, roughly, that unless one holds that actions are objectively right or wrong, and unless reasons can be given which demonstrate the rightness or wrongness of actions, rational discussion of them is impossible and a rational decision as to what should or should not be done is precluded. Such discussion does not make sense if one believes that "right" and "wrong," "good" and "bad" simply express emotions and that judgments using these terms are not objectively true or false. Hence, if people are to discuss practical questions of politics, and resolve them on the basis of facts and evidence rather than on the basis of feelings, they should, if they wish to be consistent, adopt an objectivist and rationalist position.

But the argument does not deal with attitudes, and despite it an emotivist might well produce arguments in support of a position he feels is a good one concerning taxation or welfare. His position on the meaning of the terms "good" and "bad" does not preclude his using them; nor does it preclude his trying to persuade others to join him in certain actions. He can certainly try to change their attitudes by adducing facts, describing consequences, and doing similar things, while still maintaining that none of his arguments can force others who admit the facts and the validity of his arguments to change their attitudes. A rationalist and an emotivist on the floor of the United States Senate might carry on a discussion identical to one carried on between two rationalists or two emotivists.

I am inclined to believe that Blanshard would not deny this, though he sometimes writes as if he did. He does not claim that Westermarck or A. J. Ayer are anarchists, despite the connection he finds between their theories and anarchism. There is obviously a difference between what a man's attitudes are and what his critics might claim his theory logically entails. Some emotivists are conservative with respect to United States politics, others are liberal or radical. On their own grounds their attitudes are not determined by their theories. I am inclined to believe, therefore, that Blanshard's thesis concerning the lack of any fixed connection between a philosopher's metaphysical position and his political and social attitudes can be extended so as validly to hold between the latter and one's ethical theory.

My concern is not to defend emotivism or relativism or any of the other enemies of rationalism which Blanshard has so consistently and so skillfully attacked. It is rather to examine Blanshard's own position with the hope that he may take the opportunity to write more at length on a topic to which he has paid only passing attention. Though he has expressed his faith in democracy of some sort,[4] and his opposition to fascism,[5] anarchy,[6] and communism,[7] we should not—if his own thesis is correct—attempt to explain these attitudes by analyzing his metaphysics and looking for the necessary connecting links. Nor do I see any necessary connection between them and either his ethical theory or his political theory, at least insofar as he has committed them to print. I shall consequently ignore his political attitudes and concentrate on his political philosophy.

The basic sources I shall be concerned with are the relevant portions of his book *Reason and Goodness* (*RG*,[8] especially, though not exclusively, chapter 14, "Reason and Politics") and his article "Morality and Politics."[9] My paper will be divided into four parts. In the first I shall raise the question of the object of political philosophy and try to place Blanshard's approach to it. In the second I shall investigate his view concerning the relation between ethics and politics. In the third section I shall consider the four propositions which he says constitute his theory of political obligation. Lastly I shall sketch what I think are the consequences of his theory and raise some questions, the answers to which might help fill out the political theory Blanshard has given us so far.

I

The nature of political philosophy cannot be set out a priori, nor can any one philosopher dictate to another what his political philosophy must do or what topics it must handle. Many contemporary Anglo-American philosophers take as one of their main tasks the analysis of the language of politics and of such terms as "obligation," "rights," and "democracy."

When they have broached substantive issues, political philosophers have dealt with questions on three different levels. On the first and most general level they have raised questions about society in general, government in general, and law in general; and they have sought to justify, to render intelligible, or to account for the facts that men live in society, that they are born into countries or nations or states which have governments, and that these governments have established laws to which they are subject. When, if ever, are governments legitimate? When, if ever, are laws legitimate?

The second level is built on the first. It raises the question of legitimacy or the problem of justification, not of governments or of laws in general, but of specific forms of government and basic kinds of laws. What are the different forms of government, what are the pros and cons of each type, which is the best, and what would an ideal form of government be like? On this level we find both the utopias and the defenses of kingship, or of communistic types of government, of representative democracy, of constitutional forms of government, and of specific instantiations of each of these, e.g. a defense of the political system of the United States, or of France, or of the Soviet Union. With respect to law, we find defenses of common law, or of the Napoleonic code, of the United States Constitution and constitutional law, and so on.

The third level considers specific aspects within an accepted governmental legal system. Civil disobedience to particular laws and the justification thereof have become popular issues among many American political philosophers who are willing to grant the legitimacy of the American system as a whole, while wishing to defend the right to protest certain statutes. The conditions under which such protest is justifiable, the extent to which it can go, and the compatibility of this practice with the American legal system are all "third level" problems of political philosophy.

Obviously the three levels are interconnected and related, and some questions bridge levels. It is clear, however, that though a philosophic defense might be given of government or of law in general, such an argument might well be insufficient to show that a particular kind of government or legal system is justified. And within a justified or acceptable system, an individual law or practice might be unjust or defective, and so worthy of criticism and reform.

Blanshard's writings on political philosophy have tended to stay on what I have called the first level of substantive questions. As in his ethical theory, so in his political theory, he is not primarily concerned with the analysis either of language or of concepts as such. Rather he has focused his attention on political obligation and law in general; and though he opts for a democratic type government instead of a totalitarian one, and though he prefers the American to the Soviet type of government, his arguments never justify that degree of specificity. He argues in general against anarchism, and then attempts to establish the legitimacy of governments and of law.

Now given this aim, what constitutes a justification? How does it arise, what does a justification of government or of law consist in, and by what criteria are we to judge its adequacy? The question of justification may of course arise to any reflective person as he tries to understand himself and his society. He is born into a political community which he had no part in making. As he grows up he finds himself subject to laws which he had no voice in forming, just as he is subject to parents or guardians whom he had no voice in choosing. At a certain stage in his development he may no longer choose to obey his parents; may he similarly choose to disobey the laws of his community? No. He usually cannot do so without being subject to certain penalties. And he may well ask why this should be so. Philosophers, such as Blanshard, have turned their attention to such questions and have come up with various replies.

In other instances the questions of political philosophy arise because of specific events which take place within a society—because of conflicts, threatened or actual revolutions, external pressures, internal changes, because of the actions or inaction of rulers, or because of famines or invasions or riots or wars or other social ills. Under such conditions men naturally turn to ask penetrating questions about their society and government. And in such instances political leaders and ordinary citizens may seek for philosophical grounds to defend or attack the system under which they live, and for philosophical theories in which they can express their feelings and thoughts, their aspirations and desires. The expression of these feelings and aspirations is an important function of political thought, for it is in large part these which call for justification.

We can consequently distinguish the personal political philosophy of an individual thinker from a theory which is seized by the political activist or which catches the consciousness of a people or of an age or which is used by a government to justify its actions. The latter instances, it might be claimed, are not philosophies at all. They are ideologies. For they are not thought through and held because of the validity of the reasoning processes and arguments of which they are formed; they are rather the *product* of a philosophy, the residue which can be memorized and put into slogans, charters, and preambles to constitutions, into manifestos, and civics textbooks. But they are not philosophy.

From several of his remarks[10] I am inclined to think that Blanshard would accept this division between political philosophy and political ideology. He is not interested so much in what people believe or what they have believed, as in what is true. He is interested in whether the arguments presented in defense of the divine right of kings are valid; not in whether the people of a certain age believed they were valid or whether the kings who appealed to the theory really were sincere in their appeal. Now, although I think this is a perfectly legitimate approach to political philosophy, two points in this approach should be made clear. The first is that personal political philosophies have their limitations. If they remain simply the thought of single individuals, not adopted or applied or put into practice or believed by anyone other than the individual thinkers, they have less interest than otherwise. Why? Because political philosophy is a practical branch of philosophy. Its premises and its arguments are not only speculative, they are necessarily in part practical—concerned with actual governments and people and with better and worse ways of organizing society. What is to be justified is actual systems or institutions or felt values and aspirations and goals.

Blanshard himself deals with six kinds of answers to the question of the basis of political obligation: viz. that it is "based on (1) nothing, (2) force, (3) the will of God, (4) contract, (5) self-evidence, (6) a rational will" (*RG*, 377). I presume he picked these because they have actually been held by more than one man, they have all been used practically in arguing for or against particular forms of government, they have all caught the consciousness of some sizable number of people. For if any one of them were simply the armchair musings of a solitary individual, striking no responsive chord in others, and unrecognized by anyone else as accounting for, making sense of, or grounding his feeling of political obligation, one might take this as prima facie evidence—especially if it had been published and given a chance—that it was in some way deficient.

This is compatible, I think, with what I take to be Blanshard's view of what political philosophy is. For just as one of the tests of a valid ethical theory for him is that it accounts for what the conscientious plain man thinks is right and wrong and for what he means when he says, e.g. "Murder is wrong," so must a political philosophy account for what the conscientious plain man thinks is right and wrong, and for what he means when he says, e.g. "The American way of life is worth fighting and dying for."

This leads us to our second observation. While a sound political philosophy must account for what people say and believe, its arguments must also be valid and its premises true. Though the plain man may praise the

American way of life, it does not follow that the American way of life is as wholesome as he thinks. An adequate political theory should indicate what people mean when they say certain things; but it should also indicate what they should recognize as true or as best, because it is objectively so. It is the latter that Blanshard seems most concerned with, since he attempts to present primarily a justification of government and of law, and a criterion by which they may be judged.

I shall not here rehearse his arguments against the divine right of kings and the other doctrines he briefly discusses. But consider, as he does, the doctrine of natural rights which underlay the American and French revolutions, and the sentence "We hold these truths to be self-evident, that all men are created equal, that they are endowed by their Creator with certain inalienable rights, that among these are life, liberty, and the pursuit of happiness." If we were to argue that those rights are not self-evident, that they are not inalienable, and that they are not given by a Creator (if such there be), we would have to say that the American revolutionists were at least partially incorrect in their statement, and that they were misguided in thinking that their theory, to the extent that it is false, justified their actions. Bad reasoning, mistaken information, or false beliefs cannot objectively justify anything. We can then ask whether the American Revolution was in fact justified, not in the eyes of those who revolted, but from the true, objective perspective. The best we can do, of course, is to judge from the true and objective perspective which we have been able to develop and make clear. Each generation judges history by its own light.

Blanshard's theory supplies us with an objective criterion which the American revolutionists only partially saw and inadequately expressed. If the state "becomes so corrupt as to cut us off from those [great] ends rather than further them, when it serves its purpose so badly that it is better to risk chaos for the sake of a better order than continue to suffer under the old, then resistance becomes a right and a duty" (*RG,* 401–2). This is a different criterion from his general one of judging an action "right if, and only if, it tends to bring into being as much experience that is at once satisfying and fulfilling as any alternative action" (321). For by that criterion a revolution might be justified even without gross governmental corruption. But on neither account can we tell or know if the American Revolution is justified, though we are told that this is what we should mean if we are to be consistent and objective and rational. We cannot know on the second criterion, because there is no way of knowing what the consequences would have been if there had been no revolution. On the first criterion there is enormous room for disagreement—as there was in the American colonies—whether the government was as corrupt as Blanshard's criterion requires. If Blanshard's reply is that the revolution was either right or wrong, though we can never be sure which it was, and that his criterion is as good a one as is available, the skeptic may not be entirely happy. What constitutes a justification, however, is in part dependent on what is available and at what point men are willing to stop asking questions. The American revolutionists were willing to stop before Blanshard. A skeptic will never stop.

What is interesting here nonetheless is that Blanshard is certainly espousing and putting forth a common doctrine of government and of revolution which at least many Americans would accept as true. I think he is right, therefore, in trying to account for it and for our feeling and belief that it is true, though we also have to admit that it might in fact be deficient in some way.

This I think gives some account of Blanshard's approach to political philosophy—to its object and to what he feels he must account for. Let me say one last word on his method insofar as it is rationalist. I must admit that his use of "rationalism" seems to me to have become weaker and weaker over the years. In the context of political philosophy his claim of rationalism seems to entail basically that actions are objectively right or wrong, good or bad, and that we can give reasons why they are so. We should consequently discuss and present arguments, attempt to find out the way things are, and, where we disagree, continue to seek for the truth. His rationalism is not a specific approach to political philosophy in any narrow sense of rationalism, continental or other. He does not proceed a priori or dogmatically; nor does he come armed with any set of presuppositions which determines the outcome of his thinking. He argues for the claim that value judgments can be true or false, and that we should seek the evidence and arguments by which we can learn which they are. But such a rationalism is compatible with a great many varieties of empiricism, and with almost the whole spectrum of political positions.

II

According to Professor Blanshard "all political problems are in the end ethical problems."[11] This is not a novel position to maintain, and it is not at all a surprising position for Blanshard, since he claims that "A question becomes a moral question at the moment when competing values, of any kind whatever, enter upon the scene" (RG, 324). I do not wish to press the latter statement too far, though as such I think it is false, unless it means that any situation of competing values might be considered from a moral point of view. It is certainly not what the plain man would consider moral questions to be, and consequently cannot be a reportive definition. Are there good reasons for changing common usage and adopting Blanshard's view? I think not. Consider, for instance, an artist choosing between competing aesthetic values as he paints a canvas. If his painting is an aesthetic failure as a result of a poor aesthetic choice somewhere along the line, we tend to say it is a poor work of art. We do not ordinarily—and I see no reason to start doing so—call the work morally bad, or say that when he chose this color instead of that one the artist was morally at fault. What could possibly be gained except confusion by extending the use of the term "moral" to cover all such choices? Or again, our same artist engrossed in his work may decide to skip lunch one day, giving in to his desire to work and ignoring his desire to eat. On another occasion he may do the reverse. I see no need to judge these choices from a moral point of view or to say that, because we have a case of competing values, the choice between them is necessarily a moral one.

Now if it is true that not all choices between competing values are moral choices, then the reason why all political problems are in the end ethical problems is not simply because all political problems involve choices between competing values, despite Blanshard's assertion to the contrary.[12] If ordinary usage and the plain man's opinion about what is a moral issue are not to count against Blanshard's view, either we need some argument to show why we should accept his position, or we may treat his claim as a stipulative definition of "moral." Surely, however, he does not intend to settle what he considers some of the main questions of political philosophy—which hinge on the relation of morality and politics—by stipulation.

It seems to be perfectly plausible to claim that some of the problems of political philosophy are moral problems, while holding that other problems can but need not be viewed from a moral as well as from other points of view, and that there are still other problems which are not moral problems at all.

When Blanshard claims that all political problems are in the end ethical problems, he seems to argue for two independent assertions. The first is that it is immoral to disobey any law. The second is that the ultimate justification of government is a moral justification. Now I think that the first of these is a position which we not only need not adopt but are better off not adopting. The second I think is true, though it does not entail that all political problems are ethical problems. The phrase "in the end" seems to me to serve no purpose but to put emphasis on the question of moral foundations, implying without argument that all political questions can and must be pushed to this point.

Let us first consider the claim that men have a moral obligation to obey the law.

Suppose we live in an enlightened country which has a law against murder. Now murder, on most views, would constitute a morally bad action. It is not morally bad because there is a law against it; it would be morally wrong even if there were no law against it. If someone commits murder and there is a specific statute against it, the action is both legally and morally wrong. As a consequence both legal and moral sanctions may be brought to bear against the murderer. But has he committed two morally bad acts, namely murder and breaking the law? And is he to be punished for murder and for breaking the law? I hardly think so. He is guilty of murder, which is forbidden by law; but he is guilty of one offense, not two. In this case the action forbidden is a morally bad one, and this is at least in part the reason for passing a law against it.

Consider, on the other hand, the action of overparking in a metered zone on a rainy day when there are few shoppers and when by parking I am not depriving anyone else of a parking place. Along comes the meter maid and gives me a ticket, which I pay. Did I act in a morally bad way in overparking? I must say that I do not see why I should have to say that my overparking was morally reprehensible; nor do I see what is gained by labeling it morally wrong. Under normal conditions parking is a morally neutral act. It may become a legal offense when there is a statute against parking under certain conditions. One might also claim that, if parking under certain conditions causes unjust inconvenience to others, then it is immoral in its own right, just as murder is. But where the action is not immoral in its own right, is it made so simply because there is a law against it? I cannot see why. It is immoral or not, independently of the law. But, someone might insist, though the overparking in itself is not morally wrong, the breaking of the law is. I find this not only paradoxical; I fail to see what could be gained by labeling the action morally wrong as well as legally wrong. The purpose in calling it legally wrong is to justify the fine which I shall have to pay. What is gained by calling it morally wrong? Certainly moral sanctions are not required in this or similar cases. Nor can the reason be to increase our respect for law, since whether this is at issue is part of the question.

There is, moreover, a good reason for not labeling such an action immoral: only then is it possible to distinguish adequately between the violations of laws and ordinances on the one hand and moral violations on the other. The distinction becomes especially useful in cases in which a statute commands what is morally forbidden. Without the distinction one would be morally obliged to obey a law, simply because it is a law, even though it commanded one to do what is morally forbidden. One would then be morally obliged to do what one is morally forbidden to do. This is certainly paradoxical, if not contradictory, and it is a situation which can be avoided by refusing to call every legal obligation a moral one.

Blanshard seems to me to be clearly involved in this difficulty when he claims "Ultimately, therefore, political obligation, even that of obeying a morally bad law, *is* a moral obligation; and when, as occasionally happens, it becomes a duty to disobey, the ground is still the same" (*RG,* 395). As it stands, the sentence is at least paradoxical. For one has the moral obligation of obeying a morally bad law, and occasionally one may even have both the moral obligation to obey it because it is a law and the moral obligation to disobey it. The confusion, I believe, comes from the insistence that all one's political obligations are moral obligations.

Blanshard's argument claims that the state is necessary to help achieve the good of the citizens of a society; if citizens could pick and choose which laws to obey, the society could not be run; hence, if the greatest good is achieved by a society's functioning, it is better to obey all laws than for each to decide which ones he will or will not obey. Blanshard is obviously attempting to give a moral justification for obeying the law. But there are several replies one can make to his argument. The first is that though, as he says, it is politically obligatory to obey the law, he simply assumes that obeying all laws is necessary for the best functioning of society, which is to beg the question. If political sanctions are not enough to enforce a law, and if a law is constantly flouted by masses of people, then there may well be something wrong with the law.

Is selling liquor an immoral action? Some would say yes, though a great many would say no. Surely this action was not moral before Prohibition, immoral during Prohibition, and moral again after the repeal of Prohibition, though it was illegal at certain times and not illegal at others. The morality of the action is clearly separable from the legislation passed concerning it. A government is a means to the people's ends. It seems clear to me that it cannot make something immoral by legislating against it, though on Blanshard's view it can.

A system of law may be morally justified, and if more harm than good is done by breaking a law, obeying the law may be morally obligatory. But the step from here to the claim that in fact obeying the law is always better than not obeying it, and that therefore it is always morally obligatory to obey all laws, is a step that needs justification which Blanshard has not supplied.

The apparently contradictory moral obligations would dissolve if one were willing to admit that not all political obligations are moral obligations, and if one were willing to say that one is not morally obliged to obey everything which a government chooses to promulgate as law. When is one not morally obliged to obey what is promulgated as law? Obviously one clear case is where what the law commands is immoral. In such a case one may continue to be politically obliged to obey the law, and may have to pay the consequences if he breaks the law and is caught. The extent to which a moral government would recognize an individual's moral beliefs and suspend or mitigate punishment is another question. But it is perfectly possible to handle the conflict between immoral laws and one's moral obligations in a clearer way than Blanshard does by not subsuming legal obligation under moral obligation at the outset. An alternative way is to deny that immoral laws impose any obligation from even a political point of view. But this is not a position which Blanshard takes, and since it has difficulties of its own, he is perhaps wise not to do so.

Consider now the claim that all political problems are moral problems. This too is an oversimplification and an overstatement.

Citizens in the United States who satisfy certain qualifications have the right to vote. Do they have the moral obligation to vote? Some might say so. But do they have the moral obligation to vote in a certain way? It is at the polls that they are given a choice between competing candidates, parties, platforms, and so between competing values. On Blanshard's view it would seem that when one steps into the polling booth one is faced with a moral choice. There are certain candidates whom it is morally right to vote for, presumably because those candidates would do the best job for the common good. But of course no one knows which candidates are objectively the best, and there is no way to determine this conclusively because the competitors cannot serve at the same time, face the same decisions, and so on. On this view we all make a moral choice when we vote; but we can never know if it was the right choice, or if the right candidates, from a moral point of view, were elected. One can speak this way if he wishes; but once again I see no reason to do so, and nothing seems to be gained by doing so. On the other hand, there is good reason for not doing so. If one tends to look with less favor on those who act in an objectively wrong way, even in good faith, then a Republican might well consider (rightly or wrongly) his Democratic neighbor immoral for voting differently from the way Republicans vote.

In the realm of national politics and international politics moralizing has frequently in the past led to wars, oppression, and injustice. This shows only that looking at politics from a moralistic point of view can have undesirable consequences. A morally righteous United States foreign policy which sees communism as immoral and a morally righteous Soviet foreign policy which sees capitalism as immoral, if tied to a moralistic point of view, might each remain more adamant and less open to compromise than they should otherwise. It is not Blanshard's intention to advocate such moralism. But since calling all political questions moral questions so easily slips into moralism, there should be some reasons given for adopting this view which make running the risks worthwhile.

I am not denying that there is a relation between morality and politics; I am denying that all political questions are moral questions.

I mentioned earlier that Blanshard is concerned primarily with the large, fundamental questions of political philosophy and with the moral system, or with conflicts within accepted systems. It is on these other levels, however, that cases frequently arise in which the distinction between what is political and what is moral is useful and helpful both in describing the situation and in arriving at a solution.

There are two further reasons for not subsuming political under moral obligation—at least for not doing so as readily as Blanshard is tempted to do. We can speak of morality as a social institution, we can judge people to be morally virtuous or vicious, and we can speak of acts or classes of actions as being good or bad, right or wrong—at least prima facie. Both our discourse concerning morality and the institution of morality itself have developed primarily with respect to individuals, and it is with respect to individuals that we are accustomed to use the terms "right," "obligation," "responsibility," and so forth. Politics, on the other hand, frequently has as its subject nations or institutions, and amorphous entities such as governments, rather than individuals. It cannot simply be assumed that the terms relevant to the two types of discourse are the same, or that when we speak of the moral obligation of an individual and the moral obligation of a government we mean the same thing.

It is possible to speak of an unjust war, though when we speak in this way we might mean a great many different things. Since a war is not the action of an individual, it cannot simply be assumed that it can be evaluated in the same way as an individual action. Who is the agent in such a war? Is it the leaders of a country, the generals, the fighting forces, the citizens of the country which initiates the war, or only those citizens who support the government in specific ways? Whereas all the citizens of a country may be held politically guilty for an unjust war which their country has lost—in the sense that they may all be taxed so that the country can pay reparations to another country—they may not each and every one be morally responsible. Political judgments are frequently about actions not of individuals but of masses or cliques or leaders or congresses; and to lump all political actions together with moral actions tends to confuse types of responsibility, accountability, and culpability which can and should be kept distinct. Blanshard may well object that he never meant that the two be confused. But then what is the point of assimilating one to the other?

Finally, the government of a nation, even on Blanshard's view, would be responsible first and foremost for the good of its own citizens. It is to them that it is responsible and it is to them that, in an elective system, it should be responsive. This means that when it digs into the taxpayers' pockets its charge is not necessarily to do the greatest amount of good or to produce the greatest amount of fulfillment and satisfaction possible. If it is the American government we are considering, its mandate is to build roads in the United States first, rather than anywhere in the world where roads are needed most; to care for the needs of those at home before searching out the needy abroad; to help the national economy before it seeks out the economy in direst need. And a similar feeling is undoubtedly shared by the citizens of each country, viz. that their government is not to help produce the greatest good throughout the universe but is to serve first the good of the nation and its citizens. Now to argue that the best way to produce the greatest good is for each nation to look out for itself and its own is either to beg the question or to ignore the obvious fact that this may not be the case. To judge a nation's or a government's action only from the moral point of view, which is to see if it produces the greatest good, may well be different from looking at it from the political point of view. It is not necessarily moral for a government to be responsive to its constituents, if the true moral criterion is production of the greatest good. What may be productive of greatest good might be the abolition of states and national governments in favor of a worldwide organization and the worldwide administration of goods. But if this were the case, then political obligation to national governments would not be one's moral obligation. Using Blanshard's criterion, it is only because the two can be separated that we can morally evaluate political actions and government as such. To subsume one under the other is to preclude this possibility. Blanshard argues for government per se and his argument is such that most presently existing governments could be justified in their existence by his argument, and could claim that their citizens are morally as well as legally or politically obliged to obey the laws passed by their governments. Such a general argument, however, has its obvious limitations and dangers in the political realm.

It therefore seems to me clear that though there is a relation between morality and politics it is much more complicated and less total than Blanshard maintains.

III

Let me now briefly consider the four propositions which Blanshard says constitute his theory of political obligation. He writes:

> The doctrine that does seem to me true may be expanded and made more explicit in four propositions: First, we can distinguish within our own minds between the end of our actual or immediate will, and the end of our rational will, which is what on reflection would commend itself as the greatest good. Secondly, this rational end is the same for all men. Thirdly, this end, because a common end, is the basis of our rights against each other. Fourthly, the justification of the state, and its true office, lie in furthering the realization of this end. [RG, 395]

Let us look at each of the four points.

(1) The distinction between our immediate and our greatest good seems to me a valid distinction, if taken in the obvious sense that there are certain goods I desire which I am willing to forsake if I see that they will prevent me from obtaining something I desire even more. But the distinction seems to mean more than this for Blanshard; and the concepts are somewhat confused

by his discussion of the rational will, which, so far as I can see, constitutes excess baggage not required for either his ethical or his political theory.

My difficulty with the notion of my rational will as explained by Blanshard is twofold. (a) According to Blanshard it seems that what we actually will is never the object of our rational will. Blanshard gives us the example of a man who goes to buy a car, which is not an end in itself. And if he could be shown that buying the car would lead to consequences he wished to avoid, he would not buy it. The example proves that in this instance his actual will is not self-contained. But suppose he believes rightly that buying the car will help him achieve other things he wants. Does his actual will then coincide with his rational will? It appears not, neither in the sense that the two are identical nor in the sense that the one forms part of the other. We can actually will what is rational for us to have, and get it, but we cannot actually ever achieve the object of our rational will. Why not? Evidently because the rational will is an ideal and is never attainable; it is that in terms of which we judge the worthwhileness of the objects of our actual will. But we cannot ever say what it is, because it is not any single thing or any set of goods.

To say the latter, however, seems to me false. For we do come to a stopping point in answering the question of why we want a motorcar. Blanshard himself suggests the answer elsewhere, where he says that certain things—satisfaction and fulfillment of desire—are good in themselves and desirable in themselves. If getting the car produces these and we are convinced it produces them more than not getting it (and it is therefore the right thing to do), then the object of our actual will does coincide with at least part of the object of our rational will.

Now either this is the case or our rational will is never fulfilled even in part. But if the latter is the case, then our fulfillment and satisfaction—which are intrinsically good for Blanshard—are in fact not rationally intrinsically good, even when such fulfillment and satisfaction are what ought to be produced. If actual goods are not the object of my rational will then only chimera are; but since they are not satisfaction and fulfillment, then the rational will is not intrinsically good.

The reply might be that my rational will is what would make me completely satisfied and fulfilled, and obviously no one thing or set of things could do this. But equally obviously, no empty set will do this either. The rational will on this interpretation simply seems to mean that men are never completely satisfied and that they can judge between the worth of competing goods and satisfactions. What is gained by the reification of these facts into a rational will escapes me.

(b) The rational will has no specifiable object or set of objects. Yet in a choice between this and that, the choice is always between specifiables. If to save the life of the President, I jump on a hand grenade thrown by a would-be assassin, then I choose the President's life over my own. If such an action is rationally defensible it might be because I see his life as more important than mine to more people. If I give up buying an automobile because I am suddenly forced to see that I cannot pay for it and that to buy it will just involve me in difficulties with the finance company, then once again I may have acted rationally. In both instances Blanshard, if I follow him, would be inclined to say that the object of my actual will—staying alive (or in this case is it saving the President?) or having the car now—was overridden by the object of my rational will, and that I did what I would in some sense have preferred to avoid—dying or going without a car. But notice that in each case the content of my rational will was different. The reasons why I do or defer doing different acts vary. There is no one reason; so there is no one object of the rational will. And consequently to treat it as if it were one thing seems to me to be a mistake.

The difficulty, moreover, lies not simply in the use of the term "will." For if we were to speak about my "greatest good" as if it were one thing, we would fall into the same difficulty. My greatest good is not any one particular good. What is good for me may change, and constantly does change. In the above instance I find it difficult to see how my giving up my life for the President's involves *my* greatest good at all.

This consideration leads me directly to Blanshard's second proposition.

(2) Is this rational end the same for all men? I have argued above that my greatest good is not consistently the same for me except perhaps on the most abstract level. It seems to me even clearer that my greatest good is not the same as your greatest good. And this for two additional reasons.

(a) In order for my greatest good and your greatest good to be identical either it would have to contain no specific goods or the goods which it contained would have to be such that they constituted the greatest good for all men. In the first instance it would be difficult to know that they were identical, since there would be no specific goods which we could compare to decide whether they were identical. In the second instance it would have to be shown that my greatest good consisted in something that was shared by all men.

In arguing for his first proposition Blanshard showed only that we do sometimes defer gratifying our present desire because of considerations which transcend the moment. But we saw that this can be explained in terms of other specific goods, and that this deferral did not require an unknown and unspecifiable good. What could be shared by all men might be the desire for the greatest fulfillment and satisfaction on the whole. But is this really my greatest good? If it were better for the race for all blonds to be exterminated, and I were a blond, would I believe that my greatest good was being achieved as I was led to the oven? Someone might. But I do not think that it is self-evident, and I think it requires a good deal of argumentation, which Blanshard fails to produce.

(b) Blanshard presents two arguments in favor of the proposition, neither of which seems to me adequate. The first is that unless we assume that there is a truth to be found, and that it is our common end to find it, we could not so much as argue. This shows that when we argue we have this end in common. But this can be admitted without admitting that all men have a common end. Suppose that all men want to find out the truth, and that in virtue of this common characteristic they can argue, communicate, and engage in mutually supportive research. Well and good. Can we conclude that the common rational end of all men is to search for the truth? Well, no, that is not all, since the rational will goes beyond any specific end. Also, one's devotion to truth may well be secondary to one's devotion to chess or to polo or to beer. The fact that men in general seek the truth can at best show that men have a specific characteristic in common with others. But it cannot show that all men have a common end in the sense that all men have a common ideal in terms of which we would in our rational moments all choose that the same satisfactions and fulfillment be realized, or in terms of which we would all evaluate particular goods in the same way.

Blanshard's second argument claims that "Unless there is some broad agreement on the ends that are worth pursuing, neither of us would have any purchase on the thought of the other" (RG, 399). To assume that every man has purchase on the thought of every other is to assume more than may be warranted. But let us admit that it is the case. It does not follow that our greatest good is the same as everyone else's. I may have certain overlapping interests and ends with you, other overlapping interests and ends with someone else, and a somewhat different set with someone else. My desire for my survival may not be shared by someone bent on doing away with me for noble reasons of eugenics. To say that we both want the greatest good and that mine and his coincide, even if I ignobly want to live despite the greater good to be brought about by my demise, seems to me to be gratuitous.

That most people want certain ends—such as survival—for themselves, does not mean they want them for all others, and hence they do not necessarily all want either the same goods or the same good. That certain nations want certain ends—such as peace for themselves—and that this makes it possible for the United Nations to function does not mean that all nations necessarily want peace for all other nations. And to assert that all nations, like all people, if rational, necessarily want the same ends or the same set of ends, labeled the common good, seems to me neither necessary nor true.

This does not mean that communication or cooperation is impossible. It does mean that we can discuss with those who desire to arrive at truth in certain ways which we agree on, and that we can cooperate with certain people when our individual ends are either the same or complementary. It also means that sometimes we may have difficulties with others which we do not know how to resolve. We should act on the assumption that if we keep trying long enough we may arrive at a solution; for unless we try we will not arrive at one. But this is different from claiming not only that all men have something in common but that all men have the same thing in common, namely their general common good, which on inspection turns out to be no particular good and something that varies as the subject at issue varies.

If one had an organic view of mankind, it might be plausible to maintain that the end of the organism is the end of each of its parts and in this sense each of the parts shares the same end which transcends it. This, I take it, and the metaphysics which it supposes, are not what Blanshard gives as reasons in support of his view, and there is no reason to attribute them to him. Without such a view, however, the leap from my greatest good to the claim that the greatest good of all men is the same is a feat which I cannot follow.

(3) If it is the case that men have no one common end, then it cannot be the case that this common end is the basis for our rights against each other. But interestingly enough, when he argues in favor of this latter proposition Blanshard uses an example in which Jones claims the right to repayment of money which Smith borrowed from him. When pressed, Jones finds that the basis for the right to repayment consists in both parties agreeing that a society is better in which promises are kept and debts repaid than one in which they are broken and repudiated. "That this common end is the basis on which Jones is urging his right may be clearly seen by his helplessness if Smith rejects it" (*RG*, 400). I think this is a correct assessment of the situation. It implies the possibility that Jones may not have the same view of society as Smith, and it centers on a particular end which they both hold, viz. a certain kind of society which both would presumably prefer. But this particular end is not some vague single common end which always goes beyond particular ends.

Blanshard finds the basis for rights ultimately in morality and in the production of the greatest good, though he puts it in terms of common ends. He holds that "The good, in the sense of the ethical end, is the most comprehensive possible fulfilment and satisfaction of impulse-desire" (*RG*, 311),[13] and that the summum bonum "is prescribed by human nature itself" (332). I have already indicated my objection to the notion of a single common end for all men. But I do not think it is essential for Blanshard's approach to rights, which in other ways I find most attractive. I have no objection to calling an action right which produces the greatest good nor to saying that what constitutes good for man is dependent in some way on man's nature or makeup. And if we join this with Blanshard's seeming acceptance of the notion that "human nature is almost unbelievably malleable" (*RG*, 357),[14] we are, I believe, on the right track toward explaining the origin of rights, their derivation, and the fact that the list of rights grows and changes and varies—just as the conditions in which man finds himself change and vary. What we need to add is that human rights are also the result of man's historical and social development, and that they result not only from his capacities but also from the ways in which he conceives himself. They can be defended by showing that only in acknowledging them can men achieve the kind of life and society they each desire for themselves.

(4) Lastly, Blanshard holds that the state is the greatest instrument in achieving the common end and hence has rights over its citizens.

That some sort of government is useful and perhaps necessary for most men to live in relative peace and security, and that some sort of government is probably also necessary to build roads and provide for similar common goods, I can easily agree. The argument is a defense of every type of government, except the most corrupt. I think, however, that Blanshard gives us only two choices in dealing with a government, when in fact there are more. For he claims that either it is our moral duty to obey the laws of a government or (to quote this sentence once again) "when it becomes so corrupt as to cut us off from those ends rather than further them, when it serves its purpose so badly that it is better to risk chaos for the sake of a better order than continue to suffer under the old, then resistance becomes a right and a duty" (*RG*, 401–2).

The two choices, I submit, are not derived from Blanshard's general moral criterion. For if we take that seriously, there is no reason not to hold that the production of the greatest good should operate continuously, and that one should prod, goad, protest, and if necessary be civilly disobedient in order to reform and change government at every stage of its career. Before complete revolution is attempted many efforts at change on a smaller scale may be justifiably tried. Moreover, if a system is basically unjust, even if it is reasonably efficient in promoting the general welfare of its citizens, it might be morally right to change it by the resistance which Blanshard seems to reserve only for the completely corrupt.

The principle that what is right is the production of the greatest good should remain a critical principle and be used not only to justify governments but constantly to evaluate and criticize them. Blanshard's move from this principle to a general defense of government in all except extreme circumstances goes farther and gives government more benefit of doubt than is warranted by his arguments or by the facts of history.

IV

What then are we to say of Blanshard's political philosophy as a whole? As he himself says, there is probably nothing novel in it (*RG*, 402). It does nonetheless seem to me to be correct in several of its basic thrusts. On all levels of political life—local, national, international—a rational temper of the type Blanshard describes facilitates discussion, cooperation, and often necessary compromise. We do have reasons for what we do in the political as in other spheres, and the crucial issues are better decided by reason than by unregulated emotion or by force of arms. This does not seem to me to rule out many approaches to political theory; but those that it does rule out will not be sorely missed by most people.

Secondly, I think that Blanshard is correct in maintaining that ultimately the justification for government and for laws is moral. I have indicated that I do not agree that all political questions or problems are moral questions or problems. But I think it is correct to say that governmental systems and the actions of governments should be subject to continual moral scrutiny. In a society, national or international, where there are many varying views on what is right and what is good, absolutism in morality as a rule does more harm than good. I would therefore opt for a government which made possible the greatest amount of freedom on the individual level and allowed individuals the greatest scope possible in developing their capacities and reaching their fulfillment and satisfaction. This goal, I take it, is compatible with Blanshard's position, despite the fact that his emphasis is on what is objectively right. A government cannot give individual fulfillment or satisfaction; it can merely make it possible for individuals to achieve it. Though no man or country need compromise its values, it may well come to see that more harm than good is done by attempting to impose them on others.

Thirdly, Blanshard is correct, I think, in seeking the basis of rights in human nature. We have the rights we do because we have the duties we do; and both our duties and our rights are what they are because we are the kinds of beings we are. This means not only that we have the drives and impulses that we do but also that we have developed socially the way we have. To deny that we have the rights we now acknowledge would be to conceive ourselves as different and to choose different patterns of action and a different quality of social life from that which we presently have. If human nature is indefinitely malleable, however, it is possible for man to seek other goods than those we seek; and men have certainly lived in societies which did not recognize the rights we feel are so central.

I have indicated some of my misgivings about specific details of Blanshard's presentation of his political theory. In many instances I can only wish that he had pursued the topic further. The theory he leaves us with, as I have indicated, can be used to justify any except the most pernicious governments. Though his sympathies are obviously with some type of democratic government, he does not venture into the second level of political theory to defend or evaluate any particular types. Nor does he engage in utopian dreams, describing what his elusive greatest good, if achieved, might require in the way of social organization.

There are, however, two final points, central to any political theory, to which it seems Blanshard has paid too little attention, and without which his theory is open to abuses to which I am sure he would be unhappy to see it put. The first concerns justice, the second the worth of the individual person. It is true that Blanshard lists justice as an attribute of the rational mind. But it seems to me to be of paramount importance with respect to the functioning of a state or government. In our imperfect world a government cannot bring about ideal conditions for fulfillment and satisfaction; its leaders will surely blunder here and there; and the goods it can produce for the use of its citizens will be bought at the expense of other goods or activities which it could not produce or make available. But in all this, justice is not simply on a par with the other virtues or with the other characteristics one seeks to embody in a government or a legal system. The question of distributive justice has frequently been considered one of the central topics in political theory. I am uncertain whether Blanshard feels that the question of justice will automatically be taken care of if men and governments adopt the rational temper, or whether he feels that the general principle of the production of the greatest good adequately handles the question of justice. If, however, government is not so much a producer of goods as an arbiter among conflicting claims and impulses and desires, justice is a key factor which cannot be assumed.

Secondly, I am uneasy about Blanshard's failure to discuss the function or status of the individual person within the state. It is not without reason that the first ten amendments to the United States Constitution were felt necessary by our forefathers. If a government takes as its charge the production of the common good, and if, as Blanshard claims, no rights are inalienable, it seems completely compatible with this line of reasoning that certain people might simply be sacrificed to the greater good, should the occasion arise. I am not saying that Blanshard would advocate such action; but it seems to me perfectly possible to justify such actions on his scheme, providing one balances the scale with enough future satisfaction and fulfillment. Hitler's attempted extermination of the Jews and Stalin's extermination of the kulaks both were defended by some versions of the argument that more good would be produced by such actions than would be otherwise available. Similar arguments have been used in favor of sterilizing morons or people with certain diseases or deformities. Not only does Blanshard build in no explicit defense of the individual person; he is also liable to misinterpretation as an elitist, for the only right he guarantees all is the right to be considered. Once consideration is made, those with higher capacities are to be preferred—and reason stands very high on the scale of values. An argument for an intellectual elite to decide on the common good is not a far step from his position, though one that Blanshard would not, I think, himself advocate. Lacking from his view is a defense of the person and his rights against the majority and the common good, and a consideration of the claim which every person has not only to be considered but to share to some extent in the allocation of goods.

Professor Blanshard has chosen to avoid the murky empirical tangles of the second and third levels of political philosophy and has instead adopted and refined some classic lines of political thought. He can hardly be faulted for having attempted no more. In the essay entitled "Can Men Be Reasonable?" he noted that "the most practical service that any philosopher can render" is to help prepare the way for "a popular trust in reason, a pride in its private exercise, a general demand that the issues between man and man, race and race, nation and nation, be settled in accordance with it."[15] That he has taken this general task extremely seriously is evident to anyone who has read his books and articles.

RICHARD T. DE GEORGE

DEPARTMENT OF PHILOSOPHY
THE UNIVERSITY OF KANSAS

NOTES

[1] Brand Blanshard, "Metaphysics and Social Attitudes," *Social Frontier* 4, no. 30 (1937):79–81; see also Brand Blanshard, "Metaphysics and Social Attitudes: A Rejoinder," *Social Frontier* 4, no. 34 (1938):219–21.

[2] Brand Blanshard, "Morality and Politics," in *Ethics and Society,* ed. Richard T. DeGeorge (Garden City, N.Y.: Doubleday, Anchor Books, 1966), 1.

[3] Ibid., 3–9; Brand Blanshard, "Can Men Be Reasonable?" in *Our Emergent Civilization,* ed. Ruth Nanda Anshen (New York and London: Harper & Brothers, 1947), 26.

[4] "Morality and Politics," 18.

[5] "Metaphysics and Social Attitudes," 80.

[6] See the citations in n. 3 above. See also *Reason and Goodness (RG),* 377–79, for Blanshard's arguments against anarchism. In this instance he not only expresses his attitude but presents arguments in defense of his negative evaluation of anarchism.

[7] Brand Blanshard, "Reflections on Economic Determinism," *Journal of Philosophy* 63, no. 7 (1966):169–78.

[8] The chapter "Reason and Politics" extends from p. 375 to p. 408. The last five chapters of his book contain the positive statement of his own ethical position.

[9] This article recapitulates and summarizes Blanshard's political philosophy as presented in *RG*. It is interesting as much for what it leaves out from the earlier statement as for what it includes and reworks.

[10] Blanshard, "Reflections on Economic Determinism," 174–75; "Metaphysics and Social Attitudes: A Rejoinder," 220.

[11] "Morality and Politics," 1.

[12] That the view cited above is not simply a slip of the pen but a position Blanshard truly holds seems to be reinforced by his similar claim in "Morality and Politics," 2: "I should suggest that any question is a moral question whose decision depends on a choice between values. A non-moral question becomes moral the instant values are introduced."

[13]The sentence is italicized in the original.
[14]Quoted from Margaret Mead.
[15]Blanshard, *Our Emergent Civilization*, 48.

8. RICHARD T. DE GEORGE

Blanshard's Political Philosophy

Mr. De George's paper is the only one in this book that deals with my political theory, and I may fittingly comment on it here; for my political theory, such as it is, grows directly out of my ethics. Mr. De George does not think this transition from the one theory to the other is made successfully. Indeed he thinks the ethical foundation pretty sandy and the political house constructed on it a very wobbly structure. When he has finished with it, not much remains but rubble; even the four pillars that I fancied as giving it at least a pleasant façade lie about in pieces like the broken columns of the Parthenon. It is true that Mr. De George finds some points of agreement at the end, and my spirits revive a little as I review his objections. For many of these seem to be objections not to the theory I thought I was advocating; they are arrows shot at some other theory that is strutting about in my clothes and wearing a mask. Mr. De George takes aim with deadly effect at a Mr. Hyde who is standing front center on the stage, while all the time Dr. Jekyll (meaning me) sits near by feeling curiously composed. I am afraid, therefore, that much of this paper will be devoted, not to attempts at healing mortal wounds, but rather to disengaging myself from the figure that Mr. De George has so effectively demolished.

The political material I have provided Mr. De George is very scanty, consisting of a chapter in *Reason and Goodness* and a few scattered articles. These are all discussions of general principles; in none of them do I say where I stand in practical politics, nor do I suppose this a matter of much interest to such readers as I may have. But since Mr. De George has intimated an interest in this, let me say a word about it now. In my youth I was inclined to socialism, like so many others of that time; I once substituted for Norman Thomas on the radio in a presidential campaign; and I supported the insurgent cause in the war against Franco vigorously enough to hope for notice by the F.B.I., though I apparently proved too inconsequential. My socialist sympathies suffered a severe frost as a result of developments in Russia, especially the trials of 1936. Such study of Marxism as I have made has convinced me of the falsity of its main principles, though I think it should be studied by philosophers in the way in which Mr. De George has given an admirable lead. I am a member of the Society for the Study of Dialectical Materialism, and helped the society to gain admission to the Federation of Philosophical Societies at the congress in Venice. Before America entered the First World War, I served in the somewhat unheroic capacity of an army Y. M. C. A. secretary with the British troops on the Tigris, and was in uniform later with the American army in France. I hated Hitler so cordially that, though a Quaker, I supported the White Committee in its attempt to involve America in the war long before Pearl Harbor. I was an ardent supporter of the League of Nations, and still think that if it had been equipped with the necessary force to resist the Japanese aggression of 1932 and the Italian invasion of Ethiopia in 1935, the Second World War would probably not have occurred. I am a supporter also of the United Nations, though I think the antipathy that has developed in the less civilized world toward the more civilized (I dislike mealy-mouthedness in these matters) bodes ill for the future. To complete these short and simple annals, I have voted the Democratic ticket for the last forty years.

Ethics and Politics

Mr. De George in his opening pages raises a further question of a more general nature. He refers to a discussion I had with Sidney Hook long ago in the pages of *The Social Frontier,* in which Mr. Hook argued, as I recall, that rationalism had usually been conjoined with conservatism and empiricism with liberalism. I argued that, on the contrary, no fixed relation was discoverable between a thinker's metaphysical or epistemological outlook on the one hand and his political attitudes on the other. Bacon and Hume, for example, combined political conservatism with empiricism; Spinoza, Green, and Bosanquet combined liberalism with rationalism. Mr. De George wonders whether I think a philosopher's ethical theory sits equally loose to his attitudes in politics. No, I do not think it does or should. When Hitler gave to Mussolini as a birthday present a finely bound set of Nietzsche, the gift was surely symbolic; both men, I think, found in the ethics of the superman some sanction for what they were doing. I heard H. H. Asquith once remark that Mill's essay on *Liberty* was the charter of the Liberal party in England. Can one doubt that the treatment accorded by early New England to witches and heretics came straight from the ethics of the Old Testament, as incorporated into the Massachusetts theocracy? Ethics, as Frank Chapman Sharp used to say, is an attempt to set up the goalposts of life; and it obviously makes a difference to one's attitudes, both personal and political, whether one's goal is one's own pleasure, the greatest pleasure of the many, the fullest self-realization for all, the support of an elite class, or the achievement of personal or national power. A man's convictions on these ultimate ends bear directly and importantly on his political votes and values. If one wants contemporary instances of how incompatible ethical theories can drive their holders in different political directions, I should suggest a study of John Dewey and Ayn Rand.

Mr. De George would apparently disagree. He points out that emotivists in ethics argue their political issues very much as the rest of us do. "I am inclined to believe, therefore, that Blanshard's thesis concerning the lack of any fixed connection between a philosopher's metaphysical position and his political and social attitudes can be extended so as validly to hold between the latter and one's ethical theory." Now emotivism is a special case; it belongs to metaethics rather than to ethics proper; it does not commit one to any view of the ends or means of the good life; it is essentially a denial that good and evil, right and wrong, are matters of knowledge at all; such words express only favoring or disfavoring emotions. Revolutionary as this theory is, Mr. De George thinks that it exercises little or no influence on the emotivist's social views or ways of arguing. "His position on the meaning of the terms 'good' and 'bad' does not preclude his using them, nor does it preclude his trying to persuade others to join him in certain actions. He can certainly try to change their attitudes by adducing facts, describing consequences, and doing similar things, while still maintaining that none of his arguments can force others who admit the facts and the validity of his arguments to change their attitudes."

To some extent I can agree here with Mr. De George. Men like Ayer and Russell, who have adopted an emotivist theory, do often argue political issues exactly as if they thought there was an objective truth to be discovered and argumentation might bring it to light. Russell, though an emotivist, was a passionate rationalist in politics, perpetually arguing for a rational solution to issues of political right and wrong. But what does this prove? That emotivism is irrelevant to political convictions? I think not. All it proves is how illogical an eminent logician can be. Russell was offering these pleas for rationality in politics at the same time when he was urging that issues of right and wrong were outside the province of reason altogether. As an emotivist, he could not believe there was an objective right and wrong to be found about American intervention in Viet Nam, but he called together a convention of European intelligentsia in Stockholm to pronounce impartial judgment on President Johnson's policies. He must have known that this was inconsistent with his emotivism, and indeed he confessed his dissatisfaction with his own ethical theory. My objection is not to Russell's case against the war, which had much force, nor that the jury he selected was not impartial, though indeed it was far from being so, but that the very idea of an impartial tribunal is precluded by emotivism. An impartial judgment is one that expresses exclusively the requirement of the evidence; an ethical judgment for the emotivist is one that exclusively expresses feeling. And how could any tribunal, a world court, for example, pass solemn judgment on conflicting feelings? The judgment itself would be the expression of a third set of feelings. This is frivolous. The weight of such a judgment about, say, the Arab-Israeli struggle may be imagined.

The tendency of emotivism in politics is therefore toward an appeal to force. If there is no objectively right solution to a conflict, it is idle for reason to attempt to find it, and where a rational settlement is impossible, the resort to force becomes more tempting. Mr. De George says that the emotivist can still argue with his opponents; he can still "try to change their attitudes by adducing facts, describing consequences, and doing similar things, while still maintaining that none of his arguments can force others . . . to change their attitudes." What is the meaning here of "force"? In the context it must mean "provide logically compelling evidence." But if no argument or set of arguments can be logically compelling, it is presumably because evidence is not relevant to feelings as it is to propositions. No evidence will show a feeling to be true. And in that case it is hard to see the difference between argument and propaganda. To surround the Chinese with Chairman Mao's picture proved a highly effective means of changing the Chinese attitudes toward the Chairman and his party. Is there anything wrong with it? I do not see how an emotivist could protest against it with any weight, for that would merely vent one's feelings against what the Chinese people, by their different attitude, have shown to be right in the only sense in which right now has any meaning. Why indeed should not such manipulation of feeling become the standard method of political argument? In a world in which there is nothing right or wrong but feeling makes it so, the proper maxim would seem to be that nothing succeeds like success.

Mr. De George regrets that I have not dealt more seriously with "attitude" and "good reason" theories of ethics. I have in fact dealt with some of them and found them wanting in the chapter on "The Linguistic Retreat from Emotivism" in *Reason and Goodness*.

My conclusion is that, men being what they are, one cannot be sure how much their ethical conviction will affect their political conduct, but that it will affect that conduct profoundly if they attempt to make theory and practice consistent.

Mr. De George divides his main discussion of my politics into four sections, and it will be convenient in my own discussion to follow suit.

Why Should I Obey the Law?

In the attempt to classify my political theory, he distinguishes three types of political philosophy in descending order of generality. The first deals with such questions as: What is the justification for having government or law at all? On the second level such questions are asked as, What is the justification for this or that special form of government? On the third level are such questions as, What is the justification for this particular law and under what conditions would civil disobedience to it be justified? Mr. De George rightly takes my work to belong on the first of these levels. The question I set out to answer was Why should I obey the law?, which resolves itself after a moment's reflection into What is the ground of the government's claim to my obedience? And after another moment that becomes, What is the justification for having government at all? This is the fundamental question of political philosophy.

Mr. De George finds these questions meaningful, but he also finds two dangers in their discussion. The first is the danger of the armchair approach. Philosophers need to be reminded that "political philosophy is a practical branch of philosophy." A political thinker should be in touch with people's actual thought and feelings about politics; for if his thoughts are "simply the armchair musings of a solitary individual," they are unlikely to have any common sense rootage or practical flowering. I think Mr. De George would classify me not only as a philosopher of high generality but also of the armchair type; he says of me, "He is not interested so much in what people believe or what they have believed, as in what is true." I admit this happily, for I think it is what a philosopher ought to be. Am I also an armchair philosopher? Yes; and I am inclined to think that this too is what a philosopher should be. At any rate, I cannot see that it is of any great advantage to a thinker on ultimate questions to have stood on the barricades or to have engaged in the toil and sweat of practical politics. If one looks back on the thinkers who have written the classic books on political theory, were not most of them armchair philosophers? Hobbes, Spinoza, Locke, Rousseau, Hegel, Bentham, Green, Sidgwick—which of these men ever held a responsible political office? Mill did hold a seat in Parliament for one term and was thrown out at the end; Disraeli's sardonic comment on hearing him in Parliament was "Ah, the finishing governess!" I am of the Platonic way of thinking about philosophers; they are contemplators, not doers; men of thought rather than of action; and though, if one is writing on the second or third level of generality, as Mill did, practical experience probably helps, it is of little value on the first and highest.

The second difficulty Mr. De George finds with my account of political ends is that it is too general to provide guidance, and may even misguide.

Were the American colonists laying down the right lines for their new state when they wrote: "We hold these truths to be self-evident, that all men are created equal, that they are endowed by their Creator with certain unalienable rights, that among these are life, liberty, and the pursuit of happiness"? I pointed out that these rights cannot be "self-evident" and "unalienable," for then they would be without exception, whereas the colonists themselves would not extend the right of life to murderers or the right to freedom of speech and action to Benedict Arnold. Mr. De George reminds us that to deny this theory of natural rights is to say that the founding fathers were acting on a mistake. So they were. But then he wants to know how anyone, on my theory, can justify the Revolution at all. In *Reason and Goodness* I state as clearly as I can my views of the ethical end, of the function of the state as a means to that end, and of the conditions under which it is legitimate to attempt an overthrow of the state. Mr. De George thinks these conditions too vague to assure us even that our own Revolution was justified.

I admit this, though with equanimity. No statement of the end of man, or of his political end, or of the general conditions that make resistance justifiable, can supply sufficient directions for the particular case. I took the line, following Green, that since even a bad government is better than anarchy, revolt against one's government, as distinct from the endeavor to reform it, is justified only in extreme cases such as corruption so firmly entrenched that the risk of anarchy through civil war would seem more acceptable. Were these conditions fulfilled by the American Revolution? Were they fulfilled by any of the other three great modern revolutions, the French, the Russian, and the Chinese? Certainly I should not feel able myself to give a confident answer in any of these cases. For in every such case there are scores of considerations making for each side and involving various degrees of good and evil, so that the actual decision will depend on an intuitive sense of the comparative weights of two vast aggregates of factors. General rules are helpful, even in cases like these, but their value is rather to suggest the kinds of consideration that are most important to a decision, not the decision itself. So the generality of my theory here, though it is to be regretted, is unavoidable.

Mr. De George thinks that my test for the rightness of a revolt differs from my general test of rightness. It is not meant to differ, and I do not see that it does. Government is a means to good; so is conduct generally; and when, in either a personal or a political case, the means are inappropriate to the end, they should be changed. People will of course differ widely as to what should be done, particularly when, as in political issues, class and business as well as personal interests clash. But that does not make it any the less true that there is one course which, in any given case, it would be best to follow. Men will have recourse to different means in different circumstances. Still, their end is, or should be, the same, the good of mankind, whether they act as persons or also as citizens. Mr. De George remarks in criticism that even when that end is carefully defined, it still does not tell us with certainty what to do, either as persons or as citizens, since we can never know that some alternative might not have been better. True. But no ethics can ever tell us this. As C. D. Broad has said, "On any ethical theory which attempts to do justice to all the facts, estimates will have to be made in comparison with which those demanded by Hedonism would be child's play" (*Five Types of Ethical Theory,* 239).[1] Professor Prichard, a distinguished moralist, said that he was not sure he had ever done a right act. He said this, of course, not because he was an exceptionally wicked man—he was an exceptionally good one—but because he knew, as a reflective moralist, the enormous difficulties of discovering the one act whose consequences would in the long run prove best, or as he would prefer to say, most obligatory. Morality is a continuous struggle to do the impossible, to find the right act and to do it. It is one's duty, nonetheless, to try.

Moral Choices as Choices between Values

In his second section, Mr. De George considers three propositions of mine:

(1) All problems involving a choice between values are moral problems.

(2) All political problems involve a choice between values.

(3) All political problems are moral problems.

(1) It is easy to see why I should subscribe to the first of these. The objectively right act in any situation I hold to be that which will produce the best consequences on the whole, that is, the greatest amount of intrinsic value. This means that a morally right or wrong act is *defined* by reference to a choice between amounts of value. If a choice involves no apparent difference between values at all, as when I decide to take my walk at 2:00 instead of 2:30, it would be generally admitted that the choice is not a moral one. But if I recall that I agreed to pick up Smith as a companion at 2:15, everyone would admit that the choice has become a moral one. Why? Because now values have come into the picture. If I go at 2:00, I shall be able to pick up Smith as I promised; if I go at 2:30, I shall not only break an agreement but give rise to frustration, disappointment, and loss of time to another. It seemed obvious to me in the light of such considerations that the best criterion of whether an action fell within the moral sphere was whether it involved either an increase or decrease of value.

Mr. De George cannot accept this. "It is certainly not what the plain man would consider moral questions to be . . . ." This is probably true. The plain man is inclined to reserve the term "moral" for problems where values of importance are involved, and would hardly condemn himself for moral wrongdoing if he failed to answer a letter quite promptly or bought a meal consisting entirely of desserts. But the plain man and his usage are not authorities in philosophy, and he would certainly give us no clear guidance as to where the line should be drawn between important and unimportant values. It seemed to me better, therefore, not to try to draw this wavering line at all, but to adopt the course required by the logic of the situation, and to class all acts as moral that affect the amount of value in the world. This would indeed place nearly all our acts under the headings of moral or immoral. If it is objected that this would place a premium on priggishness, the answer is that it does not in the least compel us to take all acts with equal and solemn seriousness; it leaves plenty of room for the morally trivial as well as the morally important; it insists only that they all may be regarded legitimately from the moral point of view.

Mr. De George suggests that this would lead us to the absurd result of charging a painter with moral wrongdoing if he put a patch of color in an aesthetically unfitting place. And it is true that no one would blame him for this, if he were engaged in play or experimentation. Would one still refuse to do so if he did it deliberately and with the knowledge that it would lower the work's value to the person who may have commissioned it or to an exhibition in which it was to be hung? Of course the putting in of the obtrusive patch might be a mere mistake as to what was aesthetically fitting. We need here to be clear between two meanings of "wrong" that are current among moralists. An act may be "morally wrong" in the sense that it springs from a bad motive; it is objectively wrong in our sense if its consequences are worse than those of some alternative open to the agent. A man may with the best of intentions do something that turns out disastrously. It would be absurd to call a mistake of the painter "morally wrong"; but if his action led to the bad consequences we have mentioned, what he did would remain wrong in the standard, technical sense in which we have used the term. I do not see that with these explanations there need be any confusion.

Political Choices as Value Choices

(2) My second proposition was that all political problems involve a choice between values. By a political problem I mean one that may suitably be dealt with by government or its agencies, or which affects the structure or functions of government. Random examples are: whether a legislative body should pass a law regarding taxation or immigration or the post office, whether a voter at an election should vote for the conservative or the liberal party, whether a court should condemn a certain property for use as a public road, whether banks or railroads or mines should be publicly or privately owned. I do not

see how it can be denied that these are problems affecting the public welfare, which means the advantage or disadvantage of persons; and on my view that makes the problems moral. Mr. De George demurs, though he does not pursue the matter at length. "It is at the polls that they [the citizens] are given a choice between competing candidates, parties, platforms, and so between competing values. On Blanshard's view it would seem that when one steps into the polling booth one is faced with a moral choice. . . . But of course no one knows which candidates are objectively the best, and there is no way to determine this conclusively. . . ." But to say that a problem is not one of values or morality because it cannot be determined conclusively is, as we have seen, a non sequitur. The way to refute my second proposition is to adduce instances of political problems that do *not* turn on results in the way of value to the persons affected. And no such instances seem to be forthcoming.

Are All Political Problems Moral?

(3) Mr. De George pays little attention to the second proposition, because his interest is fixed chiefly and rightly on the third, that all political problems are moral. We could not expect him to accept the conclusion of a syllogism whose major and minor premises he rejects, and on that conclusion he directs his strongest fire.

I am puzzled by his line of argument. "When Blanshard claims that all political problems are in the end ethical problems he seems to argue for two independent assertions. The first is that it is immoral to disobey any law. The second is that the ultimate justification of government is a moral justification." Now the first of these propositions I have never held; indeed I have explicitly supported its opposite. I have written (*Reason and Goodness,* 401): "Does it follow that since the state is a necessary means to our major ends, we should in all circumstances obey it, that we never have the right to rebel? Not at all. Our view would not only justify disobedience in some cases; it would require it." But this point has already been touched upon. Of the second assertion, that the ultimate justification of government is moral, Mr. De George says he thinks it is true with the reservation added, "though it does not entail that all political problems are ethical problems." But I think it does entail this. Suppose one were maintaining to a skeptic that one ought to use one's privilege of voting, or ought to pay one's income tax, or to urge an enlargement of the police force. "Why?" asks the skeptic. My own answer would be, "Because it helps the state to do its work more efficiently," and no doubt I should go on and try to specify the ways. The skeptic can argue that these ways are ineffective, but if by this he means "ineffective in promoting human good," he seems to be admitting that such promotion is the end of the state. Suppose that, seeing this, he plays his last card and questions the need of a state at all. Mr. De George admits that at this point he would resort to a moral justification of the state. But can he afford to do this? If all political actions are designed to help or hinder the state in performing its functions, and these functions are to be justified by their promotion of the moral end of its citizens or mankind, then every political action is in the last resort to be justified in the same way. "In the last resort" does not make the argument merely formal or trivial; it makes it fundamental.

Mr. De George has further difficulties with the thesis that all political acts are moral. In a civilized community, murder is of course regarded as an immoral act; it is also an illegal act; is the murderer therefore committing two different offenses, one of which is to be punished by moral disapproval, the other by a legal penalty? The answer is surely No. He is committing one offense which is so grossly immoral that the community has seen fit to make it illegal also and to attach severe penalties to it. I doubt if there is any real difference here between Mr. De George's view and mine.

He adduces another instance, however, in which he thinks there is such a difference. Is it morally wrong to violate a parking regulation and to leave one's car in a given space longer than the regulation permits? Normally I think it is. The law was laid down because people who took liberties of that kind were restricting the freedom of others, and that is something one should try to avoid. But suppose, Mr. De George persists, that it is a rainy day, and there are plenty of alternative spaces to park in. I agree that if the "offense" is a moral offense at all, it approaches the vanishing point. Further, it does not even violate the spirit of the law, since that law was not imposed to meet conditions of this kind. But is any wrongdoing at all involved? Mr. De George thinks one can say that only if one holds that there is something wrong in breaking the law as such. Now I have admitted that it is not always wrong to break the law; sometimes it is a necessity. But I persist in thinking it a moral duty to *respect* the law, even where the public advantage of obeying it is, as here, at the vanishing point. What does this mean? It means that one is not at liberty to violate the law "other things equal," i.e. public and private advantage being equal; it means that one should assume the burden of proof, and that if one feels a violation to be called for, one should commit it with reluctance. Further, one is not free to disobey a law simply because one dislikes or even disapproves it; if the citizens of a country could pick and choose which laws they cared to obey, chaos would be the result. In a country like ours, law represents what the people, through their representatives, regard as the minimum that the community should demand of its members to promote the welfare of all; and the very fact that they have legislated a certain line of conduct is a prima facie reason for obeying it. If one disobeys it, the disobedience should be confined to the exceptional case in which the greater good itself clearly supports the violation.

Mr. De George quotes from me the statement: "Ultimately, therefore, political obligation, even that of obeying a morally bad law, *is* a moral obligation; and when, as occasionally happens, it becomes a duty to disobey, the ground is still the same." This seems to him a paradox at best. But there is no inconsistency in it. Law deals with classes of cases; it lays down how people generally or members of some large class should act if the good of all is to be promoted. But it cannot provide for the unique cases and for every contingency. Ordinarily one should heed red signals; but if a man is trying to get a friend with a heart attack to a hospital, the very thing—the greater good—which dictates obedience to the rule of not driving through a red light may dictate an exception to it. There is no sort of inconsistency here.

I have said that in general it is one's duty to obey law, even a law that one disapproves. One may disapprove the income tax as eloquently as Edmund Wilson did, but I do not think that this justified him in persistently ignoring it and complaining loudly when the law caught up with him. Mr. De George says that there is an alternative to my view of the general duty of obedience to law, an alternative which he does not develop but which, for all I know, may be his own. This is "to deny that immoral laws impose any obligation from even a political point of view." The alternative does not seem to me eligible. "Immoral" may mean either what certain disaffected citizens take to be immoral, or what is really immoral. (a) If it is the former, suppose a group of narcotics peddlers think a ban on heroin an immoral invasion of their freedom. They would then not only be morally justified in breaking the law but, since they have no political obligation to obey it either, have committed no crime in disobeying it; and the police and the courts would have to keep hands off. (b) "Immoral" more probably means here objectively wrong in the technical ethical sense. Now many if not most of our laws are immoral in this sense, the sense, that is, of not serving the public good as well as some possible alternative law. There would in that case be no obligation, even of a political kind, to obey them. This is surely an extreme position. Furthermore, it would make legal obligation depend on morality to an extent that not even I had thought of.

My tendency to regard politics as applied ethics is rendered implausible to Mr. De George by the further fact that while ethics deals chiefly with the relations of man and man, politics must deal with the relations between state and state. When one state takes advantage of another by excluding its products or its emigrants, or takes control of another by colonization or by war, to whom exactly does the supposed moral blame attach—the head of the offending state, its parliament, its army, or the people as a whole? It is often impossible to say. And when it is thus impossible to bring home to its perpetrators any definite responsibility for wrongdoing, does it make sense to talk in moral terms about the rights and duties of nations?

It makes excellent sense. Indeed it is perhaps in international affairs that we can see most clearly the relation of law to morals, and observe on the most impressive scale the emergence of law from ethics. In a strict sense international law scarcely exists, for there is no world government to promulgate or enforce it. But because of the frequency and growing destructiveness of war, and the increasing dependence of nations upon each other for food, fuel, and the tools of civilization, nations are little by little framing explicit agreements in which those practices which a moral consensus of mankind regards as most intolerable are prohibited. There is no enforceable law governing genocide, or colonial exploitation, or the torture of prisoners, or unprovoked aggression, or the extinction of the tuna fish or the whale, but in the United Nations at least one can fairly feel the moral indignation against such conduct crystallizing itself into codes that have almost the force of law. What are they based on? They are based unambiguously on the sense, among great powers and small, that certain kinds of conduct must be outlawed by the good of mankind. This does not mean that nations and groups of nations do not at times make treaties that are cynically selfish. It does mean that the moral opinion of the world is making itself felt with increasing power and definiteness against the inequity of such treaties and in favor of a greater fairness in new ones. And the need of a world government with power to enforce these agreements is coming to be felt more keenly. In recent decades we have been able to see with our own eyes the process of ethics transforming itself into something like law.

If statesmen are to be governed by moral considerations, Mr. De George asks, whose good is to be consulted, that of their own people or that of mankind? I think it would be generally agreed that their first duty is to their own people. But no civilized statesman would say that his duty stopped there. There is a growing sense that a wealthy nation should not allow a poorer neighbor to starve without sacrifices in its behalf, but national practice in these matters has condoned a degree of indifference that lags behind individual ethics, and it is safe to say that no clear consensus has yet emerged as to where the line should be drawn between national self-interest and the obligation to others. All one can say with confidence is that when it finally is drawn it will be drawn by an awakened international conscience.

The Actual and the Rational Will

In his third section Mr. De George considers what I regard as the four cardinal points in my political theory, and, I am sorry to note, rejects them all. To develop my case for them in full would require more space than can well be afforded, but I shall try to deal briefly with the main objections.

(1) My theory is a modified form of the theory of a general will first stated by Rousseau, but worked out in far more acceptable form by Green, Bosan-

quet, and Hobhouse. It turns on the distinction in each person between his rational will and his actual will. His actual will is easily described; it is for what he immediately wants. The goal of his rational will is a more speculative notion. It is what his reason would prescribe as his proper end in the long run; and I argued that this was to make the world as much better as possible. It is obvious that the rational man will often place a veto on his actual will because he will see that to indulge it will retard rather than advance the achievement of his rational will.

To this Mr. De George objects (a) that the rational will "constitutes excess baggage not required for either his [Blanshard's] ethical or his political theory." Excess baggage! I had supposed it was the keystone of the arch, without which both my ethical and political theory would fall to the ground. If the objection had taken a psychological turn and held that there was no such will, I should have been in trouble with some psychologists. For the end of this desire is admittedly not on a level with those of other desires, but a rational construction; it is what we should desire as an ultimate end if our desires were governed by our reason. When that question is raised, one answer alone seems to me acceptable, namely the greatest good of sentient beings. It is the indispensable, ideal test of the rightness of any act.

(b) It is objected that "what we actually will is never the object of our rational will." Nor can it even form part of our rational will. But if the two then fall hopelessly apart, how can we take even the first step toward our end? Now it is true that the person who has completed only part of a journey is never at the end of it. There is always a good lying beyond anything actually achieved, a duty never done; the actual never overtakes the ideal. But even the remotest goal must be approached step by step, and all that can be asked of us, because it is all that we can do, is to take the next step in the right direction. The next step, though not the goal itself, is still a means to it and therefore prescribed by it.

(c) It is objected that the rational good is a chimera. The only existing values are those actually experienced; the goal of the rational will is not experienced, and presumably never will be; so it is not strictly a good at all. We must admit that this and indeed all other ends are unreal, since by hypothesis they are unrealized. But if the rational good is by hypothesis unrealized, it is also by hypothesis that which if realized would be the greatest of all goods. A goal or end is not rendered illusory by being unattained, or even by being unattainable, but only by being misconceived. The goal of the rational will remains ultimate and valid if approximation to it would bring more good than approximation to any alternative end.

(d) "But we cannot ever say what it is, because it is not any single thing or any set of goods." This too is true, but I do not see that it raises any great difficulty. We cannot at present know definitely what would fulfill any of our faculties in the end, for humanity is evolving and our powers are evolving with it. What satisfied the physicist's impulse to know in the seventeenth century does not satisfy it today. One can to a certain extent plot the trajectory of advance, but never very far. Still, we can see that in the realm of knowledge, for example, we are driving toward a coherent system, and that is definite enough to provide both the outlines of a goal and a useful working test. To be sure, we cannot fill in the detail. But to insist on knowing the detail in advance could virtually disqualify all ends at once, for we can know that detail only as the ends vanish into their realization.

Is There a Common Good?

(2) I have argued not only that there is a rational good, but that it is the same for all men. This does not mean that we all want to occupy the same ground, or to own the same house, or eat the same bread. In that sense your good and mine can never be the same, since you are a different person, whose fulfillments and satisfactions must obviously be yours alone. Where is the sense, then, in saying that we do, or might, seek the same ultimate good? It lies in recognizing that our desires are not confined to our own experiences. A father can desire the good of his children, a patriot the good of his people. Though we cannot share the same immediate good, we can desire the same ultimate good. When the interests of two persons conflict, there is therefore a better solution than fighting it out. If they both have, beyond their interest in their own advantage, an interest also in the general good, this shared interest may and often does solve their problem. Is it unreasonable to ask of a reasonable man that he should consider which claim would better accord with the general good? It may be that if he does so consider the matter, he will be called upon to modify his own claim. But he can hardly object to such modification if it would plainly subserve his interest in the largest good. There is probably only one adjustment of the two claims that will most subserve this common end, and if the two claimants are reasonable, they will both have an interest in finding it.

(a) Mr. De George puts his finger here on an ancient difficulty that has troubled some moralists seriously. If a father sees that only a sacrifice on his own part can fulfill the needs and ambitions of his son, he might of course take the line, "Why should I sacrifice my own goods for others that I shall never know? *I* am giving up goods whose loss I feel acutely: *I* shall never experience those goods that will be purchased by my sacrifice; I am being asked to give something for nothing." This argument is sometimes taken by the egoist as showing that altruism is unreasonable. That is just what it does not show. If one can see that good A is intrinsically better than good B, reasonableness lies in producing A, whether A falls in one's own experience or another's. Mr. De George takes exception to saying that the duty of self-sacrifice is "self-evident," particularly if the sacrifice is great. He writes, "I think it requires a good deal of argumentation, which Blanshard fails to produce." But on the logical side, I do not see that argument is necessary; it *is* sometimes self-evident that one good is greater than another, and that one has a duty resulting from that insight. The real difficulty is rather psychological. Such a victory of rational insight over the weakness of the flesh may seem like a miracle, or at the least sheer saintliness. But the testimony to its possibility is overwhelming. There are numberless parents who have sacrificed their own good for that of their children. And one likes to think it was not mere heroics that led Nathan Hale to say he regretted that he had but one life to give for his country.

(b) Mr. De George is inclined to admit that men do have one end in common, namely truth. It seems clear enough that unless they were jointly interested in truth, they would not wrangle with each other about it, and that unless they meant the same thing by it, they would have no measure that they could jointly apply. But it does not follow, Mr. De George points out, that the ends of their other impulses are similarly held in common, or that they have the same conception of the end of life as a whole. Now it seems to me that in one sense this view is obviously true, and in another sense almost equally obviously false. The set of experienced goods that would mean fulfillment for Mrs. Siddons would not mean fulfillment for Dr. Johnson, and their life plans were correspondingly different. But if they found these plans good, it was because by means of them they were able to fulfill their differing bents and capacities. It would of course be impossible for anyone to list all the bents and capacities evinced by the billions of persons that are beginning to overrun the earth, or to enter by imagination into the myriad goods of mankind. But if even the most general sketch of the goal of our theoretical impulse enables us to direct our search and measure our progress toward it, so a general knowledge of what makes experience good makes progress toward it practicable and roughly measurable. And I have argued that this general character or constitution of intrinsic goodness is known to us. It is the joint presence in experience of the fulfillment of human need and desire and the satisfaction or happiness that attends this. We do not have to show that this conception of human good is explicit in men's minds, or forms for most men a conscious and dominating goal. All I should contend is that it *is* the inevitable goal, and that as men advance in rationality it is bound to become more explicit and more dominant.

A Common End as the Ground of Rights

(3) My third political thesis is that the possession of a common end is the basis of men's rights against each other. If Smith borrows from Jones, and Jones asks repayment, on what can he base his claim? Only on the assump-

tion that Smith, like himself, prefers a society in which debts are repaid to one in which they are not. If Smith declares that he has no interest and sees no superiority in such a society, Jones's argument will fall on deaf ears. Mr. De George seems to agree so far. He would agree that Jones's right to repayment rests on the two men's having as a common ideal a society in which debts are repaid. "But this particular end is not some vague single common end which always goes beyond particular ends." It is something closer at hand and relatively specific.

Now I do not think it is. Suppose Smith refuses to admit that a society where loans are repaid is any part of the life he regards as ideal; is Jones without further resources? Not at all. If Jones accepts such a society and Smith does not, it is presumably for reasons; a kind of state is always to be defended, I have argued, by being itself instrumental to the good. Jones can show to Smith that a state in which loans are repudiated will naturally be one in which promises are not kept, property is not respected, and distrust is general. And this society will be less secure, less prosperous, less happy than one in which the common moral rules are respected. Jones asks Smith whether he favors a society in which security, prosperity, and happiness prevail or one in which they do not. If Smith may be presumed to be sane and honest, he will desire the former. Jones can then point out to Smith that if he is to act consistently with his own ideal he will repay his debt. The ultimate lever on which Jones must rely is not an immediate political agreement but an ultimate ethical identity of end.

The State as an Instrument to the Good

(4) The last of my cardinal theses runs as follows: it is because the state is the most useful and powerful of instruments to the common end of its citizens that it has rights against them. If we are to attain that end, we need roads, schools, police for the protection of life and property, an army and navy for defense, and courts to settle disputes; only the state can supply these; therefore, we should support it as the indispensable means to our common end. The argument is as powerful as it is simple.

Mr. De George agrees with it in principle, but says that as I present it, it offers only two alternatives—to obey the laws of the state or, if it is sufficiently corrupt, to try to overturn it. My language must have been careless if it suggested this. A chisel is a useful tool. But if it is dull, I am not confined to using it with all its dullness or else throwing it away; I can put a better edge on it. A state is a tool, though a much larger and more formidable one. It would be a most irresponsible way of using it if, whenever a president proved incompetent or a judge corrupt, we were to jettison the whole system and try another. Small ailments call for limited remedies. Democratic systems of government have the provision for such remedies written into their charters, for if the people are dissatisfied with the performance of their governors, they have in their hands the machinery for periodically replacing them. Not only is government dictated by the ultimate moral end, but so also are the means of amending and improving it.

Justice

At the close of his paper Mr. De George mentions a difficulty that has haunted many a teleological moralist, the difficulty of defending justice as primarily a means to the general good rather than a good in itself. So far as justice concerns the distribution of goods or the conditions of achieving good, two different principles seem to be at work, equality and distribution according to merit. The principle of equality is based, I think, on self-evidence. If all that is known about a group of persons to whom food, for example, is to be distributed is that they are human beings, the rule that none should get more than any other unless a reason can be adduced for the difference does not seem to me to require argument. When the question is of the distribution of rewards and punishments, the principle that common sense adopts seems to be a combination of self-evidence and consequences. The fittingness seems evident of recognizing good dessert with honors and privileges and ill dessert with their withholding. But when the magnitude of either rewards or punishments is in question, this principle is modified by the appeal to consequences, particularly where punishment is involved. What will deter or reform the criminal, or contribute to the community's safety, often overrides considerations of dessert. Since I accept the validity of some self-evident propositions, there is no conflict between these commonsense rules of justice and my own position, though I have no doubt that in a thorough study of justice many thorny questions would arise. I have had something further to say about justice in commenting on Mrs. Beardsley's and Mr. Johnson's papers.

Lastly, Mr. De George thinks I pay too small a regard to the rights of the individual; they get lost in the promotion of the greatest good on the whole. I might reply that I have been accused of concerning myself too exclusively with the rights and duties of the individual and too little with those of institutions and states. But that would not answer this specific criticism. To be sure, I have not neglected the problem wholly; I have insisted on equality of consideration, that is, the equal right of each man to have his needs and capacities taken into account in distributing the conditions of the good life. Mr. De George reminds me that my principles could be used to support what might be called elitism and also for a cruel sacrifice of the unfit. As for the first count, that of elitism, it is perhaps dealt with sufficiently in my comment on Mr. Freeman's essay on my philosophy of education. As to the second, that of cruelty, I can reply, first though a little irrelevantly, that if there is anything in the world that I hate unwaveringly, it is the cruelty of man to man and man to animal. On the other hand, I confess that I should be encouraged by my theory to carry farther than many what they would call a cruel invasion of individual rights. In our hospitals are large numbers of normal adults whose lives are spent in caring for persons who are hardly persons at all, but organisms bereft from birth of all hope of normal consciousness. I think the time will come when the painless and early exit from life of these tragic creatures, under the joint sanction of parents and medical men, will be socially approved. It ought to be now, and my ethics of the general good would support it.

I have written little on political philosophy, and was surprised when I did come to write on it what a definite and rounded political theory my ethics had committed me to. I am grateful to Mr. De George for having inspected my small acreage with so strong a telescope from his joint eminence as an airplane pilot and an analyst of the intricacies of Soviet political thought. If the rest of my work had been examined in like detail I should probably have been kept writing for the remainder of my days.

---

1. C. D. Broad, *Five Types of Ethical Theory* (London: Kegan Paul, Trench, Trubner; New York: Harcourt, Brace, 1930), 239.

IV   PHILOSOPHY OF EDUCATION

9 THE COMMITMENT TO EXCELLENCE IN BLANSHARD'S PHILOSOPHY OF EDUCATION
Eugene Freeman

Introductory Note

I first met Brand Blanshard in 1959, in my role as the editor for Open Court of his Carus Lectures, *Reason and Analysis,* and we have been friends ever since.

At the time the present Library of Living Philosophers volume devoted to his philosophy was being planned, and I was invited to write a critical study of Blanshard's views on education, his publications on that subject consisted, for the most part, of a rather large number of formal addresses to students that he had delivered over a period of many years at ceremonial occasions, such as commencement exercises or inauguration ceremonies for the installation of college presidents. These had been published in a scattering of relatively inaccessible periodicals or monographs; and when I agreed to write the paper, Blanshard was kind enough to send me a sheaf of reprints to spare me the labor of tracking down his papers.

While these addresses were not sent to me to be considered for publication by Open Court, I could not help seeing them first through the eyes of an editor, and my immediate response was that they belonged together in a book, which could be produced with hardly any more editing than, first, the judicious pruning required to minimize repetitions of thought or phrasing, and second, the occasional freshening of an out-of-date example. A careful reading confirmed my initial response that the papers were too valuable to be left in their scattered form, where they could not exert the influence they deserved to have. What made them so notable were two things, first, his superb literary style, which combines the poetic grace of Bergson or Santayana with the clarity of Russell or William James, and second, the importance and timeliness of his powerful counteroffensive against equalitarianism, relativism, and mediocritism as guiding principles for transmitting the values of our culture through education.

Blanshard accepted my suggestion that the papers be published in book form by Open Court, and he and his wife Roberta, a former editor for the Yale University Press, cooperated patiently and with unflagging good humor in the rather tedious and protracted editorial chores required to publish the volume. Blanshard accepted appreciatively those of my editorial suggestions which he considered reasonable, but he was adamant in rejecting others, especially my proposal that we call the book *Reason and Education.* Such an obvious echo of his Gifford Lectures and his Carus Lectures he thought would be inappropriate and misleading in an unpretentious volume addressed not to scholars but to the general reader. He suggested a more modest title, *The Uses of a Liberal Education,* and this was the title under which it was duly published, in 1973, by Open Court. Even though as a pragmatist I cannot accept some of Blanshard's rationalist premises, I am confident that in time this book will take its place alongside of Whitehead's *Aims of Education* as one of the classics in its field.

After the manuscript for *The Uses of a Liberal Education* had been sent to the printers, and while the present paper was in preparation, I spent several very pleasant days as the guest of Blanshard and his wife at their home in New Haven. At my suggestion, we made tape recordings of our discussions of his philosophy, with the understanding that I could quote from the tapes for my paper wherever I found them relevant. (The transcript is cited as Tr.)

Part I: Three Main Themes or Principles of Blanshard's Philosophy of Education

In our discussions, I mentioned to Blanshard that the preliminary criticism I was prepared to make of his views on education from my reading of the manuscript of *The Uses of a Liberal Education* was that he seemed to me to be advocating a kind of elitism tinged with snobbery which was displayed, I thought, in his characteristic practice of measuring the excellence of a college or university by only one criterion, that of counting the number of superstars it had produced, and apparently ignoring the kind of job the institution might be doing for the overwhelming majority of its students, who were not superstars and never would be.

In reply, Blanshard stated that

> I doubt that my theory is subject to that criticism. My feeling is that everyone has faculties that are peculiar to himself. I wouldn't prescribe anything like the same education for Babe Ruth that I would for Bertrand Russell or T. S. Eliot. . . . as things are, no two people have exactly the same faculties or therefore the same ends. And on my theory of education, we'd have all sorts of schools and colleges and technical institutes and liberal arts colleges, and what we would have to do is to find the sort of education that was best fitted to the individual capacities of the man. Now I don't think

that theory is open to your criticism. [Tr., 27] . . . You say that all through
the book my emphasis is on turning out stars or superstars. To which my
reply is that my aim is to elicit from each person the sort of achievement that
that particular person is capable of. So I'd send Babe Ruth to an athletic
school, I'd send the local carpenter's son, if he wanted it, to a carpentry institute, and I'd send Asquith and Gilbert Murray to Oxford. I don't think
that's elitism. [Tr., 29]

I don't think this reply meets adequately my objection to Blanshard's
determining the excellence of a college or university by counting the number
of superstars it has "produced," and ignoring completely the performance of
the *nonstars* the institution also produces. I think that no adequate evaluation
of the *quality* of an institution of higher learning can be made without taking
into full account the quality of the performance of its nonstars as well as its
superstars, and this Blanshard fails to do.

But he does acknowledge that an institution has a responsibility not only
to its superstars but to its nonstars also. One of the major principles or
themes which pervades Blanshard's philosophy of education is suggested in
the remark just quoted from our conversations, namely, "my aim is to elicit
from each person the sort of achievement that that particular person is
capable of." I name this principle his *Commitment to Democratic Self-
Realization* (CDSR), i.e. his commitment to the discovery and cultivation,
through education, of the natural talent or faculty with which each person has
been the most abundantly endowed, and the concentration of efforts on the
achievement of the highest possible excellence in the area of the talent or
faculty, even though the. development in other areas considered to be higher
in intrinsic value may need to be subordinated or neglected.

The second major theme or principle in Blanshard's philosophy of education is a basic commitment to excellence that characterizes not only his
philosophy but his life as well. Blanshard's commitment to excellence is expressed in four ingredient subordinate themes or principles that collectively
define the main theme that I call by the generic name of Blanshard's *Commitment to Excellence* (CE). These are:

(1) Blanshard's *Aristocracy of Values* (AV); i.e. his commitment that
some values are better than others;

(2) his *Objectivity of Values* (OV); i.e. his commitment that there are intrinsic values, which are not merely relative but objective, despite the fact that
they can be realized only in human experience;

(3) his *Elitism of Values*; i.e. his commitment to the importance and
superiority of what he considers to be the better or higher values; less pejora-
tively called his *Preference for Humanistic Values* (PHV);

(4) his *Perfectionism of Performance* (PP); i.e. his commitment to perfectionism in measuring performance, of individuals and of institutions, in all
areas, by comparison with the best as the standard.

The Commitment to Democratic Self-Realization (CDSR)

This is an admirable principle in what it affirms, namely that the full resources of our educational systems should be used to help each individual achieve the maximum excellence in the area of his chief talent or principal faculty.

It would be considered, however, to be a pernicious principle by those who are not ready to concede either (1) the self-evident superiority or inferiority of one area of human excellence as compared to another; or (2) the self-evident preferability of producing persons who have achieved maximal realization of one talent combined with minimal achievement in every other area of human life. During my last quarter of residence in graduate school I shared a large sitting and study room which separated my monkish cubicle from one belonging to a nineteen-year-old mathematical genius who was getting his Ph.D. at the end of the quarter. He was a gentle and rather unworldly young man who was as underdeveloped in other areas as he was precocious in mathematics. He was naive, unsophisticated in a childlike fashion, relatively illiterate outside of mathematics, likable but incredibly raw and ignorant and devoid of social graces (he had never had a date), and he could talk with animation about nothing but mathematics. He went directly to the Rand Corporation after he got his degree and I don't know what happened to him after that. To me he represents the embodiment of the kind of person who would be produced if the principle of CDSR were carried to its logical extreme by concentrating all efforts on the realization of the fullest potential of the major talent or faculty without any responsibility for the realization of any other lesser talents or faculties, especially when we are considering persons like engineers, inventors, banjo players, and carpenters.

The Four Ingredients of Commitment to Excellence (CE)

1. Aristocracy of Values (AV). I distinguish between the broader contention that *some* values are better than others (AV) and the narrower contention that it is the *humanistic* values that are better than others (PHV). For it is possible to accept AV and at the same time reject PHV. This is done by those who evaluate the practical values as being superior to the humanistic values, *Preference for Practical Values* (PPrV).

2. Objectivity of Values (OV). Blanshard's contention that values are objective is riddled with a paradoxical ultimate subjectivity of value. The claimed objectivity of value is based on his flat and unsupported assertion that values are what they are regardless of what the person in whose experience they are encountered *wants* them to be. On Blanshard's view, all persons who are qualified to experience values, and appraise them, will grade them as better or worse in proportion to their expertness. The objectivity of values thus turns out to be intersubjective agreement among experts about the ranking of values. That he believes values are *not* objective, in the naive realistic sense of their having an independent being, Blanshard makes unmistakably clear. For him values can have being only in the experience of a subject; were all experiencing subjects annihilated, all values would also be annihilated.

Thus the first condition of being reasonable is that there be an independent common rule. The second condition is that this common rule should at times control the course of our thought. We must sometimes be able to say: If I thought as I did, it was because my mind was under the influence of an independent pattern, the pattern of an objective truth. This is only to say that thought, if it is to be reasonable, must be like perception when it is accurate. Suppose we look at a checkerboard. If there is to be any such thing as accurate perception at all, there must be, in a sense "out there," a certain number of squares related to each other in a certain way. That corresponds to our first condition. Secondly, we must be able to say: If I see them in this way, that must be because they *are* this way, because that independent order acts upon my mind and makes me see it so. If this arrangement presents itself, not because it is there, but because my mind is being pulled about by wires from within, then there are no grounds for believing that we ever do or can see accurately; if we did, it would be sheer luck. I am happily not concerned with the mechanism of perceiving, but with a principle. If, when we perceive things, we never perceive them so because they are so, then perception is a cheat. Similarly in thinking, unless at times we think as we do because the real relations of things are controlling our thought, laying it under constraint, governing its movement, then knowledge must be an illusion from first to last. [*Uses*, 130–31]

Will you carry out with me another little philosophical experiment? Imagine successively three kinds of world. First, our modern world with all its gadgets, and scattered around them its notable men and women, Churchill and Charlie Chaplin and Eleanor Roosevelt and you and me. Secondly, imagine a world with all our modern gadgets subtracted—with no electricity or steam or motors or railways or radios or telephones, with no printed books or newspapers, no means of preserving food, no anaesthetics, no science of medicine or surgery, no sewing machines, reapers, typewriters, even spectacles. One feels at once that such a world would be shrunken and impoverished, for so much that we are and do is made possible by these things. Would life in such dreary poverty be worth living at all? Well, let me remind you that this *was* the world of Socrates and Sophocles and Aristotle, of Virgil and St. Augustine and Dante. There was nothing poverty-stricken about these minds; indeed it is to these minds precisely that men in other times turn when they want to escape from their own poverty. Carlyle once raised the startling question, Which would be the greater loss to England if it had to part with one or the other: Shakespeare or India? With all respect to India, how that question lights up the worth of one great spirit!

But now imagine the third world. Instead of subtracting the machinery of civilized life, let us leave it all standing, or rather multiply it to the limit, with superskyscrapers on every horizon and, within them, push-button resources for every want. And let us subtract just one thing, consciousness. It is a paradise of gadgets, lacking only persons. And the question I want to ask is, What would be the value of such a world? The answer is, nothing at all. Without its persons the worth of the world would vanish utterly. It is for persons, for better and more sensitive persons, for the knowledge and love and goodness of persons, that all the machinery of civilization exists. There may be great persons with little or none of this machinery. There can be greater ones, I am convinced, with the aid of this machinery. But the machinery without the persons has a value of precisely zero. [*Uses*, 165]

Here, I think, Blanshard's view, to which he has held steadfastly for a great many years, could be very much improved if he were to add to it the insight offered in one of the most recent and most original conjectures about these matters, Karl Popper's account of what he calls *his* third world. The third world is a world of objective being, Platonic forms, numbers, essences, etc. which mediates between the first world—the physical world—and the second world—the world of psychophysical brain-mind activity. Third world objects are created as second world products, but once they are brought into being as living thoughts, once they are transferred to records like books and other artifacts, their *continued existence* becomes independent of the mind that created them—as the continued existence of honey is independent of the continued existence of the bees that made it.

As against the common dualistic view that there are really two worlds, the world of matter and energy and the subjective world of conscious experience, Karl Popper has proposed three worlds as follows: (1) the *World of matter and energy*, which is the material world, both inorganic and organic, and including machines and all living forms—even our own bodies and brains; (2) the *World of conscious experiences*, not only our immediate perceptual experiences—visual, auditory, tactile, pain, hunger, anger, joy, fear, etc., but also our memories, imaginings, thoughts and planned actions that he refers to as our "dispositional intentions"; (3) the *World of objective knowledge*, which would include the objective contents of thoughts, as he calls it, especially of the thoughts underlying scientific and artistic and poetic expression. In particular, he stresses the World 3 status of all theoretical systems and of problems and problem situations and critical arguments. The importance of World 3 will be readily appreciated when we come to consider its relationship to Worlds 1 and 2.

In fact we can state that in World 3 are all arguments and discussions and records of human intellectual efforts, and in particular there are the records preserved in libraries and museums either as written records or as paintings, sculptures, ceramics, ornaments, tools, machines, etc. However, it is important to recognize that in World 3 there is only the objective knowledge that is coded symbolically in the actual structures . . . . carrying the codes such as books, pictures, plastic art forms, films and even computer memories would be of course in World 1.[1]

It seems to me that if values were objective in the same sense that sensory qualities are objective—which in a word is what Blanshard's claim comes to—disagreement about values between qualified experts would be virtually impossible; or, when one expert was found in disagreement with the prevailing opinion of his peers, a disqualifying defect in his ability to perceive and rank values would be suspected and he would be sent to an expert on value-blindness for an examination to disclose the particular variety of value-blindness with which he has been so severely afflicted as to cause him to disagree with the experts.

But the claimed self-evidency of Blanshard's contention that the experts would agree, as I see it, reduces to either a tautology or a false claim about the nature of things as they are found in our everyday world. His claim that values are objective in the sense that similar value judgments would be made by equally qualified experts means operationally that like-minded people are like-minded people—that is, they have the same value criteria and they make the same gradings in their value judgments—a tautology that is not particularly enlightening, and which is what is meant in ordinary language by "occupational bias." How would Blanshard account for a difference of opinion among experts in their value judgments? Would he say that only those are experts who agree with him, or rather, that only those are experts who agree with the view that humanistic values are higher than any other? He could then account for any disagreements as being due to inexpertness, which I think is the view he is compelled to accept, since the only other alternative which would account for a different grading of the same values by two experts of equal skill would be that values are *not* objective, but are relative to the person who experiences them and who decides how valuable they are in terms of how valuable they are *for him*. And this is a conclusion, of course, which Blanshard rejects as being incompatible with one of his primary assumptions.

3. Elitism: Or Preference for Humanistic Values (PHV). Blanshard's elitism, or preference for humanistic values as higher than any others, is both the expression of one of the primitive propositions or assumptions on which his philosophical system rests and the expression of his occupational bias as a rationalist philosopher. As Plato and John Stuart Mill before him did—and he is in very good company here—Blanshard considers it self-evident that intellectual humanistic values are better than less intellectual nonhumanistic values, that the "useless" or rather *intrinsic* values are *better* than the useful ones, i.e. those values that are realized merely as means to other values. He offers no more proof than Mill did, namely, that those who experience both prefer the intellectual pleasures; therefore since they are preferred, they are preferable.

I question, however, both (*a*) the premise that those who experience both actually do *prefer* the humanistic pleasures, and (*b*) the conclusion that therefore they *ought* to do so.

(*a*) I deny the premise on the grounds that most people get more pleasure from doing what they can do *well* than doing what they can do only poorly—and the values that they *do* prefer are not the intellectual ones but the nonintellectual ones. This is rather conclusively proven by the relative preference of the public not for the "better" TV programs but for the poorer ones.

(*b*) I deny the conclusion, since on Blanshard's view farmers, and mechanics, and carpenters, and banjo players who are not intellectually equipped to achieve success as intellectuals either are *incapable* of experiencing intellectual values—which is just not the case—or they *have* at various times experienced both intellectual and nonintellectual pleasures. Then on Blanshard's view of the objectivity of values, they should be compelled to agree with him, which again is simply just not the case, they do not agree.

Advocates of Blanshard's and John Stuart Mill's position would argue that the carpenter who goes to his first concert is incapable of experiencing the music that Bach offers him because he hasn't had years of training. For the same reason, however, they themselves are just as incapable of experiencing the rhythms and harmonies of modern banjo playing or rock music the first time they hear it as anything but just so much noise. And this is even more so in the case of the strange sounds which an ear attuned to the music of modern Western culture would hear without experiencing the music if confronted with the music of cultures like those of the North American Indians, or of Asian cultures like those of Japan, India, and China.

4. Perfectionism of Performance (PP). One of the most straightforward and consistent ways in which Blanshard's CE is manifested is in his perfectionistic standards. The achievement of excellence is a laudable aim, and I applaud it. But as John Gardner has shown in his clear and provocative book, *Excellence,*[2] the aim of achieving excellence in a democracy comes into head-on collision with the equalitarian aims of a democracy, and this raises grave problems that demand wisdom and reasonableness for their solution. Gardner's view is that the achievement of excellence is not incompatible with the full realization of democratic principles—and I would agree.

My criticism of Blanshard is that his concern for excellence is directed, as I interpret his writings (perhaps most unfairly), exclusively toward the cultivation of excellence in those who are naturally excellent. To translate my point into the context of classroom teaching, for Blanshard the A students pass, and the B and C and D students have failed. And of course in a real sense they have failed, namely, to achieve excellence; but in another sense—and Blanshard too would put it this way—they have not failed if they have realized their full potential. I know there are, as William James has said, "middle-aged bald-headed and bald-hearted ruins of what could have been good farmers in our graduate schools"—I too have met them there. My revered teacher, George Herbert Mead, referred to them on occasion as "squatters in the temple of education." But there are also frustrated Sinclair Lewises reading and correcting manuscripts and galley proofs in publishing houses by day and writing and rewriting their own unpublished masterpieces in their lonely rooms at night.

"No two human beings have the same potential," says Blanshard. What this means for Blanshard, as Plato would have agreed, is that talents and faculties are distributed unequally at birth. Some persons are abundantly endowed, others are sparsely endowed, and all persons are differently endowed. It is the gene pool that ultimately determines who will achieve excellence, and in which areas. I will return to this below in my consideration of the conflict of principles in Blanshard's theory.

Commitment to Reasonableness

The third major guiding principle or theme which I found running all through Blanshard's philosophy of education, equal in importance to his principle of Commitment to Excellence, is his *Commitment to Reasonableness* (CR). Reasonableness is the quality of mind and temper which Blanshard considers to be, in the final accounting, one of the most desirable products of a liberal education.

> In sum, my philosophy of education is one of fulfilment on the sides of both knowledge and value, and in widest commonalty spread. That is the end of education, as it is of life. It may be thought that this is less than consistent with another theme that runs throughout these addresses, the theme that the end is reasonableness. There is no real inconsistency here. To me the good life and the reasonable life are synonymous terms. Reason or intellectual insight is for me the ultimate court of appeal in questions of taste and morals as well as in questions of truth. The judgment that intense happiness is intrinsically better than intense pain seems as truly a self-evident rational insight as a judgment of mathematics. The judgment that I ought to make the world as much better as I can seems to me also a rational insight, one indeed on which the whole of ethics is founded. The weighing of my competing goods against each other, the weighing of my own goods against those of others, the ultimate decision as to what is right between conflicting claims of any kind, all rest with reason. Thus for me the reasonable life is not only one in which the mind follows with its understanding the structure of the world; it is also one in which rational insight selects the goods one is to pursue and governs both will and feeling in the pursuit of them. I have argued that the best product of education is the rational temper. It is an attitude in which self-respect is identified with the living of a rational life. The use of reason, to be sure, is a means, not an end, but rationality, the habitual appeal to reason in belief and practice, is so intimate a condition of the good life that means and end are practically one. [*Uses*, p. xvi]

Ethical Foundations of Blanshard's Theory of Education

This admirable summary statement which Blanshard has made in *Uses* for the general reader may be supplemented by another valuable summary statement intended for the scholar, which I quote at length from my tapes of our discussion. Here Blanshard summarizes the way he arrived at the ethical theory on which his educational theory is based.

> I really started from my theory of human nature. I've been very much influenced by the dynamic psychology of McDougall, who left Oxford just about the time I did and came to Harvard where he was teaching during my year there. I think that McDougall's psychology is peculiarly illuminating from the point of view of understanding human nature.
>
> My ethics has had a rather curious history. I was really bowled over by G. E. Moore. I thought his ethical theory was just about inexpugnable, just about beyond criticism. But when he left, after living with me for six months, I began to think more critically about his view, and finally I was unable to accept it. That is, I was unable to accept the abstract goodness which he thought was present in every experience that was intrinsically good, and which was indefinable because it was absolutely simple. It was intuitable by a special faculty, but it was wholly indefinable. Well, I kept looking for this character in my experiences of chocolate eclairs and listening to music and understanding philosophy, but I couldn't find it. And I came to the conclusion that Moore had been deluded about that simple quality. Then I fell back on Aristotle, who seems to me to give an explanation of why it is that we find some things good; we find them good because they're fulfilling of our natural capacities. We do not find good what an earthworm or an arthropod would find good. It seems to me that the great intrinsic values of life, such as food and drink and sex and knowledge and so on, are all of them satisfactions of fundamental drives of human nature. Aristotle was surely right that goodness is essentially related to human faculty. It isn't true, as Dean Inge and Hartmann thought, that goodness and other values are eternal essences that somehow embody themselves in things; their goodness is a quality that belongs to an experience in virtue of its being fulfilling.
>
> Now my educational theory is a direct outgrowth of that. I said, as Moore did, that the end of life is to achieve the great intrinsic goods, but that these intrinsic goods in turn are fulfillments of human faculties. . . .
>
> I'm trying to make my theory of education hang together with my ethical and my epistemological theories. Whether I've succeeded I can't know until these criticisms come in. But if you can find loopholes in it, I'd be grateful if you'd go after them vigorously, and I'll either amend my theory or defend it as seems called for. [Tr., 37–38]

Part II: Harmony and Conflict in Blanshard's Principles

The Problem

As Blanshard has noted, the two major themes or ingredients of his philosophy of education which run through *Uses*, his Commitment to Excellence (CE) and his Commitment to Reasonableness (CR), are not inconsistent with each other. CR is also consistent with the supplementary principle of Commitment to Democratic Self-Realization (CDSR) which is elaborated in the transcript of our tape-recorded discussions.

Thus CR is consistent with both CE and CDSR. However, a major problem, in fact the major problem considered in the present study, is the apparent incompatibility of the demands made in the name of CE and those demanded by CDSR. Can we establish standards in education based on the performance of the very best in our very best schools as perhaps required by CE? In that case, what about the masses of ordinary people who will be failed because they cannot meet these standards, but must be given the opportunity to try, as required by CDSR? Shall we lower our standards sufficiently so that the masses of ordinary people can get an education, as required by CDSR? In that case, what would happen to the quality of education which CE requires us to maintain?

Perhaps the demands of CE and CDSR are so incompatible with each other that these two principles cannot coexist in a single theory of education, but must be championed in separate, rival systems.

Or perhaps it might be possible, by an application of CR, to modify the demands made by CE and CDSR and put them into a form that would permit a "reasonable" compromise to be made in their otherwise incompatible demands? This is the principal question that I wish to raise in this paper, and it is the central question of John Gardner's optimistic book, *Excellence*. I hope Blanshard will also address himself once more to this question in his Replies.

Commitment to Reasonableness (CR)

Some logicians, like Carnap, have had the ideal or dream of an absolutely precise language, logical, and thus totally free of ambiguity, with one and only one meaning for each word in the language. At the other extreme, poets like Karl Krause (and Goethe before him)[3] dream of a language which is so poetic and thus essentially vague that a word in it may achieve so rich a meaning that it has a universal reference or universal ambiguity,[4] a universal range of meanings changing kaleidoscopically as the context rotates around it.

Blanshard tends to use the word "reasonable" as a poetic rather than a logical term, with a range of meanings in which the "reasonable" is the synthesis that resolves the contradiction between the "rational" and its antithesis, the "irrational." The primary or root meaning of "reasonable" is, of course, "rational," that is, being guided by reason, and in fairness to Blanshard, most of the time he does use the term in its root sense. But he finds it convenient on occasion to use a word which has a broader meaning, containing all of the virtues of the rational, and in addition, some of the practical advantages of adding just enough "irrationality" to the rational to rid it of extremism or even fanaticism, and thus make a commonsense (or "reasonable") compromise possible. For this purpose Blanshard's term "reasonable" is, I think, admirably chosen, and means, I think, essentially "the rational insofar as the rational is tempered with commonsense wisdom and philosophic insight and judgment"—and, in the pattern of Karl Krause, even this does not exhaust its meaning. What intrigues me the most about Blanshard's use of the term is the paradoxical way in which the term "reasonable" on occasion becomes richer and more practical than the term "rational" by adding to its meaning what, in fact, is literally *irrationality*. For example, it is quite rational for a person to refuse to compromise his principles and to refuse to agree to do something which he is convinced is wrong for him to do. But it may be unreasonable of him to refuse to negotiate a dispute in which both sides are convinced of their own rightness, as in, say, a labor dispute, but a dispute which if not resolved would result in disastrous consequences to both sides. In such cases, it is better to give up the unreasonable for the reasonable, which combines what is essentially the rational with just enough of a concession to the wrong or the irrational to make it acceptable to both sides.

Thus one of Blanshard's goals in education is the production of people guided by a wise and judicious reasonableness, which tempers rationality and enables them to resolve the many conflicts of authorities and values that confront us in everyday living, in contrast to persons who, like Kant and our Puritan forbears, were guided by a narrower strict rationality.

But there is a more fundamental difficulty here. The problem, as Sidgwick pointed out, is that it is unreasonable for a person not to prefer his own good above that of others, but it may be right for him to do so where duty and self-interest conflict. Ultimately it is not reason but the intuition of the good, and consequently of what is right to do, that becomes the supreme guiding principle of ethics; reason or the reasonable is retained as a principle of subordinate authority. Blanshard's Commitment to Reasonableness is very much like the similar commitment of his revered predecessor, Sidgwick, and of the teleologist and deontologist heroes who were his teachers, Carritt and Moore and Rashdall and Joseph and Prichard and Ross. Like them, he has accepted as one of the consequences of his position a baffling problem which they discovered they could not solve without abandoning their rationalism or their teleology. Blanshard cheerfully acknowledges this, and remarks that if his heroes couldn't solve the problem, he is not unduly frustrated by the fact that neither can he.

I think that question is one of the most difficult in ethics. I don't know that Moore ever dealt with it successfully. I was saying that Sidgwick and Moore and Rashdall all struggled with it, and all of them failed to come up with a perfectly clear solution. If I fail where Moore, Sidgwick, and Rashdall failed before me, I don't think I have much grounds for beating my breast. [Tr., 10] . . . I've never been satisfied with my own thinking on the point. I suspect that the best attack on these problems is made in H. W. B. Joseph's book, *Some Problems of Ethics*. I heard him give those lectures, and Prichard was sitting right under his nose as he delivered them in New College. He was arguing against the Prichard theory. Prichard would say, "Where you see that an action is just, or you see that it is right, then you do it for that reason, and sometimes it is your duty to do the right or the just act even though that act fairly clearly contributes less good than some alternative act that you might do instead. . . ." Well, I'm not content with that. It seems to me that Moore is right. When Moore was sitting opposite to me at luncheon one day in my house, and I quoted some of the arguments of Ross to him, Moore's reply was: "It still seems to me clearly to be my duty to make the world as much better as I can." Now if you ask Moore whether he ought to do the just act rather than some alternative act, I think that the only way he could answer would be to say, as Joseph does, that justice belongs to a system or frame of action, "a form of life," to use Joseph's phrase, following Plato, which is intrinsically more good than the form of life to which the other act is essential. . . . I don't think you can solve the problem of justice without falling back on something like this Platonic idea of one form of life being as a *whole* intrinsically better than another. Suppose that you were confronted with two acts, one of them the act required by justice and the other the act which, as far as you can see, would produce the largest amount of intrinsic good. Which would you do? Ross, Carritt, and Prichard would all say that you should, in many cases at any rate, even if not all, do the just act—and there's no way of reconciling that obligation with traditional utilitarianism. Now if there is a *single* act of obligation of that kind, it is enough to refute the view that you should always so act as to produce the greatest good. Joseph was fully alive to the force of that objection. And his reply was that you can't justify such an act in isolation. He would agree that you sometimes ought to do the just act, even though you were *apparently* producing the less total intrinsic good (and he was really quoting Plato). To justify the act you must take into account the form of life to which it belongs. . . . He has an obscure idea there but he attempts to make it plausible, and I think he succeeds. But it makes a great difficulty for a person like me who tries to hold that the only intrinsic good lies in the experience of persons. I'm inclined to be an Aristotelian, you see, but I think this problem with justice is the most difficult one for an Aristotelian or for a Moorean theory. And I'm very close to Moore—I'm almost a Moorean except, I think, in the one great problem of intrinsic goodness. [Tr., 10–12]

The Demands of CE versus the Demands of CDSR

One of the interesting consequences of Blanshard's theory of education which results from accepting the criterion of the *reasonable* as the *preferable* is that it raises the crucial problem for Blanshard of how he can reconcile the demands of CDSR with those of CE. The demands of CDSR require him to assure Babe Ruth and Ty Cobb that it is better for them to develop their natural talents and make the Hall of Fame in Cooperstown than it would have been for them to try to become, say, poets or philosophers.

> I hope that the traditional education—the ideals of traditional education—are sufficiently attacked to make impossible the inference that I would approve training Ty Cobb and Babe Ruth on the same general pattern on which I would train Gilbert Murray and Asquith. Babe Ruth could hit a baseball farther than anyone else in the world, so far as known; that was a capability which deserves development, and fortunately, Ruth had it. If Ruth had been sent to Harvard, for example, or Oxford, he might well have never had an opportunity to develop his greatest power and make it part of his image to himself and the world. . . .Yes, and I want to make the banjo player a better player of banjos. [Tr., 33]

But Blanshard's Commitment to Excellence (CE), as expressed in his sub-principle, Commitment to Aristocracy in Values (AV) and his Preference for Humanistic Values (PHV), also requires him to explain to them, and to Eddie Peabody, the banjo king of their day, that the values which could be gained from activities of low cultural esteem such as the ones they were engaged in were lesser in real or intrinsic value than those which could be gained (Blanshard does not specify *by whom,* I presume he means by those who have the capacity to realize them) by humanistic activities like poetry or philosophy or music or art or literature or mathematics or history, which "stretch and enrich" the mind and the personality.

The following remarks made by Blanshard in our discussion reveal rather clearly several of Blanshard's themes, e.g. CDSR, and two of the themes of CE, particularly the PHV.

> Now let's suppose on the one hand that you have a group of engineers and on the other a group of Arts people. And let's suppose the Arts school turns out people like some of the heroes I've talked about—Gilbert Murray, Asquith, John Buchan, T. S. Eliot—that type of person—and suppose that the practical arts school, the Engineering school, turns out people very able in engine construction. Is there any educational criterion by which one could say that one rather than the other of these two types of institution is intrinsically superior to the other? Would you say, no, there isn't any such criterion?
>
> [E.F.: No, no, of course not. As a matter of fact . . .]
>
> Now, Gene, you see that I am an elitist in one sense, I want to admit that.
>
> [E.F.: I am too, by the way.]
>
> I thought you probably were. [Laugh.] I don't know if it is in the same sense that I am. But I would say that if you had to choose, to take a classic example, between having the mind of Shakespeare, let us say, and having the mind of Charles Kettering, it would be better to be Shakespeare. Obviously, the intrinsic values that he realized made life more worth living for him than

Kettering's values did for *him*. So if one had to choose, if one were God and had to choose whether to create William Shakespeare or Charles Franklin Kettering it would be obligatory for the deity himself to produce Shakespeare. [Tr., 32–33]

While there are great technological difficulties which are yet to be solved, it is now not too soon to anticipate some of the conceivable advances in human technology which are in the blueprint stage, one of which is "cloning." Cloning, when perfected, will be a gift to man from our science laboratories which will give him the power to make choices that up to now could only be made by God. What shall we do when we have this power? Shall we make none but superstars? Who will collect the garbage? Shall we make robots for this? Then shall we make more robots for everything else that can't be done except by Shakespeares, Beethovens, and the like? For example, shall we make audiences to appreciate them and to applaud at the right things and the right places and the right times?

Shall we clone the experts who agree and not those who don't?

As I play with these fancies, I am glad I am not God; and the panel of bioethical experts who decide what our future generations will be like have my deepest sympathy. Blanshard's fanciful speculation concerning the choice God would be forced to make if He had to choose between creating Shakespeare or Kettering is a bit of whimsy, and it would be silly to take it seriously as though Blanshard had intended it to tell us something about God. But it does tell us a great deal about Blanshard—namely, how strongly he prefers the humanistic values above all others. As far as God is concerned, if I were to speculate about Him I would be more likely to observe that if Blanshard meant by "God" a divinity who actually did create Shakespeare, then I presume that at least two implications follow directly from this premise:

(1) If it is the case that God had the power to create Shakespeare, and that He did use this power to create him once, isn't it highly probable that He also had the power *to do so again if He had wanted to*?

(2) But He has not done so again; therefore He did not want to.

More than that: God has not only not cloned Shakespeare and his environment but as far as we know He has never replicated the genes and the environment He has used to produce any great superstar in any field of human accomplishment. Instead, every superstar in every field stands in solitary splendor not only as a testament to God's power but as proof of His respect for uniqueness and originality—that He prefers to make each man *one of a kind* rather than a copy. Not only has there been only one Shakespeare but there has been *only one Kettering*. Apparently God, who presumably had the power to do otherwise, thought it was better to have a Shakespeare and a Kettering in the world rather than to have two Shakespeares and no Kettering. Kettering enriched the world with something

Shakespeare couldn't give it. Through his inventions he provided the means that made available a great deal of intrinsic good that man would otherwise have had to forgo—and I am not as certain as Blanshard is that his life was not as intrinsically worth living for himself as Shakespeare's was for Shakespeare. Each time he invented another of the thousands of successful inventions he gave to the world, he shared in the intrinsic values of intellectual discovery. This may well have given him the same kind of euphoric delight and expansion of mind and spirit—and even as much of it—as Shakespeare might have gained from creating and contemplating his literary inventions. As a matter of fact, if we play another round of Blanshard's whimsical game of thinking as God might have thought, then I think that it is at least as likely that He would have envisioned Himself as an inventor rather than as a writer if He were forced to restrict Himself (per impossible) to creating a man who reflected only *one* of His images. It is just as plausible that he would have created a Kettering, whose visions and dreams became actualized in a world of concrete reality, rather than a Shakespeare, whose inventions were fated to be never more than visions and dreams. And God not only actualized His inventions, but botched up enough of them so that He could well have recognized in Kettering a kindred spirit—in man alone there are over five hundred congenital defects which bear witness to how badly the job of actually making a man was done!

One of the major critical comments I have to make on Blanshard's view is not so much a difference with him about what he *does* provide for in his theory as what he apparently *does not*.

To quote from the transcript,

> [E.F.: I can see your position with respect to an intelligent effort to develop the actual potential that an individual brings. Are you saying you want to make the baseball player a better baseball player?]
>
> Yes, and I want to make the *banjo* player a better player of banjos. I would insist that if I had to choose between allotting public money to train a banjo player and to train Bertrand Russell I would prefer Bertrand Russell, because I think there is a difference in intrinsic value between mathematical insight and the ability to pick a banjo. . . . I'm not maligning banjo players [laughter] nor am I maligning Babe Ruth. [Tr., 33]

For an educator who cherishes humanistic values, as Blanshard does, it might reasonably be expected, it seems to me, that he would have exhibited more concern here for sharing these values with the banjo player, and helping to make of him a more complete person. A banjo player like Eddie Peabody, for example, may not need help to become a better banjo player as much as he may need help to become something *more* than a banjo player.

Eddie Peabody, my boyhood idol, was both a gifted violinist and an even more gifted banjoist—a superstar of world rank. I think Blanshard might have been somewhat frustrated if he had tried to explain to Eddie Peabody that violin playing was *really* better than banjo playing but that *for Eddie* banjo playing was *really* better than violin playing, or to Babe Ruth that writing philosophy or poetry was *really* better than playing baseball but that *for Babe* baseball was *really* better than either. Blanshard is confronted here with two alternative choices. (1) He could renounce the objectivism of intrinsic values (OV) to which he has been dedicated for a lifetime, for a facile relativism; or (2) he could be an elitist, and this is, of course, his choice. Thus he could assure them that whatever was better for them was *really* better than that which was not better for them, which is what they might like to hear, but which it would be against his convictions to assert; or he could frankly and perhaps brutally tell Eddie and Babe that as a matter of fact violin playing was *really* better than ball playing and that writing philosophy was *really* better than banjo playing but that with their markedly inferior talents for philosophy and the violin they would be *better advised* to concentrate their major efforts on achieving superstardom in the areas of inferior worth for which their native talents and faculties had so richly been given to them. He could warn them that they were destined for frustration and failure if they tried to make a vocation of the fields in which their talents were limited; that their wisest choice would be to make their living at the activity or trade of lower intrinsic value for which their talent or natural capacity was the greater, and to make a hobby, if they wished, of the activity of higher value for which their talents or natural capacities were lesser.

The first alternative, of choosing to be a relativist, may indeed be a logical possibility, but for Blanshard it would be an unthinkable one. He would *never* agree that banjo playing was better than violin playing or that baseball was better than philosophy, even if it were wiser for people like Eddie Peabody or Babe Ruth not to try to become violinists or philosophers. Accordingly we can safely dismiss this alternative as viable for Blanshard, since he would never choose it.

Blanshard's Elitism

The second alternative, of elitism, which is chosen by Blanshard, subjects him *to the risk* of being called a snob, especially by those who do not agree with his valuations. It is true that, if you tell people they are inferior, you are in danger of having them accuse you of snobbery. In today's culture it is highly likely that to declare any person, *rightly or wrongly*, to be inferior *in any respect* may well produce the same kind of conditioned response of a maddened head-down charge that is triggered by waving a red cape at a bull. But in fairness to Blanshard, as well as to all those who, like Blanshard, are committed to the maintenance of the highest possible standards in education (Blanshard's subprinciples AV and PP, Aristocracy of Values and Perfectionism of Performance), an impartial and objective appraisal of relative degrees of competence or lack of competence in a candidate who aspires to enter a field can hardly be considered to be snobbish, even if it is sharply negative, provided it is made by a person who is a recognized authority in or on that field. The phrase which is of key importance here is "rightly or wrongly." The importance of this distinction is hinted at in Webster's *Third New International Dictionary* (unabridged), in the use of the word "especially" in one of its definitions of the word "snob" as "one rightly or esp[ecially] wrongly convinced of his superior knowledge or taste within a field or of the intrinsic superiority of his field of interest or hobby." Accordingly, I would prefer to sharpen the meaning of the word "snob" by restricting it to designate those who are *mistaken* in their judgments concerning who or what is better or worse, and I would restrict the word "elitist" to those whose judgments on values are generally *respected* even when they may not be agreed to. We would then distinguish more precisely between "snob" and "elitist" and their derivatives by classing as snobs those whose judgments of their superior knowledge or taste within a field, or of the intrinsic superiority of their field of interest or hobby, are *prima facie mistaken,* and as elitists those whose judgments are *not prima facie mistaken.* Most persons who are qualified to make judgments of grades of excellence of individuals in their fields, and are thus qualified to be called elitists, are also likely to display an occupational bias, as I think Blanshard clearly does, and are very likely to be convinced, as Blanshard is, that his field is intrinsically superior to any other. To distinguish this kind of snobbery from mistaken judgments about individuals, I call it institutional snobbery. Would an anthropologist agree that "For the understanding of human society, political theory and intellectual history are important, while drum and trumpet history, the marriage customs of the Melanesians, even social case work, are not"? (*Uses,* 215). My son James, who is an anthropologist, and who speaks with the bias of his profession, does not think so. As he has observed in one of our conversations about Blanshard's view, "An anthropologist would argue that the marriage customs of Melanesians make understandable important aspects of human society which are completely neglected by political theory and intellectual history. You cannot possibly speak authoritatively about human society unless you consider cross-cultural variations in human societies."

Where Blanshard is making judgments of comparative performance within a single category, as for example, one violinist compared to another one, one poet compared to another poet, one philosopher compared to another philosopher, he is relatively the least vulnerable and the most successful. In making these judgments, he is a perfectionist; and as such he may be called appropriately an elitist, but *not* a snob.

However, when he compares performances in different categories, granting for the sake of argument that the performances are equally competent, especially if they are the performances of superstars in the respective categories, then he is not an elitist but a snob. Examples of his snobbish cross-categorial comparisons are his comparisons of violin playing versus banjo playing (or philosophy versus science or engineering).

When Blanshard recommends sending the son of the local carpenter to a carpentry school, I wonder if he would make such a recommendation without first studying the boy's school records and College Board scores. I presume that what Blanshard meant here was that, if the carpenter's son *expressed a desire* to be a carpenter like his father, Blanshard would want to see that he is sent to an appropriate vocational school. But there is a hint of unconscious snobbery here in the implied presumption that a carpenter's son would *want* to be a carpenter. What if he wanted to become a philosopher? I am quite certain that Blanshard would not send him to a carpentry school, but would help him get scholarships and fellowships at Yale, if his school records and College Board scores showed high promise, *regardless* of his father's occupation.

A second definition offered in Webster's dictionary for a snob is "one who tends to rebuff the advances of those he regards as inferior." Here again, the important distinction between what the dictionary speaks of as "rightly or especially wrongly" is just as relevant for distinguishing between the snob and the elitist in the narrow senses of the terms. In addition, we need to comb out the unduly pejorative terms found in the second definition, like "inferior" and "rebuff" and "advances." These pejorative terms are highly charged with emotive social connotations which are admittedly important in social and political discourse but can lead only to misunderstanding if they are used in an otherwise impartial and dispassionate discussion and appraisal of individual differences in human talents, abilities, and achievements.

There is a world of difference between, on the one hand, (1) the setting of high standards in education with the purpose of maximizing excellence of achievement, and accordingly distinguishing realistically and frankly between those who meet the standards and those who do not, and, on the other hand, (2) the practicing of social snobbery, which presumes that persons of inferior social or economic class (or so-called inferior fields of endeavor) are inferior in ability, or disciplined drive, or both. The former is elitism, as I use the term here, and the latter is snobbery in the everyday sense of the term. As far as his attitudes toward persons are concerned, Blanshard is not a snob but an elitist.

Institutional Snobbery

In his grading of educational institutions, just as in his estimation of his own field as compared to other fields, Blanshard has slipped into a position that is tinged with snobbery. His hero worship of superstars is transferred to the institutions which, as he would put it, "produced them," but which I would rather refer to as those "from which they came."

Even though I admire much that Blanshard says, I would not go along with what I consider to be his unduly firm separation between vocational and liberal education. As I see it, the greatest weakness in Blanshard's theory is that he does not make adequate, or even *any*, provisions for "stretching the mind" of persons in *vocational* schools by means of humanistic studies, nor does he indicate any concern or feeling of responsibility for including, to whatever degree might be considered practicable, some minimal humanistic training for entrance into a vocation—*any* vocation—whether such training be pre- or postvocational, or integrated into the vocational curriculum. I am fully aware that a humanistic curriculum and a vocational curriculum have different ends and need to be fundamentally different. But I am not ready to grant that the education of a person in today's culture should be limited to *either* curriculum.

Blanshard seems to consider that the humanities curriculum and the vocational curriculum need to be distinguished not only in theory but in practice, so that you turn the job of preparing a person to make a living over to a vocational school, while you turn the job of stretching the mind and preparing a person to live the good life as a cultured, humanistically educated person over to the liberal arts college.

It is no longer the case, however, as it once may have been, that our liberal arts colleges could assume that their students for the most part had independent means and had no need to be concerned about the question of how they were to make a living. On the contrary, today one of the most pressing challenges which the liberal arts colleges face is the demand that they justify the cost to their students and their families of a very expensive education in terms of vocational benefits which students expect an education to give them.

At the same time, our vocational schools are recognizing that more humanistic training is desperately needed for the persons who are being trained for a vocation, especially for those vocations which are honorific professions. This is particularly true in engineering and medicine—most dramatically so in the latter field, where the explosively innovative advances in technology in recent years have opened up a Pandora's box of social, ethical, religious, political, and legal problems that the relatively inadequate humanistic training of the physician does not prepare him to cope with adequately. This is a problem which medicine is facing honestly and dealing with intelligently, by calling in philosophers, theologians, economists, lawyers, social workers, and elected and appointed political officials as consultants, and by restructuring the medical curriculum to include humanistic courses such as bioethics as well as medical ethics. Preprofessional curricula

need to be reexamined to make sure that they are not used just as an extension of the time to be spent on technical courses in the discipline, but rather
on the kind of humanistic courses that liberal arts training is ideally suited
for. An admirable example of a preparatory program that is designed very
simply and I think quite successfully to accomplish just this very purpose is
the requirement for admission to the school of architecture at Yale University, namely, an A.B. degree in preferably a humanistic and nontechnical major.

I can find no trace of *social* snobbery in Blanshard, and no one with his
own personal history, which he tells about so simply and eloquently in his
Autobiography, could ever be so snobbish as to think that in order to become
a superstar one had to have parents who were themselves superstars. But he
does not seem to be wholly free of a very similar prejudice that I call institutional snobbery—namely, the feeling that a boy of gold whose parents
were of brass and iron had better be sure to go to Harvard or Yale or
Princeton, or better yet, to Oxford or Cambridge, if he wanted to have the
best chance of becoming a superstar himself. I think Blanshard's hero
worship for the superstar institutions results in his giving more credit to the
institution for producing a superstar than it deserves. What he does not take
sufficiently into account is that potential superstars are more likely to be attracted to an institution that has an illustrious reputation for producing
superstars than to any of its lesser rivals. UCLA, for example, for the past
decade has been attracting high school All-American basketball players, who
are duly turned out by UCLA as college All-Americans. I think it would be
rather unconvincing to argue that it is highly likely these persons would not
have become All-Americans had they gone to lesser colleges.

When I suggested this criticism to Blanshard during our discussion, he
replied:

> I think I would agree with you about that. It is only in case the two schools
> have essentially the same kind of raw material to work with that you could
> measure them by the number of superstars they produce.
>
> You see my criterion is not the production of superstars. It is the produc-
> tion by an educational system of products who are disciplined in the ways
> best suited to their particular talents and capacities. And from this point of
> view I think that the American system is better than the English. The
> English system traditionally has been to skim from British youth a very
> thick cream in the way of literary and mathematical capacity. Send your
> literary geniuses to Oxford, send your mathematical and scientific boys to
> Cambridge, and let the rest go—let them struggle along as best they can,
> finding some local institute or carpentry apprenticeship which will help them
> out. I should add that things have changed greatly since the last war. Well, I
> think our system of education is more imaginative than that. We are
> developing community universities and colleges—two-year colleges as op-
> posed to four-year colleges. We have a lot of technical schools like MIT and

Cal Tech, and I think that's the direction in which a democratic system of education should be going. [Tr., 31]

As Blanshard reviewed with me his educational theory and my preliminary criticisms of it, he suggested that there was another rather important loophole in his theory which had been overlooked. He then indicated what he would say if his theory were attacked because of this loophole.

> Well, my theory is at any rate a simple one, and I think you'll probably find it easy to shoot at. It is that probably no two students have the same capacities or the same interests, and that the aim of education should be to enable each of them to live the fullest and the richest life that his natural constitution makes possible for him. . . . There's probably something wrong with that theory but just as a generalization I don't see what it is. Someone might suggest that it is entirely selfish. "You are telling people to get the most out of life for themselves; you haven't taken into account the sort of training that would make them of service to humanity. And we used to hear that that was the most important thing in education." Well, I'm inclined to think that a person does the most for the world by being his own self in the fullest measure. . . . I think we ought to aim in education to make each person fulfil himself most completely *on the grounds* that by making people more completely themselves we equip them best to be of use to the community. [Tr., 35–36]

I suggested to Blanshard that these remarks, if I were to quote his own words from the tapes, would afford the reader an admirable supplement to the statement of his theory as found in *Uses*. He not only agreed that I might quote them, but added an important summary of his position which I have also quoted in full above [p. 431] since it is available nowhere else.

> Certainly. I'd be glad if you would supplement it. I realize that for the most part the emphasis throughout that book is on personal self-realization, rather than contribution to the community. And I have raised a question or two myself—the question whether my theory isn't too individualistic and subjective and too nonutilitarian in the larger sense. My answer would be, in general, that I think that each person does the most for the community by being himself most completely. Margaret Mead has done much more for the community by making herself into a good anthropologist than she would have if she'd become an ordinary Middle Western housewife, which she seemed headed for at one time. [Tr., 36]

I am grateful to Blanshard, and I am sure that the reader will share my sentiment, for the clarification of his philosophy which the supplementary remarks I have quoted here afford. His added principle which I call his CDSR is important as a reply to my criticism of what I found to be an omission or oversight in his theory as presented in *Uses*, namely, his apparent unconcern with any but superstars. One important loophole, however, as I have suggested above, still remains, I think, unplugged in his theory. While the principle of CDSR does provide *either* vocational or liberal training for everyone, it does *not* ensure that those who receive vocational training will receive *any* humanistic training (and I think that this needs to be remedied), nor does it ensure that those who receive a liberal education will be able to earn their living, which I think is also deplorable, but correctable.

Since the goals of liberal education and vocational training are different in kind, it may well be that Blanshard will not agree with my suggested solution of combining the two kinds of education, but if he were to agree, it should be a very simple matter for him to revise his theory and plug the loophole which otherwise, on my view, would remain at this point.

Conclusion

It is my feeling that where Blanshard's theory is the most vulnerable is in his occupational bias as a rationalist and his preference for the humanistic values of our culture as being better than any other values in our culture or any other culture.

I would question, for example, the implication by Blanshard that the lives of the "scientific boys" from MIT and Cal Tech (I presume Cambridge is not included because Blanshard does not consider it a mere vocational school) are inferior in intrinsic value to the lives of the boys from Yale or Oxford (see Tr., 31 as quoted above, p. 442). It is not only philosophy, and poetry, and music, and literature, and history, and pure mathematics that "stretch the mind and enrich the spirit of man," but pure science as well, and yes, applied science and engineering also. When cloning becomes an established procedure, as a result of the cooperative endeavors of pure science, applied science, and engineering, can anyone deny that it too will stretch the mind and enlarge the horizons of man? Nor do we need to wait for the fulfillment of what today is still largely a science-fiction dream for an example of how science stretches the mind. Think of Newton, of Darwin, of Einstein, of Watson and Crick.

Blanshard's own grading of values rests on certain assumptions for which he claims self-evidency, some of which I can grant and some of which I cannot.

(1) Grades of better or worse in comparing performances in the same category of value can be made intuitively with reasonable agreement about who is *very* good and who is *very* bad, by the experts in that category—e.g. comparing one violin player to another, or one poet to another, or one banjo player to another, or one baseball player to another.

Self-evidency granted.

(2) A similar degree of self-evident accuracy can be achieved by experts in cross-categorial value comparisons where they are comparing performances of comparable proficiency, at least to the extent that these are the performances of the best in their respective fields, such as a superstar in philosophy

compared to a superstar in baseball or engineering or banjo playing, or the best graduates of MIT or Cal Tech compared to the best liberal arts graduates of Yale and Harvard and Princeton.

Self-evidency not granted.

I am willing to grant that a strong case could be argued for the contention that the violin or the human voice is intrinsically more valuable as a musical instrument than the piano or the guitar or the banjo, because of the unsurpassable quality of the *solo voice* of the violin or the singer. However, I think a strong enough case could be made out for an opposing view to warrant the denial of self-evidency for the above claim. The piano (or to a slightly lesser degree the guitar, and to a slightly still lesser degree the banjo) offers the listener the rich and complex musical experiences *afforded only by harmony*—experiences which are minimally presented in the voice of the solo violin, and not at all in the voice of the solo singer. I do not, of course, refer here to the harmonic structure that serves as the scaffolding on which a melody is built, and which is recognizable in the melody heard alone. I do not wish to belabor the point, but merely to explain why I think self-evidency cannot be claimed for either position.

Despite my numerous criticisms of Blanshard's views, many of which are intended primarily to prompt him to expand and clarify his views in further detail, I have found his philosophy to be extremely stimulating, rewarding, and provocative, and I am grateful to him for his unique and invaluable help in stretching my mind and helping me to see more clearly where we are in agreement and where we are not.

EUGENE FREEMAN

DEPARTMENT OF PHILOSOPHY
EMERITUS
SAN JOSE STATE UNIVERSITY
SAN JOSE, CALIFORNIA

NOTES

[1] J. C. Eccles, "The World of Objective Knowledge," in *The Philosophy of Karl Popper,* ed. Paul Arthur Schilpp (La Salle, Ill.: Open Court Publishing Co., 1974), 1:350–51.

[2] John W. Gardner, *Excellence: Can We Be Equal and Excellent Too?* (New York: Harper & Row, 1961).

[3] "Das ist die wahre Symbolik wo das Besondere das Allgemeine representiert (vertrift), und zwar nicht als leerer Ausdruck, sondern. . . ." *Gesamte Werke,* IX, "Maximen und Reflektionen," no. 314.

[4] As Erich Heller puts it, "The work of Karl Krause is rich in words. And every single word is of the greatest possible precision. It is precise through its infinite ambiguity." Erich Heller, *The Disinherited Mind* (Cleveland, O.: Meridian Books—World Publishing Co., 1964), 240.

9. Reply to Eugene Freeman

The Commitment to Excellence
in Blanshard's Philosophy of Education

Mr. Freeman knows more about my views on education than anyone else. It was he who urged me to put together into a book the addresses I had given in this field; he edited the book and published it; he asked me to write on education for the *Monist* and we have had some interesting conversations about it. Happily he agrees with much that I say on education, and he likes my way of saying it. But there is one critical theme that runs through his essay in this volume as a theme of Beethoven's runs through one of his symphonies. Sometimes it comes in very faintly as an echo from off stage; sometimes it is insinuated explicitly but gently, like a passage for the flutes; at other times it is a blare of accusing drums and trumpets. The theme is: Blanshard is an elitist. Educationally he is a snob—not a personal snob with his nose in the air, nor a social snob who avoids hoi polloi, but an intellectual snob who uses his own subject as a standard for all others, an academic snob who prefers that you should come from the right college or university, a snob in the arts, who holds that in literature, art, and music there are white woolly sheep and soiled and hairy goats, who forgathers with the sheep and keeps an aseptic distance from the goats. Along with many gratifying and fortifying things that Mr. Freeman says in his critique, this seems to stand out as its dominant and recurring theme, and obviously it is this in its varied forms that I must try to meet.

Whether "elitist" is the correct word for me or not, Mr. Freeman is right that I am out of tune with much that goes on in American education today. I believe in more exacting standards and more rigorous discipline than are accepted in most of our schools and colleges. I believe that some subjects are far better than others for providing discipline and enrichment of mind. I believe that some artists and musicians, some poets and prose writers, are better than others, and can be known to be better. I believe that education should acquaint one with the best in each field, and should pay little or no attention to the second and third rate, even though writers and artists on these levels may be the heroes of the day. I believe that our popular literature and our radio and television shows have given much too large a part to violence, vice, and vulgarity. I believe that in a democracy it is important to give special honor to thinkers and artists of genuine distinction, if only to counteract the advantage of those who cater to the lowest common denominator of popular taste. I believe in promoting what W. C. Brownell bravely called "democratic distinction in America," even though the phrase seems to some a contradiction in terms.

An Objective Better and Worse

It is obvious that all this assumes that there *is* an objective better and worse. The plain man has no doubt of this; it seems to him a truism hardly worth repeating, however hard he might find it to give grounds for his preferences. Nevertheless the truism is widely denied today. Members of minority groups often sense in it the claim of the "wasp" or some other group to superiority for itself and inferiority for all others. The denial has received more formidable support from certain philosophers and anthropologists. The logical empiricism of the thirties and forties, whose theory of value is still followed by many philosophers, questioned the existence of value judgments altogether; an apparent judgment of this kind was the expression of an attitude or emotion, generally of liking or disliking, and as such was neither true nor false. Among anthropologists, Sumner and Westermarck both held to a subjectivism in morals according to which "the mores can make anything right"; and the later "cultural relativism" popularized by Ruth Benedict held that there was no objective or international standard by which one culture could be judged better or worse than others.

I share the plain man's conviction that this is nonsense. I am much more certain that Shakespeare was a greater poet than Edgar Guest—*objectively* a greater poet—than I am that the analyses purporting to discredit the statement are sound. If I am wrong on this point, if such a comparative judgment is nothing but the expression of a personal liking, then any educational system that calls for an exposure to "the best" is the demand of some muddled and self-important ego that others should bow to his personal prejudices. My first business, therefore, is to show that "the objectivity of value judgments" means something definite and credible.

When we call a fact or a value objective, our primary meaning is that it is independent of our judgment about it; it is what it would be if we had judged differently or had not judged at all. That the sun is at the center of the solar system, that three and one make four, that Shakespeare was a great poet, are true whether we think of them or not, and regardless of what we may think of them. Granting, however, that these three facts do not depend on my thinking of them, can I say that they are equally independent of human experience as such? Most persons who have considered the matter would say that the first two facts were thus independent, while the third was not. The sun would still be at the center of the solar system and a group of three stars plus one would make a group of four, whether there were human observers or not. On the other hand, Shakespeare would certainly not have been a great poet if human experience had not existed, if only for the reason that reading or writing poetry is experience. Mr. Freeman would, I think, agree with this view; more particularly, he would agree that in a world without consciousness there would be no place for beauty or ugliness, good or evil.

Granting now that Shakespeare's being a great poet does depend on experience, does it depend on my experience? Suppose I had never heard of Shakespeare, and therefore made no judgment on him at all; would that have affected his quality or rank as a poet? If we may brush aside abstruse doubts about internal relations, most of us would say, "not in the least." Suppose I am in fact acquainted with the poet and judge him as disparagingly as Darwin, Tolstoy, and Shaw did; would that affect his quality or rank? No again. The intrinsic value of a poet's achievement remains what it is, regardless of the ups and downs in his reputation. If we say that Shakespeare was a minor poet in the eighteenth century and a great one again in the nineteenth, we certainly do not mean that his greatness rose and fell as did the current opinion about it, and therefore that both ages were right about him, however contradictory. What then are we asserting? When we say that Shakespeare's work had an objective intrinsic value, not dependent on our judgment or even that of the critics, what do we mean?

We mean, I think, that Shakespeare's work has the potentiality for those who read him or see his plays of inducing experiences that are themselves of great intrinsic value. I have explained already what, in my view, makes an experience valuable. It is the fulfilling and satisfying of the impulses, urges, or drives of human nature. Shakespeare's quality manifested itself in the first instance in his own experience of creation, with its extraordinary range of character and plot, and its unexampled power of expression. But the greatness of a poet lies not in his own experience only, but also in his ability to convey it to other minds. And Shakespeare had that gift in prodigious measure. He could throw back the horizons of other people's thought and feeling. He could make them live in imagination in minds near enough to their own to deepen their self-understanding, yet far enough away to widen the bounds of their experience of life. He revealed to them the possibilities of their own nature, which he enabled them to realize vicariously. Everyone has tendencies in him that would, if actualized, make him a little Jacques or Hamlet, a minor Falstaff or Portia or Othello; in Shakespeare we can see the tendencies of our own nature incarnated and developed before our eyes. And anyone with a love of expression, of the fitness of word to fact and feeling, must take delight in the inexhaustible verbal magic of a master. In sum, the greatness of Shakespeare lies in his power to supply his readers with a rich imaginative fulfillment together with the pleasure that comes from such fulfillment, the whole intensified by a rare aesthetic delight.

Does it make sense to compare works of literature, art, or music and attempt to rank or grade them? The attempt is often deplored as philistine, presumptuous, and impracticable. And comparisons are indeed often odious. But if they are called impossible in the sphere of value, there is a reply that seems to me decisive. The reply is that unless intrinsic values can be weighed against each other with some degree of assurance, not only does humanistic education become a farce but morality itself becomes an imposture. The rightness or wrongness of moral alternatives depends on precisely this weighing of consequent intrinsic values, and unless one can say that one group of such values, A, is more worth having than another, B, right and wrong become indistinguishable. Similarly, unless one can say concerning a student with certain interests and abilities that the study of Shakespeare will be more rewarding than that of Edgar Guest, or the study of Greek civilization than that of the Dobuans or the Kwakiutl, the pretensions of the liberal arts college are mere presumptions. Their studies are not the deposit of past wisdom preserved for the guidance of youth, but fogeyisms, the impositions of past prejudice. This view has recurrent surges of popularity, particularly among educational misfits who must manage to rationalize their failures. The true product of refusing to differentiate an objective better and worse is not sophistication but, as Arnold pointed out, anarchy.

One who takes this line must be prepared for *ad hominem* replies: So you claim, do you, the right of universal arbiter? There have been heated altercations among musicians as to whether Bach should take precedence over Beethoven or Beethoven over Bach; if the partisans will beat a path to your door, you will be kind enough to hand down judgment. That is most gracious of you. Henry James, Dostoyevsky, and Norman Mailer have all been made compulsory reading for students; you will no doubt be ready to tell us their comparative educational value. In a class in freshman English, the instructor is pondering whether to prescribe *In Memoriam* or Pound's *Cantos;* he will be relieved to know that all he needs is your telephone number. Is Gibbon or Macaulay the greater historian? Is Boswell, Lockhart, or Trevelyan the better biographer? Let us not go round the point; what you are really saying, with discreet abstractness, is:

"I am Sir Oracle
And when I ope my lips, let no dog bark."

All this is utter misunderstanding. I make no claim, of course, to be able to answer these questions. I doubt if there is anyone alive who has the knowledge requisite to answer them with certainty, and there are numberless questions of a similar kind which no one who ever lived could answer with certainty. But that is irrelevant to the thesis I am maintaining. That thesis is that the question whether an experience is intrinsically good, or better than another, is a question with an answer, and an answer that is objectively true, whether we are in a position to know it or not.

I have briefly sketched what I think we mean when we say that Shakespeare was a great poet. That he had the qualities that would justify the term seems clear enough, and if some critics have judged otherwise, we can discern the quirks in their thinking that led to their dissent. When it comes to comparative judgment—whether Shakespeare was a greater poet than Homer or Dante, whether Gray's "Elegy" was a greater poem than Eliot's "The Wasteland"—we face a harder kind of question, because it requires a broader range of understanding and imaginative sympathy. The critic would have to grasp completely the meaning and intention of each writer and then say whether a full response to this meaning—intellectual, emotional, and aesthetic—would provide a richer fulfillment of human nature. The more disparate the products compared, for example Eastern and Western music, the more unlikely it becomes that any critic, living or dead, has had the necessary diversity of responsiveness to make the comparison competently. But even here I do not see that the question, especially if asked about particular pieces, is meaningless, or that it is not in principle capable of definite answer. Suppose there were a critic ideally acquainted with both Eastern and Western music, and able to enter completely into the experiences intended by the two composers; suppose, further, that he listens with full receptiveness to the two pieces under comparison; and suppose that he then asks himself which of the two experiences he would be the more reluctant to forgo. I do not know why such an answer should not be given, nor why, if tendered, it should not be accepted.

Mr. Freeman's Doubts about Objectivity

These remarks may suffice to answer, at least by implication, several of Mr. Freeman's difficulties with my theory of objective values. (a) "Blanshard's contention that values are objective is riddled with a paradoxical ultimate subjectivity of value." This charge of "subjectivity" reduces to one or both of two subcharges. (i) It may mean that values do not exist apart from experience. To this, of course, I plead guilty. Though values are not reducible to pleasures and pains, they seem to me to have the same ontological status. To say that Smith is suffering from a pain is to say that he is experiencing a disvalue. The two judgments are objectively true because he is in fact suffering pain, and pain *is* a disvalue. These facts are in no way dependent on my judgments about them, though they are both dependent on Smith's consciousness, which is their only place of residence. (ii) There is another meaning for the charge of subjectivity. "The objectivity of values thus turns out to be intersubjective agreement among experts about the ranking of values." To this charge I plead not guilty. On the question whether the "Elegy" or "The Wasteland" is the greater poem critics may, for all I know, be divided to the end of time, but that would not shake my belief that the question is an intelligible one and has an answer. And if there is an answer waiting to be found, critics who find it will of course agree; but it does not follow that if they agree, they have found it, for there may be unity in error; or that if they disagree, it is not there.

(b) Mr. Freeman has a further case against my account of objectivity: it is a tautology. "His [Blanshard's] claim that values are objective in the sense that similar value judgments would be made by equally qualified experts means operationally that like-minded people are like-minded people—that is, they have the same value criteria and they make the same gradings in their value judgments—a tautology that is not particularly enlightening, and which is what is meant in ordinary language by 'occupational bias.' " But there would be no tautology in my own use of "like-minded," for the term would be seen to have different senses. On the value of the "Elegy," for example, two critics may agree because, having entered completely into the meanings and intentions of the author, they agree on the fulfillment and satisfaction derived from the experience. They are like-minded because their judgments are under the control of the same object. The "like-mindedness" that Mr. Freeman describes as "occupational bias" is an agreement of a very different kind. It is an agreement controlled by the subjects rather than the object, a likeness of their likings, a likeness of emotional disposition and appreciative habit. To say that two critics who like the same thing like the same thing *is* tautology. To say that two critics who enter fully into the meaning and intention of a poem will tend to assign it a like value is very far from being a tautology. It is one of the disputed theses of my much disputed theory of value.

(c) "How would Blanshard account for a difference of opinion among experts in their value judgments?" The only thing that puzzles me about this question is why it should be supposed to present any difficulty. Even in that most dehumanized of mental processes, the adding of a column of figures, there are dozens of ways of going wrong to one of going right. In the appraisal of a poem the traps are more numerous and more insidious. One of two critics may capture in its entirety the meaning and intention of a poem and therefore may have before him the right object to appraise. Another may fail either (i) to get the right object before him, or (ii) so to exercise his judgment as to appraise it adequately. And each of these processes may itself fall short in many ways. The critic may fail to reach the right object because his imagination is too limited, or because his ear is insensitive, or because the language is unfamiliar, or for any number of other reasons. And even if one does enter fully into meaning and intention, one may misjudge from "professional bias," or from too narrow an experience to make comparison feasible, or from a touch of half-conscious antagonism to the author's personality. To follow with assurance the abstract thought of another may be easy enough; but the grasp and appraisal of a poem, with its unique blend of feeling and idea, each of them tinged with the idiosyncrasy of the author's mind, may involve one's personality as a whole. In such a task, we can hardly hope for more than approximate success.

The Charge of Elitism

Still, unless such success is open to us, the distinction of a really better from a really worse is impossible, progress is impossible, education is impossible. And it is time we returned to education. Mr. Freeman charges me with elitism. This term again has more than one reference. One is to the belief that among the many subjects of study in American schools and colleges some are of great and others of small educational value. If this is elitism, I am deeply dyed with it. The aim of education I take to be what the word etymologically suggests, the disciplined drawing out or development of the student's powers. By the time a youth reaches the college or university, his powers have begun to show themselves, and the business of a higher education on its liberal side is to clarify the ends toward which these powers should be directed and to carry him as far toward them as possible. The best way to get a student to do good work in any field is to expose him to the best in that field and induce him by any available means to fall in love with it. "We needs must love the highest when we see it," the poet tells us, and he is right if we really do see it, though too many of our students complete their university work without ever catching a glimpse of it or knowing the lift of heart that such a glimpse affords. Still, the business of higher education remains, I think, what a great tradition has declared it to be. It is to bring home to the student, as Arnold would say, "the best that has been thought and said in the world"; it is to put before him, as Whitehead would say, "the vision of greatness"; or, as Dr. Hutchins would have it, to acquaint him with the classics, meaning by "classics" those books that are "contemporary with every age."

In discussing whether these phrases have any meaning, I have drawn my examples from literature because it is in the field of taste that the objectivity of values has been most widely and plausibly attacked. We are forever being told that *de gustibus non est disputandum,* though arguments about matters of taste continue to flourish and to prove illuminating. But while responsiveness to the arts is an important part of liberal education, it is not the only or the most important part. That part is intellectual; it is the awakening and discipline of reflective thought. The greatest achievement of man's intellect is modern science, and there is no very significant difference of opinion as to who the leaders have been in the fields, for example, of mathematics and physics, biology and economics, and—we may add—of logic and philosophy. I am not suggesting that the best way to study science is to study the classics in its history, a very dubious proposal. The most original intellects are often not the best expositors of their own work. Further, what the liberal student needs is not so much the facts that the masters discovered as the habits of mind that led to their discovery—precision in observation and statement, self-criticism as well as readiness in inference, the love of truth for its own sake. Such habits can be acquired in the pursuit of any of the sciences, and especially through those expositors who best exemplify these habits in their own writing. Take an example from the field of philosophy. Hegel, Whitehead, and Heidegger are assuredly thinkers both profound and important; but if a young man wanted to learn what clear, precise, and connected thinking meant, I should not recommend to him *The Phenomenology of Mind* or *Process and Reality* or *Being and Time.* On the other hand, if he were able to give himself a course in McTaggart's *The Nature of Existence,* along with Broad's *Examination* of it, he would have before him at once the work of two masters of reflective analysis who were also masters in the art of stating a case.

The end of intellect itself is the understanding of the world, and the aim of education on its intellectual side is both to form in the student the habits that would further that end and to help him toward it as far as his talents allow. It is part of the elitism with which I am charged that I think some subjects of study much more fitted for this end than others. If we take the three great areas into which existence seems to fall—matter, life, and mind—we must admit that some sciences provide a much more comprehensive understanding of them than others. Physics tells us more about the nature and behavior of matter than crystallography does; general biology tells us more about living organisms than entomology does; psychology tells us more about how the mind operates than does parapsychology. To those who would introduce into the liberal arts curriculum a great variety of practical subjects from shoemaking to motor repairing one can only say, without any disparagement of these subjects, that they do not belong among the liberal arts; they are not pursued for their own sake or for the sake of liberating and enlarging the mind, but for the sake of acquiring a practical technique.

The Place of the Humanities

I have been defending "elitism" in that most broad and innocent sense to which anyone is committed who holds to objectivity among values, namely that some books, authors, and subjects are really better than others. I can hardly believe that Mr. Freeman would dissent from such a thesis, though his difficulties with my objectivity theory seem at times to suggest it. He does, however, press me on my elitism in a more specific sense when he criticizes my preference for the humanities. "Blanshard's elitism, or preference for humanistic values as higher than any others, is both the expression of one of the primitive propositions or assumptions on which his philosophical system rests and the expression of his occupational bias as a rationalist philosopher. . . . He offers no more proof than Mill did, namely, that those who experience both prefer the intellectual pleasures; therefore since they are preferred, they are preferable."

Of this argument Mr. Freeman denies both the premise and the conclusion. He says, with truth I think, that the great mass of people prefer not the television programs that make some demand on intelligence but those that make no such demand. My answer here would be the same as Mill's; such preference is not a genuine rejection of the "higher" for the "lower" after full exposure to both, for the persons judging have not experienced the higher at all. One does not experience a Shakespeare play by merely sitting in front of it; one must respond to its ideas, characters, and music; and this the ordinary viewer is ill prepared to do. When he rejects Shakespeare, therefore, he is hardly in a better position to judge than were the Puritans, who rejected him without having exposed themselves to his contamination. What Mill (and I following him) would take as the court of last appeal would be the judgment of one who responded to the two types of presentation with equal understanding and responsiveness, so as genuinely to absorb what each had to offer. If under such circumstances a man finds *Charley's Aunt* to be intrinsically more valuable than *Macbeth* or *Lear,* I have no more to say, except that I have never met this man.

So much for the premise that with equal understanding of both some men prefer the "lower" to the "higher." Now for the conclusion from the premise, namely that those who find the study of the humanities more valuable *ought* to prefer them. This seems to me so obvious as to be very near tautology. But Mr. Freeman finds in it a different meaning. He takes me to conclude that persons who have been exposed to both types of product and continue to prefer what I should regard as the lower "should be compelled to agree" with me. Now Mill (of all persons) certainly drew no such conclusion, nor do I. Each person, of course, has a right to his own view, though in controversial matters he also has a duty to expose himself to opposing views. In any case, private thought is beyond the reach of coercion, which is not, I think, implied in anything I have written.

If I show a preference for the humanities as instruments of education, it is not a wholly unreasoned prejudice. Anyone who holds, as I do, that value itself consists in the fulfillment and satisfaction of powers is bound to support studies which promote that fulfillment and satisfaction, and I can think of no studies that promote these as effectively as the humanities. The natural sciences provide admirably for the discipline of the intellect, but for the most part they keep to one type of value, the cognitive, and are without professional interest in beauty or ugliness, in good or evil, or in the persons of the world and their strivings. In the study of literature and art, of history and morals, of religion and philosophy (commonly accounted a humane study) these values cannot be ignored, and they are values firmly bound up with human happiness. I would go further and say that even on the cognitive side many persons will gain more from rigorous study in the humanities than they would from an equally rigorous study of science, and this for the very reason that in the former values and facts are so intermixed. Physics and chemistry are not as a rule battlegrounds of bias, and the "personal equation" can be fairly easily allowed for or excluded. But a genuinely fair history of Ireland or Israel is almost impossible, and true objectivity in the study of religion, race, or sex is notoriously difficult. Considering how many of the problems of practical and political life are similarly bias-charged, the discipline gained through the humanities in sailing an impartial course through seas mined with explosive emotions seems to me invaluable.

Perfectionism of Performance

Another way in which my elitism seems to show itself is in my "perfectionism of performance." The criticism is not that I am committed to excellence, which it is granted that any educator should be, but that, "to translate my point into the context of classroom teaching, for Blanshard the A students pass, and the B and C and D students have failed." Now there are three very different points involved here, and in self-defense I will briefly state my view on each.

(i) I believe strongly in grades and examinations; I believe in Phi Beta Kappa and the kind of honorary degrees that reward scholarly and scientific achievement; there is too little rather than too much recognition in this country of intellectual distinction. There are vast differences in human ability, and if outstanding talents are not recognized in institutions specially commissioned to discover and develop them, education is abdicating its office. I have no sympathy with the student movement to abolish grades except that which is born of my forty years' desperate struggle to assign them with some measure of justice. (ii) While a university teacher should take his stand unequivocally for intellectual excellence, he should be able to recognize that there is no grading system which reflects human power and promise adequately. He may well recall that Arthur Balfour took a second class and Darwin only a pass degree at Cambridge; that Arnold and Bradley and Saintsbury took seconds at Oxford, and Newman a third; that Housman was failed altogether; and that Whistler, lamentably deficient in chemistry, was thrown out of West Point. ("If silicon had been a gas," he remarked, "I would have been a general.") A teacher may quite consistently hold that examinations are significant without holding that failure in them is necessarily due to stupidity or that they can test a personality as a whole. (iii) A teacher who is a good human being—and if he is not, he has missed his calling—should be interested not only in his A students but in his D's and E's and why he had to attach to them these telltale tags. He should be aware that a man who is a dunce in one department may be a genius in another. If some of Whistler's teachers had seen the young man's drawings, and Darwin's Latin teachers had seen the significance of his coming to class, as is alleged, with beetles in his mouth, they might have given their young charges more far-seeing advice.

When these three corollaries of my educational creed are made explicit, I doubt whether my "commitment to excellence" merits the charge of elitism.

Sometimes Mr. Freeman puts my humanistic elitism in a form that may unintentionally mislead. The casual reader is likely to get the impression that the humanist and his studies *as such* are put on a pedestal outtopping all others. But value *as such,* goodness as such, the goodness of the humanities as such, have no existence anywhere. Value exists only as it is realized in the fulfillment of particular minds, and such realization is always a matter of degree. If comparisons are to be made, therefore, they must be made between specific experiences that carry values in determinate amounts. What could it mean to say that humanistic values are better than those of carpentry or plumbing? Against any such statement there could be cited many cases of scholars living meager and frustrated lives and many of carpenters and plumbers who were comparatively unfrustrated and happy. It is part of my theory of the commensurability of all values that no type of good as such outweighs any other in the sense that any amount of the former, however small, outweighs any amount of the latter, however large. That was the sort of doctrine that Newman preached when he made religious and secular values incomparable and said that it would be better for all mankind to die in extreme agony than for one man to commit the smallest venial sin. That inhuman doctrine is the logical result of isolating one class of values as of incomparable importance.

One of Mr. Freeman's subheads is "Blanshard's Institutional Snobbery." I am glad to note that he absolves me from social snobbery, but he thinks I am prone to a kind of hero worship of those institutions that are prolific mothers of "superstar" sons. In a sense he is no doubt right. I confess that I do not see how anyone can pace the quadrangles at Oxford or Cambridge or cast even a tourist's glance at the portraits on their dining hall walls without becoming something of an institutional hero-worshiper; I have expressed my own feelings on the matter in earlier pages of this book. Mr. Freeman points out that a university may be illustrious as much because of the human clay it has had for the moulding as because of any skill it had in moulding it. And no doubt this is possible. The influence works both ways; if a university has students of high average ability, it can set its standards high, and if its standards are known to be high, it attracts students of ability. There are no institutions in this country that stand out from their rivals with the antiquity and prestige of Oxford and Cambridge in Britain, and in a country as populous as ours this is a healthy situation. But while we have scores of colleges in which an admirable education can be acquired, we have scores of others that are hardly more than magnified high schools, so that an arts degree has a highly variable value. Mr. Freeman infers that I would fix that value for any university by the number of "superstars" it turns out. It would not have occurred to me to use a term so suggestive of neon lights and Hollywood, that arch-perverter of values, for the best products of a university, but I did say that the quality of a university could be measured by the quality of the persons who walked out of its doors, and I would stick to that. I was thinking of the intellectual and personal quality of a college's *typical* graduate—his habits of thought, speech, taste, and character—as gauging the success of the institution, not merely of names that appear in headlines.

Reasonableness

In *The Uses of a Liberal Education,* I say that the quality I value most in the educated man is reasonableness, the rational temper. Mr. Freeman thinks I use the term "reason" and its derivatives in different senses in different contexts. This I certainly do. When I discuss it in epistemology, I usually mean by it a priori apprehension of necessity, though in the discussion of "the movement of reflection" I allow that inferences falling short of necessity may be genuine cases of reasoning. This is in full accord with usage. When discussing theology and the contrast between reason and faith, I commonly mean by reason what supernaturalist theologians mean by it, natural knowledge as distinct from revealed. I make no apology for these variations; they are called for by the context; they are not ambiguous in that context; there is no inconsistency in so using them. Mr. Freeman thinks I use the term so loosely, however, as to make the rational cover what is actually irrational.

> What intrigues me the most about Blanshard's use of the term is the paradoxical way in which the term "reasonable" on occasion becomes richer and more practical than the term "rational" by adding to its meaning what, in fact, is literally *irrationality*. For example, it is quite rational for a person to refuse to compromise his principles and to refuse to agree to do something which he is convinced is wrong for him to do. But it may be unreasonable of him to refuse to negotiate a dispute in which both sides are convinced of their own rightness, as in, say, a labor dispute, but a dispute which if not resolved would result in disastrous consequences to both sides. In such cases, it is better to give up the unreasonable for the reasonable, which combines what is essentially the rational with just enough of a concession to the wrong or the irrational to make it acceptable to both sides.

I do not see that either my philosophy or my usage involves me in confusion here. Suppose, as in the given case, that you are an arbitrator in a labor dispute. And suppose that, of the two sides, the management, A, and the union, B, you soon see that B is altogether right in its claims. If you are honest, you say so. But you also see that A is so unwilling to concede this that it is ready to close the plant and dismantle it rather than yield an inch to B's claim. What, as an arbitrator, would you recommend? The answer of my own ethics seems to me unequivocal. The only absolute principle in that ethics is the rule of rightness itself, the principle of the greatest good. And it seems to me very probable that in this case the greatest good would be achieved, not by advising B to stick to its righteous claim at the cost of closing the plant and throwing all the employees together out of their jobs, but to compromise the minor principle—to be sure to the smallest feasible extent—in the interest of the major one. Sometimes one must give up a genuine good or abandon a legitimate claim if the larger good is to be achieved. Kant's inflexible rigidity of principle may be a sort of moral rigor mortis, in which human good is sacrificed remorselessly to abstractions. This is not my notion of rationality in morals. It is true that one ought at times to stand on principle, even some minor principle, and fight it out. But it is only reason that can tell you whether in this case you are doing right or playing the fanatic, the man whom Santayana describes as redoubling his effort when he has forgotten his end. In a world full of unreasonable people, compromise with unreasonableness is often the most reasonable course. I doubt if Mr. Freeman disagrees here, but he finds this position more of a paradox than I do.

Quality versus Democracy

Mr. Freeman's main difficulty with my educational theory, however, is neither with my stress on reasonableness as the prime desideratum nor with my hydra-headed elitism, but with the consistency between my elitism and my democracy. He writes: "the major problem considered in the present study, is the apparent incompatibility of the demands made in the name of CE [Commitment to Excellence] and those demanded by CDSR [Commitment to Democratic Self-Realization]." The problem raised here is difficult, pressing, and important. It is as follows. The commitment to excellence demands high standards, most obviously in our institutions of higher learning. But the more those standards are raised, the larger is the proportion of would-be students who are turned away. And this seems to conflict flatly with the demand that the youth of the nation generally should be given the privilege of realizing their powers in the fullest possible measure. As I put it in a recent address: "In education there seems to be an inverse ratio between democracy and distinction. Quantity is at war with quality."

What makes the conflict practically so important is that it reveals a collision between two tendencies both of which run deep in American life. Democracy means that in some sense we are all equal and have equal rights to education. On the other hand we are strong believers in higher education; we have, at the time of this writing, some 1,900 colleges and universities. And higher education is by nature exclusive. There are persons in plenty to whom advanced courses in mathematics, economics, or epistemology would have little meaning and less interest, and who would be wasting their own time and the public's money in attempting them. Some persons have argued that to democratize higher education the standards for getting entrance into our universities and getting diplomas from them should be lowered. This would be deliberate debasement of the educational coinage; a B.A. open to everyone would be of little value to anyone. The two ideals of democracy and of intellectual distinction pull against each other.

Now *The Uses of a Liberal Education* was directed to college students, and made little reference to these problems of educational statesmanship, nor do I have the resources to say much about the practical issues involved. A remark or two must suffice.

(1) We must insist on the maintenance of standards in our higher education, if for no other reason than that modern life requires it. Life in this country has become so complex that even the ordinary citizen finds adjustment to it an exacting process. Positions of responsible leadership in a civilization like

ours impose a strain on the greatest of abilities. And it is from the colleges and universities that the leaders must chiefly come. To navigate our huge and floundering ship of state through the maze of rocks that lie in wait for it will require all the political economy and political wisdom, all the history and philosophy, intelligence and character, that our best brains can bring to bear on it.

(2) It is often said that there is a general right to higher education. This is about as true as that there is a general right to run the mile in less than four minutes. It would solve a great many problems if we were all born equal and education could make of us what it would. This was believed by no less a man than John Stuart Mill, who said in all sober humility that any healthy boy or girl in England could have done what he did if provided with the instruction he had received. We know now that this was a touching and mistaken dream. Some persons can do, without practice, what others could not do with a lifetime of practice. This, I take it, no longer needs to be argued. Higher education is designed for those of higher endowments, and these persons of greater gifts have rights that the rest of us do not. Compassion urges that highest priority be given to those to whom nature has been most niggardly. No doubt they have the right to compassion. But ability too has its rights. Let us remember that a right is a duty seen from the other end; that if a person has a right against society, that means that society has a duty to accord him a certain kind of treatment. And what is it that determines duties? I have argued that it is the prospect of the greatest good. Society has an obligation to treat those of great gifts in such a way as to promote that good. This way surely lies in developing their abilities to the fullest practicable extent. Hitler's mad hatreds drove out of his country some of its best brains, and by a strange justice these brains devised the nuclear equations that assured his and his country's downfall. If intelligence can destroy, it can also save.

(3) If men are not born equal and do not have equal rights to education, in what sense can they claim equality? Rashdall seems to me to have answered that question as well as anyone: what they are entitled to is equality of *consideration*. This means that when privileges are being distributed they must not be passed over; their existence, their needs, their capabilities must be taken into account. This suggests my own answer to Mr. Freeman's reiterated complaint that I reserve my solicitude for the select few. My reply is that everyone qualifies for some education. If the state demands literacy as the price of the vote, it has the duty of providing the means to that literacy. But what about that vast mass of American youth, forming probably its majority, who can qualify for literacy but not for the college or university? I have no experience that would give me competence outside the college field. But I can perhaps venture on an opinion or two.

My ethical theory and therefore my theory of education call for the fulfillment of those capacities with which a mind happens to be endowed. If a student is not qualified by interest or capacity for the liberal arts curriculum, he will be wasting his own time and that of others by seeking entrance to it. But I quite agree with Mr. Freeman that to confine education to the liberal arts would be myopic. A student with little capacity for economics or mathematics may be a future master with the piano or the violin, with stone or bronze, with motors or television sets, in wood carving or scout directing or steel working or a hundred other things. I recall from my own undergraduate days at Michigan a boy who wanted in a rather wan way, I think, to be an engineer. But I saw him play baseball occasionally and felt that here was a youngster who was as definitely a genius in that special field as Steinmetz was in electricity or Dylan Thomas in writing verse. Fortunately the coach at Michigan in those days was Branch Rickey, who saw that the boy was indeed a genius and took him competently in hand. This boy, George Sisler, soon came into his own as one of the most perfect players who had ever graced the national game and who was placed by his rival Cobb on his own team of baseball immortals.

The liberal arts curriculum is made for those with gifts above the average of scholarship, analysis, and abstraction. These are great gifts, and colleges should cultivate them to the full. But there are numberless other gifts, the gifts of the Fords and the Edisons, the Fred Astaires and Charlie Chaplins, the Calders and the Bobby Fischers, and our collegiate schedules are not drawn up with these people in mind. If their talents are to be encouraged, there should be a variety of technical, vocational, and specialized schools where they could find programs relevant to their needs. In mediaeval times, when schools were reserved for scholars, guilds of workmen and merchants made express provision for apprentices who gradually mastered their trades by working with their elders. Management and unions might well give more consideration to such arrangements now.

But greater hope lies in other directions, unless indeed the hordes of illegitimate immigrants that yearly swarm across our borders do not swamp that hope completely. Instead of the constant multiplication of liberal arts colleges that has occurred in recent decades, there should be a proliferation of community colleges with shortened courses in which training is given to those whose powers lie outside the borders of the liberal arts. I do not think that even here those arts should be ignored, for everyone needs them as part of his own humanization. But the emphasis would be on those studies that would at once elicit the talents of the unacademically minded, prepare them for filling their own niches in society, and so contribute to their earning a living. It may be objected that such persons would wear the badge of a second-class education. I doubt if there is any answer that would satisfy such a complaint short of reconstituting nature herself. For men are not born equal in any respect, nor would their gifts, after all the honing and polishing that education could apply to them, be of equal value either intrinsically or as a means to social good. If that is elitism, it is the tragic elitism that springs neither from indifference nor from snobbery, but from fact.

10 Brand Blanshard: Philosopher of Education and Teacher

James Gutmann

BEING a rationalist," Blanshard writes in the preface to his collected papers on education, *The Uses of a Liberal Education,* "I am inclined to think that the world is a system in which every fact and event is connected necessarily with every other" (*Uses,* p. ix). Walking in the footsteps of his rationalist predecessors, especially those in the tradition of British Hegelianism, Blanshard holds that the system of causal relations studied by science corresponds to the system of intelligible relations discerned by metaphysics. The function of philosophy is to establish this correspondence and "It is the business of the philosopher to approximate his thought to this system as closely as he can" (p. x).

These are, of course, the views which Blanshard has developed and elaborated systematically in his major writings. In *The Uses of a Liberal Education* they constitute the background of his thought. This is here set forth without technical argument, often in the form of commencement addresses or talks on other academic occasions. Though popular in presentation they are carefully reasoned documents on important themes such as "The Test of a University," "Education as Philosophy," "What Is Education For?" or "The Specialist and the Humanist." There are also, in this volume, more casual talks to groups of students, "Homilies" on topics such as Courage, Admiration, Conformity, and Serenity. While casual and occasional, these papers are, nevertheless, expressions of Blanshard's abiding interest and preoccupation with the nature of thought and its relation to science and to the humanities, discourses on reason and reasonableness and the threat of irrationality, on discipline and the emotions, on detachment and wisdom, knowledge and understanding. These themes appear again and again in his reflections on education. Here is an intellectual fabric with varying patterns but with a firm and coherent texture well worn by years of practice and experience.

One recalls Blanshard's contributions to the 1945 report on *Philosophy in American Education (PAE)*, the collaborative study done with Curt Ducasse, Charles Hendel, Arthur Murphy, and Max Otto. There Blanshard wrote:

> The very world of the modern mind, with the freedom it carries with it from irrational fanaticisms and fears is due, in the main, to the rise and influence of that rationalism, that insistence on reasonableness in belief and conduct, of which philosophy is the purest exemplar. That at any particular time philosophers have been less than unanimous in their rejection of charlatanism and folly may well be true; rationality is always a matter of degree. But it remains true that the very spirit of rational inquiry which has made them so ready to differ among themselves has tended in every age to draw them together into a united and formidable front against the darker varieties of contemporary unreason. [*PAE*, 105–6]

Blanshard distinguishes his conception of education from two other views which he characterizes as giving priority to the acquisition of information or knowledge for its own sake or, alternatively, as training for the practice of a profession or vocation. Contrariwise, for him "The great point is that education, on its intellectual side, is the quest not of knowledge, not of facts, but of illumination or understanding" (*Uses,* 104). Moreover in seeking this understanding, this enlightenment at which liberal education should aim, Blanshard believes that he parts company with pragmatists and with those whom he calls "permissivists" in education. The latter are identified with advocates of the "elective system" in colleges. This, according to Blanshard, implies the equal importance of all university subjects. However, it should be pointed out that not even President Eliot of Harvard, among the earliest and most ardent proponents of free election of courses, ever advocated this view in his attacks on a uniform curriculum based on rigid traditions which failed to recognize the importance of individual differences among students. Despite his criticism of "permissiveness" it must be said that Blanshard is by no means a defender of blind traditionalism. He is sensitive to the values of rich variety; such sensitivity is, indeed, his constant concern. But he seems to disregard its application to the problems which are the primary concern of "permissivists."

Blanshard's opposition to pragmatism in education is less absolute than at first appears. William James is one of his intellectual heroes, and there are pages in *The Uses of a Liberal Education* which recall James's *Talks to Students on Some of Life's Ideals.* Moreover, though he is critical of some views he ascribes to John Dewey, Blanshard writes that "most of his thought on education I can gratefully accept" (*Uses,* p. xi). His attacks on the extreme behaviorism of B.F. Skinner most educational pragmatists might well echo, just as reasonable "permissivists" would presumably consent to a student's proposals for his own course of study on grounds which Blanshard himself would probably approve.

More serious differences of outlook, it seems to me, would be entailed by Blanshard's conception of the role of the natural sciences in liberal education. In terms which recall Snow's "Two Cultures" Blanshard identifies the humanities as "the soil in which imagination grows" (*Uses,* 9). Though he proclaims his recognition of "the importance of science," the dichotomy which is pervasive in academic tradition is everywhere prevalent in Blanshard's discussion. "Great art," he writes, ". . . fills and stretches the mind; we have the sense, after exposure to it, of being larger persons" (p. xv). Granted; but does not "great science" have comparable effects? Though Blanshard admits that the contribution of scientific training is of the utmost importance to intellectual discipline, this seems limited to "a habit of orderliness, clearness, persistence and precision" (104).

Again Blanshard declares that "On the importance of science, both theoretic and practical, there will be no great difference of opinion. It is on another issue that the debate with the humanist arises. Considered simply as educational instruments, as disciplines preparatory to a full life, does the advantage lie with the sciences or the humanities?" And he goes on: ". . . My own conclusion, for what it is worth, favors the humanities" (*Uses,* 197). Indeed Blanshard's advocacy of a privileged position for the humanities in a liberal education occasionally leads him to uncharacteristic extremes of alarm. For instance he writes that "We are at the mercy of these scientists and we know it. They stand for something before which we are helpless, as we are before the surgeon with his scalpel and his masked face" (161). This sounds too much like Dracula!

Again, Blanshard writes:

> In recent years and for obvious reasons the claims of science in education have been forced upon our notice, and indeed forced down our throats. There is no doubt that we need more science . . . ; the scientific way of thinking is part of the equipment of any educated mind. But if anyone says that a scientific education by itself is a liberal education , and just as liberal as one in the humanities, I beg leave to differ." [*Uses,* 22]

Is this dichotomy inevitable?

It is in the discovery of the proper relation of means to ends that Brand Blanshard finds the full expression of genuine understanding at a level appropriately designated "wisdom." Writing in *The Encyclopedia of Philosophy,*[1] he considers the "components of wisdom" and identifies "Two traits [that] appear to stand out—reflectiveness and judgment. By reflectiveness is meant the habit of considering events and beliefs in the light of their grounds and consequences," he goes on, and adds: ". . . There is a wisdom of ends as well as of means, which is here denoted by 'judgment' " (*Encyclopedia,* 8:323).

Blanshard's theory of intrinsic value reenforces his conviction that "it is only courses in the humanities that take appreciation, as distinct from knowledge, as a prime goal." Seeking constantly to relate means and ends, he holds that "In our gadget-ridden culture, the distinction is important, for much of the trouble in our hurried and harried lives arises from neglecting that distinction" (*Uses*, xiv). Recognition of the intrinsic values embodied in the humanities, and of the intrinsic excellence of experiences such as great art affords as being good in themselves, provides the basis of Blanshard's philosophy of education. The good life, so conceived, is for him synonymous with the reasonable life. His rationalism leads to the judgment "that the best product of education is the rational temper." His analysis of the means-end relationship eventuates in the conclusion that though "The use of reason . . . is a means, not an end . . . the habitual appeal to reason in belief and practice . . . is so intimate a condition of the good life that means and end are practically one" (*Uses*, p. xvi).

Blanshard's rationalism leads him to distrust what he takes to be the essence of romanticism. "Romantics," he asserts,

> do not like rational bits and bridles; "Those who restrain desire," said William Blake, "do so because theirs is weak enough to be restrained." But one may restrain passion not because one feels less, but because one loves sense and reason more. And "it is by no means self-evident," as T.S. Eliot notes, "that human beings are most real when most violently excited." [*Uses*, 10]

Clearly Blanshard is not to be identified with the rationalist neatly pinioned in the parody of Walter Savage Landor's "Dying Speech of an Old Philosopher," he who "loved reason and next to reason, doubt—who warmed his hands before the fire of life—and put it out."

The perennial issue of the relation of reason and the emotions has been discussed by Blanshard in many contexts. In the Howison Lecture at the University of California in 1954 ("The Impasse in Ethics—and a Way Out") he raised the question of the objectivity and subjectivity of good and evil:

> Goodness *is* dependent on the feeling and impulse of conscious minds. It consists in the satisfaction and fulfillment of human nature. Does this destroy the objectivity of our judgments of good and evil? On the contrary, it provides a clear meaning for their objective truth and frees that truth from any dependence on individual thought or feeling. It bridges the chasm between fact and value. It enlists science, especially psychology, in the service of morals. It answers sensitively to our reflective judgments of better and worse. It naturalizes duty, and rationalizes its authority. It offers a standard responsive alike to men's deeper identities and to the surface differences of nature and desire. In a time when skepticism about personal morality and pessimism about international morality seem to be the order of the day, it holds that to be moral is in the end to be natural and reasonable and sane. ["IE", 112]

Echoing T.S. Eliot, Blanshard holds that one thing a student should seek in his education is self-discovery. "Besides self-discovery," he writes, "it may give us self-discipline. It may impose upon us a regimen, intellectual, aesthetic, and practical, that will enrich our spirits and add to our force, wherever our special calling" (*Uses,* 119). The self to be discovered and disciplined is an active, willing and feeling human being. "To educate a human mind is not merely to add something to it, but to do something to it. It is to transform it at a vital point where its secret ends reside. Change what a man prizes and you change him as a whole, for the essential thing about him is what he wants to be" (42–43). And, again: "We sometimes forget that feeling is as educable as intelligence and that, so far as happiness is concerned, its cultivation is even more important. What does the education of feeling mean? Someone has given the answer in the remark that culture is the adjustment of feeling to its objects and that education is learning to like and dislike the right things" (107). One may find all this a bit too simplistic, the person being educated all too passive and the "right things" too readily assumed to be obvious and easily identified. But one must recall Blanshard's constant conviction that the end of liberal education is richness of spirit and ripeness of judgment.

In *Philosophy in American Education,* Blanshard identified the philosopher's best contribution as "a ripe and impartial judgment" and detachment as "the condition of such judgment." And he added, "if he sacrifices his detachment and the largeness of view made possible by it for the sake of immediate influence, he is abandoning the only thing which in the long run can maintain that influence" (*PAE,* 111). Indeed for Blanshard the philosopher "is governed by the sort of attachment that requires detachment from the causes and enthusiasms immediately around him. Not that he is indifferent to these, nor that, in the capacity of citizen or churchman he may not return to them with added fervor as a result of his detachment. It is merely that his first allegiance is to reason" (87).

The detachment required of philosophers as educators implies no separation from practical life. Writing in *The Encyclopedia of Philosophy* Blanshard asserts that

> Wisdom in its broadest and commonest sense denotes sound and serene judgment regarding the conduct of life. It may be accompanied by a broad range of knowledge, by intellectual acuteness, and by speculative depth, but it is not to be identified with any of these and may appear in their absence. It involves intellectual grasp or insight, but it is concerned not so much with the ascertainment of fact or the elaboration of theories as with the means and ends of practical life. [*Encyclopedia,* 8:322]

Throughout his reflections on education Blanshard's emphasis is on the understanding, insight, intellectual grasp which are the true objectives particularly, as has been said, of the humanities. He eschews both elaborate theorizing and, with few exceptions, pedagogical advice. An exception, which delighted me, occurs in the preface of *The Uses of a Liberal Education.* "One suggestion as to method," he writes, ". . . I can make with some confidence." Looking back on his long career as a teacher he declares: "The best results have been gained with small groups of four to six, meeting for two or three hours, and conducted in Socratic fashion" (*Uses,* p. xiii).

It was in just such a group that I first met Brand Blanshard almost sixty years ago. In 1917 he came to Columbia University as a graduate student and was promptly appointed to teach an undergraduate course, a senior seminar in metaphysics. It was my good fortune to be one of the four students in that class. Our teacher was not many years older than his students but he already had the qualities and qualifications of a master of philosophy though he did not receive his M.A. degree until the following June at the same Commencement in which I was awarded my B.A. The skill and authority with which he conducted our small seminar sessions remain vivid in my memory, doubtless reenforced by the fact that in manner and method of communication he was then almost the same expert interpreter and analyst he has continued to be throughout the many intervening years. Others among his students may have noted different aspects of his teaching which they particularly admired, but I was impressed by and have continued to esteem his thoroughness of preparation, the clarity of his thinking, and the precision and elegance of his presentation.

Our text was F.H. Bradley's *Appearance and Reality* and Blanshard brought us not only the careful reading and reflection of his meticulous preparation but also something of the intellectual atmosphere of Oxford University where he had been a Rhodes Scholar from 1913 to 1915. I do not recall his speaking of the two years, 1915–1917, when, before the American entrance into the war, he served as a Y.M.C.A. secretary with the British army in the Far East; but his recollections of Oxford were vivid and illuminating. He gave us not only a sense of the Oxford of his teachers, Joachim and Joseph, but for me, at least, he made Bradley step out of his pages, a living figure, as we read and discussed our assignments. Blanshard was, of course, helping us to recognize the contents of a masterwork as vital forces. He himself was then and, as I have been stressing, has remained an exponent of the Bradleyan rationalist tradition, but he was able and willing to weigh and understand other viewpoints and criticisms of his author's position. We, his students, reared in the Columbia traditions of philosophic naturalism as expounded in the writings of James, Santayana, and Dewey, found Blanshard's outlook stimulating though sometimes insufficiently appreciative of that naturalism particularly as advanced by Dewey.

My classmates in the Blanshard seminar included a gifted young poet, Francis Kimball, and my lifelong friends and colleagues in the Columbia philosophy department, Horace L. Friess and John H. Randall, Jr. When, in

1959, at a meeting of the American Philosophical Association, I introduced Blanshard as speaker for one of his Carus Lectures and mentioned the 1917 seminar and its members, he twitted me saying that I had made his subsequent career seem a decline from that, his first, teaching assignment. Whatever it was for him, it has remained for me a high point in my long academic experience.

In his Carus Lectures, and indeed in all his lecturing and writing of which I know, Blanshard has, as already indicated, maintained the highest levels of clear and lucid thinking and precision of expression, which at times attain the aesthetic values of poetry. This is true not only of his public utterances, whether written or oral, but also of his participation in more informal discussion. In the New York Philosophy Club, a group formed early in the century by Felix Adler and of which Blanshard was long the senior active member, his contributions were notably characterized by the qualities I have mentioned. Obviously this would be so with regard to the papers he himself presented to the Club, but it was equally true of his participation in the round-table discussions which followed the monthly papers. I have often watched him with something approaching fascination as he wrote his notes in a small loose-leaf notebook in the neat calligraphy which perfectly matched the neatness of his comments.

That term seems appropriate even with the special connotation which "neat" has gained in current idiom. It occurs to me, moreover, as an apt adjective to apply to Brand Blanshard's attire and appearance on all occasions, whether social or academic, in urban or in rural surroundings. In Peacham, Vermont, where he long had a summer home, he stood out in this way as well as in more important ones among the residents and visitors waiting for the daily mail in the country store, at a church supper, a picnic or other gathering.

In Brand Blanshard the outer and the inner man have always seemed to me to be essentially at one. He has possessed that integrity for which Socrates prayed in the *Phaedrus*. Blanshard himself brings this relationship into focus in the concluding paragraph of his little book *On Philosophical Style:*

> The more perfectly one's style fits the inner man and reveals its strength and defect, the clearer it becomes that the problem of style is not a problem of words and sentences merely, but of being the right kind of mind. "He who would not be frustrate in his hope to write well in laudable things," said Milton, "ought himself to be a true poem."

And Blanshard ends in agreement with Professor Raleigh that "to write perfect prose is neither more nor less difficult than to lead a perfect life."

Above I have quoted from Blanshard's article on "Wisdom" in the *Encyclopedia of Philosophy,* and conclude with words from that same essay:

. . . the judgment of the wise man may carry a weight out of all proportion to that of anything explicit in his thought or argument. . . . Experience . . . leaves its deposit, and where this is the deposit of long trial and error, of much reflection, and of wide exposure in fact or imagination to the human lot, the judgment based on it may be more significant than any or all of the reasons that the judge could adduce for it. [*Encyclopedia,* 8:324]

JAMES GUTMANN

DEPARTMENT OF PHILOSOPHY
COLUMBIA UNIVERSITY

NOTE

[1]*The Encyclopedia of Philosophy,* Paul Edwards, ed. (New York: Macmillan Co. and Free Press; London: Collier-Macmillan, 1967).

10. Reply to James Gutmann

Blanshard as Philosopher of Education and Teacher

Mr. Gutmann is so generous both in his estimation of my work in philosophy and in his memories of my first blundering efforts as a teacher that any sort of polemical reply would be out of order. His paper has two parts. In the first he offers gentle demurrers to some of my more unguarded remarks on educational theory; his recollections, in the second, of my attempts at teaching give me an excuse for setting down some impressions I have formed on the teaching of philosophy.

"Permissiveness"

Mr. Gutmann thinks I link the elective system too closely with "permissiveness." He is probably right. Certainly there was nothing irresponsible about the elective system introduced by President Eliot; it was chiefly designed, as I recall, to give the natural sciences (and Eliot was a chemist) an equality with such venerable stand-bys as Latin, Greek, and mathematics. But through the crack that Eliot opened a formidable intruder soon got his foot in the door. To what absurd lengths the new license could be carried was revealed by Abraham Flexner in a scorching chapter of his book, *Universities*, published only four years after Eliot's death. And between Flexner's book of 1930 and the present the tendency to load the liberal arts curriculum with new courses, each counting officially as much toward a degree as the others, has been carried to questionable lengths.

The term "permissiveness," as applied to a college, may mean various things. Sometimes it means a lenient attitude toward student dress, manners, and morals. Sometimes it means latitudinarianism in the courses a student may combine and present for a degree. Sometimes it means allowing students to decide, or participate in deciding, the major policies of the college, academic and other. It is hard to say anything about these matters without such large qualifications as to destroy all distinctness of impression, but it may be worthwhile to indicate the direction in which my own prepossessions lie.

Permissiveness in dress, manners, and some important areas of morals reached its height in the turbulent years of 1966 to 1972. Waves of discontent were sweeping across the campuses, the more idealistic of them concerned with civil rights for blacks and with our costly national involvement, under cover of self-defense, in an essentially civil war on the other side of the earth. Distrust of the "establishment" extended to prevailing values and ways of living, and a rash of innovations appeared on American campuses—patched blue jeans, strumming hippies, experimentation with drugs, strange religious cults, Eastern mysticisms, sloganeers demanding student activism in opposite directions, the devaluation of conventional studies, and adventurism in sex. I am grateful not to have been an administrator in those days; I should probably have been a bad one, for the good and ill of the new demands were mingled so inextricably as to defy disentanglement. It would be enlightening to know how the students who invested so much of their time on these innovations now feel about their investment. My impression is that not a few regret it, and feel that apart from advancing racial equality and helping to discredit an irrational war—genuine achievements both—they might better have devoted themselves to gaining what higher education had specially to give. Scholarship cannot flourish in an atmosphere of disruption. Intellectual discipline, if it is to achieve its best results, must have a base in another and humbler kind of discipline. William James said that the more one could surrender one's lower freedom and turn over the petty decisions of life—sleeping, eating, dressing, etc.—to the control of habit, the more freedom one would have for the life of the mind. This seems to me sound advice. That is why, though I disliked nearly everything else about the army, I prized its discipline. I should like to see an adoption, voluntary if possible, of some minor academic reforms—more neatness of appearance, more regularity of hours, more self-critical speech, more regard for physical fitness, more economy of musical decibels, more time for quiet thought and reading. All these are combinable with more individualism of thought and interest.

As for unrestricted freedom of election in studies, it has, I suspect, been abandoned wherever tried. In the Oxford of my undergraduate days there were many who would have said that the best education lay in a thorough discipline in the classics. That may have made sense in the sixteenth century; it makes none in the twentieth. A characteristically thorough and discerning critique of it was offered in Sidgwick's "Theory of Classical Education" in his *Miscellaneous Essays and Addresses*. Though the demand for relevance has come to have a sinister narrowness of meaning, it is not wholly without point; and even so devoted a classical schoolmaster as H. W. Fowler could say of a former generation of Eton boys that they carried away not so much a mastery of Greek and Latin, or an ability to apply them, as "a profound conviction that there are such languages." The modern world has become far too complex in its politics and economics, its science and its technology, to say nothing of its need for communication in modern tongues, to justify spending even as much time as I did on the aorist tenses of Greek verbs and the heavy humor of Aristophanes. I wrote a paper once arguing that the subjects of most worth in education are those that go farthest toward giving one an understanding of the world one lives in. Such understanding cannot be achieved, even in an elementary form, without an exposure to history, literature, and art, to philosophy and religion, to economics and politics, to both the natural and the formal sciences. I think our curriculum makers in America are converging toward a sensible program in which special competence in some one field is combined with "distribution requirements" which insist on some acquaintance with each of the main divisions of knowledge. One must specialize if one is to learn what thorough work means; one must also have breadth of contact in order to adjust to an increasingly complicated world.

In the half dozen years of student turbulence administrators found themselves faced with "nonnegotiable demands" to which some of them felt they had to capitulate. Students wanted a more audible voice about what they should study, a part in the appointment and promotion of teachers, in allocating college investments, in fixing the college rules; they were admitted in some cases to the boards of trustees. For all this I admit that I had such limited sympathies that I have sometimes thought I was born old. Burke has always been one of my heroes. There has been incorporated into our colleges and universities, as into our Constitution, an immense amount of selfless reflection; and for inexperienced young revolutionaries who would refashion them overnight I could feel little affinity, partly no doubt because I could recall so vividly the callowness of my own youth. It is tempting to exclaim, with Shaw, what a pity it is that youth should be wasted on the young. They are brimming with health and hope, energy and buoyancy, but wisdom is slower in coming. Students, because of their inexperience and generous impulsiveness, are the ready prey of Pied Pipers and the man on a white horse. This century has shown that they can be mobilized with dismaying ease to fight, always of course in the name of freedom, for regimes that lead to the destruction of freedom. So I am not an enthusiast for students' "activism." It is best, for them, as Walter Lippmann said to the students of Amherst, to stick to their studies in college years and equip themselves to play responsibly the roles that time will thrust upon them.

Pragmatism

Mr. Gutmann thinks my distance from pragmatism in education to be less than it appears to be. Perhaps; though I think this would apply to

Deweyan ethics more clearly than to Deweyan educational theory. Pragmatism on its intellectual side never seemed plausible to me, and to read Dewey's criticism in his *Reconstruction in Philosophy* of the life of reason as lived by Plato and Aristotle was a shock to me. I thought that Dewey's own obvious loyalty to truth as such stood in strange contrast to his teaching that there was something pathological about the pursuit of knowledge for its own sake and that thought was to be appraised by its outworking in action. The examination of my own thought to see whether Dewey's account of it was true now seems, as I look back upon it, to be one of the main factors that drove me to rationalism. It forced me to the conclusion that while thought may be instrumental to any end, it had an end of its own that had nothing in essence to do with practice; and it is disagreement on this fundamental point that has prevented my becoming a Deweyan in education. On the other hand, I have more in common with Dewey's ethics than I realized in writing *Reason and Goodness*. I could accept his emphasis on consequences in morals; and his insistence in *Human Nature and Conduct* that the good life lay in fulfilling human impulses and desires so far as they did not conflict with each other was close to the theory that I arrived at myself in the end. Of course I always admired him as a man and a mind, and when I consider how much of a maverick I was in the Columbia of sixty years ago, I am grateful to its distinguished department for the uniform kindness and considerateness with which it treated me.

The Humanities

Mr. Gutmann thinks that in my comparison of the educational value of the humanities and the sciences I tip the beam too strongly in favor of the humanities. Since this is an impression he shares with Mr. Freeman, there is no need to repeat what I have already said in reply to it. But it may be well to fill in a little more of the background of my conviction on this issue. I am concerned about what seems to me a slow decline of American taste, and indeed of our scale of values generally. Our great-grandfathers were enthusiasts about the diffusion of literacy because they thought that with its achievement the best in the way of literature would be brought within the range of nearly everyone, and that this best could be trusted to do its leavening and transforming work in the general mind. That hoped-for course of things has gone awry. Other forces, unanticipated and powerful, have blocked the realization of their hope. Hollywood has pushed its vulgarity and violence into our very living rooms. The brave and just attempts to assimilate minorities into our schools have aroused storms of prejudice as well as legitimate concerns about standards. Public taste as determined by the important index of paperback sales and even by the list of best sellers, is stolidly undiscriminating. The lines between good and evil, the wholesome and the morbid, reason and fad, are becoming blurred. We are often told, and I suspect with truth, that the sovereign cure for all this would be healthy and intelligent homes in which children could grow up in an atmosphere of affection, considerateness, and a certain play of ideas. But the American home is notoriously breaking down. Some people say that since morals are rooted in faith, what is needed is a revitalization of the church. But the termites of modernity have eaten away the creedal foundations of the church, and when that has happened it is beyond reconstruction.

This is the background of conviction out of which my shrill cry for the humanities emerges. Where in such a scene of disintegration are we to find a refuge and defense for those fine fragilities of life which, once they are lost, are so hard to restore? If not in the colleges and universities, then where? English literature, and certainly English poetry, is the greatest in the world, and no one can really enter into it without being mellowed and matured in spirit. Any college with a Walter Raleigh in it, or a Quiller-Couch, or a Saintsbury, or a Chauncey Tinker, or a John Erskine, is a little city set on a hill in the great American plain. The power to enter imaginatively into a wide range of experiences plus the judgment to see among these experiences which are of enduring worth is at once our cultural need and our cultural short-coming. The average American is surrounded by more gadgetry, more of the technological means to comfort, a higher "standard of living" than anyone else. Has his standard of life kept pace with his standard of living? Judged by what he produces and what he subjects himself to in the way of prose and verse, art and music, stage and screen, the answer has to be No.

I do not mean to belittle either science or technology. I do mean to say that I differ with the advice of Lord Snow's famous *The Two Cultures,* written in the aftermath of the Sputnik. His advice may well be sound in India or China, where science and technology are sheer necessities for survival; but in a country that leads the world in science and technology yet whose values are in chaos, it is not the advice we most need. It is not that I think a renewed stress on the humanities, particularly if taught by pedantic inter-preters, themselves aping scientific method, would compensate for a declining home and church; but at least it would help to keep alive the waning convic-tion that in books and drama and music and art there are really a good and a bad, and that it is part of the business of the educated man to be in touch with the best that has been thought and said.

Mr. Gutmann has faithfully searched out my views on education as ex-pressed in scattered sources such as a Howison Lecture of 1954, the chapters I contributed to the report on *Philosophy in American Education* of 1945, and an article on "Wisdom" in the *Encyclopedia of Philosophy* of 1967. Since he approves on the whole of the views there expressed, what I obviously owe him here is not criticism but appreciation, both for a diligence beyond the call of duty and for his moral support.

Teaching

He concludes his paper with a vivid picture of my first venture into teaching, a seminar on Bradley given to four seniors at Columbia, three of whom became professors of philosophy at the university. His comments on my teaching are too generous by far, but they do give me a peg of excuse on which to hang a few impressions I have formed about the teaching of philosophy.

(1) The seminar method is best. Philosophy in its essence is the attempt to arrive at or defend a position by argument, and in a seminar of four or five, lasting two or three hours, the dialectical resources of each student can be probed, drawn out, and disciplined. Perhaps my most successful teaching of this kind was done at Swarthmore, where, under the "honors" system, such seminars were standard fare for selected juniors and seniors. My seminars at Yale, though I much enjoyed them, were too large to admit of the same intimacy.

(2) When I did come to Yale, I was given charge from the beginning of introductory courses. I had contracted a prejudice against the lecture method, but in dealing with classes of 300 to 700, one could only capitulate to it, and I devoted some pains to acquiring a lecturing technique. Little by little I learned that the best result was secured by first thinking the lecture through in detail and writing it out in part or whole, then coming back to it and running through the argument in my head on my walk to the campus, and finally delivering it without notes at all, leaving the phrasing to the moment. I had a fairly good ear for the rhythm of speech; I hear everything I write. But I found I could not talk as I wrote. My aim in writing is simplicity, clarity, and rapidity of movement. That was too exacting an ideal for impromptu speech, and not the best for the student, who wants not only to follow the argument but to get down the gist of it in his notebook. So I deliberately developed a second style, slower in pace, more formal and bookish in manner, concerned continuously with the sequence of the argument, and free in the use of summary and illustration. My early investments in public speaking now brought some tardy dividends. I recalled that some of the greatest masters of the spoken word in modern times had been philosophy professors, and I often found myself (laugh if you will) tuning my mind for the hour ahead by reading a few paragraphs from John Caird or Dean Mansel, both models of spoken exposition. Absurd or not, the method worked for me, and if response meant anything, for the students too. I finally brought my lecturing somewhere near to the point of satisfaction with it, but by then I had repeated my introduction about forty times; I was sixty-eight years old; and I realized sadly that I was giving the course for the last time.

(3) This introduction was always a problems course, never a history of philosophy. The history of philosophy does not give a good start to the or-

dinary beginner, for he probably has never raised the questions to which the philosophers give their answers; so these answers are likely to seem like a series of arbitrary speculations, all of them up in the air and equally pointless. This is perhaps particularly true with the early Greeks and the mediaeval schoolmen, whose problems grew out of mental soil so unlike our own. Philosophy is more likely to take hold of the student's mind if it starts where he happens to be and helps him along in directions where he is already groping his way.

(4) What is the outlook for teachers of philosophy in the United States? One can only guess. The analytic philosophy that developed after Wittgenstein is a very different discipline from the older philosophy. It eschews world views; it is more given to isolated questions, not always obviously important, which it discusses with much technicality and precision; it has found a new preoccupation with language, which has not however improved its ways of expression; it reports itself chiefly through articles in philosophic journals, which are proliferating greatly in number, rather than through books; it places more stress on virtuosity in a purely formal logic. The divisions among philosophers seem to be as deep as ever, though they are now between analysts on the one side and existentialists and phenomenologists on the other, between whom there is little communication. Public interest in philosophy has visibly declined; the *New York Times,* for example, for which in old days I reviewed many books on Russell, Dewey, and Santayana, now regards philosophy as almost too remote and esoteric for notice. I should have expected a somewhat similar decline of interest in the colleges, but it has not taken place at Yale, and may not at other institutions either. Since the great issues of philosophy are perennial, it is my hope that new leaders will appear who can combine the sharpness and precision of the analysts with qualities in too short supply—the humanity of James, the authority on public questions of Dewey, and something of that force and grace of expression so marked in Bergson and Santayana, in Broad, Taylor, and Bradley. Philosophy may then be publicly heard again. I dare say that Mr. Gutmann agrees with me in all this. He plainly looks back a little wistfully to the days on Columbia Heights sixty years ago, when large causes like naturalism and idealism, materialism and pragmatism, were fighting their epic battles. And now that he reminds me of them, so do I.

V THEORY OF KNOWLEDGE

I

F OR philosophy, the essential interest of the study of perception is epistemological, and the central epistemological question concerns the criteria (if there be more than one) by which knowledge or truth can be identified, and can be distinguished from what is false, deceptive, and merely apparent. The philosophical account of perception, therefore, should establish the criterion which distinguishes veridical perception from illusion and misperception; and the demand that it should do so is inescapable if any satisfactory philosophical theory of the matter is to be reached—a demand frequently overlooked by contemporary writers on the subject, perhaps because of the difficulty of meeting it adequately.

That Blanshard, in his treatment of perception in *The Nature of Thought,* is clearly aware of the essentially epistemological character of the inquiry is apparent from the definition of thought that he gives at the outset: "Thought is that activity of mind which aims directly at truth" (*NT,* 1:51). His theory of perception, throughout, rests on the contentions that perception is a form of thinking, if only rudimentary and imperfect, and that it can be either true or false (1:86, 107). The epistemological character of the inquiry, therefore, is unmistakably established from the outset, and we should expect his account to elucidate the relation of perception to reality and to reveal the criterion by which the true and the false in perception can be distinguished.

Yet, oddly enough (though, as we shall see, not altogether without good reason), Blanshard never directly addresses himself to these questions in his treatment of perception, as such. He examines its origins, discusses its main epistemological character, and describes the perceptual structure of its objects, material things; he examines the nature and composition of perceptual meaning and the manner of its functioning. In all this he confessedly pays a great deal of attention to psychological analysis and description as both illuminating and important for philosophic understanding; and in doing so he is undoubtedly right. But the major part of this excellent exposition, even though it includes much critical examination of numerous theories (both psychological and philosophical), is descriptive; and we never find, in Book I of this work, a direct answer to the question: How is the perceptually veridical distinguished from the perceptually deceptive? The distinction, nevertheless, is clearly recognized, and the assumption (we shall see) that we know, or can discover, the true state of affairs in cases which are initially deceptive is unhesitatingly made.

Blanshard is far from neglecting the problem of the criterion of truth. The whole purpose and achievement of the book is the full and detailed exposition of that criterion given in its final chapters. His reasons for making no definitive pronouncement, in the earlier portions, on the means of discriminating veridical from illusory perception are palpable enough. First, his teaching is that perception is inferential in essence and that to perceive is to judge. The criterion of its truth will, therefore, be the criterion of the truth for all judgment, and that is what we find elaborated and defended at length in Books III and IV. Secondly, he holds that perception is, at best, an elementary, haphazard, and rather halting form of thought, the more developed and adequate forms of which are to be found in the realm of free ideas and reflection. Accordingly, any account of truth and its criterion in perception would be premature and could only be provisional. Or, to state the same thing somewhat differently, perceptual thinking is the first step in the endeavour of the mind towards a goal which can be attained only in the higher echelons of conceptual thought. The form and character of this goal is set out in the final chapter of the treatise and could not adequately have been explained with reference to perception alone.

Nevertheless, and despite these weighty reasons, one cannot help feeling that something required by epistemology is missing from Blanshard's treatment of perception. We shall find that he makes statements and evident assumptions concerning our knowledge of the difference (in many cases) between the object of perception and the perceptual judgment made (what the object is perceptually taken to be) which inescapably raise the question of a criterion of discrimination between these two poles of the perceptual relation. And though the answer—in my opinion, the right answer—to that question is implied in many passages, it is never plainly stated or overtly explained. This is to be regretted, for it is a possible source of misunderstanding which may have misled some of Blanshard's critics. Before giving special attention to this matter, however, I propose to review his treatment of perception in brief summary, in order to bring out some key points about which his critics have been mistaken or for which they have failed to give him credit.

II

First, Blanshard gives an account of the genesis of perception. The description is in large measure psychological and draws upon the writings of psychologists, but its aim and intention is epistemological. For it establishes first that perception, which is an awareness of objects, cannot develop out of a process, either physiological or merely sensory, which could not possibly be an awareness of an object—an intentional experience—or even the germ of any such form of consciousness. From this it follows (as a reference to Bertrand Russell brings out) that the perception of objects cannot originate in a simple "acquaintance" with bare particular data. Secondly, and almost as a corollary, it is maintained that from the very beginning perception is concerned with universals. Blanshard's detailed account of universals comes later, and here it is not made clear what precisely the universal character is of the objects with which perception must be concerned from the very outset. All that Blanshard says (and, perhaps, provisionally this is enough) is that they must be repeatable in different contexts and so capable of recognition as the repetition of a general character.

He stresses that in the original sensory experience, from which perception develops, however, no characters are apprehended as such (in other words, no perception has yet occurred). The characters are present, but are not cognized as such until further conditions have been fulfilled, for the initial experience is sheer confusion. To bring to cognition the universal characters which it contains (as it were, in suspension), they must be identified and distinguished, and this is done by the activity of the perceiving mind itself, attending to certain features of the primitively immediate, which, through their intensity, their appeal to certain inherited instinctive interests, or their insistent repetition, or all of these together, attract special notice.

Thus the primitive experience is not an experience of anything like sense-data, as that term is understood by C. D. Broad, G. E. Moore, or H. H. Price. Anything approaching the distinctness and definiteness of such objects (if they exist) would be the product of the selective activity of attention leading to identification and distinction of characters. Yet, again, while the primitive sentient awareness (if that is an appropriate term) is not itself a form of perception, it is difficult to identify—and, of course, impossible properly to describe—a stage of awareness the content of which is not already invested with relational properties and does not already presuppose categories of the Kantian type.

Blanshard goes on to maintain and defend the view that perception is implicit judgment and is inferential in character. With this I shall deal more fully below. He then describes the structure of perceived material objects, which, he says, we put together out of sensed qualities according to certain general and not too precise rules of grouping, of which the main determining principle is convenience. The account given is again largely psychological and leaves something to be desired, for "convenience" is a slippery term. It is not clear for what purpose the described groupings are convenient. It seems on the whole to be the practical manipulation of material things. But why just these structures are convenient for this purpose, and how they could be unless the things to be manipulated had a corresponding structure,[1] is not explained.

We then proceed, in two admirable and illuminating chapters, to the nature and organization of perceptual meaning and the functions that it performs. Here we find that perceptual meaning always goes far beyond what is presented directly in sense and that it consists in the activation of dispositions not themselves brought into the focus of consciousness but moulding the actual content of that focus by influence from beyond it. This influence is admittedly mysterious and inexplicable, but its operation is an inescapable presumption. The dispositions which constitute perceptual meaning are not haphazardly associated but are related systematically; and it is by being integral to a system of meanings that the focal content of awareness is what it is cognized as being.

The structure of this system of meanings is the subject of chapter 6, and here, once more, Blanshard gives a psychological rather than a logical description of the structure. He does not neglect logical relations altogether; identity in difference is not overlooked. But he describes the structure in terms of "depth" and "integration." The first of these seems to be largely a matter of accumulation, though he says that it is hierarchical and that meaning grows by "climbing down the tree of Porphyry," a progressive specification of the general. The second, strictly, is systematization of acquired experience; but Blanshard reveals little of the actual structure of the system and speaks mainly of the psychological influences that aid and direct the course of its construction—the desire to understand, the dominant interest, capacity for recall, and the like. He then considers the effects on perceptual thinking which the structure of dispositions may have, by way of accuracy, complexity, and flexibility, and how this dispositional background of meaning forms a bridge to the emancipation from sense of free ideas.

Though there is much here that calls for comment, I shall pass over the details of the exposition in order to draw attention to those salient points which have been the subject of attack by some of Blanshard's critics.

III

Blanshard is an exponent of the coherence theory of truth, and the critics of that theory commonly castigate it for cutting our experience loose from the solid base of sense, which is our only reliable and intimate link with the external world that we seek and claim to know. The accusation is, of course, in general baseless; for no adherent of the coherence theory does this, though views of the solidity of the base and of the nature and reliability of the link between sense and the external world vary significantly. In Blanshard's case the indictment would be wide of the mark, for he traces the origin of perception precisely to the welter of undiscriminated sensation in the infant mind which James described as "blooming, buzzing confusion" (*NT,* 1:61). Blanshard's definition of perception is: "that experience in which, on the warrant of something given in sensation at the time, we unreflectingly take some object to be before us" (1:52). Something must be "given in sensation," and Blanshard insists throughout that perceptual thought is tied to sensation and that reflection can begin only when ideas break free of this and can be entertained in the absence of the sensuously given.

But "given" is a controversial term. Is Blanshard asserting here that there are "sense-data" on the warrant of which we take some object to be before us? If so, his doctrine would seem to be hardly consistent with itself and to have ominous affinities to those of C. D. Broad and H. H. Price, with which he is at pains to express his difference—not in all respects, but in certain very important essentials, to which I shall presently turn. Nevertheless, even with reference to these very essentials, R. J. Hirst[2] has accused him of inadvertently adopting the very position for which he (Blanshard) criticizes Price, and of dealing in something very like sense-data, though they are not admitted as such. Indeed, there are passages in which Blanshard's language strongly suggests that Hirst is right; but I shall argue that this suggestion is spurious and that to interpret Blanshard's language in the same sense as that of Price or Broad is to misunderstand him.

First, there is the passage in chapter 2 (*NT,* 1:81) on which Hirst lights, where Blanshard writes, "Suppose that, glancing up at the sky, I see a tiny cross-shaped object and hear a certain pervasive hum. I at once recognize an aeroplane. . . ." Are not the "tiny cross-shaped object" and the "pervasive hum" sense-data? Price would undoubtedly say that they were, and Blanshard seems to regard them as something similar. But note that he refers to the first as an "object" and not as a datum. Yet, elsewhere, he uses the word "sense-data" quite freely in analogous cases (cf. 1:109 f.). He quotes with approval Köhler's example of the sound, represented by "eagle" in English and by *Igel* in German, which, nevertheless, has very different meanings in the different languages: "here it is obvious that we have to discriminate between a genuine sensory experience which is the same in both languages, and two different meanings . . ." (1:110). Is the sound, the "genuine sensory experience," not a sense-datum? Elsewhere Blanshard speaks of "appearances" (shapes and sizes) in much the same way as Price speaks of data, and even approves (by implication) of Price's treatment of them (1:145 f.)

Hirst is one of the modern opponents of the sense-datum theory, who has marshalled a number of interesting arguments to throw doubt on their occurrence, so his criticism of Blanshard is two-edged. First, he criticizes Blanshard adversely for alleging an inferential element in perception, a doctrine to which I shall shortly turn, and, secondly, for (by implication) presupposing sense-data in exactly the same way as the philosophers whom he opposes for doing precisely that.

I believe Professor Hirst to be wrong on both counts and, further, to have gone too far in his critique of sense-data. Many of the reasons for which he rejects them are, to my mind, the wrong reasons, as is the case with several other contemporary critics. This is not the place to go into a detailed discussion of this matter; I shall say only that it is false and futile to deny (as many critics seem to do) that we can and do distinguish in our perceptual experience coloured shapes, sounds, tastes, smells, premencies, after-images and the like, and that the precise relation of these sensorily perceived objects to the material things (if any) to which we ordinarily attribute them is open to question. H. H. Price has recently assembled convincing examples and cogent arguments in support of these facts.[3] To allege that such objects do not exist simply because some philosophers have called them "sense-data" (a technical term) and have distinguished them from the material entities that we perceive by means of them would be rash, to say the least. Further, it is undoubtedly the case that any set of such sensorily experienced objects presented at one time falls far short of the perception of any physical thing that we may claim at that time to be aware of. To this extent Blanshard and the sense-datum theorists are at one, and surely any candid thinker must agree with them.

What Blanshard denies, however, and the sense-datum theorists assert, is that these sensorily perceived qualities are simple, hard, irreducible, passively received *data*. For Blanshard they are the products of sophisticated analysis requiring far more than mere sensing. If we are to be aware of them at all we must distinguish them from their background and from others of like kind, and identify them with those of like quality by a process of thought, implicit or explicit, which mere sensing cannot provide. They are, for Blanshard, "data," and he uses the term, though only in a relative sense, as the cues[4] or jumping-off points from which further inference takes place (in ordinary perception implicit, but explicable in some cases theoretically), and must take place if there is to be perception of a material world. The sense-datum theorists admit the possibility of inference from, imaginative supplementation of, and construction of complex objects out of, sense-data. But these they consider to be mental activities falling beyond and subsequent to the simple apprehension of the data as such. Blanshard denies this. The process of interpretation is for him fused in the apprehension of the "data," even as "data." He writes: "Nor is it suggested that sensed qualities are discriminated before things; the two kinds of discrimination grow up together" (*NT,* 1:75, cf. Hirst, 238). And this is no *merely* temporal or psychological relationship (though it is both temporal and psychological). The relation is also logical (in Kant's sense of "transcendental" logic), for in both cases the discrimination depends a priori on the operation in perception (*Anschauung*) of certain universal categories (e.g. identity and difference; cf. *NT,* 1:76).

"Such terms" (as "visible size" or "sensed patches"), he tells us,

> are likely to suggest that the visual sensum in perceiving a tree is as sharply and clearly defined as the coloured country I see on a map, and that to apprehend an area as being of a particular shape and size is a matter of mere sensing. Neither suggestion is true. My interest when I perceive is generally so fixed upon the object and so careless of the sensory cue, that "the meaning tyrannizes over the image" and buries it, sometimes too deep for recovery. The "patch" I use in perceiving a tree is very difficult to describe, and to think of it as standing out . . . , like a patch on a patch-work quilt, is certainly an error. And in just the degree that it does gain describable features, it is not the object of mere sensing; the classifying and relating intelligence has begun to get in its work. [*NT,* 1:140]

Bare particulars Blanshard rejects, supporting his denial of them by a whole sheaf of closely knit argument (*NT,* 1, chap. 17, secs. 9–11 et seq.). One reason for postulating them is the false belief that they can be sensed, whereas the sense-qualities we perceive are, Blanshard maintains, all of them universals, despite their particular context—which is particular simply in virtue of its contextual (relational) character. Simple, hard, elementary, particular, sensed data, therefore, such as are postulated by writers like Russell, Moore, Broad, and Price, are mere fictions. "To be sure," writes Blanshard, "we lost belief long ago in what are called particulars, and we have expressed doubts whether the 'sense-data' in the form of red patches which figure largely among contemporary writers are either so sensory or so plainly given as their name implies" (*NT,* 2:230).

What is barely sensed is, for Blanshard, preperceptual. It is something we probably can never reach in cognitive apprehension at all, even when our consciousness is reduced to its lowest level of clarity. So far from being hard, precise, and definitively particular, the objects, if there are any, of *mere* sense, are vague, confused and obscure in the extreme—as for Kant, a mere manifold, which for perception proper is virtually as good as nothing. Nevertheless, it is sensation that lies at the base of perception and so at the origin (or below it) of all cognition; and how cognition arises from sense Blanshard is at pains to demonstrate in chapter 1.

It is, therefore, a misconstrual of Blanshard's theory that leads Hirst to attribute to him a belief, if only tacit, in barely sensed data; and his criticism of the theory of implicit inference in perception, as we shall shortly discover, fails likewise. Before we turn to that, however, there is one more point of interest arising out of Blanshard's opening chapter, to which attention must be drawn.

Among modern pronouncements on the subject, few have been received with more approval and acclaim than Gilbert Ryle's identification of verbs of perceiving as "achievement verbs" in distinction from "task verbs" (like "seek," "listen," "examine," etc.). To perceive an object, says Ryle, is to achieve something. He also says elsewhere that perception is a kind of skill.[5] Now all this clearly implies that, whatever else it may be, perception cannot possibly be the immediate, passive acceptance of unprocessed data, that it must involve some activity or operation of the mind, that it is the outcome of an endeavour on the part of the percipient subject to achieve something, success in which requires skill and practice and perhaps even training.

Despite deep differences between Ryle's views and those of Blanshard, the latter would endorse all the implications of Ryle's theory listed in the last sentence. He rejects the doctrine of unprocessed data, he insists on an activity of thinking involved in perception (though Ryle voices some serious strictures on the nature of "thinking" and the part it plays). Blanshard asserts further that perception, like all thinking, is a teleological activity aiming at an end which it is trying to achieve, and that if it is to succeed skill must be exercised, and practice as well as training may be needed. "Perception," he says,

> is an experience in which, on the warrant of what is given in sensation, we take some object to be before us. It is the sort of experience we have in the apprehension of red as red, or of an orange as an orange. Such experience is an achievement, since in the unbroken continuum with which we start, nothing is grasped *as* what it is. [*NT*, 1:76]

IV

The skill involved in perception is that of judging as a result of inferential thinking. Neither the judgment nor the steps of the inference, or, if it has no steps, the nexus between premise and conclusion, are explicitly set out or even brought clearly to consciousness. They are implicit in the achievement of perceiving. This is Blanshard's view and it is, perhaps, the most controversial part of his theory, one that has been the butt of the most widespread criticism. Some of this criticism I shall here consider, as well as some of the arguments and the evidence which seem to me to dispose of it.

It must, of course, be borne in mind that the theory does not originate with Blanshard, who makes no such claim. One may say without error that it goes back to Kant, was advocated by Hegel, expounded by F. H. Bradley, Bernard Bosanquet, and H. H. Joachim, and has been recently defended, very convincingly, by C. A. Campbell.[6] The criticisms levelled against it, therefore, are not always directed specifically at Blanshard's writing, but we are concerned with the arguments on both sides rather than with their authors.

First we must consider what is meant by "implicit." Blanshard lists three meanings, two of which he rejects as inapplicable, and he adopts the sense in which the word is used when we say of a sailor that he knows implicitly that a storm is imminent. The point is that, whatever may be the sensory cues on which the perception rests, they are not by themselves the whole (if more than a minute part) of what we perceive. The rest is supplied by dispositions, whether innate or acquired or both. A disposition, whatever sort of entity it may be, whether physiological or mental, is by general consent not always operative and may exist nevertheless in unconscious dormancy. A perceptual disposition, moreover, is an apperceptive structure that need not be, and perhaps never completely is, in the focus of consciousness. In some cases it cannot be made explicit, or hardly at all; in others it may be brought to articulate awareness to some extent. Yet even when it remains wholly unconscious its operation in perception (especially in skilled or expert perception) must be presumed. The trained physicist presented with a Wheatstone bridge recognizes it immediately for what it is. Place it in the hands of an untutored layman and he is totally at a loss. This is because the physicist, in the course of his training, has acquired perceptual dispositions, the product of experience, which are immediately activated by the sensory appearance of the instrument. And these dispositions the layman lacks. We must hold them to be operative in the expert perception if we are at all to explain its difference both from that of the layman and from that of the physicist himself at the start of his apprenticeship—say, the first time he was confronted with the electrical gadget.

But in his expert perception the physicist need not and does not recall explicitly the course of his past training or previous occasions of experience with Wheatstone bridges. The dispositions which have formed in his mind remain below the level of focal awareness even while they are operative in his recognition of the apparatus. And it is this sort of operation in explicit perception of dispositions not displayed in the focus of consciousness that Blanshard calls "implicit."

So far, perhaps, all or most theorists would be in agreement, however they might differ concerning the inferential character or otherwise of perception. But if inference is involved in perception and is nevertheless *implicit* in this sense—which is what Blanshard alleges—all counterarguments based on the assumption that the supposed inference is *explicit* are ruled out of court. Blanshard emphatically denies that any syllogistic formulations are in any way involved. There is no suggestion that in simple perceiving, the sequential steps of a deductive chain are being set out *in debito ordine.* We may, therefore, summarily dismiss the following arguments:

(i) That perception is not inferential because in perceiving we do not deliberate, we do not consider or weigh evidence and its bearing upon a conclusion, we do not wonder, or entertain doubts, or raise questions about the ostensible object.[7] It is agreed on all hands that we do not, for these are forms of explicit thinking, and the inferential element alleged of perception is implicit.

(ii) That perception is not inferential because it does not involve "pondering, reflecting or putting two and two together."[8] Nothing so ludicrous is in the least contemplated.

(iii) That judgment, to be judgment, has to be expressed in a statement[9] (or some other symbolic form), and inference to be recognized as such must be set out syllogistically or as a sequence of mathematical steps.[10] In perceiving we do not make statements or frame arguments; therefore perception is not inferential.

These are the chief arguments that have been brought against the doctrine and others frequently depend on them. For instance, it is alleged that inferential process takes time, and perception is instantaneous, allowing no time to formulate propositions and arguments.[11] The reason why it is assumed that inference takes time is that it is conceived as in the foregoing arguments—as explicit. Hirst complains further that we have no "awareness of assessment of evidence" and that the inferential theory goes "flatly against the introspective evidence" (233). Of statements and syllogistic arguments in perceiving we certainly have no awareness, and if we seek them in introspection we shall not find them. But by these facts and contentions Blanshard's withers are unwrung, for what is not explicitly in consciousness is not to be sought or found by introspection, nor could we have any awareness of it; and no time is needed for what does not occur.

But more is to be said of these two criticisms, for they make allegations which are false. Blanshard himself has pointed out one of these (*NT,* 1:87). Inference does not necessarily take time, for it consists essentially in grasping a connexion; and that is an achievement (as Ryle says all perceiving is) which does not take time. If I know that, of two roads, one goes to New York, and if only one is sign-posted, with the legend "Philadelphia," I know in a flash that the other road is the one to New York—and this is an inference.

Again perception is never instantaneous, though it commonly seems so. This has been experimentally demonstrated by psychologists. M. D. Vernon writes: ". . . perception is never instantaneous. If we show people an object for a very short time, perhaps one tenth of a second or less, they may not be able to identify it. They may guess the kind of thing it is, but they may be mistaken. It is possible to halt or retard the perceptual process in various ways, and thus to study its gradual development."[12] And inferential processes can be, and have been introspected. Consider the following passages:

> A large number of experiments has been carried out in these various ways, to investigate the perceptual processes of adults. It has been found that people are first of all conscious that there is "something there," something standing out from and different from the general background of the field of view. Next, this "something" begins to assume a shape; first the outline is perceived, then the main interior features, their colour and brightness. And then begins *the process of classification and identification* [my italics]. The observer may say "It looks like such-and-such a type of thing"; or "I got the impression it might be an object of a certain kind." Then he may say: "Yes, it *is* so-and-so"; or "I made a mistake, it is really something quite different." If what he is looking at is not a familiar and easily recognizable object, but rather a complicated and unfamiliar thing, perhaps a picture, he may say: "I think it is a picture of such-and-such, but I must look at it for longer to be quite sure." Then he may need up to two or three seconds of central vision in a good light before he can make up his mind. But almost invariably he will want to go on examining the object or the picture until he is quite sure what it is and what it means to him; and he will end by naming it or describing it in words.[13]
>
> All the structural relationships illustrated were constantly described as "felt": "I had an impression that the figure was symmetrical"; "I had a feeling that the figure was growing more complex"; "I had an unconscious assumption (this subject seemed to mean precisely what others meant by 'impression' or 'feeling') that the figure was progressive." The plan of construction and of successive change, being thus "felt," was readily used as a basis of inference, and hence as a guide to observation: "I got an impression that the figure was symmetrical, though I did not notice the details. I built on that, looking for an addition or an omission, and then inferring others in other parts of the figure."[14]

The subjects here are not describing *what* they perceived but *how* they perceived it.

We may conclude, therefore, that lack of time is no obstacle to inference, and that, even if it were, as perception is never instantaneous, time would be available. Moreover, that perception is inferential has been demonstrated by psychological experiment, and subjects have reported introspective evidence of the occurrence, in perceiving, of inferential activity.

The same prejudice, that inference must, to be inference, be explicit, lies behind the objection that "implicit inference" or "implicit judgment" smacks of self-contradiction. How, it is asked, can one judge or infer without knowing that one does so? This argument no longer carries weight. Certainly, the old psychological theory of unconscious inference, due to Helmholtz, fell into disrepute, but a large and influential body of modern psychologists have revived the idea, specifically with reference to perception. Moreover, the sting

of the rebuke has been drawn, that to speak of unconscious inference or judgment is to contradict oneself, by consideration of the numerous phenomena,
long known to psychologists, of high-grade intellectual activity performed
completely unconsciously. Of this the feats of calculating prodigies are but
one familiar example. Others, most remarkable and numerous, Blanshard
has quoted in chapters 23 and 24 of *The Nature of Thought*. In fact few persons occupied in intellectual work have not had the experience that the most
difficult problems with which they have been faced have been solved, not by
conscious ratiocination, but in the intermissions between their conscious efforts of thinking, when they have been asleep or have turned their minds to
other, irrelevant matters. For my own part, I find that I can no longer (as was
my practice in the past) think out consciously the exposition of an extended
argument before writing it. But after having formulated the question or thesis
and having disregarded it for some time (days or weeks), I am able to sit
down and write out the entire exposition as if from dictation by another person.

   With one small exception, I shall pass over other arguments against the
implicit inference thesis.[15] Hirst claims that not only can judging occur
without perceiving (which nobody wishes to deny) but that perceiving may occur without judging. He then gives four examples, though he thinks that his
"idealistic" opponents can plausibly dispose of all but the first. That is the
case in which we simply watch or listen—e.g. watch a cat playing on the lawn
or listen to music (*Problems of Perception,* 227). Now, here again it seems
clear that Hirst's belief that in such cases we are perceiving ("one can hardly
listen to a concert without hearing it or watch the cat without seeing it") [228]
without judging is based on the assumption that any judgment must be explicit (e.g. "The violins are ragged," actually stated to oneself or out loud).
Clearly we cannot listen to a concert without hearing *it*. We should not simply be hearing, but should be distinguishing as music what we hear. We should
implicitly be distinguishing it from other sounds and identifying it as
music—possibly, without making any explicit assertions at all, as Beethoven,
or as the second movement of the *Emperor* Concerto. This recognition of
music, as distinct from e.g. the noise of the traffic, this identification and distinction, is quite indispensable to our just listening to it. Indeed, we cannot do
that without perceiving; nor can we perceive without the implicit discursive
activity of identifying and distinguishing which is the essence of judging. The
simpler case of the cat is no different in principle. I cannot watch it play unless I recognize it as a cat and am aware that it is playing and not fighting or
sleeping. I need not *say,* even to myself, "There is the cat; it is playing on the
lawn." But, unless I am *not* watching it or taking in the scene at all, I must be
perceptually aware of these *facts;* and I could not be aware of them unless *im-*

plicitly I were identifying, distinguishing, classifying, recognizing, activating dispositions (not merely reviving images or anything of that sort), the operation of which in present awareness has the essential form of judgment.

V

Blanshard's theory can survive criticisms such as those above, but his own presentation of it still leaves something to be desired. The greater part of the chapter on the inferential character of perception is devoted to disposing of arguments to the contrary and very little to any direct account of the nature of the inference involved.[16] So we are left with awkward questions unanswered. It may be accepted without demur that if perceiving involves some form of inferring, the perception itself will be of the nature of judgment. But inference, as Blanshard agrees, is passage from ground to consequent, from premise to conclusion. What, in perceiving, serves as ground? What could be the premise from which the inference is made? We are told that, in perception, "on the warrant of something given in sensation at the time, we unreflectingly take some object to be before us." Is the premise the "something given in sensation"? But what is this? It is not a datum or a bare particular—and if it were, how could it function as a premise?. Is it a sensed quality (or group of such)? But, if so, how could redness, or this-red, serve as a ground for anything further? From the beginning, we are assured, we are dealing with universals; but at this stage it is not clear what universals are or how they might function as premises. Sense qualities are said to be universals because they are repeatable. Very well, but what can be inferred from the present occurrence of a repeatable red, or a repeatable $C\sharp$, beyond the fact that it has occurred before or may occur again? How do I get from the red, or from the tone, to the fact that some object (presumably other than the red, or the tone, itself) is before me?

Blanshard's answer to this question seems to be: "through past association of this universal with other universals" (cf. *NT,* 1:89–90). But the past perceivings of universals and their association would, presumably, also have been inferential, and we should still be facing the same difficulties with respect to them. Red, in the past, may have been associated with roundness and hardness and bounciness, from which qualities, given in sense, I may unreflectingly have taken a ball to be before me. If so, not only do the grounds of my conclusion seem inadequate, but also the whole presumed inference is exactly that, the nature of which is being questioned. What, strictly, are its premises and how do they function as such?

Again, these sensory qualities are not themselves data in any ultimate sense. They are already objects of perception involving (presumably) judgment and inference. Must we go further back to find the grounds from which *they* are inferred? If so, are we not involved in the infinite regress which

James, Price, and other opponents of the doctrine impute to it? Blanshard says that no such regress is necessary: "that the perception of *things* involves quasi-syllogistic reasoning, does not at all commit us to the view that the perception of *qualities* involves this" (*NT,* 1:90). This is a very puzzling statement. If qualities were merely sensed it would be true, but that has been denied, and they are here said to be perceived. Is there, then, noninferential perception after all, and, if so, how does it differ from the immediate apprehension of data? Or is some inference syllogistic, some quasi-syllogistic and some neither? Nowadays, most logicians would agree that not all inference (perhaps not any) is syllogistic, and to hold this would even be congenial to Blanshard's doctrine. Nevertheless, the way in which qualities are perceived is not explained, and how they function as grounds for inference is left obscure.

Can we escape this difficulty by going back all the way to the blooming, buzzing confusion of infant consciousness? At first sight, it would seem unlikely. What promise does sheer chaos hold as a ground for inference? Can a mere manifold function as a premise? Does it give any warrant at all for taking any object to be before its bewildered percipient? It would hardly seem so. Yet if the regress is not to be infinite, this must surely be its nether limit.

The solution of this problem is, however, not far to seek and is largely adumbrated in Blanshard's opening chapter. The blooming, buzzing confusion is not so barren as we might be inclined to think, for it is not blank uniformity, but contains differences which are subsequently distinguished. In its initial primitive form it is confused and indefinite but it is not contentless. Features within it are emphasized and attention is drawn to them by factors in the physiological or psychological make-up of the organism. These may be inherent or purely fortuitous, but once something has been singled out from the chaotic mass of feeling and attention begins its restless activity of selection, we have a figure-ground structure—a complex object in which A is distinguishable from B (where B may be no more than the otherwise indefinite background). The cognition of A-not-B[17] is, however, immediately the germ of judgment. It is the product of an analytic-synthetic discursus, at once distinguishing and relating (or uniting into a Gestalt), which is precisely what judgment does. It is the construction of a schema. So even the cognition of "simple" qualities, which can never be less than an awareness of some such contrast as has been described, already involves a discursus and holds judgment inchoate in its very possibility.

From here on, the process is continuous developing organization, the distinction from one another of different and more complicated schemata, as well as their combination into more complex structures. Within these, similarities and identities as well as differences become detectable, and the developing process emerges recognizably as the activity of thinking, of which judgment and inference are continuous phases. They are the tracing out of connexions within systematic structures, and, when these are stated in symbolic (or linguistic) form, we have explicit reasoning. As Blanshard maintains, perception is simply the earliest phase in consciousness of this systematizing process. And for all we can tell, the prior purely sentient phase, upon which it works, may be the product of a not dissimilar process operative at lower levels in organic activity.[18]

In all this, we have been, so to speak, on home ground; for Blanshard was a pupil and is a follower of Harold H. Joachim, who demonstrated cogently and at length in *Logical Studies*[19] that no data can be found in explicit consciousness which are not the product of an analytic-synthetic discursus. C. A. Campbell, who espouses the same doctrine of cognition, maintains that its minimal object is "this-not-that," the germ of judgment. And the notion of schemata subconsciously at work giving meaning to perceived objects and providing implicit grounds for recognition is not foreign to Blanshard himself, for this is what he says of dispositions and the way in which their systematic interrelation constitutes the structure of perceptual meaning.

VI

When he turns to the consideration of perceptual meaning and its offices. Blanshard explains how the constantly growing organization of dispositions supporting particular instances of perceptions directs, reinforces, intensifies, limits, and distorts what is actually perceived. In all this he quite uninhibitedly presumes a distinction, even an antithesis, between "what is there to be perceived" and "what we do perceive." "It often happens," he says, "that with an object before our eyes we fail to perceive it at all. When we do perceive it, we may each perceive it differently. Even when we perceive it in the same way, we perceive it with different degrees of adequacy" (*NT*, 1:92). Clearly, here we have on our hands the issue of veridicality. The object that is "before our eyes" we do not see, or different percipients perceive it differently, suggesting that at least some of them may misperceive it, for we are explicitly told that some perceive it more adequately than others. All these statements clearly presuppose a difference between the object itself and what some or all percipients perceive; and no such difference could be presumed unless we could presume also some means of detecting it or even of knowing just what it was. How then do we determine that there is such a difference and what it is? To do so we must, obviously, have some means of discovering the existence and (at least to some extent) the nature of the object itself *other than* the actual perception with which we contrast it. If we do not see it when it is before our eyes, it cannot be our failure to do so that apprises us of its presence. Though by comparing our several perceptions we may become aware of their differences, we cannot, by this means alone, become aware of their degrees of adequacy. That requires a comparison of each and all of them with some standard—presumably the object itself.

As I have said above, Blanshard does not, in these chapters on perception in Book I, address himself directly to this question. In fact, so far as sense perception is concerned one may say he does so *directly* nowhere. When he is describing the architecture of the perceptual object—the thing—he explains psychologically how we come to associate diverse qualities and attribute them to things believed to exist substantially and independently of our knowing them; and he explains how we come to attribute to them incompatible qualities of like kinds, which each of them, in different perceptions, appears to possess. He explains how we select some of these as really belonging to the thing and others as "mere appearances" or perspectival distortions. He says (following Price) that we choose the constructible spatial properties as nuclear and assign the rest to distortion series. But for all this, he maintains, we have no better reason than "convenience," which, by his own admission, is no reason at all (*NT,* 1:141). We regard certain conditions of perceiving as "normal" and take what we perceive under these conditions to be what the objects really are; but our selection of the "normal" is largely conventional for certain purposes and may be different for everyday practical concerns from what it is for, say, astronomy or microbiology. Such identification of "the real thing" as results from this selective and constructive process is for the most part arbitrary and cannot be logically, much less metaphysically, justified (1:147 and 149–50).

While this might explain in part (though it is not Blanshard's explanation) how different percipients see objects differently, it cannot explain why or how their perceptions differ from a real object rather than one concocted by themselves on rather haphazard principles. And when Blanshard is speaking of perceptual meaning and its evolution, he does not seem to be referring to these haphazard constructs as "the real object" or the "object before our eyes." It is not merely the nuclear solid which we perceive more or less adequately, but something much more fundamentally and defensibly "real."

What the touchstone of this reality is for Blanshard has to be sought elsewhere. We do not find it in perception but rather in or through ideas; for perception is only the beginning of thought, and the very nature of perceptual meaning takes us further, to free ideas. Thus our question about veridicality is really a question of the relation of the idea to its object more aptly than one of the percept to the thing. But this needs, perhaps, more detailed explanation.

The dispositions which constitute perceptual meaning and are triggered into activity by sensuous presentations are built up in the course of experience. In perception they are tied to sensation but are by no means confined to what is presented. When I perceive, say, a house, all that is available to direct vision is at most one or two sides, but I perceive a house, not a façade merely. Its other views and properties are supplied "subconsciously" or implicitly by the activation of dispositions, which, though not identical with, obviously involves some sort of recall (not necessarily explicit), and *may* include imaging. The very fact that in perception what we are aware of goes far beyond the deliverance of sense implies that ideas are involved in it, though, being tied to sense, they are not free. "When I perceive a house, I take what I sense as continuous with what is beyond, and this reference to what is beyond belongs to the heart of the perception. . . . It comes as the completion of what is given, and forms an unbroken whole with this, so that in perceiving a house I seem to be merely seeing it and not thinking at all" (*NT,* 1:258). But it *is* thinking, if only implicit, and thinking is distinct from sensing in that its medium is idea.

"The real object," therefore, is certainly not to be found in sense, and we must seek it in the realm of free ideas, or at any rate in relation to these. It is therefore understandable that Blanshard does nothing in his account of perception, as such, to solve the problem of veridicality. The question is one of the criterion of truth, and that he confronts in chapter 25, giving it full and detailed treatment.

Various candidates for adoption as the test of truth are tried and found wanting: the pragmatic test (practical success), authority, mystical revelation, self-evidence—none of these proves adequate or even self-consistent. Correspondence is also considered for it is a favourite of common sense (to say nothing of various types of realist philosophy). Here, of course, correspondence between "the real thing" and our idea of it is the main issue. "The real thing," however, may be an event and is usually termed "the fact." Nor need it be present fact, for it may have occurred in the past. So historical judgments also come under scrutiny. But when the appeal is to correspondence between idea (or judgment involving ideas) and "the fact," the truth of historical judgment is usually traced back to eyewitness accounts, and so involves of necessity the issue of perceptual veridicality. Of course, even on the assumption of a correspondence test the matter of historical truth is far more complex. Quite apart from perceptual veridicality is the question of the honesty and reliability (in other relevant respects) of the witnesses; and, as we usually have before us only the records of their reports and not the reports themselves, records the authenticity of which has to be established, the application of the test is far from being a straightforward matter of comparison between judgment and fact.[20] When the test of historical truth is at issue, therefore, Blanshard is able in short order to reduce "correspondence" to coherence.

Our concern in this essay, however, is not with historical truth but with the criterion of perceptual adequacy, and in this same context Blanshard turns at once to the case of presently perceived fact, expressible in a judgment such as "That is a cardinal on the branch yonder." Here, then, we might expect a direct answer to the question how we discriminate between "what is really there" and "what we perceive"; but again we are disappointed. What Blanshard argues, with much justice, is that the criterion cannot be correspondence, but exactly what it is does not clearly emerge (though we are left to infer that it must be coherence).

What Blanshard shows very convincingly is that there is no "solid chunk of fact, directly presented in sense," with which any judgment can be compared or theory made to "correspond." In short there are no "hard data." Whatever we perceive is already judgment. It is saturated through and through with "theory." We cannot pare it down, by closer observation or in any other way, to bare sense-given indubitable "fact." If we could, we should have given up our alleged criterion for all but the very simplest and least interesting of judgments. But even so, and in their case too, we fail.

All this I believe to be entirely sound and correct. But what seems to have been overlooked is the possible alternative that the relevant correspondence must be between the real thing and the judgment, whether it be a judgment of direct perception or something more elaborately theoretical. And this seems to be assumed by Blanshard himself in one passage. The brute-fact view of perception, he says (*NT,* 2:229), is untenable, because perception may be mistaken. And if it is mistaken it must somehow diverge from the fact. How is this discovered? How do we decide when it occurs, and on what conditions may we be assured that it does not? The answer must be sought in the relation between the idea and its object. For if all perception is theory-laden, its truth or falsity will depend upon the adequacy of the ideas which constitute the theory. By implication, therefore, if coherence is the test of theoretical truth, it is ipso facto the test of perceptual veridicality. What is lacking in Blanshard's exposition is a clear account of how it is applied in the latter case.

VII

Ideas may be of several different types. (i) There are those which, in perception, supplement the sensory given to constitute the object perceived; though what is available at any one moment to sight or touch is only a small fraction of the total object (e.g. a table), the table as a whole is perceived. What is not immediately sensed is grasped implicitly in idea. But these ideas are so closely and intimately involved in the sensory appearance that they are not "free" ideas. (ii) The same is true of certain aspects or properties of the perceived object which are not, but could be, discriminated from its other characters. For instance, spatial extensity, or successiveness of perceived changes, numerability, brightness, and the like are perceived but not, in perception, differentiated from the concrete totality of the object. They could, however, be abstracted from it and, as such, are ideas. In perception they are tied to sense. (iii) Implicit in the percept, likewise, is the dispositional background that gives the sensory presentation meaning. This is mainly sub-conscious, but so far as it can be and ever is brought to consciousness, it is ideal.

In perception thought is immersed in the sensuous presentation, but thought of an absent object involves free ideas. How ideas, such as those listed above, come to be freed from dependence on sense Blanshard explains in terms of conflict between expectation and occurrence, between desire and its frustration, between remembered past experience and present fact. On these conditions and the process of development of free ideas we need not dwell, though later references to them will be pertinent to our theme. What we are concerned with is the relation of the idea to its object.

Blanshard develops his theory of the idea by criticizing and rejecting alter-natives. It is not to be wholly identified with image (though in some special cases it is); much less is it to be identified with muscular movement or neural discharge. It is not the same as mental act; nor is it an essence common to the mind and the external thing. It may not be unreservedly identified with men-tal event, and it is not a mere adjunct to practical activity. All such theories lead to insurmountable difficulties and contradictions. What Blanshard proposes is the only view he can conceive which will both satisfy the legitimate demands of these rival views and still avoid the difficulties they en-tail. His solution is not a little surprising and has difficulties of its own. "Thought," he maintains, "in its essence is an attempt to attain, in the sense of achieving identity with, a special end of its own. . . . the idea is a purpose which the object alone would fulfil, . . . it is a potentiality which this object alone would actualize, a content informed by an impulse to become this ob-ject" (*NT*, 1:473).

This doctrine is difficult to understand and prima facie incredible. The idea is said to be "a content informed by an impulse to become" an object. It is, presumably, a mental content, but not necessarily image. If "informed by an impulse" it is, presumably, conative while at the same time, and primarily, it should be cognitive. Its impulse is to become its object; and we are told un-ambiguously elsewhere (*NT*, 1:488 and 490) that its object is (or includes) "the features of an independent world"—"the nature of things"—"the out-side world." So the idea is said to be identical with, yet different from, its ob-ject, in the same way as the seed is identical with yet different from the tree which grows from it. Applied to perception, does this mean that when I see the moon my perception of it (for the most part idea) *is* the moon in the same sense as an embryo is the child it will become? If so, does the moon exist in two ways, embryonically as my idea and actually as itself? Or is it only em-bryonic and ideal in my thinking and in itself nothing until my thinking attains its end? I hardly think Blanshard would want to maintain either alternative, or that many would agree with him if he did.

He is fully aware that the theory is unlikely to command immediate assent, and faces up to difficulties without delay. But the way in which he deals with some of them leaves one still bewildered. He anticipates the objection that the theory requires us to believe thought and physical thing to differ only in degree, whereas they differ in kind (*NT*, 1:499). But when he replies to the objection (1:500 f.) he seems to reduce the physical thing to sensation ("one who advances the first objection would probably take as characteristic the difference between sense-data as typical existences and images as typically mental"), and proceeds to show that sensation and ideation do differ in degree and not in kind. How relevant is this to the real difficulty? The objector, surely, is denying that physical things are sensations, which he would put on the side of the mental, and is asserting that sensations, as much as images or ideas, differ from physical things in kind, not merely in degree. How can any of these mental "contents," however developed, become identical with physical things?

Again, Blanshard imagines a critic objecting that he can refer to something and have an impulse to know it (e.g. the great pyramid) without either wanting to be it or succeeding in becoming it (*NT*, 1:508). Then in the answer the ground is shifted. To seek to appreciate the *beauty* of the flower is not to seek to be the *flower*, but to realize its beauty in our experience. To seek to solve a quadratic equation is to seek to get the solution itself into my experience, not to become, "personally and as a whole," a quadratic equation. The same holds for all knowing. "To the extent to which I know the great pyramid, it does enter into the content of my experience." But does this prove that the content of experience can become identical with—can actually *be*—the great pyramid itself, or vice versa? The implications seem to be (i) that the object even when fully realized would still be "an experience," whereas it is taken by most, and has been declared by Blanshard, to be an independent and outside world;[21] (ii) that unless "physical thing" is to be interpreted wholly in terms of mental contents (as by Berkeley), the object of knowledge, whether perceptual or conceptual, can never be a physical thing. Once more, such implications would be as unwelcome to Blanshard as to the sort of critic he takes himself to be answering.

That the objects, at least of perception, are part of an "outside world" is again supported by the examples Blanshard gives of the circumstances in which ideas become freed from sense. When there is conflict, he tells us, "between an implicit idea and what is given in fact," the idea is forced into explicitness and recognized as an idea. The child, having found that a puppy is pleased when it wags its tail, caresses a cat in like circumstances and is scratched. By this shock of defeated expectation the idea of an animal as pleased is prised from its perceptual setting of tail-wagging. The presupposition persists (and is surely legitimate) that there is something in the real world (viz. the angry cat), other and different from the child's formed perceptual dispositions, which conflicts with these and so with his expectation, and that he can come to discover what this recalcitrant reality is and why it conflicts.

Yet when Blanshard comes to apply his special theory of idea to this example, he substitutes the cat's anger—a feeling—for the actual cat as the object of the idea; and, of course, a feeling can be actualized in one's own experience in a sense that a cat cannot. Similarly he chooses, as another example, the idea of Othello's despair, and maintains that the aim of our thought is to relive the actual feeling (*NT,* 1:550–51). Shakespeare's superiority as a playwright consists largely in his ability to do this and actually to become the character he imagined. There is a sense (still qualified, however) in which this is true; but once again what is being actualized in my or in Shakespeare's thought in such a case is itself an experience—a feeling—despair. But what of Shakespeare's idea of Cyprus, where the event is imagined as occurring, or the child's perception of the dog kennel?

VIII

To all these awkward queries Blanshard can give a perfectly consistent answer, though one which may yet leave us partly dissatisfied, in particular with respect to perception. The examples cited above are unfortunate, and one could wish that he had chosen others, for these seem to make his self-defense too easy. But if we take his various statements in the light of his theory of knowledge as a whole, we shall find that they fit together and can be sustained.

Blanshard insists throughout that the mind is essentially teleological and all its activity is purposive. The aim of thought in all its forms is truth, and the idea is the medium of thought. It should rather be described as an activity than as a state of mind, for it is an endeavour to realize the truth—its object. This endeavour has an immanent aim, which is what will satisfy its own demands—the requirements of the principles on which it operates. These are principles of order, system, self-consistency, and coherence. It also has a transcendent aim—knowledge of the real world. In their ultimate realization, these two aims coincide: either can be attained only in the attainment of the other. Both issue as the comprehension of a complete, self-contained and self-maintaining, system of mutually necessitating relationships which *is* the system of the real world. This, then, is the ultimate object which in all ideas is inchoate and of which every idea is a relatively germinal stage of development. Hence idea and object are related as potency and actualization. How then should the awkward questions I have pressed be answered in the light of this doctrine?

(1) Is the moon potential in my thought of it as well as actual in itself? Or is it potential merely in my thought and to be actualized only when I realize the object of my thinking? If the latter were the case, the moon would seem to be simultaneously at different stages of actualization—in the perception of it by the dog that bays at it, in that of a child, in my conception of it, and in the knowledge of it possessed by an astronomer. If we may continue the series up to God, then the former question must be answered in the affirmative as well. This roughly might be Blanshard's answer. What, after all, is meant by "the moon itself" but the best and most complete conception we can form of it? It is futile to protest that we know, or must presume, that, quite apart from any conception we can form, there is a real moon away in space independent of our thinking. Our knowledge or presumption of this is only the repetition of that best and completest conception of the moon that we can muster. The moon itself is that individual body which has precise relations to the earth and the rest of the solar system; which has certain precise physical and chemical properties; which has a certain definite and determinate history—and so on, until its exact determinate relations to everything in the universe have been set out; and these include its relation to knowing minds, mine, the dog's, and the astronomer's among the rest. Our ideas of it are partial developments, in varying degrees, of that system. If they could be completed to the full they would coincide with what God's would be—that is, with the reality—the transcendent aim of thought.

(2) The same is true of any physical thing and its relation to our ideas of it, and the question whether they do not differ in kind rather than in degree could well be answered by saying: Both. For differences in degree when they pass certain critical points become differences in kind. The objection raised above to Blanshard's treatment of this problem was that he reduced the physical thing to sensations and then showed that the difference between sensation and thought *is* one of degree. This, of course, would reverse the relation, for neither Blanshard nor his supposed critic is taking the object of the idea to be sensation. Nevertheless, the physical thing *as it really is* cannot be wholly independent of our idea of it, for what it really is is the system of its relations to everything else, and that includes its relations to our bodies, their sense organs, and to our minds. Our sensations, therefore, our perception and our idea of the physical thing are part of what it really is (*NT,* 2:485–87). And, as Blanshard insists, they relate to it teleologically; that is, they have a *nisus* to realize and become the whole. Blanshard rather more than hints, but does not adequately show (as, I think, it can be shown), that the *nisus* is the whole, working immanently in the developing part.[22] Thus the immanent and transcendent objects of thinking are identical in yet another way. And they are different both in degree and also in kind.

(3) Is "the outside world" not something other than "experience"? When challenged we found Blanshard speaking always of the object (which he con-

fessed to be an independent world) as an experience of some sort. But, it was alleged, the independent world must surely be *outside* experience. Of course, it could not be wholly "outside" and still be known. The world we seek to know is the world in which we ourselves are members. It contains us and our thinking. Our knowledge of it is hopelessly incomplete if it does not include this fact. It cannot be wholly "outside," for, as it is in itself, it is the world revealing itself, at least in part, to our knowing. To deny this is to deny the possibility of knowledge altogether.[23] Though Blanshard does not dwell on this aspect of the matter, he is not unaware of it.

> But if the question is not whether logic is applicable to some unexperienced *Welt-an-sich*, [he says,] but whether our known world of persons and things might with a keener wit be understood or intelligibly construed, we have suggested that an affirmative answer can be established as at least probable. . . . An answer in the negative would mean that the enterprise of thought was doomed from the outset, since the conditions of understanding could not be fulfilled. . . . [*NT*, 2:475]

The immanent and the transcendent ends of thought would not coincide.

Now, however, we seem to be saddled with a further consequence of the theory that is as unwelcome as the difficulties we have been trying to combat. If we accept the above must we not hold that the object of every idea—that which is potential in it and which it is tending in development to become—is always the same? It is the entire system of the universe. Whether it be my idea of the great pyramid, the child's idea of the friendly cat, Shakespeare's idea of Othello's despair, or the astronomer's idea of the solar system, the ultimate object of each and all is the total system, of which there can be but one, of necessary (internal) relations. This is not a consummation devoutly to be wished; and it is not obvious how it can help us to decide when our present perception is veridical or illusory, reliable or mistaken.

To this position Blanshard does seem, in the last resort, to be inevitably committed. Whether or not he himself would regard it as an embarrassment, there are many who would; and it is not much mitigated by his contention that everything is not equally relevant to everything else, but that relevance is a matter of degree. For the object of any idea is what the idea is potentially, and until the process of development is fully completed, all we have is another, no doubt better, idea, not the real object. It is open to Blanshard to argue, as with justice he probably would, that the structure of the systematic universe is hierarchical and that there are lesser systems—lesser "universes of discourse"—within it, which, though still necessarily related one to another, are relatively self-contained and independent. Within these lesser and provisional spheres of interest our ideas do have different objects. Yet, again, these "objects" would be only provisional. They would be more fully developed ideas with higher degrees of truth, but they would not satisfy the demand that the plain man and many philosophers believe must be made:

that there is, for each and every idea which is true in any degree, a real object, relation to which is the foundation of whatever truth it may have. Blanshard would acknowledge this demand, but can meet it consistently on his own theory only, in the last analysis, by identifying the real object with the universe as a whole.[24]

Now, I believe there is a better way open to the coherence theory of knowledge of meeting this demand; and that is to recognize that the teleological relation exemplified by the development of ideas in knowledge extends downward below the realm of consciousness and mind, as well as upward within it.[25] Then we can assert that there actually is, in the physical world, an object (say a mountain) which, being really what it is by virtue of its relations to everything else, is in necessary relation to living organisms, some with conscious minds. Through these organisms their relations to physical things (like the mountain) are brought to consciousness, which is thus at once the consciousness both of the organisms, as one term, and of the physical things, as the other term of the relations, as well as the consciousness of the relations themselves. I have tried to develop this theory elsewhere and shall not elaborate it further in this place.[26] It requires, however, a modification of Blanshard's conception of the relation of the idea to its intentional object. We should have to say that the idea was a phase or degree of realization of what was potential in the physical object (following Hegel and Aristotle) but that what the physical thing really is can be fully comprehended only when the idea has been developed to its ultimate extent.

IX

We seem to be no nearer to an answer to our original question concerning the criterion of the perceptually veridical. But here we do find some help in the suggestion that truth is a matter of degree and knowledge has progressive states of development. The ultimate system is not and probably could never be explicit as a whole to any mind (short of the divine). In our knowledge it develops through a series of lesser, more imperfect, and provisional systems, of which the perceived world is the earliest and least satisfactory. Perceptual truth is thus the lowest form, and perceptual knowledge only a very rough approximation to what will satisfy the intellect. It is, so to speak, only the ground floor of the edifice of knowledge—not, however, to be scorned on that account, for it is of fundamental importance as the ground on which the upper storeys are built. This level of knowledge is the common awareness we enjoy of the perceived world, and within this sphere we can and do distinguish between true and false perceptions. How we do so and what determines our normal perceptual assurance I shall now try briefly to explain.

It has been maintained above that anything at all informative or apprehensible that is given in sensation is already the product of an analytic-synthetic discursus with which interpretative judgment is continuous. The recognition in perception of objects is dependent upon the construal of sensory cues in terms of schematic, or organized, dispositions, some innate and some built up in the course of our growing experience. It is possible only if these cues are interpreted by reference to the system of that experience, which is our progressively developing awareness of a world of perceptual objects. Blanshard has given an admirable account of how this experience develops, how the perceived thing is constructed, and how the body of dispositional meaning grows. Our skill in discriminating and interpreting the sensory material increases to the point at which recognition is effortless and apprehension seems to us instantaneous. But it never really is immediate, and what we are doing when we perceptually identify objects is subconsciously trying to fit the present cues into the schemata at our disposal. The process certain psychologists have described in terms of subliminal adoption and testing out of hypotheses.[27] If we are to be successful we must be able to fit together our interpretations of the cues without mutual conflict, and place the resulting construct in the system of other presented objects and the awareness we have already built up of the perceptual world.

When cues conflict we are bewildered and at best we can only hazard guesses as to the nature of the present object, unless and until we can resolve the conflict. When no conflict is apparent, and we succeed, or think we have succeeded, in fitting together our interpreted cues consistently, we accept the result as veridical and do not question it unless some subsequently discovered contradiction raises doubts. If this occurs we conclude that the first perception was a mistake—that we had misperceived. We then either try to reinterpret or seek new evidence in the interpretation of further sensory cues and attempt to integrate them into the hitherto constructed system, until we can form a judgment which makes the whole coherent.

Thus coherence is as much the test of perceptual veridicality as it is of the truth of theoretical constructs. It is the coherence, not of explicit judgments, but, in the first instance, of the ultrarapid construal of sensory cues to form a presented object, and, in the second place, of the object recognized with the structure of the experienced world. How then are we to understand the distinctions between "what is there to be perceived" and "what we do perceive," between the "given fact" and the mistaken object, between more and less adequate perceptions of the same object—and the like?

In the first instance, the accepted result of perceptual interpretation is, for us, the "given object." It is one we have constructed, but not arbitrarily, for we have followed sensory cues, the original source of which is our body's organic relationship with the physical world (though this is not itself revealed in direct perception, but only discovered later by scientific investigation). Also, our construction of objects has been made, not by any isolated mind, but in perceptual and verbal communication with other people, a communication without which the developed awareness of a perceived world would hardly be possible. The perceived world is thus a common world, though its common character is subject to the limitations already set out and explained by Blanshard in his account of the growth and structure of perceptual meaning. If, having thus interpreted the sensory cues, we take an object to be before us, we take it, in the first instance, as what is actually there; and only if our doing so contradicts, openly or implicitly, something else that we know or perceive, do we entertain doubts about the reality or the character of the object. If further investigation produces a reinterpretation of the appearances more conformable to the accepted system of the perceived world, we regard our first judgment as an error and our subsequent correction as true to "given fact."

So when the child mistakes the angry cat for a friendly pet, he is interpreting the sensory evidence in the light of his experience. His elders, who know better, realize that "the given fact" is other than the child takes it to be; and when he is scratched, his interpretation of the subsequent sensory cues modifies the system of his world so as to make wagging tails on cats consistent with anger, and on puppies with pleasure. It must be noted that the new sensory material must be interpreted before it can be seen to be discrepant with past experience and before it can be integrated into a modified system. The reactions of the cat have to be recognized as angry (as, of course, the animal has to be recognized as a cat), and the pain of the scratch has to be perceived as caused by those movements. If the child took the pain to be otherwise caused, he could not learn wisdom by the experience. But "the given fact" is no less an interpretation than the initial error, and the adult recognizes it as fact because it fits into his experience of the world, which is wider and more fully integrated than the child's, while the child comes to recognize it as his experience develops.

The explanation of more and less adequate perception of the same object, by different percipients or the same percipient at different times, is not in terms of approximation to some *Ding-an-sich* beyond perceptual reach. Obviously any such criterion would be inaccessible to judgment. The criterion again is the scope and articulation of the system to which the sensory presentation is referred and by which it is interpreted. So the physicist perceives a Wheatstone bridge more adequately in the light of his training and knowledge than the layman. He does so by reference to a system of physical theory which is unknown to the layman, who cannot, therefore, perceive it as the instrument it is. Of course, there is a level of interpretation on which both physicist and layman would agree (though even here the perception of the former must be richer). They would both see a material object of definite shape, colour, and construction. But what it would mean to each would be very different. Here, however, the question of veridicality is not at issue, but rather of understanding.

Where veridicality is involved the criterion does not differ in principle. When one sees the lines in the Müller-Lyer illusion as unequal, one is interpreting sensory cues in terms of spatial schemata. As they look unequal, so, for the uninitiated and untried, they are unequal. But let him measure them, and he then reinterprets the cues in reference to a more carefully specified system in which comparisons are made more exactly. This results in a new judgment conflicting with the first; and, because the more elaborate system is more articulated and includes a wider range of experience—for our rule measures and determines more precisely any number of lines, wherever they occur and however they appear, and retains consistency throughout—the new judgment is preferred and the lines are said to be *really* equal. But they still *look* unequal, because the evidence of the Gestalt in which they are presented is still there. Nevertheless, with practice and new insight we can train ourselves to discount these effects of the visible context and can come to perceive them as equal, when we know that they are.

Hallucinations are identified in exactly the same way. When they occur some element in primary sentience, whatever its source or cause, is picked out by attention and interpreted in accordance with the percipient's prevailing dispositional tendencies. These may be weighted or even deranged by emotional stresses or chemical effects of drugs upon his neural activity. Whatever such causes are acting, they are not immediately relevant to the epistemological issue. The interpreted sensory cues, if sufficiently vivid, may be taken as real presented objects so long as they fit together reasonably well and do not conflict with the perceived background too violently. Usually, however, there is some inconsistency of which the subject is vaguely aware so that the apparition seems somehow queer or abnormal, and the perception is hesitant and questioning. Macbeth asks "Is this a dagger that I see before me?" He does not assert "This is a dagger." The subject of hallucination is usually in this uncertain frame of mind, and the emphatic assertions of the insane are often unconscious compensations for the subtle doubt or knowledge that they entertain about the reality of the alleged objects. The hallucination is distinguished from the reality by its conflict with evidence more widely gathered which is more fully coherent both in itself and with the known world in general. The percipient looks for other sensory confirmation, perhaps by seeking to view the object from a different viewpoint or in a different light, or he may attempt to support the evidence of sight by that of touch, as Macbeth tries to grasp the apparent dagger. This evidence includes the reports of others: Gertrude sees nothing of Hamlet's ghost, nor do Macbeth's guests see Banquo's. When the conflict of the evidence is recognized by the subject of the hallucination (which need not occur if he is strongly paranoiac), he knows it as a delusion and seeks exceptional causes to explain its appearance ("Is it the weakness of mine eyes that shapes this monstrous apparition?"). Or if he has deliberately taken drugs he may know the cause beforehand.

The criterion of veridicality is still the same, namely, it is the degree of systematic coherence of the available evidence over the widest possible field. The sensory cues as interpreted implicitly must first be mutually consistent to constitute for us an object we are prepared to accept as (at least possibly) real; and then the body of related evidence, as it is extended to include background and temporal context (what is perceived immediately before and after the alleged object), along with our acquired knowledge of world to which we refer this evidence, must form a system sufficiently comprehensive and self-supporting to preclude our denying the presence of the object and to assure us of its reality.

The question whether we perceive physical things as they really are is triply ambiguous depending on how we understand the terms "real" and "physical thing." If we mean by the latter "perceived material objects," and by the former "what, in the light of our perceptual experience, we have determined them to be," then, of course, we cannot but perceive them as they really are when we perceive them veridically. If, however, by "physical things" one means the objects of inquiry of the physical sciences, and by "real" the minute molecular (or other) constitution the physicist discovers them to have, then we do not perceive them as they really are; so Sir Arthur Eddington was able to speak of two tables, the solid-coloured one presented to ordinary perception and the one conceived by the physicist as consisting mainly of empty space peopled by unimaginably minute electrical charges dashing about in all directions. But the scientist's conception is the fruit of a sustained endeavour to systematize the conception we form in common sense of the perceptual world, by removing the contradictions that arise within it because of the relatively haphazard manner in which we construct our objects—as Blanshard says, largely by convention and primarily for practical convenience. It is these contradictions that give rise to scientific questioning, and the theories that result, after long and arduous analyses, experimentation, and research, are efforts to construct more precise, more articulate, and more closely integrated systems of interpretation, which, so far as they succeed, should by our criterion be nearer to the truth.[28]

If, however, we mean by "what the physical thing really is" what it is apart from and independent of our knowing, then whether we perceive it as it really is, in Hume's words, " 'Tis vain to ask." For the possibility of an answer would contradict the presupposition of the question. We cannot compare what we perceive with what by hypothesis we cannot know. All we can know is what we can learn by pursuing the immanent goal of our thinking towards more comprehensive, more definite, more precisely detailed and more completely unified system.

That Blanshard might have given a more explicit account of perceptual assurance such as I have sketched above is obvious. He does, in fact, often suggest, and at times even go some way towards, such an account. His reasons for not doing more I have suggested in Section I above. The omission, such as it is, can be filled in simply by developing corollaries of his stated theory. Whether he would approve of the way in which I have tried to do this is a question only he himself can answer.

ERROL E. HARRIS

DEPARTMENT OF PHILOSOPHY
NORTHWESTERN UNIVERSITY

NOTES

[1]The "architecture of the thing," as Blanshard describes it in chapter 3, is the form and structure that we give it in organizing our sensuous experience. But that this is the actual thing which we are called upon to manipulate in practice, or just how that is to be identified or related to others, is not immediately apparent.

[2]Vide *The Problems of Perception* (London: George Allen & Unwin, 1959), 234.

[3]Vide "Appearing and Appearances," *American Philosophical Quarterly* 1, no. 1 (1964).

[4]Hirst is not above admitting such "cues" in his own theory.

[5]"Sensation," in *Contemporary British Philosophy,* 3d ser. (London: George Allen & Unwin; New York: Macmillian Co., 1956).

[6]Cf. "The Mind's Involvement in 'Objects,' " in *Theories of the Mind,* ed. J. Scher (New York: Free Press, 1962), and *On Selfhood and Godhood* (London: George Allen & Unwin, 1957), Lect. III.

[7]Cf. Henry H. Price, *Perception* (London, reprinted Methuen, 1964), 141; Hirst, 230.

[8]Cf. G. Ryle, "Sensation," 437.

[9]Cf. Price, *Perception,* 167; Hirst, 233.

[10]Cf. William James, *Principles of Psychology* (New York, 1923), 2:112.

[11]Cf. Ryle, "Sensation"; Price, *Perception;* and Hirst, *Problems of Perception.*

[12]*The Psychology of Perception* (Harmondsworth, Middlesex, and Baltimore, Md.: Penguin Books, 1962), 31.

[13]Vernon, 31–32. Cf. also *A Further Study of Visual Perception,* by the same author, chap. 3 (Cambridge: at the University Press, 1952).

[14]Sir Frederick C. Bartlett, *Remembering: A Study in Experimental and Social Psychology* (Cambridge: at the University Press, 1932), 24.

[15]For some further discussion see my *Hypothesis and Perception* (London: George Allen & Unwin, 1970), chap. 8, sec. xi.

[16]Possibly Blanshard considered that this matter had already been adequately dealt with by Bradley, Bosanquet, and Joachim.

[17]A simple disjunction, A-or-B, modern communication engineers call a "binary digit" (bit.) and use as the unit of "information." The unit of cognition, or minimal object, seems to be much the same thing.

[18]Cf. Susanne Langer, *Philosophical Sketches* (Baltimore: Johns Hopkins University Press, 1962) and *Mind: An Essay on Human Feeling* (Baltimore: Johns Hopkins University Press,

1967), chap. 1, and my *Foundations of Metaphysics in Science* (London: George Allen & Unwin, 1965), chap. 16.

[19]London: Oxford University Press, 1948. Vide chap. 2.

[20]Cf. Collingwood's account of historical knowledge in *The Idea of History* (Oxford, 1946), pt. V.

[21]We shall see anon that this cannot be taken without qualification.

[22]Cf. his quotation from Joseph (*NT*, 1:481–82).

[23]For fuller discussion see my *Hypothesis and Perception*, chap. 12 and "Is the Real Rational?" in *Contemporary American Philosophy*, 2d ser. (London: George Allen & Unwin, 1970).

[24]Cf. *NT*, 2:180: "Our view, so often repeated, is that thought in its very nature is the affirmation through the mind of that system which is truth, the realization, in degree and partially always, of a purpose whose fulfilment would be truth complete."

[25]Blanshard seems to reject this possibility. At least he does not pursue it (cf. *NT*, 1:480), in his determination to exclude all suggestion of mechanistic explanation from the realm of mind, and his apparent suspicion that it cannot be excluded from the physical.

[26]Cf. *The Foundations of Metaphysics in Science*, pt. IV, and passim; *Hypothesis and Perception*, chap. 12; "The Mind-Dependence of Objects," *Philosophical Quarterly* 6 (1956).

[27]Cf. Egon Brunswik, J. S. Bruner, Adelbert Ames, W. H. Ittelson, H. Cantril, in various works listed in *The Foundations of Metaphysics in Science*, 404–6. The theory is variously known as "probabilistic" and "transactional functionalism."

[28]Cf. Blanshard, *NT*, 2, chap. 27, on "Degrees of Truth" and my *Hypothesis and Perception*, pts. II and III.

11. REPLY TO ERROL E. HARRIS

Blanshard on Perception and Free Ideas

My theory of knowledge has suffered a barrage of criticisms, many of them formidable and some of them certainly sound. Most of them concern *The Nature of Thought*. The earlier parts of this book were written some forty-five years ago, and some of my colleagues think I have been reiterating its themes ever since, that my thought is like a block of granite on the Maine coast on which the waves of change could beat indefinitely without producing any visible effect. That is not quite true. Any person whose thought could remain unaffected by the revolutionary coups in philosophy that have occurred in recent decades would be stupid as well as stolid; and though I think the larger contours of my thought have remained the same, it will be evident that my position has changed on a number of important issues.

The earlier chapters of *The Nature of Thought* deal with the genesis and structure of perception. The account of its genesis was influenced by those of James, Ward, and Bradley. Perception begins not with distinct sense-data of color, sound, and touch, which are then put together into a thing; our first experience of the world is more like a London fog in which nothing is distinct or distinguishable. I attempted to explain the process by which the familiar world of things emerges from this fog, and stressed five factors as of prime importance: (1) the coming into joint prominence of certain qualities, such as the brightness and shape of the moon, (2) the joint movement of qualities, as in a rolling red ball, (3) joint change, as when a distant figure becomes on approach a man with discernible arms and legs, (4) joint utility, as in the qualities of a knife or fork, and (5) the native tendency, stressed by the Gestaltists, to fasten attention on figures that are simple, regular, and symmetrical.

In his admirable essay on my account of perception, Mr. Harris has offered a variety of strictures which carry the more weight because of his general sympathy with my position. He thinks my study of perception is made too exclusively from the inside; it is a report by an introspective perceiver of his own states of awareness. The physiological machinery of perception is ignored. I allow myself to become so engrossed in perception as a mode of consciousness that I lose sight of its relation to that outside world which it is supposed to reveal. And while I insist that all perception is judgment, and that judgment aims at truth, I say almost nothing in my analysis of perception about the relation of the percept to its object or how we are to distinguish true perceiving from false.

There is much point in these criticisms. Mr. Harris gives me credit indeed for assuming that the standard of truth developed in my second volume was already waiting in the wings, and that I could have applied it to perception convincingly if I had cared to. But he thinks quite rightly that the reader of volume I may become impatient with so long a lingering within the cocoon of consciousness. How is that consciousness related to the world outside? I insist that perception involves thought and thought must be true or false. But what is the worth of this unless some standard is provided by which that truth or falsity may be determined? I admit that people perceive the same object differently, and that some persons perceive it more fully and accurately than others. But that object itself never puts in an appearance. And if it does not, how can anyone tell how nearly his percepts are approximating to it? Is there a "real object" at all, and if so, how are we to reach it?

These are straightforward questions to which I shall try to give straightforward answers, though they may not be quite simple ones. In truth, there are three objects competing with strong claims for the place of "real."

(1) First there is the real object of common sense. I look at an airplane overhead. What I actually see may be little more than a cross-shaped speck in the sky. But if anyone asked me what I was looking at, I should not say "a speck" but "an airplane." What I see is a speck; what I perceive is a plane. Obviously there is something in my perception that enables me to use the speck as the cue of a plane. This is what I have called the inferential element in perception, and it consists in the set of half-conscious dispositions, usually acquired from experience, which enable me to interpret what I see as really an airplane. What would be included if such a set of dispositions or half-conscious expectations were made fully explicit? The answer is: what you or I would perceive if we could do so with full clearness and under the most favorable circumstances. The real plane is what ordinary men and women who are familiar with such objects would see and feel if they could observe at close hand, if they could walk around it and explore it at will. Probably no one who saw it in the sky would say on seeing it land that it fulfilled his anticipations in every way, but if there were any conflict between the characters he assigned it at a distance and those it presented to close inspection, he would unhesitatingly take the latter as the real ones. And if there had been a dispute between two observers as to what the plane was "really" like, they

would no doubt agree that their dispute would be most decisively settled by their observing it under these same circumstances, that is, under the best conditions for normal inspection.

This is the "real object" of common sense. It is this sort of object that the plain man takes as the real table, the real tomato, the real "unidentified flying object." As one walks round the table, indeed, one sees a variety of lozenges, rhomboids, and rectangles, and attempts have been made by extreme realists to make the real thing into a "family" of correlated shapes, sizes, and other appearances radiating out from a single center. But common sense stubbornly refuses to accept most of these appearances as more than seemings. The real table is the one at the center which, seen under ideal circumstances, has a square brown top and four legs, and is smooth and hard to the touch. And it continues to exist, just as we perceive it, when we leave the room.

If Mr. Harris asks me what the "real table" is by which in fact we commonly test the competing claims, this is the answer I should give. I should extend it to perception generally. The "real" color of the road signal is green, not gray, and the one man in twenty-five who says it is gray is set down as unable to see the real color through color blindness. The man who reports that he saw the saucer-shaped UFO land in his back yard and a crew of green men look out at him from its windows is set down as deluded because none of his neighbors saw anything of the sort and because the similar claims of other observers have so often turned out delusive. Hence these objects are probably unreal. It must be admitted that our idea of the "real object" does not supply a very rigorous test, for it depends on agreement of normal perceivers under the best conditions, and in some cases these requirements may be unobtainable or ambiguous. Nevertheless this, I think, is what the plain man—that is, all of us when away from our desks or laboratories—would accept as "the real object of perception."

(2) Mr. Harris has written an excellent book on *The Foundations of Metaphysics in Science,* and it is not likely that such a writer would be content with this account of the rise of perception. It is too one-sided. It still leaves out altogether the physical basis of perception. We are trying to perceive what exists in nature, and we forget that between our percept and the thing in nature there is a chain of causes which makes identity impossible and even resemblance unlikely. Between the physical table and our percept of it there is first the reflection of light rays from the surface, then the focusing of these rays by the lens of the eye, then their impingement on the rods and cones of the retina, then the passage of an impulse of a quite different frequency along the optical nerves to the occipital region of the brain, then finally the appearance in consciousness of a percept of the table. That the percept is never identical with the thing is proved by two simple considerations,

namely that this causal process occurs in time and in space. The speed of both light rays and nervous impulses is pretty exactly known, and though it is rapid in both cases, the state of the thing that we think we see is always over, however briefly, by the time we "see" it. Similarly, the first and last links in the causal chain are always at some distance from each other in space. What we see, or want to see, or at least think we want to see is the thing in nature, the thing that exists out there independently of us, whether perceived or not. It is clear from these simple considerations that this thing we never see at all.

Here is where the second "real object" enters the picture. It is the real object of the physicist. The physicist takes a tomato in his hands and asks himself what is really there. He admits that the redness, smoothness, and softness that he senses are effects produced in his mind, not existents in the physical world. Even the shape of the tomato, its sharply traced rotundity, is a boundary to which nothing in nature truly conforms. Yet Price, maintaining that what we directly experience is sense-data, insists that in the space between his hands as he holds the tomato there is a "physical occupant" distinct from anything perceived; and Russell and Broad, also proponents of the sense-data theory, say likewise that the real physical object is not something seen or felt, but the material thing or things that give rise to these sensations.

The time has gone by when Hume could say that there was but one kind of real thing, and that this was comprised of sensed qualities, or when Berkeley could say that if there was anything out there beyond our percepts it was volitions in the mind of God. The cool way in which some idealists held at once that consciousness had evolved from matter and that the matter from which it had evolved was itself a state of consciousness no longer carries conviction. Yet if the world of physical science exists, our access to it is precarious in the extreme. Many philosophers have seemed to forget how precarious it is, and have fallen into incoherence as a result. By way of discrediting the identity theory between percept and thing, they could point out the causal chain in perception as if they had direct and certain acquaintance with brain, nerves, and light rays. This is of course self-contradiction, and if we talk about percepts as distinct from physical things, we must stick to this position, and admit that no one has ever directly verified the events of this causal chain. Either we must grant, as Berkeley and the later Russell did, that we never immediately experience anything but mental phenomena, and then we must admit also that the physical world lies at the end of an inference, or else, if we hold that we can directly observe our own nerves and nerve ends, we must hold that we can also directly observe physical tomatoes, planes, and stars. This thoroughgoing realism has been dealt with by Lovejoy, I think decisively.

Now I do hold, with Locke and Berkeley and Hume and Mill and the later Russell, that we never sense anything that is not mental content and mind-dependent. Does this mean that we are enclosed in "the iron ring of ideas"? I do not think so. The verifiability theory of meaning which would restrict the meaningfulness of any statement of fact to what might be verified in sense, although it was offered by positivists in the name of science, was seen before long to make nonsense of much of the science in whose name it was offered. We cannot sensibly verify the neutrons and positrons, the protons and electrons, the quanta of energy or the pulsations of light that are commonplaces of the new physics. But to say that they are the product of irresponsible fantasy is absurd. If hypotheses can be formed about them from which we can draw precise inferences as to what we shall see or hear, if by manipulating them we can produce results from the barely visible to nuclear power plants and Hiroshimas, it is idle to say that they are fictions or that we know nothing about them.

What then is the "real object" of perception for the physicist? Not the group of qualities that is immediately before us, for he would be the first to insist that this percept is removed in time and space from the physical object. No, he would say that the real object consists of the things or events that act upon our nerve ends to produce the percept. The tomato that we hold between our hands is something that bears only a remote resemblance, if any, to the percept of it. Of the things or events that compose it our knowledge is inferential and fragmentary, and what we know of their qualities as distinct from their relations and behavior is apparently nothing at all. In the physical space occupied by the tomato there are millions of submicroscopic X's rushing about at high velocities and behaving so oddly as to suggest that they are not individually governed by laws at all, but can be dealt with only as large populations are, by statistics. Russell, in his *Human Knowledge: Its Scope and Limits,* has offered some promising hints as to how the sense qualities of percepts may be correlated with parts of the physical thing. But such correlation is schematic and speculative, and perhaps will always remain so.

(3) Besides the real objects for common sense and for physics, there is the real object for metaphysics. Whether one believes in such an object turns on whether one believes in internal relations, and since I continue to believe in them, I must take note of this further object. Let us see why the belief in internal relations entails the metaphysical object. Joachim has somewhere used the illustration of a schoolboy's conception of Caesar's crossing the Rubicon. The boy may have in his mind's eye the picture of a man in Roman armor riding a big white horse into the waters of a great river—that and nothing else. Let the boy grow up. Let him go the whole way to becoming a Roman historian. At sixty, will his conception of this event be what it was at six or

sixteen? Plainly not. Traditional logic would say—not very clearly—that the denotation had remained the same while the content or connotation had changed. Which of the changed conceptions of the event comes closest to what actually happened? Undoubtedly the mature one. And this is not merely because of the correction of detailed mistakes in the schoolboy's picture. It is also because in maturity he sees the act in a wide context of relations that characterize it as truly as the armor and the white horse, and reveal it as far more rich and complex an affair. To mention one kind of context only, consider it in the light of its causes and effects. So regarded, it is a turning point not only in the career of Caesar but in that of the Roman republic and in the history of the world. And the new relations are not mere additions made from without to a nucleus that remains the same. The understanding of Caesar's purposes, as an expression of his character, of their legality or illegality, of who his opponents were and what they stood for, of the prodigious effects of his act in ushering in the empire and even affecting its decline and fall—these relations belong to the event and transform its very nature for the understanding mind. Nor is it credible that the transformation should end with the context supplied by the historian. His knowledge too is limited. Where then should we draw the periphery within which the relevant knowledge is confined? I follow an old tradition in thinking that we can draw no such boundary short of infinity, that to know the individual fact or event completely one must apprehend it in its infinite context. This is of course a disputed point to which we must return when we come to the critics of internal relations.

Meanwhile, what has all this to do with Mr. Price's tomato? A great deal. His views of the commonsense tomato and of the physical tomato—his "physical occupant"—would not, I think, be far from those just offered. But his interest does not take him so far afield as to a metaphysical tomato. In our philosophy however, if one follows the argument where it leads, that is often where one finds oneself. To understand the perceived tomato, one must understand the physical tomato, the pattern, for example, of its molecules and their component atoms that make the tomato a living, vegetable thing rather than a lump of wax or clay. To grasp these arrangements fully one would have to understand how they came to be out of a lifeless environment. This small but living structure has a role in the physical universe that one will not fully understand until the pageant as a whole is understood; it is related, as the physicists tell us, by time, space, and gravitation to all the fixed stars of the galaxies, which means that the reciprocal influences between it and them are the conditions of its being what, when, and where it is.

In short, the metaphysical object is the object as it would present itself to an understanding that grasped its nature in the light of all its relations. No one of course has ever achieved this, and the second law of thermodynamics will probably have had its genocidal way with us before anyone does achieve it. But that the relations exist and that in the light of them our perceptual and physical tomato would be transformed seems clear enough. If you ask, therefore, what the real tomato is in the ultimate sense, the sense that would complete that career of thought of which our perception is the tentative beginning, we must answer that it is the object that would be revealed to an understanding that grasped its place and office in the universe.

This is my answer to Mr. Harris's question what the "real object of perception" is, against which the truth of our percept must be measured. Mr. Harris, unlike most of my critics, would, I think, accept the notion of a metaphysical object which it is the goal of thought to apprehend. But he points out a genuine difficulty in it. Does it not make the object of every judgment, and therefore of every percept, the same? The real tomato, the real airplane, the real Julius Caesar, is not the immediate object, but what it would appear to be to a mind that understood it completely, that is, understood its relations to the universe as a whole. Now there is just one universe as a whole. Hence it is this same universe that we should really be contemplating in every judgment we made, whether about a tomato, an airplane, or Caesar. Apparently then we are always thinking about the same object. "To this position Blanshard does seem, in the last resort, to be inevitably committed."

Mr. Harris is right. To be sure, he anticipates my reply and agrees that the reply involves no inconsistency. My theory of knowledge is an evolutional or spiral theory, in which we move up from level to level in interconnectedness and range of knowledge, the meaning of what we know being in course of continual modification. When will these modifications end? Only, if at all, when the spiral has reached an altitude from which all things can be surveyed in their reciprocal relations. Mr. Harris, I think, would agree that this is the end all thought is pursuing, and the standard by which the truth of every particular judgment must finally be assessed. It is perfectly consistent to say this without committing ourselves to anything so absurd as that we carry the issue of every moment to the Supreme Court. As Emerson might say, there is no need of a mountain to crack a nut. Almost all our perceptions and indeed other judgments are made at the level of common sense, and it is by their consistency on that level that we test our truth. "This is my hat." "How do you know? It looks very like John's." "Well, it is the hat I wore here and hung on this peg, it is my size, not his, it was bought at Simpson's where he never deals, and it has a lining that I put in a month ago." These are the sort of considerations by which we should make out our case in a private difference of opinion. Any mention of Bradley's Absolute or Spinoza's Substance would arouse mystification or a laugh. But this is no argument against the view here taken. All it means is that while we live in a boundless universe the boundaries of ordinary life and thought are contracted and we can satisfy our everyday intellectual needs without going outside them.

This appeal to a limited test would be my answer to another of Mr. Harris's questions. He notes that in my discussion of "The Thing and Its Architecture" I appeal at certain points to mere "convenience" to account for our original grouping of qualities into things. He asks what I mean by such "convenience."

I mean utility, ease in use, as contrasted with the necessity with which we often take the qualities of one thing to be cemented. The most readily recognized things are human artifacts like tables and chairs, knives and forks, because their qualities, when combined, have so obvious a joint purpose. There is nothing, so far as we know, that would of necessity bring the silvery glint of this spoon into combination with this particular weight, shape, and size; from the logical point of view the combination seems arbitrary. To the ant or to the horse the spoon would probably not be a thing at all. What makes us take it as one thing is the usefulness which its special combination of qualities fits it to serve. I do not deny, and have tried not to neglect, other considerations that are also at work, and have specifically denied James's overstress on utility in teaching that "the meaning of essence is teleological." But it does seem significant that Roger Fry, who, as an artist, must have been specially inclined to note Gestaltist configurations and aesthetic wholes, should have said that "The subtlest differences of appearance that have a utility value still continue to be appreciated, while large and important visual characters, provided they are useless for life, will pass unnoticed" (*Vision and Design*, 47).[1] This stress of mine on utility was largely designed to show how little our commonsense world is a logical construct in spite of the lines of necessity that crisscross it throughout. The fact is that if it were rebuilt along lines of necessity the present order would vanish.

Mr. Harris also asks what I mean by "the given," the immediate element in perception. He summarizes his understanding of my view: "In short there are no 'hard data.' Whatever we perceive is already judgment. It is saturated through and through with 'theory.' We cannot pare it down, by closer observation or in any other way, to bare sense-given indubitable 'fact.' "

This is correct except for the possibly misleading statement that "whatever we perceive is already judgment." If I perceive my own headache, is the ache itself a judgment? One is caught here in a dilemma. If one agrees with this, if a pain or a sensation of blue is already a judgment, it looks as if sensation as such had vanished and the first twinge of pain in an earthworm is already cognition. If one rejects this view as overintellectualizing sensation, let us have one good example of pure sensation. A headache? Not if one perceives it as an ache in the head, for this is surely to characterize it in a way that is beyond sensation. It seems absurd to deny that there is any such thing as sensation, but equally hard for a mature person to introspect a case of it, since all his sensations have become barnacled over with interpretations, or mossed over with such emotions as fear, delight, and repulsion. We can say perhaps that we approach pure sensation in a pain so intense that the whole of consciousness seems to be absorbed in it, or when, in going to sleep or waking, we seem to see or hear things without recognizing what they are. But there is something paradoxical in the very notion of hunting for pure sensation, for if we find it, that is proof that we haven't found it, since the finding of it would transform it into something else.

Still, it would be absurd to deny the fact of sensation. Bradley and James are surely right in holding to a period in our early experience in which there is a welter of sensations not yet objects of actual awareness or invested with the memories of past associations. And there seems to me something artificial in analyzing such sensations into act and object—an act of awareness on our part and an object perhaps existing independently in nature. If the infant experiences at once pain, red, indigestion, and a fetid odor, these seem to me all alike elements in his state of consciousness, with no existence except in that state and possessing various intensities because of the differing strengths of the physical stimuli. We know what these stimuli are and know that because of their intervention between the sensation and any external thing there is no possibility that these sensations are sense-data composing part of the character of that thing and only a low probability of their resembling it. This fact offers ground enough in itself to reject the sense-data theory of Hume and the phenomenologists.

These pains, odors, and colors are sense-data nevertheless. The term sense-data usually connotes two characteristics in what it refers to: immediacy and certainty. Sense-data are immediate because not arrived at by inference or any other conscious steps, but are gifts ("data") presented to us by nature. If I step on a tack and feel a pain, the pain is not a construction of my own but an immediate experience forced on me from without. Secondly, sense-data commonly carry with them a higher degree of assurance than the perceptions of physical things. One may wake up at night hearing the wailing voice of a child, which turns out a moment later to be the caterwauling of a neighbor's cat. The perception of a child's voice was a mistake, but not the hearing of a sound; of that one may be quite certain, whatever its right interpretation was. Even if there is nothing external at all in the way of stimulus, and the sound, like Schumann's haunting high A, is classed as a hallucination, it is still a sense-datum, and one about which there may be a dreadful certainty.

Sensation, then, exists, and because it results from a causal chain there is no good reason to regard its quality or content as an existent in nature. Am I then to be included in the honorable company of Broad, Price, and Russell as an advocate of the sense-datum theory?

The disappointing answer must be both Yes and No. I believe there are such things as sense-data, but I do not think that the object, either as perceived or as it exists in nature, consists of them. I believe in them because we can approximate to them, if not capture them in introspection, and because there are clear indications that perception is not the first stage but the second in the growth of our minds. I can accept them also, with a qualification Mr. Harris would expect, in their use in the sense-datum theory. The holders of this theory say that when we walk round a square table we see a great variety of shapes. That all these shapes should be actual existents in nature seems incredible; they are to be eliminated by Occam's razor if by nothing else. But that I do experience such things seems to me undeniable. Professor Hirst, in his forceful attack on sense-data, seeks to dispense with them by substituting the language of the object "looking" so-and-so for the language of seeing distorted versions of it. If there is a round dish on the table, the walker around it "sees nothing which is elliptical, for there is no elliptical existent or sense-datum; there is only a round dish" (*The Problems of Perception,* 48).[2] Similarly, of the stick in water; the right account is that it "looks bent," and to the color-blind man "a red object looks grey" (ibid., 49). I have no objection to such language. But I do not know what it means unless so interpreted as to admit what are meant by sense-data. For the walker around the dish, its "looking elliptical" means that what is immediately given to him, what he directly sees as distinct from what he takes to be there, is something elliptical. Similarly of the stick's "looking bent." The child who sees this for the first time would report unquestioningly that he was seeing a bent stick, and we still see it with full clearness even when we know what correction to make. For a stick to "look bent" means that the content of what one is seeing is a bent stick, whether that content is illusory or not. And the gray that the color-blind man sees is just as good a datum as the red seen by the normal eye.

But is not this a simple acceptance of the sense-datum theory? Why go so far with the theory and then draw back? The reason is that the sense-data accepted by the theory are not strictly what they are taken to be, for they are not data given exclusively to *sense.* Consider the cross-shaped speck seen in the sky and taken to be an airplane. Mr. Harris would protest that if this speck is seen as cross-shaped it is not a pure datum; it has already passed the threshold of perception; the moulding hand of theory or of conception has already been at work on it. In this Mr. Harris is surely right. If I had seen no crosses in the past, I should have seen nothing that I could recognize or describe as a cross-shaped object now; my mind is employing a conception in interpreting the given. Similarly in the other cases. The ellipses are not taken merely as ellipses; they represent various approximations to a circle, which gives them a conceptual character. A bent stick in water is not a mere sense-datum, even to a child: and to the color-blind man who sees a gray signal, the gray is not a datum purely; it is one shade distinguished from another and probably carrying a special meaning by reason of this distinction. These are all data whose modification by conception has already begun, and are therefore more than *sense*-data. They are themselves low-grade percepts.

This view has reminders of Kant. Sensation was for him an undifferentiated "manifold," corresponding to our field of undiscriminated qualities. As soon as a quality was identified as gray, the concepts of identity and difference were being applied to it. As soon as a cross-shaped or elliptical pattern was discerned in the manifold, the "forms of pure perception," space and time, which were not themselves sensed, were being imposed as frames, as they were in due time on the other offerings of the manifold. Thus in the Kantian manifold the sense-data of the theory would find no place. In another respect our own theory follows both Kant and Plato. Men commonly suppose that it is in the direct awareness of sensation, that is, at the bottom of the epistemological scale, that they gain their most accurate glimpses of the world out there. On the contrary, it is at the top, where the categories of logic lie, that the revelation is most exact. There is no good reason to suppose that any of the colors, sounds, or odors, any of the softnesses, smoothnesses, or tastes that I may now be sensing, or indeed anything that resembles them, exist in the external world. But Plato insisted, and Kant held in spite of himself, that the world beyond our experience was governed by intelligible law, that the universe could not, for example, be so inconsistent as to compel us to say we ought unless it also allowed us to say we can. In our own theory likewise it is argued that while sensation tells us nothing qualitatively about the external world, we do know something of its structure through such highly general categories as logic and causality. Rationalists have traditionally argued that the universe is a system; they have gone further and held that it is intelligible because its parts are bound together both causally and necessarily.

If I am asked, then, whether I accept sense-data, the answer is Yes, because I clearly find introspectively the sort of data that Broad, Price, Moore, and Russell are talking about. But it is also No, because these data seem never to be data apprehended merely by sense, but always data that have been conceptually moulded already. But what is meant by "conceptually moulded"? Not merely the being placed in a spatial and temporal framework, or dealt with according to the law of contradiction, but also, according to the view developed in *The Nature of Thought,* by use as a ground of inference. The perception of the speck in the sky as an airplane involves, I maintain, a movement of thought from something given to its interpretation. Here Mr. Harris comes effectively to my aid by dealing with some of the often repeated objections to this theory. The objection, for example, that perception is instantaneous while inference takes time he dispatches trenchantly by citing psychological experiments by Bartlett and others showing that perception does take time, and by adding that in any case inference need not be time-consuming; it does not start from A and move to B, but may be an instant grasp of the nexus between them. Mr. Harris thinks, as I do, that such arguments against perceptual inference as that perception does not involve doubt, question-asking, reflection, or the explicit use of propositions fall short of conviction.

I should be repeating myself if I went over these again. But there is a point or two in Mr. Hirst's able criticism of the theory held by Mr. Harris and me in common that may well be further noticed. One of my main reasons for attributing to perception an element of judgment or inference is that perception may be in error, and that in order to be true or erroneous any mental content must have risen to the level of judgment. Mr. Hirst replies by denying that perception is true or false at all. "Perceiving may be proper, correct, clear and accurate, or indistinct or incorrect, but not true or false. . . . I cannot see truly or hear falsely; I may be mistaken *about* what I see or hear, but I do not see mistakenly. . . . Truth is a relation between statements or propositions and the world they are about . . ." (Hirst, 232–33). This is not, I think, a tenable position. (1) When Mr. Hirst says, "I cannot see truly or hear falsely," he is of course right if he means by seeing and hearing merely having the respective sensations; a sensation of color or sound is neither true nor false. But (a) that is not the point at issue. That *sensation* is neither true nor false does not prove the same about perception, for the two stand on different levels of experience. And (b) note that Mr. Hirst says "perceiving may . . . not [be] true or false." Perceiving is an act or event, and I suppose no act or event, even judging or concluding, is itself ever true or false, any more than the act of jumping or the event of falling down stairs. What is true is the *content* judged or asserted, or *what* is concluded. Hence (2) Mr. Hirst must also, I think, be mistaken in saying that "Truth is a relation between statements or propositions and the world they are about . . . ." It is obviously not a statement or proposition considered as a string of words—noises or marks on paper—that is true or false, but what these words express. We are thus brought back to the asserted content as that which is true or false. The question then becomes whether this sort of content is present in perception.

Surely it is. When the observer perceives the speck as an airplane, or the red bulgy object as a tomato, or the man ahead of him as his friend John, no words may be spoken, even to himself. But if the speck turns out to be a kite or the red round thing to be a wax model or the man ahead to be a perfect stranger, it is idle to say that one has made no mistake in perception. One has taken A to be B when it is not B but X. And one need not, in any of these cases, have explicitly distinguished A from B, or had the slightest doubt, or raised any prior question, or been conscious of any transition of thought. One has done what everyone would call perceiving and everyone would recognize as making a mistake.

Mr. Harris agrees with me here. But now he raises a difficulty of his own. I have spoken about the thought in perception as involving ground and consequent, and he wants to know what serves as the ground. He can understand passing from cross-shaped speck to airplane, but then that speck is not a mere sensum. Somewhere, he suggests, I must start with what really is a sensum, and it is not clear to him how a mere sensation of red or soft, itself unidentified *as* anything at all, could supply a ground for any sort of inference. Mr. Hirst suggests a similar difficulty in saying that my theory is faced with an infinite regress; anything that could serve as a ground turns out not to be a sensum, and I must renew the quest.

The roots of perception are lost in the mist, and where neither introspection nor retrospection is practicable, and a behaviorist approach is irrelevant, dogmatism is not in order. But one can at least suggest an account of what goes on that seems eminently natural. The child is in the midst of James's "buzzing, blooming confusion." The soft nipple of the bottle is put to his lips, and is at once followed by the pleasant taste of warm sweet milk. Here is one sensation followed by another and pleasant one. Neither is singled out; and I agree with my critics that it would be ridiculous to attribute inference to the first experience of a temporal connection of this kind. Yet the material for it is there. The presentation of one quality has been followed by another, and the first vague expectancy has presumably been induced before either the touch or the taste has been definitely discriminated. After a few experiences of the sequence both sensations are moving toward explicit notice, and on the presentation of the first the second is a little more definitely expected. Such expectation is an example of what I mean by "the inferential element." My critics are of course right that saddling the infant with a process of explicit deduction from explicit premises would be absurd. That is not what I am doing. I am saying that associations are in process of being established within the preperceptual manifold, that these associations give rise to connections of varying degrees of firmness, and that when full perception supervenes, the expectation and its sensible ground are so fused that the experience does not seem like a process at all. The soft touch at the lips is dominated by the expectation of what has habitually come with it. This process from something given to associated expectation is the commonest form of perceptual inference. Why anyone should find it strained or paradoxical I do not understand.

Not only is it the natural way of describing the rise of perception; it is the natural way of explaining error in perception. If some day the child's bottle is filled with acidulated lime juice, he will put it to his lips just as eagerly, but the cry that follows will show clearly enough that expectation has been thwarted. The thwarting of such expectation is the first form of error. It is not of course the taste of lime that is in error, but the expectation of something else. And that expectation is reached by rudimentary inference.

The word "inference" suggests to many the following of a necessary connection. And inference at its best is exactly that. But it would be pedantically narrow even for a rationalist to confine inference to such relations. Most scientific inferences are based not on necessity but on association, yet we do not hesitate to accept them as genuine acts of reasoning. It must be admitted, however, that mere association gives nothing really intelligible. And the world of common sense that is constructed in accordance with it is bound to appear something of a cloud castle to the reflective eye. We have no idea *why* sugar is sweet or wormwood bitter, why snow is white or water wet, and we forget how arbitrary are the sizes we assign to gnats and Everests, to earth and sun and galaxies. I have said that the test of truth most commonly used is coherence within this commonsense world of things. But if the mind in search of necessities were to see all things as it wants to see them, if qualities now grouped for convenience' sake were strung along lines of necessity, and human sensation, disease, and genius were seen in the light of causes that are in the end themselves necessary, the world we live in would be transformed in unimaginable ways. Even the inferences of our men of science might bear an astonishing resemblance to the fumbling inferences by which the child constructs his world.

Mr. Harris has contributed many suggestions that are so close to my own views of perception that I can accept them as corrigenda as they stand. One important criticism is directed against my theory of the idea as the potentiality of its object, but since this carries us beyond perception and is a target of criticism by Mr. Bertocci as well, I reserve it for my reply to him.

1. Roger Fry, *Vision and Design* (London: Chatto & Windus, 1928), 47.
2. R. J. Hirst, *The Problems of Perception* (London: Allen & Unwin, 1959), 48.

12 BLANSHARD ON UNDERSTANDING
Alburey Castell

BRAND Blanshard has published three substantial books to date (1971), has edited or contributed to many more, and has produced enough professional papers to make a further volume. These books, chapters, and essays have provided, for upward of thirty years, an interesting and valuable commentary on philosophy in this country and Britain. Mr. Blanshard's own "position" in these writings has, I suppose, been less widely shared than his writings have been read. There is no easy label for the position which he has been expounding and defending. To call it "idealism" is to flourish what has become essentially a term of abuse: it tells you little about the position beyond indicating (usually) that it is a position which the speaker does not share. He has, upon occasion, referred to himself as a "rationalist," and his position as "rationalism"; sometimes "unrepentent rationalism." But that does not get you much closer to the heart of the matter. The fifteenth chapter of his *Reason and Goodness*, "The Rational Temper," will give you more than any ism-label. Whatever the position should be called, you can say that, in the interests of certain things which he values, and certain claims which he considers to be beyond reasonable dispute, it has constrained him to keep a sharp watch on empiricism and its derivatives, and on materialism and its derivatives. These derivatives may be several times removed from their parent doctrines but, if the connection is there, and if they threaten things about which Mr. Blanshard is philosophically protective, he launches an attack.

These stakes have kept him busy. Between 1925, when he began teaching at Swarthmore, and 1962, when he retired from teaching at Yale, most modish positions in philosophy have incited him to criticism. Realism, pragmatism, critical realism, logical atomism, logical positivism, emotivism, associationism, behaviorism, naturalism, physicalism, existentialism, have been typical examples. As I have read his essays in criticism it has seemed to me that his claim has usually been that, "pushed to their logical conclusions," these positions turn out to be "internally incoherent," or that they threaten the attempt to think coherently with reference to matters about which Mr. Blanshard is philosophically protective. These may be two ways of saying the same thing, but that is a point on which it is not easy to be sure.

That is one-half of the picture. It can be caught sight of by reading any of his volumes, or a sheaf of his professional papers. Perhaps the best single introduction to Mr. Blanshard's thinking in philosophy is Volume Two of *The Nature of Thought*. There you see him expounding and guarding something, and attacking positions which threaten it. But there is another half to the picture. I refer to his comparative silence about contemporary writers and doctrines which, it might seem, are in one way or another supportive. A single reading of Volume Two of *The Nature of Thought* will alert you to the fact that, on diagnostic matters, he will be constrained to settle accounts, then or later, with Russell, Dewey, Santayana, Lewis, Ayer, Nagel, Stevenson, Watson, Skinner, Ryle, Carnap, and (had they arrived by then) Smart and the Australian materialists. But with whom would he smoke a pipe of peace? Among philosophical thinkers whose *floruit* falls between 1920 and 1960, it is not easy to say. Bradley, Royce, Bosanquet are too early. Joachim and Joseph are too cloistered to represent what I have in mind. This is not a trivial or irrelevant point. Mr. Blanshard has expounded and defended matters which have needed a protracted hearing and a sustained defense. This he has persistently and impressively provided. And, like most energetic defenders, he has seen that attack is often the best defense. These are grounds for congratulation and gratitude. But those matters, whatever they are, which constrain a person to an interest in philosophy, to holdings in philosophy, and to criticism in philosophy do just as surely involve him in alliances, appreciations, overlapping commitments, hurrah-moments for others in the field. It is good business for a person to say "My position is X. It constrains me to search out and destroy Y, because Y is not compatible with X." But it is also good business for a person to say "My position is A. It constrains me to appreciate and defend B, because B is connected with, or supportive of A." It should be possible to mention half-a-dozen writers for the period 1920–60 who would provide Mr. Blanshard with this sort of opportunity. Sustained and closely reasoned criticism is good. Let there be no question about that. But sustained and closely reasoned appreciation and defense is also good. Both cause the position from which they proceed to stand out clear, to be more intelligible. "You have some stakes driven in. Whom do they constrain you to speak out against? But equally whom do they constrain you to speak up for?"

Mr. Blanshard's two volumes on *The Nature of Thought* were published in 1939. They were reviewed by Gilbert Ryle in the July 1940 issue of *Philosophy*. The review contained a good send-off, enthusiastic, perceptive, yet with reservations appropriate to the future (1949) author of *The Concept of Mind*. The book was not only a critical hit for that year; it invited favorable comparison with the best that philosophy had produced in this country in any year as far back as you cared to go. It is still possible to recall its impact on those who were privileged to read it during the first years of its existence. Whether you shared or despised the position which it expounded, you were constrained to acknowledge that here was a book with some claims to greatness. It had an important and unifying theme. It had a timely, indeed perennially timely, intention (see preface). It was written with grace, wit, urbanity, and a learning which did not cause the author to become pedantic. It had charm, but a relentless tenacity. By the time you reached the last chapter of the second volume, you realized that the work was, what many books are not, a labor of love. It had taken twelve years to write, but it bore no signs that the author had wearied of his assignment. Differences of subject matter and doctrine to one side, its virtues as an impressive human artifact invited favorable comparison with James's *Principles of Psychology* or *Varieties of Religious Experience,* with Royce's *World and the Individual* or *Problems of Christianity,* or with Santayana's *Life of Reason.*

We use the term "rational" in two senses. One of these cues you in on the theme of Mr. Blanshard's book. We speak of the solar system as a rational order, meaning that it can be reasoned about, that it can be found out about by reasoning. This is an important sense of that term. It applies to the subject matters of human inquiry, from mathematics to science to history. But we also speak of man as a rational animal, meaning that he reasons and can be reasoned with. This is also an important sense of the term. If, in this second sense, it had no referent, there would be no subject matter for logic and the theory of knowledge. Now, Mr. Blanshard's theme is rationality in this second sense: man considered as a rational animal, an animal which reasons and can be reasoned with. When he speaks of the nature of thought he refers to the ways in which rational animals behave when they perceive, have ideas, and reflect systematically. Their world is rational in sense I. They are rational in sense II. What account is it necessary to give of rational animals in a rational world? As I understand it, that was his twelve-year assignment; not unlike a famous earlier eleven-year assignment.

We use the word "thought" in two senses: sometimes as a noun; e.g. "Here's a thought—stay over and take an early plane." In this sense "thought" refers to the outcome of thinking. We also use it as the past tense of *think*; e.g. "I thought my way through the difficulty." In this sense "thought" refers to a mode of behavior, an activity performed. At first glance, Mr. Blanshard would seem to be using "thought" as a noun in the title of his book; and I have no doubt that he did. In that case there is a conventionality about the title which becomes apparent as soon as you get into the book; because it seems to me, at all crucial points he is concerned with thought as a mode of behavior; that is, with thinking. This is not a trivial or irrelevant point. It is not merely that his book is in fact an attempt to give a systematic account of the nature of thinking: its intentions, its levels, its vicissitudes, its criteria, its presuppositions. In this respect it resembles Dewey's *How We Think*. It is that his overall intention, as stated in the preface, refers to a mode of behavior which rational animals perform. And this intention, it can be argued, sustains the book.

Mr. Ryle's attention was caught by the opening sentences of Mr. Blanshard's preface:

> What I have attempted in this book is an analysis of thought that will neither be instantly repudiated by the psychologist nor indignantly disowned by the metaphysician. That is a higher aspiration than some may think. Between the account of ideas and inference supplied by the psychologists, eager to construe their study as a natural science, and that of the epistemologist and logician, there has gradually appeared a chasm that is now all but impassable. This chasm, nevertheless, I have set myself to bridge.

That is straightforward enough. A chasm has emerged between psychology and philosophy in reference to the nature of thinking. The book aspires to bridge this chasm. The chasm is *not* that psychologists are concerned with thought as a mode of behavior, whereas philosophers are concerned with thought as the product, outcome, result of such behavior. It is that psychologists propose to construe thought, as a mode of behavior, in one way, whereas philosophers propose to construe it, as a mode of behavior, in another way. This is a celebrated chasm. William James said it was the widest and deepest chasm which faces a person who has given hostages to both psychology and philosophy. That this is the chasm to which Mr. Blanshard refers is made clear in sections four and five of chapter 14. These sections spell out two ways of construing the behavior of a rational animal when he is thinking: one is common (perhaps not universal) among psychologists; the other is common (again perhaps not universal) among philosophers.

Once this chasm has been formulated, the overall plan of *The Nature of Thought* is clear. There are four books. Book One deals with perceiving; Book Two with thinking that is not tied to perceiving; Book Three with thinking in the more specialized sense of getting to know, or coming to understand, or explaining; Book Four with necessity, or necessary connection, or necessary truth, as the goal or ideal with reference to which a rational animal regulates his thinking as described in Book Three. This is an intelligible progression. You can see what the author is up to, even though you may not wish him well in his assignment. However, what is *not* apparent is why Mr. Blanshard ever thought that this project, if carried through and successfully defended against attackers en route, would constitute a bridge between psychology and philosophy. One might be convinced that, successfully completed, it *ought* to be accepted by psychologists as a bridge between themselves and philosophy. But that would be to underestimate the determination of psychologists to give their own account of the behavior of a rational animal when he thinks, and to have this account be acceptable as a piece of natural science. With perhaps a few distinguished exceptions, I cannot imagine Mr. Blanshard's project, no matter how successfully carried through, making any important difference to the way in which academic psychologists think about psychology, and, as psychologists, think about thinking. Mr. Blanshard speaks of his two-volume project as a "modest eirenicon." He misleads himself. It is not modest: it is ambitious, magnificently and commendably so. It is not an eirenicon: it will bring no peace. He says, speaking of distinguished predecessors ("the great tradition," as he correctly calls it), that "they have not succeeded in awakening the psychologist to any conviction of sin." He is correct. But does he have no faith in induction, where psychologists are concerned? Or is he hoping for a miracle?

Since 1939 the prevailing tides have been against any bridge in his sense. On the one hand, Watson has been succeeded by Skinner; and cyberneticism and computerism have increased, among most academic psychologists, the conviction that they do not need Mr. Blanshard's bridge. On the other hand, among philosophers, Ryle and the Australian materialists and others have sponsored the notion that any bridge building that is needed will be on terms laid down by natural science, and by psychology thought of as a natural science. Perhaps this is the way it should be. Perhaps philosophy is not an autonomous enterprise. Perhaps it is parasitic upon mathematics, and science, and history, and art, and religion, and economics, and politics, and psychology. I do not think it is. I think it is possible to learn more about the behavior of a rational animal when he is thinking, or trying hard to think, from Mr. Blanshard's volumes, especially when he is concentrating on this matter, and forgetting about bridge building, than from volumes written on the presupposition that thinking is a "natural process," and the study of it a "natural science."

For many years, almost since 1939, I have recommended that students planning to become teachers read the seven chapters in Book Three of *The Nature of Thought* in which Mr. Blanshard gives an account of "how we think" when we are getting to know something or coming to understand something. These seven chapters (18–25, omitting 22) contain an excellent, relatively straightforward account of these matters. I do not know of a better one. If these seven chapters were published separately, as a small volume, they would get effectively into the liberal education of many persons who might otherwise never hear of Mr. Blanshard's two large volumes. In his review Mr. Ryle said that Books One and Two (which make up Volume One) contained the most valuable part of the entire work. The reasons which he gave suggest that, in his judgment, Books One and Two would be a more effective "bridge" between psychology and philosophy than Books Three and Four. Since I doubt that any such bridge is possible, I am not persuaded by Mr. Ryle's judgment on this matter. Whereas Mr. Blanshard's seven chapters in Book Three giving an account of how rational animals think in getting to know and coming to understand speak to the intellectual experiences of any person who will reflect upon his own activities in these matters. My point about these chapters, as President Hutchins said of the University of Chicago, is not that they are perfect but merely that they are the best you can get. Mr. Blanshard's account is not exhaustive, nor guaranteed to stir up no disagreements between himself and a reader; but, for the job he intended, I do not know as good an account in any other book. I would add that its virtues give point to the remaining chapters in Volume Two, in which Mr. Blanshard sets himself to defend certain outlying doctrines presupposed by his account, and to criticize certain others which are incompatible with his account.

Thus, when Mr. Blanshard has completed his account of how we think in getting to know and in coming to understand, he reminds himself that his account presupposes, for example, a coherence theory concerning the nature of truth, a theory of degrees of truth, a theory of internal relations, and a theory of concrete universals; and that his account is incompatible with associationism, behaviorism, pragmatism, empiricism, logical positivism, and a number of other outlying doctrines. He therefore writes a series of substantial and highly argumentative chapters in defense of the theories which are presupposed by his account, and similar chapters in criticism of the theories which are incompatible with his account. What is one to say about these substantial and argumentative chapters?

This is a delicate question. The point is not that Mr. Blanshard may be mistaken when he says that his account of how we think presupposes certain doctrines and is incompatible with certain other doctrines. He is shrewd at diagnosing such connections. The point is not that he mismanages his defense of the presupposed doctrines or his criticism of the incompatible doctrines. In the management of these matters, in the production of supportive arguments where he needs them and destructive arguments where he needs them, Mr. Blanshard is well able to look after himself. In these respects he is reminiscent of McTaggart and Broad and other masters of philosophical contention. The point is not that he overlooked certain doctrines (pro or con) which he should have dealt with; or that, since 1939, new doctrines (pro or con) have arisen which he had now better deal with. The astuteness, the patience, the vigor, the clarity with which he has defended or criticized these outlying doctrines suggest that, confronted with neglected doctrines or new doctrines, he would do an excellent job for them or against them as the need might be. The point is not that his seven-chapter account of how we think is, relatively speaking, easy and pleasant to read; whereas his defenses and criticisms of the outlying doctrines are, by comparison, difficult and demanding. Both claims are true, but neither is relevant to my point in all of this.

Mr. Blanshard's treatise, it will be remembered, was written to build a bridge across a chasm. The chasm is between the ways in which psychology and philosophy propose to construe the behavior of rational animals. I agree with Mr. Blanshard that there is this chasm. I question his belief, or his hope, that a bridge satisfactory to the parties separated by the chasm can be constructed. There are certain modes of behavior—getting to know and coming to understand are among them—which are not "psychological processes." They are rational activities. Mr. Blanshard's chasm is between those who construe rational activities as psychological processes and those who do not. If you do that, as a first step to giving an account of a rational activity, little or nothing that you say thereafter will have any relevance. We grant the converse of this readily enough when we say, "Don't personify the process." Mr. Blanshard's chasm is between those who thingify rational activities and those who do not. My first point, therefore, is that, if an adequate account of a rational activity is to be produced, it will be produced by those who believe that there are rational activities, and that such activities are not identical with or reducible to psychological or physiological or chemical or physical processes. If that is a "philosophical" belief, then, to return to Mr. Blanshard's chasm, it will be a philosophical task to produce an adequate account of rational activities, including the activity of which he gives a seven-chapter account in Book Three. Philosophy may have other assignments, but none of them is as primary as this one. If there are no rational activities in the world, or if we cannot get an adequate account of them, who is going to philosophize and what is there to philosophize about? In this sense, you might say, philosophy must provide its own primary data; namely an adequate account of the nature of rational activities. In his seven-chapter account of how we think, Mr. Blanshard is doing philosophy in this primary sense. Philosophizing beyond this (e.g. his subsequent defenses and criticisms of outlying doctrines in the rest of Book Three) is parasitic on philosophy in this primary sense. This is not bridge building; it is providing something which makes his substantial and argumentative chapters possible, and our evaluation of them possible. If we cannot produce an adequate account of such rational activities as getting to know and coming to understand, then questions about empiricism, positivism, behaviorism, etc. do not arise; and if, *per impossibile,* they did, there would be no way to settle them. You do not *begin* with these and similar outlying doctrines, and go on from there to produce an adequate account of such rational activities as getting to know and coming to understand. Would that not be putting the cart before the horse? To prolong that metaphor, an adequate account of rational activities is the philosophical horse, whereas those outlying doctrines are the philosophical cart. If, for example, someone says: "I am an empiricist. Let me give you an account of the activity called getting to know," how can you be sure that he is not giving you a "party line"? On the other hand, if he says: "I have performed the activity called getting to know, for many years, with reference to an important and demanding subject matter. I have reflected on the character of this activity. Let me give you an account of it," should we not be prepared to listen carefully, checking what he says, as best we can, against what, by practice and reflection, we have found out about the activity in question?

As a title for Book Three, and especially for the seven chapters to which I referred, Mr. Blanshard uses the phrase "The Movement of Reflection." Reflection, or reflecting, is a mode of behavior. It is something people do; not a "state" they are in, and not something which "happens" to them. It is behavior in the performance of which they can succeed or fail, and if they are sufficiently alert to what they are doing they can usually tell which. It is behavior appropriate to the realization that there is something you do not, or do not fully and clearly, understand. A person so circumstanced might say: "There is something about those northern lights, the shade or perhaps the intensity of their color, which puzzles me. I'll have to look into it." If he goes ahead with his intention, trying to "figure out" what it is about them that he does not understand, and why they don't look as they usually do, he will do some "reflecting." There is ignorance in the context of knowledge, puzzlement in the context of understanding. If either of these components (ignorance-puzzlement or knowledge-understanding) were absent he would not start in reflecting.

Mr. Blanshard's seven chapters aim to provide an account of this mode of behavior, its component behaviors and its normal stages or itinerary. He supplies some vivid locutions; for example: To apprehend something in terms of a system which renders it necessary. The theoretic impulse, meaning the impulse to theorize, to produce theory. The challenge of fragment to system in the domain of theory. Mainland and island as metaphors for fragment and system. I see no virtue in summarizing his seven chapters. Each is an excellent job. Taken as a set they provide a more than usually adequate account of coming to understand or getting to know. However, I would make three general points about his theme.

(1) To begin, I think it well to remind ourselves of the importance of this mode of behavior. Taken in little and in big, it is one of the most characteristic modes of human behavior. Go from your home to your office to your classroom, scan the front page of a metropolitan daily, attend a church service or the showing of a new-style movie, and, in Mr. Blanshard's sense, you will find yourself "reflecting": challenged by something you don't

know or don't understand. He speaks for the most part of "coming to understand." There are some points that may be easier to make if I speak of "getting to know." Either way, you can say that it is a mode of behavior which is of considerable importance to both the teacher and the taught. If human beings had never done any getting to know, the human world would be vastly different from what it is, and the teacher's world might not exist at all. If humans lost interest in this behavior, what we call civilization would be transformed into some form of barbarism. Its loss or any considerable reduction would make an immediate and continuous difference to our other behaviors. It is pervasive in the life of rational animals.

If you are a teacher, it is likely that you have a subject matter; e.g. mathematics, a natural science, history, geography, etc. These subject matters exist because people have performed this behavior intentionally, persistently, carefully, expertly, over a protracted period of time. If you are among the taught, you want access to organized portions of this human heritage, and in some instances you want to sharpen your understanding of the character of the behavior which produced it. This business of getting to know can be called "scientific" provided you do not confuse two senses in which we use that word: "produced by science," and in the phrase "a scientific cure for measles," and "productive of science," as in the phrase "scientific method." Getting to know can be scientific in this *second* sense. In the root meaning of "theory," it can also be called *theoretical,* in the sense of "productive of theory."

What questions can we profitably ask about this widely practiced and highly productive behavior? Can it be performed on itself? Can we get to know about getting to know? It is noticeably performed by rational animals. Is there anything about it that would overtax the natural powers of subhuman animals? Or the contrived powers of human artifacts? It is performed by different persons, at different times, with reference to different matters. Do any of these differences make a difference? Or is getting to know, in any sense, the same regardless of who does it, or when or where or with reference to what he does it? Aside from saying that getting to know is important, and that it consists in getting to know, is there anything else we can say? That, in a general way, is Mr. Blanshard's question in his seven chapters on these matters.

(2) In the history of the human race I suppose the astronomer, as successor to the astrologer, has been one of the most striking and colorful practitioners of getting to know. Reflecting on some of their far-reaching claims, Bernard Shaw once described them as imaginative and abandoned liars; and, referring to the astrophysics of the 1920s, Mr. Chesterton said, "If there is one thing I despise, it is the solar system." These exasperated remarks are ample testimony to the impressive outcomes of the investigative

behavior of astronomers. It may be that the investigative behavior of chemists runs a close second. In casting about for unquestionably prestigious practitioners of investigative behavior, it is not easy to do better than these. They enable you to point up a distinction which is fundamental to Mr. Blanshard's account of "the movement of reflection." I mean the distinction between the investiga*tive* behavior of chemists and the investiga*ted* behavior of chemicals, or between the investigative behavior of astronomers and the investigated behavior of the planets and the solar system. If you emphasize this distinction you sharpen your perception of, and you lend status to, what he means by "the movement of reflection." What can be said here?

(3) What does investigative behavior consist in doing? Is it complex? If so, what are some of its component behaviors? Has it, for a given question, a beginning, a middle, and an end? That is, are there detectable stages? If so, where and how and why does it begin? How does it proceed? Where does it reach a temporary closure? In short, is there an itinerary in getting to know? Using Mr. Blanshard's account, possibly supplementing it at minor points, I would say:

(a) It would seem to begin with what you already know. If you knew nothing at all, what would give rise to a question? If you have no question, how would you begin investigating? If you know that a man signs himself "John X Jones," you can ask what the X stands for. But if you have *no* knowledge, if you are totally ignorant, what starts you off? The notion of "idle curiosity" is no help here. If you don't know that he signs himself "John X Jones," if you don't know that "John" is usually a first name and "Jones" usually a last name and an intervening letter usually an initial, how would idle curiosity give you the question, "What does X stand for?" The word "idle" is intended to suggest that you do not attach much importance to the question, or to getting an answer; not that the question arises in the absence of all knowledge, or even all relevant knowledge. It takes a fact to raise a question, at least the sort of question that forms an essential component in getting to know. In this sense, getting to know consists in adding to what you already know.

(b) A second step is to diagnose your relevant ignorance. You must use what you already know to delimit the area of ignorance upon which you will work. No person, beginning a particular investigation, proposes to liquidate all of his ignorance by this particular investigation. "He signs himself *John X Jones,*" you might say; and proceed, "What does the X stand for?"

(c) A third step is to formulate a question which clearly expresses that ignorance. This step is important. If the question is misformulated—e.g. vague, obscure, ambiguous, misleading, too general, too particular, not precisely relevant—you are not clear what, among all the things you do not know, it is your present intention to find out.

(d) A fourth step is to propose or suggest a thesis which, if true, would be an answer. There would be no point in proposing a thesis which, if true, would not be an answer. If your question is "What does X stand for in his signature?" there would be no point in proposing the thesis, "X is the 24th letter in the alphabet." And there would be relatively little point in proposing the thesis that X stands for Xantippe, since that is a woman's name, or for Xerox, since that is not a person's name at all. The point is that, in getting to know, you are not footloose and fancy-free. If you are no respecter of limitations, the outcome of your investigative behavior may be continued ignorance or error. It is important to note that in proposing a thesis you are transcending the given. The power to do this is called imagination. No imagination, no power to transcend the given, then no getting to know. These apparent platitudes—some knowledge to start with, some ignorance, a well-formed question, a thesis which if true would be an answer, the power to transcend the given—are essential components in the investigative behavior called getting to know. They stake out what Mr. Blanshard means by "reflecting." If there is to be any speculation about knowing-machines and brain-behavior, it is of the first importance to make clear what investigative behavior consists in doing.

(e) A thesis having been proposed, it remains to discover whether you are entitled to assert it. This is crucial. To propose is one thing; to assert is another. When you propose, you put it up to people: will they consider this? When you assert, you serve notice on people: you prescribe, you assume responsibility. Are there grounds that entitle you to do this? The language of hospitality, customary at this point, is not misleading: you "entertain" your thesis as a hypothesis, with a view to discovering whether you will add it to what you already know. The prefix "hypo" conveys this notion of something "laid down" with a view to examining its credentials.

(f) Can you, then, "make good" on your proposed thesis? Can you demonstrate or establish or substantiate or validate or verify it? There is no avoiding a basic platitude at this point. You can warrant your hypothesis by showing that it is required by what you already know. The phrase "required by" is stronger than the phrase "compatible with." You do not achieve your purpose by showing that the hypothesis is compatible with what you already know. That will only show that it is possibly true. The connection must be stronger than that. There is nothing irrelevant or trivial about the question, "Is your hypothesis required by anything you already know?" If that question floors you, you are not in the business of getting to know. You are among the persuaders. You are "begging" the question. In answering that question you reason from what you already know. That is what makes assertion responsible: you are able to respond on its behalf. This, I think, is what is at stake in Mr. Blanshard's elaborate defense of coherence as the test of truth.

(g) There may be a further step. There may be a rival hypothesis. If so, it must be disposed of. A hypothesis cannot claim to express the outcome of getting to know, if there is a rival hypothesis which cannot be disposed of. What is called for is simple enough in principle. The case *for* a hypothesis is that it is required by what you already know. The case *against* a hypothesis (the rival) is that it is *incompatible* with what you already know. The point is that either way you are reasoning from what you already know. If you do not already know anything, you cannot sit in on this game.

These half-dozen points are included, along with others, in Mr. Blanshard's account of the movement of reflection. There is something which you see no way to deny; yet you realize that it is not required by anything you already know, or that it is incompatible with something you already know. This is "the challenge of fragment to system in the domain of theory." This is the goad to reflecting about it. The purpose is to discover what it will cost you to "apprehend it in terms of a system which renders it necessary." The system (what you already know) must require (render necessary) the challenging fragment (something you see no way to deny). These things being so, it is understandable that Mr. Blanshard should write a substantial and argumentative chapter in defense of coherence as the *test* of truth. But matters did not stop there. He added a second such chapter in defense of coherence as the *nature* of truth. Mr. Blanshard will forgive me if I say that I do not see that he was constrained to do that. That X is the "test" of Y, that X is evidence of Y or the form taken by evidence of Y, does not, I think, require you to go further and argue that X is the "nature" or "meaning" of Y. If A and B are constantly conjoined, you can say that this is evidence that they are causally connected. If they are causally connected, you would expect them to be constantly conjoined. But this does not require you to say that constant conjunction is the "nature" of or the "meaning" of causal connection. It is enough that constant conjunction is a "test" of causal connection. If C and D are similar in every detectable respect, you can offer this as evidence that they are identical. If they are identical, you would expect them to be thus similar. But this does not require you to say that unbroken similarity is the "nature" of or the "meaning" of identity. It is enough that it is a "test" of identity. Instances of this "reductionism" could be increased, but the point would be the same in each instance.

(4) There is another way of apprehending the character of investigative behavior. You can ask whether it has any diagnostic features. I suggested under point (2) the distinction between the investigative behavior of chemists and the investigated behavior of chemicals. That distinction may enable one to isolate important features of investigative behavior in Mr. Blanshard's "movement of reflection." Much of what I shall say here is explicitly stated in Mr. Blanshard's chapters. Perhaps all of it is implicit in those chapters.

Consider the following as a lead-in question: What can be said about the investigative behavior of chemists that cannot be said of the investigated behavior of chemicals? In the context of some philosophical issues, and in many of Mr. Blanshard's substantial and argumentative essays in criticism, this is a potentially important question. Are there any claims it would be wise to make about the behavior of a chemist that it would not be wise to make about the behavior of a chemical? I do not know of any list that is exhaustive or canonical or surprising. What features of investigative behavior could, at this late date, be surprising? Nothing you had better say about chemists and had better not say about chemicals would have any of the piquancy which marks a number of doctrines proposed between 1920 and 1960, and criticized by Mr. Blanshard in one place or another. That is a virtue in many of his essays and chapters: for the most part they contain few claims which lead you, on thinking them over, to wonder why he makes them or why you should accept them. What, then, about the investigative behavior ("reflection") of chemists? I would suggest such features as the following:

(a) The chemist's investigative behavior is fallible. He can make a mistake and not realize it. The etymon here is *fallere,* meaning to deceive. He can deceive himself into imagining that he is not mistaken when he is. This is an essential feature of his investigative behavior. It is not even an accidental feature of the behavior which he is investigating.

(b) It is corrigible. If it were only fallible, and not also corrigible, he would be in a bad way. But it is not essential to error that it cannot be detected. It can be detected, and revision can be instituted. Does that tell you anything about the behavior of a chemical?

(c) It is intentional, purposive. The aim is to overcome ignorance, to get to know something not presently known. That, in highly general terms, is what he is trying to do. If you limit your claims about chemicals to what chemistry tells you, you will not say that *their* behavior is intentional. They have no desires, and no relevant beliefs on which to act.

(d) It is critical, guided by reference to certain criteria; e.g. consistency, parsimony, falsifiability, etc. If he did not regulate his behavior by reference to such criteria, the upshot would, in great likelihood, be ignorance preserved or error entertained.

(e) It is reasoned, or reasoned-out. If you break in at any point and ask "Why this step?" or "Why this conclusion?" you would, normally, get a reason. In this respect his behavior is normative. As a rational animal, a chemist deals in reasons. He reasons and can be reasoned with. But you would be ill-advised to say this about chemicals.

(f) It is, or may become, experimental, tentative, exploratory. He may know what he wants but not always see clearly how to get it. So he tries this and tries that; a mode of behavior appropriate to fallibility and partial ignorance. This is a built-in feature. Does it correspond to anything in the behavior of chemicals?

(g) It is, or may be, response to a challenge. This is not to be waived aside. Response to a challenge is more than "response to a stimulus." The latter is automatic and "mechanical." The former is deliberate and critical. This, surely, is a difference which makes a difference. It may be that chemicals "respond" to "stimuli," but except in metaphor, can it be said that they respond to challenge?

(h) It is value-bound. If he placed no value whatever on anything whatever, would he, or would he be able to, function as a chemist? If he did not value knowledge, nor anything which knowledge makes possible, nor anything which makes knowledge possible, his investigative behavior would grind to a stop. In respect to something or other it is value-bound. It does not matter in what respect, because if it is value-bound in *any* respect, it differs from what chemistry authorizes us to say about the behavior of chemicals: *their* behavior, unless you speak in metaphor, is value-free.

(i) It is responsible, in the sense that he can answer for what he does. It would be a damaging criticism to say that, in his behavior as a chemist, he was irresponsible. In different ways he may be confronted with alternatives, between which it is his professional business to choose. It is not nonsense to say of an investigator (one who is "reflecting"), "Do not trust him. His thinking is irresponsible." What does the responsible-irresponsible distinction enable you to say about the behavior of chemicals?

(j) It requires detectable removable ignorance as a condition for its performance. If you are to get to know, you must be detectably ignorant about something. If you were omniscient, or if your ignorance was not detectable, or not in principle removable, what would you investigate? The notion of detectable removable ignorance does not cue you in on any aspect of the behavior of chemicals.

(k) It has presuppositions. To be unaware of these is not the same thing as not having any. To be aware of them is to grasp more clearly the character of the behavior which they facilitate. To be unable or unwilling to presuppose anything is hazardous for a chemist; but the point is, chemicals have no presuppositions because they do not make any, because presupposing is not a condition for any of their behavior.

Here are one-short-of-a-dozen features of the investigative behavior of a chemist, no one of which, except you speak in metaphor, is a feature of the investigated behavior of chemicals. The list is not complete, but it is representative; and it will not do to find any other features that are incompatible with these. These are in no sense peculiar to the chemist's investigative behavior; you will come upon these features in the investigatings of mathematicians, astronomers, physicists, historians, and other investigative groups.

There are at least these two modes of behavior. I shall refer to the first as activity or activity-behavior; and to the second as process or process-behavior. You can then say that some human behavior is activity; that Mr. Blanshard's seven chapters give an excellent account of the activity which he calls "reflecting"; and that the intended outcome of performing this activity is to achieve understanding. I see nothing new or strange in the claim that there are activities which are performed, and processes that occur or go on. I see no way of questioning that there are activities, because it would take some investigating to authorize the question. If we are sure that there are processes—and who is not?—then we had better be sure that there are activities, because it takes activity to discover and identify processes. If you construe a process as an activity, you personify it; and it is better not to do that. If you construe an activity as a process, you "thingify" it; and, by parity of reasoning, I should say it is better not to do that. These matters are basic platitudes. That is no count against them. In philosophizing, the piquant doctrines must be measured against the basic platitudes. When that is not done the piquant doctrines ride herd on us; and we verbalize, and try to think, fantastic notions. Mr. Blanshard's account of human understanding ("the movement of reflection") informs you, or reminds you, of certain basic platitudes which it is important not to lose sight of; because then you have nothing against which to measure piquant doctrines which get proposed, blaze up like prairie fires, and die out.

Up to this point I have suggested that Mr. Blanshard's account of coming to understand, getting to know ("The Movement of Reflection," Book Three), includes at least two claims as essential. First, that such behavior depends crucially on the notions of "required by" and "incompatible with." Second, that such behavior is an "activity," not a "process." If I am mistaken in these suggestions, then my concluding remarks are irrelevant. If I am not mistaken, then I would further suggest that Mr. Blanshard, despite any "unrepentent rationalism," may have to live with some "awkward questions." This further suggestion is not intended as a criticism. Indeed, it seems to me that a philosopher who is oblivious of "awkward questions," or unwilling to live with such questions, is open to criticism.

(1) If you warrant a hypothesis by showing that it is required by what you already know, and torpedo a hypothesis by showing that it is incompatible with what you already know, then you may be asked how you first get into this business of dealing pro and con with hypotheses. Presumably there was a time when a person first entertained a hypothesis with a view to examining its credentials. If so, then he already knew something; otherwise he could not proceed with his examination. This ur-knowledge, which he brings to bear on his first hypothesis, did not itself originate as a hypothesis, and was not

warranted by showing that it was required by what he already knew. He must have some knowledge before he can get into business showing that hypotheses are required by or incompatible with what he already knows. Now, it can be asked how he came by this original knowledge-capital, necessary if he is to get into business. I think this a fair question. I also think it is an awkward question. I see neither means of grace nor hope of glory in repudiating the question. If it is, as I think it is, a price tag on Mr. Blanshard's excellent account of the movement of reflection, and if there is no answer to this question which would not raise another awkward question, why should he not, as a lover of wisdom, learn to live with it?

(2) If the investigative behavior, of which Mr. Blanshard gives an account in Book Three, is an "activity" and not a "process," then it may be asked how (as an activity) it is related to the associated processes which go on in the investigator's brain and nervous system. Within the last dozen years vigorous papers and books have urged that "mental events" are "identical" with brain events. More than one of Mr. Blanshard's chapters suggest that he would not be satisfied with this "identity" answer to the question. There are other "answers" available if it is an answer you want. But each of these alternatives gives rise to notoriously awkward questions. I know of none that does not. If an awkward question, at one point or another, of one sort or another, is the price tag on the distinction between activity and process, and on the claim that activities are "somehow" related to processes, what is to be said against acknowledging the distinction and learning to live with the awkward question? Must there be no awkward questions for rational animals? Is this not one of them?

(3) If what Mr. Blanshard's Book Three gives an account of is an activity, not a process, then you can at least ask whether it implies an agent; and if so, what the relation is between an agent and the activity which he performs. This is a second dualism, not to be confused with the dualism of process and activity. If you take their printed word for it, there are writers who are prepared to provide a sympathetic hearing for the process-activity dualism; but, confronted with this second, activity-agent, dualism, they turn a deaf ear. Their hesitation, based on misgivings, is understandable. The second dualism is more "expensive," more demanding, than the first; so they slow down. But what are you left with if you concede activity and deny agent? Despite all the no-agent people, what is an activity that is not performed by an agent? If you are a process-advocate the answer is, I suppose: a machine without a ghost in it. But I see no reason to believe that Mr. Blanshard is a process-advocate. So the question has point: Does activity imply an agent? An activity is transient: as it is performed, it moves into the past. If it did not, the present would be much more crowded than it is. But the agent does not pass with the passing of his activity. In contrast to it as transient, he is a continuant, in at the finish.

For twenty minutes he works at a proof in geometry, or conducts an experiment in chemistry or plays a sonata by Beethoven. When the twenty minutes are over, his activity has "receded" into the past, manifesting its built-in transience. But he is still "there," able to go to work again if need be: a continuant. But a continuant in respect to what? Having performed a complex and demanding activity for twenty minutes, or twenty hours, or twenty days, there is no suggestion that he is now in *all* respects identical with himself then. But the suggestion is that he *is* identical in some important and essential respect. This much would be presupposed if we asked him "How long did it take you?" The awkward question here may be double-barreled: Does activity imply an agent? If so, what can, or must, we say about agents? For example, how are they related to their bodies? What is the "bearer" of their agent-identity? Given Mr. Blanshard's Book Three, I do not see how *not* to ask these questions. Their "awkwardness" imposes no veto to acknowledging them as questions. The phrase "awkward question" is not a contradiction in terms, no matter how "awkward," provided it is implicit in your claims. I think Mr. Blanshard would agree with me that what his Book Three gives an account of is an "activity," not a "process." I think he would entertain the question: Does activity imply an agent? I am not so confident how he would answer it. He might, like William James, insist that thoughts do not need any thinker; that, in a manner of speaking, they think themselves. James did not claim that there was nothing obscure, nothing awkward, about this notion. He seems to have made his peace with what he referred to as his "anti-substantialism." My point is not that no thoughtful person can admit activity and deny agent: I have met too many who do. I have no doubt they realize that an activity which does not imply an agent is a source of awkward questions. These they learn to live with; or they stop thinking in these terms, or about these matters. Except when he is writing colloquially, Mr. Blanshard is wary of the notion of agent. Perhaps he took warning from Hume's opening paragraphs on personal identity. But, at one point or another, in one way or another he has thought about this activity-agent dualism, and has realized that any way you deal with it, you let yourself in for an awkward question.

ALBUREY CASTELL

DEPARTMENT OF PHILOSOPHY
WOOSTER COLLEGE
WOOSTER, OHIO

12. REPLY TO ALBUREY CASTELL

Blanshard on Understanding

Mr. Harris has given chief attention to the first six chapters of *The Nature of Thought;* most others of my critics who have written about this book have concerned themselves with the later chapters of the second volume; only two, Mr. Castell and Mr. Minor, have chosen for examination Book III, with its account of the movement of reflection. Mr. Castell thinks that chapters 18 to 25 form a unit by themselves and might with profit be printed independently with some such Deweyan title as *How We Think*. It is a suggestion which I shall consider, particularly since this part of the book, hidden away in the middle of a much larger work, has been all but inaccessible to students, and Mr. Castell reports having used it profitably on his reference shelves for college classes. Indeed Mr. Castell was one of the first to recognize the book and put it to academic use, and I am grateful for the generous encouragement he has given me over the years.

In view of this feeling on my part, one of his early comments gives me pause, and, I admit, some pain. He says that I have been very ready in criticism of my contemporaries, but slow to recognize the achievements of others who were working along the same line. He draws up an impressive list of philosophers of note whom I have criticized severely, but wonders whom I should name as philosophic friends. In the years between 1920 and 1960, he points out, there must have been a fair number of philosophers with whom I could find some community of outlook, and "smoke a pipe of peace." Why then my "comparative silence about contemporary writers and doctrines which, it might seem, are in one way or another supportive?"

I know that this criticism, made by an old and valued friend, would not be made groundlessly. There must be force in it. But it did take me by surprise and is not quite easy to appraise, since one is not a good judge of one's warmth or coolness toward others. I think the appearance of coolness *is* largely an appearance, but Mr. Castell's words make it clear that I did produce it and lead me to wonder how I did so. Some autobiographical reference seems unavoidable.

I have always been something of a "loner," not in philosophy only, but in general. Though there are few people whom I am aware of disliking, neither am I gregarious; I have never been able to throw off a feeling of unease and constraint in the presence of others, and I have not sought out company, as many do. This may be owing to a lack of assurance, a kind of "inferiority complex" from which I certainly suffered in my youth. The result has been a tendency to do my work alone. I wrote the 1,174 pages of *The Nature of Thought* without submitting a page to any philosophic colleague or publishing any of it in article form. When I trundled the manuscript into Allen & Unwin's office in the fall of 1938, I had not only no letter of introduction, but no one who could testify as to the form or substance of my writing. I was teaching in a small college without graduate students, and the book did not grow out of my courses there. I enjoyed going off on vacations or sabbaticals and writing quietly away at my own pace, sometimes in a Vermont farmhouse, on occasion in the Bradley Library at Merton, often at the British Museum in London. My only intimate friend except Edgar Carritt, who lived with us for a year in Ann Arbor, was my wife, who as a rule, was happily engaged on books of her own. My later writings were produced in much the same way, though the Gifford and the Carus lectureships provided fresh and strong stimuli. There is perhaps nothing I enjoy so much as writing and reflecting by myself, feeling an argument growing under my hand and moulding it into harmony with such standards of clearness and consecutiveness as I have.

This may give some background for an answer to Mr. Castell's criticism. I had opponents in plenty; they were all who sought to put down the rationalism that seemed to me the only plausible philosophy; but of collaborators I had none. It is true that Joseph gave me some useful suggestions which I acknowledged cordially in my book; I honored the stimulus and example of Joachim by dedicating my book to him jointly with Carritt. Joachim died, to my sorrow, in 1938 without seeing any part of what I had written. The influence of Bradley was apparent and acknowledged, and there were appreciative references to Sir William Mitchell, Norman Kemp Smith, and Alfred Ewing. Bosanquet, Taylor, and Royce I never knew. One important distinction in *The Nature of Thought,* the distinction between the internal and external meanings of an idea, I worked out in laborious independence, only to find something so similar in Royce that I thought I must unconsciously have borrowed it from him, and I acknowledged the debt.

This first book appeared in England in 1939, a month or two after the outbreak of the Second World War. Naturally enough, little notice was taken of the work; and half the publisher's supply of it was destroyed by a German bomb. When the war was over, the interest in this type of philosophizing had largely disappeared. The strange new meteor of Wittgenstein was shooting into ascendancy, and one by one the chairs in Britain, and then those in America, were filled with philosophers who believed that systems of philosophy were undesirable and impossible, and had no time for the sort of thinking they supposed I stood for, namely the Bradley-Bosanquet-Royce type of idealism. I read these new philosophers with interest and some profit, but with deep disagreement. The grounds for my dissent I stated as best I could in my three later volumes on Reason.

Meanwhile, where were the people who were traveling my road? They had almost ceased to exist. Brightman in Boston had hailed my book early, and I have made some small recompense for his encouragement by writing an introduction to a volume of his selected writings; but his personalistic and theistic idealism lay rather far from my own path. Peter Bertocci gave me further encouragement by using my books in graduate courses in Boston, but his written work, valuable as it is, lay chiefly in fields somewhat other than my own. W. H. Werkmeister took my book seriously in his *Nature and Basis of Knowledge,* and I responded by going to Southern California in 1966 and giving a series of seminars in his honor. Though I have made little reference to Alburey Castell's own work, I have introduced many hundreds of undergraduates to the subject through his lucid *Historical Introduction to Modern Philosophy.* Everett Nelson's pointed criticism of the Russellian logic I used with acknowledgment, and on his retirement participated in a symposium in his honor at Columbus. When Errol Harris produced his *Nature, Mind and Modern Science,* which I reviewed with cordial appreciation, I recognized a kindred philosophical spirit and invited him from South Africa to take my place at Yale during a leave of absence. It is pleasant to add that he decided to settle in this country. With C. A. Campbell at Glasgow, my Gifford successor at St. Andrews, I expressed my sympathy in print and in correspondence; and to Sir Malcolm Knox, whose writing in both philosophy and theological criticism I admire, I dedicated *Reason and Goodness.* The eminent Hegelian scholar, G. R. G. Mure, who was a student under Joachim at the same time I was, and later became Warden of Merton, was good enough to send me the manuscript of his own pointed criticism of the new fashions in philosophy, *Retreat from Truth,* for such comment as I could offer. A. C. Ewing and I reviewed each other's work; I lived for a summer in his house in Cambridge, and he visited me repeatedly in America. Personal trivia? Admitted. But they are hardly to be avoided if I am to meet the criticism under discussion except by unpersuasive generalities. I did appreciate and acknowledge, however inadequately, the work of the scattered few who in those chaotic years would care to be recognized as coconspirators with so arrant a heretic.

I have noted that Mr. Castell fixes his eye chiefly on my account of the movement of reflection. There is a reason for this concentration. He has seen with uncommon clarity the divergence between philosophers and psychologists on this topic. The distance between them has greatly increased in my own lifetime. In my youth psychology and philosophy were often pursued in the same department and by the same men. James, Royce, Miss Calkins, and Dewey, if I remember rightly, were all presidents of both the Philosophical and Psychological Associations. In Britain the leading psychologists, Ward at Cambridge and Stout, first at Oxford and later at St. Andrews, were both philosophers; G. E. Moore lectured on psychology, and Bradley contributed notable articles to *Mind* on such subjects as "the definition of will." Wundt, whom I went to Leipzig to hear in 1913, could be described with about equal propriety as philosopher and psychologist.

Early in the century psychology seceded from the union. It wanted to be a science, and a natural science, dealing with what was objectively verifiable and quantitatively exact. In this movement the American psychologists took the lead. Some of them, in the interest of these two ideals, danced after the cap and bells of John B. Watson, who announced to the world that he had found no trace of consciousness in his test tubes, so there was presumably no such thing. Others followed E. B. Titchener, who made sensation the chief subject matter of psychology, and accordingly when he came to *The Psychology of the Thought Processes*, produced a book of dreary sterility. McDougall, with his full recognition of the purposive character of mind, made more profitable reading, but he was not at his best on the processes of thought. To complicate matters further, Freud was soon stirring the waters with a psychology that paid little attention to either objectivity or measurement and yet was too illuminating to disregard.

Psychologists of the thought processes found themselves compelled to choose between a psychology that was "scientific" but was condemned to studying moral choice and rational reflection through bodily reactions, often those of rats and pigeons, in order to unlock the secrets of the human mind, and on the other hand a psychology that frankly abandoned the ideals of natural science and admitted consciousness and purpose as prime agents in human conduct. To take the first course was to break with Western culture itself, to abandon a tradition as old as Socrates, to commit oneself to a "psychology without a psyche," and perhaps also to place oneself, as Professor Skinner deliberately did, "beyond freedom and dignity." To take the second course was to admit that there was in some sense a "ghost in the machine," which the scientific observer could not get his eyes or his hands on, and to talk the venerable jargon of the schoolmen about man as "rational animal."

As for myself, I read enough of the "scientific" psychologists to sample their quality and to make an early choice. I was lucky enough in my twenties to stumble on Green's *Prolegomena* and his *Introductions* to Locke, Berkeley, and Hume. I read the rather hilarious account in Bradley's *Logic* of the associationist version of inference, and a little later Mitchell's admirable *Structure and Growth of the Mind*. These books frankly recognized that intellectual ends such as necessity and relevance operated within the activity of thinking to keep it on a track of its own independent of association or conditioning. To pass from books like these to the accounts of the thinking process given by Watson or even by Titchener meant a thorough disillusionment about "scientific" psychology. The philosophers told me something I could check about the workings of my mind and what I was trying to do in thinking. The "scientists" were attempting to make up by a white-coated show of exactness about the functioning of the nervous system for an untutored naiveté about the ends and means of the intellectual life.

Mr. Castell is alive to all this. He sees that reductionism in psychology has nothing worth saying to offer about the activity of thinking. He believes, as Plato did, that man is at least a brokenly rational animal, and that so far as he achieves rationality he does not learn, nor does he think, in the manner of rats and pigeons. Thought, at least as the philosopher knows it, is dominated by an end, and that end is understanding, the satisfaction of a distinct impulse and interest within the organism's attempt to adjust itself to its world. Mr. Castell draws a sharp distinction between activity and process, which he illustrates vividly by the difference between the *processes* studied by the astronomer and chemist and the *activity* by which the scientist studies them; and he enumerates eleven significant differences between them. To conclude that the world consists of processes is really to contradict oneself, since the concluding is itself an activity that cannot be construed as a process.

I of course agree with Mr. Castell's line of argument here, and if I am to criticize, can only peck at details. He thinks that the gap between philosophy and psychology is now too broad for leaping, and that psychologists are committed to a long and dogged trek down a desert trail. He may be right, particularly about American psychologists, who are singularly ready to practise their science as if it were a branch of biology. But there are two facts that seem to me to offer some grounds for hope.

One is the refusal of many leading biologists to accept their own science as "natural," if that means its assimilation, even in ideal, to such sciences as physics and chemistry. The recent joint volume *Beyond Reductionism*[1] gives much evidence of this resistance. Biology is coming to recognize purposive or quasi-purposive behavior not only at the top but at all evolutional levels. Hence psychologists who exchange a philosophical for a "scientific" study of thought may find themselves among heretics moving in a direction the reverse of their own. Secondly, the breach in Britain has never been so sharp as in this country. "Philosophical psychology" is rising to a new acceptance and popularity there, with some notable contributions from both sides of the line. These developments bode well. So I am a little more hopeful than Mr.

Castell that the two disciplines will not continue to be ships that pass in the night.

Mr. Castell has taken a deep interest in education, and I am pleased to note that he thinks my account of how we come to know is of some importance in educational theory. Education is not, of course, a merely intellectual affair; but so far as it is, he thinks, as I do, that the understanding of the world one lives in is its major end, just as the formation of instructed habits of inquiry is its major means. From this notion of the end of education, it follows that not all subjects of study are of equal importance, a point that seems hardly worth making until one takes note of the chaos among present educational "experts." It is not true that meteorology contributes as much to the understanding of the physical world as physics does, or that studying the minds of Kwakiutl and Dobuans contributes as much to one's becoming or understanding the cultivated mind as the study of Greek civilization. On such points Mr. Castell and I would be in pretty complete agreement.

One fact about the structure of Book III of *The Nature of Thought* Mr. Castell regrets. He thinks that after I have made my case for coherence as the test of truth, it was superfluous to add a further chapter on coherence as the nature of truth. "That X is the 'test' of Y, that X is evidence of Y or the form taken by evidence of Y, does not, I think, require you to go further and argue that X is the 'nature' or 'meaning' of Y." In a sense this is no doubt correct. Our interest is in finding what is true, and if we have in our hands the Geiger counter by which we can detect its presence, most inquirers would be content. But if you happen to be a metaphysician, you will not be content. You will want to raise the further question whether it is coherence that *makes* something true as well as making you know that it is true. Mr. Rescher has devoted an essay in this volume to proving that one can accept coherence as the test without accepting it as the meaning of truth; and Father Owens argues that one may accept coherence as the test in science without accepting it as the test in theology. So there is evidently a real question here. I agree with Mr. Castell that the question of the nature of truth is of little practical importance. But it has metaphysical importance, and at moments I am a metaphysician. We shall return to it later.

Mr. Castell concludes his essay with three further questions that arise out of my Book III. The first is how, on my theory, inquiry could start at all; the second is how I conceive the relation between purposive activity and the mere "process" out of which it seems to arise; the third is whether I believe in a self that exercises the activity and endures through the course of it. The latter two questions Mr. Castell recognizes to be ancient and baffling metaphysical problems with which a philosopher may "learn to live," even when he has no confident answer to them, and I suspect he will find me to fall under this description. In any case, what I have to say about them is best said in the metaphysical section of my replies. The first question should be dealt with at once.

Mr. Castell, while approving in all too generous terms my account of the movement of reflection, or in his own words "coming to know," does feel that it needs supplementation. The distinctive end of reflection, I suggested, is understanding, and what needs to be understood is some fact or event that stands over against one's body of present knowledge as unassimilated and puzzling. That knock at the door; what can it mean in midmorning? That bill for fuel; why has it doubled in the last month? Reflection is the answer to a challenge and requires a conjecture, a theory, that will fit the challenging element into our familiar world. A recurring simile I used was that of a continent with a fragmentary island offshore, and the problem is how to build a bridge to the island so as to join it to the mainland. But of course there has to be a mainland to start from, and Mr. Castell asks how this mainland was ever formed in the first place. In my account, it is itself a structure of thought. But how did thought get started if it needed a mainland to begin with?

I think an answer to this question is at least present between the lines in the relevant section of my book. The world of common sense is a world of judgments that give rough support to each other. It is built up piece by piece. At the outset there is no judgment at all. It makes its first appearance in implicit form in perception, and we have seen something of how perception emerges from the mist of infancy. Perceptions become explicit judgments as the result of shocks to expectation, and these explicit judgments are slowly connected with each other by association and by logic till we have a great network of mutually supporting judgments. This network forms our commonsense world. It also forms the continent from which the bridge must be thrown out to any acquired territory. Mr. Castell's question, however, may have a somewhat different intention. If he is asking, How did the first mind to break loose from mere sentience achieve the break? my answer would in principle be the same. If the question is, How and why did the theoretical interest first appear in the world? I am afraid the answer is that with present knowledge we cannot even make a profitable conjecture.

1. Arthur Koestler and J. R. Smythies, eds., *Beyond Reductionism,* The Alpbach Symposium, 1968 (Boston: Beacon Press, 1971).

13 BLANSHARD'S RATIONALISM AND THE CRITIQUE OF EMPIRICISM
Andrew J. Reck

I. Introduction

BRAND Blanshard is a rationalist—in fact, the leading proponent of rationalism in Anglo-American philosophy today. In the final paragraph of his first major work, *The Nature of Thought,* written as the storm clouds of World War II gathered over Europe, Blanshard declared that his philosophy is not new but a variation of *philosophia perennis,* the "ancient doctrine of 'the great tradition,' . . . the doctrine of the autonomy and objectivity of reason, the doctrine that through different minds one intelligible world is in course of construction or reconstruction"; and he expressed the wish that his own "insistent and reiterated emphasis . . . on the membership of minds in one intelligible order may serve, however minutely, to confirm the belief in a common reason, and the hope and faith that in the end it will prevail" (*NT,* 2:519, 520).

The defense of reason has been the guiding theme of Blanshard's philosophical enterprise. His presidential address to the Eastern Division of the American Philosophical Association, which was not delivered orally because meetings of the Association were suspended during World War II, defends reason against the behaviorists, the psychoanalysts, and the logical positivists.[1] Two series of Gifford Lectures presented at St. Andrews in 1952 and 1953, and the Carus Lectures presented before the American Philosophical Association in 1959, afforded him the opportunity to prepare a trilogy on reason. The first volume, *Reason and Analysis* (*RA*), based on the Carus Lectures, is not only a sustained polemic against the logical empiricists and the linguistic analysts for allegedly undermining reason; it also constructively restates Blanshard's philosophical rationalism. The second volume, *Reason and Goodness,* based on the first series of Gifford Lectures, criticizes recent movements in moral philosophy, such as subjectivism and emotivism, which minimize or deny the role of reason in morality, and advances the view that reason is central to morality. The third volume, *Reason and Belief,* stemming from Blanshard's second series of Gifford Lectures, sharply criticizes the revolt against reason by recent theologians of the neo-Thomist, neo-orthodox, and existentialist schools.

True to the thesis of "the autonomy and objectivity of reason," Blanshard has projected the ideal of a rational system of necessary knowledge representing the world as an intelligible whole of internally related parts. At the same time he has insisted that in the practical area of morality reason plays a central role, since moral judgment expresses knowledge, and since good consists in the most comprehensive possible fulfillment and satisfaction of desire, which for humans is intimately bound up with thought. Nevertheless, Blanshard's rationalism, conceiving the world as a rational system of logically necessary parts in which thought is satisfied, does not identify being and goodness. Finding no reason to suppose that this world as a whole merits the attribution of goodness, Blanshard affirms, first, that "between the rational as the logically necessary and the rational as the morally right, there is an abyss of difference," and, second, that "to pass from 'everything is rational,' in the sense of necessity, to 'everything is rational,' in the sense of right, is to stultify one's moral perception" (*RA*, 491).

Blanshard's philosophical rationalism, drawing upon arguments in philosophical psychology, philosophical logic, epistemology, and metaphysics first elaborated by British Hegelian philosophers, propounds the traditional rationalist conception of the supremacy of reason in knowing reality. This rationalism is in profound conflict with the prevalent modes of philosophizing in the twentieth century. Certainly in the Anglo-American philosophical world at present the dominant philosophy is empiricism. Empiricism may be roughly defined by contrast with rationalism. Whereas rationalism holds reason to be the central faculty of knowledge, knowledge to be representative or identical with an objectively real system, and the objectively real system to be a whole of necessarily related parts, empiricism regards experience to be the exclusive route to knowledge, knowledge to be restricted to experience, and the elements of experience to be contingently related to one another, if related at all.

II. Empiricism

Historically, empiricism has been wedded to the theory of knowledge. In an earlier period, in the days of Locke and Hume, for example, theory of knowledge was treated primarily as a field for psychological investigation. Psychological empiricism holds that all ideas originate in direct experience and considers knowledge to be an elaboration of given elementary states of experience by means of a few mental activities or mental habits of association. Today empiricism generally eschews its psychological beginnings, and is grounded instead on theory of knowledge as epistemology.

The evolution of empiricism from psychology to epistemology has been stimulated by three facts. First, philosophy differs from psychology in being more critical. Psychology assumes that as a science it can find truth without reflecting on what truth is, just as the other natural sciences do. However, the critique of knowledge, examining prior topics, such as the nature and tests of truth, constitutes a major task for the separate philosophical discipline of epistemology. Second, psychology became critical of its own methods and evidence. Introspection, the method of psychology when empiricism was young, has been generally abandoned, because of its subjectivity, by American psychologists, who favor objective experimental methods. Associationism has yielded to behaviorism as the basic system of empirical psychology. Third, natural science has, as a result of its successes, captured the attention of philosophers as the model for knowledge.

Natural science claims, at least, to be empirical, although scientific empiricism differs from early psychological empiricism. The natural scientist does not qualify "empirical" as "psychological." The term "psychological" too often connotes "subjective," whereas the natural scientist endeavors to eliminate or reduce subjective factors in knowledge. Scientific empiricism is evident in the experimental method which employs physically objective instruments and requires repeatable test conditions to assure objectivity of knowledge. Moreover, natural science accepts the results of logic and mathematics without questioning their origin in reason or experience. The significant issue for natural science is whether these results find application to factual data available experimentally.

Epistemological empiricism, therefore, ostensibly abandons the concern of psychological empiricism with the sources and genesis of knowledge. It focuses instead on the basis of knowledge. In this regard epistemological empiricism seems to follow the lead of scientific empiricism. Just as scientific empiricism grounds scientific theories in facts given in observation under the control of objective experimentation, epistemological empiricism affirms that all knowledge rests ultimately on basic experiential facts. Epistemological empiricism goes beyond scientific empiricism on at least one major point. While epistemological empiricism maintains, in principle, that all informative knowledge about facts rests on empirical foundations, it also adds that all the formal elements in knowledge, conspicuous in the formulas of logic and mathematics, must be accounted for in a manner which assures that experience is the exclusive foundation of knowledge.

Traditionally epistemological empiricism held that the principles of logic and mathematics are generalizations from the experiences of individuals or that they are the inheritance of present individuals stored up in their minds or brains from the past experiences of the human race. In either case, the sort of necessity characteristic of mathematics and logic was lost. Contemporary epistemological empiricism, perhaps more appreciative of necessity in logic and mathematics, has preserved necessity, but at the price of restricting it to systems of logic and mathematics. This form of epistemological empiricism, often termed "logical," embraces a variety of positions. But what is common to all forms is the insistence that the foundation of all knowledge is empirical, whether expressed in sense-data statements or physical object statements, and that, as a corollary of the theory of empirical foundations, statements in logic and mathematics are not statements about empirical matters, although they may be applied to such matters. When so applied, however, logic and mathematics lose their character of necessity. When not applied but purely formal, logic and mathematics possess necessity, but of a wholly analytic nature, whether conceived as linguistic or in terms of sense meanings. Plainly logical empiricism, in any of its varieties, implies a number of metaphysical theses, but one common to all varieties is the contention that the relations holding between the empirical facts that constitute the world, whether interpreted phenomenalistically or physicalistically, are all contingent. Necessity is no property of the world.

Epistemological empiricism as a critical theory of knowledge cannot occupy for long the naive position of scientific empiricism from which it has derived so much of its prestige. Ironically, when epistemological empiricism advances beyond scientific empiricism, which could just as well be embraced by philosophical rationalism, it has reverted, perhaps unwittingly, to psychological empiricism, although within the context of a quite different conception of psychology as a natural science. Thus despite its endeavor to liberate itself from psychological empiricism, epistemological empiricism has a certain kind of psychology at its very center. Simply stated, this psychology traces the elements of knowledge back to sense-data or observations of physical objects, and considers developed knowledge to be a logical construction from these basic elements. The key to the principles of logical construction is no rational faculty, but rather language and linguistic behavior. Epistemological empiricism finds its logical fulfillment in the constructional theories of Rudolf Carnap and Nelson Goodman

III. Philosophical Psychology

Better than any living philosopher Brand Blanshard has recognized the centrality of psychology to philosophy. Elsewhere I have stated that he is the greatest living philosopher of mind, and that his contributions to philosophical psychology merit placing his works beside those of William James, George Herbert Mead, and John Dewey in American philosophy and those of F. H. Bradley and Bernard Bosanquet in British philosophy.[2] Now philosophical psychology is not to be confused with psychology as a natural science. The latter is fundamentally uncritical about its theory of knowledge and is committed to the experimental method which has been so successful in the other natural sciences. Scientific psychology, moreover, is naively hostile to metaphysics, so much so that it has conspicuously succumbed to a primitive naturalistic metaphysics, and has perhaps been victimized by the intrusions of this metaphysics, well favored by nineteenth-century physics, into contemporary behaviorist theories of cognition and of action.

Philosophical psychology, by contrast, is critical. As critical, it defines psychology as a science, clarifying its basic concepts and its methods. It also explores the metaphysical issues that bear upon psychology, and while it may guard psychology as a science from dogmatic metaphysical doctrines which often masquerade as science, it should, insofar as it is philosophical, pursue these metaphysical issues to their ultimate resolution in a fully coherent and comprehensive metaphysics. In philosophy, to refuse to speculate when speculation is requisite is to be uncritical. Philosophical psychology, so to speak, stands between scientific psychology and philosophy proper, whose heart is metaphysics. Philosophical psychology specifies the conditions which make possible the former and discovers principles fundamental to the latter. Blanshard's *Nature of Thought* is, in my judgment, an exemplary work in philosophical psychology. Only William James's *Principles of Psychology* merits comparable attention, although a major difference of direction should be noted. Whereas James's *Principles* is directed to the establishment of psychology as a science, Blanshard's work aims at the solution of the metaphysical issues uncovered in the investigation of the human mind. Blanshard himself has acknowledged the differing emphases of his work when he said that a stress on empirical psychology marked the earlier chapters of *The Nature of Thought*, only to be superseded later "by a more metaphysical interest, which in the end becomes quite dominating" (*NT*, 1:14).

What is also noteworthy about Blanshard's philosophical psychology is that, beginning with empirical psychology, it proceeds critically to present a justification of—not empiricism—but rationalism. It is beyond my purpose here to consider at length Blanshard's arguments for rationalism. A major part of his case for rationalism consists in his case against empiricism. No student of philosophy today can deny that some of Blanshard's most significant contributions to recent philosophy are his sustained criticisms of current doctrines, although some may add that his unrelenting dialectic may be marred by the fallacy of *ignoratio elenchi*. Certainly Blanshard's polemics against empiricism constitute a singular contribution to contemporary philosophical controversy. But even an examination of his entire critique of empiricism, requiring what is tantamount to a survey of the major developments in Anglo-American philosophy during the past half-century, is beyond my compass now. Rather I propose to focus on his treatment of the given, of the idea, and of reason. Again my focus will be selective. It is my aim to show how Blanshard, beginning with materials basic to empiricism, uncovers elements which prepare the case for rationalism. Questions critical of his enterprise will emerge. Simply put, the question is: Is Blanshard's philosophical psychology adequate for his philosophical rationalism? The answer I shall suggest is that although this philosophical psychology suffices to reveal the inadequacy of empiricism, it is not adequate to support philosophical rationalism.

IV. The Given

Historically empiricism has looked to experience as the basis for knowledge. It has, moreover, analyzed experience into ultimate data, usually sensuous in nature, which the mind or understanding passively receives. These ultimate data are considered to be particular reports of the external senses of the eye, ear, nose, etc., and sometimes also of internal reflection on thoughts and feelings. These data make up what is called the given for traditional empiricism. The given is a mass of atomic data of sense from which knowledge is a construction.

Blanshard accepts an important part of the empirical theory of the given. He concedes that "the qualitative character of sensations can only be accepted passively; we cannot create at will new and other types of sensa; colours and sounds are not mere whims" (NT, 1:213). Still Blanshard never concedes to empiricism that knowledge is anchored in a pure given, unaffected by thought. Theoretically sensation may be distinguished from thought, but Blanshard observes that probably "we never in practice succeed in reaching a datum unaffected by thought" (1:118).

Blanshard's account of the given differs from that of traditional empiricism in other significant respects. Whereas traditional empiricism considers original or primitive experience to be the given of discrete particulars of sense, Blanshard views primitive experience to be "the unbroken continuum" (NT, 1:76). Here his description of primitive experience owes much to the stream of consciousness of William James and to the perceptual patterns of the Gestaltists. Thus the given of traditional empiricism proves to be no original given but rather the product of analysis. Accordingly, a distinction may be drawn between the preanalytic given and the postanalytic given. The unbroken continuum of primitive experience is the preanalytic given, that stream of sense and thought prior to analysis. By contrast the given of traditional empiricism is a postanalytic given, a result of analysis and susceptible to judgmental error. In basing knowledge on a postanalytic given traditional empiricism lacks the secure foundations it seeks. It also fosters a false theory of perception and thought, one which stresses elements rather than structure.

Blanshard offers his own analysis of the preanalytic given, and his postanalytic given is markedly different from that of traditional empiricism. Where the traditional empiricist finds sensory particulars, Blanshard uncovers universals. "From the very first," he writes, "universals are present" (*NT*, 1:77). These universals are what Blanshard calls specific universals. A completely specific color (green) or odor (the rose's fragrance) or taste (bitter) is a specific universal. These are not to be confused with greenness or fragrance or bitterness, the qualitative universals which exist only in the mind. Of course it is tempting to hold that Blanshard's specific universals are just particulars by another name. Blanshard, however, explicitly rejects this temptation. A specific universal, while it is as vivid as empiricism regards a particular to be, is repeatable; it "may be identical with itself in various contexts" (1:624).

Blanshard's replacement of empirical particulars by specific universals has paradoxical metaphysical consequences. It is consonant with his reconception of particularity as "the uniqueness achieved by *exhausting* a thing's relations" (*NT*, 1:651), leading to the startling conclusion that "The only true particular is the absolute" (1:639). Further, since all elements of the given are universals, even spatial and temporal relations are universals—i.e. are repeatable in different contexts, rather than being the principle that locates and fixes all other existing qualities, relations, and things. Finally, specific universals are repeatable in different contexts because they remain the same despite differences of spatial and temporal relations. Hence, for Blanshard, a contradiction arises between the principle of identity and our spatiotemporal structure. To resolve the contradiction, he denies the reality of space and time as they appear. He states: "It is, no doubt, a shock to common sense to hear that spatio-temporal arrangement cannot be real just as it appears, but at least this is not nonsense or inconsistent with itself. On the other hand, a general denial of identity would be both" (1:649).

Blanshard not only analyzes the given into specific universals; he also acknowledges concepts and categories as given. This marks an important confirmation of the traditional rationalist thesis of innate ideas. For Blanshard's postanalytic given includes, in addition to the sensory given of empiricism, a categorial given. What we do with the sensory given, he observes, is done under "limits rigidly fixed; our construction always proceeds under the charter and constitution laid down by the categories" (*NT*, 1:213). Although Blanshard never offers a table of categories, it is clear from various passages that by "category" he means such traditional concepts as substance, causation, relation, quality, and so on. Nor does he provide a justification of the categories by reference to some transcendental principle or logic from which they may be deduced. Rather they are given at the start, and become explicit as what is given is analyzed empirically and articulated dialectically. At this juncture philosophical psychology can advance no further, for no psychological explanation can illuminate the categorial given. Consider Blanshard's comment on the elusiveness of substance when we seek to dissect a physical thing to find what *it* is ultimately. He writes:

> Even when the search for the "it" of a physical thing has baffled us, and we can find nothing but qualities, we continue to use "it" of the qualities. "It (this orange colour) is redder than that (a yellow colour)." "It (this difference in colour itself) is greater than that (another difference)." What the substance-attribute relation really is is a matter often disputed among philosophers, but this much would seem to be clear, that it is too fundamental to our ways of thinking to admit of psychological explanation. We cannot start with the thought of a state where things were *not* related in this manner and then show how we came to suppose they were so related, for we cannot conceive what such a state would be. Any explanation of how we came to think as we do is balked at the universal forms of thinking, for these forms determine the structure of any world we can think about, and thus to contemplate their emergence from a state in which they were not is beyond our powers. [*NT*, 1:154]

Mention has been made that Blanshard's categorial given lends support to the rationalist thesis of innate ideas. It would be wrong, however, to equate the two. The innate ideas of traditional rationalism are discrete entities directly amenable to reflection. They seem to display the characteristics of passivity and atomicity possessed by the sense-data of traditional empiricism. By contrast, Blanshard's categories are structures and dispositions which pervade our thinking. Consequently, while they are universal and necessary for our thought, they are not originally clear and distinct. Unless thinking occurs, the categories do not appear; but once thinking does occur, they begin to operate on the sensory given. Whereas traditional rationalism is mistaken to suppose that the categorial given consists of clear and distinct innate ideas, each discrete and definable at the beginning of knowledge, traditional empiricism, from Blanshard's standpoint, commits the more serious error of circumscribing the given to sense and of assuming that there is nothing in knowledge that cannot be reduced to the sensory given except a few mental activities and habits subject to psychological explanation.

Thought for Blanshard intrudes into the preanalytic given. What is thought? It is an activity of mind. Mind, which is not to be reduced to consciousness for Blanshard, is essentially purposive. "Mind is purposive to its very roots; it is in its essence a set of wants cropping out into desires and of desires pressing for their fulfilment" (*NT*, 1:195). Thus mind is fundamentally conative.[3] Among its many desires is the theoretic impulse, the desire to think, to reason, to understand. Thought is the activity of mind displayed in rational consciousness. It is "that activity of mind which aims directly at truth" (1:51).

The simplest form of thought is judgment, since "nothing simpler could yield either truth or falsity" (*NT*, 1:51). And the simplest form of judgment is perception, for perception is "the barest and vaguest apprehension of anything given in sense *as* anything . . ." (1:51–52). Blanshard frames the following definition:

> Perception is an experience in which, on the warrant of what is given in sensation, we take some object to be before us. It is the sort of experience we have in the apprehension of red as red, or of an orange as an orange. Such experience is an achievement, since in the unbroken continuum with which we start, nothing is grasped *as* what it is. [*NT*, 1:76]

Those contemporary empiricists who, seeking to avoid a thorough epistemological analysis of the given, uncritically follow natural science in accepting statements about physical objects as the bedrock of knowledge fail to note what Blanshard rightly stresses, namely, that the perception of physical objects involves thought and its categories. Empiricism adhering to the physicalist thesis naively yields a crucial issue between rationalism and empiricism to the rationalist.

Let us sum up Blanshard's critique of empiricism in regard to the given. As we have observed, the first thesis of empiricism is that the bedrock of knowledge is the sensory given. Blanshard shows that this thesis is untenable. The starting point of knowledge is a preanalytic given into which thought has already intruded, bringing its own categories with it. The sensory given is but one part of the postanalytic given; the other part is the categorial given. The categorial given is consonant with the rationalist thesis that knowledge begins with elements or forms which cannot be reduced to sense but originate in thought. When empiricism appeals to sense perception of physical objects as the alpha and omega of knowing, with all theory construction beginning and ending there, it unwittingly abandons a major issue between empiricism and rationalism. For perception is a complex affair in which meanings imparted by the mind operate on the sensory given to constitute objects, among which physical objects are constructions at a late stage in the development of thought.

Blanshard's critique of empiricism in regard to the given raises further issues. His analysis of the sensory given into specific universals has paradoxical metaphysical consequences. And his treatment of categories and of thought, as that which is implicit and which requires explication, leads beyond the given to its complete articulation in a system of philosophy. Whereas empiricism holds that all knowledge can be translated back into the sensory given, Blanshard presents a rational system in which the sensory is transformed into the perceptual and the perceptual into the conceptual by the activity of thought in pursuit of the truth.

V. Idea

While Blanshard's theory of the given is at odds with empiricism, his theory of the idea presses the opposition further, He draws upon some rather settled theories and facts of genetic and comparative psychology. The advance from perception to ideas, he comments, "marks our escape from the mind of the animal" (*NT,* 1:257). First there are "tied ideas" which are the component parts of perception, implicit but serving thought in significant ways, as the unsensed grounds of perceptual inferences. In human consciousness, ideas, instead of being wholly tied to perception, may be free, their development paralleling the evolution of language. An idea is "free" when it "is an explicit thought which is independent of what is given at the time in sense" (1:258). In addition, Blanshard subjects the leading theories of the idea in philosophy and psychology to detailed criticism. Finally, he oversteps psychology to propound his own metaphysical theory of the idea. While this theory inevitably contradicts the main theories of traditional and contemporary empiricisms, it also deviates remarkably from traditional rationalism.

Traditional empiricism considers an idea to be a mental image. Accordingly, ideas are said to copy sensations or impressions, or they are deemed to be pictures of things which the senses report. Blanshard demolishes this theory. Although he accepts the introspective evidence that images exist in consciousness, he denies that the final form of the idea is an image. He considers the image-idea to be essentially an image of something. Since, therefore, it has a meaning which transcends itself, the image is not wholly tied to sense. While Blanshard concedes that images often play useful roles in thought, he stresses that they do not exhaust the character of the idea in its full expression. As he argues, "for most thinking, imagery is inadequate, irrelevant, and uneconomical" (*NT,* 1:565). He employs introspective evidence to demonstrate that "1) The thought often grows better as the image dies away, and 2) when the image is most perfect, the thought may be most inadequate" (1:260)

Although the definition of the idea as a mental image has few, if any, advocates in psychology and epistemology today, it prevailed until fairly recent times. Not only was it the established theory of empiricism, it also was adopted by rationalism for all ideas except those cardinal pure concepts, or imageless ideas. Even William James, as sophisticated a philosophical psychologist as has ever lived, was inclined to regard ideas as images with a "fringe." Whenever Blanshard's critique of the definition of the idea as mental image seems to be a case of flogging a dead horse, it should be remembered just how long and how deeply this definition has been entrenched in the history of thought.

Contemporary empiricists do not link their position to the definition of the idea as image. Bertrand Russell, who defended the image theory of the idea, may nevertheless be cited as the transitional empiricist philosopher when in his *Analysis of Mind* he suggested that ideas take two forms: the form of images and the form of words.[4] Respectful of science, contemporary empiricists accept the view of behaviorism in psychology. According to this view, thought is reduced to behavior—to linguistic behavior, in particular. Psychological behaviorism has arisen because of the alleged unreliability (subjectivity) of the evidence of introspective methods. To establish psychology as a science, the behaviorist disregards consciousness and directs inquiry to what can be observed objectively and is amenable to experimentation—namely, behavior.

Blanshard's polemic against behaviorism has appeared in several installments.[5] Adamantly he refuses to abandon introspection. His reasoning is partly an appeal to common sense: to deny consciousness is to deny what is most obvious the moment we reflect. It is partly dialectical: the behaviorist theory, to make a truth claim, must be thought and not behavior, since only thought can be true or false, behavior cannot. And it is partly expressive of his concern with the procedure of experimental method in psychology: the explanation of mental phenomena by means of physiological and behavioral processes supposes that there exist mental phenomena for which physical correlates are sought. But what is most germane to the present discussion is Blanshard's incisive attack on the narrow behaviorist formula that thought is language.

Blanshard's denial of the reduction of thought to language may have no target in behaviorist psychology today, but it is relevant to certain prevalent attitudes in recent philosophy—in particular to the conception of logic as the formal study of language alone. Assuming the validity of the introspective method to reveal the existence of thought, Blanshard launches a fourfold argument to demonstrate the difference between thought and language (*NT*, 1:320–24). First, language may vary while thought remains the same, when, for example, persons using different languages assert the same proposition. Second, thought may vary while language remains the same, as in William James's example, *Pas de lieu Rhône que nous* expressed orally suggesting "Paddle your own canoe!" Third, language may be present while thought is absent, as in the case of non-sense syllables. And fourth, thought may be present without speech, as in perception, in reading, or in motor aphasia.

Plainly Blanshard's gravamen against behaviorism is more effective against its primitive and metaphysical forms than it is against more recent methodological and philosophical forms. From the perspective of empirical science it may be admitted that consciousness exists and still contended that the investigation of consciousness by the introspective method results in little significant knowledge. The study of behavior, neglected until recent times, opens up a more promising route to the understanding of man. In epistemology, however, methodological behaviorism, the theories of which are influential in contemporary empiricism, must be counted as uncritical. The fundamental questions concerning the nature and the tests of truth are begged.

Blanshard does not avoid the ultimate questions. On his account, the purpose of thought is the truth, and both the nature and the test of truth are coherence. Later, more will be said concerning this theory of truth. Now it suffices to remark that for Blanshard thought is purposive in two senses: "It aims at revealing the outside world; it aims equally at satisfying an inner demand" (*NT*, 1:490). Thought, then, has two ends: an immanent end and a transcendent end. The inmanent end consists in the fact that the mind "seeks fulfilment in a special kind of satisfaction, the satisfaction of systematic vision" (*NT*, 2:262). The transcendent end consists in the fact that thought "seeks fulfilment in its object" (ibid.)

Blanshard's theory of the idea is at one with his theory of thought. Indeed, idea and thought are the same, except that ideas perhaps may be considered psychological determinates in the ongoing and momentarily indeterminate process of thought. In any case, an idea, like thought of which it is a part, is purposive. For Blanshard, then, an idea not only has a content available to introspection; it is "on the wing" toward an object. Hence the relation of an idea to its object is teleological. As Blanshard writes:

> Thought in its essence is an attempt to attain, in the sense of achieving identity with, a special end of its own. The relation between idea and object must be conceived teleologically, as the relation of that which is partially realized to the same thing more fully realized. When we say that an idea is *of* an object, we are saying that the idea is a purpose which the object alone would fulfil, that it is a potentiality which this object alone would actualize, a content informed by an impulse to become this object. Its nature is hence not fully intelligible except in the light of what it seeks to become. Mind, in taking thought, attempts to pass beyond its present experience to what it would be but is not yet, and so far as it has the thought of this end, it already *is* the end *in posse*. The idea is thus both identical with its object and different from it. It is identical in the sense in which anything that truly develops is identical with what it becomes. It is different in the sense in which any purpose partially realized is different from the same purpose realized wholly. [*NT*, 1:473]

The teleological relation of an idea to its object calls for clarification. Two remarks may be helpful. First the relation is complex, involving both identity and difference. As Blanshard says, "The idea can then be *both* the same as its object *and* different; the same because it *is* the object *in posse;* different because that object, which is its end, is as yet incompletely realized" (*NT*, 1:494). In this sense, the idea is "a half-way house on the road to reality" (ibid.). Second, the relation is approximative. An object is meant by a particular idea when the idea is directed toward the object, and the object is known when the purposive cognitive impulse crystallizing in the idea is satisfied. Ideas vary in the degree to which they adequately identify with their objects: "Truth is the approximation of thought to reality" (*NT,* 2:264).

Blanshard's definition of the idea and his clarifications reveal critical problems. Ambiguity surrounds his statements. First, it seems that the idea, analyzed as content plus potentiality, is potentially its object; it is a potentiality which is realized in its object as its actuality. Then it appears that the idea's object is a potentiality. And, perhaps as a corollary of the status of the idea's object as a potentiality, it also seems that the idea is its object, but its object as potentiality.

To define an idea as content plus potentiality is to raise questions concerning the status of potentiality in consciousness. To define the object of an idea as potentiality is to do the same in regard to the external world. Potentiality is one of the most elusive types of being for empiricism.[6] Consider its status in consciousness. To affirm the existence of consciousness on the basis of introspective evidence does not warrant the acceptance of potentiality as a constituent of consciousness. Whereas the content of an idea may exist psychologically as a mental image, the aspect of the idea as potentiality has no such existence. It cannot be found by introspection, just as it cannot be observed in the external world. It may, of course, be inferred. But if inferred entities are to be allowed at all, they are justifiable only if they are required for the purposes of explaining what is observed or may be observed.

It is difficult to grasp how potentiality as a constituent of an idea is justified, although it may be useful for the purposes of some scientific explanations to predicate dispositions of the nonconscious mind—i.e. the purposive physical organism. Indeed, in view of Blanshard's critique of the mental image, it is difficult to grasp how the potentiality of an idea would be affected or guided by the content of the idea. Even if potentiality in consciousness is admitted, it may yet be doubted that each idea has a distinctive potentiality. It is more plausible that, instead of a multiplicity of potentialities corresponding to a multiplicity of ideas, there is a singular potentiality pervading or underlying all thought. Blanshard seems to be suggesting such a singular potentiality when he states that "there are really *no types* of idea at all, but only stages in the development of a single function" (*NT,* 1:567). But then the distinction between categories and ideas of lesser orders collapses, a distinction sharply made in traditional rationalism and seemingly affirmed in some of Blanshard's statements concerning the basic concepts, such as the substance-attribute relation, which are given.

Blanshard's presentation of his theory of the idea is a major part of his critique of empiricism. At the same time this theory displays an irenicism which embraces empiricist conceptions. An idea, Blanshard states, "refers to an object, yet is not the object; . . . calls words and images in aid, yet is itself neither word nor copy; . . . changes with bodily changes, but is more than any bodily change; . . . is always a means to an end, though not always to an end that is practical" (*NT*, 1:473). Doubt arises as to whether it is a rationalist theory. Blanshard, who worked this theory out on his own without being aware of any predecessors, eventually saw, by his own admission, "that something very like it was the common property of metaphysicians of the Platonic turn of mind from the father of the great succession down to Bradley, Bosanquet, and Royce," and he singled out Royce as the philosopher "whose agreement may be claimed more confidently and in more detail" (1:518). Unnamed is the genius of the school—Hegel, for whom every idea is but a passing moment in the dialectically unfolding Idea. To analyze an idea into content and potentiality, as Blanshard does, is to present it as a Hegelian *Begriff*, a notion of which one part is discernible and the other, a larger part, is submerged in a relentless dialectic that terminates only in its object—the Absolute. The discernible part, amenable to reflection, is wholly at the mercy of the submerged part, which itself is a mere part of the great whole which emerges on the surface of reflective thought only now and then. Hegel chose to call the whole Reason. Inasmuch as it undermines as well as underlies all ideas of which we are conscious, it is tempting to call it Unreason.

VI. Reason

Central to Blanshard's philosophy is the theory of reason. In his quest for a definition of reason he explores the various conceptions to be found in the history of philosophy and examines critically the contemporary revolt against reason. He concludes that reason "is the grasp of law or principle. Such a grasp is intellectual; it is not a matter of sensing or perceiving, but of understanding. The principles thus understood are assumed to be valid independently of our grasping them, and therefore to be valid for all men alike" (*RA*, 26). Reason, briefly defined, is "the power and function of grasping necessary connections" (382).

Rationalism at least posits the existence of reason as defined. But rationalism affirms more. It is not enough to grasp necessary connections; it is essential also that the truths they represent be considered most certain, applicable to our experience both theoretically and practically, and informative of reality. To be a rationalist, as Blanshard says, is to "hold that the truths apprehended through the intellect are the most important and certain that we possess, and probably also that they reveal, at least in fragmentary fashion, an intelligible structure in the world" (*RA*, 26).

Empiricism historically has rejected this view of reason. With perhaps the sole exception of John Locke, traditional empiricism has been "committed by definition to scepticism of the claims of reason as an independent source of knowledge" (*RA*, 91). For empiricism, experience is the sole source of knowledge, and "necessity does not exist at all; it can be, and has been, explained away" (*NT*, 2:335). In its traditional form empiricism treats necessities in thought as generalizations or habits, and it is indicted by Blanshard for failure to account for logic in deductive and inductive reasoning. The formal laws of logic and mathematics are neither psychological habits nor empirical generalizations. In its contemporary form empiricism concurs on this point. However, contemporary empiricism treats logical and mathematical necessities as analytic and tautological. Whereas traditional empiricism has no place at all for reason, contemporary empiricism accords it so modest a position that, despite its grasp of necessities, it knows nothing about the world.

Contemporary empiricism, commonly known as logical positivism or logical atomism, is the direct antithesis of Blanshard's rationalism. For logical positivism radically alters the role of reason in philosophy. Reason no longer has as its task the tracing of necessities between facts and the understanding of the world as a coherent system, for no necessities exist between facts; nor, for that matter, is the world intelligible as a whole. Thus logical positivism demotes reason to "a highly specialized function which could be properly performed only by experts, the function of identifying the logical or linguistic equivalences that appeared in mathematical systems" (*RA*, 145).

Blanshard's case for reason was undertaken first in his *Nature of Thought*, although surprisingly the index of this work lacks an entry for the word, probably indicating that his own concerns had not yet fully come to focus. In *The Nature of Thought*, reason seems to be equivalent to the entire movement of reflection culminating in understanding. Reflection is defined as "a movement toward self-completion on the part of an imperfect system of ideas" (*NT*, 2:98) and understanding as "apprehension in a system" (2:33). Further, Blanshard endeavors "to supply in outline an account of the reflective process in which the presence and operation of the logical ideal are recognized as clearly as the logicians have a right to demand, while the process is still regarded as a psychological one, consisting of a series of steps . . ." (2:35–36). He traces the reflective process from its initiation, triggered by something outside a system of ideas challenging the system, through four stages. First, the problem, originating in the challenge, is specified. Second, the basis for suggesting a theory to meet the challenge is broadened by observing, consulting, and reading. Third, there occurs "the leap of suggestion" which advances a theory. Finally, understanding comes, and the coherence between the experience initiating the reflective process and a theory proposed by the leap of suggestion is seen. Now in this early account of the reflective process one step at least is not characterized by necessity—namely, the leap of suggestion.

When in *Reason and Analysis* Blanshard defines reason as the grasp of necessity, he seems to restrict it to the moment of understanding in the reflective process, i.e. apprehension in a system. So far as reason is described as a grasp or an insight, it is akin to intuition. But intuition suggests mystic insight and self-evidence, and Blanshard explicitly rejects both as tests for truth. While traditional rationalism is incompatible with mystic insight, it has nevertheless often appealed to self-evidence as a test for truth. But Blanshard attacks self-evidence in its own stronghold, in the area of mathematical axioms and logical laws. These axioms and laws, he argues, are seen to be valid not simply in isolation but rather within a system of judgments to which they belong. Even the ultimate laws of logic, e.g. the law of contradiction, are justifiable by the coherence test, insofar as their denial entails intellectual paralysis.

The status of reason becomes problematic. On the one hand, it is the entire reflective process, including a stage which is not necessitated. On the other hand, it is but a moment in the process, the moment which grasps necessity. Hence reason is menaced by contingency. Psychological causes may frustrate its eventuality. And when it appears, it may be uncertain about its principles. Worse still, a pseudoreason, certain about falsehoods, may masquerade as reason.

Yet Blanshard's theory of coherence as the test and nature of truth affords a measure of security to reason, for this theory promises the convergence of the immanent and the transcendent ends of thought.

The immanent end of thought is the satisfaction thought seeks; it is achieved when understanding occurs; and understanding is "systematic vision, so to apprehend what is now unknown to us as to relate it, and relate it necessarily, to what we know already" (*NT*, 2:261). It is achieved in a coherent system of knowledge. Such a system of knowledge is "knowledge in which every judgment entailed, and was entailed by, the rest of the system" (2:264). It is unfitting here to suggest that some thinkers do not agree that this is the sort of satisfaction thought seeks immanently; but it is fitting to note, as Blanshard would agree, that the immanent end of thought has not yet been attained. It is an ideal the realization of which is dependent on psychological events.

The transcendent end of thought is its object. "To think of a thing is to get that thing itself in some degree within the mind. To think of a colour or an emotion is to have that within us which if it *were developed and completed*, would identify itself with the object" (*NT*, 2:261–62). Now if such an identification is possible in principle, it follows that the object of thought must be identical with the immanent end of thought in that this object must be perfectly coherent. "Perfect coherence would mean the necessitation of each part by each and all of the others" (2:429). Still for Blanshard it is not certain that the world is such a necessary and coherent whole, although no reason can be adduced to deny that it is. As Blanshard says, "Though one cannot without some absurdity say that anyone has ever *proved* the world to be a necessary system, one can still postulate it and then examine how far the actual exercise of reason goes toward justifying the postulate" (*RA*, 383). In regarding concrete, cosmic necessity as a postulate, Blanshard acknowledges that it is not necessary. It is not, therefore, the kind of truth that reason grasps, since by definition reason grasps necessary truths. What, then, is it? One may be tempted to say that it is the wish of a thinker who has been immersed in a certain vision of the world, who desires that the actual world conform to this vision, and—lo!—he affirms that his vision is the world. But this temptation should be resisted.

Blanshard not only postulates the world as an intelligible whole; he also proceeds to adduce arguments to show that it is. His contention that the world is a necessary system the parts of which imply each other pivots on his theory of internal relations and his theory of causality. Here it is unnecessary to restate his arguments,[7] nor need Ernest Nagel's extensive criticism and Blanshard's response thereto be considered.[8] What is germane is Blanshard's contention that one major argument for the doctrine of internal relations is the principle of causality, for this principle illuminates not only his theory of cosmic necessity but also, and more pertinently, his theory of necessity in reasoning.

Causality is for Blanshard a cardinal postulate of science and rational investigation. It is held to be universal, all things being causally related, either directly or indirectly. Moreover, he argues that "being causally related involves being *logically* related" (*NT*, 2:492). Admitting that it is impossible to grasp logical necessity in most causal relations, Blanshard nevertheless rejects the regular sequence theory of empiricism as ultimately unintelligible. The regular sequence theory is of course conceivable, but it is unreasonable, since, if it is true, then no conclusion in a line of reasoning is ever necessitated by the evidence (*RA*, chap. 11). The empiricist, accepting regular sequence as the nature of the causal relation, must treat the series of psychological events that make up a line of reasoning as a sequence. The empiricist, therefore, has a chasm between his formal sciences of logic and mathematics, on the one hand, and his contingent psychological processes subject to regular sequence, on the other. For empiricism the necessity of the formal sciences, although purely tautological, stands apart from the contingent psychological events that constitute the actual reasoning which grasps the formal necessities. By contrast, as Blanshard views the psychological process of thinking, "The rational man . . . does not always stumble and grope in darkness till he arrives at conclusions by luck, and then for the first time exhibit his rationality by accepting them. Necessity aids in the process and not only at the end" (*Philosophical Interrogations,* 240).

Thus Blanshard insists that causality involves an irreducible element of logical necessity. Again, however, his position falls short of demonstration. The postulate of causality is accepted because in his words, "It is the part of reasonableness to accept a conclusion, even when indemonstrable, if it makes sense of things and no alternative does" (*RA*, 471).

Unfortunately Blanshard's argument for necessity in reasoning as the grasp of necessity is problematic. That the world, including man's own mental processes, is a logical whole of internally and necessarily related parts is not necessary; it is a postulate. It is not known as certain. If true, moreover, it has serious implications for the nature of mind and of thought. On Blanshard's definition, mind is purposive, and so is thought. Now to affirm that thought is necessitated and necessitated logically is to raise questions about the character of mind's purposiveness. Necessitated as a part within a cosmic intelligibility, human reason risks losing its independence and purposiveness. However it functions, it is necessitated. Causation construed as inherently logical permeates the whole of which a rational man's thinking process is but a mere part. As postulated, the world as an intelligible whole assures that everything that is is necessitated: Blanshard's vision of a coherent system of knowledge that satisfies the immanent end of reason as well as the logical atomists' antithetical vision, rational as well as irrational thought, truth as well as error. But then the distinction between rational and irrational thought collapses, and Blanshard's position risks being reduced to absurdity. Every kind of thinking, since it is necessitated, is logical, whether or not it is logical.

VII. Conclusion

Blanshard presents a powerful critique of empiricism. He shows that the given, which the empiricist takes to be the bedrock of knowledge, is not purely sensory but has a conceptual or categorial side. Having in effect demolished the epistemological foundations of empiricism and discovered mind's activities in sensation and perception, Blanshard has further demonstrated how the theory of the idea as image, a favorite doctrine of traditional empiricism, will not do. Against behaviorism, the basic system of psychology adopted by contemporary empiricists who eschew introspection as a method, Blanshard has launched a series of devastating criticisms. Finally, he has attacked the empiricist's denial of necessity, his attempt to reduce it to tautology, and his theory of causation in the real world as mere regular sequence. Blanshard's gravamen against empiricism has sprung from his philosophical psychology, his theory of mind and thought, and his description of the processes of perception, reflection, and understanding. Although his philosophical psychology is empirical and introspective, it ironically uncovers the errors of empiricism.

Blanshard defends reason and makes a case for rationalism. So far as his arguments are critical of alternative positions, they are extremely telling. So far as they attack the arguments used against reason and rationalism, they are perhaps invincible. Nevertheless, Blanshard's own philosophy is less than persuasive. His philosophical psychology, so useful an instrument in detecting the defects of empiricism, proves less helpful in constructing his own rationalism. His theory of the idea as teleologically related to its object contains the concept of potentiality, and difficulties surround this concept. While he alludes to categories as the most fundamental ideas, he never elaborates a theory of categories, but suggests that all ideas are on the same footing, except that within the context of his developing dialectic certain ideas—i.e. of substance and relation—play basic roles and others do not. Clearly Blanshard's philosophical rationalism should contain a theory of categories. Similarly, his theory of reason is less than adequate. As the mere grasp of necessity, reason lacks the substantiality of a faculty and sinks into the fleeting moments of insight that erupt in the reflective process. Sensitive to the consequences for his view of reason if these moments are contingent, he advances a theory of necessity. According to this theory logical necessity runs through causal necessity, and all psychological states, like everything else, are necessitated.

Thus Blanshard leaves philosophical psychology for metaphysics. But it is in philosophical psychology that he must discover the nature of reason. It is one thing to assert that reason grasps necessities, grounding or seeking to ground every element in a coherent system. It is quite another thing to demonstrate that reason's grasp is necessitated. Failing to find such rationality in the mind, Blanshard postulates it in the world, a world conceived in consonance with what the mind desires as its theoretical satisfaction—an absolutely coherent system. In justifying the rationality of the mind by appealing to the postulated intelligibility of the world, Blanshard engages in circular reasoning. More gravely for his argument, he jeopardizes "the autonomy and objectivity of reason." All actual reasoning, no matter how erroneous, is necessitated, and furthermore, according to Blanshard, that means it is logical.

What is requisite to advance the case for rationalism is a return to philosophical psychology, but one which is not so bound by the empirical evidence of introspective psychology. Such a psychology may uncover a transcendental faculty of Reason making possible the very existence of knowledge, experience, and reality. Or it may be part of a more comprehensive anthropology which studies the basic structures of language and thought.

Be that as it may, Blanshard's philosophical psychology does not suffice to make reason sovereign.

ANDREW J. RECK

DEPARTMENT OF PHILOSOPHY
TULANE UNIVERSITY

NOTES

¹Brand Blanshard, "Current Strictures on Reason," *Philosophical Review* 54 (July 1945): 345–68.

²A. J. Reck, *The New American Philosophers: An Exploration of Thought Since World War II* (Baton Rouge: Louisiana State University Press, 1968), 85–86.

³Brand Blanshard, "The Nature of Mind," in *American Philosophers at Work,* ed. Sidney Hook (New York: Criterion Books, 1956).

⁴Bertrand Russell, *The Analysis of Mind* (London and New York: George Allen & Unwin and Macmillan Co., 1921), 241; cited in *NT,* 1:284.

⁵*NT,* 1, chap. 9: 313–40; "The Problem of Consciousness—A Debate," *Philosophy and Phenomenological Research* 27 (1967): 317–37; and "The Limits of Naturalism," in *Contemporary American Philosophy,* ed. John E. Smith (London and New York: George Allen & Unwin and Humanities Press, 1970), 21–53.

⁶Hence the endless discussions of natural connections, dispositional properties, and contrary-to-fact conditions. I know only one recent work which has sought to establish that power (or potentiality) is empirically observable: Andrew Paul Ushenko, *Power and Events: An Essay on Dynamics in Philosophy* (Princeton: Princeton University Press, 1946). See my sympathetic exploratory essay, "The Philosophy of Andrew Ushenko," *Review of Metaphysics* 11 (1958): 471–85 and 673–88.

⁷See my *New American Philosophers,* 115–17.

⁸See Ernest Nagel's essay, "Sovereign Reason," which has appeared in *Freedom and Experience,* eds. Sidney Hook and Milton R. Konvitz (Ithaca, N.Y.: Cornell University Press, 1947); Ernest Nagel, *Sovereign Reason and Other Studies in the Philosophy of Science* (Glencoe, Ill.: Free Press, 1954); and A. C. Ewing, ed., *The Idealist Tradition: From Berkeley to Blanshard* (Glencoe, Ill.: Free Press, 1957). For Blanshard's response, see Sydney and Beatrice Rome, eds., *Philosophical Interrogations* (New York: Holt, Rinehart & Winston, 1964), 224 –41.

13. Reply to Andrew J. Reck

Blanshard's Rationalism and the Critique of Empiricism

Mr. Reck has done for my theory of knowledge what he has done in his various books for the philosophy of many other contemporaries. He has provided a remarkably clear, accurate, and balanced account of that theory as a whole. Though he has been merciful in criticism, he has disclosed in an almost casual way a number of apparent chasms in my thinking that go deep. Several of these he reserves for his conclusion. The honey bee carries its sting in its tail. I shall try to pick out and comment on the most serious of his strictures.

Mr. Reck, like Mr. Harris, is not at all content with my theory of the idea; neither am I. What looks at first like a fairly easy problem proves the more baffling the farther one goes. I approached it through my favorite zigzag route, trying out alternately the most plausible theories in the field, dismissing them as inadequate in this or that respect, and then trying to construct a theory that would avoid the pitfalls of the others.

I began with the commonsense notion that an idea is a mental copy or replica of its object. This notion collapsed almost immediately. There proved to be no relation between the clearness and exactness of one's thought and the wealth or vividness of one's imagery; and there were many objects of thought such as justice or the causal relation that were incapable of being imaged at all. I examined Mr. Russell's defense in his *Analysis of Mind* first of images and then of words as substitutes for meanings, and the results were equally negative. I then turned to behaviorism in its Watsonian form. Behaviorism has cropped up again since then in various other forms—in Skinnerism, in Australian materialism, in Ryle's *Concept of Mind*. I still think, rightly or wrongly, that the case I made against Watsonianism is in principle effective against these other behaviorisms. With the pragmatic notion of ideas I took more trouble, though ending again with rejection. The attempt by Moore, and for a time by Russell, to substitute an *act* of awareness for the idea was not accepted because I could not convince myself by introspection that there was any such thing; and the "essences" with which the critical realists replaced ideas seemed obscure and ambiguous. I seemed to be traveling down a blind alley.

A way out suggested itself when I was puzzling over the general idea and its ancient logical analysis into connotation and denotation. I was astonished to find that over whole ranges of general ideas the connotation, supposed to be a distinctly conceived set of common qualities, was simply not to be found. When I thought of color, there was supposed to be in my mind a concept of color or coloredness that was not any particular color but an abstract essence of color possessed by every color alike. I could not find it. When I thought of animality, I was supposed to think of traits common to Plato and an earthworm, which formed an abstraction emaciated to the vanishing point. I discussed my difficulty with H. W. B. Joseph, who reminded me of a suggestion of Cook Wilson's that the idea of a class stood to its members in a relation very much like that of the potential to the actual, of the undeveloped to its developments. In thinking of the class of animals, we were not extracting a wraithlike essence from a range of wildly varying individuals; we somehow achieved the reference without the wraith. If someone pointed to a snail or a zebra and asked if this belonged to the class we had in mind, we should say at once that it did. That is the paradox of the general idea. We can think of the members of a class, even though the connotation that is alleged to be there is conspicuously missing. What I wanted to find was the mental content of such an idea. But when I searched for it introspectively, I found myself looking into something very like a vacuum. I have sometimes wondered whether such behaviorists as Gilbert Ryle have not been turned in the direction they took by the empty-handedness of their introspection of thought that was obviously operating at high levels.

In this impasse I was driven to take seriously the notion of dispositions, a notion that has also seemed unavoidable to Bradley and Broad. Dispositions are often thought of as unconscious persisting tendencies, the tendency for example to be rude or to be courteous. But if the general idea expressed by "animal" is to be called a disposition, it must be described also as "occurrent," not continuous, and conscious, not unconscious. "The wolf is gregarious." One may know very well what one means by both these terms, though one has in mind neither a definition nor an image of either. One can say little of the content of the general idea except that it is a conscious disposition sufficiently definite to enable one to recognize members of the class as part of what one meant. Whether this account of the general idea is true or not, it is at least quasi-true; that is, the idea behaves like this in mental practice. We can think at once comprehensively and accurately with nothing in mind but a disposition which we know could be developed, and if developed, would be the experience of certain individual things.

I went on too precipitately, I think, from the general idea to ideas in general. How is one to conceive the relation of an idea as such to its object?

My suggestion was that the idea *is* the potentiality of its object, a potentiality that if developed would *be* the object, that is, get it literally within experience. Mr. Harris complains that in testing this theory I chose examples that gave it an unfair plausibility. Touché. One may think of the color orange by noting that it falls between red and yellow in the spectrum of colors, but this would mean nothing to a blind man; in order to realize fully what any of these names refers to, one must have the color itself in consciousness, either in percept or in image. I instanced Othello's jealousy, and argued that the thought of it involved feeling in some degree its own special quality of that emotion; a person incapable of that feeling would be "feeling-blind" in his attempt to think of it. This may be well enough, says Mr. Harris, when the object of my thought is an experience of some kind. But take the moon or the Great Pyramid as the object of thought, and the plausibility vanishes. Does it make sense to say that the astronomer is trying to be the moon, or that the historian of the Great Pyramid is trying to maneuver that somewhat awkward object into his consciousness?

No, I must agree that it does not. (See, farther, my reply to Mr. Bertocci.) The target of the theoretic impulse is not things or events or persons themselves but the truth about them, as I said in the first sentence of my book. Of course this does not affect the purposive character of thought. But it does affect our account of the end of thought. That end is not identification with, but knowledge or understanding of, its object. The person who sets out to know the Great Pyramid thoroughly will need to know the motives of those who built it, the history of its construction, the nature and origin of the great stones that compose it, and so on. Such apprehension to be complete would include in its grasp not only some of its relations to other things but, we have agreed, all of them; in the widening circles of relation which knowledge may reach, there is no perimeter at which we can say here relevance ceases; what is beyond it can contribute nothing to knowledge of the object at its center. And the mind may rightly be said to expand as its comprehension of the object does; or to put the same thing otherwise, it approximates more nearly its goal of total understanding. But that goal is total understanding, not bringing of the object literally within itself or vanishing into the object. Bradley has a chapter on "Thought and Reality" (*Appearance,* chap. 15) in which he argues that the very essence of thought is to be *about* its object, and that it can never vanish into it. But he also argues that it does vanish into it, preserving his consistency by saying that it is then no longer thought; it is part of a higher immediacy in which the relations that thought has followed have vanished too. This mystical disappearance of thought when it has reached its summit is not part of my own vision of things. The end of thought is truth, but truth about the world does not exhaust the world itself. About this we shall have more to say later when we come to discuss the nature and test of truth.

I turn to some other points made by Mr. Reck. "Clearly Blanshard's philosophical rationalism should contain a theory of categories." Mr. Reck points out that I do in fact treat certain ideas as if they were categories, e.g. substance and relation, but I never attempt a systematic account of them or of their connections with each other.

Now I suppose that what we mean by a category is a concept that is necessarily present in our thought, implicitly or explicitly, whenever we think about anything. And there are a number of concepts—identity, relation, consistency, substance, causality, for example—that I have been inclined to treat as categories, though about substance I have had reservations (cf. my essay in the Broad volume in this series). I agree that the project of such a list would be interesting, and that its members would probably be interrelated in important ways. But when one considers how widely philosophers of the first rank have varied in the lists of categories they have presented—Aristotle, Kant, and Hegel come first to mind—one is not encouraged to propose still another list. Many years ago I gave a course in the logic of Hegel, but having given it once, I decided never to give it again. I found myself doubting whether any single step by which Hegel descended his formidable ladder of categories was quite valid. Nor am I sure that in my own writing I have treated consistently as a category any concept but consistency itself. I do not know why a philosophy operating with this single category and using it as a critique of all other applicants for the place should not be possible.

Mr. Reck finds me more than once flying in the face of my own main requirement. He raises the very serious difficulty, which I am going to defer for the moment, how if all causal processes are necessary there can be such a process as illogical thought. And he finds further difficulty in seeing how purposive behavior could be more than a delusion in such a wholly determined world. "On Blanshard's definition, mind is purposive, and so is thought. Now to affirm that thought is necessitated and necessitated logically is to raise questions about the character of mind's purposiveness. Necessitated as a part within a cosmic intelligibility, human reason risks losing its independence and purposiveness."

Philosophers have often thus taken necessitation and purposiveness in mental processes to be exclusive of each other. I do not myself see any conflict between them. Take a random example. I notice in the evening's paper that a highly praised performance of *The Pirates of Penzance* is to be offered at a local theater next Friday night. Liking Gilbert and Sullivan and having the evening free, I decide to go to the box office and get a ticket, which I do. Here is a typical case of purposive behavior. The essential elements in it are having an end and adopting some means to it. Now it seems to me that the more closely these elements are studied the plainer it becomes that both had antecedents from which they necessarily followed. I like Gilbert and Sullivan because I have heard a number of their comedies and invariably enjoyed them. That I should want to hear more is therefore eminently natural. Since I want to hear more and there is no alternative way of spending that evening which holds an equal attraction, it is again natural that I should take steps to secure a seat. The analysis is, of course, far from exhaustive, but I see no reason to suppose that if it were made exhaustive any element either in my entertaining of this particular end or in my adoption of this particular means to it would be left dangling without any explanatory antecedent. Would this necessitation entail that I was any the less genuinely moved by purpose? I do not think so. Would it mean that I was any the less free in my behavior? Yes it does, if that means that in my holding of the purpose and adoption of a certain means to it there was some element that had no antecedent whatever from which it necessarily sprang. But I do not think that this kind of indeterminism is essential for ethics, and if determination means causal determination, the view would conflict with the major assumption of science. Mr. Reck is right in holding that my view of mind and of thought are thoroughly teleological and that I am also a determinist. If the two positions are incompatible with each other, my view of things has a large and sinister rift in it. But the two positions have been held together by many reputable philosophers like Rashdall, Ross, and McTaggart, and I am content to follow in their path.

At the end of his essay Mr. Reck suspects that at a vital point in my argument I have proceeded in a circle. "Failing to find such rationality in the mind, Blanshard postulates it in the world, a world conceived in consonance with what the mind desires as its theoretical satisfaction—an absolutely coherent system. In justifying the rationality of the mind by appealing to the postulated intelligibility of the world, Blanshard engages in circular reasoning." Now if I had argued that the world is rational because that answers to the mind's ideal, and that the mind holds this ideal because the world is rational, I should have been arguing in a circle. But the argument is a little more self-critical than that. That rationality is the end which thought is seeking is a conclusion, as Mr. Reck correctly points out, which is based on my philosophical psychology; it seems to me in a broad sense an empirical fact. That the world answers to this ideal of thought and is really intelligible is not, I think, demonstrable in any satisfactory way. But there is no harm in postulating that intelligibility so long as one remembers that it has not been proved; indeed the philosopher always assumes it when he takes his next step; he assumes that, whenever and wherever he raises the question Why?, there is an answer to be found, whether he finds it or not. In arguing, therefore, to the governance of the mind by a rational ideal, I am not deriving this, my premise, from my conclusion, namely the general rationality of things. My premise is an independently based empirical generalization.

There is indeed another sense of "rational" in which "the mind is rational" *is* inferred from the rationality of the world. If all events are intelligibly interconnected, then mental events too must be intelligibly conditioned throughout. Whether this makes sense is a point I have explicitly deferred for later discussion. But it is not the product of a *circulus in probando*. For while the necessitation of mental events is inferred from the rationality of the world, this latter is in no sense derived from the necessitation of mental events. It is a postulate derived in the manner described from what I take to be empirical fact.

There are other criticisms in Mr. Reck's paper that remain to be dealt with. But to a paper so largely expository and appreciative rather than critical of my position, I hope this fragmentary reply will be considered enough.

14 BLANSHARD AND THE COHERENCE THEORY OF TRUTH
Nicholas Rescher

1. Coherence as the Definition of Truth

THE earlier coherence theorists tended to view coherence as a characteristic mark of the truth without any very specific and definite commitment as to the exact nature of the "mark" at issue. Is coherence a somehow necessary feature of the truth—is it a part of the definition of truth or even the whole of it? Such questions did not generally receive close attention. After F. H. Bradley, however, the issue could not readily be avoided, and Brand Blanshard faced it squarely in his characteristically hard-headed fashion. His answer is clear and emphatic: truth *consists* in coherence; coherence is not just a feature of truth, but its nature.

The critical defect of this approach to the definition of truth in terms of coherence is that it leaves the link from truth to factuality not just unrationalized but unrationalizable. The linkage surely cannot be of *contingent* character. But yet how can the step from coherence to factuality possibly be a necessary one? Upon what sort of logical basis could one possibly erect an airtight demonstration that whatever satisfies conditions of maximal or optimal coherence must indeed be the case in actual fact? Surely this poses an insuperable difficulty.

Blanshard himself is, seemingly, perfectly ready to grant this. He writes:

> Suppose that we construe experience into the most coherent picture possible, remembering that among the elements included will be such secondary qualities as colours, odours, and sounds. Would the mere fact that such elements as these are coherently arranged prove that anything precisely corresponding to them exists 'out there' [i.e. less eccentrically formulated, *is actually the case*]? I cannot see that it would, even if we knew that the two arrangements had closely corresponding patterns. . . . It is therefore impossible to argue from a high degree of coherence within experience to its correspondence in the same degree with anything outside [i.e. with what is in fact the case]. . . . In the end, the only test of truth that is not misleading is the special nature or character that is itself constitutive of truth [viz., coherence]. [*The Nature of Thought (NT)*, 2:268]

Given my (perhaps somewhat tendentious) reading of this argument against a correspondence theory, it would seem that Blanshard is fully prepared to regard the step from "coherence" to "correspondence with the facts of the matter" as problematic and potentially fallible.

We once again encounter the difficulty that has been brought forth so often, and from so many different angles of approach, as to merit classification as a central problem—if not *the* central problem—of the coherence theory of truth. I have in mind the difficulty which, in one form, has been put by Bertrand Russell as follows:

> . . . there is no reason to suppose that only *one* coherent body of beliefs is possible. It may be that, with sufficient imagination, a novelist might invent a past for the world that would perfectly fit on to what we know, and yet be quite different from the real past. In more scientific matters, it is certain that there are often two or more hypotheses which account for all the known facts on some subject, and although, in such cases, men of science endeavour to find facts which will rule out all the hypotheses except one, there is no reason why they should always succeed.[1]

The point is, that even if one utterly rejects the core thesis of the correspondence theory that truth *means* "correspondence to fact" (*adaequatio ad rem* in the old formula) one is still left, in any event, with the impregnable thesis that a true proposition is one that states what is in fact the case. The link from truth to factuality is not to be broken, regardless of one's preferred conception of the definitional nature of truth. Even the most ardent coherence theorist must grant, certainly not the premiss of the correspondence theory, that truth *means* correspondence to the facts, but merely its consequence, that truths must correspond to the facts. Even if we follow the coherentist in rejecting the definitional route from the former to the latter, we must still be able to link them mediately, via coherence. And the standard problem as put forth in the Russell passage is simply: How can this be done? How can coherence of itself ever guarantee factuality? Cannot the clever novelist make his tale every bit as coherent as that of the most accurate historian? Given the (relatively clear) fact that the products of creative invention and imagination can be perfectly coherent, and given that alternate coherent structures can always be erected from given elements (as scientists frame different hypotheses to account for the same body of data), how can coherence possibly furnish a logical guarantee of fact? So runs one of the standard objections to the coherence theory of truth, one which, to all appearances, tells also against Blanshard's formulation of the theory. In seeking to impugn the correspondence theory by insisting that there is infallible linkage between coherence and correspondence-to-fact, Blanshard succeeds less in invalidating correspondence as a standard of truth than in highlighting a fundamental difficulty of the coherence theory of the type he espouses, one according to which coherence represents the very *nature* of truth.

2. The Criteriology of Truth

Blanshard emphatically recognizes and stresses the critical difference between a criterion or *test* of truth and a *definition* thereof:

> It has been contended in the last chapter that coherence is in the end our sole criterion of truth. We have now to face the question whether it also gives us the nature of truth. We should be clear at the beginning that these are different questions, and that one may reject coherence as the definition of truth while accepting it as the test. It is conceivable that one thing should be an accurate index of another and still be extremely different from it. There have been philosophers who held that pleasure was an accurate gauge of the amount of good in experience, but that to confuse good with pleasure was a gross blunder. There have been a great many philosophers who held that for every change in consciousness there was a change in the nervous system and that the two corresponded so closely that if we knew the laws connecting them we could infallibly predict one from the other; yet it takes all the hardihood of a behaviourist to say that the two are the same. Similarly it has been held that though coherence supplies an infallible measure of truth, it would be a very grave mistake to identify it with the truth. [*NT*, 2:260]

Recognizing in general the potential difference between a criterion and a definition, Blanshard argues that in the special case of truth this difference cannot be maintained: here definition must collapse into criterion once coherence is recognized as the criterion of truth. The argument is set out in the following terms:

> As we saw at the beginning of the chapter, there have been some highly reputable philosophers who have held that the answer to "What is the test of truth" is "Coherence," while the answer to "What is the nature or meaning of truth?" is "Correspondence." These questions are plainly distinct. Nor does there seem to be any direct path from the acceptance of coherence as the test of truth to its acceptance as the nature of truth. Nevertheless there is an indirect path. If we accept coherence as our test, we must use it everywhere. We must therefore use it to test the suggestion that truth *is* other than coherence. But if we do, we shall find that we must reject the suggestion as leading to *in*coherence. . . .
>
> Suppose that, accepting coherence as the test, one rejects it as the nature of truth in favour of some alternative; and let us assume, for example, that this alternative is correspondence. This, we have said, is incoherent; why? Because if one holds that truth is correspondence, one cannot intelligibly hold either that it is tested by coherence or that there is any dependable test at all. Consider the first point. Suppose that we construe experience into the most coherent picture possible. . . . Would the mere fact that such elements as these are coherently arranged prove that anything precisely corresponding to them exists "out there"? I cannot see that it would, even if we knew that the two arrangements had closely corresponding patterns. . . . It is therefore

impossible to argue from a high degree of coherence within experience to its correspondence in the same degree with anything outside. And this difficulty is typical. If you place the nature of truth in one sort of character and its test in something quite different, you are pretty certain, sooner or later, to find the two falling apart. In the end, the only test of truth that is not misleading is the special nature or character that is itself constitutive of truth. [*NT*, 2:267–68]

The structure of this argument can be presented as follows:

(1) A coherence theory of truth cannot do less than take coherence as a, nay *the prime,* test of truth.

(2) Now if the definition of truth finds the nature of truth to reside in something other than coherence, something which—like correspondence—is not logically tantamount to coherence but can potentially diverge from it, then coherence cannot qualify as a failproof guarantor of truth.

(3) But since a coherence theory of truth must take coherence to be the prime test of truth (Premiss 1), it must see in coherence a failproof guarantor of truth.

(4) But then it follows (from Premiss 2) that a coherence theory of truth must take coherence to represent the nature of truth, and not merely to provide a test-criterion thereof. For only what is essential to its very nature can provide a conceptually failproof guarantee for a thing, and not any mere test-criterion.

The upshot of Blanshard's argument is that a recognition of coherence as the test-criterion of truth forces the conclusion that coherence must represent the definitional nature of truth.

This argument seems to be perfectly unexceptionable: Given its premisses, the conclusion must be granted. But what is to be said about its premisses? Of the essential premisses (1)–(3) of this Blanshardesque argument, it seems clear that (1) and (2) are effectively beyond cavil. Only (3) is potentially vulnerable—and indeed actually so. For *why* must the coherence test be seen as providing a *failproof guarantee* of truth?

From the very outset, any discussion of tests and criteria does well to recognize an important distinction: that between a *guaranteeing* criterion and an *authorizing* criterion. The issue is posed by the question: "What is the relationship between passing-the-criterion-for-being-an-X and actually-being-an-X?" When criterion satisfaction *logically precludes* the failure of feature possession, when the criterion is absolutely decisive for the feature, then we have a guaranteeing criterion. (Among plane figures, triangularity, for example, provides a guaranteeing criterion for trilaterality.) On the other hand, if criterion satisfaction at best provides a rational warrant for the claim of feature possession—without giving a logically airtight guarantee—then we have an authorizing criterion. Satisfaction of an authorizing criterion provides a *presumptive* assurance of feature possession, and constitutes a reasonable basis for claiming the feature. Now a *guaranteeing* criterion is certainly very closely linked to the issue of definition; indeed it might be viewed as simply an aspect of the question of definition in its larger sense. With an *authorizing* criterion, however, we leave the logico-semantical issues of definition sufficiently far to enter a distinct, genuinely criterial realm.

Recognizing this distinction, we may note that, on Blanshard's approach as enshrined in premiss (2), the partisan of coherence as the criterion of truth is committed to regarding coherence as a *guaranteeing* criterion. He is committed to regarding the link from coherence to truth as inevitable and necessary. Now subject to this presupposition, Blanshard's position is unquestionably a strong one. But why need this presupposition be made? Why could not or should not the coherence theorist intent on taking coherence as a criterion of truth regard it as an authorizing rather than a guaranteeing criterion? Why, in short, should coherence not be accepted as *a generally effective test* of truth rather than *an inescapable aspect of its nature*?

This prospect of taking coherence as an authorizing or presumptive standard of truth rather than an inevitable aspect thereof is prima facie attractive and certainly deserves exploration. But in any case, it must be stressed that the orthodox mainstream of idealist thought from F. H. Bradley to A. C. Ewing[2] accepted coherence as a *test* of truth while rejecting it in favor of correspondence as an explication of the *nature* of truth. The distinction between authorizing and guaranteeing criterion however remained undrawn and latent in their discussions.

3. Truth-Criteria as a Rational Warrant

The distinction between a definition and a test-criterion of the authorizing variety, established and familiar in other contexts, is also operative with respect to truth. The criterial approach to truth is decision-oriented: its aim is not to specifiy in the abstract what "is true" *means*, but rather to put us into a position to implement the concept by instructing us as to the circumstances under which there is rational warrant to characterize or class something (i.e. some proposition) as true.

Why bother with a criterion once a definition is at hand? The answer is obvious in the light of the preceding example. To know the meaning of a word or concept is only half the battle: we want to be able to *apply* it too. The courtier knows perfectly well what "pleasing to the king" *means;* what he strives to know is where it applies. When it eventuates that the meaning-specification is ineffectual for constituting the rules of application, the criterial problem remains an important issue—even for "meaning" itself, though in a broader sense. It does us little good to know how terms like "speed limit" or "misdemeanor" are defined if we are left in the dark as to the conditions of their application.

This line of thought applies to "is true" as well. Thus even if it turns out that certain conceptions of truth do not qualify as definitions, and so do not answer the question of meaning, there remains the significant task of examining their prospects from the criterion angle of approach.

And yet if we do take a criterial perspective upon truth, a critic might object: "You are not really grappling with the core issue of *what it is to be true* but with the merely epistemological question of what *is thought or taken to be true.*" To this we reply: Our concern is *not* merely with what "is thought or taken" to be true, but with what is *reasonably and warrantedly* to be so thought or taken. In this area the themes of definition and criteria come close. With some things there is virtually no difference at all (What is a chair? What is reasonably to be thought to be a chair?); with others a gap does open up (What is an insoluble problem? What is reasonably to be regarded as an insoluble problem?). The criterial question can be important in its own right, and can even be a significant aspect of the question of "meaning" in a sense broader than the strictly definitional.

Criteriological theories of truth share one very important common feature contrasting them with a definitional theory of truth. To bring this out it is helpful to introduce some abbreviative symbolism. Let P be an otherwise unspecified proposition and let us write:

$D(P)$ for "P conforms to a definition of truth"

$C(P)$ for "P conforms to a certain criterion of truth"
    (one that may be merely an authorizing criterion)

$T(P)$ for "P is true (in actual fact)."

Then not-$T(P)$ will be *logically incompatible* with $D(P)$; the failure of $T(P)$ in the face of $D(P)$ would simply reveal that the definition at issue is improper and incorrect. There can be no logical gap between $D(P)$ and $T(P)$. *It must be a point of logical necessity that*

$D(P)$ iff $T(P)$.

With the entrance of a criterion, however, one that need not necessarily be a guaranteeing criterion, a logical gap does open up. Precisely because C need not be tied to a definition, there will be a potential difference between the criterial and the definitional conformity. The logical fit is now incomplete: it is no longer logically necessary and inevitable that

$C(P)$ iff $T(P)$

once C can be an authorizing rather than strictly guaranteeing criterion. Definitional conformity is an *unfailing guarantee* of truth; criterial conformity may at best provide a *rational warrant* to justify the claim of truth and does not yield a certainty beyond the possibility of mistake.

Now, of course, *our* adopton of C as an at least *authorizing* criterion of truth is essentially an adhesion to the policy that *we are never to claim* T(*P*) when C(*P*) fails, and that *we will always claim* that T(*P*) when C(*P*) holds. In short, we subscribe to the *regulative precept:*

to-assert-that-T (*P*) iff C(*P*).

Unlike a definitional theory of truth, a criteriological theory of truth is regulative because it is fundamentally decision-oriented. One does not decide what *is* true, but one must decide upon the implementation of a truth-criterion: viz., to class (or to "accept") something as true. An "act" at issue, though, to be sure, a purely *cognitive* one. Actions, of course, can be rational or irrational, prudent or rash. A proper criterion must have a rational foundation. It does not provide a necessary and sufficient condition for a proposition's *being true;* that would carry it over to the definitional side of the border. Rather, it seeks to present a necessary and sufficient condition for a proposition's *being rationally and warrantedly classed as true.*

With any genuine criterion, however, we must be prepared to recognize that, at least in principle, our assertions may be wrong—even our rationally well warranted assertions. Whereas D(*P*) must logically entail that T(*P*) and so have it as a *deductive* consequence that *P.* C(*P*) does no more than to *commit* us—subject to an acceptance of the criterion C—to endorsing T(*P*) and thus to asserting (maintaining) that *P.* The inference from D(*P*) to *P* is one of deductive logic, that from C(*P*) to *P* one merely of logico-epistemic policy. Given D(*P*), it is *impossible* that T(*P*) should fail to be so; but given C(*P*), it is certainly *possible* that T(*P*) should fail to be so, though an adoption of C puts it—ex hypothesi—beyond our power to *claim* that T(*P*) does fail.

A real definition—one that purports to capture the meaning of a term possessing a fixed preestablished usage—is either correct or incorrect, and that's the end of the matter: its correctness may need to be pointed out, but it does not need argument or justification. A criterion of truth on the other hand—above all an authorizing criterion—definitely requires justification. In closing the logical gap between C(*P*) and *P* it takes a step that can be made well or badly, wisely or foolishly. It represents the adoption of one among alternative procedures, and here, as in all such cases, the question of the rational justification of adopting one specific alternative is in order. This is a question to which we must eventually give attention.

One of the tasks of the theory of statistics is that of devising "acceptance rules" for hypotheses. In employing such a rule it sometimes happens that false hypotheses are accepted (according to the rule), and sometimes that true hypotheses are rejected. Adopting a usage proposed by the statisticians Jerzy Neyman and Egon Pearson, the rejection of a true hypothesis is generally designated as a *type I error* and the acceptance of a false hypothesis a *type II error*. This usage is readily extended to our context. Given the existence of a logical gap between $C(P)$ and $T(P)$, a criterion of truth can commit errors of two corresponding kinds:

(1) A *type I error* when $T(P)$ obtains—i.e. when P is in fact true—but not-$C(P)$, i.e., P fails to satisfy the criterion.

(2) A *type II error* when $C(P)$ obtains, so that P is acceptable according to the criterion, but not-$T(P)$, i.e., P fails to be true.

Or look at the matter from another perspective. The criteriological rule

$T(P)$ iff $C(P)$

has two forms:

(i) If $T(P)$, then $C(P)$.

(ii) If $C(P)$, then $T(P)$.

When (i) leads us into trouble because $T(P)$ and not $C(P)$, the error is of type I. When (ii) is the source of difficulty because $C(P)$ but not $T(P)$, the error is of type II. With authorizing criteria of truth—unlike definitions—the prospect of both of these types of error opens up. It is an inherent feature of any essentially criterial approach to truth that a logical gap remains between $C(P)$ and $T(P)$, and that while "*P* satisfies the criterion" provides a *rational warrant* for "*P* is true," it need not provide an *unfailing guarantee.*

In developing a criteriological theory of truth, we do not want to have it be a matter of *logical* validity that the inferences

from $C(P)$ to infer P,

from P to infer $C(P)$

must be warranted. This requisite would be far too restrictive. A criterion C conforming to it might be adequate as definition but would be too restrictive to serve as a viable criterion. It would mean that in the order of demonstration we would be called upon to settle the question of the truth of the proposition in order to bring our criterion of truth to bear upon it. One reason why the Tarski condition regarding truth,

(T) $T(P)$ iff P,

is best looked upon as definitional rather than criteriological in nature is that it leaves no room for any looseness of fit. Here there cannot be a type I error where $T(P)$ & $\sim P$ or a type II error where P & $\sim T(P)$ (or—equivalently?—P & $T(\sim P)$). It is improper (senseless) to affirm the truth of something in conjunction with an assertion of its contradictory. When $C(P)$ is simply P itself—that is when we have $C(P)$ iff P—then the tightness of fit between $T(P)$ and $C(P)$ is complete (logical). In giving prominence to this distinction between a definitional theory of truth and a criteriological theory our aim is not to make a virtue of a defect but to recognize that a criteriological theory has a job to do fundamentally different from that of a definitional one.

Thus in accepting the reality of errors of types I and II we maintain *on the metasubstantive level:*

$$(\exists p)[T(p) \ \& \ C(p)]$$
$$(\exists p)[C(p) \ \& \ \sim T(p)].$$

But it is obvious that we must not regard the *substantive* replaceability of $C(P)$ by $T(P)$ as warrant for maintaining: $(\exists p)[T(p) \ \& \ \sim T(p)]$. Our insistence that the regulative replacement principle in view is an epistemically warranted policy does not drive ad absurdum a recognition of occasional errors of the two types.

The point is this: $C(P)$ *approximates* to $T(P)$, and in *substantive* contexts we can proceed to treat the approximation as "the real thing." But this regulative procedure must never blind us to the essential fact of logical gap between $C(P)$ and $T(P)$, a gap which must be carefully maintained in higher-level, metasubstantive contexts.

As this discussion shows, there is no reason of principle why any criteriological theory of truth—such as the coherence theory or the pragmatic theory—need pick any quarrels with the Tarski condition (T). At the *abstract,* metasubstantive level any such theory can endorse this principle in full. But at the *applied* substantive level where the regulative precept

(P) to treat $C(P)$ as amounting to $T(P)$

enters in the context of *substantive* applications, the conclusion that (P) applied to (T) entails

$C(P)$ iff P

must, and can, successfully be resisted, with the justification that (T) is not a substantive context in which (P) can be applied. The very recognition of C as an authorizing criterion blocks acceptance of the substantive equivalence in the wake of the regulative precept (P).

The pivotal point here is, after all, operative in any situation where approximations come into play. Whenever Q' is introduced as approximation for Q, the range of equivalence of these quantities must be restricted. For example, we will generally know perfectly well that $Q' \neq Q$, but we would not be prepared to substitute Q' for Q in *this* thesis. The criteriological approach to truth simply proposes to apply this universal truism about approximations to the special circumstance of $T(P)$ and $C(P)$.

But if these considerations are to apply to the coherence theory, if coherence is taken to provide a presumptive and authorizing rather than a guaranteeing standard of truth, then we must resolve the questions: How can coherence considerations be made to work so as to provide a rational warrant for truth-claims? How does coherence operate to yield a reasonable basis for imputations of truth?

4. Basic Problems of the Coherence Theory of Truth

The time has come for a close look at the concept of coherence. Just what is "coherence" and what does it involve? The two key questions are: (1) What is it to cohere? (2) What does the cohering?

"Fully coherent knowledge," Blanshard tells us, "would be knowledge in which every judgment entailed, and was entailed by, the rest of the system."[3] He goes on to observe:

> It is perhaps in such systems as Euclidean geometry that we get the most perfect examples of coherence that have been constructed. If any proposition were lacking, it could be supplied from the rest; if any were altered, the repercussions would be felt through the length and breadth of the system. Yet even such a system as this falls short of ideal system. Its postulates are unproved; they are independent of each other, in the sense that none of them could be derived from any other or even from all the others together; its clear necessity is bought by an abstractness so extreme as to have left out nearly everything that belongs to the character of actual things. A completely satisfactory system would have none of these defects. No proposition would be arbitrary, every proposition would be entailed by the others jointly and even singly, no proposition would stand outside the system. [NT, 2:265–66]

Coherence is thus a feature of propositions, a contextual feature that characterizes them in the wider setting of a system of propositions. One proposition coheres with the rest if what it says is said also, explicitly or implicitly, by all the rest.

Thus if P, Q, and R are three independent propositions, the set

P, Q, R

represents a highly incoherent system, whereas

P & (Q & R), Q & (P & R), R & (P & Q)

is altogether coherent. Here every proposition, being placed explicitly into the context of all the others, can be derived from any one of the rest. To be sure, the concept that in a coherent system every proposition entails every other is not, for Blanshard, a feature essential to the very definition of coherence. But he follows H. H. Joachim in regarding this as the definitive characteristic of a *perfectly* coherent system. Coherence, from this angle, is seen in the light of a condition of redundancy, and full coherence is maximal redundancy. This, surely, is not a very satisfactory conception. What great philosophic merit can possibly issue from the redundant formulation of information? And, above all, it is, to say the least, obscure how this can possibly have a helpful bearing upon the issue of truth. With Blanshard's explanation of the nature of coherence—an explanation not unique to him, but also to be found in other coherence theorists[4]—we are given an explication of the nature of coherence which leaves it very unclear how this concept is adequate to the truth-determining role for which the theory has cast it.

This problem leads to our second question: Just what is it that is to do the cohering when coherence is deployed as a standard of truth? It is clear enough, both in itself and in Blanshard's discussion, that it is judgments or propositions that are at issue. When coherence is intended as a test of truth, and the locus of truth is seen in the realm of judgments or propositions, it is patently these that must do the coherence. But *which* propositions? Where are we to search out coherence? In the realm of *all* propositions, the grossest fictions as well as the plainest facts? This family of questions poses an issue that Blanshard does not face as squarely as he might. He comes close to suggesting that not all possible judgments or propositions are at issue, but only *those we believe,* viz. "our beliefs."[5]

On this approach, coherence might well serve as a standard of rational evaluations for determining which of our beliefs should be accepted as "actually true": viz. those that "best cohere" with the rest. But this view is hardly consonant with Blanshard's settled position that coherence represents the meaning of truth. For it is plain that only beliefs themselves—i.e. select elements among "our beliefs"—will count as coherent propositions in *this* specified sense. But if coherence is confined to beliefs it cannot possibly represent the meaning of truth. Nobody would—or at any rate should—want to maintain that only those propositions that are *believed* can possibly be true.[6]

In another passage, Blanshard approaches the issue from another angle. He writes:

> Granting that propositions, to be true, must be coherent with each other, may they not be coherent without being true? Are there not many systems of high unity and inclusiveness, which nevertheless are false? We have seen, for example, that there are various systems of geometry each of which seems to be as coherent internally as the others. Since they are mutually inconsistent, not more than one of them can be true, and there are many mathematicians who would say that *none* of them are true; yet if truth lies merely in coherence, are we not compelled to take all of them as true? Again, a novel, or a succession of novels such as Galsworthy's *Forsyte Saga,* may create a special world of characters and events which is at once extremely complex and internally consistent; does that make it the less fictitious?. . .
>
> This objection, like so many other annihilating criticisms, would have more point if anyone had ever held the theory it demolishes. But if intended to represent the coherence theory as responsibly advocated, it is a gross misunderstanding. That theory does not hold that any and every system is true, no matter how abstract and limited; it holds that one system only is true, namely the system in which everything real and possible is coherently included. How one can find in this the notion that a system would still give truth if, like some arbitrary geometry, it disregarded experience completely, it is not easy to see. [*NT,* 2:275–76]

This key passage, intended to answer a basic objection, leaves matters in an unsatisfactory state. Just where and over what range is coherence to be operative? In "the system in which everything real and possible is coherently included"? But here, in this all-inclusive system, there is no difference drawn or to be drawn between the actually real and the merely possible: this exactly is the force of the objection. On the other hand, if the coherence at issue is not a matter of "coherence with *everything*" but rather of "coherence with *experience*" (as the final part of the passage suggests in despite of what has preceded), then there must surely be some further indication of how this conception is to be implemented—particularly because "experience" itself is not given as a consistent and coherent unit for other things to cohere with.

Blanshard's discussion thus leaves in an unsatisfactory state the crucial question of exactly which propositions are to represent the domain over which the selective processes of a coherence analysis are to be deployed.

5. A Contrast with Bradley

The vulnerability of Blanshard's version of the coherence theory of truth can be highlighted in a comparison with the (in my view essentially correct) version of the theory espoused by Bradley—at any rate the Bradley of the essay "On Truth and Coherence."[7]

To begin with, Bradley confines the role of coherence to that of a criterion of truth rather than a definition. He is quite willing to have *truth* defined along the traditional lines of correspondence with the facts: "Truth, to be true, must be true of something, and this something itself is not truth. This obvious view I endorse."[8] Thus Bradley is able to preserve without difficulties the essential linkage of truth to factuality. Coherence, in his view, does not give us the *nature* of truth but merely affords a testing procedure for discriminating presumptive truths from presumptive falsehoods.

With regard to the key question of what does the cohering, Bradley gives a relatively clear answer in terms of a peculiar and characteristic conception of "facts." In his essay "On Truth and Coherence," he introduces the concept of a *fact* so as to have it play a role closely akin to that of a truth-candidate or *prima facie* truth. For Bradleyan "facts"—let us call them B-facts—differ from everyone else's facts in not necessarily being factual, i.e. true. Typical, for Bradley, are the "facts of perception and memory," which need not, of course, be true, but are at best purportedly or presumptively veridical:

> ... these facts of perception [and memory], I further agree, are at least in part irrational [and so false]. ... [Yet] I do not believe that we can make ourselves independent of these non-rational data.
>
> But, if I do not believe all this, does it follow that I have to accept independent facts [i.e. facts true independently of all other considerations]? Does it follow that perception and memory give me truths which I must take up and keep as they are given me, truths which in principle cannot be erroneous? This surely would be to pass from one false extreme to another. ... I therefore conclude that no given fact is sacrosanct. With every fact of perception or memory a modified interpretation is in principle possible, and no such fact therefore is given free from all possibility of error.[9]

Bradley thus espouses—with respect to the limited range of perception and memory—a notion of "fact" according to which the facts do not automatically qualify as truths at all but at best as possible or potential truths.

Bradley's special conception of "facts" puts him into a position to answer in a relatively satisfactory way the question of just where the coherence considerations are to be applied. Moreover, since he conceives the coherence standard along criterial rather than definitional lines, the internal tensions that develop in Blanshard's treatment of this issue are avoided entirely.

Bradley also gives a more viable account of the nature of coherence. Basically, he conceives the coherence theory as maintaining "the claim of system as an arbiter of fact."[10] He formulates the matter as follows:

> The test which I advocate is the idea of a whole of knowledge as wide and as consistent as may be. In speaking of system I mean always the union of these two aspects, and this is the sense and the only sense in which I am defending coherence. If we separate coherence from what Prof. Stout calls comprehensiveness, then I agree that neither of these aspects of system will work by itself. . . . All that I can do here is to point out that both of the above aspects are for me inseparably included in the idea of system, and that coherence apart from comprehensiveness is not for me the test of truth or reality.[11]

On a Bradleyan approach, the coherence theory takes a position altogether different from Blanshard's definitional line. We begin with a family of competing truth-*candidates*: the propositions we are disposed to maintain on the basis of sense, memory, reports, or whatever other sources of putative information may be at our disposal.[12] And the analysis of coherence considerations provides the screening procedure needed to determine us to accept as true certain among these conflicting competitors, to wit, that maximally comprehensive subgroup among them whose overall coherence adjustment to one another is of the highest order. Here coherence (construed to embrace comprehensiveness) functions as a testing procedure to determine which among conflicting candidates are best qualified for acceptance as true.

This explication of the workings of the coherence concept in terms of a combination of the logical factor of consistency and the factual factor of comprehensiveness gives a more plausible and applicable construction of the nature of coherence than the redundancy considerations operative in Blanshard's conception. For on Bradley's approach we can see how a linkage from coherence to truth can be maintained, not—as with Blanshard—as a definitional connection, but as a matter of epistemic warrant.

6. Conclusion

From this perspective upon the workings of coherence, the difficulties encountered by Blanshard's version of the coherence theory of truth stem from its getting off to a bad start. It goes amiss at a very fundamental point, owing to the fact that Blanshard insists on seeing in coherence the *very nature* of truth, and is not content with having coherence play the more restricted part of a test-criterion for truth-determinations. This deprives him of the prospect of making sense of the ancient thesis that it is necessary that a true proposition agree with the facts of the case, a thesis not to be abrogated merely by abandoning a definitional correspondence theory of truth, but rather one that must survive any such abandonment.

Blanshard is inexorably forced to this insistence that coherence represents the definitional nature of truth by two considerations: (1) the (in my view essentially unproblematic) premiss that coherence is a key criterion of truth, and (2) the argument that the necessary linkage of truth-criterion to truth-definition cannot be preserved unless the criterial factor (viz., coherence) is taken over as definitional. Blanshard's *argument* here is perfectly correct, but his position is not. For it is neither necessary nor desirable for the adoption of coherence as a (or even *the*) criterion of truth to construe this as a *necessitating* or guaranteeing criterion rather than one that is *presumptive* and authorizing. And once this insistence upon a linkage of necessity is abandoned the argument "coherence-as-criterion entails coherence-as-definition" becomes abortive.

Had Blanshard not started down this necessitarian path in his articulation of the coherence theory he would, presumably, have arrived at a less vulnerable (and in my view more useful) version of the theory, one articulated along the lines of the conception that coherence provides a presumptive rather than guaranteeing criterion of truth.

NICHOLAS RESCHER

DEPARTMENT OF PHILOSOPHY
UNIVERSITY OF PITTSBURGH

NOTES

[1] Bertrand Russell, *The Problems of Philosophy* (New York: Henry Holt; London: Williams & Norgate, 1912), 191.

[2] See F. H. Bradley, *Essays on Truth and Reality* (London: Clarendon Press, 1914) and A. C. Ewing, *Idealism: A Critical Survey* (London: Methuen, 1934). Even J. M. E. McTaggart, who is at bottom a correspondence theorist, is prepared to concede coherence the place of a test of truth.

[3] Coherence can be defined without this point, which, as Dr. Ewing remarks (*Idealism*, 231), makes the case harder to establish. In no mathematical system, for example, would anyone dream of trying to deduce all the other propositions from any proposition taken singly. But when we are describing an ideal, such a fact is not decisive, and I follow Joachim in holding that in a perfectly coherent system every proposition would entail all others, if only for the reason that its meaning could never be fully understood without apprehension of the system in its entirety.

[4] E.g. H. H. Joachim, see his *Logical Studies* (Oxford: Clarendon Press, 1948).

[5] "Now I think it can be shown that coherence *is* our test, the final and invariable test, when our beliefs are under pressure" (*NT,* 2:215).

[6]Not—in any case—without a theological postulate that salvages the thesis by a deus ex machina. Nor will it do to attempt to save the thesis by a distinction between actual and possible beliefs. For unless the concept of a possible belief carries us back to the sphere of *all* propositions (and then good-bye coherence), it enmeshes us in a hopeless conundrum.

[7]Bradley, *Essays on Truth and Reality,* chap. 7, "On Truth and Coherence," 202–18.

[8]Ibid., 325.

[9]"On Truth and Coherence," 203–4.

[10]Ibid., 219.

[11]Ibid., 202–3.

[12]Ewing justifies this proceeding on Bradley's behalf in the following manner: "The principle of accepting as fact what one immediately experiences can itself be justified by the coherence theory . . ." (*Idealism,* 239).

14. Reply to Nicholas Rescher

Blanshard and the Coherence Theory of Truth

Mr. Rescher has written an able book on *The Coherence Theory of Truth* in which he makes a far more intensive and extensive examination of the theory than is made in anything I have written. That he comes out in the end in favor of the coherence criterion has given me unexpected technical and moral support, for which I am genuinely grateful. He has criticized my theory at various points, but in view of the amount of agreement between us it is tempting to cry "Kamerad," to refer the reader to his book for a detailed defense of the criterion we hold in common, and to pass on. But that would be unfair. His points of difference with me, though less radical than those of some other critics, are still important. He rejects coherence as the *nature* of truth, and though he defends it as the *criterion,* his defense differs in some respects from mine. And as his essay indicates, he differs in other ways too significant to ignore. I will confine myself for the most part to the criticisms made in his essay, though the reader may fairly be warned that his essay is little more than a collation of some considerations offered in the first two chapters of his book and in my opinion gives an inadequate idea of the strength of his case either in the defense of his own theory or in the criticism of mine.

Coherence as the Nature of Truth

Let us turn first to our theories of the *nature* of truth. Though Mr. Rescher entitles his book *The Coherence Theory of Truth,* he holds that the nature of truth lies not in coherence but in correspondence. This is in accordance with a tendency, at work for many years, to move away from coherence and toward correspondence as what truth essentially is. McTaggart, for example, in spite of his devotion to idealism and to Hegel, defended the correspondence theory in *The Nature of Existence.* Ewing, who gave an admirable exposition of coherence as the nature of truth in his early work on *Idealism,* did not accept the theory, and in the end abandoned it as supplying either the nature or criterion of truth. Mr. Rescher, who takes me as an adherent of both theories, thinks that my argument attempting to link the two theories is not a success and that my espousal of coherence as the nature of truth is clearly a mistake. It will be well to consider first the latter and more fundamental criticism.

In *The Nature of Thought,* published some thirty-five years ago, I did take my stand for coherence as supplying both the nature of truth and its criterion. But I admitted that if one asks what is the relation between (say) the body of propositions that makes up our commonsense world and the ultimate system of things that constitutes reality, "coherence" is not an accurate word for it. The relation seemed more like that of an undeveloped organism to the fully developed one which would be its consummation; the relation of the sapling to the oak, for example. This relation could perhaps be as well described by "correspondence" as by "coherence," though neither description hit the mark.

My mind has not stood quite still during those thirty-five years. My views on the appropriateness of "correspondence" and "coherence" as descriptive of the nature of truth have undergone some change. I still think of ultimate truth as an ideal that would consist in the apprehension of a coherent whole in which every component was consistent with and necessarily connected with every other. But that system of thought would not constitute the whole of reality. Thought is *of* something; it has an object; it refers to something beyond itself. What would this something be? It would be the set of facts and events constituting the real world. This also would be a consistent set, whose members would be related in the same systematic order. Thought would be coherent because it would be the apprehension of a coherent reality; it would *reflect* reality without *being* it. We may say if we wish that such thought coheres with its object, but this coherence would not be identical with that which it exhibited within itself. Both kinds of coherence would be necessary to ultimate truth, but if anyone prefers to describe the coherence of such thought with its object as correspondence, I shall not object. I shall have more to say about this shortly.

Mr. Rescher apparently considers my chief argument for coherence as the nature of truth to be that this conclusion is implied in the use of coherence as a criterion. But truth as coherence is more deeply and variously rooted than that in the soil of my thought. Its roots are both psychological and metaphysical.

In an M.A. thesis written at Columbia in 1917–18, I dealt with Hume's theory of judgment. In a B.Sc. thesis written in 1919–20 at Oxford, I dealt with Dewey's theory of judgment. In a Ph.D. dissertation written the following year at Harvard under C. I. Lewis, I tried to deal with the nature of judgment generally. In the course of these inquiries I became much interested in the factors governing the thought process. I paid some attention to Watson's behaviorism, which seemed to me a sustained *ignoratio elenchi,* since it was obvious that thought was a conscious and purposive process; and how anyone could bemuse himself into believing that there was no such thing as consciousness I could not and still do not understand. I was ready to believe with Dewey that thought, at least reflective thought, was commonly aroused by some block to instinctive or habitual activity, but it seemed clearly contrary to fact to hold that its aim was always practical, the finding of some mode of action that would surmount the obstacle. Thought was not merely instrumental to practice; it had its own distinctive end; and that end was understanding, or explaining to oneself. And what did such explanation consist in? After examining my own thinking on a wide variety of problems I concluded that explanation lay in linking the unexplained fact to its context, in such a way as to show that this context required it. To explain it was to assign its place or function in a whole. Reflective thought might of course concern itself with all sorts of questions, but its ultimate, central, and characteristic question was Why? And that question could only be answered by taking the context into account—at first the immediate context and then, as further questions arose, ulterior contexts, so that any such question, if pressed, called for an indefinitely inclusive system, as the dropping of a stone in the sea led to indefinitely expanding circles of waves. I will not stop to give illustrations, since I have supplied and analyzed a variety of them in the opening chapter of the second volume of my book. The upshot of this self-examination was what seemed to me a clear insight that thought from the beginning was a drive toward understanding, and that this drive could in the end be satisfied by one thing only. This was the achievement of a system of thought in which the question Why? had been pressed through to the end in all directions. Such a system would be at once all-comprehensive and so related internally that nothing unintelligible remained. In short, thought was a distinctive drive in human nature in which from the very beginning the end of a coherent system was immanently at work and became clearer in conception and firmer in its guidance as the development progressed.

A coherent intelligible system, then, was the only end in which thought could find full satisfaction. But how could one argue from psychological satisfactoriness to objective truth? There is a drive in all men toward the moral ideal, but to conclude, as some philosophers have, that therefore the real world is ideally good is surely groundless; I have attempted to show why in *Reason and Belief.* There is a drive toward the satisfaction of our aesthetic sense, but that the real world must therefore present an object of perfect beauty unhappily does not follow. But the three arguments are not parallel. The endeavors after goodness and beauty are attempts to mould given facts into accordance with inward aims. The endeavor after truth is the attempt to mould inward thought into adjustment to the nature of things. The aim at intelligible system would thus be a source of continual delusion unless the world that it sought to understand was also an intelligible system. Could anyone prove that the world was such a system? *That* I have not maintained. What I have maintained is that there are good grounds for proceeding upon it as a postulate. It is an eminently natural postulate, for what it assumes is that answering to our desire to understand there is an understandable world. By a postulate I mean a proposition which, while unproved and incapable of present proof, is progressively confirmed in experience. And there are grounds for accepting this postulate other than its success.

Coherence in the cosmic order means for me two things. First, in the world of facts there are no inconsistencies. Whether this is the case turns on the status of the law of noncontradiction. If it is merely a convention of ours, as some recent logicians have contended, it is idle to talk of consistency as a feature of the real. But I have argued in *Reason and Analysis* that the law must be interpreted as a statement about the nature of things, and I have seen no reason to retract or modify that argument. The other element in cosmic coherence is the logical interdependence of all facts and events. One way of showing this is to point out that the relation of difference is a necessary and internal relation, but I feel a certain distrust of arguments of such extreme abstractness, just as I do of the manipulations of some contemporary symbolic logicians. I have fallen back instead on the universality of the law of causation, which seems to me to connect all events, directly or indirectly, with all others. I then argue that the causal relation is not contingent but necessary, in spite of our inability, at the present level of knowledge, to analyze out this necessity in most cases. The result of these lines of argument is not a demonstration that the world is a coherent system, but it provides, I think, a justification for postulating that it is.

Coherence as the nature of truth thus holds a double root in my ways of thinking. It is the immanent end of man's cognitive drive, which seeks an understanding of things. It is also the postulate on which we must proceed if the immanent ideal of thought is to be regarded as even in theory achievable.

Correspondence

To anyone who may have read my books, there is in all this nothing new. I have held, I think consistently, that coherence is an essential part of the notion of ultimate truth. In what way, if any, does my present thought show a change of emphasis? Chiefly perhaps in a disposition to include correspondence along with coherence as a component of truth. There are several points worth mentioning.

(1) I have already remarked that between that coherent thought of the world which would constitute its ultimate understanding and the world that

would form its object, the relation is perhaps as well described by "correspondence" as by "coherence."

(2) It is clear that what the plain man normally means by "truth" is correspondence with fact. When he says, "That is a table," "Jim Thorpe was a great athlete," "Whales are mammals," he thinks he is saying something that accords with the facts, and he would accept "accordance" or "correspondence" with fact more readily as describing what he meant by "true" than "coherence" with anything whatever. Now I am no idolater of common sense, and still less a worshiper at the shrine of ordinary language. What the plain man means here by facts are really the perceptual judgments which he or others would make if placed in the presence of the "facts" referred to, and the relation between his present judgment and these perceptual judgments is one of coherence. And if he were asked what the facts were to which a negative or a hypothetical judgment corresponded, or still worse, a contrary-to-fact hypothetical, he would probably be at a loss. Nevertheless the general insistence of plain men, particularly when they are making statements about the existent, that they mean by the truth of their statements conformity to the facts is not something to be easily waved aside. Anyone who denies it must accept the burden of proof.

(3) Regarding commonsense judgments of fact I have pointed out that the "facts" against which they are commonly checked are themselves judgments of perception. And if one believes, with the idealistic tradition in whose shadow I grew up, that the world contains nothing but mind, indeed that it *is* a mind, and that all true thought on our part may be described as the thinking of this greater mind in and through us, the notion that truth consists in the coherence of our own thought with a thought continuous with though more comprehensive than our own is at least an inviting suggestion. It is less inviting if the world is not conceived as mind or consciousness. And I have already acknowledged that the development of modern science, while providing no confutation of that theory, has rendered it less plausible. When the physicist talks about radiation waves or packets of energy which no human eye can hope to see, or the astronomer talks of galaxies beyond the range of the most powerful telescope, or the geologist talks of the surface of the earth before the first sentient life appeared on it, he would think the suggestion exceedingly queer that he was talking about judgments or propositions in another mind, with which his own might, with good fortune, cohere. He believes himself to be talking about nonmental things and events occupying determinate places or occurring at determinate times, and he believes that his ideas correspond more or less faithfully to these things and their behavior. Is such language to be merely scouted? I do not think so.

Not that these unexperienced entities do exist "out there" as he now conceives them. He is, after all, speaking from a level of scientific knowledge that is far from final. What really exists out there is what a mind of infinite knowledge, apprehending these things and events in all their relations, would know them to be. The truth of our present judgment lies in the relation between our present thought and that ultimate reality. Is this relation one of correspondence or of coherence? Neither term is adequate, though I should be reluctant to dispense with either. I continue to think that truth is a matter of degree, and that this degree turns on the extent to which the present judgment would require alteration in order to fit into the wider knowledge. This view is a commonplace among the defenders of coherence. I do not see why it should not also apply to correspondence.

In saying this I am not aware of abandoning anything of importance that I formerly held, nor alas of saying anything that has a precise meaning. "Correspondence" is an impossibly elusive term. Every attempt to analyze or define it seems to have ended upon the rocks. The least enlightening attempt of all is perhaps that of Tarski, who informs us that "It is snowing" is true when it is snowing. Some rash souls had indeed ventured so far already, but as a way of stating the problem, not of solving it; what they wanted to know was the sort of relation obtaining between the judgment (not of course the sentence, for the same judgment could be expressed in a variety of sentences) and the event. Wittgenstein proposed a picture theory which, as I argued in *Reason and Analysis,* is strangely naive. The copy theory, relying chiefly on images, is dead. Ewing, who was himself inclined to correspondence, admitted that he could find no satisfactory analysis of it, and reluctantly thought of it as probably undefinable. I fear that I must reluctantly do so too. What I should now say is thus that truth does have an element of correspondence and that this is different from coherence, but that what exactly it is has not yet been determined.

From the Criterion to the Nature of Truth

I turn now to that argument of mine for coherence as the nature of truth to which Mr. Rescher pays chief attention. I tried to show that coherence as the criterion implies coherence as the nature of truth. Mr. Rescher sets out the structure of my argument as follows (I abbreviate slightly):

(1) A coherence theory of truth cannot do less than take coherence as a, nay the prime, test of truth.

(2) Now if the definition of truth finds the nature of truth to reside in something other than coherence, something which ... can potentially diverge from it, then coherence cannot qualify as a failproof guarantor of truth.

(3) But since a coherence theory of truth must take coherence to be the prime test of truth (Premise 1), it must see in coherence a failproof guarantor of truth.

(4) But then it follows (from Premise 2) that a coherence theory of truth must take coherence to represent the nature of truth, and not merely to provide a test-criterion thereof. For only what is essential to its very nature can provide a conceptually failproof guarantee for a thing, and not any mere test-criterion.

Given the premises, Mr. Rescher takes the conclusion to be beyond cavil. If there is a weak point in the argument, it must lie in the falsity of one of the premises, and he thinks the culprit is no. (3). It says that the coherence criterion of truth must give a failproof guarantee of truth. This Mr. Rescher denies. A criterion for something, he holds, need not *guarantee* the presence of that something; it need only provide "a presumptive assurance" of it. What we ask of a criterion of X's presence is not the certainty that X is present, but a *reasonable warrant* of its presence. There are thus two different kinds of criterion. One *assures* us that X is present. The other is weaker and merely "authorizes" or "warrants" our belief that X is present. The argument I offered from the criterion to the nature of truth is perfectly valid if by criterion I mean that which will *assure* us of truth; it is not valid if a criterion need give only a *presumption* of truth. And coherence, Mr. Rescher says, is the latter sort of criterion.

Whether one can accept this view depends, I think, on how wide a departure from strictness such a "presumption" would allow. The normal aim for seeking a criterion for the presence of anything is to remove doubts and disputes about that presence. If A is to be a mark of the presence of B, the link between A and B must be close and strong. A physician who suspects a patient of having tuberculosis, or pregnancy, or hepatitis, or cancer needs a criterion that will at least give him a high degree of confidence that the suspected condition is present. A jury trying a suspected burglar needs a criterion by which it can tell whether the person on trial was present at the scene of the crime; they hesitate to accept his own testimony, for a man ready to burglarize would presumably be ready to lie out of it; but they will accept the testimony of his fingerprints, for these point to his presence with virtual certainty. But if the criterion A could be present while the B it was supposed to indicate was absent, and the criterion be absent when the thing indicated was present, the connection would be intolerably loose. A surgeon who operated or a jury that convicted on evidence of this kind would in most men's opinion be acting irresponsibly.

What troubles me about Mr. Rescher's proposed criterion is that it possesses this kind of looseness. Between the two terms of the relation there is a "logical gap" that permits two types of error:

(1) A *type I error* when $T(P)$ obtains—i.e. when P is in fact true—but not-$C(P)$, i.e. P fails to satisfy the criterion.

(2) A *type II error* when $C(P)$ obtains, so that P is acceptable according to the criterion, but not-$T(P)$, i.e. P fails to be true.

Now a "logical gap" so broad that a criterion and what it is supposed to indicate may each be present in the absence of the other surely falls short of the trustworthiness required of a criterion.

To this criticism I find implicit in Mr. Rescher's essay three lines of reply. (1) One lies in the distinction between our saying that something *is* true and our justifiably *classing* it as true. In applying the "authorizing" criterion to a proposition, "One does not decide what *is* true, but one must decide upon the implementation of a truth-criterion; viz., to class (or to 'accept') something as true. . . . [A proper criterion] seeks to present a necessary and sufficient condition for a proposition's *being rationally and warrantedly classed as true*." This sounds too much like a distinction without a difference. The criterion is supposed to supply evidence that something is true. If it is not sufficient to enable us to say that this *is* true, how can it supply evidence warranting a *belief* that it is true? Mr. Rescher seems to be saying that though an "authorizing" criterion cannot assure us that a given proposition is true, it supplies an adequate warrant for our "classing" or "accepting" it as true. But is not this a recommendation that belief should run beyond the evidence? If what the criterion provides is only evidence that a proposition may be true, or is probably true, or is true with a certain degree of probability, that is surely what we should believe; we have as yet no warrant for "classing" or "accepting" it as true.

(2) Secondly, it is contended that the application of a criterion of truth is a matter of practice, and that practice requires a less rigorous criterion than theory. "Unlike a definitional theory of truth, a criteriological theory of truth is regulative because it is fundamentally decision-oriented." Now it is certainly true that in practice we must often be content with criteria that are less than sure; we must get along with such imperfect tests as we happen to have. But practical decisions may be extremely demanding, and where they are of high importance the use of loose criteria would be regarded as gambling with destiny. A surgeon who operated upon a diagnosis known to be very ambiguous would not get much support from the surgical fraternity; and a jury presented with merely "authorizing" evidence would have no choice but to acquit. A decision to act does not *as such* sanction a looser criterion than a question of theoretical assent. By general agreement the criterion for the use of an atomic bomb should set an all but insuperable hurdle.

(3) There is a puzzling passage in which, after defining and defending his "authorizing" criterion, Mr. Rescher says that he adopts it only as a "policy." But the policy is one in which the permissiveness granted to the criterion is explicitly withdrawn. The policy is that when the criterion is fulfilled, the proposition in question is always to be taken as true, and when it is not fulfilled, truth is never to be claimed. But this is a double departure from what "authorizing" in theory means. In forgoing any claim to truth when the criterion fails, it discards a privilege which the theory would under

some circumstances confer. And it claims what the theory disallows, namely that when the criterion is fulfilled it always gives us truth. What puzzles me is why one should carefully develop the theory of an authorizing criterion only to announce that one will not be guided by it as a policy.

The "Data" of Coherence

It is hardly fair, I realize, to carp at particular passages in Mr. Rescher's paper without seeing them against the larger background of his book. I lack the space to discuss the many points of agreement and the few of disagreement that I have with that book. However, there is one position developed in it for which I should like to express my appreciation, since it meets ingeniously one of the commonest objections offered to a coherence theory. The objection is that there may be extended and coherent systems that merely float in the air. Suppose that Trollope's Barchester series made such a system; would that offer the slightest evidence of its truth? If you have one proposition you know to be anchored in fact, you may accept the truth of other propositions that form a system with it; but that one proposition is not itself true by coherence; its truth must rest on other grounds. To which the answer generally given by coherentists, including myself, has been that they would not dream of taking any system at random as true; the system so taken is the one system that coherently includes actual experience. The reply was seldom developed, however, in a way that seemed to the critics convincing. One of the prime merits of Mr. Rescher's book is that he finds a way to make it convincing.

His method is not essentially different from that of Bradley's essay on "Truth and Coherence" of 1909, though it replaces Bradley's "facts" with "data" and works out the theory more formally and in more detail. What is it that a judgment must cohere with to earn the title to truth? If you answer, "With propositions already known to be true," you obviously have your criterion already; if you say, "With propositions not known to be true," how can you extract the true from the doubtful? Mr. Rescher's reply is to seize the second horn of the dilemma. He introduces the notion of "data" which correspond roughly to Bradley's facts of common sense, i.e., propositions not known to be true but possibly and presumptively true. We have no hesitation in attaching some presumption of truth to the perceptual judgments of ordinary life, a higher presumption, for example, than to those of dreams, though such judgments are based on diverse and uncritical grounds. One has to start somewhere, and if one takes the high line of Descartes and dismisses everything as illusory except that which is absolutely certain, one will never get a criterion that is usable.

On the other hand, if one is willing to attach some degree of credibility to ordinary memories, perceptions, tentative generalizations, and the reports of others, we have a body of evidence that coherence can work with. Taken singly, none of these "data" might command assurance; but if, taken together, they form a body of judgments that are not only consistent but implicated with each other, the credibility attaching to any of them is increased enormously. This is the principle on which the coherence criterion proceeds. It rules out factual truths of an absolute kind not only at the beginning but anywhere along the route of its application; for the body of provisional truth by which a new candidate is judged is always limited, and inconsistencies may develop within that body that may require the dismissal of some of its members. But that truth is relative to such a body and is a matter of degree is part of the coherentist tradition that Mr. Rescher, wisely I think, accepts.

Final Criticisms

In the latter part of his paper he takes me to task for several views that he thinks unwarranted. One is that in an ideally coherent system not only will any given proposition be inferable from the rest of the system, but the rest of the system should be inferable from any part. He rightly points out that I do not take this as part of the definition of coherence, and he thinks it redundant to include it even in the ideal of a system. And certainly in no system of any extent that we know of is so extreme a condition met. If any proposition in Euclidean geometry were deleted from human memory, it could be reinstated by deduction from the rest of the system, but no geometer would claim that from a single proposition the rest of the system could be reconstructed. I should myself be content with Ewing's terms: a coherent system is "a set of propositions in which each one stands in such a relation to the rest that it is logically necessary that it should be true if all the rest are true, and such that no set of propositions within the whole set is logically independent of all propositions in the remainder of the set" (*Idealism,* 229–30).[1] At the same time I think I can see why writers like Joachim should have gone further in their thought of the ideal. They conceived of the universe as organic and even superorganic, a system in which the influence of the whole so permeated every part that the integration was complete. One could see any part as it really was only as one saw its unique part in the whole, which involved, of course, that the grasp of the whole was implicated in the grasp of the part. The process was somewhat like that of the modern comparative anatomist who, given a piece from the jawbone of a brontosaurus, will reconstruct the skeleton as a whole. I cannot, now at any rate, go this far myself, since I do not think the internal relations theory can be carried all the way through. But I would remind the reader that when we are speaking either of the kind of systematic understanding that would satisfy the intellect in the end or the kind of system that may be postulated for the actual world, we cannot fairly demand exactitude or finality. We are like climbers on a Himalayan peak that has never been ascended; we cannot be expected from lower plateaus to map the terraces, ridges, and furrows that may crisscross the summit.

Secondly, Mr. Rescher says that my discussion "leaves in an unsatisfactory state the crucial question of exactly which propositions are to represent the domain over which the selective processes of a coherence analysis are to be deployed." This means, I take it, What judgments or propositions are to be included in the "coherent" system which at any given time is to serve as the base for judging a proposed candidate? I do not think I could do better here than to refer to Mr. Rescher's meticulous discussion of this question in his book. My own language on the point was, I agree, too loose and ambiguous, but I am not aware that in aim it varied in any important way from the system of "data" whose construction Mr. Rescher has studied so carefully.

In a third criticism Mr. Rescher contrasts my theory of truth unfavorably with Bradley's. "To begin with, Bradley confines the role of coherence to that of a criterion of truth rather than a definition. He is quite willing to have *truth* defined along the traditional lines of correspondence with the facts: 'Truth, to be true, must be true of something, and this something itself is not truth. This obvious view I endorse.' " But to take this as evidence that Bradley accepted the correspondence view in its ordinary sense of correspondence with facts is surely wide of the mark. As Mr. Rescher points out, Bradley did not believe in the reality of these facts; when placed in the context of a completed reality, they, *as such,* disappeared. How are we to know what that completed reality is like? Only by thought, thought that is at once comprehensive and necessarily related, part with part. Only thought of this kind could be true without qualification, only such a whole is wholly true.

Bradley did tip his hat to correspondence, as he realized that he had to. But the reality to which thought corresponded, if true, was not "the facts" but the Absolute, and the only thought that corresponded to the Absolute was a thought that was all-inclusive and perfectly coherent. Bradley's treatment of correspondence is of the sketchiest and obscurest kind; his emphasis on coherence is reiterated constantly. To say that for him correspondence gave the essence of truth *rather than* coherence is to misconstrue him radically. And it was because he thought that ideal truth lay in systematic apprehension of the whole that he adopted the criterion he did. Because truth is one coherent whole, the test of truth at any stage of our progress toward it is the degree to which we achieve this system, or to put it in another favorite way of his, the degree to which our thought could stand without alteration if incorporated into that system. In short, Bradley did precisely what Mr. Rescher so deplores in my own treatment; he made coherence part of the very essence and definition of truth, and derived his criterion from it. To be sure, I cannot follow Bradley into his final mysticism, in which all relations including that between thought and its object are transcended, a position in which coherence itself becomes meaningless. But the special points in which Mr. Rescher thinks Bradley's theory so superior to mine involve either (as in the definitional character of coherence) a misunderstanding of Bradley or (as in the method of forming a group for provisional testing) a position where I supposed my view and Bradley's were one.

For all this, a paper from outside the Bradleyan tradition, and from a writer as competent as Mr. Rescher, in support of the coherence criterion of truth is an auspicious omen and one that is seen in some conjecturable quarters with rejoicing. The new wine that Mr. Rescher so skillfully pours into old wineskins seems to have the pleasant property not of bursting them but of adding to their resilience and strength.

1. A. C. Ewing, *Idealism: A Critical Survey* (London: Methuen, 1934).

15 DOES BLANSHARD ESCAPE EPISTEMIC DUALISM?
Peter A. Bertocci

*T*HE *Nature of Thought* (1939) opens with the sentence: "Thought is that activity of mind which aims directly at truth" (*NT*, 1:51).[1] The exploration and defense of this thesis has produced a monumental work, a model of sustained and systematic philosophizing. Together with the Carus Lectures, *Reason and Analysis* (1962), it exposes a mind sensitive to dominant alternatives in British and American psychology and philosophy, and unwilling to accept a solution without giving opposing views their due. With exemplary patience, firmness, and grace, Brand Blanshard constantly lays bare the problems he and others face on their way to truth.

It is the problem of epistemic dualism upon which I wish to focus in this paper. For me this problem takes on new urgency as I study Blanshard. I find myself saying *yes* to so much he opposes, *yes* to so much as he moves to his own solution, that I often wonder whether my disagreement does not spring from failure to grasp exactly what he has in mind. In this situation, it seems wise to set forth the epistemic situation as I see it and as Blanshard sees it, so that the grounds for my hesitancy about accepting his solution will be clear at least.

1. Thinking and the Nature of Mind

While the nature of mind is not our theme here, we cannot neglect Blanshard's own verdict: "One's view of thinking and knowing is closely connected with one's view of the agent who does the knowing," and "any theory of thought will entail much about the nature of the mind" (1:474). I mention this here because I wonder, in passing, whether Blanshard's ontology of mind is not governed more than it should be by the analysis of cognitive demands—with far-reaching consequences for his final theory of value, God, and freedom. In all of his writing, and not the least in *Reason and Goodness* (1961), Blanshard has much to say about the affective-conative and other nonrational factors in the life of mind. A glance at his view will stand us in good stead.

Blanshard's theory of mind as a whole develops a thesis stated in "The Nature of Mind" ("NM").[2] Having argued that all mentality is purposive, and having emphasized the creative, aesthetic, and ethical dimensions of mind, he adds: "Our best clue [to the end of mind in ourselves] is gained from studying that function which of all our mental functions has gone farthest toward its goal, the intellectual." Nowhere is there any doubt that "mind . . . is not a single process, but a set of processes, a quiverful of arrows of desire" ("NM," 216, 215).

True, Blanshard has no intention of having some abstract reason dictate the ends of conation other than the theoretical. He would follow "the loadstones of the spirit where they lead." Yet, he expresses his conviction that these will support each other as "the implicit demands of the different sides of our nature are all realized so far as consistency will allow" ("NM," 216). All the more important is it, then, that we understand the demands of the theoretic impulse.

2. Thinking—Autonomous but Not Independent

The activity of thinking is never reducible to sensing, feeling, imagining, associating, or to any other activity or experienceing. To think is to judge ("a special impulse of the mind"; NT, 1:467 ff). And any judgment must be true or false.

Clearly, then, we must distinguish experiencing "as such" from experiencing as knowing or judging. "All objects come to us bathed in personal feeling and they are probably barnacled too with irrelevant ideas" (NT, 1:466). But whence the norm of relevance; whence the norm of truth? No experiencing, no problem of knowing. Thus, the problem of knowing begins with the distinction whether the judgment upon which it is based is true or false. Accordingly, Blanshard rivets attention to that form of experiencing which is not only a "fighter for ends," as James described mind, but a fighter for truth. To be a thinking mind is to be able to experience the intrinsic and irreducible satisfaction that comes only as the theoretic impulse realizes itself.

This experience constitutes Blanshard's underlying ground for rejecting mechanistic and atomistic views of mind. On either view an "ideal of cogency" is impossible, since events simply happen. Truth, on the other hand, never just happens. "It is a main contention of this work that unless thought is recognized as the pursuit of such an ideal [cogency], and the ideal itself is defined, neither logic nor the psychology of thinking can do its work" (NT, 2:24).

At the moment I am not concerned with the nature of the ideal of cogency. More important, Blanshard does not simply intuit this ideal and then impose it on the data. As he faces problem after problem, he finds that "what understanding means is apprehending something in a system which renders it necessary. The degree to which reflection is really reasoning, or on the other hand mere random association, is determined by the extent to which the immanent ideal of system has assumed control of the process" (*NT,* 2:24). Accordingly, no hasty conclusion satisfies Blanshard. Beginning with the simplest perceptual judgment, he notes that the growth of meaning is not the random association which brings disparate "elements" together, but the interrelating in which every part is seen to make a difference to every other part.

Knowing, then, never begins as a mere reaction or response. For example, the response, sound, if it is to be experienced *as* sound, calls for a sound-less activity of mind—which enables us to infer that any mind has its own "bony framework as truly as his body" (*NT,* 1:66). A further and basic contention is involved here. We cannot construe the mind of an infant or the nature of the world we live in as if they ever were "one great blooming, buzzing confusion." If we do, then escape from confusion may be promised, but never achieved (cf. 1:57 and 61). Why? Neither a baby nor an adult can "perceive the loud sound *as* loud, or as a sound . . . without placing it in a scale where it is opposed to the less loud, and at the beginning there are no less louds. . . . To perceive a sound *as* a sound, you must perceive it as *a* sound . . ." (1:61). Still, why? "To *be* for thought at all is to be distinct, and to be distinct is to be related to something else through space, time, degree, or otherwise . . . . to think involves the relating of the object thought of to something else within a system" (1:65).

I have purposely selected passages which pose a basic epistemic thesis—whether or not we accept Blanshard's own final theory of internal relation, universals, or coherence. I myself must agree that if we think of mind and knowing as a collection of pieces in which parts may be added or subtracted without any effect on the rest, we have painted ourselves into a corner. I agree that an occurrence must remain an inarticulate experience unless we recognize a theoretic impulse that demands and finds connective tissue. While I shall not pursue the matter here—and am not quite satisfied with Blanshard's positive articulation of a theory of the knowing agent—I would further urge that the cognitive phase of personal being is a distinguishable but not separable activity of a self-identifying yet changing person.

But I see all this as supporting rather than opposing Blanshard's main contention. We cannot move from sheer pluralism or atomism in the cognitive agent or in the cognitive process to such connection as is asserted *prima facie* in any conception of truth and falsity. To be sure, at this point it is not clear what the connection is. Blanshard from the beginning focuses attention on the satisfaction of the theoretic impulse, and, I think, interprets the process of knowing within the context of that demand. That may be the best way. But in order to leave no stone unturned in the attempt to appreciate what is involved in a person's knowing, I shall state in a slightly different way what it is that differentiates knowing from any other kind of experience and thereby, hopefully, emphasize factors that need also to be taken into account as we try to understand how epistemic dualism arises.

3. The Epistemic Claim in Personal Experiencing

In what human undergoing do we find the claim to knowing taking place? In the mind's experiencing of *objective reference*. That is, as Blanshard so clearly sees, in knowing the mind is undergoing one arrow of desire, if you will, but this undergoing is distinguished from other undergoings by the fact that the knower reaches to, or for, what is not this undergoing. I can express this "reach" only by saying that the agent *refers* to something beyond the state he is undergoing, by virtue of what is "present" in this undergoing. Thus, the conscious "undergoing," be it an experiencing of *red, justice, anger,* or *image,* is one thing; it is no different *as* undergoing from snow melting or tomatoes ripening. It is not *knowing.* For any undergoings or experiencings, as such, cannot be true or false; they are what they are. The knowing-experience, on the other hand, is one in which the agent refers his experience to something other than itself, and claims that this undergoing "presents" or "corresponds" to something other than itself. I am trying to express an "ultimate" here, for this knowing-experience is unlike any other experience. It is an irreducible kind of undergoing or experiencing, in which I refer to an object, in which I "propose" something about what is not the experience as such. The experience of proposing, the objective referring, cannot be true or false. *What* I propose can.

Now, if I am reading my experiencing here aright, I must report that *in* the experiencing there is no ideal of knowing given; nor am I told how I am related to what it is of which my proposal may be true or false. Yet, as Arthur Lovejoy (*The Revolt Against Dualism*) says, we are "inexpugnable realists." That is, I assume that the yellow is, as I am aware of it, there in *x* (book, or flower). So strong is this *psychological* conviction that I would never make the distinction between experiencing and knowing if it were always the case that what I now call the proposal is true. Inexpugnable realist I would remain if, for example, the tracks that "clearly" are experienced as meeting in the distance *did* meet, or similarly, if the object I saw "right there" did not turn out to be a mirror object.

These errors force me to distinguish what appears as the real object from the epistemic object, or "appearance" from "reality." But the moment I distinguish appearance from reality I must continue to ask what the relation of the knowing agent is to what he can now only say he claims to know. Inexpugnable realism may remain, but we must now call in question a view of knowledge assumed at the moment of our inexpugnable realism, namely that what I am experiencing is the real rather than the epistemic object. The new question is inescapable: What is the relation of claimant as knowing-experient to what, other than the experience of referring, he claims to know?

Here there is no sure-fire, final answer; we can proceed only by hypothesis. But if there can be error, then the experiencing claimant cannot be identical with the object (what I shall call the "referral object"). Blanshard grapples with the issue and thinks that some sort of identity is required. I am suggesting, as we await that argument, that we set aside the relation of identity and say something like this. Granted that the knower and the known are related in such a way that the referral object known may make a difference to the knower, knowing involves making a claim or proposal that is then found to be supported or unsupported by further claims or actions. (I am trying to avoid words like "correspondence," "presentation," "representation," "identity," because these are particular answers to the question we are asking.)

To be concrete: When I claim: "My automobile engine is running," I am psychologically certain that something other than my experience (engine running) is making the experienced difference to me. My initial act of objective reference is always of the sort: "Of course I am experiencing engine running." But when I remember that I can err, I say, much more cautiously, that I am experiencing an epistemic object which may or may not turn out to be the referral object. Since it is, initially, far from obvious what the relation is between claimant and referral object, I cannot readily settle what the relation is, or what model or norm I can have for knowledge or truth.

At this point, I am very much aware of the fact that I cannot get outside of the knowing relation in order to describe it. Every statement by which I depict the knowing relation must be made from within it. I am further embarrassed by the fact that such clauses as "depict the knowing relation" seem to assume that I can describe it truly, when in fact I still cannot assume a norm for knowing. I must still refrain from stipulating what the relation is between the knower and what he claims to be depicting, revealing, or identifying. However, I am not saying that I know nothing at all, but only that I cannot select a paradigm for knowing without allowing for the fact that I err. As knower, then, I am forever *in mediis rebus,* aware that I may well not be entitled to the psychological certitude that I constantly experience in objective reference.

In other words, to apply an earlier discovery in reverse, I must not construe the knowing relation in such a way that I cannot account for the occurrence of error as well as knowledge. I cannot here accept R. Chisholm's guideline that in knowing I should assume that a statement is innocent (true) until I can show it is guilty (false). I must remember that as a knower I am never antecedently justified either as innocent or guilty. The only guide-rule that I cannot escape is that contradictions are unacceptable, since they bring a line of reasoning to a dead stop. But I am not contradicting myself when I say: In my experience of objective reference, I do not yet know what the relation is that supports the particular claim I find myself making in referring beyond the experience itself.

4. Error, the Mind, and the Cognitive Relation

I have said that I experience objective reference, that I am psychologically convinced that the *room* is as hot as I experience it, and that the *pin* is painful. But further experience and thought indicate that these certitudes are hollow; I am startled by my errors and must learn to make "appropriate allowances." This situation involves something about the knower as such and favors a hypothesis about his relation to the referral object.

First, if what I experience is not there "in" the referral object, where is it? It makes no sense at all to say that it's "in" my brain, for an event or string of events in the brain is no more true or false than are psychological events as such. Second, if error (on this view) is to be possible, there must be a kind of being which can be itself, at the same time refer what it experiences beyond itself, *and* identify itself as the being who can so refer. A knowing being, or mind, then, is the kind of self-identifying being that is continuant in the referring, whether the referring is eventually "in error" or "in truth." The heat or cold that is not in the room is nevertheless being experienced as my experience and being referred beyond this experience. The truth *or* error is, accordingly, *mine* since I was and am *the proposer*. Third, *the error is uniquely mine* since I can explain it ultimately only as my proposal that turned out to have no basis beyond my experiencing.

Error, therefore, in a special way suggests that there is a kind of being whose undergoing is different from that of any other we know, for it is one that can undergo or experience, can refer that experience beyond itself, *and* remain as the "revealer" (in some sense) of the referral object, and as the being whose own referring experience remains his despite the fact that there is no referral object. The existence of error reinforces what is also suggested, but not so forcefully, about the general nature of what it means to know: a self-identifying knower, his epistemic object, and the referral object are all involved in relations that are far from immediately obvious.

The general framework I have been trying to articulate is not inconsistent with Blanshard's analysis, although he will find reason for suspecting the epistemic dualism of the sort I think the above analysis justifies. Thus, in rejecting direct realism, Blanshard says:

> . . . We admit that "I am aware of blue" is not the same as "blue exists"; we admit that to describe a mental event as blue is an absurdity; we admit that many objects of knowledge are permanent, and that our knowledge of them is not. [But he goes on:] How far do these admissions carry us? Do they show

anything more than this, that knowledge, in one of its aspects, is an event that happens in time? If I am to know that the diameter and circumference of a circle are incommensurable, that fact must not merely be; it must present itself to my mind; at some moment of time it must enter as a component part into my "field of consciousness" or total experienced mass; . . . [*NT*, 1:407]

Some sort of epistemic dualism is asserted here. What needs further clarification is the exact relation between knower and known; of idea to thing (referral object). In replying to concerns of several "interrogators" about possible difficulties in his hypothesis about the relation, Blanshard has said: "I was driven to this view not by its initial plausibility, but by the failure of its alternatives. If you say with realists that what we immediately apprehend is the object as it is in nature, you run into the old and insuperable difficulties about error."[3]

Thus the existence of error moves Blanshard toward epistemic dualism, but another factor that weighs even more with him comes out in the next statement, contra dualism. "If, with dualists, you take the representative view, you never *know* at all, for you can never check the correspondence of idea and object. Our knowledge of nature seems to require that the object itself be present in experience, not merely some surrogate for it, and yet that the object should fall beyond thought, as something to which this must conform."[4]

At this point I am not asking whether dualism *must* involve representative or surrogate, or whether Blanshard's proposed view *will* come closer to his ideal of knowing. I am saying that at least initially both he and I hold to *some dualism*, that is, to reference to some object that "should fall beyond thought." It may be that this dualism is relatively innocuous since it results initially from the definition of the cognitive situation. Indeed, at this point I shall accept Blanshard's contention that "the right procedure is to assume your task [of knowing, in Blanshard's sense] to be possible until you have reason to think it impossible. . . ."[5] It remains to be seen whether Blanshard's hypothesis about the thought-object relation does succeed in avoiding the inadequacies of realism and the disaster, as he sees it, of dualism.

5. The Realistic Predicament

If, says Blanshard, a realist holds that a mental act "directly engages" its object (say a red ball in the physical world), then how is he to explain the fact that the object in the physical world is removed from his mental act by the series of processes and events, physiological and psychological, media which clearly make direct knowledge impossible? (*NT*, 1:413, 414).

Such considerations lead Blanshard to depict the situation he is inveighing against. When one is comparing Saint Peter's and Saint Paul's for example, first one object, then the other appears at the focus of consciousness. In such cases of comparison, "I am active in some sense ... there is a mental process. . . . But it is a *process within the content*, not a process in which I station myself outside and look at the content, as if the field of consciousness were a tapestry hung on the wall, and knowing were the beam from a lantern . . ." (*NT*, 1:409; italics added). Over and over again Blanshard expresses dissatisfaction with this *searchlight* or *camera* metaphor. In a partly different context, he himself says:

> whenever we know, we are aware ... of something that is not in the ordinary sense an object, *but is as certainly there as objects themselves*. My mind, when I am aware of a tree, is not exhausted in this awareness. The knowing by mind of its objects is not like the taking of a camera picture, where the details of a sharply delimited field are all recorded in equal light. For beyond or below the margin of explicit awareness, there are masses of vague sensations, fluctuating pleasures and pains, wellings of obscure emotion, which form a pulsing sense of life that is easier to recognize than describe. [He continues:] These are certainly present; our awareness of them is clearly different from our awareness of a tree; *and they are bound up in a peculiarly intimate way with the sense of self*. Nothing would be easier than to take this obscure, subjective, living, changing experience as an experience of the changing activities of the self. But it is not really such. [*NT*, 1:399–400; italics added]

In these and other passages, one finds Blanshard denying a soul-substance view of mind as he describes the knowing process. As I see it, in contrast to my self-identifying actor-knower, mind for Blanshard is a complex of events and changing experiences. I accept Blanshard's case against the realistic act-object epistemology and a substantialistic soul-psychology. But does Blanshard hold that a person has no intrinsic unity of which the theoretic impulse is one very significant phase, and without which the development of a "sense of self" surely is unintelligible?

I must not pass by an ambiguity here, for Blanshard is clearer about what he rejects than what he affirms. Thus in 1941 he says: "Mental activity is the sort of activity everywhere whose reach exceeds its grasp." He adds, mind is "*a process in which the potential realizes or actualizes itself*. It is the sort of process in which that which is to be determines, in part, the course of its coming to be. Mind acts as it does because pressing in and through the present is a world that clamors to be born" ("NM," 209, 211).

Now it is one thing to say that one cannot tell what a mind is apart from reference to what it is becoming, but it is another to say that to the degree that "ends are in control;" to that degree mind is present. Again, to say that "mind is a set of processes distinguished from others through their control by an immanent end" ("NM," 216) suggests that mind is not a self-identifying unity-continuity of *its* processes, and that it therefore does not control its theoretic, aesthetic, moral, and conative impulses, but depends for its unity upon the degree of order and harmony developed.

Does Blanshard, then, deny that, as I should suggest, there is an intrinsic, *ontic* mental unity—not soul-substance, but unity in activity—whose task is to find as much *fulfillment*-unity as possible? "My" view is suggested by his contention that the human consciousness is "restlessly *transforming itself* under the spell of a secret end" ("NM," 216; italics added). Still, I am plagued by opposing statements such as "mind is really mind to the *extent that it achieves an experience at once comprehensive and ordered*" (ibid.; italics added).

As we saw earlier, what is at stake is both the nature of the relation of the mind to its object, and the nature of mind itself as its *reach exceeds its grasp* in aiming at truth. Blanshard seems to hold both that what the mind is does depend on what it grasps and that what it grasps depends upon the mind's own telic nature, theoretic and otherwise. Thus, for him the problem of the relation of thought and idea is also the problem of the inner structure of mind and its relation to the world. All the more important, then, is it to see in exactly what way epistemic dualism does and does not pervade his thinking.

As we have already noted, for Blanshard the object as known cannot be entirely unaffected by the process of knowing. The knower and known cannot be completely independent of each other or completely identical with each other. If identical, error becomes unintelligible; if separate, the process of thought or knowing becomes "a series of snapshots of an alien world produced by fortuitous changes in the brain" or in the mind (*NT*, 1:438). We agree that in knowing commerce must be going on between the event in the person and the "object to which this event somehow points" (1:445). But how can we keep from being "confined in the iron ring of our own ideas" (ibid.) or get beyond them without *being* the object known?

The answer cannot be in any copy theory, for any imprint made upon our minds would be influenced by our nature (*NT*, 1:455). Where, then, shall we look? First at our own theoretic impulse. "Thought, looked at from the inside, is not a mechanical succession of ideas. . . . It is a restless seeking for a satisfaction of its own, and it is only when we stand inside it and see things through its own eyes that . . . it is then apparent that the moving agent is *as much the goal which thought is seeking* as any event which came before to push it along . . ." Thinking "is self-development of ideal content under the control of an immanent end" (1:459; italics added). What is that end? It is "to see things within a system which renders them necessary" (1:466) and which in practice proceeds "by comparing what satisfies more with what satisfies less" (1:467).

To comment: I would hardly deny that the ideal of a necessary system is a highly satisfying norm, or that in practice we do settle for a hypothesis which is more comprehensive than others. But the question remains: On what grounds may we say that the necessity which satisfies the theoretic impulse is to be discovered in the realm to which ideas point?

We seem to be bound for trouble. Can we say that in thinking we are trying to submit our minds "to the control of something beyond," as the realists say, and say *also* that the end which will satisfy our theoretic impulse "is as truly fixed by our nature as the sort of food and drink that will satisfy us"? (*NT,* 1:490). Furthermore, if every stage of cognitive achievement brings dissatisfaction at a higher level, we can hardly have at any one stage in knowledge more than probable assurance that we are under the control of something beyond. How, then, can we escape a less innocuous dualism, if what presumably is in our grasp turns out later to be erroneous even in part? Only a dreadful intellectual and practical crisis would be required to place epistemic dualism beyond bounds. But, as Blanshard sees it, we *are* confronted by such a crisis.

6. Blanshard's Objection to Dualism

Flatly, for Blanshard, dualism and the "absolute skepticism" it entails wrecks the knowledge venture. What becomes increasingly clear is the norm which defines the success of the knowledge venture. If anything but the full satisfaction of the theoretic impulse is failure—as in his view—then we are all condemned to dualism and skepticism. Still, Blanshard cannot be easily turned aside. If we say, to begin with, that the end of knowledge and the impulse to know never can meet, we are claiming skepticism, in advance, as known. It seems to me that this argument is by no means sophistic. The skeptic is indeed saying that he knows that there is no knowledge.

Yet, until the skeptic has told us what his norm of knowing is we cannot know what he is asserting. If the skeptic means that self-contradictory propositions may be true, then the contradiction of his own proposition could be true. But, as we have seen, such a position gives the mind no place to go. Logical self-contradiction is untenable for any proposer; this need be debated no longer. But in the debate between the monistic and dualistic epistemologist, the question is whether "absolute skepticism" is involved if the dualist does take the position that Blanshard describes thus:

> If the immanent and transcendent ends of my knowledge are really independent of each other, then their coming together at any point is a matter of chance and their continuing to coincide is incredible. [*NT,* 1:491]

Again, if

> there is nothing in the fact that a certain structure satisfies my knowing impulse to show that it coincides with anything beyond . . . [then] Experience would be a sustained paranoia, which, even if it made occasional contacts with a world outside, would leave us uncertain what was dream and what

fact. If the real world on the one hand and the immanent end of knowledge on the other are curves plotted on different bases, we could never count on their intersecting: and to suppose that by reaching the end of knowledge we should arrive at reality would seem about as reasonable as to suppose that the desire of the moth creates the star. [*NT*, 1:492–93]

In short, the kind of dualism Blanshard finds horrendous is the contention "implicit in common thought" that "the immanent end to which knowledge must conform, and the object to which it must somehow also conform, are independent variables" (1:491).

Let us set *this* definition of skepticism and dualism aside for the moment. Given Blanshard's denial of direct realism, and of copy theory, we cannot be said to know normatively unless our knowing is "at once a revelation of the object and a realization of ourselves . . ." (*NT*, 1:491). Knowing must involve identity, but not a kind of identity which renders the very idea of truth and error impossible; thought must still be "a half-way house on the road to reality" (1:494).

What kind of identity, then, will serve? Blanshard's answer: one which allows ideas to be potential objects, in which the end of thought is present but incompletely realized. Here, at any rate, thought and reality will not be independent variables forever at possible odds with each other. In his own words: "The real object . . . is present in person in our thought, even when we are thinking about the absent; but it is there, not in that flesh-and-blood actuality which would make thinking something monstrous, but in various stages of realization" (*NT*, 1:497). The various stages of realization allow for the only kind of difference between object and idea that Blanshard thinks will give realism a viable defense against the dualist.

In all this Blanshard might be said to be making an important concession to realistic theories of knowing. But Blanshard's view of likeness is as different as his view of identity is. Thus he says: "Ideas *are* like their objects but with a special kind of likeness . . . the likeness of a mind half grown to that same mind fully grown; of a purpose partly realized to the purpose fulfilled" (*NT*, 1:495). This view of likeness alleviates the "great weakness" of copy theory, namely: "the interval between idea and object was a chasm between different orders of existence" which left the assumed resemblance "arbitrary and ungrounded" (ibid.) and thus made knowledge impossible. Nor will the contention of the critical realist stand as long as he insists that we know "the whole nature of the object" directly or literally. We must indeed, if there is to be knowledge, have actually in our minds the character or, normally, some fragment of the character (1:496). But "this presence is a matter of degree, and . . . it is entirely possible to think of the character with no part of its content directly present to all" (ibid.).

To illustrate: On Blanshard's view we can bridge the chasm between the mountain and such knowledge of it as we have if the mountain has potential being as idea, and the idea is fulfilled in the mountain (*NT,* 1:503). But are not ideas universals, whereas the mountain is a unique, particular existent? *This* chasm is in fact nonexistent, for *that* mountain can be specified as unique and determinate only as we exhaust the relations which we can attribute to it as a part of the universe as a whole. "This is the only uniqueness that the object possesses" (ibid.). And the "continuing sense of discrepancy between the generalities actually gained and the individual thing referred to" (1:504) is itself the expression of the immanent demand of our searching minds. The uniqueness itself is the goal of thought, but not as an object foreign to universals that would adequately define its place. Thus the individuality of any "one" thing becomes the completeness of the universe; but the completeness of the universe would be incomprehensible apart from the individuality that all of its relations define.

7. Does Blanshard's Theory of Idea Escape Dualism?

(a) We now see that Blanshard's cure for the weaknesses in both realism and dualism is indeed a metaphysical theory of the knower, the idea, and the object known. If they are completely identical, there is no meaning for "know"; if they are utterly independent variables, the claim to know becomes fraudulent. I can appreciate Blanshard's concern that the factors in our epistemic situation be so related that such knowledge as we have can be forthcoming. What is debatable is whether our knowing and our erring require the revised theory of identity and difference. Since I find no internal consistency in this revised theory, my basic query is: If this theory is developed in order to escape the horrendous skeptical consequences of dualism, does it in fact do so?

First, despite the union between mind and its object, at any moment there remains the difference between what is in mind partially and the total nature of the object. Thus "the mountain" is the temporary resting place for my theoretic impulse, which has stopped there for practical purposes. Once I give my theoretic impulse free rein, I realize how truncated the "mountain" is. Granted. But it is ever thus! At no moment will I ever know to what extent what I (claim to) know is as I assert. If skepticism means that I can never know the referral object as it is, then how can I escape it even on Blanshard's terms?

Nor will the distinction between the practical and the theoretical help. For within either my practical or my theoretical journey, at any one moment my dilemma exists: Do I have in what is before me any more than a promissory note that the remaining relations will be such that they will justify my present psychological assurance that what I hold to be so *now* is in fact so?

Second, to carry the same idea further, why may it not be that the immanent thrust of my mind, satisfied temporarily, has such a fragmentary portion of what transcends its present grasp that, as is often the case, I later see how little ground I had for my assertion? Why doesn't *knowledge,* in Blanshard's sense now, still remain a miracle, since what is to come may be so transforming of my present claim? Indeed, is it less an appeal to miracle to assume that at the end of the rainbow, beyond my vision, the promise would be fulfilled that my idea and the referral object are indeed one? Isn't the chasm between *any now* and the *final end* as devastating as the supposed dualistic chasm of idea and referral object?

To be sure, on Blanshard's view, there is systematic growth in interconnection which goes on apace in knowing. But this alternative is open to the dualist as well. Blanshard seems to think that all the difference is made by holding that in this systematic growth there is no metaphysical chasm between the object *in posse* (my idea) and the referral object. He finds satisfaction in thinking that "To the extent to which I know the great pyramid, it does enter into the content of my experience, and the impulse to know it could never be satisfied absolutely while any part of it was left out" (1:508–9). Still, does it not remain the fact that I do not know, at any given step of my theoretical advance, whether future discoveries will render my assertions about the pyramid so fragmentary that the assurance of knowing, even in Blanshard's sense, is indeed more psychological than reasonably probable? Is the specter of skepticism destroyed by *this kind of identity* between idea and reality? In any case, is the psychological assurance that may well come from such identification not equally open to the epistemic dualist? In this context, it is appropriate to reexamine the case for dualism.

(b) The dualist, we recall, argues against his *psychological,* inexpugnable realism because he finds that what seemed so psychologically certain in his experience of objective reference is not confirmed by further experiences. Let us say that I am psychologically certain that the budding tree in the field is a maple, or, to use Blanshard's example, let us suppose that I think there was a Persian victory over the Greeks at Plataea. I later discover (think, or judge) that there was a battle won by the Persians but not at Plataea, or that the budding tree is there but is not a maple. The question is: What is the status of the (erroneous) "battle-location of Plataea," and of "maple tree is budding" *at the time* I was asserting it? I was convinced that these objects were true, but now I know that I was mistaken at least in part. Can I say that *what I know now* was mistaken *was then* the object in posse?

Basically, if I accept Blanshard's view, I do not know how to understand the notion that the idea *was* budding maple tree or battle at Plataea potentially in some metaphysical sense, when in fact these ideas were false. Their existence as epistemic objects is undeniable, but I know not where to locate ideas as objects *in posse* especially when they turn out not to be correct in that specific sense. If I can say, as "my" version of dualism allows, that the idea, existent as *my* idea, is not the referral object, then I have a "home" for error. But if every idea is metaphysically the referral object *in posse* the existence of the falsity of the idea can have no "locus." I simply do not understand how Blanshard on his view of mind and of idea can find a home for epistemic reference that is not the identity even *in posse* of thought and its object.

Accordingly, I see no way of avoiding dualism of thought and thing by the route Blanshard offers. Once he has admitted that "The full character of what one refers to is never known at the time of reference" (*NT,* 1:511), the fact remains that I do not know that what I am referring to (with psychological certitude) does in fact exist as referred to.

The potentiality is all mine, not of the object, for, again, on Blanshard's view I can never know what part of the judgment I am entertaining is "undeveloped," "premature," "unexplicit." At the time of reference what was later discovered to be the "premature" part could not *be* even potentially identical, or partially identical, with the object referred to. Granted that we may explain any error as consisting in a "discrepancy between the end of thought and a premature formulation of that end" (1:512), there remains to be explained the very possibility of the mind's having a discrepancy which by definition is not the object *in posse.* One cannot ever know immediately what is and what is not discrepant. Accordingly, the discrepancy "between what we really mean and what we take ourselves to mean" (ibid.) forces upon us not only a *differentiation* between the underdeveloped and the developed but a *dualism* of the sort which Blanshard suggested made knowledge miraculous.

(c) It might seem that we escape dualism if with Blanshard we take seriously Bradley's contention that "there are no 'floating ideas,' no predicates entertained by thought that are utterly homeless in reality . . ." (*NT,* 1:512). For then "every distinguishable reference in the thought—to Greeks, to Persians, to a battle, a victory, etc.—is a reference which, if developed, would bring us to something in the real world" (ibid.). Again, I do not see how this can be an escape from dualism *at the time when* reference is asserted as true. Granted that ideas of maples, victories, budding tree, Persians, Greeks, and so on may well be found to have *some* degree of truth and reality in them (as Blanshard would hold), this does not help me to understand what the status of the idea is at the time when I judge the room to be very long (and later discover it is extended only by the use of mirrors); or when I bite the wax apple, perceiving it as the Baldwin. These epistemic objects (idea-objects, not objects *in posse*) exist, I suggest, as my thoughts, whether or not they are ever known to fit into a coherent system. Dualism does not consist only in the difference between the partial and the whole. It consists in the dualism between epistemic object that points beyond itself and the referral object.

8. A Summary and a Dualistic Proposal

I began this essay by indicating (and Blanshard would agree) that the epistemic situation involves a knower whose cognitive claims are events different from any other event insofar as they refer beyond any experiences—to past, present, or future occurrences—and be it via perceptual or nonperceptual judgments. This *prima facie* inexpugnable realism may well suggest some sort of identity between knower and known. But this conviction cannot stand as is. The relation between the knower and the transcendent object, which the cognitive agent is claiming to know, must remain open to hypothesis. But even first reflections suggest that if the knower is in error, at the same time that he is claiming to know the object as it is, there must be a mind capable of entertaining an epistemic object—an object whose existence, whatever else, depends upon its being sensed, perceived, or thought. This still leaves open the question of the relation between the agent-knower and the transcendent object.

The special challenge of Blanshard consists in his clarifying so effectively what he thinks to be the strengths and weakness of basic realistic and dualistic analysis of the knowledge situation—and his analysis is particularly challenging to me because I think that he presents an alternative which cannot be neglected. In analyzing Blanshard's alternative, I cannot escape the conclusion that while his theory provides a way by which the knower is united with the transcendent object, the assurance that this will protect us against such skepticism as dualism (supposedly) involves is more tenable psychologically than reasonably. The basic reason for this is first that the knower at any point must at best remain satisfied with a fragment of the transcendent object, the knowledge of which can be so changed by further understanding that the word *know,* in Blanshard's sense, can hardly be applied to it. Secondly, unless ideas be "in" the mind, there is no locus for that specific idea which turns out not to be the object which it presumably was *in posse.*

There are other issues that would need independent treatment in an adequate discussion. I am prepared, for example, to grant that to know is to relate ideas, rooted in experience or logical possibilities, in a system of coherent relations that is not accidental or fortuitous. But if the analysis above is correct, it is to claim more than the epistemic situation justifies to assert the total pervasiveness of necessary system and internal relations, especially of the sort involved in the relation of idea (and mind) to referral object. If some sort of epistemic dualism is in order, then the relation between knower and object falls short of the norm for knowing Blanshard has in mind, but it does seem to render the possibility of such truth (and falsity) as we have understandable and worthy of action. What seems clear to me now is that dualism cannot be escaped with adequate justification, and that the norm of knowing in terms of which it is accused of hopeless skepticism must be set aside. Perhaps *reasonable probability* (do we ever have matter-of-fact knowledge other than this even on Blanshard's view?) can be supported along the following lines.

First, why should we not say that we as conative-cognitive persons (with greater initial, intrinsic unity than Blanshard seems to allow for) are in commerce with, or interacting with, each other and with the constituents of the world, without ever being identical, either partially or wholly, with them?

Second, if this be granted, then our total conative natures and our abilities are affected in their development by a transcendent environment. They—our total natures—make their own claims on it, and it does fall to the theoretic impulse to connect any of a person's experiences and ideas in whatever network seems at once dictated by all of experience including the ongoing interaction of his life with the transcendent world.

Third, the fact of error, and our inability ever to know finally that we do have a face-to-face confrontation with, or actually experience identification with, the transcendent world, mean that even if the referral realms did not have their own natures and make "demands" on their own terms, we can never know the transcendent world with the certainty of immediacy or logic. We might add, in a longer account, as F. R. Tennant has put it, *entre l'homme et le monde, c'est l'humanité.* But it suffices here to say that all interpretation of objective reference is *ad modum recipientis,* and *anthropic.*

Fourth, I would emphasize that we have not laid the specter of skepticism to rest if knowing means immediate certainty, logical implication, or involves some sort of metaphysical identity of thinker and transcendent object. For, if our analysis is correct, such certainty is promised but not delivered; we remain always in probability—that is increased as any judgment fits more *reasonably than any other judgment* in a mutually supporting system. Hence, why not settle for this kind of reasoned probability, grounded in the (postulated) mutual interaction of known and "transcendent" world?

Fifth, if I am asked how I get out of a fortress of immediate experiences and thought, my answer is that solipsism is less reasonable (but not logically impossible) than the view that, since there is much in my world which I must accept on terms that are refractory to wants and my will, my epistemic objects are probably joint products of my interaction with referral realms or objects in the transcendent world. But again has any more actual certainty been vouchsafed on Blanshard's view?

Sixth, I simply do not know to what degree what I claim to be most coherent does actually render what the world independent of my knowledge would say if, as it were, it could speak directly to me. The view of truth I am suggesting is not pragmatic in any sense that amounts to the conclusion that my ideas and action determine truth. It seems clear that I must postulate realms in which both claims about my existence and about my thoughtful action are checked—realms of being which at the same time challenge, discourage, support, or "guide" such claims as make it possible for me to speak at all of them. (The philosophic task is to relate such "realms" to each other as coherently as possible.)

Seventh, obviously, there is much filling-in that needs to be done. But one possible merit of such a dualistic view of the epistemic situation is that, at the epistemic level, one need not claim more for the nature of the metaphysical realm than that it constitutes a "realm of eligibility and ineligibility" in relation to our total natures and the claims they make. What the nature of this realm, as a whole, is remains open to reasonable hypothesis.

On this view, then, the epistemic situation does not *prejudge* the kind of relations that bind the knower-agent to the cosmos. All it seems to me that is required is that the knower be an agent of dimensions suggested by Blanshard, that the growth of his knowledge be taken seriously as a response to promptings from within and without, that the knower be a mental being who can experience his own activities, refer them beyond themselves, and then proceed to define the further reaches open to him in the realm of eligibility. So much of what is here suggested is consistent with Blanshard's view as indicated, and consistent with much else that his philosophy includes. But it contains what he no doubt would consider a fatal flaw, the denial that the idea (and, I think, the knower) is the object *in posse*.

PETER A. BERTOCCI

DEPARTMENT OF PHILOSOPHY
BOSTON UNIVERSITY

NOTES

[1]Unless stated otherwise, all quotations will be from *The Nature of Thought* (*NT*).

[2]*Journal of Philosophy* 38 (April 10, 1941): 207–16. "For in my view mind *is* conation; all mental processes reduce to it" (212).

[3]See *Philosophical Interrogations*, eds. Sydney and Beatrice Rome (New York: Holt, Rinehart & Winston, 1964), 249.

[4]Ibid.

[5]Ibid., 250.

15. Reply to Peter A. Bertocci

Does Blanshard Escape Epistemic Dualism?

There can be few persons who know my *Nature of Thought* more thoroughly than Mr. Bertocci. He has led a succession of graduate seminars critically down its roads and even its bypaths; and he agrees with enough of my position to make his divergences of exceptional interest and weight. He is himself an epistemological dualist, holding that the object of knowledge is not identical with our experience of it; and his essay is designed to show that I have not avoided such dualism myself, nor the partial skepticism that attends it. He is largely right in this criticism. But both my dualism and my skepticism would today be regarded as fossil species of these genera, and since in the book mentioned I wind into my conclusions through hundreds of weary pages, it may be well to begin by stating in outline how I view the relation of thought and its objects. I can then turn with a better chance of being understood to Mr. Bertocci's pointed doubts and dissents.

First a point or two about terms. The issue between epistemological monism and dualism is often taken to be whether sense-data are identical with the qualities of physical things. That is not the present issue. The question is not whether we sense physical things directly, but what is the relation of thought to its object. And in discussing that question it is well to talk of judgments rather than ideas, since the judgment is the simplest mental act that can attain either truth or falsity. Judgment always has an object about which its assertion is made and which is assumed to be distinct and independent of our reference to it. This is what Mr. Bertocci calls the "referral object." That there is a difference between this object and the judgment or thought about it seems to me, as it does to him, obvious, indeed so obvious as to be hardly worth debating, particularly when the object falls in the past or the future. The question of interest, therefore, is whether the admitted dualism between thought and its object is such as to imply skepticism, that is, to cut us off from genuine knowledge of it. If our unit of thought is the judgment, the referral object will, I take it, be what is referred to by the subject term, and our problem will be how the content asserted is related to that subject.

Three Kinds of Subject

I follow H. W. B. Joseph in distinguishing three such subjects. First there is the grammatical subject, the subject usually named in the grammatical subject of our sentence. "That bird is a nuthatch"; "Shelley was drowned at thirty"; "This mushroom is not of the edible kind." Here we are asserting something about a person or thing singled out by our subject noun. But the logical subject, that of which we mean to assert, may not be the grammatical subject. "Trial by jury is the fairest kind of trial." Here, if our statement is an answer to the question "What is your opinion of trial by jury?" then trial by jury is the logical as well as the grammatical subject. But if we are answering the question, "What kind of trial is the fairest?" then our subject is the fairest kind of trial, which we assert to be that of a jury. But there is another and third subject that lies beyond both grammatical and logical subjects. For in judging we are not only asserting a character of some limited subject we have singled out; we are ascribing the content of our judgment as a whole, subject and predicate in union, to the real world. That is why a logic divorced from ontology is a superficial logic. Reality is the subject—the metaphysical subject—of every judgment. It is the relation of the judged content as a whole to this ultimate subject that constitutes its truth or falsity.

What is this metaphysical subject? Since my answer, such as it is, has been repeated many times, I can afford here to be brief. Suffice it to say that the world is not a set of atoms, whether sensa, as Hume thought, or substances, as Aristotle thought, but a system of facts and events in relation, a system so firmly integrated that its every member is related necessarily to every other. My ontology is that of the thoroughgoing rationalist. When in judgment we assert something to be true, we are claiming to have an insight into some area, however limited, of that vast but ordered whole.

Let us turn from this ultimate subject of thought to the thought itself. The point of importance here, though to see its importance a wide perspective is needed, is that it belongs to a certain plateau in the evolution of understanding. The impulse to know is one drive of human nature, as old as the instinct of curiosity itself, which means that the impulse arises far below the human level. In the course of its advance, cognition constantly remodels the object of perception through observing it in more detail, classifying it with increasing accuracy, and grasping its relations to a widening circle of other things. "That bird is a nuthatch," "Trial by jury is the fairest trial" are judgments whose asserted content is relatively clear to us, but would not appear in the same way in the mind of primitive man, nor again in all probability in a mind a few millenniums further up in the long ascent of human knowledge. The ascent, on its cognitive side, is governed by an end which emerges into greater explicitness and therefore into greater utility in guidance as knowledge advances. That end is understanding. And understanding proceeds through an insistent pressing of the question Why? The answer to that question lies in seeing that the fact or behavior which puzzles us is what it is because it is necessitated by its relations within a system that includes it. The system to which at present we take our appeal is the system of science as a whole, or perhaps we should say our *Weltanschauung,* the philosophy in which the areas of our knowledge are fitted together with the greatest consistency. The end of the impulse to know or understand would obviously be a system that was at once all-comprehensive and so fully integrated that the question Why? would no longer have point. Now when Mr. Bertocci asks me whether in my theory of knowledge I am a dualist in a sense involving skepticism, I can only answer: in the main, yes; in some cases, no.

Take first the grammatical and logical subjects, which for convenience may be dealt with together. Regarding some such subjects, dualism does not imply skepticism, for the subject need not be anything falling beyond experience to which experience seeks to conform; it may fall within one's own consciousness, as in "This pain is intense." Even here there remains the duality between subject and predicate, but that does not affect the present issue, for both are equally in consciousness. "That noise sounds like a roll of thunder." "That rainbow is very bright." Is the plain man here a dualist in the sense that his thought is of something independent of consciousness? The question places him in a quandary. He would say that the sound and the rainbow are both objects out there in nature, not private to himself, for other people too can hear and see them. That suggests that between thought and thing there is a complete difference of ontological status; and if he were asked whether what he heard or saw was something in his consciousness, he would undoubtedly say No. Yet he seems to be engaging in the subject not through a film of other sensations or ideas, but directly. The fact is that he is straddling the fence; he is a dualist and a monist about the same subject. While he thinks the subject he is talking about is something out there in nature, it is not. Though he does not know it, it is a part of his own field of consciousness, about which skepticism would be groundless.

Now take a subject that is a little more complex. "That bird is a nuthatch." What do we take the subject to be? Certainly something that exists apart from us in nature. But does it, in the form in which we perceive it? We see its shape and color, and from our experience of birds, assume that its other side is like the one we see. Now this bird of common sense is largely a construction of our own. The color we see and also the shape (though I know that this is a controversial point) belong in our own consciousness, and so does the construction of its other side. I do not mean that when we see a natural object—a stone, a tree, a bird—there is nothing out there at all. There is and must be, to account for our perceiving what we do. But what exists in physical space is not the object that we partly see and partly construct; it is what the physicist would find there, a cloud of billions of atoms, with nothing like the sharp outline we see, and none of the color or other sensible qualities that might be given to our sight, hearing, or touch. On reflection, therefore, we must say that the commonsense bird, the bird we partly see and partly construct, exists only in our own experience. But we clearly do not suppose it to be. We take the perceptual object to have a being wholly independent of our seeing or thinking about it. In this we are wrong. Yet we are not altogether wrong, for there must be a being out there which gives rise to our percept and to which that percept in some degree conforms. Regarding the commonsense order of things, then, we are referring to what is largely our own experience and construction, about which skepticism is hardly possible. Regarding the truly physical object there is a gap which makes skepticism inevitable.

The Metaphysical Subject

To Mr. Bertocci's question whether in the theory of knowledge I belong to the camp of dualistic skepticism, I should thus give a mixed answer as regards both the grammatical and logical subjects of judgment. What of the metaphysical subject? Here I am of course a dualist. What are the two sides between which the relation of truth or falsity obtains? On our own side there is the asserted content of the judgment, the universals in union that constitute the subject and predicate terms. On the other side is the universe as it really is, the reality to which every judgment must conform if it is to be true. And we can see from considering the two sides that it never does conform. The bird as it exists in reality is not the bird of common sense, which is largely a structure of our own and limited in every detail by our ignorance, nor is it the bird of the physicist, whose knowledge, though more technical than ours, is also fragmentary in the extreme. The bird as it really is is that which would be apprehended by a mind that grasped its nature and structure in detail, its relations *in toto* to all the other genera and species of the bird and the animal kingdom, indeed its place in the scheme of things as a whole. This account of the real bird depends on the thesis that the bird as we know it, whether of common sense, ornithology, or physics, is related internally to the rest of the universe and cannot be known in its full reality until these relations are exhausted. The best that present knowledge can reveal is but a tiny fragment of what a completed knowledge would contain. I have argued this out in ways with which Mr. Bertocci is familiar. Regarding our knowledge of the metaphysical subject we are bound to be epistemological dualists.

Some readers have felt that my line of argument at this point is not wholly clear. I have spoken of an inner and an outer goal of thought as if in the end the two became one. The inner goal is satisfaction of the theoretical impulse in completeness of understanding; the outer goal is the adjustment of thought to things as they are. The inner or immanent goal is at work in the process of thought throughout its long advance, but what *guarantees* that the nearing of this immanent goal will bring us nearer to the outer goal? I have discussed this question in commenting on Mr. Rescher's paper, but Mr. Bertocci and others raise it too, and I must be as clear about it as I can.

I should say: (1) We have no *guarantee* at all. We might come at any time upon a fact or an event that was a sheer miracle in the sense of remaining an island in the world, to which no bridge of explanation could ever connect it. (2) No unambiguous case of this kind has yet come to light, and sufficient progress has been made in the direction of systematic knowledge to give us hope that none ever will. (3) So long as this progress continues, we are justified in postulating that an intelligible system is there to find. (4) The practical test we apply when a new claimant to truth appears is consistency with the present body of knowledge. This does not imply that the body of truth already gained is absolute; it never is. Often the old theory itself must be partially reconstructed if it is to accept without inconsistency a strongly supported new theory; the classic examples are the displacement of the Copernican theory by the Newtonian, and of the Newtonian by the Einsteinian. (5) The ultimate test for any theory lies in the answer to the question, How largely would it have to be modified if it were to be fitted into that system of truth which is our journey's end? (6) What would be the relation of that system which constitutes our immanent end and that system of facts and events which forms the system to be known? Would it be one of coincidence, as Bradley suggests, one in which thought disappears into a unity with its object that can be only mystically apprehended? That is not my view. The thought that understands the world would not lose its character as thought because of the magnitude of its object. And as I have said in replying to Mr. Rescher, the link that relates the two embraces both coherence and correspondence.

Mr. Bertocci may complain with some justification that this is not the doctrine of *The Nature of Thought*. There has indeed been a change, and he will want my own statement of the extent of that change. (1) It does *not* consist in any change in the relation I conceive to hold between present thought and the immanent end of all thought. That relation is still conceived to be one of potential to actual, of partially realized to fully realized purpose. The immanent end is rather the ultimate *objective* of the pilgrimage of thought as a whole than in any ordinary sense the *object* of thought. (2) There is some change in my conception of the remote and speculative relation holding between the completed system of thought and its object as the system of reality. I am now more ready to accept correspondence as well as coherence as describing that relation. It is not one of copying or picturing, and so far as it is correspondence, I have not succeeded in analyzing it. (3) The relation of potential to actual that I offered in my first book as the nexus between the idea and its object, in Mr. Bertocci's sense of "the referral object," has been given up except in special cases. My thought of certain colors and perhaps of certain emotions still seems to me essentially an attempt to get the object within consciousness. To apply this doctrine to objects in the physical world, particularly if they are in the past, to say for instance that my idea of the emergence of the earth from the sun is an attempt to identify itself with the object, seems to me now rather a suggestive metaphor than an account to be taken literally.

Skepticism

Mr. Bertocci wants to know whether, and if so to what extent, my theory of knowledge commits me to skepticism. If to know anything as it is requires seeing it in its relation to the whole of things, is not skepticism inevitable? Yes, unfortunately it is. I see no prospect, even if the immense explosion of knowledge that has occurred in the last century should continue until human life becomes extinct on the planet, which also seems inevitable, that the ideal of a universal and integrated knowledge should be achieved. Furthermore, if the truth of our thought varies inversely with the degree of alteration required for incorporation into such knowledge, we shall never know with finality what degree of truth we have achieved, for the criterion would not be in full possession until we reached the end of the road.

But this, after all, is far from being total skepticism. We can see even now that the truth of some of our judgments is affected less than that of others by the context of increasing knowledge. The beliefs of a theologian disciplined in science and philosophy have changed almost beyond recognition from those of his predecessor of a few centuries ago. Our thought of man's place in nature has not been the same since Darwin; our thought of the structure of the human mind has not been the same since Freud. On the other hand we possess some insights into the structure of the world that have been little affected by the increase of knowledge, and may be expected to retain their high stability. The law of noncontradiction seems to be an indispensable part of any logic, and I am not aware that the validity of the multiplication table has been undermined by any additions made to our knowledge. We have no doubt that two stars and two stars made four stars before human life appeared on the planet. As Mr. Bertocci knows, I thoroughly disbelieve in the conventionalist view of such insights; the issue has been argued out in *Reason and Analysis*. I should say, then, that we do possess some highly important and secure knowledge of the nature of things. Even of the entities dealt with by the physicist we are not quite committed to skepticism. When I talk about my desk, I am not sure whether Mr. Bertocci would take as my "referral object" the desk I have described as a construction of common sense or the physical desk of the scientist. If it is the latter, we must grant that our knowledge of it is meager, and since we cannot make direct contact with it, is likely to remain so. But, as Russell has pointed out, if we admit distinguishable causal lines leading from parts of the physical thing to parts of the object perceived, we can form isomorphic theories that can be largely confirmed by predicting what will follow in observation if they are true. I hold also that among values we have relatively certain insights; we can see, for example, the greater intrinsic value of some experiences than of others. The argument is stated in *Reason and Goodness*. I do not, therefore, consider myself a skeptic, even though I think that our knowledge is and will probably remain severely limited.

The Self

So far I have been occupied exclusively with the main thrust of Mr. Bertocci's questioning, which concerns epistemic monism and dualism. But in pursuing this inquiry he has raised certain cognate questions too important to be passed over. One of these is a question on which Mr. Bertocci is himself a specialist, and I have little hope of satisfying him with such answer as I can give. Nevertheless I shall give it briefly and, as is unavoidable, somewhat dogmatically. Mr. Bertocci repeatedly notes that I use such phrases as "I think," "I desire," "I remember," and he wants to know what I mean by that "I." In short, what is my theory of the self?

First, let me dismiss some well-known theories that I do *not* accept. I cannot accept any theory that would place the self outside the field of consciousness. The self is not a pure ego, an atom, a monad, that accompanies and owns a series of experiences but is distinct from them and may precede or outlast them. Nor is it a substance in which experiences inhere but which never puts in an appearance among them—for example the "something I know not what" of Locke. The self is not the *Selbst-an-sich* of Kant, which is an unknowable outside the phenomenal order. All these are rather attempts to explain the unity of the varied experiences that appear simultaneously in the conscious field and the continuity that holds the successive experiences together. But we do not and cannot know what these selves are or how they operate; they do not explain; they are scarcely more than nods in the direction of an explanation, like the famous account of why a pill puts one to sleep: it has dormitive powers. Hume was right, I think, in insisting that the self must be found in the stream of consciousness or nowhere, though his inventory of the contents of that stream was lamentably limited. Bradley's suggestion that the self falls within the field but is that part only which is unobjectified would leave out of the self that which seems most obviously part of it, the brightly illuminated focus of sensation, idea, and desire. The self is not a fragment of the field, above all not a peripheral or subliminal part of it.

Subject to a qualification shortly to be made, the I of the present moment is the field of consciousness connected with the body I call mine. It includes a vast number of assorted items—percepts of rows of books, the pens, calendar, and sheets of paper distributed on my desk, and concentric circles of dimmer percepts fading out toward the limits of the field of vision. There is the persistent bodily coenaesthesia that is always present in waking life. There is the controlling interest, namely in the self, that now dominates my thought, and passing interests in other things that carry my thought from time to time away on vagrant courses. The items in the field are unified in a unique way which James and Bergson have described in masterly fashion; the components seem almost to interpenetrate each other, and the whole may be suffused by a sunny or somber mood. Does this field exhaust the present self? Hardly, and here comes the qualification. It seems necessary to include dispositions which, though not necessarily present in consciousness at all, may be present as tendencies or incipient impulses to go off on tangents, impulses to hum tunes, to worry about the state of my finances or my health, to think with concern about unanswered letters, to watch with pleasure the gyrations of a squirrel in a tree outside my window, or to remember with sorrow that my old friend X died last week.

Indeed the field of consciousness is not a static field. It is rather a massive stream, as James described it, a stream carrying on its surface many little wavelets of impulse and many larger ones of desire, together with the casual flotsam and jetsam that our environment throws into it. What is it that gives this moving stream its identity? Chiefly memory, which enables us to recognize that much in the stream was present a minute or hour ago, and which may retain the "far away and long ago" with a warmth and vividness that leaves us no doubt of its having been part of our earlier self. (I agree, however, with Mr. Penelhum in his article on "Personal Identity" in the *Encyclopedia of Philosophy* that any sure test of the sameness of the person must call in bodily identity to supplement memory.) A main source of continuity lies in the conative and purposive character of the self, the fact that it is virtually a bundle of impulses seeking realization. In each of us there are impulses to love, to flee from danger, to fight, to associate with our fellows and influence them, to construct things, to acquire things, to know. Of all these—and there are many more—the most important is the impulse to know, for it is through the exercise of this impulse that we set before ourselves the ends of all our impulses. The impulses, drives, or desires of human nature are distinguished by their ends, and the stream of consciousness of a given moment *is* a partial realization of a set of ends.

The I or self, then, is for me a stream of consciousness whose direction is fixed by a group of drives, partly native, partly acquired, which are themselves enhanced or inhibited by success or failure and supplied with defined goals by thought operating within desire. Though the cognitive drive seems to me the most important, I cannot single out anything within the stream or anything outside or below it that can be identified with the self. There are changes in the direction of my attention, changes in the closeness of my observation and in the intensity of my interest, that seem introspectively to be volitions issuing from some central citadel, but these can be explained more cogently by other conscious or subconscious factors, many of which can themselves be caught introspectively. All this, I fear, will be pretty unsatisfactory to Mr. Bertocci. But for the moment I can find no better way of sketching what H. D. Lewis has so appropriately called "the elusive self."

Error

There is another issue that rises insistently in the concluding pages of Mr. Bertocci's paper, namely the way I deal with error. In the course of my struggle in *The Nature of Thought* to develop a viable theory of the relation between idea and object, I proposed to take that relation as one between potential and actual. The idea was essentially a purpose to identify itself with its object. The ground for this theory was my conviction that neither subjectivism nor realism was tenable, and that a middle position must be found. But Mr. Bertocci points out quite rightly that what he calls the "referral object" may be so different from the idea of it that to describe the object as what the idea is seeking to become, or the idea as the object *in posse,* is to border on the absurd. I agree with him, and, as indicated in one or two other of these replies, I no longer hold this theory as stated in my first book. The chief reason for giving it up was my doubt whether the entities of modern physical science could be reasonably described as mental. If they could not, the notion that an idea could become identical with them by self-development seemed no longer plausible.

But the larger theory of which this formed a part still seems to me sound. Let me try to make this clear. I accept Bradley's later view that there are no floating ideas, that every idea forms a component in a judgment. Now every judgment falls within what I have called the cognitive drive or the theoretic impulse in human nature. That is a drive toward understanding the world, and it would achieve this fulfillment only when complete comprehension were attained. In such comprehension the "referral object" would for the first time be fully known. Thus if we mean by "the object" the referral object, and describe the ultimate aim of thought as its "objective," it will remain true that only by fulfilling the potentiality of thought through attaining its last objective shall we ever see the object of thought as it is. If it is replied that even so thought would not become identical with its object, I grant this. I cannot agree with Bradley that thought and its object "somehow" become one in the absolute.

I do think, however, that seeing the relation of thought and its object in this light goes far toward explaining the nature of error. For error is the byproduct of our "broken rationality," as Plato has it, or, to put it more specifically, it is an inference gone wrong. Descartes charged all error to a defect of will, an impatient acceptance of something as true before we had taken the pains to see the truth clearly and distinctly. This was at least a move in the right direction. To reflect is to attempt to see something in the light of its grounds or consequences or both. Error occurs when these grounds or consequences are wrongly used. Take the examples that Mr. Bertocci cites. "The budding sapling yonder is a maple"; but it turns out to be really an oak. Why did you take it for a maple? Judgments do not issue out of a vacuum. You saw something in the tree, perhaps its shape as a whole, perhaps the angle or the height at which the branches left the trunk, from which you drew the suggestion "maple," though the inference proved unwarranted. What you saw was not a set of true marks of the maple; perhaps you did not observe them carefully enough; perhaps you did not know the true marks at all, but were moved by someone's remark that maples were the commonest tree hereabout. Given the data before you, which were insecurely hazy, and given the psychological pressures working on you consciously or subconsciously, you could be pushed in a dozen directions besides the correct one. Descartes therefore was essentially in the right, even though he overestimated our power to resist deflecting influences. We err because we draw from the data before us, and under nonrational pressure, inferences that do not follow.

The other example Mr. Bertocci cites may be dealt with in the same way. "The Persians defeated the Greeks at the battle of Plataea." The truth is, of course, the other way about; the Greeks defeated the Persians. The error consists in a discrepancy between the fact and what one judges to be the fact; but how did the error come about? One is not, as in the other case, making a perceptual judgment, but a judgment it clearly is, and it is made from some ground which one must have misused. One has perhaps read that the Persians destroyed Plataea in B.C. 480 and inferred that this *was* the battle, though that occurred a year later. Or one may know that in the Graeco-Persian struggle the Greeks were not always successful, and remembering that Marathon, Salamis, and other engagements were Greek victories, think that Plataea was probably one of the defeats. Some clue or other has been misconstrued.

Mr. Bertocci's objection is that the referral object cannot generally be described as the fulfillment or realization of the idea. I am conceding that he is right. While granting, however, that my thought of the moment is not the potentiality of the referral object, I think I can still consistently hold that it is the potentiality of the metaphysical object. For my thought is seeking an end which, if obtained, would reveal the true nature of both the tree and the battle by placing both in their full context of relations. And this would provide the truth about two objects at once, one about the referral object, the other about the metaphysical object. The referral object in these cases is presumably what an observer on our level would experience if he were placed at a point of vantage for his observation. But even this kind of observation would not give him the ultimate truth about the object, but only carry him nearer to it. Such truth *would* be provided in the completed understanding that forms the fulfillment of the cognitive impulse. Error in all cases is due to our imperfect rationality, to inferences improperly grounded or nonrationally diverted. Of course this imperfection is a flaw that runs deep in human nature, and the consummation that would remove it is hardly to be hoped for in any finite future.

I must strike another note in conclusion. *The Nature of Thought* appeared at a most unpropitious time. It was published in England in the fall of 1939 and in the United States a few months later. World War II had just broken out, and people's minds were naturally and anxiously engaged elsewhere. The book was little noticed on either side of the water. But like everything else in philosophy, it fell under the eye of Edgar Brightman, Mr. Bertocci's predecessor in the Bowne chair at Boston University, who read it, thought well of it, and brought it to the notice of his students. Fortunately for me, Mr. Bertocci inherited his interest as well as his chair, and this interest, both critical and sympathetic, together with his examination of my work in many classes of Boston students, has been a source of constant encouragement to me. It is a pleasure to add this note of gratitude.

16 UNDERSTANDING AS SEEING TO BE NECESSARY
Charles Hartshorne

M Y basic comment on the doctrine implied by the title will be, "To understand is not necessarily or in all cases to see to be necessary." But first I want to make clear that I think there is a large class of cases to which the doctrine correctly applies and in this application expresses an important and often neglected truth.

The class of cases in which intelligibility is necessity includes most obviously abstract necessities, such as those of arithmetic or formal logic. To understand "greater than" or "implies" is to see that these relations are *necessarily* transitive.

Much less obviously but truly, the dictum applies to certain classes of temporal-causal relations. Hume, we know, denied this. But (to mention only one of his oversights) he did not sufficiently distinguish between relations of antecedent causal conditions to subsequent results or outcomes, and the reverse relations. Conditions are in principle knowable from results far more than results from conditions. From a tree stump much of the history of the tree is inferable. By contrast, from a seedling comparatively little about the future of the tree follows, upon any biological laws known to us. One may attribute this to our ignorance. And it is true that, although physics suggests (since Heisenberg, and indeed since Maxwell) that there is an element of chance in nature, it does not in any clear way support the biological analogy I have just used. Competent physicists, some of them to their dissatisfaction and puzzlement, fail to find a clear indication of asymmetry, of time's arrow, in known laws. So Brand Blanshard seems to have a plausible ground for holding that we must choose between a lack of necessity in either direction—later to earlier, earlier to later—or a necessity both ways. I find both of these options most unattractive, and hence cannot believe that physics in its present state gives us the literal truth about the world process.

How can we argue this issue? I first wish to make clear that symmetrical necessity is not universal even in the abstract realm and that contingency and necessity are equally at home in this realm. The symmetrical form of necessity is the biconditional, p entails q *and* q entails p. But this is plainly a special case of entailment. Otherwise entailment and equivalence would be the same. What logician finds this a natural way to think? The normal case of entailment is one-way: p entails q but not conversely. In special cases the distinction disappears. Symmetry is always a special case in which difference reduces to zero, at least for some purpose (see chapter 10 of my *Creative Synthesis*).[1] Note that "p and q are equivalent" is an unordered relation compared to the one-way case. For p & q, q & p, it is all the same if the "&" stands for equivalence, but not the same if it stands for entails. Thus the order drops out in the symmetrical case. Were all true propositions equivalent, they would form a totality in which no particular order had any significance. Is this supposition an aid to understanding? I fail utterly to see it.

To grasp that "this is a fox" entails "this is an animal" is a part of understanding the relation of the two propositions. But to see that "this is an animal" does *not* entail "this is a fox" is just as good a part. To understand the conceptual relations, both insights are equally necessary. Contingency is as necessary as necessity!

This does not mean that necessity swallows up and abolishes contingency. Rather (see chapter 6 of *Creative Synthesis*) contingency is the inclusive aspect. It is the contingent specification *fox* that includes *animality,* not the other way. Again, universals must have instances, but the whole point of universal concepts is that, although to grasp them one needs *some* instance, yet given any instance, or set of them, another instance or set would also have done. We understand numerical concepts by considering examples, but the unique features of the particular examples are irrelevant.

I agree with Blanshard that relations to the past are necessary, given a certain present. To be what I am now it was necessary to have the childhood I actually had. But that child might have matured differently and might have been killed before maturing. (It very nearly was, more than once.) This second or nonnecessary aspect is an issue between Blanshard and me. I shall argue the case by showing that the retrospective necessity is intelligible in a way that does not apply to the prospective.

We remember the past. There are claims to foresee the future, but they do not compare with our everyday experience of remembering, at least in frequency of occurrence, even in the most abnormal individuals. But not only do we remember the past, we perceive it. The heard terrestrial explosion took place a little before the hearing, the seen stellar explosion took place a long time before the seeing. Whitehead has given metaphysical grounds for generalizing this. Peirce had similar views. All experience, it may for definite reasons be held, has previous events as its data. Hence to say that an experience could have been the same had the data been otherwise is to say that there are no data. (Obviously experiencing x differs from not experiencing x.) And Hume in fact never tells us what it is to experience something. His impressions are either experiences of nothing, or somethings that are not experienced. Experience is a relative term, whereas Hume treats it as standing for an absolute, something which could be what it is no matter what else there was or was not. True, Hume pluralizes the absolute, but that does not get rid of the absurdity.

Another step: in some cases at least the past is the experienced; either this does or does not give the very meaning of "past." A great simplification of problems, if nothing else, results if we can take the affirmative option. One must, with Leibniz, Whitehead, Bergson, and Peirce (in some passages), admit that most of the data of experience are not accessible to conscious introspection. But since one can define deity (in one of many equivalent ways) as infinite introspective power, it may not be so shocking to say that we lack such unqualified power of self-knowledge. So I hold: the entire past is given (though not known) to man and all creatures, and therefore it is necessary to the reality of the present.

Is the future equally given and necessary? Apart from special claims to precognition there seems no serious ground for affirming this. And for many reasons, some of them suggested above, it is reasonable to hold that becoming is freely creative rather than deterministic.

As has often, but not often enough, been pointed out, the standard expression "necessary and sufficient condition" is a biconditional. For "sufficient," as usually interpreted, means: sufficient to guarantee, necessitate, the outcome. The bland assumption that this symmetry is the universal truth is like the assumption, which almost no formal logician makes, that all conditioning is biconditioning. The opposite extreme, or Hume's position, that there are no necessary connections, at least none that we can know, is like the assumption that all propositions are logically independent of one another. Translated into ontology, we have a choice between the block universe and a chaos of unconnected atoms. Clearly these extremes do not exhaust our options. Just as in logic we have one-way implication, necessity in one direction and contingency in the other, so there is good reason to look for both necessary and contingent connections in reality. In that case the sufficient cause is one that makes what subsequently occurs possible, but does not guarantee it. To the obvious objection that we do often need guaranteed outcomes, the answer is that what we thus need is not what actually happens in its full concreteness, but something more or less abstract. The full concreteness of events is not conceptualizable anyway, and transcends science in principle. We need to predict, not what happens, but whether or not it will involve such abstract features as the bridge falling into the stream, the vehicle reaching the moon, and the like. Always there is a gap between any reasonable prediction and subsequent events.

I salute Blanshard for his long skillful fight against the atomistic, radically pluralistic view, opposite to his monistic view. But I submit that discrediting one extreme is far from justifying the opposite one. Blanshard is not the only philosopher who has seemed somewhat unaware of this point of logic. I believe very deeply that the golden mean ideal fits immensely more cases than Aristotle realized. Mere pluralism, mere monism; mere contingency, mere necessity; these are not forced options.

I anticipate some of Blanshard's probable forms of reply. He may say that ethical responsibility implies strict determinism. He may say that the ideal of science is entirely deterministic. I hold that both of these statements are overstatements, that a reasonably qualified or limited determinism is all that either ethics or science needs, or even can genuinely use. But I have argued these matters elsewhere at such length that I do not wish to repeat the arguments here.

Blanshard accepts the contention of Bradley that likenesses and differences must be internal or necessary relations. If A resembles B in a certain respect, neither could be what they are did this relation not obtain. Well, I resemble Shakespeare in having something like the feeling he expressed in, "We are such stuff as dreams are made on/and our little life is rounded with a sleep." (I have this feeling partly because Shakespeare wrote these lines.) Did this relation obtain when Shakespeare was alive? I hold that it did not, for there was then no such entity as Charles Hartshorne, and no relations to that entity either. You may object that I was already a part of the total universe, the inclusive whole in which, according to Blanshard, everything has its necessary place. But this way of conceiving the total or inclusive reality, or "all that is," "the universe," "the truth," begs a principal question of metaphysics. According to process philosophers there is no cosmic totality, complete once for all, of all events and all things, but instead a new totality, with partly new constituents, and a new inclusive truth, with every new instance of creative becoming. If so, expressions like "the universe" or "what exists" mean the present universe, or "what exists now," or still better, "what has happened up to now." The argument from the internality of likeness presupposes the resolution of this issue in favor of the anticreationist view. Over and over I seem to find Blanshard not even envisaging the theory that creativity is the most concrete aspect of reality. On this point I never cease to admire Lequier, Bergson, Peirce, James, and Whitehead, who, knowing what they were doing, eloquently defended the creationist view. (It should be added that Blanshard is a worthy and eloquent defender of the opposing conception.)

That truth is timeless is a familiar doctrine held by some distinguished logicians. However, Peirce and Whitehead took the other side, and among more recent or contemporary logicians Prior and Storrs McCall have shown how it can be formalized.[2] Also some intuitionists have defended the doctrine that the partial indeterminacy of the future must be taken into account in logic. I am rather happy to be in such company.

My likenesses and differences from Shakespeare are indeed (here Blanshard is nobly right against a fashionable doctrine) aspects of my nature, some of them vividly so, but not even in the depths of his unconscious was relation to me, or to the reader of this essay, anything at all for the poet of Avon. So a creationist believes. I freely grant that an opponent could, with some plausibility, appeal to reported cases of precognition as counterinstances. But this topic also I do not wish here to investigate.

Blanshard says that, although necessity holds strictly in all directions, this does not prevent us from knowing what is important for a given purpose about an item without knowing all other items. Everything makes a difference, but not everything makes a great difference, to a given item. However, I hold that this subtly begs the question. For when we distinguish the important from the unimportant difference, we presuppose contingency. "Had X been different Y would be sufficiently the same as it is, but had Z been different, Y would not have been sufficiently the same." But talk about what *would have been if* makes sense only because of contingency. If X could not possibly have been different, how can talk about this impossibility be relevant? If all truth is mutually, symmetrically, implicative, then alternatives to what is actually true are absurdities. And the respect in which Y would be the same in the two cases repeats the problem: is it sufficiently the same respect, the same universal, in two mutually exclusive cases? Either we have a vicious regress or I do not know what is going on. Incidentally, I do not in the least accept Blanshard's equation of a particular with a set of universals. And it seems to me an oddity in a doctrine of universal necessity. I prefer Spinoza at this point.

Blanshard is in some sense an idealist. To be is to be perceived. And indeed if everything depends upon everything else, everything depends upon my present perception. I agree that everything depends upon perception, but not that (if it is a past event or system of past events) it depends upon being perceived by me, or any particular set of actual perceivers. A different set would have done. (Even God as the necessary perceiver of all is no *particular* perceiver—as I have explained elsewhere.[3])

The basic role of one-way dependence appears in connection with at least six important ideas: implication or entailment, inclusion, universality vs. particularity, causality, experience as remembering or perceiving, and deity. If p *implies* q, it is not normally the case that q implies p, that the two propositions are equivalent. If X *includes* Y, Y does not normally include or necessarily depend upon X. A whole could not be what it concretely is, lacking a single part or constituent, but—except in the special case of organic wholes, whose analysis, I have tried to show elsewhere, is into one-way relations between events—entities may become constituents of new wholes without any internal change whatever. The letter pair XY cannot appear anywhere without X appearing there, but X may appear by itself. (Hume missed this only because he assumed absolute simplicity for the final constituents of the world, a view Wittgenstein came rightly to reject.) We mean by a *universal* precisely something which is independent of particular instances, but not conversely. Whiteness can be without this white paper, the number two can be without my two eyes. But the paper and the eyes cannot be if whiteness and two are not. To *remember* or *perceive* is to depend for one's experience upon antecedent events, which it is too late to influence. Events have antecedent *causal conditions* and depend upon them, but not vice versa (according to our natural causal idea, perverted by thinkers wittingly or unwittingly distorting the meaning of that idea). The tree depends upon the soil in which its seed sprouted, but that soil as it then was did not depend upon the tree as it now is. And "God" refers to the (nonparticular but still individual) being upon whose existence all particular existence depends, but not vice versa. (God may depend upon particular creatures for some of his qualities, and indeed I hold that God and the creatures form an organic whole. But this is God not merely as barely existing, with his essential properties of unsurpassability by another and the like, but God as dealing with the particular world that does exist. With another world God would still have been God, though with concretely different experiences or states. Thus symmetrical interaction and one-way dependence are both involved, as in relations between individuals generally.) The full account of the foregoing, I hold, is possible only by making unit-events, rather than unit-substances, the final terms of analysis.

When Hume said that what is distinguishable is (symmetrically) separable, he proved that he did not know or had forgotten what implication, inclusion, universality, causality, experience, or deity might be. And when Bradley held that relations, so far as real, must be (symmetrically) internal (internal at both ends), he showed the same thing.

I hope that my airy dogmatism will be forgiven. The floor is Mr. Blanshard's.

CHARLES HARTSHORNE

DEPARTMENT OF PHILOSOPHY
UNIVERSITY OF TEXAS

NOTES

[1] *Creative Synthesis and Philosophic Method* (La Salle, Ill.: Open Court, 1970).

[2] Arthur N. Prior, *Past, Present and Future* (Oxford: Clarendon Press, 1967), 113–36, 172. Also Storrs McCall, "Time and Physical Modalities," *The Monist* 53, no. 3 (1969): 426–46.

[3] See my *Anselm's Discovery* (La Salle: Open Court, 1965), 124.

16. Reply to Charles Hartshorne

Understanding as Seeing to Be Necessary

One-Way Necessity

Mr. Hartshorne holds that my philosophy is flawed by one large and rather obvious mistake. When faced by the two extremes of atomism and monism, I have elected one of the extremes, monism, rather than steered a middle course between them. As against atomism, he is on my side. He thinks it absurd to say that *nothing* is necessarily connected with *anything* else. But he thinks it equally absurd to say that *everything* is connected necessarily with *everything* else. A monism so extreme has little or no plausibility.

What has led me to accept this improbable view? Apparently a simple oversight about entailment and causality. Take any two facts or events, A and B. What I am suggesting is that A entails B and that B entails A, because if A were different B would have to be different, and if B were different A would have to be different. But that overlooks the fact that entailment is normally a one-way relation. "P entails q" does not entail "q entails p." If being a fox entails being a mammal, that does not entail a mammal's being a fox. From the hypothetical judgment, "if A is B, C is D," you can, by affirming the antecedent, derive the consequent, but you cannot, by affirming the consequent, derive the antecedent. If A has sat at an open window and in consequence caught cold, you cannot argue that when he again catches cold it must be because he sat at an open window, for colds are produced by various causes. In short, A's necessitating B is normally a nonreciprocating relation.

Mr. Hartshorne points out that a favorite argument of mine for monism is to show that everything is connected causally with everything else. A storm on the sun, to be sure, is not directly connected causally with anything happening on earth during the next eight minutes, for no cause travels faster than light. But the two events are connected indirectly nevertheless, for the present storm is linked by a causal chain with the upheavals on the sun at the time it threw off the earth, and that event started chains of events that have had their influence upon everything happening on earth today. Mr. Hartshorne demurs at this arguing both ways along the lines of causation. "Conditions are in principle knowable from results far more than results from conditions. From a tree stump much of the history of the tree is inferable. By contrast, from a seedling comparatively little about the future of the tree follows, upon any biological laws known to us. One may attribute this to our ignorance. . . . So Brand Blanshard seems to have a plausible ground for holding that we must choose between a lack of necessity in either direction—later to earlier, earlier to later—or a necessity both ways. I find both of these options most unattractive." Mr. Hartshorne opts for a necessity backward but not forward. "I agree with Blanshard that relations to the past are necessary, given a certain present. To be what I am now it was necessary to have the childhood I actually had. But that child might have matured differently and might have been killed before maturing."

I cannot accept this view of causality. It seems to say that, looking back from the present, I can see that this present is determined, but that looking forward from it, I can see that my future is not determined. But if, when I look back an hour later, I can see that the apparently free decision and the events that followed it *were* determined, I am left with a contradiction on my hands. Retrospective determination and prospective freedom are not both possible if applied to the same events. I cannot accept both accounts, and if I must choose, it is surely the determinist account based on memory that is the better informed, since both causes and effects are there laid out before me, while in looking forward from the present, so much is veiled. It may be recalled that Sir Francis Galton once characteristically attempted to deal with the issue of determinism empirically. He noted in his diary decisions that at the time of making felt perfectly free, and then after a short interval (perhaps at the end of each day), tried to recapture the situation that had existed just before each decision. It was so easy to bring to light pressures of which he took no conscious thought in making the decisions that he adopted a determinist conclusion. Of course determinism, like indeterminism, admits of no empirical *proof,* but the conclusion becomes harder to resist the more the empirical evidence is studied. It is worth remembering that such archempiricists as Hume and Mill were both determinists.

But the issue that Mr. Hartshorne is pressing here is somewhat different; it is whether or not the causal relation is reciprocating. If, given A, B must happen, may I also say that given B, A must have happened? And if I say that given B, A must have happened, may I say that given A, B must happen? Mr. Hartshorne, as I understand him, accepts the former and denies the latter. He therefore denies that the causal relation is reciprocating; one cannot argue with necessity in both directions.

Two-Way Necessity

He refers here to the analogy of formal logic, in which from affirmation of the antecedent you may affirm the consequent, but not vice versa. Formal logic, however, has nothing to say about the meaning of causality. The real authorities, if there are any, are the philosophical logicians, such logicians, to name a few only, as Joseph and Joachim, Bradley and Bosanquet. I would recommend to Mr. Hartshorne Joseph's admirable chapter on non-reciprocating causal relations, in which he explains why, though there are no such things, we should have come to believe there are. Again, I agree with Joachim that "scientific thinking endeavours to eliminate, from the contents which enter into its judgements, all matter irrelevant to the necessary nexus which they affirm. . . . It moves towards a formulation in which the two contents are so purified that each necessarily involves the other . . ." (*The Nature of Truth*, 86). "The given fact, if you will look at it," says Bradley, "contains the aspect of 'A before B' and of 'B after A' each at once and in one. And the presence here of but a single 'asymmetrical' relation is an assumption which to me is monstrous" (*The Principles of Logic*, 2d ed., 2:697).[1] Bosanquet put the same doctrine less belligerently. "Every B that is conditioned by A is the condition of A being such as to condition B, i.e. of A being what A is; and if the being of A were wholly relevant to B, this would be equivalent to saying that the existence of B involves the existence of A. In other words, if there is nothing in A beyond what is necessary to B, then B involves A just as much as A involves B" (*Logic*, 2d ed., 1:248).[2]

Though it is reassuring to have names like these on one's side, no question of philosophy is to be settled by authority. And I should have thought it plain enough that the end which thought has constantly in mind as it analyzes the causal nexus is reciprocity. Mill's "plurality of causes" and "intermixture of effects" are natural halting places on the road, but they are surely not the end of the road. When one wants to drive a nail, there are many things that will do in lieu of a hammer: a stone or the back of a wrench or a piece of lead pipe. But this does not mean that for the sinking of a nail there is a true plurality of causes; what sinks it is something common to all these "causes," the application in a certain direction of a certain amount of force. The main value of Mill's "methods" is precisely to pare away irrelevancies, to show that since the result can occur without the use in particular of a hammer, a stone, a wrench, or a pipe, none of these things as such is the cause, though each may serve as the vehicle of the cause. Similarly of what Mill calls the "intermixture," and Joseph more happily the "diversity of effects." The same dose of penicillin, administered to different persons, produces very different effects; so we are justified, when we speak practically, in saying that the same dosage of the same drug has a diversity of effects. But we forget that if there are included in the cause, as strictness would require, all the conditions that affect the result, then we are *not* applying the same cause, for what produces the result in one case is penicillin plus, say, organic allergies in the patient, and in another the drug without the allergies. Now the object of these parings away and fillings in is to eliminate irrelevancies and get the connection pure;

and they are all based on the assumption that if we do get the connection pure we shall have a law that holds without exceptions. It is obvious that with such a law we could argue with equal certainty from cause to effect and from effect to cause.

The case, it may be held, is otherwise in formal logic. In his able book *Creative Synthesis and Philosophic Method*, Mr. Hartshorne has a chapter on "The Prejudice in Favor of Symmetry" in which he maintains that the standard form of necessary reasoning approved in formal logic is a one-way rather than two-way inference, and that reciprocity is a departure from that norm. This raises too large an issue to be dealt with in passing, and if I did enter upon it, it would not be through the Russell-Whitehead logic, in which "implication" has little relation to its ordinary meaning; it is defined as "either p is false or q is true." In such a logic a proposition may imply another where there is no apparent connection between them at all; "the cat is on the mat" implies "Hannibal committed suicide"; and to crown the absurdity, such logic would say that this nonrelation runs both ways. But it may be worth pausing for a moment to see that at least in many cases where traditional formal logic insists that necessity is irreversible, it is nevertheless reversible if one looks below the surface. Perhaps the logical form that seems most obviously one-way is that of the hypothetical syllogism, whose well-known law is that from an affirmation of the antecedent you may affirm the consequent, but not vice versa, and that from a denial of the consequent you may deny the antecedent, but again not vice versa. But it is easy to offer examples of perfectly valid reasoning in which both these rules are broken at once: "If a triangle has three sides equal, it is equiangular." Here the necessity is clearly reciprocal. One can argue with equal propriety from denying the antecedent or affirming the consequent on the one hand and from affirming the antecedent or denying the consequent on the other. The reason is that the triangle forms a little system of its own in which one can see that the two properties of equality of sides and equality of angles are necessary to each other. These little systems are not present only exceptionally and rarely, even in the hypothetical syllogism; I should say that they are the standard basis of such inference. "If the moon rotates exactly once in the period of its revolution round the earth, it will continue to show the same side to the earth." Get the little system of relations between earth and moon clearly in mind, and one can see that the identity of the periods of rotation and revolution is not only the condition of the moon's presenting the same face, but that it is the unique condition, and therefore that one may argue in either direction. Much depends, as in causal argument, upon the purity of the apprehended connection, that is, on the absence of irrelevancies. "If this patient has scarlet fever, he will show a red rash." Scarlet fever is an interconnected set of changes in the organism which would enable us with sufficient knowledge to argue from one to another in either direction. Is the above judgment true? Not quite, I find from Sir William Osler's *Principles and Practice of Medicine,* for both rubella and puerperal scarlatina may show a rash so similar to that of scarlet fever as to be practically indistinguishable from it. It is therefore unsafe to take the rash alone as diagnostic. It should therefore be taken in conjunction with certain other symptoms. "McCollom lays stress upon the appearance of a punctate eruption in the arm pits, groins, and on the roof of the mouth as positive proof of scarlet fever" (op. cit., 8th ed., 335). The system of symptoms constituting the disease is less than perfectly known, but if to the rash these other symptoms are added, the inference is universal and reciprocal. Not only does scarlet fever necessarily display these symptoms; these symptoms display reliably the presence of the disease. Every diagnosis, even the safest, is a technically illicit argument from affirmation of the consequent.

Formal logic is supposed to supply the most general conditions of arriving at truth through reasoning, and if it loses sight of this end, as it often has, it becomes frivolous. As an organum for finding truth, it may easily lead one astray, as we have seen of the hypothetical syllogism. I am inclined to think that if we carried our analysis through to the end, we should find in all hypothetical reasoning a case of reciprocal necessity or, if not that, a more or less impure approximation to it. I am inclined to think also, as Mr. Hartshorne justly suspects, that my heresy would not stop there. If our thought were wholly clear and exact, should we not find all necessary reasoning to be reciprocal? I do not know, but at least the "prejudice" in favor of symmetry does not stand in my own mind for a prejudice at all. It stands for an ideal, an ideal seldom realized in commonsense thought, frequently approximated in logical and scientific thought, always exerting its immanent pressure within the logical sense.

Mr. Hartshorne contemplates ruefully the "block universe" in which his well-meaning but misguided colleague Blanshard lives. But to Blanshard, his Spinozism seems not an abnormality but the natural outgrowth of commonplace reflection. Start anywhere. Start from a pebble on the beach. It has a shape of its own, which probably differs, if considered minutely, from that of every other pebble in existence. These differences are internal and necessary relations, for unless the pebble possessed them, it would not be the pebble it is. Again that shape has a place in geometry; it has relations both within and without, which if formally stated and developed would involve the whole of geometry and an inexhaustible number of geometrical relations between itself and other existent things; these relations are necessary too. Look at the pebble in relation to the past. It marks the convergence of lines of causation, millenniums long, which determine every detail of its being. Look at it in relation to its present environment. It exercises a reciprocated gravitational influence on every other pebble on the beach of every ocean, and an influence, similarly reciprocated, on all the fixed stars. It seems to me that without going further in this catalogue of determinations we can see that this pebble is no island. In a sense the whole universe is engaged in forming it, in polishing it, in determining its smallest roll in response to the incoming wavelet. If that is living in a block universe, I fear it has no escape.

All that has been said so far has gone on the assumption that Mr. Hartshorne presents to me at the outset, that a block universe is bound together by cords of a necessity that runs both ways. But is this assumption true? Suppose that all the necessities converging on the cribbed and cabined pebble were one-way determinations, would that release it from the relentless grip that holds and moulds it? I do not see that it would. It is true that the question Why? would no longer be universally answerable and that the completeness of understanding that philosophy aims at would have to be abandoned as its goal; but that would not yield by itself the contingency that Mr. Hartshorne seems to desire. Indeed he seems at times to admit this. ". . . I hold: the entire past is given (though not known) to man and all creatures, and therefore it is necessary to the reality of the present." Presumably the same could be said of any future present. If so, then the world which is a flux for the process philosophy is a flux in which every breath of air, every darting of a star or an idea is mandated by the past. To say that past futures have been so mandated but that future futures are not seems to me incoherent. And even a world governed by one-way necessity cannot afford inconsistency.

Obiter Dicta

In the course of his main argument, Mr. Hartshorne makes a number of interesting observations which, though he could not develop them in so closely packed a paper, serve to mark the divergence of our positions and to admit of useful comment. They are of varying degrees of importance.

(1) Mr. Hartshorne remarks that "the full concreteness of events is not conceptualizable" and that it "transcends science in principle. . . . Always there is a gap between any reasonable prediction and subsequent events." It is true that the properties even of a pebble are beyond exhausting, and so too are the laws governing those properties. But when it is said that a knowledge of either would "transcend science in principle," I am not clear what is meant. If it means that the properties and their appropriate laws are so numerous that we shall never in practice overtake them, I agree. But if it means that there is a line up to which we shall find the attributes of the pebble governed by law but beyond which our search would be flouted, I do not know how or where this line would be drawn. I do not think Mr. Hartshorne has in mind here the Heisenberg principle; but if he has, it may be pointed out that physicists are still divided on what exactly this principle implies, and that it is too early to leap to a suspension of causality in the subatomic realm.

Again, if "transcending science" means that below all the attributes of a thing there is an "it" that owns the properties but is itself completely characterless, I should not only question the existence of any such will-o'-the-wisp, but add that if it did exist it would be unknowable, since knowledge proceeds through the connecting of characters. The attempt to characterize or to predicate fully remains always incomplete and always more or less flouted, but I see no reason to believe that this is because of the fickleness or lawlessness of nature. It is rather because of our invincible ignorance.

(2) I am inclined to hold that everything is connected by the relation of difference to everything else, and that since this relation is necessary everything is necessarily so connected. Mr. Hartshorne replies that when Shakespeare was alive he was not related by this difference to Charles Hartshorne because Charles did not then exist. But I do not think that a doctrine of internal relations need limit itself to the physically existent. Charles Hartshorne, with all his encyclopedic knowledge of birdcalls, was in 1600 a future possibility with its causal foundations already actually laid. A mind sufficiently powerful—that of the traditional Christian God, for example—could have foreseen him in detail. And Shakespeare was in 1600 different from that theoretically foreseeable figure in this respect and in that. And who can deny that without these differences he would not have been the man that he was?

(3) This raises the question of the relation of the actual to the possible. My own doctrine is simply stated. If whatever is is necessary, then at any given time only the actual is possible. To say that what existed a moment ago is the sufficient condition of what is happening now, and yet that what is happening now might have been otherwise, is self-contradictory, for a sufficient cause is one which is not only necessary to the effect but in which nothing thus necessary is absent. To suggest that it may rain in New Haven tomorrow is to suggest what is either necessary or impossible.

Does this mean that the language of "may" and "might" is meaningless? Not at all. It is perfectly legitimate, given the knowledge that we have, to say that it may rain tomorrow. But the statement is then about the extent of what we know. "It may rain tomorrow" means "I know that some of the conditions producing rain exist, but not that all of them do, and I know of no condition that would preclude rain." "If Booth had missed Lincoln, reconstruction would have been much hastened." For a metaphysical monist to argue in this way with full responsibility is no easy matter. For to take responsibly the supposition of Booth's having missed Lincoln would involve denying the conditions that led to his succeeding; these conditions ramify out over an indefinitely large area; and who knows what would have happened if the conditions had departed so widely from the actual? One is reminded of the difference between Russell and Bosanquet over such a proposition as, "If a donkey is Plato, it is a great philosopher." To this formal logic raises no objection. Bosanquet commented that in a world so different as one would be in which a donkey were Plato, one could not say what would follow. "The hypothesis scatters your underlying reality to the winds, and what I should call the basis of implication is gone" (*Logic,* 2:41 and n.). Bosanquet seems to me right.

(4) Mr. Hartshorne thinks that in a world where everything was necessarily connected with everything else it would be idle to talk about any change being more important than any other. "Everything makes a difference, [according to Blanshard,] but not everything makes a great difference, to a given item. However I hold that this subtly begs the question. For when we distinguish the important from the unimportant difference, we presuppose contingency. . . . talk about what *would have been if* makes sense only because of contingency." There is something here that I have failed to follow. I agree that in a completely interconnected world it is extremely hard to determine the amount of difference that any event did make, will make, or might have made. But I see no inconsistency in recognizing degrees in the massiveness or importance of the effects produced. It is not unreasonable, I think, to say that if Churchill had been killed by a bomb in the London blitz it would have made more difference than if Mr. X, the eighty-five-year-old green grocer, had been killed. And I do not see how the admission of either degrees of truth or degrees of importance involves contingency. We say indeed that it was a matter of mere chance, mere luck, that the bomb took Mr. X and not Mr. Churchill, but that surely does not mean that there was any contingency in nature. Relatively to our knowledge it was an accident, but if an accident is an event not governed by causal law, accidents are myths.

"If X could not possibly have been different, how can talk about this impossibility be relevant?" Mr. Hartshorne asks. But scientific men constantly do use it as relevant, permissible, and useful. "What if I had tried streptomycin in that case? The patient might have recovered. I'll bear that in mind in the next such case." Regret may be pertinent about the past, even for the determinist, and efficacious for the future. "If I had served God as diligently as I have done the king, He would not have given me over in my grey hairs"; Wolsey was right to be sorrowful about his faults whether they were inevitable or not. There is an engrossing little book on *The If's of History* by Professor F.J.C. Hearnshaw speculating on what might have happened if—. Suppose that Callimachus, chairman of the Greek Council of War, had voted otherwise when the Council divided five to five on the eve of Marathon on whether to engage the enemy. "On that vote, in all human probability," wrote Sir Edward Creasy, "the destiny of all the nations of the world depended" (*Fifteen Decisive Battles,* 23).[3] Gibbon speculates that but for Charles Martel at Tours, the Moslem call to prayer might today be heard from the minarets of Oxford. We can never be sure what would have happened if what did happen had not happened, but it may be very enlightening to speculate on it, particularly if the argument is carried forward rather than backward. There is some truth in Bolingbroke's "History is philosophy teaching by examples."

(5) ". . . I do not in the least accept Blanshard's equation of a particular with a set of universals." What does Mr. Hartshorne mean by a universal? My own meaning is this: a quality or relation, or a set of qualities in relation, that does or might appear in a diversity of contexts. Let us return to our particular pebble. It has a perfectly specific shape, color, weight, hardness, smoothness, and so on. Could these singly or collectively appear in other contexts? I can hardly conceive that Mr. Hartshorne would deny this. But if so, they are in my sense universals. What is left over when such qualities are exhausted? Existence? But I have confessed that I do not know what a characterless existence means. Perhaps, then, the relations of these qualities to other things. But are not these relations also universals? They too conform to the definition. But if you exhausted the thing's relations to everything else in the universe? Would you not then have something unique and unrepeatable, particular and individual? Yes, you would, for then you have reached the universe, which is unrepeatable by definition. Mr. Hartshorne says that he prefers Spinozism to my doctrine. But I supposed my line to have been essentially Spinozism. There is only one thing in the world that is quite particular, unique, and individual, namely God, Substance, or the Absolute.

(6) "Blanshard is in some sense an idealist. To be is to be perceived." In none of my writings, so far as I know, have I accepted this argument of Berkeley's, and it still seems to me unacceptable. I am an idealist in the sense that I think everything immediately apprehended is mental. I am not an idealist in the sense of supposing that I have some substitute proof that everything is mental. The earth existed before human life appeared on it, but if Berkeley's *esse est percipi* is denied, in whose mind did it exist? In that of Berkeley's God? But there seems to be no good proof that his kind of God himself exists. If someone could prove to me that universals are necessarily mental, I should have a right to the name of idealist. But I know no proof for that either. So I must apparently be content to be a gypsy philosopher, an absolutist and a rationalist but unacceptable in any idealist camp.

I am not so sanguine as to believe that these replies will satisfy Mr. Hartshorne. His criticisms spring directly out of a process philosophy whose roots ramify so widely that to excavate and examine them in detail would run beyond my space, and also, I must add, beyond my competence. Those roots are deeply entangled with Whiteheadianism, and of that philosophy I must confess a rather disgraceful ignorance. In my years at Yale I was surrounded by such hedgerows of Whitehead experts—Northrop, Lawrence, Margenau,

Weiss, Christian, Fitch—that I felt absolved from following their example; I could refer any inquirer to any of them for counsel with far more confidence than I could give it myself. Not that I made no effort to patch my ignorance. I made repeated attempts on *Process and Reality*. But when I sat down before that great work, contemplating its meaning darkly through the glass of that Brobdingnagian terminology, I could not help thinking that the book was long, very long, and that life was fleeting. So I kept deferring my education. I cannot deal with Mr. Hartshorne's work with anything like the intimate knowledge with which he has honored mine. For any injustice that may have sprung from this, I am sorry and ask his pardon.

1. F. H. Bradley, *The Principles of Logic*, 2d ed. rev., 2 vols. (London: Oxford University Press, 1922).

2. Bernard Bosanquet, *Logic; or the Morphology of Knowledge*, 2d ed., 2 vols. (Oxford: Clarendon Press, 1911).

3. E. S. Creasy, *The Fifteen Decisive Battles of the World from Marathon to Waterloo* (New York: A. L. Burt, n.d. [Preface dated 1851]).

17 CREATIVITY IN BRAND BLANSHARD
William S. Minor

THE specific focus of creativity in the philosophy of Brand Blanshard is found in his faithful commitment, during a period of more than a half-century, to *rational thought* as the way toward that ideal and all-comprehensive system which is the ultimate whole, timeless or eternal, self-caused, and intelligible in that all of its parts are not a mere aggregate, but that every part is necessarily connected with every other part. Furthermore, this ideal system is changeless, complete and wholly real. In this commitment, reason is focal as "a drive toward intelligibility under the guidance of the implicit ideal of system" (*Reason and Analysis* [*RA*], 388). At the end of *The Nature of Thought* this commitment is confirmed: ". . . the writer would like to think that the insistent and reiterated emphasis, maintained throughout this work, on the membership of minds in one intelligible order may serve, however minutely, to confirm the belief in a common reason, and the hope and faith that in the end it will prevail" (*The Nature of Thought* [*NT*], 2:520).

Blanshard's commitment to reason has been made and maintained in the context of massive opposition to it. Not only has he been aware of the opposition but he has addressed it analytically and critically, as in *Reason and Analysis*, where he says, "The purpose of this book is to inquire whether the revolt against reason has made out its case" (*RA*, 49). He sees *movements* against reason which "have little in common except the object of their dislike" (48). He makes a summary statement, at the close of his introductory chapter, of the "replacements for reason" by these movements:

> In philosophy, the appeal is commonly from reason to convention, perception or practical consequences; in theology it is to revelation; in psychology to the requirements of our instinctive nature; in sociology to men's diverse feelings and desires; in politics to the demands of class or nation; in art to a taste disburdened of principle. But on this they are united, that they must reject the pretensions of any reason which would hand down canons of necessary and universal validity. [*RA*, 48]

Both popular and scholarly articles now appear which not only confirm Blanshard's earlier critical analysis of the revolt against reason but also indicate its increasing range and intensity. Melvin Maddocks's essay in *Time* magazine entitled "The New Cult of Madness: Thinking As a Bad Habit," clearly indicates the trend. In this article, *The Thinker*, in cartoon form, ". . . sits slumped at the end of a labyrinth of drunkenly tilting stakes. His eyes stare out of focus in the general direction of his knees. His forehead wears its frown like a cross." This forlorn figure says: "I will review my thoughts just once more." His thinking "seems less and less likely to solve his problems." Even worse, "thinking seems to have become the problem."[1]

Maddocks documents with excellence of form and content both historic and current trends in the revolt against reason. He sees no age as "a true Age of Reason," in which "everything makes sense," but he observes that "we have become the first people to proclaim their age as the Age of Unreason." "Reason" and "logic" as death words are replaced by life words, "feeling" and "impulse." The irrational becomes more interesting than the rational. "Madness threatens to become the fashion in the arts." The theater of the absurd is used to illustrate the fact that one no longer bothers to speak of it "as if it were an exotic fringe entity." The new cult of madness exceeds the judgment of Nietzsche who said: "All that is now called culture, education, civilization, will one day have to appear before the incorruptible judge, Dionysus" ("New Cult," 100).

In the conclusion of his essay, which vivifies this current revolt, Mr. Maddocks suggests that "the time is coming when judgment must be passed on the Dionysiacs themselves." He shares with unique insight what he thinks this judgment will be:

> The irony is that as absolutes, Reason and Unreason commit the same mistake. The ideology of Reason was an attempt to escape human complexity by rising above it. The ideology of madness is an attempt to escape by plunging beneath it. . . . What the Madness Revolution finally demonstrates is that man cannot even go mad without organizing committees and writing books about it—without sitting down and repeating, God help us, 'I will review my thoughts just once more' ("New Cult," 100).

In the context of this massive revolt, the philosophical works of Brand Blanshard clearly stand forth as a refusal to compromise with the ideology of madness in its attempt to escape the complexity of man by plunging beneath it. Yet, in some sense, Blanshard's ideology of reason is an attempt, perhaps involuntarily and even unconsciously, to escape the complexity of man by rising above it. In this essay we shall project and examine that hypothesis.

In pursuing our study of creativity in the rationalistic philosophy of Blanshard, we shall examine: (1) the context of creativity in the history of rational thought; (2) rational thought as the locus of creativity; and (3) creativity as creative interchange between novelty and necessity.

Context of Creativity in the History of Rational Thought

Blanshard's philosophic context is the tradition of rationalism. We shall present a brief summary of some of his main perspectives on this tradition, as they relate to creativity, in order to gain further understanding of the root conditions from which his philosophy emerges.

The Western history of rational thought from Plato forward is especially significant for Blanshard. Its great source is classic Greek thought. In commenting on it as the main source of rationalism, he says: "To be sure, none of the great rationalists have accepted the Greek idea of reason entirely. Yet, directly or indirectly, their rationalism has in every case stemmed from it" (RA, 69). Basic "in the Greek mind lay the conception of form" as "identity of structure" which "maintains itself through diversity and change." A common referent for reason was "relation or order" which is not sensed but is apprehended by intelligence. "Reason is rather like an X-ray that penetrates through the fleshy outside of things to the skeleton underneath, that sees the abstract in the concrete, the universal in the particular—an insight, furthermore, that has so freed itself from the inner forces of liking and disliking as to be influenced only by the logic of the case" (55).

Blanshard points out that "the Greeks were the first to conceive of this sort of reason" whose objects seemed to be remote and austere, but "they were able to conceive of it because they had the idea of form" (RA, 55). Their subideas of form include: (1) essence or thinking in terms of universals; (2) end or the over-arching purpose of the whole; (3) law, "a connection of concepts that was certain, fresh, non-sensible, universal, objective, unalterable"; and (4) system as "an understanding that grasped things as timelessly complete and necessary." This, says Blanshard, is what Plato "was reaching for in his ultimate idea of reason." It is that system "in which everything was made intelligible through the part it played in the whole." In this all-comprehensive conceptual system, intelligence answers intelligence and the reason of the creature greets the immanent reason of the creator (56–67).

Blanshard finds in Plato and Aristotle not only theoretic reason which influences conduct indirectly but also practical reason whose influence is "more direct and permeating." "It appears in the list of virtues under the name wisdom. In Plato's familiar image, it is the charioteer, keeping a firm and equal rein upon the black horse and the white, the appetites and the passions" (RA, 68).

Following his treatment of classic contributions of the Greeks, Blanshard surveys further works on reason in Western philosophy. For a thousand years, during the medieval period, "reason had been the handmaiden of faith," but with the rise of modern philosophy, "Descartes made it autonomous" (RA, 70). Following Descartes in the tradition of rationalism came Spinoza, whose "reflection on the end of human endeavor led him to the conclusion that this was knowledge itself, in the form of rational understanding. . . . Reason, for Spinoza, was thus the very essence of mind; a mind was a mind in the degree to which this immanent end was realized" (74–75). When reason attains its consummatory end, "human knowledge would have fused itself with God's, and man have risen into unity with the divine. . . . God *was* the universe considered as a single system, at once fully comprehensive and fully comprehensible; . . . . 'Philosophy . . . , in its highest form, is to Spinoza . . . the life of religion'"[2] (*RA*, 77).

Blanshard sets forth the social consequences of rational thought as Spinoza saw them:

> . . . in a fully necessitated world there can be no undetermined choices. But. . . . There is no conflict between freedom and necessity if the necessitation is by reason. . . . To be free is to be . . . determined by one's real self. And one's self is real just so far as it is rational. . . . Growth in rationality means being increasingly laid under constraint by rational law. But surrender to such necessity is the open secret of freedom.[*RA*, 78]

In Leibniz, the "great successor" of Spinoza, Blanshard sees the beginning of a retreat in the rationalist tradition. "Leibniz held that logic and mathematics were thus intelligible, but little or nothing else" (*RA*, 81–82). The retreat went much further in Kant. ". . . reason for Kant was both more and less than it had been for his rationalist predecesors. It was more, because it was now the artificer of nature as well as its contemplator. It was less, because it paid for its creative power the price of total ignorance of things as they were in themselves" (83). Between Kant's and Hegel's conceptions of reason, Blanshard sees "a long leap." Hegel's originality was profound in that his "new conception of reason required a reconstitution of logic" as a rhythmic process from the most abstract to the most concrete concepts. For Hegel, "reason is a continuous process operating at many levels." He "regarded necessity, truth, and reality themselves as matters of degree." He was trying "to trace the career of the theoretical interest by itself." Blanshard concludes that its main outlines give "an illuminating account of the actual advance of thought" (86–89). The advance, for Blanshard, seems to be expressed in the thought of Bradley and Bosanquet. For them, reason was the presence in experience of something described variously as a "nisus towards wholeness," "the spirit of totality," and "logical stability." . . . "Wholeness meant two things: completeness and interdependence of parts. In all experience we find a pressure towards such wholeness" (90).

It is the tradition of rationalism, here tersely delineated in terms of its more significant perspectives, that provides the context from which creativity in Brand Blanshard's thought emerges. In this context, he identifies the opposition to the tradition of rationalistic thought in the following summary statement: "The most formidable attack ever made on reason as an independent source of knowledge has come from those positivists and analysts who are the present-day successors of Hume" (*RA,* 92). He then confronts this opposition by making a careful critical analysis of it in his Carus Lectures. We get the fuller impact of this confrontation in six chapters, 3–8, in *Reason and Analysis.* A clear-cut summary response to the opposition appears in a single sentence: "We found no good ground whatever for regarding necessity as arbitrary or conventional or linguistic, nor again as analytic merely" (423). Following his bout with the wide-ranging opposition which pervades much of the field of philosophy, he calmly returns to the great tradition of rationalism, not merely to reaffirm its basic nature but also to analyze it further, clarify it, and supply some needed correctives.

Rational Thought as the Locus of Creativity

For Blanshard, thought is a purposive activity with both an inner and an outer end. The inner end is "intellectual satisfaction" or understanding. The outer end is "the revelation of its object," which is ultimately truth itself or the complete system. These two ends of thought coincide in that "an idea is a potentiality which, if fulfilled, would *be* its object." In fact, these two ends of thought converge and operate implicitly "throughout the career of thought, from its first tentative appearance in perception to the flights of speculative reason." . . . In this career of thought, "there is a single continuous drive toward intelligible system, a system which, as all-comprehensive, is logically stable, and, as perfectly integrated, leaves no loose ends" (*NT,* 2:428).

Creativity in rational thought, in Blanshard, is characterized specifically as "invention and discovery" (*NT,* 2:98). Thinking as reflection "is an attempt to answer a question, . . . a struggle for relevance, . . . an effort to surmount some difficulty" (2:194–95). In this sense, reflection is problem-solving. The nature of invention, for Blanshard, is clarified from this context, for he says: "Every solution of a problem is invention" (2:136). So creative invention in problem-solving is a wide-ranging process extending from its root conditions in reflection and what gives rise to reflection to ultimate fulfillment in explicit understanding. The complexities encountered in this process have been a main source of continuing research throughout the history of philosophy. But, however great the difficulties which obstruct the movement of reflective thought toward explicit understanding, Blanshard maintains the faith that this movement of mind "is not lawless, that even in the coming of new insights there is nothing magical or capricious which would put the mode of their coming quite beyond our discernment" (2:100).

Problem-solving, for Blanshard, involves not merely the effort of persons to deal effectively with the multiplicity of more or less significant problems encountered day after day; it entails as well isolating and focusing upon a fundamental problem which is the real ground for understanding creative invention in problem-solving. This fundamental problem arises with "the impulse to bring within the system of experience some isolated fact that challenges it." He calls this impulse "the mainspring of reflection" (*NT*, 2:428).

Even the plain commonsense person, whose thinking is not disciplined for careful analysis and criticism, has a system of experience however unexamined and incomplete. But the theoretic impulse for further understanding and for further expansion of the limited and fragmentary system of experience is present. "The course begins in every case with a shock to the system of thought already present. Something is offered so alien to the present circle of ideas, so unassimilable by it, so tantalizingly isolated from it, that the impulse toward integration is stung into action" (*NT*, 47). This something alien is like an island separated from the mainland. It is felt that the gap should be bridged. This island is *novel* to the main system—the "rock of routine perceptions and beliefs" one lives on. "Intelligibility is not evenly diffused" through the system, "but it is by no means a chaos." The system "is organized on principles;" . . . . "And the principles of structure of the plain man's world are also the rules that govern his thinking. If he is to extend his world to include the novel it must be by bringing the novel within the domain . . . ; if it stands out and defies assimilation, intelligence has collapsed" (2:53).

We see this fundamental problem of closing the gap between whatever system of thought one has attained and what is novel to this system as basic to our understanding of creativity in Blanshard. This issue seems to pervade Blanshard's thinking, for it recurs again and again in his writings in a variety of forms of expression.

In his effort to deal effectively with this problem, he accepts novelty as instrumental to the advancement of systematic thought and also to the ultimate completion of the all-comprehensive rationalistic system. He sees that "The powerlessness of the rational impulse to break by itself the fetters of established belief is a familiar fact of social history" (*NT*, 2:58), and that it is incredibly difficult to encourage the principle of originality. "Thought will not work in a vacuum. And even where material is abundant it will not reach the level of reflection if it can appropriate this material automatically. It must be presented with what is foreign enough to be challenging, yet not so foreign as to make assimilation hopeless" (2:60).

He concludes that the mainspring for creative invention in problem-solving is "a tension within thought itself between an immanent but unrealized end, in the form of intelligible system, and the relatively incomplete and disorderly state of present knowledge" (*NT*, 2:63). The "immediate stimulus" is the island of novelty off that mainland of thought which is the

present accepted system. The problem is the integration of that novel
something with the intelligible whole.

With this understanding, "that reflection is always an attempt to solve a
problem" (*NT,* 2:78) and that "every solution of a problem is invention," we
see clearly the significance of Blanshard's claim that invention "lies at the
heart of the reflective process" (2:79). This leads us to the conclusion that
reflection is invention in-the-making, and that the basic problem encountered
by reflection as invention in-the-making is the integration of some alien
novelty with what is systematic in rational thinking.

In Blanshard's more thoroughgoing analysis of invention, his association
of "discovery" with invention is clarified. "The scientist who has discovered
a new law has thought creatively just as truly as the novelist has; and the
novelist who traces the development of a character has discovered something
just as truly as has the original scientist" (*NT,* 2:98). The artist does not make
the psychological laws at work in his character any more than the scientist
makes the laws of nature. In each case he discovers these laws and must conform to them. "The more profoundly he conforms to the laws of his spiritual
realm the greater at once are his discovery and his creation. Thus invention is
not in essence different in science and in art. The artist discovers when he
creates; the scientist creates when he discovers" (2:99). In either case,
whether it be discovery or invention, creativity is its essence. Blanshard
suggests that there are laws which govern invention in reasoning:

> . . . what governs invention in reasoning is the requirements of a whole
> already present implicitly and seeking explicit completion. The laws that
> govern this whole are not in the ordinary sense psychological laws, nor are
> they, in that sense, empirical or natural laws; they are laws of what ought to
> be rather than what is—rules prescribed by the nature of those wholes,
> moral, aesthetic, or logical, which thought is seeking to achieve. [*NT,* 2:109]

Within rational thought there is "the *nisus* of an implicit system to complete itself coherently . . ." (2:119). It is in this nisus from what is present in
the incomplete rational system to what ought to be in the complete rational
system that we find the moral, aesthetic, and logical aspects of the rational
process. The nisus is "the groove of necessity" (2:127). Blanshard says that
"the prime office of reason" is "the discovery of necessary connections"
(*RA,* 422). The connections are between universals. "Reason . . . involves the
grasp of a necessary relation between characters, and these characters are not
particulars, but qualities, or complexes of them, that might occur elsewhere;
and hence they are universals" (392). He defines a universal as "a quality or
relation or complex of these that may be identical in diverse contexts." He
denies the existence of both a "qualitative universal . . . whose instances are
qualities or characters of one kind" and a "generic universal . . . whose instances are individual things or persons, for example, man, horse, or stone."

He accepts the existence of a "specific universal . . . as a quality or character that is incapable of sub-division into kinds, for example, this shade of red or this degree of loudness in a sound" (392–93). He concludes that "our immediate experience is of *nothing but* specific universals" (399) and that "the work of reason is to lay bare the connections between universals" (401–2). This work is done by "dissecting out the nerves of necessity that run through the body of nature" (421). What Blanshard means by these "nerves of necessity" is not in accord with the formalist tradition of "flat either-or's" (*NT*, 2:469). They function differently in different contexts. "But we must remember . . . that necessity, whatever our first impressions, is a matter of more and less, and that between a complete demonstration and a mere accidental conjunction it may be present in very many degrees" (2:499). So "identity in diverse contexts" means, for Blanshard, what "concrete logicians have called 'identity in difference.' " It exists "in and through its differences, it resists abstraction from them" (2:471). The nerves of necessity operate by means of implication in connecting specific universals.

Implication is to be distinguished from inference in that implication is a timeless and objective logical relation which "holds whether we recognize it or not." Inference is a temporal, psychologically subjective "passage from one judgment to another." It may or may not include implication (*RA*, 461 –62). Logical coherence is the ultimate test of implication, and also of truth, which is our ideal end in our quest for understanding. "Certainly this ideal goes far beyond mere consistency. Fully coherent knowledge would be knowledge in which every judgment entailed, and was entailed by, the rest of the system. Probably we never find in fact a system where there is so much of interdependence" (*NT*, 2:264). The all-comprehensive system is that ideal end which is the metaphysical embodiment of complete fulfillment of this system of interdependence.

Our ancient but unfulfilled fundamental drive in Blanshard's philosophy of creativity is the ordering of experience in terms of necessity. It is the drive of reason toward intelligibility and understanding "under the guidance of the implicit ideal of system" (*RA*, 387–88). We have seen that this drive is a problem-solving process and that the real problem encountered, as distinguished from the relatively more insignificant problems, is the integration of something which appears as alien to the incomplete coherent system moving toward completion. This alien something is characterized as novel. The coherent system in-the-making is orderly. It operates in rational thought by implication as logical necessity. It is a nisus or thrust toward complete intelligibility, complete understanding, the completion of the rational system in which every part fits into every other part in the fulfillment of interdependence within the whole as truth itself. The novel character, as related to necessity, is a disturbance, for novelty and necessity are not integrated. So long as this novel character remains outside the system, the disturbance is felt by the nerves of necessity. The need for connecting novelty and necessity is imperative.

Furthermore, we have seen that the connection to be made between novelty and necessity, according to Blanshard, is through universals, but not any kind of assumed universals or pseudouniversals which are called "generic" and "qualitative" universals. These will not do. It is only through what he calls "specific universals" that effective connections can be made between novelty and necessity. These specific or concrete universals function as more-or-less rather than as either-or within the logic of "identity in difference," or as "identical in diverse contexts."

This change from either-or to more-or-less identical in diverse contexts seems to be an opening for solving the real problem of integrating novelty and necessity, but we suggest that further analysis of the basic issue is needed. We see this basic issue to be invention as creativity in problem-solving.

Creativity as Creative Interchange Between Novelty and Necessity

Creativity is an abstract universal, but, to use Blanshard's phraseology, it becomes a specific and concrete universal when it is identifiable in diverse contexts, as in creative interchange. Its logic is the logic of identity in difference. Creative interchange is the specific universal which connects novelty and necessity, for the principles of novelty and necessity are interdependent in their operations within the actual body of the natural world of events and their connections. Without novel events, rational necessity would be denied its basic function as the agent in the creative integration of novel events. And without rational necessity as an operative principle for ordering novel events, the activity of novel events may well be characterized as sheer madness, anarchic and chaotic. Recognition of the factual interdependence between the principles of novelty and necessity is an opener for a dramatic new awakening in the minds of men. This new awakening is the observation of creative interchange as an actually operative and identifiable creative process which connects creatively novel and necessary events within the body of the natural world. Novelty and necessity are each equally relevant for creative interchange. Neither principle is to be discounted in favor of the other. Each event of the natural world carries and embodies the principle of operative novelty. Furthermore, each event of the natural world carries and embodies the principle of order as rational necessity yielding coherence and intelligibility. Without the ultimate principle of novelty in nature, the principle of rational necessity could yield nothing but an established order of dead routine. Without the principle of order, the novelty of individual events would be self-destructive. Therefore, the principle for ultimate human concern and commitment is neither novelty nor order but creative interchange between novelty and the rational order of necessity. Creative interchange between novelty and order is the key to creative invention. Within the process of creative interchange, both novelty and order are creative. But there is a significant difference between the key to invention as we see it and Blanshard's clear-cut claim. He says: "What controls the process of reflection and provides the key to invention is the operation within the mind of that system which forms its end, ... " (NT, 2:428).

We have found in Blanshard that what operates "within the mind of that system" is "the nerves of necessity" by means of coherent rational implication rather than by mere inference. Implicit within rational thought is the nisus toward completion. The ideal end exists within the incomplete system and also transcends the incomplete system. Complete and all-comprehensive fulfillment of the ideal end is dependent on the complete integration of novelty, as alien to the system, with the system itself.

However, we see in Blanshard a richly meaningful creativity. It has classic content. There is no discounting of the purposive nature of reflection. Reason is implicitly creative of further rational activity, although the operation of our rational thought is not perfect. There are devious detours and complex obstructions to rational thinking, but the career of reason is not a hopeless process. It is not flimsy. It has laws of its own to be discovered and obeyed. Disobedience of its basic law of coherence is self-destructive for those who violate it. The law of coherence is as relevant for the development of ethics as for the attainment of knowledge.

> And if we ask as to the place of reason in the moral life, we find this to be analogous to its place in the theoretical life. Reason is in neither case a form imposed from without on a content alien to it. It is already working immanently in desire just as it is at work in perception. Its business in the moral life is to order and unify desires, just as in its theoretical career its business is to order into a coherent whole the world of the perceptually given. [RG, 343]

So creativity which operates in rational thought also operates in the moral life. Furthermore, the relation of reason to the good is clarified as follows: "It is thus absurd to say that reason and goodness are extraneous to each other. So far as thought enters into desire, it is the architect of the good" (347). Reason is the source of coherence in the moral life. It "operates not only within desires, but between them" (349). It is also effective in the transformation of society: "Men who believe in a common end and a common reason will naturally seek to make them prevail; and that such prevalence would transform society needs no arguing" (407).

Creativity operative in rational thought, for Blanshard, expands and enriches life in accord with whatever capacity for fulfillment it may have.

"The really good in anything," as an expanding creative good, "is that which would give the appropriate powers of our nature their fullest and most satisfying play" (*RG*, 420). Reason as it operates in human life is not a bleak and cold calculating analysis separated from feeling.

> Human beings never merely think, and never merely feel; all the main sides of their nature are at work in everything they do. Adequate criticism, therefore, cannot be offered from a single point of view. It must surround and enfold the work with a comprehensive knowledge and a generous understanding of comparative values. [*RG*, 434]

In this study we do not see creativity in Blanshard as something to be cast aside. His philosophy of rational thought in the context of philosophy of creativity is worthy of maintenance and further fulfillment, for irrational thought is indeed obstructive to creative advance in human life. Blanshard has offered radical correctives for this classical tradition. His basically modest claims for his own contributions are an invitation for further creative correctives and fulfillment. In closing *Reason and Goodness* he says:

> And if great numbers of our most important beliefs are thus held with confidence on a basis which, if produced, would be inadequate, does not this suggest that the appropriate attitude toward any of our beliefs that may be called in question is one, not of dogmatic assertiveness, not of feeble self-distrust, not of touchiness at correction, but of impersonal readiness to amend, withdraw, or reiterate as the evidence requires? [*RG*, 441]

In concluding our study of the stimulating and interesting philosophy of creativity in Brand Blanshard, we offer the following correctives for further possible fulfillment of it:

We sense an over-all imbalance between novelty and necessity in his philosophy of creativity. Blanshard does recognize the presence of novelty. Furthermore, he accepts its significance as a source of stimulation for further rational system-building. But his main emphasis, which creates the imbalance between novelty and necessity, is on rational necessity. Not only is what appears as novel subordinate to system in-the-making, but rational system, as the ideal complete and perfect end in which every part fits perfectly and harmoniously with every other part in the all-comprehensive whole, is the kind of ideal structure of thought which does not embody or even permit the emergence of novelty within or from it. This ideal end reveals Blanshard's perfectionism. Creativity in Blanshard is clearly evident in rational system in-the-making, but it is not present in the ideal end, for the system is finished.

The basic corrective for this negation in Blanshard's perfectionist metaphysics is recognition of the significance of naturalistic creative process metaphysics determined by the world of nature, inclusive of its past, its present, and its future possibilities, which is ever in-the-making. Since novelty is an ultimate characteristic of nature, the future is open. It is not a closed system. The past is open to reinterpretation. The present is eternally the locus of creativity in which there is ongoing creative interchange between the reinterpretation of history and the projection of further possibilities for actualization and increase of value in the eternal present. This creative process metaphysics is a dynamic life-giving metaphysics of continuous experimental adventure which stands in sharp contrast to Blanshard's envisagement of an ideal, all-comprehensive, and complete rational system.

Creative experimental adventure thrives on novelty as an ultimate principle operative in the nature of events and their relations. Novelty is expressive of all of nature's events and especially so in the individuality and autonomy of human nature. The overplay of system and the subordination of novelty to it is a fit context for human rebellion and revolution.

However, we are not suggesting the underplay of rational system in-the-making. Rational necessity as an ultimate principle of order and coherence operative in nature is no less deeply rooted than is the principle of novelty. But the imbalance of these principles renders each a major source of tragedy. Creative interchange between them yields growth of meaning and value. Natural events function naturally, not in a complete rational system as a closed order, but within a continuously creative novelty-producing order.

The principle of creativity implies continuity. Creative interchange can never be complete since both novelty and necessity are ultimately characteristic of the events and their relations in the world. A functional fixation within the human self, a fixated habit in the relations of marriage which obstructs creative interchange between husband and wife, or the fixation of an institutional policy which resists creative interchange in national or international relations is due in each case, not to the creation of the self, the marriage, the institution, the nation, or international organization, but to some obstruction to the continuity of creative interchange within or among these unitary functions or events. Basic in these obstructions is the imbalance between novelty and necessity, and, more specifically, between the consequent autonomy and order of events.

The projection of an ideal, all-comprehensive, and complete rational system in Blanshard's philosophy is undoubtedly an outcome of his analytical and critical thought. We do discover side effects in the creative technology of our economy which are anything but creative. A new discovery or an invention may greatly increase unemployment, or even good and expensive tools may be rendered obsolete, with consequent waste of materials and labor. Are not these uncreative displacements due to creative innovation? Is not creativity in the growth of technology or even in the growth of the economy to be mistrusted or even feared as a source of human tragedy? Is not the ideal end for all of us a complete all-comprehensive system in which each part fits into every other part and means every other part, yielding a perfect whole? Our response is negative, for the tragic side effects attributed to creativity are not an outcome of creativity at all. They are, instead, the consequence of bifurcation of novel innovation from system fixation. Again we see that an imbalance in our evaluation of either pole of creativity is basically obstructive to creativity itself. That which is worthy of ultimate concern and commitment is creative interchange between these two poles of creativity. The clue to creative continuity in technology and industry, as well as in other institutions, is commitment to creative interchange between their novel innovative discoveries and inventions and their formal ordering principles and policies.

We have seen that Blanshard is committed to the development of rational thought as coherent theory, and to theoretical knowledge, and truth for its own sake as opposed to basic concern for its use in practical situations.

> Understanding is useful, enormously useful, but this is largely because those who own it have kept their eye on truth rather than on usefulness. If they have succeeded in understanding and in seeing things as they are, that is because seeing things as they are has itself been a passion with them. [*RG*, 436]

Blanshard is clearly referring here to the effort to describe the world as it is. To know the truth in this sense is to describe as accurately as possible the operational nature of events, regardless of how we may think they ought to operate, or how we may make use of them. To confuse the aim of description with the aim of valuation and use is a common source of introducing various forms of bias and prejudice into the quest for truth. This is especially so if the interest in use and the process of valuation are based on unanalyzed and uncritical commonsense opinion rather than evidence. But Blanshard, in his effort to protect descriptive knowledge from prejudice, uses the coherence of rational thought as the ultimate test of truth. This is consistent with his acceptance of theoretical knowledge as ultimately the highest form of knowledge to be attained for its own sake.

We concur with his concern that descriptive knowledge, and, in fact, all knowledge, be as free as possible from prejudice. But we believe that the ultimate test of the truth of a hypothesis which is formulated for the purpose of describing the way certain given events operate in the world is the test of determining by experimental procedures the correlativity or lack of correlativity of the given hypothesis with the operation of the events in question. The test of the hypothesis is not merely to assure its coherence with other well-tested hypotheses, but more significantly to determine the workability of the hypothesis in its performing or failing to perform operationally what it is meant to perform in terms of the correlativity of causal factors as related to effects.

In turning to another level in the quest for knowledge, namely the level of valuation and criticism of given situations to determine what is better or worse in their operations, and also how conditions may be supplied for increase of value, we discover a significant inadequacy in Blanshard's analysis of the relations between instrumental or extrinsic and intrinsic values.

> To ask the good of a thing *is* to ask the use of it; the assumption is that if it has no use, it has no value, that value *is* usefulness. And this is untrue. The intrinsic value of things *never* lies in their usefulness; to say that something is useful is to say that it is valued as a means to something else which itself has intrinsic worth. [*RG*, 423]

We see clearly and accept the common distinction which Blanshard makes between instrumental and intrinsic values. The cup used as an instrumental value to quench one's thirst for water is an instrumental value. Or again, language skill, including formation, critical analysis, and reconstruction of language in the interest of precision and clarity in the use of language, is an instrumental value as related to the communication of meaning as an intrinsic value. But after acceptance of this distinction, we see that it is inadequate as a basis for providing necessary conditions for the transformation of situations in the interest of improving them.

The root problem at this valuational level of knowledge is not merely to see things as they are by getting accurate descriptions of them, but to see, first, the contrast between what they are and what they might become in terms of their possible improvement. Secondly, there is the problem of discovering conditions which may be supplied to yield improvement, as increase of value, in the situation in question. Thirdly, positive correlation between the conditions supplied and the end or ends desired, including ends regarded as having intrinsic value, is necessary for growth of value. But merely positive correlation of the conditions with some desired end or ends does not yield evidence that increase of value is occurring. In fact, the consequence may be an increase of disvalue. For example, positive correlations may be expanded into a vast complex network for effective destruction of nations and cultures. The possible disvalue in correlativity is discovered by determining its limitations with regard to its capacity for creative continuity. Creative continuity is an implicit characteristic of creative correlativity which is the generative source of value.

We have seen that Blanshard's metaphysics as the ground for both descriptive knowledge and valuation includes the ideal end as a complete, all-comprehensive, timeless, intelligible rational system in which every part is necessarily connected with every other part. We find that this ideal end is a symbol of *complete* correlativity, but not of *creative* correlativity. The perfectionism of the system prevents it from being creatively correlative. His system has correlativity in terms of the mutual support of the relations of all the parts within it. It is a perfect harmonization of parts within the perfect whole. What is lacking is the mutual enhancement of parts and the growth of meaning and value. But to correct this deficiency would require a radical transformation of Blanshard's metaphysics from perfectionism of mere mutual support to a creative process metaphysics which discovers creativity as its ultimate valuational principle.

However, we are not discounting the value present in the coherent mutual support of ideas in Blanshard's metaphysical system. We mean only to open this system for creative continuity, not only for the further production of creative novel insights and ideas but also for the growth of rational, coherent, and dynamic creative *action*. We suggest that this transformation of Blanshard's metaphysics can be effected, not by the destruction of it, but by correctives for continuously creative fulfillment of it.

The suggested transformation requires that in the process of valuation there be complete commitment to creative interchange between extrinsic and intrinsic value. This kind of commitment opens the way for growth of understanding of the creative exchange which goes on in the process of creative correlation of value activities. Within creative process metaphysics, as axiology of valuation, we see that conditions which have been regarded as merely instrumental really become intrinsic, and that these intrinsic values in turn become, in the context of creative continuity, instrumental for further increase of value. Thus, again, we see from this context the import of the fact that creativity implies continuity.

However, we are aware of obstructions to creative interchange between extrinsic and intrinsic values. The vast complexity of determinings from historical situations, of determinings from future possibilities projected, or not projected, and of creative current determinings within the eternal present—all are constitutive and interrelated determinings in the process of valuation. Since these three types of complex and interrelated determinings are so difficult to analyze and describe clearly, many scholars accept failure to treat the whole value situation by the methods of scholarship, and dismiss it as mainly emotive rather than cognitive. But Blanshard is not doing this and neither are we. For we see clearly that creativity as creative interchange between the nerves of novelty and the nerves of necessity is an actual creative process at work within and among the events of nature including human nature, and that this process is most worthy of human concern and commitment because it generates the growth of meaning and value.

We do not deny the actual and ultimate existence of conflict between the nerves of novelty and the nerves of necessity operative in the world of nature, including human nature and human thinking. Instead of denying it, we affirm it. The innovative expression of the novelty of events makes conflict ultimate and inevitable. The basic question which arises from our affirmation is: "How can we respond to this ultimate conflict?" Our reply is: "We can respond either destructively or creatively." We can respond destructively by ultimate commitment either to novelty or to necessity, or to both ambivalently. We can respond creatively by learning how to provide the necessary conditions for release of creativity within the human self and among people, and also in the wider context within and among ecological systems. This process of learning is not a merely theoretical ideal. It is ongoing as research, including experimental application, especially in the context of education. Extension and improvement of this process of learning deserve to be recognized as worthy of our support.

We who have experienced a clear vision of creative interchange, as operative in dealing with ultimate conflict, are impelled by its lure to pursue it further because of its aesthetic attractiveness. Creative interchange in its inseparable formative-expressive-functional aesthetic nature is the essence of beauty. The release of creative interchange in us, and in nature generally, cannot be forced. Its aesthetic quality is a sufficient lure for those who experience it.

Art which becomes classic or which lives on with creative continuity is demonstrative of the acceptance of ultimate conflict without destruction of the conflict, but with creative inclusion and transformation of the conflict within the aesthetic situation. In great art, conflict serves creativity through creative interchange between its principles of form and expression. The expressive principle gives the art object its fresh novel character. The formative principle gives it structural order. Without structural integrity, the art object is sentimental and melodramatic. Without novel expression, its structure is mechanically rigid and, consequently, boring. Great art is produced by creative interchange between form and expression.

But our philosophy of art which we are presenting here in the form of some brief introductory statements is not Blanshard's approach to art. The goal of the logical or theoretic impulse is, for him, "nothing short of a system perfect and all-embracing. . . . or better perhaps, a system that would include and order all lesser systems" (NT, 2:438). The aesthetic impulse of the artist is not satisfied by rational system, but by aesthetic feeling. These two impulses "require for their satisfaction different types of whole" (2:439). After suggesting that each type of whole may well possess something characteristic of the other, he subordinates the novelty of aesthetic expression to "full systematic necessity" (2:449). However, before effecting the subordination, he demonstrates the versatility and comprehensiveness of his thought in dealing with the great variety of forms and expressions encountered within the compass of reality, a quality of his thinking which we greatly appreciate. Yet, we must acknowledge radical differences in our perspectives on art and aesthetics. For us, the artist at best demonstrates through the practice of his philosophy of art the operation of creative interchange between novel expression and systematic necessity. In this sense, aesthetics is indeed useful in developing a philosophy of creativity.

Finally, we shall examine that hypothesis which we presented in closing the introduction to this paper, namely: that Blanshard's "ideology of reason is an attempt, perhaps involuntarily and even unconsciously, to escape the complexity of man by rising above it" (supra, p. 647).

Certainly Blanshard is not attempting to escape the complexity of rational thought, for this is the matrix of his creativity. His analysis of the complexities of perception, implication, necessity, universals, and the ultimately real—to mention only a few of the main issues in the vast network of rational thought—and his showing that the multiplicity of these complex relations is subject to the drive of reason as coherent rational system for complete intelligibility and understanding are indeed clear indications that he is not and has not been attempting, throughout his distinguished working career of more than a half-century, to escape the complexity of rational thought.

However, we do find that Blanshard moves through and beyond rational thought in-the-making, beyond the various different systems, and into an ideal rational system of systems which is the arrival, the finished product of rational thought in-the-making.

> The inference from degrees of knowledge to degrees of reality may be objected to on other grounds. It may be taken as implying that, since there is no absolute necessity in knowledge, there is none in reality. But there is no force in the alleged implication. The immanent end of thought is a system at once perfect and all-embracing; in such a system necessity would be complete; and it is the working assumption of thought that reality *is* such a system. For the aim of thought is to explain things; its assumption is that things are explicable; and explicability *means* full systematic necessity. [*NT*, 2:449]

Blanshard's assumption that reality is an all-comprehensive, complete, and perfect system of systems is the basis for our saying that ultimately his metaphysics is a negation of creativity.

In this context, the main question is yet to be examined: Is Blanshard's ideology of reason an attempt to escape the complexity of man by rising above it? Our response to this question is affirmative, since his ultimate commitment is to the kind of understanding which is an exercise of rational thought, finally as complete all-comprehensive systematic necessity, a system of systems for its own sake, rather than the kind of understanding which involves ultimate commitment to creativity as creative interchange between coherent rational action and the innovative production of novel activity yielding continuity in creative action.

We see our understanding as an intelligible commitment to creativity as creative interchange between the principles of novelty and necessity operative within the ecology of nature, including human nature. We see the operation of creative interchange as basic therapy both for the poverty or loss of creative meaning in the routine of established systems, with consequent boredom, and for despair generating nihilistic rebellious and revolutionary violence against fixated habits in persons and institutions, now called "the establishment." We see the operation of creative interchange as basic therapy for the madness of the struggle to be different from the establishment, to break the boredom and to experience something refreshing, something novel, even though the experience may become an adventure in chaotic anarchic behavior. We see that insofar as the implicit beauty of creativity as creative interchange becomes clear and vivid in the vision of persons and peoples, its impelling aesthetic attraction will increasingly negate punishment and purify our human ecology.

WILLIAM S. MINOR

FOUNDATION FOR CREATIVE PHILOSOPHY
CARBONDALE, ILL.

NOTES

[1] Melvin Maddocks, "The New Cult of Madness: Thinking As a Bad Habit," *Time,* 100, no. 3 (March 13, 1972): 51–52.

[2] Blanshard quotes H.H. Joachim, *A Study of the Ethics of Spinoza* (Oxford: Clarendon Press, 1901), 181.

17. Reply to William S. Minor
Creativity in Brand Blanshard

I noted some way back that only two of my critics had specially concerned themselves with my study of the movement of reflection. Mr. Castell's interest in this study grows out of his conviction that "scientific psychology" does not and cannot give an adequate account of this movement, and here he found me in agreement. Mr. Minor approaches the same subject with a very different interest. His dominant concern as a philosopher is with "creativity," and he naturally raises the question whether my account of intellectual invention is in accord with what he considers genuine creativity to be. Much of his paper is a generous and careful statement of what he conceives me to be saying, and since this is in the main accurate, it hardly calls for discussion. In the last half of the paper he offers a number of "correctives" designed to make my theory acceptable, and I shall shortly turn to these.

There is an obvious step, however, that must be taken first. What does Mr. Minor mean by that all-essential word "creative"? He must be painfully aware of its ambiguity; it is actually used in both laudation and derision. When one speaks of Bach or Rodin or Goethe as a creative genius, no one dissents; the connotation seems clear enough. But when one hears of "creative cooking," "creative exercise," "creative play," and "creative photography," one begins to be puzzled. Residents in academia have heard of courses in "creative writing" in which nothing but fiction is regarded as creative; and the spontaneous gush of an undisciplined imagination would be classed as "creative" while an exposition of relativity by Broad or Russell, or Macaulay's account of Glencoe, would be brushed aside as clearly not "creative," which seems merely absurd. Mr. Minor would no doubt agree in deploring such usage. But what does "creative" mean to *him*?

We may note first that "creativity" applies to a much larger range of events in Mr. Minor's thinking than "invention" does in mine. What I was studying was the way reflection goes about it to solve problems; what Mr. Minor is concerned with is something that appears in all the events of nature, conscious or not. Nature, he says is governed throughout by two principles, that of necessity and that of novelty. Between these two principles there is a "factual interdependence," and we should have a "new awakening" if we recognized the "creative interchange as an actually operative and identifiable creative process which connects creatively novel and necessary events within the body of the natural world." Every event in nature manifests the presence of both principles.

> Without the ultimate principle of novelty in nature, the principle of rational necessity could yield nothing but an established order of dead routine. Without the principle of order, the novelty of individual events would be self-destructive. Therefore, the principle for ultimate human concern and commitment is neither novelty nor order, but creative interchange between novelty and the rational order of necessity.

What is the meaning here of "novelty," which is again an all-important term? Its literal meaning is "something new," and in this sense it would certainly apply to all events, since any event, taken as something that happens at a given time, has never happened before. But this cannot be the meaning, for if it were, all events would be equally creative, and Mr. Minor does not wish to suggest this. It is not therefore the production of novelty as such that is creative, but the production of some special kind of novelty. What kind? The answer is, novelty possessing value. Goethe's work would be considered creative because that work produced experiences in the minds of his readers that were of great intrinsic value. Edison's invention of the electric light was creative because, though the light bulbs themselves may have had little if any intrinsic value, their extrinsic or instrumental value was immense. Further, a creative event may have "side-effects." "A new discovery or an invention may greatly increase unemployment, or even good and expensive tools may be rendered obsolete with consequent waste of materials and labor." These, Mr. Minor says, are not strictly to be attributed to creativity: "They are, instead, the consequence of bifurcation of novel innovation from system fixation." Whether an event is really creative is to be judged, I understand, by weighing against each other the goods and evils it produces, both designed and undesigned. By intelligent planning we must provide for "creative continuity," in the sense that not only will the immediate results have positive value but they will produce similarly positive values in their turn. If we were generally committed to this kind of creativity, life would be a far richer experience than it is. Indeed humanity would recognize in creativity "its ultimate valuational principle."

It is necessary to give this résumé of Mr. Minor's theory of "creativity" because it is the basis of his criticism of my own theory of invention. Much of his account I can accept, though I should no doubt put it rather differently. There are also important points in it that I have either failed to understand or failed to find convincing. Let me set down some of my difficulties.

(1) How can "creativity" be assigned to the events of nature generally? Consider one point only. So far as we know, life and sentience exist only on one small satellite in the universe, and are apparently bound to be snuffed out within a calculable time. After that time, the astronomers tell us, the universe will go on as before. But would a nonsentient universe be at any point creative? Only, says Mr. Minor, if productive of value. But could there be any value in a universe without sentience? In my own view it would be impossible. For value is dependent on experience, such experience as the fulfillment of desire and the satisfaction or pleasure that attends this. There would be no goodness or badness, extrinsic or intrinsic, in the movement of a glacier on Neptune or even in the crash of a meteor into a lifeless earth. I have stated the argument for this view in *Reason and Goodness*. The position is not an eccentric one; it is, I suppose, the majority view of those who pursue the theory of value. But if it is true, then it cannot also be true that nature generally is creative. Creativity must be confined to that portion of nature in which there is experienced striving followed by experienced fulfillment and experienced enjoyment.

(2) If we accept this view, we must next ask how Mr. Minor's theory of creativity applies to it. If we would be creative, he holds, we must seek "neither novelty nor order but creative interchange between novelty and the rational order of necessity." I am afraid I still do not understand.

(a) It is clear that to be creative we must produce something novel. But novel to whom? To human beings generally? Then an act of reflection, for example, will be creative only if it adds to the sum of human knowledge. But that would make such acts extremely rare and extremely hard to verify. Leibniz and Newton were both working on the calculus at the same time, and there was a bitter dispute as to who developed it first. Its discovery was certainly a creative act, but on the theory before us, if Leibniz had already discovered it when Newton did, Newton's discovery was not creative, because it was already known. But this seems absurd, for if Newton's great achievement was not creative, what act can hope to be?

Furthermore one could seldom be sure whether an act was creative or not. We seldom know, when we deal successfully with a challenging situation on the chess board or a peculiar breakdown in the carburetor of our car, whether our achievement is really a new one or not. It is very unlikely, therefore, that Mr. Minor would confine the name of novelty only to that which is new to the race.

The most natural alternative to this conception of novelty is novelty to the inventor himself. If this is the meaning, both Leibniz and Newton were creative, and our adventures on the chess board and under the hood of the car are also creative. There is no objection to that except that the term now becomes as broad as in the former meaning it was narrow, so broad indeed as to be virtually useless. Since we shall be acting creatively whenever we deal successfully with what to ourselves is a new situation, the most creative person will be the child, who faces such situations daily; and the stupid man will be more continually creative than the intelligent one, since the intelligent man recognizes in the "new" situation only a version of an old one, while to the stupid man it appears entirely new. I do not suppose that Mr. Minor conceives of novelty in either the restricted or the loose way; my complaint is that he does not provide us with any definite meaning of this essential term.

Nor do I think that people generally attach any definite meaning to it; and perhaps for that reason it is best avoided. I should agree with Mr. Minor that if it is to be used at all it should be reserved for acts productive of what is new and valuable, but I should take "new" to mean new to most workers in the same field, and "valuable" to refer to value that was distinctive in kind or great in amount. The term would still be vague, but not so vague as to be useless. Leibniz and Newton, Goethe and Edison would undoubtedly qualify; the ordinary child, chess player, or car repairer would not.

(b) We now come to what is to me the most puzzling part of Mr. Minor's theory of creativity. If we are to be creative, what we should aim at is "neither novelty nor order but creative interchange between novelty and the rational order of necessity." Mr. Minor thinks of order and novelty as two distinct "principles" which are in some sense opposed to each other. The principle of order is that of universal and necessary law, by which rationalists from Plato to so remote a camp follower as myself have supposed the facts and events of the world to be bound together. But peeping through the cracks of this vast and rigid structure there are tender buds of novelty which save the structure from rigor mortis. These it is our duty to nurture and cultivate. Sometimes Mr. Minor sounds as if working in the back of his mind there were a conception of the universe a little like that of the political order as it appeared to reformers in the turbulent years of 1966–72. Many thought of "the establishment" in those years as a rigid, inhumane system that stood heartlessly for "law and order" at any cost, while a humane and forward-looking few made their desperate bid for freedom and innovation. Mr. Minor seems to feel similarly that in a nature governed completely by necessary law novelty and creativity would have no chance. "Without the ultimate principle of novelty in nature, the principle of rational necessity could yield nothing but an established order of dead routine."

Now I have never been able to see why necessity should exclude novelty. When a novelty does appear in nature—a comet unlike any that has appeared before, a two-headed calf, a new variety of orchid or tulip—no instructed person supposes the event to be a matter of chance or the work of a "principle of novelty" at odds with the principle of law. Even if a natural scientist had no notion what caused the new phenomenon, it would not occur to him that it might have had no cause at all, or that it was due to some factor of lawlessness in nature. He would have no doubt that it issued from a cause in accordance with law, and that if it was a surprise to us that was only because we did not know the laws governing it. Nor is the case really otherwise when we turn to human invention or creation. If one is suddenly converted to determinism, one does not need the next morning to deny that Newton or Goethe ever produced anything of novelty or value. Their work would retain the value it had before, however it was produced—whether by the operation of law in a gifted mind or by an unpredictable explosion of free will, or by a "principle of novelty" that worked independently of law. Indeed when Mr. Minor himself explains to us how creativity is to be appraised, he does not do it in terms of antecedents but exclusively in terms of the value of the thing produced or which it produces in turn.

I find myself doubting whether there is any such thing as a "principle of novelty" at all. There is of course the *fact* of novelty; things new to oneself, new to the community, new to the race do undoubtedly appear. But Mr. Minor means more by the "principle of novelty" than any such truism as this. He appears to mean that there is some power or drive in nature that resists law and necessity, but not presumably in any lawful or necessary way. And I must confess that as a rationalist I see no need or ground for such a principle. I admit that events are happening daily which no one could have predicted and which no one understands. But I see no need of assuming that these events fall outside the realm of law and are therefore unintelligible even in theory. Why not follow the course of scientists generally and attribute such opaqueness in events not to caprice in nature but to our own invincible ignorance?

Mr. Minor may reply that the principle of novelty never acts alone. Where creativity occurs, there is always "a creative interchange." Mr. Minor regards this as important, since he returns to it again and again in a variety of forms. Sometimes the interchange is between novelty and necessity or law; sometimes between intrinsic and extrinsic values; sometimes, as in art, between form and expression. In the latter case it has a clear meaning. A Shakespearean sonnet has a definite form which exercises constraint upon the expression, and the expression not only fills the form but modifies it to its own purposes. But in the other two cases operation of this "interchange" is very dark to me. Mr. Minor speaks of the "interdependence" of novelty and necessity. Such interdependence implies that novelty is acted upon by necessity or law. But we have been told explicitly that as far as anything is the product of necessity it is neither novel nor creative. Why interaction with necessity should be not only allowed but required for creativity is puzzling. Again, we are told that we should commit ourselves to producing the conditions out of which creativity will emerge. But what can this mean unless creativity and novelty *are* linked by law to antecedents? If they were not, how could we prepare "conditions" for them?

In much the same way I am puzzled by the "interchange between intrinsic and extrinsic values." If Mr. Minor has in mind that we should try to give processes of purely extrinsic value like the drudgery of laundering clothes some intrinsic value in the way of gleaming and pleasant washing machines, and that the values we look for in books should not be intrinsic only, such as pure enlightenment, but also extrinsic, such as one gains from do-it-yourself manuals, I agree. But he seems to be saying something profounder than that, and I am not clear what it is. In any given process, I do not see how the intrinsic value of the product could act on the extrinsic value of its cause, for that would make the line of causation run backward. Yet he seems at times to suggest this. The paper cup used to quench one's thirst seems to gain intrinsic value if there is really an interchange. But this is hardly borne out if the cup is thrown at once into the discard. Where is the *intrinsic* value of the cup, unless in some mysterious way the end adds some of its intrinsic value to the extrinsic value of the means, a transaction for which there seems to be no evidence.

There is much in Mr. Minor's theory of creativity, then, that I do not understand. The result may be less than justice to the criticisms which he directs from this base upon my own position. However I will comment as best I can on what seem to be the most important of these criticisms.

One that is made repeatedly is that I escape the multiplicity of the world by rising above it—not by showing how the diverse facts are related but by rising above them to an abstract unity that does not in truth relate them at all. Now there is one way of reaching unity that is indeed open to this objection. Starting from the rich diversity of physical things, for example, one may classify them by increasingly abstract resemblances, first into dogs, cabbages, stones, etc., then into animals, vegetables, and minerals; then into material objects, then into substances, and finally into mere beings. The concept of being will thus be the most comprehensive of all concepts; and since everything is at least a being, everything will be unified under it. Now I have argued at length in *The Nature of Thought* that such a concept is a "false or abstract universal," that far from being the richest of all ideas it is the thinnest and most meager. It unifies nothing since it is reached by leaving out everything that is distinctive of anything. Thus if I am charged with unifying my world by abstracting from its differences, I can only plead not guilty.

It is true that I have held the world to be a unity, both causally and logically. But I have held in both cases that the unity would be lost if a single ripple on the sea or a single grain of sand on the shore were to be left out. My world is a system, but an all-inclusive system in which, if a single grain or ripple were excluded, the lines of causality and implication leading to it would be left dangling in the air. If Mr. Minor thinks I lose the trees in the wood, the diversity of the world in its unity, I suspect that it is because he is classifying my thought under the wrong kind of monism—that of Parmenides, Plotinus, and Bradley. All these thinkers run out in the end into mysticism. If you carry your monism so far as to deny all plurality and to reject all relations as self-contradictory, the diversity of the world will of course vanish. But with it will go the law of contradiction itself, since this implies different and related terms, and with it also will go necessity and coherence, since these two are relations. For Bradley the pilgrimage of thought begins in an immediacy that is below relations and ends in an immediacy above them. But though I accept much of Bradley, I cannot see how one can use the law of contradiction, which clearly involves terms and relations, to show that terms and relations are unreal, and suppose that one escapes such incoherence by diving into a mystical pool of unity in which language and logic are submerged together. I remain a rationalist; I am not a mystic.

Nevertheless Mr. Minor thinks my rationalism exhibits a grave "imbalance." Indeed he suggests that "The overplay of system and the subordination of novelty to it is a fit context for human rebellion and revolution." He believes, as we have seen, that we should recognize in nature, just as we do in society, a strife between law and order on the one hand and burgeoning innovation on the other. But one cannot "overplay" what is universal. The rationalist metaphysician has traditionally assumed, with the natural scientist, that he is living under the reign of law. His most persistent opposition on this point has come from certain moralists who have held that unless the self can make choices which somehow issue from no cause and in accordance with no law, moral responsibility vanishes. They have not always considered that this would make psychology impossible, and while I agree that a mechanistic or a behaviorist psychology would be no great loss, I cannot agree that mental events occur without any causes at all. Persons who think they do should read Sir David Ross on determinism in *The Foundations of Ethics*. And if one is justified in assuming that causal law holds everywhere without exception, then to say that anyone is "overplaying" the part of law or necessitation in the world seems to be meaningless. It implies that one is finding such law where it does not exist, that there are regions where novelty eludes causality and pops up out of nothing. If a person maintains that such things happen, he should be prepared to supply examples and also to provide a criterion by which one could distinguish events that are necessitated from those that are not. Unless I have missed something important in his essay, Mr. Minor has not provided either. Until he does, I do not think I can appropriately be charged with overplaying necessitation. To such a charge it seems fair enough to reply: I shall accept it as soon as you show me one event that has *not* issued from any past events in accordance with law.

Mr. Minor suggests that I think of creativity in exclusively intellectual terms, that is, in terms of solving problems. It is true that in *The Nature of Thought* I was dealing specifically with the intellectual life, where creativity does, I think, take the form of solving problems. In saying this I do not of course think of a problem as merely a set puzzle in arithmetic or chess; I mean a challenge to bring some anomaly that is not now understood into intelligible relation with one's normal world. I have implied that such creation always involves an ideal of system actively at work in one's mind.

Is the ideal of system or coherent whole similarly at work in creation in other fields? Without attempting to develop the thesis in detail I have suggested that it is. In the composition of music, for example, or in the construction of a drama, a coherent whole is also in course of creation. There is room for useful work here in considering whether differing kinds of necessity are at work in the aesthetic and moral fields. I have argued in *Reason and Goodness* that in moral creativity it is of the first importance to take account of consistency among prospective ends or values. To be sure, "creativity" is not a term I commonly use. But if it is taken roughly to mean the production of what is novel and important, I do not think my treatment of it has been confined to its intellectual form. What I can justly be charged with is having used the pattern I found in intellectual invention or discovery as a key to unlock the creative process in other fields.

On the whole my theories seem to me to come out rather well from Mr. Minor's scrutiny. One of his criticisms, however, is far more serious for the sort of theory I was stating in *The Nature of Thought* than any so far considered. He charges me with holding to a "block universe" in which nothing novel could ever appear. He could have pursued this criticism farther and maintained that in such a universe nothing could ever happen at all, since such a world lies beyond time and change altogether.

Now it is true that in certain passages of my book I did accept either explicitly or by implication the view that time cannot be real, and for anyone who does that, the whole course of evolution, of history, of the development of his own thought must also be appearance only. The rationalist seems to be committed on the one hand to the advance of his own thought under the guidance of an ideal. But that ideal, assumed to reflect the real, is of a system in which every detail is connected necessarily and timelessly with the others. Thus he finds himself holding, as Green and Hegel did, to a timeless universe in which nevertheless the history of thought is clearly a process in time. This obviously will not do. The thinker can hardly mean that the activity of his own reflection never occurred. Some thinkers like Bradley and McTaggart have stoutly held, nevertheless, to the unreality of time. Their arguments, so far as I have understood them, do not now seem compelling.

But *need* a rationalist deny the reality of time? Causation is a temporal process governed by laws, and I have held that in the end these would be found to be necessary laws connecting the nature of the cause with that of the effect. Indeed in a sense time can be taken up into the statement of the law itself, expressed in hypothetical form: "If abc . . . occurs in a certain combination at time t_1, ABC . . . will occur at time t_2." If it is complained that there is some hocus-pocus about this, that an abstracted law is not an actual sequence, that an indescribable but essential element of flux is left out, I must confess to uneasiness. But the uneasiness is in part an uncertainty as to what the criticism amounts to. The critic, if challenged, cannot say *what* is being left out, since any what that he might mention will include characters or universals, and he is trying to go below these. The difficulty is one that is hard even to state, let alone solve. But it does raise the ancient speculative problem of the relation between permanence and change, between timeless law and transient occurrents. An event, like an individual, seems to me to be made up of universals, and these universals are connected with others by timeless law. What is the *it* which has the characters and suffers the change? Anything further that I have to say on this ancient puzzle will be more suitably said in my reply to Mr. Hahn, who has chosen to press the question home.

18 BLANSHARD'S CRITIQUE OF PRAGMATISM
John E. Smith

I T would be difficult to find, or even to construct, a form of thought more thoroughly at odds with Blanshard's rationalistic idealism than pragmatism, especially if one focuses on those features of the position which stress action, transformation of the environment, and individual satisfaction. Blanshard recognizes this point himself on numerous occasions throughout his extensive analysis of pragmatism in *The Nature of Thought* ([*NT*] 1:341–93).[1] And, in fact, so total is his opposition that one has the distinct impression that should a pragmatist have asserted any proposition which Blanshard could accept, that proposition could not possibly express any doctrine distinctive of pragmatism. Yet in his characteristically generous manner of conducting philosophical discussion, Blanshard ends his critique with the noting of one point of agreement between his and the pragmatic view. "Thought," he writes, "*is* a means to an end; it is in its essence instrumental; it may be described not illegitimately as a kind of intention or purpose" (1:393). But as he continues, it becomes at once clear that the focal point of difference concerns the character of this purpose or intention. "Where the pragmatist is wrong," he claims, "is not in his insistence that thought is a means, but in what seems to us his perverse refusal to recognize that thought has an end of its own" (ibid.).[2]

The issue is clearly put; pragmatism is seen as making thought serve as an instrument to an end (or ends) not of its own making, whereas a correct view of thought is that it has its own goal, one end which it alone specifies as that which realizes itself. And, as I shall suggest, Blanshard is so sanguine in his demand that there be *the* goal of thought that he is led to suppose that when the pragmatist specifies any function for thought, he must be claiming that it is *the* function for thought. Why may thought not at times function in such a way that its ideas are "plans of action" without our having to say that *the* essence of thought is "a drive toward practice"? (*NT,* 1:350). Such a position is that held by Peirce; for him, all thought except for certain logical and mathematical instances (see *Collected Papers,* 5.27 ff.)[3] involves distinctions in practice, but Peirce denies that all thought is for the sake of action. Blanshard, on the other hand, seems to require of pragmatism, if it is to have something "new to say," that it assert nothing less than that *the* function of thought is to be instrumental to physical change. Even if Dewey could be interpreted as asserting this thesis, it is far from any assertion which Peirce would accept. Moreover, we should not forget that James acknowledged a purely theoretical purpose for a thinker as long as it is seen as one purpose among others, and this acknowledgment fits in consistently with his own scientific pursuits.

As a prelude to considering Blanshard's critique with respect to this issue, and several others to be introduced later, it is necessary to indicate the perspective and purpose of this essay. To begin with, I do not propose to offer a knock-down defense of pragmatism in the face of Blanshard's incisive criticisms, partly because I agree with some of them, and partly because the enterprise would be too unwieldy. The term "pragmatism" denotes a substantial and extensive intellectual territory, a territory which would have to include the doctrines of Peirce, James, and Dewey, to say nothing of Mead and Lewis. Blanshard bases his examination of the position largely on carefully culled quotations from the writings of James and Dewey, introducing Schiller's extreme views at just those points where total demolition is called for. No reference is made to Peirce except insofar as he is quoted by others; and this fact, while understandable,[4] is not without significance, because Peirce's version of pragmatism has within it resources—especially his view of concepts, his theory of science, and his Scotistic realism—for meeting some of Blanshard's objections. Moreover, Blanshard, it seems to me, fails to take seriously some of the motives behind the pragmatic movement precisely because he views it uncompromisingly in the light of the standard furnished by his own conception of thought as having but one essential goal—the attainment of one coherent, theoretical insight into the nature of the real.

Let us begin with the fundamental idea of the goal of thought, bearing in mind what was said above about the difference between thought having its own goal and thought being subjected to a goal which it does not determine. The first question is, What does it mean for *thought* to have a goal?, and further, If thought does have a goal, does it have but one goal which can readily be recognized as *the* goal of thought? Would it not be more in accord with our common experience to say that persons have goals or purposes, that persons have intentions and ends in view, and that whereas it is conceivable that *one* of these intentions may be the attainment of a total, rational comprehension of what there is, some further warrant is required for endowing "thought" itself with this one intention or goal as if it could not exist except as having or being subject to this goal? The point can be clarified by means of an illustration drawn from a quite different philosophical context. Kant, in his analysis of the antinomies of pure reason, viewed the incompatible or dialectical assertions as stemming not from doctrines expressed in books and systems but from the nature and development of reason itself. But after having assured us that theoretical reason comes to a standstill in the face of these antinomies and cannot resolve them in objective terms, Kant introduces, with dramatic suddenness, the idea of the "interest" of reason in the dialectical conflicts, by which he means that if our purpose is that of attaining scientific knowledge, we shall come down on the side of the antitheses and if our purpose is moral and religious we shall come down on the side of the theses. But if theoretical reason is brought to a standstill in the face of the antinomic assertions, what can it possibly mean to attribute the two different "interests" to reason? Is it not clear that it is man, the thinker, who has the interests or purposes in question, and that these purposes direct rational activity even if they do not entirely determine the structure of that activity. My purpose obviously is not to discuss Kant, but only to use this example to elucidate a point germane to Blanshard's view. The question how reason as such comes to have an interest for Kant is analogous to the question how thought as such comes to have a goal for Blanshard. Is the answer not, in both cases, that it is the person and not the abstract "reason" or "thought" which has the interest and the goal? Peirce, James, and Dewey, regardless of other features of their thought, were all prepared to admit, and in Peirce's case to insist, that *one* of our human purposes is that of seeking a purely theoretical account of the real, which for all of them meant the enterprise of science. I am not saying that Dewey's thoroughgoing instrumental conception of science represents a final or adequate account, but even he acknowledged the reality of the enterprise which aims at disclosing an intersubjective world of public fact through the recurrent use of experimental procedures. Peirce's account of science seems to me on the whole more satisfactory than that of Dewey, and there is no question that it allows ample place for the theoretical ideal.

What Blanshard does is to identify this one theoretical purpose with *the* purpose or goal of thought, and the result is that all other human purposes involving thought must inevitably appear as the subjection of thought to an alien goal. That thought does indeed arise or is a reality in its own right is too well attested to be in doubt. That thought, moreover, has structures not to be derived from the surrounding conditions or occasions when it does make its appearance is something I would insist upon. But is it necessary to guarantee this autonomy of thought by endowing thought itself with the one goal of attaining not only the purely theoretical account of reality which we attribute to science but a total scheme of rationality—coherence accompanied by necessity—representative of a philosophical ideal? Is it not clear that what Blanshard has done is to identify the goal of thought itself with his own philosophical vision of what rationality means? I suspect that what Blanshard has in mind, and what leads him to regard the pragmatists as archenemies, is that he believes that thought "left to itself," as it were, would inevitably lead to the goal he specifies, whereas the pragmatists were not inclined to view thought in this way but to take it instead as an activity which is never unrelated to the purposes of the being whose activity it is. But who can say where thought "left to itself" would go? Is it not in fact the case that every conception of thought's goal based on a conception of its autonomy is not actually a discovery of where thought *would* end but rather the expression of a doctrine of where it *must* end, which is to say, a philosophical theory of its true nature? Can we determine from the inspection of all the elements of thought—ideas, judgments, universals, logical principles—and *quite independently of human purpose*, what *the* goal of thought must be? If thought is to have one goal, is that goal not rather the expression of a human purpose and the projection of a philosophical ideal on the part of a thinker (or even many thinkers) that thought should have that one goal because it is believed that a true view of the nature of thought requires it? Neither Locke, nor Hume, nor Mill, nor Russell can readily be interpreted as pragmatists, and yet no one of them would accept the thesis that *the* goal of thought is identical with the one which Blanshard specifies. This fact suggests that every conception of thought's goal is rooted in some doctrine of the nature of thought which purports to express its essential nature. If one examines Blanshard's own account of the nature of thought starting with his theory of the idea, one sees at once that the analysis is *intentional* throughout, and that it presupposes a thinker who has already adopted as his purpose for thought the one theoretical ideal which he projects. In expressing his theory "in briefest compass," Blanshard says, "Thought in its essence is an attempt to attain, in the sense of achieving identity with, a special end of its own" (*NT,* 1:473). But again, is it not obvious that what we have begun with is not "thought in its essence" but the thinker who has, from all of his purposes, selected that of gaining a purely theoretical apprehension of what there is and who has in addition identified the nature of that with the main thesis of philosophical idealism? What troubles me about this identification of the thinker's theoretical purpose with the essence of thought as such, and further with a specific reading of that essence, is that, for the life of the individual, all other purposes not expressive of the theoretical ideal but still involving thought—moral, religious, aesthetic—must then be regarded as cases where thought is being subjected to an alien end. What the pragmatists were trying to do becomes relevant precisely at this point. They envisaged man as having a multitude of purposes, one of which embodies theoretical ideals to be realized in logic, mathematics, and bodies of science, but which, just because it is one purpose among others, has to be intelligibly related to those other purposes in a continuum of living experience which is by no means structured solely in accordance with the one purpose or ideal that says, "All men by nature desire to know." The pragmatists, to be sure, got into many difficulties and perplexities in their attempt to connect both theoretical activity and its fruits with the other activities which constitute ongoing experience; and I would agree with many of Blanshard's criticisms, especially of Dewey's thoroughgoing instrumentalism. However, it remains unclear to me how, once the thinker's theoretical purpose has been projected far beyond him and identified with the goal of thought itself, other human purposes and activities where the theoretical ideal does not predominate—making things, arriving at moral and political decisions, believing in God, appraising aesthetic creations, seeking to correct injustices, etc.—are to be related both to the intellectual activity aimed at reaching the goal of thought and to the truth which, as it appears, is known only at the end.

A further consequence, as it seems to me, of Blanshard's rather too simple presentation of the situation as one in which we have to choose between his conception of thought's goal and a number of alternatives involving the denial of thought and its autonomy altogether, is that the ingredience of thought in purposes where it is inappropriate to regard the theoretical ideal as either exclusive or dominant ipso facto becomes a case of thought being subjected to an alien goal. My suggestion is that, on the basis of this consequence, not only should Blanshard's conception of the goal of thought come up for reconsideration, but also the matter of the interrelation between man's many purposes and especially how we are to understand the implications for thought of the fact that man's theoretical purpose is but one among others, even if it be, in a sense, the most important.

I go on to another focal point in Blanshard's critical examination of pragmatism: his claim that when thought is viewed as the instrument of an organism, or a means to satisfaction, it follows that the self is confined to its own series of experiences. For the pragmatist, says Blanshard, "it is inevitable that for 'experience' we should read 'my experience' " (*NT*, 1:375). I believe it would be generally agreed that James placed very considerable emphasis on individual judgment and the need for a person to make his own appraisal of the extent to which the outcome of believing or acting in a specific situation was satisfactory or not. Even allowing for this, however, I doubt that it is correct to interpret the pragmatic conception of experience in a way which implies that an individual is confined to *his own* ideas, sensedata, impressions after the fashion of the entire British empirical tradition stretching from Hume to Russell and beyond. In fact even James, who was closer to that empiricism than either Peirce or Dewey (both of whom rejected it outright), argued in his "radical empiricism" that for "pure experience" the content is primary and the consciousness, i.e. the distinction between that content and the awareness that the content is "mine," comes by way of addition through reflection. Two minds can thus know the same thing, since we do not start with the assumption that initially each has "his own" idea which is his alone and then have to look about for a way of transcending this privacy in order to reach the "external world."[5]

But suppose we allow that there is in James's thought a strong individualistic thrust; the question still remains as to the correctness of Blanshard's claim that experience has to be "my experience" when one considers Peirce and Dewey. The former beyond all question (see esp. 5.402 nn. 1, 2, 3) held that the experience which counts for the pragmatist is "ours" and maintained that the disclosure of the real is accomplished only through the efforts of a community of knowers in which the purely individual thought or opinion is filtered out by the convergent opinion of many inquirers.[6] The same holds true for Dewey; and the very fact that many critics have raised precisely the question as to *whose* experience is meant by Dewey when he writes of "experience" as method, and as the funded results of many inquiries, casts suspicion on Blanshard's thesis that the pragmatist is encapsulated within "my experience." I am suggesting, of course, that there has been no unified tendency among those who have commented on Dewey to suppose that for him experience meant "first person" and nothing more. How is it possible for Blanshard to have arrived at his thesis when so many others have wondered whether Dewey's thoroughly biosocial understanding of man does not in fact cast doubt upon the reality and autonomy of individual experience?[7] Blanshard has, I believe, been led astray at this point in his interpretation of pragmatism by one of his own assumptions, an assumption which is at the root of classical empiricism and proved so powerful that even a dialectical master like Bradley who sought to overturn that empiricism could not escape from its influence. I have in mind the assumption that in one form or another experience is primordially of "experience," that is, a certainty of an ideational content which is grasped as *internal* and thus as somehow separated from an objective world beyond. As I shall point out, it is not pragmatism but classical British empiricism which encapsulates us within "my experience."

To begin with, I agree with Blanshard that much of what Dewey writes about experience requires reference to experience as had by some individual, and I am supposing that this holds true for what any philosopher writes about experience. The central question, however, is whether from this alone it follows that experience never means more than "my" or some other individual's experience; my view is that it does not follow. What is there in Dewey's thought which leads Blanshard to suppose that pragmatism is forced to remain within the confines of purely individual experience? I believe that Blanshard comes to this conclusion because he misunderstands the main point of Dewey's objection to classical epistemology. On numerous occasions, Blanshard points out that Dewey rejected epistemology *only* because he did not want to admit the dualism between the mental and the physical which that tradition of thinking engendered (see *NT,* 1:369–70 esp.). But while I agree with Blanshard's incisive criticism of Dewey's attempt to avoid the introduction of an idea as a vehicle for meaning (1:367 ff.),[8] I do not see that Dewey's objection to the epistemological approach is entirely summed up in the dualism issue and the reality of the mental. Dewey was uncertain about modern epistemology precisely because of the prevalent view that experience is knowledge and that this knowledge takes the form of an immediate certainty, not only of some content, but also that that content is confined to our own series of experiences. Were this not the case it would be difficult to explain why the entire "empirical" tradition from Hume to Russell had to solve this problem: given some immediate certainty about our own internal "experience"—i.e. ideas, sense-data, etc.—how can we reach the external world? But the fact is that Dewey did not accept this way of constructing the problem, and Peirce accepted it even less.[9] For neither is there any immediate certainty that the direct object of consciousness is merely internal or confined to the individual who has it alone, and on this account it becomes difficult to see how either could be accused of confining experience to "my experience." Blanshard, curiously enough, calls attention to this point himself (1:375–76) and says that "this reply has sometimes been taken as decisive" (1:376) but he goes on to claim that the issue is not whether thought is mental or not, but rather that as long as pragmatists continue to maintain that the essence of thought is "a means to successful behaviour on the part of an individual organism" (1:376) they are encapsulated within individual experience. I agree that, at this juncture, the issue is not that of the mental, but Blanshard's way of posing the real problem is surely redundant. If we are talking about an "individual organism" *and nothing else,* then, of course, we are talking about individual experience and nothing else. But this assertion by itself does not support Blanshard's larger claim that for pragmatism experience must be "my" experience. And in fact it is quite clear that both Peirce and Dewey were unconditionally opposed to the classical view of experience[10] according to which experience can be nothing other than "my" experience, even if custom and the uniformity of nature were invoked to persuade us otherwise.

Blanshard objects to attempts to escape limitation to the individual by including, or appealing to, the social dimension of a situation. I agree that the form this appeal takes in the statements by Moore which Blanshard cites (*NT,* 1:376–77) is not very strong, but the point can be made in a far stronger way. At the risk of repeating what has been said, I shall restate the essential point briefly. The central idea is that, for Peirce and Dewey at any rate, experience, while always realized in and for an individual, is not confined to either the momentary or singular consciousness, but aims at being a critical, funded, and intersubjective disclosure of an objective Nature (Dewey) or of independent Reals (Peirce). The "social" element enters when we consider that critical experience is a product or result of a methodical enterprise embracing the experience and activity of many individuals who are sharing and comparing experiences for the purpose of sifting out what is wayward and idiosyncratic and of retaining what withstands critical testing. It is in this sense that for both Peirce and Dewey the cognitive enterprise is understood in terms of a community of investigators each of whom is committed to the following of certain procedures aimed at disclosing a critical and intersubjective result. The important point is that standing behind this essentially discursive conception of experience and knowledge is a firm denial on the part of Peirce and Dewey that experience is primordially an intuitive affair rooted in the certainty of impressions, ideas, or data of sense which are known to be internal to, or the exclusive possession of, an individual consciousness. In short, for the pragmatist experience is not essentially a doubling back on consciousness, least of all on individual consciousness, but rather a many-sided interaction or encounter between a sign-using being and what there is such that the outcome of this encounter assumes cognitive status when certain critical conditions are satisfied. In view of the foregoing, I find it difficult to understand why Blanshard insists that for pragmatism "experience" always means "my experience."

Another point at which Blanshard attacks pragmatism has to do with the much discussed question about knowledge of the past. The problem emerges for the pragmatists because of their doctrine that the meaning of an assertion is identical with some conceivable and expected *future* events that at the same time are to serve as evidence for the assertion, and it seems paradoxical indeed to claim that an assertion about, say, Anselm's deliberation over whether to publish his *Proslogion,* means that such and such *will be* experienced if one carries out certain investigations.[11] Here I believe that Blanshard's critique is essentially correct, especially as it concerns Dewey's attempt to show what knowledge of the past could mean on an instrumentalist view. The discussion of this issue, which Blanshard reviews (*NT,* 1:359 ff.) with characteristic precision, turns on the possibility of there being an idea or judgment which refers to the past. Blanshard is right in his contention that Dewey must admit the existence of judgments as distinct from "esthetic fancies" about the past and that a proposed judgment about, for example, Abelard's attitude toward Heloise is intended as a judgment about a past state of affairs at the time it is made and does not change its status from a "fancy" to that of a judgment merely by the actual adducing of what would verify or disconfirm it. The intended judgment about the past, that is to say, focusing or selecting its object is, if clearly enough formulated, either true or false, and the fact that, from the standpoint of the knower, the process of testing or finding evidence is a serial one which has a *future terminus* does in no way alter the intended past reference. From within the actual knowing process it seems clear that all the *evidence for* a past event must be found later than that event and therefore as something future to it, even if the evidence itself were contemporaneous with the event referred to, as when a chronicler records an event as it is taking place. Difficulties need arise only if it is insisted that what the judgment about the past *means* is identical with a description of the future evidence which would either support the judgment or render it precarious. If, for example, I were to put the question, Did Luther experience doubts about the wisdom of appearing and delivering a manifesto at the Diet of Worms? and if I located in the future, evidence, say his own diary, which expressed such doubts, on this basis I could assert "Luther entertained doubts about . . . ," and my reference would be to the man and his experience, not to the diary. The evidence is evidence *for* something other than itself, and when I make an assertion on the basis of evidence, "Luther entertained doubts about . . . ," I do *not* mean there is future evidence in the form of Luther's diary containing such and such statements. What I do mean to assert is that "Luther entertained doubts . . . ," and in support of the assertion I cite the future evidence which precisely as evidence is evidence *for* something other than itself, and that something is a past occurrence. The fact that, within the knowing process, the evidence is always found "in the future" with respect to any past event gives no ground whatever for denying that the present judgment refers to that past event. Dewey says, "Only when the past event which is judged *is a going concern having effects still directly observable are judgment and knowledge possible*,"[12] and I would agree with Blanshard in accepting this statement, if it is taken to mean that the evidence though in itself future to the event and, in the nature of the case, present to us, is evidence for a judgment about a past event. My own view is that confusion is created when the purported meaning of the judgment about the past event is identified with the sort of consequences which, if they occur and are available to us in some present, can serve as evidence for the truth or falsity of the judgment. This identification confuses the evidence with what it is evidence for.

There is a final point raised by Blanshard's question as to whether Dewey is in fact offering a theory of the nature of thought as such, and this question will serve to bring us back to the opening topic: *the* goal of thought. First, I believe that in fact Dewey regarded his instrumental account as, so to speak, covering the whole ground and thus as expressing not one alternative among others but the fundamental character of reflective thought in opposition to other positions. Blanshard, of course, has a dialectical reason for taking Dewey's position in comprehensive terms because, like Royce before him, he aims at pointing out that should a universal truth claim be advanced in behalf of a pragmatist or instrumentalist conception of thought, that claim would involve presuppositions either inconsistent with or even excluded by the conception itself. As Royce put it, if the pragmatic theory of truth is itself true, it is not true in its own terms. Persuasive as the objection seems prima facie, I do not believe that the self-referential argument is entirely conclusive, but an extended discussion would be required and that is not possible here. I would like instead to concentrate on this question: if (1) we object to Dewey's attempt to characterize the nature of thought in terms of the problematic occasions on which it is said to arise and thus to identify it as essentially instrumental or problem solving, and (2) we argue that this approach either fails to allow for or even destroys the *autonomy* of thought, what is it which gives us the warrant for supposing that there is the one goal of thought which alone expresses that autonomy? I believe with Blanshard that describing the rise of reflection as, in Dewey's own terms, "response to the doubtful as such"[13] does not of itself serve to establish the thesis that the whole nature of thought consists in the resolution of the sort of problems raised by the occurrence of Dewey's problematic situation. In short, I would not only allow, but even insist, that thought has intrinsic structures manifested in, for example, mathematics, logic, physical science, and in philosophical reflection itself which are not uniquely derivable from actual occasions when disappointed expectations call forth reflective thought. On the basis of a principle of functional autonomy, recognized in science no less than philosophy, activities can come to have structures far more complex than those involved in their initial or immediate appearance. When our automobile breaks down and frustrates our habitual responses, reflection on the problem and its resolution is in order. But the structure of that reflection is by no means entirely determined by its operation in that instance. We can examine the structure of that reflection itself and discover in it a logic which far transcends in generality not only specific instrumental uses but even the logic of inquiry itself.[14] Blanshard would, I assume, agree with all this, but then, if I understand him correctly, he would take the step with which I have difficulty; once the autonomy of thought is acknowledged, he would go on to express that autonomy not only in structures of thought but also in *the* aim or goal of thought which takes the form of an internal relations idealism.

And it is this move which brings me back to my initial question: How does thought get an aim? Structures it has, to be sure, but how does thought acquire an aim which is not that of the human thinker and especially how does it acquire the specific aim which Blanshard envisages for it? In my view, what Blanshard does is to endow thought itself with the ideal human purpose of achieving a comprehensive, theoretical understanding of the whole of reality. I am willing to admit the reality of this purpose as *one among others* in the spectrum of human purposes, but then the achievement of this purpose has to be related to our other purposes, which means, among other things, that we shall need principles of relevance and selectivity enabling us to decide on specific occasions exactly what items of knowledge gained as a result of purely theoretic activity do actually "count" or have bearing on the specific occasion which concerns us. It was precisely this consideration which James had in mind when he pointed to the encyclopedia on the shelf as the symbol of a total knowledge and asked: "When do I say these things?" And it is the same consideration that gives me pause when I contemplate the special reading which Blanshard gives to the goal of thought. In accordance with his ideal, *every* item of knowledge and possible knowledge is relevant—for the purely theoretical ideal—if thought is to achieve its goal, but how are the relevances for this or that specific situation to be determined if *the* aim of thought is such that these specific relevances (*precisely what the pragmatists had in mind*) have to be transcended in order not to interrupt and relativize the autonomous advance of thought itself?

My point is that once you extract from the spectrum of human purposes the purely theoretic one and identify it with *the* goal of thought in the form of the one system of necessity and internal relations, you can no longer take seriously other human purposes and the specific temporal occasions upon which they come into play; these other purposes must then be regarded as no more than obstacles or hindrances to the operation of thought bent on attaining its one goal. The pragmatists may well have gone too far in their attempt to connect thought with, or to show its relevance for, all the contingent, immediate, and often quite mundane events and situations arising in human experience. But if their attempt was not entirely successful, it does not follow that the problems they sought to resolve do not still exist or that we can simply ignore them. The most superficial assessment of the contemporary climate of opinion will serve to call attention to the urgency and even the explosiveness of the human concerns to which the pragmatists addressed themselves. After decades of scientism, and of technical philosophies that ignored the difficult human problems of life and death in order to concentrate on the theory of knowledge, the quest for purpose and significance by modern man has finally turned into the desperate pursuit of the wondrous and the near-miraculous. The return of astrology, fortune-telling, fascination over speaking in tongues, excursions into the world of expanded consciousness, reaching out for new and mysterious gods and wisdoms, all bear witness to the lengths to which men go when their questions and concerns are ignored by professional wise men whose conception of thought is either too narrow or too austere to permit them to discuss speculative questions that have practical bearings in a rational and controlled way.

Blanshard, to be sure, has a broad and rich conception of thought, and I am far from identifying his position with any form of scientism or analysis; that would be too absurd. Nevertheless, the question may still be raised as to whether Blanshard's conception of thought with its one all-embracing theoretic goal may not in the end also exclude the "problems of men" insofar as these problems are not resolvable in terms of a complete system of internal relations. If we, as philosophers, have doubts about the validity of some of the ideas, practices, and doctrines to which many of the younger generation are turning in their attempt to face themselves and the world, we must seek to discover what it is that they find in these new ideas and practices not to be found in current philosophical thinking. Then we must address ourselves in a critical and constructive way to those issues. But if we fail to do so for fear of sullying thought or of endangering its purity, we must not be surprised if thought comes to be rejected altogether as not germane to present concerns.

JOHN E. SMITH

DEPARTMENT OF PHILOSOPHY
YALE UNIVERSITY

NOTES

[1] I am taking this discussion as the *locus classicus* of Blanshard's view. I do not know whether he would still subscribe to the whole of this critique of some thirty years ago, but my suspicion is that he would, especially in view of the chapter on "Instrumentalism" (161 ff.) in *Reason and Goodness* (1961). At any rate it is one of the purposes of this volume to provide him with an opportunity to answer the question.

[2] It is worth noting that this was precisely the issue which separated Bradley and James, reflected in that part of the correspondence which we possess. See *Mind* 75, no. 229 (July 1966): 309–31. James accused Bradley of launching thought from the platform of immediate experience without demanding that it return to that experience from time to time for corroboration or correction. And, James added, it is precisely because of the view that thought has its goal entirely immanent in itself that Bradley saw no need for thought to have "perching places" in its flight once it has taken off.

[3] *Collected Papers of Charles Sanders Peirce*, eds. Charles Hartshorne and Paul Weiss (Cambridge: Harvard University Press, 1931–1938).

[4] The papers of Peirce were making their appearance in the 1930s in the edition of Hartshorne and Weiss, and although Peirce's writings were available to Blanshard, it is only fair to say that at that time Peirce was not widely recognized and studied as he has been in the past twenty years.

[5] See *The Meaning of Truth* (New York: Longmans, Green, 1909), 49 n., where James argues that the "same object" can appear "in the mental history of different persons. . . . It thus ceases to be the private property of one experience, and becomes, so to speak, a shared or public thing."

[6] See Peirce, *Collected Papers*, 5.234–35, for the view that ignorance and error are precisely what distinguish the private self.

7See Gordon Allport, "Dewey's Individual and Social Psychology," in *The Philosophy of John Dewey*, ed. P. A. Schilpp (Evanston and Chicago: Northwestern University [now published by Open Court], 1939), 265–90; and 554 ff. of the same volume, where Dewey accepts Allport's charge that he had not given an adequate theory of personality and explains that he was trying to avoid "spiritualistic" theories about the nature of the individual self.

8Blanshard is right in maintaining that you cannot make a physical object "function" referentially without an intelligence which grasps this unique "function" and understands its meaning through an idea.

9See 5.213 ff. "Some Questions Concerning Certain Faculties Claimed for Man."

10See Dewey's "An Empirical Survey of Empiricisms," in *Studies in the History of Ideas*, vol. 3 (New York: Columbia University Press, 1935), and "The Need for a Recovery of Philosophy," in *Creative Intelligence*, by John Dewey et al. (New York: Henry Holt & Co., 1917).

11Peirce, on the whole, distinguished the meaning of a historical assertion from the reference, and maintained that such an assertion about a past event does in fact refer to it. But there is at least one place (5.461) where he has the belief about a past event *referring* to the future. On the other hand, 5.459 and 8.195 support the view that historical assertions refer to past events.

12Quoted by Blanshard (*NT*, 1:365) from *Journal of Philosophy* 19 (1922): 311. Italics in original.

13"The Need for a Recovery of Philosophy."

14It is important to notice that Dewey agrees with at least part of what I am saying; logic exists as the *theory* of inquiry, which means essentially as *methodology*, but presumably he would refuse to admit that there are logical forms not derivable from or exhibited in inquiry.

18. Reply to John E. Smith
Blanshard's Critique of Pragmatism

Mr. Smith, who writes with authority on American pragmatism, thinks that my criticism of that philosophy in *The Nature of Thought* was too narrow in the range of writers considered and too idiosyncratic in its interpretation. There is point in both these strictures, though on both heads I can offer some pleas in extenuation.

He reminds us that when my criticism was being written in the thirties much of Peirce, Lewis, and Mead, and not a little of Dewey was still unpublished or inaccessible. The three accepted leaders of the pragmatic movement were James, Dewey, and Schiller, and these I took as the subjects of my study. Dewey I chose for special attention as the most thorough exponent of the theory.

As for Peirce, though I said nothing about him in my first book, I did deal with his "pragmaticism," as he preferred to call it, in *Reason and Analysis*. If the theory as there developed in his early essays is typical, I cannot think that his inclusion in the earlier study would have done anything to bolster the pragmatic case. He says that a belief is a rule for action, which it is not. My belief that India has more than 500 million people is not a rule for any kind of action. Peirce says that we can determine the difference in beliefs by determining the difference in action to which they lead, which is clearly untrue. I may believe firmly that Caesar was a greater commander than Napoleon without ever revealing it in anything I say or do. He says at times that belief reduces to a "habit" of action. But a belief held once and then forgotten is as truly a belief as an acceptance of an article of the Creed which is recited every Sunday. He says: "our idea of anything is our idea of its sensible effects." This contradicts itself. For if our idea of anything is our idea of its effects only, what is the "it" that is alleged to have the effects? When we are clearing our ideas, we are to look to the consequences of our belief in the way of action; but then we are also to look to the consequences of the objects in the way of sensations. Neither of these directions is reliable, and they are inconsistent with each other. Peirce's "pragmaticism" was far too sandy a foundation for James or anyone else to build on.

The work of George Herbert Mead, who died in the early thirties, was published fragmentarily and posthumously by various editors and at various times, which made any adequate critique of his theory difficult during that decade. Lewis's pragmatism departed so widely from that of any of the others that he is hardly to be called a pragmatist at all. He was not a pragmatist, for example, regarding empirical propositions, but only regarding the a priori. I have briefly discussed this type of view, though not in special connection with Lewis, in *Reason and Analysis.*

More serious than the suggestion of too contracted a coverage is the suggestion that I misconstrue the pragmatists that I do deal with. There are two chief reasons for this misconstruction. First, I have imposed on thought an arbitrary end of my own, from whose point of view I am bound to judge the pragmatists unfairly. Second, as a result of so misconceiving the end, I have misconstrued the true relation between thinking and the other purposive activities of our nature.

The arbitrariness in my account of thought lies in my imposing on it from its earliest appearance an end prescribed by the metaphysics of absolute idealism. ". . . is it not obvious that what we have begun with is not 'thought in its essence' but the thinker who has, from all of his purposes, selected that of gaining a purely theoretical apprehension of what there is and who has in addition identified the nature of that with the main thesis of philosophical idealism?"

As to the charge of arbitrarily selecting for thought the end of "a purely theoretical apprehension of what there is," I shall say something in a moment. Meanwhile I must demur to the suggestion that my analysis of thought on its lower levels has been twisted by a preconceived absolutism. *The Nature of Thought* was a genuine exploration, which, as explained in the preface, began as a study in psychology. I think the reader could traverse several hundred pages without guessing what I took as the ultimate end of thought. It was only gradually that I came to see this end myself. What I felt sure of was that the current psychological accounts of thinking were wrong because they did not admit the pull or presence of necessity in thinking. But it was not until the opening chapter of the second volume that I was ready to delineate with any clearness the sort of system in which thought could come to rest, and from there on the influence of the goal is strong. That my studies of Spinoza, Green, and Bradley had something to do with this delineation is no doubt true. But how did these philosophers themselves reach their conception of the end? It was by traversing in their own way the route that I did; if one doubts it, let him look at Spinoza's *Improvement of the Understanding,* Green's *Prolegomena,* or Bradley's *Principles of Logic,* a book which, if I may compare a work of doggedness with a work of genius, was also a climb from one plateau to another. Bradley started in the psychology of thinking and, as reflection ripened, moved inevitably on into metaphysics.

Is it replied that these men too were misconstruing the goal of thought by reading back into its earlier stages the results of speculation? I answer: What else could they have done? If you are to understand any purposive drive in human nature, you must look to its end, and that may well require speculation. It may require the drawing of a graph running through introspectively apprehended acts of thought on different levels of development, and the projections of this line into the future. One will hardly understand an acorn without grasping its destination as an oak. The lowly egg is more than a pleasing oval, for it is also a potential chicken. I admit that it seems absurd at first to see in the child's connection of tail-wagging in dog and cat with different dispositions an attempt to understand the universe. But if understanding anything means seeing it in the light of its conditions, one cannot say with each petty conclusion that the intellect is satisfied and the case closed. If understanding in common life means seeing things in the web of necessitating conditions, when would the expansion of this webwork be arrested? Only, I contended, when the web became all-inclusive. This idea is indeed a projection of the line of past and present thought. But I see nothing arbitrary about it, nothing but a straightforward inference from an examination of what I have been doing when I try to think. It would probably be truer to say that my absolutism grew out of my analysis of thought than the other way about.

More important, of course, than the question how I arrived at my theory is whether it is true. Mr. Smith thinks it fails. It fails because it does not catch the actual relations between the cognitive impulse and the other impulses of human nature, an enterprise in which the pragmatists have done better. Let me quote the crucial passage:

> What troubles me about this identification of the thinker's theoretical purpose with the essence of thought as such . . . is that, for the life of the individual, all other purposes not expressive of the theoretical ideal but still involving thought—moral, religious, aesthetic—must then be regarded as cases where thought is being subjected to an alien end. What the pragmatists were trying to do becomes relevant precisely at this point. They envisaged man as having a multitude of purposes, one of which embodies theoretical ideals to be realized in logic, mathematics and bodies of science, but which, just because it is one purpose among others, has to be intelligibly related to those other purposes in a continuum of living experience which is by no means structured solely in accordance with the one purpose or ideal that says, "All men by nature desire to know."

It is important to avoid some conclusions to which a reader might be led by this passage. I do not deny the variety of human impulses; indeed my theory of human nature and human goods is based on this variety. I do not hold that anyone should pursue exclusively the theoretical ideal, and have criticized severely its overemphasis in "intellectualism." I admit that thought enters into noncognitive desires "in a continuum of living experience," and in *Reason and Goodness* have spent much time in detailing how this occurs. I have agreed that thought is used constantly and rightly as an instrument to practical ends. Where then, exactly, do I differ from the pragmatist? I differ in holding (1) that the theoretical impulse is sharply distinct from all others, and (2) that its contribution to ends other than its own is irrelevant as a measure of its own success. Let me try to be clear.

(1) The first sentence of *The Nature of Thought* is "Thought is that activity of mind which aims directly at truth." This seems to me an empirical statement, which can be easily confirmed introspectively in any act of thought, whether theoretical or practical in its dominant interest. A man wants to buy a hat, thinks that he could get one at Macy's, and does so. The dominant aim here is not cognitive; it is to get a hat; but the thought that he can get one at Macy's is not a volition or "plan of action," but a judgment that is true or false, as a plan to act is not. If "theoretic impulse" makes such judgment too speculative, the name does not matter; what is meant could quite well be called "cognitive interest," "the urge to know," "curiosity," or even "the love of truth." The impulse manifests itself with all degrees of complexity from the child's engrossed inspection of a caterpillar to Hegel's conclusions about an infinite rational order. What is at work is one continuous interest exercised on countless objects and on countless levels.

Mr. Smith says that the pragmatists clearly recognize this theoretical interest and object only to giving it an undue primacy. In a somewhat curious sense this is true. When Montague objected to Dewey that he made thought a means to action rather than to truth, Dewey replied: "What I have insisted on is quite a different point, namely that action is involved in thinking and existential knowing, as part of the function of reaching immediate non-practical consequences" (Montague, *Ways of Knowing,* 135n.).[1] This too is strange doctrine. It is hard to see that when one sits and thinks about free will or universals anything like action in the ordinary sense is involved. And this teaching can hardly cancel Dewey's long insistence that the immediate concern of thought is always with action. An idea, he says, is an "intention to act so as to arrange them [things] in a certain way" (*Essays in Experimental Logic,* 310);[2] "Knowing is itself a mode of practical action" (*Quest for Certainty,* 104);[3] "ideas are statements not of what is or has been but of acts to be performed" (ibid., 133); they are really "plans of action." Dewey's addition that the action planned is itself an instrument to some later immediate experience beyond it will not save this analysis; judgments of the past, judgments in logic and mathematics, judgments of taste, are too obviously not concerned with action at all. The main tenor of Dewey's *Reconstruction in Philosophy,* as I read it, is that philosophy must get away from the sterile theorizing of the Greeks and make philosophy an instrument to the remoulding of nature and society.

James, like Dewey, protested against the imputation of overlooking the theoretic interest, and he did give it perfunctory recognition. But this was quite inconsistent with the main thrust of his pragmatism. It would be easy to document this main contention with many passages, but a single typical one will perhaps serve: "the tangible fact at the root of all our thought-distinctions, however subtle, is that there is no one of them so fine as to consist in anything but a possible difference of practice" (*Pragmatism,* 46).[4] To say that the meaning and test of all our beliefs about God and the Absolute, about causality, about implication, about the self and matter, reduce to differences in practice is in effect to deny altogether the theoretical interest as it is here conceived.

(2) But Mr. Smith's main criticism of my account of pragmatism is that, if it is true, "all other purposes not expressive of the theoretical ideal but still involving thought—moral, religious, aesthetic—must then be regarded as cases where thought is being subjected to an alien end." Let us see exactly how pragmatist and rationalist differ here, and let us take a field in which Mr. Smith is notably at home, the field of religion. How are we to justify a belief in God? This belief is notoriously bound up with interests other than cognitive, with reverence, love, fear, hope, and the longing for security. The rationalist would say that these attitudes, however involved historically with the belief in God, are irrelevant to the truth or falsity of that belief, that if a man believes in God because he takes satisfaction in revering a loving and ideal person, or because he hopes for another life, or because he wants to avoid punishment, or because he needs security in this life, he is deluding himself. His belief may be true or not, but it is not true for these reasons. The belief in God may further these ends, but they are "alien ends" in the sense that furthering them does not supply or confirm knowledge that God exists.

This firm distinctness of ends the pragmatist would break down. One can see the gradual movement toward what to me is philosophic tragedy in the changing thought of James. When he wrote *The Will to Believe* in 1896, he took the line that if the evidence—evidence in the ordinary logical sense—clearly favored or disfavored the belief in God, one should order one's belief accordingly. But if the decision were "living," "momentous," and "forced" or unavoidable, one was justified in accepting as true the belief most conducive to the peace, vigor, and security of one's mind. This was the thin edge of a very large wedge, and it raises acute questions about the ethics of belief to which we shall have to return in discussing Mr. Ferré's paper. It does seem to imply that if a belief gives one peace, vigor, and a sense of security, that is somehow relevant to its truth. And in his later full-blown pragmatism James seems to accept this frankly. When talking about the verification in practice of theological beliefs, he says: "Other than this practical significance, the words God, free-will, design, etc., have none. Yet dark tho they be in themselves, or intellectualistically taken, when we bear them into life's thicket with us the darkness *there* grows light about us" (*Pragmatism*, 121). If a belief in God helps us to get through "life's thicket," that so far verifies its truth.

Dewey, who had little of James's sympathy with traditional religion, gave him a gentle rebuke for this way of thinking. He saw that if God were conceived as theologians had commonly conceived him, his existence could not be proved by anything as irrelevant as the satisfactions attendant on believing. So he took the bold step, taken also a little later by the positivists, of denying that the idea of God held any meaning at all except certain changes in present and future experience. Dispensing with theological belief altogether, he defined "religiousness" as devotion to long-run human good.

I cannot think that Mr. Smith would subscribe to either of these views. Would he accept the view of James that satisfying the heart, giving courage and confidence in shouldering one's way through "life's thicket" is really evidence for the God of Aquinas, of Luther, of Tillich? My guess is that he is too committed to common sense and rationality for that. Would he follow Dewey in converting "religiousness" into practical devotion to the moral ideal? Again, I think not. But if not, why does he suppose that pragmatism, with its mixing up of the cognitive with the other impulses of our nature, shows special insight into their true relation? For my own part the rationalist, with his clear distinctions between human ends and his insistence that however the paths to them may crisscross they should never be confused, shows a far clearer insight into the actual structure of man's mind.

Mr. Smith's next criticism is that in my account of pragmatism "the self is confined to its own series of experiences." He agrees with me (and with Dewey) that experience occurs only in some individual mind, but continues: "The central question, however, is whether from this alone it follows that experience never means more than 'my' or some other individual's experience; my view is that it does not follow." Mr. Smith is right. The fact that it is I who am thinking does not restrict what I mean to my own experience. Nor would I impute any such argument to Dewey. He obviously believed in our power to think of bodies and minds not our own, and in our power to cooperate with them in inquiries which were settled by "objective" results. What I did say about him was that his account of the reference of thought was ambiguous, and that on one interpretation, plainly stated by himself, he was not entitled to any reference beyond his own experience. What was that interpretation?

It was the "naturalistic" interpretation. By naturalism here I mean what Dewey meant by it, namely that there was not to be found in the world anything in the form of a mental, spiritual, nonphysical existent. Such naturalism has always seemed to me nonsense, and it seems so still. Consciousness seems to me to exist more undeniably than any physical state and to be self-evidently irreducible to it. Yet Dewey announced himself a behaviorist. This meant that thinking was a physical process performed by the physical organism. In his desire to deny anything distinctively mental, he went so far as to say that smoke, even in the absence of any observer to interpret it, meant fire. This too seems to me nonsense, as I am pleased to note that it does to Mr. Smith. Now an organism is a physical thing, composed we now know of some billions of "wavicles" moving about among each other at tremendous speeds, and thinking is presumably identical with certain movements occurring in the brain or with movements of the organism as a whole.

The behaviorist, as I understand him, maintains that some of these movements *are* meanings or ideas, thoughts of Julius Caesar, for example, or of disestablishmentarianism. All the other experiences we call mental will similarly be changes in the position of matter. When I said that for this kind of naturalist his experiences must be confined to himself, I was, I think, speaking accurately. Dewey said that when matter functioned in a certain way, as when the smoke meant the fire, it was functioning mentally, and when the organism functions in this way, it too may be called mental. Some of its movements, whether of the lips, of the organism as a whole, or more probably of particles in the brain, mean Julius Caesar; their moving in that way *is* the function of meaning Caesar. Now I think one can see by introspection that one's reference to Julius Caesar is *not* the movement of particles in one's head, or any other movements of matter, that one is not talking about the same thing when one uses these differing phrases. Nor can movements, either neural or muscular, *refer* to anything. If Dewey is really a behaviorist, as he claims to be, then our ideas and all other forms of consciousness are for him within our skin and even in thought we cannot get out of it. It was in this special interpretation that I held Dewey's pragmatism to confine his experience to himself. Behaviorism, as Lovejoy said, is a kind of intradermal philosophy.

Mr. Smith corrects me on one point of some interest. I said that Dewey's notorious distaste for epistemology as traditionally pursued was due to its recognition of "mental" ideas; he felt that to accept it would commit him to some form of dualism. Mr. Smith points out correctly that his reaction was against the whole tradition of British empiricism from Locke to Mill, which insisted that our immediate experience is of sense data conceived as mental existents. I must add, however, that if he thought it necessary to escape from such empiricism in order to retain the possibility of referring beyond his own experience, he was going to unnecessary pains. I myself hold to the Berkeleian position that all our immediate experiences are of mental content—as Russell himself at last held. Yet it is perfectly possible for one who holds this to believe in other minds and bodies and, as far as meaning goes, in God and demons and archangels. Dewey's reaction against dualism in epistemology was no more necessary than his reaction against the dualism of body and mind.

I have mentioned the oddity of holding that a bodily change can be a reference to Julius Caesar. But the fact is, and here Mr. Smith agrees, that thought about the past in general cannot be dealt with on Deweyan premises. If thought is a plan of action regarding the future, the judgment of the past must remain something as undigestible as it is undeniable. Some of the early positivists, holding with the pragmatists that the meaning of a judgment lay in its mode of verification, found in this judgment an insuperable stone wall. The judgment that Elizabeth swore rich oaths became a statement to the effect that if one turned the leaves of Green or Lingard in the library one would find verifying sentences there. Unfortunately the sentences themselves were verificatory only if both author and reader were doing successfully what the theory declared impossible, and genuinely thinking of the past. The historical judgment has proved intractable for pragmatist and positivist alike.

Mr. Smith doubts my view that if the pragmatic analysis of judgment is offered as universally true it is inconsistent with itself, though he does not argue the case. I continue to think that the inconsistency exists, and for two quite simple reasons. (1) It seems clear to me that when Dewey and James analyzed the judgment as they did, they meant to say something about judgment as such, and therefore universally true. If so, they were taking truth in its ordinary, not in its pragmatic, sense. I do not think that when they said "truth is working" they merely meant that this judgment worked. I think they meant to report the facts about the nature and structure of thought. They talked and they offered evidence very much as other philosophers would, and assumed that this evidence would be taken as relevant in the ordinary sense. It was as if they felt that a pragmatic defense of pragmatism, which on their theory would alone be valid, would be unconvincing, and so fell back on the conventional meanings. Indeed this was inevitable if the defense was to be at all persuasive. For what people wanted to know was what thought was like essentially and generally, and if pragmatism was to be accepted and "the object of knowledge is prospective and eventual" (*Quest for Certainty*, 173), then pragmatism was only a hypothesis as to how thought would behave in the future.

(2) The theory breaches consistency in another way. It offers itself as a general theory of thought, though it is bound to consider any general statement in the scientific sense as meaningless. It is meaningless because it is unverifiable by any human experience however extended. I do not see, for example, how a pragmatist could attach to the law of gravitation, still less to the

law of causality, the meaning, indifferent to time, assigned to it by the scientist. For this meaning is valid timelessly, that is for the whole of the past and the future. In like manner, it could not offer a *general* theory of thought. It is interdicted by its own express analysis from offering what it nevertheless purports to offer.

Mr. Smith's final difficulty with my position is that it does not provide room for the unpretentious problems of everyday thought. If all thought for me expresses a sustained endeavor to understand the world, and in the end everything is relevant to everything else, what room is there for my simple attempt to think where I have mislaid my pen? Is that an attempt to understand the universe?

This question distresses me less than perhaps it should. The answer seems straightforward enough. A man is more than an intellect. He is a being of innumerable wants. I want to get in touch with my friend David by writing; for writing I need my pen; by thinking I can perhaps recall where I laid it down. If by thinking I can find it, that is all I want of my thought at present. I could, no doubt, continue my thought about the pen, its relations to my mind, its causes and effects, into the farthest reaches of speculation, but philosophy under the circumstances would be folly. I have argued in another place that the whole world of *things* is the product of thought that has been directed and halted by convenience; all the artifacts of daily life, knives and forks, tables and chairs, are the product of thought in the service of ends other than its own, ends in the way of food, comfort, and enjoyment. There is surely no difficulty in holding *both* that thought has an ultimate end of its own in the understanding of its world and also that one can postpone that quest in the interest of instant need. A philosopher who was a philosopher only would be insane.

Does that mean, Mr. Smith asks, that the rationalist philosopher uses different standards of relevance in his ordinary thinking and in his speculation? Yes, he does. When I am trying to think where I laid my pen, it is highly relevant that I signed a check with it last evening and was at the time wearing my brown coat, for this suggests that I shall find it in the pocket of that coat. These facts are relevant as means to the immediate end of finding my pen; they would be of small interest to a philosopher considering whether the pen consists of sense data. Not that these facts would be wholly irrelevant for the philosopher; no facts are. Every event in the pen's history is both a cause and an effect, and I hold myself that if any one of them had been different the world as a whole would have been different. But there is no inconsistency between being at times a philosopher reconstructing a logical whole and at other times a practical man in pursuit of food and drink.

Mr. Smith thinks, however, that the very ideal of the rationalist philosopher tends to wither his humanity, and he concludes his paper with a plea for the sort of philosophy that is willing to concern itself with "the problems of men." One suspects that it is his own humane interests that have cast a glow for him over a philosophy otherwise so unpersuasive as pragmatism. At any rate he is surely right in saying that a philosopher who can immure himself unconcernedly in his cell while outside it there swirls a sea of crime, misery, delusive fads, and drug-induced nirvanas is a man who is morally deformed. And any philosophy which encourages him in it is deficient even as a philosophy.

Here too I agree. But I suspect that Mr. Smith, in taking to task the metaphysic of rationalism, has overlooked its exacting ethics. Rationalism seems to me to prescribe a standard that is almost impossibly high. In *Reason and Goodness,* indeed, I identify the good life with the reasonable life. In another book, *The Uses of a Liberal Education,* I have argued that reasonableness, "that great gray virtue," is the chief end of education and respect for it the chief need of our time. By reasonableness I do not mean, of course, the acceptance of a rationalist metaphysics, but rather a temper of mind that ought to follow from it. I mean the respect for reason which leads one to follow, as best one can, what reason dictates, whether in theory or practice. The man who acquires that temper of mind has, I should say, the best of all antidotes to the fads, fanaticisms, and imbecilities of our chaotic times. Here at last I am at one with Dewey. The general application of intelligence to "the problems of men" is a strategy that he said had never been tried. And though I differ from him as to how exactly intelligence proceeds, I agree that a general adoption of the respect for reason and the effort to be reasonable would be the most helpful as well as the most radical of revolutions.

1. William P. Montague, *The Ways of Knowing* (London: Allen & Unwin, 1925).
2. John Dewey, *Essays in Experimental Logic* (Chicago: University of Chicago Press; Cambridge University Press, 1916).
3. John Dewey, *The Quest for Certainty* (New York: Minton, Balch [1929]; London: Allen & Unwin, 1930).
4. William James, *Pragmatism* (London: Longmans, Green, 1907).

19 Blanshard's Critique of the Analytic Movement
Robert J. Fogelin

1. The Historical Problem

ANYONE who attempts to assay the worth of the analytic movement is immediately faced with a complicated task, for, as Blanshard clearly sees, it has been "a disorderly and sprawling development" (*Reason and Analysis* [*RA*], 11).[1] Thus he is quick to renounce any claim that he has written "a history of the analytic movement" (*RA,* 11). In order to deal with the complexity of the analytic tradition, Blanshard makes two decisions. The first is to concern himself with this development only to the extent that it bears upon his special interest in the place of reason in philosophy. This is fair enough and explains his neglect of significant technical achievements (for example, Carnap's remarkable work in formal semantics).

Blanshard's second decision is both more important and problematic: he chooses logical positivism as his major subject for attention. Furthermore, he does so on at least partially historical grounds: "The historical trunk of the widely spreading tree was logical positivism or empiricism. This clearly formulated position served as the rallying point in the twenties and the thirties and the point of departure for new developments in the forties and fifties" (*RA*, 99). This metaphor of a trunk carries with it the intentional implication of roots and branches. Thus the Tractarian Wittgenstein is seen as a protopositivist and many (though not all) recent analysts are detected as cryptopositivists.[2] This view of the analytic tradition establishes Blanshard's strategy: if the citadel of logical positivism can be successfully stormed, then its outlying camps may be easily mopped up. In *Reason and Analysis* Blanshard dedicated two hundred pages to the refutation of positivism, leaving less than eighty pages for his treatment of linguistic philosophy in what he calls its earlier and later forms.

This approach to the analytic tradition raises a number of questions, some more important than others. Given the conceits of the early seventies, this emphasis upon the positivist standpoint may seem one-sided. Positivism has been off center stage for about two decades, and the avant garde analyst—to use Blanshard's phrase—is likely to treat it as just another form of traditional philosophy (even *metaphysics*) that we have now learned to despise. At the same time, when Blanshard spoke before the British Academy in 1952, positivism still represented a viable force in philosophical thought, and if it now seems that he overvalued its significance, it is probably also true that many now undervalue it. Indeed, there is probably more cryptopositivism still about than is usually acknowledged. In any case, we can leave these questions of *significance* to the historians of philosophy who will write in the next century.

More substantively, we can ask whether Blanshard, through taking logical positivism as his point of focus, has given the analytic tradition both a *fair* and an *accurate* presentation. I do not think that he has always done this. Wittgenstein's *Tractatus,* as I shall argue later in detail, is badly mauled by having positivistic dogma imposed back upon it, and the main thrust of much postpositivistic analysis is often missed through Blanshard's tendency to warp new doctrines back into familiar positivistic shapes. This, I believe, has had unfortunate philosophical consequences. Blanshard is certainly right that analytic philosophy, in virtually *all* of its forms, has challenged the approach that dominated British philosophy in the early decades of this century. Where he has recognized such a challenge, he has always replied in a way that is clear, nonevasive, and—I'm bound to say—almost always decisive. The question remains whether, in his zeal to refute positivism, he has met all, or even the most decisive, challenges to the sovereignty of reason. Perhaps a negative answer to this question will spur him on to do so.

2. The Main Theses of Logical Positivism

Recognizing the existence of variations from the norm, Blanshard characterizes the logical positivist (or empiricist) position by four main theses:

> These four theses . . . are: (1) logical atomism, the doctrine that all complex statements of fact depend for their truth on simple statements about what may be sensed, and that none of these simple statements entail any others; (2) the verifiability theory of meaning, which holds that a statement means what would verify it in sense; (3) the analytic character of a priori knowledge, i.e., that all necessary statements unfold the contents of our ideas rather than report truths about nature; (4) the emotive theory of values, i.e., that statements of value are neither true nor false, but expressions of attitude. [*RA,* 99–100]

Of course, none of this is quite accurate as it stands. The last three theses were given any number of formulations that cannot, without some injustice, be captured in brief rubrics. Blanshard, in fact, realizes this, and shows enormous patience in spelling out these variations, subjecting each to searching criticism. The first thesis, that of logical atomism, is a less obvious member of the packet, for to a really tough-minded positivist it might seem all too metaphysical. Blanshard seemed to recognize this in his British Academy lecture, where he takes only the last three theses as central to positivism—an instinct which I think is rather more sound. Given the full slate of four theses, he goes on to say that ". . . Hume anticipated all [these] positions." Allowing for a certain looseness of fit, especially with emotivism, logical positivism is then presented as Humean empiricism with the doctrine of Relations of Ideas made more respectable by means of the techniques of modern logic. Thus Blanshard's critique of logical positivism is presented as a continuation of the traditional confrontation between rationalism and empiricism, transposed into its contemporary form. I propose to examine Blanshard's treatment of each of these positivistic theses, getting emotivism out of the way first, since it is least important to our present concerns.

3. Emotivism

I shall touch only lightly on this subject, since other contributors will certainly discuss Blanshard's views on ethics in detail. In *Reason and Analysis* Blanshard connects the second and third theses of logical positivism with the thesis of emotivism.

> Only two types of statement were recognized as meaningful, as we have seen, statements of sensible fact on the one hand and statements of analytic necessity on the other. Into which class did statements of value fit? They seem clearly not to be statements of empirical fact; when we say, for example, that lying is wrong, the word 'wrong' does not seem to point to any attribute that can be seen or heard, or otherwise sensed. Nor is the statement a necessary truth, for if it were, there could be no exceptions to it, and most of us do not mean this. But if the statement is neither empirical nor necessary, what is to be done with it? The alternative before the positivists was either to revise their theory of knowledge or to deny that statements of value were in the ordinary sense statements at all.
>
> They took the latter course. Statements of value were held to assert nothing whatever; they were neither true nor false; they were pseudo-assertions, which had no cognitive meaning. [*RA*, 124][3]

Here Blanshard argues, quite explicitly, that theses (2) and (3) of logical positivism imply the nonassertive character of judgments of value. This is not correct. In order for the positivists to legitimately derive this conclusion, theses (2) and (3) must be supplemented by something like Moore's critique of naturalism in ethics. This can be seen at once by reflecting upon the fact that there is no incompatibility between theses (2) and (3) and an old-fashioned form of hedonistic subjectivism. Naturalism is, then, an option open to a logical positivist, and, in fact, Schlick adopted a naturalistic standpoint in his own ethical writings.[4]

Yet, if someone accepts Moore's critique of naturalism, then it does seem that theses (2) and (3), supplemented in this way, do entail the nonassertive character of value judgments. For the moment, let us accept this much and see what follows next. Are we at once committed to an emotivism? Of course not, for as Blanshard is quick to point out, "there are other sentences than indicatives and other meanings than cognitive; words may be used by a speaker to express his attitudes; exclamations express his feelings; imperatives express his commands" (*RA*, 124). Fair enough; Blanshard does not suggest that abandoning the idea that value judgments are assertions commits one at once to a Boo-Hurrah emotivism. Yet he seems to suggest that it commits one to some form of emotivism however sophisticated:

> . . . it has undergone many further modifications, not so much by way of abandoning its central contention that statements of value are not assertions, as by way of developing the many types and shades of attitude that these statements may express. It is clear that to all objectivists in morals, i.e., those who believe that the rightness or wrongness of an action does not depend on our attitudes toward it, this theory is a sharp challenge. For it implies, *prima facie* at least, that there is and can be no objective standard of morals, . . . [*RA*, 124–25]

I'm afraid that I do not see the force of this prima facie implication. I do not see, that is, how abandoning the idea that value judgments are assertions eo ipso ties them to the expression of *attitudes*. To take one of the possibilities cited by Blanshard, suppose we hold that value judgments (down deep) really express commands (or better, prescriptions). Does this tie values to attitudes and thereby destroy the objectivity of values? Surely not, for the notion that value judgments *express* commands carries no greater subjective implications than the parallel claim that we use indicatives or assertions to *express* our thoughts. Nor do I think that the plain man believes that commands, as such, are not capable of objective assessment. The plain man, in fact, believes just the opposite. In sum, the inference from the nonassertive character of judgments of value to the conclusion that there could be no objective standard of morals does not go through.

Of course, many positivists (though not Schlick) did deny the objective status of values, and many philosophers who would reject the label of logical positivist have followed them in this. But the point that I am trying to make is logical, not historical. If theses (2) and (3) together led to the conclusion that values are not subject to rational assessment, then this would count as a fairly strong reductio ad absurdum argument against their *joint* assertion. But Blanshard's argument involves two steps: first, that (2) and (3) jointly imply the nonassertive character of value judgments, and second, that accepting the nonassertive character of value judgments compromises the objective status of values. I do not think that he has established either of these inferences.[5]

I should like to add one general remark before moving on. I think that it is deeply characteristic of Blanshard's position to connect rationality (objectivity, etc.) with judgment. Not only is the real rational (and conversely), but only what is assertable is rational, and everything rational is (at least ultimately) assertable. The first half of this dictum makes him unsympathetic to patterns of analysis using prescriptions, performatives, and other nonassertive ways of doing things with words. The second half of the dictum excludes from his world doctrines of ineffability, a subject I shall discuss in detail later on.

4. The Verificationist Theory of Meaning

Blanshard's critique of the verificationist theory of meaning is painstakingly thorough, almost always fair and accurate, and, in the end, completely decisive. Of course, it is possible to pick about at the edges of his critique, noting an indecisive argument here and a flawed interpretation there, but this would be wasted effort. Verificationism has been refuted, and refuted largely for the reasons that Blanshard suggests. I wish to make this acknowledgment clear from the start to avoid misunderstanding of the point of the discussion to follow. I shall not question Blanshard's critique of verificationism, but I shall express reservations about some of the philosophical conclusions he derives from this critique.

To simplify matters, I shall divide his criticisms of verificationism into three main kinds:

(i) He shows that the proposed criterion—in one form or another—is inadequate even within the positivist framework.

(ii) He shows that the proposed criterion—in one form or another—leads us to treat as meaningless expressions that are commonly thought to be perfectly meaningful.

(iii) He shows that the criterion—again, in its various formulations—cannot be applied back upon itself without self-destructive consequences.

I shall examine these patterns of criticism one at a time.

(i) In a rough-and-ready way, we can divide the expressions of our language into three categories:

(a) The meaningful expressions of empirical science and mathematics.

(b) The meaningful (or at least apparently meaningful) expressions of everyday life that hardly seem scientific or mathematical in character.

(c) Expressions acknowledged, presumably on all sides, as transparently meaningless.

The logical positivists' task was to formulate a criterion of meaning that simultaneously captured everything in group (a) without admitting anything from group (c). With this done, they could then set about constructing a plausible justification for the division imposed upon group (b) by their derived criterion.

One of the striking features of the positivist movement was the difficulty it had in completing even the first step of this program, and here Blanshard, in his criticisms, moves on perfectly sure ground. In well known ways,[6] each proposed criterion either excluded items from category (a), thus proving too strong, or admitted items from category (c), thus proving too weak. Furthermore, these difficulties did not turn upon making subtle decisions concerning borderline cases. Each proposed criterion in turn, when its implications were worked out, was shown to miss its intended mark by a mile.

What are we to think of the positivists' inability to satisfy even their own philosophical prejudices? I believe that the conclusion Blanshard wishes to further is that this exhibits the untenability of a narrowly conceived *empiricist* criterion of meaning. By confining experience to sense experience, "... logical empiricism has not been empirical enough. If it had been, it would surely have recognized that we do in fact think of many relations ... whose nature makes it impossible to sense them" ("P of A," 48). But another diagnosis is available; instead of arguing that a (narrowly conceived) *empiricist* criterion of meaning is not empirical enough, we can say, instead, that any attempt to formulate a *criterion* of meaning exhibits an unwarranted rationalist bias. The fault lies not in the manner of the quest but in the nature of the quest itself.

This view is, of course, characteristic of Wittgenstein's later writings where he attempts to show that the concept of meaning is so diverse a notion that all attempts at definition are doomed from the start. "Meaning" is one of those odd-job words in our language that plays a number of different roles, as is illustrated by the diverse forms that actual explanations of meaning can have. Of course, Wittgenstein takes much the same attitude toward other concepts that have been philosophical favorites: knowledge and value, to mention just two.

How shall we decide which moral to draw: was the verificationist quest faulty in its one-sided empiricism or faulty in its assumption that some definite criterion must exist, an assumption which is all too rationalistic? Of course, if the defenders of rationalism could succeed where the positivists have failed, i.e. if they could produce a satisfactory specification of the necessary and sufficient conditions of meaningfulness, then the issue would be settled in their behalf. As it is, I do not think that the friends of reason have even tried this, at least in a sufficiently straightforward manner to allow assessment. It thus can come to seem that rationalism and empiricism gain their chief support through the mutual exploitation of weakness. Such a suggestion carries a challenge to philosophy far deeper than anything even hinted at in the philosophy of logical empiricism. This more radical attack suggests that both the empiricist and the rationalist are posing questions that do not exist in the form that they are asking them. To such questions as "What is meaning?" "What is knowledge?" or "What is value?" no essentialist answer is forthcoming. Not that these notions are empty, meaningless, or useless; quite to the contrary, they are immensely important notions whose significance is fully appreciated only after we give a sympathetic and open-textured taxonomy of their employment.

I think that we can now see why the positivists command Blanshard's respect. They share with him a central commitment to the clear straightforward elucidation of philosophical concepts in propositional form. Yet this commitment may be wrong and has been challenged (e.g. by Wittgenstein among others).[7] I don't think that Blanshard has faced this challenge, and thus (to return to the central point) it is hard to decide whether he has presented a defense of reason or a tacit critique of reason in one of its manifestations.

(ii) The logical positivists' first problem was to fashion a criterion of meaning to match *their own* philosophical prejudices, something, strange to say, that they seemed never able to do. This provides the basis for what I take to be the best criticism of this development. Another set of criticisms arose because the empiricist criterion of truth, especially in its stronger versions, offended against commonsense notions of meaningfulness. This happened in at least two ways: (1) sometimes the positivists were led to reject as meaningless expressions whose meaningfulness (and, indeed, whose *cognitive* meaningfulness) seems quite beyond question. For example, at one stage they were forced to declare *all* empirical laws meaningless since they were not subject—even in principle—to complete verification.[8] (2) Somewhat differently, the positivists were sometimes forced to produce very curious accounts of the meaningfulness of a set of expressions in order to accommodate them within the bounds of their theory. Past tense judgments, for example, which certainly seem to be about events in the *past,* must be reconstrued as predictions about the character of data that will turn up in the *future* (*RA*, 206–8). This hardly seems plausible.

I shall not shoulder the burden of answering these criticisms derived from commonsense belief and commonsense understanding. In Austin's words, "we set some limits to the amount of nonsense that we talk, or at least the amount of nonsense that we are prepared to admit we talk. . . ."[9] Yet Blanshard must walk a very thin line in his appeal to the *truth* of the plain man's beliefs and the *sense* of the plain man's talk. If he were to make common belief his touchstone, then he would join G. E. Moore in the defense of common sense—something his own substantive position will not allow him to do. Common sense gets its hearing and cannot be dismissed lightly, yet it too is subject to philosophical interrogation and revision. Nor can Blanshard accept the plain man's linguistic practice as a touchstone for meaningfulness. This would reduce his position to the "ordinary language" philosophy that arose after the Second World War, a position that he treats gingerly as a strange and foreign object, yet plainly as something he wishes to reject.

I do not know what principle Blanshard uses in appealing to the plain man, but I shall not raise any objections on this score. My difficulties with Blanshard's appeal to common understanding derive from another source: I sometimes find him confident of the meaningfulness of an exotic remark and, at the same time, cannot discern the source of this confidence. A single example will illustrate my worries.

> [Schlick] took the seemingly trivial case of my looking at two pieces of paper and saying "this has the same green colour as that." Is this statement meaningful? Yes, of course, since I could verify it by looking. But now complicate the statement a little. Another person is looking at the pieces, and he too calls them green. Does he see the same colour as I do? That, says Schlick, is a question I cannot hope to answer. I can offer him a series of shades, and note whether he reports that the shade he has been seeing falls in the same place in the series as I do, but beyond that I cannot go. Why is this psychological curiosity worth our attention? Because it presents a crucial case to the present theory of meaning. If it is true that I cannot, even in principle, verify the statement that you are seeing the same colour as I do, must not the very suggestion be meaningless? Schlick saw that this was involved, and drew the inference unflinchingly. "The statement that two experiences of different subjects not only occupy corresponding places in a systematic order, but also resemble each other qualitatively, has for us no sense. Note that it is not false, but senseless (sinnlos); we have no idea what it means."
>
> Now this is not very convincing. That I cannot *verify* your having the same sensation as I have seems clear enough, but that such a suggestion conveys nothing to me at all seems merely absurd, for the meaning is surely as definite and intelligible as its verification is difficult. Here is a case in which meaning and verifiability fall apart, and hence to identify them must be wrong. [*RA*, 209–10]

Before turning to the main issue, a subsidiary problem demands attention: I do not think that Blanshard has represented Schlick's position accurately. Schlick does not deny that two people can see the same color, and it is certainly not part of his intention to deny the meaningfulness of sentences of the following form:

(a) A and B are seeing the same color.

Instead, Schlick denies the meaningfulness of quite a different remark:

(b) Two experiences can resemble each other qualitatively.

It might be thought—and Blanshard seems to assume this without argument—that (a) and (b) come to the same thing or, at the very least, (a) entails (b). Two people cannot be *seeing* the same color, as opposed to merely *looking at* the same patch of color, unless they have qualitatively identical, or at least, qualitatively similar, experiences. In fact, it is the whole point of Schlick's position to reject this analysis of (a) in terms of (b).

He offers an analysis of (a) roughly along the following lines. Our color space contains a set of formal relationships subject to logical articulation. When two people see the same color, their respective experiences are not cross-identified by some felt qualitative feature, but instead, through some isomorphism of place within the formal system of colors. This, to my mind, is not a very plausible account of the meaningfulness of (a), yet it does show why Schlick thought he could accept the meaningfulness of (a) while, at the same time, treating (b) as meaningless. This is all worth insisting upon, since it blunts the immediate edge of Blanshard's criticism. (a) is a common un-problematic expression whose exclusion from the domain of the meaningful would constitute a serious loss. (b), on the other hand, is a philosopher's remark and, setting aside questions of job security, we might adjust ourselves to its loss with less difficulty.

But now to get to the main point: the intelligibility of (b). Schlick thinks it is meaningless to claim that two people's experiences are qualitatively the same, whereas Blanshard finds the meaning of such a claim both definite and intelligible. Blanshard seems to be saying something like this: just as it is in-telligible to claim that this patch of green is qualitatively the same as that patch of green, it is also intelligible to suppose (however difficult the problem of verification might be) that my experience of the patch of green is qualitatively the same as yours. To cite another example: can I significantly wonder if another hears middle C an octave higher than I do? Blanshard, it seems, would answer this question yes, whereas Schlick would plainly answer no.

Faced with this disagreement, I think that our first instinct is to side with Blanshard against Schlick. A charge of meaninglessness suggests gibberish, a category mistake, internal incoherence, a schizophrenic word-salad, or, perhaps, unbridled metaphorical extravagance. In comparison with such mis-demeanors, the claim that someone else hears middle C an octave higher than I do or that you and I have qualitatively similar experiences when we look at a green patch seems a model of good sense. Perhaps the charge of meaninglessness has given a faulty impression by suggesting such misleading comparisons.

Yet there is an important conceptual issue here. Questions of meaningfulness cannot always be settled straight off. An expression may *seem meaningful* yet not *be* meaningful, and a decision on this matter may in-volve a careful investigation. We can grant, then, that a claim of similarity between two persons' experiences certainly seems meaningful. It should, however, strike us as significantly fishy that no verification procedure of *any* kind suggests itself: no empirical test, no logical deduction, and, for that matter, no transcendental deduction either. The judgment seems to exist in a curious isolation; to use a Wittgensteinian figure, it is rather like a crank that seems to be a part of the machine but is attached to nothing.

At this point, I think that the controversy takes a rather strange turn. I believe that Blanshard, given his general philosophical commitments, would also agree that a judgment which is completely cut off from other judgments that might support it is, in fact, no judgment at all. As matters stand, this seems to be the status of the claim that two person's experiences are qualitatively the same. Yet the feeling remains that such a judgment is, after all, meaningful and therefore must, somehow, enter into the evidential web of other judgments. One strategy, then, is to stand by our primitive feeling of meaningfulness even if we cannot, at present, give an account of this meaningfulness. This, I think, is Blanshard's strategy.

Quite another strategy is to attempt to exhibit this feeling of meaningfulness as an illusion. A beginning of such an exhibition might take the following form. We can notice that the two following judgments are largely unproblematic:

    (a) Patch X and patch Y are qualitatively the same.

    (c) A and B are experiencing the same patch of color.

I say that these judgments are largely unproblematic for we have at least some idea of how we might check upon them. Sensibly aware of human fallibility, and expecting difficult and deviant cases to arise, we usually settle (a) by looking at the patches and we settle (c) by discovering what A and B themselves are looking at.

At this point, we generate a new expression—a version of our old friend (b), by crossing (a) with (c):

    (b) A's experience of the patch of color is qualitatively the same as B's experience of the patch of color.

Certainly (b) *seems* meaningful, but now we account for this by pointing to the similarities between (b) and (a) on the one hand and between (b) and (c) on the other. At the same time, we should be deeply suspicious of the apparent meaningfulness of (b) since none of the connections that tie (a) and (b) to other judgments carry over to (b), and (b) seems unable to supply these connections from its own resources. However much an object may look like a crank, the coherence theorist, at least, ought to be wary of giving it that title until he is sure that it is somehow connected to the mechanism.

Blanshard believes that the claim that your experience of a green patch and my experience of a green patch may be similar is "as definite and intelligible as its verification is difficult." For my own part, the more I reflect upon such a claim—the more I attempt to put this claim into systematic relationship with the meaningful components of my thought—the less able I find myself to make sense of it. In this case, and in a number of others, I do not share Blanshard's confidence concerning meaningfulness. Nor am I able to detect the source of his confidence.

(iii) The third, and perhaps Blanshard's favorite, criticism of the verifiability principle depends upon turning it back upon itself. The argument here is short and seemingly decisive. On their own principles, the positivists must treat the criterion either as an a priori truth or an empirical generalization. If it is an empirical claim, then it would be necessary to show empirically that all synthetic judgments are empirically based, and that seems impossible, or circular, or, anyway, wrong. On the other side, if the principle is considered a priori, then, by another important tenet of the positivist position, it must be treated as a tautology and thus devoid of informative content. As Blanshard puts it, the criterion seems "doomed to die by self strangulation" (*RA*, 239).

Some positivists attempted to live with this consequence by acknowledging that the verifiability principle was neither an analytic nor a synthetic proposition and thus not a proposition at all. One line was to call it a *recommendation* for the use of the term "meaningful." But this does not seem to help much, for we immediately want to ask why we should accept this particular recommendation. If it is simply arbitary, then it is of no interest to anyone, including the positivists. If it is more than arbitrary in *truly* marking out the difference between the meaningful and the meaningless, then this assertion in its support is subject to just the self-referential criticism that we are trying to avoid. Although Blanshard is more careful in stating this criticism, I have, I think, captured at least its gist.[10]

I think that Blanshard's argument—or, rather, my shortened version of it—is totally convincing except for one nagging doubt. It is well known that curious things happen when we allow propositions to refer back to themselves: in particular, paradoxes (such as the Liar) are apt to arise. Furthermore, these paradoxes are not curiosities to be solved by a clever undergraduate of an afternoon. They prove to be strangely intractable and their significance runs deep, as illustrated by the works of Gödel, Tarski, and Church. Here we might wonder whether our difficulties came from attempting to apply a criterion of meaning back upon itself rather than from any material shortcomings within the criterion we have formulated.

Schlick, in fact, gave this line of thought serious consideration. He held that the verifiability principle "has always been followed and used by science as a matter of course, at least unconsciously, and in the same way it has always been acknowledged by commonsense in everyday life."[11] Yet at the same time, this principle actually could not be put forward in the form of a theory. "A 'theory' consists of a set of propositions which you may believe or deny, but our principle is a simple triviality about which there can be no dispute. It is not even an 'opinion,' since it indicates a condition without which no opinion can be formulated. It is not a theory, for its acknowledgment must precede the building of any theory."[12] Here Schlick produces something like a transcendental deduction of the inexpressibility of *and* general theory of meaning.

I don't think that Schlick has worked these ideas out with any great clarity, but, at the same time, I do not think that this notion that a completely general criterion of meaning is nonformulable (ineffable) should be dismissed as a mere lapse into mysticism. The significance of self-referential paradoxes, as I have said, runs deep, and any philosophical theory with a claim to generality must take them seriously. In particular, it will not do to dismiss these paradoxes as the special problem of the formal logician, arguing, perhaps, that the logician has brought these problems on himself through the barrenness and abstractness of his methods. The striking thing about these difficulties is that they arise at a very rudimentary level of language formation, and instead of disappearing as the language is enriched, they become more and more deeply entrenched. If we establish as the goal of reason a *fully articulated, self-contained, completed system of necessary connections,* we may, in fact, have established for ourselves a goal that is conceptually impossible.

But let me come down from these airy heights of speculation and summarize this discussion of Blanshard's critique of verificationism. It is certainly true that the verifiability principle, in each of its formulations, has encountered overwhelming difficulties, and Blanshard has been unstinting in pointing this out. Furthermore, I have little to say in response to the main core of Blanshard's criticisms. Yet after the criticism is complete, the moral remains to be drawn, and here there is considerable room for disagreement. Blanshard wishes to further the conclusion that the fault with verificationism lies in its narrowly conceived empiricist base. That, surely, is one possible diagnosis. Along the way I have suggested two others. (i) That the concept of meaning is so diverse in its structure that it defies definition of any kind. This is a line associated with Wittgenstein's later writings, in particular, with his *Philosophical Investigations.* (ii) The very structure of language—the very character of meaning—precludes the *formulation* of a completely general criterion of meaning. We have noticed that doctrine in the writings of Schlick, but of course its original home is Wittgenstein's *Tractatus Logico-Philosophicus.*

It makes a difference which of these diagnoses we accept. If we follow Blanshard, then reason is elevated by the defeat of its traditional enemy. But if we accept either of the other two diagnoses (which, incidentally, stand poles apart),[13] then reason avoids verificationism only to face a specter more awesome in its visage than the demon just exorcised.

5. Logical Atomism

The mention of Wittgenstein's *Tractatus* leads naturally to the topic of logical atomism. From the start, it is important to distinguish two very different theories that have gone under the name of logical atomism: one concerns the nature of experience, the other concerns the nature of propositions. Hume's *Treatise* is usually taken as an example of the first kind of atomism and is described, not altogether fairly, along the following lines: All complex ideas can be divided into intuitable simple ideas, and these simple ideas stand in only external relations to one another. It is this kind of atomism that Blanshard is thinking of when he uses the following phrasing: "if we break up the world as we know it into its ultimate components, it will be found to consist of an enormous aggregate of sensory simples" ("P of A," 54).

Another kind of logical atomism, and here the name is more appropriate, concerns the nature of propositions. The main idea, which is at least suggested in Descartes's *Discourse on Method,* is that complex propositions can be analyzed into a set of independent basic propositions, and that (somehow) the truth-value of the analyzed proposition is a function of the truth-values of the propositions into which it is analyzed. Of course, a given philosopher may be an atomist in both ways at once (this seems to be true of Russell at one stage in his career), and we may even feel that the two sorts of atomism naturally go together. Yet they are different theories with different intentions, and mixing them up can only generate confusion.

This then, leads me to the sharpest charge that I shall make about Blanshard's treatment of the analytic tradition: I think that he gets Wittgenstein's *Tractatus* by the wrong handle by attributing the wrong sort of atomism to it. It is perfectly clear that Blanshard connects the *Tractatus* with the proto-Humean view sketched above. This is exhibited in any number of passages. I shall cite just one:

> Wittgenstein was a logical atomist, and the atomists held, as we have seen, that all such statements resolved themselves on analysis into statements about atomic facts. [So far, so good.] And these facts were of a type that could be presented through sense perception; they were all particulars characterized by an attribute or connected through a relation; our nearest approach to them in expression was something like "here—red" or "this brighter than that." [*RA,* 197–98]

I believe that G. E. M. Anscombe has shown that this view of the *Tractatus* is wholly wrong.[14] The *Tractatus* does not contain a doctrine of sensory simples, nor are atomic propositions identified with protocol sentences. The few passages that vaguely suggest this are easily shown not to bear such an interpretation, and if it is suggested that an empiricist doctrine shines out between the lines, then it is just as easily established that the explicit text excludes such a reading. Wittgenstein was attempting to produce a *pure* theory of representation from which everything empirical was not only absent but wholly out of place. How this or that creature forms his representations or goes about checking their veracity was, from Wittgenstein's lofty standpoint, a contingent issue and thus a matter for empirical science, *not* for philosophy. Questions concerning the material character of representations were, in Wittgenstein's opinion, psychological questions, and about psychology he said: "Psychology is no more closely related to philosophy than any other natural science" (*Tractatus Logico-Philosophicus* [*TLP*] 4.1121).[15]

In sum, the *Tractatus* attempts (to use traditional language) a transcendental deduction of the pure conditions of meaningfulness or representation. Of course, any intrusion of empirical considerations into such an argument leads to grotesque inconsistencies. Blanshard finds the *Tractatus* inconsistent at almost every turn. My suggestion is that these inconsistencies that he points to are largely the result of imposing empiricist dogmas upon a text explicitly intended to exclude them.[16]

Wittgenstein, I have said, was interested in the structure of propositions. I shall try to sketch his position very briefly. Our everyday language depends for its significance upon certain deep structures hidden from us by the superficial grammar of our language. This deep structure contains three basic mechanisms that generate significant discourse. There are names or simple signs that refer to objects or basic individuals. The meaning of such a simple sign is just its reference (*Bedeutung*). This deep structure also contains elementary propositions which are composed solely of simple signs, and the way in which these signs are put together *pictures* the way in which objects are fitted together in an atomic fact. The meaning (*Sinn*) of an elementary proposition is the (possible) atomic fact it pictures. Furthermore, naming and picturing (*Bedeutung* and *Sinn*) are mutually exclusive notions, for that which can be named cannot be pictured (i.e. objects cannot be pictured)[17] and what can be pictured cannot be named (i.e. situations cannot be named).[18] Finally, the sentences of our everyday life derive *their* meaning through being truth functions of elementary propositions.

This is certainly a curious theory and, as Blanshard remarks, its total elaboration is surely obscure. Yet its broad outline seems plain enough, and I'm afraid that Blanshard just gets it wrong. Let me cite a single striking example of this: "Again, what becomes of the idea of *picturing* on this theory of the particular? In Wittgenstein's view, the meaning and truth of every atomic proposition lay in its mirroring of atomic fact. It now turns out that the subject in any such fact is incapable of being mirrored, since there is no content there to mirror" (*RA*, 174). Here Blanshard plainly inverts Wittgenstein's position as a preface to criticizing it.

I don't think that any useful purpose will be served by pursuing this criticism further. Yet before moving on, I would like to make two general remarks. At the beginning of this essay, I suggested that Blanshard's heavy emphasis upon the logical empiricists has led him to misrepresent other forms of analytic philosophy. I think that this is nowhere more apparent than in his criticism of Wittgenstein's *Tractatus*. The second remark is rather more difficult to make articulate. Blanshard, I think, participates in that great epistemological tradition that has characterized modern philosophy. For him, questions of knowledge occupy a primary place. Following Frege, Wittgenstein attempted to break with this tradition. Conceptual issues come first; questions of knowledge, which presuppose conceptual commitments, come next. Perhaps this is the source of Blanshard's difficulty with Wittgenstein: he continually charges him with giving bad answers to questions he has not asked.

6. Necessity

Since I have already sketched the Tractarian view of propositions, this can provide a basis for introducing the problem of necessity.

We have already seen that Wittgenstein held a curious doctrine about the nature of propositions. He thought that the way in which the signs were put together in a propositional sign was intended to show (not immediately, but through the deep mechanisms of language) the way things go together in the world. More exactly, any particular arrangement of signs gains its significance from being one selection out of a possible range of selections. Thus by putting signs together in this way rather than in that, we assert that things stand to each other in this way rather than that. Now if drawing such a contrast is essential to the very nature of a proposition, it follows at once that all propositions are contingent.

This result, of course, poses a problem: what are we to say about so-called necessary propositions? More accurately, since we now find ourselves stuck with the consequence that there are no necessary propositions, how are we to account for those propositions that at least *seem* necessary?

Suppose we begin with tautologies, for however boring they may be, they at least provide an example of putatively necessary propositions. It has been argued (by positivists in particular) that all *necessary* truths are tautologies and, quite differently, that all a priori truths are tautologies. Rather a large fuss has been made over both these theses (Blanshard, for example, is anxious to reject them both),[19] but a more important issue comes first: what are we to say about tautologies themselves?

Whitehead somewhere says that tautologies are the intellectual amusement of the Absolute. However this may be, they do lead us into very deep issues. Philosophers commonly say two things about tautologies: they are devoid of content and they are necessarily true. But it seems that if tautologies are true, they must be true *of* something, while, on the other side, if they are devoid of content, they are not *about* anything at all. It thus seems that being true and being devoid of content are mutually exclusive notions.

Here various choices present themselves. I think that most philosophers have, in one way or another, attempted to save the propositional status of tautologies by supplying them with a content. But the options in this direction hardly seem inviting. We can take as our example an instance of the law of excluded middle: John is my father or he is not. One line is that this is *really* a proposition about our language, that is, it is an unperspicuous way of stating that such and such is a convention of the language which I am speaking. Of course, on this approach, both the necessary character and the a priori status of the proposition are compromised. Blanshard is, I think, wholly convincing in his attacks on all such *linguistic* reductions of the a priori and the necessary.

But if the law of excluded middle is not about the conventions of our language, then we seem forced to say that it is about the structure of reality. Yet this seems puzzling as well. Wittgenstein was not being counterintuitive when he suggested that the general form of a proposition was: *this is the way things are.*[20] Yet if a proposition tells us that *this* is the way things are, this plainly presupposes that things *might* have been otherwise. But a necessary proposition seems to destroy this needed contrast by excluding even this *might have been.*

Early in his career, Wittgenstein came to the conclusion that these so-called propositions of logic demand a radically different interpretation from that given to other propositions. His basic insight (he calls it his "leading idea") was that logical terms were not representative; i.e. they did not *stand for* or *refer to* anything at all. From this it followed that propositions whose truth depended solely on considerations of logic were, strictly speaking, true *of* nothing and thus not propositions. When I assert that John is my father or he is not, I am not making a remark about the conventions governing the words "or" or "not." I am not even making an assertion about the concepts of disjunction and negation. We might say that I have produced a *failing* attempt to make an assertion about my lineage.

Are we then to forget about the necessary truths of logic? Somehow they seem too important to be ignored. Here Wittgenstein hit upon the remarkable idea that this very inability of the laws of logic to *say* anything about the world *in itself showed* something about the world. This self-annihilating quality involved in trying to say something as fundamental as the law of excluded middle at once shows us something about the fundamental structure of language (thought) and the world. We thus arrive at three fundamentally exclusive notions: Names *name* objects, propositions *picture* situations, and the formal structure of our language *mirrors* the formal structure of the world.

Wittgenstein's solution to the problem of logical necessity sets the pattern for his solution of the status of all kinds of necessity. Passing from logic to ontology, consider the claim that there are objects (or, more generally, that something exists). According to Wittgenstein, it is of the very essence of propositions to refer to things and indicate that they are disposed to one another in a given way. Of course, it is plain that the (transcendental) assertion that there are objects (that something exists) cannot be made out as an assertion that objects are disposed to one another in a given way. Once more, then, we encounter the unsayable. Again, however, what cannot be said can be shown: that there are objects is shown by the occurrence of substantive terms (names) in our language.

A tautology, on Wittgenstein's view, shows us what it intends to say by saying nothing. A similar status is assigned to all the formal propositions that comprise the *Tractatus*, and this, I take it, is the point of the remark that Blanshard finds puzzling, even offensive:

> My propositions serve as elucidations in the following way: anyone who understands me eventually recognizes them as nonsensical, when he has used them—as steps—to climb beyond them. (He must, so to speak, throw away the ladder after he has climbed up it.)
>
> He must transcend these propositions, and then he will see the world aright. [*TLP*, 6.54]

If we get some distance from the text, we are at once struck by the strangeness of the Tractarian world picture. It is strange, however, in precisely the same way in which Plato's theory of forms, Leibniz's notion of monads, and Kant's pure categories of the understanding are strange. Each of these philosophers senses a deep underlying unity beneath the disconnected surface of the manifest world. Each in his own way was led to posit certain fundamental ontological structures to provide a basis for this unity that he sensed.

In reading Blanshard's account of the *Tractatus*, however, very little of this development seems to come through. He realizes, of course, that Wittgenstein, in the end, must declare his own work to be devoid of sense. But Blanshard seems to attribute this to some kind of empiricist (verificationist) scruple. This is not correct. More interestingly, Blanshard even seems to miss the general thrust of the *Tractatus*. For him, the *Tractatus* presents the world as one vast heap of disconnected facts. In contrast, Wittgenstein himself looked back upon the *Tractatus* in a wholly different way: he saw it as a pure crystalline structure—eternal and unchanging. It was this necessary structure *within which* the set of unrelated facts could display themselves that was the subject matter of the *Tractatus*. Blanshard's treatment of the *Tractatus* is rather like a presentation of Spinoza where all is *natura naturata* without *natura naturans* or like a treatment of Hegel that makes his system into a "Bacchanalian revel where not a soul is sober" but *not* "at the same time a transparent calm."

In fact, given a correct reading of the *Tractatus,* fundamental *agreements* between Blanshard and Wittgenstein emerge that lay the basis for an examination of further interesting *disagreements*. They certainly both take the system of necessary connections as the proper object of philosophical contemplation. This is the deepest similarity. Beyond this, they both hold to a monistic conception of propositions. Let me try to explain this. Wittgenstein came to the conclusion that it made no sense to speak of two different kinds of propositions: some that are contingent, others that are necessary. Necessity and contingency are too wholly different to be expressed in the common vehicle of a proposition. For the reasons sketched above, Wittgenstein decided that only contingencies can be formulated in a propositional content, and was thus led to his notion of inexpressibility relative to necessary connections. Starting from much the same position (i.e. a monistic view of propositions), Blanshard reasons in the reverse direction. In a thought, the propositional content is presented in an intelligible unity, and thus a wholly contingent proposition would be no proposition at all. Indeed, in the long run, all contingency must be eliminated and the world presented to us in a coherent system where everything is exhibited as internally related to everything else. The embarrassment of the contingent proposition will, eventually, disappear.

I think that the deepest disagreement between Wittgenstein and Blanshard might be this: Wittgenstein thought that there were *two* ways that language could reveal things about the world: through formulating contingent relations in a propositional content and through mirroring the necessary structure of the world within the necessary structure of language. This, of course, is the difference between saying and showing, and everything important to philosophy is cast into the second category. Blanshard, it seems, holds that there is only *one* way that language can reveal things about the world and that is through expressing them in a propositional content. Thus Wittgenstein and Blanshard not only disagree concerning what is sayable and what is not, they also disagree about the worth of these categories. For Wittgenstein, everything significant for philosophy, and perhaps for the significance of life, falls into the category of the unsayable; for Blanshard, nothing whatsoever falls into this category.

7. Linguistic Philosophy—Earlier Forms

Under this general heading, Blanshard discusses a number of matters, but most important, I think, is his examination of Moore's *commonsense* philosophy. Blanshard is certainly right in saying: "For the analyst, Moore's most important essay was 'A Defence of Common Sense,' published in 1925"[21] (*RA*, 311). Blanshard sketches this essay in the following words:

> He gave a long list of propositions, often challenged by philosophers, of which he claimed to be absolutely certain, such propositions as that the earth existed long before he was born and that material things now exist. . . . No argument philosophers offered against such propositions seemed to Moore to have anything like the certainty of the propositions themselves; so he proposed that instead of philosophy's setting up as the critic of common sense, common sense should serve as the touchstone of philosophy. . . . ["P of A," 61]

Although this may be a place where reasonable interpreters may disagree, it seems to me that Blanshard has here overextended Moore's claims. Moore surely held that the list of propositions he presented was known by him to be certainly true. He also constructed a second set of propositions that he was sure others would find certainly true. He considered all of these as propositions of common sense, and further argued that whenever a philosophical position came into conflict with these commonsense propositions it must be the philosophical theory, not common sense, that is wrong.

But a striking feature of Moore's list is the care with which he constructs it. Furthermore, he argues that any philosophical theory that comes in conflict with *these* propositions must be wrong. It would certainly be possible for Moore to continue his list of commonsense propositions, perhaps indefinitely, but all the same, he never sets up the faculty of common sense as the infallible judge on all matters. Common sense may itself be muddled and confused in various ways. Even so, there are certain propositions of common sense that we certainly know to be true and it is these propositions whose truth may not be transgressed.

If this reading of Moore is correct, then Blanshard's critique of the *general* competence of common sense (*RA*, 314 ff.) is quite beside the point. The theory that time is unreal, for example, implies (or seems to imply) that it is false that the world has existed for many years before I was born. If it implies this, then it is simply wrong, for however dubious and muddled common sense may be elsewhere, here, at least, it is on firmer ground than any philosophical argument. If, on the other hand, the doctrine that time is unreal does not carry this false implication, then, I think, we have the right to suspend our semantic goodwill and ask the proponent of the theory that time is unreal exactly what he *means* by this claim.

This reference to meaning leads to the second, and more important, feature of Moore's "A Defence of Common Sense": we can know that a given proposition is true (and know this with complete certainty) without at the same time being able to offer an analysis of this proposition. Blanshard explains Moore's position in these words:

> For the strange fact was, he said, that we could understand a belief, and know that it was true, without knowing what it meant, in the sense of knowing the right analysis of it.
> Now there is something very odd in saying that you can be sure a proposition is true before you know what it means. ["P of A," 61]

Now *exactly* what is so strange about the circumstance that Moore envisages? Of course, if someone utters a sentence in Urdu then it will certainly be strange for someone else, who knows no Urdu, to be able to recognize its truth. Recognizing the truth of an assertion normally presupposes a certain level of linguistic competence. Needless to say, Moore does not deny this plain deliverance of common sense. We can put Moore's position in this way: a person might have the linguistic competence and the intelligence to recognize the truth of some assertion without being able to give an account (an analysis) of *his* linguistic competence. Is this a *strange* fact? Far from it, for it is a general feature of a competence that it may be acquired without at the same time acquiring a second-order ability to describe this competence. I know (and know for certain) that red and green are different colors, yet if someone were to ask me to elucidate the conceptual status of colors, I would quickly become lost in difficulties. Even so, this philosophical embarrassment casts *no* retroactive doubt upon my original knowledge claim.

Blanshard will have none of this:

> ... what this implies is that one can see what one is saying to be true—indeed Moore says "wholly true"—without knowing just what it is that one is saying. How strange this doctrine is may be seen from Moore's own practice. He devoted vast pains and patience to reflecting on what we mean when, looking at an inkstand or a match-box, we say that this is a material thing. After a characteristically minute consideration, he concluded that there were three and only three possible answers to this question . . . . [Yet] Moore admitted that to each of these answers there were "very grave objections"; he professed himself unable to choose between them, and went so far as to say that "no philosopher has hitherto suggested an answer which comes anywhere near to being certainly true." Now is it not odd to say that the plain man can be perfectly sure of his answer when the meaning of that answer, as correctly stated, breaks up into a set of alternatives none of which he has ever heard of, and all of which remain uncertain under the most thorough examination? What Moore is suggesting is that beliefs entertained at one level, that of unreflecting assent, should be accepted as answering questions raised at a very different level, that of reflective criticism. [*RA*, 315–16]

It is clear that a presupposition of this argument against Moore is that to *know* what something means involves being able to *say* what it means. Given this assumption, Moore's position does, of course, collapse in just the manner that Blanshard indicates. If, after a long and careful philosophical search, we find ourselves unable to state what the plain man means by certain of his remarks, then we ought to entertain serious doubts that the plain man himself understands, *in any sense,* what he is saying, and then, needless to say, we should also doubt whether we can accept, without further ado, the idea that what he asserts is *wholly true.*

Blanshard's challenge to Moore's position encompasses most of the non-positivistic analytic tradition. As *meaning* became associated with *use,* it became a cardinal doctrine that one could know *how* to use an expression (and in this way know its meaning) and not at the same time be able to give an accurate description of this use (i.e. not be able to offer an analysis of this meaning). Now, in his response to such a position, it is important to notice that Blanshard is not unfairly trading upon the plain man's[22] inability to elucidate the meaning of his discourse. His charge is that the reflective mind, after the most careful scrutiny, is often unable to find any clear sense in what the plain man says or any obvious ground for accepting his claims as true. Why, at this point, should we side with unreflective confidence over against thoughtful doubt?

In sum, Blanshard has ingeniously turned the tables on Moore. Moore believed that at least *some* of the judgments of common sense are *wholly* true, and being wholly true must also be meaningful. The philosopher's task, then, is not to bother about the truth of these claims (since this is already settled), but rather to undertake the difficult task of elucidating the meaning of these claims. Blanshard's reply is that the most careful investigation has revealed no coherent sense to these commonsense beliefs, therefore our initial confidence in their truth has been quite undermined. Since the emphasis has now shifted from the undeniable truth of these judgments to their now questioned sense, perhaps it will be more appropriate to pursue this topic under the new heading of Linguistic Philosophy—Later Forms.

8. Linguistic Philosophy—Later Forms

Blanshard is not at ease in discussing the developments in linguistic philosophy since the Second World War. One problem is that it is again Wittgenstein who emerges as the dominant figure, and between Blanshard and Wittgenstein there seems little chance for communication. I have already charged that Blanshard misreads the Wittgenstein of the *Tractatus.* The same charge cannot be made against the Blanshard treatment of Wittgenstein's later writings. Blanshard neither misconstrues nor construes Wittgenstein's *Philosophical Investigations*: he chooses not to discuss this work at all:

I have chosen Ryle rather than Wittgenstein because I seem to be able to understand him. I have not dealt with the *Philosophical Investigations* because
any critic of that work must face the facts (a) that its most admiring exponents do not agree on its interpretation, (b) that no matter how effective
one's criticism, it will be dismissed as having failed to catch the profounder
meanings of the prophet. [*RA*, 348 n.]

It is easy to share Blanshard's impatience with Wittgenstein's idolators, but
even so, his unwillingness to confront the Wittgensteinian challenge straightforwardly must be counted as one of the major weaknesses of his critique of
the analytic movement. Wittgenstein's writings are difficult, perhaps un-
necessarily and even perversely difficult; but they have constituted the major
influence in analytic philosophy over at least the last fifty years, and an
assessment of the analytic movement that ignores this influence must be
radically incomplete.

Setting aside his invidious comparison, there can be no complaint with
Blanshard's decision to take the writings of Gilbert Ryle seriously. Ryle has
written brilliantly over a wide range of subjects, and even if there is room to
disagree with him concerning the treatment of particular problems, there is
no question that he has exemplified the spirit of postpositivistic analytic
philosophy.

Blanshard's account of Ryle seems sometimes slightly out of focus. This
begins with his overall characterization of Ryle's position:

Moore thought that if we took the statements of common sense about tables
and chairs, time and space, with their ordinary meaning, we had statements
which, in their truth and certainty, provided touchstones for philosophy.
Ryle holds, on the contrary, that ordinary language produces confusions
that are the prime source of philosophical perplexity. Not that it produces
these in the plain man himself. When he says "Satan does not exist" or "the
arrow flew through the centre of the bush," he is not in the least confused,
nor is he using words in a questionable way. He is talking on a pre-
philosophical level on which neither the questions nor the answers of the
philosopher have yet appeared, nor therefore the muddle philosophers fall
into. The difficulty arises when the philosopher does arrive on the scene.
[*RA*, 343]

First of all, it is rather difficult to grasp the contrast that Blanshard is trying to draw between Ryle's attitude toward everyday language and Moore's.
Moore thought that certain claims of common sense are known to be wholly
true. I do not think that Ryle would dispute this. Moore also thought that the
philosopher's task was to give a proper account of the meaning of these
claims. Again, I think that Ryle would agree. Furthermore, Moore saw quite
clearly that the surface grammar of our language was no sure guide to the
proper analysis of a proposition. Indeed, he went beyond this to suggest that
the surface grammar of our language may be positively *misleading* in its in-

dications about the proper form that an analysis should take. It is better then to view Ryle's position as a *systematic* extension of some of Moore's basic insights rather than as a competing doctrine.

Ryle's leading idea was that language is misleading in certain standard ways that are capable of characterization. In his remarkable essay "Systematically Misleading Expressions" he examines three main categories of such expressions under the general headings:

I. Quasi-ontological Statements

II. Statements Seemingly about Universals, or Quasi-Platonic Statements

III. Descriptive Expressions and Quasi-Descriptions

Under each of these headings further cases are listed, and an enormous effort is made to avoid oversimplifying generalizations that would, in their own way, be misleading.

> I do not know any way of classifying or giving an exhaustive list of the possible types of systematically misleading expressions. I fancy that the number is in principle unlimited, but that the number of prevalent and obsessing types is fairly small.[23]

Again, his conclusion concerning the status of this investigation relative to philosophy as a whole is stated with great caution:

> But, as confession is good for the soul, I must admit that I do not very much relish the conclusions towards which these conclusions point. I would rather allot to philosophy a sublimer task than the detection of the sources in linguistic idioms of recurrent misconstructions and absurd theories. But that it is at least this I cannot feel any serious doubt. [*L&L*, 39–40]

I believe that Ryle's "Systematically Misleading Expressions" is, in the richness of its insight, in the openness of its approach, and in the modesty of its pretensions, one of the masterpieces of the analytic movement.

Ryle's name, of course, is usually associated with *categories* and more particularly with *category mistakes*. In his important essay "Categories"[24] he seems to adopt a narrow and somewhat inflexible approach to philosophical problems, for he declares that

> not only is it the case that category-propositions (namely assertions that terms belong to certain categories or types) are always philosopher's propositions, but, I believe, the converse is also true. [*L&L*, 281]

Here Ryle gives his thesis a "linguistic turn" by speaking about "category-propositions" rather than simply of "categories," and this may lead to the charge that he is either just factually mistaken about the history of philosophy or being high-handed, co-opting the name *philosophy* for one thin line that runs through it.

Certainly Ryle did not suppose that philosophers (when doing philosophy) invariably raised their problems *as* problems concerning category-propositions. He seems to think that this is what philosophers have *really* been doing even if they have not been fully aware of this. More modestly, we can say that viewing the philosopher's task as dealing with category-propositions is one way of illuminating the philosopher's enterprise, in contrast, say, to that of the empirical scientist. This, I think, does not overly distort the character of the philosophical tradition. It has generally been thought that it is not the philosopher's *particular* concern to decide whether a given object is red, although it is his concern to give a conceptual analysis of perception. Again, it has generally been thought that it is not the philosopher's *particular* concern to decide whether one symphony is better than another, yet the analysis of aesthetic judgment falls squarely into his domain. If it is agreed that the philosopher's task is not to ascertain the truth of particular claims or to form empirical generalizations from them, then calling his enterprise a categorial enterprise does not seem far from the mark.

I think, however, that it is a mistake to dwell too long on slogans; instead, we should look at Ryle's detailed use of the notions of categories and category-propositions. He suggests that we hitch ourselves up and become interested in categories for two main reasons:

> (1) There are concepts with which we are perfectly familiar and which we are perfectly competent to employ—incessantly occurring, for instance, in questions which we know quite well how to solve. Yet whole classes of ordinary propositions embodying one or more of such concepts, some of which propositions we have perfectly good reasons for accepting as true, are ruled out as false by other propositions, no less well authenticated, embodying other equally familiar concepts. In a word, we are confronted by antinomies. [*L & L*, 295]

Surely Ryle is correct in supposing that this is one of the main reasons that our first-order ease is interrupted and we become forced to take a reflective turn.

A second and new kind of type-riddle emerges after the philosopher begins to reflect upon the categories employed in his everyday affairs.

> (2) Then, when we have begun to explore the mechanics of some of our concepts and propositions, we find ourselves embarrassed by some purely technical perplexities. We are not quite sure how to use our own professional implements. [*L & L*, 296]

Thus, the technical terms of philosophy are capable of type-crossing (and other forms of abuse), and so philosophy can become the source, not just the result, of categorial perplexities. Ryle mentions the problem of internal relations as one that the philosopher generates from his own technical concerns. Problems about sense-data, universals, intentional entities, prime matter, etc., would, presumably, also fall into this class.

Now if we combine the earlier idea, that the role of philosophy is (at least) the detection of systematically misleading expressions, with this newer idea, that philosophy is a categorial study, we arrive at the notion that (at least) a main task of philosophy is the detection and resolution of *type-riddles* and *category mistakes*. I don't think that Ryle anywhere explicitly limits philosophy to this single task, yet much of his actual practice shows him working in this way; and so I do not think that Blanshard is far from the mark in saying, for Ryle, "such confusion . . . is the beginning of philosophy; its end and special business is to clear up the confusion" (*RA*, 347). Then we naturally want to ask, with Blanshard, whether such a view of philosophy "covers the ground, that is, whether it applies to philosophical problems generally" (348).

Blanshard believes that it covers very little of the ground indeed. To show this he examines a "few random samples" of philosophical issues that do not, in his words, show "a continuing family resemblance to . . . category confusion." Because of lack of space, I can examine only one of Blanshard's samples; in any case, I am inclined to say much the same thing about each of them.

> A young man has enough savings for a car or a year at the university; which should he take? If he is of a reflective turn, he may well go on and ask, What things are most worth having, and how can one judge between them?, which are of course ancient ethical questions. Do such questions arise from a confusion of categories? Some ordinary language philosophers would protest that this is an idle inquiry, since ethical questions are not in the relevant sense questions at all. To say that the enlightenment gained from a year of study would be more worth having than the pleasure gained from the car is not to assert anything, but only to express a feeling or an attitude of one's own. This is of course a possible ethical position, but I do not think it is possible consistently with respect for ordinary language. Whether he is correct or not in doing so, the plain man certainly does not mean, when he calls something good or right or a duty, to express merely his own feeling or attitude toward it, and I think that the ordinary language philosopher who says he is has already abandoned ordinary language as his guide. If he does take such language as his guide, and recognizes ethical problems as genuine ones, he will not find much plausibility in saying they arise from confusing categories. The problem what things are most worth having surely springs not from conflicting categories but from conflicting desires, the desires of the young man, for example, both for education and for pleasure. The suggestion that his problem arises out of his attempt at some point to combine incongruous sentence or proposition factors seems to bear no relation to fact. [*RA*, 348–49]

I have cited this passage at length for it illustrates Blanshard's criticisms at their best, but also, I'm afraid, at their worst. Let me begin with the worst. I do not know why emotivism is cited in this context at all. It certainly has nothing to do with the issue at hand: in this case, whether philosophical problems in ethics are categorial problems. The passage also carries the broad suggestion that ordinary language philosophers have characteristically held to some version of emotivism. I do not think that this is true. In any case, it is hard not to feel peevish about Blanshard's tendency to hang the albatross of emotivism about the neck of every philosopher with an analytic head.

Of course, what is good about the passage is that it confronts Ryle's approach with a very tough example. It surely doesn't seem that the question What things are most worth having, and how can one judge between them? arises out of category confusions. But instead of stopping at this first impression, we can ask why this question has, as it certainly does, a philosophical ring. That is, why does it have a feeling of depth and why does the issue seem so peculiarly intractable? A traditional answer is that this question *feels* deep because it *is* deep: it concerns the fundamental structure of the moral life. On this view it is not surprising that the issues involved should prove intractable.

An alternative response is that the question seems deep because we are really at a loss to know how to go about answering it. The young man choosing between a car or a year at the university operates with a whole set of value commitments in hand. His decision is made against this standing background that may shift over time, but only very slowly. In contrast, his reflective query, What things are most worth having?, calls these background commitments into question, and thus his standard way of dealing with questions of value is wholly displaced. The two questions:

(a) What shall I have, a car or a year at the university?

(b) What things are most worth having?

may seem similar. (b) might be thought of as the most general form that questions like (a) can take. What I am now suggesting, very tentatively, is that (b) is a question of a wholly different type from (a) and that a failure to fully appreciate this type difference is one source of philosophical perplexity.[25]

Does Ryle's approach cover all of the ground? I do not think that it covers *all* of the ground, but I think that if we stop to consider the distinctive quality of many philosophical problems, the idea that they turn upon categorial issues does not seem grossly narrow in its conception.

Philosophers, it seems, are always involved in trading one thing off for another. If a philosopher is committed to clarity and straightforwardness, then subtleties and complexities must be suppressed and a charge of superficiality and oversimplification is always available. In contrast, a philosopher may have an unstinting commitment to do justice to the phenomena in all their richness: suppressing nothing, regimenting nothing. This can invoke the charge of unintelligibility and pointlessness. Wittgenstein, especially in his later writings, exemplified this second approach and it is for this reason, I think, that Blanshard finds his philosophy wholly uncongenial.

Ryle seems altogether different. He writes with the clarity, elegance, and directness that have characterized much of British philosophy. At the same time, I think that it is a misunderstanding to suppose that Ryle was doing more than presenting specimens (good specimens) of how philosophical inquiry should proceed. Speaking of Plato, Ryle has remarked that "He was too much of a philosopher to think that anything that he had said was the last word. It was left to his disciples to identify his footmarks with his destination."[26] At the risk of embarrassing the emeritus Waynflete Professor of Metaphysical Philosophy, I think that the same description fits his own philosophical career.

Conclusion. From the start, Blanshard recognizes that the philosophy of analysis does not constitute a school whose essence can be captured under a few easy rubrics. This, of course, presents him with a difficult task of assessment. These same difficulties carry over to my efforts to assess his assessments. I have found myself standing on one foot, then on the other, in order to respond to arguments aimed at varying targets.

If I may now venture an overall evaluation, I think that it would be this. Blanshard's greatest strength lies in his meticulous examination of logical positivism. The positivists share with Blanshard a commitment to clarity and argumentation, and I think that it is for this reason that he can combine sharp criticism with respect. On the other side, I do not think that Blanshard is at home (and thus not nearly as trenchant) in dealing with the nonpositivistic dimensions of the analytic treatment. Philosophy will certainly benefit if he renews his efforts in this area. I would like to think that the nonpositivists in the analytic movement will be able to hold their own against his criticisms, but as a student who has witnessed his remarkable ability to deflate pretension, I must confess to a genuine uneasiness on this score.

Robert J. Fogelin

Department of Philosophy
Yale University

NOTES

[1]Setting aside issues of analytic ethics, which are more carefully discussed in *Reason and Goodness, Reason and Analysis* represents Blanshard's most sustained and careful examination of the analytic movement. I shall, therefore, key my discussion on this text. On occasion, however, I shall also cite the remarkably compact and elegant address that Blanshard gave before the British Academy under the title "The Philosophy of Analysis" (hereafter cited as "P

of A"; *Proceedings of the British Academy* 38 [1952]:39–69). Restrictions on space preclude an examination of further relevant discussions in both *The Nature of Thought* and his numerous journal articles.

²". . . these theories, particularly those central to positivism, remain very much alive, despite their depreciation and disavowal by many *avant garde* analysts" (*RA*, 11).

³Substantially the same argument occurs on p. 59 of "P of A."

⁴See Moritz Schlick, *Problems of Ethics*, trans. David Rynin (New York: Prentice-Hall, 1939).

⁵It should be clear that none of this bears upon Blanshard's detailed criticisms of various forms of noncognitivism found in his *Reason and Goodness*—most of which I accept. I am only trying to break the conceptual link between emotivism and the other components of the positivist's program.

⁶They have also been detailed by Carl Hempel in his justly famous essay "Problems and Changes in the Empiricist Criterion of Meaning," *Revue internationale de philosophie* 4, no. 11 (1950).

⁷It will not do to take this commitment to clear definitions as *definitive* of philosophizing. A look at the tradition will show that a surprisingly large number of philosophers (of various stripe) do not share it.

⁸Blanshard discusses this difficulty in *RA*, 226–27.

⁹"Performative Utterances," *Philosophical Papers* (Oxford: Clarendon Press, 1961), 221.

¹⁰I think that there is another way of dealing with the recommendation dodge. If self-reference is taken seriously as a criticism, it does not help a bit to switch from propositions to recommendations. Although the positivists did not pay sufficient attention to the problem, some account must be given that sorts out the meaningful from the meaningless in the area of recommendations themselves. ("Assume that the absolute is lazy!") When they thought about this, the positivists usually suggested something along the following lines: a recommendation (or imperative) is meaningful if its counterpart indicative is verifiable. Thus, "Close the door." is meaningful because the indicative counterpart "The door is closed." is verifiable. But now if the meaningfulness of recommendations rides piggyback on the meaningfulness of the counterpart assertion, then switching from propositions to recommendations to avoid a difficulty will never work.

¹¹Moritz Schlick, *Gesammelte Aufsätze, 1926–36* (Vienna: Gerold & Co., 1938), 246–47.

¹²Ibid., 246. In the same vein Schlick remarks: "It is not necessary to make hypotheses about meaning, and they would come too late, because we must presuppose meaning in order to formulate any hypothesis" (182).

¹³In his later period, Wittgenstein viewed meaning as too mundane and vulgar to conform to definition; in his earlier period, he viewed it as too sublime to undergo such submission.

¹⁴See especially the first chapter of *An Introduction to Wittgenstein's "Tractatus"* (London: Hutchinson, 1959), where she examines a passage from Karl Popper that is strikingly similar to the passage just cited from Blanshard.

¹⁵*Tractatus Logico-Philosophicus*, trans. D. F. Pears and B. F. McGuinness (London: Routledge & Kegan Paul, 1961).

¹⁶Urmson defends an empiricist reading of the *Tractatus* on the grounds that "it was the sort of interpretation I have given, right or wrong, which was accepted in the period under examination, and which has therefore been of historical importance and influence. For our purposes it is what Wittgenstein was thought to mean that matters" (*Philosophical Analysis* [Oxford: Clarendon Press, 1956], pp. ix–x). But such a line is not open to Blanshard since he speaks directly about the text itself, viewing it, strange to say, with the eyes of a logical empiricist.

¹⁷"Objects can only be *named*. Signs are their representatives. I can only speak *about* them: I cannot *put them into words*" (*TLP*, 3.221).

¹⁸"Situations can be described but not *given names*" (ibid., 3.144).

¹⁹See chapter 6 of *RA*, which exhibits Blanshard's critical skills at their best.

²⁰This is not to suggest that his working out of this idea was also intuitively plausible.

²¹Interest in this essay¹ has been stirred anew by the appearance of Wittgenstein's *On Certainty*,² which subjects this work, together with Moore's "Refutation of Idealism"³ to the very closest scrutiny.

[1]in *Contemporary British Philosophy,* 2d ser. (London: Allen & Unwin, 1925).

[2](New York: Harper & Row, 1970).

[3](*Mind,* n.s. 12 [Oct. 1903]).

[22]Anyway, the plain man is not some statistically selected segment of society (the vulgar), but just ourselves naturally engaged in unreflective activity.

[23]In *Logic and Language: First and Second Series* (*L & L*) ed. Antony Flew (Garden City, N.Y.: Doubleday, Anchor Books, 1965), 39. The quotations from Ryle that follow are from "Systematically Misleading Expressions," pp. 39–40, and "Categories," pp. 281, 295, and 296.

[24]It is important to remember that the problems concerning categories have generated a wide-ranging discussion within the analytic movement, and this essay itself does not constitute Ryle's position on the matter but one important stage in the development of this position.

[25]I am not saying, nor do I believe, that questions of type (b) are pseudoquestions, although that is a possibility worth examining. Of course, these remarks do not constitute an argument; they are only a vague gesture in the direction of an argument.

[26]*Dilemmas* (Cambridge: At the University Press, 1956), 14.

19. Reply to Robert J. Fogelin

Blanshard's Critique of the Analytic Movement

My criticisms of the analytic philosophy have not, so far as I know, had much attention from the analysts themselves. To them my voice was a faint one, crying from a discredited past or from some wilderness where the new conquering empire of light and analysis had not yet penetrated. This was not quite my own view of how I stood in relation to them. Many of them I knew, liked, and respected; I was for many years American treasurer of *Mind* and tried hard to increase its circulation in this country. I admired the clarity of Ayer and Ryle. Though clarity is not enough, it remains in philosophy a cardinal virtue, and in my criticism of the analysts I tried to be not less clear than they were, indeed to apply the kind of analysis to their own position that they used, often I thought with success, upon the kind of philosophizing in which I had been brought up. But I do not think my criticism had much effect.

Mr. Fogelin's essay is so far as I know the only attempt by an analytic philosopher to meet my strictures in systematic fashion. With much of what I have written I am happy to note that he agrees. But this is in part because I directed my critique so largely to logical empiricism rather than the linguistic philosophy which succeeded it and which he holds in higher respect than I do. I agree that a thorough examination of this latter philosophy is due. I venture to think it would be left by such a scrutiny about where Sir William Hamilton's philosophy was left when Mill had finished with it; but however that may be, the work will have to be done by someone with more time, patience, and learning than I have at command.

In placing the logical empiricists in the center of my picture, I do not feel that I was gravely mistaken. After all, it was their theory that made the historic breakthrough; its theses, at least as stated in Ayer's classic little book, were put with an attractive lucidity; it was they who dropped the big rock into a relatively placid sea, and their influence is apparent not only in the tremendous splash they made but also in the succession of waves and wavelets of analysis that have been lapping on our shores ever since. Not of course that I thought them right; indeed I thought that in getting the fly out of the bottle, to use a favorite illustration of theirs, they were taking a thoroughly unsound line. My own line in criticizing the philosophy of analysis was simple enough; it was to break the bottle neck, which I conceived logical positivism itself to be. How much, if anything, this strategy contributed I do not know. At any rate the imprisoned fly of philosophy seems to be out again and buzzing cheerfully about with a slowly renewing animation.

The four theses of logical empiricism that I thought most important were (1) logical atomism, (2) the verifiability theory of meaning, (3) the analytic character of a priori knowledge, and (4) emotivism. Mr. Fogelin begins with my attack on emotivism. He does not criticize the substance of that attack, but confines himself to two questions that lie on its periphery: (A) whether emotivism is a deduction from the positivist theory of knowledge, and (B) whether attitude theories surrender objective standards in ethics.

Emotivism

(A) Emotivism seemed to me an unlikely theory to have emerged from an objective study of ethics. As I looked at it more closely, I felt a little like those astronomers who observed an unnatural bump on the orbit of Uranus; there must, they thought, be some extraneous force pulling the planet out of its orbit. The force, as yet undiscovered, proved to be Neptune. The Neptune of emotivism must, I thought, be the positivist theory of knowledge. Consider theses (2) and (3) above. Thesis (2), the verifiability theory of meaning, says that factual propositions, if they are to have meaning at all, must be verifiable in sense experience. No. (3) says that a priori propositions are universal and necessary only because they are analytic, that is, because their predicates are already included in their subject terms. And these two kinds of proposition are the only kinds there are, since they alone are capable of being true or false. Where, as between these two, did the statements of ethics fall? A typical ethical statement would be that an act is *right,* that an experience is *good,* or that one *ought* to do something. Now does "right," or "good," or "ought" refer to anything that can be verified in sense? Clearly not, I thought. Ethical statements evidently fell, then, in the other class; they were a priori statements, and therefore universal and necessary. Very well; "thieving is wrong"; is that universal and necessary? No again, stealing is normally wrong, but if a life depended on getting a drug from a drugstore that was closed, would it still be wrong? Ethical rules are not always, or even usually, exceptionless. But if ethical statements fell neither in the one class nor in the other, they could not be propositions at all. Still they surely had some meaning; they were not just noises or marks on paper. Such meaning as they had must be noncognitive and presumably emotive, the kind of meaning that lay in exclamations of liking or disapproving. This, I concluded, must be the way in which the positivist mind was working.

In this I still incline to think I was right. None of the leading positivists was primarily a moralist. They all came into philosophy from science, and the philosophy of science was their dominant interest. Propositions about value were not in the range of their normal concern, and to relegate these to an emotive status was the most natural course. Mr. Fogelin points out that this is to attribute to them an illogical conclusion. One may hold the verifiability theory of meaning and still believe in a cognitive ethics *if* that ethics so defines its terms as to make sensible verification possible. In this he is clearly right, and in supposing that the positivists' theory of knowledge committed them logically to noncognitivism I was clearly wrong.

I hope there is no weaseling, however, in saying that I was not wholly wrong. The positivists' epistemology, though not necessarily excluding cognitivist theories, did confine them to a narrow range of such theories, namely those forms of naturalism which can accept verification in sense as their basis. Apparently only one of the positivists attempted to work out a theory of this kind. Moritz Schlick, in his little book *Problems of Ethics,*[1] devotes himself to the proof of the following proposition, which he calls "a fundamental ethical insight": "the moral valuations of modes of behavior and characters are nothing but the emotional reactions with which human society responds to the pleasant and sorrowful consequences that, according to the average experience, proceed from those modes of behavior and characters" (78). This, to be sure, sounds like another version of emotivism. But Schlick did not intend it to be. He believed that moral statements were really judgments, and says: "the verification of a proposition concerning value" is "simply the feeling of pleasure" in which "the *essence* of value is completely exhausted" (105). This is, in fact, pure hedonism. And I doubt whether even this is genuinely open to the positivist. The happiness or unhappiness of others is certainly not verifiable by any sense observations of mine; nor is it clear that my own happiness or unhappiness is subject to the sort of sense observation that positivism requires of factual propositions. And even if they are, hedonism is a most insecure refuge. It has been refuted by so many moralists from Butler forward that no rehearsal of its case seems necessary. In sum, though the positivist epistemology did not, as I wrongly said it did, require an emotivist theory in ethics, it did confine the positivist to a choice between noncognitivism and an untenable kind of naturalism.

(B) In more than one of my discussions of emotivism I have gone on to say that the "attitude theories" that succeeded it shared its more serious shortcomings, and notably the absence of an objective standard in morals. Mr. Fogelin takes exception to this view, and it will be well to have his words before us.

I do not see . . . how abandoning the idea that value judgments are assertions *eo ipso* ties them to the expression of *attitudes*. To take one of the possibilities cited by Blanshard, suppose we hold that value judgments (down deep) really express commands (or better, prescriptions). Does this tie values to attitudes and thereby destroy the objectivity of values? Surely not, for the notion that value judgments *express* commands carries no greater subjective implications than the parallel claim that we use indicatives or assertions to *express* our thoughts. Nor do I think that the plain man believes that commands, as such, are not capable of objective assessment. The plain man, in fact, believes just the opposite.

This passage bristles with difficulties. I will indicate a few of them without developing the case as I would if there were more space.

(i) Mr. Fogelin does not see how rejecting moral judgments as assertions commits one to making them expressive attitudes, and he takes imperativism as an example which is neither the one nor the other. But in my own thought and treatment of the matter, imperativism has always counted as one of the attitude theories. To issue a command, to announce an imperative, to recommend or urge an action (Mr. Hare, the chief representative of the theory, uses all these terms) *is* to take up an attitude toward an action. The point is rather more than a verbal one, for if the imperativist theory may be so classed, it must share with other attitude theories the heavy burden of having no objective standards.

(ii) Does it really lack such standards? Mr. Hare is solicitous to show that imperatives can be supported by reasons, and if by these reasons he could establish that an action is really the right one to take, I should have nothing further to say. But how does the rational defense proceed? It proceeds, Mr. Hare tells us, by showing that the judgment, or rather the command, in question is consistent with and required by other commands which, taken as a whole, make up a way of life. Thus the particular command has an entire system behind it. The argument here is admirable. But the question of course is bound to arise, What is to decide the right course if two ways of life as a whole conflict? Mr. Hare is a Christian and a liberal, and he would defend the making or obeying of a particular command by showing that it was involved in the life-plan of a liberal in politics and a Christian in morals. But suppose he is arguing with a communist who rejects Mr. Hare's particular command because it is inconsistent with the communist life-plan as a whole. At this critical point, as I understand him, Mr. Hare gives up the hope of a rational defense. The choice between ways of life must be made by an act of will, a commitment for which no further reason can be offered (*The Language of Morals*, 69).[2] Now I do not see how it can be held that a theory provides an objective standard of conduct when it admits that between conflicting ways of life there is no ground for choice. To say that both communist and Christian have justified their cases in the fullest possible way, though these cases remain in conflict, seems to me equivalent to saying that in the most fundamental of moral problems there is no rational court of appeal and no objective standard at all.

(iii) Consider next Mr. Fogelin's statement: "the notion that value judgments *express* commands carries no greater subjective implications than the parallel claim that we use indicatives or assertions to *express* our thoughts." This seems to me to conflict with our actual meanings. The implicit claim of every judgment is to be true, that is, objectively true, and that this is of its essence is shown by the fact that without it what is expressed would not be considered a judgment at all. A command makes no such claim, either to truth or to rightness. The command of a mafia leader to his henchman X to "rub out" Y carries no claim to rightness; so far as it makes an objective claim, it is that it would be more convenient to the gang if Y were dead. Thus while judgment as such is a claim to objective truth, all that a command or imperative need express is subjective desire. To say, then, that interpreting moral statements as commands or imperatives carries no more implication of their subjectivity than interpreting them as thoughts or judgments is to draw a misleading parallel. Indeed the desire expressed in an imperative may be for what one knows to be wrong; the intention expressed by judgment is always to express truth.

(iv) "Nor do I think," Mr. Fogelin adds, "that the plain man believes that commands, as such, are not capable of objective assessment. The plain man, in fact, believes the opposite." I agree. But that does not put the plain man on the side of the imperativist. He certainly does not interpret his own moral judgments as commands. He does not believe, for example, that in judging that John Wilkes Booth did wrong in shooting Lincoln he is really saying, "Booth, desist!" That he would regard as a fantastic suggestion. What he believes is that commands may be moral acts, and that when they are, they should be judged in the same way as other moral acts. He would say that when Hitler ordered the invasion of Poland he was acting immorally, and if you asked him why, he would say, "Because that order started an aggressive war," an act that he regards as objectively wrong. He is not confusing judgments with commands. No doubt Hitler judged "the Polish government is one that deserves overturning," but if you asked the plain man whether it was that that he was condemning, he would surely say, "No; a man has a right to his own opinion, even if that opinion is badly mistaken. What I am condemning is not the opinion, but the *act* of ordering an aggressive war." The plain man is thus implying his conviction that a judgment is one thing and a command, even if it grows out of that judgment, is another.

Mr. Fogelin's modesty has kept him from mentioning that he has written on this problem himself. In his *Evidence and Meaning*[3] he has developed with clarity and acuteness an ethical theory of his own with most of which I find myself in agreement. He holds that moral judgments are really judgments and rejects noncognitivism; he is a naturalist who finds Moore's nonnatural good to be undiscoverable; he finds that values are connected in an intimate way with human needs and desires; he believes that some conduct is rational and some not, and that there are objective standards of conduct. In all this I agree and applaud. He has developed the interesting and ingenious view that a value statement declares that an evaluation is in some degree warranted, making the reference to evidence an essential part of the statement.

Where then would I differ? It would be in the emphasis he places on the evaluative element as a "prescription" or an "imperative." "Subject to certain qualifications," he writes, "let me suggest the following warrant schema for evaluations involving the term 'good': There are adequate grounds in behalf of the prescription: Choose A" (*Evidence and Meaning*, 149). Similarly "the evaluation 'A is better than B,' when used in a context of choice, may be interpreted as follows: There are adequate grounds on behalf of the prescription: Choose A rather than B" (ibid., 148). Now this reading of a value judgment as advising a choice is no doubt applicable in cases where one is buying a suit or choosing a candidate; and Mr. Fogelin is very liberal in his interpretation of what choice means. "Thus under the heading of choosing I shall include such diverse activities as buying, tasting, seizing, joining, etc." (ibid., 152). But I should have thought there were many cases in which value judgments made no reference to choice or prescription or imperatives of any kind. If I say, "Intelligence is good," or "Being 6 feet 4 inches tall like Mr. Fogelin is good," an imperative element would be pointless, for intelligence and height are not within the range of things that can be prescribed or chosen. The difficulty that one cannot prescribe to the past he meets by exchanging present for past prescriptions. Thus the judgment, "It was better for Caesar to cross the Rubicon quickly rather than to wait and allow his enemies to consolidate their position," reads in his reformulation, "There were, at the time, adequate grounds in behalf of the prescription: Caesar, cross the Rubicon quickly, etc."! (ibid, 159). Regarding this I can only comment that when I say "It was better for Caesar to act so," I do not find in my own mind this reference to an ideal or possible prescriber. I should add that Mr. Fogelin carefully disavows making all value judgments prescriptive, but it is not clear where the line lies between those that are prescriptive and those that are not. My own feeling would be that having recognized value judgments as cognitive and some of them at least to be nonprescriptive, it would be better if he dropped the troublesome prescriptive ghost altogether.

The Verifiability Theory

Mr. Fogelin agrees for the most part with my criticism of the verifiability theory of meaning, and does so in terms that I much appreciate. But he adds certain comments that call for remark.

(1) He says that if empiricists have failed to define "meaning" adequately—or the notions of knowledge and value either—so have rationalists. What is the significance of this failure on both sides? Is it that we are asking unanswerable questions? Regarding the first notion, meaning, I suspect we must say what Wittgenstein does, and concede that it has too many and various senses to be crystallized in any one definition. As in attempts to define "religion," the definition would inevitably leave out some of the uses or, if it covered them all, it would be so thin and vague as to be worthless. Not that the term "meaning" should be discarded, but that if confusion is to be avoided, one should note which of its many senses is being used; cognitive meaning and emotive meaning, for example, are not to be interchanged. As for the other two terms Mr. Fogelin mentions, I am rather puzzled by his suggestion that rationalists have failed to lay their cards on the table. That the definitions they have offered are not universally agreed upon is no doubt true, but on such questions unanimity is hardly to be expected. If I may volunteer as a sample rationalist, I do not feel guilty of hanging back on these notions. I have written, not wisely perhaps, but lengthily about the nature of both knowledge and value. Knowledge I take to be belief that is at once justifiable and true. In *The Nature of Thought* I have placed the justification of belief in coherence with experience, and attempted explanations of these terms; truth I also found to lie in coherence, though in replying to Mr. Rescher in the present volume I have admitted that such coherence does not stand alone; it needs supplementation by correspondence, however hard that term is to define. In *Reason and Goodness* I have held that value lies exclusively in such experiences as fulfill and satisfy impulses. These theories are offered, I hope, with due tentativity, and they may all be wide of the mark. But they are witnesses against the view that rationalists have sat serenely on the fence while empiricists at least committed themselves to the fray.

(2) Mr. Fogelin next expresses a doubt about my success in a brief passage at arms with Schlick. In accordance with an extreme form of the verifiability theory, Schlick had held that when another man and I both look at a patch of color and I say that he sees the same color that I do, I am talking meaninglessly. "The statement that two experiences of different subjects . . . resemble each other qualitatively, has for us no sense. Note that it is not false, but senseless (*sinnlos*); we have no idea what it means." When I wrote *Reason and Analysis* this seemed to me preposterous, and I confess that it seems so still.

It is important here to be clear what exactly the issue is. Suppose you and I are sitting in a room where there is what would commonly be called a green bowl on the mantelpiece, and that we are both looking at it. There are of course epistemological difficulties in saying that we are seeing the same bowl, but since this is not quite the immediate issue, I pass them over. At least our eyes seem to be focused on the same spot; and let us say that we both remark,

"That bowl is green." Does the fact that we are looking at the same bowl entail that we are seeing the same color? Obviously not. The sensitivity of your retina may be slightly different from mine, so that even if light waves of the same form and frequency fall on our two retinas, the result may be sensations of somewhat different color qualities. Now suppose that I judge, "You are seeing the same green color that I am." Schlick's position commits him to saying that if there is any way in which I can verify this statement, it is meaningful; otherwise not. Very well; *can* I verify my statement? Schlick answers that in one sense I can, but in a second and more important sense I cannot. First we can compare color "frames," which I interpret as follows. Taking each color in turn, I can construct series ordered according to brightness, saturation, or hue. I can then ask you whether you place the color of the bowl at the same point in each of these series as I do. Schlick would say, I gather, that if you do, we can say that you are seeing what I do in the sense that you are putting what you see in the same place in your framework of color relations that I do in mine. But does that assure me that you see the same quality that I see? No, for every color in all the scales may be slightly different for you and for me. Thus the statement about similarity of the two greens remains unverifiable, and is therefore meaningless.

Schlick's cleverness has let a wire-drawn epistemological theory run away with his good sense. We must grant that there is no way of my assuring myself that you see the same quality as I do, but to say that the very suggestion that you do is meaningless is absurd; we all think such notions daily and without doubt or difficulty. Schlick could not consistently even use color frames as tests, for the suggestion that your color qualities might differ systematically from mine is on his theory as meaningless as the notion that they are the same.

Mr. Fogelin reminds me that I am here paying a respect to common sense that I do not always show, and he wants to know how I can be so sure. If his question is how I can be so sure that the color seen by another *may* be like mine, my answer is that I can conceive this possibility with what seems to be perfect clearness, and that no further consideration has made this conception seem obscure or confused. If the question is why one should believe that the color seen by you *is* the same, the answer is a little more complicated. It rests on the enormous mass of evidence provided by daily life of the general similarity of our perceptions. Unless your experience of shapes, odors, tastes, feels, and colors were similar to mine, our dealings with each other would be distorted everywhere; we could not agree about what we were buying or selling, or about the food we were eating, or the rugs, curtains, and books in our living rooms. Regarding colors we are constantly though implicitly testing each other by comparing informally our color frames, by agreeing that this is a darker blue than that; our scarlets, crimsons, and pinks seem to stand in the same relations with each other. And this is important. Mr. Fogelin says of the judgment of similarity between your colors and mine that it "seems to exist in a curious isolation; to use a Wittgensteinian figure, it is rather like a crank that seems like part of the machine, but is attached to nothing." But Schlick could not afford to use such an illustration. For if he believed that we agree as to where a color fell in our color frames, he would also have to admit that there was no great dissimilarity in our color qualities. Why? Because he admitted that color relations were internal relations. "These relations which hold between the elements of the system of colors are obviously *internal* relations" in which "the relation is necessarily implied by the very nature of the terms" (*Gesammelte Aufsätze,* 162). Even, therefore, if the color that lay at the point of intersection of our color series were blank, we could presumably fill it from a knowledge of its relations. It will be remembered that even Hume thought we could construct a missing shade from such a color series, even though this ran counter to his whole theory of the origin of ideas. The belief that other minds see approximately as we do is no detached crank, and in making it so analysts like Schlick and Wittgenstein sacrificed their common sense to a skeptical oversubtlety.

The Verifiability Principle as Inconsistent

(3) I have argued, with Ewing and many others, that the verifiability principle is inconsistent with itself. For if taken as a universal principle applying to all statements of fact, it is itself unverifiable and therefore meaningless. The positivists soon recognized this and remoulded the "principle" into a "recommendation." Mr. Fogelin shows that if thought out, the recommendation goes the way of the principle. But he confesses to a "nagging doubt" whether we have not disposed of the verifiability principle too easily, and he quotes Schlick in support of this doubt. Schlick writes that "our principle is a simple triviality about which there can be no dispute. It is not even an opinion, since it indicates a condition without which no opinion can be formulated. It is not a theory, for its acknowledgment must precede the building of any theory" (ibid., 246). One must agree that all judgment has presuppositions, which it is the business of philosophy to drag to light; and the most essential of these is that a judgment must be self-consistent. Schlick's "principle," besides being clearly false in fact, is also self-refuting, for on its own showing it must be meaningless. To say that it is so fundamental that it is inexpressible as either opinion or theory is also very close to being meaningless; and not knowing what precisely, if anything, it does mean, I shall not attempt criticism. Neither shall I raise the question whether in making a self-referential proposition meaningful one is involving oneself in

Russellian and other paradoxes. I agree with Mr. Fogelin that such questions are important, but they are questions I must leave to logical specialists.

Logical Atomism

It is at this point that Mr. Fogelin makes what he calls his "sharpest charge" against my criticism of the philosophy of analysis. He thinks I have confused two kinds of atomism, the experiential atomism of Hume and the logical atomism of Wittgenstein. Hume was concerned with the analysis of experience, whose ultimate elements he found to be simple data of sense, standing in external relation to each other. Wittgenstein's concern was rather with propositions. "The *Tractatus* does not contain a doctrine of sensory simples nor are atomic propositions identified with protocol sentences. . . . Wittgenstein was attempting to produce a *pure* theory of representation from which everything empirical was not only absent, but wholly out of place. . . . In sum, the *Tractatus* attempts (to use traditional language) a transcendental deduction of the pure conditions of meaningfulness or representation."

What is one to say to this charge? Mr. Fogelin knows his Wittgenstein far better than I do, and if he says I have misinterpreted him, he is no doubt right. But how far wrong I have gone I do not know. I shall confine myself to a few comments.

(1) If the charge is true, I err in a large and goodly company. Mr. Fogelin himself quotes Mr. Urmson, whose book on *Philosophical Analysis* accepts the empiricist reading and points out that it was the interpretation generally accepted in the twenty years or so between the two world wars. This interpretation has been denied roundly by competent exegetes. I can hardly imagine stronger evidence for my own finding of Wittgenstein's extreme obscurity. Equally devoted students spend years in studying him only to come to opposite conclusions not merely on the details of his theory but on its main intentions.

(2) An account of the conditions of representation can hardly be appraised unless one has some idea of what is to be represented. What propositions represent, according to Wittgenstein, is facts. Now among these facts a large proportion certainly consists of the sort of facts Hume had in mind, such facts as that the sky is now blue or that this spot is black. Anyone who tells us that a proposition, to be true, must represent such facts correctly must tell us what the correct analysis of such facts is. How Wittgenstein could do this and yet ignore the whole empirical realm I do not see. Neither did Wittgenstein, and of course he did not ignore it entirely. However unhelpful the *Tractatus* may be with illustrations, it does tell us how empirical facts are to be analyzed. We must begin by realizing that though we think in terms of propositions, usually complex ones, every complex proposition can be broken

up into atomic ones, and each atomic proposition represents an atomic fact. "An atomic fact is a combination of objects" (2.01); "The object is simple" (2.02); the atomic proposition pictures the atomic fact, and "The elements of the picture stand, in the picture, for the objects" (2.131).[4]

Let us take a simple atomic proposition and see how, on Wittgenstein's theory, our thought represents it. "This spot is blue." Unfortunately this will not do, for it contains two different assertions, "This is a spot" and "This is blue." Very well; we simplify it, and say "This is blue." But that is still unsatisfactory, for the word "is" seems to stand for a characterizing relation, and Wittgenstein insists (though constantly violating the injunction) that one must not speak of such relations in words; they can only be reflected or mirrored in the structure of the proposition itself. So we reduce our expression further to "this-blue." On Wittgenstein's theory each component of a proposition stands for an "object." What, then, does "this" stand for? It cannot be a spot, or an area, or a surface, for these are all characters, and the reference to any of them would involve us again in two propositions rather than one. He concludes that the "this" is characterless, which can only mean that it is a bare particular. What does "blue" stand for? One would ordinarily suppose that it is the "object" blue, the experienced blue that is referred to in the predicate of the proposition. But Wittgenstein, as so often, takes us by surprise; he denies that it is any such thing. "objects are colourless," he says (2.0232), apparently meaning here not only that objects are not to be identified with colors, but that they are not to be identified with qualities or properties of any kind. Objects can be named; they cannot be described (3.221). Need one add that he does not hold to this consistently? He writes: "This blue colour and that stand in the internal relation of brighter and darker eo ipso. It is unthinkable that *these* two objects should not stand in this relation" (4.123). Colors, then, *are* objects. But he also writes: "It is clear that the logical product of two elementary propositions can neither be a tautology nor a contradiction. The assertion that a point in the visual field has two different colours at the same time, is a contradiction" (6.3751). I. M. Copi has quoted this passage and added: "It follows that colour predications are *not* elementary propositions, and the implication seems clear that objects are not properties."[5] If this is true, not only the referent of "this" but *both* the objects embraced by the fact are bare particulars.

When I gave an account in *Reason and Analysis* of the logical atomism of the *Tractatus,* I tried to interpret it in such a way that it would be applicable to our actual knowledge. What of this other account that tries (though inconsistently again) to keep clear of empirical involvements? It seems to me that most of my strictures still hold, and that the present theory, whether truer or not to the author's intention, is in some ways worse than the other. It would make empirical knowledge impossible. The reasons may be simply stated.

(1) A fact is now two bare particulars standing in a certain relation. But what kind of relation? If objects had qualities like color, sound, or shape, their relations would be of definite kinds appointed by the character of their terms. But characterless particulars can appoint no relations. Indeed it is difficult to see how they could have any relations at all, even of difference, for they have no characters to differ; and Wittgenstein waves aside the identity of indiscernibles without argument.

(2) The picture theory, already difficult, becomes impossible. For whether the entities in relation that are supposed to provide the picture are taken as the terms of the proposition, the parts of the propositional sign, or the words of the sentence (and Wittgenstein seems, however incoherently, to say all three), the relations between these items are clearly dependent on their character, and therefore cannot picture or show or mirror the relations between characterless particulars, even assuming that these *could* have relations.

(3) It seems to me that this prolegomenon to all knowledge would rule out science as well as philosophy. For more obviously than philosophy, science deals with empirical facts, and if in truth these facts have no empirical filling, then science, which is an attempt to find the connections among the characters of things, must be dealing in systematic illusion. The proper business of science, according to Wittgenstein, is the clarification of scientific terms, but if the facts of the world are really nonstatable relations between characterless points, what is there left for science to do but to distort them?

(4) If the scientist does proceed with his impossible task, how is he to communicate his results? Many or most of the statements of science are statements of causal connection. But in the new cognitive regime, the statement that lightning causes thunder would violate the canons of correct expression. "Lightning" and "thunder" ascribe characters to objects that are really characterless; "causes" gives a verbal name to that which is unnamable and admits only of being "shown." Besides, to suppose that causality operates in nature is an illusion. "Superstition is the belief in the causal nexus" and vice versa. Thus there appears to be no way in which so simple a scientific statement as "Lightning causes thunder" can be made without radically distorting the truth.

These remarks could be much extended. But I have perhaps said enough to show that the empirical *Tractatus* is not to be saved by transposing it into the key of a transcendental deduction. It may have been built, as James said of absolutism, as a shining temple on a hill, but the architect neglected to provide a flight of steps by which one could descend from it to the plain of empirical fact.

Necessity

Mr. Fogelin writes: "Wittgenstein was not being counter-intuitive when he suggested that the general form of a proposition was: *this is the way things are*. Yet if a proposition tells us that *this* is the way things are, this plainly presupposes that things *might* have been otherwise." (This is not clear to me, but let us proceed.) If propositions do carry this presupposition, what are we to say about statements like the laws of logic, which say that in certain respects things *could not* have been other than they are? Clearly we must deny them to be propositions at all.

> His basic insight (he calls it his "leading idea") was that logical terms were not representative, i.e. they did not *stand for* or *refer to* anything at all. . . . Here Wittgenstein hit upon the remarkable idea that this very inability of the laws of logic to *say* anything about the world *in itself showed* something about the world. . . . [It helped him to] arrive at three fundamentally exclusive notions: Names *name* objects, propositions *picture* situations, and the formal structure of our language *mirrors* the formal structure of the world.

This formal structure supplies "a deep underlying unity beneath the disconnected surface of the manifest world." Mr. Fogelin thinks I am deplorably unperceptive in failing to see this. "For him [Blanshard], the *Tractatus* presents the world as one vast heap of disconnected facts." Again several comments are called for.

(1) The *Tractatus does* "present the world as one vast heap of disconnected facts." It tells us on its very first page: "The world divides into facts. Any one can either be the case or not be the case, and everything else remain the same" (1.2, 1.21). Where would one look for a more uncompromising statement than this of the independence of all facts from each other? It is true that when we talk of scales of sounds or colors, Wittgenstein tells us, necessary relations enter in. But it is the very point of Mr. Fogelin's protest that I made the *Tractatus* talk about such empirical things though it insisted that the components of facts were characterless. Now one cannot have it both ways. One cannot say at once that the world is shot through with necessary relations because for example middle C is connected internally with all other notes, and at the same time say that the facts of the world sit so loose to each other that any of them could be removed without affecting any other. To be sure, Wittgenstein takes both lines, but note that it is on Mr. Fogelin's own nonempirical line that the world becomes a ragbag of independent facts.

(2) When Wittgenstein says that the formal structure of our language mirrors the formal structure of the world, I am at a loss as to what he means. He cannot mean that what mirrors the world is the structure of actual languages, for these languages differ too widely; he cannot mean ordinary

English, since it would be absurd to claim that the syntax exhibited in our dependent clauses, our "ands" and "buts," and our more or less dangling participles are reflections of nature. Does he mean, then, that our statements will mirror nature when we have reduced them to their strictest logical form? This too is unfeasible, for there is no necessity linking the symbols in our proposition, though there must be if their relation is to mirror another necessity. As for mirroring by relations within the sentence or the propositional sign, I have dealt with it sufficiently, I think, in my book.

(3) The mirroring doctrine about necessary propositions seems to be connected in its author's mind with a mere mistake in psychological fact. He thought we could not name or in words refer to a necessary relation. But in fact we do so continually, successfully, and unambiguously. I believe, for example, that the causal relation is necessary; and to show what I mean, I find it both possible and helpful to discuss in words what distinguishes this relation from that of physical compulsion or regular association. We can discuss in words the differences between material, formal, and strict implication. Musicians find necessities in music and artists in painting, and they have often contrasted these with the necessities of logic and mathematics. Wittgenstein would say that if tone C is higher than B, and B than A, then C is higher than A, but he would not try to sing this bit of reasoning; the three relations of "higher than" are conveyed quite clearly through words. Further, in spite of the obscurity of the *Tractatus* and its author's admission that it was chiefly nonsense, he achieved more intelligibility than would have been possible if his own theory were true.

(4) The laws of logic, according to Wittgenstein, say nothing about anything. They seem to me to say something important about everything. To say that X cannot at once be and not be A tells us something about every Chihuahua, chimpanzee, and chimney sweep in existence; it tells me, with complete clearness, that there is something they cannot be; and there is no relation in the proposition in which I express this that mirrors that impossibility. Incidentally, just how would one go about it to mirror an impossibility?

Linguistic Philosophy

Mr. Fogelin considers that I have been less than just to Moore's "Defence of Common Sense." In that essay Moore listed a series of propositions that had been held false by many philosophers but true by common sense, such as that time and space and physical things are real. Regarding these propositions Moore maintained that common sense was obviously right and the philosophers wrong. I therefore said of the essay: "he proposed that instead of philosophy's setting up as the critic of common sense, common sense should serve as the touchstone of philosophy . . ." ("The Philosophy of Analysis" ["P of A"], 61).

Mr. Fogelin protests that Moore ". . . never sets up the faculty of common sense as the infallible judge on all matters." And this of course is correct. Moore never exalted common sense to this height, nor did I intend to suggest it. What he did hold was that on many of the important philosophical issues we could profitably appeal to common sense as against philosophy. This was both true and something of a paradox; and it seemed to me worthwhile to examine how far it could be carried. I do not think I said or implied that Moore would defend common sense against philosophy *everywhere*. If I did, I was certainly mistaken.

Mr. Fogelin thinks I also missed the mark in my main criticism of Moore. Here I cannot agree. I pointed out that on one of the issues where Moore himself carried the appeal to common sense, this proved a broken reed. When the plain man looks at his inkstand and says, "I am seeing a material thing," he has no doubt that he is right. But when Moore analyzed the statement, he found it very ambiguous; in fact he found in it three different meanings among which he could not to the end make up his mind. Now it seemed to me capricious to say that common sense supplied the truth of the matter when he found it impossible to accept as true any of these various meanings. It will not do to answer that what common sense is unclear about is the meaning rather than the truth of that meaning, or that we cannot expect of the plain man a second-level analysis of what he means. For what I am saying is that the plain man thinks he knows what he means and thinks that this is wholly true, whereas on both points he is mistaken. If so, he cannot be a trustworthy guide even on the issues on which Moore would appeal to him. I think this argument stands.

Mr. Fogelin thinks the main defect of my treatment of linguistic philosophy is that I did not attempt a critique of Wittgenstein's *Philosophical Investigations,* and this opinion would no doubt be concurred in by other analytic philosophers. But I am glad Mr. Fogelin agrees that Ryle is a philosopher of stature who is well worth dealing with.

Ryle is with justice called a linguistic philosopher because he held that many or most of the problems of philosophy arise from linguistic confusions. Philosophers follow false scents and wrong analogies in the use of language, and because they fail to notice these, they say things that do not answer to the structure of facts. Mr. Fogelin thinks I overstate the part played by the detection and rectification of such defects in Ryle's view of philosophy. So it is worth quoting a sentence near the end of "Systematically Misleading Expressions," an essay which Mr. Fogelin regards as a masterpiece: "And I am for the present inclined to believe that this is what philosophical analysis is, and that this is the sole and whole function of philosophy."[6]

It is important to see what Ryle meant by searching out and clearing up category mistakes. His categories differed widely from what either Aristotle or Kant meant by the term; indeed his list is inexhaustible. A category for Ryle is really a "sentence-factor," that is, "any partial expression which can enter into sentences otherwise dissimilar."[7] In "Socrates is wise," "Socrates" and "wise" exemplify categories or sentence factors of certain types. Each of them will fit into a sentence with some other such factors and will repudiate others; one can only tell which by trying. The compatibilities and repugnances of a term or phrase Ryle describes as its "logic," and I think that he is here making a useful protest against the confinement of logic to purely formal relations; you cannot tell what "Socrates" or "wise" will go with unless you take into account the specific meaning or content of the term. Now philosophers have all too often supposed, for example, that because they can say "My life began at a certain time" they can say "The world began at a certain time," or even "Time began at a certain time." This sort of error Ryle calls a "category confusion."

How much of philosophy consists of the exposure of such confusion? In *Reason and Analysis,* chapter 8, I argued that Ryle had much overestimated this amount, and I listed some of the old and leading problems of philosophy which, so far as I could see, neither rose out of such confusions nor could be solved by removing them. Mr. Fogelin examines one of these, the problem of making a choice between two prospective types of experience. A young man has to make a choice between buying a car and having a year at the university, and he asks which of the two will open up to him experience of the greater value. He is easily led on to ask, "What things are most worth having?" which is perhaps the most important question the moral philosopher can ask. Mr. Fogelin thinks it is probably a confusion to regard these questions as of the same type. The young man makes the first decision in the light of "a whole set of value commitments in hand"; the second "calls these background commitments into question and thus his standard way of dealing with questions of value is wholly displaced." This does not seem to me convincing. In both cases one is balancing against each other the intrinsic goods and bads of differing kinds of experience, one's own and others'; and while in the second the range of candidates in the way of value is much wider and one's powers of imagination and judgment less adequate, the type of problem and the mode of solution seem to me the same. For other problems that resist the Rylean type of analysis I must refer the reader to pp. 347 ff. of my book.

Most of my criticisms of Ryle Mr. Fogelin passes over without remark, but there is one that I should like to emphasize because it applies widely to linguistic philosophy. Mr. Ryle is reluctant to talk about categories as entities in nature, since this would threaten continually to carry him across the dreaded threshold of metaphysics. He prefers to talk of "sentence-factors," as we have seen. One can say "Socrates is wise," for the two factors here go together; one cannot say "Socrates is a triangle" or "the number 7," or "the year 1492," for then the sentence-factors do not jibe. True, but why? It is because what they mean does not jibe, because one can see that a human individual like Socrates cannot also be a plane figure or a number or a stretch of time. It is as if linguistic philosophers thought they could avoid talking about the things and relations in nature by talking about words and sentence-factors instead, even when the only way they can classify their words and phrases is through the things and relations these refer to. They do not thereby escape reference to the real world, and their language is made needlessly roundabout.

But enough of this. In spite of taking issue with Mr. Fogelin at so many points I am grateful for the painstaking attention he has given to my critique of the analytic philosophers; indeed he is one of the very few of them who have taken notice of it. It is a pleasure to deal with criticisms that are so acute, so clearly stated, and so obviously enveloped in good will.

1. Moritz Schlick, *Problems of Ethics* (New York: Prentice-Hall, 1939).

2. R. M. Hare, *The Language of Morals* (Oxford: Clarendon Press, 1952).

3. Robert J. Fogelin, *Evidence and Meaning* (London: Routledge & Kegan Paul; New York: Humanities Press, 1967).

4. Ludwig Wittgenstein, *Tractatus Logico-Philosophicus* (London: Kegan Paul, Trench, Trubner; New York: Harcourt, Brace, 1933).

5. I. M. Copi, "Objects, Properties, and Relations in the Tractatus," *Mind* 67 (April 1958): 162.

6. Gilbert Ryle, "Systematically Misleading Expressions," in *Essays on Logic and Language*, ed. A. G. N. Flew, 1st ser. (Oxford: Basil Blackwell, 1951), 36.

7. Gilbert Ryle, "Categories," *Logic and Language*, ed. A. G. N. Flew, 2d ser. (Oxford: Basil Blackwell, 1953), 68.

20   IDEALISM, HOLISM, AND "THE PARADOX OF KNOWLEDGE"
Richard Rorty

1. Introduction

IF one rereads Blanshard's *Nature of Thought* in the light of philosophical developments in the thirty years since its publication, one may be struck by two things. First, many of the particular points which Blanshard makes against sense-data theories, logical positivism, and reductionistic theories of meaning are the same points which were later to be made all over again by, for example, Wittgenstein, Quine, Austin, and Sellars. In the endless war between philosophers who wish to analyze things down into their least parts (smallest units of meaning, of knowledge, or of reality) and those who stand out against such attempts in the name of "system" and "context," the pendulum has recently swung toward holism. Blanshard's work of 1939 is a storehouse of holistic arguments. But, second, the overall project of *The Nature of Thought* seems very remote from the preoccupations of the philosophers I have just mentioned. The very notion that "thought" has a "nature" is alien to most contemporary Anglo-American philosophy, as are such Blanshardian conclusions as "To think of a thing is to get that thing itself in some degree within the mind" (*NT*, 2:261–62).

To understand those similarities and differences we must distinguish at least three quite different sets of tacit presuppositions of philosophical inquiry.

The first is the reductionist and atomist presuppositions common to Hume, Russell, Wittgenstein's *Tractatus,* and Ayer. These are the target of criticism from Blanshard and Quine, Blanshard and the Wittgenstein of the *Investigations,* etc. The second set is presuppositions common to what Quine has called the "idea idea," the tradition which encompasses not only Hume but Leibniz, Locke as well as Hegel, *The Analysis of Mind* as well as *The Nature of Thought.* Finally, there are the metaphilosophical presuppositions which Blanshard, in *Reason and Analysis,* thinks of as common to himself and to most of his predecessors (Hume as well as Kant, Russell as well as Bradley) but sees as having been abandoned by recent "linguistic" philosophers. These latter philosophers have on Blanshard's view abandoned what he calls "reason," through having given up the notion of philosophy as a search for necessary, a priori knowable, truths about important matters.

Blanshard views the reaction against the second and third sets of presuppositions, and, more generally, the reaction against traditional conceptions of philosophy and its problems, as stemming from the reductionistic and positivistic epistemological presuppositions of the first set. I have argued elsewhere[1] that, *pace* Blanshard, these metaphilosophical debates over the third set can be separated from controversies about objectionable epistemological theses of the first set. I shall try to avoid going over this ground again. Instead, I should like to focus more sharply on the contrast between the first two sets of presuppositions. I shall argue that repudiating the first ("atomistic," "reductionistic") set does not necessarily lead one to preserve the "idea idea" and the associated Cartesian doctrines which recent philosophical trends have taken as their target. Indeed I shall be arguing that Blanshard's own contextualizing leads to a position from which the notions of "thought," "idea," "meaning," and "necessity" look very dubious.

Two topics have divided the gods from the giants, the rationalists from the empiricists, and Blanshard from the majority of his contemporaries: the question of what, if anything, is "known with necessity" by "reason," and the question of what, if anything, "is given indubitably" to "the senses." As Dewey rightly pointed out, nine-tenths of modern philosophy has revolved around the quest for certainty, or abjurations of such a quest. The indubitability of the given and the stark clarity and rigor of demonstration are the two great candidates for certainty. The Hegelian tradition, from which both Dewey and Blanshard stem, set its face against the notion of the "given"—especially in Hegel's critique of "sense-certainty" in the *Phenomenology* (a *Haupttext* for T. H. Green and for Royce in their criticisms of empiricism and naive realism). But this tradition set its face also against the Platonic notion of "abstract universals" generating unmodifiable necessary judgments, and thus against the notion of mathematics as a model for philosophy. Hegel's historicist notion of "dialectic," the fullest expression of the contextualism which was intended to displace Platonic and Cartesian paradigms of philosophy, was too rich for the blood of such English idealists as Green and Joachim. There is little trace of it in Blanshard himself. But Blanshard's work does offer a continued polemic against the notion of meanings conceived of as "hard little nuggets," and a continued insistence on the need to recognize degrees of necessity, to view necessities as modified by context and particularly by increasing knowledge, and to insist that we never fully grasp the meaning of any concept until we have gone through all its species—a potentially infinite process. The same holism and contextualism which Blanshard employs to attack Humean notions of givenness and, more generally, against what Bennett has recently described as the empiricists' besetting sin of "assimilating the sensory far too closely to the intellectual,"[2] is here turned against the Platonic-Cartesian notion of "simple natures" which exfoliate necessary truths and chains of demonstrations of such truths. The root fallacy of both British empiricism and pre-Hegelian rationalism was, on this view, the "atomist" notion that isolated bits—images flashed on the retina, simple natures poised before the eye of reason—were by themselves capable of offering knowledge and certainty.

In what follows, I shall compare Blanshard's critique of these pre-Hegelian paradigms of certainty with criticisms offered by Quine and Sellars, in order to illustrate the similarities between Blanshard's position and theirs which I noted at the outset.

2. Degrees of Necessity and Shades of Gray

Quine's attack on the analytic-synthetic distinction is often viewed as denying the existence of necessity—a revival of John Stuart Mill's attempt to view the truths of mathematics as well-confirmed empirical generalizations. Blanshard's insistence on the internality of all relations is often viewed as denying the existence of contingency—a revival of the traditional Leibniz-Spinoza thesis that so-called "mere empirical generalizations" are merely "confused (or incomplete) representations." So it would seem that no views could be more opposed. I want to claim, on the contrary, that once one admits there is no way to draw a line between propositions which express pure necessities and those which express pure contingencies, the effect is to make the necessary-contingent distinction obsolete. When one has a distinction whose whole dialectical role has been to draw a hard-and-fast line between two classes of entities—a line which has generated endless debate about which side a given entity goes on—then one simply cannot attach the same sense to the contrary predicates once the distinction is collapsed into a difference of degree. To say that "everything is really necessary" or "everything is really contingent" can only be a way of saying that the necessary-contingent distinction itself is dubious—perhaps of saying that some other distinction ("central" versus "fringe," "confused" versus "clear," "partial" versus "total") should take its place.

Blanshard himself uses the terms "concept," "meaning," and "universal" almost interchangeably. Thus it seems reasonable to take his discussion of concrete and abstract universals as, mutatis mutandis, a discussion of the meanings of terms, and to connect it with recent discussions of "meaning" and in particular of "truth in virtue of meaning." Philosophers like Quine and Putnam who have attacked the latter notion have criticized the notions of "meaning" accepted by the logical positivists, for example, in two ways. The first is roughly behavioristic—the argument that once one leaves the "circle" of interexplicable terms ("synonymous," "analytic," "meaning postulate," etc.) and looks for a behavioral criterion which, applying to speech-dispositions, will segregate utterances into types along the traditional analytic-synthetic line, no such criterion will appear. This argument has often been criticized as question-begging. The friends of analyticity can rejoin that no one claimed that meanings could be handled in terms of behavioristic criteria, and that it is no disgrace, but a commonplace of scientific theorizing, to find a relatively small circle of interexplicable terms of the sort Quine deplores. Blanshard would doubtless be sympathetic to this criticism of Quine, but I take it that he would find congenial the second, broader and more basic, point which Quine, Putnam, and many others have put forward. This is simply that the notion of necessary and sufficient conditions for the application of a term built into the term's meaning is a fake. It rests, as Harman puts it, on assuming "a type of distinction between dictionaries and encyclopedias that does not exist."[3] To use Putnam's way of putting the point: all terms which are the subjects of sentences stating natural laws are "cluster-concepts," in the sense that there are as many interlocking criteria for their application as there are such laws. This gives practically all philosophically interesting terms the "open texture" which Waismann described, and frustrates any hope of finding the necessary and sufficient conditions which would be required to make viable the notion of "true by convention" or "true by virtue of meaning." The point is generalized further when Quine emphasizes the relevance of practically every statement to every other, including the "laws of logic," as in his dictum that "the unit of empirical significance is the whole of science," with the implicit addition that there is no clear line to be drawn between "science" and the banalities of the layman's daily life.

This sort of holism is just what Blanshard is insisting on when, for example, he treats singular conditionals, laws of nature, and laws of logic as on a par in respect of conditionality. In a passage which, except perhaps for its penultimate sentence, Quine might have written, Blanshard says:

"If I leap from the top of the Empire State Building, I shall be a sorry mess at the bottom." Why yes, *if* I carry no parachute, *if* my body retains its mass, *if* the law of gravitation continues, and so on. It never occurs to us to state such conditions expressly, because that is unnecessary; we know that they will be taken for granted without reminder. But conditions merely assumed to exist are as truly conditions as those expressly stated. "If a beam of light is reflected from a surface, the angle of reflection equals the angle of incidence." Yes, *if* the space is Euclidean, *if* the influence of gravitation on the beam is discounted, *if* no other distorting factors enter in. . . . "If Marathon came before Thermopylae, and Thermopylae before Salamis, then Marathon came before Salamis." It may seem here at first sight that nothing is needed to warrant the inference but the two temporal relations, taken in bare abstraction. But consider first, that the implication is only seen as the result of a construction in which the three terms are placed in an arrangement and the relation between the extremes is read off from that. And consider, secondly, that every temporal connection is asserted subject to the laws of identity and contradiction, which get their warrant in turn from the whole of experience. [*NT*, 2:433]

Blanshard is carried toward this final sentence by the whole drift of his holism, and as a fellow holist I think he is right. But this sentence, and much of his doctrine of degrees of necessity, is, I believe, inconsistent with his polemic against Mill and those empiricists who do wish to conflate the laws of logic with empirical generalizations. When attacking these philosophers, Blanshard drops his Hegelian holism and contextualism for a pre-Hegelian rationalist "intuition of simple natures" view according to which

A mind of normal intelligence does not have to wait for experience of circles of various sizes and colours in order to see that these things are irrelevant; it penetrates straight through to the connection between circularity and the property entailed. . . . It does not have to try its conclusion with circles of different sizes, because it sees that circularity is in the nature of the case independent of change in size. . . . [*NT*, 2:346]

This latter passage is in the context of an attack on the empiricist notion that the laws of logic are validated by regularly repeated conjunctions, which Blanshard sometimes regards as the only possible view of their epistemological status except the true view—that they are self-evident. But "self-evidence" is just the sort of notion that makes no sense unless one holds the doctrine of the "false, or abstract, universal," which Blanshard sums up as follows:

The theory that there is a little, hard, abstract, unchanging essence of colour or triangularity or humanity, absolutely identical in all colours, triangles, or men, absolutely unaffected by its context, and capable of being compounded with foreign elements into a mosaic, which is then describable as a species of it—this was a theory that we found unverifiable. . . . Matter invades form. And therefore necessity cannot be secluded in the abstraction of pure form. It cannot be lifted from concrete argument by clean excision and without remainder. [*NT*, 2:369]

Unless a necessity can reside in pure form, one will have to say that the necessity of the laws of logic does not reside in a grasp of the meanings of "is" and "not" but rather, as Blanshard said in the passage quoted earlier, in "the whole of experience." If one says *that,* however, then it is hard to see how

Blanshard's position can differ from that of the empiricists whom he criticizes for suggesting that "the inner relations have become what they are precisely because the outer relations have pressed themselves for countless generations upon the plastic matter of our minds"—a view which Blanshard envisages as being put forward to avoid the skepticism about "even our simplest judgments of perception" which would follow from admitting that the laws of logic are "no more than firmly fixed habits" (*NT,* 2:349, 348). The "evolutionary" defense of the laws of logic—the claim that their claim to belief is to be justified pragmatically, in the way in which our use of our present "quality spaces" for projecting predicates might be justified—is, Blanshard says, insufficient because "the possession of survival value without any mirroring of nature is both possible and common." "Survival value is clearly possible without resemblance, and hence the mere fact that certain rules and connections have come to prevail in our minds does not prove that they also prevail in nature" (2:349). But Blanshard is in no position to use an argument which makes truth lie in resemblance and in the "mirroring" of nature. For him, the only sense in which ideas must resemble their objects is "the likeness of what exists in potency to the same thing actualized . . . of a purpose partly realized to the purpose fulfilled" (1:495). But in this sense of "resemblance" it is hardly clear that survival value *is* possible without resemblance. For what purposes could the thought have save just that quest for coherence and explanatory power and a sense of the union of all things which the laws of logic have aided so conspicuously for so many generations? I do not see any way in which a full-scale abandonment of the "copy theory" which Blanshard rightly views as the origin of most bad epistemologies can be reconciled with this sort of attack on a pragmatic and evolutionary sort of justification.

To sum up this point, I think that Blanshard's Hegelian contextualism moves him in the direction of Dewey and Quine at the same time that his pre-Hegelian notions of "reason" as the detection of "necessity" lead him in the opposite direction. Blanshard could reconcile the view that "to understand is to lay hold of necessity" (*NT,* 2:412) with his abandonment of the copy theory if he were willing to view necessity as unconnected with certainty. If, with Quine, he viewed necessity simply as "an explanatory trait, or the promise of it,"[4] then he could not argue that the laws of logic were somehow inviolate, and thus paradigmatic of knowledge. To develop consistently the important and deep point that "Necessity is not a single golden thread that in all fabrics remains the same" (2:438) we should have to allow that an evolutionary justification of the laws of logic was quite as good a justification as we could get, and quite as good an explanation of our certainty about them. For if one holds that "To exhaust the meaning of necessity we should have to exhaust the varieties of whole which imposed upon their parts any sort of interdependence" (ibid.), one should not view the difference between an ingrained habit and a "self-evident truth" as important. Once the "formalistic" view of necessity which is deplored by both Blanshard and Quine—necessity as a feature of the "abstract, non-sensible, unchanging framework of things" (*NT*, 2:356)—is overcome, the difference between Hume (as improved by Goodman) and Hegel (as diluted by Green) seems less important. The difference between a habit of association and a sense of the interdependence of parts in a whole is not really very great.[5]

To offer a still more broadly stated interpretation of the dilemma I believe Blanshard illustrates, let me make some remarks about the usual picture of the history of philosophy as moving vertically from Hume to Hegel by way of Kant (who was, so to speak, halfway up or down the slope, depending upon one's point of view). On the view I want to suggest, Kant shared with Hume two great misconceptions: the psychological atomism which led him to talk about a manifold of unsynthesized intuitions even while granting that intuitions without concepts were blind, and the notion of a kind of "objective" necessity which science claimed (rightly for Kant, wrongly for Hume) to possess. The former was overcome by Hegel, but the latter unfortunately not. Hegel continued to take seriously the notion of "objective necessity" and to draw a distinction between higher and lower kinds of cognition in terms of it. He thus perpetuated the view that to avoid a naturalism which degrades our reason to the level of the beasts one must cling to a notion of necessity which "science" exemplifies but mere unreflective common sense does not. Dewey's naturalism, like Quine's, shows how necessity as unification and explanatory power is compatible with an epistemology which recognizes no such difference in kind, but only differences in extent and utility of unification. Blanshard, however, even after rejecting the Kantian intuition-concept framework, continues, like Hegel, to associate necessity with certainty and self-evidence, as well as with unification. He thus is in the position of having to use Kantian objections against Hume's empiricism while simultaneously using Hegelian objections against Kant's formalism. He has to condemn positivists for not establishing a distinction between kinds of cognition on the basis of certainty and lack of certainty, while simultaneously condemning such neo-Kantians as C. I. Lewis for neglecting the sort of holism which will not countenance such a distinction. From the point of view of such a holism, as from Dewey's, the attempt to analyze all necessity as stemming from "the meanings of terms" or "convention" or "categories of the understanding" or "conceptual structure" (or even to say that there are two forms of necessity—logical and physical—or three, or four) is, to be sure, just misguided. But Blanshard does not carry through this train of thought to its limit. His Hegelianism abandons him at the point at which he feels constrained to insist, against Mill, behaviorists, positivists, and their ilk, that it is just a mistake to deny the existence of necessity. While admitting the concreteness of the universal he is discussing, and insisting on the ubiquity of its application, he attacks those whom he takes to hold that it has *no* application. But the appropriate reply for these opponents to make is that once the concept is softened enough to be thought of as applying everywhere, they no longer have any interest in attacking it. The appropriate attitude for Blanshard would, I think, be to insist that no one *could* deny the existence of necessity; that one could only rechristen it (as "centrality," "pragmatically adopted convention," "taken-for-grantedness," or the like); and that such rebaptisms do not greatly matter.

3. The Paradox of Knowledge

In the previous section I have argued that if one finds necessity everywhere then one is not really quarreling with those who find it nowhere. I shall shortly argue that if, like Blanshard, one holds that there is at most one particular—one object of knowledge—and that all else is more or less universal, then one is not really quarreling with those who think that there are no universals. Before reaching this topic, however, I need to discuss the problem which drives Blanshard toward his paradoxical conclusions.

Blanshard comes to hold that there "are no particulars" (*NT,* 1:631), or that the only particular (if one likes to call it so) is the Absolute (1:639), as a result of an analysis of the nature of ideas. The analysis is motivated by the assumption that knowledge will be possible only if thought can be in some sense identical with its object (cf. 2:261 ff.). On this assumption, all theories of representative perception, all copy theories, all theories of sense as a source of knowledge (in addition to thought or in combination with thought), must necessarily fail. Since thought deals with universals, any theory which takes the objects of thought to be a multiplicity of particulars will lead to skepticism. ". . . if thought and things are conceived as related only externally, then knowledge is luck" (2:261). Since understanding must hold of necessity and yet must also hold of an object, the only object which will do is the whole. Only the whole—the nexus of everything's internal relations to everything else—will be the sort of thing which an object of knowledge must be. For only thus can we have an idea which can be "at once the same as its object and not the same": "If thought can be seen as a stage on the way to its transcendent end or object, as that end itself in the course of becoming actual, the paradox of knowledge is in principle solved" (1:494).

What paradox is this? Here again we come to what may well seem an unbridgeable opposition between Blanshard on the one hand and recent critics of traditional empiricist dogmas (Quine, Austin, Sellars, Wittgenstein) on the other. For the latter philosophers would agree that only the Lockean representationalism which Blanshard deplores makes knowledge seem a paradox, and the relation between ideas and objects a genuine problem. Consider, for example, what Lovejoy calls the "natural and spontaneous epistemological creed of mankind" which incorporates "diverse aspects of the one mystery of the presence of the absent, the true apprehension, by a being remaining within certain fixed bounds, of things beyond those bounds."[6] On the view of these philosophers, this "creed" is a seventeenth-century invention, unknown to the ancients or to the plain man. For Blanshard, this attitude toward Locke's ideas—"whatsoever is the object of the understanding when a man thinks" (*Essay*, I: 1,8)—confuses the claim that "ideas are not to be thought of as copies" with the know-nothing claim that there are no ideas. Blanshard's discussion of the theories of New and Critical Realism (*NT*, 1: chaps. 11, 12), which try to substitute "acts" or "essences" for ideas, as well as his attack on behaviorism and pragmatism (*NT*, chaps. 9, 10), argue that commonly received views about knowing will not permit us to get rid of what Quine calls "the idea idea," despite the epistemological skepticism which this idea has always seemed to entail. Rather, the notion of something "before the mind" must be preserved and purified, in the hope of resolving the paradox of the identity of idea and object.

There is indeed an unbridgeable opposition here, but it does not concern the claim that there are no particulars, or no ideas, or no minds. It concerns the picture of knowledge illustrated by such a thesis as "To think of a thing is to get that thing itself in some degree within the mind" (*NT*, 2:261–62). If one thinks of truth and knowledge as relations between mental entities and objects, and if one is sure that any copy theory of ideas will lead to skepticism, then the only thing left to do is, like Blanshard, to remodel the object of knowledge so that it too can fit into the mind rather than sit about outside it waiting to be copied. The recent anti-Lockean and anti-Cartesian reaction, however, is not just against ideas as copies nor yet against mental entities in general, but rather against the notion that the "relations to the object" of such entities determine the presence or absence of knowledge. For this anti-Cartesian view, thoughts and perceptions are not "universals" which might be woven together into a more or less coherent whole (which could then be identified as the goal, and hence the object of thought) nor are they "representations" of an object. Rather, they are a series of particulars which go to make up an introspectible stream of consciousness. Concepts are not introspectible, but they too are not representations. Rather they are what one has when one knows how to use a word (or, perhaps, when one knows how to do certain things, e.g. discriminate objects of different colors). A *belief* is the closest thing to a "representation" which this view recognizes, and it is not an introspectible mental content—although it may be the sort of thing had only by beings equipped with minds.

In the long run, the question between Blanshard and recent holistic critics of empiricism comes down to the plausibility of such a picture of the mind—one in which nothing is "before" the mind and in which the correspondence between beliefs and facts is not a matter of mental entities either "copying" or being "identical" with nonmental entities. Although I think that this picture is (simply because it skirts traditional epistemological perplexities) preferable to the Cartesian "mental eye" picture, I shall not debate the issue here. Rather, I want to argue that if one abstracts from this more fundamental disagreement concerning the existence of a "paradox of knowledge" and looks simply at Blanshard's holistic arguments against particulars, then the same sort of conciliation between Blanshard and, e.g. Sellars and Wittgenstein is possible here as is possible in connection with necessity and contingency.

4. Sensed Particulars and Congeries of Universals

Much twentieth-century metaphysics has revolved around the attempt to keep the subject in "immediate relation" to something other than its own ideas, while nevertheless granting to Hegel and Kant that only where there are concepts can there be meaning and knowledge. Thus Peirce's "secondness," Bergson's "intuition," Whitehead's "prehension in the mode of causal efficacy," Heidegger's *Zuhandenheit,* C. I. Lewis' "expressive language," and the like are so many names for that ineffable connection with the object which prevents our beliefs being merely "subjective," and our philosophy from being "idealist." But, obviously, one will only yearn for such an ineffable connection if one thinks that the paradigmatic object of knowledge is a particular which is somehow "nonideal" in character. One will probably only have this notion of the object of knowledge if one believes that the senses are a channel for knowledge, independent of thought, and that "conceptualization" produces some sort of synthesis of the respective contributions of thought and of sense. Blanshard stoutly resists the notion of sense as a source of knowledge, and has no qualms about treating "sensed particulars" as a philosopher's fiction. "Scientific realists" and "physicalists" like Quine and Sellars, on the other hand, spend a great deal of time explaining away universals, propositions, meanings, and the like, in the interests of nominalism, unified science, atoms, and the void. Yet Quine and Sellars are as scornful of traditional empiricist epistemologies as Blanshard himself. To see how the battlefields have shifted, one must see the way in which nominalism and naturalism are, in these latter writers, disjoined from empiricism.

Sellars's basic criticism of traditional empiricism is that it glosses over the distinction between particulars and facts: "it is *particulars* that are sensed. . . . [but] what is *known,* even in non-inferential knowledge, is *facts* rather than particulars, items of the form *something's being thus-and-so* or *something's standing in a certain relation to something else.*"[7] This criticism is the same as that phrased by Bennett as the empiricists' attempt to assimilate "the sensory far too closely to the intellectual." Sellars elaborates upon it in the context of a contrast between Thomism and the Cartesian tradition.[8] It is described by Green, in his discussion of Locke and Hume, as:

> the fundamental confusion, on which all empirical psychology rests, between two essentially distinct questions—one metaphysical, What is the simplest element of knowledge? the other physiological, What are the conditions in the individual human organism in virtue of which it becomes a vehicle of knowledge?[9]

Blanshard says that in Green's "classic criticism the old bridge from acquaintance with sense particulars to knowledge of actual things was damaged beyond repair" (*NT,* 1:63).

On Sellars's view of the matter, however, the fact that sensation is not knowledge is no ground for denying that what we know are particulars. We know facts, and many facts are *about* particulars—and, indeed, about sensed particulars. For Blanshard, on the other hand, there is no way in which a fact can be "about" anything but more facts—no way in which an idea can be about anything except its own fuller and more concrete realization. Once again, the reason is that Blanshard thinks knowledge involves getting an object inside the mind. Since sensing (*pace* empiricists) is not going to put a particular in there, the mind will know no particulars unless and until the Absolute takes shape as a result of weaving universals together. For Sellars, however, no roads lead from epistemology to ontology, for science is the measure of all things. Thus no roads run from the "paradox of knowledge" to the Absolute (or to such metaphysical novelties as those cited above from Peirce and Whitehead). The putative ontological gaps between universals and particulars, facts and values, minds and brains turn out, on Sellars's view, to be simply the irreducibility of various nondescriptive language-strata (semantic discourse, moral discourse) to descriptive discourse. But, within descriptive discourse, nothing philosophical can hinder science from explaining (and thus providing improved descriptions of) everything there is as so many arrangements of atoms.

When one focuses simply on the question "Who is right about particulars—Sellars or Blanshard?" the question tends to dissolve under one's eyes in the same way as does the question "Who is right about necessity—Quine or Blanshard?" Once again, the problem is that when one takes contrasting terms such as "particular" and "universal" and asserts that one term of the contrast is empty—that it not only applies to nothing but cannot be coherently taken to apply to anything—then little force is left to the assertion that the other term is comprehensive. If there are no particulars, we might well ask, just what is a universal supposed to be? If everything we have always described as a particular turns out to be a batch of universals whose internal relations to all other universals are not yet completely grasped, then perhaps we should just say that the universal-particular distinction was a bad way of dividing up the world in the first place. Perhaps, like the necessary-contingent distinction, it was simply a misleading way of getting at the distinction between complete and incomplete knowledge, or between stages in the development of inquiry.

But, it may be said, the term "universal" does not acquire its meaning simply by contrast with "particular" but also from the fact that it is recognizable as the appropriate object of thought. The trouble, of course, is that the sense-thought distinction is in the same difficulty as the particular-universal distinction. Once sense as a cognitive faculty goes, what exactly is "thought"? To see thought as the making explicit what was implicit, in the manner of Hegel and Blanshard, rather than as synthesizing or abstracting from sensory intuitions, is to force the term "thought" to cover everything remotely cognitive. Just as we must now force the notion of "congery of universals" to cover even the object of the most unmediated confrontation with brute opposing forces, so we must stretch "thought" to cover the confrontation itself. In the process of stretching these terms, we must somehow save the appearances by recapturing the old contrasts we used to make when we thought that sense, a cognitive faculty which took particulars for its objects, actually existed.

5. Conclusions

I shall not try to compare or evaluate the various ways in which one might attempt to annul those old distinctions while saving the phenomena. Rather, I shall end by reiterating and developing a point made in section 3 above. Whereas Blanshard sees the task of philosophy as given by a set of Socratic questions ("What is necessity?" "Thought?" "Knowledge?") which can be raised *semper, ubique, et ab omnibus*, the recent holists I have discussed see themselves as occupying a particular point in history and as reacting to a certain set of notions which originated at a certain time. What Quine calls the "idea idea," the distinction between primary and secondary qualities which underlies the distinction between Sellars's "scientific and manifest images of man," and the textbook Cartesian puzzles about knowledge and mind which amused Wittgenstein and which are thrown in doubt by his remarks on "privacy" are all parts of a world view which cannot with any confidence be traced back before 1600. Although these latter philosophers have quite different attitudes toward the relations between philosophy and the history of philosophy, and although only Sellars can be thought of as self-consciously historicist, nevertheless the spirit of their work is not antiempiricist nor antiatomist but anti-seventeenth century. By contrast, Blanshard stands well within the problematic set by that century. He takes its distinctions, and thus its questions, as given, and works out elegant and sustained criticisms of certain answers to these questions and closely reasoned defenses of his own answers. Given the seventeenth-century picture of the mind, knowledge is indeed a paradox, common sense is only a beginning on the way to wisdom, and heroic efforts are necessary to resolve the paradox and assign common sense its proper place. But if one doubts this picture of the mind, then one will doubt that common sense need be transcended. One may then, with Wittgenstein, wish to leave everything as it is. Or, with Quine, one may brusquely turn to science, leaving common sense to sink or swim without the benefit of philosophical defense, mediation, or adjudication. Or, with Sellars, one may see philosophy as working out a complex set of distinctions which will enable one to dissolve the problems that the apparent opposition of science and common sense seems to engender. But one will in any case be sufficiently "distanced" from the contest between common sense on the one hand and philosophical-reflection-stemming-from-science on the other to be skeptical about the philosophical questions which the seventeenth century propounded. Blanshard has little distance from these problems, and in *Reason and Analysis* he has forcefully expressed his suspicions concerning the easy way in which recent philosophers have attempted to "dissolve" them.

Whether one draws Blanshard's neorationalistic morals from one's holism, or rather what Blanshard sees as the anti-intellectualist morals drawn by many practitioners of "analysis," will therefore depend largely upon one's way of seeing the history of philosophy. In particular, it will depend upon whether one sees the problems discussed by Hume, Kant, Green, and Russell as problems which anyone might discover by taking thought about his own thought, or as problems developed in a particular time in reaction to particular intellectual and social developments. It will have been obvious that I incline to the latter, historicist, view. But I have no defense of that view to offer, and I have tried to offer some reconciliatory and mediating ways of looking at the matter which do not demand a choice between these two general points of view.

RICHARD RORTY

DEPARTMENT OF PHILOSOPHY
PRINCETON UNIVERSITY

NOTES

[1]See my review of *Reason and Analysis* in the *Journal of Philosophy* 60 (1963): 551–57.

[2]Jonathan Bennett, *Locke, Berkeley, Hume* (Oxford: Clarendon Press; London and New York: Oxford University Press, 1971), 25. Bennett's point here is that the empiricists, in their use of "idea" to cover both sense-data and concepts (just as Descartes had used *cogitationes*), were able to pretend that sense, unaided by reflection, inference, or learning, produced knowledge of fact, and that the having of an image was automatically the grasp of an essence. Green, in his criticisms of Locke and of Hume, spends a great deal of time making this same point. Cf. T. H. Green, *Works* (London: 1885), 1:13–19.

[3]Gilbert Harman, "Quine on Meaning and Existence, I," *Review of Metaphysics* 21 (1967): 136.

[4]Willard V. O. Quine, *Ways of Paradox* (New York: Random House, 1966), 56.

[5]In particular, Hume's atomistic notion of sense images as rudimentary bits of knowledge may be dropped under the pressure of Green's criticisms without admitting any of Bradley's criticisms of traditional logic—rather than running Green's and Bradley's criticisms of Hume together as Blanshard does (*NT,* 2:383 f.), and thus insisting that to adopt a truth-functional view of propositional logic is to grant that "the attempt to *understand* is hopeless from the beginning" (2:384) because the attempt to grasp *necessity* has been abandoned.

[6]Arthur O. Lovejoy, *The Revolt Against Dualism* (La Salle, Ill.: Open Court Publishing Co.; New York: W. W. Norton, 1930), 15.

[7]Wilfrid Sellars, *Science, Perception, and Reality* (London and New York: Routledge & Kegan Paul and Humanities Press, 1963), 128.

[8]Cf. ibid., 41 ff.

[9]Green, *Works,* 1:19.

20. Reply to Richard Rorty

Idealism, Holism, and "The Paradox of Knowledge"

Mr. Rorty's acute and closely packed paper is a reassessment of some of the main theses of my theory of knowledge in the light of the philosophic changes that have occurred since I wrote *The Nature of Thought*. He points out that some of my ideas, instead of being antiquated survivals, reappear in the van of thought; that there has been a swing of the pendulum from minute philosophy to holism, from the attempt by Wittgenstein and the positivists to isolate the simplest objects of knowledge to the attempt to see things in context and eventually in the light of the whole. He thinks that the criticism of the atomists has been effective and fatal; atomism and positivism are lost causes. On the other hand these criticisms have proved boomerangs. The very arguments used by myself and others against atomism undermine my own kind of holism. If I apply the doctrine of internal relations to sense-data, I must apply it equally to concepts, the concepts I seek to connect by strands of necessity. And then the concepts and the linking strands lose all their distinctness and become a blur. What I want to be, Mr. Rorty suspects, is not a Hegelian; he rightly finds little direct influence of Hegel in my work; he thinks of me rather as a seventeenth-century rationalist, a Spinozist or a Leibnizian, whose webwork of necessities has definite concepts as nodes and clean lines of connection. At least he thinks that this is what I tried to be, but that my doctrine of internal relations drags me back again into the vast Hegelian fog where all cows are gray.

Necessity

This criticism is fundamental, and I will venture to draw it out in my own way, though without sparing myself. I argued in my early work that the simple "ideas of sense" talked about by Locke, Berkeley, and Hume were largely fictions. Whatever our sensory experiences were like at first, it is unlikely that we have any of them in pure form now; they have become so barnacled and encrusted with associations, so caught up in spatial, temporal, causal, and other frames, that their nature has been deeply affected; I held that even in so simple a report as "I now have a toothache," every word shows a conceptualizing of the ache that must render it different—though how different we do not know—from the experience of an animal mind, where it is presumably unmodified by the halo of concepts it wears for us.

Now if I take this view about sense-data, Mr. Rorty reminds me, I must take it also about concepts. Do I? Yes, but he thinks quite inconsistently. I both do and do not. I inveigh against the abstract universal and yet use it uninhibitedly; I talk about self-evidence as if it connected concepts as clear and distinct as those of Descartes. My arguments for necessity in causation imply that the attributes connected can be sharply singled out, and when I talk of the laws of logic, I talk of them as if I had forgotten all about internal relations and indeed as if the laws could be lifted cleanly out of all contexts and be considered like gems in their hardness and purity. At the same time I insist on concrete rather than abstract universals. I try to show that there are no "hard little nuggets" such as a "manness" identical in all men and no abstract "color" or "coloredness" to be found in all colors. Now if necessity links abstractions, and the abstractions that it links are not to be found either in thought or in nature, has not necessity gone down the drain? How can you deduce what is entailed by triangularity if there is no such thing as triangularity? What is entailed by Socrates' being a man if the common humanity of men is a myth?

All this suggests to Mr. Rorty that I am tending in the same direction as another philosopher in whose company I am honored but astonished to be found. For Mr. Quine also has been developing dismaying doctrines about necessity. He has called into question the traditional distinction between necessary and empirical propositions. Necessary propositions cannot be distinguished sharply from empirical ones; the difference is only of degree; so it is best to put all propositions on an empirical slope reaching up toward but never achieving clear analytic necessity; if Mr. Quine abandons the "two dogmas of empiricism," and puts all propositions in the same class, he becomes an outright empiricist. Mr. Rorty suggests that my own inquiry ends in much the same way, though not by leveling necessities down to contingencies, but by leveling contingencies up to necessities. By finding rational connections everywhere I make all propositions, even those that seem most innocently empirical, like "snow is white," into necessary propositions. Thus Mr. Quine and I both end by dropping an old and fundamental distinction and tossing all propositions into one capacious bin. Our bins wear different labels, but does that really matter? In both our cases, "the effect is to make the necessary-contingent distinction obsolete."

This is pointed criticism which raises a number of knotty questions. What Mr. Quine would say about this comparison I shall not try to guess. But I must at least try to set down the points required to make my own position clear.

Necessities and Contingencies

(1) Mr. Rorty is right that I hold the view, paradoxical at the first glance to the point of absurdity, that no actual judgment is purely contingent. This is rooted in my view of the nature of thought and of the place of logic within the enterprise of reflection. Thought is an attempt to understand; to understand is primarily to answer the question Why?; and that question is answered adequately only by showing that X is what it is because it is in some sense necessitated by something else. X may be the equality of the angles of a triangle to 180 degrees, or John's catching cold yesterday, or the roughness of an oak's bark, or the student unrest of the sixties. My conception of necessity is empirical in the sense that it arises directly out of an examination of what in fact satisfies the theoretical impulse. It has none of the remoteness from actual thought of the notion of implication on which *Principia Mathematica* is founded, in which "Keats assassinated Shelley" implies "Blanshard is wiser than Socrates" because their "truth value" is the same. Logic for me is chiefly an attempt to set out the forms or structures of those inferences that our theoretical sense finds compelling.

Now if the end of thought is understanding, it is clear that we are a long way from that end. We are brokenly and imperfectly rational, as Plato said; we know that snow is white and that John caught cold yesterday, but we do not fully know why, and the same is true of the greater part of our knowledge (indeed all of it if we press the point). But if understanding is the special end and aim of thought, it will be found at work, however feebly, from the beginning. In the child's first discernment that dogs bark and cats purr, there is more than a mere registry of items given together, for an active mind is noting that it is dogs, not cats or tables, that bark, and cats, not dogs or tables, that purr; and whether the question Why? is asked or not, as it probably will be, the spirit that prompts it is implicitly at work. That dogs bark is no accident; and if dogs do while cats and tables do not, there must be something in the nature of the dog that makes him bark, even if the groping mind has no idea what it is. John caught cold yesterday; he does not know why; perhaps the doctor does not know either; but children are natural philosophers, and John is not likely to be long put off by the suggestion that he caught cold for no reason at all. He is soon aware that that is not the way things happen.

It follows that when I say all judgments can be put in one bin marked "necessary" I am doing so on a different ground and in a more tentative way than Mill or Quine. Mill said that all judgments are empirical because the only exceptions, namely necessary ones, proved on examination to be no exceptions at all; they were the product of psychological habits, now unbreakable because of an association that was exceptionless and indefinitely long. This explanation was prima facie plausible. Mr. Quine says that all propositions are empirical because if you take the same exception, the necessary proposition, and ask why it is necessary, you are told that it is because it is analytic; if you then ask what "analytic" means, you are told that it cannot be defined without reference to "synonymy"; and if you ask what that means, you find you cannot define it without going back to "analytic." And since a criterion circularly defined is logically unsatisfactory, you give up the attempt to separate out a class of necessary propositions.

My own way of dealing with the two classes is different from either of these. I begin by admitting that at least ninety-nine out of every hundred judgments we make are empirical in the sense that we come to make them in the way empiricists describe. But I do not stop there. I go on to inquire, not of symbolic logic but of myself, what I am trying to do in thinking. To which the old answer returns: I am trying to understand. And it is plain that in saying merely "dogs bark" and "cats purr" I am *not* understanding, though I have put a first timid foot on the steps that lead to it. There must be some connection between dogs and barking and between cats and purring. If I could isolate that in the dog which made the barking inevitable, and that in the cat which made it purr, I should understand, and not till then.

"This is all very well," it may be said, "as an explanation of why you want to find necessity, but what makes you think it is there to be found? Wanting something is no guarantee of its existence." This I of course admit. "Are you then merely appealing to faith?" No, not in the sense presumably intended. I have stated my answer to this question more than once, for example in *Reason and Analysis,* chapter 6, and more briefly in *Reason and Belief,* pages 72 ff. The gist of the argument is (i) you cannot deny the validity of logical law, e.g. that of noncontradiction, for in denying it you are assuming that its falsity excludes its truth, which is to accept it; (ii) this law is not a linguistic or other convention, but a statement about the nature of things; it says that whatever is true about the world is consistent with itself; (iii) there is a "sufficient reason" for every fact or event. This, while perhaps not provable, is a necessary postulate of philosophy. For the philosopher is trying to explain, and unless he could believe that to his persistent question Why? an answer was there to be found, his vocation would be gone. There is no pretense of certainty here; the rationalist should be ready to admit that he *may* at the next step meet an insuperable block to his inquiry. But it would be absurd to carry on an undertaking with the postulate that it could not succeed, particularly when the opposite postulate has been confirmed by a long series of successes.

When I put all judgments in the same bin, then, I not only put them in a different bin from that of Mill and Quine, but put them there for very different reasons. I cannot claim as much of a *rapprochement* as I should like.

(2) Though I hold that our present range of necessary insights is lamentably small, it is much wider than Mill or Quine would probably entertain for a moment. Mr. Quine takes as his example of a necessary statement "All bachelors are unmarried," and concentrates his fire on it. This is not a sort of statement in which I am particularly interested, since nobody talks or thinks that way except when explaining to someone the meanings of the words. No one normally talks tautologies; "The rose is red" may be worth saying, but not "A rose is a rose"; and even "A rose is a rose is a rose" adds nothing except in Steinese. "Snow is snow" is not a judgment at all, for no distinct predicate is being asserted.

It is a mistake to confine necessities to logical and mathematical tautologies. The fact is that our experience is shot through with necessities of other and more interesting types. Mr. Ryle thinks that these types, as accepted in his informal logic, may be inexhaustible: "Socrates cannot be the figure 9" and "Time cannot begin at a point in time" are perfectly good necessary propositions. So, in my view, are the following: "In the scale of colors, orange comes between red and yellow"; "The same surface area cannot be variously colored at once"; "If A occurs before B, and B before C, then A occurs before C"; "Happiness is of greater intrinsic value than unhappiness"; "If A is north of B, and B is east of C, then A is northeast of C"; "Grief is appropriate at the loss of a friend"; "The 'Ode to a Nightingale' is a greater poem than 'John Gilpin's Ride' "; "The gratuitous infliction of pain on another is wrong." These are not, of course, propositions of logic; they are not true by virtue of their form, logical or syntactical; they are true by reason of their content or intension, the special character of their terms or relations. Similarly if A causes B, it is because the character of A is specially connected with the character of B; every causal law connects "as suches." It is incredible that these connections should express mere associations, though the analysis that would excise irrelevancies and exhibit them as pure necessities has not yet been effected on all of them. This admission will make my meaning clearer when I say that I am not a rationalist in the sense in which Mill and Quine, on their differing grounds, are empiricists. They are empiricists by a *fait accompli*. I am a rationalist *ambulando*. My rationalism is not an achievement but a program. I admit that in most cases of causation our understanding has hardly outstripped Hume's, though I do think advances have been made; the physical analysis of white light has narrowed the causal analysis of why snow is white; and the detection of necessity as one of the determinants in rational inference is a small but immensely significant breach in the Humean generalization. Meanwhile the wholesale reduction of either class to the other is no more than an extravagant claim; the necessary and the contingent remain for our knowledge diverse and profoundly so.

"Holism" and Inference

(3) Mr. Rorty thinks that my "holism" is at war with my theory of necessary connections. For necessary connections link essences or attributes or properties, in short, abstractions, and is it not precisely these abstractions that in my polemic against "the false or abstract universal" I have denied to be either existent or strictly thinkable? Mr. Rorty quotes from me a passage about the abstract universal: "The theory that there is a little, hard, abstract, unchanging essence of colour or triangularity or humanity, absolutely identical in all colours, triangles, or men, absolutely unaffected by its context, and capable of being compounded with foreign elements into a mosaic, which is then describable as a species of it—this was a theory that we found unverifiable." But if such abstractions cannot be singled out and linked with other such abstractions, what is it that the threads of necessity are supposed to connect?

I know of no logician who deals with this question adequately. There is little profit in appealing to the formal logicians either of the older or the newer schools, for their conception of a class disregards the delicacies of the genus-species relation which lie at the heart of the problem. The conception of man is not some abstract outline with everything that differentiates the species of men left out, and it would be of small value in inference if it were. What would follow from such a wispish and vanishing conceptual skeleton? What *is* present to the mind is harder to say. It is scarcely more than an active potentiality felt as developing in one direction or another depending on the interest of the moment. If that interest is in human evolution, one may find one's thought specifying itself upon primitive Chinese or African skulls which lie at the threshold of human emergence. If the interest is in the human future, one may find oneself contemplating the numbers of the Chinese or Indian population. It was in attempting to deal with the content of a general idea that I hit upon my theory of the idea as a potentiality of its object, and though that theory does not hold for all ideas, here it is surely close to the truth. The concept of a genus is a mental disposition ready to develop itself on call into the thought of the species and individuals covered by that genus. Such concepts as being, animality, even manness, do not lend themselves readily to inference, for as abstractions they are too thin and as dispositions they are too ambiguous to be of much use. Even generalizations about narrower classes—women as such, Frenchmen as such, musicians as such—are notoriously unreliable. In science it is not until one reaches definite attributes that one feels comfortable, and even these, in order to yield laws, need usually to be dealt with as quantities varying together. If it can be shown that the probability of having lung cancer varies with the number of packs of cigarettes consumed daily, the scientist rubs his hands; this is the sort of connection that approximates law.

Now I do not see that this singling out of attributes and their strands of connection is inconsistent with my kind of rationalism. It is true that I hold that terms change in acquiring new relations, and that as one goes from person to person one should therefore find that neither cigarette smoking nor lung cancer remains precisely the same thing. This, I suspect, is strictly true, and to that extent any inductive correlation of attributes falls short of precise law. But the likenesses in the terms in their varying environments clearly outweigh the differences; smoking is a determinate practice and lung cancer a determinate disease, even though the forms they take may not be identical in any two persons. Things do change in acquiring new relations, but I have never held that all new relations induce changes of equal importance. The soldiers' epitaph to their mule tells the story eloquently: "Here lies Lizzie, who kicked two captains, three lieutenants, sixteen sergeants, and one gelignite bomb."

I have insisted, indeed, that not all relations are equally relevant; some, like the relation to smoking, may be found to determine the very existence and character of the disease to be explained, while others, like the patient's dietary or sleeping habits, may have no appreciable influence. I have held, and continue to hold, that every event is connected directly or indirectly with every other, that every fact is in like manner connected with every other, and hence that any alteration anywhere would register itself everywhere. A *complete* understanding of anything would involve the whole. Some critics have said that we should therefore talk of nothing till we saw it in its absolute context. But that would mean abandoning the attempt to understand. We are finite; we must walk in semidarkness and "proceed as way opens." It is only by suspending ultimate considerations for the time, only by singling out and following the lines of necessity that we can ever hope to apprehend the webwork of necessities which for the rationalist constitutes the world order. We never understand wholly any judgment we make or any term we use. But as we do use them and come to see their implications, the darkness lightens.

Self-evidence

(4) This brief discussion may help to make intelligible what I have to say in answer to Mr. Rorty's criticism of my handling of "self-evidence" and "in-

tuition." In my view, he says, the laws of logic are self-evident. "But 'self-evidence' is just the sort of notion that makes no sense unless one holds the doctrine of the 'false, or abstract, universal' . . . ." If this kind of criticism were pressed home against me, I should be cut off at once from all speech and all thought. For in saying anything about anything I am speaking of parts or fragments of a whole, and on my theory I shall not have seen these as they are until I see them in relation to the whole, which I admit that I do not. The conclusion would seem to be that I should keep my lips sealed till I am ready to speak absolute truth. I cannot accept this restriction. I do not know why an absolutist and a rationalist should not be granted the privilege of thinking and speaking like an ordinary human being. The tables and chairs among which he moves, his grumblings at the editorial in the morning paper, the rough-and-ready analyses he makes of his political, ethical, and religious views—his judgments in all these cases are less than quite true as they stand. Granted. But he must start somewhere if he is to think at all. If he is to reason, he must reason discursively; and to do that is to analyze, to isolate attributes and connect them as best he can. His analyses will be provisional only, and if he continues thinking, he is bound to revise them and go beyond them. But go *through* them he must. There is no other way. If he tries to lift himself by his own bootstraps directly into the absolute, he is acting not like a rational man but like a dervish.

This brings me to self-evidence. It is important, but it is not final. To reject it would be to reject all mediate or discursive reasoning too, for if one says that p entails q, and q entails r, and r entails s, and hence p entails s, every link in the chain is an appeal to self-evidence, and unless some reliance can be placed upon it, the chain comes apart. But my use of self-evidence is not Cartesian. There is no self-evident starting point on which I hang my deductions, nor is my acceptance of any intuition dependent on self-evidence alone. There have been innumerable insights that have offered themselves as self-evident only to turn out illusions. Even the law of contradiction I should not allow to rest merely on self-evidence. "Unless a necessity can reside in pure form," Mr. Rorty writes, "one will have to say that the necessity of the laws of logic does not reside in a grasp of the meanings of 'is' and 'not' but rather, as Blanshard said in the passage quoted earlier, in 'the whole of experience.' " But the ultimate defense of the law of contradiction *is* precisely that experience as a whole depends on it. The full force of the law is not apprehended in nodding assent to "X cannot both be and not be A." As Locke said, God did not make man merely two-legged and leave it to Aristotle to make him rational. The rule that every affirmation involves a negation was operative in every field of man's thought long before it was formulated in the law, and what made it so compelling when it did receive formulation was not merely the distinctness of the skeleton, but the realization that unless it were conformed to, all judgment and all truth were at an end. The defense of the law is thus, as Bosanquet says it is of any other proposition in the end, "this or nothing."

Propositions taken as self-evident do often lay bare the nerve of connection between the terms connected, and it is tempting to say that no expansion of context would affect either their meaning or their certainty. This is a mistake. "2+2=4"; "A straight line is the shortest line between two points"; "Stealing is wrong." It would be absurd, I agree, to suggest that by an enlargement of context we might see that 2+2 equaled not 4 but 4.2768. But I doubt if our certainty is not enhanced when we see that unless it is true, the number system as a whole would be destroyed; nor do I think that we grasp its full and true significance unless we see the place occupied by the number system in the whole of things. I agree with Bradley that all categorical statements are implicitly conditional. "A straight line is the shortest line." We commonly mean that to hold of actual space, but then we must add "if actual space is Euclidean." "Stealing is wrong." Kant thought that if this was not self-evident, it was at least demonstrable by a self-evident step or two. In this he was in error, as we can see when the statement is put in the context of our moral values generally; when the purloining of a letter would avert a murder, the theft may be a duty rather than a wrong. In sum, the rationalist may and must use self-evidence; indeed, to see that a certain proposition is consistent with the whole of things would presumably itself be such an insight. But an isolated linkage of two terms, while it may be revealing, can never be taken as final truth.

Necessity and Certainty

(5) Mr. Rorty writes: ". . . I think that Blanshard's Hegelian contextualism moves him in the direction of Dewey and Quine at the same time that his pre-Hegelian notions of 'reason' as the detection of 'necessity' lead him in the opposite direction." He thinks I should do better if I were "willing to view necessity as unconnected with certainty," and to put all propositions on a single inclined plane differing in explanatory value but without insistence on inviolable necessities. Mr. Rorty is right that I am drawn in both these directions. But there is no inconsistency in being so drawn if one accepts what is sound and rejects what is amiss in these differing ways of thinking. I do put all propositions on one inclined plane if that means that I regard all of them as reaching after necessity, however gropingly, and all of them as approximations to it in degree. But to ask me to drop necessity and its attendant certainty altogether is to ask me to sail without compass or pole star. That I cannot do. I cannot do it because I am too much of an empiricist. I try, that is, to stay close to what experience presents to me, and if it presents anything clearly, it is surely that some propositions can be seen to be necessary and

that others cannot. It is futile to gloss over the difference between "2+2=4" and "Grass is green." Not that the former exhibits perfect understanding, but that we can see *why* 2+2 cannot be 3 or 5 in a way in which we cannot see why grass should not be blue or orange. Further, I think we can extrapolate the sort of ideal whole that would give us the full necessity, and therefore the understanding and certainty we seek. A schedule exhibiting more or less "explanatory power" I can accept if such power means approximation to this ideal of necessity. If it does not, then either the persons who offer such schemes or I have failed to catch correctly the animating end of thought. Perhaps I may add that it is because Bosanquet's *Logic or the Morphology of Knowledge* traces so firmly the development of thought as governed by this end that it throws so much more light on the processes of actual thinking than the comparatively mechanical deductions of *Principia Mathematica*. Not that it is much easier reading; as Bradley once remarked to me, Bosanquet's style has stood in the way of his recognition. But he could deal from the inside with the levels of thought because he saw what at all levels it was seeking.

Returns to Naturalism

(6) Mr. Rorty finds in recent philosophy tendencies to resuscitate some moribund theories of an older time, particularly certain forms of naturalism. He mentions (i) a return to evolution for an account of the adoption of logical law, (ii) a return to pragmatism for its validation, and (iii) a return to behaviorism to escape the nebulousness of conceptual analysis. And he thinks that my theory of knowledge might be more acceptable to younger philosophers if I could see my way to reconsidering and perhaps adopting these theories. I must confess that, no doubt to my loss, I have been unable to keep abreast of the breathless and kaleidoscopic changes in recent philosophy and cannot pretend to do them justice. But even if I had kept abreast, I doubt if I should have abandoned the convictions I reached on these points, not without struggle, long ago.

(i) (a) First a few comments on evolution and logical law. The law of contradiction, to take an old friend, is not only true; it is also such that we cannot conceive its contradictory. Now the uniform finding through countless generations that two propositions which are inconsistent with each other were not both true could no doubt establish a firm habit of expecting that such inconsistency would be attended by untruth in the future, but it is not clear how this alone would deprive us of our power to think otherwise. Presumably fire has been found hot and water wet since the race began, but I have no difficulty in conceiving a flame as freezing my fingers and water as feeling dry as flour.

(b) The evolutionary case is circular. It offers an argument to show how the law achieved its validity, but unless the law is already accepted as valid, the argument is without force. It reaches its conclusion by assuming the truth of that conclusion.

(c) The argument also seems to assume that there might have been other environments which would have impressed upon our brains and minds logics other than and inconsistent with those we have. But since, whatever our disability rests on, we cannot think that which contradicts our present laws, the theory can be given no definite meaning. It may be replied that this overlooks the actual discovery of alternative logics. I answer that there are no such logics if that means logics that deny, for example, the law of contradiction. A logic that denied that law would hold that a statement and its contradictory could both be true, in which case the denial of its validity would be on the same footing as assertion of it, and then what is being contended? I have discussed this matter more fully and more than once elsewhere (see, e.g. *RA*, 269 ff.).

(d) I agree that our logic is that which obtains in nature, and that our conformity to the logic of nature is one reason for our survival. But I see no reason for giving what may be called a biological accident priority over the clearest of present insights. If I accept the law of contradiction, it is because I see (or think I see) that two contradictory statements about the world cannot both be true; and to make the validity of that insight depend on a controversial suggestion in biology is to muddle the priorities of our thinking.

The debate here is of course an old one. The evolutionary explanation of logic was stated forcibly by Herbert Spencer; it was criticized, as I think still more forcibly, by Cook Wilson in his inaugural lecture at Oxford in 1889 (see his *Statement and Inference,* 2:616 ff.).[1]

(ii) Any appeal to pragmatism as testing the truth of either empirical or logical statements rests on their contribution to an end. When the test is put in this general way, I am myself a pragmatist. Thought *is* the pursuit of an end; that end is truth; it can be reached only through greater fullness of understanding; what gives that understanding is so far true. But if pragmatists meant nothing more than that, they would never have taken themselves off as a splinter group from the rationalist camp. Dewey, James, and Schiller did not believe in intelligible system as either the end of thought or the nature of truth; they held to another end of their own which was described as working, or success in practice. This seems to me, to use Ryle's term, a "category confusion." It confuses the aim at truth, in the traditional meaning of that term, with the aim at something which, however important, is totally different. It is not easy to define what is meant by "working" or "success in practice." Let us define it in the most generous way as contributing to the richest or completest fulfillment of human desires. That means that the truth of beliefs is to be chiefly determined by how useful they are in furthering what we should commonly call noncognitive ends. It seems to me plain that contributoriness to these other ends, whether happiness, power, professional achievement, or anything else, is irrelevant as a test of truth. Not that knowledge is useless as a means to these ends, or that men do not often pursue it with these other ends in view, or that they are not justified in that pursuit. What I am saying is simply that the attainment of knowledge is one thing and the attainment of these other ends quite another thing.

"But are you not being dogmatic? Surely the pragmatist has every right to define truth in his own way. Are we not free to use words as we wish?" That depends. Fowler tells us that "gorse" and "furze" mean the same thing precisely, so I suppose we have freedom of choice; and one may write, if one wants, "Whenever in the following pages I say 'the City of Brotherly Love' I shall mean Brooklyn." But one is not at liberty to confuse definition as a report of one's usage and definition as describing an object. And what I mean by truth is the object that people are aiming at when they try to think or know. That object is clearly different from the object of the desire for any noncognitive good, such as long life, or power, or wealth, or success in any sense but one. The truth about the world has a structure of its own, and the law of consistency is a central girder. To test them by their use for some alien end is a radical confusion. A belief may work because it is true, but it is never true merely because it works.

(iii) Mr. Rorty points out that anyone who tries, as I do, to analyze concepts, meanings, and universals, and to distinguish necessary from non-necessary statements is walking among mists and quicksands. This is painfully true. He then reminds me that Quine, Putnam, and others have approached these distinctions in a behaviorist way and used "the argument that once one leaves the 'circle' of inter-explicable terms ('synonymous,' 'analytic,' 'meaning postulate,' etc.) and looks for a behavioral criterion which, applying to speech-dispositions, will segregate utterances into types along the traditional analytic-synthetic line, no such criterion will appear." Mr. Rorty suggests that if I were to adopt a similar criterion many cobwebs would be swept away. No doubt they would. But I can only assure him that here there is no hope at all. I have studied Watson's and Skinner's behaviorism and Carnap's physicalism, all with astonished disbelief, and have long ago said my say about them. Of course I do not doubt that the attempt to correlate the various forms of consciousness with nervous and cortical changes is an important enterprise. But to identify consciousness with its physical correlates is like saying that catnips are cats, or that when common sense and other such non-sense has been dispensed with, being square is really the same as being blue. So far as I know, there are no two things in the universe more deeply different from each other than a sensation of pain and a movement of physical particles across a cerebral synapse. Indeed the attempt at identification can proceed only by the *correlation* of the pain with the cerebral change, that is, by admitting that *two* changes are before us, not one.

Even if the correlations had been worked out with much greater completeness than they have, the value of studying conceptual distinctions through their physical correlates is approximately zero. Suppose that Kant is sitting in his study wondering whether his judgment, $7+5=12$, is synthetic or analytic. Are there any observable bodily twitches, nods, or jerks that would give us the slightest help in answering this question? Watson would suggest that we listen to those under-the-breath mutterings which constituted his thought processes. But even if they occurred, as they might not, and we managed to overhear them, they would still be irrelevant, since the question is not whether Kant thought his judgment synthetic, as he did, but whether it really was so. And to that question no physical answer can be given, for the reason that it is not a question about physical behavior at all. If this is denied, we are back to the original assertion that catnips are cats, and with it the ultimate parting of the ways. Perhaps I may be allowed to refer to my debate with Mr. Skinner on this general issue at the meeting of the American Psychological Association in 1965 ("The Problem of Consciousness," *Philosophy and Phenomenological Research,* March 1967, 317–37). I can understand how my respected mentor of Harvard days and a predecessor in this series of volumes, C. I. Lewis, felt when confronted, in his "Replies to Critics," with the new physicalism of the positivists: "And now that I seem to see a third wave coming in, with emphasis upon a behaviorist vocabulary, in order to lay even this ghost of experience which still haunts them, I find nothing for it but the other side of the street. To my jaundiced eye, this behaviorist dialect is a somewhat muscovite methodology for disallowing any mention of the obvious facts of life which they perversely refuse to recognize" (*The Philosophy of C. I. Lewis,* 664). In short, the cure for pragmatism and behaviorism alike is an empiricism that takes experience seriously.

The Paradox of Knowledge

In the final section of his paper Mr. Rorty gives a good exhibition of his ability to look at issues with the eye of the philosophical historian. He sees me in the ranks of seventeenth-century dualists about knowledge, fighting a rearguard action against the overwhelming though somewhat disorganized forces of modernity. To some modern philosophers, Locke seems to be the arch sinner who "brought death into the world and all our woe." He held that what we are immediately aware of is our own "ideas," and that it is through their mental veil that we must manage, if at all, to know what lies beyond in the external world. The obvious objection to this view is its implicit skepticism; for how can we compare our own ideas to their objects if we are forever confined to one side of the comparison? Sensations are effects produced in consciousness by the action of stimuli on our nerve ends, and with such a mode of production there is no guarantee of resemblance between inner effect and outer cause. Concepts were still more obviously mental, and the gulf between them and their object, if possible, even deeper. Philosophers of the present are trying to rid themselves, Mr. Rorty tells us, of these mental intermediaries, and with them, of the blight of skepticism.

Now on the main point at issue here I hold unrepentantly that Locke was right. While rejecting many of the arguments he and Berkeley offered, I hold that the colors and sounds, the tastes and smells, even the shapes and sizes that we directly engage in perception belong in consciousness, not in the subject matter of physics. The attempts of the early Russell and the new realists to make them parts of nature failed signally, and Lovejoy's *Revolt against Dualism* is the enduring tombstone that marks their burial place. Russell himself came finally to concede that all these objects are mental. So also are our concepts of man and justice and democracy. It would be fantastic to say that in using them we were in immediate contact with their objects. What about the multiplication table? Here the problem is more difficult. It is tempting to believe with the mathematician G. H. Hardy that in mathematics we are directly in contact with a realm that is independent of us but is neither physical nor perhaps mental.

> I believe that mathematical reality lies outside us, that our function is to discover or *observe* it, and that the theorems which we prove, and which we describe grandiloquently as our "creations," are simply our notes of our observations. This view has been held, in one form or another, by many philosophers of high reputation from Plato onwards, and I shall use the language which is natural to a man who holds it [*A Mathematician's Apology*, 123–24].[2]

I think Hardy was right that these structures are not created but discovered by us. I should go farther and say that in successfully following them our thought is in some measure under their constraint, and carried along the line of its inferences by their timeless structures. But even here it is doubtful if our inference ever follows the nerve of necessity in its purity; and certainly in our reasoning about everyday affairs, where that nerve is always embedded in extraneous matter, our judgments are burdened with irrelevancy. Whether moving on the perceptual or the conceptual level, therefore, we must recognize a mental content that, however hard to dissect in introspection, is indubitably there.

All this the new linguistic analysts are trying to dispense with. "Concepts," "meanings," "universals" are superfluous baggage, and as philosophers we should travel more lightly and economically without them.

What is put in their place? The answer is: *language*. So long as we must peer at the world through a complicated mental apparatus, we shall never see it; furthermore the apparatus is a myth which forces us to misconceive the problem of knowledge. Let us stop talking about our "concepts" of the "nature" of knowledge, of thought, of truth, which for many centuries has produced nothing but controversy. Let us instead ask the much simpler question how these words are used. We shall then at last have problems we can hope to answer.

The trouble here for the critic is that just as he could find no agreed-upon meaning of verifiability among the positivists, so now he can find no agreed-upon interpretation of "the new way of words." Sometimes we are told that we must construct an ideal language that will cut philosophers off from both the temptation and the power of talking nonsense about the unintelligible. The new language will contain no words that refer to objects that cannot be given in perception. But this too obviously begs the question in favor of an empiricist epistemology; the ideal language does not exclude philosophy; it is itself based on a philosophy and a highly questionable one. Sometimes the proposal is to stick to ordinary words in their ordinary senses. But that would contract the range of our reflection drastically. A question freely canvassed by linguistic philosophers, for example, is whether necessary statements are analytic or synthetic. This is (or may be) a perfectly definite and legitimate question, but not if one follows the usages of the plain man. "Necessary" is not being used in his sense; "analytic" and "synthetic" are either not used by him at all, or used in senses that would muddle the question, not clarify it. The thought and language of common sense make excellent starting points for philosophy, but unless it can play free from them they soon impose crippling reins and blinders. Sometimes the misuse of words alleged to engender philosophical perplexity is dealt with in Freudian fashion; rationalists talk about an Absolute because they need the security and repose that comes of dwelling on such a being. But this is itself a venture into philosophy which presumably springs from Freudian roots, and therefore tars itself with its own irrational brush. Sometimes the imperative to the would-be philosopher is put with a no-nonsense sharpness and brevity: "Don't look for the meaning; look for the use."

What is plainly needed here is a critic of unwearying patience who will plough through the vast literature of linguistic theories, give them some order, and subject them to a rigorous examination. Mr. Rorty himself has made a useful start toward this in the preface to his anthology on *The Linguistic Turn*. I must content myself here with the briefest of comments. "Look for the use," if followed faithfully, takes us straight back into epistemology. Words themselves, words as sounds or as marks on paper, mean nothing. They acquire a use or a meaning only as they are used by a person. And what does "used by a person" mean? If he is using the words cognitively, he is thinking of, or referring to, some object. This does not mean that he is pointing at it with his finger, or muttering about it under his breath, or focusing his eyes upon it. People may say, if they wish, that this is all it means, but in saying it they are not only violating common sense and common usage; they are descending to a cruder philosophy than any of the philosophers they are trying to set right. To *use* a word, in this context, is to *mean* something by it; and to mean something by it is an act of mind. What sort of act? To gain competent help with that question, where shall one turn? I can only report that I get most light myself from logicians with a special interest in the theory of knowledge like Bradley, Cook Wilson, and Joseph, from philosophical psychologists like Stout, Ward, and Sir William Mitchell, and from analysts who are not wedded to linguistics, like Broad and Price. Such persons seem to me to have a firmer grasp of the facts of mental life than those who take a detour around them by the path of language. That the theory of the idea as the potentiality of its object which I worked out thirty-five years ago requires amendment I acknowledge in my reply to Mr. Bertocci. But unless one sees that there is a genuine paradox of knowledge of the kind Lovejoy insisted on, "the mystery of the presence of the absent," the paradox of ideas that go beyond themselves to lay hold of external fact, I do not think the problem of knowledge has been clearly seen.

Universals and Particulars

Mr. Rorty ends his paper, as he began it, with an eirenic suggestion. He says that just as the thesis that everything is contingent comes to about the same thing as saying that everything is necessary, so the contention that everything is universal amounts to about the same as saying that everything is made of particulars. Thus, just as I have something in common with Mr. Quine on one side, I have something in common with Mr. Sellars on the other. I am flattered by this suggested *rapprochement* with views of a former colleague whose subtlety in these matters I much admire. But if there is a resemblance between my thought and that of Mr. Sellars, it lies, I suspect, not in this homogeneity of constituents in our respective worlds, but rather in the roles played in both by particulars and universals.

In his essay on "Being and Being Known"[3] Mr. Sellars writes: "Philosophers have been fascinated by the fact that one can't have the concept of white without being able to see things *as white,* indeed, until one has actually seen something as white. But this can be explained without assuming that sensation is a consciousness, for example, of white things as white." Sensation, though essential to knowledge, is not itself knowledge. It is not until perception supervenes, and something of the form "this is white" is affirmed, that anything we can call true or false, or therefore knowing, emerges.

Now this is my own view exactly. Where then do we differ? It is in the status assigned to the objects of sensation. Mr. Sellars would say, I take it, that in sensing white we are sensing a particular; I hold that it is a universal. This seems to be considered an eccentric view. But how does one define a universal? For me a universal is a character or relation, or a group of these, that does or may occur in diverse contexts. So far as I know, there is nothing unorthodox in that definition. But if the definition is accepted, the white one senses must surely be called universal. For this precise shade plainly *could* appear elsewhere. It may be replied that it is not white as such that is being sensed, or even a special shade of white, but an *instance* of a special shade of white, and that this is a particular. But as Mr. Sellars says, it is not sensed as an instance. Why then say it is an instance? Presumably because someone else, or ourselves at a later time, can say that the white that was sensed by us was sensed at a certain time and place. Now time and place are indicated by specifying certain relations—before and after, to the right of, to the left of, and so on. And what is the status of these relations? I have argued that they too are obviously universals. But if that is true, not only the particular but that which is alleged to particularize it is universal. If space and time were absolute, I suppose presentation at a certain point would particularize; but are they? However that may be, I have taken the view that only the specification of an object's relations to everything else in the universe would guarantee its uniqueness. The only thing that is fully particular or individual is the whole.

I agree (and differ) with Sellars about universals in a somewhat similar way. Mr. Rorty describes me as holding that "Since thought deals with universals, any theory which takes the objects of thought to be a multiplicity of particulars will lead to skepticism." But it is in such a multiplicity of particulars, he also tells us, that Mr. Sellars' thought comes to rest. For "within descriptive discourse, nothing philosophical can hinder science from explaining (and thus providing improved descriptions of) everything there is as so many arrangements of atoms." Now a reader might easily get the impression that since I hold the object of sensation to be universal, I must a fortiori hold that the object of thought is universal. But I do not hold this view in any conventional form. I have argued both in *The Nature of Thought* and in *Reason and Analysis* that generic universals like manness and qualitative universals like color exist neither in thought nor in things. The traditional intension of the class term I have been unable to find either in our thought of such classes or in the classes themselves. In the latter of these books I have argued that the concept of such a class is a reference not to an identity but to a range of similars. Thus, like Mr. Sellars, I have sharply criticized the traditional theory of universals. But that does not lead me to hold that either all men or all colors are particulars. Colors are all universals; and an individual man is a congeries of universal attributes, each of which can be dissected out by analysis and each of which has logical and causal relations that connect the man with everything else in the universe.

Of course all this will not satisfy Mr. Rorty, or Mr. Sellars, or anyone who takes as seriously as they do "the new way of words." There is much in this new "way" that seems to me very strange indeed, no doubt in part because of my failures to understand. But I have such respect for its practitioners as to be grateful to Mr. Rorty for having brought to light some areas of coincidence between my thought and theirs.

1. John Cook Wilson, *Statement and Inference*, 2 vols. (Oxford: Clarendon Press, 1926).

2. G. H. Hardy, *A Mathematician's Apology* (Cambridge: Cambridge University Press, 1969).

3. Wilfrid Sellars, "Being and Being Known," *Proceedings of the American Catholic Philosophical Association* (Washington, D.C., 1960).

VI METAPHYSICS

21   BLANSHARD'S THEORY OF MIND AND FREE WILL
Francis V. Raab

I

S INCE Brand Blanshard's views about freedom of the will are best understood in the light of his interactionist dualism, I shall first discuss his
views about mental states and their relation to brain states and behavior.

Blanshard opposes both scientific and philosophical behaviorism on the
grounds that they fail to provide an even approximate analysis of the nature
of mental states. To whatever extent both verbal and motor behavior are involved in mental states, they are not what the plain man has in mind when he
ascribes some mental state to himself or others. When the plain man says the
thought occurred to him that his engine might be low on water, he is not saying anything about any actual or possible behavior. And he is not just saying
that some subvocal speech occurred which he is now uttering out loud. Nor is
he merely saying that he has a disposition to act or speak in certain ways under certain conditions. Blanshard claims that mental state terms do not stand
for any of these things and that the meaning of a mental state term is
something different from the meaning of the terms used to describe motor
behavior and speech. Most psychologists and philosophers today agree with
him on these points. However, the scientific behaviorist while agreeing still
feels free to construct a behaviorally defined terminology, and then to discover laws connecting stimulus to response (speech or motor behavior).
Numerous S-R theories have been suggested in the past decade that show
that behavioristic psychology is not going to be easily frustrated by the strictures against earlier behaviorism. The new S-R theorists believe that if their
models can in principle explain human behavior, the effect will be to rule out
the reality and efficacy of nonneural entities over and above the stimulus and
response events and the laws connecting them. Charles Taylor in perhaps the
most acute study of this problem[1] has concluded that S-R theories fail
because they do not allow for the notion of purposive, intentional, or goal-
directed behavior. Taylor says[2] that while peripheralist (S-R) theories cannot
succeed without these notions it is still possible that a "centrist"

(neurophysiological) theory might succeed in explaining behavior without these notions. This leads us directly into the issues of the classical mind-body problem—the problem whether a mental state and some neural state are one and the same.

In *The Nature of Thought* (*NT*, 1:336–38) Blanshard argued against reductive monism, a position now discarded by experts on the mind-body problem. That was the view that mental state terms were analyzable into brain state terms because the former were obviously meaningful and could not be analyzed into behavioral terms. Such a view was usually part of the position called "naturalism." It became evident to most philosophers who were sophisticated about the nature of meaning that mental state terms did not *mean* the same as the terms of the brain physiologist. With the failure of reductive monism and scientific behaviorism there were only two alternatives left: dualism or the denial that mentalistic terms "referred to anything real." For some philosophers this was intolerable, and it was this impasse that among other things may have stimulated the appearance of philosophical behaviorism. Philosophical behaviorism had a very brief career because it too made claims about the meaning of mentalistic terms that were not borne out by later analysis. Once again matters were back to either dualism or the non-referentiality of mentalistic terms.

In 1956 U. T. Place,[3] followed quickly by H. Feigl[4] and J. J. C. Smart[5] formulated a new variation on monism—the identity theory. They insisted that monism could not be established by an appeal to meaning considerations. Nevertheless, a statement of the type "Mental state X *is* brain state Y," which means that "Mental state X and brain state Y are one and the same state," is a synthetic, identity statement which can be established once correlation laws have been discovered connecting the mental states with brain states.

In a recent essay, "The Limits of Naturalism,"[6] Blanshard attacks the identity theory on several counts, but he doesn't attack the argument made by Feigl and Smart, which is the theory's strongest positive argument. And he doesn't challenge a strong point they make against dualism. Feigl says[7] that dualism would give us very peculiar correlation laws connecting mental states with brain states because what would be correlated would be something very simple, like pain, and extremely complex neural events. Such laws are "nomological danglers" and would be like nothing else in science. The other point is that if we accept the dualistic ontology of mental events we would have a double ontology in our explanatory system. For every mental event there would be a corresponding complex of neural events, and these mental events would be nomological danglers from the standpoint of science, which would not accord them any efficacy because the true cause of any behavior would always have to be some neural events. Such an ontology strikes Smart[8] and Feigl as being very queer. Their ontological sensibilities are offended, just as James's and Watson's ontological sensibilities were upset by dualism. Mental entities have been regarded as queer by twentieth-century philosophers, and those who have accepted dualism have done so either because they were convinced by what seemed to be cogent arguments or because monism upset their humanistic sensibilities and/or their belief in immortality and freedom of the will. Blanshard, in not dealing with this problem of nomological, ontological danglers, leaves himself open to traditionally troublesome reflections.

But his neglect of the identity theorists' most important argument—the argument from theoretical reduction—leaves one wondering what his response to it would be. Their argument is simply this: Suppose that we have a high-powered neurophysiological theory which enables us to describe and explain everything that happens in the brain. Suppose also that the neurophysiologist succeeds in correlating a type of brain event that invariably accompanies pain as ascertained either by personal report or by the observation of someone's overt behavior. Furthermore, suppose that using these correlation laws he can deduce from his theory any commonsense and psychologically established laws about human pain, e.g. that when people have migraine pain they experience nausea. Thus, on the neurophysiological theory, the occurrence of pain can be deduced merely from a knowledge of some immediately prior brain state, without observing the person's behavior. Furthermore, all the speech and motor behavior connected with pain can be deduced. Under these circumstances it would be proper to say that the pain and this brain state were one and the same state. This type of reduction was twice accomplished in nineteenth-century physics: the reduction of molar gas theory to statistical mechanics and the reduction of physical optics to electromagnetic theory. Since then we have been able to say, for example, that the temperature of a gas and its mean molecular momentum are one and the same state. Such, in brief, is the central positive argument of the identity theorist.

I would also like to know what Blanshard would say to a futuristic version of the identity theory offered by Hilary Putnam.[9] He agreed that today the statement "Pain *is* C-fiber stimulation" is semantically deviant in English. But would it be deviant in the English that will be spoken several centuries hence, when the correlations between mental states and brain states will have become a matter of common knowledge? May it not come to pass that people will use the expressions "pain" and "C-fiber stimulation" interchangeably? And when they do, won't these expressions gradually become synonymous? If this happens then indeed it will not be deviant to say "Pain and C-fiber stimulation are one and the same state of a human being." Later on "pain" might be dropped from common usage and become an archaic word. If

Blanshard thinks this is too far-fetched to take seriously as having any bearing upon questions concerning the ontological status of mental entities, he might consider the fact that many of our mentalistic expressions are synonymous with various kinds of head, brain, and heart talk. Very likely the head and brain expressions have come into use because of the common belief that the head region or the brain is the "seat" of mental activity. And it is quite possible that heart-talk is a survival from ancient times when the heart was thought to be the organ of emotion because of its more rapid beating under various kinds of stress. Among the Homeric Greeks,[10] mentalistic language was unknown. What we say with mentalistic language they said by reference to the change or movement of bodily organs or regions. One type of example is the expression "His heart was in his throat," for "He was terrified." The Homeric Greeks had only the former kind of expression in their language. Some examples in common use today are:

It's all in your head.
Once he gets it into his head to do something, he'll carry it through.
He racked his brains for an answer.
He has plenty of brains (a good head on his shoulders).
Use your brains (head)!
Get it out of your head that you can always talk your way out of a jam!
It went clean out of his head.
His head was filled with ideas.
He has a head filled with nonsense.
He's too cerebral.
He's empty-headed.
He has a clear head.
What put that into your head?
Don't trouble your head with it!
In all the commotion he alone kept his head.
His staff has plenty of brain power.
That never once entered his head.
The tune kept running through his head.

For each of these expressions there is some mentalistic expression which has the same conventional criteria of application and is synonymous. Suppose we consider whether just one fact or two facts are true of Smith when we say, "He racked his brains for an answer" and "He tried very hard to think of an answer." Surely we will not say that there are two things true of Smith, two things taking place in Smith. If the equivalent mentalistic expression were dropped from English, we would not be deprived as long as we kept the former. Thus it seems that at some future time an advanced neurophysiological theory might be able to replace mentalistic ways of speaking. A psychologist once told me that in the presence of his children he would say things like "Mom's adrenalin titer is going up" instead of "Mom's getting angry." Suppose the former is taught to them in the same circumstances as the latter, so that the criteria, behavioral and otherwise, are the same as for the latter. Why couldn't the former replace the latter totally? Would literature and history, which Blanshard is acutely concerned to protect against the desuetude of mentalistic language at the hands of the materialists, be deprived of anything except a simpler expression? And we would now have an expression which would not lend itself to the problem of other minds. We could in fact verify whether a person's adrenalin titer was rising by a blood assay. It would be interesting to have Blanshard set forth his reflections on these speculations.

These speculations by no means exhaust the possibilities within materialism for bringing dualism into question. Paul Feyerabend[11] advocates a materialism which is not susceptible to the standard criticisms of the identity theory. One of his criticisms of the identity theory, and by implication all forms of dualism, is that when we speak of correlating brain states with mental states, what reality do these mental states have that makes a correlation possible? All that the scientist has to go on is his observations of the motor behavior and the verbal reports of his subjects. This sort of thing he might be able to correlate with brain states. But he has not got hold of anything else he can correlate with the subjects' brain states. These mental states can have no reality for him as an observer, and so mental state—brain state correlation laws are as mythical as laws correlating the presence of phlogiston with oxidation of metals. It would be like trying to find a correlation between certain lethal biochemical processes taking place in a man's brain and his soul leaving his body. Today we ridicule the idea of such a correlation because we have rejected the idea that there is such a thing as a soul. While it might be objected that we have very definite criteria which make it impossible for desires, intentions, and decisions not to exist when these criteria are fulfilled, it was equally true that people once had criteria for a soul leaving a body—usually when the body showed no sign of life. Today these criteria are only criteria of death. Likewise our current criteria for ascertaining the presence of desires, intentions, decisions, etc., might in the future become criteria of the presence of brain states, although they would not be the only criteria available, because we could develop elaborate equipment to ascertain the brain state of the person.

Feyerabend says that we have no way of telling just how good mentalistic language is as a description and explanation of human behavior until we have a rival theory. And as things stand today we have no way of knowing whether we are entitled to give a realistic interpretation to mental terms or whether they are purely instrumental—a point made by James[12] and Russell,[13] especially about the notion of consciousness. The heart of Feyerabend's materialism is the contention that there is no logical barrier to the possibility of a materialistic explanation of everything that is now described and explained in mentalistic terms, as well as of many things about human behavior that it is unlikely mentalistic concepts ever could explain. This is the challenge that dualism will have to face.

I shall formulate the traditional mind-body problem in a new way. The ontological import of the mind-body problem has been the question whether there are such things as mental entities over and above their concomitant neural processes in the brain. Thus the question has been posed in the form: "Are mental events neural events or are they numerically different events?" I shall try to show that this question is no longer a fruitful one to seek an answer to. We have been forcing a complex philosophical issue into an identical-or-not-identical dichotomy. The traditional issue should be reformulated in terms of the principle: Our ontological commitment should not extend beyond what it is necessary to postulate to provide an adequate explanatory theory. One of the marked characteristics of philosophy in the third quarter of the twentieth century is that it tends to see problems of ontic commitment in terms of this principle. One thinks here, pre-eminently, of Quine.

My complaint against the traditional formulation of the mind-body problem is that it tries to answer a question that is semantically deviant. It asks the question whether a mental state is one and the same state as some state of the brain. Now this may sound like a sensible question, but there are reasons for thinking it is not. According to the molecular theory of matter, material objects or space-occupying objects are composed of molecules. A scientist who assumes this theory in his particular studies, say, on the magnetic properties of metals, will try to understand why a bar of iron becomes magnetized when it is stroked by a magnetized bar. He will try to explain the behavior of the magnetized bar, such as its causing a deflection in nearby compass needles or affecting the patterns of iron filings placed on glass just above it, and the induction of an electric current in a wire coil by a magnetized rod oscillating inside the coil. And this explanation will have reference to the behavior of the electrons in the atoms of the molecules which the iron bar is composed of. He would assume that any changes in the intensity of the bar's magnetic properties will be simultaneous with the changes in the molecules which the bar is composed of. Now let us suppose he turns philosophical and assumes, like those opposed to philosophical behaviorism, that the magnetization of the bar is something more than its behavior with compasses, iron filings, etc. He might then ask: "Is the magnetized state of the bar one and the same thing as the state of the electrons in the molecules of which it is composed?" How should we answer this question?[14] If we insist on taking seriously the difference in meaning of "is magnetized" in contrast to the meaning of "the electrons are spinning" then we will say that no matter how absolute the correlation between being magnetized and the behavior of the electrons, a reduction is not permitted, and the identity question must be answered in the negative. We will then think that there are two different things occurring simultaneously, a double ontology of physical states; and we will wonder whether there are two-way causal interactions between the two states of the bar or whether the magnetic phenomenona are mere epiphenomena of the underlying electron behavior. Since the iron bar is composed of molecules, are the molar- or macro-properties of the bar one and the same, or numerically different from, the simultaneous behavior of the molecules which compose it? How can this question be anything but semantically deviant when it is wholly unlike typical identity questions?

To answer this question we have to be certain that there are indeed such things as magnetized states of an iron bar, and that these states of the bar are not just its behavior and its behavioral dispositions. So long as we insist that there are magnetized states of the bar because we have definite criteria for ascertaining them, we are plunged into macro-micro dualism. The only way we can be released from this conclusion is to question the existence of magnetized states on the grounds that molecular type explanations allow us to explain and describe the behavior of the bar without postulating magnetized states. But if we allow theoretical reduction to eliminate the notion of magnetization from our explanations, it does not follow that the answer to the identity question "Is magnetization = electron states of molecules" is "Yes." Indeed, it cannot be, because what theoretical reduction shows is that there is nothing about the magnetized bar that the electron states of the atoms can be identified with.

The parallel with the mind-body problem is obvious. Only the puzzles surrounding the issue of how correct first-person mentalistic statements can be made without criteria prevent a perfect analogy. If I may be permitted a pair of paradoxes: The only way we can identify mental states with brain states is by showing that mental states do not exist! And the only way we can show that mental states exist and are numerically different from brain states is the same as the way of showing that all molar- or macro-states of all material objects and organisms exist and are numerically different from the molecular states with which they are concomitant. Accepting this latter paradox is bound to give credibility to all sorts of false beliefs about what exists so long as we have conventional criteria of application for molar- or macro-concepts. For example, suppose that the conviction among so many physicists in the first half of the nineteenth century that there was an ether led to its existence being taught in elementary school. Instead of saying "The apple fell from the tree," children were taught to say, "The apple parted the ether beneath it," the conventional criteria being kept the same for both sentences. Now suppose two generations speak in this way about the terrestrial movements of objects. At the end of the nineteenth century physicists deny the existence of the ether. Would we as philosophers have had to concur in the newly established ways of speaking and say that because there are conventional criteria for all these movements of objects in the ether the sentence "The apple parted the ether beneath it" will be true whenever its criteria are satisfied; or even that it will have to be accepted as an *observation* sentence? An example even closer to our concerns is to be found in our everyday mind-talk. We have an elaborate repertory of such talk, and each specimen has the same criteria as the equivalent sentence in mentalistic talk. For example, "I made up my mind to go to Mexico" means the same as "I decided to go to Mexico"; and "It never crossed my mind that he might be injured" means the same as "The thought never occurred to me that he might be injured." Does it follow that there exists in a human being an entity which is capable of becoming involved in so many changes, doing so many things, etc? In short is there in man something answering to the concept of mind in everyday speech which is neither a cluster of behavior nor behavioral dispositions, nor some neural processes? To pose this question is to have it answered in the negative by most philosophers. And finally, suppose we taught children in an isolated community to say "His lind wound around his quind and passed thru his zind to go to Mexico" instead of "He decided to go to Mexico." And instead of teaching them "He is of two opinions on that issue" we taught them "His quind cleaves his zind on that issue" and so on. These children would have criteria of application for each of these and the many others we could invent. Would it follow that *there are* linds, quinds, zinds, which might possibly be correlated with neural states; and that these entities are non-neural because the very meaning of the terms that denote them is different from the meaning of the neurophysiological terms? John L. Austin said that ordinary language contains "superstition and error and fantasy . . . it can everywhere be . . . superseded."[15] I think our everyday mind-talk is a case in point. But why should our doubts cease when we come to mentalistic language? It too was introduced long before anything was known about the physiology of the human body, and even before Hippocrates, who was one of the earliest men of the ancient Greek world to hold that our intellectual processes were seated in the brain and not some other organ like the heart, liver, lungs, tongue, or diaphragm.

I doubt that Blanshard would honor any ontological commitments that might appear to be imbedded in ordinary language. Idealism has notoriously advocated positions that went against ordinary speech. Perhaps Blanshard would agree that the truth of statements containing denoting expressions "requires" (in suitably defined senses depending upon the kind of statement—excepting negative existentials) that the denoting expressions denote something which exists. And in order for us to know that this is true, someone must know that its denoting expressions denote something which exists. If we cannot impose both these conditions on our use of "true" and "know" then we shall be opening the gates to an intolerable amount of myth in our ordinary and scientific language. "True" would degenerate into something like "is helpful" or "is satisfying to believe." Blanshard does not tolerate this corruption of "true," for even if one's criterion of truth is coherence, as Blanshard's is, the rationality or justification for relying on coherence as a test for truth must be that it is the only way we have of knowing whether the denoting phrases in our statements do in fact denote something which exists.

In order to try to solve the mind-body problem in its traditional form as a question whether mental states are identical with brain states, we must be able to ascertain that there are such things as mental states and brain states. But then we must have some criterion of their existence which would be acceptable. This criterion must not itself be a matter of controversy or doubt, otherwise we haven't yet reached the point where we have a clarified identity question. The defenders of the existence of mental states appeal to the fact that such things as intentions, desires, decision, thought-occurrences (but not thoughts, because a thought as something that occurs to a person is neither mental nor neural, just as *what* I said when I uttered something is neither mental nor physical)[16] cannot sensibly be held not to exist because for each of these mental states or occurrences there are behavioral or verbal criteria whose satisfaction entails the existence of the relevant mental state. As Malcolm says: "It is preposterous to think it could be shown that people do not have desires, purposes, fears, or goals . . . ."[17] By parallel reasoning he should say that it is inconceivable that iron bars which behave in certain ways are not really magnetized. But we have already indicated that such a judgment regarding magnetized states is not completely secure from attack. I think what is going on here is that in ordinary language there are at least two kinds of truth: truth, a sufficient condition of which is that conventional criteria for a term's use are satisfied, and truth, a necessary condition of which is that the denoting expressions in a statement denote something which exists. Malcolm and the materialists are opposed on the issue whether statements whose truth is a function of the satisfaction of conventional criteria relevant to the mental predicates under consideration are unassailable, or whether what is predicated of a person does not necessarily denote something which exists, because we can construct an explanatory theory which will ignore these predicates in favor of purely physical predicates. And denoting phrases containing these latter predicates will, in true statements, denote something which exists. There is little doubt that both criteria of truth are appealed to in our everyday thinking. But in the mind-body problem they are in head-on conflict.

The materialist does not yet have clear sailing even if we grant precedence to the denotational conception of truth. He has still to meet the challenge of a third criterion of ontological commitment, i.e. immediate experience. This is the problem of how to deal with the reality of our own pain or other sensations like dizziness, itches, tickles, nausea, tingling in the hands or feet, ringing in the ears, etc. Here we appeal only to cases where we know our own sensations without criteria. How could a theory whose descriptive terms all belong to physics or neurophysiology explain away the reality of the pains we feel?

In discussions of the mind-body problem philosophers debate what is, or should be, the dominant criterion for deciding questions of ontological commitment.[18] At this point someone might suggest that it begins to look as if we have an insoluble problem, because how could we settle the question which criterion is, or should be, overriding? Or they might even suggest that ontology may be a bogus enterprise because there is no rational way of settling on any one of the three criteria in dealing with questions like: Are pains irreducibly real? Are occurrences of thoughts irreducible to any other kind of occurrence?

However, I think Blanshard is quite open to the suggestion that the criteria of direct experience, and satisfaction of conventional criteria for truthfully applying a certain predicate, must yield to coherence. He would say that direct experience has not shown itself to be trustworthy enough for conclusive verdicts based upon it. And we cannot slavishly trust that something exists simply because conventional criteria for saying it does have been satisfied in a given case. Having this as a final court of appeal would leave the way open for ignorance becoming enshrined in our common ways of speaking and thinking. If Blanshard agrees with me on this, he must heed the materialist who is also appealing to coherence. Blanshard like his idealist predecessors has little time for the existence of the nonintelligible or that which falls outside of a fully coherent system. Thus if he is to be consistent with his most basic commitments in metaphysics and epistemology, he will, like the materialists, conclude that *if* we can explain all of human behavior in terms of their ontology, then no rival ontology is correct. For Blanshard, there cannot be two rival systems equally coherent and fully comprehensive.

Since Blanshard is an interactionist, he holds that mental states are not only real but efficacious. He presents many arguments against epiphenomenalism, which denies their efficacy ("Limits of Naturalism," 26–30). However, even if mental states are efficacious he cannot hold that they are immediately efficacious. He would not say that a decision or desire acts directly upon the muscles of the arm in bringing about some gesture. He then must hold that the desire which supposedly causes the gesture acts upon some group of neurons. But how are we to discover which ones? Here we are back to the Cartesian mysteries—almost too high a price to pay for committing oneself to the double ontology of dualism! But no matter for the moment. If the desire brings about a change in some neurons, which in turn causes some activity in motor neurons, which in turn activates the muscles of the arm, we could have a physical theory that would explain my gesture in terms of its immediate physical antecedents without reference to the desire. Blanshard would then have to propose a plausible empirical argument to the effect that without the desire the gesture would not have occurred, and he would have to do this without implicitly appealing to an argument from ordinary usage to the effect that desires are efficacious. If he claims this, he is claiming that although the desire was not a sufficient condition for the explanation of the gesture, it was at least a necessary condition for the occurrence of the gesture; without it, the immediate neural conditions for the gesture would not have existed. But how can we be sure that desires do play such a role? And even if it is granted that they could, the appeal to them for the purposes of explanation has already been watered down. We just aren't impressed with a theory which purports to provide us with explanatory concepts that, when appealed to, refer to nothing more than a single necessary condition which is prior to the immediately efficacious or determining conditions. Yet this is all that a dualistic ontology can provide for explaining overt motor behavior and speech.

The dualism which Blanshard defends has the advantage of being entrenched in mentalistic language. Take all of the terms of our mentalistic vocabulary, with the complex meaning of each and the various behavioral implications of so many of them, and one has a formidable task in trying to generate a critique of dualism. It is difficult because our mentalistic terms exhibit a complexity of meaning that defies an analysis of the kind proposed by philosophical behaviorism. At the same time this meaning prevents us from saying that these terms *mean* the same as neural state terms, and from saying that whatever is denoted by denoting expressions containing mentalistic terms can be identified with what is denoted by denoting expressions containing neural terms. Nevertheless grammar does not prove that anything exists which corresponds to it. However, even if the materialist is correct that a purely physical language can successfully explain all of human behavior with the ontological consequence that there are no mental states, it does not follow that in using mentalistic terms for the description and explanation of human behavior we are talking about ourselves in sublime ignorance. Surely not even the materialist would say that if, beginning today, children were no longer taught mentalistic language they would not be in the least impoverished in their attempts to understand themselves and others. This being so, mentalistic language has got hold of some kind or degree of truth—apparently without denotation. How it manages to accomplish this would be a large and worthwhile topic and one that encompasses the success of most of our molar- and macro-physical concepts.

It is not clear how one can proceed to develop a successful critique of mentalistic language without having a successfully applied physical language which threatens to replace it in detailed ways. But something can be said against mentalistic language without its being confronted by a high-powered rival. Mentalistic language is troublesome in the following ways:

1) Trying to predict human behavior in mentalistic terms is quite unreliable. Too often even the shrewdest observers of human nature, with much data on their subject, cannot predict, nor is it possible to retrodict after the subject has acted or spoken in a certain way. This indicates that there are variables not accounted for in mentalistic terms.

2) When causal explanations in mentalistic terms are given, we seldom have any way of checking up on the assumed causes. If a man says that the thought of his mother's death caused him to become depressed, we have no way of knowing (nor has he) whether this thought was the cause and not some other thought, or some drug, brain condition, or incident.

3) Serious definitional problems have existed for nearly a century and these problems are not due to the open-textured character of the terms themselves.

4) For a long time there has been considerable doubt or at least uneasiness about the referent of mentalistic terms. In science doubts about the referent lead to conceptual revision.

5) The other-minds problem exists because of the peculiar nature of the verification of mentalistic terms. If neural terms replaced them, the verification would be public. I could know whether another person's neurons were firing in a certain way and whether it was this that caused him to mispronounce a word, without being limited to a scrutiny of his motor and speech behavior.

6) Occurrences of thoughts and images are not locatable in space or anywhere in the brain, yet their necessary and sufficient conditions supposedly *do* occur in the brain. Also, the nonspatial occurrences of thoughts are supposed to bring about spatially locatable events in the brain.

The dualist says that purposive, intentional behavior cannot be explained by purely physical laws—that no answer to the question: "Why did he deliberately raise and lower his arm?" can be given in purely neurophysiological concepts and laws. However, of those dualists who say this, none except the parallelists have noticed that it would be equally difficult for them to explain how a mental occurrence such as having a thought can be accounted for neurophysiologically, or how intentions, purposes, and goals can come into existence from a purely physiological set of circumstances. For example, the dualist will point out that certain sentences which can be used to "report" or "express" thoughts that occur to us have certain marks of intentionality.[19] Then he goes on to say, if he is not careful, that if the occurrences of these thoughts did have these marks then they would be something non-neural because nothing neural could have such logical characteristics. But if so, how could neural processes have ever brought into existence the occurrence of a thought? This cannot help but be an ultimate mystery for the dualist, and for that reason is a strong argument against him. And it undermines his insistence that since actions are goal-directed, a characteristic not shared by neural processes, they could not be explained by reference to these neural processes.

I think both Blanshard and the materialist have common cause in denying that we are ontologically committed to the objects of sensations just because they are "directly experienced." Blanshard has been no friend of "the given." Both he and Feyerabend could agree that the feeling of certainty I have about being in pain is a result of the fact that my concept of pain is not a rich, theory-laden concept. Blanshard would say that the lines of inference running from it to the concepts of brain states and biochemical conditions of an injured finger have not yet been established. But once they were, it would not be easy to be so certain that we felt a pain when so many other judgments would have to cohere with this judgment. In what follows I shall try to provide additional reason for not abandoning the coherence theory in the face of ontological claims made by some dualists who would use an argument from direct experience to establish the existence of mental states.

I shall have to say rather dogmatically that we do not directly experience the occurrence of the thoughts that occur to us. Whatever we are talking about when we say that a certain thought occurred to us, it is very elusive—a slippery customer. Just because we can "report" on its occurrence does not prove that we can clearly "see" what sort of thing we are reporting. If the thought we report having is complex enough, we can easily make a mistake and say "No, it was not quite that way." The same is true of very complex intentions. We are not quite sure just what we directly experienced or are directly experiencing when we say that we intend to do such and such. It is very easy to feel certain that a particular mental episode occurred to us or that we are in a particular mental state. Philosophers may come along and erect epistemologies of inner awareness, direct experience, or acquaintance to account for our commonsense certainty. Suppose English were totally divested of its mentalistic language and used only mind-talk like "I made up my mind to go to Mexico," and "It's been in the back of my mind to go to Mexico," "I changed my mind about going to Mexico," "It never crossed my mind that I wouldn't want to go to Mexico," and a hundred other mind-sentences. What credibility would these epistemologists have if, in order to preserve the apparent certainty of these utterances on a given occasion, they held that they were directly aware of the existence of their own minds, and that they inwardly apprehended the states of their minds, the changes in their minds, etc.—all the while the rest of us are convinced that there is no such thing as a mind? Thus I wish to leave a trail of doubt that we know that there are such things as thoughts and intentions because we directly experience them. But the question of the ontological status of pains is another matter, because they are considered to be paradigms of things "directly experienced."

It would seem that there is no logical barrier to giving a neural description of people who wince, groan, curse, and clutch the finger they just hit with a hammer. In such circumstances they now might say, "I am experiencing severe pain." But they could just as well be taught neural talk—and say, "I am experiencing neural state X." The use of "experiencing" here would not differ substantially from that of a heart specialist who says, "I am experiencing coronary occlusion." He is not required by constraints upon the use of "experiencing" to say merely, "I am experiencing pain in my chest, a pain which is invariably associated with coronary occlusion." Likewise, instead of saying in certain circumstances, "I am experiencing anger," a person could be taught to say in these circumstances, "I am experiencing a rise in my blood adrenalin titer." To the physiologically uneducated these sentences would be virtually synonymous, but to the others they would not mean the same thing once the expression "blood adrenalin titer" had been defined. Furthermore, the above behavior which the child learned to consider as criteria for saying "He is experiencing neural state X" would, unlike the case of the criteria for "pain," be nomologically connected with neural state X. If so, we can dispense with the concept of pain and the ontic commitment to something which is non-neural. No one could still reasonably insist: "But you are experiencing something besides neural state X. So you must introduce a word to describe it!"

We shall have also left behind the irritating problem of other minds—whether for example, despite their behavior, other people feel pain. Whether or not another person is experiencing neural state X can be determined either by reference to the nomologically connected behavior or by equipment designed to ascertain brain states. A person's neural events will be no more private than a horse's, nor more private than his liver metabolism, though far more difficult to predict.

It is not necessary that the children who are taught the expression "I am experiencing neural state X" understand the meaning of "neural state X," whatever complex state this might denote. They no more need to understand "neural" and whatever words are substituted for "X" than they need to know what the word "mind" means in "I made up my mind to keep my room cleaner" or "It was in the back of my mind all the time." At least when the child becomes an adult he can learn how these neurophysiological terms are defined or what sort of entities they stand for. Philosophers have not been so fortunate with "mind," "pain," "thought," "image," and "belief."

The upshot of our inquiry is: Will mentalistic concepts be indispensable to a rigorous scientific explanation of human behavior? Will it turn out that the neurophysiologist will be unable to explain everything that happens in the human nervous system because he has failed to consider the action of mental entities upon certain parts of the brain? I think there is considerable hesitation to answer "Yes" to the second question. This being so, the hesitation must extend to the first, for the second is the cash value of the first. Whether the materialists' ontology is sufficient is an empirical matter and thus cannot be legislated against a priori or by some presently "incontestable" empirical considerations. Blanshard himself wrote: "It is hard to set clear limits to what an apparatus as complex as the human body can do without purposive guidance" ("Limits of Naturalism," 26).

II

Blanshard is both a dualistic interactionist and a determinist. His criticisms of epiphenomenalistic dualism are numerous.[20] His determinism asserts four principles, only two of which are important to his views on free will: (1) that every event has a cause, and (2) that the cause of any single event necessitates that event. Consequently, every event is necessitated, which entails that whatever happened, be it a physical event or an action, is the only thing that could have happened or could have been done. This is where Blanshard would seem to be negating our common sense belief that we do on many occasions act of our own free will—which seems to imply that in some sense we could have done otherwise. Later, I shall try to show that unless this sense of "could have" is exactly specified, there are plenty of counterexamples to the thesis that free will implies "could have done otherwise." Blanshard himself supplies some of these. I shall try to show that free will implies "could have done otherwise" when this is properly understood, and yet it does not contradict the apparent implication of Blanshard's necessitarianism, that no one "could have done otherwise" than what he did.

Given Blanshard's interactionism and determinism, he would allow for the following possibilities: that a mental event can be caused or determined by preceding mental events and/or neuro-chemical events, and that the latter can be caused or determined by preceding mental events and/or neurochemical events.

There is one further contention of Blanshard's that, as far as I know, is the first attempt[21] in recent discussions to make the very possibility of acting of one's own free will dependent upon a particular solution to the mind-body problem. I do not agree with his interactionism, but I do applaud his perception that a solution to the free will problem depends upon a solution to the mind-body problem and/or a correct theory of the nature or status of mental states. Other writers on the free will problem, including myself, have failed to connect the two problems. Blanshard has put this point simply: determinism does not threaten free will, but mechanistic determinism does. As he is using "mechanistic," it is equivalent to "purely neuro-chemical causation or determination of actions." For him, mechanism also means that the action was not caused by reason, desire, or attended by intention—which for him belong to the mental realm. Insofar as these determine an action and are not identical with neuro-chemical process, Blanshard would say the action is free even though a huge number of neuro-chemical processes are the final determinants of an action.

Contrary to mechanistic determinism, Blanshard holds that actions are done of one's own free will only when the ideals of morality, beauty, and knowledge enter into the highest levels of psychic causality and supervene upon the lower levels.[22] I take this to mean that something like a Platonic Form enters into our higher mental life (via causality?), which in turn causes psychic phenomena at a lower level, which in turn cause neuro-chemical reactions, which in turn cause actions which are done of one's own free will. Of course, if action is not involved, these Ideals cause higher levels of mental phenomena like the recognition of beauty and morally right action and logical connection between thoughts. Blanshard thinks a man is most free when these ideals are the determinants of his behavior.

Blanshard is not alone in thinking that mechanistic determinism negates free will. Skinner is not only a determinist, but a mechanistic one who denies free will. Of course, many determinists have denied free will (the hard determinists). Some, like R. E. Hobart,[23] argued that the free will, by requiring agency and authorship, in turn requires deterministic relation between a person and his act. A dualist could be a hard determinist and deny free will of any kind, and there are the compatiblists like myself who, unsure of determinism at the macro- or micro-level, still say that an act may be determined and yet be done of one's own free will, of one's own accord or volition, or voluntarily.

In opposition to Blanshard's attempt to reconcile free will with determinism, I am going to present an alternative view of how to reconcile the two. In my entire discussion of mind-body theories in Part I, I went along with the familiar talk of most of today's mind-body theorists, Blanshard included, who speak of the causes of mental events, the causes of brain events, of causal chains of brain events, psycho-physiological causation, psychosomatic causation (the psychological causation of bodily pathology—ulcers, paralysis, etc.). I think it is time to bring into question the sense of all of these phrases. Does anyone really think that a propositional attitude like belief, with all its complexity, is the *cause* of a host of other states, processes, and behaviors that are themselves extremely complicated? Might it not be more correct to speak of a belief as being one of the many *determinants* of a person's action, so that we have as a model statement "Action A was determined by states B, C, D, E, F, . . . n"? However, I am not going to leave this way of talking unchallenged either.

I start with some distinctions that I hope will not change the ground rules. Secondly, instead of accepting Blanshard's thesis that Ideals of morality, beauty, and knowledge enter into the higher levels of psychical causality, I am going to offer a view of mental states that is just as metaphysical, though not as "Platonistic."

First, something about the meaning and truth of determinism. It is standard practice in philosophical writing to define determinism as the thesis that every event has a cause. I depart from this practice by calling this thesis causalism. Determinism is the thesis that every event is determined. Our intuition tells us at once that these two theses are not logically equivalent. Causalism might be false and determinism true, or vice versa. Both could be true, both could be false. Specifically, it is possible that the notion of cause is a low-level concept, a practical concept useful when we are for the most part ignorant of what other states of affairs or conditions existed at the time of which we speak when we say "the dropping of a lighted match caused the forest fire." If we knew a great deal more of the specific chemistry and thermodynamics of that entire situation, and if we had no practical concern in imputing fault to someone, we would express our thoughts about this situation in a deterministic singular, such as, conditions A, B, C, D, E were the determinants of the fire. Such a person might deny ontological status to causal relations, but affirm the ontological status of determining relations. Since I speak of their truth or falsity, you would ask how I can speak in this way without knowing what it is for an event to be caused and what it is for an event to be determined. Now the trouble is that no one knows the answer to either of these questions. Beginning with Hume, Kant, Mill, Ducasse, Blanshard, Hart, and Davidson, attempted to answer the first question only. Using current vernacular, the question became: "What is meant or implied by a causal singular like

> The tremor caused the bridge to collapse

and the variations of the definite and indefinite article depending upon specific information about the tremor and the bridge, held by the listener or reader?" To a listener who knows nothing of a tremor or a bridge in the area, the correct statement is "A tremor caused a bridge to collapse," and to a person who knows about the tremor and who believes that there is only one bridge in the area, this latter statement could be misleading, for he might infer that the speaker was talking about still another tremor and another bridge not known to the listener.

Now the Hume-Mill analysis is that causal singulars entail no connection but regularity between the tremor and the collapse of the bridge. This analysis is disputed by some of those who claim that some kind of necessity is being asserted. One may hold that a causal singular entails both a necessary connection and one of regularity. But necessitarians have not made their case either—the appeal to the supposed counter-factual implication of a causal singular being insufficient.

Hart[24] and Honore deny both points of view. They claim that a causal singular picks out the atypical feature of the environment, in this case the tremor, and relates it to an atypical occurrence, the collapse of a certain bridge which has not collapsed since it was built fifty years ago. Without the necessary embellishments, suppose we accept this view of what a cause is—an atypical event that makes the difference between some normal condition such as the stability of the bridge and the atypical state of its being collapsed. Would we now want to say that in this sense of "cause," every event has a cause? I think not. I jump to the conclusion that in none of the analyses of "cause" by philosophers do we want to say that every event has a cause. This has been the shortest route I could take to present to Blanshard this question: would he want to claim that in his ontology or what *exists* for him *some causal* relations exist even independently of human knowledge? If he accepts the distinction I made between a causal relation and a determining relation, then I think he must pause before answering "yes." For one thing, it is not clear that the statement

The tremor caused the bridge to collapse

entails a necessary connection like: given the tremor, the collapse of the bridge was necessitated by it. Now it has been very tempting to say that the second statement is incomplete. Thus the first statement entails "Given the tremor and all the other (necessary?) conditions, the collapse of the bridge was necessitated."

Now I suggest that the first statement does not entail this amended statement and that those philosophers who thought it did had in mind a deterministic singular of the kind used in physics and astronomy, like "ϕ was determined by α, β, γ," where the warrant for this was some equation where independent variables had been exactly measured, the equation solved, and the value of the dependent variable ϕ was deduced, and thus ϕ, some magnitude, was determined in the physical world. More specifically, such deterministic singulars are like "position and momentum at t_1 were determined by position and momentum at t_0" in accordance with a law-formula. Here *all* the relevant variables are made explicit. There is no picking out one of them, calling it "the cause," and speaking of whatever else is relevant to an outcome or effect as "the other conditions." By and large, people who assert causal singulars do not know what other conditions are relevant. When people first said, "Lightning caused the forest fire," they knew nothing of oxygen. When flint and steel were struck to light a fire, the cause was known, but "the other conditions," "the background conditions" like O_2, the temperature of the spark, were unknown. The tinder *had* to be dry—a necessary condition, but this is not a background condition. And just how dry it had to be was not quantitatively established, so it had to be "dry *enough*," as could be established by touch or smell. Of course if it caught fire, then it was dry enough, sufficiently dry.

So I think Blanshard is far more likely to choose to hold that every event is determined rather than caused. In his ontology, in his theory of what relations exist between events, he would choose determining relations rather than causal relations, because determining relations seem to be necessary relations. Take our position and momentum example. If we can deduce position and momentum at t_1 from position and momentum at t_0, then it is entirely natural to say that position and momentum at t_0 determined or necessitated position and momentum at t_1. We may use the words interchangeably, though the former probably entails the latter in this law-formula context. Having said that position and momentum at t_1 were necessitated, it is awkward to add: "and so were caused—caused by position and momentum at t_0."

One final point. Causal singulars like "The nail caused the puncture" do not entail "given the nail, the puncture could not have helped but occur." But a deterministic singular in law-formula cases like "ϕ was determined by α, β, γ" does seem to entail that given α, β, γ, no other outcome in place of ϕ *could have* occurred. I suppose we didn't need this accessory example of a deterministic singular entailing that something could not have happened, since we have already argued that such a singular might entail that some event was necessitated. But the separate appeals to our linguistic intuitions seem to strengthen the case that two modal notions are entailed by deterministic singulars where a law-formula has a high acceptance and the values of its independent variables are known. But beyond this I plead ignorance. Other kinds of deterministic singulars which I shall briefly consider do not seem to imply that an outcome which is determined is necessitated, or that nothing other could have happened instead of it. Of further possible interest to Blanshard is the fact that while for the most part a causal singular links but one event to one other event, law-formula-type deterministic singulars tell us of the plurality of events or states of affairs that determined some outcome. An oceanographer has told me that some 340 variables are relevant, in varying degrees, of course, to the behavior of tides. Many independent variables may determine a single state of affairs at a given instant—within a specifiable system, I hasten to add, for we may not know or there may not be any consequences at that very instant outside the specified system, whether it be the solar system or a thermodynamic one set up in a laboratory.

I have not brought out the many differences between the meanings of causal and deterministic singulars, but one important difference should be mentioned. No one would contend that deterministic singulars can be established by a single observation; laws or generalizations together with some or a large number of data are required. But causal singulars can be established by one observation, e.g., "The icicle striking the window caused it to break." Now it is important to note that very many causal singulars transform in a regular way into a transitive verb singular where the verb links the two events referred to by definite or indefinite descriptions. Thus the above causal singular transforms into "The falling icicle broke the window." Since I can establish the truth of this singular with one observation, it follows that its causal transform can be so established. This is not always possible with causal transforms, e.g., "The drug depressed him" cannot be established by one observation, and therefore neither can its causal transform "The drug caused him to become depressed." An interesting point of comparison is that while there are many concrete transitive verbs linking events, states of affairs, and facts, that transform into causal singulars, none of them transforms into a deterministic singular. Nor do any of the less concrete transitive verbs when used in singulars transform into deterministic singulars. Obviously, we are dealing with a new breed of cat.

I distinguish two kinds of deterministic singulars—those based on well-established laws and accurately measured independent variables where deductions are quite explicit, from those deterministic singulars where plausible but rough generalizations are used together with a large number of non-quantitative data and perhaps some quantitative data to warrant these singulars. For example: Despite the entirely and yet inconclusively circumstantial evidence against the defendant, the guilty verdict brought in by the jurors was determined by a concert of factors—the jury was all-white, the defendant black; the defendant's prison record, which every juror knew about because of newspaper publicity; the feelings among some of the more dominating jurors that blacks have to be put in their place; and the lack of a credible witness to give him an alibi.

This sort of deterministic singular almost wears its warrant on its face, especially to seasoned lawyers, judges, court reporters, and social psychologists. We see plainly the appeal to rough sociological and psychological generalizations considered true, as well as to facts like the last one, which implies that when a defendant has no alibi but the words of a not-too-credible witness, the jury will not accept the defendant's alibi. It is interesting to note that causal singulars are not usually justified in this way, but by the assertion that in the past occurrences of type A were followed by occurrences of type B under varying circumstances. I have in mind the causal singular "The drug caused him to become depressed," and not those causal singulars verifiable by a single observation.

Another example of a deterministic singular used by knowledgeable people does not link numerous states of affairs to a single outcome: "The nature of American diplomacy from 1930 to 1960 was determined by the structure of the State Department." This claim can be warranted only in the manner of the preceding example. Unlike some causal singulars, no type of deterministic singular can be confirmed by a single observation. And like causal singulars, my last two examples of deterministic singulars do not seem to entail that the state of affairs which was determined was necessitated, or that no other outcome could have occurred.

I think I have said enough to indicate that determinism is different from causalism. This distinction is crucial to any discussion of Heisenberg's indeterminacy principle, to a discussion of the distinction between statistical vs. deterministic laws, and statistical vs. causal laws, which as usually understood are relatively rare. Measles is always caused by virus is acceptable as a generalization, but virus doesn't always cause measles. Decapitation of a mammal always causes death (if the mammal is normal and doesn't have its brain in its chest). It is of course crucial to Blanshard's ontology to ascertain what sort of relation a determining relation is and whether *there are any* true deterministic singulars. Blanshard may conclude that there are no deterministic singulars and thus there is no case of one or more facts determining another fact or facts. He may well hold that the kind of relation he believes to link every fact or event with all other facts or events is not properly described by verbs like "to cause" or "to determine." He can say this and allow that causal and/or deterministic singulars state incomplete truths about relations between events, the linkages between events. I use the word *linkage* here as the most neutral of all to talk about fact- or event-linking verbs such as cause, determine, regulate, control, maintain, destroy, bring into being, produce, stimulate, force, elicit—all very general—and other fact-linking verbs, the very concrete transitive verbs like melt, clean, tear, break, which can appear in fact-linking singulars like "The sun melted the snow," or "The broken-off wing of the plane tore off the roof of my house." I have previously indicated that all of these can be transformed into explicit causal singulars. The semantics of the concept of event-determination dogs us at every step and thus complicates the problem of knowing the truth of any deterministic singular and the truth of the thesis of determinism itself. Appeals to so-called deterministic laws in macro-physics is no help. It hides the question whether in a comprehensive philosophic grasp of such matters there are any deterministic laws.

I raise these problems because Blanshard, in particular, believes that the facts and events of the world are linked, and his most basic perception of this linkage is that it is a logical one, and therefore a necessary one. But he has also used the verbs "to cause" and "to determine" to talk about this linkage.

I am, however, unable to find support in the meanings of these fact- or event-linking verbs, or any support from an analysis of causal or deterministic singulars to accord with his basic notion of the kind of linkage between events he most cares about affirming. So I think he should renounce his claims that this or that event is caused by some other event, or that all events are determined. To express his basic convictions he is using words that fail to do so. Of course he can give any meaning he arbitrarily chooses, but Blanshard has, like Moore, avoided exercising those rights. So often he says "what the plain man means" when he commences the analysis of a philosophic concept. Blanshard has told us that the fact-linkages he believes in are logical linkages; and what appeals most to him about such linkages is that in principle they are the most luminous, therefore the most intelligible, linkages. Thus, for him, the intelligibility of the world consists in the logical linkages between the totality of facts or events.

Now if Blanshard will tolerate my depriving him of the use of words like "cause" in "to cause" or "determine" in "to determine" when speaking of *factual* linkages, I wonder whether he is willing to give up interactionism as he has formulated it. He says that mental states can and do cause other mental states and brain states; and brain states can cause mental and/or other brain states. He has also said that "there are levels of causality," and "the ideals of morality, beauty, and knowledge . . . enter into the highest levels of psychic causality and supervene upon the lower levels."[25]

If I am right, Blanshard is not entitled to make any such claim in trying to analyze the notion of acting of one's own free will. Nor is he entitled to talk about "levels of determination," "psychic determination," "enter into," and "supervene upon." What could these last two expressions mean if he is not allowed to translate them into causal or deterministic language? I am baffled about the passage even if it is fully explicated in causal or deterministic terms.

However, I want to concede to Blanshard that we understand what it is to say that human actions are determined by antecedent mental and neurochemical states and that in some cases we do know a causal singular concerning an action to be true. Naturally, I cannot think of any true statements of the kind "His action was determined by antecedent states α, β, γ." If such a statement were true it would follow, we have for the sake of argument agreed, that the person's action was necessitated by states α, β, γ, and, of seeming importance for the free will problem, the consequence that he could not have acted otherwise.

Those who think of necessitarian determinism as destroying free will have a model before their minds of a set of determining conditions as exacting an action from a person, or of forcing him against his will to do certain things or of making him do what he does not want to do. After all, the necessitarian insists that a man's desires are the chief determinants of his behavior, and where this is so the model of human action his critics construct is one he is not in the least compelled to accept.

Let us agree, then, that mental states, brain states, and bodily states constitute a deterministic system. Their doing so, however, will not guarantee that we will ever fully understand such a system, one reason being the extraordinary complexity of the brain, with its 10 billion neurons, each neuron having an average of 100 axon connections with the dendrites of at least 100 neurons. The number of chemical reactions within the neuron and at the locus of an axon-dendrite bridge on the occasion of our having a certain mental occurrence makes it wildly improbable that when Blanshard and I are thinking the same thought there is any identical pattern of neural firings occurring in our brains. If this is so, then there is no correlation law holding between my thought and my brain state which also holds between Blanshard's thought and what is going on in his brain. I am not merely saying we will be unable to establish such a law, though even if there is a law it would be difficult to establish it. I am saying that for our higher mental states—the propositional attitudes—there are no correlation laws between shared mental states and some neural concomitants. Not only are there no deterministic laws relating the mental and the neural, there are no strong statistical laws.

Secondly, only unreflective common sense has led me to suggest that Blanshard and I could ever share exactly the same mental state. Blanshard's metaphysics entails that this could not happen, because each mental state is unique because it is constituted by its relations with all other mental states, brain states, and physical states of the external world. Another line of philosophical analysis leads to a roughly similar conclusion to that entailed by Blanshard's metaphysics. It is that our propositional attitudes such as doubts, beliefs, thoughts, desires, preferences, decisions, and intentions are conceptually linked to a large number of other beliefs. Likewise, one desire is related to many others and conceptually to many beliefs, doubts, and intentions. Also each of these mental states is causally related to other mental states, brain states, and behaviors in such a way that when a person has a certain desire or intention there are a staggering number of conditional statements that would be true of him—true statements about other mental states and about his behaving in certain ways—if he were to be in certain circumstances which he is not now in. I have to reject our unreflective view that two people can ever share exactly the same mental state. I arrive at this conclusion via the conceptual analysis of each of these propositional attitudes. If because of the complexity of our brains we do not have identical brain states, any more than we have identical fingerprints, and if because of the complexity of higher mental states we do not and cannot have exactly identical mental states, why should there be any correlation laws holding between mental states and brain states, determined and necessitated though each may be by other mental and brain states? These points do not tell against Blanshard's dualism, nor against his necessitarian determinism. They do tell against all type-type identity theories that assume that correlation laws hold between mental and neural states. Nevertheless, I am an identity theorist, a monist, a materialist, a mechanist, but my monism is particularistic. It says that each person's mental state just *is* a very complicated neural state he is in at that time. This view preserves the sanity of the type-type identity theorists who would not allow that mental states can be non-spatial while their necessary and sufficient conditions or neural determinants were spatially located. My view also preserves what interactionism and identity theorists share, namely a desire to hold a theory that accords efficacy to mental states. My view says indeed that they are efficacious because they *are* brain states—desires can explain actions because they can cause or be determinants or at least partial determinants of actions. And my view denies what every neuro-physiological researcher denies—namely that there could be chemical processes in the brain that could only be explained by resorting to phantom events; that is, mental events as conceived by the dualist. For me the most important necessary condition for an act to be done of one's own free will is that the act be done in accordance with (or determined by) a desire; and I want my desires to be flesh-and-blood realities, which dualism couldn't admit. Blanshard has said that *mechanistic* determinism negates freedom. I disagree. I want to grant him his determinism of human behavior, but assert mechanism too, because in Blanshard's sense of "mechanistic" my particularistic monism or particularistic identity theory is assuredly mechanistic, in that it holds that the very highest mental states, the propositional attitudes, are perhaps just terribly complex states of protein molecules, and terribly numerous chemical reactions at perhaps millions of synaptic junctions. We have never known such a complicated system. We know what the geniuses of the race have done. We have no knowledge that anything was involved in their creations except the activity of their brains—adding non-physical mental states and processes adds nothing to our understanding of Mozart. I give anyone all of the mental states—dualistically conceived—to play around with so that by using them he can try to construct a theory to explain Mozart's musical accomplishment. No one will take my offer, because we already sense the bankruptcy of this approach. Even Blanshard does not try to use mental states to explain Mozart's musical intuitions. Instead, he reaches beyond the mental entirely into the highest levels of psychic causality. Well, he does this to explain what a person's highest freedom consists of. My alternative is to say that his ordinary everyday acting of his own free will is acting in accordance with desires (this does not translate into "doing actions that are caused or determined by desires"—only a psychological theory can propose and justify that translation)—and in accordance only with those desires his system of desires or values approves of his possessing or acting on in certain circumstances.

I don't see how I act of my own free will if something outside of me enters into the highest levels of psychic causality and supervenes upon the lower levels (of psychic causality and/or neural processes—or do these lower levels of psychic causality determine neural states, which in turn determine certain kinds of actions which we say we did of our own free will or voluntarily or quite willingly?). If Blanshard's account thus far contained no mysteries, he would still have to add that every free action was an action done in accordance with one or more desires (or, I'll grant him, "was an action *determined* by one or more desires along with many other psychic and neural determinants").

Not only is every free action done in accordance with one or more of one's desires, but these desires themselves, and acting on them in appropriate circumstances, must be approved by more basic desires or by one's system of desires and values. This is, I think, the most important necessary condition for acting of one's own free will. Of course, one must be conscious and must know what one is doing, and intend it, and no internal or external condition such as psychosis or torture must be a partial determinant of one's action.

For me desires are persisting, extremely numerous, and complicated neuro-chemical states or processes. They are formed from experience together with past conditioning and/or genetic physiological endowment. My desires for truth, righteousness, and beauty do not originate in me because certain abstract ideals or Platonic Ideas enter or ingress into the highest levels of psychic causality. Their origin is far more pedestrian—I am reared in a culture which through teachers, books, moral training, and exposure to the arts produces these desires in me; and what has been produced in me are these vastly complicated, persisting neural states in which, under circumstances that our culture tries to make possible for its citizens, I perform acts of my own free will such as studying, trying to write philosophy, or trying to do what I know to be the morally right thing. In doing these things I am most free because my actions are done in accordance with desires which, all other desires considered, I desire to act upon. That all of this is brain at work demeans it not one whit.

Thus for me a man acting of his own free will is a vast system of molecules acting of its own free will. I once nearly included in an essay the statement: A person's being depressed is matter (highly unusual matter and arranged in ways as yet too complicated for our understanding) in a state of depression. I thought it acerb, but now I believe it to be apt.

To this line of thought it might be objected that since acting of one's own free will is understood in my materialistic way, we may someday know all the neuro-chemical concomitants of this kind of action, and thus drop "free will" from our vocabulary. First, I doubt that the neural "concomitants" are the same for any two freely acting persons. But even if they were, it does not follow that we would have to learn and use the neuro-chemical vocabulary, nor would we have to change our views that one important necessary condition to having acted freely is that we did what we desired to desire to do. So mechanistic determinism is no threat to acting of one's own free will. Mechanism could only be a threat to our concept of free will and our use of that term if it entailed that we do not act in accordance with the desires we desire to possess (desires being construed as neural states). If mechanism entailed that desires do not exist even as neural states, then it would threaten freedom. But instead of entailing that desires do not exist, it insists that they do. Again, mechanism could threaten free action if it could show that our ordinary concept of desire is mythical, like the concepts of phlogiston or ether, or that the concept was self-contradictory. But mechanism or particularistic monism entails none of these and thus does not compromise free will. Could mechanistic determinism compromise our belief in free will by showing that desires, considered as neural states, are incapable of being incorporated into a neural theory which was extremely powerful in explaining those human actions which the appeal to desire never completely explains, while also explaining a vast variety of human phenomena, speech learning, Mozart's productivity, etc.? In other words, this neural theory can do without the concept of desire; thus from the standpoint of this theory, desires do not exist. And where desires do not exist, there can be no actions done of one's own free will. And if no free actions can be asserted in this powerful neural theory, what happens to the common-sense reality of such actions? The ontological difficulties that arise here are severe and complex. This is why I said earlier that the solution to the free will problem depends upon a solution to the mind-body problem.

What about the "could have done otherwise" supposedly implied by free will and the "could not have done otherwise" supposedly implied by the concept of event-determination? I am not wholly convinced that the supposed implications hold. Perhaps when we understand the meaning of these implications better than we now do, we can be more certain that they do or do not hold. I am, however, willing to go along with today's philosophical majority in agreeing to these implications. Apparently Blanshard does too, since his concept of event-determination, which I have urged is closer to his metaphysical outlook than event-causation, entails that nothing could have happened except what did happen. And this is his reason for denying free will as ordinarily understood to imply that a person could have acted otherwise under the very same circumstances under which he did act. I am sufficiently close in my sympathies to event-determination so that the difference between that thesis and the kind of probabilistic Pythagoreanism which I do espouse makes little difference to the free-will issue. I think that the latter metaphysics, allowing for Peircean "gappiness" as it does, would be consistent with the view that if there were strong statistical laws of human behavior, we might easily say: "given the antecedent conditions, he couldn't have done otherwise." It might be said that we are changing the meaning of "couldn't have done otherwise," but I answer: "not very much." Practically this means that if out of a sample of 10,000 men who under specified conditions of torture, only one failed to yield to his captors, it would not be inappropriate to say of any of the others who yielded that they could not have done otherwise, and of the 10,001st man who yields under the specified torture that he could not have done otherwise either.

Those who think that the notion of acting of one's own free will implies that one could have done otherwise have to explain apparent counter-examples that somehow do not bother us. If someone jumps into a torrent and saves a child from death, he might say: "I couldn't have stood there and watched that child drown." I don't think we can say that he didn't act of his own free will unless we have information that he was "beside himself" with anguish. Rather, we interpret his statement to mean that it would have been contrary to his conscience and sympathies to have made no effort to save the child. Again, a young man very much wants a Jaguar sports car within a certain price range. He locates one that has all the features he desires, and the price is right. He buys it and says to a friend: "I just couldn't have passed up this baby." Are we to infer that he did not act of his own free will? No, we say that what he means is that it would have been contrary to reason to desire something having certain features and then not satisfy that desire when he has the unimpeded opportunity to do so. Again, there is the historically controversial case of Luther's saying before Emperor Charles V: "*Ich kann nicht anders.*"[26] Who would argue that this implies that Luther did not act of his own free will? Instead, we would interpret him as saying that his action flowed from his entire moral, theological, philosophical nature—that it was an act that flowed from his very essence—that to act otherwise would have been in contradiction to his entire nature or his most essential nature. So it is apparent that saying "He could not have done otherwise" does not always entail the denial of free will, which supposedly entails "could have done otherwise." In fact, we may even say that Luther's behavior was determined by his principal desires and values, and still say he acted freely, and I believe that, apart from other metaphysical commitments, Blanshard would agree with this analysis of the Luther case.

What then might be meant by the "could have done otherwise" supposedly implied by free will? Either we deny the implication altogether, or deny our analysis of the Luther case, or try to show that the "could not have done otherwise" of Luther and Blanshard is not the true contradictory of the "could have done otherwise" implied by free will. This last option is typically compatibilist. Since Moore, the line of reconciliation taken by the compatibilist has been to analyze "could have done otherwise" into a conditional statement like "If I had wanted to, I would have done otherwise." The determinist would agree that such an analysis reconciles the "could not have done otherwise" of determinism with the "could have done otherwise" of free will. But the determinist and others have severely criticized this analysis.

When we say: "I could have done otherwise," we often intend to make a categorical statement which is the exact contradictory of that use of "could not have done otherwise," not as this is entailed by event-determination, but as it is used in everyday life by those who have tried desperately hard to do otherwise and failed, or by one who says: "I know that no matter how hard I had tried to succeed in doing it, I would have failed," and the more general: "No matter how hard anyone had tried to do otherwise, he would have failed." Failure in the face of a great effort not to fail or in the knowledge of the fact that great effort would not have averted failure is the best ground anyone can ever have for saying "I could not have done otherwise." This is sometimes the entire ground we have for excusing tortured or brainwashed or severely coerced persons from wrongdoing. We say they could not have done otherwise. *This* is the "could not have done otherwise" which contradicts the "could have done otherwise" of free will. When a man is in circumstances, like torture, that lead to his confessing to his captors, and we know he has *tried* to avoid the confession, tried to intercept or cancel the influence of the torture upon his actions, we conclude that his confessing was inevitable, i.e., that which will happen despite efforts to prevent it. Tidal waves, hurricanes, and earthquakes are inevitable because no known human agency can prevent their occurrence. The belief that they are determined does not entail that they are inevitable. Nor does the fact that a man's action is determined entail that it was inevitable. But we do say his action was inevitable when he tried hard to avoid doing it and that no matter how hard others had tried to help him avoid confessing, they would not have succeeded.

So when we say that we acted of our own free will and thus could have done otherwise, we are denying not that our action was determined, but that it was an inevitable action—that it is the case that we tried to avoid doing it but failed. On the contrary, we may have made an effort to do it, since doing it was what we most desired at that moment. Our criterion for saying "he could have done otherwise" in the sense in which this is supposedly entailed by "He did A of his own free will" consists in the absence of the inevitability of his doing A. Apart from beliefs in determinism, we have criteria for saying that a man could not have done otherwise, and asserting this on the basis of these criteria is a practice more ancient than our belief in determinism. These primary criteria are: he tried hard and failed; had he tried hard he would have failed; and, no matter how hard anyone had tried, he would have failed. I cannot imagine better reasons for saying that someone could not have acted differently. Our notions of the extent and limits of human capacity are based upon what people have done when they made an effort, and what they failed to do even when they tried. These primary criteria have been employed to yield secondary criteria for saying that someone could not have done otherwise, e.g., when he is tortured, brainwashed, coerced by threats to his life, acting in a state of gross panic, etc. Thus the criteria for saying that a man could have done otherwise are the negations of all of these primary and secondary criteria. It is this sense of "could have done otherwise" which is always implied by saying "He did it of his own free will." I do not believe there is another sense implied by free will.

Blanshard's views on moral responsibility are ones I share. The fact that I become angry and resentful toward those who act wrongly speaks more to my un-Spinozistic training and the failure to make my feelings conform to my philosophical views. I don't think any philosopher believes that his feelings of anger, resentment, envy, and retribution should dominate his moral philosophy, moral psychology, or his metaphysics. I am thinking here of those who argue from the "fact" of a man's moral responsibility to the falsity of determinism.

Of course, there is a difference in a murder committed by a madman, a hired killer, and one who murders his beloved wife because of a rage started by an inauspicious quarrel. As Strawson says,[27] we can and do take different moral stances toward these three cases, and it would be a pity if because of a belief in determinism, we treated the last two the same as the madman—with no resentment. He argues that when we no longer view a person's bad actions with resentment, we think of him as less than a person. Perhaps we now do, but although Strawson makes a strong case for this, I see no necessity in this if we were trained differently. In any case, I am not impressed with the concept of a person in societies that garrote, hang, and electrocute people who have violated laws, or that send them to brutalizing and filthy prisons.

The test case is this: suppose a man commits a crime, and in scientifically reconstructing the independent variables of the action, we conclude that anyone who instantiated those variables would have acted as he did. Where is the basis for *blaming* the murderer? Yes, he did it freely, knowingly, intentionally, and in accordance with his desires, but if everyone in that total situation were also to have acted freely, etc., in committing murder, how can we single out one person for blame? This argument has more force if we find out that 50 percent of the population are committing some crime, say tax evasion, in the face of severe penalties for the many who are caught and convicted. Because of the high percentage of evaders from all social and economic classes, and particularly the more influential economic classes, what would happen to the severity of the penalties? They would decrease just as the penalties for smoking marihuana decreased markedly when it became commonplace among the children of the upper economic classes. Our approval of punishing certain offenders is closely tied to our beliefs about the probability of our performing a criminal act. If we thought the probabilities were high that we or our spouses, children, close relatives, and friends would perform criminal acts and would go to jail, we would lower the penalties to fines or we would abolish that punitive law altogether. But those who make the laws and influence law-makers for the most part believe that the probability is very low that *they* will ever commit a crime, and so they are unconcerned about the penalties inflicted on those who do commit crimes, persons mostly from the lower classes with whose problems they cannot empathize. In this kind of context it is easy to speak of a man's blameworthiness for his crimes. In the former kind of case, we would expect to hear less about the blameworthiness of the tax evaders who constitute 50 percent of all those who fill out tax forms, and who are economically powerful enough to influence judges, legislators, all the media, and thus public opinion.

Now I have assumed a case where science has discovered the determinants of a certain type of crime and one then asks: where is the moral blameworthiness of a man who does exactly what anyone else instantiating his internal and environmental variables would have done? Well, Blanshard as a determinist and I myself generalize from this case by saying that whatever crime a man commits, there were determinants for it such that if they were instantiated in anyone else, he too would have committed a crime of that type. If blameworthiness is problematic in the scientifically analyzed case and we also make the supposition that 50 percent of the population will at one time or another instantiate crime-producing determinants and will thus commit a crime, then from the determinist's point of view, blameworthiness is a philosophically and morally disreputable concept to apply to human beings.

FRANCIS V. RAAB

DEPARTMENT OF PHILOSOPHY
UNIVERSITY OF ARIZONA

NOTES

[1]*The Explanation of Behavior* (Atlantic Highlands, N.J.: Humanities Press, 1964), see esp. chaps. 6–11.
[2]Ibid., 269.
[3]"Is Consciousness a Brain Process?" *British Journal of Psychology* 47 (February 1956).
[4]*The 'Mental' and the 'Physical'*, Minnesota Studies in the Philosophy of Science, vol. 2 (1958).
[5]"Sensations and Brain Processes," *Philosophical Review* 68 (1959).

[6]"The Limits of Naturalism," in *Mind, Science, and History,* eds. H. E. Kiefer and M. K. Munitz (Albany: State University of New York Press, 1970), 3–33.

[7]*The 'Mental' and the 'Physical',* 428.

[8]"Sensations and Brain Processes," 142–43.

[9]"Minds and Machines," in *Dimensions of Mind,* ed. Sidney Hook (New York: New York University Press, 1960), 166.

[10]R. B. Onians, *Origins of European Thought,* 2d ed. (Cambridge: University Press, 1954). Bruno Snell, *The Discovery of the Mind* (Cambridge: Harvard University Press, 1953).

[11]"Problems of Empiricism," in *Beyond the Edge of Certainty,* ed. R. G. Colodny (Englewood Cliffs, N.J.: Prentice-Hall, 1965), 186–206.

[12]"Does 'Consciousness' Exist?" in *The Writings of William James,* ed. John McDermott (New York: Random House, Modern Library, 1968), 169.

[13]*The Analysis of Mind* (London: George Allen & Unwin; New York: Macmillan Co., 1921), 23.

[14]I discuss this problem in detail in "Of Minds and Molecules," *Philosophy of Science* 32 (1965): 63–68.

[15]"A Plea for Excuses," in *Philosophical Papers,* eds. J. O. Urmson and G. J. Warnock (Oxford: Clarendon Press, 1961), 133.

[16]I owe this analogy to my friend and colleague Henry C. Byerly.

[17]"Explaining Behavior," *Philosophical Review* 76 (Jan. 1967): 104.

[18]For an interesting discussion see H. Hochberg, "Of Mind and Myth," *Methodos* 11 (1959).

[19]Take the sentence: "The thought occurred to me that there is a sick tiger in the baggage car." This sentence has three marks of intentionality. Neither this sentence nor its denial entails (1) the existence or nonexistence of tigers or (2) the truth or falsity of the embedded "that"-clause. (3) Even though tigers are the largest carnivores in India, it does not follow from the truth of the quoted sentence that "The thought occurred to me that there is a sick specimen of the largest carnivores of India in the baggage car." For amplification on these marks see R. M. Chisholm, *Perceiving: A Philosophical Study* (Ithaca: Cornell University Press, 1957), chap. 11.

[20]"The Limits of Naturalism."

[21]Given in February 1957 as an address entitled "The Case for Determinism," and published in *Determinism and Freedom,* ed. Sidney Hook (New York: New York University Press, 1958).

[22]Ibid., 14–15.

[23]"Free Will as Involving Determinism and Inconceivable Without It," *Mind* 43 (1934).

[24]*Causation in the Law,* chap. 2 (Oxford: Clarendon Press, 1959).

[25]"The Case for Determinism," 14–15.

[26]D. B. Terrell and Gareth Mathews simultaneously called my attention to this example.

[27]In "Freedom and Resentment" in *Studies in the Philosophy of Thought and Action,* ed. P. F. Strawson (New York: Oxford University Press, 1968).

21. Reply to Francis V. Raab

Blanshard's Theory of Mind and Free Will

The persistence of behaviorism in the twentieth century is an anomaly and an anachronism. In its robuster forms the theory affirms that consciousness does not exist, and all that does exist is matter. It seems to me, on the contrary, that everything we immediately experience has been successfully shown to be mental. Most people would admit that their loves and hates, pains and pleasures, hopes and fears, memories and expectations, purposes and decisions, images and dreams, are mental. I think it has also been shown that perceptions and percepta are mental. Some objects of sensation, such as colors and sounds, shapes and sizes, were taken by "new realists" in the early days of the century to be independent of mind. The leading figure among them, Bertrand Russell, had reversed himself on this point by 1948 and concluded that everything of which we are directly aware is mental. Here I agree. When someone tells me that consciousness or experience is unreal and that the only reality is matter, he seems to me to be talking the language of irresponsible metaphysical paradox. The material world, the world of electrons and ions, of quanta and sound waves and light waves, lies at the ends of numerous and often fragile inferences from experience; it is an epistemological "dangler" hanging somewhat precariously from the stable world of common sense, every bit of which is mental.

Anachronistic Behaviorism

Why this unseasonable resurrection of a theory refuted times without number? The main reason, I suspect, is the general prostration before natural science. That such science is worthy of respect, admiration, enthusiasm, I of course agree; it and its stepchild, technology, have made the world we live in possible. And if science could get rid of consciousness, it would have disposed of the only stumbling block to its universal application. Scientific method offers its results as open to public verification. If a person alleges that he has discovered a stripeless zebra, or a ghost, or an inflammable asbestos, he must be ready to submit his results to the critical observation of others. Now when he claims to have a headache or to be thinking of Socrates or feeling dejection, no other persons can verify his claim. They could verify it only if his having a headache or thinking of Socrates or feeling dejection could be identified with some perceptible bodily movement such as a grimace or a movement of the lips or at the worst some change in the brain or nervous system. If such identification cannot be made, consider the strange position in which the natural scientist finds himself. If a man claims to be in converse with Satan or the Archangel Gabriel, the scientist cannot disprove his claim; if a man says he felt a pain because he stepped on a tack, the scientist will say a neural chain of events occurred that can be followed to the brain, but there it will end in a realm that is publicly invisible; if the man claimed to have lifted his arm because he wanted to remove his pipe, the scientist, if he accepts it, must suppose that a causal movement began in the brain with nothing that is even potentially observable to start it. All this, to the natural scientist, sounds like a fairy story. And it could all be dispelled by the simple expedient of identifying psychical process with physical change.

To this there is only one objection, though a rather important one, namely that it is nonsense. By this I do not mean that it is nonsense like saying that the moon is made of green cheese, which seems at any rate logically possible, or like taking a man for his twin, which needs no ingenuity, or like saying that the morning star is the evening star, which is not nonsense at all, but the assigning of differing attributes to the same thing. I mean that behaviorism is nonsense in the way in which Christian Science is nonsense when it denies that anything is really evil; it is nonsense logically, and therefore ultimately and abysmally; it is nonsense in the way in which it would be nonsense to say that the color blue was in A-sharp, or that a loud explosion occurred in silence. One can deny the existence of matter without, so far as I see, committing oneself to any self-contradiction, though the argument for it is less than conclusive. But one cannot deny the existence of consciousness without at least implicitly contradicting oneself in a peculiarly conspicuous way, since the judgment that there is no consciousness is so obviously a conscious act. Obviously? Yes. That such conscious acts are different from any sort of matter in motion is, I should hold, self-evident.

Mr. Raab well knows my views on behaviorism, to which I have returned repeatedly in the past forty years. But he has meditated long and acutely on the problem of body and mind and has convinced himself that in some of the newer identity theories the nonsense of the older theories can, with the aid of logical and linguistic subtleties unknown to the Watsons and the Skinners, be effectively evaded. Clearly my main business here is to ask if this is so.

New Attacks on Dualism

Mr. Raab's opening statement of what these new theories are attempting to establish puzzles me. He says: "a statement of the type 'Mental state X *is* brain state Y,' which means that 'Mental state X and brain state Y are one and the same state,' is a synthetic, identity statement which can be established once correlation laws have been discovered connecting the mental states with brain states." But any proof of identity that depends on correlation laws is surely self-contradictory. Only if X and Y are admittedly different can correlation laws be established between them; a course of events cannot be related by laws of correlation to itself. Again, the main thesis regarding identity is said to be "a synthetic, identity statement." This seems to me self-contradictory again. If the statement were described as analytic, that would leave room at least for identity of denotation, as does "A bachelor is an unmarried man." But in a synthetic judgment the predicate is by definition neither the same as the subject nor included in it.

Mr. Raab goes on, however, to explain why, in the opinion of the proponents of identity, dualist ways of thinking must be given up. He gives three reasons. First, "dualism would give us very peculiar correlation laws connecting mental states with brain states because what would be correlated would be something very simple, like pain, and extremely complex neural events." Why should this be regarded as "peculiar"? There are many examples of it even on the purely physical level. A billiard ball may be struck simultaneously by a large number of marbles; the result may be simple; it may move off in a straight line; but its cause is very complex—the impact of a large number of smaller bodies coming from many directions. Secondly, laws of correlation would in this case be "nomological danglers," which means, I take it, that they would be without further effect on the physical order. But this assumes a one-way body-mind causation which is both improbable in itself and at odds with common sense. Thirdly, dualism is to be ruled out since "science . . . would not accord [these events] any efficacy because the true cause of any behavior would always have to be some neural events." But this begs the question against interactionism, and since interactionism seems to common sense (and to me) the only plausible position, I will not for the present linger over it.

Mr. Raab next proceeds to state "the identity theorists' most important argument." It runs as follows: Suppose we have a superneurophysiologist who finds that a certain type of brain event is always accompanied by a certain type of pain, which he discovers "either by personal report or by the observation of someone's overt behavior." From the correlation laws so discovered between nerve processes and mental processes he can predict when the pain will occur and even what mental processes, for example nausea, will follow it. "Under these circumstances it would be proper to say that the pain and this brain state were one and the same state." I confess that I cannot see even a tendency in this sort of argument to prove the conclusion suggested. That one series of events uniformly accompanies another series, so that one can predict from a knowledge of the one series what will happen in the other, does not imply that we do not have two series but one. Secondly, we are told that the pain and the brain state are correlated; but once again, an event cannot be correlated with itself. Thirdly, that the subject is experiencing pain is discovered, we are told, by personal report or by the observation of the patient's overt behavior. But if the pain *is* the event in the brain, why should our superneurophysiologist have to rely on such methods? In knowing the brain event he would know all there is to know.

Mr. Raab seeks to render the identity theory more plausible by adding: "This type of reduction was twice accomplished in nineteenth-century physics—the reduction of molar gas theory to statistical mechanics and the reduction of physical optics to electro-magnetic theory." Since he says a little more about the first than the second, let us confine ourselves to that. We thrust our hand into a hot oven, get the sensation of intense heat, and say that the air inside has a high temperature. Now what is temperature? Mr. Raab gives us the physicist's answer, that "the temperature of a gas and its mean molecular momentum are one and the same state." Now it is undoubtedly true that the physical temperature of a gas, what makes the mercury rise or fall in a thermometer, is the speed with which the particles of the gas are moving. But this does not mean a "reduction" of felt hotness to molecular motion. If this example proves anything, it is the opposite of what the identity theorists are maintaining. When one thrusts one's hand into the oven and says it is very hot, one is talking about an intense but familiar kind of sensation; when one says, with the physicists, that the temperature is high, one means that the air particles are moving with high velocity. "Hot" in the experienced sense and "hot" in the physical sense are as different as two things could be. If the example is to be relevant, it must show that these things have somehow been reduced to identity; and they clearly have not been. That heat in the physical sense is the *cause* of heat in the experienced sense is of course true, but to say even that is to give up the case for identity, since an effect cannot be reduced to its own cause.

The Linguistic Approach

Mr. Raab next explores the linguistic approach to the problem. He points out correctly that much of the language we use about mental events is physical language: "He is empty-headed"; "he has a clear head"; "the tune kept running through his head." Though this is physical language, it is used metaphorically, and everyone understands it as referring to mental facts. But suppose mentalistic language were to disappear completely, and we used physical terms exclusively; would not the old mentalistic meaning disappear too? He borrows an example from Hilary Putnam, who agrees that the statement " 'Pain *is* C-fiber stimulation' is semantically deviant in English," which means, I take it, that it violates our actual and ordinary meaning. But look several centuries ahead, when "the correlations between mental states and brain states will have become a matter of common knowledge. May it not come to pass that people will use the expressions 'pain' and 'C-fiber stimulation' interchangeably? And when they do, won't these expressions gradually become synonymous? . . . Later on 'pain' might be dropped from common usage and become an archaic word." Now I am quite ready to entertain the hypothesis that we might come to use the phrase "C-fiber stimulation" whenever we wanted to refer to our own or another's pain. What is the inference that Mr. Raab draws from this? It is one or other of the following: (a) that by changing the word by which we refer to pain, we may change the reference of the word, so that whereas before we referred to a type of consciousness, we now refer exclusively to a physical event, or (b) that by the change in the word we abolish the difference itself between the mental and the physical events. If the inference is (a), it seems to me fantastically improbable. For the plain man, the only importance or interest attaching to "C-fiber stimulation" is that it is associated with an intensely disagreeable experience; and the suggestion that he should cease to think about or mention that experience because the word used to refer to it also refers to a physiological event about which as such he cares nothing plays fast and loose with human nature. If the inference is (b), it is no more persuasive. There have been physicalists, to be sure, who thought (i) that mental events could all be correlated with physical events; (ii) that statements about mental events could somehow be "translated" into statements about physical events; (iii) that translatability meant identity of content; and therefore (iv) that mental events *were* physical events. I have considered the logic of this procedure in *Reason and Analysis* (212–20). It is based on the theory that one can change the nature of things by changing the words in which we refer to them. Since I cannot believe that Mr. Raab would take such a theory seriously, I shall not stop to refute it again.

He does seem to think, however, that another variant of the identity theory is worth discussing which makes even shorter work of dualism. He cites Mr. Feyerabend as having held that if you are to discuss whether two things are identical you must at least start with two things, and that in this case there are no two things to start with. You are a scientist considering whether the organism commonly called Jones is conscious or not. You can hear this body talk and see it move (whatever these mean to a materialist), but even with your best observations you never observe its so-called mental states. The scientist, therefore, in his proud intellectual rigor, will say that "These mental states can have no reality for him as an observer, and so mental-state brain-state correlation laws are as mythical as laws correlating the presence of phlogiston with oxidation of metals." There were persons who actually took this position when "logical" positivism was in its first bright dawn; they would not professionally admit that their wives or children were conscious because they did not and could not observe any such consciousness in them or attached to them. Of course these philosophers were kindly human beings who would never dream of acting on their shrewd discovery that other human beings were automata. But if I knew that a certain person did practically believe this, I should give him a wide berth. I do not see why, if he got me alone, he should not proceed to cut me into small pieces; my pain would be as truly a myth to him as phlogiston, and the suffering my death produced in others would be likewise pure myth. I am no worshiper of common sense, but I am far more certain that the man of common sense is right in insisting that his human and animal friends have feelings than that any logical prestidigitation is valid which "proves" the nonexistence of other minds.

An Argument from Analogy

After these preliminary explorations of identity theories, Mr. Raab comes to his own theory, which turns out to be very close to them. His aim, he says, with a sound sense of economy, is to find a theory that explains the facts with the simplest and fewest postulates; and he thinks the theory that best achieves this aim is a thoroughgoing scientific materialism. The great objection to this theory, he considers, is the obstinate conviction of plain men that entities like pains and thoughts are irreducibly different from entities like knee jerks or electrochemical movements in nerve fibers. He therefore sets out first to show that seeming differences of equal depth have appeared in the past and have been intellectually overcome. As his prime example he takes two apparently different meanings of the magnetization of a bar. The physicist strokes a bar with a magnet, and finds that the bar has acquired new properties. It will now deflect the needle of a compass that is near it and rearrange the iron filings on a plate that is above it. How is such change of behavior to be accounted for? The plain man will probably say vaguely that it is by a "state of magnetization" newly achieved by the bar. The physicist, on the other hand, knows that it is the result of a certain "spin" of the electrons in the atoms composing the bar. The question then arises, "Is the magnetized state of the bar one and the same thing as the state of the electrons in the molecules of which it is composed?" The plain man and the physicist will give different answers. The plain man, knowing nothing of the physics of the case, will attribute the new behavior of the bar to the state of magnetization, which will be for him quite different from the overt behavior which evinces it. The physicist will realize that the state of magnetization *reduces to* or *is* the spin of the electrons, which is enough in itself to give a full explanation of the bar's new behavior. The indefinite state of magnetization assumed by the plain man is quietly dispensed with, and the behavior of the bar, microscopic and macroscopic, is seen as one continuous event.

The parallel here with mind and body seems to Mr. Raab illuminating. Because of the intelligent responses of a certain organism, we attribute to it a mind which, though unobserved, is taken to account for them. The physiologist, however, knows that whenever this macrobehavior occurs certain changes are taking place in the cortex of the organism. Are there two processes here or one? The plain man will naturally say "two," since he knows nothing of the cortical conditions of the macrobehavior he has observed. He is thus attributing to the organism a state that no more exists as a separate entity than the "magnetization" he attributes to the iron bar. The scientist knows that such an entity is superfluous, and that what arouses the intelligent behavior is not an invisible and intangible mind, but the functioning of microscopic changes in the nervous system.

I am sorry to say that this elaborate analogy seems to me of little help, since it breaks down at the vital point. The reduction of the "magnetization" of the bar to the action of electrons that partially compose it is a reduction that occurs wholly within the physical order, and once the physicist has had his say, the supposition of an unobserved special state to account for the behavior of the bar is plainly gratuitous. But the ascription of consciousness is not in the least gratuitous. Though we cannot observe it in other organisms, we have the most vivid awareness of it in ourselves, and every reason to infer that similar states occur in others. Indeed there is no more intense reality in the world than that of an agonizing pain, and for anyone to abolish this by identifying it with the howls and grimaces that may evince it or with the electrochemical pulsations that condition it is, in argument, impermissible. Mr. Raab seems to concede this when he says of his analogy: "The parallel with the mind-body problem is obvious. Only the puzzles surrounding the issue of how correct first-person mentalistic statements can be made without criteria prevent a perfect analogy." Unfortunately these "first-person mentalistic statements" not only prevent "a perfect analogy"; they ruin it altogether. The plain man's "magnetized state" is a mere improvisation, like the "dormitive power" ascribed to sleeping pills to explain their putting one to sleep. Consciousness is, both psychologically and logically, the most undeniable reality in the world.

Varying Criteria for Truth

Mr. Raab has just spoken of the puzzles attending first person statements of conscious experience "without criteria" for the truth of these statements. And he suggests that perhaps these puzzles prove so difficult because there is no agreement about the criteria for their truth. He points out that at least three different criteria are in use, the "conventional" or commonsense one, which he does not further define, the criterion which accepts a proposition as true if and only if its denoting terms point to what actually exists, and finally the criterion of coherence. Now I do not see that this diversity of criterion has any significance here. I should be willing to let Mr. Raab choose his own criterion, for as applied to the existence of mental states they all give the same result. If it is the conventional criterion that is used, an unambiguous answer is returned, as Mr. Raab agrees; the plain man would simply say, "*Of course* I have pains and pleasures, and I have no doubt that the people around me have them too." What then if we apply the second criterion, that of the existence of denoted terms? Here a great to-do is possible as long as one is concerned with the question of other minds. But I should be content to say with Mr. Malcolm, as quoted by Mr. Raab, "It is preposterous to think that it could be shown that people do not have desires, purposes, fears or goals." But we do not have to depend on the inference to other minds, however certain, to assure ourselves of the existence of denoted conscious states. If someone asks how I know that what is denoted in "I now have an intense and throbbing toothache" actually exists, I should say (after a pause of astonishment at being asked such a question): "Because I am directly sensing and feeling it in the most vivid way." If the questioner is a Christian Scientist and insists that I am suffering an illusion, I should reply that the illusion of pain may be as painful and is as certainly a mental existent as the pain itself. Of course if one means by existence the sort of existence possessed by chairs and tables in the physical order, this reply would lack force, but then so would the argument, since it would beg the question outrageously. So let us turn to the third criterion, the appeal to coherence. The result will still be the same. Try to deny the existence of conscious events and see how consistent your position is. You will contradict yourself implicitly in your very first statement, since denial itself is a mental event. If the materialist replies that this begs the question, since on his own view all is physical, ask him just what is the movement of matter with which a logical negation is identical, and according to whether he has more sense or less, he will capitulate at once or take cover under the sophistries of physicalists in the forties, who finally abandoned the theory themselves. And if you recognize that denial is a mental event in yourself, how can you consistently withhold such events from others? If you attempt it, you will find yourself riddled with incoherences, ethical as well as logical. The conclusion is that on any of the criteria Mr. Raab offers us for the truth of judgments of mental existence, the result is the same—their unambiguous ratification.

Interactionism

Mr. Raab turns next to the interaction theory, which is held by common sense and some form of which seems to me inescapable. His objections to the theory are two: (a) that if a decision affects the body, it must do so in a very strange and indirect way, and (b) that at best it can provide only a necessary, not a sufficient, condition.

(a) It is true that when I deliberately lift my arm, though the volition seems to take effect directly on my arm, this cannot be true. The volition acts, if at all, through a certain region of the cortex, as becomes evident if that region is paralyzed. And how the volition affects the nervous process no one has the least idea. But our ignorance of how consciousness affects behavior does not show that it has no influence at all. For (i) as Mr. Raab would admit, we are in virtually complete darkness as to how causes produce their effects generally; but that does not lead us to deny causation. (ii) An interaction of this kind, though moving in the opposite direction, is one of the commonest of occurrences. If I open my eyes for an instant on a landscape, I take in a large assortment of items at once. How the waves striking my retina give rise to an impulse, and how this impulse is transmitted to a small region at the back of my head can be traced in some detail; but how the nervous webwork in the back of my head gives rise to the perception of the landscape is utterly unknown. Nevertheless few scientists would deny that such production of mental states occurs constantly, however different in quality the cause and effect may be. If it occurs in one direction, what difficulty is there in principle in its occurring in the other direction also?

(b) It is true that all the interactionist would claim is that the volition is a *necessary* condition of lifting the arm, not a *sufficient* one. (i) But Mr. Raab would probably agree that necessary conditions are all that is provided by any causal law at all. As Mill pointed out, the cause in any actual case is the convergence of many different lines of causation, though in causal explanations the efficient cause alone is commonly mentioned. In freely admitting that the psychical cause does not act alone but must cooperate with physical causes in order to produce its physical effect, the interactionist is thus only following a universal practice, not admitting a special defect. (ii) It may be insisted: how do you know that the volition is even a necessary condition? Here I think we must listen to the voice of common sense. The plain man would say that he can sometimes "see" with something approaching certainty that the angry words he spoke to another would not have been uttered if he had not felt angry; that he would not have bought that shirt in the store window if he had not felt a desire for it. It is perhaps conceivable that he would have marched into the shop and bought the shirt even if he had been an automaton, but he knows he is not an automaton; and one of the reasons he knows it is that he makes conscious decisions which his body follows up with a high degree of regularity. If the same regularity were found between two physical phenomena, we should not hesitate to ascribe a causal connection. Why should it be denied when the antecedent happens to be mental?

Objections to "Mentalistic Language"

Mr. Raab enumerates in rapid succession a series of brief objections to the use of "mentalistic language." To deal with these in detail would take more space than can be afforded here, but it is perhaps better to reply briefly than not to reply at all.

(1) "Trying to predict human behavior in mentalistic terms is quite unreliable." True, but this is only what is to be expected in view of the hidden character of the cooperating causes, which consist largely in subconscious mental states and inexactly known physical ones. And consider how much has been done to meet this objection within the last generation or two; one need only mention Freud.

(2) We cannot check mental causes. "If a man says that the thought of his mother's death caused him to become depressed, we have no way of knowing (nor has he) whether this thought was the cause and not some other thought, or some drug, brain condition, or incident." I should have thought that the man's report in a case like this could be accepted fairly safely on the strength of Mill's method of difference. But apart from this, the variety and comparative inaccessibility of the causes, and the limitations placed on experiments with human beings, are enough in themselves to account for the difficulty in checking causes.

(3) "Serious definitional problems have existed for nearly a century and these problems are not due to the open textured character of the terms themselves." I am not clear as to what terms are here in question. If they are such terms as "consciousness," "experience," and "pain" they may be admitted to be indefinable, but no more so than "time" and "space," which figure freely in physical contexts. If they are the images, memories, and feelings of another mind, which are private to him and no doubt qualitatively different from our own, we can seldom be quite sure about them, but this uncertainty applies rather to their precise character than to their existence.

(4) "For a long time there has been considerable doubt or at least uneasiness about the referent of mentalistic terms." Such doubt is due in part to genuine differences in experience; it has been alleged that behaviorists can

skim with such facility over imagery because they lack it themselves; but it is also due in part to a stubborn conviction that for "the unity of science" all but physicalistic terms must be excluded. But the "unity" is factitious and arbitrary, and unless it is scientific to ignore inconvenient facts, the "science" is unscientific.

(5) "The other-minds problem exists because of the peculiar nature of the verification of mentalistic terms. If neural terms replaced them, the verification would be public." (a) It would certainly not be public in any very practical or usable way. How accessible to my observation are the neuronic changes in your cortex? (b) I do not myself believe that if a surgeon and I were jointly to inspect your brain, what we saw would even then be public in any strict sense. Neither the act nor the object of his perception is identical with mine, nor is either identical with what the physicist means by an event taking place in nature. (c) To suppose that I am verifying the presence in your mind of a feeling or an image by looking at the neuronic movements is, from my point of view, to beg the question yet again.

(6) "Occurrences of thoughts and images are not locatable in space nor anywhere in the brain." True. Neither is the proposition $2+2=4$, yet it has its own kind of being; it is a reality which we can contemplate; and we cannot justly ignore it because of its ontological oddity. Nor can we ignore for similar reasons such entities as thoughts and images.

Near the end of Section I, Mr. Raab reminds us of the difference of clearness that we have about differing mental states. Thoughts, for example, have become so heavily barnacled with theory that it is very difficult to see them for what they are, or in Mr. Raab's case, to be sure they exist. "Thus I wish to leave a trail of doubt," he says, "that we know that there are such things as thoughts and intentions because we directly experience them." He finds it harder to deny, however, that we do directly experience pain. Now it must be admitted that some mental states are much more difficult to introspect and describe than others. But if someone were to ask me whether at the present moment I am entertaining the thought of a friend I saw yesterday or am intending to take a certain journey at the end of the month, I could say yes to either question with the utmost confidence. I have written a book about thought which involved me in much introspection, some of which, as I owned, I found difficult and baffling. But the notion that one cannot with clarity and profit introspect a thought or a train of thought is so much at odds with my experience that I find it difficult to follow Mr. Raab's "trail of doubt" about them. Instead of being dubious and exotic entities they seem to me among the staples of common life.

Pains, he says, are another matter; the claim that they are directly experienced is accepted by almost everyone. To meet this formidable consensus he returns to a linguistic argument which he has used before, and in which he feels a confidence that puzzles me. He thinks that even with people who "wince, groan, curse, and clutch the finger they just hit with a hammer" there is "no logical barrier" to giving a completely neural description of what they are going through, and that "instead of saying in certain circumstances, 'I am experiencing anger,' a person could be taught to say in these circumstances, 'I am experiencing a rise in my blood adrenalin titer.'" Such a person might come to lose the very idea of what we now call pain. "If so, we can dispense with the concept of pain and the ontic commitment to something which is nonneural. No one could still reasonably insist: 'But you are experiencing something besides neural state X.'"

I suppose it shows how hopeless is my "ontic commitment" to "mentalistic events" that I cannot take this argument seriously. As I have intimated already, even if you were to train a boy to use nothing at all but physical expressions, so that when he brought the hammer down on his finger he would describe the incident in the coldest language of Gray's *Anatomy,* he would still mean by that language primarily that he was suffering an intense pain. He would have no particular interest in the physiological event in his finger if it did not happen to be connected with the aggressive and engulfing experience of this pain. And if people insisted on taking him to mean nothing but the physiological event, he would show a Shakespearean inventiveness in language to make others understand what he was talking about.

I hope I have not offended Mr. Raab by repeating this "everlasting No" to his extension of his hand toward the identity theory. If it will ease his feeling about my intransigeance to know that I should also repudiate a Cartesian dualism of substance, I shall gladly do so. But that mental characteristics are not the same as the movements of matter in my body seems to me as clear as that chalk is not cheese. How my cortex gives rise to these thoughts of mine, why I should see blue when I look at the sky, why I should hear sounds or feel delight when someone at the keyboard plays Brahms, I confess—with the memory of reassuring similar confessions of Adrian, Penfield, and Sherrington—that I have not the flimsiest idea. But that is neither here nor there. My thought on this subject is not a northeast movement of an electrochemical current through my frontal lobes at 100 feet per second; my sensation of blue is not the same as any motion in my retina, optic nerves, or occiput; the Brahms that I hear and enjoy is not the blows of the hammer bone on the anvil bone in my ear. And Mr. Raab, as I have known him, seems to me much too clear a head to go on playing with a theory so incredible that only a clever man would ever have thought of it.

Determinism

Mr. Raab thinks that anyone with my views on matter and mind should have strong views on determinism too.

He is right. Unless my desire to comfort a friend, which is *not* an electrochemical swoosh across a synapse, can move me to say certain words conveying kindness to another, we may as well emigrate at once to Mr. Skinner's Utopia of Anaesthesia-upon-the-Lethe, where we are beyond dignity and all other values. But I am surprised at the form my determinism takes when applied to moral action. Having supposed I was a determinist of the old simple-minded variety, without any ifs or buts, I suddenly find myself espousing a theory of formidable sophistication.

What I thought I was saying was: "I am a determinist in the old sweeping sense in which all events have causes. I add, to be sure, one important qualification. These causes *logically necessitate* their effects."

(a) Mr. Raab accepts my generalization; he does not accept my qualification. One psychic event causing or necessitating another is out; I can point to no observed instance of anything of the sort. I can point to Mill's strings of single effects. Instances of uniform or varying concomitance can be gathered in plenty. But I can adduce no instances of causing, let alone causing with logical necessity. Mr. Raab seems to think it even contradictory to try, since an observed example would be a sensible one, and a necessitating relation would not be an object of that kind.

To which my reply is an ever-respectful "Nonsense!" I have been producing instances to the precise specification of my critics for years. My stock instance, though a crucial one, is the case where, from what is given, an inference is completed. You can sometimes see clearly that the relation of necessity between premise and conclusion is an essential part of the cause why the conclusion appears. (I will not be put off by the question-begging reply that you have seen the conclusion to be entailed by the premise, and that is why the conclusion appears. You cannot explain the appearance of a conclusion by assuming that it has already appeared.) Or suppose you are getting the eighth power of two by successive multiplication. The process is plainly necessary; its guiding pressure of necessity can be felt at each step; it is a causal process in which necessity, *logical* necessity, contributes. It is just what Hume and Mr. Raab declare impossible, a causal process whose steps are seen to be necessary.

(b) "Now if Blanshard will tolerate my depriving him of the use of words like 'cause . . .' or 'determine . . .' when speaking of *factual* linkages, I wonder whether he is willing to give up interactionism as he has formulated it. . . . He has also said that 'there are levels of causality,' and 'the ideals of morality, beauty, and knowledge . . . enter into the highest levels of psychic causality and supervene upon the lower levels.' "

The answer to Mr. Raab's wonder is No. I do not think I have been deprived of my sense of "necessary cause or determination," and in talking about my insight causing action, or causation acting on higher levels, I think

I am talking sense—far more sensible sense than my critics. Suppose that an amendment is presented to the Constitution at the polls. Suppose I see (or think I see) that the goods accruing from the amendment far outweigh its evils, and that in consequence it is my duty to vote for the amendment. Here is a case in which insight into comparative value actually determines my choice. Of course Mr. Skinner says the sense of duty or the feeling of romance or the soldier's sense of honor never makes a difference to what is done. For these are figments of the unscientific imagination.

(c) Mr. Raab is willing to admit that he has free will in the sense that he sometimes does what he desires. He admits that desire is massively connected with the self. A desire may be connected with a hundred other likings, repulsions, prejudices, hopes, and fears, and what backs a certain choice may be a host of feelings linked in an unravelable tangle. But it is to be remembered that this is the plain man talking, and not Mr. Raab. For Mr. Raab now admits, I wince to realize, that when he talks about desires he is not talking about desires at all. He is really talking about the cerebral conditions and correlates of desire. The brain consists, he tells us, of some ten billion neurons, and each of these neurons is connected to its neighbors by numberless synapses over which energy flows in endless flux and reflux. When Mr. Raab speaks of a desire, he is really speaking of an immensely complex set of material particles in motion. He is quite ready to describe this as a mechanical system, governed of course by mechanical law. In such a system consciousness plays no part: ". . . adding nonphysical mental states and processes adds nothing to our understanding of Mozart."

What has happened to my good friend Raab? Partly, I suspect, he has suffered a sunstroke of the current mania about words. He thinks we can change the meaning of "chalk" to "cheese" if we keep at it sedulously enough and for enough generations. And so we *can* change the meaning of our words. Whenever we speak about a desire, we may mean a million neurons firing across a million synapses. But that won't make chalk into cheese or desire into moving particles. Sometimes brooders over these matters seem to think that while it is palpable nonsense to say that one neuron or one passage across a synapse is a desire, it just might be that a million of them milling about might make a desire. Sheer confusion again.

Mr. Raab seems to think it makes no difference whether we recognize the distinct existence of a desire or not. It reminds me of James's "mechanical sweetheart" of seventy-five years ago. James had been reading some of Watson's lurid literature about these things, and it occurred to him to ask what a sensible American girl would have to say on the point. She suddenly realizes that her lover, though enfolding her in the same dulcet sounds, though expressing every care for her preferences and her comfort, though exchanging professions of undying love for her, is really a machine without one kindly feeling, sensation, or thought. James is surely right. This is not her lover. She would flee from the horrid thing in terror, made more terrible by the thought that what was pursuing her was not a lover but a death's head.

And what a shambles all this would make of the moral life! We are monsters of many kinds; but that Mr. Raab is not a machine of this kind I am sure. He is not a programmed computer, even IBM's brightest and best.

22 BLANSHARD'S THEORY OF CAUSATION
Richard Taylor

A critic of Blanshard's thought can hardly begin with anything but admiration, even though, as in the present case, he may find himself quite at odds with the philosopher's basic approach. Blanshard stands as a model of what a philosopher ought to be—always lucid, free of dogmatism and contentiousness, profound, and above everything else, intellectually courageous, never yielding to the solicitations of intellectual fads, never seeking simple and trite solutions, never losing sight of his great goal of rational comprehension or doubting its attainability.

If we look at Blanshard's thought in the general context of philosophy in America, then try to fix the significance of philosophy in the larger context of the intellectual life of our nation, I think it is fair to say that while the latter—art, music, literature, jurisprudence, social and political theory—has flourished, simultaneously giving to and taking from the cultural revolution in which we have been living, academic philosophy has in the meantime withdrawn into almost total irrelevancy and decay, no longer heeded by anyone except as an object of derision and, when not pitied by those who have chosen more promising paths, simply ignored. It would hardly occur to anyone today to turn to philosophy for understanding and light on anything. Even philosophers have largely abandoned the intellectual aspirations of an earlier decade, and retreated into fastidious problems of logic and language having significance to none but themselves, and rather little even of that, beyond the exigencies of livelihood. Within this overwhelming philosophical prosaism and Philistinism, Blanshard's philosophy stands with the constancy of gold, and its author can still declare with unabashed sincerity that all he is trying to do is "understand the world,"[1] which he does not for a moment doubt is a rational system ("Internal Relations" ["IR"], 228).

The Theory of Causation

Blanshard's opinions on causation are fundamental to his philosophy. He believes that everything in the universe, throughout its infinite space and time, is connected with everything—indeed, that everything is thus connected with everything else by relations of *logical necessity,* which is precisely what renders the world intelligible ("IR," 228ff.). Given this rather awesome metaphysics, it is not difficult to surmise what his theory of causation is going to be.

Blanshard believes:

(1) that every event in the universe is causally related to every other, such that (a) given any two events whatever, however remote from each other in space and time, if either had not occurred, then the other would not have occurred exactly as it did ("IR," 228 ff.); and (b) given all the events that have occurred up to any time t_1, any event that occurs at t_1 could not fail to occur—which is simply the thesis of determinism (*Reason and Analysis* [*RA*], 453, 467);

(2) that the connection between cause and effect is not merely one of invariant concomitance but of logical necessity, such that with sufficient knowledge and acumen one could rationally deduce from either what the other *must* be ("IR," 232);

(3) that the link of necessity between cause and effect can be neither seen, felt, tasted, detected, nor otherwise apprehended by sense, but it can nevertheless be "surmised" (with "probability") that some "filament" or "trace" of it is always there (*RA,* 449, 453, 454, 456, 465, 466, 471; "IR," 223, 230, 234);

(4) that the cause of any given event is not merely some other one event that is conspicuous, novel, or within our control, but rather the entire totality of those conditions, each of which is *necessary* for the occurrence of the event in question (the *conditiones sine quibus non*), this totality then being *sufficient* (*RA,* 453); and

(5) that if there were not this filament of necessity connecting all causes with their effects, then the constancy or invariance of familiar causal connections would be a sheer miracle, an "outrageous run of luck," comparable to having an honest die turn up the same throughout millions of throws (*RA,* 465 ff.; "IR," 234).

I am going to comment on these opinions in the order (1), (3), (4), (5), (2), saving the second until last because it is the most important and most controversial, and will need to be studied with the greatest care.

(1) The universality of causation. The view that everything in the universe causally affects or is affected by everything else can of course neither be proved nor disproved, either scientifically or metaphysically. The law of universal gravitation suggests it (see "IR," 231), but then there is no way of proving that this law expresses a literally true assertion. It may be that the housefly now resting on my desk top is causally related to a minnow now resting in a

pond in China (see "IR," 229), but nothing could be more plainly impossible than a proof of this. No empirical test would be likely to yield any proof of it, or indeed, even the smallest hint of it. The assertion that it is true, therefore, could only be made on the basis of the sweeping general statement that *every* item in the universe is thus causally connected with any other item whatever; and of course the statement about the fly and the minnow does logically follow from this one. But then it is, after all, precisely that sweeping statement whose truth is in question. *It* can neither be proved nor disproved. There are considerations, such as some of the suppositions of physical science, that certainly suggest it to a philosophical mind, and Blanshard has pointed these out (e.g. "IR," 231–32), but supplied nothing more.

I think the same may be said with respect to the assertion of causal determinism. This too is an opinion that has been widely held in philosophy, and also among scientists, even though there never has been or could be a non-question-begging proof of its truth, because of the very character of the assertion itself. It is an opinion concerning *every* event that ever has or ever will happen in the history of the universe. This is not the sort of thing one attempts to establish by an inspection of cases. One instead tries to show how it follows from certain other statements, which must of course be no less general or sweeping, if they are to do what is needed here. But then, just in case there should be an event—just one—which happens not to be causally determined, not only is the thesis of universal determinism overthrown *but also the very premises from which it was deduced.* And no one can show that there is *not* such an event. (I happen to believe that such events are fairly common.) Obviously, then, no one *knows* that this thesis is true. It cannot be proved empirically, for obvious reasons, and every argument must in the nature of the case be question-begging.

Suppose, for example, that a tiny amoeba, advancing in its characteristically protean way through its environment, gradually moves off to the right. Is it permissible to suppose that, under precisely the circumstances in which it veered off to the right, it might have moved to the left instead, or continued more or less straight, or stopped, or even perhaps have reversed course? *Impossible,* the determinist has to say, and Blanshard even says such a thing is *logically* impossible. With sufficient knowledge and acumen, he claims ("IR," 228, 230–32), a rational mind could see that the animal *had* to go to the right. Anything else was logically impossible.

Now my question is, how could anyone know that?

There are, it would seem, only two ways this could be known. First, one could actually *find what it was* (if anything) that caused the rightward motion—some obstacle in the amoeba's path, for example, that permitted of no other course; or some irritant, from which it could escape in only this way; or some attractant, causally sufficient for the motion observed—something of that sort. But suppose, as is common enough, that the most careful inspection of the situation reveals nothing like this, discloses nothing at all that would suggest, even to the most prodigious intellect, this particular direction of motion rather than any other.

In that case, the philosophical determinist has to declare: But this event *had* to have *some* cause, after all (see *RA,* 467); it couldn't just *happen;* and the fact that we cannot discover what it is does not show that it is not there.

We can of course concede the third of these statements, and perhaps the second; but what reason has Blanshard or anyone for affirming the first, namely, that it *had* to have *some* cause? It seems clear that the only basis for that declaration is the presupposition that *every* event, and hence this one, has a cause. But that, after all, was the question at issue.

(3) *The invisibility of the filaments and traces of necessity.* Blanshard frequently concedes that the necessary connection between cause and effect can be neither seen, felt, tasted, nor otherwise detected by sense, and must therefore be surmised or inferred (with probability), at least to the extent that there must be "filaments" or "traces" of it present (*RA,* 449, 453, 456; "IR," 230).

I am deeply puzzled by the concession that the causal connection between events, considered as a relation of necessity, cannot be seen, felt, tasted, and so on. What on earth would it be like to *see* it or *feel* it?

In fact, the commonest and least controversial relations between things can be neither seen, felt, nor tasted, and yet no one supposes that it takes a metaphysician to infer filaments or traces of them.

Consider, for example, the relationship consisting of one thing *being taller than* another. Suppose there are two trees, A and B, standing side by side; B is completely overshadowed by A, being, let us suppose, only about ten feet high, while its neighbor is perhaps sixty. Now we can surely say: (i) that A is taller than B; (ii) that this is an observable fact, that is, something easily confirmable by observation—one needs only to look, to see that the one tree is taller than the other; and yet (iii) that the relation *being taller than* can neither be seen, felt, nor tasted. One can see (or feel or taste) the trees. One can see that the one is taller than the other—though in a different sense of "see," it should be noted. But one cannot in *any* sense see some third thing there (perhaps hovering between the two trees someplace?), a thing which is named "being taller than." Nor can one feel it. Or taste it.

Clearly these observations would provide no occasion for a philosopher gravely to discourse: "I will concede that the relation *being taller than* can neither be seen, felt, nor tasted. Yet I think there are considerations which enable the rational mind to surmise or infer, at least with probability, that it is there, or at least that there is present some filament or trace of it." Against such an imaginary philosopher, two points would be in order.

The *first* would be that the expression *being taller than* denotes not a thing but a relation of things: its invisibility therefore results not from its being something hidden, recondite, esoteric, or metaphysical, and thus inferable only with probability from metaphysical considerations, but from the most elementary understanding of the distinction between *things* and the *relations* of things.

The *second* point would be that, in seeing two trees, one of which happens to be much taller than the other, one can *also* (normally) see *that* one is taller than the other, without this requiring (absurdly) that one be able to see (or feel or taste), in addition to the two trees, *that very relation itself.*

Having made these two points, in response to the fanciful metaphysician who talks about the relation *being taller than,* shall we not make the corresponding points to the real metaphysician, Blanshard, who talks about the relation *being causally necessitated by*?

Thus, *first*: The expression *being causally necessitated by* denotes not a thing or event but a relation between things or events; its invisibility therefore results not from its being hidden, recondite, esoteric, or metaphysical, and thus inferable only with probability from metaphysical considerations, but from the most elementary understanding of the distinction between things or events and the relations of things or events.

And *second*: In seeing two events, one of which happens to be caused by another, one can also (sometimes) see *that* one is causally necessitated by the other, without this requiring (absurdly) that one be able to see (or feel or taste), in addition to the two events, that very relationship itself of causal necessitation.

Thus: Suppose that, holding a nice straight, strong nail, point down, against a block of soft wood, the way one normally would if he wanted to drive the nail into the wood, I then deliver to its head a strong, square blow with a good hammer. The nail sinks into the wood, as I was pretty sure it was going to.

Concerning what has transpired, we can say: *First,* that I can *see* the hammerhead coming into violent contact with the head of the nail, firmly and squarely, and I can also *see* the nail sink into the wood. Those are both events. I do not also see something called "causal necessitation" relating these two events. But the reason I do not see this is *not* (a) because it does not exist, i.e. because the blow of the hammer did *not* necessitate the nail's sinking into the wood, for it most assuredly did; nor (b) because it is something obscure, hidden, esoteric, some metaphysical "filament" connecting the two events, and inferable (only with probability) on the basis of certain a priori considerations drawn from metaphysics.

The reason I do not see (or taste or feel) this relationship of causal necessitation between the two events is simply because it is a relation, not a thing or event.

But *second*: We can say that I can see *that* the nail's sinking is causally necessitated by its being hit by that hammer in just that manner. It is perfectly obvious, to anyone who knows what a nail is, what a hammer is, and what a soft block of wood is. If anyone were to ask, What made the nail go into the wood? we would only need to describe what we had seen, *and the question would be answered* (see *RA*, 465). If the questioner, being shown the nail, hammer, and wood, were then to ask to have the relationship of causal necessitation laid out alongside these, for him to see (or feel or taste), this would only indicate, not that he possessed great and subtle philosophical sophistication, but that he had quite stupidly failed to understand the description just given.

So it can be seen that I hold about the same opinion as Blanshard concerning the necessitation of an effect by its cause, but I arrive at it by a rather less circuitous and metaphysical route.

Finally, however, something should be said about Blanshard's choice of such expressions as "filament" and "trace" as applied to anything like a relationship of necessitation (*RA*, 453, 456; "IR," 230). Necessity, whether it be causal or logical or whatever, either *obtains* or does *not*. It cannot hold tenuously, in filaments or traces. Indeed, the very notion of a *filament* of logical necessity, which can only invite comparison with a big thick glob of the stuff, seems utterly bizarre.

(4) The multiplicity and complexity of causal conditions. Blanshard points out that the cause of an event can be considered as nothing less than the sum total of all the conditions causally necessary for its occurrence, rather than some one or more of these that happen to be conspicuous or novel, and he cites J. S. Mill's well known argument for this (*RA*, 453). The cause of the nail's sinking into the wood, for example, is not merely the blow of the hammer; it includes also the softness of the wood, the hardness and sharpness of the nail, and other things as well.[2]

This is surely true, and worth saying often. A correlative point Blanshard makes, however, that is less plausible is that the conditions necessary for the occurrence of an event are in sum total *sufficient* for its occurrence (*RA*, 453). I think neither he nor anyone else knows that this is true, and I think it is probably false. Consider, for example, some event (perhaps our aforesaid amoeba motion) for which, let us suppose, sufficient conditions do not obtain, or one which is such that, in precisely the conditions in which it occurred, it might have failed to occur. (Blanshard thinks no such events ever happen, but that is neither here nor there. I think they are fairly common, but that is likewise irrelevant here.) Assuming such an event might occur, there must nevertheless be conditions *necessary* for its occurrence, and hence a sum total of such conditions—which falls short of sufficiency. A necessary condition of the amoeba's turning right just as it did, for example, was its being alive. Another was its being unhindered in that direction. And so on. But just in case there was no set of conditions sufficient for that event, as we for the moment are supposing, then the sum of those necessary conditions was *not* sufficient.

If, incidentally, one says here, as Hobbes did, that the sum of the conditions necessary for an event's occurring *must* be sufficient, *because, admittedly, no more are necessary,* then he commits a delightful fallacy; but I am not aware that Blanshard has ever fallen into that one.

(5) *Necessity versus tychism.* Blanshard sometimes invokes an argument that seems at first a vast oversimplification of the issues. He is obviously fond of it, and while my first reaction to it was utter disbelief, I have since concluded that it is apparently correct. I am not sure it proves that the connection between causes and their effects is one of *logical* necessity, as Blanshard believes, but it does appear to support the idea that causes do necessitate their effects, that is to say, render them inevitable. Perhaps the difference between Blanshard and myself is that he has a wider notion than I do of logical necessity, such that, for him, it would comprehend what I call inevitability, in which case any dispute would be merely verbal.

Blanshard's argument is that there must, surely, be a necessary connection between causes and their effects, for if there were not, then the constancy and invariance of familiar causal relations would be nothing but an "outrageous run of luck" (an expression taken from Montague), comparable to getting the same result in millions of throws of an honest die (*RA,* 471; "IR," 234). Either there is this necessary connection between the hammer blow and the nail's sinking, for instance, or there is no telling *what* might happen the next time someone bangs a nail with a hammer; it might ignite, melt, or turn into a fairy. But since we feel pretty sure that nails are going to go on responding to hammer blows the way they usually do, there must be this trace of necessity in that causal relation. And the same with all other causal relations. Or at least, Blanshard says, we may consider it probable ("IR," 234, 236; *RA,* 471).

At first this seemed to me altogether too easy. Blanshard's opponents, I thought, do after all recognize invariance as at least part, perhaps all, of the causal relation; and this is quite enough to ensure the invariance which Blanshard seems to think is imperiled by their view. But *this* is what is too easy, and Blanshard, I think, is dead right.

All that follows, from the mere fact that events of kind A have always, in similar circumstances, been accompanied by events of kind B, is that there has been this invariance. If we suppose that such a conjuction is the result of a causal connection between A and B, then we are supposing that had A *not* happened in one of those instances, given only the other things that did happen, B would not have happened either, and moreover, that given that A *did* happen in all of those instances, then, given the other things that did happen, but those only, B *had* to happen. And to put the thing that way is certainly to assert a stronger relationship between causes and their effects than mere constant conjunction. It is to affirm that, given a certain event A (e.g. the blow of the hammer on the nail head, under the conditions previously considered), then another event B (viz. the sinking of the nail into the wood) *cannot fail* to occur; and that, given that the event A does *not* occur, under precisely those conditions and no others, then the other event, B, *cannot* occur.

But again, it can be doubted whether these modal terms express a logical necessity. I am accustomed to think of it as simply a causal necessity, which seems to me quite enough. Blanshard's basic point, however, does remain.

(2) The necessity of the causal connection. I turn finally to what appears to be Blanshard's basic argument for his opinion: that there is a *logically necessary connection* between every cause and its effect.

I have already indicated that I concur in this view, though I omit the qualifier "logically," as I do not know what it means in this context. That is, I am quite sure, as Blanshard is, that causes necessitate the occurrence of their effects, or render them inevitable. I do not believe, however, that Blanshard's favorite argument for this proves what it is supposed to prove.

The argument, so far as I know, is Blanshard's invention, and he obviously considers it a trenchant one. If it is, then I have surely missed something. I have turned this argument over and over in my mind, until I feel quite certain that I have got it straight, and it still appears to me simply invalid.

I shall quote in its entirety the clearest version of it that I have found, then exhibit where it seems to me to come apart. The argument is this:

> Reasoning or inference is a series of events in time in which one passes from judgment A, a psychical occurrence, to judgment B, another. The emergence of judgment B is an event which, like other events, has its cause. I suppose no one would question that part of this cause is the presence to one's mind of the premiss or premisses a moment earlier. Suppose someone points out to you that no insects have eight legs and that a spider does; the rather surprising conclusion darts into your mind, "Then a spider is not an insect." To say that the presence of the premisses had nothing causally to do with the appearance of the conclusion would be absurd. To say that this causal relation resolves itself into one of regular association seems to me equally absurd; the association may never have presented itself to you before. I think you can see, as the conclusion appears, one condition why it did appear, namely that the premisses logically required it. The nontemporal relation of necessity linking the contents of the judgments was a condition that channeled the temporal process of inference in the course it took. One cannot

give an adequate causal account without including necessity as a part of it.
["IR," 233]

Let us consider in a somewhat systematic way the things that are being said
here.

Let A be an event consisting of the judgment, that is, the psychical occurrence, occurring in your mind at a certain time t_1, to the effect that spiders
have eight legs but that no insect does.

Let B be another event, consisting of the judgment, that is, the psychical
occurrence, occurring in (or "darting" into) your mind at a certain time t_2, to
the effect that a spider is not an insect. (The darting of this thought into your
mind might be accompanied by a feeling of surprise, as Blanshard suggests;
this does not matter.)

And suppose that the cause of A, the first psychical occurrence, is
someone's "pointing out to you" (presumably uttering the words) that no insects have eight legs, though spiders do. That is, you are caused to make this
judgment, at t_1, by someone doing something, namely, pointing something
out to you, whatever that might consist in.

Now concerning what we are supposing has here transpired, Blanshard
says:

(a) That B, a certain (psychical) event occurring at a certain time, was at
least in part caused by A, which was a different (psychical) event at a time
presumably preceding the occurrence of B. He expresses this by saying that it
would be "absurd" to deny that the premises have something causally to do
with the "appearance" of the conclusion.

This point appears unexceptionable.

(b) That this causal connection between these two psychical events in your
mind cannot be resolved into a connection of regular association, for "the
association may never have presented itself to you before."

This point too seems unexceptionable, and it can be illustrated, as
Blanshard has himself illustrated it elsewhere (*RA*, 458), in this way: If I say
to myself, "do, re, mi" then it is almost inevitable that "fa" will at once pop
into my mind, simply because of the association that this concatenation of
syllables has acquired in my mind from past repetitions. The relationship of
A and B in the present case, however, cannot be of this kind, for the reason
given. It is obviously a stronger connection.

All this, I think, we should grant.

(c) That the two premises and the conclusion of the argument cited here
for illustration are logically connected; that is, that between the two
statements,

(i) No insects have eight legs,

(ii) Spiders have eight legs,

and the third statement,

(iii) A spider is not an insect,

there is a logical connection. And of course there is; the first two statements logically entail the third. It is a valid syllogism.

So we should grant this.

(d) That this logical connection between (i) and (ii), on the one hand, and (iii), on the other, was *one* of the causal conditions responsible for the occurrence of B, that is, the psychical occurrence consisting of the "darting" into your mind of the very thought expressed in statement (iii).

Blanshard expresses this idea in several ways, perhaps the clearest being that this relationship of logical necessity connecting what is expressed in the statements (i), (ii), and (iii) was one of the causal conditions that "channeled the temporal process of inference in the course it took."

And this, too, seems unexceptionable. It is, no doubt, the very fact that (i) and (ii) entail (iii)—or perhaps more precisely, the fact that you believe this entailment to hold, and also believe what is expressed in the premises—that induces you to accept the conclusion.

And finally,

(e) That a causal account of the series of events described—certain psychical occurrences in your mind—cannot therefore be given "without including necessity as a part of it."

And this, too, seems unexceptionable. There *is* a logical necessity uniting (iii) to the conjunction of (i) and (ii), and it has something to do with your assenting to (iii).

On the basis of all this Blanshard says, on the page following, that this one example "is enough to show that Hume was wrong," wrong, that is, in denying that there is any necessary connection between causes and their effects—*between, for example, events A and B in the description just given.*

But *now* we ask, Where is the thing that was going to be proved? We were going to be shown two or more events occurring in time, two psychical events, A and B, occurring in one's mind, in the present case (these we have been shown), causally connected with each other (this, too, we have been shown); and then we were going to be shown that this causal connection between these two events A and B, occurring in time, is one of *logical necessity.* This, so far as I can see, we have *not* yet been shown. Instead we have been shown that the argument about spiders is a logically valid syllogism (which of course it is), that the premises of this simple syllogism have a logical connection to the conclusion, enabling the latter to be validly drawn from the former (which is another way of saying the same thing), and that the validity of this syllogism is one of the causal conditions for the emergence (darting) of B into one's mind (which it doubtless is).

But none of this, however interesting and unexceptionable, adds up to the further claim, the sort of claim denied by Hume, that the two psychical occurrences A and B, occurring at different times in someone's mind, admittedly related as cause to effect, are *also* related by logical necessity. This conclusion, so far as I can see, has yet to emerge; and I do not quite see how it is going to make it.

It seems to me that what has happened here is this: A syllogism has been presented, and its validity noted; two psychical events of judging have been presented, related to each other causally; and then these two things—the syllogism, on the one hand, and the mental illation, on the other—have been jumbled up together as though they were one and the same thing, the sole justification for this being, truly but irrelevantly, that sometimes the validity of an argument can causally influence a reasonable man in drawing the conclusion he in fact draws.

RICHARD TAYLOR

TRUMANSBURG, N.Y.

NOTES

[1]"Internal Relations and Their Importance to Philosophy," *Review of Metaphysics* 21, no. 2 (Dec. 1967): 227. Henceforth referred to as "IR."

[2]It being, I believe, Blanshard's view that everything in the world is necessary to everything else, such that, if anything were different, everything else would be different too, then the cause of an event must on this view, I believe, be considered nothing short of the entire world together, just at or just prior to the occurrence of the event in question.

22. Reply to Richard Taylor

Blanshard's Theory of Causation

My philosophy must be an irritant to Richard Taylor at many points, for my views on ethics, metaphysics, and the theory of knowledge differ deeply from his. Yet he combines this depth of difference with an appreciation of what I have done or tried to do that is generous in the extreme. I will not argue with him about that, but take it as evidence, which is occasionally needed and is always refreshing, that philosophers can differ profoundly without losing respect or even affection for each other.

It is my theory of causality that Mr. Taylor has chosen for attention, and causality has been a special interest of his on which he has written a number of illuminating papers. He raises five questions about my theory, of which the last is the most pointed. I will follow his order of treatment in my reply.

The Universality of Causation

1. I have ventured to hold that every event in the universe is causally connected, directly or indirectly, with every other. This Mr. Taylor thinks a bare possibility, though he also thinks the evidence overwhelmingly against it. He even questions the law of causality itself, namely that every event has a cause, which is the main ground of determinism. Let us consider the latter point first.

The determinist holds that every volition is caused. Why does he hold this? Not, of course, because he has inspected every act of will and found a cause at work, nor even because in any single act he could show that its every component was caused. He believes what he does because he knows that a volition is an event and believes that all events are caused. But what right has he to believe *this*? If it is hard to prove that all acts of will are caused, it is surely much harder to prove the vastly more general proposition that all events whatever are caused. No doubt we assume the truth of this proposition continually and successfully in the work of science. A new and strange disease breaks out in a community, and physicians begin to search at once for the cause. How do they know there is a cause to be found at all? They don't, Mr. Taylor replies. What they implicitly argue is that whenever the body has in the past begun to behave queerly, a cause of some kind has been brought to light for it, and hence a cause must be at work here too. But that clearly does not follow. It follows only if the major premise is supplied, and we get the syllogism: All events have causes; this case of disease is an event; therefore this disease must have a cause. And that major premise is still unproved. Hence every attempt to prove inductively that a given event has a cause begs the question scandalously.

This has been clear since Hume, and Mr. Taylor thinks it would be well if scientists took it more seriously. They forget that the law of universal causation (every event is caused) is only an assumption or a postulate, and that there is nothing illogical in supposing exceptions to it. He takes the case of an amoeba weaving its devious way through a liquid. Watching it through a microscope, one sees it veer off to the right. "Is it permissible to suppose that, under precisely the circumstances in which it veered off to the right, it might have moved to the left instead . . .? *Impossible,* the determinist has to say. . . . Now my question is, how could anyone know that?" And more particularly, how could anyone know it when the most careful and exhaustive inspection reveals nothing whatever that points in one direction rather than another?

If the argument is stated in this way, I see no good answer to Mr. Taylor's question. His case rests on the belief that the law of causation is purely inductive, and that to such generalizations exceptions are always possible. But is our support for the law inductive solely? In *Reason and Analysis* (466 ff.), I cited with agreement several propositions of C. D. Broad about causation that he considered a priori. The first two of these were "Every change has a cause" and "The cause of any change contains a change as a factor." These propositions seemed to him, and they seem to me, self-evident. Consider the case of the wayward amoeba. Let us suppose, with Mr. Taylor, that the circumstances are those in which the amoeba would ordinarily turn left. It does in fact turn right. Now I find it hard to believe that Mr. Taylor is suggesting that precisely the same cause that made the amoeba turn left yesterday makes it turn right today. But if this is not what he means, then his meaning must be that the amoeba changes its course for no cause at all. And this would violate both the propositions that Broad, and I following him, are inclined to think self-evident. After considering the instance further, I continue to think so. It is entirely imaginable, as Hume pointed out, that a motionless billiard ball should suddenly move off on its own, or leap straight up in air. But what is imaginable may not be clearly thinkable. To say that a motion can occur without any cause at all is to say that something can come from nothing, that in a vacuum without form and void there could suddenly arise an amoeba, or the change of motion in an amoeba, or Venus on a half shell. I know that it is notoriously easy to take a prejudice for an intuition. With this in mind, I am still inclined to take as a self-evident intuition that *ex nihilo nihil fit*. And if I am correct in this, the major premise of the determinist is not a merely inductive generalization.

This conclusion, we may note, has some bearing on the doctrine of creation. It has sometimes been maintained that God created the universe out of nothing. If my conclusion is true, this could not have happened. There would have had to be something prior to creation, out of which the universe was made. One can hardly say this was God himself, for that would place God outside of or apart from the universe, which is self-contradictory. And the vital question would still remain, How did God himself come into being? Surely not out of nothing. This line of argument seems to run out to the conclusion that the universe did not begin in time at all.

Along with my determinist view that every event has a cause, Mr. Taylor considers my more extreme view that every event is causally connected with every other, that, to use his example, the movement of a housefly on his desk is connected causally with that of a minnow in a pond in China. Together with most other sensible people, he regards this as pretty wild. And of course I admit that any empirical proof of it in the particular case is out of the question. But he can no doubt anticipate what my answer would be, and indeed he suggests it in part. If there is any law of science that could claim to be well established, it is that of gravitation. Now gravitation is a law connecting all masses, and though the strength of the pull approximates zero as the masses become smaller and the distance greater, the operation of the law itself is not thereby suspended. If the motion of the moon affects the tides, the motion of the fly must affect the minnow.

This is a direct causal relation, however trivial. But then I do not depend on direct causal relations. Events are causally related indirectly as well as directly, and these relations may be such that if one of the events indirectly related failed to occur, the other would also fail to occur. Neither the minnow nor the fly would be what or where it is if at a remote point in space-time the earth had not detached itself from the sun. Both the movement of the fly and that of the minnow are connected with this remote event by straight lines of causation, and I do not see how it can be logically denied that if the movement of the fly or the minnow had been different every causal link in the immensely long chain that led to it would have had to be different, including the arbitrarily chosen first one, the detachment of the earth from the sun. But *that* change would involve a change in every necessary step leading down to the second event, so that the V-shaped connection, each of whose sides is millions of years and miles long, would connect fly with minnow as inevitably as if the minnow were to gobble the fly. And if two events like these, chosen for the very improbability of their being causally connected, can be shown to be so nevertheless, I cannot think that the mere oddness of my conclusion is sufficient to refute it.

Causation as Non-Sensible

2. Mr. Taylor is puzzled by my insistence that the causal relation, which he agrees is in some sense necessary, is one that cannot be seen or otherwise sensed. He wonders who ever supposed that it could. I seem to be forgetting the nature of a relation, which is not a third bead on a string connecting two others, but is obviously invisible and intangible.

> Suppose there are two trees, A and B, standing side by side, that B is completely overshadowed by the other, being, let us suppose, only about ten feet high, while its neighbor A is perhaps sixty. Now we can surely say: (i) that A is taller than B; (ii) that this is an observable fact, that is, something easily confirmable by observation—one needs only to look, to see that the one tree is taller than the other; and yet (iii) that the relation *being taller than* can neither be seen, felt, nor tasted.

Mr. Taylor thinks I must mean that the relation is not observable, but that "there are considerations which enable the rational mind to surmise or infer, at least with probability, that it is there."

I agree that this would be a most unconvincing account of our grasp of relations. Happily it is not mine. I do think, however, that our way of knowing relations is a difficult and obscure problem. Several comments are called for.

(a) *Are* relations observable in the same sense as colors and tastes? Mr. Taylor says in the same sentence that we can see that one tree is taller than the other, but that we cannot see the relation *taller than*. Clearly the word "see" is being used here in different senses, as indeed Mr. Taylor recognizes. When we "see that" A is taller than B, we are making a perceptual judgment. When we say that we do not see the relation, we mean that we do not visually sense it. Now if I am asked why I make a point of the relation's invisibility, I answer (in part): Because there is a genuine problem here. If the terms can be seen, but not the relation between them, by what sort of apprehension is the relation grasped?

(b) It is plainly not "surmised," or "inferred," or assigned some "probability," as Mr. Taylor thinks I may be saying. It is laid hold of directly and as one part of the perceptual judgment. Here we may profit by borrowing an insight of Kant. For him the sensing of the green colors and the apprehension of the relation were perceptions, but differing kinds of perception; the greens in the percept are apprehended by sensation; the relation between them is apprehended by "pure perception." Pure perception was a unique kind of knowledge whose objects are relations of space and time. We know immediately, though without seeing it, that the relation *taller than* holds between A and B; we know immediately, though without hearing it, that the relation of before and after holds between two notes that have just been sounded. Both perceptions are really judgments. The intellect must be already at work, for concepts of identity and difference are already being employed. But Kant was right, I think, in holding that space and time are relations of a unique kind, bound up with perception in a special way. To mark the uniqueness of this grasp was another reason for my insistence that spatial and temporal connections cannot be seen or felt.

(c) There was a third reason. Empiricism commonly says roundly that all our knowledge comes from sense experience. Of course as a rationalist I do not accept this. And what better examples can one cite to show its falsity than our knowledge of relations? If they are necessary relations, like those of logic, the case against empiricism is doubly strong, since neither the relational nor the necessary character is itself presented in sense. In dealing with causal relations, we are dealing with relations that are not obviously necessary. Hume saw this, but he seems not to have seen with equal clearness that our grasp even of a causality that lacked necessity was enough to undermine his empiricism. I wanted to make that also clear.

Necessary and Sufficient Conditions

3. Mr. Taylor welcomes my insistence that the cause of an event is not, as is often supposed, the precipitating cause, that is, the most conspicuous change in the vicinity of the event and just preceding it. The true cause is rather the assemblage of conditions that may be so described, and they are usually numerous. Here I follow Mill. But when I go on to say that the assemblage of necessary causes constitutes the sufficient cause, Mr. Taylor demurs. Whether this demurrer is correct or incorrect depends, I suggest, on whether one is speaking of the causation of all events of a certain kind, or the causation of some one event. Suppose one asks what is the cause of malaria. Most physicians would stop with the necessary and precipitating cause, which is the bite of the anopheles mosquito. But there are other causes equally necessary to producing the condition of the patient, for without gravitation, the distance of the sun, and the presence of air, the effect would not have been what it was. These conditions are universally present and universally necessary for the production of what happens to any patient. Put them together; do they then constitute the sufficient condition for the disease in a given individual patient? Clearly not. The disease as it manifests itself in John Jones is a unique affair, exactly like no other; and to account for it, one must go into the particular state of his body at the moment of the bite, the amount of poison injected, the degree of his resistance to such poisons, and many

other things. It is obvious, therefore, that the sum of the necessary conditions of the disease generally is *not* identical with the sufficient condition in the individual case. So understood, Mr. Taylor's demurrer is justified.

But suppose that in the individual case we could and did exhaust the necessary causes; would their union give us the sufficient cause? Yes, I think it would. If every condition necessary to the event is present, that means that no condition is absent that is needed to produce it, and in that case the event must surely occur. To say that every condition required for the production of an event is present and yet the event does not occur would be equivalent to denying the general law of causality itself. In the individual case, then, the unity of the necessary conditions does give the sufficient condition.

Causation versus Luck

4. I was reassured to find that on the next point, though Mr. Taylor began by thinking I must be wrong, he ended in substantial agreement. My argument was that if there was no relation between cause and effect except one of constant conjunction, as Hume supposed, that conjunction itself would be incredible. We always assume that if one draws cards from a fairly shuffled pack, and draws the four of clubs a hundred times running, the result is not a matter of chance. Now men have observed the rising of the sun followed by the illumining of the earth every day without any known exception for millions of years. On the Humean theory we have no right to infer anything closer than a repeated chance togetherness in this protracted series. But this is not only thoroughly at odds with common sense; if taken seriously, it would undermine the science of statistics. If the sun's rising, followed by the illumination of the earth, is a matter of chance, then there must be many other alternative states that are equally likely to follow. Now try to calculate the probability, under such conditions, of getting the same result from the sun's rising a million times in succession. The odds against it would flout the capacity of any known computer. What does this prove? Mr. Taylor doubts whether it would show any logical necessity between the cause and the effect, and on that he may be right. But it does show, we agree, that there is some bond of connection between cause and effect that is much closer than association. Such continual association cannot be chance. A further bond is required to account for it.

Necessity in Causation

5. Though Mr. Taylor's agreement with me here is encouraging, he disagrees with me emphatically in his next criticism. Even here, however, it is only at the final stage of the argument that we part company. The argument to which he takes exception is one I have used repeatedly, and I confess that it

has seemed to me decisive; so I am troubled that it seems to him in its final stage to break down.

Hume holds that in no case of causation do we see any relation closer than one of association. His contention fails if we can cite a single case in which cause and effect are linked by logical necessity. I claim that there are many such cases, and for convenience I will take the case Mr. Taylor cites from me. Suppose that at moment t_1 I think the thought that all insects have eight legs, though spiders do not. At time t_2 I think the thought, "Then spiders can't be insects." These two thoughts are psychical events, the first preceding the second and serving as at least a part cause of the second. The contents of the two thoughts, when put together, form a syllogism:

All insects have eight legs
A spider does not have eight legs
A spider is not an insect.

On these things we agree; and we agree that the conclusion follows logically from the premises. Mr. Taylor goes even further by agreeing that "the validity of this syllogism is one of the causal conditions for the emergence (darting) of [the conclusion] B into one's mind." But then he parts company sharply. "It seems to me that what has happened here is this: That a syllogism has been presented, and its validity noted; and that two psychical events of judging have been presented, related to each other causally; and then these two things—the syllogism, on the one hand, and the mental illation, on the other—have simply been jumbled up together as though they were one and the same thing, the sole justification for this being, truly but irrelevantly, that sometimes the validity of an argument can causally influence a reasonable man in drawing the conclusion he in fact draws."

Now if it is read in my own way, this last clause of Mr. Taylor's has granted all that is essential to my case. The issue is why the conclusion darts into one's mind, and I am maintaining that in some instances it does so because the logical necessity relating the contents of two judgments itself enters into the causal process. Why this should be regarded as irrelevant I do not see, for it is the nub of my position.

Perhaps Mr. Taylor regards it as irrelevant because, like other critics, he has confused my position with another that is deceptively like it. These critics have supposed me to argue that the conclusion comes to my mind not because its content is necessitated by the joint premises, but because I *see* that it is so necessitated. But that explanation would move in a circle. The question is why a certain proposition presents itself to my mind. If I say that this is because I see that the premises entail that proposition, then the appearance of the proposition is accounted for by a cause which already includes its presence. Obviously I cannot explain the thought of B by saying that I think of A as entailing B, for then the appearance of B is made a cause of itself. It is not, therefore, the *seeing* of the entailment that enters into the causation, but the entailment itself.

Such a theory seems odd to present-day thinkers, for it introduces a kind of cause that they commonly rule out by definition. A cause, we are told, is an event, and the relation of entailment is not an event but a timeless relation between propositions. Still, I can only suggest that my critics examine their own thinking and ask themselves how likely it is that the thought that a spider is not an insect would have risen in their minds when it did if the premises entailing that proposition had not been there just before. I do not see how any candid person could say that it was in the least likely. The logical connection made the decisive difference. How then is one to avoid admitting that the objective entailment of content by content is at least sometimes a sine qua non for the appearance of the conclusion?

It may be replied that entailment holds not between thoughts, which are psychic events, but between the objects of thought, presumably propositions. But then the propositions are parts of the thoughts. A judgment is an assertion *that p*, or, as it used to be said, that S is P. A judgment that judged nothing would be no judgment at all. Now I am reluctant to get involved in the tortured question of the ontological status of propositions. We can hardly say that as they stand they are parts of truth or reality, for they may be mistaken. They seem to be mental presentations whose contents and relations reflect more or less faithfully the arrangements of things in nature. These contents can be prescinded or abstracted from their psychical setting in the events of which they form a part, and their relations considered independently. The multiplication table or Euclidean geometry presents a set of such propositions all interlinked by necessity, and when we think within these systems, we have no sense of arbitrariness in the movement of our thought, no sense of manufacturing the relations and terms with which we are dealing. A mathematical deduction is not the telling of a whimsical tale. There is a sense in which these propositions and their relations have a being of their own, and a sense in which, as we move from point to point among them, we are surrendering to the guidance of lines of connection that are there in our subject matter. The more rigorously logical our thought becomes, the less do we feel the process to be one of making, and the more to be one of discovery. As we succeed in surrendering ourselves more completely to the structure we are trying to apprehend, the more our thought seems to be controlled by the necessary connections that hold its parts together.

Mr. Taylor generously credits me with having originated this argument for the partial logical control of psychical process. I cannot accept the credit. The argument is implicit in Spinoza and in T. H. Green's great introduction to Locke, Berkeley, and Hume; and it breaks out explicitly in Bradley's *Logic*. It has often been suggested in vaguer forms by writers who are religiously and mystically inclined, in A. E. Taylor's "initiative of the eternal," for example, or in Emerson's "I look up, and put myself in the attitude of reception, but from some alien energy the visions come." But I see nothing visionary or mystical in my own statement of it. It seems to me a position demanded by any broadly empirical psychology, by which I mean a psychology that looks steadily at all the relevant facts, not one which like the behaviorist's dispenses with all the more interesting facts, nor one that like associationism fails abjectly when it comes to the higher processes. Ever since making the studies necessary to *The Nature of Thought,* I have been convinced that the mind is not the sort of agency that can be understood by "scientific" psychology, even when eked out by an extensional logic. It is essentially a state of consciousness under immanent purposive control. On the cognitive side it is a drive toward understanding, and understanding means the grasp of something as necessitated by its context. Perhaps the most illuminating thing ever said about the human mind was said by Plato when he remarked that it was something rational, but brokenly and imperfectly so.

This is the sort of conviction that lies behind my argument for the participation of necessity in the causation at work in valid inference. Mr. Taylor would go much farther with me in this unorthodox and unpopular direction than would most philosophers of the present day. I am grateful to him for his support at a number of moot points, for the candor and fairness of his present criticism, and for his own significant contributions to the study of purpose in mental behavior.

23 BLANSHARD'S RATIONALISTIC REALISM
Ervin Laszlo

I am entirely in sympathy with Blanshard's epistemological and metaphysical aspirations. I am somewhat less in sympathy with the arguments he advances to back them up; I do not follow him to the full extent of his rationalistic realism. However, this paper is not a critical but a supportive one. There is an unfortunate tendency among philosophers to be clever at each other's expense, and in such practice it is the body of ideas under discussion that is the loser. I shall not engage in criticisms of Blanshard's arguments to the detriment of the cause itself: the basic epistemological and ontological positions he champions. These I take to be too important to bandy about for the sake of matching wits concerning individual points and arguments. Indeed, the kind of systems-oriented holistic position maintained by Blanshard is greatly in need of serious consideration today, as the atomizing analytical trends of contemporary philosophy face bankruptcy and young thinkers search for new paradigms.

In this paper I shall affirm Blanshard's ideal of intelligibility as an interconnected system of knowledge. I shall voice some skepticism on the score of imputing a matching systemicity to nature, although I shall affirm that such a view continues to be the most cogent construction of empirical reality. I shall proceed by first outlining some of Blanshard's relevant conclusions (without being able to reproduce the many finely honed arguments he presents in their support), then expose the grounds for my differences with him, and finally sketch out the reasons for my basic agreement with the holistic, systems-oriented approach that lies at the core of his thinking.

I

Blanshard himself admits that he is a rationalist of what is commonly taken as an extreme form. In epistemology he holds that there is a priori knowledge of the existent; in metaphysics he holds that all events are causally and all facts logically interconnected.[1] The key concepts of his positions are coherence and internal relations.

Blanshard's epistemological position is dominated by the idea that all knowledge aims at intelligibility, and intelligibility means the coherence of terms within an interconnected body of thought. All ideas, judgments, and processes of reflection, he tells us, are directed toward the goal of intelligibility; understanding itself can be understood only if we are clear about its ultimate end, and that is the achievement of intelligibility. Unless thought is recognized as the pursuit of such an ideal, and the ideal itself is defined, neither logic nor the psychology of thinking can do its work (*The Nature of Thought* [*NT*], 2:24).

To understand something is to incorporate it in a system. Inasmuch as we understand anything, we form a system of our ideas. In such a system the terms are mutually related thus, that one term necessitates—to some *degree* of necessity—the others. There is no knowledge in the absence of system. Learning, i.e. the acquisition of new knowledge, proceeds by assimilating "islands" of facts into the "mainland" of systematic knowledge. Thereby the mainland is enlarged. At the end of the process of gradually unfolding understanding lies the full system: the universe of terms where each necessitates all others, and none is left out of account. The construction of such a universal system starts with the presentation of a problem—something that does not fit into our existing system—and proceeds bit by bit, as challenges are overcome and problems solved. The fresh islands are interconnected by bridges from the mainland, and all experience becomes the continent of the interconnected system.

Blanshard joins his epistemological rationalism with a thoroughgoing metaphysical realism. For him the two ends of thought are one: constructing the logically perfect system, and attaining to empirical truth. The most coherent body of thought is also true. Coherence not only defines an ideal of thinking but constitutes a test and a definition of the nature of truth.

Blanshard argues that if we assume there is an answer to the question "Why?" we are committed to the assumption that there are no accidents, no loose ends, no facts or events in the universe that are ultimately unintelligible ("Internal Relations").[2] Accepting this rationalistic postulate thus commits us to a definite type of structure in the world. It commits us, says Blanshard, to the view that the world is rational in the specific sense that every fact and event is connected with every other fact and event in a logically necessary way. He thus moves from an argument for intelligibility as an ideal of knowledge to an argument for internal relations as characterizing the real world.

Blanshard does not disregard the objection that, while coherence may function as an ideal of knowledge, it may lead to empirical falsehood. Where is the guarantee, he asks, that when I have brought my ideas into the form my ideal requires, they should be *true*? (*NT*, 2:261). He seeks the guarantee in the concept of coherence itself. It is incoherent to agree to take coherence as the test of truth while assuming that a coherent body of knowledge fails to correspond to empirical reality. In other words, it is incoherent to assume that the world itself is incoherent whereas our knowledge continues to be guided by coherence. Thus at the pain of self-contradiction, we are enjoined to admit the coherence of the real.

The completely satisfactory system, for Blanshard, is one wherein no proposition is arbitrary, but every one entails all others. The integration would be so complete that no part could be seen for what it is without seeing its relation to the whole (of reality), and the whole itself could be understood only through every part.

Blanshard counters with great skill various types of objections, and ends by affirming that perfect knowledge forms a system, of which the object is also a system. Thought is a potential, of which the fulfillment is the object—the real world. Intellectual satisfaction (the "inner end" of thought) coincides with the revelation of truth (thought's "outer end"). Only the notion of potentiality, as fulfilled in the grasp of the object through systematic thought, would make this coincidence other than a miracle.

> Indeed it is a major part of our contention that the chaotic and fragmentary character of experience belongs not to the nature of things but to our knowledge in a transitional stage, and that our knowledge loses this character precisely in the degree to which it approximates, or rather achieves and embodies, the real.[*NT*, 2:448]

Reality, for Blanshard, becomes intelligible only if it is grasped as a system, all-inclusive and perfectly integrated, such that all its parts are internally related. Such relation means that the knowledge of each part presupposes a knowledge of all others; that each part is what it is in virtue of its relations to all others, and that each part necessitates, for being what it is, all the other parts. All events are causally, and all facts logically, interconnected.

> Let *a* and *x* be *any* two things in the universe. They are then related to each other causally. But if causally, then also intrinsically, and if intrinsically then also necessarily, in the sense that they causally act as they do in virtue of their nature or character, and that to deny such activity would entail denying them to be what they are. [*NT*,2:516]
> ... with approximation to its immanent end, the achievement of systematic necessity, thought is also approximating its transcendent end, the apprehension of the real." [*NT*, 2:516–17]

Herewith we reach the ultimate conclusion of Blanshard's realism-cum-rationalism.

II

Nothing would please me more than to accept the above conclusion with a clear conscience. It would endow the type of philosophy I have been at pains to develop over the past several years not only with cogency but with empirical certainty. For the world would be shown to be *necessarily* a total system of internal interdependence—the ultimate implication of the metaphysical superstructure of systems philosophy.[3] However, despite the attractiveness of this prospect, I feel compelled to take a more modest stand. I shall not claim that we can assert with either logical or empirical warrant the systemic nature of the world; I shall merely claim that we can reasonably and fruitfully construct it under that perspective. My differences with Blanshard thus concern the degree of certitude we claim for our positions. The positions themselves are strikingly similar. I shall now explicate in more detail the reasons for my more modest (and skeptical) stand and hence the grounds of my differences with Blanshard.

I argue that certainty of any kind concerning empirical matters of fact is excluded in virtue of the very situation of the human knower. Now the basic epistemological position of human beings can be assessed on phenomenological as well as on naturalistic grounds. The phenomenological analysis would take the individual knower as the criterion of truth; the naturalistic position would bring in factors concerning the human situation, assembled by means of prior acts of knowledge, held valid.

(A) In the "purer" phenomenological approach, we conceive of knowledge as based on experience that had its beginnings in the past of the experiencer. Experience forms a "duration" or "stream" which includes all elements going on in the mind: perceptions, feelings, volitions, memories, abstract thinking, moods, and so on. From this welter of differentiated experiences we evolve a knowledge of ourselves and the world around us. Initially in our personal history, "I" and "world" are merged in a continuum. Gradually the concept of the self is formed, and to it we attribute our concept of the body. Self and body are then contrasted with the world around them, including objects and other embodied selves.

The question whether any such construction of reality corresponds to reality itself has puzzled philosophers for centuries. We need not rehearse here the historical examples of empiricism and rationalism, materialism and idealism, skepticism and dogmatism. Rather, we can reassess the situation of human knowledge in the phenomenological perspective by using some concepts of empiricism. According to them, certain segments of experience we construct as referring to internal processes in us, the experiencer. At the least, these are our moods, memories, and feelings. At the most, they encompass all perceptions including our "sense-data" (on the doctrine of secondary qualities held by Locke and Hume and used as the basis for an idealistic metaphysic by Berkeley). Because of a continual matching of certain elements in our experience with certain others, we come to impute some elements to the world around us. The matching involves our perceptions of colors, shapes, sounds, odors, textures, and tastes (the data of our "external senses") with perceptions of body-schemes indicating the disposition, functioning, and behavior of what we come to regard as "my body" or "myself." By manipulating our proprioceptive sensations through acts of volition (which appear to be at our disposition: I can move my finger or turn my head if only I decide to do so), we get matching modifications in the exteroceptive sensations. But the latter are not entirely under our control: things which we perceive through colors, shapes, and sounds also seem to have a will of their own. Hence we attribute them to "the rest of the world" rather than to "myself."

With further scrutiny it becomes evident that although some of our proprioceptive sensations (i.e. our feelings of bodily functioning and disposition) are under our control, they too appear to obey laws of their own, and hence we cannot conceive of them as being some pure center of consciousness or ego. Rather, we conceive of the body as "belonging" to myself, but as being-in-the-world and subject to its laws and vicissitudes. There remains only the center of consciousness, the transcendental "I," as constituting the core of my being. While the many elements which constitute it—feelings, moods, abstract thinking, projects, self-reflections, etc.—change over time, they do have a day-to-day continuity. They permit me to conceive of myself as a unity persisting over the stretch of time (a "duration") that elapses between vague beginnings of experiencing in childhood and the not-yet-experienced but seemingly inevitable end in old age.

This account, while imperfect in many respects, does reflect some of the essentials of the empirical-phenomenological approach to the human situation with respect to knowledge. Thus construed, this situation presents us with insurmountable barriers. How could we be certain that the knowledge of the world we derive in the course of our daily stream of experience gives us a "true" picture of the world? On the correspondence theory, which holds that knowledge is true if it corresponds in some way to an independently existing reality, we should have to obtain proof of sound knowledge by inspecting both the independently existing world and our knowledge of it, and seeing whether they correspond. But we cannot inspect the world independently of our knowledge of it. Hence any correspondence we postulate remains an article of faith, even when backed by empirical or logical, abstract or intuitive arguments. On a skeptical theory we end by renouncing the quest for certain knowledge and content ourselves with constructing more or less complete and more or less satisfying edifices of thought, which we impute with uncertain justification as characteristics of the real world. On the rationalist theory we hold that whatever we conceive of clearly and distinctly, obeying the laws which govern systematic thought, is also true. In an idealistic variant, the real is contained in the sphere of the ideas we entertain, either because the world of experience that constitutes our life history is held to be all there is (or all that is truly knowable) or because our experience is a segment of some universal experience (mind or spirit) which makes up all there is of reality.

There is, however, an in-between position which, while seemingly a compromise, is the one that appears to me the most reasonable. It may be termed constructivism or perspectivism. In this position we hold that out of the stream of experience that makes up our conscious life we can and do construct various concepts and theories of reality. We cannot ultimately and finally verify—or even falsify—any of them. But this does not condemn us to rest content with any concept or theory we happen to stumble across. There are noteworthy differences in regard to consistency, generality, simplicity, elegance, and similar factors, which must not be disregarded.[4] To be sure, these do not condemn the inconsistent, special, complex, and inelegant world view to falsehood nor do they guarantee that the consistent, general, simple, and elegant one is true. We can never get outside our system of experiencing to inspect the world to which we impute our constructions of experience. The "real" world "out there" is unknowable except through experience, and experience presents us merely with the building materials, and not with the blueprints, for constructing a knowledge of it. That world may well be incoherent, complex, and inelegant in its haphazard construction. Or it may constitute (as Blanshard holds) a system where every element is tied through internal relations of causal interdependence and logical necessity to every other. I hold that, by scrutinizing our personal experience, we can never ultimately and finally decide this. But we can, it seems, strive to perfect our *constructions* or *perspectives* of reality. Such striving is in accordance with almost all of our constructions of reality as encompassing ourselves: it is self-consistent. For example, on a *biological* construction (of which more later), the organization of thought gives man a selective advantage over other species. It enables him to control his environment and bend its forces to his own purposes of survival, well-being, and reproduction. The more coherent and inclusive man's conception of the world around him, the more reliable and full his mastery over his environment. Such constructions regard even "pure" theoretical science under the aspect of control, gained through the experimental verifications of predictions. On a *psychological* construction, man is seen as having also an emotional need to organize experience. We need a coherent picture of the universe to show what we can hope for and what we must fear. The world around us must be emotionally significant for our existence. A tie-in with art and aesthetics can occur here. Motivated by the emotional need to render the world meaningful, we create unities of experience through which to apprehend its aspects. These we call works of art (and, in a more general aesthetics, also fantasies, imaginary self-expressions, and other meaningful but extrascientific thought processes). Finally, on a *pragmatist* construction, our knowledge is tested by its consequences; and man in a complex environment finds himself confronted with a welter of intricately connected consequences. The more he makes use of his physical, biological, and social environment, the more he is called upon to construct coherent knowledge systems to evaluate the consequences both with regard to the validity of his knowledge and with respect to the realization of his goals and purposes.

Hence whether we adopt a biological, a psychological, or a pragmatic perpective, the ideal of systematically organized encompassing knowledge remains valid. This ideal ultimately forces us to examine the *internal* coherence of alternative perspectives, making us into self-reflexive philosophers. It is perhaps natural that while engaging in such pursuits we should also wish to extend our ideal of systematic coherence to the concept of empirical truth. In Blanshard's terms, we are tempted to affirm that when our knowledge corresponds to our ideal of intelligibility, it also grasps (grows into, coheres with, or becomes) its object: the universe as a whole. Although assuming this may be coherent, and thus satisfy the ideal of knowledge, it remains an article of faith. On consistent empirical-phenomenological premises the proposition that our knowledge system is perfectly all-embracing and systematic, and yet false, is neither contradictory nor falsifiable. When the ideal of knowledge is recognized for what it is, namely a regulative principle of *thought* but not necessarily of *reality*, its affirmation does not commit us to anything about the latter.

(B) Can we extricate ourselves from the skepticism inherent in the empiricist-phenomenological approach by choosing a more naturalistic point of departure? We may take experience as not only "mine" but as typical of members of my species. Naturalism could warrant a biological or psychological perspective by imputing knowledge to a historical, natural entity, with an evolutionary past and a contingent future. But naturalism does involve, *sensu stricto*, circular reasoning. It assumes that what we know about ourselves as a system in the real world is a valid framework of our inquiry into the nature of knowledge itself. It disregards the fact that any such framework is itself derived from prior processes of knowing. Hence the conclusions to be proven are smuggled in as tacit premises. This is true also of Blanshard's justification of his thesis that all events in the universe are causally connected, in terms of the theory of gravitation ("Internal Relations," 231). That theory presupposes a naturalist perspective in which we *assume*, without prior grounds, that there is a physical universe which obeys certain types of laws. We then construct our concept of that universe in reference to postulated laws, validated with respect to their deduced consequences in experience. Hence no theory of the empirical sciences rests directly on untainted observation (as Blanshard himself recognizes). But if the nature of empirical knowledge is hypothetical, it cannot be made to support a world view claiming truth for its postulates. Our world views must remain hypothetical and can hope at best to satisfy internal ideals of knowledge.

The naturalism characterizing the philosophical foundations of the natural sciences is not, by itself, sufficient to warrant the concept of an internally related universe. Suppose that we do not go as far as Blanshard in assuming that in the universe there are no accidents, no loose ends, and no facts or events that are ultimately unintelligible, but assume merely that there exists a physical universe which is temporally prior both to our personal and to our species experience and constitutes the object of our empirical knowledge.

Does this type of account entail Blanshard's concept of the world? No, since alternative concepts remain equally compatible with it. For example, the naturalistic assumption (the leap beyond the *sole ipse*) does not forbid the inference that the world is a giant clockwork obeying the laws of Newtonian mechanics, and living things are accidental configurations in the aimless concourse of molecules. It does not forbid the interpretation of all nature as a projection in the mind of an Absolute Spirit, or as the self-evolution of the Absolute Idea. Naturalism leaves all metaphysical options open except consistent skepticism. Blanshard's logically necessitated and causally interconnected universe is but one of several metaphysical options which could follow from a naturalistic perspective.

III

The above remarks keynote my differences with Blanshard. These are small, however, in comparison with the areas of our agreement. I do not believe that the issue of certainty with respect to our knowledge of the empirical world is a ground for concern. Born men, not gods, we must put up with hypothetical constructions. Yet we can distinguish between constructions that are more or less satisfactory, not on grounds of empirical truth or falsity but on those of ideals of knowledge. Lack of certainty does not deprive attempts to understand reality of cogency. Hypothetical foundations that satisfy universal cognitive ideals are sufficient grounds to persevere. Only the impatient young men of philosophy, who want certainty or nothing, will give up the ship in disgust or discouragement, and turn to more "concrete" pursuits.

Today there emerges a new paradigm of scientific philosophy that satisfies Blanshard's knowledge ideals to as great an extent as any metaphysical construction of the past, and it grows out of common elements in the new theoretical developments in the empirical sciences. This philosophy may be the most informed guess we can presently make as regards the nature of reality. It is based on the concept of hierarchically interrelated, self-maintaining, and evolving dynamic open systems. Such systems are researched in fields as diverse as biology, ecology, psychology, sociology, international relations theory, and cybernetics. The theories of biological, ecological, psychological, social, political, and cybernetic systems exhibit basic invariances. These constitute the foundations of a general theory of systems. Such theory in turn is fraught with implications for our concepts of man and his knowledge. The elaboration of the implications of the systems sciences, via the general theory of systems, constitutes systems philosophy.

The metaphysical superstructure of systems philosophy approximates Blanshard's concept of the world. It does not do so, however, on his rationalistic grounds. We can conceive of the world as a complex hierarchical system, not because we can deploy logical strategems, such as the argument from difference, or psychophysiological ones, such as the causal basis of inference, but because such construction is at once the simplest, the most consistent, and the most elegant general theory currently available. It corresponds to our ideals of systematic thinking: it endows the myriad products of the contemporary scientific knowledge explosion with intelligibility. Its characteristics have been explored by the writer elsewhere, and here merely the relevant metaphysical statement will be repeated.[5]

Rejecting the assumption that one and only one type of metaphysics can be inferred from the scientific bases of systems philosophy, I argue for a monistic rather than dualistic or pluralistic framework as according, with least extraneous assumptions, with the postulates of this mode of thought. In the light of the scientific theories that form the foundations of systems philosophy, the most indicated conception is one of the universe as a giant matrix out of which arise the many phenomenally distinctive entities. We need conceive of no radical separation between forming and formed, and between substance and space and time. We do not have existing substantial things, located at discrete points in space and time. Rather, the universe is conceived as a continuum, defining both space and time, and the spatiotemporal events which disclose themselves to empirical observation. The latter can be thought of as stresses or tensions within the constitutive space-time matrix, emerging within the phenomenal field as tips of an iceberg above water. Hence there will be no action-at-a-distance, despite causal or functional correlations of spatially and temporally distant events. The connections are propagated within the cosmic matrix, limited by a constant, such as the speed of light in vacuo. Interaction can thus be defined by the light cones of Minkowski and Weyl.

Within the range of interaction defined by the cones, the cosmic matrix evolves in patterned flows, one actualized flow conditioning the emergence and development of the rest. Some flows hit upon configurations of intrinsic stability and thus survive, despite changes in their evolving environment. The flows represent recurring sets of events which jointly constitute the invariance of the flow: these we call systems. The actualized configurations of stability—acting as constraints in the systems—are realizations of possibilities intrinsic to the cosmic matrix. Likewise, the constraints acting on the systems, and both limiting their degrees of freedom and providing their vital medium, represent possibilities actualized in the continuum, externally to the systems. Hence the possibilities in the cosmic continuum become actualized in the selective evolution of systems, adapted to their environment. The evolution of systems is the evolution of the continuum into increasingly adapted, and (in part) increasingly complex and individuated, modules. This process is but the accommodation of the singularities of flows in the continuum, within its general flow patterns. In the final analysis, it is the matrix which orders itself, bringing about a buildup of organization in some sectors, at the expense of smoothing out complex flows in others. But in those areas where flows complexify, the matrix forms multidimensional fields, with elaborate hierarchical patterning.

The events which engage our attention are the observable points of the continuum, and especially those where flows are either constant or complex. Constant flows of relative simplicity furnish the events investigated by physics, such as the many radiations, including light and quantized energy transfers. Complex flows with high levels of cybernetic stability are the objects of biological, psychological, and sociological inquiry. In each instance flows are mapped by a theoretical model insofar as they exhibit an invariance. The self-maintaining invariances give us the concept of "entities"; in addition, those with perceptually observable properties furnish the referent of "things." We, of course, as cognizant human beings, are likewise flows, of a highly complex, self-maintaining, and organizing kind. This consideration can explain why some flows are perceptually observable for us and some are not: those which are, are relevant to the maintenance of the flow invariances we ourselves incorporate, while the unperceivable ones are not.

The present doctrine incorporates possibility in actuality, rather than placing it on a separate, transcendent plane. What is, is a partial realization of what can be. The latter is the sum of the potential strata of stability within the cosmic matrix. Within that matrix we find the properties which come to be realized, one after another and in sets, as the actualization of one possibility conditions the actualization of others. The last vestiges of the passive "neutral stuff" or "inert matter" conceptions of classical thought are hereby discarded. The universe is *causa sui*. The manifest orders represent the perceivable phases of its self-evolution, not determined by any outside force. There are only internal relations. Platonic ideas, or Whiteheadian eternal objects, are rejected as uncalled for; likewise the notion of a transcendent God or other Deity. Ordering is from within, but proceeds from the non-perceivable continuum toward increasingly discrete particulars. The latter are not fully discrete (since systems are but individual sets of points along the continuum), but are increasingly perceivable as such since, in the course of their evolution, they acquire integrated properties which can interact with human sense organs.

Thus the metaphysics based on the conceptual framework of systems philosophy accords with Blanshard's concept of the world as an internally related, encompassing system. Let me make clear, however, that the validity of this metaphysics does not rest on Blanshard's rationalism: it does not involve the assertion that its warrant lies in the mutual logical necessity of terms in its statement. Rather, the systems philosophical metaphysics is content to rest on contingent grounds and be presented as the most consistent, general, simple, and elegant metaphysical construction of the most consistent, general, simple, and elegant theory of man and nature presently to come out of the empirical sciences. Since absolute certainty in matters of empirical knowledge is, in the nature of the case, excluded from the human knowledge situation, the best we can do is to adopt the most satisfying perspective for constructing our concept of the world. As Whitehead said, a theory must be judged not only by its truth but also by its measure of satisfaction. Ideals of knowledge are immanent in the situation of knowledge and they can be explicated and obeyed. We cannot press beyond them with certitude. Blanshard's ideal of knowledge is convincing, and it endows the new philosophy based on the general theory of systems with all the cogency any empirical theory can legitimately claim. In turn, the current popularity and growth of this theory[6] demonstrates that the ideal of knowledge as an interconnected system is not the figment of an isolated mind, or the product of a small group of rationalistic thinkers, but a widely recognized and increasingly powerful factor in contemporary science and philosophy.

ERVIN LASZLO

NOTES

[1]Personal communication, Aug. 5, 1973.

[2]Brand Blanshard, "Internal Relations and Their Importance to Philosophy," *Review of Metaphysics* 21, no. 2 (December 1967): 227–36.

[3]See Ervin Laszlo, *Introduction to Systems Philosophy: Toward a New Paradigm of Contemporary Thought* (New York: Harper Torchbooks, 1973).

[4]For more detailed discussion, consult Ervin Laszlo and Henry Margenau, "The Emergence of Integrative Concepts in Contemporary Science," *Philosophy of Science* 39, no. 2 (June 1972).

[5]The next paragraphs are excerpted from my own *Introduction to Systems Philosophy*, 292–94.

[6]For overviews, see Ervin Laszlo, ed., *The Relevance of General Systems Theory* (New York: George Braziller, 1972); *The Yearbook of the Society for General Systems Research*, eds. L. von Bertalanffy and A. Rappaport, 16 vols. (The Society for General Systems Research, 1957–71); and W. Gray and N. Rizzo, eds., *Unity through Diversity*, 2 vols. (New York and London: Gordon & Breach, 1973).

23. REPLY TO ERVIN LASZLO

Blanshard's Rationalistic Realism

In the controversy between the rationalism to which I subscribe and the theories that have dominated philosophy in recent years, I am glad to find Mr. Laszlo on my side. Without deprecating analysis, he thinks that analytic philosophy is in danger of "analyzing itself out of existence" by devoting itself to increasingly minute issues without regard to their importance for a wider understanding of man and his place in nature. He believes, as I do, that any fact is to be understood by seeing its part in a system of which it is a member, and is to be understood fully only by seeing its part in that ultimate order of which the world consists. But he holds his view more tentatively and skeptically than I do mine, and so is inclined to think that I have taken the rationalist bit in my teeth and run away with it. In spite of a broad sympathy with my position, generously expressed, he issues some modest and probably well based warnings about my speculative headstrongness.

The philosophical worlds in which Mr. Laszlo and I live may be initially distinguished by the names they bear. I subscribe to a system of rationalism; Mr. Laszlo's outlook he describes as a "systems philosophy." For me the drive of reflective thought is toward a single goal, a system which is all-comprehensive and whose facts are related to each other by intelligible necessity. For Mr. Laszlo the world is full of systems, ordered on different principles and differing vastly in their scope.

Systems Everywhere

Take the human body as a starting point. That body is a biological system whose parts show a high degree of interdependence. But it is only a midpoint in a series of systems that extend indefinitely above it in comprehensiveness and indefinitely below it in minuteness. Above it is the terrestrial system of the planet that it inhabits, with which its ecological relations have become such an anxious matter in recent years. But the planet earth is itself a small member of a much larger solar system. And this solar system, as is now well known, is a rather insignificant part of an enormous galaxy consisting of millions of stars. Astronomers are beginning to understand that galaxies themselves are but parts of farther-flung groups of galaxies that form systems of their own. Somewhere beyond these unimaginable vastnesses is a whole or universe whose nature is too dimly known, Mr. Laszlo thinks, to make scientific statements about it at this stage profitable.

Just as the body is a subsystem within systems of wider inclusiveness, so it is a Chinese box containing a succession of smaller boxes within it, each of them a system in itself. It is an organization of countless cells with highly differentiated functions but working together in such a way that the functions of each serve the requirements of the whole. A cell commonly contains such simpler organizations as crystals and colloids, while these in turn are composed of molecules. The developments of this century have carried the hierarchy of systems still farther down, for molecules have turned out to be systems of atoms. And the atom is another system, consisting of both a nuclear structure, itself revealed as normally complex, with a set of electronic entities apparently revolving around it. Are these entities themselves systems? We do not know. Without dogmatism regarding either end of his hierarchy, Mr. Laszlo cuts off his pyramid of systems with the atoms at the bottom and clusters of galaxies at the top.

In this tremendous structure, where does mind come in? As manifested in man, it is itself a highly integrated system of mental events, characterized by "adaptive self-stabilization." It is to Mr. Laszlo's credit that he has broken completely both with the Humean notion of consciousness as composed of sensory elements held together by bonds of association, and equally with the reductionism that would assimilate consciousness to bodily behavior. Mind with its unique new element of consciousness has emerged from matter, and its chief effort is to survive by adapting itself to matter, but neither its elements nor its structures are material. Mr. Laszlo recognizes, as I do, a distinguishable drive toward understanding, though he describes this in the scientific terms that spring from his own approach to philosophy. Speaking of the cognitive drive, he says: "The fundamental reward in the feedback effect is intelligibility, attained by means of the input-construct match. Overt behavioral responses may not be produced at all if no immediate reward is expected of them; intelligibility is the goal, and that will nevertheless have been gained. Thus motivation is assessed here as a striving toward meaning, rather than toward behaviorally obtained reinforcements" (*Introduction to Systems Philosophy,* 131).[1]

How successful can this drive toward knowledge hope to be? Mr. Laszlo suggests that the soundest assessment of its prospects lies in a double account of the search for knowledge, one from the inside, through which we can study the movement of ideas introspectively, another from the outside, in which advance is regarded as a process of organic adjustment. He has looked at my account of thought from both these points of view, and it will be convenient in my comments to follow suit.

The Internal Account of Knowledge

Mr. Laszlo holds, as probably most psychologists now do, that consciousness begins in each of us with a state in which no self or objects yet exist. Little by little those sensations that are under our control (muscle-joint-tendon sensations, for example) are set on one side, and those of objects beyond our control (tables, chairs, trees) on another. I have spent a good deal of time in *The Nature of Thought* in studying how *things* emerge, and I am happy to think that Mr. Laszlo would go with me most of the way. But he speaks of the self in a manner that puzzles me. He thinks of "the transcendental 'I', as constituting the core of my being." But he immediately adds: "While the many elements which constitute it—feelings, moods, abstract thinking, projects, self-reflections, etc.—change over time, they do have a day-to-day continuity." But surely the "transcendental I" has no presented content at all. It is the "pure ego," supposed to lie behind the scenes and preside over the coordination of sensory and other content without ever putting in an appearance in person. If there is such a being, which seems to me questionable, it is clearly not the same as the series of experiences, some enduring, some momentary, out of which philosophers have sought to construct an empirical self. If only on the grounds of his empirical leanings, I should hardly expect Mr. Laszlo to pursue this transcendental will-o'-the-wisp.

In any case, out of the materials provided in experience we soon come to form "constructs" consisting of things and groups of things. Do these things of common sense—chairs, tables, clouds, and rocks—exist in nature or not? Mr. Laszlo would take both their qualities and their relations as "phenomenal," with little regard for the old distinctions between primary, secondary, and tertiary qualities. Can we have any assurance that these "constructs" of ours resemble, either in their qualities or in their patterns of combination, what belongs to physical nature? His answer is No. The truth of our constructs lies in the fidelity with which they correspond to the "things" in physical nature; if we are to determine that correspondence, we must compare our constructs with what is "out there"; to do that we should have to observe nature directly; and this we can neither do nor hope to do. Hence as regards our knowledge of nature, Mr. Laszlo professes a pretty thoroughgoing skepticism.

But when he talks physics or biology, in both of which he is at home, he certainly does not sound in the least like a skeptic; he speaks of other bodies and other minds, of cells and molecules and atoms, with a confident competence. What has happened here? I suspect Mr. Laszlo has been victimized by his own empiricism. If the only way to reach a knowledge of the external world were really to compare our percepts with what is forever inaccessible, we should indeed have to be skeptics. But while I agree that all objects of perception are mind-dependent, I am not myself a skeptic, and chiefly for two reasons.

(a) I think we have a priori knowledge of the nature of things, and in *Reason and Analysis*, Chapter 10, have reviewed some of the forms of this knowledge, such as logic and arithmetic. I know that alternative logics have been offered us, and I should be sorry to think that the only logic at our command was the extensional logic of *Principia Mathematica*. But I incline to believe in an Ur-logic essential to all valid systems and showing itself fragmentarily in such indispensable laws of our present logics as that of non-contradiction. The validity of such laws in the real world is not a matter of faith in the ordinary sense, for the assumption that they are not so valid is a meaningless hypothesis. Here it is clear that I must part company with Mr. Laszlo. Of the world outside our knowledge he says: "That world may well be incoherent. . . ." "On consistent empirical-phenomenological premises the proposition that our knowledge system is perfectly all-embracing and systematic, and yet false, is neither contradictory nor falsifiable." But to say that such a system is "systematic" in my sense, namely that its parts are interconnected by necessity, nevertheless *is* both self-contradictory and falsifiable. It is self-contradictory because such a system excludes self-contradiction from the outset; it is falsifiable in the sense that what is genuinely necessary cannot be false; what is necessary within an all-comprehensive system is necessarily true. I think we can also see that the law of causality, if strictly formulated, is an a priori insight, not holding only, as Kant said, of phenomena, but also, as he really thought, between phenomena and their nonphenomenal causes. Since I am also inclined to take causation as a connection possessing and occasionally exhibiting logical necessity, I hold that we have a greater a priori knowledge of the structure of the real world than Mr. Laszlo would admit.

(b) I am nearer to him about our qualitative knowledge of things. Colors, sounds, tastes, smells, itches, pains, the feelings of rough and smooth, hard and soft, are all, I think, mind-dependent, nor do we have reason to believe that anything like them exists in the physical world. The primary qualities are more troublesome. When one holds in one's hands a sphere of a certain size, it is hard not to think that the exact size and shape one feels exist in the physical world. Furthermore, if one denies this conclusion, one has to deny that the space we directly experience is that of the physical world. Nevertheless I do not see how to avoid this denial. And it makes the establishment of a correlation between sensory quality and external cause extremely difficult. To escape from this difficulty through the somewhat naive theology of Berkeley or the radical skepticism of Hume would be far more rash in this heyday of physical science than it was for them. It is possible, as the later Russell showed, by postulating causal lines connecting specified components of one's mental content with distinct external causes, to mark out an order of physical entities and a quasi-spatial arrangement of them, which gives us at least some idea of the patterns in nature even though everything of qualitative interest remains within the conscious realm.

The Naturalist Approach

We have been considering the first of Mr. Laszlo's approaches to knowledge, that which studies its structure and growth from within. But he sketches briefly an alternative and naturalist account. This account is essentially that of the working scientist who assumes that observation brings us into direct touch with the nature of things and is impatient of epistemological puzzles. He pays the price of his nonchalance; for, as Mr. Laszlo clearly sees, his system is all too simple; argumentatively it is a circle. It explains the appearance of mind in the world by assuming that the framework it finds in nature is really there, forgetting that this framework may be, and certainly in part is, supplied by the perceiving mind. The theory explains the emergence of mind by unexamined assumptions about nature, and explains nature by assuming unexamined capacities in the mind. "Hence the conclusions to be proven are smuggled in as tacit premises." Mr. Laszlo adds, however: "This is true also of Blanshard's justification of his thesis that all events in the universe are causally connected, in terms of the theory of gravitation." This is not, I think, quite accurate. For (a) though I do assume the universality of the law of gravitation, I do not offer it as a proved conclusion, but as the sort of extrapolation from experience to which an exception is always possible. At the same time an assumption resting on so broad a base of exceptionless confirmation is clearly entitled to hold the field and is not merely a tentative hypothesis. (b) The assumption that the law is universal is strengthened by the insight that gravitation is a causal law and the further insight referred to earlier that causation has an a priori warrant. We know that if a ball falls to the ground there must be some reason for its acceleration. We do not know with the same certainty that the cause lies in the action of gravitation; but if the law of the inverse squares fits the circumstances exactly, and with no plausible alternative, the presumption of its necessity is strong.

Again, "Naturalism," says Mr. Laszlo, "leaves all metaphysical options open except consistent skepticism." The universe might be, as I take it to be, a whole of necessarily related parts; but naturalism "does not forbid the inference that the world is a giant clockwork obeying the laws of Newtonian mechanics, and living things are accidental configurations in the aimless concourse of molecules." Now, if a naturalist theory of knowledge is one that holds to the contingency of every assertion about existence, this clockwork view of the world is a possible conclusion. But then so much the worse for naturalism. So far as the Newtonian laws do really hold in nature, they are not contingencies merely; and while some configurations are "accidental" in the sense that with present knowledge they are unpredictable, the notion of objective accident will not, I think, survive analysis. While Mr. Laszlo stands stoutly and with a clear head against many of the fashionable philosophies of the day, he does not seem to me to have quite escaped from those empiricist philosophies of science that have flourished, along with other empiricisms, since the thirties.

The Interrelation of Systems

After concluding the statement of his chief differences from my outlook, he says: "These are small, however, in comparison with the areas of our agreement." Needless to say, it is reassuring to me to find a philosophical school which insists, as I do, that the understanding of the world must be through wider and wider systems and which brings to the support of this view a far larger acquaintance with the sciences than I can claim. If I may venture on a criticism which, for all I know, may have been adequately met already, it would be that the relations between the many systems that have been brought to light seem less clear than the internal relations within the systems themselves. There is a great variety of bases on which systems may be formed: it is not merely molecules and human organisms that are systems, but also works of art, cities and states, the activities of the "economic man," the set of our moral duties, and the complicated webwork of the United Nations. Plainly the kinds of articulation that hold together the parts of a painting or a sonata are not those that hold together the citizens of London or the stars in the Milky Way. How can systems so diverse be synthesized into one? The aesthetic constraints that organize the elements of the picture or the sonata do not extend themselves to atoms or galaxies, and the mechanical laws of the galaxies will not explain the peculiar constraints of composing a work of art. Are we limited to an empirical study of how these systems are put together? They are organized, Mr. Laszlo says, hierarchically. If that means that as one studies wider and wider groups of them one finds certain principles that apply to all, and that these principles are those of greatest explanatory value, the rationalists and the systems philosophers are converging toward a single cosmology. These systems are not accidents. Given the world outside any one of them, the emergence of that system is a necessity, a necessity that I have not hesitated to call logical. I gather that the systems philosophers are not ready for so rash a leap into metaphysics. But a rationalist can only hope that with their admirable stress on system they will come to recognize in the cosmos the most perfect system of all, that which is fully integrated because fully intelligible.

1. Ervin Laszlo, *Introduction to Systems Philosophy* (New York, London, Paris: Gordon & Breach, 1972).

24 Blanshard's Theory of Universals
Marcus Clayton

P ROFESSOR Blanshard's original and carefully considered theory of universals has not yet received the critical attention which it deserves. He distinguishes three kinds of universals and holds that universals of one kind exist in nature while those of the other two exist only in thought. A "generic universal" is "one whose instances are individual things or persons, for example, man, horse, or stone." A "qualitative universal" is "one whose instances are qualities or characters of one kind, for example, colour, sound, or shape."[1] Universals of these kinds, Blanshard holds, have a purely conceptual status. A specific quality or character, such as a color which one can point to, or a number which one can name, is held to be capable, at least theoretically, of being the same in diverse contexts and thus to be a universal. Universals of this kind are held to exist in nature. In this article, I shall consider, first, Blanshard's theory of generic and qualitative universals and then his theory of specific universals.

Regarding generic and qualitative universals, he has at different times held different views. He once held, in *The Nature of Thought*, when considering the question "What is the object of a general idea?" that such universals exist and that the question of importance concerning them is how they are to be conceived (*NT*, 1:580 ff.). He denied, first, that the universal of a genus is an abstract from its species (1:583 ff.), and then that it is coextensive with them (1:609). He concluded that since it is false that the universal of a genus is something distinct from the special characters of its species, it must be true that it is identical with them, it must be true that it is distinct from them (1:609–10). These seemingly impossible conditions could, he thought, be met by holding that the universal is a partial realization of its species, a potentiality which its species actualize (1:610). Having elaborated and defended the theory that an idea is its object *in posse* (*NT*, 1: chap. 14), he concluded that the universal of a genus is existent only in and as idea (1:611 –12). To the question "Do you mean to say . . . that the universal does not exist in nature at all . . . ?" he responded that if "nature" means "the order of things and persons dealt with by common sense," then the answer is no; for the world is "not more than a half-way house between the ideal and the fully real" (ibid.). In *Reason and Analysis* he switches from an identity theory of qualitative and generic universals to the resemblance theory and denies that either exists. (*RA*, 409 ff.).

What were Blanshard's reasons for committing himself to an identity view of generic universals (by "generic universals" I mean both what he calls "qualitative" and "generic" universals); and what were his reasons for later rejecting it in favor of the resemblance view? The first question is easy to answer. He once supposed that only an identity theory of generic characters can explain the fact that we perceive things, make judgments, and draw inferences in the way we do; and that without an identity view of generic characters, the truth claims of thought would be without theoretical justification and would be left unwanted and unconfirmed (*NT*, 1:580–81).

Is this supposition true? Blanshard no longer thinks so. I suspect that it is. Clearly it would not be true if the task of explaining and confirming perceptual judgments, etc. can be accomplished by either the identity theory or the theory of resemblance equally well. Again, it is not true if the task can be accomplished by neither. Certainly it is not true if the identity theory cannot perform the task and the resemblance theory can. It is true only if the identity theory can perform the task but the resemblance theory cannot.

What is my objection to the theory of resemblance? Is it that the theory commits one to the acceptance of at least one universal of the kind which the theory denies, namely that of resemblance? Blanshard answers this objection by asserting that there is no reason why one cannot hold that resemblances resemble each other (*RA*, 414–15). But is my objection that if resemblances resemble each other then the resemblances between resemblances also resemble each other, and that the view entails an infinite regress of resemblances and of levels of resemblances? This objection would have weight only if it could be shown that the infinite regress is vicious. John Kearns, in "Sameness and Similarity," has attempted to show that it is.[2] Blanshard easily shows, I think, in "A Rejoinder to Mr. Kearns," that the attempt is not a success.[3] Do I object that things that resemble each other always do so in some *respect*, and that this *respect* must be recognized as an identity? No, the issue between the identity theory and the theory of resemblance is precisely whether or not the *respect* in which two characters or individuals resemble one another *must* be recognized as an identity or not. What then is my objection? It is that something about the theory of resemblance which seems to Blanshard to be part of its strength seems to me to be a fatal weakness.

In behalf of the theory of resemblance, Blanshard argues that it explains cases of classes with uncertain boundaries, whereas the identity theory does not (*RA,* 417; cf. 406). Now a theory which explains cases of classes the boundaries of which are *uncertain* cannot also explain cases of classes the boundaries of which are *certain*. We cannot, as Blanshard maintains, say precisely where in a series of shades the genus red ends and the genus purple or the genus orange begins; but the genus color does not shade into other genera such as shape or sound in the way that red shades into purple or orange. Two colors may resemble each other more closely than either resembles a third. The three colors resemble one another more closely than any one of them resembles a sound. But each color is connected with other colors by intermediaries. There are no intermediaries between a color and a sound. This fact the resemblance theory leaves unexplained.

But can the identity theory do what the resemblance theory cannot? This question can be more easily answered if one considers Blanshard's reasons for abandoning the identity view.

In *The Nature of Thought* Blanshard regarded the main question concerning generic identities as being that which divides defenders of the abstract from those of the concrete universal (*NT,* 1:576; cf. 1:581). He began his attack on the abstract universal by opposing the view that the universal of a genus is distinct from the special characters of its species in nature and distinguishable from them in thought (1:583 ff.; cf. *RA,* 401 ff.). He later opposed the view that the universal of a genus remains precisely the same through the range of its different species (1:601 ff.). To deny that a generic character is distinct from the special characters of its different species and maintain that it remains precisely the same in each of them involves an obvious difficulty which Blanshard wished to avoid (1:609; cf. *RA,* 413–14). To admit that the universal of a genus does not remain precisely the same and maintain that it is an identity and really a universal involves an even more obvious difficulty which Blanshard also wished to avoid (1:607). He attempted to replace the abstract identities which he rejected with a different sort of identity—that of a potentiality which remains the same throughout the different stages of its own development (1:610–11). Unfortunately this view of identity involves a difficulty which Blanshard at first did not see. The identity theory of generic characters was initially accepted by him because he thought it was required to explain the fact that in perception we recognize different characters as species of a single genus, as exemplifications of something which might be exemplified elsewhere and in other ways. We believe that in such cases our judgments are true, and an identity theory of generic characters was thought to be required if our judgments are to be confirmed. But if one holds that the universal of a genus is the *thought* of its species, this thought being conceived as a potentiality which the species actualize, he must accept an awkward consequence. To the question Why does one recognize a specific character which he calls blue as a species of the genus color and not of the genus sound? the only possible answer is that the specific character actualizes the potentiality which is the genus color but not the potentiality which is the genus sound. What one needs is a theory about the world which answers questions about ourselves. What Blanshard offered was a theory about ourselves which explained, if it explained anything at all, certain facts about the world. It thus required a further theory about the world for its completion, which in *Reason and Analysis* he apparently sees.

But why did he reject formal logic's view that the universal of a genus is distinct from its differentiations in nature or at least distinguishable from them in thought? In *The Nature of Thought* he offers a number of objections, and I shall consider the two which seem most important.

(1) We recognize blue as a species of color and square as a species of shape. For special purposes we would perhaps be willing to say that a certain object which happens to be blue is a member of the class of square things. Or that an object which happens to be square belongs to the class of blue things. Should anyone argue that since blue may be round, elliptical, or square, square blue is a species of blue; and that since a square may be blue, red, or yellow, blue square is a species of square, we would probably all think this odd. We take square rectangle to be a species of rectangle, but for some reason we do not take blue square to be a species of square. We see that the genus rectangle includes the character square, but not the character blue.

What is the difference between the two cases? Evidently we see that the genus rectangle includes the character square, but that the character square does not include the character blue. The view that a generic identity is *distinct from* the special characters of its different species provides no justification for our saying that square is a species of rectangle but that the blue square is not a species of square. The fact that we do say this is neither justified nor explained. (*NT,* 1:585–86).

(2) We can distinguish the blue of a blue square from the squareness, but can we distinguish from the colors blue, yellow, and red the generic character color, or from the shapes square, circle, and triangle the generic character shape? The view that a generic identity is distinct from the special characters of its species implies that we can. The fact is that we cannot. We cannot think of color that is distinct from all colors, nor of shape that is distinct from all shapes. The view that implies that we can could never serve to explain the plain fact that we cannot (*NT,* 1:583–85).

Unless these objections can be met the defender of an identity theory must hold either that a generic character, although not distinct from the special characters of its different species, is yet the same in each; or hold, as Blanshard once attempted to do, that the universal of a genus is identical with its differentiations and also distinct from them (*NT,* 1:597–98). But either view seems inherently paradoxical, and the only remaining course would be to abandon the identity theory and accept the resemblance view. Can these objections be met? I believe that they can, and I shall indicate briefly the direction in which I think hope might lie.

In *The Nature of Thought*, Blanshard anticipates various questions concerning his objections to the abstract universal. One is: May not the universal be a genuine object of *implicit* apprehension? His answer is that it is not. But in later discussion he reveals, I think, that it is.

Blanshard thinks that it is easier to see in the case of color that a generic character is not something distinct and thus distinguishable from the special characters of its species than it is in the case of triangle (*NT*, 1:593). Kemp Smith had argued: "If triangularity be defined as the type 'three-sided rectilinear figure,' then through all variations of type the number, straightness and closedness of the sides remain unvaried. In these respects the type is absolutely uniform and identical in all triangles, however otherwise they may vary."[4]

Blanshard's response is that "if triangularity consisted simply of threeness *plus* straightness *plus* closedness, there would be force in this; but it does not. It consists in a combination of these things, an arrangement which in no two species of triangle is the same" (*NT*, 1:602). But what is the basis of Blanshard's confident assertion about what triangularity *is*? Has he mentally surveyed a range of similar plain figures? It is possible that he has. I think it more likely that he has not. But if not, then what has he done? Apparently he has added to his explicit apprehension of the elements threeness, straightness, and closedness the implicit apprehension that what a triangle is is not the elements themselves but always the elements "combined." If so, then he has proven that a generic character may be at least in part a genuine object of implicit apprehension.

I turn now to Blanshard's theory of specific universals. The defense which he offers of an identity theory of specific qualities or characters consists partly of an argument for universals and partly of an argument against particulars. My thesis is that the principle that two things cannot differ solely numerically is affirmed by the argument for universals but inadvertently contradicted by the argument against particulars; and that if the argument for universals is retained, the argument against particulars must be given up.

The basic issue concerning specific universals is regarded by Blanshard to be that of identity versus exact likeness. Taking as an example "two patches of white which are indistinguishable in their shade," he argues: "If the shades are exactly similar, then so far as their *quality* is concerned, they are one. If they are not one, where do they differ? To point to some difference other than one of shade would be irrelevant, for it is only shade that is in question. And if we keep to shade, it is admitted that no difference is there. Either, then, the shade is literally one, or we are contradicting ourselves" (*NT*, 1:631; cf. *RA*,

394). This argument, Blanshard acknowledges, commits him to the principle that two things cannot differ only numerically—otherness is always based on dissimilarity, never dissimilarity on sheer otherness—and in *Reason and Analysis* he concludes the argument by considering an alleged example of a purely numerical difference proposed by Max Black.

We are asked by Black to conceive of a universe consisting solely of two spheres, each a mile in diameter and with their centers two miles apart. Every attribute and relation possessed by the one, he argues, would then be possessed by the other, but they would still be two. Two things may therefore be other while also exactly alike. Blanshard recognizes that neither sphere could be said to be to the left or right or above or below the other because such relations could only exist from the point of view of an observer outside both (*RA*, 396). Any basis on which one sphere could be called "this" and the other "that" is excluded by hypothesis. Blanshard writes: "Now we . . . hold . . . that where you have nothing on which you could base a 'this' and 'that', you cannot have two things; and hence to begin by saying in effect, 'Take a world consisting of two things that do not even differ as this and that', is asking us to do what we are maintaining we cannot do" (397).

Part of Blanshard's defense of specific universals consists of an attempt to maintain the thesis that "There are no particulars." He writes, ". . . what gives apparent particularity to any character or complex is itself always universal" (*NT*, 1:631). To the argument that spatial or temporal relations serve to confer uniqueness, his reply is that such relations are themselves repeatable and are, therefore, universals. Such relations as *to the right of* and *later than* are found at different places and at different times. To the argument that even if a thing's spatial and temporal relations taken singly are repeatable and cannot confer uniqueness, the totality of its spatial and temporal relations could not be repeatable and thus does not confer spatio-temporal uniqueness, his reply is that the totality of a thing's spatial and temporal relations is repeatable. He writes: "There is no reason in principle why there should not be two spaces, both infinite in extent and one the duplicate of the other, just as there is dream space and waking space. And though time in its greater abstractness is always harder to deal with than space, there seems again no reason in principle why there should not be more than one time series" (*RA*, 401; cf. *NT*, chap. 17, sec. 13).

But in arguing thus, Blanshard raises the question: What would make two spaces two? They could not differ solely numerically any more than two qualities or characters could. On what sort of difference then could the numerical difference of two duplicate spaces be based? What would prevent two duplicate spaces from being simply one self-identical space? We may rule out any qualitative difference between the content of one space and that of another, for if what we mean by space includes such content, then a difference between the things and events of one space and those of another might provide a basis for numerical difference, but the two spaces would then not be duplicates. On what sort of dissimilarity could the otherness of two *duplicate* spaces be based? One might, I suspect, on the basis of an identity theory of the content of consciousness and processes or states in the brain, hold that two private spaces are related in one public space. If so he would have to admit that the totality of a thing's spatial relations in both private and public space confers uniqueness, or assert the possibility of duplicate public spaces as well as duplicate private spaces and then confront the same question: What makes two spaces two?

Blanshard once wrote in a letter to me that "there is no super space in which possible spaces are themselves all included." Presumably he holds that if two spaces are spatially related, they are actually parts of one space.

Perhaps two duplicate spaces may be thought to differ in time. An illustration which Blanshard offers would seem to suggest that they may. He writes: "Suppose we were so made that we spent half of each day in dream and the other half 'awake,' and that all the things and events in one half duplicated the things and events of the other. . . . the two orders would have equal title to real existence. But note that there would be no spatial uniqueness, not even if the orders were extended to infinity; for however far the determination of a thing were carried in one order it could be paralleled in the other" (*NT,* 1:638). But an alternation between two spatial orders in one temporal order would entail different relations of before and after between the two spatial orders and these different temporal relations would serve to particularize each. Only in an infinite temporal series without beginning or end, without any past, present, and future, could the relations of one spatial order within the series be the same as those of another. But such a time series would be in principle timeless. In a real temporal succession a sequence of consecutive spaces would contain spaces with different relations of before and after to one another, and different and ever-changing relations to first one and then another present space.

Should one suggest that a space in one temporal series could have the same relations as a space in a different temporal series, the question arises: In what way would one temporal series be different from the other? We may rule out difference in quality and also difference in time. Just as different spaces might be contained in one temporal series, so different temporal series might have different locations in space. But, if so, then the spaces in one time series and those in another time series would be all contained in one space.

The argument for specific universals begins with a denial of the possibility of exact likeness. The argument against particulars ends with what amounts to an assertion of the possibility of two spaces exactly alike. Thus, one of the two arguments must be abandoned. The argument for universals cannot be abandoned since, as Blanshard insists, identity is a condition of thought. "... to abandon identity generally would be to abjure all reasoning, since inference moves through identity; ..." (*NT*, 1:649). Since Blanshard would not wish to give up universals, he must accept particulars as well.

MARCUS CLAYTON
DIVISION OF PHILOSOPHY AND RELIGION
PAINE COLLEGE

NOTES

[1] *Reason and Analysis (RA)*, 393; cf. *The Nature of Thought (NT)*, 1:624.
[2] *Philosophy and Phenomenological Research* 29 (1968–69): 105–15.
[3] Ibid., 116–18.
[4] *Mind* (1927), 416 (quoted in *NT*, 1:601).

24. REPLY TO MARCUS CLAYTON

Blanshard's Theory of Universals

By a universal I mean a quality, a relation, or a pattern of qualities in relation, that may exist in diverse contexts. Such entities are essential to thought at every level. They are essential to perception, for when we perceive something before us as a dandelion or a man or a Ford car, we are classifying the object, that is, recognizing it as one of a kind: and a kind is a universal. When I argue that this tree, being a maple, will have red or yellow leaves in the fall, I am arguing through a universal; for I am saying that the character of being a maple normally carries with it the further character of having in the fall leaves that are so colored. Scientific inquiry consists largely in the search for causal laws; and a causal law connects events of one kind with events of another; a special kind of malady, hay fever, is caused by a special kind of pollen, for example, that of the ragweed. The existence of universals is therefore of the greatest practical importance; and since they are a mainstay of thought at every level and in every field, their analysis is of the greatest theoretical importance.

Abstract Universals

Accordingly in both *The Nature of Thought* and *Reason and Analysis* I gave much time and effort to their examination. What particularly marked my treatment in the earlier book was a criticism of the traditional logical doctrine of the abstract universal. It was thought to supply the key to all classification. Suppose you are confronted by a range of colors that includes every color in the spectrum, and given the task of classifying them. You would probably begin by grouping the shades together under a few salient or familiar colors, such as red, green, and yellow. You would include under red all the shades from a deep crimson to a light pink, under yellow all the shades from a deep orange to a light lemon, and so on. Now according to the traditional theory, this grouping is done by extracting from the range of reds an identical redness possessed by all the reds in common, an identical yellowness from all the yellows, and so on. These are universals that form the species of which a range of shades are instances. Can these species be grouped together in a class? Yes. For when one compares red, yellow, and green, one can see that they themselves are all kinds under a higher genus, color. How does one recognize this? In the same way as before: one sees that in all these colors there is an identical abstract character, color as such, or coloredness. But when I fixed my attention on the abstraction red, or the higher abstraction color-as-such, I found myself gazing at a blank. When you leave out all that differentiates the various reds, you have not reached an invariant redness, common to all reds; and when you try to isolate (not of course physically, but conceptually) the color-as-such in all colors, which is nevertheless no color in particular, nothing recognizable as color is left. The same seemed to be true of other sensory qualities, such as smells, tastes, hard and soft, rough and smooth, hot and cold. The alleged identity to be found in such ranges of qualities I called the "qualitative universal." And because I could not find any such identity, I called it a fiction, a "false universal."

I had much the same experience with classes of which the lowest members were individuals rather than qualities—such things as plants, men, and animals. You may define the essence or universal of man, for example, as "rational, two-legged animal." But that obviously will not do. It implies that an amputee would lose his humanity along with his legs, and that Emerson, when his mind had gone, would cease to be a man. Besides, as you climb the ladder of classes from man to animal, you should find yourself rising from the essential to the quintessential when instead you find yourself at the top with the thinnest figment of all. Shakespeare and an animalcule are both animals, but can you lift from the two of them an essence identical in each, a hard and unchanging central core which, with due additions, becomes now a snail, now a snake, now a dinosaur, and now the bard? That is certainly not the way things are constructed, nor is it the way we think about them. I did not dismiss this kind of universal with the confidence that I did the qualitative universal, but I ended by doing so nevertheless. This universal whose members were individuals I called the "generic universal."

Specific Universals

Did it follow that there were no universals at all? No, that would not do either. I found them, however, not at the top of the scale of abstractions but at the bottom. Take, not red or color, both of which denote classes of colors, but the specific shade of this rose leaf. Is it, or is it not, possible that this precise shade should be presented elsewhere? Of course it is. If it did not appear in some other petal of the same rose, it may well have done so in some flower of the tenth century B.C. or A.D. But suppose it were never duplicated at all; would that affect its status as a universal? Surely not. We can see that in the nature of the case it might be; and this is all that is needed. Or take the specific number six. Does not that remain the same in six matches, six sisters, and six planets? Does it make any kind of sense to say that as it appears in six matches it was perhaps a little less than six and in six planets a little more? The question answers itself. In such absolutely specific characters as this shade of red or the number six we have identities that are clearly repeatable. These I called "specific universals." I called them so because they could not further be divided into kinds. There are no kinds of this specific shade, and though there are divisors of six, there are no kinds or species of it.

This theory of universals still seems to me to accord well with our use of universals in thought; and it is only just to remember that I was approaching the subject from this side. The "inverse variation of intension and extension" had little relation to the actual content of our concepts. On this theory the word "triangle" should mean less to the geometer who had studied the varieties of triangles and their properties than to the beginner in the study; and to the old salt who had sailed in every kind of ship the term "ship" should carry the most meager figment of meaning. That this was not true seemed manifest from the instant and competent way such people dealt with mistakes. Say something mistaken about the triangle, and the geometer at once points out that in the scalene triangle this is not the case; say something about sailing ships, and the old salt will point out that your remarks do not apply to brigantines. The grasp of the universal goes down among the species over which it ranges, even though these species are not regarded as an explicit part of the genus. In actual thought the concept, or grasp of the genus, seems to hold the thought of the species within itself, though in implicit or dispositional form. It was this that suggested the notion of the concept as the potentiality of its range of objects. I do not suppose that this notion will hold literally; it is probably better taken as a metaphorical sketch of the relation between a general thought and its objects; but if so taken, it seems to me close to the truth.

When I came to deal with the problem of universals and particulars in *Reason and Analysis*, I felt the same difficulties as before. There was no identical red in the range of reds.

But it did not seem accurate, either, to say that the range of reds was implicit or potential in the thought of the genus. What united the range of reds was similarity or resemblance. Again, though Shakespeare and the animalcule were extremely unlike, it seemed more sensible to connect them through a long line of resembling organisms differing in complexity than by some kernel of animality that was present changelessly throughout. Did such resemblance imply identity? Bradley said it did; and I made a careful study of the debate on this question long ago in the pages of *Mind* between Bradley and James. I began with the presumption that Bradley, being the more formidable logician, was probably right. I came slowly to the conclusion that he was wrong. Colors were united with colors and odors with odors, not by any discoverable identity, but by a similarity that must be taken as ultimate. When Bradley was pressed in such cases, he fell back on the conviction that the identity *must* be there, whether he could elicit it or not. This carried too strong a suggestion of whistling in the dark. The upshot of my reflections was that the case for identity in the specific universal was overwhelmingly strong, but that both the qualitative and the generic universals seemed most accurately interpretable as references to ranges of similars. I say "references" advisedly. For regarding the existence of the universal in nature I held to my old view; these universals were concepts existent in the mind of the thinker.

I have ventured on this summary account because my theory of universals has received so little attention that I cannot assume familiarity with it, and because some summary is therefore needed to bring us to the point at which Mr. Clayton starts his criticism. He has given my theory, and even the modifications of it, a long, generous, and careful study, under which the original theory comes out more happily than its later developments. He particularly deplores my abandonment of the identity for the similarity theory. I am pleased to note, however, that he refuses to adopt either of the two commonest grounds for rejecting the similarity view. One is that of Russell, who argued that even on the similarity view one must accept at least one universal based on identity, namely similarity itself; and if we have to admit one such universal, we may as well admit others. But why this one universal should be irreducible never appeared. Surely similarities may be as truly united by similarities as any other class; the similarity between Caesar and Napoleon is surely not identical with that between romantic and Christian love. Similarity, as a universal, may therefore be dealt with in the same way as qualitative universals. The other common objection is that if similars resemble each other, they must do so in a certain respect, and this respect must itself be a universal of the identical sort. But as Mr. Clayton sees, this is to beg the question, for whether this alleged common element is an identity or a range of similars is the very point at issue.

The Resemblance Theory

So he begins his attack at another place. He thinks the resemblance theory plausible enough so long as it deals with classes that lack sharp edges; red shades over so gradually through purple into blue that it is more or less arbitrary where the class line between red and blue is to be drawn. Mr. Clayton admits that this cloudiness at the borders answers to the facts, and that the resemblance theory squares with it well. But what about the higher universals of color and sound? Here the edges are of the sharpest. We may admit that "each color is connected with other colors by intermediaries. There are no intermediaries between a color and a sound. This fact," says Mr. Clayton, "the resemblance theory leaves unexplained."

I am puzzled by this objection. For one thing, it hardly belongs to the theory of universals to "explain" why the classes we find in the world are as they are, why the classes of colors shade into each other while those of color and sound, or sensations and atoms, do not. This is a problem for the ontologist, not for the logician. But further, why should classes that are sharply divided from each other give special difficulty to the advocate of resemblance? He will find no more difficulty than before in relating by resemblance the ultimate members of his classes, and the very lack of similarity between certain classes as wholes, such as sounds and colors, eases his task rather than complicating it. It does for him just what it does for the identity theorist, namely give such classes a desirable sharpness of outline.

Mr. Clayton next raises a point of much difficulty, to which I doubt if I have given or can give an answer satisfactory even to myself. He says that in spite of my attack on the abstract universal, I admit it and use it. Take the case of triangularity. Kemp Smith maintained that the intension of triangle, defined as "a three-sided rectilinear figure," remained identical through all triangles, since the number, straightness, and closedness of the sides were all invariant. I replied that a triangle consisted not simply of threeness plus straightness plus closedness, but a union of these three in which there lay already the potentiality of variance. The most obvious mode of division was into triangles where all the sides were equal, two were equal, or none were equal—the equilateral, isosceles, and scalene. Could triangularity as such, the union of these three attributes in no particular manner, either be or be conceived? H. W. B. Joseph thought not, and with Mr. Joseph I seldom found it possible to disagree. Triangularity was *not* quite the same thing in the various species of triangle. To grasp triangularity as such is to grasp the possibility of taking certain diverse forms, and then the clean-cut division between genus and species has been blurred. Mr. Clayton charges me with coming down on both sides of this blurred line. On the one hand, as a critic of the abstract universal, I maintain that there is no abstract identity running through the variety of triangles. On the other hand I admit that geometers continually and successfully talk about "the triangle" and report properties that hold of it "as such," i.e. equally in all species. I doubt if these views are really inconsistent. It is possible, I suppose, to take a given triangle as standing for all varieties of the figure, and to see in deriving one's theorems about it that its being equilateral, isosceles, or scalene would not affect the truth of the theorem. If it were not possible to direct or divide one's attention in this way, fixing it upon fundamental resemblances and dismissing irrelevant differences, science could not do its work.

The Identity of Indiscernibles

Mr. Clayton turns next to my treatment of specific universals, such as this shade of red and the number six. His argument here is more complicated. He holds (1) that my defense of the specific universal commits me to the identity of indiscernibles, which is a controversial thesis; (2) that the principle of individuation I adopt commits me to a denial of particulars; and (3) that my defense of this principle involves me in an admission of the particulars I deny. There is a force worth considering in each of these allegations.

(1) That the number six does not differ in six spots on a die and in six apples, muses, or planets is, I think, self-evident. If more evidence were wanted, it could be pointed out that unless this identity were granted, no calculation into which the number entered could be relied upon as valid; and since what held of six would no doubt hold of other numbers, no measurements could be made, no grocery bills added up, and no bank accounts kept with confidence. The identity of this shade of red with that must be defended differently. If someone said that two stamps of the same issue differed in shade, we should probably resort to inspection. But seeing them as the same hardly proves them the same, for some people can see differences where others cannot; and even proof that the two wavelengths were the same would not be enough, since wavelength is not color, and even to the same wavelength two persons may differ in their response. But I think we can see that there is no sort of reason why two sensings of mine, or of yours and mine, should *not* be of the same shade precisely; and this is all that is contended.

Why not say that in such a case the shades you and I are seeing are not identical but exactly alike? Of course the sensations, as events occurring in different minds, are at best similar, not the same; but if it is held that the *content* of sensation, the shade of color sensed, is precisely similar though different, that seems to me nonsense. Remember that in *shade* the colors admittedly do not differ, and if their shades do not differ, these are not merely alike; they are the same. That is what is insisted on by "the identity of indiscernibles"; if things are two that must be because they differ; they do not differ because, though indiscernible, they are somehow two. In short, there is no such thing as a merely numerical difference. Numerical difference is based on otherness, not otherness on a prior difference in number. Being two is based on being other, not being other on being two. The principle has been disputed by Mr. Black in an example in which the world is reduced in imagination to two spheres which are alleged to have none but a numerical difference. I have dealt with that example in *Reason and Analysis* (396 ff.), with a result that leads me to say, with Sir Alfred Ayer: "in spite of all that can be urged against it, I am still inclined to hold that the principle of the identity of indiscernibles is necessarily true."[1]

The Principle of Individuation

(2) Suppose one holds that the two stamps are of exactly the same shade and shape; they are still admittedly two. What makes them two? A traditional answer has been that they are two different instantiations or particulars of the same character. Now what is it that particularizes? The traditional reply has been that the identical character belongs to two different substances, two different *its* that possess the character in common. What sort of entity is this "it"? That question, we are told, is unanswerable, because the *it* has no characters of its own by which it could be described; its office is to possess characters without being anything characterizable in itself; it is a mere and bare particular. In a proposition it may stand as the logical subject, never as the predicate. Thus what differentiates the two stamps is real but wholly indescribable. Now I doubt the existence of these will-o'-the-wisps. They cannot, of course, be verified in sense; they seem to be ad hoc figments invented to explain why the characters of a thing stick together and are counted as one thing. For that there are other and more plausible explanations. And it is hard to see how so transparent and characterless an entity as a bare particular could provide either the transient glue or the permanent foundation of anything.

But if not this pure particular, what is it that individuates? I have held that it is the differing relations in which characters stand. We say that stamp A is different from B because it stands to the left of B, three inches farther away than the pen, and ten inches nearer than the envelope. These relations are all different in the case of B. It has been acutely pointed out by Mr. Meiland that one cannot escape individuating through relations by falling back on particulars, since the only way in which particulars could differentiate is to have different relations themselves.[2] It is interesting that Russell, from *An Inquiry into Meaning and Truth* forward, was moving toward this same conclusion, that what individuates is not particulars, but relations.

This carries us to an unconventional conclusion. If what individuates is not particulars, but relations, and relations are universals, then particulars seemed to have been dispensed with altogether. That is the conclusion I reached in *The Nature of Thought*, and I have still found no conclusive reason for abandoning it. Perhaps the most natural reply is as follows: We admit that the relations "to the left of," "farther," and "nearer" are themselves universals. But suppose one continues the process of adding relations until one has exhausted all the relations of the given stamp to everything else in space. Surely that is something absolutely unique. But is it? A universal is not necessarily what is repeated, but what might be, and I do not see why in principle there should not be two spaces or more, in which one repeated the contents of the other.

(3) In suggesting such a reply, Mr. Clayton thinks I have gone too far and fallen into self-contradiction. For should I not be admitting the possibility of duplicate spatial realms without providing any principle of individuation which would make them distinguishable? Am I not left in the position of admitting at least two particulars, or realms of particulars, that are distinguishable only numerically?

That there are differing spatial orders seems evident from the fact of a distinct space in dreams. Mr. Russell has argued that this distinct space may exist at a point in one's head, which itself is in waking space. I find it difficult to make this notion clear. But the fact remains that we do live in different spaces in the dream world and the waking world, and there seems to be nothing logically impossible in duplicate spatial orders. The two worlds might be experiences or aspects differently related to an absolute, as were the "attributes" of Spinoza, or phases of an eternal cyclical recurrence distinguishable in time. And it should be pointed out that the difficulty of finding a satisfactory principle of individuation in this highly speculative case does not make more intelligible the alternative notion of that which is identical being really two.

Why all this animadversion against the barely particular? Chiefly because it is unverifiable in experience and unnecessary in logic, a sort of *asylum ignorantiae*. But there is another reason that Mr. Clayton has no doubt surmised. The bare particular is a road block to the understanding of things. Existentialists can talk profoundly about it, and point out that rationalists are skating on thin ice that covers unplumbed depths of the existent and the unintelligible. The rationalist finds it not quite easy to reply. It is only too true that his intelligence is a feeble instrument and that all the knowledge that it has acquired amounts to a few pebbles on the beach of an unexplored sea. If people tell him that his reason is too frail a craft in which to launch out upon that sea, he wants to know why. If they tell him he will never reach the Indies and that if he did, they would prove a different land from any he hoped to find, he will reply that this is probably true, but that if there is a chance in a thousand of his even seeing in the distance the gleaming port of understanding, he will take the risk. But if they tell him that the port itself is an illusion, and that his craft must founder at its very launching on rocks of irrationality in the nature of things, this is a more serious matter; the very search after understanding will then be futile. He must try to find for himself whether the rocks are there, whether below the surface of patterned characters that his mind can deal with there lies an assortment of jagged existents, the more destructive for their concealment, and which are beyond examination or analysis by intelligence. Mr. Clayton has suggested that I look again and make some reconnaissance of these dangers, and I am grateful to him for the warning. I have followed his advice; I have looked again; and can only report that I still find nothing. So, foolhardy or not, I am out on the sea again.

1. A. J. Ayer, "The Identity of Indiscernibles," in *Universals and Particulars*, ed. M. J. Loux (Garden City, N.Y.: Doubleday, 1970), 224.
2. Loux, *Universals and Particulars*, 260.

25 BRAND BLANSHARD'S WORLD VIEW
Lewis Edwin Hahn

ALTHOUGH Brand Blanshard has been more concerned to apply his general philosophy or world view to problems of knowledge and moral conduct than to set it forth explicitly and systematically, it is clear that he offers a fresh and lucid version of Absolute or Objective Idealism, a view exemplified also by Hegel, Bradley, Bosanquet, and Royce. The main thrust of this view is toward integrating experienced material in larger and larger wholes, each more inclusive, more determinate, and more coherent than the level before, until the Absolute is reached; and then it turns out that in a sense the Absolute has been present all along guiding the movement of thought or reason toward fulfillment in a comprehensive intelligible system of necessarily related parts. The features of any organic or integrative process and its achievement, on this view, as one commentator puts it, are:

> (1) fragments of experience which appear with (2) *nexuses* or connections or implications, which spontaneously lead as a result of the aggravation of (3) *contradictions,* gaps, oppositions, or counteractions to resolution in (4) an *organic whole,* which is found to have been (5) *implicit* in the fragments, and to (6) *transcend* the previous contradictions by means of a coherent totality, which (7) *economizes,* saves, preserves all the original fragments of experience without any loss.[1]

Blanshard does not set forth this system as demonstrably true. Rather he insists that it is a hypothetical or postulational affair, something to be judged in terms of empirical consequences. He suggests that it is neither self-evident nor certain; but if we do accept it provisionally, we can then see how well the facts fall into illuminating order and how far the exercise of reason goes toward justifying our postulate (*Reason and Analysis* [*RA*], 383). Proceeding on this assumption, we may be surprised at how well things fall into place. This is not to say that his world view is without its problems, but which of its alternatives is free from difficulties?

Blanshard has developed this position with resourcefulness and verve and with such attention to details, problems, and relations that one may be sure the difficulties have not escaped his attention. Accordingly, if he has nevertheless maintained his position, he undoubtedly has his reasons and good ones, growing out of the logic of the materials and ideas involved; and our questions will come as no surprise to him. But, hopefully, they may afford him an opportunity to shed further light on some aspects of his world view and to direct our attention to the lines of evidence pointing toward, perhaps even necessitating, his conclusions.

My questions fall into four main groups: first, some queries concerning Blanshard's explanatory ideal and his account of explanation; second, some misgivings concerning the place of change and novelty in his view; third, some questions concerning his treatment of the many finite individuals; and fourth, some inquiries as to values and the relation between the intelligible and the valuable for him.

1. Cosmic Geography: Islands, Continents, and Central Mass of Experience

Before turning to these questions I should like to outline in somewhat greater detail some key features of his view, beginning with his account of the integrative process. For Blanshard this process is developed in large part in terms of thought, not surprisingly for an idealist; but if we remember that for him thought is in process of identifying itself with or becoming its object and is already this object *in posse* (*The Nature of Thought* [*NT*], 1:473), we see that he is talking about the full range of facts and experiences in the world and not simply about the psychological as opposed to or apart from things. On his view, as we have noted earlier, thought moves in the direction of increasing comprehensiveness, determinateness, and coherence.

For Blanshard, the ultimate reason why thought moves is "because the system of ideas which at any moment *is* the mind on its intellectual side is incomplete and fragmentary, and because that completed system which is immanent and operative within it impels to explicit fulfilment" (*NT*, 2:45). The course of thinking in any given case begins with a shock to the present system of thought. What we find conflicts with the system. "Something is offered so alien to the present circle of ideas, so unassimilable by it, so tantalizingly isolated from it, that the impulse toward integration is stung into action" (2:47).

Typically in any given situation thought starts in the following way:

There comes, as in Macbeth, a knocking at the door by something that the mind is not prepared to receive, but must find a place for. The unity of thought is shattered; outside the continent that forms its mainland—to use a

very useful figure—there appears an island that ought to be attached to it
and yet is not; and this disunion on the surface sets in motion a force below,
which by upheavals and rearrangements seeks to unite the fragments to the
mainland. [*NT,* 2:48]

These fragments have connections, implications, or "logical filaments"
which lead on toward a complete whole or totality. Nothing is irrelevant to
anything else. Everything has relevance for something. Everything has
referential strands pointing beyond itself toward something else. As
Blanshard and Bosanquet agree, a "nisus toward wholeness," or a "nisus
toward completion," is everywhere the spring of thought (*NT,* 2:129). The aim
of understanding "is to achieve systematic vision, so to apprehend what is
now unknown to us as to relate it, and relate it necessarily, to what we know
already" (2:261).

The dynamics of the world situation are such that there is no stopping
short of the Absolute. So long as any possible unattached island remains in
thought there is a restless surge toward tying it firmly to the mainland. The
drive toward necessary, intelligible system, as Blanshard interprets it,
struggles against the unstable, the incoherent, the incomplete, the inarticulate, the indeterminate, the partial, the contingent, and the changing. The
presence of any one of these—and some would hold that they are present
throughout our world—is a sign of the need for greater logical stability, more
coherence with more inclusiveness. The goal of the theoretic impulse "is
nothing short of a system perfect and all-embracing" (*NT,* 2:438). It "cannot
rest while anything in the universe is outside the web of necessity" (1:654).

The drive toward completeness and necessary coherence culminates in an
absolute organic whole, "a system which, because subject to no further conditions, can alone be self-subsistently real" (*NT,* 2:427). This intelligible
whole or system, "as all-comprehensive, is logically stable, and, as perfectly
integrated, leaves no loose ends" (2:428). It is "a system at once perfect and
all-embracing" (2:449), fully determinate, and fully real. As something
beyond the potential, it is also beyond time and thus unchanging. Or to take
Blanshard's phrasing in his *Encyclopaedia Britannica* article on "The Absolute," the Absolute "is timeless or eternal," "not subject to change."[2] It is
the one and only true particular (*NT,*1:639). In short, then, for both Blanshard
and Bosanquet, "the world is a single individual whose parts are connected
with each other by a necessity so intimate and so organic that the nature of
the part" depends "on its place in the Absolute" (*RA,* 145).

Once the Absolute is reached it is seen to have been implicit in the
fragments, in the islands, of experience from the beginning. It has been
"there" all along (*NT,* 1:516). Although our comprehension of it may change
from time to time, the Absolute is unchanging. So in spite of all the talk of

development, growth, fulfillment, realization, advancing, and the like, in reality the Absolute does not need to have developed; it has been there throughout in its perfection, in its completeness, of necessity, guiding our search for the all-comprehensive, coherent system. Blanshard, however, describes the search in terms of two major ends of thought, "one immanent, one transcendent. On the one hand it [thought] seeks fulfilment in a special kind of satisfaction, the satisfaction of systematic vision. On the other hand it seeks fulfilment in its object. . . . these ends are one" (2:262). The more fully we realize the immanent end, the more adequately we characterize the transcendent reality.

All the contradictions, fragments, incoherences, and contingencies are transcended in the Absolute, and the various fragments are preserved without loss in the totality, the system of systems. All the parts or lesser wholes are combined and integrated into an intelligible structure, a coherent totality, without omitting what is distinctive in each (*NT*, 2:442). In superseding lesser systems the Absolute as the perfect and all-embracing system absorbs and extends their gains (2:438). It is "an all-inclusive system in which everything is related internally to everything else" (2:453), which is to say that everything is so integral a part of its context "that it can neither be nor be truly conceived apart from that context" (2:452). Blanshard explains that a relation "is internal to a term when in its absence the term would be different; it is external when its addition or withdrawal would make *no* difference to the term" (2:451). Thus the parts are fully coherent in the double sense of being consistent throughout and mutually entailing each other (*Philosophical Interrogations* [*PI*], 212). Every part coheres perfectly with every other and is thus necessarily related to every other (*NT*, 2:429).

2. Knowing, Understanding, and Explaining

What is it to know something? To understand something? To explain it? To render it intelligible? To analyze it? These are questions which, understandably, may be answered differently by representatives of different world views. These notions, as Blanshard and I agree (*RA*, 382), may well be interpreted differently in terms of their different conceptual frameworks. Accordingly, an Aristotle, a Peirce, or a James may answer the questions differently from a Blanshard. Whereas for Blanshard any deviation from the notion that everything in the universe is logically necessary and intelligible marks a retreat from rationalism (81–82), an Aristotelian may argue that there is in nature a material surd factor which it is only reasonable to recognize. Or again, though Blanshard conceives of reason as "the power and function of grasping necessary connections" (382), a Peirce or a James would find it eminently reasonable to emphasize contingency in our world. For the latter pair there is a place in the real world for the almost, the not quite, the imprecise, the aleatory, and the maybe so. But not so for Blanshard. And we might well ask how much evidence or what kind of evidence, if any, he would need to shift these from the realm of appearances into the real world. Perhaps nothing short of a radical transformation of his conceptions of reason or the intelligible and the real would do.

Blanshard's explanatory ideal is based on the Absolute. It is not until we see things in their necessary place in the Absolute that we understand them and they become intelligible. Understanding means "apprehending something in a system which renders it necessary" (*NT,* 2:24). Something becomes intelligible "only when it is seen in context, and seen as required by that context."[3] Stopping with a limited context, moreover, will not satisfy Blanshard's version of reason or the theoretic impulse. Accepting the rational postulate "commits us to the view that the world is rational in the specific sense that every fact and event is connected with its context, and ultimately with every other fact and event, in a way that is logically necessary" ("Internal Relations," 228). This, in turn, "implies that every fact and event is ultimately connected with all others by internal relations" (ibid.).

For Blanshard there are many types and degrees of necessity or requiredness—causal, means-end relation, logical, and so on; and as a contextualist I can see, with Dewey, that the needs or requirements of different problematic situations are varied. The types of explanation may vary accordingly, and although the philosopher may use all types, as Blanshard sees it,

> only the logical type seems wholly satisfactory. For only when a proposition is self-evidently true, or is seen to follow from something else that is, can the question Why? be so conclusively answered that it is meaningless to raise it again. When one sees that a proposition, thing, or event *must* be what it is, it is idle to ask Why? again, for one already holds in one's hands the clearest and most conclusive answer that is possible. ["Internal Relations," 227–28]

If only the logical type of explanation or necessity seems wholly satisfactory, is the reason cited above the appropriate one for an objective idealist? Is self-evidence the reason why? This seems contrary to Blanshard's usual emphasis on a coherent, comprehensive system and to the basic categories of objective idealism. I should think that for him the reasons would have to be given, if possible, in terms of the requirements of the Absolute as a comprehensive system of necessarily related parts.

There are, however, some problems with this too. Our experience is with far more restricted contexts than that of the Absolute. Our problems are many and varied and grow out of specific situations and contexts, and their solutions require something far short of the totality of things. Although it may be possible to trace connections between any two things one may happen to mention, with many or few intermediary links, the degree of relevance for any given problem may vary from crucial to practically insignificant; and to hold that all things are parts of the absolute web of necessity may go beyond both our evidence and our needs for any given problem.

The vision of a tidy universe with no litter, no loose ends, and no contingencies may have a certain aesthetic appeal, but is it required by reason or the intellectual impulse? And if our world is shot through and through with change and contingency, do we understand it better by calling these features unreal? Do we understand the imperfect better by treating it as perfect? Does not understanding anything involve seeing it as it is, both in actuality and in potential, rather than converting it into what would be crystal clear for human reason?

Will nothing short of perfect all-embracing totality satisfy the theoretic drive and the requirements of reason for Blanshard? And if the answer is that only the Absolute will do, is this so by stipulation or definition? For that matter, is a counsel of perfection required by or even in accord with what he sometimes refers to as the good gray virtue of reasonableness? Are we identifying the theoretic end with a partial system which, though "informed by the genuine theoretic aim, still falls so far short of the end as to present this only in abortive form" (*NT*, 2:440–41) if we suggest as a whole appropriate for the theoretic interest anything short of the Absolute? Is a system or whole partial if it is sufficient for the purpose in hand but not all-embracing?

It seems clear that for Blanshard a nisus toward wholeness is central for the theoretic interest and that this involves both inclusion of appropriate materials and organic interrelatedness of parts. The intellectual impulse is always one to integrate (*NT*, 2:49), to apprehend things in a system or whole. But how extensive must the system or whole be? The normal requirements of action become manifest in and apply to relatively specific situations, a fact which, according to Blanshard, has blinded pragmatists like Dewey and James to the important truth that "the drive of reason . . . presses . . . far beyond the point at which utility ceases . . ." (*PI*, 257). Thought, "even when in the service of action, has an interest or aim of its own," namely, that of understanding the nature of things, apprehending them in a system (*NT*, 2:33).

If we carry the intellectual drive to the cosmic context, there are at least two ways of developing world views or attempting to do justice to all there is. One of these is the way of the objective idealist who attempts to advance from fragments, or lesser wholes, to more inclusive wholes to the Absolute, the all-embracing totality of necessarily interrelated parts. This has the disadvantage that the finite knower never arrives at the absolute view of things, never achieves the world as seen by the Absolute. It would seem to go beyond the kinds of systems we finite humans have experienced. It also makes the world in which we find ourselves a vast domain of appearances, perhaps pointing toward reality, perhaps constituting from the Absolute's view a fragmentary, distorted version of the real. But if it is valid, it has everything wrapped up in one great system.

A second way of developing a world hypothesis is to attempt to provide a set of categories which will apply to each and every thing or situation. It is an effort to achieve a distributive comprehension of the full range of things rather than to apprehend everything at once as an all-embracing totality or whole. As William James suggested, reality may exist as a strung-along, incomplete, or unfinished world in time, not as a totality of internally related parts but rather as an indefinitely numerous set of *eaches,* coherent in all sorts of ways and degrees but with a large measure of contingency. There is obviously an element of risk in such a world. Even if its categories seem to apply in illuminating fashion to everything so far, who can be sure what tomorrow will bring? But it has the advantage of doing less violence to common sense than the totalistic view. There may be as much connection as one finds between things, but there is no commitment to the notion that everything is connected by strands of necessity with everything else. Indeed, we may find more and more connections, referential strands, between things; and each and every situation will doubtless have connections with others; but from this, as James saw it, it does not follow that all of them are necessarily interconnected in an Absolute.

One may wonder, for that matter, whether some one of the innumerable forms of chaos is the only alternative to Blanshard's version of logical unity or system as the appropriate object of the drive for understanding. But granted that the notion of organic wholes is crucially significant for his world view, is the way of the Absolute the only fruitful one which can satisfy the theoretic interest? Are there not at least two different ways of making significant use of the notion, one emphasizing wholes and the other *the* whole? In Aristotle's philosophy, for example, there is a place for many organic wholes; in Hegel's there is but one. But in aesthetics both of them, along with Bosanquet and A. C. Bradley, make use of many wholes, each work of art constituting such a whole and exemplifying balance, order, and harmony of parts. The degree of integration and the amount of material integrated are significant for the work.

Blanshard, however, warns us that we must distinguish between the aesthetic and the logical or intellectual interest (*NT,* 2:438–40), and the fact that idealistic aestheticians commonly agree that we can have not one but many organically related wholes or systems fully satisfying aesthetically does not show that the theoretic interest can be satisfied in this way. It may be enough, nevertheless, to raise some question as to the necessity of a single all-embracing whole for reason. What human context requires this? For understanding? Understanding for what? Does apprehending the nature of things require that we comprehend not simply more and more different things as problems arise but the totality of things all together and all at once? But, according to Blanshard, the intellectual impulse cannot be satisfied with a plurality of wholes. So long as there is the slightest possibility of some unattached island the intellectual drive requires that we go on. But must we deny the oceans to recognize the land?

At any rate, the dominant trend in Blanshard's thought appears to be an absolutistic emphasis, but from time to time there is a suggestion that we can put our questions to nature on a more limited scale. The questions may arise from the materials of a specific situation, and the immanent goal of satisfying the impulse responsible for them just possibly may be met within that context and that not simply for sloppy minds. For example, if a mathematician puzzles "over his problem until he arrives at an insight that brings its elements into a certain order" and then stops because "he has found in this final order what satisfies the desire that moved him" (*NT*, 1:489), it would appear that on occasion specific questions have a specific answer and the theoretic impulse does not have to move on to the Absolute. But how far is the mathematician's quest, as Blanshard sees it, an authentic instance of reason's being satisfied within a limited context?

In terms of his criticism of the claim of the logical atomists that a full knowledge of the world pulverizes it into atoms (*RA*, 145), I gather that both Blanshard as an objective idealist and I as a contextualist have misgivings over the type of analysis that seeks to break something up into discrete elements or atomic units. Perhaps we agree that analysis, far from being a matter of reducing a whole into indivisible units, is rather an affair of tracing connections or strands of reference from a given texture into control textures. If so, for him the ultimate control texture is the Absolute. For me less extensive control textures are feasible. We agree that human thought and action are purposive and that it is important to note the end or goal being sought. Analysis may proceed by delineating the initiating conditions, the stages or phases of development, and the end aimed at.

One further set of queries may be posed concerning Blanshard's notion that knowledge requires absorption of thought in its object. According to him, when "we say that an idea is *of* an object, we are saying that the idea . . . is a potentiality which this object alone would actualize, a content informed by an impulse to become this object" (*NT*, 1:473). And there are systemic reasons for his adopting such a theory of knowledge. But does not this raise doubts about both the theory of knowledge and the metaphysical system? Are the alternatives—say, for example, the view of Dewey and the pragmatists—that bad? Is to understand something to become identical with it? Must I become a rotten egg to tell that one is rotten?

3. Change?

We are surrounded by the contingent, the indeterminate, the inarticulate, and the changing; and yet there appears to be no place for them in the real world described by Blanshard. If thought is always implicitly identical with its object, which is ultimately the Absolute, how is it that, say, change is a conspicuous and pervasive feature of the world we live in and yet has no place in the ultimately real? Change, novelty, and contingency are all around us. Are they only appearances?

Change and contingency are troublesome notions on Blanshard's world view. On the one hand, his dynamic or progressive categories, the ones characterizing the movement from fragments or lesser wholes to more inclusive wholes on the way to the Absolute, seem to require them. The realization of the immanent end is a gradual process, taking time to work itself out. The potential and contingent idea of one stage changes, develops, grows into one with a greater degree of necessity. If a problem is solved, this is done not instantaneously but sometimes slowly, with one's knowledge growing more adequate from one stage to a later one.

On the other hand, his ideal categories, the ones characterizing the Absolute in its completeness, present it as beyond time, changeless, unchanging, completely necessary, and not subject to change. So once we have arrived at the Absolute, we see that it has been present at least implicitly all along. At this point the idea has become one with, is fully realized or absorbed in, the Absolute, and it is realized that the Absolute has been present in it all the while. The fragments, the changing, the incomplete, the contingent, the indeterminate are transcended in a fully determinate, completely necessary, all-embracing totality. And what we thought were indications of change, development, growth, fulfillment, temporally successive stages, and the like are said to be logical terms, ways of expressing a logical rather than a temporal relationship. Such a nontemporal teleology may indeed be, as he claims (*NT,* 1:520), a perfectly clear notion, but is it therefore acceptable? Can all real change be disposed of in this way?

If we say that the Absolute is not subject to change, how does this square with the doctrine of internal relations and the internal relation between myself or my idea and the Absolute? Initially, my idea attempts to pass beyond its present content to what it would be but is not yet. The search, the striving, for identification with that end seems to be predicated on the assumption that in some sense the idea is not now one with that end. If later my idea becomes one with that end, the Absolute, it may then be seen that the Absolute was present all along, necessarily implicated in the idea, and the seeking was really unnecessary. But whether the search was necessary or not, at one stage I thought I was seeking and at another I saw that I already had what I sought. There is at least a difference in level of comprehension in me between the two stages, a change in the extent of my understanding. Does this make no difference to the Absolute? To say that it does not appears to deny the internality of the relation between myself or my idea and the Absolute. To say that it does is to admit change in the Absolute.

At any rate, it would be good to have something more from Blanshard on his view of the ontological status of change. He sometimes gives the impression that he thinks being rational is like being pregnant: one either is or is not; there is no such thing as being somewhat or partially pregnant. But is any change a sign of the not fully real or rational? And does reason require that there be either a fully necessary world or an anarchic, chaotic one with no connections between things? Is there nothing in between? Is there no place for some mixture of contingency and necessity? Why should there be no possibility of any necessary connections or requirements except in a fully determined, completely necessary world? Is there no place for real change in an intelligible order?

4. Pots, Pans, and Persons

The search for the Aristotelian substantial bearer or carrier of qualities, on Blanshard's view, is bound to be a frustrating one (*NT*, 1:122). For there is but one true particular, and that is the Absolute (1:639). According to Blanshard, "all that we commonly call particulars, pots and pans, mountains and rivers, are . . . seen to be universals" (ibid.). Indeed, neither individuals nor instances or particulars can avoid being dissolved into universals (1:626 –27). For both the argument that particulars are directly apprehended in sense and that they are required by difference of position in space and time prove to be confusions rather than cogent arguments (1:631). Hence his position is that "there are no particulars," presumably except for the Absolute. "For what gives apparent particularity to any character or complex is itself always universal" (ibid.). What happens, then, on this view, to pots, pans, and persons? They would appear to be clusters of universals, characters in relation (*PI*, 255).

This account raises some questions as to the status of individuals and poses once more ancient questions concerning the one and the many. Which is primary in our world, unity or multiplicity? What constitutes an individual, and how many such individuals are there in our world? It seems clear that for Blanshard all minds are members of one intelligible order (*NT*, 2:520), and that for him and other absolutists all things and all minds are components of a single mind (1:377), that of the Absolute; and if for Blanshard, Bradley, Royce, and company the true subject of every judgment is not this or that finite person or thing but rather the Absolute (1:647), the one is certainly preserved, but what about the many? Are they simply swallowed up in the Absolute? How junior is their membership in the one? Does one do justice to the individuality of the many finite persons and things in holding that there is only one particular, only one subject, the Absolute? Does it do justice to, say, Blanshard, Bosanquet, Bradley, Royce, Hegel, and Plato to treat them as only modes of the one ultimate reality?

For Josiah Royce the Absolute may be interpreted as the great community of intercommunicating, mutually interpreting persons or minds; an interpretation which he hoped would maintain the reality of both the one and the many. But what is the case for Brand Blanshard? Would Royce's version, in whole or in part, be acceptable to him? For Blanshard how are the many related to the Absolute, or what is the Absolute's relation to them? Is the relation that of reality to appearances, reality to potentialities, real to ideal, fully real to partially real, reality to realities, whole to parts, subject to predicates, less actual to fully actual, construct to constructs, substance to modes, determiner to determined, or what?

5. Can the Absolute Be Bad?

Not even a sketchy account of Blanshard's world view would be complete without some consideration of the place of value in it and the relation between the most real and the most valuable, the more especially since traditionally the objective idealists have had something distinctive to say in this regard. In spite of the fact that he has written extensively and illuminatingly on problems of moral conduct, moreover, I have found relatively little in Blanshard's writings directly concerned with the relation between the intelligible order of the world and the shoring up of values in it. In addition, his brief discussion of this topic in the final pages of *Reason and Analysis* suggests that he may be taking a different turn than his idealistic predecessors; it would be interesting to see whether this is definitely the case and if so, how much of a break he is making with them. So I am eager to hear something further from him on this topic.

Traditionally, the objective idealists have held that the notion of an organic whole of internally related parts, supremely illustrated by the Absolute, is central for an account of the good and the beautiful as well as of the true and the real. The Absolute is the peak of perfection, the culmination at once of value and of the intelligible and the real. It provides the standard of what truly is as well as of what is valuable. Accordingly, Bradley, for example, as Blanshard notes, held that "The best life, like the truest thought, is that which approaches most nearly the Absolute."[4]

The Absolute exemplifies the ideal of the fully integrated whole, embracing the totality of facts and events in a logically necessary system, each fact and event internally related to or implied by every other. Whatever the materials, whether judgments, acts, feelings, or something else, the ideal of integration or organization of diverse contents into a unified whole remains the same. The higher the degree of integration and the larger the amount of relevant material integrated, the more nearly we approach the Absolute: the more real, the more true, the more intelligible, the more valuable. In Bosanquet's words, the basic method of philosophy is everywhere the same, namely, "to expand *all* the relevant facts, taken together, into ideas which approve themselves to thought as exhaustive and self-consistent."[5]

If "intelligence finds an answering intelligibility" in our world,[6] is there no answering chord for our value aspirations and hopes, or, in Jamesian phraseology, could only a tender-minded yearning for a moral holiday lead us to ask? If necessity "holds in degree everywhere," being "the characteristic, not of special forms, but of a whole or system into which everything apparently enters" (*NT,* 2:335), is value somehow exempt or inoperative in this framework? If in accepting the rationalist's postulate we are committed to a world in which "every fact and event is connected with its context, and ultimately with every other fact and event, in a way that is logically necessary" and "every fact and event is ultimately connected with all others by internal relations" ("Internal Relations," 228), can this system be limited to logical connectedness? Does not the presence of values in it make a difference?

If all the contradictions, fragments, incoherences, and contingencies are transcended in the Absolute and all the parts or lesser wholes are combined into an intelligible structure, a coherent totality, without omitting what is distinctive in each (*NT,* 2:442), will this be without regard to value content? When the Absolute as the perfect and all-embracing totality supersedes lesser systems, absorbing and extending their gains (2:438), does this apply only to the intellectual gains? William James somewhere says that since the Absolute contains all errors and mistakes and silly things as well as the true and the real, it must contain more rubbish than desirable content; but if nevertheless all this is transcended in the perfection of the Absolute, giving us truth and reality in their completeness, is there no comparable transcending and maximization of values?

Blanshard sees the theoretic drive as having far greater sweep than, say, the moral or aesthetic interest. And in a rational world reason, far from being simply a slave of the passions, enters into everything and exerts a shaping influence. So it is that for him our goods "lie in the fulfilment not of bare impulses, but of desires into whose nature thought has entered once for all, with its own demands for consistency, integration, and expansion" (*Reason and Goodness,* 347). He defines the good in the sense of the ethical end as "*the most comprehensive possible fulfilment and satisfaction of impulse-desire,*" and by comprehensive fulfillment he means "one that takes account not only of this or that desire, but of our desires generally, and not only of this or that man's desires, but of all men's" (ibid., 311). If these desires are rational, is there no place in the nature of things for them? Indeed, is there not a logically necessary place for them, one which assures the conservation and optimalization of values in the universe? If the world is, as Bosanquet, for example, maintained, "a single individual whose parts are connected with each other by a necessity so intimate and so organic that the nature of the part" depends "on its place in the Absolute" (*RA*, 145), does not this insure an optimal place for values? Or could such a world be bad?

Blanshard concedes that many persons have found in the belief that the world is a necessary system, and thus in a sense rational, "a source of ethical and religious reassurance"; but he questions whether this reassurance is warranted. He argues, first, that "between the rational as the logically necessary and the rational as the morally right, there is an abyss of difference," and secondly, that "to pass from 'everything is rational,' in the sense of necessity, to 'everything is rational,' in the sense of right, is to stultify one's moral perception" (*RA*, 491). I am not disposed to deny that there are significant differences between the senses mentioned, but whether in terms of the implications of his general view the differences are so abysmal I am less certain. Blanshard's characteristic tendency to face up to facts squarely is, of course, admirable, but one wonders why one who can in effect deny the reality of change should have this much difficulty with the problem of evil. Is reason somehow more fully manifest in logic and the causal structure of nature than in art or morals?

At any rate, philosophers differ in their characterizations of the Absolute. Some, as Blanshard notes in his *Encyclopaedia Britannica* article on "The Absolute," agree with Royce in holding that it is morally good whereas others side with Spinoza, great naturalist and rationalist, in affirming that it is above all distinctions of value. How would Blanshard describe it? As neither good nor bad? Would he hold with Bosanquet that the highest and most appropriate value characterization of the Absolute is perfection? Is the world a perfect whole logically but not morally?

LEWIS EDWIN HAHN

DEPARTMENT OF PHILOSOPHY
SOUTHERN ILLINOIS UNIVERSITY
AT CARBONDALE

NOTES

[1]Stephen C. Pepper, *World Hypotheses: A Study in Evidence* (Berkeley and Los Angeles: University of California Press, 1942), 283.
[2]*Encyclopaedia Britannica* (1967 edition), 1:50.

[3]"Internal Relations and Their Importance to Philosophy," *Review of Metaphysics* 21, no. 2 (Dec. 1967): 227.

[4]Brand Blanshard, "Francis Herbert Bradley," *Journal of Philosophy* 22, no. 1 (Jan. 1, 1925): 15.

[5]Bernard Bosanquet, *Three Lectures on Aesthetic* (London: Macmillan and Co., 1915), 3.

[6]Brand Blanshard, "Current Strictures on Reason," *Philosophical Review* 54, no. 4 (July 1945): 361.

25. REPLY TO LEWIS EDWIN HAHN

Brand Blanshard's World View

Mr. Hahn's critique of my "world view" is written, I take it, from the point of view of a Jamesian pragmatist and pluralist. He has the Jamesian gift of entering appreciatively into points of view other than his own, and begins his paper with an attractive account of the drift of my argument in *The Nature of Thought*. He admires the industry I have brought to the fabrication of my rather ambitious cosmic astrodome, the unflagging optimism with which I have heaved its beams and girders into place, and the wariness with which I have hedged and moated it against philosophical trespassers. But when he stands and looks at it from the distance that lends detachment, he feels very much as James did when he viewed the pretentious edifice of the Bradleys, Bosanquets, and Royces. It was handsome and imposing, James thought, this "marble temple shining on a hill," but something hardly meet for human habitation. It seemed to bear no relation to the grubby human life going on around it. It was really the product of intellectualism run amuck. Plain men would not think of going to it for answers to the questions that arose from common life. Mr. Hahn thinks, as James did, and as in fact I do, that this is a serious criticism of any philosophy. And he comes to me with a number of plain questions in his hand, questions that he admits are old, and more often asked than answered, but still so central and imperative as not to brook evasion. For one or two of them I am afraid I have no answer that will satisfy either him or me. He divides his essay into four sections, dealing respectively with four topics: 1. Understanding, 2. Change, 3. Individuals, and 4. Values. I will take them in the same order.

1. Understanding

(1) Is there not in nature an absurd or unintelligible element that reason cannot hope to deal with? Such an element has been recognized over and over again in the history of philosophy, not merely by lovers of mystery and of mysticism but by philosophers of weight. Aristotle recognized it in the

primordial matter upon which intelligence imposed form. Locke recognized it in the "something I know not what" which owned predicates but was not a predicate itself, and in the *I* that could sense and imagine but could not itself be sensed or imagined. Wittgenstein recognized it in the bare particulars that served as the subjects of his atomic propositions. The existentialists recognize it when they insist that essences do not exhaust the nature of things, that there is a reality lying below them, and that reason is therefore doomed to skate upon the surface of the world. Plotinus's ineffable real, Kant's thing in itself, Spencer's unknowable, and countless other inconceivables litter the pages of frustrated speculative inquirers.

The question is not, of course, whether there is much in the world that man does not know, and presumably never will. The universe divided by human reason, as Goethe said, will always leave a remainder. The present prospect is that the second law of thermodynamics will make an end of us and our questions long before we find their final answers. The question at issue is more subtle. Can there be a characterless existent? To use Bradley's case of the lump of sugar, is there an "it" which owns the attributes square, white, sweet, and hard, without being itself a character or a relation or a set of these? If so, reason cannot deal with it, for reason can deal only with characters and relations. One may ask the proponent of such a faceless entity what he means by it, but he is likely to answer that this begs the question by its very form, since the entity he means has no *what*. Its only character is that of being a subject of characters and relations. Now I have argued elsewhere (in an essay in this series on *The Philosophy of C.D. Broad*, 237 ff.) that this suggestion does not stand up under criticism. A mere featureless "it," a bodiless embodiment of the verb "to be," a something that is not anything rather than anything else, is an asymptotic approach to epistemological zero. If the "it" of the lump of sugar can support the quality sweet and exclude the quality sour, if it can move through space and time and sustain relations to other entities in these frames, there must be some ground in its nature which distinguishes it from entities that lack these powers. Either that, or the entity itself is an illusion. I incline to the latter view. All that we actually find in the lump of sugar is the qualities and their relations, given in a framework of space and time. This will not disprove the existence of the it for one who can believe in bare particulars and whatless somewhats, in *x*'s that can sustain characters and relations without any nature or content of their own. If it is replied that in dismissing such entities I am begging the question in favor of the rationality of things, I plead guilty. I would merely urge that anyone who admits a breach in rationality at this point will probably go on to admit further breaches which will not be so harmless.

(2) The rationalist holds that everything in the world is in the end intelligible. Mr. Hahn reminds us, however, that "a Peirce or a James would find it eminently reasonable to emphasize contingency in our world. For the latter

pair there is a place in the real world for the almost, the not quite, the imprecise, the aleatory, and the maybe so. But not so for Blanshard." Now these intransigeants are not all on the same level. There remain plenty of "almosts" and "not quites" in my real world; though there is nothing imprecise in it (the density of the deepest fog is a matter of precise degree); and there are no "maybe so's," since for a completed knowledge no uncertainties remain. Are there any "aleatories"? The word comes from the Latin for a game of chance played with dice, which Horace sensibly warned against as a perilous business: *periculosae plenum opus aleae*. But Horace could hardly have doubted that there were laws determining how a die, when thrown in a certain way, would impinge upon the table, and what side would be up when it came to rest. There is no chance, except to our ignorance, in the fall of a die. Nor are there any objective accidents in history. Sir Edward Creasy begins his account of the battle of Hastings: "Arletta's pretty feet twinkling in the brook made her the mother of William the Conqueror. Had she not thus fascinated Duke Robert the Liberal of Normandy, Harold would not have fallen at Hastings, no Anglo-Norman dynasty could have arisen, no British empire" (*Fifteen Decisive Battles*, 192). The course of history hangs on numberless "chance" meetings of this kind. George Herbert Palmer held, if I remember rightly, that while there was no chance in a single causal line, if two such lines intersected, as when a tile fell from a roof on the head of a passer-by, the point of intersection was a genuine matter of chance. But surely it would not be so to an intelligence that could grasp both lines together. A more formidable claim for chance has been made by Heisenberg. So far as his indeterminacy principle involves a suspension of the law of causality in the submicroscopic realm, I have dealt with it inadequately but as best I can in *Reason and Belief*, pp. 485–86. My own view, to put it simply, is that there are no *mays* in nature; when we say it *may* snow tomorrow, we are expressing our imperfect knowledge of the presence and absence of determining grounds. But except in this sense there is no chance about its snowing tomorrow. That it will snow is either necessary or impossible.

(3) Mr. Hahn next quotes a passage from a paper of mine in which I accept a self-evident proposition as a final step in explanation, i.e. one in which the question Why? cannot be raised again. This seems to him inconsistent with my usual position. He is right. There are, for me, no incorrigible self-evident propositions, either perceptual or abstract. I have argued that in so simple a proposition as "I have a toothache," there is a variety of conceptualizations any one of which may need to be modified. As for the Cartesian type of "self-evident" proposition, I will, to avoid repetition, refer to my treatment of this topic in my reply to Mr. Rorty.

(4) Mr. Hahn, like Dewey and James, thinks that most of our problems are immediate and specific, and that to drag in the Absolute by way of answering them is to use a mountain to crack a nut. Most of our problems

arise out of practical frustrations and are solved when those frustrations are removed. The drain in the sink is clogged; what can I do to free it? We ought to entertain our new neighbors, the Wilkinsons; who will make the more pleasant party with them, the Jacksons or the Jordans? Even where the question is purely intellectual, the limited solution is usually satisfactory, as when the mathematician solves an equation. He feels no need of pressing farther. There is no reason for calling "a system or whole partial if it is sufficient for the purpose in hand but not all-embracing."

Again I agree. Most of our problems are those of today or of the days just ahead, and anyone who involves "the eternities and immensities" to solve them is impractical and a bore. It is a part of rationality not to be forever obtruding one's rationalism. The pragmatist is right in holding that our commonest concerns are, and must be, with practical problems of health and comfort, of adjustment to our jobs and our families; and as our thought is normally aroused by difficulties in practice, so it normally comes to rest when the practical end is reached. But as I have insisted so often, our practical and theoretical ends are not the same. For some persons at some times it is altogether fitting and proper to give their thought freer rein, and we may be grateful that in some scientists and philosophers the theoretic and practical interests have reversed their usual priority. Indeed one may pass with no sense of a barrier from common sense or science to philosophy. The mathematician who has solved his equation may wonder whether the arithmetic or algebra he is using is continuous with logic, and why logic should be regarded as a safe guide; and in raising such questions he is a philosopher already. It is the philosopher's special business to press such questions as far as he can; and if he is a rationalist he sees, or thinks he sees, that in his quest for understanding there is no boundary short of the whole. And he stops with the whole only because an attempt to explain the whole by going beyond it would be self-contradiction.

(5) Mr. Hahn asks why *the* whole should be the only satisfactory one? There are many wholes, which have many different degrees and kinds of unity, and persons of different interests will be content to work within the particular unity of their subject matter. To the physician the body is a unity that is distinct and self-maintaining, and if he can control its delicate balance of input and output and aid the *vis medicatrix naturae* to do its work, he is quite ready to leave to others the relation of the organism to the cosmos. The painter who is doing a landscape is concerned with another whole in which the parts are all so intimately related to each other that a change in one may require changes in the others; but these relations are not set out in any textbook of logic. And what of the physician's or the painter's *mind*? Is not that too a whole of still another sort, in which relations of every variety, from the most casual association to the most rigorous of inferences, are all included in one

heterogeneous assembly? These are the wholes we actually live with and struggle to maintain; each has its own kind of unity, though none of them is a logical unity; they may be studied in relative isolation from each other; and the professional man may be an expert in the maintenance of any of them without ever giving a thought to its place in the world at large.

This, I think, would be Mr. Hahn's position, and that of James in his *Pluralistic Universe*. It is my position too until I come to look at things from a particular point of view. The special concern of the philosopher is with understanding, and he will examine both the internal and external relations of these wholes with that interest dominating his thought. The self-maintenance of the body, its diseases, and their treatment are governed by causal laws, and the physician rightly considers that his work is done when he masters and successfully applies them. Some of these laws are clearly mechanical; some of them are mysteriously teleological; and it is the philosopher's business to point out that neither kind gives us a fully satisfactory understanding. The painter may feel that there is something wrong about his picture both in balance and in color; it occurs to him to put a green canoe on the river's bank to the left, and with the addition all comes right. He is bowing to aesthetic necessity, whether he could formulate this or not. It is the philosopher's business to distinguish this sort of necessity from the kind he chiefly works with, which is logical. The psychologist knows that there are laws governing the most whimsical lapses of memory and professorial absence of mind; sometimes, as in Freud's explanation of dreams and slips of the tongue, he must reconceive the mind philosophically in order to find the laws. It is the philosopher's business to consider what unity belongs to a mind, as distinct from other wholes, and in what sense a changing mind is the same.

Just as the philosopher must consider these types of internal unity, so he must try to see the place of these minor wholes in the more comprehensive whole. Granting that for the special student the organism, the painting, and the mind are all relatively self-contained wholes, it is impossible to understand any of them fully without going far beyond them. If a body is really the product of "a fortuitous concourse of atoms," it is a very different kind of thing from the product of a Bergsonian élan vital; and though the place of the human organism in nature is still a battleground of philosophy, it is philosophy that will ultimately fix that place. In evaluating the picture we can hardly stop within its own four corners; our thought is naturally carried on to the place of aesthetic good among goods generally, and then to the question whether there are objective goods at all, and what their status is in the world. The place of mind in nature is a problem still more fundamental. Consciousness is of course not reducible to physical change, but it is connected with it as effect and apparently also as cause; and though its flow of ideas can in some measure be explained by association, it rises at times in reasoning to feats that suggest direct control by the rational structures it is following. In short all these minor worlds are dependent on a wider world in ways that must be understood if these fragmentary wholes are themselves to be understood.

"But why understood only by necessary relations? You have admitted that these wholes are not logical wholes as they present themselves to us; why ride over them and flatten them out with your intellectualist bulldozer?" I have no desire to flatten them out; indeed unless the rationalist can see them as they appear to those who work in them, his explanations will be without interest. Nor do his explanations supersede or replace those of the scientist or the artist. He is not saying that ultimate understanding is the only human desire or for all men the most fulfilling; he is saying that it is legitimate, and for him absorbing. He admits that in large areas of philosophy itself his thought falls short of necessity—in dealing with body and mind, for example, or the relations of sensa, percepts, and concepts to their objects, in the philosophies of law, religion, and politics. He admits that he must often rely on the two other standard modes of explanation, the causal and the teleological. Both indeed are enlightening, but the first is still generally opaque to us and the second limited in its application. It is only when he sees that something not only is so but *must* be so that the intellectual question is answered, and only when the must is imposed by the whole that it is answered once for all.

(6) Is it the invariable aim of thought to identify itself with its object? In my reply to Mr. Bertocci I admit that my view here has altered and try to say how.

2. Time and Change

Mr. Hahn observes that throughout *The Nature of Thought* there run two inconsistent assumptions. According to the first, change is presumed to be real, for I am studying intellectual development as it proceeds, under the control of an immanent purpose, from one level to another of understanding. But all through this process the ultimate object of understanding, a complete and fully interrelated whole, is somehow already there, waiting to be understood. This whole is assumed to be static and changeless. Now this world view, says Mr. Hahn, is incoherent. If the process of development is real, then the real world cannot be changeless. If the absolute is changeless, then the process of development which falls within it must be an illusion. One or the other must be given up, for the world cannot be both changing and changeless.

The point is obviously well taken. The contradiction is one that has haunted many rationalists; it cannot be denied and it ought not to be dodged. I fear that it *is* being dodged when it is dealt with merely by some dark Hegelian profundity such as that the difficulty is transcended in the absolute consciousness. I think it is also dealt with unsatisfactorily by denying the reality of time. Bradley's arguments at the beginning of *Appearance and Reality*, which once seemed to me formidable, now seem very unconvincing. He takes time as a relation between terms which are themselves times; he then finds each term dissipating itself into a relation between further times, and he is launched on an infinite regress. But the terms related by "before" and "after" are not primarily stretches of time but events. Bradley cannot accept this either. If A is related by C to B, he seems to think of C as a third thing which must be related to A on the one side by another relation D, and to B on the other by a still further relation E. And then the infinite regress breaks out again. Now this analysis is artificial and inapplicable. The business of a relation is to relate, and though the relation of succession is often causal and capable of further analysis, it is not to be analyzed by patching new pieces without limit onto its ends. This would destroy not only succession but all other relations, and with it all knowledge, for to know *is* to grasp relations. And to deny knowledge altogether is a kind of contradiction Bradley could hardly have intended.

The most sustained attack I know on the reality of time is that of McTaggart. In *The Nature of Existence* he distinguishes a series of events, B, which are related as before and after, from another series, A, whose events are past, present, or future. He holds that the B series involves the A series, and that unless the A series can be accepted as real, both series must be set down as unreal. The crucial question, therefore, is whether the A series can be consistently maintained. McTaggart holds that it cannot. The reason is that any given moment M must then be judged to have at once the characteristics of being past, present, and future, and that this is inconsistent. But surely, we reply, what we are saying is that M *has been* future, *is* present, and *will be* past, and in this there is no contradiction. But McTaggart will not accept this analysis. He insists that the only correct analysis is that M is a moment that, either simultaneously or timelessly, *now has* the characteristics of pastness, presentness, and futurity. Why he should have held that there is any such moment or event it is not easy to see. If indeed there is such a moment or event, he is right that its possession of the three characteristics would be self-destructive. But as Broad shows with his usual clarity (*Examination of McTaggart's Philosophy*, 2:313), there is no reason whatever for analyzing temporal statements in this way. To say that a given event or moment M *has been* future, *is* present, and *will be* past is perfectly consistent, since the event or moment in question has these characters successively and not at once. The analysis that would make any event or moment possess them all at once has no correspondence with our actual meaning.

The mass of our experience that comes to us under the form of time and change is so vast that any abstract formula designed to expose it as unreal must be very skeptically scrutinized. Life and death, progress and decline, memory and learning and inference, eating and drinking, indeed all history and even one's own specious present, must be illusory if time and change are declared unreal. That is too high a price for me at least to pay, particularly when the arguments designed to show their contradictory character collapse so quickly under examination. The question then becomes whether, if time and change are admitted realities, the rationalist can still hold to a system in which all facts and events are necessarily interconnected.

I do not know why not. His system will not, indeed, be a closed system, for the tide of events will be moving the line of the present farther and farther up the sands of time as it annexes more of the future. But that does not affect the necessity of the events that have already occurred, or of the events that are still to come. If the causal relation is necessary, as we have held it to be, and all the events of the past are causally connected with each other directly or indirectly, the world of both past and future remains a single necessary system. It is an open system in the sense that the stream of events has not reached its end and, if infinite, never will; but it is not open in the sense that the future is contingent and that anything may happen. There is no reason to believe that the future will be less rigorously governed than the past by causal law.

Let it not be supposed that by granting the reality of time I have joined those process philosophers who follow Heraclitus in holding that everything is in flux. I follow Plato, rather, in holding that we live in two realms, one of change and one of permanence. We are so obviously immersed in change that I need insist on it no further. But it should be noted that even the changes in the universe are connected with each other by relations that are themselves timeless. In each galaxy in the sky, for example, there is a certain number of stars, and between these numbers there is a vast complex of arithmetical relations, some of which have been noted by arithmeticians and astronomers, others not. The patterns of arrangement of these bodies exhibit innumerable geometrical relations, and the laws that govern these patterns are again, like those that govern the numbers, valid timelessly. The propositions that in a scale of colors arranged in order of likeness purple comes between red and blue, and that the same surface cannot be diversely colored at once, are timelessly true in the sense of true at all times and irrespectively of whether the colors are seen or not. A's causing B is an occurrence in time, but the causal law connecting anything of the kind A with anything of the kind B is not itself an occurrence; it is again something that is true regardless of the time of judgment. For that matter, there is a sense in which it is true at every moment that what happened, or is happening, or will happen at any moment, did happen, is happening, or will happen just as it did, does, or will. "Once true, always true."

Does it make sense to say that something is true when no judgment to that effect is being made? If so, *what* is it that is true? Some philosophers, convinced that it is timelessly true that Charlemagne was crowned in A.D. 800, and knowing that it would be ridiculous to say that every moment someone or other is making this judgment, hold that what is true is a proposition which subsists timelessly. And there must be as many distinguishable propositions that are thus true as there are distinguishable facts about which they may be made. On the grounds of Occam's razor, this infinite multiplication of entities is to be avoided if possible. I suspect that it can be avoided; McTaggart and Broad have both suggested methods of doing so. I shall be content if it is recognized that there is some sense in which it is true, for example, that Charlemagne was crowned in 800 even at times when no judgment about this event is being made. This seems to be recognized in the belief that there is an immense number of implications of a true occurrent judgment that must also be true, even though they are not included in the affirmed content of the judgment.

With regard to our joint occupancy of the two realms of the changing and the timeless, there is a further point to notice. Progress depends on the degree of our emergence from the one into the other. The aim of the philosopher, according to Plato, is the vision of all time and all existence, and that aim can be retained as theoretically possible even by one who has small hope that the race will ever attain it. But progress depends on this emergence in another sense. It is through the mastery of their timeless laws that we become masters of temporal events. To give one example only: the race has achieved a bare beginning of the understanding of the dependence of mind on body. As the grasp of this dependence becomes greater, the development and control of a mind over its body and therefore over itself is bound to be facilitated and accelerated, so that the length and the enrichment of human life should be expanded indefinitely. We are not wholly the slaves of change, for in the degree to which we understand it at crucial points we may become its masters.

3. Individuals

To Mr. Hahn, my explanation of individuals is more truly described as a process of explaining them away. And to anyone who holds the view that a thing is a substance with attributes, that impression will be well founded. Locke's "something I know not what," which is itself characterless while supporting a variety of characters, seems strictly unthinkable. So does the idea of a pure particular. A rock or a mountain is to me a synthesis of attributes. These attributes, as we experience them, seem very loosely connected with each other; there is no evident reason why a certain shape in the rock should be associated with a certain color, hardness, and weight. In the "pots and pans" Mr. Hahn inquires about, the ground of unity is clearer; for the attributes, when put together in a certain pattern, so plainly subserve a purpose. In the chapter on "The Architecture of the Thing" in *The Nature of Thought* I have considered the reasons why, out of the chaos of qualities that present themselves to us whenever we open our eyes, we group qualities as we do, rather than in the countless other ways that are theoretically possible. These reasons are curiously arbitrary in the sense of being physiological, psychological, and practical rather than logical. How largely the demarcation of things is dependent on considerations within ourselves is suggested by the speculation whether the rock would be a thing at all to the insect that crawls across it. To the reflective eye, the rock is a congeries of qualities, the presentation of each of which is the result of long converging causal lines, and the meeting point of long lines of similarity.

When we come to living things, and above all to human minds, the case is different. A human mind is a unity because its conscious components are held together by a pervading, immanent purpose. This purpose may itself be ill defined and inharmonious; for a human being, at least as I conceive him, is a set of drives whose fulfillments may conflict. But such a being is the only one known who can coordinate his drives toward a remote and reflectively unified end. Individuality is a matter of degree. The rock has it in a degree slightly above zero; the chimpanzee has it in a very much higher degree; a Churchill or an Einstein has it in a degree almost incomparably higher still.

My interest in human development has been chiefly on the cognitive side. Here the end for which human nature is reaching, as I have said so often, is simply the understanding of its world. The achievement of this understanding is not a process merely of being pushed from behind; I conceive it also as a process of being drawn from ahead. I do not think that G. H. Hardy was talking nonsense when he insisted that the mathematician was discovering rather than creating, nor was it wholly nonsense for Kepler to exult that he was thinking God's thoughts after him. The world for me is a necessary system, and in the degree to which the thinker can surrender his thought to that system and follow it, he is in a sense participating in that which is timeless or eternal. This has been part of the thought of all the great rationalists from Plato through Aquinas and Spinoza to Hegel and McTaggart. So when Mr. Hahn asks me whether the individuality of these minds is as arbitrary and unreal as that of the rock, I answer No. A human mind has entered in some measure into that "logical stability" which for Bosanquet was the very "principle of individuality" and which is realized to the full in only one individual, the absolute itself.

When I wrote my first book, however, I took the purpose of thought to be identification with its object. Plato seems to have thought that in apprehending the ideas the mind was itself achieving the timelessness that belonged to them. This I should like to accept, but cannot. The judgment that contemplates the timeless is itself in time, and like all other events is carried away down the river. The place of the human mind in the general economy of things is not so grotesque as to leave a piece of that mind in eternity while the rest of it goes the way of all things mortal. For a full understanding of the place of any mind in the world we must grasp how its processes are related to those of the body, how the unplumbed depths of its subconscious portion affect those processes, and how in its higher reaches the mind is actually guided along logical channels by the rational structures it engages. There is nothing in such determination to prevent the mind's achieving a high level of individuality, value, and that kind of freedom that issues from rationality. On the other hand I see no good reason for believing that an individual mind persists either as a substance (since it is not a substance) or as a disembodied field of consciousness.

4. Values

The last sentence in Mr. Hahn's essay runs: "Is the world a perfect whole logically but not morally?" My answer to this question, such as it is, is given in *Reason and Belief*, a book that appeared too late to be of use to Mr. Hahn. He is of course right that in the idealist tradition of the last century the absolute has usually been regarded as not only a perfectly integrated logical whole but one that was also morally and even aesthetically perfect. The tendency has been to regard human nature as a many-sided effort after fulfillment and to conceive the absolute as the harmonious fulfillment of all these strivings alike.

In *Reason and Belief* I broke with this tradition, not, to be sure, on the intellectual side but on the moral. The main reasons, I suppose, were these. (1) The postulate of moral judgment is extremely different from that of the judgment of fact. The assumption of the latter is that the ideal of thought in regard to consistency and intelligibility obtains in the actual world; if it did not, the enterprise of thought would be doomed from the beginning. But the assumption of moral judgment is not that the moral ideal is similarly realized. Indeed if it were, the world would already be morally perfect and the effort to change it could only be immoral. Morality would therefore be pointless and self-defeating.

(2) That the world is not morally perfect is not only assumed in judgments of obligation but confirmed further by any unprejudiced survey of the distribution of good and evil. There is an immense amount of evil in the world that to the best of our knowledge is purely pointless, particularly in the vast field of human and animal suffering. No doubt suffering produces at times a good that outweighs it, but it is irresponsible and frivolous to say that the suffering of all the animals that have been torn limb from limb in biological history produced a counterbalancing good, or that a being powerful enough

to control the course of nature could find no more economical way to produce that good. It may be that for reasons beyond our conjecture it was necessary, if good were to be maximized, to produce mongoloid and disease-ridden children, to apportion among men the powers of achievement and enjoyment without regard to equality or justice, and to make most of the known universe uninhabitable by sentient beings like ourselves. But I know of no consideration that makes this belief plausible. The usual defense of it is to fall back on faith, but this is commonly a tacit admission that mere evidence fails. If one had to judge by known facts whether the absolute is concerned about the maximizing of good, I do not know how an affirmative answer could be supported.

(3) Furthermore, from my point of view this very question is an inappropriate one, since it implies a misconception about the intrinsically good. In *Reason and Goodness* I have argued that there is no good apart from experience, and that what makes any experience intrinsically good is (a) its fulfilling of a human impulse-desire and (b) the satisfaction or positive feeling tone that normally accompanies such fulfillment. I have been fortified in this conclusion by noting the surely significant coincidence between the great goods of human nature and its fundamental drives. Knowledge, beauty, friendship, love, the goods of the table, reputation, professional success are all prized by us because they are ways of fulfilling ourselves through the pathways of natural desire; and for beings of a quite different equipment of desires a very different spectrum of goods would be recognized. Now is there any reason to suppose that the absolute is animated by these desires of ours, or indeed by any desires at all? When it is remembered that the absolute is the whole ordered universe, only one answer seems credible.

This detachment of morality from its old theological and metaphysical status does not affect the real goodness of its goods or the objective validity of its judgments. It merely makes ethics a relatively autonomous science—I say "relatively" because no science is or can be wholly autonomous in the sort of world in which we live. But subject to those ultimate modifications to which all finite judgments must submit, moral judgments are as objectively true as those of any other science. The objective rightness of an act depends on its productivity of the greatest possible amount of intrinsic good, taking into account all its effects in the way of value upon those affected by it—or, with a modification I owe to Plato by way of Mr. Joseph, all the goods of the way of life in which this sort of action is a necessary part. This mode of conceiving rightness no doubt needs further definition, which is given, though inadequately, in my book on ethics. I have also sought to defend myself there against the charge that this view of ethics subjectifies moral judgment and trivializes the moral life. In fact it frees that life from many restrictions imposed upon it by its entanglements with irrational theologies.

That Western ethics and religion are in conflict seems to me clear. The tradition of Western religion is that the ultimate power in the world is a Deity personal and good, and therefore that all things come together for good to those that trust him. The moralist who looks at the facts objectively finds it hard to endorse either the premise or the conclusion. And I am trying simply to look at the facts. I do not claim that the divorce of ethics from theology would lead to more happiness; indeed, the relatively gray world of a neutral absolute may well be less happy to live in than one believed to be undergirded by a Deity who notes every sparrow's fall. But I think the person who believes for that reason is either confused or intellectually immoral.

While I do not think that either the nature of goodness or its distribution supports the view that the world is governed by it, the fact that the world has produced it is surely significant. So far as we know, anything good has appeared only at one pinpoint in the universe, but that appearance was no accident, and, given the materials and the laws governing them, life and mind may appear in many places and have a career both longer and more impressive than on this planet. Values, like the lives that support them, are ephemeral, but the quality of life of a Plato, a Shakespeare, or a Bach is none the less exalted because its embodiment was brief. And if in my own treatment of the moral life I have insisted so strongly on the work of intellect, it is in part because it is our main reliance for adding quantity of life to quality. We are only beginning to learn the conditions, congenital and environmental, bodily and psychological, that make fullness of life possible. If this fullness of life is to be attainable by the many, or enduring for anyone, it will be only through a mastery of those conditions by a trained and devoted intelligence, not by intervention from outside the sphere of nature. Whether the reason that has brought us such civilization as we have will be used to destroy it or to perpetuate and disseminate it rests with ourselves.

Note on Internal Relations

In his book *Sovereign Reason* (Glencoe, Ill.: Free Press, 1954), Professor Ernest Nagel wrote an important criticism of my theory of internal relations. Since it is the policy of the Library of Living Philosophers not to publish what has already appeared in print, and Mr. Nagel, to my regret, was unable to contribute a further essay to this volume, I have made no attempt here to reply to his criticisms. Readers who would like to have my lines of reply may find them, however, if they are willing to refer to the following somewhat scattered sources: *Philosophical Investigations*, eds. Sydney and Beatrice Rome (New York: Holt, Rinehart & Winston, 1964), 219–41; my *Reason and Analysis*, 459–65; 478 ff.; and a symposium on "Internal Relations and Their Importance to Philosophy," *Review of Metaphysics* 21, no. 2 (Dec. 1967): 227–72. In this symposium I first state my view, am subjected to criticisms by Professors W. H. Doney, Bruce Aune, W. F. Kennick, and Alice Lazerowitz, and then offer my replies to each.

VII   PHILOSOPHY OF RELIGION

26   BRAND BLANSHARD ON REASON
AND RELIGIOUS BELIEF
Frederick Ferré

T HE writings of Brand Blanshard on religious belief range widely over the
theological landscape, but the banner he plants wherever he ventures is
unmistakably the same one: it is the ensign of reason, in whose name he
claims every territory on which he treads. Unlike many philosophers of
similar persuasion, however, Blanshard grapples at close range with the
theologians whose challenge to human reason is sharpest. Out of this struggle
emerges a positive doctrine, an ethic of belief, which in some ways serves him
as a religious creed and leads, in turn, to further questions that I shall put to
him about the nature of religion and the logic of belief in general.

I

In Blanshard's critique of four major Protestant voices—Martin Luther,
Søren Kierkegaard, Emil Brunner, and Karl Barth—which appears in
Reason and Belief [*RB*], we find the essential notes of his theme developed.
His fundamental objections to each will repay attention as the basis for my
later examination of the common creed from which these objections spring.

Luther, the earthy and volatile founder of Protestantism, made no secret
of his loathing for "whorish" reason. His grounds for this distaste were at the
very center of his theological vision of man and his desperate situation: man,
since Adam's Fall, is in a state of sinful corruption; his reason, of which he is
so inordinately proud, is no less hopelessly corrupt; salvation for man is in no
respect possible through his own works, but only through the supernatural
(and unearned) gift of God's grace "through faith alone"; reason, by inspiring
false pride in man's own powers of achievement and by casting itself in the
arrogant role of critic over matters of divine truth, leads to loss of faith and
damnation. If to doubt is to destroy a soul eternally, reason is the Devil's fair
accomplice in worse than murder.

Blanshard acknowledges the power of Martin Luther's spirit and the intensity of his conviction on these matters. But precisely in the throbbing con-

viction that made Luther's religious vision so widely effective, Blanshard finds the basic confusion that weakens the Lutheran case for truth. This confusion is between the certainty of feeling (the "emotion of conviction") and the certainty of knowledge proper ("in which there may be no discernible emotion at all"); the former certainty too often ignores or violates the indispensable standards of the latter.

> The patriot, for example, "knows" his country to be right, and the lover "knows" his beloved to be beautiful and good in rare degree. In the same way the man of strong religious feeling tends to believe that the framework of dogma which has served since childhood as the great firm trellis of his emotional life must be true. That life would hang in a void if the dogmas were untrue; therefore they are and must be true. If a weaseling intellect brings in a verdict of not proven, then it must be denied that in the realm of truth the intellect has exclusive rights. [*RB*, 178]

But, alas, no matter how great the intensity of such certainty may be, says Blanshard, "that intensity bears no relation to the truth of what is believed" (ibid.). Luther's great mistake was in allowing himself to be ensnared by his passionate convictions.

Behind this mistake, Blanshard suggests, may have been two others. First, Luther seems to have implicitly supposed that feeling may be an avenue to knowledge; but this, Blanshard insists, is not the case. We may think propositions, believe them, disbelieve them, deny, opine, suppose, or doubt them—but feelings (in the proper sense of emotions or affections) simply do not have to do with propositions, i.e. what may be true or false. Hence as Blanshard puts it: "the phrase 'I feel that—' cannot be correct. . . . One may, to be sure, have a profound 'knowledge of the heart' in the sense of knowing the shades and causes and ways of working of human emotion, but this is knowledge *of* the heart and not *by* it" (*RB*, 178).

Second, Luther may have slipped, argues Blanshard, by assuming that the presence of intense conviction is somehow evidence for the truth of what is so intensely believed. But "there is no reason to think that our desires, however powerful, carry with them any guarantee of fulfilment" (*RB*, 179). On the contrary, among the plainest facts of life are the frustration of even passionately held hopes and beliefs. "One cannot," concludes Blanshard, "even in religion, argue that the depth and generality of men's desire that a belief should be true has any relation to its being in fact true" (ibid.).

Whether or not, historically, Martin Luther actually ever made such assumptions as Blanshard criticizes is beside the present point. Luther's vision of man's sinful situation was neither built nor buttressed by the warrants of rational discourse. And as a consequence, Blanshard points out, serious violations of morality and integrity flow in the breach. Morality is violated, for example, when punishment is recommended for theological dissent, despite the very limited degree to which our beliefs are under our voluntary control, even (or especially) on Luther's own view that faith is a supernatural gift from God. And integrity is broken when standards of intellectual virtue practiced in most areas of life become inexplicably intellectual vices in the area of religion:

> It was thus admirable for Copernicus to follow his evidence rather than his heart till he collided with the book of Joshua, but thereafter he must follow his heart and reject the evidence. Luther would no doubt explain to the critic that the feeling which may be trusted to guide religious belief is something quite different from the feeling which is dangerous to secular belief, for the first is divinely prompted and the second a mere natural feeling. But how one is to distinguish the first from the second is not made clear. [RB, 181]

In this bifurcated situation the love of truth for its own sake is threatened, and even (judging from Luther's vicious polemical practice against his rivals) the respect for simple justice in the stating of an opponent's position.

On these grounds Blanshard finds in the thought of Martin Luther a sobering object lesson in the dangers of depreciating reason anywhere, emphatically including the vital realm of religious belief. Even Luther's primary premise, human depravity and the corruption of the intellect, is an unwarranted starting place: "it is a libel based on a myth" (RB, 186).

Turning to Søren Kirkegaard, Blanshard extends and sharpens his criticism of irrationalism in religion. Kierkegaard, he suggests, is particularly significant because of his place in shaping theological strategy. In Blanshard's military metaphor, "It is Kierkegaard's part as a staff officer in the anti-rationalist campaign that we are to study" (RB, 191).

The strategy perfected by Kierkegaard is simple: refuse to use the weapons—or to fight on the field—of reason. Once one frankly embraces paradoxicality as essential to religious passion[1] and proclaims his religiously motivated behavior to be "by virtue of the absurd,"[2] there is no purchase left for the rationalist. As soon as one scorns objective considerations[3] and even dismisses the possibility of communication,[4] one has achieved invulnerability in advance to any attack from philosophers demanding evidence and logic.

Blanshard acknowledges the difficulty of dealing with such a strategy. It is evident, he admits, that "if an appeal is taken to the unintelligible and the irrational, it is begging the question to protest against it on any grounds of sense or reason" (RB, 236). There can be no direct disproof of the irrationalist position if the concept of proof itself has been utterly repudiated. "But we can at least point out," Blanshard notes, "that the irrationalist defence is double-edged" (ibid.).

The strategy of Kierkegaard wounds itself first in its relations with rival irrationalisms: "If it undercuts its opponents, it also undercuts itself, in the sense that it has foregone all right to the rational criticism of others. If opponents claim a divine warrant for the opposite of what Kierkegaard proclaims, all he can do is denounce them as impostors" (ibid.). This characteristic recourse to polemic and abuse, which was noted in Luther's practice earlier, seems powerfully tempting once the controls of reasonable argument have been thrown off. And in this there seems to be a moral defect of some importance.

Still more striking, in this connection, is the moral nihilism that Blanshard finds to be an inevitable consequence of Kierkegaard's perverse demand that the highest level of religious life—that of the "knight of faith"—be lived outside the boundaries of ethical universal norms which might justify and make intelligible the "knight's" choices. Kierkegaard insists that Abraham, his prime example, was right in being willing to murder his beloved son on the basis of no justifying principle whatever, simply "by virtue of the absurd." But if anything so obviously vicious can be approved, if inflicting meaningless pain and destroying possible good is potentially part of saintly duty, then no meaning remains for our moral terms and the moral life is reduced to a shambles.

Finally, on the level of theological belief once more, Blanshard criticizes the Kierkegaardian attack on objectivity and communicability as, in effect, the undercutting of theological content itself. What is meant by "believing" the logically self-contradictory? What is left to believe when, as Kierkegaard urges, a man has learned "to relinquish his understanding and his thinking, and to keep his soul fixed upon the absurd . . ."[5] Blanshard replies:

> The difficulty with this claim is to attach any definite meaning to it. If we were told that though a certain belief was improbable we should try to make ourselves believe it, that would be intelligible, whether ethical or not. If we were told that a belief, though beyond our present understanding, was vouched for by others who did understand it, and that through provisionally accepting this assurance we might come to understand it ourselves, that too would make sense. But if we are told that although a belief is both unintelligible and self-contradictory we shall see that it is absolutely true and certain if we commit ourselves to it passionately enough, we can only question whether the proposer knows what he is asking of us. The law of contradiction is not a principle that is valid in some cases and not in others; if it is invalid in any case, it is invalid *as such* and therefore in every case. But if it is thus universally invalid, then in no case does the assertion of something as true exclude the truth of its denial, and *nothing* is true rather than untrue. And that makes assertion meaningless, for *what* could one be asserting? Just as Kierkegaard's ethics implies the denial of a realm of value, so his translogical truth undermines truth as we know it. [*RB*, 241]

Reason appears the one bulwark against nihilism in both life and thought, then, as Blanshard rests his case against Kierkegaard. The strategy of irrationalism is bought at a fearful price.

Even if this price is paid, the costly strategy turns out to be in fact unworkable, Blanshard argues, as he examines the theology of Emil Brunner.

Brunner's approach, growing from the same theological root as Luther's and Kierkegaard's, requires the separation of the sphere of reason from the sphere of revelation. Behind this recommended isolation is the premise that human reason is simply incompetent (due to the depths of human depravity and the heights of divine truth) to deal with revelation. Either we have been given faith in revelation, in which case we shall not want to criticize what we believe; or we have not, in which case we may not properly criticize what is in principle beyond rational scrutiny—so Blanshard depicts the dilemma proposed by Brunner.

But the second horn fails, Blanshard argues, since reason in principle is always relevant wherever thought and discourse are present. How could it be otherwise? The very activity of the theologian in choosing one word over another, in affirming some statement rather than denying it, in alleging dilemmas against his opponents—all this does not deny logic, it exemplifies it. Even when Brunner attempts to escape into a "nonpropositional" revelation, he fails.

> He says in his striking simile that life is like a wheel whose spokes all radiate from a certain centre, but that where the hub should be there is for the natural man a blank and a mystery. But on his own showing, the hub is neither a blank nor altogether a mystery. It is filled with manifold attributes—love, mercy, justice, truth, forgiveness, repentance, happiness, submission, aspiration, and many more. [RB, 267]

"Success" would entail the cessation of attempts at communication altogether. Theology would be at an end, and even silent thought in such matters would be impossible.

Fundamentally it is the inescapable character of reason that frustrates every theological attempt to subordinate it to (or isolate it from) faith. The authority of logic is the necessary condition of every thought's being what it is rather than something else. Logic in this fundamental sense is not optional; reason at this level is prerequisite for faith's very possibility. But the reverse is not the case:

> This is not true of faith. Brunner admits that most men are without it and that, however miserable their lot and prospect, they somehow manage without it. But without logic they could not take a step or make a remark. . . . When Brunner denies the authority of logic in the sphere of revelation, his very denial takes its significance from the logic he is questioning; for unless this logic is valid, the denial of its validity would not exclude that validity, and he would be saying nothing. In short, conformity to logic is the indispensable condition of experience, the opposite of which is strictly unthinkable. [RB, 276]

If this is so, then anything that might be considered a responsible human action must also presuppose reason ("logic") in this basic sense. To choose

Christian revelation over the multitude of competing claimants for one's faith (if choice enters into the matter at all) needs to be an act of reason in order to be a responsible choice (*RB*, 277). Thus in theory and in practice reason is prior to any of the specifics of religious commitment. It may seem, Blanshard admits, that arguing for this priority is circular.

> But the objection is pointless by now; indeed it is one more nail in the irrationalist coffin, for it is further evidence that the appeal to reason is beyond escape if one thinks at all. Any argument on the ultimate test of truth that was *not* circular in this sense would invalidate itself by its own canons. We conclude that when the natural man has to choose between two claims to truth, one admitted to be meaningless to him, the other the implicit basis of all his experience, one answer only is responsible. We cannot ask him to lay his reason, and with it his common sense, his science, and his philosophy, upon the altar of a God admitted to be unknown and unknowable to him. [*RB*, 276–77]

The alternative would be moral nihilism again. If man's only available standards are held to be totally corrupt, if our best-attested truth is falsehood, and if foolishness is somehow supposed to be the wisdom of God, then man "must believe that his faculties are so deeply perverted that his right may be really wrong, and his wrong, right" (*RB*, 279). In this situation one concludes (at best) to utter moral skepticism. An even harsher but no less just conclusion would be to despair of the moral goodness of God himself, who on this theological view is depicted as capable not only of teasing and befuddling his helpless creatures with faculties that prove delusive, but also of horribly punishing a large (but arbitrarily selected) number of them merely for trusting the powers with which they were equipped by him. Even these grim alternatives are entailed and are intelligible only because logic abides, whether we like it—or acknowledge it—or not. "It looks increasingly," Blanshard concludes, "as if reason, which in Brunner's picturesque universe figures only as a broken reed, may have to be reconceived as the head of the corner" (*RB*, 287).

Thus far Blanshard has argued that the abandonment of reason in religion (1) confuses the "heart" with the "head," intensity of conviction with certainty of knowledge (Luther); (2) destroys meaning of every sort (Kierkegaard); and (3) defeats itself, both theoretically and practically, when attempted (Brunner). In each case, as we have seen, a most serious moral failure follows. All these deep defects are found, finally, in the position of Karl Barth, as Blanshard scrutinizes his writings; and in addition Blanshard notes twin faults of what might be called "theological attitudes."

First, Barth's polemic against the applicability of critical rational methods to theology is directed, as Barth alleges, against "pride." Man's proper response, Barth holds, is humble obedience to the word of God.

Testing, examining, pressing for proofs—this is the manifestation of sinful self-assertion, Barth claims. But Blanshard finds Barth's polemic astonishing. The shoe of pride fits on the other foot. What could be more arrogant than to claim obedience, in the name of God Himself, to one's own theological position? Has the theologian been so blinded by his own self-identification with "God's point of view" that he is unable to see that heaping accusations of "pridefulness" on his opponents is a comic reversal? Such a theological attitude is a poor advertisement for the product that gives it rise.

Second, and in summary, the Barthian attitude toward rational method in all areas of thought runs counter to civilized man's growing sense of what constitutes intellectual virtue. We find ourselves in a world largely created by science. Theological attitudes of hostility toward scientific ways run against a rising stream that must carry them away. True, we need not be bound to what Blanshard calls a "fundamentalism of science." Theologians need not accept reductionistic materialism, for example, as the basis for all their thinking. "Science, however, means more than a set of conclusions; it means also a set of methods and intellectual habits. The most important of these habits is adherence to a rule that is felt to be at once intellectual and moral, the rule of adjusting one's assent to the evidence" (*RB,* 313). Here emerges the root defect of the theologians covered by Blanshard's critique: each grossly violates the "principle of intellectual rectitude" that would chain belief to evidence and bind assent to reasonable warrant. And in this violation each has flung open the door to absurdity, obscurantism, fanaticism, and cant at the deepest level of life, the level of religious belief. Luther, Kierkegaard, Brunner, and Barth would scorn such a "principle of intellectual rectitude" and reject Blanshard's ethics of belief. The issue itself, therefore, sharpens into one of defining more precisely what are the rights and responsibilities of reason in the area of religion. As Blanshard becomes more explicit on this crucial question we shall find topics for debate.

II

The positive position from which Brand Blanshard directs his previous criticisms against theologians who minimize or oppose the use of reason in matters of religious belief is best approached through examination of his essay, "The Ethics of Belief."[6] Before proceeding further into the domain of fundamental value intuitions, however, any writer should in fairness expose his own sympathies. I shall do this in the present section as frankly as possible.[7]

Like Brand Blanshard, I am a partisan of reason in religion—as in all of life. Without the controls of some criteria, life drifts or staggers aimlessly. Without concern for consistency and coherence among the aims of life, one's policies of action are likely to defeat one another and, even at best, will lack integration and the benefits of mutual support. Without insistence on adequacy to the many demands of life, integration itself may be purchased, by the resolute exclusion of relevant value claims, at the high cost of fanatical narrowness.

Reason in life, in other words, guards wholeness and fullness against ad hoc randomness, self-defeat, and one-eyed loss of perspective. Religion, as the domain of life's fundamental values, is a fortiori in urgent need of reason at every level: reason is needed, that is, not only in analyzing *particular assertions* and practices as to their success in performing their appropriate function within the total scheme, but also in assessing those *propositional networks* by which religious thinkers attempt to articulate and relate the beliefs that are implicit within their religion's basic values—and is needed even in weighing for wisdom the fundamental *value-orienting imagery* on which religions rest.

Consequently the easiest—but perhaps the least illuminating—formulation of the issue is stated through Blanshard's polemic against the historical strand of Protestantism most hostile toward intellectual responsibility in matters of religious belief. Luther, Kierkegaard, Brunner, and Barth all took positions sufficient to draw Blanshard's fire; thus if the issue is set in their terms my response is obvious. If the issue, as Blanshard phrases it, is whether or not we should tolerate "a hard requirement that no matter what the evidence one might suppose one had, assent must be given to certain tenets of the creed. . . . ("Ethics of Belief," 84), then my answer, like his, must be an unambiguous negative. Such a formulation calls for a barbarous self-mutilation of the mind. I share Blanshard's deep moral revulsion from it. The demand for belief *no matter what* the evidence has no more ethical than intellectual justification; on the contrary, its ethical defects are equally fatal, and any religion requiring such dehumanization of its devotees stands condemned on both counts.

The issue is less clear-cut, however, on another passage wherein Blanshard phrases his question: "Ought we to believe where we do not see?" ("Ethics of Belief," 86). On one interpretation of "not seeing," of course, the image of "blind belief" is evoked, and what I have just said against Kierkegaard's brand of theological obscurantism remains pertinent. Call this the "do not see *at all*" interpretation, and classify it with the "no matter what" view as clearly unacceptable. But this is only one (rather extreme) reading of the question. Another interpretation (equally extreme) might be phrased: "Ought we [ever] to believe where we do not see with perfect clarity?" Call this the "do not see *perfectly*" interpretation, and it is clear, I think, that the subject has been significantly changed. Between not seeing perfectly and not seeing at all there is a wide range of possibilities. I may see less well without my eyeglasses than with them, but being without them will not prevent me from coping adequately with some kinds of activities. How well I need to see depends upon my purposes and the circumstances. On a foggy day I shall drive my car more slowly and doubtless, unless in urgent circumstances, I shall give up hopes of flying my airplane at all. The crucial questions are, however: *how great the restrictions* on the visibility and *how large the risk* that is warranted by my purposes. If I were trapped at an airstrip in the center of a rapidly closing forest fire with my airplane, and if my only chance of survival lay in taking off into conditions I would normally avoid, I suspect that even quite low visibilities would seem a blessing.

But this is all a metaphor. Its epistemological application would seem to be that belief without *any* appropriate warrant, on the one hand, and belief with *perfect* certainty (which presumably occurs only in connection with self-evident or logically necessary truths), on the other hand, are far from exhausting the relevant alternatives. Our normal situation, I suggest, is somewhere between these extremes. We have some grounds, but far from enough for complete certainty, for most of our beliefs; and the question of whether it is reasonable for us to believe or not under those conditions depends upon our circumstances: including the accuracy of our assessment of the risks in being wrong and the rewards of being right. Blanshard asks: "Ought we to believe where we do not see?" My answer is: "It all depends." It depends on how imperfect our vision is, how urgent the need for decision, what sorts of things *need* to be "seen" under the circumstances. In all of this, of course, I am including not merely religious belief but any sort of beliefs. I am, in brief, calling for a richer notion of "reasonableness" than Blanshard has yet given us for weighing the merits of affirming or withholding assent.

A third formulation of the issue before us is proposed by Blanshard in a way that might lead to just such an enriched notion if pursued. He contrasts withholding belief till the evidence warrants with "the embracing of belief, whether intelligence is satisfied or not" ("Ethics of Belief," 82). The question is well raised: Just *what* "satisfies intelligence"? Must intelligence be *fully* satisfied prior to the adoption of any belief under any circumstances? *Whose* intelligence, by the way, are we discussing? Just as I am confident (with Blanshard) that reasonableness does depend somehow upon satisfaction of intelligence, so also I suspect that intellectual satisfaction is not irrelevant to persons, times, and places. We all know that this is the case actually, inasmuch as different intellects are in fact differently satisfied. And even ideally, it would at the very least be extremely difficult to specify an absolute standard of intellectual satisfaction—one that demonstrably has and continues to have the power to convince every intellect exposed to it of its satisfactory character. The most I look for, therefore, are general criteria of good thinking set within a larger context of values and purposes. But this should be enough for finite human thinkers. This means, of course, that various intelligences may be legitimately satisfied without necessary agreement with each other. It further means that the genuine hunger many men feel for intellectual satisfaction is set within a multiplicity of basic human hungers, also genuine and deserving, that may sometimes be in competition with one another. Seen in this light, it is at least possible that under some circumstances other interests than intellectual ones should *reasonably* be served *along with* intellectual interests and even before the intellect is completely satiated in its demands (if satiation is possible even in principle, which might well be debated). If persons were exclusively intellects, disembodied and eternal, no other satisfactions would count. But since this is not the case it may be *unreasonable,* in the fullest sense, to defer feeding all other hungers until the intelligence is gorged.

Thus far I have been pressing toward an enriched conception of "the reasonable" as it pertains to the giving or withholding of assent by living human agents. Another skein of questions is brought to the fore by Blanshard in a fourth statement of the issue: "Is it true that even in religion," he asks, "beliefs should be accepted only on logically relevant evidence?" (Ibid., 86). Here the main concepts that may require some enlargement are "logical relevance," "evidence," and "religious belief" itself.

What is it to be "logically relevant" to some possible belief? Is there some absolute standard of logical relevance for all types of belief and all domains of thought? Is one and only one kind of evidence designated by the modifier "logically relevant," or is it a normative relationship that Blanshard has in mind? Assuming the latter in view of the endless variety of the subject matter of human beliefs, what sort of relationship constitutes logical relevance? Blanshard suggests that "logical relevance" must in principle always exclude consideration of feeling or of human fulfillment, but surely this cannot be so. If I am inclined to believe, for example, that Bach's music is greater than Saint-Saëns', a part (though probably not all) of my evidence will have to do with the quality of my own—and others'—musical experience, essentially including affective as well as cognitive dimensions. Likewise data about human fulfillment or frustration cannot without great loss be ruled logically irrelevant to ethical beliefs. Indeed, what counts as logically relevant evidence for beliefs in mathematics, physics, or astronomy excludes, for the most part, direct reference to the value claims of human life (though even here I would not want to forget the relevant—and unavoidable—part played by aesthetic, moral, and religious convictions in shaping scientific belief); but as subject matters differ, so also, I submit, does the character of what may be taken as logically relevant. My answer to Blanshard's question, then, so far is: "Yes, even in religion beliefs should be accepted only on logically relevant evidence; but we still must determine *what sorts of evidence* this allows in view of *what sorts of belief* are included in religious beliefs."

A detailed analysis of the crucial concept of "evidence" is far beyond the scope of this chapter. Suffice it to say that while the general function of evidence is to count for or against the reasonableness of giving some degree of assent to a possible belief, its specific nature is field-dependent and thus relative to the logical character of the sort of beliefs at issue. Evidence is either logically relevant, that is, or it is not evidence (within that field of thought) at all. In practice, furthermore, what makes some datum or other evidence is not some absolute characteristic inherent in it but, rather, the considered judgment of those who work and think in the field that it needs to be taken into account in the weighing of their beliefs. Thus evidence becomes evidence, I submit, by a kind of ruling made—often not without debate and never incorrigibly—by those most intimately concerned. Evidence is provisionally granted its evidential status by being acknowledged as properly pertinent to the resolution of the issue at hand; it is ruled in order by those seized of a question; it is admitted into court, as it were, by those most interested in reaching a fair verdict.

Such a view as I have expressed reminds us to be cautious about challenging the logical relevance of what is taken within some field to be significant evidence for or against beliefs that concern that field. My view raises no absolute prohibition: it is always in order (both for "insiders" and "outsiders") to ask that the rules of evidence in some domain be explicit and carefully examined. Decisions on these matters are always subject to appeal. But if those most concerned continue to insist on considering as evidence for or against their beliefs what seems to others logically irrelevant, it is well to remember that it is always possible for critics to misconstrue what kind of belief is really at issue. If religious beliefs are logically more similar to astronomical beliefs than to moral beliefs, for example, then surely it is true, as Blanshard argues, that considerations of human fulfillment are logically odd when adduced. Here even William James is in full agreement: "The future movements of the stars or the facts of past history are determined now once for all," he asserts, "whether I like them or not. They are given irrespective of my wishes, and in all that concerns truths like these subjective preference should have no part; it can only obscure the judgment."[8] Granted. Here everyone seems in sweet harmony. But since many thoughtful religious believers do persist in pointing to considerations of human fulfillment—considerations that would obviously be irrelevant in astronomy—I propose we take seriously the possibility that at least some important types of religious beliefs are quite unlike the astronomical ones with which Blanshard appears implicitly to compare them.

Finally, I turn to a fifth statement of the issue presented by Blanshard. He says that "while the scientific mind has on the whole, though with many lapses, held it wrong to exceed the evidence before it, the religious mind has held that there is one great exception, and that in this exceptional case it is not only a right but a duty to give one's belief a freer rein. The question before us is whether this is true" ("Ethics of Belief," 86).

My main concern, having already touched on the need for an enlarged concept of reasonableness in risking assent, a more flexible concept of evidence, and a revised analysis of religious belief, is now with the ethical notion of "rights and duties," particularly within the domain of religious belief. Religious beliefs, in my view, as I have hinted, form a complex fabric whose threads are of many quite different kinds. There are doubtless some beliefs which function very much like the beliefs of historians (or astronomers), but I take these to be quite subsidiary to the fundamental function of primary religious beliefs which serve not mainly to describe finite states of affairs but to organize, elicit, and express ultimate values.

My role here is not to expound on this view. Rather, entertaining it as a mere hypothesis, I am curious to see its implications for the question whether there are ethical grounds for giving "freer rein" to the religious beliefs we adopt than could be appropriate in the sciences or in other primarily descriptive discourse. The outcome, I think, tends to confirm the intuition of what Blanshard calls the "religious mind" that there are significant points of difference in both rights and duties.

The "right" to give freer rein to religious than to scientific beliefs is derived from the different functions played by the two. The scientist, through his enterprise, has taken on an obligation to describe finite fact as it is with the utmost dependability. In reality he does much more, and it is not my intention to reduce the nature of scientific thinking to sheer descriptive accuracy; that, however, must await later discussion (below, 922–23). What is important here is that the rights and obligations in thinking be seen as relative to purposes and values in life. One of the main purposes of empirical science is dependable reporting; thus one of the key values of this enterprise is precision in statement coupled with humble subservience to the actual. The religious believer, by contrast, is part of a different enterprise, is consequently under a different set of obligations, and is thereby in a context of different rights. In affirming a religious belief he is not (on my hypothesis) necessarily attempting to report accurately on the actual; he may well be celebrating his intuition of the ideal. His central purpose is to maintain and increase consciousness of the most intensely worthy and most extensively relevant object of reverence of which he is aware; thus one of the key obligations of this enterprise is the avoidance of hypocrisy in speech, coupled with humble self-scrutiny against idolatry in ideals. In saying this I am not intending to suggest that the religious believer has absolutely free rein (values are not irrelevant to what is the case and vice versa), nor am I attempting to reduce religious thinking to sheer prescriptive expression. Such additional complexities would have to be supplied in a fuller account.[9] My quick sketch here is merely to suggest a basis for an affirmative reply to Blanshard's question whether the "religious mind" has a right, somehow, to a freer rein (not a totally absent rein) in affirming a religion's most crucial beliefs. If those beliefs centrally deal with what is most worthy of worship rather than (in the first instance) with what is most probably actual, then they should be allowed that right.

What, though, of the "duty" to give freer rein to religious beliefs than scientific ones? I agree with William James that the purely defensive posture in life—the attempt to avoid all risks by refusing all uncertainties—is both impossible and, when attempted, self-defeating.[10] We are obliged by the facts of finite life to accept risk, whether we like it or not (or acknowledge it or not); the refusal to make a positive choice is to make a negative one. Thus if (as on my hypothesis) religious beliefs primarily have to do with value commitments rather than matters of cool, objective fact, there will be no avoiding religious issues—implicit in our ways of living, at least, even if never uttered or examined.

The question of a "duty" to religious belief, therefore, has two facets. In one sense, since there is no avoiding living so as to exemplify some values or other, we are obliged—but not in any moral sense—to give freer rein to religious belief in my proposed sense of the word. We literally cannot suspend judgment, while going on living, on all matters of relevance to religion so understood. But in this sense we have no "duty" to accept *implicit* religious belief of some kind since we cannot help ourselves and "ought" implies the possibility of doing otherwise.

There is another side to the question, however, on which it makes good ethical sense to speak of a "duty" to give freer rein to religious belief: this is the duty to articulate, openly affirm, and thereby make *explicit* for examination the fundamental value structures of one's life. Whence comes this duty? Is it externally imposed by philosophers of religion to enhance their prestige or their market value? No, if there is a duty to be self-conscious and reflective about one's functioning religious beliefs, it arises from a common duty to our full humanity. We are more than disembodied intellects, that is true; we are lovers, haters, builders, destroyers, artists, poets—people who feel and fear and need and all the rest. But we do think, since we are human; we are rational agents, intelligent organisms, and we diminish ourselves if we fail to use our frail powers of reflection to their best advantage in all aspects of our lives. Most profoundly of all, then, we have a duty to make explicit and to examine that valuational core from which our policies, our sense of self, our vision of the meaning of our world extend. We may shirk our obligation to reason in religious belief; but if we do, the sanctions fall upon ourselves as well as others. As I said at the start of this section, practical unreason—the neglect of consistency, coherence, and adequacy as general guides in weighing the wisdom of one's policies of life—invites randomness, self-defeat, and one-eyed loss of perspective. The duty to explicit and examined religious belief is the duty we all share to enhance intelligence in human existence. This duty to be reasonable, in turn, is ultimately grounded in the ideal of a full and integrated life.

III

In the light of these more general remarks about the role of reason and religious belief in life, I should like to put some questions to Brand Blanshard about his own commitments, especially as they compare with the commitments of the more traditional theologians he has taken to task. These questions, I hope, may serve to clarify the nature of the struggle in which Blanshard is engaged.

First, I should like to know whether he will acknowledge what I believe to be the case: namely, that his defense of reason is in fact a type of religious apologetic. By this I do not mean to imply that he covertly requires supernatural sanctions for his position—religions, as I have suggested above, need not involve any such supernaturalistic beliefs—but, rather, that for Blanshard the service of reason (rather specifically defined) is the value above all values, the life-organizing ideal, which commands his unconditional assent.

Religious beliefs differ so vastly, as we look at the range of actual and historical religions, that it is futile to look for necessary and sufficient conditions of religion in the area of doctrine at all. Instead, I have suggested that what distinguishes all religions is the sense of limitless worth and unbounded relevance pertaining to some focus of values for the devoted community or individual. In the Judeo-Christian tradition this focus has been God: holy, transcendently important, inescapable, before whom man's right response is unconditional reverence.

The passionate intensity which Blanshard correctly sees in Martin Luther's attitude toward God is a paradigm. It is no coincidence that Luther is remembered as a giant (for better or for worse) in religious history. Nothing, neither popes nor princes, neither personal safety nor social sensibilities, could be more important to Luther than obedience to the God upon whom his faith was cast. No area of life could be beyond the scope of this God's service. In qualities both of intensiveness and of comprehensiveness, in other words, supremacy in all Luther's valuing was commanded by his God alone. Precisely by virtue of the intensiveness and comprehensiveness of valuing—and by approximation to it among his followers—the religious character of Lutheranism is assured.[11]

Blanshard's temper and tone are, of course, universes removed from Luther's. The specific character of what they supremely value accounts for much of this difference. But is it not the case that in his way Brand Blanshard intends to be as wholehearted in the cause of reason as Martin Luther was in obedience to God? Nothing for Blanshard is more comprehensively relevant. Nothing for Blanshard commands a higher allegiance. In action no less than in thought, reason inescapably is pertinent and reason universally is supreme. The modes of expression demanded by reverence for reason are different in kind from those appropriate to the Lutheran God, as we should expect from such different foci of value; and the forms of life built on such different bases look, feel, and are quite unlike. But intensiveness of valuing does not always express itself in roarings and rendings; only a specific sort of intensity expresses itself in bulging eyes and foaming lips. Commitment to reason is shown in other ways.

May it then be granted that Brand Blanshard qualifies as a "theologian" of reason if we now take "theos" to stand for the supreme focus of value, the ideal object of devotion? If so, this does not entail any weakening of his philosophical case (which, like that of any philosophical theologian, must stand or fall on its own philosophical merits), but it helps to locate Blanshard and his adversaries more certainly within a common arena. More than this, it exposes certain limitations beyond which Blanshard's arguments cannot in principle carry him and thereby illuminates the logical character of this and other disputes over ultimate beliefs.

My second question, then, is whether Blanshard is prepared to acknowledge the irreducible elements of risk that are involved in his, as in any, religious commitment. He objects, as we have seen, to Kierkegaard's emphasis on the "leap of faith"; but, poetic license and its exaggeration aside, Kierkegaard was usefully pointing up one of the unavoidable features of the human situation, one from which Blanshard's appeal to reason in no way escapes.

There is an unavoidable risk, for example, in deciding just how well one needs to "see," given the vast range between what I earlier called "do not see *at all*" and "do not see *perfectly.*" In matters of urgent practical import we cannot be assured in advance just what degree of clarity we should demand as a standard of reasonableness fit for just these circumstances. We know, in general, that if we hold out for too much clarity we may miss our goal just as surely as if we plunge ahead rashly without adequate clarity. But such general knowledge serves simply to underscore the risk that cannot in principle be evaded by holding out for greater clarity. When the appropriate degree of clarity is itself the issue, the demand merely for more of it is no solution. A decision must be made, a risk accepted—a "leap" taken, if you will—in advance of any assurance that in this case one sees well enough what seeing "well enough" would entail. Of course one wants as much clarity as possible—here is where Kierkegaard's rhetoric, seeming to revel in darkness, needs firm opposition—but the business of living never allows as much as, ideally, one might like. Kierkegaard tempts us to ignore the little light we may have; Blanshard tempts us to remain immobile until all the shadows have fled. Neither extreme is without its risks; neither is well designed to maximize one's chances of finding an abundant life in the chiaroscuro of this universe.

Another, related, risk run by Blanshard's evangelical stress on intellectual satisfaction in all areas of life is failure to find due proportion for the other legitimate satisfactions that make life rich and fully human. His tendency to treat religious belief as though it were simply a matter for metaphysical speculation rather than the emotion-filled poetry that fashions (or threatens) community and shapes (or shatters) lives, is not wholly misguided but is partial. Men turn to religious imagery for more than explanatory functions because religion touches the whole of life and men are more than intellects. Kierkegaard's stress on passion and his contempt for the madness of "objectivity"[12] are, as usual, overblown; but he reminds rationalists of their limits. I would argue that the intellect must be a constitutional monarch: ruling, indeed, but with recognized restraints against totalitarian domination of life. Intelligence, in the enriched sense I have attempted to describe, should rule life in order to serve it. The ever-present risk in giving ruling power to any person, group, or faculty, however, is tyranny. There would be no need for concern if the only goal in life were understanding, but since that is not the case Blanshard should be alerted to possible conflicts of legitimate interests in religion as in life generally.

Still another risk entailed by Blanshard's commitment to reason as he defines it is the possibility of losing precious opportunities in life simply because of what might be called "procedural inhibitions." When the rules themselves become sacred, what the rules are intended to protect may be missed. The principle of universalizability, for example, may be the soul of moral consistency, and moral consistency the mother of justice, but how often among the bureaucratically minded one finds opportunities for human justice lost because of myopic preoccupation with universalizability. "If I do it for you, I should have to do it for everyone" may become the worst barrier to the performance of possible good, even in special circumstances wherein no one would actually be harmed by making an exception. Kierkegaard, though carrying the point perversely far, saw at least this possibility of breaking the rules for the sake of something higher as he portrayed his "knight of faith" venturing out dangerously, with appropriate fear and trembling, where the rules become a temptation to settle for something less than the best in the unique situation. The dangers of moral nihilism, Blanshard points out, are ever present (as Kierkegaard himself, too, clearly saw);[13] but the risks of moral mediocrity, or worse, stand on the other side as a warning against the worship of proper procedure.

Intellectually no less than practically, the mind may sometimes leap ahead of its warrants to convictions which, though not rationally justifiable under present circumstances, are true and important. Men of science have risked their careers and devoted their fortune, at times, on such convictions—sometimes not being vindicated until long after their deaths, if at all. The rules Blanshard stresses would chain them closer to their evidence; but fortunately for advance in thought, those rules are more honored in retrospect than in practice by the pioneers who accept such dangerous exception-making as the acceptable price for grasping new truth. May not religious thinkers with some justice claim a similar right? Their hopes for confirmation cannot be of the same sort as the scientist's, but their vision, dimly articulated though it must be, of valuable truths beyond present powers of proof may no less deserve respect.

Finally, Blanshard's theology of intellect entails one more risk of which he must be aware if his faith in reason is to be adequately self-critical: this is the risk that human faculties may not be so trustworthy as he assumes. We must of course make do with the powers we are given. But we have learned much—through these very powers, admittedly (and therefore fallibly)—of the limits of human intelligence and, even more vividly, of the unreliability of human consciences. Blanshard rejects as a "libel" the pessimistic view of man shared by his Protestant adversaries, but the risk remains that man is less enlightened, less trustworthy at heart, than Blanshard's confidence in moral intuition and human intelligence requires. Human as we are, we cannot be sure. Perhaps Blanshard is right in his optimism; I frankly hope that his myth of human nature is nearer to the truth than is Luther's, but this is a judgment that in its very nature must outrun proof, since it is precisely the reliability of the proof-judging process itself that is at issue.

Blanshard may reply that trusting human reason minimizes, at any rate, the risks of loss over the long run, since reason will adjust its assessment of the reliability of various beliefs (including belief in its own trustworthiness) according to the evidence it continues to find. And in this strategy I frankly join him since I share in such large measure his basic faith. I accept this, and I trust that I can give "reasons for the faith that is in me." But I do recognize it as a faith, a risk-laden commitment with ontological implications that are by no means self-evident. This explicit acknowledgment is one I invite Brand Blanshard also to make.

My third question arises from my earlier reminder concerning the field-dependence of evidence and the relativity of intellectual satisfaction (above, 915ff.). Granting, as I do, that Emil Brunner's approach to "revelation" is unduly bifurcationist, is there not more to be said for the legitimate role of committed community in the shaping of thought—particularly, though not exclusively, thought about ultimate matters—than Brand Blanshard has typically recognized?

Blanshard writes against Brunner (above, 912ff.) as though "reason" were an individual's possession quite apart from the social context in which that individual has been provided his language, his standards, his general goals, his admired paradigms, and (to some degree) his particular projects. But this intellectual privatism is not the case even in the sciences,[14] to which Blanshard appeals as his own paradigms of good thinking. What constitutes acceptable scientific method, logically relevant evidence, a scientifically convincing solution—even what counts as a legitimate scientific problem—all these are deeply dependent upon the shared convictions of the scientific community, including the interlocking and overlapping groups of persons who are editors of technical journals, judges on applications for grant support, graduate degree committee members, as well as researchers, experimentalists, and theoreticians. Recognition of this fact does not in any way demean science or its rationality; it simply requires a broadening, a humanizing, and a socializing of what "rationality" really entails. And such a recognition carries with it a sense of the necessary limits within which human beings, however well-meaning, scientific, and devoted to reason must work and think.

If this is true even in those empirical domains of thought open to relatively cool tests and confirmation procedures, then we should not be shocked or surprised to find theologians, who work deeply within the molten core of human conviction, warning against the too facile supposition that someone's individual intellect, however cautious, profound, and sincere, should be expected to stand in supreme judgment upon the historic deposit of the relevant religious community. I heartily agree with Blanshard's insistence that churchmen have no right to claim a special exemption from the best thinking of which they and their critics are capable. Needless obscurity, intellectual provincialism, encrusted superstitions could otherwise not be cleansed to make room for more adequate articulations of profoundly important intuitions. But what is essential in a religious intuition is by no means exhausted by those past attempts at giving it some specific doctrinal expression. Perhaps the priority of this essential value-laden intuition over any of its doctrinal articulations is what Brunner was attempting to convey in his appeal to the "non-propositional" character of "revelation" (above, 912). True, no full articulation of the intuitions of the worshiping community will be possible apart from some propositional expression, and such expressions will then be properly vulnerable to full examination by pertinent standards. But clearly the appropriateness of the articulated doctrine to the prearticulate "sense of the community" is a judgment that must be left to the community's own decision-making processes. And in like manner the pertinent standards of examination themselves cannot be wholly divorced from the consensus of the community whose thinking and valuing is involved. (a) What *sorts of evidence* are deemed relevant to a claim, for example, clarifies the meaning of the claim itself. To the extent that a community has the right to determine for itself what it means to say (to itself and to other listeners), it must have the logically related right to rule on the types of evidence that would be pertinent to supporting its intention. (b) What are the acceptable *limits of literal consistency* within a mode of discourse, again, shows to a large extent how much precision of reference and how much syntactic rigor is expected of that discourse by the community employing it. To the degree that a speech-forming community has the right to articulate its intention according to its own purposes and values, the community of speech-users must show logicians by its performance how its expressions are to be interpreted.

To recognize all this is not, of course, to side with Brunner against the competence of reason in matters of "revelation." But it is to press Brand Blanshard to notice more clearly the complexities involved in performing the needful and appropriate rational assessment of the utterances of a living religious community. As in any community, including the scientific (and philosophical), theological standards and utterances are simultaneously forged in the heat of value and on the anvil of purpose. Their literatures are similar, that is, in being shaped by purpose; they may be different, however, in the specific purposes they serve. A too quick assumption that religious statements are primarily aimed at serving scientific-descriptive functions or at accomplishing philosophical-clarifying purposes may lead the unwary into forced interpretations, misapplications of standards, and misplaced hostilities. I do not dispute the fact that there have been and are many good grounds on which lovers of intellectual integrity may wish to take up the cudgels against religious irrationalists, past and present. I hope, however, that Brand Blanshard will also agree that wise men in all communities should do their best to guard against the absolutizing of—and thereby the fanatical pursuit of—limited visions of intellectual integrity, and should do their best, instead, to foster the generosity and tentativeness appropriate to our shared human condition.

My fourth question has to do, finally, with "theological attitude" as this affects the quality of relations first with rival theologians and then more generally with the contemporary world. Blanshard, we recall, strongly objects to Karl Barth's presumptuous attitude in calling men to obedience, in accusing the reluctant or the critical of sinful pride, and in outraging modern man's growing acceptance of scientific thinking as normative (above, 913f.).

I have little desire to defend Barthian attitudes in these matters, but I believe that in all fairness another dimension should be added that may clarify the situation and thereby mitigate the offensiveness of attitudes on both sides. Barthian attitudes, without doubt, are offensive to critics. They are sometimes indeed deliberately designed to offend. But it is crucial to remember that in principle such offense is always given "in the name of the Lord." Barthian theologians, that is, do not conceive of themselves as arrogantly demanding obedience to their own thoughts. The obedience of faith is to be given only to the Word of God, of which they as theologians are merely humble servants. This is why Barth was able to characterize his theology as preeminently a "modest" theology: the theologian, in his own view, has no right to ask for obedience or demand belief on his own behalf—he is wholly bound over in the service of the Word. His commitment has been claimed by God, and God permits no other gods before Him, not even the enticing idol of intellectual respectability.

Blanshard, as I have tried to suggest, is no less deeply committed. He, too, is in the service of a master greater than himself. He, too, asks obedience not to himself but to the omnirelevant focus of his most intense valuation, to reason in thought and life. He, too, demands this obedience in the name of the inescapable and the fundamental. And he, too, may have the very human difficulty of distinguishing between his own call for obedience to reason in general, on the one hand, and agreement with his specific doctrinal descriptions of what this must entail, on the other. There is therefore little wonder that rationalists, too, may sometimes appear to their theological adversaries as stiff-necked and prideful.

Both sides are in error, however, in trading charges of pride. Each should recognize the other as—in intention, at least—speaking on behalf of values that far transcend such ad hominem considerations. Of course there is the constant danger of forgetting these distinctions and of identifying one's person with one's position. We all are guilty to some extent of such confusions, especially when our deepest values are in contest. But this human fact should not blind us to the logical situation, which is one of competing visions of the transcendently valuable.

This logical situation would be more plainly seen, I believe, and the attitudes of mutual respect appropriate to ambassadors from different sovereignties could be more readily cultivated, if Brand Blanshard were more explicit about his devotion to reason as, precisely, a form of religious devotion. Will he do so and thus take a step to improve the sour attitudes that prevail? This would by no means end the conflict, but it might give the debate a healthier context in which all parties acknowledge one another as fellow mortals fallibly engaged in service to what is sincerely seen as of ultimate value. Out of such mutual acknowledgment a basis might eventually be found for respecting even irresolvable differences in an amicable pluralism of competitive coexistence. Perhaps, in view of the disappointing history of religious conflicts, this hope is too high. But such a hope is at least not unworthy as a religious eschatology devoutly to be worked for. Brand Blanshard is, I think, in a position to help create a climate in which such a hope may grow.

With regard to climates of thought, my concluding note to Blanshard is that he consider more seriously the fading of the consensus he claims in support of the scientific ethic of belief. The argument *ad eram* is always dangerous, especially in a time of swiftly passing "eras." If the Barthian attitude against rationalism was a cultural liability a few years ago (as Barth fully recognized, by the way), it may soon be a cultural asset in a time of growing hostility among the young to science and to rational restraints generally. A new romanticism, heedless of the values of the intellect, may be rising largely against what is perceived as the dessicated lifelessness of scientific "dehumanization" and the "system" ruled by passionless thought. Evidences of these trends abound at this writing, and seem on the increase.

What does this matter? Does it in any way prove Blanshard wrong? Of course it does not. What it calls for, rather, is new tactics—and with them a new attitude—on the part of those who wish to challenge and turn this cultural stream. We who love reason must wear our hearts more openly on our sleeves, denying in convincing ways that thought excludes feeling and that science is inhuman. We must show, in sum, that reason can become religious.[15]

In part, at least, the turn away from intelligence is motivated by a commendable thirst for vitality. Intelligence has not been perceived as sufficiently vital, and for good reason. Its advocates have tended to speak a language that emphasizes control over expression, objectivity over the immediacy of personal involvement, and impersonal principles over the rich concreteness of human community. But these dichotomies are false ones. Intelligence appears most truly when it permeates all of life to enhance it in every aspect. Reason properly conceived is no less vital a candidate for centering a life or a community than its rivals.

Brand Blanshard has at least a part of this vision. He speaks and argues eloquently for reason's centrality in every domain. Might he not commend this vision still more effectively by plainly acknowledging its roots, its risks, and its rewards?

FREDERICK FERRÉ

DEPARTMENT OF PHILOSOPHY
DICKINSON COLLEGE

NOTES

[1]S. Kierkegaard, *Philosophical Fragments,* trans. David F. Swenson (Princeton: Princeton University Press, 1936), chap. 3, and Appendix.

[2]S. Kierkegaard, *Fear and Trembling,* trans. Walter Lowrie (Garden City, N.Y.: Doubleday, Anchor Books, 1954), 46 ff.

[3]S. Kierkegaard, *Concluding Unscientific Postscript,* trans. David F. Swenson and Walter Lowrie (Princeton: Princeton University Press, 1941), chap. 2.

[4]*Fear and Trembling,* e.g. 70–71, 86–89, 122–29.

[5]*Concluding Unscientific Postscript,* 495.

[6]"The Ethics of Belief," *Philosophic Exchange* 1, no. 2 (1971): 81–93.

[7]The remainder of this section is a revision of a comment first published in *Philosophic Exchange* 1, no. 2 (1971): 95–100, and used here by kind permission of the editor.

[8]William James, "The Sentiment of Rationality," *Essays in Pragmatism,* ed. Alburey Castell (New York: Hafner, 1957), 27.

[9]See, for such an account, my *Basic Modern Philosophy of Religion* (New York: Charles Scribner's Sons, 1967), esp. pts. I and III.

[10]*Essays in Pragmatism,* 106.

[11]For a fuller discussion of these qualities as they relate to religion, see my *Basic Modern Philosophy of Religion,* chap. 2 and 3.

[12]Kierkegaard, *Concluding Unscientific Postscript,* 174.

[13]Kierkegaard, *Fear and Trembling,* 88, 106.

[14]See supporting arguments, from quite diverse starting points, in Thomas S. Kuhn, *The Structure of Scientific Revolutions,* 2d ed. (Chicago: University of Chicago Press, 1970); Michael Polanyi, *Personal Knowledge* (New York: Harper Torchbooks, 1964); and Harold K. Schilling, *Science and Religion: An Interpretation of Two Communities* (New York: Charles Scribner's Sons, 1962).

[15]Cf. Nels F.S. Ferré, *Faith and Reason* (New York: Harper & Row, 1946), Appendix B, "Reason Must Become Religious."

26. REPLY TO FREDERICK FERRÉ
Brand Blanshard on Reason and Religious Belief

Frederick Ferré gives us an excellent example of the spirit of fair controversy over an issue where feelings are strongly engaged. And it is encouraging to find a theologian who has whetted his mind on analytic philosophy agreeing with so much that I have to say. He is repelled, as I am, by the hostility to reason shown by the Luthers and the Kierkegaards of the world. He agrees that you cannot consider God as "wholly other" than man in intellectual and moral standards without courting moral nihilism. He agrees that theology is a rational study that should be pursued with as scrupulous a regard for the evidence as science itself. He would even agree that reason should be the supreme arbiter of life in matters of practice as well as theory. And yet when he considers the application to religion of my simple rule for the use of reason, "Equate your assent to the evidence," he finds that he cannot travel with me down the final stretch. Respectful as he is of reason, a full assent to my kind of rationalism would stick in his honest throat. Fortunately he has been at pains to make clear where and why he feels bound to part company.

He is able to accept my maxim only with many reservations. The first is that the rule "Equate your assent to the evidence" is interpreted too narrowly; it would require us to answer the question "Ought we to believe where we do not see?" with an unambiguous No. Mr. Ferré is ready to accept the rule in cases where we see clearly or do not see at all. We can see that 2 and 2 *must* be 4, and we should therefore grant our assent absolutely. We cannot see what is self-contradictory to be true, no matter how hard we try, and hence we should withhold assent absolutely. But these, Mr. Ferré holds, are extreme cases. Most matters where belief is called for do not admit of absolute certainty, one way or the other. If I hold that the Democratic party should be voted into office next November, or that an investment in Xerox would be more profitable than in IBM, or that my overcoat will last out another winter, there will be some evidence pointing each way and a certain Yes or

No may be impossible. Mr. Ferré, in the intervals between meditations, flies an airplane of his own about the country, and he illustrates his case vividly. Suppose one is on an airstrip with a forest fire rapidly closing in and the visibility extremely low. Shall we stay on the strip, hoping that the fire will halt its advance, or take off into the smog? In such circumstances neither alternative has a clear case. We must decide nevertheless. To wait for certainty might well prove fatal.

It is true that Mr. Ferré gives this as only one meaning of a rule that he considers ambiguous, but what puzzles me is how he ever supposed this even a possible meaning of my rule. Everyone knows that few of our beliefs, if any, can be held with absolute certainty and that most of them are matters of more or less probability. "Oh what a dusty answer gains the soul/ When hot for certainties in this our life!" It is probability, as Butler said, not clear vision, that must be our guide. That is the state of things for which my rule was framed. There would be no point in saying "Equate your belief to the evidence" where that evidence amounts to zero or certainty, for there we have no problem. It is where the evidence is divided that an ethics of belief is needed, and there our maxim tells us to adjust our belief to the probabilities of the case. It tells the voter, the investor, the overcoat owner to consider the pros and cons, and to follow where the balance of evidence leads. And I take it that this is exactly what Mr. Ferré would do if caught on that airstrip in a fire. He would calculate however hurriedly the comparative chances of escape by standing pat and by taking off. And I have no doubt he would provide us with an admirable illustration of how our rule should be applied. One is following the major maxim of belief just as truly when one adjusts one's belief to the probabilities as when one grants it to a certainty.

Secondly, Mr. Ferré thinks that my stress on adjustment of belief to evidence tends toward an arid intellectualism. He reminds us that human beings have many other needs and interests besides the cognitive; "the genuine hunger many men feel for intellectual satisfaction is set within a multiplicity of basic human hungers, also genuine and deserving, that may sometimes be in competition with one another," and it may at such times be wise to defer intellectual satisfaction to that of other needs. "If persons were exclusively intellects, disembodied and eternal, no other satisfactions would count. But since this is not the case, it may be *unreasonable*, in the fullest sense, to defer feeding all other hungers until the intelligence is gorged."

Whose position is here being corrected I do not know; it is certainly not mine. I expressly pointed out in "The Ethics of Belief" and stressed at length in *Reason and Goodness* the variety of human impulses, needs, and goods, and made it clear (as I thought) that intellectual goods *ought* at times to be sacrificed to others. The student sometimes rightly lays down his books and answers a call to national service; the philosopher who cannot support his family by his philosophy must try to support it in other ways; and for the Charlie Chaplins and Babe Ruths and Pavlovas of the world to desert what they were clearly made for to become seekers after truth would serve neither the world's good nor their own. I have argued against intellectualism as against other forms of fanaticism, and I hope I should be incapable of the advice "to defer feeding all other hungers until the intelligence is gorged." I have argued, it is true, that decisions between values are made by genuine judgments and therefore by the intellect. But by making the intellect arbiter in such cases one is not stipulating that intellectual values alone shall count. In my philosophy, at least, it is reason itself that denies the claim of knowledge to be either the sole or always the primary good.

In the same paragraph in which the above objection is offered, two further suspected ambiguities in my theory are noted. When I deprecate "the embracing of belief, whether intelligence is satisfied or not," Mr. Ferré asks, first, "Just *what* 'satisfies intelligence'? Must intelligence be *fully* satisfied prior to the adoption of any belief under any circumstances?" The answer of course is No. I have argued in *The Nature of Thought* and again in *Reason and Analysis* that to satisfy intelligence fully is humanly impossible. The theoretic impulse would be satisfied completely only by complete understanding, and such understanding, I argued, could be achieved only by seeing the place of a fact or event in the universe as a whole. That sort of insight no one has ever achieved or presumably ever will. The full grounds and implications of any belief run out into the universe at large; even what we call the "certainties" of logic and mathematics belong to systems, and we understand them better when seen in the light of the system than when they stand alone. To require such understanding before we are permitted to believe would paralyze thought entirely. Hence if we are to believe or act at all, it must be on grounds that are *not* wholly satisfactory.

How firm a ground we should require before committing ourselves to a given belief will depend, as Mr. Ferré agrees, on circumstances. The plain man, who may be unequipped in either talent or knowledge to thread his way through speculative issues, will depend, and rightly depend, on others who are better able to do so. The professional philosopher or theologian is in a different case. It is his business to see for himself and to apply as best he can the full exactions of the rule; and those whose thought is profoundest will probably be least inclined to dogmatism. How far one is to press an inquiry before coming to a decision will depend for the most part on such common sense as one can muster. On the one hand, one does not want to be a Hamlet or a Flaubert, who could say "la bêtise consiste à vouloir conclure"; on the other hand, one does not want to be a flibbertigibbet. I suppose the only rule that can be given here is that just as one should proportion one's belief to the available evidence, so one should proportion one's demand for evidence to the importance, practical and theoretical, of the issue in question. It would be absurd to explore as painstakingly the question whether one should have custard for supper as the question how one should draw up one's will or what one's vocation should be.

This brings us to Mr. Ferré's second question in the paragraph under consideration. When we speak of satisfying intelligence about a belief before committing ourselves to it, "*Whose* intelligence . . . are we discussing? . . . different intellects are in fact differently satisfied. And even ideally, it would at the very least be extremely difficult to specify an absolute standard of intellectual satisfaction—one that demonstrably has and continues to have the power to convince every intellect exposed to it of its satisfactory character." This seems to me a dangerous way to put the matter. It may be, and in Mr. Ferré's case certainly is, an expression of tolerance and charity. But it carries the suggestion of a relativity of standards that I cannot accept either in knowledge or in conduct. The issue is not one of what men in fact do but of what they ought to do. Mr. Ferré is quite right in saying that a belief with which one man will rest content will leave another thoroughly dissatisfied. But that does not mean that their views should have equal respect, still less that there is anything relative in truth itself. The knowable world stands over against us like a great mountain range, massive, jagged, infinitely varied, but definite in every detail. That man will be best able to report about it accurately whose special ability and training qualify him most completely for seeing as they are the things in his field. What this means for a given field is not impossibly difficult to specify. The applicable principles of logic and scientific method have been worked out with high precision; nor is it very difficult to test whether a claimant to new truth has conformed to them.

Of course in any field democracy, if that means that one man's vote should count for as much as another's, is unsound. Even as applied to government, Churchill could only call it the least absurd procedure available. On the question whether the earth moved, Galileo had against him the people, the Popes, and the Bible itself, and Galileo was right. He was right because he had the requisite intelligence to see the relevant data and what they implied. His one vote outweighed millions on the other side. If Mr. Ferré asks, "Whose intelligence should be satisfied as the condition of accepting a belief?" I answer: The intelligence of those most skilled in grasping and interpreting the evidence. In the degree to which anyone has this skill himself, he is entitled to an opinion of his own. If he lacks it, he can only turn for guidance to those who, in his best judgment, have it. Most of us have enough of this skill to order our affairs with some degree of prescience and prudence, though all of us need more of it. We all need more, as well, of the ability and willingness to select the true authorities when we lack clear vision of our own.

These remarks seem obvious, and I doubt whether there is much difference about them between Mr. Ferré and me. The next point also suggests misunderstanding rather than disagreement. It concerns what is "logically relevant" to a belief. "Blanshard suggests that 'logical relevance' must in principle always exclude consideration of feeling or of human fulfillment, but surely this cannot be so." When Mr. Ferré judges that Bach's music is greater than Saint-Saëns', his emotional experience of the two is clearly relevant, he thinks, to the decision. "Likewise data about human fulfillment or frustration cannot without great loss be ruled logically irrelevant to ethical beliefs."

It is no doubt unfair to expect one's critics to have read one's writings generally, but Mr. Ferré could hardly have written these lines if he had read my *Reason and Goodness*. For among the main theses of that book are (1) that moral judgment is an intellectual function, (2) that the objective rightness or wrongness of actions depends on the intrinsic values they produce, and (3) that the fulfillment of human nature enters into the very definition of intrinsic value. I hold that values, far from being irrelevant to moral judgments, are the most relevant and essential evidence that can be adduced. Similarly of aesthetic judgment, I should say that if Bach is better than Saint-Saëns it is because his music better fulfills and satisfies the aesthetic (or more specifically the musical) sensibility of persons of educated taste. To abstract from the content and quality of the musical experience involved would render any such judgment baseless. When Mr. Ferré therefore argues for "an enriched conception of 'the reasonable,' " I am at a loss to know what this means. He suggests at one point that my conception of the reasonable is suited to astronomy but not to matters where human fulfillment is concerned. But how could reasonableness be further enriched than by including all values in its province and by defining these values in terms of satisfaction and fulfillment?

Mr. Ferré's fundamental difficulty with my position, however, begins to appear only in the latter half of his paper. It springs from his conception of the special character of religious belief. He thinks I have misunderstood that character. I have assimilated it to beliefs regarding matters of fact, such as we find in astronomy or history. "There are doubtless some beliefs," he says, "which function very much like the beliefs of historians (or astronomers), but I take these to be quite subsidiary to the fundamental function of primary religious beliefs which serve not mainly to describe finite states of affairs but to organize, elicit, and express ultimate values." Of the religious believer he says: "In affirming a religious belief he is not (on my hypothesis) necessarily attempting to report accurately on the actual; he may well be celebrating his intuition of the ideal." Again: "those beliefs centrally deal with what is most worthy of worship rather than (in the first instance) with what is most probably actual"; and once again: ". . . religious beliefs primarily have to do with value-commitments . . ." And if they are commitments of this kind, it is most inappropriate to treat them as if they were scientific hypotheses. "We literally cannot suspend judgment, while going on living, on all matters of relevance to religion so understood."

This interpretation changes the issue radically. I will try to say plainly where I stand regarding it. I agree with Mr. Ferré in two respects. (1) He seems to me right in saying that for many present-day Christians the expression of belief is more an expression of their dedication to an ideal than of their assent to a proposition. A man may stand in church and sing a hymn or recite the Creed with scarcely the shadow of an idea crossing his mind. But with or without an idea, he leaves the church convinced that he has given and gained support for a better life.

(2) And so he has. The dominant note of the Christian ethics is that of love and service to others, and it is safe to say that this marks an ethical level superior to any he is likely otherwise to occupy. The Christian morality is an exalted one whose attitudes are hard to achieve, let alone sustain, apart from joint and fervent rededications to it. And in the minds of most worshipers, this morality is bound up intimately with such creeds as they have. In a vague way this morality speaks the will of God himself, and, again in a vague way, they feel that in neglecting it they are incurring incalculable risks regarding their future. I should agree, then, that the moral influence of religious belief, at least in the country we know best, is in fact beneficent. And if this is admitted, what more is there to say? Why niggle with beneficence?

Because there is more to be said about it, in the light of which this amalgam of idealism and belief loses something of its glow.

(1) The place Mr. Ferré assigns to belief in this compound is far from that of historical Christianity. The Christian church has not been an institution for promoting morality in which belief has been secondary and somnolent. It was certainly not so for its founder, who is reported to have said, "he that believeth not shall be damned." It was not the attitude of St. Paul, who said, "if Christ be not risen, then is our preaching vain." It was not the attitude of Augustine, or Aquinas, or Luther, or Wesley, or Newman, or Barth. The central affirmation of Christianity for some 1500 years has been the Apostle's Creed. That creed states that Christ was "conceived by the Holy Ghost, born of the Virgin Mary, suffered under Pontius Pilate, crucified, dead and buried, descended to hell, the third day rose again from the dead, ascended into heaven, seated at the right hand of God the Father Almighty, whence he will come, to judge the living and the dead." These statements do not sound to my ears like the celebration of an ideal of practical living; they have the ring of

unequivocal statements of fact; and those contemporaries who take them as primarily bowings of the head toward a moral ideal are departing widely both from the Christianity of the New Testament and from that of the historical church. These beliefs have been at the center of Western religion. They must therefore exemplify what Mr. Ferré means when he says that "religious beliefs primarily have to do with value commitments." Does this really give the meaning of these fundamental dogmas? I cannot think so. They seem rather to be statements of the ultimate and most important facts, the facts of the relations of God and man. I agree that there are many Protestants and some Catholics who regard their creed as a bit of picturesque historical baggage that carries a modicum of truth but is of secondary importance to a church that is primarily an ethical society. But such persons can be described as Christians only in an unhistorical and heretical sense.

(2) Though we have admitted an association between Christian belief and the tendency toward virtuous living, such living does not depend on the belief. A great many people think it does, and are therefore inclined to look upon critics of theology as if they were attacking goodness itself. But the two are so far independent of each other that either can exist without the other. Socrates was a good man, though he never heard of Christianity; Marcus Aurelius was a good man though he persecuted it; John Mill and John Morley repudiated Christian belief, and one only wishes that more Christians could claim their standards either of belief or of morals. On the other hand, Louis IX and Joan of Arc, Chinese Gordon and Stonewall Jackson could presumably sign every article of the Creed, but so far as it is part of Christianity to "seek peace and ensue it," they were not wholly exemplary. But there is no need to develop this theme, which I have argued elsewhere. The good man's aim is to produce as much as he can of what is intrinsically good, and if he is also a free mind, what he takes as intrinsically good is so taken not because some authority says it is but because he sees it to be so with his own eyes. The dependence of morality on creed is not nearly so close as believers have commonly supposed.

(3) In this compound of belief and moral commitment, Mr. Ferré is inclined to stress the second as primary, while I take the first as primary both historically and analytically. I suspect Mr. Ferré is moved to keep the element of dogma in belief somewhat elastic and nebulous, since he is keenly aware what controversies rage around it and he is himself so good-tempered and eirenic. That brings me to my third point of criticism. To a rationalist this mode of defending belief sounds too much like a siren's song. We are urged to accept beliefs because of the moral values that cling to them, and since no one wants to traduce moral goodness, we allow tatterdemalion beliefs to enter our doors because of their highly respectable escorts.

The greater part of *Reason and Belief* is an attempt to inspect these tatterdemalion guests. It is a scrutiny of the towering but rickety supernatural architecture which ecclesiastics have constructed on sandy historical foundations. In the chapter on myth in religion I tried to show how easy it is for myth which at the start is perfectly natural to harden into rigid dogma, and the process was illustrated in some detail through the formation of Catholic thought about the Virgin. We saw that the central Christian dogmas originated at a time before critical standards of research, either historical or scientific, had emerged. To offer the mind of the twentieth century the sugar coating of an exalted morality to induce it to swallow dogmas that are intellectually indigestible is bound, after a time, to arouse suspicion and even bitterness; it is calculated, as Mill pointed out, to cause a distressing internal conflict between the love of truth and the love of goodness. And there is less warrant for this tactic when we consider that the sugar coating is itself not wholly assimilable. We fully agree that the Christian morality is a noble one, but it is not perfect, nor indeed is it adequate for modern life. It takes no sufficient account, for example, of either aesthetic or intellectual goods. In short to the rationalist neither the dogma that is pressed on him by the fundamentalist nor the moral coating supplied to it by the liberal turns out what it seems to be.

Mr. Ferré concludes his paper by putting to me three pointed questions to which he thinks plain answers would clear the air. I welcome these clearly put questions, and will answer them as straightforwardly as I can.

First, am I not advocating a religion myself? Not, of course, a religion of the supernatural, but a religion in this broad sense, "that for Blanshard the service of reason (rather specifically defined) is the value above all values, the life-organizing ideal, which commands his unconditional assent"? To this my answer is Yes. In the last chapter of *Reason and Belief*, which was still unpublished at the time Mr. Ferré wrote, I suggest that religion may be understood as devotion to what one takes as ultimately true and good. This would of course be a mockery for Newman or Barth, and it does stretch the current meaning of religion, vague and ambiguous as that is. I conceive of the mind as a struggling purposive agent, seeking at once to realize its powers and to adjust itself to a world it did not make. Reason seems to me the faculty which at once reveals to us the nature of our world, defines the ends in which our other powers would find fulfillment, and passes judgment on their comparative value.

The word "God" seems to me in a different case from that of "religion." "God" has come to mean, at least for Westerners, a being personal like themselves and with a scale of goods and evils like their own, only vastly more powerful and wise. This term I do not feel entitled to use. I accept an Absolute, however, in the sense of a world whose facts and events are bound together by causal and logical necessity, forming an intelligible whole. The service of reason *is* therefore in a sense my religion. That service calls for the use of one's own reason to embrace as much as one can of the reason implicit in the universe, and its use at the same time to define and harmonize the ends of practical life. If devotion to theoretical and practical rationality can be called a religion, I should like to think myself entitled to be called "religious." I can conceive no higher vocation.

Mr. Ferré asks, secondly, whether I have counted the risks that belong to so uncompromising a rationalism. "In matters of urgent practical import we cannot be assured in advance just what degree of clarity we should demand as a standard of reasonableness fit for just these circumstances." The classic temperament has its disadvantages as well as the romantic; for while the romantic leaps ahead of the evidence and falls into unforeseen bogs, the classic may see so many difficulties that he does not move at all. This danger of course exists; as Royce said, philosophy is not for everyone.

The answer to the objection is twofold. In the respect in question, there are far more romantics than classics in the world, far more people who act on impulse to their hurt than suffer paralysis because of excessive thoughtfulness. Among Americans particularly, "the Latin branch of the Anglo-Saxon race," the emphasis needed is on reflection rather than on restless activity. In the second place, it is part of the very meaning of rationality to acquire judgment in these matters. Aristotle considered it a test of the trained mind to know how much evidence to insist on; in mathematics one should be satisfied with nothing less than certainty while in politics a low probability might be all that was possible. It is precisely the seeker after understanding and its application who is most likely to know how much understanding to insist on before acting. "Kierkegaard," says Mr. Ferré, "tempts us to ignore the little light we may have; Blanshard tempts us to remain immobile until all the shadows have fled." But Blanshard realizes all too well that he is creeping up a narrow path through a dense forest in something like an Egyptian night. He has no apparatus to guide him except a precious flickering taper. He would not dream of standing still until "all the shadows have fled." All he insists on is holding the taper high and walking cautiously by such light as it gives. It is the only light he has.

A further risk run by the rationalist, Mr. Ferré says, is "failure to find due proportion for the other legitimate satisfactions that make life rich and fully human." But this is again to confuse rationalism with intellectualism. To order life rationally is not to repress all but the cognitive demands of one's nature, and on my theory of value that would be precisely to kill the layer of the golden eggs. Mr. Ferré thinks that these noncognitive demands should be recognized and fulfilled, but in "due proportion." So of course do I. But what faculty or organ of human nature is to fix the meaning of "due proportion"? I submit that the only eligible candidate for this office is that reason which is here charged with being alien and repressive.

A still further risk of my rationalism is that "human faculties may not be so trustworthy as he assumes." "Blanshard rejects as a 'libel' the pessimistic view of man shared by his Protestant adversaries, but the risk remains that man is less enlightened, less trustworthy at heart, than Blanshard's confidence in moral intuition and human intelligence requires." The trust in reason is described as "a faith, a risk-laden commitment."

In essentials I think I agree here with Mr. Ferré, but I am anxious to make the point of agreement clear. I cannot concede that the risk I run makes my position a "faith" in the sense that Luther's position, or Kierkegaard's, or Barth's was a faith. In demanding a "leap of faith" that set reason at defiance, they were, I hold, taking a risk that was suicidal, for a leap into self-contradiction is an abandonment of intelligence altogether. My own faith in reason is no risk at all if that means that there is some alternative to it that might involve smaller risk. There are no such alternatives. To think truly but in defiance of logical law is a meaningless expression. In this sense, then, a trust in reason is not a faith but a necessity. At two points, however, it does fall short of certainty. To believe that the world is intelligible, if not a matter of faith, is a postulate whose truth is not satisfactorily provable. Secondly, there is clearly a risk in trusting to the advance of reason. Whether human nature will in the future prove as corrupt and base as Luther believed it to be or as capable of rational insight and self-improvement as I incline to think, is admittedly "on the lap of the gods." With my own optimistic conjecture I am glad to note that Mr. Ferré agrees.

Still under the heading of his third question Mr. Ferré asks whether I recognize "the legitimate role of committed community in the shaping of thought." "Blanshard writes against Brunner as though 'reason' were an individual's possession quite apart from the social context in which that individual has been provided his language, his standards, his general goals, his admired paradigms, and (to some degree) his particular projects. But this intellectual privatism is not the case even in the sciences, to which Blanshard appeals as his own paradigms of good thinking." The answer here is (1) that I recognize the role of the community in determining how people do think, but (2) that I do not consider that this role counts for much in determining how they ought to think.

(1) Practically all who have religious beliefs have derived these from the people around them. That the Catholicism of a peasant in South Ireland, or the Buddhism of a Burmese businessman, or the religious indifference of a Moscow commissar is a position independently elaborated by himself is most unlikely. It is impressed on him by his community. And one has only to visit one of the great cathedrals of England or France, such as Chartres, to realize

how powerfully religion served to unify the people, how it expressed and impressed the common beliefs not only through words from the pulpit but through the images that filled the niches and the great windows glowing with Biblical stories. That power of the church in unifying and expressing the communal belief has largely gone. But it remains true, as Mr. Ferré suggests, that most of our religious beliefs are absorbed from our religious community, and indeed that most of our other beliefs, political, social, and even scientific, are breathed in from the atmosphere around us.

(2) When Mr. Ferré speaks of "the *legitimate* role of committed community in the shaping of thought," he is going beyond the question of fact and raising the question of right. The question of fact I have conceded; religious beliefs *are* for the most part community-determined. But what of standards of truth and canons of relevance? Does the community have the right to set these too? Mr. Ferré seems to be saying Yes when he writes: "To the extent that a community has the right to determine for itself what it means to say (to itself and to other listeners), it must have the logically related right to rule on the types of evidence that would be pertinent to supporting its intention." Here I must demur. Has Mr. Ferré considered what this implies? The Catholic church appeals to the "marks of the true church" as conclusive evidence of its divinely directed character; the Mormon community accepts as evidence a Scripture alleged to have been handed from a divine source to its founder, Joseph Smith; the Moslem community accepts as evidence a wholly different Scripture believed to have been written under supernatural inspiration by Mohammed; the community of Christian Scientists regards the statements of *Science and Health with Key to the Scriptures* with a somewhat similar veneration. Now if it is legitimate for a community to set its own standards of truth and relevance, the beliefs of all these communities are accepted legitimately, for they are accepted on rules of evidence pronounced by the respective communities as adequate. But they cannot all be adequate, for they lead to contradictory dogmas. Assuming that truth is the goal, it is therefore not the case that a community has the authority to fix its own standards of evidence. Authorities that are real authorities cannot nullify each other.

Where, then, is a religious community to go for its standards? The answer may be unwelcome but it is not far to seek. Since the sixteenth century the understanding of the world has moved forward at a precipitate and accelerating pace. The knowledge that has been attained is not opinion merely; in large part at least it is verified, exact, and securely established. The rules of logic and scientific method by which it was attained and tested have been codified in detail. They are not arbitrary rules, for not only has their reliability been tested times without number but they are in truth formulations of the way a rational mind works when it is at its best and clearest. Since they wear this fundamental character, they are not the products of any group resembling a religious community. They are the rules that are followed, consciously or not, by everyone who is conducting a responsible inquiry into fact. The committees that award Nobel prizes in mathematics, physics, and chemistry do not pause before assessing the achievement of a candidate and ask whether the Austrian or Argentinian scientific community may have different standards of evidence or of relevance which must be consulted before their candidate's achievement can be appraised. Throughout the civilized world these standards are the same.

It is by these same universal standards that religious statements must be judged. We must admit that there are dogmas like those of the creation and the Trinity to which the methods of physics, for example, are clearly inapplicable; but methods of rationality are not confined to physical science, and speculative thought may be as rigorous as scientific. And in any case a surprising proportion of religious dogmas deal with matters of fact. Whether the raising of Lazarus or the walking on the water actually occurred, whether the devil or witches exist and demons enter human bodies, whether the cures effected at Lourdes and Fatima are contraventions of natural law, are matters of fact. Like most of the statements of the Apostle's Creed, these are claims so definite that it is idle to demand the interpretation by varying sects before considering them as allegations of fact. That ingenious scientist Sir Francis Galton once proposed to test empirically the efficacy of prayer. He suggested that two wards of a hospital be occupied by persons suffering from the same diseases, warranted by competent physicians to be in similar stages of advancement. For the occupants of one ward the religious people of England would offer prayers, for the other not. The suggestion was rejected indignantly by the religious community. This has never seemed to me a convincing response. If persons firmly believe that prayers are answered, and that God is eager to strengthen the faltering faith of others who say, "Lord, I believe; help thou mine unbelief," then why should they not welcome the scientific confirmation that they would naturally expect? It may be objected that even a "confirmation" would meet with so many religious interpretations that we should still be where we were. I doubt that. And I doubt that to the religious community belongs, in Mr. Ferré's words, the "right to rule on the types of evidence that would be pertinent to supporting its intention." When Paul VI returned to the field of Fatima to confer his sanction on the "miracle," the press reported that he was surrounded by about a million of the faithful. I suggest that that entire million had less right to set the standard of evidence for what had really occurred there than one open-minded observer instructed in psychology and the philosophy of science.

Mr. Ferré has a fourth question to put to me. Would not my polemical attitude be more persuasive if more eirenical? He agrees with me about the irony of Karl Barth's speaking in the name of the Most High and then accusing of pride men who speak in the name of their own reason only. But he suggests that none of us is in a position to throw the first stone. If Barth descends from Sinai and sounds like Moses delivering the Ten Commandments, it must be remembered that the authority he appeals to is not his own; he does not present himself as the authority but only as its humble mouthpiece. And is his critic not after all in a similar position? He certainly can make no claim to be incarnate Reason. The best he can offer is a set of fragmentary glimpses that are always distorted and colored by the mind that catches them. And surely it is the part of wisdom for persons who live in glass houses to be chary about throwing stones.

Some of this gentle reproof is certainly deserved and is accepted. I have often written with an air of confidence that I did not feel and had no right to feel. But this falls short, I think, of being a mortal sin. Philosophers can speak thus with the less presumption because they know that no one takes them as infallible; all their hearers, including themselves, are aware that what they are offering is their own opinion only. Indeed in confronting theologians they have often been perhaps too diffident. "At the midnight in the silence of the sleep-time,/ When you set your fancies free," the cold fear has at times crept over me whether men so clearly cleverer than I as Pascal or Newman or Barth may not after all have been right. And then the horror of their position strikes me again and I say No, no, it is impossible. Here are men who are telling me that a God infinite in love and mercy has chosen to throw countless millions of men into appalling and hopeless misery for the ill luck, arranged by himself, of their never having heard of the bloody self-sacrifice of his son to save them from his own wrath. Pascal said that in view of such a fate awaiting the unbeliever it would be better to brutalize one's mind into believing; Mill, with a courage that McTaggart said was a turning point in religious history, said that rather than prostitute his intellect by accepting such a being as good, "To hell will I go." Brave words indeed; but, as Mill well knew, they constitute no proof, and the dreadful possibility seems to remain that the world of Luther, in which the hosannas of the saved are lost in the screams of the multitudinous damned, is the world we really live in.

Mr. Ferré thinks that in arguing with theologians like Luther we should both recognize in humility that we are merely trying to speak for a great authority standing behind us, and thus stand on similar grounds of logic and courtesy. But I must point out again that the authority I appeal to, which I have ventured to call Reason, is not an authority in the sense in which the Pope or the Lutheran Bible is an authority. It is not the property of any man, or any book, or any school, such as that of rationalism. It is simply the authority of our native faculty of cognition, which is always appealed to without question except when challenged by something disorienting, like an alleged inroad from a nonnatural world, which throws it temporarily off balance. As I have argued elsewhere, human thought is a continuous process from the first stirrings of perception to the giddiest heights of metaphysics, and through the whole process one continuous purpose runs, namely to grasp reality as fully and as consistently as we can. In that quest the laws of logic, and more specially the law of consistency, are always our ultimate touchstones. In so using them, we are doing nothing arbitrary; there is no sane alternative to doing so. In appealing to such an "authority," I am not going outside the process of thought to introduce some alien monitor of our natural thinking. I am only doing what nature makes me do.

What of the authority on the other side, that of Lutheran revelation, to which I am invited to pay equal initial respect? For one thing, there is nothing inevitable about it; it has gone unrecognized by the vast majority of the living and the dead. For another and more important thing, we cannot responsibly accept it if we try, and much of the argument of my *Reason and Belief* will be lost if this point is not seen. If we accept the Christian revelation as understood by the Lutheran succession, we have to abandon both the canons of logic and the canons of ethics, and while we can do this in words, we cannot do it in thought. We cannot, with Luther, believe that in following the logical light that is within us we are—to use the language natural to him—going whoring after false gods. We cannot, with Kierkegaard, glory in murder divinely ordained; we cannot, with Brunner, take as final truth both that we can and that we cannot contribute something toward our own salvation. We cannot, with Barth, assert that God is a being so "wholly other" as to be ineffable and inscrutable, and then devote ten thousand pages to talking about him.

Perhaps I should summarize this slightly complicated answer to Mr. Ferré's fourth question. Humility is the obligation of every controversialist, since the evidence of human wrongheadedness leaves no one untouched. Appeals to authority, however, do *not* have equal right to respect, any more than do the rules of evidence offered by differing communities. Reason, if it can be called one among authorities at all, stands unique. It, and it alone, cannot be denied without self-stultification. The authority we have been criticizing cannot in fairness claim parity with such a position. It has no inevitability; there are many alternatives to it. And it asks an initial sacrifice that no rationalist could accede to, a sacrifice of the very rights and powers that might threaten it. The refusal of this concession is not a discourtesy; it is a necessity, for the concession would surrender the powers that make us thinking men. So I am less sanguine than Mr. Ferré as to the prospects for "an amicable pluralism of competitive co-existence."

May I add that I have enjoyed this bit of jousting with so urbane an opponent, an opponent to whom one can speak one's mind without danger of misconstruction of feeling or motive.

27 BLANSHARD'S VIEW OF CHRISTIAN ETHICS
George F. Thomas

T HE question Brand Blanshard seeks to answer in his chapters on Christian ethics in *Reason and Belief* is the following: "Is Christian ethics also a rational ethics?" (*RB*, 324). In view of the "tensions between reason and faith" with respect to Christian morality, he wishes to determine whether the latter is merely a matter of faith or is also supported by reason. Although he recognizes that it is bound up with Christian theology, "love of man" with "love of God," he believes that it can be distinguished from the latter and considered by itself. It soon becomes clear that he has adopted this method because he has rejected the religious beliefs associated with Christian morality but is convinced that certain elements of Jesus' ethical teaching, as he interprets them, are both rational and important.

Unfortunately, this procedure cuts off Christian ethics from beliefs concerning God, man, and their relations to one another, upon which it depends for both its content and its power to transform human lives. Jesus' purpose was primarily religious. He was not a moral philosopher and had little to say about many questions that have been discussed by moral philosophers. Of course, a moral philosopher such as Blanshard can for his own purpose separate Jesus' ethical teachings from his religious beliefs and purpose, and can incorporate some of them into his own ethical theory. But if he does so, their meaning will not remain the same and they will not have the same power to affect the wills and acts of men.

It is also unfortunate that Blanshard virtually identifies Christian ethics with the ethical teachings of Jesus. Although he refers from time to time to later Christian thinkers, he generally treats Jesus' teaching on a particular point as *the* Christian view, mentioning later views only briefly to indicate developments and modifications of Jesus' teaching. It is easy to see why he does this. As he says, Jesus' teachings have been accepted by all Christians as having an authority above that of later Christian thinkers, e.g. Aquinas and Calvin, whose authority has not been recognized in all branches of the

Church. Also, the historical development of Christian ethics is a complex subject and would require a more lengthy treatment than the two chapters Blanshard has written.

However, Christians in every age have sought to interpret the meaning of Jesus' teachings for their lives and to apply them to the new situations and problems they have had to face. In doing so, they have interpreted some of Jesus' teachings in different ways. For example, pacifists and nonpacifists have interpreted his saying "Resist not the evil one" very differently and have disagreed on the application of the saying to the problem of war. Moreover, modern Christians have seen implications of Jesus' teachings which earlier ones had failed to see, e.g. that love of neighbor is incompatible with slavery and other forms of social injustice. Hence, Christian ethics cannot be identified simply with Jesus' ethics, supplemented by occasional brief references to later thinkers on certain points. It is also the ethics of the Christian community as developed in the various branches of the Church and in the different periods of its history.

In addition, Blanshard seems to ignore the critical work which has been done by generations of scholars on the Gospels, particularly on the sayings of Jesus. Consequently, he usually accepts uncritically Jesus' words as reported in the Gospels, whether in the Synoptic Gospels or the Fourth Gospel. Since he is concentrating on Jesus' teachings in the Gospels on the assumption that they have always been normative for Christians, it is important to observe that many modern Christians have not been so uncritical. They have recognized that some of the teachings ascribed to Jesus were probably not his teachings at all or were not reported correctly.

The Kingdom of God and Ethics

Blanshard deals very briefly with Jesus' teaching concerning the Kingdom of God, although this provides the religious framework of his ethics. At his baptism by John the Baptist, "a voice spoke from heaven" and said to him, "Thou art my Son, my Beloved; on thee my favor rests" (Mark 1:11).[1] Shortly afterward, he began to proclaim the Gospel or "good news": "The time is come; the Kingdom of God is upon you; repent and believe in the Gospel" (Mark 1:14, 15). The belief that he had been called by God to proclaim the imminence of the Kingdom or Reign of God accounts for the sense of urgency with which he sought to prepare men for its coming by persuading them to repent and amend their lives. It also accounts for his stern warning that those who were unprepared for the Kingdom would be excluded from its blessings, as the foolish virgins without oil in their lamps were shut out from the marriage feast when it began (Matt. 25:1–13). For he believed that the *eternal destiny* of every man was at stake in his decision as to whether he would submit to the Reign of God in his life, believing in Him and obeying His will.

Blanshard is aware of this "eschatological" aspect of Jesus' teaching, but he seems to be interested only in its possible *negative* implications for his ethics, e.g. the question whether it negates or at least limits the claim of his ethical teachings to truth. He raises again the question of Albert Schweitzer as to whether Jesus' ethics constituted only an *Interimsethik* for the short time before the coming of the Kingdom. He also asks whether Jesus' mistaken belief in the nearness of the Kingdom affected his values and hence puts in doubt the permanent validity of his teachings (*RB,* 326). With respect to the first question, almost all New Testament scholars have rejected Schweitzer's view. Jesus clearly believed that his ethical teachings were valid for any and every time because they describe the way men should act who seek to obey God's rule in their lives, whether His rule was to be consummated by the coming of the Kingdom soon or be indefinitely postponed. Hence, despite the disappointment of the hopes of the early Christians that the Kingdom would come soon, later Christians have sought to live their lives as members of it, recognizing that the time of its consummation must remain unknown to men. After all, although Jesus had said, "this generation will not pass away before all these things take place," he had added "But of that day or that hour no one knows, not even the angels in heaven, nor the Son, but only the Father" (Mark 13:30, 32).

As to the second question, Jesus' belief in the nearness of the Kingdom may well have influenced his conduct and that of his disciples in certain ways. For example, he expected his disciples to abandon their homes and follow him at the risk of their lives. Also, his belief in the imminence of the Kingdom probably affected his ethical teachings on certain issues, as we shall see. However, the substance of his teaching was clearly derived from his understanding of God's eternal will for men and was quite independent of the time of the consummation of God's Reign.

But the *positive* importance of Jesus' belief in the Kingdom of God is that it provided a *perspective* in which moral conduct could be viewed, a perspective very different from that of moral philosophers. Ethical theories since the time of Aristotle have usually been based upon a rational analysis of man's nature and desires as known through experience. They have sought to determine the goods man should seek and the duties he should perform by means of such an analysis. This is a legitimate and valuable task, and it has been faithfully performed by philosophers such as Blanshard. But Christian ethics has a different basis and aim. Its basis is the will and purpose of God as interpreted by men of prophetic insight and above all by Jesus of Nazareth. It begins not with the nature of man as he actually is but with man as he was intended to be and should be, a being made in the image of God and capable of living as a son of God and a brother to other men. Moreover, the aim of Christian morality is not the maximum fulfillment of human desire under the control of human reason but the attainment of blessedness through love of God and love of one's neighbors. For it is only through love that men can be delivered from the physical and mental evils that afflict them and become the whole persons they were intended as God's children to be.

This religious perspective is the source of the most distinctive features of Christian ethics. First, Christian ethics, like Jewish ethics, regards man as part of God's creation, dependent upon God for his existence and responsible to Him for his actions. At this crucial point it is sharply opposed to modern humanistic ethics of the naturalistic kind. For naturalistic humanism views man as merely the highest of natural beings, dependent primarily upon his own reason and will for his good, and responsible to no power beyond himself and other men for his conduct.

Second, Jesus' religious perspective is the source of what is often called the "*perfectionism*" of his ethics. "For I tell you," he says, "unless your righteousness exceeds that of the scribes and Pharisees, you will never enter the kingdom of heaven" (Matt. 5:20). Yet the scribes and Pharisees exemplified the highest type of goodness in the Judaism of Jesus' time. According to Matthew, Jesus also said, "You, therefore, must be perfect, as your heavenly Father is perfect" (Matt. 5:48), or, as the New English Bible translates the saying, "There must be no limit to your goodness, as your heavenly Father's goodness knows no bounds." These and other perfectionistic sayings led Reinhold Niebuhr to speak of Christian ethics as setting before men an "impossible possibility,"[2] i.e. a way of life that cannot be realized by men because of their egoism and which is possible only in the limited sense that with God's help it can be in some measure approximated in conduct. Jesus' condemnation of lust as well as adultery (Matt. 5:28) illustrates one aspect of his perfectionism, since it seems to demand a radical restraint of a powerful natural desire. His demand that each of his disciples "deny himself" and "take up his cross" and follow him (Matt. 16:24), i.e. be prepared to sacrifice his life, is only the most drastic of Jesus' "hard" sayings. Needless to say, this perfectionism with the self-denial it requires has been the main stumbling block which has always prevented men of the world from accepting his ethics, and it has led even his sincere followers to compromise with the world in different degrees.

As a result, Christians have usually interpreted Jesus' demand for moral perfection as an ideal that can never be fully realized, even by the saints, but which can serve as a goal to be sought and progressively approximated by moral striving. They have also recognized that it requires such a radical conquest of egoism or self-love that they must be constantly assisted by God's grace if they are to approximate it and that they will always need God's forgiveness for their moral failures. They know that otherwise they will be tempted into moral complacency and pride by their limited moral achievements, into what Niebuhr called "the intolerable pretension of saints who have forgotten that they are sinners."[3] Thus, it is only by God's grace and with His forgiveness that the "impossible" becomes a "possibility." But although the Christian perfectionistic ethics presents men with an impossible ideal, it is a relevant one.[4] For it provides Christians with a transcendent standard by which they can judge their moral acts and achievements and see where they fall short. At the same time, it sets before them a goal which can stimulate them to transcend their moral limitations.

It is unfortunate that Blanshard ignores this religious perspective in morality which was provided by Jesus' belief that men should submit themselves to the Reign of God in all their acts, for it is absolutely essential for a full understanding of his ethics.

Love of Neighbor

The fundamental principle of Jesus' ethics, of course, is the twofold commandment of love. The first commandment, love of God, is derived from Deuteronomy 6:5; the second, love of neighbor as oneself, from Leviticus 19:18. Before we consider Blanshard's attitude toward the first commandment, we must ask whether his understanding of the second commandment, "Thou shalt love thy neighbor as thyself," is adequate.

He realizes that love of neighbor is not merely an emotion, but "a settled good will, a permanent concern for the good of other people" (*RB,* 329–30). He also stresses the fact that Jesus "universalised" it by asserting that "it was also called for toward enemies, toward men as men, without regard to race or sex, and whether they were Jews or Gentiles" (330). Finally, he regards love of neighbor, understood in this way, as "the essence of the Christian morality," and says that the rational moralist "would perhaps agree that the core of the Christian ethics was sound and not likely to be invalidated by criticism" (331).

But the next sentence makes one wonder whether the "love of man" approved by Blanshard is really "love of neighbor" in Jesus' sense of the phrase. "At least," he says, "if love may be taken as implying benevolence, that is, being habitually solicitous for others' good as having an importance as great as one's own, it is an attitude hard to challenge on rational grounds, and in making it central to the moral life the ethics of Jesus may well be an ultimate ethics" (*RB,* 331). For the "principle implicit in it" is "the principle of benevolence," which "has been recognised by many moralists as self-evidently true." As Henry Sidgwick expresses this principle, "one is morally bound to regard the good of any other individual as much as one's own, except in so far as it is less, or less certainly knowable or attainable."[5] Of course, says Blanshard, the good achieved by a Shakespeare or a Beethoven is more important than that of an idiot or a moron. "But the principle of benevolence does not deny this; what it says is that if the intrinsic good of one man is the same in amount as that of another, the two persons must be treated accordingly; if they are treated differently, as is sometimes necessary, it must not be done arbitrarily, but on reasonable grounds" (332). Blanshard adds that "common sense" should be used in applying this principle. "There is no inconsistency," he says, "between a genuine regard for the good of all men and a recognition that this good is most effectively furthered by each man's concerning himself most with those whom he can best serve," presumably those of his "own family," as the next sentence implies.

Is this "benevolence" what Jesus means by "You shall love your neighbor as yourself"? (Mark 12:31.) It seems clear that it is not. First, it would require that before one does an act a comparison must be made to determine whether the good of each person affected by the act would be the "same in amount," "less than," or "more than" the good of every other person affected by it. Also, it would require that in making this comparison one must include one's own good along with that of all the others. This implies, of course, that one must make an estimate of the "amount" of good which would be furthered in each person affected by the act. But Jesus never speaks of the good in quantitative terms or compares the amount of good which would be furthered by an act in one person with the amount which would be furthered in another, in order to determine whether the former would be the "same" or "less" or "more" than the latter. Nor does Jesus ever seem to consider the question whether the good of one neighbor is really "as important" as "the good of another" or suggest that if it is not as important the former should be "treated differently." Second, he would not have agreed that the good of another should be regarded "as much as one's own" only if his good is "the same in amount" as one's own. For this seems to imply that one should further one's own good in preference to that of another when one estimates that it is greater in amount. Yet the picture of him in the Gospels is that of one who always served others, always furthered the good of others rather than his own. Clearly, when he said, "You shall love your neighbor as yourself," he did not mean that you should further his good rather than your own only when it is "the same in amount" as or "more than" your own.

Indeed, the idea that one should further the good of *this* in preference to the good of *that* person—or the good of *oneself* in preference to the good of *another* "less important" than oneself—would have seemed strange to him. When he himself furthered the good of others, it was usually the good of "less important" rather than "more important" persons, those whose good was considered by most people as "less" rather than "more" than that of others. When his disciples were asked by the scribes and Pharisees, "Why does he eat with tax collectors and sinners?" he said, "Those who are well have no need of a physician, but those who are sick; I came not to call the righteous, but sinners" (Mark 2:16, 17). For love, as Jesus conceived it, seeks to further the good of each neighbor as an individual person and does not consider how "important" he is or the "amount" of good that can be furthered in him. Its primary concern is not to *maximize* good, as in *utilitarianism,* but to serve the needs of each neighbor and thereby to further *his* good. And all of one's neighbors are of equal importance in the sight of God.

How, then, does Jesus conceive of love of neighbor? First, it is love based upon God's *all-inclusive* love rather than the imperfect, limited love of men for each other. "You therefore must be perfect," says Jesus, "as your heavenly Father is perfect" (Matt. 5:48). Love of neighbor must be extended even to one's enemies, as the heavenly Father "makes his sun rise on the evil and the good, and sends rain on the just and on the unjust" (Matt. 5:45). Men should act as His "sons" by imitating His boundless love, and Jesus himself sought to do so by loving the publicans and sinners despised by others.

Second, love of neighbor does not depend upon the *worth* of those who are loved. Whereas ordinary love is evoked by admirable or approved qualities of the person loved, love in Jesus' sense is to be given whether it is deserved or not. Here, again, men are to imitate God's love. According to the Pharisees, there is a sharp division between righteous and sinful men in the sight of God and man alike. God's attitude toward them is determined by their obedience or disobedience to His Law, since justice requires that He show His favor only to those who obey His will. In contrast, Jesus represents God as bestowing His love freely upon all, as we have seen. He does not measure it out according to human ideas of justice based upon the merits of men. Thus, in the parable of the prodigal son, the older brother complains that his younger brother's wayward conduct does not deserve the loving welcome shown him by the father (Luke 15:11–32). He is clearly right from the standpoint of man's idea of justice. But God's love is not given in proportion to a man's merit, and a man should love his neighbors in the same way.

Third, love of neighbor does not depend upon the *return* of love by him. Unlike the ordinary love of men, it is given whether it is reciprocated or not. Jesus contrasts this kind of love with the love shown by sinners. "If you love those who love you, what credit is that to you? For even sinners love those who love them" (Luke 6:32). Like the boundless love of God, love of neighbor does not give in order to receive; it gives because it is the nature of love to give. In this respect, Christian love, *agape,* differs sharply from both erotic love, *eros,* and friendship, *philia,* which usually last only as long as they are reciprocated.

It is obvious that love in this sense requires a conquest of self-centeredness or egoism and a willingness to serve the needs of others which goes far beyond what is usually expected of love. This, of course, is why Jesus' disciples are required to deny themselves and be prepared if necessary to sacrifice their lives. It is one of the weaknesses of Blanshard's account of Christian ethics that he has nothing to say about *self-denial,* much less *self-sacrifice.* Is this because he has separated love of neighbor from God's perfect love for men which it seeks to imitate, and because he has reduced it to a general benevolence that allows one to further one's own good in preference to that of another when the latter is "less, or less certainly knowable or attainable"?

Motive, Behavior, and Consequences

In an attempt to determine the "central stresses" of Jesus' ethics, Blanshard distinguishes three "components" of an action: motive, behavior, and consequences. He points out that there have been three main types of ethical theory, each of which regards one of them as the principal element in right conduct. The "ethics of inwardness or motive" stresses motive, "commonsense ethics" stresses behavior, and "teleological ethics" stresses consequences. Christian ethics, he holds, belongs to the first type, the *"ethics of motive."* In this respect it is similar to the ethics of Kant, although Jesus differs from Kant in that he regards the "heart" rather than the "head" as the "seat" of the motive. In support of this view, Blanshard refers to Jesus' statement in Mark 7:21, "For from within, out of the heart of man, come evil thoughts" and other "evil things." This implies that if a man frees himself from evil feelings and dispositions such as anger, lust, and covetousness he will rid himself of the evil actions which spring from these (*RB*, 328–29). Blanshard also refers to the "new inward attitudes" set forth by Jesus in the Beatitudes, e.g. "Blessed are the poor in spirit," which are "qualities of character rather than prescriptions of behaviour" (329).

Undoubtedly Jesus did emphasize the motive behind an act and did believe that evil acts normally flow from evil dispositions or feelings while good acts flow from good ones. Hence, he regarded acts that merely conform outwardly to moral laws but do not spring from right motives as morally deficient. However, it is an oversimplification to say that Christian ethics stresses motives, as if it were not equally concerned with the behavior that arises from them and the consequences that result from them. That it is as concerned with *behavior* as with motive is shown by the fact that both of the commandments of love quoted by Jesus from the Old Testament and many precepts of his own prescribe or at least counsel the doing of certain kinds of acts. Although they should be done from right motives, they are addressed to the will, as well as the feelings. Also, one should never forget Jesus' saying at the end of the Sermon on the Mount: "Every one then who hears these words of mine and *does* them will be like a wise man who built his house upon a rock. . . . And every one who hears these words of mine and does *not do* them will be like a foolish man who built his house upon the sand. . . ." (Matt. 7:24, 26; italics mine). Moreover, in the picture of the Last Judgment the "sheep" ("righteous" ones) are admitted to the Kingdom of God because they gave food to the hungry, drink to the thirsty, and clothes to the naked, welcomed strangers and visited the sick, while the "goats" ("cursed" ones) are excluded because they failed to do these things (Matt. 25:31–46). Clearly, Jesus was concerned about right acts as well as motives. He held that motive and act are bound up together, right motives normally giving rise to right acts as a good tree bears good fruit, and evil ones normally giving rise to wrong acts as a bad tree bears bad fruit (Luke 6:43–45).

Again, the fact that Jesus does not use the term *"consequences,"* as teleological moralists do, does not mean that he is indifferent to them. Love of neighbor is to be manifested in acts which serve the needs of the neighbor and hence have good consequences for him, as in the parable of the good Samaritan (Luke 10:25–37). Moreover, although Jesus does not use the philosophical term "summum bonum," he clearly held that life under the Reign of God constitutes the highest good for man and that it is accompanied by joy or blessedness. This implies that right acts not only result in beneficial consequences here and now but also will lead to the joys of life in the Kingdom of God. Even the Beatitudes, which Blanshard takes as evidence of Jesus' concern for feelings and attitudes, show that he was also deeply concerned for the blessings of the Kingdom, e.g. "Blessed are you poor, for yours is the Kingdom of God" (Luke 6:20). It should be noted that the blessings of the Kingdom will not constitute a reward that is extrinsic to and different in kind from the life of love men are to live in time. Rather, it is to be a continuation and fulfillment of the life of love in time and the joys that accompany it.

Thus, Jesus' ethics is not only an ethics of motive; it is also an ethics that requires the expression of good motives in right behavior and aims at both the attainment of good consequences in time and the enjoyment of eternal life in the Kingdom of God.

Jesus and Moral Laws

What was Jesus' attitude toward the "Law of Moses" and the "oral tradition" which had been developed by the scribes in interpreting and applying it to the many situations of life? Are the precepts and counsels that constitute so much of his own ethical teaching in the Sermon on the Mount and elsewhere a "new law" which is to be obeyed to the letter by Christians? In other words is Christian ethics a legalistic ethics? Blanshard has little to say about this important but controversial issue. In his main reference to it he asserts that, with the exception of the twofold law of love, Jesus completely rejected the effort of Judaism to regulate conduct in detail by the Mosaic Law and the oral tradition of the scribes and Pharisees.

For the Pharisees particularly, who were leaders in scholarship and piety, the Mosaic law had become a complicated straitjacket of requirements. Jesus broke this straitjacket deliberately and publicly. He broke the rules about the Sabbath, saying that the Sabbath was made for man, not man for the Sabbath. He broke the rules about ceremonial cleanliness, about eating and drinking and fasting and praying, and about association with social outcasts. . . . He saw that it was possible to achieve high standing in this ethics of conformity and still be a hollow man, etc. [*RB, 327*]

This is true, and well said. The Pharisees, said Jesus, "leave the commandment of God and hold fast the tradition of men" (Mark 7:8), and he denounced them as "hypocrites" and "whited sepulchres."

But it is essential to distinguish between the Mosaic Law which was the written *Torah* of the Old Testament, and the oral tradition, the *Halakah*, which had been elaborated by the scribes into a "complicated straitjacket of requirements." As Blanshard says, Jesus was highly critical of the "oral tradition" and of the scribes and Pharisees for demanding obedience to its regulations. But his attitude to the written Law of Moses was not so much negative as discriminating. On the one hand, he did not hesitate to set aside certain Mosaic laws. For example, he criticized the permission of divorce for men in the Book of Deuteronomy on the ground that, while Moses had allowed it "for your hardness of heart," at the beginning of Creation God had "made them male and female" and that in marriage "the two shall become one." "What therefore God has joined together, let not man put asunder" (Mark 10:2–12). He also abolished the law of retaliation in Exodus 21:23, 24, "an eye for an eye, and a tooth for a tooth," and opposed to it the precept, "Do not resist one who is evil" (Matt. 5:38, 39). Thus, although Matthew reports him as saying that he had come not to "abolish" the Law and the prophets but to "fulfill" them (Matt. 5:17), he set aside several commandments of the Law on the ground that they did not represent God's absolute will.

On the other hand, Jesus respected and obeyed the Law of Moses and corrected it only wherever he thought that Moses had lowered the absolute demands of God's will by making concessions to men's "hardness of heart," as in the case of the two laws just mentioned. There is no evidence that he meant to abolish the written Law as a whole, and in his reply to a man who inquired, "Good teacher, what must I do to inherit eternal life?" he quoted with obvious approval six of the Ten Commandments (Mark 10:17–19). And while Christians from the time of Saint Paul have not accepted as binding upon them the ritual and dietary laws, they have always regarded the moral laws as an indispensable source of moral guidance. It is not true, therefore, that Jesus had no place in his ethics for the moral laws of the Old Testament, as distinguished from the "oral traditions" of the scribes and Pharisees.

What is the place of Jesus' own moral precepts, in the Sermon on the Mount and elsewhere, in Christian ethics? Do they constitute a "new law" which supplements the "old law" of Moses? Although Matthew pictures Jesus as the new lawgiver who laid down laws that superseded the Law of Moses (Matt. 5:21–48), Luke does not view him as a lawgiver or contrast his precepts with the laws of Moses (Luke 6:17–49). For Jesus made no attempt to set forth a new code of laws which would regulate men's conduct in every conceivable kind of situation. His ethical teaching was occasional rather than systematic. Frequently, it was given in answer to questions from his disciples or others. For example, the parable of the good Samaritan was offered as an answer to the question of a lawyer, "And who is my neighbor?" (Luke 10:29–37). It is clear, therefore, that the legalistic interpretation of Jesus' ethics by Catholic thinkers like Aquinas and Protestant thinkers like Calvin has been a serious mistake, and this mistake has been largely responsible for the widespread modern reaction against Christian morality as a rigid and repressive set of rules.

But the fact that Christian ethics is not a form of ethical legalism does not imply that it can be simply identified with the commandment of love and that the other precepts and counsels of Jesus are of no importance. His many precepts, counsels, parables, and aphorisms are indispensable "guidelines" which indicate kinds of action or attitude required by the love of God and neighbor in different situations. They are to be applied by Christians to the various and changing situations that confront them, in a spirit of freedom and in a manner appropriate to each situation. Since they are guidelines rather than laws, they are to be followed only insofar as they are consistent with what love, the one absolute law, requires. In the sections of this essay which follow, we shall consider several of these precepts and counsels and shall attempt to show that they are to be taken seriously but not regarded as absolute laws.

Wealth and Poverty

Blanshard is highly critical of Jesus' "indifference toward wealth" and believes that it is "clearly opposed to the values of modern man" (*RB*, 337). Although he holds that "the quest of money in itself" is irrational, he believes that "glorification of poverty . . . as in itself a state of blessedness" is equally irrational (338). As evidence that Jesus glorified poverty, he cites the beatitude as reported by Luke, "Blessed are you poor, for yours is the Kingdom of God" (Luke 6:20). He also refers to the parable of the rich man and Lazarus, the poor man at his gate, in which the former after death is sent to Hades while the latter is carried by the angels to Abraham's bosom (Luke 16:19–31). "There is no explanation," he says, "of the disparity of treatment except that the one is rich and the other poor" (*RB*, 338). Finally, he quotes Jesus' sayings, "You cannot serve God and Mammon" (Matt. 6:24), and "It is easier for a camel to go through the eye of a needle than for a rich man to enter the Kingdom of God" (Mark 10:25). In short, "Wealth is repeatedly denounced as such, and poverty as such exalted" (*RB,* 338). In contrast, Blanshard maintains that, while "Wealth does, beyond doubt, increase the temptation to indolence, self-indulgence, and arrogance," "it does not by itself produce them, and in the freedoms it offers—freedom to educate oneself, freedom to choose one's own course of life, freedom from gnawing want and worry—its opportunities surely outweigh its disadvantages" (339). He acknowledges that, despite Jesus' "theoretical exaltation of poverty," he and the early Christians made "a noble practical effort to relieve it," but he sees this as inconsistent with Jesus' view that "the poor were better off spiritually than the rich" (339, 340).

Most modern Christians would agree with Blanshard's view that it is irrational to seek either wealth or poverty "in itself." They would also agree that a certain amount of possessions offers advantages of security and opportunity which poverty cannot offer. Although Christian monks have taken the vow of poverty necessary for their vocation and Saint Francis idealized "Lady Poverty," most Christians have always shunned it and many of them have devoted themselves like their Master to relieving it. But does Jesus really "glorify" poverty *in itself* or "denounce" wealth *in itself*?

On the contrary, when Jesus said, "Woe to you that are rich," he was not "denouncing" wealth as such; he was warning that riches tempt one, as Blanshard admits, to "indolence, self-indulgence, and arrogance," and hence stand in the way of the faith and repentance which are necessary for entrance into the Kingdom. There is no evidence that he regarded material things as evil; indeed, he clearly shared the general Hebraic view that the material world and its resources are part of the Creation and hence are good. But he held that material possessions must be *subordinated* to the eternal life of the Kingdom and must be sacrificed if they stood in the way of it. This is the point of his saying, "No man can serve two masters; for either he will hate the one and love the other, or he will be devoted to the one and despise the other. You cannot serve God and Mammon." It is also the point of his contrast between earthly and heavenly treasure: "Do not lay up for yourselves treasures on earth . . . but lay up for yourselves treasures in heaven. . . . For where your treasure is, there will your heart be also" (Matt. 6:19–21). He does not say that it is impossible for a rich man to be saved. "With men," he says, "it is impossible, but not with God; for all things are possible with God" (Mark 10:26, 27). Indeed, we have an example of the realization of this possibility in the case of the tax collector, Zacchaeus. When he repented and promised to give half of his goods to the poor and to restore fourfold to anyone he had defrauded, Jesus said, "Today salvation has come to this house since he also is a son of Abraham" (Luke 19:8, 9). However, in general riches are a peril, since they tend to *distract* man from love of God and His Kingdom.

They also make a man *indifferent* to the needs of his neighbors. This is the point of the parable of the rich man and Lazarus. We are not told that the rich man harmed Lazarus in any way, but, like the priest and the Levite in the parable of the good Samaritan, he paid no attention to his misery and made no attempt to relieve his hunger. The implication is that the luxury in which he lived had blinded him to the suffering even of those at his own gate. Hence, he was not cast into Hades merely because he was rich, as Blanshard asserts, but because he was callous to the needs of a neighbor. Again, the parable of the complacent rich man who was sure he had "ample goods laid up for many years" but whose life was taken from him that very night drives home the *folly* of accumulating material things since death may at any time separate one from them (Luke 12:16–21). Thus, Jesus does *not* "denounce" wealth in itself; he warns that undue concern for riches tends (a) to displace God and His Reign as the object of ultimate concern, (b) to make one indifferent to the needs of the poor, and (c) to foster the accumulation of material values ("treasures") that are transitory rather than spiritual and moral values that will endure.

Does Jesus "glorify" poverty? The fact that he sought to relieve it, as Blanshard admits, is strong evidence that he did not. Indeed, at the Last Judgment, as we have noted, the righteous ("sheep") are admitted into eternal life because they sought to relieve bodily needs such as hunger and nakedness which usually result from poverty (Matt. 25:34–40). Nor is this inconsistent with Jesus' saying "Blessed are you poor," as Blanshard thinks. Who were the "poor" to whom he refers? According to Luke, Jesus pictures a striking reversal when the Kingdom of God comes. Those who are "poor" will be "blessed," while those who are "rich" will suffer "woe." But "the poor" in Judaism did not denote those who were merely without material possessions; they were those who were socially "of low degree" but who "feared God," the "pious ones," while "the rich" denoted not merely those with great possessions but the "proud" and "mighty." In other words, Jesus used "the poor" in the wide sense which the term had acquired in the ancient prophets. As Joachim Jeremias has said, "in the prophets the word embraces the oppressed and the poor who know that they are thrown completely on God's help," and Jesus uses it for "all those in need, the hungry and the thirsty, the unclothed and the strangers, the sick and the captives."[6] Doubtless, Matthew is interpreting "the poor" in this wide sense when he represents Jesus as saying, "Blessed are the poor in spirit," i.e. the humble who are conscious of their need and dependence on God for help in contrast to the rich and proud who trust only in themselves. An example is the contrast between the "poor widow" who put a penny into the temple treasury, while "many rich people put in large sums." Jesus says to his disciples, "This poor widow has put in more than all those who are contributing to the treasury. For they all contributed out of their abundance; but she out of her poverty has put in everything she had, her whole living" (Mark 12:41–44).

Thus, as Jesus did not "denounce" wealth in itself, he did not "glorify" poverty in itself. Rather, he praised the humility and piety of "the poor," those of "low degree," who seemed to respond more readily to the "good news" of the coming Kingdom than "the rich," those of the ruling classes. Since he sought to relieve hunger and other effects of poverty in his time and demanded that his followers do the same, he would not condone the grinding poverty and want of hundreds of millions of people in the world today or the indifference of affluent nations like our own to their suffering.

Although Jesus did not "denounce" wealth, one wonders whether Blanshard is sufficiently realistic in his estimate of the moral and social effects of wealth. Is it adequate to say that, while wealth does "increase the temptation to indolence, self-indulgence, and arrogance . . . it does not by itself produce them," or to say that "in the freedoms it offers . . . its opportunities surely outweigh its disadvantages"? If he means by "wealth" only sufficient possessions to satisfy the needs of oneself and one's family, including the need for amenities such as "a comfortable house," "medical care," "books" and "some art and music" (*RB,* 336), one would doubtless agree. But if "wealth" means riches well beyond such a sufficiency of possessions, surely the spiritual and moral dangers stressed by Jesus outweigh its advantages. Moreover, in rich nations like our own the social evils that have resulted from the pursuit of riches—economic exploitation, the gulf between the rich and the poor, and the consequent conflict between classes—are all too obvious. And when one considers how easily men become obsessed with material comforts and pleasures and how weak is their attachment to spiritual values such as truth and goodness, one must conclude that Jesus' warnings against the dangers of riches are among his truest and most important teachings, although they have been more honored in the breach than in the observance by most Christians.

Women and Family Relations

Blanshard speaks with appreciation of Jesus' attitude toward and relations with *women,* especially of his understanding of them and his sympathy with them. He illustrates this by reference to Jesus' refusal to condemn the woman taken in adultery (John 8:1–11); his saying about the woman of the street who anointed and kissed his feet, "her sins, which are many, are forgiven, for she loved much" (Luke 7:47); the freedom with which he talked to the woman of Samaria (John 4:7–30); and his "easy familiarity" with the sisters Martha and Mary (Luke 10:38–42). He also points out that Jesus' strong condemnation of the divorce by men of their wives (Mark 10:11) manifests deep respect for them. Parenthetically, whether this condemnation is to be taken by Christians as an absolute law admitting of no exceptions depends upon whether one takes a legalistic or nonlegalistic view of his teaching.

However, Blanshard thinks that Jesus' saying, "everyone who looks at a woman lustfully has already committed adultery with her in his heart" (Matt. 5:28), indicates that he regarded as evil "the mere stirring of sexual desire" (*RB*, 354). He also sees the beginnings of the later "separation of flesh and spirit" in Jesus' saying, "there are eunuchs who have made themselves eunuchs for the sake of the kingdom of heaven. He who is able to receive this, let him receive it" (Matt. 19:12). We would point out that these two passages do not require a dualistic interpretation. The former is an example of Jesus' stress upon right desires as well as acts and is probably a warning against permitting a natural "stirring" of sexual desire to develop into lust for a woman as a mere means to one's own pleasure. The latter is surely only an assertion that, while monogamous marriage is the normal state for most men and women, there is a place for voluntary celibacy in the service of God's Kingdom. Jesus himself was probably not married, and in this saying, unless "eunuch" is taken literally as a castrated man, he was doubtless thinking of his disciples who had dedicated themselves with him to the task of preparing others for the coming Kingdom. If so, there is no condemnation of the "mere stirring of sexual desire" in the first saying and no ascetic dualism in the second. However, when read along with Jesus' approval of permanent monogamous marriage and condemnation of divorce, they constitute a strong rebuke to man's obsession with sex and a warning against the dangers of uncontrolled sexual desire.

What was Jesus' general view of *family relations*? "Christianity as traditionally interpreted," writes Blanshard, "stressing the permanence of marriage, likening the relation of man and wife to that of Christ and the church, and harbouring memories of Christ's tenderness toward children, has had important civilising influences on family life . . ." (*RB*, 368). But he follows this statement of appreciation with the charge that Jesus was "an individualist whose ultimate loyalties were to no organisation" and who believed that family ties which conflicted with the claims of the Kingdom "must be ruthlessly broken." To support this charge, he cites passages in which Jesus demanded that loyalty to himself and the Kingdom should take precedence over family loyalties. The most severe of these passages is: "If anyone comes to me and does not hate his own father and mother and wife and child and brothers and sisters, yes, and even his own life, he cannot be my disciple" (Luke 14:26). Blanshard recognizes that Jesus' stern demands for loyalty from his disciples to himself resulted from his conviction that the urgency of the situation as the Kingdom drew near "reversed the ordinary priority of duties." But he thinks it led Jesus to demand that a man "do violence to his natural feeling and even his conscience" under the influence of a delusion (*RB*, 369).

It is certainly true that Jesus' ultimate loyalty was not to any human institution but to the Reign of God. Hence, he demanded that loyalty to himself as the representative of God and His Reign should take precedence over family loyalties. It is also true that he expressed this demand at times in strong language, e.g. "He who loves father or mother more than me is not worthy of me" (Matt. 10:37). One must even "hate" the members of one's family, i.e. must break with them whenever their opposition requires it, if one is to "come to" him and enter into the Kingdom (Luke 14:26). Perhaps it was this demand that caused many of his neighbors and probably also his family to "take offense at him" (Mark 6:3), as his people had taken offense when the prophets from Amos to Jeremiah had tried to persuade them to abandon their idolatry and injustice.[7]

However, Jesus' demand for the subordination of family loyalties to loyalty to the Kingdom does not imply that he had "little regard for family ties" or "disparaged" love within the family circle. One may give one's ultimate loyalty to Christ and the Kingdom of God without ceasing to love the members of one's family. One may even break with them over their opposition to that loyalty without being indifferent to family ties. Jesus seems to have been fully aware that his demand for ultimate loyalty would cause division within families and that suffering would result from it. Indeed, there has always been tragic division within families over the ultimate issues of life. But the Kingdom is "the pearl of great price" and one must be ready to sell all one has if one is to possess it (Matt. 13:45, 46). And the suffering and sacrifice will be justified by the extension of love, which is all too often limited to one's own family, to all men and women who are children of the Heavenly Father. This is the meaning of Jesus' saying, "Here are my mother and brothers! Whoever does the will of God is my brother, and sister, and mother" (Mark 3:34—35). For love of neighbor which imitates the boundless *agape* of God can transcend the barriers that separate families, races, and nations and help to create a family that will include all of God's children.

Civic Duty and Justice

Some of the most provocative sections of Blanshard's treatment of Christian ethics are those which deal with problems of *social ethics*, especially civic duty and social justice. For example, he points out that Jesus' attitude toward *civic duty* is in sharp contrast to that of Greek philosophers such as Plato who held that an individual could attain the best life only in and through service to the state, by fulfilling the duties of his station. For Jesus says very little about the state or about the responsibilities of citizens to society. Blanshard rightly points out that the famous saying, "Render to Caesar the things that are

Caesar's, and to God the things that are God's" (Mark 12:17), says nothing about "What things are Caesar's" (*RB,* 342). However, one should not forget the political situation in which Jesus and his disciples lived. They were members of a nation that had lost its independence and was only a small part of the Roman Empire. As a result, they had no political power or responsibility, and their only "civic duties" were to pay their taxes and obey the laws imposed upon them by Rome. The Zealots, of course, were seeking to throw off the yoke of Rome by violent revolution, and there were those who wanted Jesus to offer himself as the national Messiah who was to rule over Israel. Since he was not a Zealot and did not believe himself to be a national Messiah, specific teachings about the "civic duty" of his followers might have invited misunderstanding among the people and suppression of his mission at once by the Romans. His primary purpose was not political; it was to prepare men for the coming Reign of God.

However, the principle affirmed in the saying about "the things that are Caesar's" and "the things that are God's" has been more valuable for political thought and practice than Blanshard acknowledges, because it emphasizes that there are limits to the state's authority and implies that ultimate authority belongs to God rather than Caesar. Unfortunately, Christians have often failed to follow this principle. Instead, they have usually accepted the view of Saint Paul that "he who resists the authorities resists what God has appointed, and those who resist will incur judgment" (Rom. 13:2). In doing so, they have overlooked the fact that his warning against civil disobedience was given at a time when Christians were a powerless minority in the Roman Empire and were expecting the imminent establishment of God's Reign. However, from the refusal of early Christians to burn incense to Caesar to the resistance of Bishop Berggrav of Norway to the Nazis and the participation of Dietrich Bonhoeffer in a conspiracy against Hitler, many Christians have put the authority of God above that of any earthly ruler, often at the cost of their lives.

Blanshard also believes that Jesus' emphasis upon love led him to neglect *justice.* "He taught that if one loved God and man unreservedly, all other virtues would take care of themselves, since they were all really manifestations of love" (*RB,* 360). This is an exaggeration, but there is truth in it. Jesus offered no principles of justice to guide his followers in dealing with social problems and institutions. Indeed, he sometimes seemed to think that justice is of little importance to one who governs his conduct by love, as when he refused to arbitrate between two brothers over the division of the family property and warned them against covetousness (Luke 12:13–15). Moreover, his ethical teaching almost always concerns relations between persons rather than relations between groups such as classes, races, or nations, whereas problems of social justice usually involve relations of the latter sort, e.g. between rich and poor classes or white and colored races.

Blanshard acknowledges that "justice, though often at odds with the immediate and personal demands of love, is a necessary instrument of that larger love—really a settled benevolence—which is directed to mankind" (*RB*, 360).[8] However, he does not discuss the important question as to how this "larger love," i.e. Christian love of neighbor as we have described it, has affected men's ideas of punitive and distributive justice in the past, or how it is helping to modify the treatment of criminals and the distribution of the benefits of society between whites and minority races at the present time. This is unfortunate, as the social gospel of Rauschenbusch,[9] the social and political insights of Reinhold Niebuhr,[10] the political thought of Jacques Maritain,[11] and the leadership of Martin Luther King and others in the struggle for racial justice have made Christians of our time more aware of the fact that love of neighbor must express itself in group relationships by seeking to do equal justice to the claims and needs of all races and classes. Indeed, Blanshard makes no reference whatever to the social Christianity of these and other twentieth-century thinkers for whom love without social justice is sentimental at best and hypocritical at worst.

Instead of dealing with the ways modern Christians have attempted to draw out the implications of Christian love for social justice, Blanshard criticizes what he takes to be a difficulty in Jesus' view of the relation of love to justice. He points out that Jesus regards God's goodness as perfect and holds that his followers should strive to be perfect like Him. "And yet," he says, "God is described as holding attitudes which, in those enjoined to imitate him, would be considered unjust in the extreme" (*RB*, 361). As one example, he cites Jesus' denunciation of the Pharisees for their hypocrisy. "No doubt the Pharisees did show varying degrees of hypocrisy. But in the long, sweeping, and bitter arraignment of them ending, 'Ye serpents, ye generation of vipers, how can ye escape the damnation of hell?' (Matt. 23), it is hard to discern the accents of love or justice, to say nothing of mercy" (*RB*, 362). These denunciations are difficult to evaluate, but we would make two comments about them. The first is that when the Gospels were written, many years after Jesus' death, the break between Christians and Jews had produced such bitterness against the religious leaders of Judaism that Jesus' criticisms were probably exaggerated by the writers of the Gospels. The second is that Jesus was convinced he had been called by God to prepare his fellow Jews for the coming of the Kingdom, and yet he had been bitterly opposed by the Pharisees from the beginning. Therefore, he saw God's will to save His people being thwarted by the moral pride which caused the Pharisees to reject his mission, to exclude tax gatherers and sinners from fellowship, and to insist upon strict tithing and other practices while neglecting "justice and mercy and the weightier matters of the law" (Matt. 23:23). He was not a philosopher arguing calmly with other philosophers about a theory, but a prophet declaring what he believed to be God's will and seeing it thwarted by the very religious leaders who (he thought) should be furthering it.

More telling is Blanshard's criticism of the teaching of Jesus that sins of omission such as failing to feed the hungry and clothe the naked will be punished in a *hell* of eternal fire (Matt. 25:41). As Blanshard says, eternal punishment "is clearly not in accord with human conceptions of justice." Much less, we would add, is it compatible with God's boundless love. However, it should be pointed out that punishment in hell is not at the center of Jesus' teaching and that he seems to have simply taken for granted a contemporary conception of hell. Most modern theologians, except in highly conservative circles, reject this ancient belief in a hell of eternal torment as inconsistent with the justice and mercy of God. Jesus' acceptance of it, they hold, is an example of the fact that there were limitations in his knowledge as a man. Blanshard also rightly criticizes the substitutionary theory of the *atonement,* according to which "The edge of the divine wrath against mankind is turned by the voluntary submission to torture and death of a wholly innocent person" (*RB,* 362), as incompatible with the justice of God. The writer would only add that Jesus himself never speaks of turning away "the edge of the divine wrath against mankind" by his death, that the substitutionary theory is only one of several later theories of the atonement, and that few modern Christians with the exception of Fundamentalists accept it.

Also, Blanshard argues that certain *parables* of Jesus raise serious questions about his conception of justice. The first of these is the parable of the laborers in the vineyard which represents a householder as paying the same wage to workers who began work only an hour before the end of the day as he paid to those who worked all or most of the day. When the other workers complained, he replied, "Am I not allowed to do what I choose with what belongs to me?" Jesus adds, "So the last will be first and the first last" (Matt. 20:1–16). Blanshard misinterprets this parable as a parable concerning human and divine justice. "The moral it most obviously teaches," he says, "is that a person of wealth is not called upon to obey the rules of justice in disposing of it; he can do what he will with his own . . . . nor is there any intimation that the householder has acted unjustly" (*RB,* 364). This interpretation overlooks the fact that, although the story is about a householder and his dealings with his laborers, the point of it is not that wealthy *men* can flaunt "rules of justice" but that *God* deals with those who come late into His Kingdom as He deals with others and more generously than they deserve. Since His love is not measured out to men according to their merits, it is given equally to all who come to Him, whether soon or late. Thus, the parable is not concerned with human justice but with God's love. Nor does it imply, as Blanshard suggests, "that divine and human justice are incommensurable," since nothing whatever is said about the divine justice.

In his interpretation of this and several other parables, Blanshard overlooks an important fact about the parables which was first stressed, as far as I know, by Adolf Jülicher and later by C. H. Dodd and Joachim Jeremias.[12] A parable makes only one point and therefore one should not ask for the meaning of every detail in it as if it were an allegory. Thus, when a man such as a householder is used in a parable to symbolize God, the hearer or reader is not meant to approve everything he does or every aspect of his character. The one point of this parable is that God's love is more generous to men than they have deserved by the "work" they have done for Him. The reason there is no "intimation that the householder has acted unjustly" is that the parable is not about human justice at all.

Because Blanshard has overlooked this important fact about Jesus' parables, he has also misinterpreted another parable which likens the Kingdom of Heaven to "a treasure hidden in a field, which a man found and covered up; then in his joy he goes and sells all that he has and buys that field" (Matt. 13:44). "He conceals its existence from the owner," says Blanshard, "until he can command the price of the field. He then with 'joy' gets both field and treasure from the man he has kept in ignorance of the value of his property" (RB, 364). Thus, the parable seems to recommend "a piece of sharp practice in dealing with a stranger," "a gross bit of trickery." But the one point of the parable is clearly that the Kingdom of Heaven, like a treasure, is of such incomparable worth that one should willingly and joyfully give up everything one possesses to enter into it. The details, e.g. the fact that the man "conceals its existence from the owner," are irrelevant to this point. Thus, the parable does not recommend the "sharp practice" of a man; it exalts the supreme worth of the Kingdom which justifies the sacrifice of everything else for it.

Finally, Blanshard criticizes Jesus' parable of the man who praised and rewarded two servants after they had made a profit for him by trading with talents entrusted to them but who rebuked a "wicked and slothful" servant for hiding the talent entrusted to him and returning it to his master without any gain. It is strange, says Blanshard, that although "the master is the symbol of Deity and therefore of perfect justice," "justice is being conceived as that of an avaricious and arbitrary employer rather than that of an ideal morality" (RB, 365). Here, again, he overlooks the one point the parable is making, that God requires of every man to whom He has entrusted talents, whether in the original sense of money or in the later sense of natural gifts, that he should employ them responsibly and fruitfully. If he does so, God will bless him and say to him, "enter into the joy of your master," i.e. into the

Kingdom. If he fails to do so, he will lose the talent entrusted to him and be "cast into outer darkness," i.e. excluded from the Kingdom. Thus this parable, like that of the laborers in the vineyard, is not about justice, divine or human; it is about man's responsibility to God for the effective and fruitful use of his talents. And the master is the symbol of God *only* in holding his servants responsible for such a use.

Nonresistance

One of the most difficult issues of Christian ethics is the interpretation of Jesus' saying "Do not resist the evil one" (Matt. 5:39). One's attitude toward this saying will depend to a great extent upon whether one interprets his precepts as a "new law" which allows no exceptions and must be taken literally or regards them as "guidelines" indicating ways in which the law of love may be applied in various situations. Christian sects such as the Anabaptists and Christian thinkers such as Tolstoy have interpreted the precept in the former, legalistic sense and have believed that it was meant by Jesus to apply not only to individual offenders but also to national enemies. Hence, they have adopted a pacifist position with respect to the participation of Christians in war. Blanshard seems to agree with this interpretation of Jesus' meaning and holds that Christians are consistent with his teaching only when they accept "thoroughgoing pacifism" (*RB,* 348).

It is impossible to determine whether Jesus had national enemies as well as individual wrongdoers in mind in this precept and in the saying "Love your enemies" (Matt. 5:44). The examples he gives in Matthew of evildoers who are not to be resisted are individuals who inflict injuries on other persons, e.g. one who "strikes you on the cheek" or who "would sue you and take your coat" (Matt. 5:39–41). All of the examples Jesus gives in Luke to illustrate the precept "Love your enemies" also refer to individual offenders, e.g. "those who hate you" or "curse you" or "abuse you" (Luke 6:27–30). One of the examples of nonresistance offered in Matthew, "if anyone forces you to go one mile, go with him two miles" (Matt. 5:41), may refer to the military practice of requiring men to carry baggage for an army passing through the country.

Most Christians have thought that in these precepts Jesus had in mind only individual offenders. They have also believed that they should not be taken legalistically as absolute laws but seriously as indications of the way love requires one to respond to personal injuries. On the one hand, to take them as absolute laws to be interpreted literally would lead to absurdity. What should one do if, after turning the other cheek, one is knocked down and then attacked with a knife, or if, after giving up one's coat and cloak, a demand is made for the rest of one's clothes, or if, after going the second mile, one is forced into permanent service? On the other hand, if the precepts

"Do not resist the evil one" and "Love your enemies" are not interpreted as absolute laws but as illustrations of the way one should respond to personal injuries, they are vivid expressions of the attitude of love which forgives rather than retaliates. When Peter asked Jesus, "Lord, how often shall my brother sin against me, and I forgive him? As many as seven times?", Jesus replied, "I do not say to you seven times, but seventy times seven times" (Matt. 18:21, 22). For love which extends even to one's enemies should not allow a wrong done to one by another to go unforgiven and hence to raise a barrier between them. Rather, one should forgive the offender again and again and seek to be reconciled with him. It is in this spirit that Jesus counsels his disciples not to resist one who is evil. The return of evil for evil usually provokes another evil, while the refusal to retaliate may check it, especially if one manifests goodwill toward the evildoer. This is why Saint Paul says, "Do not be overcome by evil, but overcome evil with good" (Rom. 12:21). For resistance to those who injure us does nothing to eliminate the impulses that have led them to do so. But if we are able to restrain the natural impulse to retaliate, we may be able to effect a change in the attitude of the evildoer by trying to understand and remove the cause of it.

It would be unrealistic, however, to expect all evildoers to change their attitude and conduct when treated in this way. Some may even be encouraged to continue or increase their aggression. For this reason, most Christians would agree with Blanshard that the precept of nonresistance should not be regarded as a universal law, for "there are some men in any society who take such gentleness as an invitation to exploit it to their own advantage . . ." (RB, 343–44). Moreover, if an attack is made not on oneself but on another person, "the very principle of love for others may dictate the stronger line."

Most Christians would also agree with Blanshard's criticism of absolute pacifism which extends the precept of nonresistance to aggressive nations. Although the early Christians refused to serve in the Roman legions when they were a small minority with no political power, their attitude changed after Christianity ceased to be persecuted and became a legal religion. They recognized their responsibility for maintaining a just social order and for defending it against attacks from within and without. This seemed to them necessary because of human sin and its threat to the security and survival of society.

Because of the horrors of total war and the threat to humanity from weapons of mass destruction, there has been a revival of Christian pacifism in our time. Many Christians have come to believe that the earlier concept of a "just war" is no longer applicable and that a nuclear war would be worse than any evil a nation might suffer by refusing to resist an aggressor. Blanshard feels the force of this argument. However, he insists that it does not justify the conclusion that a nation should never resist the aggression of another nation and should accept dictation at its hands. Rather, an "international government" must be organized which will be capable of taking action against an aggressor nation (*RB*, 347). Most Christians whose minds have not been corrupted by extreme nationalism would agree with this.

But something else is also needed. While Christians strive to establish a federation of nations to enforce peace, they should also actively seek to prevent war by finding ways to resolve conflicts between nations. "Blessed are the peacemakers," says Jesus, "for they shall be called sons of God" (Matt. 5:9). Christian statesmen have a special responsibility to lead in this effort, and Christian citizens should support them and oppose in every possible way those who advocate policies that may lead to war. And all Christians have an obligation to oppose unnecessary and indiscriminate killing and devastation in a time of war, as well as to work for just terms of peace that will make possible a speedy reconciliation with the enemy. Christian "absolute pacifists" can make a special contribution to this process of peacemaking and reconciliation. They can not only work diligently to prevent war but also set in motion as soon as possible after a war the forces of reconciliation. Pacifists in the "peace churches" such as the Friends and Mennonites have been among the great peacemakers of our time. In addition, "selective pacifists" who believe that a particular war is immoral can refuse to participate in it and accept whatever punishment is meted out to them. And Christian nonpacifists should support the right of both "absolute" and "selective" pacifists to follow their consciences against militarists who think that the appeal to force is the only way to deal with international conflicts. Would Blanshard agree?

Knowledge and Art

As a moral philosopher who accepts the "teleological" conception of ethics, Blanshard holds that moral acts are instrumental to human *ends* or *values*. Hence, he finds Jesus' ethics "incomplete and fragmentary" because it stresses love but says little about the ends or goods which love should promote in men's lives (*RB*, 333). It is "a truncated ethics requiring large supplementation."

Like all philosophers, Blanshard regards *knowledge* as a high intrinsic good, but he finds no support in Christian ethics for the pursuit of it. Not only does Jesus show no interest in theoretical knowledge, i.e. science and philosophy; he also says nothing about practical knowledge, "the means of implementing desire in such a way that its ends may be achieved" (*RB*, 335). Blanshard rightly points out that special knowledge of various kinds is required to discover means to our ends, e.g. "medical expertise" to make our sympathy for the sick fully effective, and the social sciences for the efficient relief of poverty. But Jesus made no use of the knowledge of experts. And Saint Paul showed "outspoken contempt" for "the Greek love of reason," as in the question, "Has not God made foolish the wisdom of the world?" (I Cor. 1:20.) Blanshard admits that Christianity has produced "some magnificent intellects" such as that of Aquinas, but is more impressed by the fact that so many intellectuals have been placed on the Index (*RB*, 334)!

Again, he contrasts the attitude of Jesus toward *art* and beauty with that of the Greeks. Although he admits that Jesus was sensitive to the beauty of the lilies of the field and the poetry of the Old Testament, he asserts that art, sculpture, and music were "left almost a blank" in Jesus' teaching (*RB*, 340). He admits that "we owe to the Christian Church the patronage of some of the most magnificent art in history," e.g. medieval cathedrals and Renaissance paintings, but he regards them as "hybrid products, due to the crossing of Christianity with the Renaissance, the Gothic spirit, and much else." More typical, he seems to think, has been the "puritanism" with respect to the fine arts of Christian leaders such as Saint Francis and Savonarola who "remained closest to the pure and primitive teaching."

Now it is certainly true that Jesus had little to say about knowledge and nothing about art. This is not surprising. It was not the Hebrews but the Greeks who put a high value on philosophical and (in some fields) scientific knowledge and had a passion for art, architecture, and literature. However, this does not mean that Jesus put a low value on knowledge; it means that the *kind* of knowledge he prized, like other Jews, was knowledge of God, of men's relation to Him, and of their conduct toward each other. Also, the "contempt" of Saint Paul for knowledge was only contempt for the "wisdom of the world" by which "the world did not know God," i.e. the philosophical speculation which had not attained and could not attain to the knowledge of God's love and His Reign in the lives of men (I Cor. 1:20–25). Similarly, while Jesus said nothing about the beauty that is expressed in art, he was deeply sensitive, as Blanshard acknowledges, to the beauty of nature and of the poetry of the Old Testament, and many of his own sayings have a striking beauty.

However, it is true that Jesus provides no analysis of the values of knowledge and art which have been recognized by moral philosophers since Plato as essential elements of the good life. As Blanshard says, if love demands that I serve the needs of my neighbors, I must know the values that will fulfill their needs, and I must accord a high place among them to knowledge and beauty. Also, I must have the practical knowledge provided by the sciences of the means which will best realize these and other values in their lives.

The conclusion which should be drawn from this is that Jesus' ethics of love is not a *comprehensive system* of ethics which includes everything Christians need to know in order to live the good life and to further it for others. The twofold law of love and the precepts of Jesus which illustrate its application to different situations constitute a *foundation* of morality but do not provide the *whole content* of morality. They define the right relationship between man and God and between man and his neighbors; and only a moral structure which is built upon that foundation, like a house upon a rock, can enable man to live in harmony with the Ground of his being, with his fellows, and with himself. For, as Reinhold Niebuhr said, "the law of love is the law of life"; it is the law which is suitable to man as a spiritual and social being and which is confirmed by man's experience as the basis of his happiness.

Upon that foundation Christians have the responsibility to build the good life. In doing so they must use the best knowledge of human nature and values which is available to them from every source. In particular, they must use the knowledge provided by moral and social philosophy concerning the values and structures of personal and social life, as well as the practical knowledge provided by the sciences of the means that will best achieve their ends. They must also develop their appreciation of the beauty of nature and the rich diversity of values and meanings expressed in the arts and literature. This many of them in every age of the Church have attempted to do, enriching their life by the culture of the ancient Greeks and the peoples of the West. Moreover, they have been creative themselves in philosophy, art, and literature. Blanshard's disparagement of Christian art in medieval cathedrals and Renaissance paintings as "hybrid products" and his emphasis upon the "puritanical" hostility of Christians to art are, to say the least, very one-sided. Doubtless Christians of the first century who were expecting the return of Christ in their time had little concern for the pursuit of knowledge or the creation of art, but as their belief in the imminence of the Kingdom faded they began to appropriate Greek culture. Later, they preserved ancient classics during the Dark Ages, and created a Christian culture in the Middle Ages.

However, Christian ethics regards the life of love as the primary end and good of human existence. While it recognizes that "intrinsic goods" such as knowledge and art are indispensable, it holds that without love they lose their worth. As Saint Paul says, one may "understand all mysteries and all knowledge," but he is "nothing" if he has not love (I Cor. 13:2). As Kant maintained that the satisfaction of desires for the sake of happiness must be subordinated to the goodwill, the one absolute good, Christians believe that love of God and of one's neighbors is the highest good and that other goods such as knowledge and art must be subordinated to it. This is compatible with the view of teleological ethics that moral acts should seek to fulfill human needs and realize human values, but it affirms that obedience to the will of God as expressed in the law of love is the highest good and that the pursuit of all other goods must be consistent with it.

Love of God

After his critical examination of Christian ethics apart from Christian beliefs, Blanshard turns to the Christian belief upon which love of neighbor depends, *love of God*. He asserts that it is difficult for the modern mind to understand the "feeling" Jesus called "love of God" and the "ethical importance he attached to it" (*RB*, 370). For God is not "near" to us but "remote" from us. Omnipotent, omniscient, and perfect, He has none of our weaknesses and frustrations. Hence, there is no "basis for intimacy" with Him. Also, since there is no "definite conception" of Him, "how can man love he knows not what?" Moreover, Jesus' own conception of God was completely anthropomorphic. In Matthew Arnold's words, He was simply a "magnified non-natural man" (371). Since nature is known by modern science to be "a fixed order of law," this anthropomorphic view is no longer possible. "Its object is too plainly a product of man's imagination in the service of his need—his need for comfort and assurance in the face of a universe that is too much for him." The love of God, Blanshard asserts, is "capable of profound philosophical interpretation" as in the theology of Paul Tillich, and therefore can be made "the essence of religion" (372). But the Christian belief in God as analogous to a father who loves his children is impossible for the modern mind.

What is the "modern mind"? Blanshard is well aware that there are millions of modern Christians for whom belief in the God of Jesus is *not* impossible, but actual. He is also aware that the "mind" of no age, even the "modern," possesses a monopoly of truth or the final truth. Again, he makes no effort to prove his assertion that God as He is conceived by Jesus has nothing in common with man which could provide a "basis for intimacy" with or love for Him. The fact is that at the heart of Jesus' view of man is the Biblical belief that man is made "in the image of God" (Gen. 1:27), and even the omnipotent, omniscient, and perfect God of Aquinas' theology is also represented as possessing attributes analogous to those of man, e.g. knowledge, will, and love.[13] But Jesus' conception of God was *not* anthropomorphic; he did *not* picture Him as a "magnified non-natural man." Although he addressed Him in intimate terms as "Father" and stressed His love for His children, he also regarded Him as Lord and King whom men should serve and obey, as Creator upon whom they depend, and as perfect as no human father is perfect. Thus, he exalted God above men, despite the fact that He possesses certain personal qualities analogous to (although far from identical with) theirs. While he claims to know Him intimately as only a son can know a father, his attitude is always one of reverence for God and complete submission to His will as Creator, Lord, and King. Finally, since God possesses certain attributes that are analogous to those of a person, man *can* have a "definite conception" of Him sufficient to inspire and sustain his relationship to Him, although he can never comprehend His essence in "clear and distinct" ideas because of His transcendence.

However, the deeper reason for Blanshard's rejection of the God of Jesus is that he seems to accept completely the modern scientific view of nature as a "fixed order of law." There is no place in this world view for a God who is distinct from (although immanent in) nature, analogous to human personality in certain of His attributes, and active in nature and history to fulfill His purposes. The question is whether the Christian belief in God should be rejected merely because it is incompatible with such a deterministic and impersonal view of the world. Obviously, this is not the place to argue the question whether theism offers a less or a more adequate view of the world than that which has been based upon Newtonian modern science, either in its naturalistic or its pantheistic form.[14] However, Whitehead in *Process and Reality* has shown that the Newtonian view of nature is incompatible with the recent revolution in physics and incapable of explaining creativity in biological evolution and human experience, while a metaphysics in which God presents "subjective aims" to actual entities as they arise and conserves the values attained by them offers a more adequate explanation of the world as a creative process. And Charles Hartshorne in *The Divine Relativity* has shown how the Christian conception of God as analogous to a personal being can be freed from the extreme emphasis of Thomistic theology on His transcendence and hence from the denial of His real relation to finite beings and of His love for men. Whatever one may think of this process philosophy, Christian belief in God should not be dismissed on the ground that it is not in accord with a view of nature as impersonal and purposeless which is rejected by many scientists and philosophers of our time.

Since Blanshard rejects the Christian conception of God, he is naturally critical of love of God as a *motive* for moral conduct. He offers two reasons for this conclusion. The first is that love of God is not an "obviously ethical" motive. If one, he says, does something from love of God simply because He has commanded it, there are two alternatives. Either one does it because one sees that God's will is righteous, in which case one's motive is "right doing itself," an ethical rather than a religious motive (*RB,* 374). Or one does it "regardless of his [God's] moral quality," i.e. whether He is good or bad, in which case the love of Him may lead to immorality, as in the case of Abraham who was prepared to sacrifice Isaac at God's command although his conscience viewed it as wrong (374–75). The second reason is that love of God is not a necessary condition of moral conduct, since the perception of values such as justice and wisdom is itself "a powerful motive to their realisation" as many examples of "purely secular goodness" have shown

(375). Thus, while love of God has often been a "supplementary" motive, it is not an "indispensable" one.

Blanshard is clearly right in saying that love of God is not a moral motive when one is led by it to do an act one's own conscience judges to be wrong. But to do what is right solely from a moral motive, i.e. because one judges it to be right in itself, is not the only alternative to this. Christians believe that obedience to the commandment of love will further the good and therefore that it is morally right. Hence, they try to obey it not only because of their love for God but also because they think it is right in itself. Thus, love of God does not and should not *replace* the moral motive, but should *support* and *strengthen* it.

Blanshard's view that the love of God is not "indispensable" as a motive for morality and that a "purely secular goodness" is possible is fully justified. It is directed against exclusive claims that have often been made for Christian ethics. Many Christians have asserted that morality which is not based upon the Christian faith is impossible because men can know what is right only through God's revelation of His will in Christ. This claim is contradicted, as Blanshard says, by the fact that many men of unquestioned moral character have been adherents of other faiths, e.g. Gandhi, or scientific humanists, e.g. Julian Huxley.

However, love of God has in fact been an effective motive for morality in the lives of Christians. When it has been freed from legalistic, puritanical, and other distortions and applied with intelligence, it has given a religious dimension to morality that has raised it to a higher level. It has provided men with an absolute principle, the law of love, but has liberated them from the necessity of conforming to a detailed code of moral laws. By awakening love for their neighbors, it has enabled them in some measure to overcome the egoism or self-love that has always been the greatest enemy of moral goodness. It has given them a broader conception of duty by making them aware that in serving the needs of their neighbors they are also helping to realize the ideal of brotherhood among all men. It has offered them hope that despite their failure to realize Jesus' perfectionistic ideal they can depend on God's help as they strive more nearly to approximate it. It can prevent them from falling into moral complacency over their limited moral achievements or into despair over their repeated moral failures. Finally, their belief in and union with Christ as the supreme manifestation of God's love and their association with those who are committed to him and his way of life can sustain and encourage them in their moral striving.

The Nature and Role of Christ

We can speak only very briefly of Blanshard's view of Christ himself. (1) Blanshard charges that Jesus did not consistently exemplify his own teaching about *humility* in such sayings as "Blessed are the poor in spirit," since he claimed the right to forgive men their sins and made other exalted claims for himself. However, it should be noted that he made no claim to be the national Messiah of the house of David who was expected by his people. Also, it is only in the Gospel of John, the latest and least historically accurate of the Gospels, that he made the claim to be divine, as in the saying, "I and the Father are one" (John 10:30). According to the other three Gospels, the central theme of his teaching was the Kingdom of God, not his own nature and claims, and he seems to have left it to his disciples to decide for themselves who he was. It is certainly true that he spoke and acted with authority, as we have seen, forgiving men's sins and making loyalty to himself at the end of his life a test of loyalty to the Kingdom. But he did so as one who had been called by God to proclaim and prepare men for the coming of the Kingdom, i.e. not as God but as God's representative. At his trial, it is true, he is reported by Mark to have expressed the conviction that he would be vindicated by "the Son of Man" sitting at the right hand of Power and coming with the clouds of heaven (Mark 14:62). However, New Testament scholars are not in agreement as to the authenticity of the saying or as to the relation of the "Son of Man" to Jesus.

(2) Blanshard asserts that Jesus must have been either *God,* "incarnate Deity," or *man,* "only a human being" (*RB,* 378). His own view is that Jesus was "a great but in part mistaken man" (ibid.). This writer is not a theologian and cannot pretend to speak for all Christians with respect to their belief about Jesus. But he would point out that many Christians, while affirming the full humanity of Jesus, believe that more needs to be said than that he was "only a human being." They have rejected the traditional view that there was a "metaphysical union" of the human nature of Jesus with the divine nature, as expressed in the formula "two natures in one person." For they hold that this view is both unintelligible in itself and inconsistent with the humanity of Jesus as described in the Gospels. But they believe that there was a unique union of will and purpose between him and God. Under the influence of God's Spirit, he freely surrendered himself to God's will. Hence, God was able in and through him to manifest His love for men, to awaken faith and love in them, and thereby to redeem them from their bondage to the sin which separates them from Him and from other men. As Saint Paul expresses it, "God was in Christ reconciling the world to himself" (II Cor. 5:19). According to this view of the nature and role of Christ, he was neither God nor "only a human being," but a man in whom God acted to overcome the estrangement of men from Himself and from each other, one who through his complete surrender of himself to God's will was a unique revelation of His love and a unique instrument of His purpose.

(3) If one accepts this view of Christ, one can affirm without reservation his full humanity and therefore acknowledge the *limitations* of his knowledge and power which Blanshard stresses. Clearly, Jesus would not have been an embodiment of God's love and purpose in a man if he had possessed unlimited power and knowledge. The charge of moral imperfection raises more difficult questions which the Gospels do not provide us with sufficient evidence to answer with certainty. Blanshard offers, as evidence to support the charge, Jesus' strong denunciation of the Pharisees. But this has been regarded by others as quite justified, for reasons we have pointed out. On the other hand, he seems not to have made a claim to moral perfection himself, and when a man addressed him as "good teacher," he said to him, "Why do you call me good? No one is good but God alone" (Mark 10:17, 18).

In short, he was "made like his brethren in every respect" (Heb. 2:17), and for this reason his ethical teaching and example are relevant for other men. But he was also a man who embodied God's love so uniquely and effectively that he has inspired countless men and women through the ages to love God and to love their neighbors.

Christian Ethics and Reason

Finally, Blanshard argues that Christian ethics is "deficient in its respect for reason" (*RB*, 394). Much of what he says on this point repeats his criticisms of Jesus' attitude toward knowledge, with which we have already dealt. But he also criticizes the Jewish cosmology of Jesus' time, which he accepted and which provides the framework for his ethics.

Most of the *cosmological* beliefs Blanshard attacks were accepted without question by both Catholics and Protestants before the rise of modern science and the development of Biblical criticism. However, these beliefs about the world and man have been either abandoned or substantially modified by Christians who have been influenced by these modern intellectual developments. For example, Blanshard asserts with respect to the view of man in the Book of Genesis, "there was no Eden, no Adam, no tempting Satan, no fall, no inherited sin" (*RB*, 395). Here he seems to assume that the story of the fall of Adam and Eve and its tragic consequences for mankind must be interpreted literally by Christians as a historical account of the origin of sin in the disobedience of the first man and woman. Yet Christians who have made a critical study of the Bible realize that the story of the fall is mythical rather than historical and should be interpreted symbolically as a description of the fall of *every* man, rather than the *first* man.

Blanshard also regards as incredible the anthropocentric view that the universe "was all fabricated as a stage for the performance of one biological species, appearing transiently on one floating grain of dust . . ." (*RB*, 395).

This is doubtless true. But while such a view has been held by many Christians, especially before Copernicus, it is not the Biblical view. The Bible represents the Creator as preserving and caring for *all* His creatures, as in Psalm 104, and Jesus affirms that the Father in His providence feeds the "birds of the air" and clothes the "lilies of the field" with splendor (Matt. 6:26, 30). And while it is true, as Blanshard says, that the Bible contains many stories of nature miracles such as that of Jesus walking on the water, stories which earlier Christians accepted uncritically, modern Christians have increasingly recognized that faith in God as manifested in Christ is not based on belief in these stories. However, since Blanshard pays little attention to the changes in Christian beliefs during the history of Christian thought, he does not acknowledge that they can be and have been expressed in terms of a modern cosmology which takes account of natural and historical science.

With respect to the *eschatological* element in Jesus' teaching, Blanshard is especially critical of Jesus' belief that "our actions carry with them an everlasting reward or penalty," because it has led to a distortion of the *motive* for moral conduct (*RB*, 397). Right conduct which is brought about by the promise of eternal happiness and the threat of eternal pain, he says, is only a "hollow shell." Also, belief in heaven and hell was in an earlier period used to justify the torturing of heretics on the ground that they would be saved if they could be persuaded to recant.

Modern Christians would agree that desire for eternal rewards and fear of eternal punishments are not the most worthy motives for moral conduct, although the desire for eternal life has been cherished from the beginning of history and there is nothing unworthy in it. But we would make two comments on Blanshard's criticism. The first is that fear of eternal pain in *hell* does not belong to the essence of Jesus' ethical teaching. The vivid and detailed pictures of hell used by later preachers like Jonathan Edwards to frighten sinners into repentance are not to be found in the Gospels. Except in Fundamentalist circles, Christian ministers in our time almost never seek to arouse fear of physical torments in hell, and most reflective Christians have abandoned belief in them altogether as incompatible with the love of God.

Our second comment is concerned with belief in *heaven*. While Jesus clearly regarded eternal life in the Kingdom of God as blessed and indeed as the highest good for men, he did not picture it in terms of physical pleasures or other external rewards. Instead, he viewed it as a continuation and completion of the life of love which begins in time. Hence, its blessings are not to be different from those which accompany that life here and now. Vivid pictures of the delights of heaven are not to be found in the Gospels, although they occur in Christian writings beginning with the Book of Revelation. Although belief in eternal life is not as strong now among Christians as it was in earlier ages, hope for it is still a reality in their lives. But it is not the primary motive for moral conduct in the lives of thoughtful Christians.

More serious, perhaps, is Blanshard's criticism of the attitude of Christian ethics to the place of *reason* in morality. "It failed," he says, "to recognise the place of reason in the moral life. It did not perceive the degree in which ethics is *autonomous* [my italics]. The principles of ethics are not derived from some authority outside itself, even theology, but from the reason implicitly at work in all morality" (*RB*, 398). Judgments of intrinsic and comparative value are not deduced from metaphysical or theological premises, but are derived from "rational insight." Blanshard does not deny that Jesus had insight into values, but he stresses the fact that Jesus spoke not as a philosopher but as a *prophet*. Since the words of the prophet come primarily from the "heart" rather than the "intellect," he says, "they are not likely to express the balanced judgement of the sage" (399).

These criticisms are an expression of Blanshard's rationalism. We can comment on them only very briefly. First, most reflective Christians would agree that judgments of intrinsic value are based upon "rational insight," provided that "rational" is interpreted in a broad way to include ethical intuitions. They are convinced, for example, that Jesus possessed "rational insight" into the truth that, in Blanshard's words, "love was better than hatred and forgiveness than vengeance" (*RB*, 398). Second, they would agree that Jesus was a prophet. But they would deny that his "vision of what life might be" came merely from the "heart," since they believe that his prophetic insight was the primary source of that vision. Third, they would agree that ethics is "autonomous" in the sense that its principles are not simply "deduced" from metaphysics or theology. For the principles of Jesus' ethics of love, as we have said, were derived directly from his ethical intuitions. But they would deny that ethics is autonomous in the absolute sense of being separated from and unaffected by metaphysical or religious views. For one's understanding of man's true nature and highest good is inevitably influenced by one's view of the nature of ultimate reality and of man's relation to it. As we have indicated, Christian ethics has been profoundly affected by the religious belief that God is the ultimate reality upon whom all other beings depend and that His relation to men is analogous to that of a father to his children. Blanshard rejects this belief, and views the world as a "fixed order of law" in which every event is determined. Obviously, in such a world view there is no place for a faith in a personal God who loves men and can be loved by them. Hence, many of Blanshard's criticisms of Christian ethics are determined by the fact that he rejects the Christian world view and maintains a world view which is incompatible with it.

We have argued that Blanshard has misinterpreted Christian ethics at a number of points, partly because he has paid so little attention to Christian ethical thinkers after Jesus and to modern Biblical criticism. Also, we have pointed out that many of his criticisms are valid only if one accepts his deterministic—and pantheistic?—world view. However, he has taken Christian ethics more seriously than many recent philosophers and has acknowledged the truth and importance of certain ethical teachings of Jesus, at least as he interprets them, e.g. love of man as a motive for conduct. Moreover, he has performed a useful service by criticizing certain beliefs of conservative Christians, although these have been abandoned by Christians who accept modern science and Biblical criticism. Also, he has reminded us that Jesus' ethics is not a comprehensive ethical theory and must be supplemented by insights of moral philosophers and others into the nature of the good life. Although we disagree with much of his interpretation and many of his criticisms, he has gone about his task with the moral seriousness and written with the candor and lucidity which have always been characteristic of him.

GEORGE F. THOMAS

DEPARTMENT OF RELIGION
PRINCETON UNIVERSITY

The writer wishes to express his appreciation to R. B. Y. Scott, formerly Professor of Old Testament at Princeton University, and John Knox, formerly Professor of New Testament at Union Theological Seminary, New York, for valuable suggestions.

NOTES

[1] Unless otherwise stated, the Biblical references are to the Revised Standard Version.

[2] Reinhold Niebuhr, *An Interpretation of Christian Ethics* (New York and London: Harper & Brothers, 1935), chap. 2.

[3] Reinhold Niebuhr, *The Nature and Destiny of Man*, 2 vols. (New York: Charles Scribner's Sons, 1941–43), 2:126.

[4] Niebuhr, *Christian Ethics*, chap. 4.

[5] *The Methods of Ethics*, bk. III, chap. 13, sec. 3; as quoted in *RB*, 332.

[6] Joachim Jeremias, *New Testament Theology* (New York: Charles Scribner's Sons, 1971), 112, 113.

[7] Some New Testament scholars think that the Gospel passages in which these severe demands are expressed reflect the experiences of early Christians, who sometimes had to break with their families and who also suffered persecution.

[8] Cf. G. F. Thomas, *Christian Ethics and Moral Philosophy* (New York: Charles Scribner's Sons, 1955), chap. 11.

[9] Walter Rauschenbusch, *A Theology for the Social Gospel* (Nashville: Abingdon Press, 1945).

[10] Reinhold Niebuhr, *Christian Realism and Political Problems* (New York: Charles Scribner's Sons, 1953).

[11] Jacques Maritain, *Man and the State* (Chicago: University of Chicago Press, 1951).

[12] Adolf Jülicher, *Die Gleichnisreden Jesu* (Tübingen: J. C. B. Mohr, 1910). C. H. Dodd, *Parables of the Kingdom*, rev. ed. (New York: Charles Scribner's Sons, 1961). Joachim Jeremias, *The Parables of Jesus*, rev. ed. (New York: Charles Scribner's Sons, 1963).

[13] Thomas Aquinas, *Summa Theologica* I, questions 14, 19, 20.

[14] I have argued in my *Philosophy and Religious Belief* (New York: Charles Scribner's Sons, 1970) that a strong case can be made for theism, based upon religious experience and supported by a rational interpretation of natural order, moral obligation, and other aspects of experience.

27. Reply to George F. Thomas

Blanshard's View of Christian Ethics

Mr. Thomas dissents from nearly all my interpretations of the Christian ethic, even where I supposed I agreed with it. How is one to deal with this kind of disagreement? If the issues were philosophical, one could argue them out. If they were historical, one could cite the evidence pro and con. But when the issue is over the interpretation of fragmentary sayings, passages seemingly contradictory, Oriental parables, and ambiguities in language, there is no satisfactory criterion to which differing critics can appeal. Mr. Thomas points out rightly that my ultimate appeal is to reason, or rather to a view of the world elaborated by philosophy and science in accord with what I take to be the canons of reason. His own ultimate appeal is to a very different view of the world, in which nature and history are governed by a supernatural being whose will for mankind was revealed in the life and words of a unique prophet. This prophet was the chosen spokesman of God, inspired by him, perfect in moral insight and action, and therefore speaking with an authority that no secular or rational moralist is competent to challenge. Mr. Thomas is not a fundamentalist, nor is he ever moved by the contempt of reason displayed by Luther and Kierkegaard; he is a philosopher himself; he cannot believe that God would endow his creatures with reason and conscience and then require of them conduct which clearly violated both. Nevertheless it is not to human faculties of reason and conscience that he takes his case in the end. It is to the will of God as taught and lived by Jesus. This will is perfect; Jesus' interpretation of it, as far as this goes, is errorless; his own life was sinless. The presence of these conceptions is felt throughout Mr. Thomas's carefully considered essay. If a parable seems to enjoin injustice, we *must* have missed the point of it; if one injunction seems to contradict another, one of them *must* have been misreported; if there is an incident that leaves a speck on the character of Jesus, this speck *must* be wiped away. Hence with all his sincerity and ability Mr. Thomas never, if I may say so with much respect, seems to achieve full freedom of mental play. Through the darkest thickets and jungles of interpretation, even through the dense mist of historical ignorance, there always lies ahead of him a vast unmistakable luminary, and so long as his face is brightened by its light, his march *must* be in the right direction.

Mr. Thomas seems to me much nearer the truth than all-or-nothing theologians like Barth, who put down opposition with an imperious "Thus saith the Lord." That is not his tone or temper. Whether he would like the description or not I do not know, but he seems to me a liberal in theology, a liberal being defined as a believer who is doing his best to keep the faith while trying also to keep it consistent with science and historical research. What puzzles the rationalist about such liberalism is how it can go as far as it does without going farther. Mr. Thomas is ready to set down much as mythical in both the Old Testament and the New; he is in sympathy with rigorous criticism of the Biblical text; he rejects the incarnation in the sense of the embodiment in a human life of omniscience and omnipotence; he would reject, I think, the virgin birth, the raising of Lazarus, and the walking on the water; he is aware that the teaching of the New Testament is heavily charged with the preconceptions of its time and place, with superstition, with ignorance of critical history or science, with legends and metaphors taken as facts; he is alive to the paradoxes of supposing nature and history to have been governed by a God of love and justice.

And yet when it comes to Christian ethics, one reads between his lines a kind of Kierkegaardian commitment. Knowing that Jesus suffered from extraordinary delusions regarding the second coming, and was otherwise limited in power and knowledge, he insists nevertheless that he was the sinless embodiment and the inspired mouthpiece of a divine will which we must accept as morally perfect. The antecedent improbability of this combination of ignorance and moral perfection makes it imperative to inquire whether the admitted fallibility of Jesus in many fields left his authority untouched in the field of morals. Mr. Thomas seems to have been unmoved by such inquiries, whether made by me or by better scholars in the past; no blot will be found on that scutcheon. And since the text is often ambiguous in the extreme, the proof that any one interpretation is *the* correct one is often impossible. I do not expect to convince Mr. Thomas. I can only offer the reflections of an interested layman on his commentary, without pretending to an equal knowledge of the field.

At the outset of his paper Mr. Thomas notes two shortcomings in my treatment of Christian ethics. The first is that I attempt to isolate the ethical teaching from the religious, of which it was an organic part, and to appraise this ethics separately. Christianity, he protests, was far more than a moral code or even ideal; it was a religion with the divine mind and will at the heart of it; and to separate its morality from the heart, which gave it its pulse and its power, is like amputating a limb from the body and trying to learn about the functioning of the live organ from dissecting the dead one. The protest has force. One who believes that through Christian faith the feeble motor of his own will is connected by a secret belt with the power controlling the universe can live with a confidence and exhilaration that in a mere rationalist would be irrational. This I have fully admitted in *Reason and Belief.* But three comments must be added.

(1) The criticism is double edged. Though the practical life may gain power and direction from a theology that is sound, it may become an engine of evil when tied to a theology that is false. Mr. Thomas quotes with respect Whitehead's view of the operation of God (i.e. Whitehead's God) in history. But Whitehead's own theology has had no effect in history, and it is interesting to note his view of those that have:

> history, down to the present day, is a melancholy record of the horrors which can attend religion: human sacrifice, and in particular the slaughter of children, cannibalism, sensual orgies, abject superstition, hatred as between races, the maintenance of degrading customs, hysteria, bigotry, can all be laid at its charge. Religion is the last refuge of human savagery. The uncritical association of religion with goodness is directly negatived by plain facts. Religion can be, and has been, the main instrument for progress. But if we survey the whole race, we must pronounce that generally it has not been so (*Religion in the Making*, 37–38).[1]

It may be thought cruelly unfair to link Christian belief with moral attitudes of this kind, and certainly the Christianity most of us have known does not deserve such a description. But Whitehead was not excluding Christianity from his review. Better by far a purely secular morality than the religion that slaughtered the Albigenses, wreaked the butchery of St. Bartholomew's day, burnt the Salem witches, and massacred the heathen red men.

(2) Mr. Thomas will reply that these are aberrations of conduct that sprang from an aberrant theology; they could not possibly spring from a belief in the God of love revealed to us by Jesus. But the religion of Jesus was not directed upon a God of love and justice only, but also on a God of implacable anger, who could cast men into an eternity of suffering even for something as innocent as unbelief. For millions who have taken this seriously, life has been haunted with fear, and death with a foreboding worse than that of annihilation.

(3) Ethics *ought* to be separated from theology. To let it become entangled with theology is to weaken, not to strengthen, its authority. Reasonable men for the most part agree on the great goods and ills of life; they do not agree on the ultimate nature or government of the universe. In chapter 12 of *Reason and Belief* I have tried to show that the theologies which take the world to be governed by a personal being with a scale of values like

our own have their root in imagination and desire, and disintegrate as reason plays more freely through them and around them. While admitting, therefore, that sincere belief in a God of love who offers mankind a splendid destiny in return for faith and obedience may add to a life both peace and power, I think that unless the belief is carefully hedged round, it will fall, and may carry with it the morality with which it is bound up. This moral collapse would be illogical, since ethics is not in truth based upon theology, but it has happened in many minds. It need not have happened if morals, of which we are far more certain than of theology, had not become entangled with it. At any rate ethics has a firm base of its own, and not only can but ought to be judged on its own merits, in divorce from any theology or metaphysics with which it has come to be associated.

Mr. Thomas's second initial demurrer is that I have confused Christian ethics with the ethics of Jesus. It is true that the two phrases may mean different things. Christianity has greatly changed both in thought and in practice. On the simple sayings and parables of the Gospels there has been heaped a tonnage of exegesis and criticism that must surely out-top any similar pile in the world. Further, Christian practice has had to adjust itself over the centuries to varying cultures, expanding knowledge, and advancing civilization, so that the Christian ethics actually practiced today is at a far remove from that which was heard and lived on the shores of Galilee. In all this I agree. But to the charge of ignoring it I can plead extenuating circumstances. (a) I did not ignore it wholly. Indeed in *Reason and Belief* I devoted the first eight chapters to what I considered the two chief interpretations which the West had given to Christianity, the Roman and the Lutheran. These chapters Mr. Thomas had not seen when he wrote, since the book had not appeared, and like the other commentators on this particular volume, he generously agreed to write on one section alone, without the book as a whole before him. But (b) the very vastness of the literature made a restriction of topic excusable and necessary. And (c) I chose to go back to the synoptics (I made little use of John) because they are after all the foundation on which the mountain of commentary is built. In the words and acts of Jesus lies the only statement of Christianity that speaks to his followers generally with full authority; and it seemed to me best to go to them directly, unhampered, if also unaided, by masses of exegetical baggage. Indeed there is some advantage in so approaching the Gospels; they have become so encrusted and barnacled with the accretions of time that their true contour is often lost to the modern reader. Their drift, their gist, their teaching of the spirit in which life should be lived, is not excessively occult or obscure; and though it is too much to hope that "wayfaring men, though fools, shall not err therein," still the modern philosopher may at least take his chance with others. In my own case, coming back to the Gospels after a long absence, I saw them with new eyes and confess that I was sometimes surprised by what I saw.

The Kingdom

After these two preliminary reservations, Mr. Thomas suggests that I place the Christian ethics in distorted perspective by paying so little attention to what was in truth its essence, a proclamation of the kingdom of God. Secular ethics, he says, grows out of a study of human nature; the Christian ethics grows out of an insight into God's will. This will is that a kingdom should be set up on earth whose head was father as well as sovereign, and whose members were brothers in the great family of the faithful. It is true that I say comparatively little about the kingdom. But then what should be said about it? What did it mean to Jesus and his followers? The answer surely is that it had no fixed meaning. Sometimes it was what Mr. Thomas takes it to be, a permanent community bound together by a common spirit of devotion and brotherhood. At other times it was something profoundly different, a kingdom to be instituted supernaturally by a second coming in clouds of glory, a judgment upon the quick and the dead, a consignment of unbelievers to hell, and the setting up of a heaven on earth for the redeemed. Now this second kingdom, promised as coming before the present generation was past, never came. And it was part of my contention that you cannot take with full seriousness the first kingdom without seeing it in the light of what happened to the second.

Mr. Thomas is quite ready to accept the statements of Jesus regarding the headship, membership, and duties of the first kingdom as expressing with complete fidelity the will of God for man. At the same time he can only admit that Jesus was making a gigantic error regarding that mind and will. "The belief," he writes, "that he had been called by God to proclaim the imminence of the Kingdom or Reign of God accounts for the sense of urgency with which he sought to prepare men for its coming . . . ." That implies that his sense of what God had called him to proclaim was at a crucial point mistaken. If so, Jesus did *not* know the mind and will of God with anything like completeness or fidelity. And my question is: How can one continue to talk of Jesus as the perfect exponent of God's mind and will in the face of this proof that he was not? Whether this error affected the details of Jesus' ethical teaching as much as Schweitzer thought it did, important as that is, is not the main issue. That issue is whether the world that Jesus lived in was the real world as we have come to know it. The inevitable answer is No. His world was a world of angels and demons, in which moral values could brush physical laws aside, a family world whose austere father was about to conclude an unsatisfactory experiment with mankind and send his children to their terribly differing destinies. And the importance of Jesus' eschatology is that it shows so clearly that he did not live in the world in which modern science has forced us to live.

Mr. Thomas suggests that to live in that world with its merely rational ethics is to miss the force of Jesus' command, "Be ye therefore perfect," a command which Reinhold Niebuhr, with his love of paradox, has called an "impossible possibility." Now if this is in truth a demand for perfection from beings limited as we are, it is not a possibility at all, and to exact it is clearly unjust. On the other hand, if it means, "Do your best to approximate perfection," the demand is reasonable, but applies to the secular moralist as well. An ethics as thoroughly mundane as the utilitarian supplies us an ideal of conduct so far beyond our capacity that no one has ever embodied it and presumably no one ever will. And the attempt of the natural man to be perfect is not aided, as is that of the true believer, by occasional accessions of divine grace, vouchsafed (according to Barth and Brunner) on no recognizable principle. He must depend upon the light of his own insights, rendered as rational and precise as possible by the study of "the best that has been said and thought in the world," a process, incidentally, that is denounced by Mr. Niebuhr as "pride." The pursuit of perfection is as open to the natural man as it is to the supernaturalist, and it is open under conditions more consonant with what we normally accept as just and reasonable.

Love and Benevolence

Christianity has often been said to be the *final* morality. I have acknowledged that at least in one respect it has a reasonable ground for this high claim; its principle of love, interpreted as a settled concern for the good of others, denotes an attitude beyond criticism. But of course this is very vague, and in order to give it the sort of clarity that reflective ethics demands, I ventured to identify it with the principle of rational benevolence. As stated by Sidgwick, this principle runs: "one is morally bound to regard the good of any other individual as much as one's own, except in so far as it is less, or less certainly knowable or attainable." Mr. Thomas thinks it grotesque to identify Jesus' principle of the love of man with so bleakly quantitative a formulation. And he goes on to raise several important points about it.

(1) Jesus, he says, did not think in quantitative terms at all. This is only too true. Because he did not, his ethics fails at times to give much needed guidance and even invites the charge of being morally undiscriminating. Love of another person is no guarantee that one will act toward him in the right way. If one loves one's mother, one may want to recognize her birthday, but if she would get far more pleasure from a teakettle than from a bunch of roses, one's love should surely be supplemented by plebeian quantitative con-

siderations. A man who makes his will without considering the comparative amounts of good his money may do through differing distributions is failing in his duty. And parable after parable of Jesus remains puzzling or positively misleading because of his failure to take amounts of good into adequate account. He suggested that a man might do what he wants with his own and might hence pay workers who toiled through the heat of the day as little as those who had worked one hour; he had only rebuke for those who thought too little was made of the son who had remained at his post as compared with the wastrel prodigal who had returned; he praised Mary, who sat at his feet, but apparently withheld any word for Martha, who was laboring for his comfort; he approved the woman who poured over him a costly ointment, and rejected the suggestion that with its value much could have been done for the poor. All these are cases that have troubled minds anxious about right doing. What makes actions right is the production of values; values must be compared if there is to be an ethics at all, and if one value is to be chosen above another, as it obviously must, quantity has to be considered.

(2) If benevolence is to be rational, it must often count one person's good as greater and more important than another's. According to Mr. Thomas, Jesus never thought in this way. "Nor does Jesus ever seem to consider the question whether the good of one neighbor is really 'as important' as 'the good of another' or suggest that if it is not as important the former should be 'treated differently.' " But this seems to be the sort of abstract equality that should be avoided. If Jesus were on a committee that had to choose whether to give a musical scholarship to the young Yehudi Menuhin or to an ambitious youth without an ear, or a Rhodes scholarship to George Thomas or some low-browed football fullback, would he consider the goods promoted by the two appointments to be equal? If he did, love would have issued in injustice; if he acted with due discrimination of the persons and goods involved, his love would not be of the kind Mr. Thomas says it was. Such discrimination between persons and values is one of the constant necessities of life.

(3) Mr. Thomas thinks that Jesus differs from the rationalist over self-sacrifice. "Clearly, when he said, 'you shall love your neighbor as yourself,' he did not mean that you should further his good rather than your own only when it is 'the same in amount' as or 'more than' your own." Jesus' practice, we are to understand, was always to prefer others' good to his own, regardless of the cost to himself, or the amount of gain to others. This sounds very much like a gospel of self-sacrifice for its own sake, and tempts me to quote the words of an eminent theologian who was a revered former teacher of mine, Dean Rashdall: "It needs little reflection to show that self-sacrifice for its own sake is always irrational and immoral" (*The Theory of Good and Evil*, 2d ed., 2:70).[2] He admits that in special circumstances we may find in it a particular "beauty and propriety," "as when a mother, not grudgingly or of

necessity but willingly and spontaneously, gives up much more for her child than he will gain by the sacrifice: but normally and apart from any special circumstances or relations of the persons, I do not think it can be said that we do on calm reflection approve the sacrifice of more for less" (ibid., 76). Rashdall was a doughty defender of the Christian ethics, but he saw that self-sacrifice had, like self-assertion, to be held within rational limits. These limits, according to Mr. Thomas, Jesus did not recognize: "the picture of him in the Gospels is that of one who always . . . furthered the good of others rather than his own." Certainly the readiness to sacrifice oneself for others is one of the glories of human nature. But to sacrifice oneself *always*, without regard to the *quantities* of good and evil involved, is to pervert nobility into fanaticism, as has often been done by Christian ascetics.

(4) Mr. Thomas offers another important thesis about Christian love. "Whereas ordinary love is evoked by admirable or approved qualities of the person loved, love in Jesus' sense is to be given whether it is deserved or not. Here, again, men are to imitate God's love . . . . But God's love is not given in proportion to a man's merit, and a man should love his neighbors in the same way." Now love of this kind seems to be (a) psychologically impossible, (b) ethically inappropriate, and (c) inconsistent with Jesus' own practice. (a) It is psychologically impossible because I cannot if I try love John Dillinger or Charles Manson as much as I do Gandhi or Schweitzer or my father. (b) One may say, "Very well, hate the sin, but love the sinner." But that is in practice a false disjunction; a man's motives are part of himself, and an extremely important part. To shower one's love equally on Himmler and Eichmann on the one hand and on their victims on the other, as God "sends rain on the just and the unjust," is to place love in blinders. (c) Jesus neither preached nor practiced this sort of love consistently. He taught the being of a God so wrathful against some sinners that he would forgive them neither in this life nor in the next; and his "love" for the Pharisees expressed itself in such words as "ye generation of vipers, how can ye escape the damnation of hell?" Which reminds us that the God we are enjoined to imitate did *not* rain his love equally on the just and on the unjust.

When I sought to classify the Christian ethics I distinguished three types of moralists, those who fixed the focus of right and wrong respectively in the motive, in the act, and in the consequences. Christian ethics I described as an ethics of motive, of inwardness, of the condition or attitude of the heart. There was nothing novel in this classification; I was surprised to find it questioned by Mr. Thomas; and I cannot think our difference about it is more than a matter of emphasis. I certainly did not intend to suggest that Jesus fixed his eye solely on the inner springs of action and ignored both acts and consequences; I meant that, compared with other moralists, he stressed the first of the three factors more and the other two less. This still seems to me true.

That he did not belong to the second group, in which adherence to rules of action is the great requirement, is well shown in Mr. Thomas's discussion of his attitude toward the *Torah* and the *Halakah* of the ancient Hebrews. He respected both, but felt free to suspend the rules of either where they seemed to him inexpressive of the spirit of love. What he substituted, Mr. Thomas points out truly, was a set of "guidelines"—counsels or precepts that were to be elastically applied; and "Since they are guidelines rather than laws, they are to be followed only insofar as they are consistent with what love, the one absolute law, requires." This is in line with what I intended to say. I admitted also that Jesus took account of the consequences of actions, as all moralists must and do. But I did take exception to the narrow range of consequences which he seemed to consider important. The state of "blessedness," of the sense of union with God and with our neighbor in love, was for him both the ideal source of our action and its ideal end in this life and in the next; what went beyond this end was of minor importance. A much more comprehensive view of intrinsic goods was essential, I suggested, for an adequate life in the modern world.

Mr. Thomas thinks I exaggerate when I say that Jesus disapproved of wealth as such and approved of poverty as such. But in both cases I felt that I was following what Jesus actually said. "Woe unto you that are rich"; "the rich hath he sent empty away"; "it is easier for a camel to go through the eye of a needle, than for a rich man to enter into the kingdom of God." When his "astonished" disciples asked him, "Who, then, can be saved?" he answered, "With men it is impossible, but not with God: for with God all things are possible" (Mark 10:23–27), which seems to mean that a rich man could enter the kingdom only by a special divine interposition. Again, "Blessed are ye poor, for yours is the kingdom of God." The man who has abandoned his house and lands and adopted voluntary poverty "for my sake and the gospel's" is promised eternal life (Mark 10:29–30). There is little discussion of the reasons for this disapproval and approval respectively, and if one goes to the recorded words, those interpreters seem to me justified who have said, as I did, that "wealth is repeatedly denounced as such, and poverty as such exalted."

Problems of Interpretation

There follows in Mr. Thomas's paper a long series of points in which nearly every criticism I have ventured to make of the Christian ethics is challenged. To take them all up in detail would distend my space unduly, and I must content myself with those cases that elicit the kind of reply theologians are most likely to make.

Sometimes the explanation given for a questionable passage is that it is merely a picturesque exaggeration. I said that though Jesus was markedly friendly to women, he said very little about the problems of sex. I quoted the troublesome statement, "there are eunuchs who have made themselves eunuchs for the sake of the realm of heaven. Let anyone practice it for whom it is practicable" (Matt. 19:12, Moffatt). Mr. Thomas says this "is surely only an assertion that, while monogamous marriage is the normal state for most men and women, there is a place for voluntary celibacy in the service of God's Kingdom." This may be true, but it seems to me a pretty bland explanation for so bold a pronouncement. I pointed out, further, that the denunciation of the Pharisees as "whited sepulchres" and a "generation of vipers" destined for hell was not the language of love. Mr. Thomas observes, as one of two comments in reply, that "when the Gospels were written, many years after Jesus' death, the break between Christians and Jews had produced such bitterness against the religious leaders of Judaism that Jesus' criticisms were probably exaggerated by the writers of the Gospels." Again this may be true. But it offers a dangerously wide option to interpreters of puzzling passages. There are many sayings in the Gospels that are out of tune with the main teaching, and it is tempting to explain them away as "exaggerations." The trouble is that by giving oneself a little freedom of rein on this road one could end up with a "bowdlerized" Scripture. One may well bear in mind Schmiedel's opposite principle, that if something is said that seems quite uncharacteristic of Jesus, the probability is in its favor, since a writer would not have attributed to him anything so far out of line unless he had firm grounds for doing so.

Another reply that is used more than once by Mr. Thomas is based on the expectation of an imminent second coming. Jesus said almost nothing about civic duty except the famous and cryptic "Render unto Caesar the things that are Caesar's," and this seems to have been interpreted by his followers very much in the manner of Saint Paul: "Whosoever . . . resisteth the power resisteth the ordinance of God; and they that resist shall receive to themselves damnation" (Rom. 13:2). This I thought an unsatisfactory account of civic duty. So does Mr. Thomas. But he explains that this "warning against civil disobedience was given at a time when Christians were a powerless minority in the Roman Empire and were expecting the imminent establishment of God's reign." Again, in dealing with Jesus' denunciation of the Pharisees, Mr. Thomas explains that "Jesus was convinced he had been called by God to prepare his fellow Jews for the coming of the Kingdom, and yet he had been bitterly opposed by the Pharisees from the beginning." Now we had already been told by Mr. Thomas that "the substance of his teaching . . . was quite independent of the time of the consummation of God's Reign." In the cases just cited his conception of civic duty and a notable departure from his central teaching of love are both connected with the expectation of the imminent coming of the kingdom. If that expectation exerted so potent an influence on his teaching in these two cases, it might surely have influenced him on many other important issues. Schweitzer was right that if this explanation is used at all it must be used consistently and on principle; it cannot be used ad hoc to meet special difficulties.

It is pleasant to note that Mr. Thomas rejects belief in a hell of eternal fire, though admitting that Jesus himself accepted the doctrine. What is his explanation for this acceptance? ". . . it should be pointed out," he writes, "that punishment in hell is not at the center of Jesus' teaching and that he seems to have simply taken for granted a contemporary conception of hell." That the doctrine was not central in his teaching seems doubtful; it is attributed to him in all of the synoptic Gospels. But suppose it is true that he simply took it for granted. Consider what this means. For surprisingly mild sins, such as saying to another, "thou fool," men were "in danger of hell fire" (Matt. 5:22), and even for sins of omission such as *not* feeding and clothing the poor. Great numbers of people, some interpreters say the entire human race except "the chosen few," were consigned to agonizing and hopeless suffering. Now if Jesus did explicitly accept this doctrine, it is idle to say that either he or the God he sought to follow was governed by love or justice in the human sense. If, knowing what the doctrine meant, he simply took it for granted, teaching it to be true but giving it little heed, how are we to explain away an apparent callousness toward human suffering which in a man would arouse moral indignation? Whether the doctrine is central or peripheral in Jesus' teaching, he does seem to have believed that far more of God's children were going to be tortured endlessly and excruciatingly than were going to be saved. Will any theologian please tell me how that belief is to be reconciled with the belief in a God of boundless and overflowing love? It should not be left to blundering laymen like me to insist that theologians talk sense on this matter.

In my study of the ethics of Jesus, I pointed out that in his concentration on love as the greatest of the virtues, he came very near to making it the sole virtue, from which all others flowed. Confident of the supreme efficacy of love, he seems to have overlooked the fact that justice has problems of its own which no amount of love by itself will solve. The result is a curious vacuum in Christian teaching where justice is concerned. Mr. Thomas thinks this a somewhat ungrateful conclusion, and he reminds us that some of the noblest movements for justice in modern history, such as the war on slavery, the social gospels of Rauschenbusch, Niebuhr, and Maritain, and the firm though temperate leadership of Martin Luther King, were all outgrowths of Christian teaching. So they were. That such leaders have had an incalculable influence for good I conceded in my book and am glad of the opportunity to reaffirm it, to emphasize it, indeed if these heroes would welcome it from such a source, to glorify it. No one can read unmoved the stories of Wilberforce, of John Woolman, of the nameless padres of the old Spanish West, commemorated by Willa Cather, whose hearts were as full of selfless goodness as their breviaries were of mythology. My only answer to criticism here is the simple one that I was not writing the history of Christian social action; I was writing on *Reason and Belief*; and unfortunately the nobility of one's life is no proof of the validity of one's creed. If it were, we could summon clouds of witnesses from the lives of Buddhists, Stoics, Moslems, and Mormons for beliefs that flatly contradict each other. My interest in Christian ethics was an interest in Christian ethical doctrine; and for that doctrine there is only one fully authoritative source. To that source, then, I would go. I wanted to find what Jesus actually thought and taught, and though that is not the whole story of Christianity, it is both the essential part of it, and a part that can be studied in independence of its checkered later history.

The Parables

Three of the well-known parables of Jesus seem to give sanction to a kind of justice that is at odds with a rational ethic. My interpretation of these parables is vitiated, Mr. Thomas thinks, by my overlooking an important fact brought to light by Jülicher, Dodd, and Jeremias, that "a parable makes only one point." It is therefore idle to study the content of the story except as it directly bears on this point. Now with all respect to Messrs Jülicher, Dodd, and Jeremias, I beg to differ with them emphatically. This view is perhaps true of childish and bumbling parable-makers who do not know how to illustrate a point without taking the mind off on mistaken scents and down irrelevant alleys. But have they forgotten whom they were dealing with here? Jesus was one of the great masters of the art of teaching by parable. Are we to suppose him to have been so inept and bungling in his rendition of these parables that in trying to make one point he inevitably distracts the attention to another? In all of these cases he could have made his point with ease through matter that was neutral and undistracting. In all of them he chose to clothe the point with matter that was not only distracting but distractingly questionable. And the distraction is too great to ignore.

Consider the cases. First there is the parable of the laborers in the vineyard. A landowner needed some workmen to harvest his crop. He went out early in the morning and hired some men to do a day's work for "a penny." He went out again at the third hour, the sixth, the ninth, and finally at the eleventh with only an hour of daylight left for work, and without specifying any fee, told the employees in each case "whatsoever is right, that shall ye receive." When the men reported for their pay at the day's end, the owner paid off first the men who had worked an hour only, and gave them exactly the same fee as those who had worked all day. The latter naturally grumbled, saying, "These last have wrought but one hour, and thou hast made them equal unto us, which have borne the burden and heat of the day. But he answered one of them, and said, Friend, I do thee no wrong; didst not thou agree with me for a penny? Take that thine is, and go thy way: I will give unto this last even as unto thee. Is it not lawful for me to do what I will with mine own? . . ." (Matt. 20:1–15). Mr. Thomas thinks that this parable makes just one point, which is "that *God* deals with those who come late into His Kingdom as He deals with others and more generously than they deserve. Since His love is not measured out to men according to their merits, it is given equally to all who come to Him, whether soon or late." This may indeed be the main point. But if so, one has to hunt for it in a story whose most conspicuous point is that the master, after promising to give "what was right," chose to pay those who had worked least at a rate twelve times that of those who had worked most. Mr. Thomas remarks surprisingly that "nothing whatever is said about the divine justice." I should have thought that the dominant note concerned God's justice, and that what it conveys is that he has the right to set aside what men call by that name. Mr. Thomas relies on the cryptic conclusion to nullify this impression: "So the last shall be first, and the first last: for many be called, but few chosen." But this leaves the issue of justice where it was.

The same kind of interpretation is given to the parable of the hidden treasure. A man finds a valuable treasure in a field owned by another. Without telling the owner, he hides the treasure, sells all he has and buys the field. About this Mr. Thomas says: "the parable does not recommend the 'sharp practice' of a man; it exalts the supreme worth of the Kingdom which justifies the sacrifice of everything else for it." No doubt this is right. But would a master of parable choose these details, which so cloud the point, if he felt as keen a reprobation of the injustice plainly involved as the modern reader does? Similarly of the parable of the talents. Mr. Thomas accepts as "the one point" of the parable that all men to whom God has given talents "should employ them responsibly and fruitfully." But I cannot keep my mind properly focused on that one point when I read that the man who merely kept his master's money for him—and so far as we know, this was all that was asked of him—was greeted as follows: "Thou wicked and slothful servant, thou knewest that I reap where I sowed not, and gather where I have not strawed . . . . Take therefore the talent from him, and give it unto him which hath ten talents . . . . And cast ye the unprofitable servant into outer darkness: there shall be weeping and gnashing of teeth" (Matt. 25:26–30). The master here is used as the symbol of a God of unbounded love and forgiveness. Mr. Thomas would have us regard his uncompromising harshness to the man who had kept his talent in a napkin as irrelevant to the teaching of the parable. I cannot think it either is or is meant to be so.

Fortunately with Mr. Thomas's discussion of nonresistance I agree so fully that comment on it seems needless.

The Place of Reason

I suppose my main criticism of Christian ethics is the very serious one that it gives no adequate account of the *ends* of life, the intrinsic values that are to be sought for their own sakes, and here too Mr. Thomas largely agrees. "It is certainly true," he says, "that Jesus had little to say about knowledge and nothing about art." "However," he adds, "this does not mean that Jesus put a low value on knowledge; it means that the *kind* of knowledge he prized, like other Jews, was knowledge of God, of men's relation to Him, and of their conduct toward each other." The kind of knowledge here referred to is a kind not recognized in secular books on the theory of knowledge; it is presumably revealed knowledge, coming directly from a supernatural source and not subject to the checks and tests used in the ordinary quest of truth. Now a large part of *Reason and Belief* is devoted to an examination first of the Catholic and then of the Protestant claim to such revealed knowledge. The unavoidable conclusion was that much of this "knowledge" could not be consistently accepted by anyone who also accepted the law of contradiction. Many eminent Protestants, including Luther and Kierkegaard, Brunner and Barth, took Emerson's high line that "A foolish consistency is the hobgoblin of little minds." Perhaps a more useful reminder to store in memory is McTaggart's "No one ever tried to break logic but what logic broke him." If this special kind of knowledge is exemplified in the truth warranted as revealed by the Roman church or in the Bible as interpreted by Lutheran theologians, I had to admit failure to find it.

I do not deny that a knowledge of God is possible by means not recognized by secular students of epistemology. There may be a "knowledge of the heart" that differs from all the cognitive processes known to the philosophers. But it would be idle to discuss them without a better acquaintance with them than I can profess to have. Meanwhile my disagreement with the attitude toward knowledge of the traditional theologian is not confined to doubts about the kind of knowledge he claims. It is largely concerned with his attitude toward the efforts of men who had only their natural faculties and a love of truth to guide them in exploring the religious field. His theological ethics of belief here seems to me to have been defective. "Blessed are they who have not seen, and yet have believed." The historical result of this attitude has been too often to place on a pedestal persons who believed without an adequate right to do so, and too often to pillory honesty of mind. Anyone who wants these statements documented will find all he needs and more in two great books, A. D. White's *Warfare of Science with Theology*, and W. E. H. Lecky's *Rise and Influence of Rationalism in Europe*. In these books the intolerance by religious authority of knowledge that conflicted with revelation is described in full and painful detail. It will be said, of course, that persons who hold my views, even though driven to them by reflection over many years, are themselves intolerant; it is wrong to impose logic upon those who resent and distrust it. In a sense this is true. If someone claimed that he clearly saw how a person could be both one and three, using the term "person" in the same sense each time, I should not accept his "insight," though I should certainly not try to silence him. If this is intolerance, there is at least nothing arbitrary in it, because the authority of logic is immanent in human thinking itself; to try to think *means* to try to think logically.

Divergent Philosophies

If Mr. Thomas is not a theologian, as he says, I am much less so. Perhaps that is why his view of the nature and person of Jesus puzzles me. He admits that Jesus was limited in power and knowledge; he apparently dismisses the physical miracles as legendary; he cannot accept the theology of John that "I and the Father are one"; he admits that at many points in Jesus' world vision and even in his moral vision he shared the provincialisms of his time and place. Was he therefore simply a very great and good man? Mr. Thomas shrinks from this, which is my own, conclusion. He holds rather that "there was a unique union of will and purpose between him and God." He was "one who through his complete surrender of himself to God's will was a unique revelation of His love and a unique instrument of His purpose." I would not reject this view as a priori impossible. In the final part of *Reason and Belief* I have argued for a view that on the intellectual side is vaguely analogous to it; I follow Plato, Spinoza, and many others in holding that man's mind is brokenly and imperfectly rational, and that so far as he achieves rationality, he could be said to be embodying an Absolute. But (1) it is not easy to see how a "union of will and purpose" with an all-wise God could issue counsel based on a delusion about the imminence of the kingdom, and could speak so fragmentarily about the true ends of life. (2) The kind of Deity that Christianity has traditionally accepted, a God of boundless love and justice, who is guiding the course of nature and history to appropriate goals, seems to me hopelessly irreconcilable with the facts of evil.

It is this speculative difference between Mr. Thomas and me that is the crucial one, as he recognizes. We have different views of the world. Many of the points stressed in his concluding pages I can agree with unreservedly: the practical values of the "love of God" in his sense of that phrase; the reassurance given to humanity by a life actually dominated by the spirit of love; the rationality implicitly present in much of the Christian ethics; the increasing rationality of "believers" about the bizarreries of the traditional faith—its hosts of angels and demons, its recurrent miracles, its eschatology of sadistic horror. But in whatever directions we travel together, we come at the end to a reluctant parting of the ways. Mr. Thomas says that I have surrendered to a world dominated by the unchanging laws of science. Yes, I suppose I have. I think that science gives us our most reliable knowledge of the world; it is the system that covers the widest area of fact and brings it into fullest consistency. Not of course that it is our only knowledge; there are logic and metaphysics, ethics and aesthetics and history. But the intellectual ideal to which science is our most impressive approximation, the ideal of a comprehensive and intelligible system, I admit to be my Grail.

There is room in that world for all aspirations that are legitimate and all "truths" that are true. It does not exclude purpose; I have held from the beginning that the whole life of mind is purposive. When Mr. Skinner tries to deny purposive action, he is obviously engaging in it while he denies it. The world we live in is in process of construction, and also revelation, through our slowly advancing rationality, working at first through common sense, then through science, then through a more adventurous and dubious but inevitable metaphysics. And if there is anything which this widening rationality brings home to us, it is that the world is one interrelated whole. There is only one nature, one cosmos of fact, one system of truth. There is no realm of supernature tacked onto it by links that are rationally inscrutable, and tenanted by beings who repudiate the logic and ethics that we know. There are not two standards of truth and right, one of them known to Locke, Mill, and Sidgwick, and another known only to God and a singularly chosen few such as Luther and Kierkegaard.

Compared with this latter precious pair, Mr. Thomas is an eminently reasonable man. What I find difficult to see, as already said, is how he can go so far in divesting himself of the old supernaturalist trappings without going farther. He accepts the results of textual criticism. He has looked soberly over the pages of history, chiefly gray or black; he knows we did not start with Adam or Eve but with a long, bloody, prehuman struggle in which life, as Dean Inge said, was "a conjugation of the verb 'to eat' in the active and the passive"; he knows that the Judaeo-Christian religion was only one of many, and was so introduced into the world that the majority ever since have had no access to it; he knows that "the starry heavens" outside our floating speck are, for all we can discover, a lifeless waste. How probable is it that these endless galaxies are the work of a loving father, a larger image of ourselves, who made it as a testing ground for one miscreant species on this vagrant dust-grain, who broods over their sins and keeps recorded in his fateful book all their stumblings and petty successes? How likely is it, in the light of Strauss and Renan, Fraser and Freud, that the heavenly hierarchy to which he and the son and his mother belonged, and the "scheme of salvation" which they mediated, are sober facts rather than the natural products of a desperate, pathetic need for some importance and security? The notion that the facts of evil can be reconciled with that of a benevolent Deity, either finite or omnipotent, seems to me to have been dealt with unanswerably by McTaggart.

Of course I do not believe that religion is bound up with beliefs like these, and at the close of my book I try to explain how much of the precious attitudes of the Christian inner life can be retained by a religion that has become less dramatic but more skeptical and more honest. Mr. Thomas had had no chance to read that explanation when he consented to write about my chapters on Christian ethics. He will, I am sure, reject it as inadequate. But happily I am sure also that it will not impair the prized friendship and respect that have held between us for almost fifty years.

1. Alfred North Whitehead, *Religion in the Making*, Lowell Lectures, 1926 (New York: Macmillan Co., 1927).

2. Hastings Rashdall, *The Theory of Good and Evil*, 2d ed., 2 vols. (London: Humphrey Milford, Oxford University Press, 1924).

28 FAITH AND REASON
Louis Dupré

A LL his life Brand Blanshard has been intensely interested in the relation
between faith and reason. As early as in 1931 he published an article on
the place of belief in religion.[1] His work *Reason and Belief (RB)*, published in
1974, is a lengthy monograph completing his trilogy on reason, that discusses
in detail the rationality, or lack thereof, of the essential tenets of the Christian
faith in the Catholic and Protestant traditions. Although Blanshard has
become increasingly critical of religious dogma, his rationalist position has
remained essentially unchanged. To him reason must be the ultimate
criterion of man's relation to the transcendent, both in its basis and in all
specific matters. The term religious rationalism is entirely appropriate to
characterize this attitude provided Blanshard's position is not identified with
that of most positivists who also consider themselves "rationalists" with
regard to religion. Blanshard explicitly rejects as too narrow a concept of
science restricted to what is given in, or may be verified by, sense experience.
To him science systematically explores every kind of facts, including such
private ones as a pain or an emotion, as long as they display some continuity
with other persons' experiences, or at least bear some generic resemblance to
them.[2]

Nor does Blanshard's rationalism reduce him to silence with regard to
religious problems. The philosopher also is concerned with the question of
transcendence and refuses to leave this entire domain to the theologians. Even
a suprarational revelation must not a priori be ruled out. But it must be able
to withstand the test of reason and be related to known facts and states.
Those conditions are incompatible with the idea of a revelation such as
Barth's, which is totally disconnected from man's worldly existence.
Blanshard is more favorably disposed toward Aquinas's idea of a revelation
which remains in harmony with, and is partly accessible to, autonomous
reason. According to Saint Thomas, the larger part of revealed truth, in-

cluding the theory of one God and the destiny of the soul, may be reached by reason alone, while those revealed truths which surpass the capacity of reason are at least coherent with what we know by reason alone. Nevertheless Thomas's approach also proves to be unsatisfactory in the end. For what "surpasses" the realm of the fully intelligible would be acceptable to reason only if there were compelling reasons for accepting it. Blanshard has devoted much space in *Reason and Belief* to proving that no irrefutable motives of credibility of the revelation exist, or, more correctly, that the existing ones fall far short of the mark. As for the revealed truths accessible also to reason, it is not clear how a person could ever accept on divine authority what is open to his own insight. Far from reinforcing understanding, revelation can only interfere with it, and reduce the rational to the authoritative.

Yet the brunt of Blanshard's attack is directed against the alleged concordance between the revealed truth and the fundamental conditions of reason. Bible and magisterial documents contain so many errors and inconsistencies that any claim of coherence and, much more, of accordance with reason would itself be irrational. Various parts of the Scripture contradict one another on essential matters of faith and morals, and even on the doctrine of God. Opinions at one time held to be revealed blatantly conflict with well established conclusions of astronomy, biology, and psychology.

Although Blanshard never denies the possibility of a revelation, his scheme of interpretation appears to leave no room for one. For any revelation either coincides with rational knowledge and is therefore redundant, or is added to this knowledge, and is therefore ultimately destructive of autonomous reason. "If such things [as the nature of the Deity and the destiny of the world] are to be known at all, they must be known by rational reflection which starts from the facts of experience and goes on to draw inferences from them; there is no quick nonrational road which, somehow skirting the infirmities of our natural powers and knowledge, conducts us to absolute truth" (*RB*, 34).

Most contemporary philosophers of religion consider it their task to explore the logical structure of the believer's claims. To Blanshard the structure itself a priori conflicts with the basic rules of logic. The very appeal to revelation excludes faith from the realm of truth. Although the notion of transcendence itself is meaningful enough, religious revelation provides us with no valid insights into its content. We should prefer a philosophical exploration, however low its yield, to the easy riches of revealed truth.

Blanshard's position displays some obvious affinities with that of seventeenth and eighteenth century rationalists. Yet I do not think that the term Deist could be applied to him, since the Deist idea of God, for all its claims of pure rationality so obviously modeled on the pattern of the Judeo-

Christian concept, proves too narrow for his philosophical taste. Perhaps a comparison with Spinoza might be more fruitful.

Students of religion will generally object to such a philosophical approach, with which they claim to be all too familiar. They will insist that the philosopher study the structure of the existing faith rather than substitute a concept of his own which no longer corresponds to the original one. However, the question remains whether the philosopher has a real alternative. If the structures of the faith proposed to the believer do not satisfy the philosopher, he can only provide a more satisfactory explanation himself or exclude the realm of the transcendent from his investigation altogether. He can hardly be expected to assume consistency where, in his expert judgment, inconsistency prevails.

Still, the believer might insist, reason in Blanshard's thought is conceived in a univocal way. Since reality is clearly manifold, man's attempt to interpret it must be complex as well. A verbal exchange between two people declaring their love for one another obviously differs from the mathematician's proof of a geometrical theorem, and so does the poet's expression of reality. Yet all three contain a truth worthy of rational exploration. No one, however, would ever apply the criteria of one to the other. Least of all Brand Blanshard, who, in his classic portrait of the rational temper, requires that the man of reason be aware of the distinctions between the various realms of reality. Ethics differs from mathematics and from poetry.

> If reason is to appraise value rightly, it must know what it is talking about, and when it is dealing with art or poetry or play or religion, it cannot know what it is talking about if it deals with them in the abstract, as if they were so many counters that could be manipulated by rule, like the symbols of mathematics. Much of the positivism and behaviourism of recent times has been ludicrously philistine about these things, not even dealing with them as abstract counters, but substituting for them "observables" in the way of behaviour that answer to the demands of a Moloch of their own manufacture called "scientific method." [*Reason and Goodness* (*RG*), 421]

It is essentially rational to approach one's subject with "imaginative sympathy," as Blanshard himself does so well in his theory of ethics.

Has he applied those principles with equal consistency to his study of faith? Before exploring this question we should be aware of the particular difficulty of the subject and the many reasons which tempt the philosopher to equate the nature of a religious tenet with that of a scientific theory. The Christian churches themselves have constantly confused the two meanings of truth, often with catastrophic consequences as in the unfortunate Galilei case or, more recently, in their strange opposition to the evolution theory. A doctrine which posits a supernatural "truth" as ultimate criterion of all knowledge inevitably ends up obstructing the advancement of science and philosophy. The history of the Catholic church in the last two centuries shows how detrimental such a confusion can be to the development of authentic thought. Apparently Blanshard takes the confusion to be inherent in the nature of a revealed faith.

His interpretation entails momentous consequences, for the concept of revelation is essential to religion itself. Archaic men as well as the ancient Greeks or modern Christians regard religion as a relation to a self-revealing transcendent reality. This revelation is primarily a disclosing event through which the divine presence is made manifest. Without revelation, then, religion becomes an impossible concept. To be sure, the philosopher may develop his own ideas about the transcendent, and he may even do so with a great deal of religious fervor, as Spinoza did. Indeed, he may have no other choice if the allegedly revealed faith lacks logical consistency. But to make sure that this is the case he must first investigate the religious concept of revelation in accordance with the rules of its specific nature. Those rules are not spelled out in dogmas or theological theories, as Blanshard assumes. They have to be discovered through a patient analysis of the religious phenomena *as the believer experiences them*. I am not sure that Professor Blanshard has adequately acquitted himself of this preliminary hermeneutic task. He seems to take too much from the very tradition which he criticizes. When he encounters the term "truth" in a religious text, he is inclined to attribute to it the same meaning which it possesses in a treatise on physics or philosophy, while only a clear awareness of the pluralism of symbolic meanings would preserve the proper identity of religious truth.

Whence Blanshard's reluctance to apply the epistemological pluralism to a subject which so obviously requires it, after he has clearly admitted the principle of pluralism? That faith itself is all too often guilty of this confusion should be no reason why the philosopher should uncritically accept its claims, for his task is precisely to bring to religion the critical reflection which it lacks. I believe the real reason to be Blanshard's negative attitude toward the philosophical apparatus which alone could accommodate a genuine pluralism within the unity of reason, namely, a philosophy of symbols. In a critical reply to Paul Tillich, Blanshard maintains that symbols fulfill no real function in a theory of understanding, since they are neither thoughts nor objects of thought. Moreover, since the relation between symbol and symbolized is often not rationally predictable, he dismisses symbols as "formed on no principle whatever." At most, Blanshard will concede that psychological associations establish some sort of relation between the symbol and the symbolized.[3] What can rational man possibly learn from such a bond without necessity?

However, I do not see how Blanshard could possibly fulfill his rationalist promise to give each experience its due without granting some objective status to symbols. Simply to declare the term truth more or less appropriate in poetry, religious dogma, and scientific theory will not satisfy the various parties involved. For all feel that each one in a unique way possesses its own truth. Yet Blanshard rejects the very structures of cognition which would support such a pluralism. Advocates of a theory of symbols might reply to his objections that, although symbols are neither thought nor object of thought, they are that without which neither one of them could originate. The symbol, like the Schoolmen's *species*, is that *through which* we know. It is neither formed "on no principle whatever" nor connected with the symbolized reality merely by "psychological associations." Symbols are formed according to necessary principles, even though this necessity is not in all instances that of logical reason. But why should it be? Is the demand for a uniform necessity not begging the very question which must be investigated? Does Blanshard himself not write that "reasonableness is not exhausted in the exercise of reasoning"? (*RG*, 411).

Only an objective theory of symbols allows us to recognize the essential differences between the mind's various cognitive structures of reality. Thus, faith may claim truth for its doctrines without directly contributing to scientific or philosophical knowledge of ourselves and the world. Such a claim can be evaluated only after one recognizes the unique character of the religious symbolization process.

Of course, the various forms of truth cannot be totally separated. Unless they share some common ground which allows them to be compared with one another, the concept of truth itself vanishes into meaningless equivocality. In this comparison priority must be granted to the primary analogue of truth, the rational articulation of the real. No assertion, in any universe of discourse, that basically conflicts with this rational articulation can still claim a truth in its own right. Some primary religious assertions must be transferable to ordinary rational language where they become subject to the strictest laws of reason. Without passing their test, faith cannot claim to be *true* in any sense at all. It is this requirement which Paul Tillich attempted to meet in his principle: *All religious statements are symbolic except the primary reference to the transcendent:* God is the supreme Being.[4] I leave aside for the time being whether the primary reference can be expressed in a single proposition, and prefer to clarify first the meaning of the term "symbolic," which, since Tillich, has been used to describe religious language.

All language is symbolic in the sense that it articulates an object of knowledge rather than merely announcing it. The complex articulation of language always surpasses the univocal relation of sign and signified. Why then should religious language make any unique claims to the attribute "symbolic"? First of all because religious symbols uniquely accentuate a primary characteristic of the symbolization process, namely, the relative independence of the symbol of its referent. All symbols signify *beyond* the given symbolic content: without this intentional quality, they would cease to signify altogether. Yet religious symbols widen the discrepancy between sign and signified. Their meaning contains the additional message that empirical appearances must be transcended altogether. Religious symbols primarily show what their referent is not. Although this is true for all religious symbols, we must restrict the present discussion to language.[5] The paradoxical and often distorted character of religious language has been pointed out often enough. The listener or reader is prevented from understanding what he would normally understand. But religious language also symbolizes in a positive sense by suggesting a *particular* structure of the transcendent. To do so it frequently recurs to images. Concepts are closely bound to the objective reality which they express and it is difficult to surpass their ordinary meanings. It is far easier to convey an extraordinary meaning through an image than through an ordinary concept. Images possess no meaning in the strict sense in which concepts do: they can convey, although less rigorously, any number of meanings related to their appearance. Hence the "typological" and to the secular mind often arbitrary interpretations of past events in the later books of the Old Testament and in the entire New Testament. Even when no deliberate typological interpretation is conveyed, the representational setting of many narratives suggests a meaning beyond the ordinary.

The negative side of this polymorphic quality of images is their elusive character. At least in an advanced culture man would feel that he has not acquired *truth* until he has *conceptualized* his ideas in the true sense of the term. To do so it is not sufficient to conceptualize one's metaphors. Nothing has been gained as long as concepts themselves are used as what Hegel calls "representations," that is, concepts which do not name the transcendent directly but merely suggest it indirectly. Today most students of religion would admit that some literal conceptual expression is needed to support all the symbolic ones. But few would accept the older thesis that concepts can directly designate God. Still, I believe the older position to be the correct one. To be sure, all assertions about God that are phrased in terms of intrinsically finite perfections cannot but be metaphorical. But not all concepts are thus restricted. Those designating pure perfections may be considered conceptual and cognitive in the strictest sense. Of course, not even they allow us to "represent" the transcendent, for what is "represented" belongs to the empirical universe, and that includes even our strict conceptualizations of the transcendent. Yet the point is not what we can properly represent, but what we can properly and directly signify. In an analogous way certain concepts refer directly to the transcendent in spite of their representations. One spokesman of the old tradition expresses the idea succinctly:

> The meaning of the term is not common to God and creature as if somehow
> embracing the specific ratio of both: the essence of God after all cannot be
> constrained and represented within any concept or name. It is rather proper
> to the creature and extended to God in the intellectual project which is
> analogical knowing. . . . The knowing itself is accomplished in a judgment
> which affirms God as an infinitely removed and unconceptualizable term,
> but within a perspective opened up by the intelligible contents of the
> concept.[6]

Because of their representational limitations, such concepts of the transcendent
might still be termed "symbolic"—as they are in Tillich's work—but
then the term "symbolic" no longer stands for what is merely metaphorical
or only indirectly related to the transcendent. It rather indicates that in
signifying the transcendent we must surpass all representations.

Returning now to our original thesis, we claim that religious assertions
are subject to the laws of rational discourse in two ways. (1) The basic
possibility of a positive affirmation of the transcendent must be rationally
justified. (2) No assertions concerning the transcendent are allowed to conflict with the principles of purely rational knowledge. It is in the fulfillment of
this second requirement that Blanshard finds religious statements most at
fault.

To declare the Bible the ultimate criterion of truth on all subjects discussed
in it is to commit oneself to pre-Ptolemaean astronomy, biological fixism,
historical primitivism, and, generally speaking, to a position which conflicts
with all major acquisitions of modern science. Nevertheless, this general
thesis as well as its application to specific issues has been presented at one
time or another as essentially connected with the Christian faith. Religious
statements of the past may have found some justification in the all-
comprehensive role of theology or of a theologically directed philosophy at
the early stages of cultural development, but since the emancipation of the
pertinent sciences, the theological intrusions in those areas can only be
regarded as blatant category mistakes. Fortunately, wherever confusion of
this nature has not been formally denounced by theological authorities, it has
long since ceased to exercise any impact upon religious thought.

Religious assertions proper have little in common with philosophical and
scientific statements: they deal with a segment of experience altogether unac-
counted for by science and only marginally related to philosophy. No scientific progress will ever eliminate its territory, and its claims are neither
verifiable nor falsifiable by scientific conclusions. Undoubtedly, some scientific discoveries may strengthen while others weaken man's belief in specific
religious tenets. Thus, modern science has made it considerably more difficult
to believe in life after death. Nor can the educated believer give a rational assent to articles of faith touching on scientific data without squaring his beliefs

with his knowledge. In the case of the afterlife, this requires an outright dismissal of the visions of heaven and hell which the pious imagination has produced throughout the centuries. Yet, although the religious mind is thus constantly forced to reexamine faith in the light of science and philosophy, the essence of that faith remains beyond the scope of scientific investigation. It concerns reality, not as it appears (which is what the positive sciences study) nor as it is in its ultimate foundation (the domain of philosophy), but ultimate reality as man is existentially involved with it.

I wonder whether Brand Blanshard, following a line of thought suggested by numerous and never-retracted statements of Christian doctrine, has not taken the entire realm of faith to be an extension of science, philosphy, and even morality beyond the limits of natural cognition. Thus, to science and philosophy, religion would simply strengthen some "truths" and add some others which are inaccessible to autonomous reason. Not surprisingly, such an extension of reason fails to satisfy Professor Blanshard, for it is not merely inadequate but contradictory. Truth in the scientific and philosophical meaning of the term is by its very nature restricted to what is rational, and what is rational is obviously determined by what is accessible to reason. In defense of faith, one might argue that this view of an "extended" truth is not the one of modern religious thought, nor was it ever a primary one in past religious thinking. The major documents of faith have, at all times, clearly proposed claims very different from those of science and philosophy. They articulate insights that could not possibly be expressed in purely philosophical or scientific statements, even though they may touch on them. Meanwhile, Blanshard's incisive criticism of the absurdities made in the name of faith force the religious mind to reflect upon what it is really attempting to express. This gadfly service may well be his signal contribution to our understanding of the logic of faith.

Louis Dupré

Yale University

NOTES

[1] "The Place of Belief in Religion," *Crozer Quarterly* 8, no. 2 (April 1931): 213–17.

[2] "Critical Reflections on Karl Barth," in *Faith and the Philosophers,* ed. John Hick (London and New York: Macmillan Co., 1964), 194.

[3] "Symbolism," in *Religious Experience and Truth,* ed. Sidney Hook (New York: New York University Press, 1961; London: Oliver & Boyd, 1962), 48–50.

[4] *Systematic Theology,* vol. 1 (Chicago: University of Chicago Press, 1951), 235–41.

[5] Language provides the basic symbolization of religion, since all other religious symbols require linguistic ones for their interpretation.

[6] William Hill, *Knowing the Unknown God* (New York: Philosophical Library, 1971), 143.

28. Reply to Louis Dupré

Faith and Reason

Mr. Dupré points a charitable finger at a variety of shortcomings in my critique of Catholicism on faith and reason. I shall confine myself to what seem the two most significant of his criticisms. The first, though he devotes little space to it, is of great importance logically. The second is of exceptional interest because it gives us a sketch of his own general attitude toward the problems we face in common. His two criticisms, then, are these: (I) my critique of the Catholic position proceeds on a theory of reason that rules out from the start the possibility of revelation, and therefore begs the question; (II) it shows an inadequate understanding of the office and value of symbols in religion, and Mr. Dupré considers a sound theory of symbolism to be essential. I shall follow his example in dealing with the first of these briefly and the second more fully.

(I) In Mr. Dupré's judgment, "the concept of revelation is essential to religion itself"; and revelation he defines as "primarily a disclosing event through which the divine presence is made manifest." Regarding such disclosures he writes: "Although Blanshard never denies the possibility of a revelation, his scheme of interpretation appears to leave no room for one. For any revelation either coincides with rational knowledge and is therefore redundant, or is added to this knowledge, and is therefore ultimately destructive of autonomous reason."

This dilemma calls for comment, but before offering it I must remark on certain other of Mr. Dupré's just quoted statements. (a) In a sense my theory of knowledge, far from "leaving no room" for revelation, leaves no room for anything else. I hold that the universe is an absolute whose parts are necessarily connected into a single whole. Every bit and fragment of our knowledge is therefore from one side a partial apprehension by ourselves of the Absolute, and from the other a partial disclosure to us of the Absolute. Theists have so preempted the term "revelation" that it is commonly taken to mean revelation by a personal Deity whose thoughts, feelings, and volitions are more or less like our own. But while I have no doubt that the Absolute, as I conceive it, would be an unsatisfactory substitute for Deity to the ordinary religious man, I do not know why a "God-intoxicated" rationalist like Spinoza should be held to exclude revelation altogether. For him the advance of knowledge was a continuous revelation.

(b) I am given pause by the statement that "the concept of revelation is essential to religion." Have there not been many men of the tribe of Gandhi and Emerson who could not accept revelation in the common meaning of that term but who were also religious in any sensible acceptation of the word? For a defense of this way of thinking, one may refer to Julian Huxley's *Religion without Revelation*.

(c) To conceive revelation as "primarily a disclosing event through which the divine presence is made manifest" seems to restrict unduly the concept as usually held. In the Catholic church, for example, the prime channel of revelation is Scripture, which makes known to us a great number of past events from the creation to the resurrection and a great number of dogmatic truths such as the doctrine of eternal life and the efficacy of baptism. In the revelation to us of these dogmas the divine presence is not made manifest in any obvious sense. Perhaps Mr. Dupré is thinking of the "primary" case of revelation as that in which the mystic feels the immediate and overpowering presence of the divine. Though it is natural enough to take this as the "primary" meaning, revelation in the traditional sense is not confined to it.

Does Rationalism Rule Out Revelation?

Mr. Dupré is substantially right in saying that a theory of knowledge like mine is bound to deny revelation in this traditional sense. But the ground and extent of this exclusion are not quite as simple as one might suppose from the interesting dilemma that he proposes; indeed the most promising way to begin is to seize it by both horns. The dilemma I am alleged to face is: "any revelation either coincides with rational knowledge and is therefore redundant, or is added to this knowledge, and is therefore ultimately destructive of autonomous reason."

Is it true that on a rationalist theory of knowledge revealed truth would be redundant? Yes and No. It certainly need not be redundant at the time of its reception. It is conceivable, for example, that we should be granted advance knowledge of the time of our death and whether or not we should survive death. These items might, as they came to us, be neither self-evident nor deducible from anything we knew, though their truth might be amply verified and even seen to be necessary after the event. There might be no plausible explanation for them except revelation. Would they be redundant? Not unless what is very useful may be a redundancy, for they would undoubtedly be of great service in the drawing up of our plans for the future. They would be redundant only in a technical sense, namely that in a rationalist metaphysic the events disclosed would be so connected by logic and causality with the rest of the world that a mind sufficiently superior to our own could in theory have seen these connections and deduced the events without the aid of revelation. Such revelations *would* be redundant in my system, though only in this very special sense.

Let us look at the other horn: if revealed knowledge were "added to" natural knowledge, it would be "ultimately destructive of autonomous reason." Everything turns here on what is "added." I do not see that the disclosure to us of the sort of truths just considered would be "destructive of autonomous reason." The rational knowledge we already had would still be knowledge, and the added insights regarding the time and survival of death would presumably be duly confirmed and assimilated to the rest of our knowledge. I do not know what would mark these insights or intuitions as revelations rather than hypotheses before they were verified, but I do not see how their possibility can be ruled out a priori; and if when tested they proved coherent with the rest of our knowledge, they could hardly be called "destructive of autonomous reason."

But what is "added" may be something very different, and if Mr. Dupré has this in mind, he is right that my theory of knowledge does rule out revelation. I must try to explain why. Knowledge for me is a long and painful clearing of the woods which surround us on all sides with a nearly impenetrable jungle. The process of clearing begins in perception, where from the outset there is an attempt to organize the material of sensation in accordance with categories already at work in it, categories of identity and difference, time and space, causality and necessity. The little clearing so made is slowly pushed outward on all sides. New land is safely won only by linking it with the clearing, which is our intellectual home, in such manner that there may be logical and causal commerce between old and new. If a man marches off into the jungle by himself, gets lost, and cannot establish connections between the things around him and the clearing that forms his base, his state is what we call insanity. We can move to new ground, but it must be integrated and continuous with the old; we cannot accept the new at the cost of making our world incoherent. Why not? Because that would render meaningless the notion of knowledge itself. If contradictories can both be true, then nothing is true rather than false, and the world built up by common sense and science is a tale told by an idiot. Incoherence is our surest gauge of unreality. There is nothing arbitrary in thus insisting on coherence as the test, for it is a standard immanent in thought itself and at work in it from the outset. So also, I venture to think, is the category of causality; we could not accept as real a province between which and the world we live in there could be no sort of reciprocity. A set of alleged existents that could not act upon our senses or our thought and to which no actions of ours could make the least difference would not be real; they would not even have the sort of reality of a DeQuinceyan opium dream, for he could in some measure control that world by taking or withholding the drug. But a world quite cut off from us causally would not belong to our real world at all.

It will now, I hope, begin to appear in what sense my theory of knowledge rules out revelation. A realm of alleged existence which, when "added on" to our home world of common sense and its scientific extension, would make nonsense of that world by the disruption of its logical structure must be ruled out because it would commit us to meaninglessness and rational suicide. Again, a realm between which and our own there could be no causal intercourse would not be a real extension of our own. Finally, a realm that could be "added on" only at the cost of sacrificing the best established empirical laws, while not ruled out absolutely, must be set down by any rational mind as highly improbable. This way of conceiving knowledge does clearly preclude our accepting as a whole the revelation claimed by the Judaeo-Christian tradition. That revelation, as accepted by Mr. Dupré's communion, embraces many clear contradictions, not merely in matters of fact, but also in matters of the utmost religious importance, such as the character of Deity and the ideal moral life. Further, it denies some of the best established conclusions of natural science. Much evidence of these incoherencies is supplied in *Reason and Belief*, and there is no need to repeat the unhappy story here. To the extent to which the acceptance of these incoherencies would logically disrupt our world, Mr. Dupré is right in maintaining that my theory of knowledge, by its very structure, must exclude the belief in revelation.

It is interesting to note the difference here between my two Catholic critics. Neither of them, if I may say so, seems to deal with my difficulties in a manner that I should suppose encouraged by their church. Father Owens dismisses some of the inconsistencies I cited as dealing with matters irrelevant to the main purpose of Scripture, and therefore indifferent, though the official teaching of the church is that Scripture is "inspired in all its parts." As for incoherencies in matter admittedly relevant, he is ready to accept the assurances of his church that they are not in the end what they now appear to be, and to turn with relief to the more exigent problems of practical life. Mr. Dupré is more troubled by these irrationalities. One of his admirations is for that arch-rationalist, Spinoza. Rationality means so much to him that he is prepared to throw out as incredible the traditional doctrines of heaven and hell. He would deny, I think, that God can be conceived both as the books of Samuel conceive him and as the book of John conceives him, though his church officially requires the acceptance of both. He evidently thinks that the church made grave mistakes over Galileo and evolution, and he dislikes its long-standing practice of trailing its robes so that science is bound to step on them. How far would he go in this direction? Would he accept the raising of Lazarus, the walking on the water, the birth of Christ with no human father, the supernatural interventions at Lourdes and Fatima? I do not know. But it would be most interesting to learn how he would justify his rejection of the church's view on evolution while accepting (if he does accept) the virgin birth and bodily assumption of Mary. My own experience is that if the nose of rationalism is once admitted under one's tent, a large and formidable camel is soon likely to follow the nose.

Mr. Dupré on Symbolism

(II) I come now to the second ground of Mr. Dupré's discontent, namely my inadequate understanding of the true office of religious symbols. He has some kind words, which I appreciate, for the way in which, in *Reason and Goodness*, I enter into the experience of moral values; and he approached my *Reason and Belief* with the expectation that I would show a similar imagination when I discussed religious values. In this he was disappointed, and he asks why my work should be so deficient on this side. He answers: "I believe the real reason to be Blanshard's negative attitude toward the philosophical apparatus which alone could accommodate a genuine pluralism within the unity of reason, namely, a philosophy of symbols." I have failed to "recognize the unique character of the religious symbolization process." Mr. Dupré proceeds to sketch what that process is. If his readers find, as I do, that his exposition is somewhat cryptic, they should know that he is compressing into it the main conclusions of his impressively learned and comprehensive work, *The Other Dimension*.[1] Having been somewhat puzzled by his brief paper, I betook myself to that work with much enlightenment as to the background and force of Mr. Dupré's criticism. In order to make clear what it is that in his opinion I have overlooked, I shall put before the reader in my own way what I conceive his theory of religious symbolism to be.

(1) First we must distinguish a symbol from a sign. A sign points to something beyond it; a symbol does this also, but besides merely pointing to its object, it *represents* it. "The symbol *shows* the signified in its own structure. . . . It truly presents what it represents . . ." (*The Other Dimension*, 149; henceforth referred to as *OD*).

(2) Religious symbols differ from others by representing what is *transcendent*. The symbols of common sense and science represent objects in the order of nature; religious symbols represent something distinct from this order, something above and beyond it. This ultimate referent of religious symbols is not the absolute of the philosophers, which is arrived at by extending and integrating the phenomenal order in thought; we become aware of the religious ultimate only in religious experience. In this experience, whatever symbols we

use point to a "beyond" that no symbol can present adequately. For these symbols are drawn from ordinary life, and God transcends that life. We may think of him through the image of a cross or a crown or a shepherd or the shadow of a great rock, but he is not like any of these things. Our symbols for him are thus used negatively as well as positively, for while they point to what is beyond them, they are also used with the implicit denial that their referent is like them. God resembles none of the finite objects or persons known to common sense or singled out by the intellect. "Once the ultimate object of the mind is defined as transcendent, the upward movement *must* eventually leave the intellectual order" (*OD*, 123).

(3) Verbal symbols are to be distinguished from imaginal symbols. Science and philosophy deal with concepts, and for singling out and expressing concepts, words are our chief reliance. Of course words and the concepts they convey are, like other symbols, inadequate to Deity, but they are necessary if we are to think about his attributes and his relations with man. Are all our words about God symbolic in the sense that they point to something beyond what the concept itself presents to us? Not quite all. For then the summit at which all religious language points would remain vacant for us and we should have no sure knowledge of what we were straining after or how nearly we were approaching it. In fairly close agreement with Paul Tillich, Mr. Dupré says that the assertion that God is the Supreme Being, if this includes the denial that he is Being in the same sense as man, is nonsymbolically true. But even such assertions as these are nonsymbolic only "to the extent that they affirm divine existence," not so far as they characterize this existence in any way (*OD*, 228–29).

(4) The meaning of a religious symbol can be understood only by the man who has faith. "Faith alone provides the key to unlock the transcendent meaning of the revealed. It alone separates the transcendent content from the immanent appearances in which it resides. By themselves symbols, ideas, or events, however unusual, cannot point beyond the immanent universe to which they belong. . . . What makes words and deeds surpass their intramundane appearance is the constitutive act of faith. Faith alone transforms events into religious events and words into revelations. Only the eyes of the believer perceive the revealed as revealed" (*OD*, 294–95). The philosopher or psychologist—William James, for example—who tries to understand or enter into the experience from the outside is bound to fail.

(5) Mr. Dupré sometimes carries the efficacy of faith still farther. "For symbolic signs and expressions actually *produce* [his italics] the signified and expressed reality" (*OD*, 183). I do not think he can really mean what this seems to say, namely that the religious man in talking about God produces God. But he does mean two extraordinary things about religious language as used by the believer. (a) Its reference to God as an existing being cannot be

mistaken. When a man is aware of the sky as blue, no one can deny that the blue he claims to see is really present to him. When the man of faith reports that he has experienced the presence of God, no one standing outside that experience is in a position to deny that he has experienced what he says he has. Mr. Dupré is not averse to using paradoxical language here, for the way in which faith apprehends God is not the way of common sense or rational reflection. "The paradox of the act of faith is that it throws a bridge by declaring the gap unbridgeable" (*OD*, 108). And again: "a volitional element definitely enters the act of belief, as appears in the fact that certainty results only from the decision to assent. It is the decision to believe which makes the partial evidence conclusive. The gap between evidence and believing assent can be bridged only by the will" (OD, 45). The commitment or decision of faith thus provides a guarantee of the reality of its object.

(b) This faith is more than a merely human achievement. It is not an attitude that can be willed, or a skill that can be acquired by practice. It is not strictly the exercise of a human faculty at all, but a gift granted by God himself, an action of God in and through him. "Revelatory 'knowledge' differs from ordinary knowledge as much by the method of perceiving as by its 'object.' When religious man claims that God has revealed himself, he means, rightly or wrongly, that he knows God through himself. Revelation, then, must be considered an essential correlate of the receptive attitude of faith. As the experience intensifies, the passivity increases. The masters of spiritual life leave us no doubt that religious awareness follows the direction opposite to that of logical reflection: instead of approaching ever greater spontaneity, it moves toward total receptiveness" (*OD*, 283).

(6) One further point. Though science, morals, aesthetics, and religion use the term "truth" in somewhat different senses, they must all recognize as primary those laws of logic that underlie "the rational articulation of the real. No assertion, in any universe of discourse, that basically conflicts with this rational articulation can still claim a truth in its own right." Even revelation must be coherent with itself.

This in outline is the theory of symbolic knowledge through want of which my own criticism of revelation has gone astray. What are we to say of it?

The Limitations of Symbols

I must confess that Mr. Dupré's learned and able work has not removed my skepticism about the value of studying anything through the symbols used in thinking of it. If the symbol really "presented" its object in the sense of reflecting its structure, as Mr. Dupré at times suggests, a study of the symbol might obviously throw light upon the object. But as I said in my paper on Mr. Tillich's theory of symbols, I can see no general relation between symbols and what they symbolize except that of association, and association of the loosest kind. The same thing may be referred to by the widest variety of symbols, and the same symbol may be used to refer to the widest variety of objects. These points are important, and it is well to be clear about them.

Take a dozen men at random and set them thinking about Franklin Roosevelt. Consider the content of the symbols by which they direct their thought to him. What I discover in my own case is the picture of him that appears on a postage stamp, with the jutting jaw, the uptilted cigarette-holder, and the eyeglasses. For all I know, this symbol may be peculiar to me, and there is certainly a wide range of other symbols that people may and do use in thinking of the same man. For one person the symbol may be a wheelchair or a set of crutches, for another an erect young man at salute in naval uniform, for another the emaciated figure that appeared at the Yalta conference, for another a figure bent over a desk at Hyde Park, for still others nothing but a name, heard or seen in imagination. Conversely, the same symbol may in different minds refer to entirely different things. The sound "eegul" means to the average American the bald eagle which has itself become a national symbol; to the German it means a hedgehog. Or take the image of a red flag with a hammer and sickle imprinted upon it. To communists it is the symbol, haloed with emotion, of a great country leading the world in its social order; to many others it means a dictatorship devoid of freedom, a sinister continuing threat to the general safety, or a set of principles laid down by Marx or Lenin.

In the chapter in *The Nature of Thought* which deals with imagery in thinking, I could find no general relation but this of association between the symbolizing image and the object symbolized. Expert psychological introspection seems only to confirm this conclusion. W.H.R. Rivers reported that in his youth he used imagery freely, but that in his scientific maturity it had disappeared from his thinking in favor of verbal symbols, with no difference to his thought except perhaps an increase in its definiteness. Galton reported cases in which certain subjects did not know what the use of images meant because they apparently did not form them at all. E.B. Titchener, in his *Psychology of the Thought Processes*, says that when he talks about meaning, the image in his mind is that of a gray trowel digging into some soft material.

Now to attempt to learn something about meaning from a study of Mr. Titchener's trowel seems to me the same sort of enterprise as that of contemporary theologians when they try to learn about the object of men's worship from the chaotic variety of symbols they use in that worship. It may be said that they can learn from the community of structure between the symbol and the symbolized. But just where lies the community of structure between the various symbols used for God and God himself? Take the cross, the crown, the shepherd, the shadow of a great rock, a burning bush, an open Bible, a

Gothic cathedral. To the worshiper these may all signify God equally, but what common structure do they exhibit that could even give us a start in the attempt to know God? Am I blind when I find nothing at all?

Indeed symbols seem especially unrevealing when they aspire to represent Deity. In my thought of Roosevelt the image on the stamp at least suggests some characteristics of the man, both mental and physical, which photographs and biographies may confirm. We have independent knowledge of Roosevelt against which we can appraise such images as we may form of him. But what knowledge of God do we have against which we can similarly appraise our symbols of him? Mr. Dupré admits that the only conceptual and nonsymbolic knowledge we have of him is that he exists and is unlike anything finite; we know that he is or has being, but the instant we attempt to characterize him further, we are assigning to him attributes which, deriving from a finite experience, must be inapplicable to him. We know so little of *what* he is that we cannot even tell the degree of approximation with which our symbols approach him. We say, "God is love," and the mediaeval theologians elaborated various kinds of analogy through which human love might be considered representative of divine love; but since one side of the analogy was forever concealed from them, they had no measure of how nearly parallel the other side was. We say God is all-wise, all-powerful, perfect, slow to anger, just, and forgiving; these are concepts drawn from our human experience, and we are expressly interdicted from applying them to Deity. The approach to God, then, through either verbal or imaginal symbols seems to be effectively blocked. Yet this is the approach, as I understand it, which would have opened up to me that "other dimension" from which my rationalism cuts me off.

"But naturally you are cut off from it," I may be told, "for you are talking about the religious experience from the outside, and only the person who talks about it from the inside, from the involvement of a living faith, is prepared to receive the revelation with its world-transforming vision." It would be easy, though all too easy, to reply that faith, on the account here supplied, is not to be achieved by human effort but is a divine gift which Providence, for inscrutable reasons, has withheld from certain persons. This would be a relevant debater's reply, but it would not express my own thought on the matter. I must in candor reply that I do not see either (1) why a person speaking from the outside should not be able to understand in some measure this "other dimension" or (2) how a person who does speak from the inside can be so sure whereof he speaks.

Faith and Certainty

(1) We may never have seen a ghost, and doubt whether there are any to see, but we can easily enough put ourselves in the position of the person who

does believe in them, and feel the shivers down our spines when someone points to a suspicious movement in the darkness. We probably do not believe, as Wordsworth did, that "our birth is but a sleep and a forgetting," and that the child's enjoyment of nature is a trailing of clouds of glory brought with him from his eternal home. But that does not prevent our reading the great "Ode" with appreciation and delight. There can be few persons, particularly among those who have had a religious upbringing, who have not had religious or mystical experiences that enable them to enter the purlieus if not into the inmost sanctum of "the other dimension." One does not have to believe that Macbeth's dagger actually existed before him in order to imagine his seeing it there. Ernest Renan, one suspects, had a far fuller and deeper appreciation of the Christian attitude, even after he had lost belief in the world it signified, than most orthodox Christians. The religious belief of William James was vague, tentative, and eccentric, but his readers will surely grant him a remarkably clear perception and understanding of the varieties of religious experience that he so vividly depicts. I can hardly agree, therefore, with the position that "All religious speech requires faith for its understanding . . ." (*OD*, 202).

(2) Nor do I find credible the view that faith confers truth and certainty on assertions that the evidence leaves questionable. "It is the decision to believe," we have heard Mr. Dupré saying, "which makes the partial evidence conclusive." Such a "will to believe" may give us certitude, but surely not certainty. This distinction of Joseph Jastrow's is essential in any discussion of belief. The partisan, the bigot, the fanatic may burn with the zeal of conviction, but we know that this emotional attitude of his, no matter how intense, makes no difference to the truth of what he believes. Certainty, on the other hand, is the sort of confidence attaching to clear intellectual apprehension, the insight, for example that if all A's are B's, and all B's are C's, then all A's are C's, or that the probability of getting three successive sixes in the throw of a well made die is 1 in 216. We should think it absurd on the part of a gambler to insist that his chance was 1 in 6 or 1 in 36 merely on the ground of his inner conviction that it was. Given the evidence before us on a certain issue, there is one belief that is warranted by that evidence, and many that are unwarranted. In writing on the ethics of belief I have ventured to hold that it is our duty (within the bounds of rational living generally) to equate our assent to the evidence and to nothing else. However difficult it may be to assess, the relation between the evidence and what it establishes is as truly objective and independent of our attitudes toward it as the pyramid of Gizeh.

In the face of all such criticism Mr. Dupré falls back, as we have seen, on a tradition that has been widely held by both Protestants and Catholics. "Hamann and Kierkegaard are basically right. Faith alone provides the key to unlock the transcendent meaning of the revealed. . . . By themselves sym-

1012   BRAND BLANSHARD, REPLIES TO MY CRITICS

bols, ideas, or events, however unusual, cannot point beyond the immanent universe to which they belong. Christians believe that Jesus was God. Yet any attempt to prove this on the basis of his deeds and words is doomed to failure. ... Faith alone transforms events into religious events and words into revelations. . . . Faith receives them as such and thereby constitutes them as revealed" (*OD*, 294–95). Now faith is an attitude existing in our own mind. What these words tell us is that a proposition, "Jesus was God," though admittedly unprovable "on the basis of his deeds and words," is nevertheless made absolutely certain by our assumption of this attitude. If we alleged that any secular belief, unsupported by the evidence, was converted into an objective certainty by a change in our own attitude, we should be scoffed at. It is only in the religious sphere and when the attitude adopted is faith, that this extraordinary claim is given any respect. Why should it have credence here and nowhere else?

The answer provided is that faith is radically different from any other attitude, indeed that it is not an attitude of ours at all but an indwelling act of God himself. But as a piece of apologetics this is obviously circular. The critic raises a question as to whether faith does reveal, as it claims to do, the presence of God. The reply is that the revelation is guaranteed by the presence of God in the very act of faith. This, I suppose, is "the slippery hermeneutic circle" that Mr. Dupré at one point recognizes (*OD*, 163). But a rationalist can hardly be expected to involve himself in so obvious a fallacy. Nor do I see how this sort of theology, propounded by such antirationalists as Luther and Kierkegaard, can avoid disaster morally. It holds that God grants to some searchers after him, on no grounds whatever that are discoverable by human inquiry, the priceless gift of admittance to the other dimension, while others, not less worthy by every human consideration, he excludes from his kingdom forever. On the theory of symbolism that has been offered us, we know that in ascribing justice to Deity we cannot mean by justice what ordinary good men mean by it. By the theology that lurks behind this we are asked to mean by it that God is in our sense positively unjust.

That Mr. Dupré, with his obvious and sincere respect for reason, should nevertheless fall back on this tradition I find puzzling and disappointing. What he defends is not, for the most part, what I attacked in Catholicism. What I attacked was an immense fabric of dogma which I showed to be at many points inconsistent with itself, inconsistent with established teachings of science, and incapable of defense by rational argument. What Mr. Dupré has offered in reply is a theory of religious symbolism. And I have not found that theory wholly convincing.

What puzzles me, finally, about Mr. Dupré's position is how he supposes his theory of symbolism to be related to the structure of dogma with which I was concerned. He pays surprisingly little attention either in his essay or in his extended treatise to those dogmas of the church which are the chief stumbling blocks to inquirers like myself. He makes it clear that our symbols all break down except the naked proposition that God is the Supreme Being who negates all finitude. Nevertheless he apparently accepts the Catholic view of the world. And, as the church's highest authorities repeatedly assure us, in that view the truth of the Bible is accepted in toto, besides the long series of dogmas that have been one by one defined in the two millennia of church history. If the Catholic is to be a Catholic in the official sense at all, he must believe in the Trinity as defined at Nicaea, in inspiration as defined at Trent, in infallibility as defined at Vatican I, in the sinlessness of the Virgin as promulgated by Pius IX, in the bodily assumption of the Virgin into heaven as promulgated by Pius XII. He must believe that Jesus was descended from David (indeed descended through two different sons, Nathan and Solomon, since Scripture plainly says so); he must believe that, as a man, Jesus grew in knowledge but that, as God, he was also omniscient; that he walked on water and turned it at need into wine; that he was free not only, like his mother, from original sin, but also from any wrongdoing of his own; that his moral and theological teachings are without defect; that he could make others rise from the dead and that he so rose himself; that we are all tainted through descent from a real Adam and Eve; that Jesus believed he would return in judgment in the time of men then living and that we should still expect him; and that when he comes, he will crown the few with eternal bliss and banish the many from his face forever.

Does Mr. Dupré believe all these things? Does his theory of symbols entitle one to believe them? I do not think so. I think that if we take his theory seriously, we come out with something like this. In speaking of the events in the life of Christ—his fatherless birth, his temptations in the desert, his healings, his raising of the dead, his feeding of the five thousand, his last supper, his trial, death, and resurrection—we are speaking through symbols which always fall short of the reality and never represent the events exactly. Perhaps none of these events happened just as reported, and some of them may never have happened at all. Furthermore—and this seems to me a point of much importance—I think that Mr. Dupré would regard the events themselves as symbols only, symbols of that other great dimension which constitutes a divine kingdom. Then what exactly do *these* symbols mean? We need an interpreter of them, and who is in a better position, Mr. Dupré would ask, than the church whose history takes us back to the events themselves? So he bows to the teaching *magisterium* of that church. But that *magisterium* denies him the privilege of reading these events themselves symbolically; these words and deeds happened as recorded and *are themselves* the revelation. Can Mr. Dupré accept this? No, and for two reasons, to both of which he commits himself firmly. The first is that all symbols, even well-known historical events, fall short, indeed immeasurably short, of the God whom they reveal. "They are but broken lights of thee,/ And thou, O Lord, art more than they." The second reason is that Mr. Dupré has accepted another standard which takes precedence even of the authority of his church. For ecclesiastical authority is itself acceptable only when it conforms to this ulterior one. This ultimate standard is indicated in the sixth point of our outline of the theory of symbolism: whatever is true in any department of experience must conform to "the rational articulation of the real." That means that it must be at least consistent; even revelation, to be really such, must be coherent. Now our own case has been based upon precisely this requirement. We have seen that the church's interpretation of Scriptural events, loaded as it is with discrepancies both with itself and with science, cannot survive an application of this rational standard.

Mr. Dupré is therefore caught, as the great Aquinas was, and such dimmer lights as Luther and Kierkegaard, Brunner and Barth, in the inevitable inconsistencies that are involved in the appeal to two differing ultimate standards. The authority of an alleged revelation requires him to believe one thing; recourse to reason makes it plain that he must believe another thing. I do not think that Mr. Dupré can accept the authority of his church about the events in the New Testament and also accept the authority of the law of contradiction. These events are not for him history to be taken literally; they are very imperfect symbols of something infinitely beyond them. What exactly, then, do they intend? Their intention throughout is God, but what certainties do they vouchsafe about him? Only that he *is*, and that he differs immeasurably from all our thoughts about him. Because our symbols are all so remote from him, we can see him only through a glass darkly. This conclusion Mr. Dupré seems sadly to admit. ". . . I see no alternative but to assume that God remains unspeakable after all has been said and that revelation ultimately manifests the impenetrable darkness of the divine mystery" (*OD*, 292). What does this conclusion itself symbolize? This, I think: that it is exceedingly dangerous for a theologian to be also a philosopher.

---

1. Louis Dupré, *The Other Dimension* (Garden City, N.Y.: Doubleday, 1972).

Joseph A. Owens

I

TO read the first four chapters of Brand Blanshard's *Reason and Belief* is
both an intellectual pleasure and a moral uplift. For the past fifteen
years strident attacks have been made on Catholic beliefs and practices from
within. The express aim has been to change them in the name of an inner need
of the Church to conform to the mentality of the age. It is accordingly
refreshing to meet from the outside—and from a competent observer—the
considered judgment that the recent Council, Vatican II, "did not change in
any important particular the corpus of Catholic belief" (*Reason and Belief*
[*RB*], 24).[1] It is moreover intellectually gratifying to see set out so clearly and
so cogently the reasons why in the name of his own way of thinking a contemporary philosopher finds the Catholic faith unacceptable, and to witness his
vivid interest in exploring the problem's many details. It is also morally
stimulating to note the earnestness and the breadth of mind with which the
task is undertaken, together with obvious sincerity in the efforts to pursue
and establish the truth.

Exactly in this last objective, however, does a fundamental difference of
viewpoint rapidly emerge. Pilate's question "What is truth?" was framed in a
setting very different from modern epistemological interests. Yet it rings
down the ages. In one form or another it keeps asking for an answer. Truth is
instinctively valued and sought by men of moral caliber. It is a prized goal in
the routine affairs of daily life just as in expensive moon voyages and in the
complications of Watergate. But over and above all the particular instances
of truth, as sought in the various disciplines and pursuits of human life, the
question what truth in itself is remains a properly philosophical problem and
calls for solution on a properly philosophical plane. If the answers accepted
as true to the many and important questions raised by Brand Blanshard
differ so radically in the carefully reflected judgment of mature thinkers who
approach them from opposite camps, the suspicion that the issues are being

gauged by two different conceptions of truth can hardly help but arise. If this turns out to be the case, the problem at issue will be basically philosophical in character, even though the materials upon which it bears are located largely in the fields of sacred theology and ecclesiastical history.

In view of Blanshard's lifelong absorption in philosophy and his remarkable success in handling its problems, a basically philosophical orientation may be expected in his approach to the present questions. In fact, his reluctance (*RB*, 33–36) to acknowledge any radical distinction between philosophy and sacred theology, even while as a philosopher giving a "respectful hearing" (Preface, p. 9) to those who make the distinction, would indicate that the discussion is meant to be thoroughly philosophical in outlook. This will sooner or later require consideration of the nature of truth itself.

No matter how open one's mind is kept in approaching this new book, and no matter how ready one is to meet new assertions at their face value, regardless of the author's previously published philosophy, the underlying presence of a recognizable theory of truth soon makes itself felt. The second chapter, in its opening paragraphs, sets down as a requirement for revealed truth, that "all parts of it are consistent with each other" and that it "form a body of internally consistent truth" (*RB*, 37). This sets the discussion unmistakably in the framework of the coherence theory of truth, quite to be expected from the author of *The Nature of Thought*, in which "Coherence is our sole criterion of truth," and coherence is regarded as "the nature of truth" (*NT*, 2:259, 260–301).[2] The fourth chapter of the present book (*RB*, 80–81, 111–18) leaves no room for any doubt in this respect. It sets up a coherence framework for the body of doctrine accepted in Catholic belief (111–12), and then proceeds to show that the details do not cohere in the pattern recognized by Idealistic philosophy.

Accordingly the first question to be met is whether the Catholic believer, in accepting the content of his faith as true, is understanding the nature of truth in the coherence manner envisaged by Blanshard. This is obviously a straight philosophical problem. The Catholic believer can of course have no objection to coherence as an accompaniment of truth. One of his firm beliefs is that the universe has been made in accord with the unitary and all-embracing wisdom of God, and that all events are governed by the one divine providence. But this involves a pattern inaccessible in its totality to man in his present state. It renders unverifiable by unaided human reason the most relevant details. It is certainly not the setting of Idealistic philosophy or of any other framework open to purely philosophical scrutiny. In those contexts, and even in another religious context, the faith on its own admission appears as a stumbling block and foolishness, prompting Tertullian's emphasis rather on its lack of coherence with such patterns—"*credibile est, quia ineptum est"*[3]—as a test of its authenticity, and giving prima facie attraction to Hegel's conclusion that "with the Catholic Religion, no rational constitution is possible."[4]

No, coherence cannot be the nature or even the ultimate test of truth as it is faced by the Catholic thinker. The overall framework of the coherence is not something that comes within the purview of philosophical knowledge. His conception of truth follows rather the correspondence view. He swears to the truth of a statement in court because the assertion corresponds to the individual facts as he knows them. On accepting as true the articles of faith about the Trinity, the temporal creation of the world, the Incarnation or the Resurrection, he means that the assertions in those articles correspond as separate judgments to a reality that actually exists or that actually took place. On the philosophical level, moreover, the notion that truth consists in conformity of intellect and thing has been traditional in Catholic thought. Even the term *correspondentia* is used in this regard by Aquinas.[5] But against a strong Aristotelian background, this conformity is understood in two ways. It may be conformity of the intellect with thing, or in the opposite direction it may be conformity of the product or conduct with intellect.

In the original Greek terminology there is on the one hand "theoretical truth," in which a judgment corresponds to reality, to what actually exists. Perhaps, though the terminology does not fit exactly, one may call this type truths of fact, including both particular facts and generalizations based on them. On the other hand there is "practical truth," consisting in the correspondence of conduct to right moral habituation.[6] These divisions may not be explicit in the thinking of a Catholic who lacks philosophical training, but they are implicit in the way he will hold as true the statements that a man has the right to life, liberty, and the pursuit of happiness, and that God is to be honored and human life respected. These are true because of correspondence not to ordinary ("theoretical") fact but to right moral orientation. His notion of truth is accordingly not restricted to realms of purely objective fact and theoretical science, but extends to the order of conduct. It is not confined to a one-way correspondence of thought to things. It includes, and has to include, the correspondence of actions to thought and purpose, both human and divine. It means that in the realm of what *should* be done, truth is not attained after the manner of the sociologist who finds out what actually *is* done. Truth about the factual situation may be thoroughly known without knowledge of the truth about what should be done. The latter kind of truth appears in the conformity of the statement "It should be done" with right moral habituation.

These differences in the basic conception of truth make themselves apparent when issues such as those of Blanshard's book are raised. The first main issue is the acceptance of all the canonical books of Scripture with all their parts as contained in the Vulgate edition (*RB*, 38–39). This is a practical, not a critical, edition of the inspired word. A Catholic accepts all the statements in the Vulgate as true. But what does he understand by "true?" Does he mean that the statements correspond to what exists or what happens in the external world? Sometimes. In regard to statements like "God made heaven and earth" (Gen. 1:1), "This is my body" (Matt. 26:26), and "Christ rose from the dead" (1 Cor. 15:20) he emphatically does. But what about statements like "Two men went up to the Temple to pray . . . But the tax-collector . . . said 'O God, have mercy on a sinner like me' " (Luke 18:10 –14)? By truth here does a Catholic reader understand that once upon a time two men actually went up to the temple to pray in that way? Would he not find the question rather odd? Two men may have done this at one time, or two men may never have done so. These alternatives make no difference to his belief in the truth the statements are conveying. The factual existence of the two men in their doings is irrelevant to the truth intended. The truth at issue is that humility should be practiced. It does indeed involve truths of fact, for instance that God exists and listens to prayer. It requires for its truth the facts that are necessary for its purpose, which is to teach that men should be humble and contrite before God. Where the type of statements is moral or practical, the truth of the statements consists in their conformity with right moral orientation in the agents concerned, even though it involves their conformity with the relevant facts.

This differs from the coherence theory of truth used by Blanshard. It is found worked out and applied in Aristotle, and accordingly is not an ad hoc device set up to meet present contentions. For Aristotle practical truth consists in conformity not with things but with correctly habituated choice, involving truths of fact only to the extent required by its purposes.[7] It is likewise the ordinary conception of truth as understood in court cases. The testimony of various witnesses may differ considerably in irrelevant factual details, but the verdict—the "true statement"—of guilt or innocence in the accused's disposition is drawn from it regardless of irrelevant factual discrepancies. Nor is this an attempt to water truth down. It is geared rather to understand what is true about truth, and in particular that truth in practical matters is not to be gauged by norms meant for nonpractical areas.

In neither of these two types of truth can the Catholic thinker afford the luxury of a coherence test. He believes that here on earth he does not have that kind of access to the overall pattern of things and of providence. He is quite receptive to Hamlet's remark that "There are more things in heaven and earth, Horatio, than are dreamt of in your philosophy." If he has training in any of the traditional Christian philosophies, he has reasoned to a cause that is infinite in being, while everything else, including his own mind, is finite. He knows, accordingly, that he can fully comprehend neither God's being nor God's designs. He realizes that there are things he has to leave to God's "inscrutable Providence" (Newman's words, quoted by Blanshard (*RB,* 581, n. 49), or, more dryly, remark with Belloc's correspondent, "How odd of God." He can approach the problems neither with a conception that makes truth depend upon philosophically known coherence nor with a conception that would limit truth to the one-way correspondence of mind to thing.

In his approach to the Scriptures, the Catholic looks upon them as documents whose sole purpose is to guide men to their supreme destiny in God. Their only intended orientation is to make men holy. They reveal the facts required for this purpose. The type of truth by which they are to be gauged is accordingly practical truth. Are their contents such that they lead men to holiness? Do their statements conform to the design and intention by which God leads men to himself, an orientation shared in man through the infused habituation of grace? If they so conform they are true, and all the parts that contribute to this conformity are true. The Catholic believes that all the parts of the Scriptures, as found in the Vulgate, are of this character. They are true, *tout court.*

Consider what should be expected of an infinitely wise and infinitely powerful agent who decided to inspire such documents. Would he envisage some sort of automatic writing, in which the writers exercised no free will and in which their personalities and their deficiencies and limitations played no role? That would hardly be in accord with their dignity as human persons or with the infinite providence of God. One would expect rather that the writers would retain completely their freedom and their shortcomings, and make these manifest. Yet, like "the mind of a king" (Prov. 21:1), the writers would be in the hand of the Lord to be turned in whatever direction he wished. How a free act rises above antecedent determination is a philosophical problem. It cannot be accounted for ultimately by the limited nature of a finite agent. To be free, the act has to be caused by an infinite agent, restricted by no limiting nature. Under that entirely open causality the determination of the free act is always made by the finite agent, even though the act in its totality is caused by the unlimited and unlimiting divine action.[8]

Accordingly the type of guidance to be expected in the writing of the Scriptures would be that of an infinite God who allows the writers and copyists to act freely and let their own limitations appear in the documents as he inspires and guides them to the purpose he has in view. He will constantly and infallibly guide the free activity of the writers in the direction intended, just as with the king's mind. The guidance to salvation given by the Scriptures will in consequence be free from error. Much factual truth, such as the assertions of God's existence and power, will be required for this guidance. Here truth will be conformity to what exists or takes place. Other factual statements, such as the exact length of temple columns, will be irrelevant to the purpose and will not come under the truth that is intended. What would be incompatible with the truth meant would be statements directing men away from their eternal destiny, such as encouragement to blasphemy or adultery, or a serious assertion of God's nonexistence or incapacity to hear and provide for men. In all their parts the Scriptures are expected to teach "without error that truth which God wanted to put into the sacred writings."[9]

This is actually the attitude with which the Catholic approaches the Scriptures. It is important to note from the start the direction of his thought and reasoning. His starting point is the living teaching of the Church, learned and experienced as a rule from early childhood, but in any case accepted through the faith infused in baptism. He does not go from Scriptures and history to present faith, but from present faith to them. On grounds of the living Church's teaching he accepts the Scriptures as inspired, and the Church as the sole competent interpreter of the truth they are meant to impart. It is with this notion of truth and with this order of reasoning that the Catholic faces the problems arising from the text of the Scriptures and the history of the Church.

II

With this approach to the Scriptures, statements of fact that are irrelevant to the overall purpose will not come under "that truth which God wanted to put into the sacred writings." They may be left for explanation by the uninvolved activity of the writer or copyist. From this solely pertinent viewpoint it makes no difference if the gold from Ophir was said to be valued at 420 talents in 1 Kings, and at 450 talents in 2 Chronicles (*RB*, 39). One is tempted to remark that this rise in price over several centuries is a mild rate of inflation compared to the jump from $35 to $157 an ounce in our own times! But the point is that such details have no bearing one way or another upon the truth of the Scriptural message. They record the changing viewpoints and inadequate expressions and the deficiencies of the writers or of the generations of scribes who did the transmitting. It is not because they are small or "trivial" (40) details. It is because they do not pertain at all to the truth intended. They do not come under its scope.

These details, in consequence, do not bother the ordinary Catholic reader, even when brought expressly to his attention. He is fully justified in declining to connect them with the truth-value of the Scriptures, and he is content to leave to the experts whatever explanation they require. In the practice of his religion he knows from experience that they do not affect the truth with which he is concerned. Blanshard (*RB*, 41–53) lists a number of ways in which Catholic exegetes have tried to account for them. Naturally specialists are moved by a laudable curiosity and a desire for clearing up discrepancies. They like a neat package. But any close observer can surely see that even they, as long as they retain their Catholic faith, accept without hesitation the truth of the Scriptures on grounds other than their own expertise. The specialized arguments on details do not sway one way or the other their basic judgment about Scriptural truth. Like Renan (575, n. 9), the Catholic exegete may have sufficient confidence in his expertise to stake his life on the discrepancies between the synoptics and the fourth gospel. But that attitude need not at all conflict with his belief that the Scriptures are in all their parts divinely inspired, nor need it offer the least reason for abandoning Catholic belief. Factual conformity in these details just does not enter "that truth which God wanted to put into the sacred writings." The objective, at least in a philosophical setting, is not to take sides or apologize for these details, but rather to *understand* their place in the Scriptural message.

One rather commonly heard argument, though, does call for comment. Some parts of the Bible, it is said, hardly edify. Blanshard (*RB*, 51) mentions commands of God to slaughter human beings. One might add the penalty paid by Ananias and Sapphira (Acts 5:1–11) for a comparatively small deception in a money matter. It is hard to see the justice of so severe a penalty. Is the answer to be sought in the progressive revelation and moral development present in the Scriptures?

There are numerous instances of such seeming disregard for men's lives in the Scriptures. Are they meant to inculcate the dominion of God over human life? Are they meant to show that at times God will assert that dominion? Private reflections may or may not verge in this direction, and may be appalled at the prospects opened for justifying crimes in an alleged holy war. But for a Catholic it is hard to see how an age in which large segments of people want to authorize the killing of unborn children in numbers incalculably greater than in the accounts of divinely ordered slaughter in the Scriptures has any cause to be shocked at assertion of sovereignty over human life. The Scriptural accounts leave the authority to the maker of life. They do not hand it over to independent human control. Even in these situations they still lead to God, leaving the unauthorized taking of human life as abhorrent as ever to the rightly habituated man. In this regard the most outstanding instance should be found in the way the eternal Father required the sacrifice of his own Son on Calvary.

On these points, however, private interpretation is, as Blanshard realizes (*RB*, 40–41; cf. 53–55), no guarantee of Scriptural truth for the Catholic. To the Church alone belongs the role of explaining definitively what the Scriptures mean, just as her teaching is the only means of distinguishing inspired from noninspired books. On factual details necessary for her religious practice, the Church is very definite in her interpretation. In her ordinary magisterium she teaches that the opening chapters of Genesis are historical in character (46). The relevant facts are that earth and firmanent were created by God in time, that man was made specially to the image and likeness of God, that the first man sinned against God with the result that the whole of mankind is tainted through this original sin, that man was punished and a Redeemer was promised. On these necessary points of historical fact (in the sense of "historical" that is appropriate here) the teaching of the Church is unhesitating. The Sunday school "apple" is mentioned by Blanshard (45), though what the Scripture speaks of is the fruit of "the tree of the knowledge of good and evil" (Gen. 2:16–17). That way of speaking is enough to indicate how "rib" and "serpent" are to be taken.

On other factual points of Scripture that play key roles in Catholic practice, the ordinary magisterium of the Church is equally clear. The Incarnation, the Virgin birth, the Resurrection, the descent of the Holy Spirit on the Apostles, the meaning of "This is my body" in the sense of transubstantiation, the role of Mary as spiritual mother of mankind, the doctrines of heaven, purgatory, and hell, and other such points are taught in all necessary clarity by the ordinary magisterium. The same holds in matters of conduct, such as the immorality of onanism, the indissolubility of marriage,[10] or the necessity of baptism. On still other points the magisterium lays down the basic doctrines without undertaking the interminable task of specifying all the consequences that follow. For instance, it teaches without hesitation the eternity and immutability of God, while continually speaking of the divine action from the viewpoint of temporal and changing effects. The step of understanding God's repentance and nonrepentance (*RB,* 39) respectively from these two viewpoints can easily be left to the reader. Problems on names in genealogies, numbers of children, identity of writers, or on additions to the original text may well be handed over to experts, though authoritative judgment on inspired truth in these areas is reserved to itself. Likewise the extent to which Christ abolished the prescriptions of the Old Law (52) and the extent to which he had "not come to do away with them" (Matt. 5:17), it sees placed under its own authoritative decision. The judgment on what is permanent and what is provisional in the Old Law belongs to the discernment of the Church.

For Blanshard, however, this overall attitude of the Church toward Scripture "implies that the Bible is hardly recognised as an independent authority at all" (*RB,* 40). This palpably understates the situation. Neither the Church nor the Bible (nor tradition) is an independent authority. There is but the one source—divine revelation, as taught through Church, tradition, and Bible—and from the pedagogical viewpoint, in that order. The Catholic learns from the Church, and approaches the interpretation of both tradition and Bible from the viewpoint of the Church's teaching. The Bible may be a book and the Church a corporate institution and tradition a process of handing down from generation to generation, but the divine revelation the three teach is the same. The Bible and tradition contain the revelation, the Church interprets it authoritatively and guarantees its truth. None of the three is independent of the others in the teaching of divine revelation.[11]

Accordingly the statement that "the ultimate authority for the Catholic is not Scripture but the church" (RB, 53) needs qualification. The Church cannot initiate doctrine. She can only explain and interpret it, and guarantee its original implications. Without the Scripture and tradition she would have nothing to explain or interpret or guarantee. In regard to content, Scripture and tradition are ultimate. In regard to interpretation of the content, the Church is the ultimate authority. But absolutely speaking there is but the one source, the God who reveals. Nor is there circularity in the Catholic's approach to this source. As noted at the end of the last section, the Catholic starts from the living teaching of the Church, experienced in his daily life, and believed in, as Blanshard notes (30–31), through the supernaturally infused virtue of faith. From that starting point he goes on to accept Scripture and tradition. This order will be exemplified in detail in the discussion of papal infallibility as raised in Blanshard's fourth and concluding chapter.

The Scriptural details collected by Blanshard in the present chapter, accordingly, do not at all establish any "disharmony between revelation and reason as such" (RB, 58), when they are approached from the viewpoints of traditional Catholic thought. To balance the rhetoric in the assertion that a discrepancy in even one such detail has as its consequence "that the book the writer wrote is not infallible, that the collection of books in which this one appears is not infallible, and that the doctors, councils, and popes who pronounced it infallible were not themselves infallible" (40), one may with equal emphasis state that a thousand or several thousand such details taken together do not involve those conclusions, since these details do not affect the truth that is being proclaimed and guaranteed. It is interesting, and instructive, for a Catholic to have put before him in so clear and trenchant a way the logical sequence of an Idealist's conclusions from the latter's accepted premises. Given the coherence theory of truth, given the failure to distinguish practical truth from truth of mere fact, given the sphere of supernaturally unaided reason as the standard for measuring truth, those conclusions effectively close the door to any knowledge of man's supernatural destiny as revealed through the Scriptures. In refusing to accept the premises that entail those conclusions, the Catholic cannot help but rate himself as the true liberal. He regards his own as the mind that is open, and free to pursue the truth beyond the restrictions of natural limitations. Words have their magic. Yet they have to be used according to the prevailing acceptance. Reluctantly the Catholic sees the term "liberal" applied in this context to thinkers bound to the natural only and closed to the supernatural, in express contrast to the open expanse offered by the Scriptural teaching: "You will know the truth and the truth will set you free."[12]

III

The theme subjected to critique in the third chapter of *Reason and Belief* is the impossibility of a *vera dissensio* between revelation and natural knowledge. It is reworded more loosely in the conclusion (*RB*, 79) as the "contention that between truths of the natural and of the supernatural order there can be no conflict." Certainly there has been conflic' after conflict between the adherents of each. The chapter lists outstanding examples. These could be multiplied and extended to fields other than the natural and the life sciences. The ordinary Catholic parishioner is well aware of them in issues where his own natural knowledge brings him into conflict with the official policies of parish priest or bishop. In practice blame may usually be expected on both sides. But, though there occurs real conflict between people who focus primarily or entirely on natural knowledge and people who focus principally on revelation, can conflict between them be what is meant by the *vera dissensio* quoted at the beginning of the chapter?

Surely the nature of the question is not correctly stated in asking "whether what is offered us by the church as revealed, and therefore certainly true, does in fact conflict at any point with what scientific specialists, working in the appropriate field, would hold to be established by the evidence" (*RB*, 59). The "at any point" would suggest that one instance would establish the *vera dissensio*, quite in accord with a coherence theory of truth. But worse than that, it locates the question as dealing with a conflict between the doctrine of the Church and the authority of the experts. Even the sciences themselves cannot afford to bask in the ease of so authoritarian a principle, else there would have been no Copernicus, no Pasteur, no Einstein, no Heisenberg. Conflict with the prevailing acceptance of a scientific view does not entail conflict with natural knowledge.

The Church has had only too abundant experience of finding that the specialists had been wrong after she had followed them, as well as of realizing that she herself had been wrong when she opposed them. She accepted in her schools the Aristotelian physics, the Ptolemaic astronomy, the abiogenesis that preceded Pasteur. After being cordial to the heliocentric theory in the time of Copernicus, she reacted against it under changed circumstances during the next century in Galileo. She allowed now discarded physiological theories to pervade her ascetic literature. Although undisturbed for centuries by Augustine's version of evolution, she has been severely critical of several conclusions drawn from modern theories. What is exactly at issue here?

Over and over again the Church has experienced trouble at the impact made on her pastoral work by newly encountered tenets. The influx of Greek and Arabian ideas in the thirteenth century seemed to endanger her teachings on creation and providence and human free will. The Cartesian dualism of mind and matter occasioned difficulties in religious matters. Freudian theories were used to explain the origin of religion in a way incompatible with the Church's doctrine. Consequences drawn from organic evolution have caused people to doubt or deny the special creation of each human soul. In these cases blame can usually be attributed to both groups of people. Creation, for instance, is not a question for paleontology but rather for metaphysics. There is nothing about it that can be measured or even observed. The paleontologist is wholly unjustified in making any decisions about it, for it lies entirely outside his field. The embryologist has no instruments for dealing with the spiritual soul, since it lacks extension and perceptible qualities. When, in the name of science, writers go outside their fields to attack or discredit religious doctrines, they have to accept their share of the blame if an overstrong reaction occurs.

The Church in her on-the-spot reactions may have been inconsiderate, harsh, and at times downright criminal in her attitude. With pastoral needs urgent, there has often been no time for adequate study and appreciation of new views. The Church sees the immediate harm being done to her flock, and acts swiftly and fiercely to prevent it. Later, when tempers cool, she repents and follows wiser counsels. She becomes aware of her own crimes (*crimina*), and in her official and public prayer speaks of being joined to her spouse because they have been washed away.[13] The words of the liturgy here have a sacramental sense. But, though this is definitely not the meaning given them by the liturgy, one may well observe that in the overall record of the Church in promoting natural knowledge the crimes committed are washed away in the good she has contributed by her encouragement to pursue that knowledge, and by her own schools and institutes and universities through the centuries. She has fostered what is best and preserved what is best in pagan culture, even though her own mission focuses only on the supernatural, providing occasion for Chesterton's lines:

> . . . it is only Christian men
> Guard even heathen things.[14]

In the total perspective of her history the crimes against human progress may stand out painfully as do sore spots anywhere, but the space they occupy on the whole panorama is small in comparison with the splendor of her positive and continuing achievements. They are the blemishes to be expected wherever human passions are at work. People on both sides of the fence make their mistakes, but that should not occasion blindness to the solid contributions made by each group, nor should it impede either from allowing full rights of existence and activity to the other.

In this respect the mentality of the Church is like that of an esteemed biologist whose discoveries contributed notably to work in the area of insulin. He likes to say that he has nothing against the theory of organic evolution in

itself, but that he is afraid it may mislead him in his laboratory. In his special-
ty the animal nearest to man is the pig. If he had let himself be guided by
prevailing evolutionary theories indicating that the primates are closest to
men, he would have been led badly astray. Similarly the Church has nothing
against any kind of natural knowledge in itself. But when that knowledge is
used, unjustifiably on its own force, to cast doubt or discredit on her religious
beliefs, what type of reaction should one expect? For the Church, guidance of
her members to their supernatural destination is the all-important thing.
Natural knowledge, on her own declaration, should be no hindrance, since it
also has its source in God. But in point of cold fact, men can and do make
use, unjustifiably, of this knowledge to lead others far away from her
guidance. Evolutionary theories have been used popularly to deny creation,
and in particular the special creation of each human soul. But these are
questions that are beyond the reach of biology or paleontology, though that is
not explained or even mentioned in popular literature. The natural
knowledge, in the factual situation, becomes able to mislead people through
its use by journalistic writers. The ideal way might be to counter with adequate explanation. But that takes years or decades of research and discussion,
while the harm is being done here and now. It would also presume adequate
access to the mass media of communication, something the Church does not
have. So, rightly or wrongly, she has resorted to censorship and repression. It
is a case of prudential judgment for the protection of the spiritual interests of
her flock, and it is very easy to make the wrong judgment. The worst mistake,
from her viewpoint, would be to sit by and do nothing.

Two instances, both referred to by Blanshard, illustrate this attitude. One
is the case of St. George Mivart (*RB,* 66). His contention that though the
human soul was directly and individually created the human body
nevertheless was a product of organic evolution met with strong ecclesiastical
opposition.[15] Some fifty years later, in the *Humani Generis* (1950), section
36, this opposition was renewed, though in a much milder way. For the
metaphysics and natural philosophy of Aquinas, the difficulty here can hardly appear as more than a matter of semantics. Only actualization by a
spiritual soul can make a body human. Accordingly the human body, though
not itself created, can come into being from other matter only through the
direct and individual creation of the soul. How that is to be stated in
religiously acceptable language is a semantical question. One may say "Each
man is made individually by God," or use some similar phrasing, without in-
fringing either upon the principles of Thomistic philosophy or upon the findings
of paleontology and of embryology. Metaphysics, a field of human
reasoning to which biology has no access whatsoever, shows conclusively that
each spiritual soul comes into being through individual creation. Though "no
absolute structural line of demarcation" is biologically observable even in

principle, at the structural point where the body is to become human the direct creation of spiritual soul is required by the exigencies of nature itself. There is no interference with nature, but rather the fulfillment of nature in the development to which it itself tends. Outside this Thomistic setting the human body may be regarded as something real in itself apart from the soul, ready for the soul to be created within it. This dualism brings back the Cartesian problems, emphasized more recently by Gilbert Ryle in his caricature of "the ghost in the machine." Until these points are made clear in the popular mind, the Church may be expected to continue opposition to the unqualified acceptance, as a fact, that the human body evolved from lower forms of life. The Church does not enter into the field of biology herself, for she has no competence there. But she reacts very sensitively to the use made of biological findings to cause doubt about and denial of her teachings.

The second and much thornier instance (*RB*, 63–64) is the problem of original sin and the origin of the human race. The revealed doctrine is that "one man's disobedience made the mass of mankind sinners" (Rom. 5:19), with Eve included, Mary excepted. The *Humani Generis* (section 37) forbids the faithful to accept a polyphyletic origin. The reason is that "it is in no way apparent how such an opinion can be reconciled with that which the sources of revealed truth and the documents of the Teaching Authority of the Church propose in regard to original sin." Hardly anyone would care to quarrel with that statement! It is difficult to discuss here, since sin, in the religious sense of an offense against God, comes under the consideration neither of philosophy nor of biology nor of paleontology. But till theologians are able to show clearly how the sin of one man could cause the fall of the whole human race regardless of monogenism or polygenism, or until scientific investigation settles definitely for monogenism, the present attitude of the Church may be expected to continue, since the pastoral concerns here are grave. If and when the lack of opposition is finally made apparent to the popular mind, the opposition of the Church, just as in the case of heliocentricism (*RB,* 59), may well be "silently removed." Neither victory nor defeat in controversy is a vital concern of the Church throughout these conflicts, but rather the pastoral policy of protecting her flock from the onslaught of writers who cannot "keep out of the sacristy."

The statistics quoted by Blanshard (*RB,* 72) about the small percentage of Catholic scientists may well hold for the United States. A similar survey in French Canada, to judge from casual conversations, could be expected to show a quite different spread. But instead of "a keenly felt inner tension between scientific and Catholic thought" (ibid.), should not the conclusion to be drawn be that public and private funding in the States increase the revenues of Catholic colleges and universities to the point where they will be financially capable of carrying out expensive scientific programs on a par with their secular counterparts? Catholic scientists of my acquaintance give no sign of such "inner tension," and the historical instances to which reference has been made indicate entrance into the sacristy rather than any *vera dissensio* between natural knowledge and Catholic faith. However, the Church may make tactical mistakes in the pursuit of her pastoral policies. Tempers rise, repressive measures may become harsh and unjust, bitterness and alienation follow.

But if in pursuit of her pastoral policies the Church makes so great mistakes and is guilty of such injustice, how can she claim divine guidance? Crimes against heretics and witches aggravate this query. Perhaps the case of Joan of Arc is the most outstanding. A Church court in 1431 condemned her as a relapsed heretic, with the undisguised intention of bringing about her death through the secular arm for political purposes. In 1920 the Pope canonized her as a saint—a notable effort to wash away a crime. How can an institution that acts in these ways be the body set up by an infinitely good God to bring men to their salvation? Or can these faults be paralleled with the discrepancies in irrelevant details found in the divinely guided Scriptural writings?

In the Scriptural documents there is no question of moral guilt on the part of the writers. Here there usually is. Can divine providence, then, in causing the free acts of men in accord with the liberty of human nature, allow men to do evil while guiding them toward the good? Is not that a part of the more general problem how an infinitely good and infinitely powerful God can allow evils in the world? The Catholic doctrine is that God has constituted his Church out of sinful men. The personnel of the Church is replete with faults and deficiencies.[16] These make themselves felt, for the divine guidance does not destroy personal freedom. Yet in spite of all faults and crimes, divine providence, as with the mind of the king in the Scriptural verse, is able to guide the Church in the direction desired and through her ministry bring men to their supernatural destiny. Quite as in the Scriptural writing, the deficiency of the free instrument does not exclude the efficacy of the divine guidance.

With regard to angels and demons, the Church is definite in her teaching. She declares that both exist, though there is much metaphor and myth in Scriptural language about them. She encourages her members to pray for the help of the angels, and warns them against dealings with the devils. Since these matters of the spiritual world lie outside the scope of natural knowledge, it is hard to see how genuine opposition can arise. Possibility of pure spirits may be shown by metaphysical reasoning, but not the fact of their existence. The phenomena at seances and various psychic occurrences may at times puzzle psychology and other natural sciences, but possibility of their explanation on natural grounds and their duplication by natural means has to be left open in these sciences. They offer accordingly no scientific means of reaching the spiritual order, or for making decisions for or against its existence. If phenomena such as those upon which *The Exorcist* was based be shown to proceed from merely natural causes, they cease to be arguments for the existence of devils. The doctrine of the Church is based upon Scriptural revelation, and not upon these observable occurrences. *Vera dissensio* cannot arise in this area, though conflicts between indiscreet partisans can.

As to miracles, the Church asserts God's absolute power of doing anything that does not involve a contradiction, and his ordinate power of directing the course of events to his own purposes. The causal proposition, in this context, is not the physically observable generalization "same cause, same effect" (*RB*, 78), but the metaphysical conclusion "every event has an efficient cause." The Church accordingly encourages prayer for God's special help, and allows accounts of miracles and relics to encourage the faithful to this type of prayer, as long as the accounts remain within her very broad norms. She is well aware of the dictum "*Deus non eget nostro mendacio*"—"God has no need of deceit on our part"—and in the new liturgy, to the disgruntlement of some, she has suppressed accounts for which there was no satisfactory evidence. Where there is basic evidence, she is not so drastic. The beautiful legend of Saint Cecilia may serve as an illustration. Historians can trace the way the legend was built up from sources that had nothing to do with the Cecilia of the catacombs and of the church in the Trastevere. The evidence would give the presumption that she was neither a virgin nor a martyr, but a Roman matron. Further, one comparatively minor use of the masculine form would indicate that the saint in question was a man.[17] But in spite of all this, the basic evidence for the existence and veneration of the saint is solid, and the later accretions serve to foster the esteem for virginity and for steadfast profession of the faith even in the face of pain and death. As with Scriptural stories, the truth with which the Church is concerned is the practical truth, including the really relevant facts. From this viewpoint, other factual details may be only incidental. The fact that the vast majority of Catholics go through a lifetime without ever witnessing a miracle is beside the point. The accounts do in fact serve the purpose, and the Church considers herself justified in encouraging them within the norms she has set down. The songs of a nation, according to an old saying, are more important than its laws.

Nor is there any naturally devastating effect here on the overall course of things. From a purely physical viewpoint even the Resurrection allowed the rest of nature to continue as though no miracle had happened. To apply the term "miracle" to papal infallibility (*RB*, 77), or to transubstantiation (115), seems stretching its usual meaning. These follow the regular order of divine providence on the supernatural plane. The Church's meticulous concern with the validity of Orders makes that clear. They are not interferences with the prescribed order. Nor does the usual instance of prayer ask for any interference. Prayer for favors such as the recovery from illness or the finding of a misplaced article, or for proper guidance, merely request that the natural order of events proceed in the required direction. Divine providence is eternal and infinite, so considerations of time and difficulty do not affect the problem.

To sum up this section, the material surveyed by Blanshard does not reveal one instance of a *vera dissensio* between revelation and natural knowledge. Conflicts between adherents of the two are many, and may be expected to continue as long as hearts beat high on one side and the other. An ingrown delight seems to be experienced in using natural knowledge to discredit revealed doctrines, and churchmen seem to like telling members of the Pontifical Academy of Sciences what to say and what not to say at their meetings. A Catholic intellectual may lose his faith as easily as a nonintellectual, if he does not make use of the supernatural means necessary to preserve and safeguard it. But all this is far removed from the contention that "the orthodox Catholic does not and cannot live intellectually in the world accepted by modern science" (*RB,* 68). Actual experience shows that the properly instructed and practicing Catholic lives gladly in the world as known by present-day science, and as pressurized in modern technology.

IV

The thesis examined by Blanshard in the fourth chapter is that "the fact of revelation itself can be established rationally by considerations decisive for any open mind" (*RB,* 80). For the first time on a major point, Blanshard's statement of Catholic doctrine is not acceptable, at least in its obvious meaning. He is aware (31) that, for the Catholic, faith is a supernatural gift. Its acceptance cannot be caused by any naturally accessible evidence. The fact of revelation is not excluded. There is nothing in all the available evidence that compels assent to it, as the experience of many who have examined that evidence proves. Assent to it is a free act, made under the influx of supernatural grace. Motives of credibility are indeed required, the word of parents and teachers for the child, proportionate study of the workings and history of the Church for the adult. But these motives and marks are not premises that compel with rational cogency the assent to revelation. In that seemingly obvious sense of "established rationally," Blanshard's statement here has to be rejected by the Catholic thinker. In the ordinary Catholic the faith is alive and active long before he undertakes any critical examination of marks or motives or papal infallibility, and the articles of the creed (including the four marks) are professed unhesitatingly as matters of supernatural faith, not natural knowledge. Yet because the marks, whatever their number, form part of the motives of credibility for an educated person, Blanshard's observations on them call for appropriate consideration. But throughout one must keep in mind that Vatican I described Scriptural revelation as having taken place "in another and supernatural way" (Denziger—see infra, n. 21—no. 1785), and anathematized anyone who says "that the assent of the Christian faith . . . is necessarily produced by proofs from human reasoning" (Denziger, no. 1814). No matter how certain the external signs may be, without the aid of grace they are not decisive (Denziger, no. 1791; *Humani Generis,* no. 4).

Against unity as a mark of the Church, Blanshard (*RB,* 82–83; cf. 54–55) notes reversals of decisions in regard to condemnations for heresy. The most notorious is that of Honorius (54) who was condemned for failure to condemn other people. All this is a matter of housekeeping from year to year, decade to decade, century to century. Trouble spots keep changing, as does also the current understanding of the condemned doctrines. In our own time a papal encyclical (*Quadragesimo Anno*) of Pius XI declared bluntly: "No one can be at the same time a sincere Catholic and a true Socialist." But almost immediately Socialism as understood in England was acknowledged to be acceptable to a Catholic. In the last century, Liberalism was roundly condemned. Yet the political Liberalism of Sir Wilfrid Laurier remained untouched. The instances mentioned by Blanshard, and easily multiplied, nowhere involve anything like a definitive and formal declaration of an article of faith for all time. They exercise no particular influence on the religious life of a Catholic today, but are brought back to notice only through historians. Like the instances of Scripture dealt with earlier, each has to be studied on its own merits with all the technical methods and tools of the church historian. Each requires understanding from the viewpoint of the relevant expertise. But in no case is the unity of doctrine, as a mark of the Church, involved. That continues unchanged as the articles of the creed are professed each Sunday, while Catholic life and faith continue to be practiced and to develop on their basis.

Blanshard (*RB,* 83) is quite ready to acknowledge that suffering in hell, in the sense of "the agony of eternal fire, has been held by the church from the beginning." But purgatory, indulgences, the Immaculate Conception and the Assumption of Mary, and papal infallibility, he regards as accretions. These, unlike the points mentioned previously, are all doctrines that deeply influence the life and practice of Catholics. They are all taught formally by the magisterium. The Immaculate Conception, the Assumption, and papal infallibility have been formally defined. Purgatory and indulgences[18] are explained formally by the Council of Trent, and in the circumstances it would be hard to show that the ordinary magisterium was not being formulated. So they all may be taken as established Catholic doctrines. The one point at issue is their presence in the teaching of the Church in its earliest years.

In the documents that have come down there is no express mention of these teachings. But were they in fact contained in the doctrine of the early

Church as the oak leaves are contained in the genetic constitution of the acorn or the branches of the apple tree in the seed? The only way to find out is to look at the full-grown tree, and work back to the sources in the seed. The Catholic accepts the above doctrines in the full-blown presentation held in the Church today. That, as previously mentioned, is his starting point. Working back, he sees them contained in the doctrines held by the medieval and early Church. Purgatory and indulgences are seen in germ in the Scriptural assertion "It is therefore a holy and wholesome thought to pray for the dead, that they may be loosed from their sins" (2 Macc. 12:46) and in the suggestion of forgiveness "in the world to come" (Matt. 12:32). The Immaculate Conception and the Assumption are found contained in the Scriptural account that Mary was the mother of Christ. Papal infallibility is seen in the texts stating that upon Peter the Church was to be built, and in his commission to feed sheep as well as lambs. The consequences may not follow cogently on the strength of naturally knowable sequence. The point is whether divine providence in inspiring the statement that the dead should be prayed for meant this to include purgatory and indulgences, whether in constituting the dignity of mother of God it included the Immaculate Conception and the Assumption, and whether it meant the statements to Peter to include infallibility as defined in 1870 and as in the belief of the present-day Church. Only through the authoritative interpretation of the Church, on whose word the Scriptures are accepted as inspired, can the full and developed meaning of their original assertions be known.

The concept of a Church frozen forever in the external contours of the first century A.D., without development, without adventure, without history, causes an involuntary shudder. It would hardly be adaptable to the exigencies of human nature, calling for development in a unitary way and expressed so vividly in Tennyson's *Locksley Hall*:

Yet I doubt not through the ages one unceasing purpose runs,
And the thoughts of men are widened with the process of the suns.

In all the instances just mentioned, the doctrine in its full-blown shape had been gradually developed in the actual life of the Church in liturgy, practice, and popular prayer. Only after all this lived progress was the doctrine formally and definitively stated. This full-blown and definitive expression is the starting point of the Catholic's reasoning. He does not look for that expression, fully developed, in the primitive Church. Yet he sees thoroughgoing unity of doctrine in the different stages of development.

Infallibility nevertheless may present a special aspect of its own, from the viewpoint of development. "What exactly is it that at a given time is to be taken as infallible?" (*RB*, 90–91). But it is hard to see any difficulty here if, as the Catholic believes, the doctrine is the same no matter at which stage of development it is defined. Papal infallibility itself may in the future be formally extended to canonization of saints and dogmatic facts, but that extension would not interfere with the definition of 1870. As to "question-begging or self-refutation" (91), the study of the development starts from the present teaching of the Church. That starting point is a living fact, clear and firm. It is something not begged, but accepted on supernatural faith. On it the assessment of events in ecclesiastical history depends.

As to sanctity, the Church is totally focused upon it in intention. Her express purpose is to lead men to the beatific vision of God, something dependent upon grace. If by holiness one understands the life and workings of grace, the entire tenor of her striving is holiness. In its fullness this achievement has been realized in only one creature—"our tainted nature's solitary boast," as described in Wordsworth's sonnet "The Virgin." In numbers of others it has been realized in a fairly high degree, not only in remote figures known only through scant archeological indications and the mist of ensuing legends, but also in people whose lives are quite an open book, as with Thomas More, Thérèse of Lisieux, Maria Goretti, Pius X, and the recently (April 28, 1974) beatified Frances Schervier. The vast majority fall far short of that level. But at least it is sincerely acknowledged as a target.

Sanctity is recognized outside the profession of Catholic Faith. Saint Paul appealed to Athenians who worshiped the unknown God, Clement praised "the noble Heraclitus," Ronald Knox came to feel for the enthusiasts about whom he was writing.[19] In acknowledging today "goodness in full measure" in persons outside their fold—if that is what is meant by "without supernatural sanctions" (RB, 92)—Catholics attribute any holiness in it to God's grace, for, like the Athenians to whom Saint Paul spoke, they "are also his offspring" (Acts 17:28). No matter what abstract distinction is made between philosophical and theological viewpoints, the Catholic will always hold that in the concrete, just as in the mind of the saint, "theology and morals are intertwined" (RB, 93). In fact, the case is stronger. In practice they are not just intertwined, they are a unit. The good in any human act is caused by God, and God has set but one destiny, the supernatural, for all human activity. Accordingly "moral maturity" (92–93) does not for the Catholic isolate morality in absolutist fashion, nor can it separate "values and existence."

Highly esteemed and pursued by the Catholic in common with the secular moralist is what Aristotle called the *kalon*. The word was taken over in the New Testament from the Greeks to mean the morally good. It expresses a notion difficult to signify by a single word in English. "What is right" or "what is seemly" would approximate it. In regard to it the fact is more important and more basic than the reason why.[20] From this fundamental standpoint there is common ground. The Catholic concludes that rights belong exclusively to intelligent nature, which is not present in lower animals. Yet, if he follows the spirit of his faith, he abhors cruelty, either to animals or to men.

At the same time he has no repugnance to the slaughter of animals for food or clothing, or to appropriate punishment for criminals. His respect for human life extends to life in the womb, to life in the aged and incapacitated, to life in himself, as well as to the physical process by which it is procreated and the marriage union in which it is brought to maturity. He explains his respect for human life in terms of divine dominion over it, reasoning to the immorality of abortion, euthanasia, suicide, artificial contraception, divorce, and, in former times, of the socially accepted code of dueling. On a number of these, in degrees that vary, the secular moralist can agree on the fact of the immorality, even though his reasons differ significantly. Both prize the *kalon*. But their reasons lead at times to differing consequences.

The Church does indeed formally declare "that the celibate life is essentially superior to the non-celibate" (*RB*, 94), and her positive reasons have been fine-combed in recent discussions.[21] Wholehearted and extraordinary sacrifice for a high purpose is a recognizable *kalon,* as with a daughter who renounced marriage prospects to care for incapacitated parents. Where deep faith invites this sacrifice, next to that of life itself, should not the acceptance of the challenge be an acknowledged *kalon*? Not without deep discernment were martyrdom and virginity sought for in patrons for churches from the age of Constantine on.

The universality of the Church is her openness to all men, as Blanshard (*RB*, 96–97) notes. This universality of belief and practice is never easy to maintain. But it is striven for, and on the whole (a notion quite in accord with the derivation of "catholic") it has been manifest throughout the centuries with rather remarkable success. Never more so than today is the Church a worldwide institution, in spite of grave imbalances and deficiencies. The ubiquitous appeal in spite of strict and often difficult requirements of orthodoxy renders this universality all the more notable.

Finally, in regard to apostolicity, it is interesting to note that Blanshard (*RB*, 98–101) can read the New Testament and find very little prominence given to Peter, while another reader who recounted his experiences found the prominence overwhelming enough to change the whole course of his life.[22] Experts can argue back and forth about these points in the Scriptures and in the early Christian writings, and sufficient grounds for credibility can emerge. But these grounds are not the reason why the Catholic accepts the primacy of Peter. The reason, here as in other such matters, is the teaching of the living Church today, a teaching accepted on supernatural faith as already noted. Paul rebuked Peter, just as Saint Catherine of Sienna reproached the Pope in her day or just as a contemporary cardinal may fly to Rome for last-minute opposition to the issuance of a papal encyclical. The face-to-face encounter is quite compatible with deep living faith in the Church's teaching about the primacy. It is no argument against apostolicity. If anything, the continued tendency to rebuke the Pope might be taken as a perpetuation of apostolic practice! Paul, however, and the others just mentioned, did not desert. The most notorious instance, the Council of Constance (*RB*, 57), which set aside three papal claimants, ended with a new Pope both very much in command and allowing no right of appeal from his decisions.

The Scriptures do show strong expectations in the early Christians of an immediate second coming of Christ. Christ had spoken (Matt. 24:6–37) as though much history, including the preaching of the gospel "all over the world," was to take place first, and had emphasized that the time of his second coming was unknown. Paul (1 Thess. 5:1–2) reminded his readers that the time was unknown, and urged them (2 Thess. 2:1–2) not to be disturbed. Firm doctrinal teaching that the second coming was imminent seems incompatible with these passages. The origins of the expectations are for experts to explain. The second coming of Christ is still proclaimed each Sunday in the Nicene Creed, and preachers still stress for their own purposes the uncertainty of its time. Nor is there anything against apostolicity in the marvelous development of Christian teaching in the volumes of Aquinas and other theologians. Here again "the thoughts of men are widened with the process of the suns." The suggestion (*RB*, 107–8) of Christ's bodily presence at a Catholic Mass, unlike the parallel fantasy in the *Brothers Karamazov*, is for the Catholic an actual reality, and the words of the liturgy proclaim without hesitation that the Mass is being celebrated at Christ's command. The tenet of one true Church may be unpalatable to those outside it and seem against norms of common justice. But the gift of eternal life is far above anything to which a creature has a right, and the way in which it is to be given to men belongs to God alone to determine. As with the chosen race, one can only say "How odd of God" when one dwells on the shortcomings of the Church meant to guide all mankind, not excepting theologians, philosophers and scientists (see *RB*, 77, 115–16, 52–53).

One could go on indefinitely.[23] Blanshard's views of the medieval mind and its isolation may be questioned, for it was widely read in Greek, pagan Latin, and Arabian sources. But the overall consideration in regard to the marks of the Church remains the same. The starting point for the Catholic in matters of faith is the present-day teaching of the Church. Within that doctrine he *believes* that the Church is one, holy, catholic, and apostolic. He professes this belief publicly in the Nicene Creed. Reason shows that by the marks and signs "the Gospel teaching was rendered conspicuous" (quoted by Blanshard, *RB*, 80–81). But as rational motives they do not compel assent. The mind can resist, and in point of fact requires, according to Catholic belief, the help of supernatural grace to assent with full certainty. Unless the notion "rational" is extended to include faith, a Catholic cannot hold "that the fact of revelation itself can be established rationally by considerations decisive for any open mind." The Church does not impute either inability to reason or intellectual dishonesty to those who do not accept the fact of revelation. But it does pray that they be given faith.

V

The above scrutiny should suffice to show how Blanshard's reflections are interesting, instructive, and morally stimulating to a practicing Catholic. An appreciative understanding of their nature and of their cogent sequence upon an Idealist coherence basis of truth gives a Catholic a deeper realization of his own sources of integral reasoning, and arouses his desire to parallel Blanshard's wholehearted pursuit of truth, though now from his own twofold basis. His overall conception is too extensive to allow the use of a coherence pattern. Blanshard (*RB*, 26) is expressly aware of the twofold source used by a Catholic, and readily acknowledges that except for overall tendency there is no discernible difference, in the area of natural knowledge, "between the way in which a Catholic would go about it to establish a truth and the way of anyone else" (ibid. cf. "ninety-nine hundredths" *RB*, 73). Possibility of profitable dialogue accordingly lies open, in Blanshard's own perspective.

Here one observation is necessary. Though natural reason keeps its validity intact in the Catholic's twofold source of truth, it does not become the arbiter of supernatural knowledge. There "belief" itself, not natural knowledge, remains the judge. In spite of acknowledgment of the twofold source for the Catholic, does not Blanshard in his critique make natural knowledge the sole judge of truth in revealed Doctrine? Is not this inevitable if Blanshard is to remain coherent with his own coherence theory of truth? Aside from his rather weak recognition of (*RB*, 33–34) and undermining explanation of (110–13) the reality in the wider Catholic experience, does his approach allow the genuine understanding that in matters of faith the Catholic is speaking from a world of lived experience? The Catholic's assurance in these matters parallels the pragmatic certainty derived in natural knowledge from application in the real world. Yet Blanshard (ibid.) gives a strong impression of regarding this side of the Catholic's *Lebenswelt* as something merely abstract, as a hypothetical and unreal world. He seems rather obviously to identify himself with the "contemporary man" who would "protest that the over-world of heaven and hell, angels and demons, transcendental cures and ecclesiastically induced changes in the weather seemed to him unreal" (*RB*, 117). Until the reality of Catholic integral experience, and not only the acceptance of natural knowledge, is appreciated as a fact for the sake of the discussions, dialogue will be extensively possible but hardly effectual.[24] The Catholic will not realize how much he is dependent, even in these discussions, upon the faith in which he actually lives. His opponent, not vibrating to the chords of that lived assurance, will be baffled at the failure of the seemingly all-important details to bother the Catholic in any significant way. Blanshard's clearly etched procedure is a welcome illustration, and on the philosophical level merits warm appreciation. The task of the philosopher is not to take sides, not to play the attorney or the controversialist, but to *understand* what the situation is and how in it human freedom should pursue its high destiny.

JOSEPH A. OWENS, C.S.S.R.

PONTIFICAL INSTITUTE
OF MEDIEVAL STUDIES

NOTES

¹In the light of this statement I interpret the "almost untouched" in the first heading in the Analytical Table of Contents (*RB*, 599) to mean that the doctrine was not changed at all in any important particular, but only in some ways of external expression. This does away with the need to spend time showing how any new expression in Vatican II leaves the doctrine itself unchanged.

²For a critique of the coherence theory on the purely philosophical level, see Haig Khatchadourian, *The Coherence Theory of Truth* (Beirut: American University, 1961). The stand of this book (p. x) is that the theory is "untenable both as an account of the nature of truth and as the test of truth." A recent and brief survey of the recognized theories of truth may be found in Alan R. White, *Truth* (London: Macmillan Co., 1971), 91–127.

³Tertullian *De Carne Christi* c. 5; ed. Ernest Evans (London: S.P.C.K., 1956), p. 18.25. Cf. "revolting to the Jews and absurd to the heathen," Paul, I Cor. 1:23. A discussion may be found in Vianney Décarie, "Le Paradoxe de Tertullian," *Vigiliae Christianae*, 15 (1961): 23–31.

⁴Hegel, *Philosophy of History*, trans. J. Sibree (New York: Dover Publications, 1956), 449.

⁵*De Veritate* I. 1. c. Prima ergo. For Aquinas the proposition and the existence are the objects of two different intellectual acts, and therefore can be compared for correspondence.

⁶Aristotle *Nicomachean Ethics* VI 2.1139a23–31, b12. The expressions "truths of fact," "truths of existence," though the most acceptable, are not exclusive enough, since moral dispositions likewise are facts and are existent. A further type, artistic truth consisting in correspondence of literary product to literary form, plays an important role in present-day Scriptural interpretation.

⁷For Aristotle productive and practical kinds of knowledge involve theoretical knowledge only to the extent necessary to achieve their purposes; see *Nicomachean Ethics* I 7.1098a26–33 and 13.1102a 18–26. Moreover, Bronowski's "Principle of Tolerance" (title of a paper read to the Royal Society of Canada, June 4, 1974) extends even to truth in the exact sciences. On the topic see Jacob Bronowski, *The Common Sense of Science* (New York: Random House, n.d.), 123–35, and *Science and Human Values* (New York: Harper & Brothers, 1956), 80–94. As the high point of moral virtue for Aristotle is the mean between the extremes, so truth in its overall conception is neither extremely rigid nor at all lax.

⁸This I take to be the meaning of Aquinas in writing "according to the condition of these causes, effects are called either necessary or contingent, although all depend on the divine will as on a first cause, which transcends the order of necessity and contingency." *On Interpretation, Commentary by St. Thomas and Cajetan* I. 14. 22, trans. Jean T. Oesterle (Milwaukee: Marquette University Press, 1962), 118–19.

⁹Vatican II, *Dei Verbum* c. 3. no. 11; quoted by Blanshard, *RB*, 39. The text adds "for the sake of our salvation" immediately after "writings."

¹⁰On the sense of "false marriage" required in Matt. 5:32 and 19:9, on account of the special background in those for whom he wrote, see Joseph Bonsirven, *Le Divorce dans le Nouveau Testament* (Paris: Desclée, 1948), 38–60. The literary forms involved explain also the "stop" of sun and moon in Joshua 10:13, at Gibeon, mentioned a couple of times by Blanshard (*RB*, 61, 74).

[11] On this interdependence, see Ives M.-J. Congar, *Tradition and Traditions*, trans. Michael Naseby and Thomas Rainborough (New York: Macmillan Co., 1967), 379—424. On the Church as the "place" for the authentic reading of Scripture, see ibid., 391—92.

[12] John 8:32. Cf. the experience of G. K. Chesterton: "Becoming a Catholic broadens the mind," *The Catholic Church and Conversion* (New York: Macmillan Co., 1926), 63, and "To become a Catholic is not to leave off thinking, but to learn how to think," ibid., 86.

[13] "Hodie caelesti Sponso iuncta est Ecclesia, quoniam in Iordane lavit Christus eius crimina." Office of Epiphany, ant. ad Bened.

[14] G.K. Chesterton, *The Ballad of the White Horse*, bk. III (London: Methuen, 1911), 66.

[15] On Mivart, honored by the Pope and finally censured by his bishop, see Jacob W. Gruber, *A Conscience in Conflict* (New York: Columbia University Press, 1960), 39, 70, 188. The ground for censure, however, extended much wider than question of the evolution of the human body; see Gruber, 202—10.

[16] On person vs. personnel in the Church, see Jacques Maritain, *On the Church of Christ*, trans. Joseph W. Evans (Notre Dame: Notre Dame University Press, 1973). Using a sixteenth-century notion of person (p. 16), Maritain holds the person of the Church blameless while placing the responsibility for the evils on the personnel. This may sound like a version of the English legal dictum that the king can do no wrong, but it is open to an acceptable explanation through the way the infinite efficacy of the first cause guides men without detriment to freedom; see supra, n. 8. Maritain (p. 186) indulges in the grim humor of remarking that torture as a "cure" could be effective enough to convert the victim himself into an Inquisitor.

[17] A short account in English of the Saint Cecilia problems may be found in Vincent L. Kennedy, *The Saints of the Canon of the Mass*, 2d ed. (Vatican City: Pont. Inst. di Archeologia Christiana, 1963), 183—88.

[18] It is difficult to see how the time element referred to by Blanshard (*RB*, 87) could have meant originally duration in Purgatory rather than time of penance performed on earth. Even the latter outdated measure, however, is not used in the present discipline on indulgences; see *Enchiridion of Indulgences*, trans. William T. Barry (New York: Catholic Book Publishing Co., 1969), 21 (no. 5); 108 (no. 4).

[19] See Acts 17:22—34; Clement of Alexandria, *Stromata* II. 2. 8 (ed. Otto Stahlin [Leipzig: J.C. Hinrich, 1906], p. 117.3); Ronald A. Knox, *Enthusiasm* (New York: Oxford University Press, 1961), pp. vi and 581—90. For Justin Martyr's regard for Heraclitus, Socrates, and all who live in accord with reason, as Christians even though apparently atheists, see *First Apology* c. 46, and *Second Apology* c. 8.

[20] See Aristotle *Nicomachean Ethics* I. 4.1095b6—13; 7.1098b1—8.

[21] Interestingly, Chesterton wrote some fifteen years before his conversion to Catholicism: "I have not myself any instinctive kinship with that enthusiasm for physical virginity, which has certainly been a note of historic Christianity. . . . But the fact that I have no appreciation of the celibates, I accept like the fact that I have no ear for music. The best human experience is against me." *Orthodoxy* (London: John Lane, 1912), 288—89. The doctrine on celibacy and virginity was stated clearly by the Council of Trent; see Henry Denzinger, *The Sources of Catholic Dogma*, trans. Roy J. Deferrari (St. Louis: B. Herder, 1957), 297 (no. 980).

[22] See Vernon Johnson, *One Lord—One Faith* (London: Sheed & Ward, 1945), 115—41.

[23] Some very minor points in Blanshard's presentation call for a bit of attention. "Literal sense" (*RB*, 575, n. 1) for Aquinas (*Summa Theologiae* I. 1. 10 c) is "what the author intended; now the author of the Sacred Scripture is God." This is much wider than today's meaning of "literal sense." The context of the statement about Samuel (*RB*, 28 and 574, n. 18) is that such conclusions are not heretical till their sequence has been established as contrary to faith (*ST*, I. 32. 4. c). Restriction to five major doctrines (*RB*, 29 and 574, n. 20) is hard to find in *Contra Gentiles* I. 4, and in any case creation in time, not creation as such, would come in the list. "Insight" (*RB*, 35) hardly seems the term for the Catholic's assent by faith, for the object remains dark. In the circumstances, Loyola's advice to declare black something that appears white (*RB*, 32 and 574 —75, n. 32) on account of superior cognition through faith does not seem more drastic than declaring black the object that appears as white on a photographic negative. Infallibility (*RB*, 53) was hardly reserved to the Pope alone in 1870, even though assigned to him apart from consent

of the Church. It still belongs to general councils and to the Church, though here not apart from the Pope. Many Catholics still quarrel with aspects of papal infallibility, but if some (*RB*, 57) do not accept it as defined in 1870, it is hard to see how they can honestly call themselves Catholics. Orders are not rendered invalid by invalid papal election (*RB*, 98), though they would be by invalid episcopal consecration. The Good Friday darkness (*RB*, 61 and 577–78, n. 7) need not, even in the readings at Luke 23:45, mean an astronomical eclipse, nor is the Virgin birth (*RB*, 113) attributed by Catholics to biological parthenogenesis. The wider sense of the Greek term "eclipse" may be seen in Aristotle, *Post. Analytics* II 8.93a23; b2–6.

[24]Like a tone-deaf person in a discussion on Bach's music (see supra, n. 21), a nonbeliever has to proceed on the assumption of the reality of the supernatural for the other person, if there is to be mutual understanding and effective dialogue. In this question the overall situation has not changed since the time of Duns Scotus, in his observation (*Ordinatio,* Prologus I. I. 5) that here the controversy seems to be between philosophers who hold that nature is a finished whole, and deny its supernatural perfection, and theologians who know the deficient state of nature and its need for grace and supernatural perfection.

29. Reply to Joseph Owens

An Appreciation of Blanshard's Views on Catholicism

Father Owens is a generous commentator. When I consider what a root-and-branch criticism is made of his fundamental convictions in the first four chapters of *Reason and Belief*, I am touched by the uniform friendliness and urbanity of his reply. I shall try to follow his example in this response.

I am somewhat puzzled by his statement of the issue between us. He thinks that a main part of that issue is how truth is to be conceived. In *The Nature of Thought* I defended a view of truth as coherence, whereas the Catholic tradition is committed to truth as correspondence. Now I do not think that this difference forms any important part of the present issue. The reason for saying so is that I have based my criticism almost entirely on the requirement of consistency, and consistency is a requirement of truth for the coherence and correspondence theories alike. Would Father Owens, adhering to the correspondence theory, accept as true two statements that he knew to be inconsistent with each other? Surely he would not. But if not, he is accepting the test on which I chiefly rely for my criticism of the Catholic position. My argument, though extended, is in principle simple: (1) that the body of dogmas accepted as revealed contains inconsistencies within itself; (2) that some of these dogmas are inconsistent with established truths of science (established, that is, in the view of supporters of both theories of truth), and (3) that the appeal to the "marks" of the church to establish its authority also fails through manifold inconsistencies. Since my argument is based on a requirement for truth which is held by the two schools of thought equally, that requirement is not at issue, and I am quite content that Father Owens should hold all his assertions to be true by correspondence. What he must do, then, to meet my case is either (1) to deny the existence of the inconsistencies I hold to be there, or (2) to deny that they are important, or (3) to deny that consistency is a requirement of truth at all. I have assumed that he would rule out the last course, as I would. What he does in fact is to take partly the first course and partly the second. Some of the inconsistencies pointed out he thinks are due to our limited vision and would vanish with fuller insight. Some of them he admits, but regards as irrelevant to the main aim of the church, which is not to make philosophers of its devotees, but to guide them toward a holy life.

Nevertheless he makes one or two remarks about truth which give me pause. He says that in a certain religious context "the faith on its own admission appears as a stumbling block and foolishness, prompting Tertullian's emphasis rather on its lack of coherence with such patterns [of consistent systems]—*'credible est, quia ineptum est'*—as a test of its authenticity . . . ." If this means that there is much in the universe that will probably forever remain dark to us, I understand and agree. If it means either that there are in reality genuine contradictions of fact or truth or that statements clearly seen by us to be contradictory may both be true, I cannot agree, nor do I think that Father Owens would maintain either position. As for the first, it is a firm belief of the Catholic, he says, "that the universe has been made in accord with the unitary and all-embracing wisdom of God, and that all events are governed by the one divine providence." I venture to assume that a "unitary and all-embracing wisdom" would not contradict itself. As to the second, I have already assumed Father Owens to agree that of two propositions clearly seen to be contradictory, both cannot be true, since rational discussion would not otherwise be possible. If these two points may be agreed upon, I think the ground is cleared for going forward, without the necessity, which would take us far afield, of excursions into the metaphysics of truth.

There is another point I must remark on before getting under way. A few years ago I participated in a "dialogue" between Catholic and humanist scholars, in which I read a paper stating some of the conclusions of *Reason and Belief.* The paper was based on a study of Papal and conciliar decrees and yet it was rejected by most of the Catholics present (younger men in orders for the most part) as out of date. In their view Vatican II had opened the doors so wide for free questioning that they were ready to brush aside the most authoritative pronouncements of popes and councils. I was bewildered. I protested that Vatican II, while changing liturgical practice and permitting somewhat more freedom of scholarly criticism, had left the historic dogmas of the church essentially where they were. To my relief, Father Owens is with me here. He admits the restlessness and even radicalism that have appeared in recent years in some disaffected groups of the vast Catholic community, but he agrees that if the critic is to talk about Catholicism responsibly, he must talk about the Catholicism of history and the hierarchy, the Catholicism whose tenets and traditions have been defined by formal decrees of popes and councils over many centuries. It may be that in time these authorities will be overthrown and that one can no more discuss *the* Roman teaching than one can discuss *the* teaching of Protestantism, with its hundred differing sects.

But that day has not yet come, and in our discussion it is comforting to realize that at least Father Owens and I are in agreement as to where authority in the church is to be found.

Inconsistencies in "Revealed" Truth

In discussing my critique of Catholicism, Father Owens follows my treatment chapter by chapter, beginning with the second. The first is devoted, not to argument, but to a statement of the Catholic position on the relation between reason and faith. The fact that my critic does not raise questions about this chapter implies, I trust, that we start from a common understanding of what that position is. The next chapter is devoted to pointing out that within a body of truth which is accepted as revealed and therefore true without defect, there are numerous inconsistencies of which in each case one side at least must be false. For example, the same pillars in Solomon's temple are reported to be of different heights; the same woman is said to have been childless to the day of her death and the mother of five sons; the genealogies of Jesus in Matthew and Luke differ in many particulars; the two accounts of Paul's conversion and the several accounts of the resurrection differ in various details. How can a Catholic retain his belief in a Scripture true in its entirety in the face of such inconsistencies?

Father Owens's answer to this question is as follows:

> In his approach to the Scriptures, the Catholic looks upon them as documents whose sole purpose is to guide men to their supreme destiny in God. Their only intended orientation is to make men holy. They reveal the facts required for this purpose. The type of truth by which they are to be gauged is accordingly practical truth. Are their contents such that they lead men to holiness? Do their statements conform to the design and intention by which God leads men to himself . . . ? If they so conform they are true, and all the parts that contribute to this conformity are true. The Catholic believes that all the parts of the Scriptures, as found in the Vulgate, are of this character. They are true, *tout court*.

And again:

> With this approach to the Scriptures, statements of fact that are irrelevant to the overall purpose will not come under 'that truth which God wanted to put into the sacred writings.'

Father Owens feels free to concede most of the inconsistencies I cite because "such details have no bearing one way or another upon the truth of the Scriptural message."

Now this doctrine of a divided Scripture in which those parts that bear on the plan of salvation are inspired and true, while those that do not may be uninspired and untrue, is *not* the traditional teaching of the church. It was not, for example, the position of the Council of Trent, which said with Papal approval: "if anyone receive not as sacred and canonical the said books *entire and with all their parts* as they have been used to be read in the Catholic church, and as they are contained in the Old Latin Vulgate edition . . . let him be anathema" (my italics). This position has been reaffirmed over and over again by the highest authorities. It was taken by Vatican I (Session III, chap. 2). It was stated in the most emphatic way by Leo XIII in *Providentissimus Deus:* "All the books which the Church receives as sacred and canonical *are written wholly and entirely, with all their parts, at the dictation of the Holy Ghost;* and so far is it from being possible that any error can coexist with inspiration, that inspiration is not only essentially incompatible with error, but excludes and rejects it as absolutely and necessarily as it is impossible that God himself, the supreme truth, can utter that which is not true" (my italics). There is no suggestion here that the "only intended orientation [of Scripture] is to make men holy" and that "The type of truth by which they are to be gauged is accordingly practical truth." We are told in the most emphatic and unambiguous way that *all* the Scriptures and *all* their parts are to be taken as true without exception.

Father Owens is of course perfectly familiar with these texts and others like them. How does he reconcile them with his own teaching that there are parts of the Bible that are false, but whose falsity does not matter because they are irrelevant to the "sole purpose" of Scripture, namely guiding men toward holiness? His reliance here seems to be upon a clause in Vatican II's Constitution on Divine Revelation. The passage is as follows: "Therefore, since everything asserted by the inspired authors or sacred writers must be held to be asserted by the Holy Spirit, it follows that the books of Scripture must be acknowledged as teaching firmly, faithfully, and without error that truth which God wanted to put into the sacred writings for the sake of our salvation" (chap. 3, sec. 11). This passage is ambiguous. Does it mean that what "God wanted put into the sacred writings for the sake of our salvation" was only a certain part of the Scripture, mixed in with masses of matter irrelevant to that purpose? That this position has some plausibility is clear; for the numberless Old Testament legends, the interminable tales of kings slaying and being slain, and the dreary chapters of "begats" seem to have no bearing whatever on man's holiness or salvation. But plausible or no, this is not the position of the church, which holds that *all* Scripture is inspired. Indeed the sentence just preceding what I have quoted from Vatican II says: "In composing the sacred books, God chose men and while employed by Him they made use of their powers and abilities, so that with Him acting in them and through them, they, as true authors, consigned to writing *everything and only those things which He wanted*" (italics mine). Obviously, if the authors consigned to writing *only* those things which he wanted, then we cannot call some parts relevant and others not. Does Father Owens accept this? He does and he does not. After laying it down that the gauge for inspiration of Scriptural passages is the question, "Are their contents such that they lead men to holiness?" he goes on to say: "The Catholic believes that all the parts of the Scriptures, as found in the Vulgate, are of this character. They are true, *tout court.*"

Now Father Owens cannot have it both ways. He cannot, when pressed with contradictions in the text, reply that their matter is irrelevant to the main purpose and therefore not inspired, and at the same time insist that Scripture is inspired throughout. He cannot say that only those parts of Scripture need to be taken as true that conform to the intention of leading men to holiness and also maintain that *all* the parts of Scripture do so conform and are therefore "true, *tout court.*" He may take one line or the other, but not both.

But can he responsibly take either line? Suppose he adheres to his first position and says that inspiration is confined to those parts of Scripture that contribute to or bear on man's salvation. The Bible as we know it then ceases to be. Much of the Pentateuch would go at once. Much of Joshua, Judges, Ruth, the two books of Kings, the two books of Chronicles, the book of Esther and the Song of Solomon, and much also of the prophets from the Lamentations of Jeremiah to the book of Malachi would have to go. What would be left would not be the Bible as we know it, but a text both mutilated and truncated. On the other hand, if Father Owens were to include what the Council of Trent, and the two Vatican councils and a long succession of popes expressly insisted on including, he would have to accept as true not only the contradictions I cited and many more, but extensive tracts of "history" written no doubt in good faith by the authors, but now believed on excellent evidence to be imaginative constructions. The choice for a Catholic is not a happy one.

What led Father Owens to suggest that some parts of the Bible were irrelevant was the need to do so if inconsistency was to be avoided. It could be avoided if certain "factual statements, such as the exact length of temple columns," are placed outside the central purpose of Scripture and do not "come under the truth that is intended." Very well; suppose we confine ourselves to the truth that is intended. Will this enable us to achieve the desired escape from inconsistency? Unfortunately not. For among the truths that are undoubtedly "intended" are statements about the character of God. And is the characterization of God in Scripture a consistent one? Let us recall that according to the Council of Trent, the Catholic "accepts and venerates" "all the books of the Old and New Testaments, since one God is the author of both, with equal piety and reverence" (Session IV). Then consider the following: in the Old Testament God orders Saul, when he attacks the

Amalekites, to "slay both man and woman, child and suckling." He imposed a pestilence that killed thousands, enjoined "an eye for an eye, a tooth for a tooth," and approved the institution of slavery. A few hundred pages later we find that, on the contrary, God is grieved not only over the troubles of men but over the fall of a sparrow, that we are to turn the other cheek and forgive seventy times seven. The Catholic may, though inconsistently with the teaching of his church, contend that these two teachings merely report correctly two different conceptions of God held at different stages of moral evolution. Does he so escape the charge of inconsistent representations of Deity? Not at all. For the same difficulty is repeated at the very core and center of church teaching, that of Jesus in the New Testament. At the time when Jesus was teaching that God is love, he is represented as also teaching that for certain sins God would send men to endless torture in hell. In short, no matter how far you carry Father Owens's suggestion that pure truth will be obtained by clinging close to what is "intended" in Biblical teaching, you are defeated in the end. How can it be denied that contradiction, and therefore falsity, enter into the quintessential teaching of the New Testament regarding the character of Deity?

Father Owens's account of inspiration puzzles me not only in what it says about the content of inspiration but also in what it says about the process. The sacred writers are of course human beings, suffering from the inevitable ignorance, stupidity, and bias of such beings. How did they come to speak infallible truth? The answer is, we are told, that the writers are

> in the hand of the Lord to be turned in whatever direction he wished. How a free act rises above antecedent determination is a philosophical problem. It cannot be accounted for ultimately by the limited nature of a finite agent. To be free, the act has to be caused by an infinite agent, restricted by no limiting nature. Under that entirely open causality the determination of the free act is always made by the finite agent, even though the act in its totality is caused by the unlimited and unlimiting divine action.

This kind of causation baffles me. One of the authors of the synoptic Gospels is writing, let us say, his account of the resurrection. This, if anything in Scripture, is set down under the guidance of inspiration. The ordinary psychological account of an act of writing would be something like this: a set of events comprising a state, ABCD . . . n, some of them physical and some mental, act conjointly at time t_1 to produce a psychophysical result abcd . . . n at time t_2. The scientist would admit that he could not exhaust all the factors comprising either state, nor completely correlate its component events with those of the other, but he would say with a good deal of confidence that *if* the analysis were carried through, nothing in the second state, namely the writing at time t_2, would be left dangling and unexplained. Perhaps Father Owens is agreeing with this when he says that "the determination of the free act is always made by the finite agent . . . ." But then in the same sentence he says "the act in its totality is caused by the unlimited and unlimiting divine action." Now I do not see how an act can at the same time be "determined" by the finite agent or factors in it and yet also determined in its totality by nonfinite factors. What we have here is two causes, admitted to be quite different, but both of them said to be causing the same event. I do not suppose that Father Owens would consider this intelligible; it is a miracle, and miracles are not supposed to be intelligible to finite reason. But it sounds to me also very much like another self-contradiction, and this, though it might be welcomed with enthusiasm by Kierkegaard and his like, would not, I had supposed, be welcomed by those who had sat at the feet of Aquinas.

Father Owens's summary of his answer to my first contention, namely that the body of alleged revelation is not consistent, strikes me as typical of our failure to engage gears with each other. "Given the coherence theory of truth, given the failure to distinguish practical truth from truth of mere fact, given the sphere of supernaturally unaided reason as the standard for measuring truth, those conclusions effectively close the door to any knowledge of man's supernatural destiny as revealed through the Scriptures." My case is thus taken as resting on three premises, all of them unacceptable. As for the first, the coherence theory of truth, I am not aware of having appealed to it at all. This theory, as I developed it in *The Nature of Thought,* involves an elaborate doctrine of internal relations which it was quite unnecessary to introduce into the present discussion. What I did appeal to was the mere consistency which I supposed philosophers of all stripes would accept as a minimum requirement of truth. As for the second premise, the failure to distinguish practical truth from other kinds, I had defined carefully in *Reason and Goodness* the sense in which I took judgments of right, good, and duty to be true; and though I could not accept Father Owens's return to Aristotle in conceiving the judgment of right as asserting conformity to right habituation, I was ready to allow any plausible definition of practical truth to pass without demur. As for the third premise, that natural reason is the standard I am using, I of course plead guilty. It is the only reason I know. Father Owens tells us repeatedly that if we started with faith, as the good Catholic does, and if this mere natural reason were kept out of the Sacristy, where it does not belong, we should see the light. I must own deficiency in this kind of light. I do not deny that there are kinds of light to which I am blind, and I regret the blindness. What I should here insist on is that if something is A, it cannot also *not* be A, and that where this is denied, there can be no light at all. Nevertheless I think I have shown that over and over again in the church's interpretation of Scripture this prime requirement of light is in fact denied.

Catholicism and Science

In my third chapter on the Catholic view, I pointed out that dogmas officially accepted as revealed were in conflict with established truths of science. Father Owens's general reply to this is that such conflicts cannot occur. They cannot occur because Scriptural interpretation and natural science have different provinces which do not overlap and therefore could not come into competition. Similar statements are made by Barth, Brunner, and other Protestant theologians. I argued in *Reason and Belief* that such statements have been out of order since the appearance of President White's *Warfare* and Lecky's *Rationalism*. These books do not devote themselves to irresponsible outbursts either of local priests or of village atheists, but to conflicts between authoritatively supported dogmas on the one hand and established scientific truth on the other. The conflicts are not vague; they can be stated with precision on both sides; and the genuineness of the conflict is indubitable. Father Owens suggests that a conflict at a single point would not be a *vera dissensio*. This is true, of course, if the dogma questioned is not really "of faith," or if the scientific doctrine that is challenged is a controversial speculation. But if the dogma belongs to the content of revelation and the scientific doctrine has the full support of scientific method, then it surely does follow that a *vera dissensio* has occurred. For the truth claimed for revelation is absolute; and if it is proved not to be truth, the authority of its guarantor, the church, is reliable no longer. In my argument, I pointed to three areas in which such conflicts had actually occurred, namely astronomy, biology, and psychology.

In astronomy the unavoidable case was that of Galileo. Three popes successively condemned his "error and heresy of the movement of the earth." He was brought before the Inquisition and compelled under threat of severe punishment to recant the doctrine. I chose this case because the issue it presented was simple and clear. Galileo maintained that the earth went round the sun; the church maintained that this was untrue and that its untruth was disclosed by revelation. The scientist proved to be right. It is idle to say that this was not a conflict between religious authority and scientific truth, or that the church's authority was not committed, or that this authority had not been in error. Father Owens passes over the case without mention; I do not know why. He points out that scientific theories have often turned out to be mistaken. But if there is any scientific hypothesis that may be regarded as confirmed beyond doubt, it is that of the movement of the earth round the sun. Furthermore, scientific theories are advanced, not as dogmas promulgated by authority, but as hypotheses confirmed by the available evidence though never certain absolutely. The discarding of a scientific hypothesis is thus not the discrediting of science, for it is by science, more rigorously applied, that the old hypothesis is corrected. Unfortunately the church, when it speaks ex cathedra, has no corresponding provision for self-correction, since to correct itself would be to assert that infallibility had erred. Father Owens says that the church *has* corrected errors, and cites the case of Joan of Arc, who, after being burnt at the stake for heresy in 1431, was made a saint in 1919. But the two cases are not parallel. The responsible official in Joan's case was not the Pope, but Pierre Cauchon, Bishop of Beauvais (subject of De Quincey's famous apostrophe), and the infallibility of the church was not on trial. In Galileo's case it was.

Turning next to the field of biology, I instanced the theory of evolution. If theology and biology have entirely different provinces, the Catholic biologist, in his scientific capacity, should not labor under any restrictions from his church. Does he? I pointed out two cases in which he does. (1) He is in effect forbidden to believe in mental evolution. He holds that the soul is that in us which thinks, wills, and feels, and his church tells him that the evolution of this soul from subhuman life cannot have occurred. The biologist who conforms to its demands must hold that the soul was affixed to the body by God at some point in biological evolution and is affixed to each individual body at some point in prenatal life. Pope Paul VI addressed a group of theologians in 1966 as follows: "The theory of evolutionism will not seem to you acceptable whenever it does not accord decisively with the immediate creation by God of each and every human soul, and does not hold decisive the importance that the disobedience of Adam, universal protoparent, has had for the lot of humanity" (*N.Y. Times*, September 30, 1966). So far as I know, no biologists outside the church believe in this supernatural intromission of the soul into the body, though they have no means of disproving it. What they would say, I suppose, is that every year of research into the animal mind serves to reduce the gap between that mind and the human, and that the continuity of growth in each individual makes the idea of nonnatural intromission superfluous. Father Owens thinks, however, that though the Catholic theory receives no support from biology, it receives decisive support from metaphysics. "Metaphysics, a field of human reasoning to which biology has no access whatsoever, shows conclusively that each spiritual soul comes into being through individual creation." Since I am unfamiliar with this proof and unable to conceive how it would run, I shall not attempt to criticize it.

(2) The other restriction upon the Catholic biologist is a required belief in Adam and Eve. According to Pope Pius XII in *Humani Generis* of 1950, this belief is rendered necessary by the doctrine of original sin; unless the whole race had descended from a single, sinful pair, we could not be sure that the sin of this pair would have been disseminated through the whole race. The independent origin of the human species in different parts of the world is thus

theologically ruled out. Now I have no idea how likely or unlikely this independent origin may be. What does seem clear is that this imposition upon biologists of what I must be allowed to call a fantastic piece of mythical immoralism is an affront to their reason. It restricts the conclusions of biological research on the ground that such conclusions might lead to a loss of belief in the damnation of the majority of the race for sins they had never committed. I have said, and I say again, that this attribution to a God whom we are supposed to worship and obey of conduct compared with which that of Jenghis Khan or Attila would be merciful is a standing disgrace to theology. Theological bits and bridles on the pursuit of truth may be endured for the sake of the good the church is doing, but when they are imposed in the interest of securing reverence for immorality, silence is not the better part. Why so kindly and gentle a person as Father Owens should swallow this poisonous draft is a mystery to me unless indeed he has handed over his reason and conscience to an authority that is unworthy of them.

The third field of conflict I mentioned between revealed and natural knowledge was psychology. I pointed out that for centuries diseases which today are competently dealt with by psychiatrists were ascribed by the church to demon-possession and witchcraft. Has the church abandoned its belief in a personal devil and his minions? In answer I noted (*RB*, 67) that on December 17, 1972 "the Vatican newspaper *L'Osservatore Romano* devoted fourteen columns to Satan, which churchmen reported as part of a papal counteroffensive against attempts in the Netherlands and elsewhere to dilute traditional teaching about the devil," and that a few weeks earlier Pope Paul had said of Satan: "We thus know that this obscure and disturbing being really exists and that he still operates with treacherous cunning; he is the occult enemy who sows errors and disgrace in human history." The Pope went on to urge a return to the study of demonology. I gather that Father Owens would accept all this without demur. "With regard to angels and demons," he says, "the Church is definite in her teaching. She declares that both exist . . . ." And he adds: "Since these matters of the spiritual world lie outside the scope of natural knowledge, it is hard to see how genuine opposition can arise."

It seems to me all too easy to see how opposition has arisen and why it continues to arise. The human mind is a very complex affair whose immediate causes of behavior are largely hidden in the cortex of the brain and in the caverns of the subconscious. Little was known until recent times about the psychology of insanity, and if a person started "speaking with tongues" or acting in a manner completely out of character, it was natural enough to suppose that his body was "possessed" by some alien spirit. This view was accepted in the New Testament and elevated by the sanctions of the church to incontestable truth. The mercilessly unambiguous command of Exodus, "Thou shalt not suffer a witch to live," did its widespread and murderous work. With the coming of the theory and practice of depth psychology, the causes of these aberrations are becoming increasingly known. And those causes, whether psychical or physical, are of course taken as belonging to the natural order. The man who wants to wash his hands incessantly, the man who is convinced that he has committed the unpardonable sin, the kleptomaniac, the arsonist, the man who thinks he is Napoleon or the Deity—these are people who are mentally ill; and if some physician of the mind were to diagnose them as possessed by a demon or in league with the devil, his colleagues would think him more fitted to be a patient himself than one entrusted with the care of patients. Yet numberless pitiable women have been sent to the most cruel of deaths on just such diagnoses. Is there a conflict here between the church and science or not? The church says of a certain woman that she is possessed of a devil, and quite possibly she thinks so herself. The psychoanalyst who studies her case finds, say, that she had rigid and dominant parents who taught her that impulses of a certain kind, not improbably sexual, were wicked. She fell in love with a certain man, felt these impulses toward him, repressed them firmly as evil, and lost him to a rival. She now hates the rival, hates herself for this hatred, hates her parents though still trying to love them, and finds herself festering with wickedness. Feeling herself abandoned, she decides that she may as well be really abandoned. Here the two disciplines of demonology and psychoanalysis give incompatible explanations for the same mental state. I do not think one can disprove that demons have been active, nor do I think that any psychological analysis is likely to explain the facts completely. I would simply ask which explanation in the light of present knowledge is nearer the truth, and leave the answer to the reader.

The "Notes" of the Church

In beginning his discussion of my fourth chapter Father Owens points out a difference of interpretation between us as to the way in which the church uses these notes. Four of them are usually mentioned: the unity of the church, its sanctity, its universality, its apostolicity; and they are sometimes included in a longer list of "motives of credibility." These form a set of alleged facts about the nature and history of the church which are so extraordinary as to compel the assent of any rational and open mind to the unique position of the church as founded and guided by revelation. This I said, relying on Leo XIII's declaration in *Aeterni Patris:* "Reason declares that from the very outset the Gospel teaching was rendered conspicuous by signs and wonders which gave, as it were, definite proof of a definite truth." Father Owens tells me, however, that my interpretation is incorrect. These considerations are not sufficient to prove to *reason* the claim of the church; they are seen to be sufficient only by the person who has received the gift and insight of faith.

Now if Father Owens says this, I concede the point at once; he knows the church's position far better than I do. From the point of view of the non-Catholic, however, it places the church in a curious position. It reminds me of a story which I hope will not be unacceptable to Father Owens's sense of humor. A lady passenger was crossing the Atlantic by ship when a violent storm arose. She made an unsteady way to the Captain, and said, "Captain, would you tell us plainly what our situation is?" "Madam," he replied, "we are in God's hands." "Oh," she said in dismay, "has it come to that?" I raised the question whether the "notes" of the church prove the church's claim. As to that, replies Father Owens, we are in God's hands. It is true that reason cannot see it. But if heaven gives us the gift of faith, we somehow can. To the mere rationalist, that does not have the most reassuring ring.

Nevertheless there are many Catholics who do turn to these notes when under intellectual pressure, and do think that they give powerful rational support to the claim of the church to be the chosen channel of intercourse between God and man. It will therefore be worthwhile to examine briefly Father Owens's replies to my strictures. The unity of the church commonly means its unity through time, the changelessness of the deposit of faith which the church is given to guard. In *Reason and Belief* I argued that this changelessness is a belief without foundation. The historian has no difficulty in adducing cases in which, even in official pronouncements on faith, one Pope has contradicted another. Furthermore, the church has added many dogmas and discarded many.

Pope Innocent I denounced the doctrines of the distinguished theologian Pelagius as contrary to the faith, and excommunicated his followers. Within a year Innocent died and was succeeded by Pope Zosimus, who almost immediately declared the teaching of Pelagius to be orthodox. Such reversals of official doctrine I should have thought absolutely fatal to the alleged "unity" of church teaching, but Father Owens dismisses them as "a matter of housekeeping from year to year, decade to decade, century to century." They "nowhere involve anything like a definitive and formal declaration of an article of faith for all time." I should have thought a formal denunciation of Pelagianism as heretical and a formal acceptance of it as orthodox were both cases where the church's highest authority had committed itself definitely on a matter of faith. If these are mere matters of "housekeeping," where does housekeeping stop and responsible teaching begin? Again, we are told that the doctrines here involved "exercise no particular influence on the religious life of a Catholic today, but are brought back to notice only through historians." But when one is considering the enduring identity of church teaching, the question is surely whether a dogma is still a required belief, not whether it retains a practical influence. And who but historians are in a position to know whether the church has preserved its unity through history or not?

Father Owens's main defense of that unity, however, is the one adopted by Newman. Both in his Anglican and in his Catholic days Newman was searching to find evidence in early Christian writers of such doctrines as purgatory, the immaculate conception of the Virgin, and papal infallibility. He could not find them there. So in order to save the theory of identity in church teaching, he devised an ingenious theory of development which held that a doctrine was itself present if it was present in potency. The beliefs in purgatory, in the sinlessness of Mary, in the infallibility of Peter, were not accepted in the early church, but their seeds were present; and just as the oak is in some sense present in the acorn, so these beliefs were potentially present in many psychical seedlings scattered among the phrases of both Testaments and the writings of the Fathers. Now the identity, or at least continuity, of acorn and oak may be granted. But when applied to doctrines or beliefs the analogy breaks down. The Roman, the Anglican, and the Eastern Orthodox creeds are all developments from the same primitive seed, and therefore somehow present in it. But while the church of Rome accepts Papal infallibility, the other two branches deny it; hence infallibility and its opposite are both present in the primitive seed. But could not seed so ambiguous in its promise as this produce anything one desired? Indeed, given the theory of development, it would be a diverting and perhaps not very difficult exercise to find among the metaphors and crypticisms of the Pauline epistles, the book of Revelations, and the treatises of Tertullian and Origen whole necklaces of double helixes presaging Eutychianism and Nestorianism, Sabellianism and Erastianism, Mr. Muggleton and Mrs. Eddy. A theory that must be strained to the breaking point to support orthodoxy and may be used with ease to support heterodoxy is no very stout pillar for the unity of the church.

In dealing with the note of "sanctity," I expressed an admiration deep and sincere for the great saints of the church, for its Francises, its Xaviers, and its Damiens. But I contended (1) that morality can reach its full flowering without aid from theological belief, and (2) that the morality taught by the church has itself serious flaws.

(1) What I meant by the first contention is that morality consists of the attempt to produce certain values, and that the appreciation and pursuit of these values does not depend on theological beliefs of any kind. The perception of this independence is a matter of logical insight; for example, goodness cannot *consist* in obeying the will of God, for God is himself described as good, and *his* goodness cannot be obedience to his own will. For then if he willed pestilence and slaughter we should have to call this conduct good, and we can see that it would not be. Further, we know that many persons who have ranked high in the scale of goodness—Hume and Sidgwick, for example—lived outside the Christian fold.

Father Owens's reply is something of a surprise to me. By "sanctity" he does not mean any goodness that could be achieved by the natural man, but "holiness," which can come only through an infusion of grace. What, then, becomes of the goodness of the just named unbelievers? He answers, even more surprisingly, that this too is the work of God. "The good in any human act is caused by God, and God has set but one destiny, the supernatural, for all human activity." This seems to me a position that is irrefutable but carries no conviction. To say that David Hume, who by the testimony of those who knew him was an exceptionally good man, was really achieving a "holiness" due to the descent into him of a divine grace of which he was unaware, and that this holiness was directed to a supernatural destiny in which he disbelieved, is to make of this good man a sort of jasper meteorite lodged in the tainted clay of human nature. He was endowed with grace, though this must have been divorced from faith, for of faith he had none. And that the Deity should have passed over so many who did have faith in order to confer upon this unbeliever a holiness exceeding theirs seems merely another example of that injustice of which morality is full when once it leaves the solid ground of rational ethics.

(2) To the criticism offered of the church's ideal of morality, Father Owens is content in reply virtually to repeat the Catholic position. To me a right is the obverse side of a duty, so that if it is our duty to treat animals humanely, it is their right to be so treated. Father Owens would agree that it is *kalon,* translated fairly enough as right and seemly, to do so, but he repeats his church's attitude: "The Catholic concludes that rights belong exclusively to intelligent nature, which is not present in lower animals." "He explains his respect for human life in terms of divine dominion over it. . . ." But does man, in virtue of his "intelligent nature," have rights against the Deity? I doubt whether Father Owens recognizes any such rights. For when I instanced among other examples of apparent divine cruelty God's order to slay the Amalekites, man, woman, and child, he answered only with questions that seemed not to recognize these as cruelties at all: "Are they meant to inculcate the dominion of God over human life? Are they meant to show that at times God will assert that dominion?" And he astonishes me by saying that it is hard to see how anyone advocating the privilege of abortion "has any cause to be shocked at assertion of sovereignty over human life." He accepts without demur his church's attitude on "the immorality of abortion, euthanasia, suicide, artificial contraception, divorce," and the essential superiority of the celibate to the noncelibate life. "Not without deep discernment were martyrdom and virginity sought for in patrons for churches from the age of Constantine on." So different a standard of morality is at work here that it would probably be unprofitable to argue these issues. Father Owens derives his judgments on them straight from his church, from which he accepts them on faith. My own judgments I derive, so far as I can, from the experienced values, both human and animal, that are involved in the case, and

I have tried to show in another book that this is the rational method in ethics. It is obvious that the two methods conflict. In *Reason and Belief* I have maintained with regard to both Catholicism and Protestantism that to follow a standard, religious or other, which conflicts with the rational is logically suicidal and morally wrong. In fairness to Father Owens I should point out that when he wrote, the argument of this book as a whole was not before him. But I do not think he would have been moved if it had been, since he is confident of his access to an authority that can brush aside natural reason as though it were a cobweb.

The note of universality, to turn now to this, claims that though Catholics have flourished in many cultures, the creed has maintained itself through all diversities, and that such convergence upon a single doctrine is further impressive testimony to its truth. What other faith can describe itself in the proud language of *quod semper, quod ubique, quod ab omnibus*? I answered: this would indeed be overwhelming if the testimony were freely given by minds not under constraint. If a thousand scholars were selected at random from all the nations of the earth with the single qualification that they be minds of high intelligence and objectivity, and if all agreed that the Catholic creed were true, the argument would be irresistible. But the actual case is extremely different. Only those votes are counted that are cast by persons already in the fold; anyone who dissents is heterodox and therefore excluded. The creed is thus universal by stipulation, not by free decision, which would indeed render an opposite verdict. Father Owens's reply is: "The ubiquitous appeal in spite of strict and often difficult requirements of orthodoxy renders this universality all the more notable." In the light of my reply, the terms "ubiquitous" and "universality" do not seem warranted.

As regards apostolicity, I pointed out that the strength of the chain transmitting authority from the founder of the church to Saint Peter and thence continuously to all successive bishops of Rome is only as strong as its weakest link; and that this seems to be the first link of all. If the validity of the bestowal on Peter of the keys is made to rest on evidence—the evidence of Matthew 16, the evidence of the strange silence about this event of all the other Gospels, the evidence of the apostles, of the Fathers, of the early councils—the probability that Jesus ever spoke the decisive words or that Peter ever held the primacy assigned to him is disconcertingly low. And the notion that Jesus was intending to found a permanent hierarchy to carry the Gospel down the centuries and throughout the world is plainly out of accord with his reiterated belief that the world was coming to an end in his own generation. Father Owens reads of these difficulties and is unperturbed. He is ready to admit that for a mere philosopher or a mere historian there may be no way through or over them; but as for himself, he is reluctant to go into them and he hurries over them in what I sense as a somewhat impatient weariness. At any rate such weariness would, from his own point of view, be natural enough. Why should he bog himself down in these historical doubts and inconsistencies when he knows that they are all resoluble and cannot affect the conclusion? He knows this not by the sort of subtle but fallible deduction that Sherlock Holmes or Lord Peter Wimsey would bring to bear. They might, to be sure, fill in a few small gaps. "But the overall consideration in regard to the marks of the Church remains the same. The starting point for the Catholic in matters of faith is the present-day teaching of the Church. Within that doctrine he *believes* that the Church is one, holy, catholic and apostolic." In the light of this sweeping guarantee of how the inquiry must come out, the step-by-step process of inquiry seems a work of supererogation.

Napoleon is said to have come upon a fort in his Egyptian campaign that he wanted to remove from his path. He ordered his batteries to open up upon it, but after a time ordered them to desist. The cannon balls were burying themselves harmlessly in the thick earthen walls, and he was wasting his ammunition. I feel a somewhat similar frustration. I open up upon Catholicism with what seem to me annihilating batteries of logic, history, and textual criticism. When I am through the fortification ought to be a pile of rubble. But what do I see but Father Owens's cheerful countenance smiling at me from atop the pile. As I approach he extends a hand and thanks me for the expertness of aim and the general efficiency of the attack. "This" I say, "is as delightful as it is unexpected, but do you realize what I have done to your dogma?" "Oh, that," he replies; "I have no worry about that." "But surely—" "You see I have my secret weapon. It is a weapon you haven't discovered, which makes my position impregnable to every kind of intellectual weaponry, however advanced." And since I must confess that I do not understand nor can imagine what this really is, I can only shake my head as I shake his hand and return a smile that is less inscrutable than his own.

30 THE RATIONALIST AND THE REFORMER: A CRITIQUE OF BLANSHARD'S VIEWS OF PROTESTANTISM
Jerry A. Irish

BRAND Blanshard's appraisal of Protestantism appears in four chapters of his latest volume, *Reason and Belief (RB)*. Joining *Reason and Analysis* and *Reason and Goodness,* this work completes his sketch of the "office of reason" in the theory of knowledge, ethics, and religion.

What is the office of reason in Protestantism? To answer that question, Blanshard turns to the Lutheran tradition as represented by Martin Luther, Søren Kierkegaard, Emil Brunner, and Karl Barth. He is sensitive to the possible accusation that he has been narrow and arbitrary in choosing just one among the many strands that constitute Protestant religious thought. Certainly he cannot be faulted for choosing one tradition, but there is little justification for treating only those representatives most vulnerable to his rationalist attack. Blanshard mentions Rudolf Bultmann, Reinhold Niebuhr, and Paul Tillich as proponents of Luther's teachings. Instead of including one of them in the sample, he selects both Brunner and Barth, of whom he writes: "To many laymen they are all but indistinguishable, a pair of theological twins," the Tweedledum and Tweedledee of neo-orthodoxy. (*RB,* 249).

Blanshard's selection reveals his real intention in the chapters on Protestantism. He is carrying out a task announced in *Reason and Analysis (RA,* 26), namely, the examination of criticisms leveled at reason in theology. This is, indeed, a narrow view of the office of reason in Protestantism, but it is instructive nonetheless.

Blanshard identifies his basic themes in the chapter on Luther. Since the three succeeding chapters present variations on those themes, I have chosen to concentrate on the rationalist's estimate of the reformer. Following a review of Blanshard's exposition and critique of Luther (I and II), I will offer an alternative interpretation (III and IV). Then his charges against Luther will be taken up in detail (V).

1. Blanshard's Luther

The single-minded defense of reason that determines Blanshard's selection among Lutheran theologians also guides his interpretation of Luther. What little attention is given to Luther's life and times is intended to underscore the irrational elements in his character rather than reveal the context of his theology. Blanshard states that Scripture, not experience, was the intellectual center of Luther's pre-Copernican world (*RB*, 122). This simple antithesis blinds him to important distinctions in the development of Luther's thought. Insofar as Blanshard exhibits his own interpretive aids, the dominant influences are Julius Köstlin (*The Theology of Luther*, 1897) and A.C. McGiffert (*Martin Luther: The Man and His Work*, 1911). As often as not, specific references to Luther's works are taken from secondary sources and topical collections. One senses that the reformer has been given a role to play in the rationalist's portrayal of reason and belief.

"What was there in Luther's thought that aroused in a succession of Popes the passionate desire to see him on a pile of faggots?" (*RB*, 124). Blanshard suggests two factors. The first is Luther's extraordinary character, deeply flawed, yet in such a way as to be extremely formidable. "He was intemperate, unreasonable, violent and unfair. But it is one of the tragic facts of history that rational causes are sometimes most effectively served by unreasonable agents" (*RB*, 126).

The second factor, of primary interest to Blanshard, is Luther's conception of reason and faith. Blanshard cites emotional antipathy to reason as well as the conviction that reason was unimportant, even dangerous, as two bases for Luther's numerous disparagements of it. Since for Luther reason was our guide in the realm of the flesh, a realm corrupted by the fall, its judgments were bound to be misleading when it entered the realm of the spirit. Blanshard probes these matters further, and his recurrent objections to Luther's theology begin to emerge.

Why did Luther impose such strict limits on reason? First, his intense religious experiences were of a nonrational sort. Luther was also a follower of Saint Paul, who had a keen dislike of rational pride and impiety. "Thirdly, and for us most significantly, Luther thought that between the structure of divine and human truth there was a fundamental difference, which made any bridging of the gap by human effort impossible" (*RB*, 132). Blanshard illustrates this gap in theology and ethics.

Quoting from Luther's commentary on Galatians, Blanshard exhibits Luther's view that the most important Christian doctrines, e.g. the resurrection of the dead, the virgin birth, and the effectiveness of the sacraments, were absurd if reason be our guide. The truth of a proposition in philosophy was no guarantee of its truth in theology. In fact, one might begin from a true theological premise and reason quite logically to a theologically false conclusion. Blanshard writes of Luther, "if he had adhered to this view in practice, his works would have been greatly reduced in bulk" (*RB*, 133).

The gap between the human and the divine also appeared in morals. Once again, reason was a blind guide, and not simply because God's judgment on our conduct was comprehensive. According to Blanshard, Luther was making the much more radical claim that "the very standards by which God judges conduct are different from ours" (*RB*, 134). Thus, what we would call good, God would call bad, and some of God's conduct would, in our eyes, be evil. In fact, Blanshard accuses Luther of teaching that "God is ultimately responsible for all the evil that has ever occurred" (ibid.). In permitting our fall, God gave rise to the ensuing corruption, then he admonished us to overcome this corruption, though God alone held the only key to our escape, a key he gave out with no apparent correspondence to what we did. Our reception of grace, like our sin, was determined. "Thus, so far as we can see, God's treatment of us has no relation to what we deserve" (*RB*, 136).

With what then, asks Blanshard, are we to replace the much disparaged reason? Faith, answers Luther. Blanshard presents a five-part distillation of Luther's understanding of faith.

1. "Faith is belief" (*RB*, 136). It is a kind of knowledge, cognitive in the sense that something is believed. Blanshard asserts that confidence and trust, attitudes associated with faith by most religiously minded persons, were not admitted by Luther into his idea of faith (*RB*, 137). Here Blanshard is simply mistaken. In "The Freedom of a Christian" Luther defined the second power of faith as follows: "It is a further function of faith that it honors him whom it trusts with the most reverent and highest regard since it considers him truthful and trustworthy."[1] The centrality of trust in Luther's understanding of faith is inescapable regardless of one's interpretation, and Blanshard's second point would seem to imply as much.

2. What Luther "steadfastly holds to be the core of faith is *the belief or awareness that we are forgiven*" (*RB*, 137). Blanshard notes that sometimes Luther put this assurance in terms of essential doctrines of belief, but at other times he denied that faith as knowledge understands anything. The certainty in the midst of this rational ambiguity was the "awareness that we have been delivered by him [Christ] from sin and its penalty. . . . a sure sense that we are saved already" (ibid.).

3. Faith as the awareness that we are forgiven is not anything we achieve or even grasp by ourselves. It is an act of God apprehended by his agency in us. "The assurance, as truly as what it assures us of, is supernatural . . ." (*RB*, 138).

4. Faith is not itself a human work nor is it granted as a response to such works. Given our fallen state, good works cannot escape self-seeking. Pride in our meritorious acts is counterproductive when it comes to faith.

5. Faith issues in good works. As a good tree brings forth good fruit, so will the justified sinner seek to do good works.

Having set forth what he takes to be Luther's understanding of reason and faith, Blanshard turns to Luther's view of Scripture. Here was the check against private judgment and personal self-righteousness in matters of Christian doctrine and practice. Over against the authority of the church Luther pitted the authority of the Bible, but within the Bible itself this authority was distributed unevenly. "The central message of Scripture was that of man's redemption through the cross, and the importance of the various parts could be measured by their relevance to this nuclear revelation" (*RB*, 142). On this basis, Romans and Galatians ranked high whereas the letter of James should have been left out entirely.

Blanshard points out that though Luther himself was a biblical scholar, he made the prime qualification for understanding the text not mastery of Greek and Hebrew but faith. This position presents two difficulties to Blanshard. First, it is circular to argue the significance of faith on the basis of Scripture that receives its own warrant via that very faith. Circularity is justified in such fundamental issues, provided it can be stated with sufficient clarity to commend itself to unbiased hearers. "And the trouble is that when Luther does so state his case it does *not* commend itself to the majority of his hearers" (*RB*, 144).

A second difficulty in Luther's view of Scripture is his treatment of obvious internal contradictions and errors of fact. Blanshard applauds Luther's having admitted these discrepancies, but finds his appeal to levels of inspiration arbitrary and inconclusive. "The Protestant appeal to the authority of Scripture ends in difficulties as insuperable as the Catholic appeal to the authority of the church" (*RB*, 147).

2. Blanshard's Assessment

Blanshard's interest in Luther is that of a "speculative inquirer who, aware of the historic influence of Luther's teaching, wishes to raise the one question whether it is true" (*RB*, 148). He finds three essential points in Luther's account of reason and faith: 1. "man has been vitiated by original sin"; 2. "reason is incompetent in the sphere of religious truth"; 3. "faith as distinct from works is the key to salvation" (*RB*, 150).

1. For Blanshard, the doctrine of original sin is false. Worse, in the context of Christianity it is a "moral outrage" (*RB*, 151). Understood as the biological transmissibility of sin, the doctrine is untrue on three grounds. It

has no basis in history; there was no garden of Eden, no Adam, no Eve, etc. It has no basis in the Bible; the closest thing to an explicit reference to the hereditary transmission of sin appears in a vague passage by Paul (Rom. 12:18–19). It has no basis in biology; sin, either as an activity or a propensity, is not a genetic characteristic.

The doctrine of original sin is morally indefensible on numerous grounds. It empties justice of all meaning by making one responsible and condemnable for the sin of another, who died centuries earlier in a distant land. In assessing the human situation as one of total corruption, it allows for no middle ground, no proportion between misdeed and consequence. Surely, argues Blanshard, one may "break an engagement for lunch without incurring the criminality of starting a world war . . ." (RB, 154). The doctrine ignores the involvement of individual wills in sin by condemning persons before they are able to choose for themselves "what is known to be worse over what is known to be better" (RB, 155). It does not allow an equally arguable case that moral goodness is also inherited. If original sin, why not original goodness? Furthermore, it is inconsistent to hold one guilty for an unavoidable act. Nor does the doctrine cohere with Christian teaching about God's love and forgiveness. On the contrary, it implies a God who neither stemmed the flood of evil at the outset nor responded to the variety of evil in the present.

2. Blanshard turns from the issue of original sin to the incompetence of reason in Luther's theology, particularly the notion that a proposition false in philosophy might be true in theology. If we are dealing with literally the "very same proposition" in both cases, the results are disastrous; ". . . if self-evidence itself is to be rejected as a witness to truth, what ground is there for supposing that our reason is reliable anywhere?" (RB, 160). Reality itself takes on the incoherence of a nightmare.

If Luther meant that, when speech common to the philosopher was used by the theologian it carried a different meaning, Blanshard finds little consolation. It leads to needless misunderstanding to assign two contradictory meanings to the same word. Furthermore, Blanshard sees this double-meaning notion, as he also sees Luther's more comprehensive two-realm theory, as an evasion of the genuine contradictions between reason and theology.

Another difficulty with Luther's disparagement of reason in the realm of faith was his own inability to abide by the warning. While pushing reason away contemptuously with one hand, he was using it deftly with the other (RB, 164). Acting in opposition to his own theory led Luther into a host of internal inconsistencies, which Blanshard demonstrates by taking quotations out of a variety of contexts. Though somewhat puzzled that Luther, "not a stupid man," should have been aware of contradiction and yet not have sought to resolve it rationally, Blanshard ascribes the reformer's attack on reason to the incoherence of a person "too impatient and impulsive to be a good philosopher" (*RB,* 166).

3. Finally, Blanshard aims his critique at Luther's understanding of justification by faith. "Our question is whether his teaching on faith, regardless of its source, and regardless too of its vast historical influence, is acceptable today" (*RB,* 167). Blanshard first objects that Luther set the whole process of human salvation out of the natural world. Thus persons become pawns of the supernatural in the very enactment of their own destinies. The moral and spiritual faculties of selfhood were replaced rather than refined by such a process of salvation. Taken seriously, this view operates as a moral depressant. If our own good works of affection and kindness are as sin before God, why bother? We cannot even point to good works as a sign of our salvation because they could arise from sources other than faith. Moreover, to make the focus of salvation not our own works but the work of God in Christ becomes a moral depressant, shifting "the centre of gravity from conduct to belief" (*RB,* 170). There is a tendency here to stress what has already been done for us rather than what we ourselves must do.

Blanshard moves to a second line of criticism, arguing that Luther held belief, a form of thought, to be the effective component of faith. He makes no mention here of the "awareness that we are forgiven," which he acknowledges elsewhere as the core of faith for Luther. "To make belief the very core of a process that is also represented as supernatural and transcendent of human faculty is a paradox" (*RB,* 171). Blanshard finds Luther on both sides of the paradox, sometimes elevating the object of belief beyond human reason, at other times calling for belief in definite propositions. Taking the latter side of Luther's apparent inconsistency, belief as "knowledge of the heart," Blanshard asks whether the propositions thus held have stood up in the light of human experience. That Christ was crucified and suffered, there is little doubt, even among historians. That Christ was born of a virgin and rose bodily from the dead could not be disproven, though probability is overwhelmingly against such claims. However, one can clearly test the reliability of Luther's belief that Joshua (who commanded the sun to stand still), not Copernicus, was correct, that the devil was a power in the world, and that some women were witches. Or, if one prefers moral to scientific examples, what about Luther's belief that God allowed the hardening of Pharaoh's heart, that Abraham was ready to kill his son, that the Jews should be sent back to their own land, and that the Pope was antichrist? In all these cases, asserts Blanshard, Luther was simply mistaken. "Even fideists, if they are candid, can hardly avoid the conclusion that faith, as he conceived it, is no guarantee of truth" (*RB,* 176).

Probing deeper, Blanshard finds the roots of Luther's errors in a confusion of emotive and cognitive certainty. While both kinds of certainty have been associated with "knowledge of the heart," the emotive is primary; indeed, Luther's own intense religious emotions yielded the assurance of a patriot or a lover rather than the demonstrability of a mathematician or a physiologist. Blanshard sees two dubious assumptions at work in Luther's "knowledge of the heart." One is that feeling can know, in any meaningful sense of that word. The other is that a belief's satisfaction of a massive demand of feeling is evidence of the truth of that belief.

Blanshard's third and final challenge to the acceptability of Luther's understanding of justification by faith is that it "makes belief a moral act, and indeed the most important of all such acts, for our fate depends upon it" (*RB*, 179). But if the faith that makes belief possible is a gift of God, then how can we be punished by that God for not believing? Noting the implicit injustice of God and Luther's own irrationalism, Blanshard goes on to point out that belief is far less voluntary than Luther sometimes suggested. That is, belief is too dependent on one's own background to be treated, if it is in error, as a sin comparable to murder. Furthermore, Luther's view of belief strained intellectual integrity by appealing to different standards in realms that overlap. "It would be absurd for a scientist or historian to try to confirm a hypothesis by an appeal to the heart, but when his hypothesis conflicts with a statement in Scripture, the resort to feeling ceases to be an offence, and becomes a duty" (*RB*, 181). Luther's theology depreciated the love of truth that is characterized by respect for fact, relevance, and consistency.

In a concluding review of several of these issues, Blanshard maintains that the very facts of Luther's own experience as well as his inferences from fact were too largely determined by his theological preconceptions. Even consistency itself had no appeal in a theology that often maintained the truth of both sides of a contradiction. Such irrationalism assaults intellectual integrity. "Follow the argument, and faith protests that one is holding sacred things lightly. Follow faith, and reason protests that one is being intellectually dishonest" (*RB*, 184). The two sides are not evenly matched, for the abandonment of reason is not even a possibility. "It *is* possible for faith to adjust itself to reason. It is *not* possible for reason to adjust itself to faith, if this implies abandoning the canons implicit in any attempt to think, for then the power to assert or deny intelligibly, and therefore to say anything at all, is cut off at the root" (ibid.).

Blanshard makes some two dozen distinct criticisms of Luther's account of reason and faith. It would be far too simple to say that all fall under the rubric "faith versus reason." The rubric itself is misleading. In sum, there are two major charges: Luther's teaching fails to meet generally accepted criteria of rationality and generally accepted standards of morality.

3. The Awareness of Divine Forgiveness

Faced with what Blanshard takes to be the manifold uses and abuses of reason in Luther's theology, one cannot help but wonder if there is some underlying structure or organizing theme that makes sense out of the confusion, or, failing in that, at least reveals some points of order in the midst of chaos. Since Blanshard identified such an interpretive principle in the "awareness that we are forgiven," we should test how it might provide an alternative interpretation of Luther.

Anyone who has experienced genuine forgiveness in interpersonal relations can begin to imagine the impact of such an event between Luther and his God. First we become aware of the fact that we have wronged someone who means a great deal to us. Then we do whatever we can to make up for that wrong. We go out of our way with gifts and courtesies meant to undo or repair the harm we have done. During this process we may be offered forgiveness, but we are in no position to accept it so long as we intend to earn it by our own deeds. Should the other party sense our self-seeking attitude, the hurt may be increased.

Then there comes a time when we realize there is nothing we can do to rectify the situation. The deed that wronged another is irrevocable, and the relationship can be restored only by the other party's magnanimity. If the other does not really face the wrong that has been done, the forgiveness is likely to be shallow. It is also possible that in our inability to alter the situation by ourselves, we find the other's forgiveness repugnant. In any case, only when we realize that the situation is beyond our control are we able to receive forgiveness.

Forgiveness genuinely offered must be truly accepted. Acceptance involves forfeiting all efforts at earning forgiveness. It also involves interpreting the other party's actions as honest manifestations of the new relationship. The process here described usually culminates in an event or gesture that embodies the forgiveness and its acceptance. This embodiment may come to stand for the new stage of the relationship. Unconditional forgiveness calls on and exhibits the deepest human resources of rationality and good will. In fact, from outside the relation the process appears to break the bounds of common sense and social practice.

All the elements described here were present in Luther's struggle with God. He entered an Augustinian monastery under a vow he claims to have made when a bolt of lightning put him in desperate fear for his life. In any event, he worked hard at being an obedient monk, reportedly out-confessing, out-praying, and out-meditating all his brothers. Why?

Young Luther shared the religious world view of the conservative German peasantry in which he was reared. Even in his university training, the entire environment confronted him with God's power and the church's access to that power. This highly sensitive human being's spirit knew flights of exaltation equaled in intensity only by fits of depression. We do not need Luther's moment of fear in the face of death to understand why he entered a monastery. In that time and place there was no better way, no more certain procedure, for making one's peace with God.

But Luther's meticulous fulfillment of the daily monastic routine gradually heightened rather than diminished his sense of alienation from God. When he became a priest, he was regularly confronted with God's presence in the Mass. How could he, a mere creature, stand before such holiness? In the absence of a satisfying answer, Luther panicked. As an unfaithful lover today might resort to candy and flowers, Luther resorted to fasting and prayer. Chastity, poverty, obedience, mortification of the flesh, discipline of the mind, Luther did it all—beyond the expectations of his elders, but not to the satisfaction of his God.

Luther took advantage of all the church's various means of aiding the struggling sinner. A trip to Rome enabled him to make the rounds of shrines and basilicas and see innumerable holy relics. Routinely in the monastery, and according to the church's comprehensive sacramental system, Luther focused his piety on penance. He confessed daily and sometimes at great length. Yet no matter how long or deeply he probed his memory, he would later remember a sin left unconfessed. And what about the sins of which he was not even aware? Perhaps it was during this period that Luther began to sense that the penitential system with its focus on particular sins merely dealt with the symptoms of a disease it could not cure. He tried mystical alternatives, occasionally reaching an exalted state. But alienation always accompanied him.

At the point of despair, there was nothing he or anyone else, including the church with all its sacraments and saints, could do to merit God's favor. Like a person seeking human forgiveness, he acknowledged his utter dependence upon the offended one for the peace of his soul. In such a state, what was one to make of God's justice anyway? The proffered mercy seemed only to heighten the wrath.

> Admittedly, it gives the greatest possible offense to common sense or natural reason that God by his own sheer will should abandon, harden, and damn men as if he enjoyed the sins and the vast eternal torments of his wretched creatures, when he is preached as a God of such great mercy and goodness, etc. It has been regarded as unjust, as cruel, as intolerable, to entertain such an idea about God, and this is what has offended so many great men during so many centuries. And who would not be offended? I myself was offended more than once, and brought to the very depth and abyss of despair, so that I wished I had never been created a man. . . . [*Luther's Works* (*LW*), 33:190]

At this extreme point in his vain attempt to save his own soul Luther was told to prepare himself to take over the chair of Bible at the University of Wittenberg. From 1513 through 1518 he lectured on the Psalms, Romans, Galatians, and Hebrews. This teaching and study brought about a sharp turn in his life.

He makes several references to this period in his *Table Talk*. The important points for our purposes can be summarized as follows:

1. Luther had despaired of success in the struggle to justify himself before God. The very words "righteous" and "righteousness of God" struck his conscience like lightning. "If God is righteous, he must punish" (*LW*, 54:193). Elsewhere in the *Table Talk* Luther speaks of his terror and hostility at the words in the Psalms: "In your righteousness, free me!"[2] In another passage he relates that he had been astray for a long time, not knowing what he was about (*LW*, 54:442).

2. But then, Luther tells us, "by God's grace" he "came to the conclusion" that the very words that had terrified him meant "if we, as righteous men, ought to live from faith and if the righteousness of God should contribute to the salvation of all who believe, then salvation won't be our merit but God's mercy." Luther asserts that this meaning was "unveiled" to him by the "Holy Spirit" (*LW*, 54:193–94).

3. With this new understanding, the terrifying words "became more pleasing" to Luther and his "spirit was thereby cheered" (ibid.). He speaks of the righteousness of God as a beautiful and pleasant word.[3]

In these accounts from Luther's *Table Talk,* the analogy with interpersonal forgiveness is completed. Despairing of self-justification to the point of anger at the One who offers forgiveness, Luther came to the recognition that God's mercy renews the relationship freely and unconditionally. The depth of this recognition, the profundity of this awareness, was the experience of justification by faith. With the acceptance of God's forgiveness, one is liberated from the fruitless self-seeking of worthiness to be forgiven.

In Luther's case, even the recognition of unconditional forgiveness came as a gift, a revelation of the Holy Spirit. This understandably strikes the rationalist as the height of irrationality, to say that one has to have faith in order to be justified before God, but that faith is itself given by God. And yet here, if nowhere else, Luther was utterly consistent. If the experience of forgiveness is dependent upon a rational inference, it is not unconditional.

What generates confusion is Luther's attempt to articulate all the elements in the experience. He has become aware of unconditional divine forgiveness. But, like the forgiven one in our analogy, he also accepts that forgiveness. From this perspective one can say the forgiveness is incomplete until it is accepted. "For if God promises and there is no one who believes

Him when He promises, then surely there will also be no promise of God and no fulfillment, for it has been promised to no one, since no one has received it. Therefore faith ratifies the promise, and the promise demands faith in him to whom it is made" (*LW*, 25:40). Luther was simultaneously aware of God's unmerited grace and the necessity of his own response to that grace.

Further confounding the modern rationalist, Luther understood his experience of justification by faith in terms of God's revelation in Christ. The awareness of forgiveness did not take place in a vacuum. Luther was an Augustinian monk and biblical scholar regularly celebrating the Mass and studying the Scripture. Concentration on Christ and him crucified provided the context for Luther's experience of justification by faith, and it became the content of faith, the organizing principle whereby Luther sought to articulate an experience that exceeded the limits of rational discourse. Analogous to the embodiment of interpersonal forgiveness, the Mass becomes the embodiment or the gesture of divine forgiveness, the very presence of Christ.

As soon as Luther articulates his experience in terms of Christ he becomes vulnerable to rationalist attack. He seems to contradict his claim that justification is gracious by tying it to a particular belief. He underlines this connection and magnifies its implications by generalizing from his own experience and criticizing those who do not share it. As if this were not enough, he goes on to make claims about Christ that are unacceptable today on scientific and historical grounds. Understanding the roots of these vulnerabilities, we may be better equipped to sort them out and evaluate their significance.

4. Two Kingdoms

Justification by faith might be summarized as the simultaneous awareness and acceptance of God's unconditional forgiveness understood in terms of Christ. Thus, faith can be described alternately as a gift, a response, and a belief. Before returning to Blanshard's criticisms, we should see how some of Luther's apparent inconsistencies emerge in relation to his experience of justification by faith.

Luther came to identify his own despair before the awesome power of God with Christ's abandonment on the cross. "My God, my God, why hast thou forsaken me?" These words recorded in Psalm 22 as well as the New Testament passion narratives made sense to Luther. He found in Christ his own suffering and rejection by God. But this identification broke down, because Luther was a sinner, one whose desperation was due to his own weakness and impurity. This could be true for Christ only if he had identified with the sin of mankind to the extent that he suffered the very estrangement and alienation from God that dogged Luther. This is precisely what Luther came to believe. The identification was one in which Christ took on the estrangement of the sinner while the sinner took on Christ's righteousness. Luther writes to a fellow monk:

> ... my dear Friar, learn Christ and him crucified. Learn to praise him, and despairing of yourself, say, "Lord Jesus, you are my righteousness, just as I am your sin. You have taken upon yourself what is mine and have given to me what is yours. You have taken upon yourself what you were not and have given to me what I was not." Beware of aspiring to such purity that you will not wish to be looked upon as a sinner, or to be one. For Christ dwells only in sinners. [*LW*, 48:12–13]

Note the dualities here. The justified sinner remains a sinner; the compassionate Christ remains a righteous Lord. This makes sense on our model of human forgiveness. The one who forgives does not right the wrong that has been done or forget that it has occurred. The effect on the forgiven is twofold: gratitude for the possibility of a new relationship; heightened sensitivity to the wrong that has been done.

Similarly, as Luther describes justification by faith, sin is forgiven, not annulled. In the wake of divine forgiveness Luther was more aware than ever of his own presumptuousness and self-righteousness. Wilhelm Pauck writes: "Luther could not help viewing man, i.e. the Christian man, as simultaneously sinful and righteous, a sinner in fact and a righteous man in hope, i.e. as a repentant sinner or as a forgiven sinner."[4]

In moving out from Luther's experience of divine forgiveness, we see the growing importance of the content of faith for theological exposition. The experience of identification with the abandoned Christ places Luther under the covering of Christ's righteousness. "Is it not that they [saints] know that there is sin in them but that for the sake of Christ it is covered and is not imputed to them, so that they may declare that all their good is outside of them, in Christ, who yet through faith is also in them?" (*LW*, 25:267). The rationalist who begins to dissect Luther at this point is bound to be baffled. If the effort to understand Luther's theology does not begin with his experience of justification by faith, it will surely find absurdity in his doctrines of Christian belief.

Luther's awareness of divine forgiveness issued in a new understanding of the God he had been desperately trying to please. Once again, we find a duality. God is still awesome and holy. God alone is righteous. But the consuming fire that before his experience of forgiveness terrified Luther afterward becomes purging fire that leads to healing. The life of the justified sinner is a life of judgment *and* mercy, wrath *and* love.

But how does one understand the relation between the divine justice before which humanity stands condemned and the divine mercy by which men and women are forgiven? Does the former melt into the latter, becoming a form of leniency? And if so, what is one to make of that divine righteousness to which Scripture continually refers and before which Luther struggled so desperately? The Apostle Paul seemed to be facing this problem in Romans. In the "Preface" to his Latin writings, Luther recalls his own efforts to understand Paul on this point. The despair, revelation, and liberation we noted in the *Table Talk* accounts are present here in the context of a theological exposition. Reason tries to articulate what, for Luther, is finally beyond its grasp.

> At last, by the mercy of God, meditating day and night, I gave heed to the context of the words, namely, "In it the righteousness of God is revealed, as it is written, 'He who through faith is righteous shall live.' " There I began to understand that the righteousness of God is that by which the righteous lives by a gift of God, namely by faith. And this is the meaning: the righteousness of God is revealed by the gospel, namely, the passive righteousness with which merciful God justifies us by faith, as it is written, "He who through faith is righteous shall live." Here I felt that I was altogether born again and had entered paradise itself through open gates. There a totally other face of the entire Scripture showed itself to me. [*LW*, 34:337]

In this description of Luther's experience of justification by faith, one looks in vain for a resolution to the theological duality of God's judgment and mercy. While reason is operative before and after the experience, it is not the controlling factor in the experience itself. The move from despair to liberation is not the move of a logician. Nor is there a rational resolution of the simultaneous experience of God's wrath and love. Flood and famine, disease and oppression, remain. Innocent children continue to die; corrupt priests and princes continue to flourish. Certainly Luther's own life does not become any less tumultuous. Yet he felt as though he was "altogether born again."

The dualities we have noted can best be summarized in Luther's doctrine of two kingdoms. "For God has established two kinds of government among men. The one is spiritual; it has no sword, but it has the word, by means of which men are to become good and righteous. . . . He administers this righteousness through the word. . . . The other kind is worldly government. . . . He administers this righteousness through the sword" (*LW*, 46:99). What is here given "political" expression has its roots in the experience of justification by faith, the experience of living in a sinful world in the presence of a forgiving God. Luther's dualities manifest a fundamental distinction between nature and grace. That distinction is soteriological before it is epistemological; it has to do with how God saves before it has to do with how God is known. This is why it is necessary to take Luther's own personal experience seriously if we are to understand his theology.

The doctrine of two kingdoms represents a distinction, not a separation. Luther's Christian lives at once in the realm of nature and the realm of grace.

Flesh and spirit, for example, represent two orientations of the whole person rather than a dichotomy between body and soul. "... one and the same man is spiritual and carnal, righteous and a sinner, good and evil" (*LW*, 25:332). "... we must note that the apostle does not wish to be understood as saying that the flesh and spirit are two separate entities, as it were, but one whole ..." (ibid., 339). The person who has experienced God's forgiveness lives in the dynamic tension of these two orientations.

B. A. Gerrish writes that Luther thought of the two kingdoms as two dimensions of existence. "At one and the same time, the Christian faces towards God in the Heavenly Kingdom, and towards his neighbour in the Earthly Kingdom."[5] Grace, faith, and spiritual righteousness belong to the former kingdom; law, works, and civil righteousness belong to the latter.

These two dimensions come into focus with the Christian's awareness of divine forgiveness. So it is that Gordon Rupp can use the phrase "coram Deo" as a polestar in his interpretation of Luther's theology. Revelation shows one: "... to be 'coram Deo' a sinner, unrighteous in all his acts, under condemnation. A man can only face this truth about himself in the presence of another righteousness, which God has given to men in Jesus Christ, and which men can never deserve or achieve, but which can only be accepted."[6]

5. The Charges

Blanshard makes two fundamental accusations: (A) that Luther's teaching fails to meet generally accepted criteria of rationality; and (B) that Luther's teaching fails to meet generally accepted standards of morality. There are a number of specifications under each of these indictments.

A1. Luther disparaged reason while simultaneously making use of it himself. Blanshard is understandably distressed at blasphemy compounded by inconsistency. And yet he makes very little effort to get beneath the surface to see if there was some basis for Luther's ambivalence.

Luther himself made critical use of reason. He was involved in the epistemological debates between the realists and the nominalists, he was responsible for progressive curricular reform at the University of Wittenberg, and he was an advocate and practitioner of humanist scholarship. In his introduction to Luther's lectures on Romans, Pauck says of the reformer: "In these lectures, the "modernist" orientation of his mind is most apparent in his general view of God and the world, in his psychological conceptions, and especially in his interest in the proper understanding of terms and words, and in the interpretation of them according to their etymological meaning" (Pauck, p. li).

Luther openly praised reason as that which distinguishes mankind from the beasts. Reason was the "inventor and mentor of all the arts, medicines, laws, and of whatever wisdom, power, virtue, and glory men possess in this life" (*LW,* 34:137). Reason was among those sound natural endowments whereby we are able to build houses, hold government office, and steer ships (*LW,* 26:174). These references could be extended, but the point has been made. Luther's disparagement of reason was only half the story.

Luther distinguished between reason and its use. Reasoning, as a function of the mind, was uniformly good in Luther's view. The ability to make inferences, to distinguish, and to define was something to be exercised through training in logic, grammar, and dialectic. As Blanshard observes, Luther himself was heavily dependent upon reason as the organ or instrument of communication and argument.

But reason as a capacity or tool can be put to a variety of uses, and there the distinction between two kingdoms is crucial. Did Luther hold that reason could only be employed in the natural or earthly realm? No. This is what puzzles Blanshard. Luther used reason in the service of a theology intended to give expression to the experience of justification by faith. Reason so employed was the servant of revelation. Such regenerate or illumined reason was, contrary to Blanshard, quite competent in theology. How did it differ from reason used in the natural realm? It was free from all association with self-seeking. Here we are at the root of Luther's disparagement of reason.

Reason employed in the earthly realm of human affairs was properly self-seeking. To subdue the earth and have dominion over its creatures was for Luther the God-given task of natural reason. Reason went astray in taking its attitude of self-seeking, its sense of domination and success into the spiritual realm. When natural reason moved to theological matters without the benefit of revelation, it could not comprehend unconditional forgiveness because it presupposed that God's grace was not needed.

Luther's own experience is instructive here. As an Augustinian monk and biblical scholar he brought all his rational faculties to bear on the problem of his salvation. Yet it was finally in despair of his own faculties that he experienced divine forgiveness. Reason, autonomous in the realm of nature, could not make itself over into a servant in the spiritual realm.

In his study of these issues Gerrish concluded that Luther's disparagement of reason was fundamentally disparaging a legalism incompatible with the gospel (Gerrish, 84–99, 135–37). Under attack was not the capacity to reason, but the association of that capacity with a particular assumption, quite understandable on natural grounds, utterly mistaken on spiritual grounds. The assumption was that a just God had given the law, and those who kept the law would be saved. If a just God commanded, then one's worth before God must be in terms of obedience. Human reason and wisdom taught "if you want to live to God, you must observe the law" (*LW*, 26:156).

This alliance of reason and law opposed Luther's faith. "As soon as reason and the Law are joined, faith immediately loses its virginity. For nothing is more hostile to faith than the Law and reason; . . . the Gospel leads us above and beyond the light of the Law and reason into the darkness of faith, where the Law and reason have no business" (*LW*, 26: 113–14). In this alliance reason was employed in support of the law. Natural reason had general knowledge of God as creator and judge (ibid., 399). In keeping with its autonomy in the earthly kingdom, reason assumed this knowledge was complete and made the logical inference that creaturely merit came with obedience to the laws of the creator. Luther certainly saw the plausibility of this view. He had to meet its force in defending himself against the charge of antinomianism (ibid., 214–15).

But here reason was misguided, despite the naturalness of its position. It took humanity and humanity's rational capacity as its starting point and measure. In doing so it confused its own righteousness with God's. The legalists prescribed their own conditions for salvation. Thus, rational religion was works-religion.

In addition to making the case for legalism, reason tried to refute the opposition. If obedience to the law does not merit salvation, if justification has no regard for works, then why not ignore the law and do evil? Blanshard argues this line. Luther would respond that this position misunderstands the civil and theological purposes of the law. "God has ordained civic laws, indeed all laws, to restrain trangressions" (*LW*, 26:308). The need for such restraint reveals the wicked insanity of the world and suggests the theological purpose of the law, to reveal human sin and destroy the presumption of righteousness. ". . . the proper and absolute use of the Law is to terrify with lightning (as on Mt. Sinai), thunder, and the blare of the trumpet, with a thunderbolt to burn and crush that brute which is called the presumption of righteousness" (ibid., 310). This was certainly the effect of the law on Luther himself, driving him to that state of humility in which, having abandoned his own self-righteousness, he was able to hear the word of divine forgiveness. But such passive righteousness was an anomaly to the legalist armed with reason.

Reason, in alliance with the law, also misunderstood the office of Christ by assuming that he tells the sinner what to do to be saved. Reason could not grasp the gospel message that Christ does what is necessary for the sinner's justification. "The human heart neither understands nor believes that such a great prize as the Holy Spirit can be granted solely through hearing with faith; . . . Because such a great treasure is being offered freely, it is despised

(*LW*, 26:213). Reason, operating out of its own assumptions from the earthly kingdom, could not comprehend the unconditional forgiveness of God.

We can see that Luther approved of reason, understood formally as a capacity or instrument, in both the natural and the spiritual realms. In the former it operated with autonomy, in the latter as a servant of the Word, the gospel of Christ. Insofar as reason was understood in a material sense, in association with an attitude or opinion, it bore the stamp of the earthly kingdom and there alone did Luther welcome it. Precisely this orientation of natural reason prohibited its effectiveness in the spiritual realm.

> For grace has set before itself no other object than God toward which it is carried and toward which it is moving; it sees only Him, it seeks only Him, and it always moves toward Him, and all other things which it sees between itself and God it passes by as if it had not seen them and directs itself only toward God. . . . But nature set for itself no object but itself toward which it is borne and toward which it is directed; it sees, seeks, and works only toward itself in all matters, and it passes by all other things and even God Himself in the midst, as if it did not see them, and is directed only toward itself. [*LW*, 25:346]

Luther's disparagement of reason did not criticize reason per se but rather its alliance with egoistic legalism. On these grounds, his simultaneous disparagement and use of reason was not inconsistent, and half of the charge of irrationalism is undercut.

A2. Luther's work is internally inconsistent. This specification can only be sustained if the distinctions discussed under the first specification are understood and the inconsistencies remain. Turning to the examples Blanshard brings to support his charge that Luther's theology is "riddled with contradictions," we find a variety of statements, some from Luther, some from Köstlin, and some from Blanshard's own paraphrases (*RB*, 165).

Five of the nine examples refer in one way or another to the doctrine of predestination in Luther's theology. As with many teachings of predestination, the reformer's efforts to protect God's glory, omniscience, and immutability resulted in a singularly distasteful statement of the human situation. It is to Luther's credit that he concluded one of his discussions of predestination with this caveat: "Yet here I am issuing the warning that no man whose mind has not yet been purged should rush into these speculations, lest he fall into the abyss of horror and hopelessness, but first let him purge the eyes of his heart in his meditations on the wounds of Jesus Christ" (*LW*, 25:389).

In Luther's doctrine of predestination you have an extreme magnification of God's glory commensurate with the experience of his unconditional forgiveness. Couple it with observations about the earthly realm of human affairs, and you confound natural reason. But granting the distinctions Luther consistently employed, you do not have a self-contradiction.

" 'God is not able to deny His nature, that is, He is unable not to hate sin and sinners'; yet 'There is in God no wrath or disfavour; His heart and thoughts are nothing but pure love' " (*RB*, 165). Here Blanshard is quoting Köstlin who is in turn quoting Luther, but without citing the specific references. The second statement reflects Luther's unqualified trust in God's good will for his creation; the same will is righteously angered at distrust on the part of his creatures, thus the first statement. The combination of statements further represents the duality of divine wrath and mercy as apprehended by the believer, simultaneously sinner and saved.

"If a human court condemns a man for something done by his father, that is unjust; if God condemns a man for something done by his remotest ancestors, this is perfect justice" (*RB*, 165). Blanshard's first statement is an observation of natural reason holding true in the earthly realm. His second statement, if read literally, might be taken as a theological statement of trust in God's will, however strange that may appear to natural reason. Read with Blanshard's probable intention, it raises the issue of original sin, a topic discussed below.

"Christ was sinless, but as a man he was a sinner" (*RB*, 165). These are Blanshard's words, so the specific reference is unclear. However, the second statement probably refers to Christ's identification with human sin, his taking on or covering human sin with his own righteousness. In that case, the statements are consistent with one another, both being theological expressions of Luther's experience of justification by faith.

" 'Let no one hope to be saved through another's faith or work,' though our only hope of salvation is through the faith and work of Christ" (*RB*, 165). This combination of statements from Luther, if not very careful, is nevertheless consistent with the reformer's view that only the righteousness of Christ saves; "another's faith" refers to the order of creatures, "Christ" to the Savior. It is the failure of natural reason to comprehend the second statement that leads it to believe in such things as indulgences, thereby opening it to the admonition of the first statement.

In arguing that Blanshard's examples do not reveal internal inconsistency in Luther's theology, I am not suggesting that Luther was a systematic theologian whose work exhibits a seamless coherence. Luther's thought developed over the years, many of his writings were "occasional," and he lived in the midst of personal and social upheaval. Certainly one can find inconsistencies in his theology. But that does not justify the charge of irrationalism. On the whole, Luther's teachings are not self-contradictory. Which means we must look elsewhere for the real conflict between the rationalist and the reformer.

A3. Luther held that a proposition false in philosophy may be true in theology. This specification moves our discussion from reason to truth. Were Luther an irrationalist, he might bolt from a discussion of truth under the general topic of rationality and its criteria. However, given his respect for reason (critically employed) and the fact that his two-kingdom distinction is already before us, we need not be concerned.

In a disputation on the proposition "The Word was made flesh," Luther did say that the proposition in question is true in theology while it strikes the philosopher as impossible or absurd (*LW*, 38:239). Luther argued that two truths never contradict each other, but that the same proposition may be true in one discipline and not in another. The first assertion rests finally in God's dominion over both the earthly and the heavenly kingdoms; the second assertion acknowledges that categories and techniques differ as we move from one discipline to another. "Philosophy and theology differ from one another. Philosophy deals with matters that are understood by human reason. Theology deals with matters of belief, that is, matters which are apprehended by faith" (ibid., 262).

Blanshard responds that if "a proposition false in philosophy may be true in theology" refers to "the very same proposition," it is a disastrous teaching that "would make reason unreliable everywhere" (*RB*, 160). Though Blanshard's illustrations are somewhat confusing, he and Luther seem to be in agreement here.

Perhaps, suggests Blanshard, Luther meant that "when the theologian uses forms of speech common to the philosopher and himself, he means by them different things" (*RB*, 161). This interpretation is certainly closer to Luther's view that philosophy and theology are different disciplines with different categories and techniques, though one cannot be sure that Blanshard would grant that these disciplines also have different starting points. His dismissal of Luther's two-kingdom theory as a "well-meaning evasion" is not encouraging (*RB*, 162). Be that as it may, Blanshard argues that, although this second interpretation of Luther's position removes the necessity of a conflict, it leads to needless misunderstanding. If, for example, a theologian means by "eternal punishment" the loss of divine favor, and by "justice" accordance with an inscrutable divine will, he should use different words.

Certainly the difference between theological and philosophical usage can reach an inexcusable extreme. But Blanshard has not demonstrated such an extreme in Luther's case. In *Reason and Analysis* he has this to say about confusions of type or category:

> People think of God, perhaps, in terms of Professor Wisdom's allegory, as a world-gardener, and suppose that when they call him invisible and intangible they are using words of the same type as "immense" or "inert," whereas if they were to try these words with the word "mountain," they would see that

the types were different. With this they would presumably recognize that the beliefs were confusions, and be prepared to see them dissolve. Strangely enough, however, such beliefs have a way of persisting stubbornly, even after this difference of type is seen with all clearness. Nor is this due merely to the fact that they rest on so broad a base of desire. The fact is that the belief in God, whether warranted or not, is neither a meaningless belief nor involves of necessity any sort of type confusion. [*RA,* 349]

Assuming the same tolerance for Luther that he shows for the believer in Wisdom's garden, Blanshard must grant, at least for purposes of discussion, that something meaningful might be at stake in such a proposition as "The Word was made flesh." One cannot imagine Luther's being prepared to see this belief dissolve, and he has self-consciously acknowledged difference of type in his theory of two realms.

Blanshard argues that the "double sense" under discussion here and the "architecture of two realms" underlying it are evasive efforts to save consistency and by-pass reason in the drive for reformation (*RB,* 161–62). Luther's impatience for reform is a dubious historical judgment that need not detain us here. But "to save consistency" is a cause that will reveal fundamental differences between the rationalist and the reformer.

Blanshard inverts Luther's priorities when he assumes that the two-realm theory is an evasion to save consistency or avoid incoherence. As was pointed out above, Luther's respect for rationality put a high premium on consistency and coherence, but not so high that he could not live with contradictory experiences beyond reason's powers of resolution. The point to clarify is where the real contradiction lies in Luther's theology. Blanshard does not further that effort when he states that Luther, "faced by a contradiction between his experience and his theology, elects to commit himself to both and let the pieces fall where they may" (*RB,* 163). It is a more accurate statement of the problem to say that Luther, faced with contradictory experiences, developed a theology that acknowledges these contradictions to be beyond rational resolution.

The central contradiction in Luther is the simultaneous awareness of a world in which evil is pervasive and an all-powerful God's unconditional forgiveness and mercy. Instead of resolving this contradiction, Luther's theology seeks to articulate it. The result is teaching laden with dualities, all finally made understandable, though not necessarily true, in terms of a theory of two realms. Blanshard, in equally understandable allegiance to his rational ideal, calls the dualities inconsistent and treats the two-realm theory as an evasion of contradiction.

We have tried to come at this problem from Luther's perspective; it may now be fruitful to approach it from Blanshard's own coherence theory. ". . . the coherence of judgments within a system is our test, and our only test, of any truth or fact whatever" (*The Nature of Thought* [*NT*], 2:215). Not only is coherence the sole criterion of truth, it is the very nature of truth. This assertion rests on Blanshard's theory of the relation of thought to reality. Thought seeks a systematic vision. Guided by this ideal of intelligibility, necessity within a system, we seek to apprehend what is presently unknown so as to relate it necessarily to what we know already (2:261). To the extent that we achieve a systematic vision, thought is satisfied.

But what does the satisfaction of thought have to do with reality? Thought itself answers that thinking of an object is having that object within the mind in such a way that, were it completed, what is within us would identify itself with the object. ". . . thought is related to reality as the partial to the perfect fulfilment of a purpose. The more adequate its grasp the more nearly does it approximate, the more fully does it realize in itself, the nature and relations of its objects" (*NT,* 2:262). The satisfaction of systematic vision, thought's immanent end, is finally the fulfillment of its object, thought's transcendent end. If these ends are not identified, skepticism is the only alternative and the impressive advance of knowledge has been the result of fortunate guesswork.

Reality, then, is a completely ordered and fully intelligible system with which thought increasingly identifies in its advance. Growing knowledge is a reunion with things in their ordered wholeness. On the basis of this relation between thought and reality, Blanshard writes: "Truth is the approximation of thought to reality. . . . The degree of truth of a particular proposition is to be judged in the first instance by its coherence with experience as a whole, ultimately by its coherence with that further whole, all-comprehensive and fully articulated, in which thought can come to rest" (*NT,* 2:264).

Even such a brief statement of Blanshard's coherence theory of truth adds to our understanding of the rationalist's frustration with the reformer. It can also be used in analyzing the development of Luther's theology.

Insofar as Luther was guided by the ideal of intelligibility, his struggle for self-justification was based on a fairly comprehensive systematic vision, namely that of late Scholastic theology and the church's sacramental system. What he could not bring into necessary relation with that present knowledge was his own sense of despair. Apparently most of his colleagues, and certainly the dominant forces in his culture, assured him that the problem lay with Luther, not with the system.

Whether suddenly or gradually, Luther's experience of justification by faith confronted him with something Blanshard might call "a collision between a system or order already present in the mind and some fragment that ought to be included in this and yet remains outside it" (*NT,* 2:130). But unlike Blanshard's detective puzzling over Lord X, found mysteriously dead in the library, Luther's previous experience could not accommodate the foreign element, not even by a leap of suggestion or invention. Or, if Luther's "rediscovery" of the gospel was such a leap, it resulted in a radical modification of the previous system, so radical as to be labeled heretical by the system's defenders.

We must be careful in identifying the "continent of our knowledge" and the "island we wish to include in it" (*NT*, 2:261). If the "continent" for Luther was late Scholastic theology and the church's sacramental system, the "island" of unconditional divine forgiveness could not fit. Bridges were burned not built. But this is no threat to Blanshard's theory of coherence. Science itself is replete with instances in which the "island" leads to a dramatic reshaping of the "continent."

Yet Blanshard senses something else going on here. What if the "continent" is reason itself and the "island" is an experience reason cannot comprehend? Again we must be careful. Luther distinguished between reason as a capacity or tool and reason as an attitude or opinion. He praised the former, even took it into the household of theology. He praised the latter, provided it stayed within the earthly kingdom. He said, in effect, no bridges can be built between reason as attitude or opinion and the experience of justification by faith. What is it about reason in this sense that denied its comprehension of divine forgiveness? Precisely what Blanshard, in his theory of coherence, calls "the faith that the real is rational," the assumption that reflection's pursuit of its own end is progress toward the transcendent end as well (*NT*, 2:263). *The conflict between Luther and Blanshard is not between faith and reason; it is between faith and faith.*

To put the matter this way is not to decide the debate between the rationalist and the reformer, but only to set it in proper context. It is to acknowledge that Luther's "a proposition false in philosophy may be true in theology" is not refuted by simply repeating the philosopher's reasons for finding the proposition false. The question of truth or falsity here is not whether Luther's claims meet or fail to meet Blanshard's rationalist criteria. The question is which of two rival faiths is true. If we recognize this, other conflicts can be clarified, though not resolved.

A4. Luther's theological preconceptions too largely determined his facts and his inferences from fact. Blanshard is correct in citing the influence of Luther's theological preconceptions. As he himself states in *The Nature of Thought*: "The solid piers of fact, supposed to be standing there in broad daylight as the bases of our structure of theory, are illusion. There are no such things. The 'facts' that were to support our system are themselves relative to the system" (*NT*, 2:214–15).

What we have in the rationalist and the reformer are two opposing systems, each claiming a comprehensive perspective. Because Blanshard's coherence theory of truth is an extension of rationality and can point to the advance of science as its key witness, it has a decided advantage over Luther's theology with its appeal to the hiddenness of God and the receptivity of the inner person. But there are some other differences between the two systems that keep the debate alive.

Luther's basic question or starting point was soteriological. What must I do to be saved? Or, in somewhat more contemporary terminology, how can I be assured that my life has some enduring meaning? Blanshard's fundamental question is epistemological, though surely in the broadest sense of that word. What am I able to know? What are the limits of my systematic vision? Insofar as there was fulfillment in Luther's quest, it was in the assurance of divine forgiveness and the consequent magnification of God's glory. Insofar as there is fulfillment in Blanshard's quest, it is in the enrichment of systematic vision and the consequent satisfaction of thought.

Though each system has its own questions and answers, they overlap. From Luther's perspective, Blanshard's epistemological endeavors have soteriological implications. Blanshard's theoretic impulse "cannot rest while anything in the universe is outside the web of necessity" (*NT,* 1:654). For Luther the web of necessity was hidden in God. From Blanshard's perspective, Luther's soteriological endeavors had epistemological implications. Luther's understanding of justification by faith placed limitations on the extent of reason's domain. ". . . if thought cannot assume that to its questions there are intelligible answers, it will die from lack of motive" (*NT,* 1:653).

A5. Luther's faith confused emotive and cognitive certainty. This specification, closely related to the preceding one, arises out of Blanshard's assertion that faith is no guarantee of truth. For example, the natural and social sciences have conclusively disproven the biological transmissibility of sin as an activity. The inference that the doctrine of original sin is therefore untrue does not necessarily follow. Some would argue that the doctrine's truth lies in its adequacy as a theological description of the human situation.

The present question, however, is whether the scientific disproof of claims made in the name of faith disproves the faith as well. Blanshard takes great relish in pitting Copernicus against Joshua. Luther was neither the first nor the last Christian theologian to make mistaken assertions about the natural order. But Blanshard exaggerates the significance of these errors. Religion is not science.

Religion, at least in its Christian form, affirms the meaning of existence in a world in which such meaning seems uncertain. The Christian hopes that even death, the greatest threat to meaning, will finally be overcome. The only "reason" the Christian can muster for such a hope is the experience of divine acceptance in Christ. This experience is a highly personal, subjective awareness, encompassing all the faculties of the self. It is characterized by participation and particularity rather than by observation and universality. Insofar as it is akin to knowledge, it is what Blanshard refers to as knowledge of the heart.

Blanshard argues that such knowledge of the heart confuses emotive and cognitive certainty. This trust in divine forgiveness or confidence in the enduring value of one's life lacks "the certainty of the mathematician who has demonstrated a theorem or of the physiologist who has isolated by experiment the cause of a disease" (*RB*, 177). If any claims to truth that lack such certainty are attributed to emotional extravagance or psychological need, then there is no point in continuing the dialogue, for religion and its claims will always lack such certainty.

Blanshard's observation that a faith "justified practically and emotionally may be less than justified rationally" could conceivably imply a limitation on reason as well as on faith (*RB*, 157). The criteria of truth and the claims made by theologians and scientists may be sufficiently different to merit an exploration of the difference itself, in hopes of finding ways in which they can be constructively critical of one another. The rigidity of Luther's distinction between the earthly and the heavenly kingdoms does not encourage such an effort, but neither does Blanshard's refusal to admit that such a distinction might represent real incongruities in human experience that reason has yet to comprehend. Cognitive certainty, as Blanshard defines it, may not be the only measure of truth.

Having heard the arguments on five specifications, what verdict are we to return on the charge that Luther's teaching fails to meet generally accepted criteria of rationality? No simple verdict is possible. We have seen that Luther was not an irrationalist, unless that term applies to anyone who places limits on reason's capacity to fully comprehend human experience. If Blanshard intends such an application, then the debate is indeed between two faiths. In such a debate the rationalist can appeal to the awesome advance of science. The reformer can only appeal to a paradox, trust in the love of God hidden in a broken creation.

Blanshard's second fundamental accusation is (B) that Luther's teaching fails to meet generally accepted standards of morality.

B1. Luther held to the doctrine of original sin. The general charge is epitomized in the first specification. Not only is the notion of inherited corruption unfounded, for reasons discussed above; it is morally indefensible. "The doctrine is, if possible, even more untenable morally than factually" (*RB*, 154). It amounts to a denial of three generally accepted moral principles: one is only responsible for one's own acts; there are degrees of morality; one must have attained social maturity in order to be held morally accountable.

It is no surprise that literalistic interpretation of Adam's fall and the consequent corruption of humanity infuriates the rationalist. It is unfortunate, however, that Blanshard refuses to discuss a demythologized version of the fall and original sin. While correct in saying "One needs to walk warily here, for the dogma has been treated like a piece of putty and has been moulded by imaginative hands into very diverse shapes," Blanshard walks so warily that he misses the scenery (*RB,* 150).

Be that as it may, Luther did think of original sin as hereditary corruption. In suggesting that it might be the chief ground for Luther's disparagement of reason, Blanshard overlooks its secondary position in relation to justification by faith. But our concern here is with the morality of Luther's teachings, and whether his doctrine of original sin is offensive in the manner Blanshard indicates.

Luther's two-kingdom theory does blunt this charge somewhat. The doctrine of original sin has to do with one's righteousness before God. Personal responsibility for one's acts, degrees of moral value, and social maturity are distinctions that fail to qualify the pervasive human pride and self-sufficiency that condemn all men and women before the divine judge. Yet these same distinctions are of great importance with respect to righteousness before one's peers. The fulfillment of one's social obligations, no matter what one's role and station in the earthly kingdom, was of great importance to Luther. Yet if these actions have no bearing on one's ultimate destiny, why bother? For Luther, this very question revealed the inhibiting self-service that motivates works-righteousness. It is not, as Blanshard states, that the whole scale of natural values is denied. Indeed, those values are affirmed in the light of justification by faith.

> We do not . . . reject good works; on the contrary, we cherish and teach them as much as possible. . . . Man. . .needs none of these things for his righteousness and salvation. Therefore, he should be guided in all his works by this thought and contemplate this one thing alone, that he may serve and benefit others in all that he does, considering nothing except the need and the advantage of his neighbor. [*LW,* 31:363–65]

Christian liberty, as Luther described it, was freedom from anxiety over one's own destiny. Thus liberated, the Christian could see the needs of the neighbor and seek to fill those needs without thought of reward or punishment from God or neighbor. Here we see another expression of the two-kingdom theory: "A Christian is a perfectly free lord of all, subject to none. A Christian is a perfectly dutiful servant of all, subject to all" (*LW,* 31:344). Security of the inner self, trusting completely in God, generates openness of the outer self, turned completely to the neighbor. The dynamic of the two great commandments was stated in Luther's notion of liberation and service.

In this context, the two-kingdom theory gave religious meaning to earthly vocations while removing the special status of ascetic, monastic, and priestly vocations. If one's "person" is related to God in faith, one's "office" becomes the vehicle for fulfillment of the law, insofar as that is humanly possible. While Luther's doctrine of original sin may offend our moral sensibilities, his understanding of Christian liberty sets a high moral standard.

B2. Luther's view of justification by faith operates as a moral depressant. Blanshard holds that the negation of works as a means of winning salvation discourages acts of kindness and militates against the sense of honor and justice. An allied criticism is that persons are merely pawns in a supernatural transaction completely beyond their control. These charges are difficult to assess. The first assumes that without the prize the race is not worth running; the second assumes that the race is rigged anyway. It is hard to imagine Blanshard or anyone similarly disposed to Luther's understanding of God making either of these assumptions. And if one shares Luther's view of God, the criticisms melt away. We have seen the positive place of works as the fruit of justification. As for being human pawns, Luther would prefer to say persons are instruments of God's glory; and that, far from being a depressing view, is invigorating. One comes to personhood in fulfilling the divine will as completely as possible. For Luther, identification with Christ and magnification of God are the most appropriate expressions of humanity.

Blanshard comes closer to the heart of Luther's vulnerability when he claims that the reformer's doctrine of faith "shifts the centre of gravity from conduct to belief" (*RB,* 170). Though he exaggerates the significance of belief as a cognitive act in Luther's understanding of justification by faith, he is correct in claiming the susceptibility of Luther's position to a righteousness of belief.

In Luther's theology one of the greatest assets is also a liability. Luther's theory of two kingdoms holds in dynamic tension one's place *in* the world *before* God. The dualities we have discussed manifest this tension. The Christian must affirm life in both kingdoms in obedience to one God of judgment and mercy.

How might the Christian relate deeply personal trust in God with a forty-hour week in an assembly line placing hubcaps on new automobiles? How might the Christian relate confidence in God's providential care with the provision of a high standard of living for one's family? How might the Christian relate a profound sense of God's mercy to responsibility as a prosecutor in the district attorney's office?

As long as the tension expressed in such questions remains, there is a real possibility that the two kingdoms will interact, that Christ's presence in the soul will have consequences for the body, that God's justification of individuals will bring some measure of justice to society. But if the tension is resolved on either side of the duality, the dynamic is lost. Distinction becomes division; dialectic becomes compartmentalization.

One might agree with H. Richard Niebuhr that "it is a great error to confuse the parallelistic dualism of separated spiritual and temporal life with the interactionism of Luther's gospel of faith in Christ working by love in the world of culture."[7] Nonetheless, that error has been committed, and where it has taken the form of a righteousness of belief Blanshard's criticism is appropriate. When faith becomes the assent to certain theological propositions rather than a relation of trust in the God before whom one continually stands, then moral conduct is set free to take shape in a variety of ways.

Although clearly intended to counter the notion of works-righteousness, Luther's stress on passive righteousness has also engendered a quietism of avoiding works as far as possible.

> ... this most excellent righteousness, the righteousness of faith, which God imputes to us through Christ without works, is neither political nor ceremonial nor legal nor work-righteousness but is quite the opposite; it is a merely passive righteousness, while all the others, listed above, are active. For here we work nothing, render nothing to God; we only receive and permit someone else to work in us, namely, God. Therefore it is appropriate to call the righteousness of faith or Christian righteousness "passive." [LW, 26:4–5]

Understood without the tension of the two kingdoms, liberation to act becomes excuse to wait. A related compromise of Luther's position is to forget the tension within the soul itself. The final fulfillment of the promise is beyond this life, and the ecstasy that may accompany divine forgiveness must not erase the anguish of continuing sinfulness. Should it do so, the drive to extend the process of healing beyond the individual self is lost.

The tendency to resolve Luther's two-kingdom tension on the side of the spiritual and individual is given indirect and unintended support by Luther's view of the law. In its theological use the law reveals "sin, blindness, misery, wickedness, ignorance, hate and contempt of God, death, hell, judgment, and the well-deserved wrath of God" (ibid., 309). In this manner it crushes presumption, leading persons to despair of self-justification. If one's understanding of the law is restricted to this theological use in the spiritual realm, conservatism or even defeatism with regard to social institutions and their capacity for reformation may result.

Luther himself also defined a civic use of the law appropriate to the temporal realm. Here the offices and structures of society have their importance, and solutions to the problems of personal and corporate interaction are to be pursued. "This is why God has ordained magistrates, parents, teachers, laws, shackles, and all civic ordinances, so that, if they cannot do any more, they will at least bind the hands of the devil and keep him from raging at will" (*LW*, 26:4–5). While Luther did not neglect the law in the earthly kingdom, the restraining role he assigned it may encourage a negative attitude toward the created order and a moral resignation regarding social problems.

That Luther's theology can operate as a moral depressant in the ways described underlines the importance of maintaining the tension between an earthly kingdom oriented to humanity in its self-seeking and a heavenly kingdom oriented to God and his gracious justification. This is a fundamental point at issue between the rationalist and the reformer. The tension that Luther's theology seeks to hold is a tension that Blanshard's philosophy seeks to overcome. The discontinuities associated with Luther's interpretation of the gospel are alien to Blanshard's liberal moralism. While the rationalist would have us believe that a reformer's preference for Paul distorts Luther's vision, Blanshard has his own astigmatism. Despite his attraction to the "biographical gospel," he is surprised at an implication he draws from Barth to the effect that our jails might be "filled with Christians under aliases," and our churches and humane societies might be "filled with people suffering from sinful human kindness." (*RB*, 307).

Were Luther alive today he probably would not share Blanshard's view of an emerging world of hope "based on effort plus the increasing mastery of nature" (*RB*, 310). While not denying the importance of an extended life expectancy and an enlarged United Nations, Luther would hold this in tension with the mistrust and defensive anxiety exhibited in the erosion of values and the increasing gap between rich nation and poor. This tension is manifest in the strain on the law in its civic capacity. For Luther, however, an even stronger tension than that revealed in the current domestic and international scene is rooted in one's relation to God revealed in Christ.

Once again, it is difficult to return a simple verdict on Blanshard's charge. If we take seriously Luther's understanding of Christian liberty and vocation, it is difficult to argue that his teaching fails to meet generally accepted standards of morality. Yet, as we have seen in considering several vulnerabilities in Luther's position, he holds the entire moral order in question before God.

6. Conclusion

It would be a mistake to confuse the rationalist's estimate of the reformer with an assessment of the office of reason in religion, or even Protestantism. But some lessons can be learned from this encounter.

Religion is neither science nor ethics. It is not an extension of rationality or morality, though it contains elements of both. Religion is a richly textured phenomenon that involves personal commitment and social movement while defying identification with any one cause or institution. This is the instructive significance of Luther for the philosopher of religion. The puzzling dualities of his life and thought challenge the adequacy of any single approach to religious experience. And thus the instructive significance of Blanshard's critique. Unable fully to comprehend religion, rationalism opposes it as a rival faith. Unable fully to domesticate religion, moralism rejects it as an alien force.

JERRY A. IRISH

DEPARTMENT OF RELIGION
WICHITA STATE UNIVERSITY

NOTES

[1] Martin Luther, *Luther's Works*, eds. Jaroslav Pelikan and Helmut T. Lehmann (Saint Louis: Concordia Publishing House, 1958–74), 31:350. Wherever possible, reference will be made to this edition of Luther's works, hereafter cited as *LW*.

[2] Martin Luther, *Tischreden* (Weimar, 1919), vol. 5, sec. 5247, p. 26.

[3] Luther, *Tischreden,* vol. 3, sec. 3232a, p. 228.

[4] Wilhelm Pauck, trans. and ed., *Luther: Lectures on Romans,* Library of Christian Classics, vol. 15 (Philadelphia: Westminster Press, 1961), p. xliv.

[5] B. A. Gerrish, *Grace and Reason* (Oxford: Clarendon Press, 1962), 119.

[6] Gordon Rupp, *The Righteousness of God* (London: Hodder & Stoughton, 1953), 161.

[7] H. Richard Niebuhr, *Christ and Culture* (New York: Harper & Row, 1951), 179.

30. Reply to Jerry A. Irish

The Rationalist and the Reformer

In dealing with Protestant theologians in *Reason and Belief*, I spent much time in showing that if you start with two independent realms of nature and supernature, and two standards of truth, revelation and reason, you will never get your two realms together and will end in logical schizophrenia. The four eminences whom I considered, Luther, Kierkegaard, Brunner, and Barth, all drew the line firmly, though at somewhat different places, and argued their conclusions in somewhat different ways. I was therefore disappointed that Mr. Irish, invited to appraise my critique of this Protestant succession, decided to fix his attention on what I had said about Luther alone. Of all Protestant theologians, Luther is perhaps the most extreme, the most intemperate, the most contemptuous of reason, the most incoherent, and the most inextinguishably voluble. Mr. Irish alas invites me to return to him. Furthermore, he offers "an alternative interpretation" of him which is supposed to be proof against my criticisms. What to me is most important about this interpretation of his is that it accepts the part of Luther which I thought least defensible, the doctrine of the two realms of nature and grace. An argument with anyone who holds this view is likely to be futile, since his acceptance of it does not depend on rational considerations, but on an experience of firsthand entry into the superrational realm, where the critic, endowed with merely human faculties, cannot follow. Thus the partners in the discussion are like two ships that pass in the night. When we come to the crucial point, however eloquent Mr. Irish may be, I shall be bereft of the necessary knowledge of what he means; and however limpid and logical I may try to be, he can wave it all aside, as Luther would, as rationalist confusion and pride.

Justification by Faith

Mr. Irish begins his criticism with the "alternative interpretation of Luther's justification by faith" to which I have just referred. It is not clear to me where this interpretation supplies an alternative to the one I gave; it seems to me the same, though with the feeling-tone index changed from minus to plus. Man, as a result of his own and his ancestors' sins, has been corrupted through and through. Foul with this corruption, he faces a righteous Deity whose very righteousness requires the infliction of the most condign punishment. Man's corruption is so complete that there is nothing he can say or do to avert the divine anger, and his appropriate attitude is complete despair. There is one hope only. God has sent to earth his son, who, as the second person of the Trinity, is himself really Deity, and he took it upon him to suffer in his own person the punishment that God held in store for man. Our salvation from this punishment and acceptance into the eternal kingdom lies in faith. This faith is not an achievement of our own; we are too far gone in corruption for that; it is a gift of God, a divine activity within us. Such faith is essentially belief or awareness that our sins are forgiven. With the coming of this awareness we pass at once from helpless terror and despair to security and blessedness. And our question must be whether Luther's doctrine of justification by faith, so stated, is acceptable. I will rapidly set down the first six or eight difficulties that come to mind.

(1) The faith that saves is not, we are told, one's own work; it is God's work; the state of faith is God in us. Now if this is taken seriously, it is hard to see how the self that did the sinning is saved at all. That self has been replaced by another self which, as divine, is in no need of saving. If it is in fact the human I that is saved, a double paradox is involved. First, I cannot be saved in virtue of anything I have done; I never deserve to be saved. Secondly, if God, to be righteous, *must* punish, as Luther held, his pardon to me must be *un*righteous.

(2) Such pardons would seem to be more unjust if dealt out selectively than by a general amnesty issued to all alike. But the amnesty is not general. God selects some persons, irrespective of their works and merit, to receive the grace of justification, and denies it to others who, so far as mortal eyes can see, deserve it equally. Injustice is thus compounded.

(3) The forgiveness granted is said to be granted "unconditionally." This, when explained, turns out to be self-contradictory. For the forgiveness is granted only on the condition that the man forgiven shows faith. *Un*conditional forgiveness would be forgiveness without conditions. And this required condition, we are told as the nightmare intensifies, is one that we can never hope to fulfill by anything we do.

(4) It is to be remembered that most of the sins for which we have been forgiven are sins we have never committed. They consist of an enormous volume of sin that has been accumulating on the back of mankind ever since the theft of the apple in Eden.

(5) The state of faith is described as "cognition" or "awareness that." If this cognition is an activity of our own faculties, it is, by Luther's insistence,

unreliable, since our faculties have been totally corrupted by sin. If, on the other hand, it is God's cognition, then, though God is aware of having forgiven us, we are not. And if not, how can *we* attain saving faith at all?

(6) Mr. Irish's analysis of forgiveness seems faulty. He writes: "We may be offered forgiveness, but we are in no position to accept it so long as we intend to earn it by our own deeds"; and again, "Acceptance involves forfeiting all efforts at earning forgiveness" (Sec. 3). It is well to work with a concrete case in mind. Sir Walter Scott was a member of the firm of Ballantine & Co., publishers. Owing to some bad business ventures in which Scott had a somewhat indirect part, the firm failed, involving many of its investors in the loss of their funds. One gathers that some of them were willing to forgive Scott their loss, but he declined to claim the protection of the bankruptcy laws, set out to make up to his creditors their losses, and drove himself mercilessly for the rest of his life in the attempt to do so. Mr. Irish seems to be saying that Scott could not accept the forgiveness of his creditors while he was attempting to earn it. This is strange psychology. Scott could and did accept gratefully the forgiving attitude of his creditors, even while trying long and desperately to be worthy of it by taking full responsibility. Mr. Irish says again: "Should the other party sense our self-seeking attitude [that of trying to make up to him the hurt we have inflicted], the hurt may be increased" (Sec. 3). But *was* it self-seeking on Scott's part to make up to his creditors their losses? Surely the course of self-seeking would be to claim bankruptcy and wash one's hands of the whole business. Mr. Irish carries his view of forgiveness into theology. "With acceptance of God's forgiveness, one is liberated from the fruitless self-seeking of worthiness to be forgiven." It is self-seeking to try to be morally worthy! One would have thought that if there is anything *not* selfish it is the attempt by labor and self-sacrifice to become deserving of forgiveness.

(7) The understanding of justification is not made easier by reading that it is really an "identification" with Christ. "The experience of identification with the abandoned Christ," says Mr. Irish, "places Luther under the covering of Christ's righteousness" (Sec. 4). He quotes Luther: "Is it not that they [saints] know that there is sin in them but that for the sake of Christ it is covered and is not imputed to them, so that they may declare that all their good is outside of them, in Christ, who yet through faith is also in them?" This is an almost inextricable tangle. We must start with the assumption that all men are gross sinners. Of some men, we are now told, their sins are not "imputed" to them. If this means that God does not *ascribe* to them sinfulness, it can only mean that the Deity is in error, for their sinfulness is the admitted fact we started with. If it means that, though they are really sinful, God has transferred their sinfulness to someone else, he is doing what in men would be considered doubly unjust, saddling the innocent with guilt, and using one man's innocence to cancel the guilt of another. Seeing the paradox of

imputing man's guilt to the innocent Christ, Luther insists that Christ was *not* innocent after all, that he was really the worst of sinners since he had taken on himself the guilt of the world. But he must also be sinless, since otherwise his grace would not balance the incalculable weight of human sin. He is therefore both sinless and the worst of sinners. Luther—I am not sure about Mr. Irish—asks us to swallow this whole, on pain of perdition. Furthermore, the God who requires this of us is a God of boundless love and justice! Comment on this sort of theology, from either the logical or the ethical point of view, is hardly necessary.

(8) It seems to me that there is a simpler account than revelation for Luther's adopting of theological dogmas in which the laws of nature, ethics, and logic are all brushed aside. Like Kierkegaard, the man was absorbed to the point of pathology in his own sinfulness, "out-confessing, out-praying, and out-meditating all his brothers," as Mr. Irish says. "Chastity, poverty, obedience, mortification of the flesh, discipline of the mind, Luther did it all—beyond the expectations of his elders, but not to the satisfaction of his God" (Sec. 3). Now for a sane modern reviewer of Luther's life there is no reason to believe that he was a solid ball of putrescent and maggot-filled wickedness. He had narrowly missed being killed, we read, by a stroke of lightning, and his imaginative and terrified mind, taking with dreadful literalness the theology of the day, began to dwell on what it would have been like to stand before an angry Almighty, with the flames of hell in the offing. Is there any doubt that, as he misread the depth of his accursedness when he was in the slough of despair, so he misread the meaning of his euphoria when he was on his heights? One who could see and hear Satan at work around him would not be above finding God at work in his periods of assurance and ecstasy. His very considerable ability, combined with his utter contempt of the reason that challenged his conclusions, made the construction of a theology on the grounds of his own ecstasies and despairs a relatively easy matter. His habit of reading Scripture selectively, throwing out as un-canonical whole books that tended in the wrong direction, made the construction easier. If one asks which is the more likely, that this overwrought mind should project its exaltations and its terrors on the world or that its mazes of theological incoherence, peopled with the devil and his minions, and a Deity both kind and cruel, both just and unjust, should be truth absolute, the choice seems clear enough.

Luther's Irrationality

I. The main part (Sec. 5) of Mr. Irish's essay consists of a reply to my "charges" and "accusations" against Luther. The chief of these, he says, are two, which are certainly of major importance: that Luther's teaching is irrational and that it is immoral. Under the first head he has selected several subcharges to which he replies in order. I shall follow approximately the same order in replying to his replies.

(A1) "*Luther disparaged reason while simultaneously making use of it himself.*" The case for this I developed at some length. Mr. Irish's defense of Luther here contains several counts.

(a) He at times praised reason; admitted.

(b) He saw that natural reason was inevitably self-seeking, and that it would be impious presumption to carry such self-seeking into the realm of grace, where its function is that of servant and mouthpiece to revelation. Now this is to get things exactly wrong. The only aim of reason everywhere and always is at truth, which requires the firm repression of self-interest, and to describe this as self-seeking is to use words perversely, as we have already seen. According to Mr. Irish, Luther was a pragmatist about natural reason: "To subdue the earth and have dominion over its creatures was for Luther the God-given task of natural reason." Of course thought *can* be used in this way as a tool of practical need and exploitation, but that is not its primary function. It is one of the aims of *The Nature of Thought*, from the first sentence on, to show that thought throughout has a natural and immanent end of its own. The suggestion that as it rises to a higher level it surrenders this end and becomes the tool of something else is not only untrue; it ends in logical disaster. What it implies is that thought, in entering the realm of the supernatural, must give up the guidance of its own canons of logic, and accept as higher truth what its own immanent standard brands as false. And this double standard can only undermine thought everywhere; for if the region in which its own standards are transcended is the region of greater reality and authority, as for Luther it was, then the verdicts of thought everywhere are under suspicion. If the law of contradiction is invalid anywhere, it is simply invalid, and that means valid nowhere, since it is not the sort of law that can be sometimes true and sometimes false. For the fuller statement of this case I must refer the reader to *Reason and Belief.*

(c) Mr. Irish's third plea in extenuation of Luther's disparagement of reason is that it was associated in his mind with legalism. The Pharisees had insisted that salvation lay in obedience to the Mosaic and other laws believed to have been laid down by God himself. The presence of such law gave the legal mind a congenial field for reasoning of a casuistic kind. Mr. Irish quotes from Luther's *Tischreden*: "As soon as reason and the Law are joined, faith immediately loses its virginity. For nothing is more hostile to faith than the Law and reason; . . . the Gospel leads us above and beyond the light of the Law and reason into the darkness of faith, where the Law and reason have no business." Furthermore, stress on obedience to law is connected with the doctrine, hateful to Luther, that we are judged by our conduct rather than by our faith; so that there was an association in his mind between salvation by works, law, and reason. His hostility to the first two was thus carried over to the third. Mr. Irish sums up: "Luther's disparagement of reason did not criticize reason per se but rather its alliance with egoistic legalism. On these grounds, his simultaneous disparagement and use of reason was not inconsistent, and half of the charge of irrationalism is undercut."

This is a surprising defense. It seems to be saying that because Luther had formed a psychological association between reason and legalism, he was not attacking reason as such, but only its alliance with legalism. No doubt he was capable of such confusions, but it is hard to acquit him on such grounds here. Consider only the way in which he poured contempt on Aristotle, whose use of reason certainly had no connection with Hebrew legalism; yet for Luther he was "a blind heathen" as well as "a lazy ass." Consider his lament that instead of reading history and poetry, "I had to spend my time on devil's filth, the philosophers and sophists, with great labor and damage. . . ." But, to repeat, suppose it is true that Luther's hostility to reason *was* based on its use by Hebrew legalists to support their case; what ground does that afford for a general attack on philosophers as purveyors of "devil's filth"? One does not discredit a human faculty by showing that it is capable of misuse; *any* human power could be discredited by that argument; indeed faith itself can be discredited by it, and with singular ease. Once again, *was* the use of reason by the Pharisees to defend and interpret law a "misuse"? It did indeed lead to an emphasis on conduct rather than "the darkness of faith" as what was most essential to the Christian life; but most people would probably consider that, as I do, a far sounder and less obscurantist emphasis than that of Luther himself.

Luther's Consistency

(A2) My second mistaken charge, in Mr. Irish's view, is that "*Luther's work is internally inconsistent.*" In one paragraph of my chapter on Luther I mentioned nine points of importance at which he contradicted himself (*Reason and Belief,* 165). I will not tire the reader by going down the line of these contradictions, one by one, with the replies to them; I should prefer to ask him to read the paragraph in context, together with the replies. But it may be well to take the two inconsistencies that are dealt with most briefly in order to indicate the sort of reply that in such cases Mr. Irish thinks sufficient. I said: "If a human court condemns a man for something done by his father, that is unjust; if God condemns a man for something done by his remotest ancestors, this is perfect justice." To hold both the se doctrines together, as Luther did, seemed to me inconsistent. Mr. Irish replies: "Blanshard's first statement is an observation of natural reason holding true in the earthly realm. Blanshard's second statement, if read literally, might be taken as a theological statement of trust in God's will, however strange that may appear to natural reason." The second contradiction was: "Christ was sinless, but as a man he was a sinner." Mr. Irish replies: "These are Blanshard's words, so the specific reference is unclear. [I had already given the specific reference, with Luther's words in his own Latin, *RB*, 140, 583 n. 37.] However, the second statement probably refers to Christ's identification with human sin, his taking on or covering human sin with his own righteousness. In that case, the statements are consistent with one another, both being theological expressions of Luther's experience of justification by faith."

It will be noted that in both these cases the reply is essentially the same. One or both of the contradictory statements are moved into the sphere of theology, where we must believe that they are perfectly reconciled though our natural reason cannot see how. Look a little more closely at the first inconsistent pair. Here the first of the two statements, that it would be *un*just to convict a man of his ancestor's sins, is accepted as clear enough. The second, which says that the same action as attributed to God is *just,* is declared not to be inconsistent with the first; why? Because it is "a theological statement of trust in God's will," and such a statement does not have to be intelligible. In the second case, both statements are theological and hence do not have to be either intelligible to reason or consistent by rational standards. Thus in theological controversy, if one may be permitted to say so, God is a very present help in time of trouble. The theologian can make statements which, according to the reason employed by common sense, science, or philosophy, contradict each other flatly, and by pushing one or both into the region of divinity, make them sufficiently unintelligible to allow both to be true. It is not an operation calculated to inspire confidence in those of us confined to "the earthly realm."

Faith versus Faith

(A3) The third charge of mine that Mr. Irish considers is: "*Luther held that a proposition false in philosophy may be true in theology.*" This he admits. But he denies that it stands in need of apology. In "the Word was made flesh," for example, we have a proposition that may present itself as absurd to reason; for how could omniscience and omnipotence be embodied in a man who was clearly limited in both knowledge and power? But through faith we are enabled to see that it is true nevertheless, though how this can be is beyond understanding by our natural faculties. Mr. Irish says that "Luther, faced with contradictory experiences, developed a theology that acknowledges these contradictions to be beyond rational resolution," but he is reluctant to admit the contradictions to be as numerous as to me they seem. "The central contradiction in Luther is the simultaneous awareness of a world in which evil is pervasive and an all-powerful God's unconditional forgiveness and mercy." We do not see how a God who is loving and merciful could create a race of creatures most of whom he foredoomed to eternal misery. "The result," says Mr. Irish, "is teaching laden with dualities, all finally made understandable, though not necessarily true, in terms of a theory of two realms. Blanshard, in equally understandable allegiance to his rational ideal, calls the dualities inconsistent and treats the two-realm theory as an evasion of contradiction."

Here we are confronted by two views of the world, both alleging themselves to be based on experience, but one holding to two conflicting orders, the other to a world consistent throughout. (By way of finding what sort of world I live in, Mr. Irish quotes two of my books on the theory of knowledge, a courtesy which I appreciate.) How are the conflicts between the realms to be resolved? Mr. Irish is convinced, as Luther is, that they cannot be resolved rationally. My conviction that the world contains no inconsistencies is in the end, he says, as much a matter of faith as Luther's own. "The conflict between Luther and Blanshard is not between faith and reason; it is between faith and faith."

This is a frequently used tactic in the warfare between theology and rationalism, and if Mr. Irish has read me, he must know my answer to it. It is as follows. The rationalist's belief that the world is a self-consistent whole *is* in a sense a matter of faith, but it is faith in an utterly different sense from that of the theologian. It is a faith that the law of contradiction is true. You cannot prove that law to be true, for every step of any proof that might be employed would assume the truth of the proposition to be proved. Nor can you claim the law to be true by self-evidence, for a disbeliever in the rationalist's logic will deny the force of logical self-evidence, and insist that in using it you are begging the question. You may invite him to give an example of what he means by contradictories that are both true. He will of course fail, for though one may believe them both, one cannot see them both to be true. The law of contradiction is therefore a proposition incapable of being proved in the ordinary way, but assumed to be true in every judgment and every inference, and confirmed daily and hourly. There is no proposition in the range of human thought that can be made with greater certainty; it cannot even be denied without assuming its validity.

To compare an assertion of this kind with religious faith is irresponsible. Take the five articles claimed by Saint Thomas as necessary to salvation and certified by faith—the creation, the Trinity, the incarnation, the divine presence in the sacraments, and eternal life. Can anyone maintain that any of these dogmas, alleged to be attested by faith, has the certainty of a law of logic? The doctrine of creation is denied by all who believe that time could have had no beginning. The doctrine of the Trinity is denied by all Moslems. The incarnation is denied by all Jews. The miracle of the mass is denied by all non-Christians; eternal life is denied by all materialists. How these dogmas can be true is vouchsafed to a selected group of persons who are able to see their truth only through a partial transplantation of divinity into their minds. Luther would disdain to hold that doctrines so attested were understandable by the mere human reason that followed logic and purveyed "devil's filth"; they held a higher degree of certainty open only to the elect, and incommunicable to anyone else. If Mr. Irish says that against Luther's faith I am only offering another faith, I am content that the case should be so judged, provided that the marginalia I have introduced be kept firmly in mind.

"Preconceptions"

(A4) My fourth questionable criticism is that *"Luther's theological preconceptions too largely determined his facts and his inferences from fact."* To this Mr. Irish replies by citing a passage from *The Nature of Thought* (2: 214–15) in which, he suggests, I have myself admitted such preconceptions to be legitimate and inevitable. But again, as in the matter of faith, there is no relevant resemblance between the two meanings of "preconception." What I maintained in the passage cited was that in objects of perception such as tables and chairs there is always, besides what is given, an element of theory; a table or a chair is not given as a whole to sense, but is built up by a process of construction that carries over a deposit from past experience to meet the newly presented sensation. But to say that either an "apperception mass" or the view that it exists is a "preconception" in anything like the Lutheran sense seems to me very strange indeed. The frame of meaning into which the sensory element is fitted has a firm base in experience, and its presence and operation are facts to which I had earlier devoted many pages of analysis. To compare such perceptual meaning with Luther's preconceptions, for example, about the truth of Scripture from Adam and Eve in the garden to the Pauline second Adam is to play on two utterly different meanings of the same term.

Mr. Irish continues by arguing that my starting point is so far from Luther's that it is inevitable I should do less than justice to his view.

> Luther's basic question or starting point was soteriological. What must I do to be saved? Or, in somewhat more contemporary terminology, how can I be assured that my life has some enduring meaning? Blanshard's fundamental question is epistemological. . . . What am I able to know? What are the limits of my systematic vision? Insofar as there was fulfillment in Luther's quest, it was in the assurance of divine forgiveness and the consequent magnification of God's glory. Insofar as there is fulfillment in Blanshard's

quest, it is in the enrichment of systematic vision and the consequent satisfaction of thought.

Two comments are necessary. First, one cannot translate Luther's "What must I do to be saved?" into any such ingenuous query as "How can I be assured that my life has some enduring meaning?" Luther's question sprang straight out of the mediaeval world, out of a framework of unquestioned theological dogmas such as the existence of a rewarding and avenging Deity and the need of a dramatic intervention to save man from the wrath to come. For most modern minds that cosmic setting is absent, and the question based on it is therefore not a live one. On the other hand, to the question offered as its translation, "How can I be assured that my life has some enduring meaning?" Luther had no objective answer to give. Has anyone attempted such an answer? Yes, and here is my second comment, which may surprise Mr. Irish. I have made that rash attempt myself. Mr. Irish seems to think I am an epistemologist solely and that my answer to the question what would give a life its richest fulfillment is the "satisfaction of thought." He has evidently not consulted my *Reason and Goodness* (of which I certainly do not complain), but if he had, he would have seen that I emphatically reject the mere satisfaction of thought as an adequate human good. I do of course accept intellectual fulfillment as a part of that good, and try to explain its role in man's fulfillment as a whole. But one may be a rationalist without being an intellectualist. And whether my account is correct or not, I think I have shown that such an account can be given without presupposing at any point a theology that would doom those who took it seriously to perpetual terror.

Emotive and Cognitive Meaning

(A5) The fifth criticism Mr. Irish considers is that "*Luther's faith confused emotive and cognitive certainty.*" I had argued that the certainty belonging to Luther's vivid experiences of the presence of God and of Satan was probably better described as an "emotion of conviction" than as a genuine cognition. I supplied a series of instances in which experiences that seemed qualitatively similar to Luther's had produced beliefs that had turned out mistaken. And if a certain method of reaching beliefs leads to error, that so far disqualifies the method. Mr. Irish asks the relevant question "whether the scientific disproof of claims made in the name of faith disproves the faith as well." It does not, I agree. All sorts of absurd claims have been made in the name of faith. Many or most of them must be false, if only because they are inconsistent with each other. But that does not prove that there is no one particular faith among them that is *the* right and authoritative one.

Two comments are in order here. (a) The faith experience that is authoritative must be clearly enough defined so that it can be distinguished from others that claim truth also; it is bound otherwise to remain under suspicion. Thus far no clear identifying mark of this experience seems to have been found. When theologians like Barth and Brunner are confronted with mystical experiences that seem remarkably like that of Saint Paul or their own experiences of superrational certainty, what are they to do? Three lines seem to be open to them. (i) They may level up. They may say that the experiences of faith that are qualitatively indistinguishable as assurances of truth should be placed on the same level. But that would abandon their case, for it would mean that they would have to accept as true many beliefs that are inconsistent with their own. (ii) They may admit that of two qualitatively similar experiences one does in fact warrant the truth of the belief that issues from it, while the second does not. But then the authenticating mark of the experience is the belief itself; they would be saying that only those experiences exhibited genuine faith that issued in beliefs of the right kind. This, besides begging the question against other faith claims, would abandon faith as the decisive basis of belief, since the truth of the belief would then have to be decided on other grounds. (iii) They may level down. They may say that Paul's conversion experience and Brunner's faith state as described by himself are so like the mystical experience of the Sufis and Saint Theresa, Martin Luther and George Fox, and the beliefs they seem to warrant so far apart, that all alike must be of subjective origin. They are cases in which inconsistent beliefs have been so saturated with the emotion of conviction that they have been confused with genuine cognitive insights. That is the disillusioning view that the facts seem to make most credible.

(b) The claim of faith to validate belief is clearly discredited when untrue beliefs can be unambiguously brought home to that faith. This is sometimes impracticable, as we have seen, since one may be unable to show that the faith held by persons of differing beliefs is really the same. But there is no doubt that the claim has failed when it has been made by an individual for beliefs issuing from his own faith which have turned out false. Nor can there be any doubt that Luther supplies a case in point. It is not always clear, to be sure, when he is speaking in his own voice and when it is "God in him" that is doing the speaking; but when he speaks in a formal way and with the accent of authority on matters of religious importance, it is fair to read him as expressing the faith that is in him rather than a passing private opinion. Of what, then, did his faith give him certainty? For one thing, it gave him assurance regarding the whole theology of salvation, including God's loving-kindness and his infliction of eternal punishment, his predestination of some to receive faith and his hardening the hearts of others, both of course being perfectly just. Luther could denounce the Pope as anti-Christ and hence doomed to hell; he could urge the persecution of the Jews as having been accursed ever since their act of deicide; he could approve execution for what his faith classified as blasphemy. If Mr. Irish says that one cannot blame every kind of faith for the vagaries of some varieties of it, he is right. But if the faith of a given man issues in beliefs that are inconsistent and actions that are barbarous, that man's faith does not retain much authority as a source of truth and right.

Luther's Ethics

II. Mr. Irish has been stating what there is to be said in defense of Luther's rationality; he turns now (B) to a defense of Luther's ethics. He undertakes to answer two charges I made against that ethics.

(B1) The first is that Luther held to the doctrine of original sin. The defense is more correctly called a plea in extenuation, for Mr. Irish admits to his credit that on some points Luther is beyond defense. He adds, "It is unfortunate, however, that Blanshard refuses to discuss a demythologized version of the fall and original sin." I answer that I do not know of any demythologized version which would not destroy the theological essence of that doctrine. If it means merely that we are all sinful creatures, even as our fathers were, and that there is every prospect of our continuing to be so and paying the price, the doctrine is no doubt true, but it is hardly worth stating. As soon as one begins to add the traditional content of the doctrine, the depth of its immorality begins to reveal itself. The doctrine of hereditary sinfulness, the doctrine that God, with foreknowledge of man's misuse of his liberty, still created him as he did, the doctrine condemning man for the sins of his forefathers, the doctrine that a good man's goodness can somehow cancel a sinful man's sinfulness, the doctrine that a kindly Deity would approve a bloody sacrifice as atoning for moral evil, the doctrine that baptism can roll from our backs a load of evil, the doctrine that goodness is not hereditary though wickedness is, the doctrine that men will be consigned to eternal suffering for what they never did, the doctrine that a God who would do these things should be called "good" and "just"—all these components and more in the traditional doctrine are outrages on our moral sense. If Mr. Irish is willing to call all this mythology, as I should do, perhaps we could find some common ground on the old dogma. But I do not think he would, and the thought that dogmas on this moral level are still being taught, even with expurgations, in our theological seminaries strikes one layman with astonishment.

Mr. Irish seems to accept Luther's view at a critical point: it is by faith, not works, that we are delivered from the fear of punishment for original sin. He proceeds to explain that there is a genuine moral advantage in this theological arrangement. So long as we are without faith, we work under a double handicap: our most altruistic labors are self-serving, and our fear of damnation remains alive, for we know that our good works, however great, can never save us. But once faith is granted us and our fear for the future is removed, we can work for others with the knowledge that our old selfishness in serving them is gone, and that we are able at last to give ourselves to them for their own good alone. "Christian liberty, as Luther described it, was freedom from anxiety over one's own destiny. Thus liberated, the Christian could see the needs of the neighbor and seek to fill those needs without thought of reward or punishment from God or neighbor."

Surely this puts us in a curious position. (i) It assumes, as we have seen, that all our natural interests in others' good are self-deceptive; we are really seeking our own good throughout under the hypocritical guise of an interest in that of others. Now in ethical circles this is simply the hoary fallacy of psychological egoism, which has been examined and found wanting by scores of moralists from Butler to Broad. For anyone who knows the literature, there is no need to repeat the standard refutations. (ii) It must be remembered that the faith that enables us to be thus other-regarding has not been achieved by us at all; it has been implanted in us from on high, and, so far as we can see, arbitrarily. Why this liberation should be conferred on some and withheld from others who by human standards deserve it more is a matter that lies in darkness, but must be accepted as wholly right and just. (iii) If genuine service for others is possible only to possessors of the Lutheran type of "faith," the outlook for mankind in general is extremely dreary. All charitable organizations, for example, all civic interests, all humanitarian medicine, all societies for the prevention of cruelty to animals or infants, unless operated by the few that are chosen for the receipt of grace, are really being conducted by corrupt and selfish minds. Even Schweitzer at Lambaréné, who would have called all this nonsense and therefore was an unlikely recipient of grace, had none but a self-serving interest in his patients. If the altruistic salt of the earth is really so depraved as this, there is small hope left for us. (iv) Even the man who has been granted through grace some interest in the good of others is limited to giving them second-rate goods; he cannot even lend them a helping hand toward gaining the pearl of great price. He can help them to be healthy, wealthy, and wise; he can teach his children to aim at the high goods of morality; but these are petty things which will mean nothing at the great assize. (v) Furthermore, he will get no credit for his efforts, even if they are genuine works of love; for, as I understand it, Luther would deny that works, no matter how prompted, had any effect on one's state of grace. Our moral status is therefore curious and complex. As natural men, nothing we do that is good will count in our favor, though everything we do that is bad will be held against us. As recipients of grace, everything we do is good, since it is God in us who is acting, whether to the impartial eye it looks good or not, while for the same reason we are incapable of doing wrong. (vi) "Christian liberty, as Luther described it, was freedom from anxiety over one's own destiny," says Mr. Irish. But is it not something of a mockery to hold up before those who are in slavery the ideal of a freedom which no effort, however heroic, can enable them to attain? The great majority of men are headed, through the will of a loving Deity, to permanent misery, and that "freedom from anxiety over one's own destiny" in which Christian liberty consists is an unattainable bait dangled beyond the reach of men who live in chains.

Mr. Irish's attempt to find some advantage mitigating the immorality of the doctrine of original sin is not, I think, a success.

A Moral Depressant

(B2) The last of my criticisms of Luther that Mr. Irish undertakes to meet is that "justification by faith" is a depressant to morality. In my book I quoted a number of passages from Luther regarding the corruption in which natural man is supposed to be living. For example: "In Scripture God concludes . . . [that] 'every imagination of the thoughts of his [man's] heart was only evil continually.'" "No one should doubt that all our good works are mortal sins if they are evaluated by God's strict judgment." If such statements mean anything—and in Luther they are plentiful—they mean that nothing we can do will win approval in God's sight, and that the highest morality of which we are humanly capable is still damnable, since it is not only sin but mortal sin. Here is how Mr. Irish begins his reply:

> Blanshard holds that the negation of works as a means of winning salvation discourages acts of kindness and militates against the sense of honor and justice. An allied criticism is that persons are merely pawns in a supernatural transaction completely beyond their control. These charges are difficult to assess. The first assumes that without the prize the race is not worth running; the second assumes that the race is rigged anyway. It is hard to imagine Blanshard or anyone similarly disposed to Luther's understanding of God making either of these assumptions. And if one shares Luther's view of God, the criticisms melt away.

Unfortunately the criticisms do not melt away. Luther says that "all our good works are mortal sins"; I complain that this discourages good works; Mr. Irish replies that such a complaint "assumes that without the prize the race is not worth running." By "the prize" he presumably means either the prize of salvation or the prize of moral goodness. And Luther says unequivocally that neither of these is open to us by anything we do. Salvation is not to be won by works of any kind. And if we try to be morally good, "our good works are mortal sins," which again means, if it has any meaning, that our attempts at good works only plunge us deeper into God's disfavor. There is no denying that Luther said these things; I do not see how anyone can deny that they are morally depressing.

The second assumption I am charged with is "that the race is rigged anyway." Why Mr. Irish should find it "hard to imagine" my ascribing this view to Luther I do not know, for it is exactly what he held. He held a view of predestination according to which a few are selected, on no principle discernible to us, for the gift of grace and for consequent election to his kingdom, while the others, regardless of their effort, are denied all hope of this prize. This is rigging results on a cosmic scale. Mr. Irish answers: "As for being human pawns, Luther would prefer to say persons are instruments of God's glory and that, far from being a depressing view, is invigorating." Invigorating to whom? Perhaps to Luther himself, who was so sure that he was a chosen vessel of grace, and to a comparatively small band of the elect. But in his computations of invigoratingness Mr. Irish seems to have forgotten one group—the human race generally. It is not, I should have thought, exhilarating to realize that in all probability one is doomed to an undying torture which no effort can avert.

Mr. Irish does his best for Luther—better indeed than he deserves. I began my study of the reformer with the praises of Carlyle, which I had read in my boyhood, still echoing in my ears. But I had read practically nothing of the man's own words, and the more I read him, the more disillusioned I became. Here certainly was a formidable natural force. But how unreasonable he was—profoundly, grossly, proudly, perversely unreasonable! He was brimming with prejudices as violent as they were irrational; he even shook a big, futile fist in the face of logic; he elaborated a theology that made God both loving and sadistically cruel, both just and an ogre. By holding up as divine practice a morality that was itself immoral, he befuddled the minds and clouded the standards of generations of would-be Christians. I do not know how far Mr. Irish has committed himself to this powerful and uncouth prophet, but in a world where there are so many clear, humble, and honest thinkers to choose from, so many minds that have managed to keep faith, even in their religious flights, with their sense of decency and justice, it would be a pity if any promising young scholar still chose for hero-worship a mind so tortured and so confused.

PART THREE

BIBLIOGRAPHY OF THE WRITINGS OF BRAND BLANSHARD TO 1980
(Compiled by John Howie)

PREFACE TO THE BIBLIOGRAPHY

S OME of the graduate seminars that I have taught during the past ten years have been devoted entirely to Brand Blanshard's philosophy, others to a survey of representative American philosophies. For these seminars a list of Blanshard's writings was initially prepared and regularly revised. In the last few years he has sent me lists of the annual additions.

Many persons as well as Brand Blanshard have helped in the preparation of this bibliography. Alan Cohn and Kathleen Eads of Morris Library, Southern Illinois University, have been unreserved in their helpfulness through the years. Ira Farber of Earlham College has helped complete several entries for the Quaker publication, *Friends Intelligencer*. Roberta Yerkes Blanshard has verified many entries and dredged up others more or less forgotten by their author. The compiler's debt to all is very great.

JOHN HOWIE

DEPARTMENT OF PHILOSOPHY
SOUTHERN ILLINOIS UNIVERSITY

THE WRITINGS OF BRAND BLANSHARD

1916

The Baghdad Railway. *Young Men of India,* Vol. XXVII, September, 1916, pp. 514–521. Calcutta: Y.M.C.A.s of India and Ceylon.

1917

Young Men of India, Vol. XXVIII, [Spring], 1917.
(Exact title unknown; an appreciation of James Hope Moulton, professor of Greek, Manchester University.)

1920

The Church and the Polish Immigrant. Philadelphia: A. C. Barnes, 1920. Pp. 79.

1923

Review of J. M. E. McTaggart's *Studies in the Hegelian Dialectic.* In *The Journal of Philosophy,* Vol. XX, 1923, pp. 413–415.

1924

Review of R. F. A. Hoernlé's *Matter, Life, Mind and God.* In *The Journal of Philosophy,* Vol. XXI, 1924, pp. 191–193.

Review of Joseph A. Leighton's *The Field of Philosophy.* In *The Journal of Philosophy,* Vol. XXI, 1924, pp. 361–362.

1925

Review of Norman Kemp Smith's *Prolegomena to an Idealist Theory of Knowledge.* In *The Journal of Philosophy,* Vol. XXII, 1925, pp. 605–609.

Francis Herbert Bradley. *The Journal of Philosophy,* Vol. XXII, January, 1925, pp. 5–15.

1927

Drama and the Liberal Arts. *Quarterly Journal of Speech Education,* Vol. XIII, November, 1927, pp. 375–386.

Review of J. E. Turner's *A Theory of Direct Realism.* In *The Philosophical Review,* Vol. XXXVI, January, 1927, pp. 76–80.

Review of James E. Creighton's *Studies in Speculative Philosophy.* In *The Journal of Philosophy,* Vol. XXIV, 1927, pp. 46–50.

Review of John Cook Wilson's *Statement and Inference.* In *The Journal of Philosophy,* Vol. XXIV, 1927, pp. 525–530.

Review of James Ward's *Psychology Applied to Education.* In *The Journal of Philosophy,* Vol. XXIV, 1927, pp. 555–557.

1928

The Ethics of Imperialism. *Friends Intelligencer,* Vol. LXXXV, June 2, 1928, pp. 423–425.

Behaviorism and the Theory of Knowledge. *Philosophical Review,* Vol. XXXVII, July, 1928, pp. 328–352.

Review of James Ward's *Essays in Philosophy.* In *The Journal of Philosophy,* Vol. XXV, 1928, pp. 582–586.

1929

Review of J. M. E. McTaggart's *The Nature of Existence,* Vol. II. In *The Journal of Philosophy,* Vol. XXVI, 1929, pp. 582–587.

1930

The Seventh International Congress of Philosophy. *The Journal of Philosophy,* Vol. XXVII, October 23, 1930, pp. 589–606.

1931

The Place of Belief in Religion. *Crozer Quarterly,* Vol. VIII, April, 1931, pp. 213–227.

Style in Literature and Life. *Hollins Alumnae Quarterly,* Vol. VI, April, 1931, pp. 1–5.
(Selected portions from Blanshard's Founder's Day Address.)

1932

Review of A. E. Taylor's *The Faith of a Moralist.* In *The Journal of Philosophy,* Vol. XXIX, March 3, 1932, pp. 129–137.

Review of F. R. Tennant's *Philosophy of the Sciences.* In *The Journal of Philosophy,* Vol. XXIX, October 27, 1932, pp. 610–614.

The Purpose of a Liberal Education. *Friends Intelligencer,* Vol. LXXXIX, December 3, 1932, pp. 971–973.

1933

The Case Against Japan. *The New York Times,* March 21, 1933, p. 16, column 6.
(Letter to the editor on the Sino-Japanese situation, written from Swarthmore College, March 18, 1933.)

The Rhodes Scholars at Swarthmore. *Friends Intelligencer,* Vol. XC, June 3, 1933, p. 427.

Brains Count More in Rhodes Awards. *The New York Times,* June 4, 1933, Section #4E, p. 7.

The Swarthmore Reunion. *American Oxonian,* Vol. XX, July, 1933, pp. 139–152.

On New Year's Resolutions. *Friends Intelligencer,* Vol. XC, December 30, 1933, pp. 907–908.

Review of Second Congrès Polonais de Philosophie. In *The Philosophical Review,*
Vol. XLII, January, 1933, pp. 77–78.

1934

Talk. *Eleusis of Chi Omega* [Fraternity], Vol. XXXVI, February, 1934, pp. 72–77.
    (Reprinted, as Talk and Talkers in *The Manuscript* [Swarthmore], June, 1936,
    pp. 3–10, and published also in *Presbyterian Life,* Vol. IX, September 1, 1956,
    pp. 10–11, 28–30.)

To Prepare or Not to Prepare? *Friends Intelligencer,* Vol. XCI, March 17, 1934, pp.
163–164.
    (An editorial.)

York and Dr. Jacks. *Friends Intelligencer,* Vol. XCI, December 15, 1934, pp.
794–795.

1935

Lynching and the Law. *Friends Intelligencer,* Vol. XCII, February 2, 1935, pp.
70–71.

The Economic and the Inner Man. *Friends Intelligencer,* Vol. XCII, June 22, 1935,
pp. 390–391.

The Price of Neutrality. *Friends Intelligencer,* Vol. XCII, September 21, 1935, pp.
598–599.

1936

Christian Ethics. Review of Reinhold Niebuhr's *An Interpretation of Christian
Ethics. Friends Intelligencer,* Vol. XCIII, July 18, 1936.

Inward Light and Outward Darkness. *Friends Intelligencer,* Vol. XCIII, August 15,
1936, pp. 535–538.
    (Abstract of an address given July 9, 1936, at Friends General Conference,
    Cape May, New Jersey. The entire address was published as a pamphlet by the
    Friends General Conference in Philadelphia in 1937 (27 pages). Reprinted in
    Through a Quaker Archway; edited by Horace Mather Lippincott. London:
    Thomas Yoseloff, 1959, pp. 27–51.)

1937

Review of James T. Shotwell's *On the Rim of the Abyss. Friends Intelligencer,* Vol.
XCIV, January 16, 1937, p. 42.

Quakerism and Moral Chaos. *Friends Intelligencer,* Vol. XCIV, February 13, 1937,
pp. 108–110.

The Ministry of Beauty. I and II. *Friends Intelligencer,* Vol. XCIV, April 17, 24,
1937.

The Fruits of Neutrality. *Friends Intelligencer,* Vol. XCIV, July 31, 1937, pp.
517–518.

Metaphysics and Social Attitudes. *Social Frontier,* Vol. IV, December, 1937, pp. 79–81.
    (Reprinted as Philosophy and Social Attitudes, *Portfolio* [Swarthmore], March, 1938, pp. 11–14.)

1938

Should the Campus Be Cloistered? *Portfolio,* March, 1938, pp. 31 –32.
    (A three paragraph contribution to the discussion.)

Metaphysics and Social Attitudes: A Rejoinder. *Social Frontier,* Vol. IV, April, 1938, pp. 219–221.
    (Discussion of Dr. L. J. A. Mercier's paper in *Proceedings of the American Catholic Philosophical Association,* Vol. XIII, 1938, pp. 143–146.

1939

The Outlook in Europe. *Friends Intelligencer,* Vol. XCVI, February 25, 1939, pp. 121–122.

Educate for Internationalism. *Social Frontier,* Vol. V, April, 1939, pp. 216–218.

I Believe . . . . *Friends Intelligencer,* Vol. XCVI, May 13, 1939, pp. 311–312.

The French Take Stock. *Friends Intelligencer,* Vol. XCVI, August 12, 1939, pp. 521–522.

Reflections on Neutrality. *Friends Intelligencer,* Vol. XCVI, September 23, 1939, pp. 617–618.

The Nature of Thought. 2 Vols. London: George Allen & Unwin, 1939; New York: Macmillan Co., 1940; Vol. I, 654 pp., Vol. II, 532 pp. Present distributor, New York: Humanities Press.
    Vol. I, contents: Preface—Book I. Thought in Perception—Chapter 1 The Genesis of Perception, Chapter 2 The Inferential Element in Perception, Chapter 3 The Thing and Its Architecture, Chapter 4 The Nature of Perceptual Meaning, Chapter 5 The Offices of Perceptual Meaning, Chapter 6 The Structure of Perceptual Meaning; Book II. The Theory of the Idea—Chapter 7 The Idea as Image, Chapter 8 Mr. Russell on Ideas, Chapter 9 Behaviourism and Thought, Chapter 10 Pragmatism and Thought, Chapter 11 Realism: Acts Replace Ideas, Chapter 12 Critical Realism: Essences Replace Ideas, Chapter 13 Bradley on Ideas in Logic and in Psychology, Chapter 14 A Theory of the Idea, Chapter 15 The Elementary Types of Idea, Chapter 16 The False or Abstract Universal, Chapter 17 Universals, Generic and Specific.
    Vol. II, contents: Book III. The Movement of Reflection—Chapter 18 The General Nature of Understanding, Chapter 19 How Reflection Starts, Chapter 20 Specifying the Problem, Chapter 21 Observation, Chapter 22 Invention and Association, Chapter 23 The Nature of Invention, Chapter 24 The Subconscious in Invention, Chapter 25 The Tests of Truth, Chapter 26 Coherence as the Nature of Truth, Chapter 27 Coherence and Degrees of Truth; Book IV. The Goal of Thought—Chapter 28 Empiricism and Necessity, Chapter 29 Formalism and Necessity, Chapter 30 Logical Positivism and Necessity, Chapter 31 Con-

crete Necessity and External Relations, Chapter 32 Concrete Necessity and Internal Relations. Index (for both volumes).

Review of George Mattisse's *La Philosophie de la nature.* In *The Philosophical Review,* Vol. XLVIII, 1939, p. 232.

Review of L. Noël's *Le Réalisme immédiat.* In *The Philosophical Review,* Vol. XLVIII, 1939, p. 343.

1940

A Meditation at Chartres. *Friends Intelligencer,* Vol. XCVII, January 13, 1940, pp. 19–20.

Cynicism, A Lament. *Bulletin of the Swarthmore Student Union,* May, 1940, 4 pp.

Why I Am Not a Pacifist. *Friend,* Vol. CXIII, May 2, 1940, pp. 393–395.

Mysticism and Pacifism. *Friend,* Vol. CXIV, September 5, 1940, pp. 72–73.

Two Swarthmore Presidents: I. Frank Aydelotte; II. John W. Nason. *Friends Intelligencer,* Vol. XCVII, October 19, 1940, pp. 671–673; October 23, 1940, pp. 687–689.
(Reprinted in *American Oxonian,* Vol. XXVIII, January, 1941, pp. 1–9.)

1941

The Nature of Mind. *The Journal of Philosophy,* Vol. XXXVIII, April 10, 1941, pp. 207–216.
(Reprinted in *American Philosophers at Work. The Philosophic Scene in the United States;* edited by Sidney Hook. New York: Criterion Books, 1956, pp. 183–193. Abstract, *The Journal of Philosophy,* Vol. XXXVII, December 5, 1940, pp. 679–680.

May a Non-pacifist Be a Friend? *American Friend,* Vol. XXIX, July 17, 1941, pp. 302–303.

The Principles of Education at Swarthmore. In *An Adventure in Education: Swarthmore College Under Frank Aydelotte,* by the Swarthmore College faculty. New York: Macmillan Company, 1941, pp. 1–24.

1942

Review of *The Philosophy of George Santayana,* edited by Paul A. Schilpp. *Philosophical Review,* Vol. LI, March, 1942, pp. 213–216.

Jesse Herman Holmes. *Friends Intelligencer,* Vol. XCIX, June 6, 1942, pp. 368–369.

Non-pacifist Quakerism. *Friends Intelligencer,* Vol. XCIX, June 20, 1942, pp. 393–394; June 27, 1942, pp. 409–410.
(Reprinted in *American Oxonian,* Vol. XXX, April, 1943, pp. 80–87.)

Review of E. G. Conklin's *What Is Man?* In *The Humanist,* Vol. II, Summer, 1942, pp. 77–78.

The Religious Office of Art. *Friends Intelligencer,* Vol. XCIX, November 14, 1942, pp. 734–735.

Fact, Value, and Science. In *Science and Man;* edited by R. N. Ashen. New York: Harcourt, Brace, 1942, pp. 185–203.

In Commemoration of William James, 1842–1942; edited by Blanshard and Herbert W. Schneider. Foreword by H. M. Kallen. New York: Columbia University Press, 1942. Pp. xii + 234.
    (Reprinted, New York: A. M. S. Press, 1967.)

1943

Some Pacifist Confusions. *Christianity and Crisis,* Vol. III, May 31, 1943, pp. 2–5.
    (Reprinted in *Modern Writing;* edited by Willard and Margaret F. Thorp. New York: American Book Company, 1944, pp. 337–342.)

A Negotiated Peace. *Friends Intelligencer,* Vol. C, June 19, 1943, pp. 405–406.

Adjustment of the College Curriculum to Wartime Conditions and Needs. Report No. 9: Philosophy, by Brand Blanshard, Grace de Laguna, and Glenn R. Morrow. United States Office of Education, Federal Security Agency, n.d., mimeographed, 15 pp. [1943 or 1944].

1944

Must Democrats Have a Theology? *Humanist,* Vol. IV, Summer, 1944, pp. 79–82.

Death Comes for the Archbishop. *Friends Intelligencer,* Vol. CI, November 11, 1944, pp. 737–738.

Theology and the Value of the Individual. *Conference of May 1943 on the Scientific Spirit and Democratic Faith.* New York: King's Crown Press, 1944, pp. 74–86.

Comments on Charles W. Morris's The Social Assimilation of Cultural Relativity, and comments on Filmer S. C. Northrop's Philosophy and World Peace. In *Approaches to World Peace.* Fourth Symposium of the Conference on Science, Philosophy, and Religion in Their Relation to the Democratic Way of Life, edited by Lyman Bryson, Louis Finkelstein, and Robert M. Maciver. New York and London: Harper & Brothers, 1944, pp. 630–632, 658–659.

The Great Commandment. Philadelphia, Pennsylvania: Friends General Conference, 1944. Pp. 14.
    (Reprinted in *Presbyterian Life,* July 23, 1949, pp. 20–22.)

1945

Notice of Harold F. Cherniss's *Aristotle's Criticism of Plato and the Academy.* In *The U. S. Quarterly Book List,* Vol. I, March, 1945.

From the Commission's Mailbag. *Philosophical Review,* Vol. LIV, May, 1945, pp. 197–259.
    (Excerpts from letters received by the Commission on Philosophy edited with comment by Brand Blanshard.)

Notice of Harold F. Cherniss's *The Riddle of the Early Academy.* In *The U. S. Quarterly Book List,* Vol. I, June, 1945.

Education as Philosophy. *Swarthmore College Bulletin,* Vol. XLII, July, 1945, pp. 5–19.

    (Address delivered February 25, 1945, at the Commencement exercises of Swarthmore College. Reprinted in *Readings for Liberal Education,* Vol. I, edited by Louis Glenn Locke, W. M. Gibson, and G. Arms. New York: Rinehart, 1948, pp. 587–596. In *Perspectives,* edited by Leonard Fellows Dean. New York: Harcourt, Brace, 1954, pp. 57–67. In *Essays for Study,* edited by Maurice Baudin Jr. and Karl G. Pfeiffer. New York, Toronto, London: McGraw-Hill, 1960, pp. 501–512.)

Current Strictures on Reason. *Philosophical Review,* Vol. LIV, July 1945, pp. 345–368.

    (Presidential Address, Eastern Division, American Philosophical Association.)

A Critical Work on Logic. Review of Morris R. Cohen's *A Preface to Logic.* In *The Yale Review,* Vol. XXXV, September, 1945, pp. 170–172.

Review of Ernst Cassirer's *Essay on Man.* In *The Philosophical Review,* Vol. LIV, September, 1945, pp. 509–510.

Review of Jacques Maritain's *The Dream of Descartes.* In *The Philosophical Review,* Vol. LIV, November, 1945, pp. 611–612.

Workshop of the Unconscious. *American Mercury,* Vol. LXI, December, 1945, pp. 693–698.

The Climate of Opinion; The Opportunity of Philosophy; The Basic Courses in Philosophy: Ethics; The Basic Courses in Philosophy: Metaphysics (with C. J. Ducasse). In *Philosophy in American Education: Its Tasks and Opportunities.* New York and London: Harper & Brothers, 1945, pp. 3–42, 87–117, 221–224, 227–232.

1946

The Inner Light. *Harvard Divinity School Bulletin,* Vol. XLIII, March 10, 1946, pp. 43–64.

    (Dudleian Lecture, Harvard University.)

Do Scientists Need the Humanities? *Yale Scientific Magazine,* Vol. XX, March, 1946, pp. 7–8, 26.

    (Article three in a series of four on Science and the Humanities. The other writers: R. L. Calhoun, Henry Margenau, Hardy Cross.)

Russell on Philosophy and Philosophers. Review of Bertrand Russell's *A History of Western Philosophy.* In *The Yale Review,* Vol. XXXV, March, 1946, pp. 568–570.

Review of Luther P. Eisenhart's *The Educational Process.* In *The Journal of Higher Education,* Vol. XVII, May, 1946, p. 276.

Notice of Max Wertheimer's *Productive Thinking.* In *The U. S. Quarterly Book List,* Vol. II, September, 1946.

Current Strictures on Reason: A Rejoinder. In *The Philosophical Review,* Vol. LV, November, 1946, pp. 670–673.

    (A reply to Criticism by J. H. Groth, pp. 668–670.)

The Nature of Man. *The Journal of Philosophy,* Vol. XLIII, 1946, p. 673.
(An abstract.)

Part 2, Personal Ethics. In *Preface to Philosophy: Textbook,* edited by William Pearson Tolley. New York: The Macmillan Company, 1946, pp. 103–195.

1947

The Liberal College in An Expanding World. *The Inauguration of Martha Lucas as President of Sweet Briar College* [November 1, 1946]. *Bulletin of Sweet Briar College,* Vol. XXX, January, 1947, pp. 5–19.

Can Man Expand With Expanding Knowledge?
(Abstract of address to the American Academy of Arts and Sciences, January 8, 1947.)

An Inner Compass. In Emily Green Balch Number of *Four Lights,* Vol. VI, January, 1947, p. 2.

American Speculative Thinkers. Review of Herbert W. Schneider's *A History of American Philosophy.* In *The Yale Review,* Vol. XXXVI, March, 1947, pp. 530–533.

Notice of W. Fales's *Wisdom and Responsibility.* In *The U. S. Quarterly Book List,* Vol. III, March, 1947, p. 29.

Notice of D. C. Williams's *The Ground of Induction.* In *The U. S. Quarterly Book List,* Vol. III, June, 1947, p. 143.

Life as Art. *Swarthmore College Bulletin,* Vol. XLV, November, 1947, pp. 3–16.
(Baccalaureate address delivered at Swarthmore, June 15, 1947.)

Can Men Be Reasonable? In *Our Emergent Civilization,* edited by Ruth Nanda Ashen. New York and London: Harper & Brothers, 1947, pp. 25–48.
(Translated into Polish in Filozofia Amerykánska, East Europe Institute. Boston: Boston University Press, 1958, pp. 117–145.)

The Escape from Philosophic Futility. In *Freedom and Experience,* Essays Presented to Horace M. Kallen, edited by Sidney Hook and Milton R. Konvitz. Ithaca and New York: Cornell University Press, 1947, pp. 191–204.

1948

Limited Minds and Unlimited Knowledge. *Bucknell University Bulletin,* XLVII Series, September, 1948, 12 pp.

Notice of R. M. Grant's *The Bible in the Church.* In *The U. S. Quarterly Book List,* Vol. IV, September, 1948, pp. 281–282.

Review of A. H. Smith's *Kantian Studies.* In *The Philosophical Review,* Vol. LVII, November, 1948, pp. 607–611.

Comment on David Baumgardt's Poise and Passion in Philosophy. In *Learning and World Peace: A Symposium,* edited by Lyman Bryson and others. New York: Harper & Brothers, 1948, p. 368.

Speculative Thinkers. In *Literary History of the United States,* edited by R. E. Spiller, W. Thorp, T. H. Johnson, and H. S. Canby, 2 Vols. New York: Macmillan Company, 1948, Vol. II, pp. 1273–1296.

1949

Semantics, Relativity, Probability. Review of Bertrand Russell's *Human Knowledge: Its Scope and Limits. Saturday Review of Literature,* Vol. XXXII, January 8, 1949, p. 15.

The New Subjectivism in Ethics. *Philosophy and Phenomenological Research,* Vol. IX, March, 1949, pp. 504–511.

Notice of Martha M. Pingel's *An American Utilitarian: Richard Hildreth as a Philosopher.* In *The U. S. Quarterly Book List,* Vol. V, March, 1949, pp. 39–40.

Notice of Reidar Thomte's *Kierkegaard's Philosophy of Religion.* In *The U. S. Quarterly Book List,* Vol. V, March, 1949, p. 40.

Rationalism. Review of Samuel H. Beer's *The City of Reason.* In *The Saturday Review of Literature,* Vol. XXXII, April 23, 1949, pp. 23–24.

Notice of Otis Lee's *Existence and Inquiry.* In *The U. S. Quarterly Book List,* Vol. V, June, 1949, pp. 172–173.

Review of H. J. Cadbury's *George Fox's Book of Miracles.* In *The Pennsylvania Magazine of History and Biography,* Vol. LXXIII, July, 1949, pp. 396–397.

Dropping of the Object Everywhere. Review of C. E. M. Joad's *Decadence.* In *The Saturday Review of Literature,* Vol. XXXII, July 16, 1949, pp. 12–13.

Notice of Helmut Kuhn's *Encounter with Nothingness: An Essay on Existentialism.* In *The U. S. Quarterly Book List,* Vol. V, September, 1949, pp. 326–327.

Unraveling an Idea. Review of Philip P. Wiener's *Evolution and the Founders of Pragmatism.* In *The Saturday Review of Literature,* Vol. XXXII, October 22, 1949, p. 15.

The Why of a College Education. *Wheaton Alumnae Quarterly,* October, 1949, pp. 10–11, 24–25.
> (Condensation of the Convocation address, The Uses of a Liberal Education.)

Union or Destruction. Notice of Stringfellow Barr's *The Pilgrimage of Western Man.* In *Freedom and Union,* November, 1949, p. 32.

A Philosophical Logician. *Review of Metaphysics,* Vol. III, December, 1949, pp. 249–260.

The Heritage of Idealism. In *Changing Patterns in American Civilization,* by Dixon Wecter, F. O. Matthiessen, Detlev W. Bronk, George F. Thomas, and Blanshard. Philadelphia: University of Pennsylvania Press, 1949, pp. 82–124.

The Uses of a Liberal Education. Norton, Massachusetts: Wheaton College, 1949, 16 pp.
> (A Convocation address at Wheaton College, September, 1949. Reprinted as Hazen Foundation Pamphlet No. 26 [1950], 21 pp. Also reprinted in *Viewpoints: Readings for Analysis,* edited by Thearle A. Barnhart, William A. Donnelly, Lewis C. Smith. Englewood Cliffs: Prentice-Hall, 1954, pp. 27–41, and in *The*

Uses of a Liberal Education, edited by Eugene Freeman. La Salle, Illinois: Open Court, 1973, pp. 27–43.

Foreword. In Leonard Nelson's *Socratic Method and Critical Philosophy,* translated by Thomas K. Brown III. New Haven: Yale University Press, [1949], 1965, pp. v–vii.

Review of A. C. Ewing's *The Individual, the State and World Government.* In *The Philosophical Review,* Vol. LVIII, 1949, pp. 67–71.

1950

Notice of L. Harold DeWolf's *The Religious Revolt Against Reason.* In *The U. S. Quarterly Book List,* Vol. VI, March, 1950, p. 31.

Notice of Ray Lepley's *Value, A Cooperative Inquiry.* In *The U. S. Quarterly Book List,* Vol. VI, March, 1950, p. 31.

Notice of Ralph Barton Perry's *Characteristically American.* In *The U. S. Quarterly Book List,* Vol. VI, March, 1950, p. 33.

Notice of Joseph Haroutunian's *Lust for Power.* In *The U. S. Quarterly Book List,* Vol. VI, June, 1950, p. 165.

Review of Isabel Ross's *Margaret Fell, Mother of Quakerism.* In *The Pennsylvania Magazine of History and Biography,* Vol. LXXIV, July, 1950, pp. 409–410.

Twixt Saint & Brute. Review of David Bryn-Jones's *The Dilemma of the Idealist.* In *The Saturday Review of Literature,* Vol. XXXIII, July 8, 1950, pp. 25–26.

Notice of John E. Smith's *Royce's Social Infinite.* In *The U. S. Quarterly Book List,* Vol. VI, September, 1950, p. 297.

The Great Pragmatist. Review of Lloyd Morris's *William James: The Message of a Modern Mind.* In *The Saturday Review of Literature,* Vol. XXXIII, November 11, 1950, p. 11.

Philosophy Teaching, Past and Present. In *The Teaching of Philosophy,* edited by Frederick P. Harris. Cleveland, Ohio: Western Reserve University Press, 1950, pp. 1–12.
      (Published form of Proceedings and Addresses of the Conference on the Teaching of Philosophy, Western Reserve University, October 14–15, 1949.)

Psychology and Psychotherapy. In *The Nature of Man: His World, His Spiritual Resources, His Destiny,* edited by A. William Loos and Lawrence B. Chrow. New York: Church Peace Union and the World Alliance for International Friendship through Religion, 1950, pp. 29–36.

1951

Subjectivism in Ethics—A Criticism. *Philosophical Quarterly* [St. Andrews], Vol. I, January, 1951, pp. 127–139.

Philosopher's Paradox. Review of Bertrand Russell's *Unpopular Essays.* In *The Saturday Review of Literature,* Vol. XXXIV, March 3, 1951, pp. 11–12.

Reason and Politics. Review of George Santayana's *Dominations and Powers.* In *The Saturday Review of Literature,* Vol. XXXIV, May 12, 1951, pp. 10–11.

Review of Eliseo Vivas's *The Moral Life and the Ethical Life*. In *The Philosophical Quarterly*, Vol. I, October, 1951, pp. 464–467.

Reason and Its Critics.
    (Syllabus of the Gifford Lectures, first course, session 1951–1952; a 200-word summary of each of the ten lectures in the first series. 8 pp.)

1952

Homespun Philosopher. Review of Jerome Nathanson's *John Dewey: The Reconstruction of the Democratic Life*. In *The Saturday Review of Literature*, Vol. XXXV, January 5, 1952, p. 16.

Mankind's Conflicts. Review of Bertrand Russell's *New Hopes for a Changing World*. In *The Saturday Review of Literature*, Vol. XXXV, February 2, 1952, pp. 14–15.

Two Poets. *College Echoes* [St. Andrews], May, 1952, pp. 14–15.

The New Philosophy of Analysis. *Proceedings of the American Philosophical Society*, Vol. XCVI, June, 1952, pp. 227–230.

The Philosophy of Analysis. *Proceedings of the British Academy*, Vol. XXXVIII, 1952, pp. 39–69.
    (Also issued separately. The annual philosophical lecture on the Henriette Hertz Trust, March 19, 1952.)

Reason and Goodness
    (Syllabus of the Gifford Lectures, second course, session 1952–1953; a 200-word summary of each of the ten lectures in the second series. 11 pp.)

1953

Continental Testament. Review of George Santayana's *My Host the World*. In *The Saturday Review of Literature*, Vol. XXXVI, March 28, 1953, pp. 12–13.

Philosophical Style. *Yale Review*, Vol. XLII, June, 1953, pp. 547–578.
    (The Adamson Lecture, University of Manchester, 1953. Published as a book, *On Philosophical Style*. Manchester: University of Manchester Press, 1954, 69 pp. Midland Book Edition: Bloomington and London: Indiana University Press, 1967.)

That Which Is That. Review of H. W. Fowler's *A Dictionary of Modern English Usage*. In *The Saturday Review of Literature*, Vol. XXXVI, July 4, 1953, pp. 16–17.

1954

Review of John Wild's *The Return to Reason: Essays in Realistic Philosophy*. In *The Philosophical Quarterly*, Vol. IV, January, 1954, pp. 93–94.

The Case for Plato. Review of Ronald B. Levinson's *In Defense of Plato*, and John Wild's *Plato's Modern Enemies and the Theory of Natural Law*. In *The Yale Review*, Vol. XLIII, March, 1954, pp. 444–447.

No Time for Timidity. Review of Ralph Barton Perry's *The Realms of Value*. In *The Saturday Review of Literature*, Vol. XXXVII, May 1, 1954, pp. 36–37.

Wisdom on the Wing. Review of *Dialogues of Alfred North Whitehead*, recorded by

Lucien Price. In *The Saturday Review of Literature,* Vol. XXXVII, May 8, 1954, pp. 13, 33.

Dean Inge. *Friends Intelligencer,* Vol. CXV, June 5, 1954, pp. 311–313.

Review of UNESCO's *The Teaching of Philosophy.* In *The Journal of Philosophy,* Vol. LI, September 2, 1954, pp. 529–531.

A Faith for Academe. Review of Bernard E. Meland's *Higher Education and the Human Spirit.* In *The Saturday Review of Literature,* Vol. XXXVII, September 11, 1954, pp. 33–34.

Sources of Serenity. Buck Hill Falls, Pennsylvania: Foxhowe Association, September, 1954, 23 pp.
    (Reprinted in *Friends Journal,* Vol. II, March 3, 1956, pp. 132–133. Reprinted in part as Fear and Serenity in *Intellectual Digest,* Vol. IV, June, 1974, pp. 49–50.)

Can the Philosopher Influence Social Change? *The Journal of Philosophy,* Vol. LI, November 25, 1954, pp. 741–753.

Coherence Theory of Truth. In *Contemporary Philosophy,* edited by James L. Jarrett and S. M. McMurrin. New York: Holt, Rinehart & Winston, 1954, pp. 32–37.
    (Selection from *The Nature of Thought,* Vol. II.)

1955

Right and Wrong in 1955. Review of Bertrand Russell's *Human Society in Ethics and Politics.* In *The Saturday Review of Literature,* Vol. XXXVIII, January 29, 1955, p. 13.

Lady Wylie Visits the U. S. A. and Canada. *American Oxonian,* Vol. XLII, January, 1955, pp. 10–13.

The Morality of Self-respect. *New Republic,* Vol. CXXXII, February 28, 1955, pp. 11–12.

Philosophical Defenses of Freedom.
    (An address to the American Theological Society, April 15, 1955. Mimeographed, 7 pp.)

Nature, Mind, and Modern Science. Review of Errol E. Harris's *Nature, Mind, and Modern Science.* In *The Philosophical Quarterly,* Vol. V, April, 1955, pp. 166–174.

What Should We Get From College? *Carleton College Bulletin,* Vol. LI, June, 1955, pp. 3–18.
    (Fifth annual address of Dana Lecture Series, Carleton College, Northfield, Minnesota, delivered October 22, 1954. Reprinted in *The Purposes of a Liberal Education.* Pacific Lutheran University, n.d., pp. 3–17.)

Notice of Frederick E. Johnson's *Religious Symbolism.* In *The U. S. Quarterly Book List,* Vol. XI, June, 1955.

Philosopher through the Fog. Review of *John Dewey,* edited by Irwin Edman. In *The Saturday Review of Literature,* Vol. XXXVIII, August 13, 1955, p. 9.

Review of John Henry Melzer's *Philosophy in the Classroom: A Report.* In *The Journal of Philosophy,* Vol. LII, September 15, 1955, pp. 521–523.

Notice of Reinhold Niebuhr's *The Self and the Dramas of History.* In *The U. S. Quarterly Book Review,* Vol. XI, September, 1955, p. 360.

Wrestling with Ethics. Review of Philip Blair Rice's *On the Knowledge of Good and Evil.* In *The Saturday Review of Literature,* Vol. XXXVIII, December 10, 1955, p. 21.

The Impasse in Ethics—and a Way Out. Berkeley and Los Angeles: University of California Press, 1955.

> (Also published as University of California Publications in Philosophy, Vol. XXVIII, pp. 93–112. Translation into Spanish by José González. ¿Está la ética en un callejón sin salida? [1. ed. en español.] México, Centro de Estudios Filosóficos, Universidad Nacional Autonoma de México, 1959, pp. 45–66. Cuadernos del Centro de Estudios Filosóficos, 2.)

1956

Moderately Good Fun. Review of Bertrand Russell's *Nightmares of Eminent Persons.* In *The Humanist,* Vol. XVI, January–February, 1956, p. 51.

Notice of *The Philosophy of Jonathan Edwards,* edited by Harvey G. Townsend. In *The U. S. Quarterly Book Review,* Vol. XII, March 17, 1956, p. 12.

SR's Book of the Week. Review of Charles Frankel's *The Case for Modern Man.* In *The Saturday Review of Literature,* Vol. XXXIX, March 17, 1956, p. 12.

Quantity and Quality in American Education. Printed in two parts: Quantity and Quality in American Education and No Amount of Quantity Can Buy Quality. *Colby Alumnus,* Spring, 1956, pp. 14–18; Summer, 1956, pp. 12–15, 18.

> (The Ingraham Lecture at Colby College, Waterville, Maine for 1956. Also printed in a separate pamphlet by Colby College. Reprinted in *The Student Seeks an Answer,* edited by John A. Clark. Waterville, Maine: Colby College Press, 1960, pp. 247–272.)

Quantity or Quality? *Harvard Educational Review,* Vol. XXVI, Spring, 1956, pp. 199–202.

Comments on Walhout's Theses. In Colloquium no. 9, Donald Walhout, Judgment. *Review of Metaphysics,* Vol. IX, June, 1956, pp. 644–645.

Why Study Philosophy? *Yale Alumni Magazine,* Vol. XIX, June, 1956, pp. 16–17.
> (The general title of the article is Philosophy in the Modern World.)

Courage. *Swarthmore College Bulletin,* Vol. LIII, June, 1956, pp. 13–18.

Notice of Herbert Marcuse's *Eros and Civilization.* In *The U. S. Quarterly Book Review,* Vol. XII, June, 1956, pp. 184–185.

Review of Marie Collins Swabey's *Logic and Nature.* In *The Journal of Philosophy,* Vol. LIII, August 2, 1956, pp. 509–510.

Logician of Illogic. Review of Stuart Chase's *Guides to Straight Thinking.* In *The Saturday Review of Literature,* Vol. XXXIX, September 8, 1956, p. 38.

Absolute. In *Encyclopaedia Britannica.* Chicago, London, and Toronto: Encyclopaedia Britannica Incorporated, 1956, Vol. I, p. 64.
> (Reprinted in the 1967 edition, Vol. I, pp. 49–50.)

1957

Proof in Psychical Research. *Journal of the American Society for Psychical Research,* Vol. LI, January, 1957, pp. 3–24.
    (The third John William Graham Lecture on Psychic Science given May 11, 1956, to the American Society for Psychical Research.)

Frank Aydelotte. *American Oxonian,* Vol. XLIV, April, 1957, pp. 49–58.

America's Cultural Resources for Leadership. Address at Conference on Our Moral and Spiritual Resources for International Cooperation. Temple University, Philadelphia, Pennsylvania, April 6, 1957. Mimeographed report prepared for UNESCO, June, 1957, pp. 50–69.

The Idea of the Gentleman. *Oberlin Alumni Magazine,* May, 1957, pp. 8–11, 15.

Lord Russell Plus Shock. Review of Bertrand Russell's *Why I Am Not a Christian.* In *The Saturday Review of Literature,* Vol. XL, October 5, 1957, pp. 14–15.

The Isle of Man. Review of José Ortega y Gasset's *Man and People.* In *The Saturday Review of Literature,* Vol. XL, November 16, 1957, p. 24.

The Nature of Truth, and Concrete Necessity and Internal Relations. In *The Idealist Tradition. From Berkeley to Blanshard,* edited by A. C. Ewing. Glencoe, Illinois: Free Press, 1957, pp. 253–261, 262–279.
    (Reprinted selections from *The Nature of Thought,* (1939, 1940), Vol. II, Chapters 26 and 32.)

1958

A Contemporary Voltaire. Review of Alan Wood's *Bertrand Russell: The Passionate Skeptic.* In *The Saturday Review of Literature,* Vol. XLI, January 25, 1958, p. 15.

Theology of Power. Review article on Ernest W. Lefever's *Ethics and United States Foreign Policy.* In *The Nation,* Vol. CLXXXVI, March 22, 1958, pp. 253–255.

Frank Aydelotte (1880–1956). A Biographical Memoir. In *Year Book of the American Philosophical Society, 1957.* Philadelphia, Pennsylvania: American Philosophical Society, 1958, pp. 104–109.

The Case for Determinism. In *Determinism and Freedom,* edited by Sidney Hook. New York: New York University Press, 1958, pp. 3–15.
    (Reprinted in *Determinism and Freedom in the Age of Modern Science,* edited by Sidney Hook. New York: Collier Books, 1961, pp. 19–30.)

Review article on Leonard Nelson's *System of Ethics.* In *Ratio* (1957–58): in English, Vol. II, pp. 177–182; German translation, Band II, pp. 79–85.

Review of Mortimer J. Adler's *The Idea of Freedom: A Dialectical Examination of the Conceptions of Freedom.* In *The New York Times,* September 14, 1958, Book Review, p. 6.

1959

Review of Hannah Arendt's *The Human Condition.* In *The New York Times,* February 15, 1959, Book Review, p. 26.

Review of John Macmurray's *The Self as Agent*. In *The Philosophical Review*, Vol. LXVIII, October, 1959, pp. 545–548.

Review of Alfred North Whitehead's *American Essays in Social Philosophy*. In *The New York Times*, November 15, 1959, Book Review, p. 40.

Charles Van Doren and After. *Yale Criterion*, December, 1959, pp. 5–7.

Introduction to Education in the Age of Science. *Daedalus*, Vol. LXXXVIII, 1959, pp. 3–6.

Education in the Age of Science, edited by Brand Blanshard. New York: Basic Books, 1959. Pp. xviii + 302.
    (Blanshard is the author of the Introduction, pp. vii–xviii. The book is based on discussions in a seminar sponsored by the Tamiment Institute at Tamiment, Pennsylvania, in June, 1958.)

Broad's Conception of Reason. In *The Philosophy of C. D. Broad*, edited by Paul Arthur Schilpp. New York: Tudor Publishing Company, 1959, pp. 233–262.

1960

Is the Nation the Villain? Review of Alfred Cobban's *In Search of Humanity: The Role of the Enlightenment in Modern History*. In *The New York Times*, September 18, 1960, Book Review, p. 59.

Body, Mind and Science. *Yale Scientific Magazine*, Vol. XXXV, October, 1960, pp. 10–12.

Values: The Polestar of Education. In *The Goals of Higher Education*, edited by Willis D. Weatherford Jr. Cambridge: Harvard University Press, 1960, pp. 76–98.
    (One of the William J. Cooper Foundation Lectures at Swarthmore College, 1958.)

What Is Education For? In *Education in a Free Society*. Pittsburgh: University of Pittsburgh Press, 1960, pp. 40–62.
    (Pitcairn-Crabbe Foundation Lecture, series 2, Vol. II.)

Comment on A. J. Ayer's Meaning and Intentionality. In *Logic, Language and Communication*, Vol. IV, pp. 411–412. Firenze: Sansoni Editore, 1960.
    (Proceedings of the 12th International Congress of Philosophy, Venice, September 12–18, 1958. Ayer's paper is in Vol. I, pp. 139–153.)

1961

The Business of Living. Review of George P. Grant's *Philosophy in the Mass Age*. In *The New York Times*, February 12, 1961, Book Review, p. 34.

Review of John W. Gardner's *Excellence: Can We Be Equal and Excellent Too?* In *The New York Times*, February 19, 1961, Book Review, p. 3.

On Being Young. Yale-Harvard Hockey Program. Yale Winter Weekend, March 3–5, 1961.

The Changing Climate of Philosophy. *Liberal Education*, Vol. XLVII, May, 1961, pp. 229–254.

The Reasonable Life. *Earlham Review,* June, 1961.
> (Senior convocation address, Earlham College, April 27, 1961. An adaptation of chapter 15, *Reason and Goodness.*)

Review of Jacob Loewenberg's *Reason and the Nature of Things.* In *The Philosophical Review,* Vol. LXX, July, 1961, pp. 430–433.

Review of Richard Wollheim's *F. H. Bradley.* In *Philosophy* (London), Vol. XXXVI, October, 1961, pp. 372–374.

"Hamlet" vs. the Laws of Thermodynamics. *New York Times Magazine,* December 24, 1961, pp. 8, 16, 18.

Symbolism. In *Religious Experience and Truth: A Symposium,* edited by Sidney Hook. New York: New York University Press, 1961, pp. 48–54.
> (The published form of the proceedings of the fourth annual New York University Institute of Philosophy, October 21–22, 1960.)

The Humanities in the College of Liberal Arts and Sciences. In *The College of Liberal Arts and Sciences—Its Role in the 1960's.* Minneapolis, Minnesota: Lutheran Brotherhood Insurance Society, n.d.
> (Address at the inauguration of Chauncey G. Bly as President of Thiel College, September 29–30, 1961.)

Reason and Goodness. London: George Allen & Unwin; New York: Macmillan Company, 1961; present distributor, New York: Humanities Press. Pp. 451.
> (Based on the Gifford Lectures, delivered at St. Andrews 1952 and 1953, and in part on the Noble Lectures, Harvard University, 1948.)
> Contents: Preface, Chapter I. The Tension Between Reason and Feeling in Western Ethics—Chapter II. Stoicism and the Supremacy of Reason—Chapter III. St. Francis and the Supremacy of Feeling—Chapter IV. The Dialectic of Reason and Feeling in British Ethics—Chapter V. Subjectivism—Chapter VI. Deontology—Chapter VII. Instrumentalism—Chapter VIII. Emotivism—Chapter IX. The Linguistic Retreat from Emotivism—Chapter X. Three Theories of Goodness—Chapter XI. Human Nature and Goodness—Chapter XII. 'Good', 'Right', 'Ought', 'Bad'—Chapter XIII. Thought and Desire—Chapter XIV. Reason and Politics—Chapter XV. The Rational Temper—Index.

1962

Review of C. J. Ducasse's *A Critical Examination of the Belief in a Life after Death.* In *The Journal of the American Society for Psychical Research,* Vol. LVI, January, 1962, pp. 52–56.

Review of June Bingham's *The Courage to Change.* In *The New Leader,* Vol. XLV, May 14, 1962, pp. 22–23.

Conformity and Human Nature, and Conformity and the Intellectual Task. In *Conformity.* Indianola, Iowa: Simpson College, 1962, pp. 11–21, 54–64.
> (Two addresses delivered at the Eighth Annual Christian Liberal Arts Festival, October 8–9, 1961.)

The Pros and Cons of Conformity. *Wells College Bulletin,* Vol. XLVIII, June, 1962, pp. 9–14.

(A convocation address that is essentially the same as Conformity and the Intellectual Task. This address was presented again at Carleton College, October 24, 1962. Reprinted *The Pros and Cons of Conformity*. Northfield, Minnesota: Carleton College, n.d., 13 pp.)

Review of Charles Frankel's *The Democratic Prospect*. In *The New York Times*, October 14, 1962, Book Review, p. 30.

Review of A. C. Ewing's *Second Thoughts in Moral Philosophy*. In *Ratio*,Vol. IV, December, 1962, in English, pp. 157–161, German translation, Band 4, Heft 2, pp. 139–144.

Epilogue, A Memoir. In Arthur Pap, *An Introduction to the Philosophy of Science*. Glencoe, Illinois: The Free Press, 1962, pp. 427–431.

Reason and Analysis. La Salle, Illinois: Open Court Publishing Company; London: George Allen & Unwin, 1962, pp. 505. Open Court paperback, 1973.
    Contents: Preface—Chapter I. The Revolt Against Reason—Chapter II. The Idea of Reason in Western Thought—Chapter III. The Rise of Positivism—Chapter IV. Logical Atomism—Chapter V. The Theory of Meaning—Chapter VI. Analysis and A Priori Knowledge—Chapter VII. Linguistic Philosophy—Some Earlier Forms—Chapter VIII. Linguistic Philosophy—Some Later Forms—Chapter IX. Universals—Chapter X. Necessities in Nature—Chapter XI. Necessity in Causation—Chapter XII. Some Intimations of Cosmic Necessity—Index.

On Sanity in Thought and Art. Tucson: University of Arizona Press, 1962. Pp. 23.
    (The Annie W. Riecker Memorial Lecture No. 8. Translated into Chinese by Philip S. Y. Sun in *College Life* (Hong Kong), Vol. IX, No. 8 (1963), pp. 5–19.)

1963

Notice of Chad Walsh's *From Utopia to Nightmare*. In *The New York Times*, March 24, 1963, Book Review.

Pope John and Reunion. *Friends Journal*, Vol. IX, May 15, 1963, pp. 221–223.

Naturalism and Human Nature. *Mem. 13th Congr. Intern. Filos. III*. Mexico, September, 1963, pp. 59–71.
    (The 13th International Congress was held in 1959.)

The Test of a University. In *Man, Science, Learning and Education: The Semicentennial Lectures at Rice University*, edited by Sanford Wilson Higginbotham. Houston, Texas: Rice University, 1963, pp. 21–40.
    (Rice University Studies, Vol. XLIX, supplement No. 2.)

The Specialist and the Humanist. Providence, Rhode Island: Brown University, n.d., 28 pp.
    (Address before the graduate convocation, June 3, 1963. Brown University Papers No. 40.)

1964

Always the Great Enemy Was Orthodoxy. Review article on Barrows Dunham's *Heroes and Heretics*. In *The New York Times*, January 12, 1964, Book Review, p. 3.

Review of C. D. Broad's *Lectures on Psychical Research*. In *The Journal of the*

American Society for Psychical Research, Vol. LVIII, January, 1964, pp. 66–71.

Les Courants de la pensée Américaine. *Les Études philosophiques,* No. 2, April–June, 1964, pp. 275–281.
>(Translated from the English by Gérard Deledalle. This essay was written for publication in French.)

Four Facets of Thought. Review of Harry Prosch's *The Genesis of Twentieth Century Philosophy: The Evolution of Thought from Copernicus to the Present.* In *The New York Times,* August 2, 1964, Book Review, p. 6.

A New Way of Thinking. Review of *John Dewey and Arthur F. Bentley: A Philosophical Correspondence, 1932–1951,* edited by S. Ratner and J. Altman, with J. E. Wheeler. In *The New York Times,* October 4, 1964, Book Review, p. 6.

Review of Karl Jaspers's *Three Essays: Leonardo, Descartes, Max Weber.* In *The New York Times,* November 15, 1964, Book Review, pp. 30, 32.

The Goal Is Well-Being. Review of Henry Hazlitt's *The Foundations of Morality.* In *The New York Times,* December 27, 1964, Book Review, pp. 6, 26.

Teleology and the Self. In *Philosophic Problems,* edited by Maurice Mandelbaum, Francis W. Gramlich, and Alan Ross Anderson. New York: Macmillan Company, 1964, pp. 291–297.
>(Reprint of a section from *The Nature of Thought,* Vol. I.)

The Objectivity of Moral Judgment. *Revue Internationale de Philosophie,* Vol. LXX, Fascicule 4, 1964, pp. 361–378.

Critical Reflections on Karl Barth. In *Faith and the Philosophers,* edited by John Hick. London: Macmillan & Company; New York: St. Martin's Press, 1964, pp. 159–200.
>(This consists of material that was later published in *Reason and Belief.*)

Blanshard's Interrogation of John Wild on ethics; Interrogation of Blanshard. In *Philosophical Interrogations,* edited by Sydney and Beatrice Rome. New York: Holt, Rinehart, and Winston, 1964, pp. 123–125, 201–257 (conducted by Louis O. Mink).

1965

Critical Reflections on Behaviorism. *Proceedings of the American Philosophical Society,* Vol. CIX, February, 1965, pp. 22–28.

Eliot in Memory. *Yale Review,* Vol. LIV, June, 1965, pp. 635–640.

Review of C. D. Rollins, ed., *Knowledge and Experience.* In *The American Oxonian,* July, 1965, pp. 158–159.

Review of Mortimer J. Adler's *The Conditions of Philosophy.* In *The Journal of Higher Education,* Vol. XXXVI, October, 1965, pp. 409–410.

1966

No One To Be Ignored. Review of Arthur C. Danto's *Nietzsche as Philosopher.* In *The New York Times,* January 23, 1966, Book Review, p. 30.

Reflections on Economic Determinism. *The Journal of Philosophy,* Vol. LXIII, March 31, 1966, pp. 169–178.

(Reprinted in *Dialogues on the Philosophy of Marxism*, edited by John Somerville and Howard L. Parsons. Westport, Connecticut and London: Greenwood Press, 1974, pp. 31–42. From the *Proceedings of the Society for the Philosophical Study of Dialectical Materialism*, contributions in Philosophy No. 6.)

Reason and Unreason in Religion. *Zygon*, Vol. I, June, 1966, pp. 200–204.
(Reprinted in *Midway*, No. 28, autumn, 1966, pp. 90–97.)

The Tyrant Within. Review of Ronald V. Sampson's *The Psychology of Power*. In *The New York Times*, September 11, 1966, Book Review, p. 16.

A Remarkable Thesis. Review of Edwin A. Burtt's *In Search of Philosophic Understanding*. In *The Humanist*, Vol. XXV, September–October, 1966, p. 167.

Beyond the Fence, Green Pastures. Review of Edmund W. Sinnott's *The Bridge of Life: From Matter to Spirit*. In *The New York Times*, November 6, 1966, Book Review (Part I), p. 3.

Foreword. In Arthur Pap, *Semantics and Necessary Truth*. New Haven: Yale University Press, 1966, pp. v–xii.

A Verdict on Epiphenomenalism. In *Current Philosophical Issues. Essays in Honor of Curt John Ducasse*, compiled and edited by Frederick C. Dommeyer. Springfield, Illinois: Charles C Thomas, Publisher, 1966, pp. 105–126.

In Defense of Metaphysics. In *Metaphysics: Readings and Reappraisals*, edited by W. E. Kennick and Morris Lazerowitz. Englewood Cliffs: Prentice-Hall, 1966, pp. 331–355.

Foreword. In *New Studies in Berkeley's Philosophy*, edited by Warren Steinkraus. New York: Holt, Rinehart & Winston, 1966, pp. v–vii.

Reason and Analysis. In *American Philosophy in the Twentieth Century*, edited by Paul Kurtz. New York: Macmillan Company, 1966, pp. 477–499.
(An excerpt from *Reason and Analysis*.)

Morality and Politics. In *Ethics and Society: Original Essays on Contemporary Moral Problems*, edited by Richard T. De George. Garden City: Doubleday & Company, Anchor Books, 1966, pp. 1–23.

1967

Religion and Revolt. Review of Alan Heimert's *Religion and the American Mind: From the Great Awakening to the Revolution*, and Conrad Cherry's *The Theology of Jonathan Edwards: A Reappraisal*. In *The New York Times*, January 1, 1967, Book Review, p. 3.

The Problem of Consciousness—A Debate. *Philosophy and Phenomenological Research*, Vol. XXVII, March, 1967, pp. 317–337.
(A debate between Blanshard and B. F. Skinner at the meeting of the American Psychological Association, Chicago, 1965. Opening remarks by Blanshard, pp. 317–324; reply by Skinner, pp. 325–332; concluding remarks by Blanshard, pp. 333–337, abstract in *Review of Metaphysics*, Vol. XXI, September, 1967, p. 197.)

The Great Grey Virtue.
(Dinner address, May 15, 1967, to the Beta Association of Phi Beta Kappa, Southern Illinois University, Carbondale, mimeographed 20 pp. Translated into Chinese by Shu-hsien Liu. *The Young Sun,* Vol. XXXII, No. 4, August, 1967, pp. 17–25.)

Internal Relations and Their Importance to Philosophy. *Review of Metaphysics,* Vol. XXI, December, 1967, pp. 227–236.

Rejoinder to My Critics. *Review of Metaphysics,* Vol. XXI, December, 1967, pp. 262–272.
(For the criticisms offered by Bruce Aune, Willis Doney, W. E. Kennick, Alice Ambrose Lazerowitz see pp. 237–261 in the same issue.)

Frank Laurence Lucas (1894–1967). *Yale Review,* Vol. LVII, December, 1967, pp. 317–320.

The Life of the Spirit in a Machine Age. Northampton: Smith College, 1967. Pp. 28.
(The fourth of the author's William Allan Nielson Lectures at Smith, delivered May 2, 1967.)

William Ernest Hocking (1873–1966). *Year Book of the American Philosophical Society, 1966.* Philadelphia: 1967, pp. 149–155.

Wisdom. *The Encyclopedia of Philosophy,* edited by Paul Edwards. New York: Macmillan Company and Free Press; London: Collier-Macmillan Company, 1967, Vol. VIII, pp. 322–324.

1968

Current Issues in Education. *Monist,* Vol. LII, January, 1968, pp. 11–17.

Kierkegaard on Religious Knowledge.
(An address presented to the meeting of the American Philosophical Association, 1966. Mimeographed, 35 pp. Published as Kierkegaard on Faith. *Personalist,* Vol. XLIX, winter, 1968, pp. 5–23. Reprinted in *Essays on Kierkegaard,* edited by Jerry H. Gill. Minneapolis: Burgess Publishing Company, 1969, pp. 113–126. This consists of portions of materials that were later published in *Reason and Belief.*)

Basic Opinions. Review of Otto A. Bird's *The Idea of Justice;* V. J. McGill's *The Idea of Happiness;* Charles Van Doren's *The Idea of Progress;* Robert G. Hazo's *The Idea of Love.* In *The New York Times,* February 25, 1968, Book Review, pp. 36–37.

Rules for Readers. *Swarthmore College Bulletin,* Vol. LXV, March, 1968, pp. 12–19.
(Reprinted in *Middlebury College News Letter,* Vol. XLIII, winter, 1969, pp. 10–16.)

Reflections in a Library. *Friends Journal,* Vol. XIV, March 15, 1968, pp. 128–129.

The Liberal in Religion. *Humanist,* Vol. XXVIII, May–June, 1968, pp. 11–14.

Rejoinder to Mr. Kearns. *Philosophy and Phenomenological Research,* Vol. XXIX, September, 1968, pp. 116–118.
(A reply to John T. Kearns's discussion, Sameness or Similarity? pp. 105–115 in the same issue.)

The Final Law. Review of Reinhold Niebuhr's *Faith and Politics.* In *The New York Times,* October 6, 1968, Book Review, pp. 10–11.

Reason and Politics. In *The Development of the Democratic Idea: Readings from Pericles to the Present,* edited by Charles M. Sherover. New York: Washington Square Press, 1968, pp. 484–515.
  (Reprinted from *Reason and Goodness.*)

Retribution Revisited. In *Philosophical Perspectives on Punishment,* compiled and edited by Edward H. Madden, Rollo Handy, and Marvin Farber. Springfield, Illinois: Charles C Thomas, Publisher, 1968, pp. 59–81.
  (Comments on Blanshard's essay are offered by Peter H. Hare and Marvin K. Opler, pp. 82–85, 85–89. Concluding comment by Blanshard, pp. 89–93.)

1969

Bertrand Russell in Retrospect. *Dialogue,* Vol. VII, March, 1969, pp. 584–607.
  (Address delivered on November 9, 1968, at the opening of the Russell Collection to the public at McMaster University, Hamilton, Ontario.)

Review of Donald Cary Williams's *The Principles of Empirical Realism.* In *The Philosophical Review,* Vol. LXXVIII, July, 1969, pp. 399–402.

Lady Wylie in Memory (1882–1969). *American Oxonian,* Vol. LVI, October, 1969, pp. 215–218.

1970

Rejoinder [to Professor Oakes]. *Personalist,* Vol. LI, Spring, 1970, pp. 243–245.
  (A reply to Robert A. Oakes's comments in the same issue, pp. 237–242, Some Historical Perspectives on Professor Blanshard's Critique of Critical Realism as "Objective Idealism in Disguise.")

Review of Morris Lazerowitz's *Philosophy and Illusion.* In *Metaphilosophy,* Vol. I, April, 1970, pp. 178–185.

Tribute to Curt John Ducasse. *Journal of the American Society for Psychical Research,* Vol. LXIV, April, 1970, pp. 137–141.

The Limits of Naturalism. In *Mind, Science and History,* edited by H. E. Kiefer and M. K. Munitz. Albany: State University of New York Press, 1970, pp. 3–33.
  (This is Volume II in Contemporary Philosophic Thought of the four-volume series recording the International Philosophy Year Conferences at the State University of New York, Brockport, New York. Reprinted in *Contemporary American Philosophy,* edited by John E. Smith. London: George Allen & Unwin, Ltd., 1970, pp. 21–53.)

Frank Aydelotte of Swarthmore. By Frances B. Blanshard. Middletown, Connecticut: Wesleyan University Press, 1970. Pp. xxii + 429.
  (Brand Blanshard completed and edited this book by his wife. Editor's Preface, pp. xii–xxii; chapter 16 The Commission on Palestine, and chapter 17 The Quiet Years, pp. 343–404.)

1971

The Revolt Against Reason in Theology. *Proceedings of the American Philosophical*

Society, Vol. CXV, April 22, 1971, pp. 83–87.
(This paper was presented on November 12, 1970.)

The Ethics of Belief. *Philosophic Exchange,* Vol. I, No. 2, 1971, pp. 81–93.
(Reprinted in substance in *Reason and Belief.*)

John Dewey. William James. Josiah Royce. George Santayana. In *The Penguin Companion to American Literature,* edited by Malcolm Bradbury, Eric Mottram, and Jean Franco. New York: McGraw-Hill Book Company, 1971, pp. 72–73, 134–135, 224, 227–228.

1972

Catholicism and Revelation. *Humanist,* Vol. XXXII, July–August, 1972, pp. 25–26.
(This article is a section of Part I, Catholic and Humanist Critiques. The papers were selected for publication from the Catholic/Humanist Dialogue held in New York City, May 5–7, 1972. Part I includes papers by Paul Blanshard and Robert J. Roth, S. J., and Marvin Zimmerman's reply to Roth.)

1973

Philosophy. *Yale Alumni Magazine,* Vol. XXXVII, October, 1973, pp. 12–30.
(Four paragraphs by Blanshard, p. 12, in the Yale Faculty Symposium, How Did You Choose Your Academic Field?)

The Uses of a Liberal Education and Other Talks to Students, edited by Eugene Freeman. La Salle, Illinois: Open Court Publishing Company, 1973. Pp. xxi + 415.
(The talks are arranged under three headings—Ends, Corollaries, and Homilies. In addition to reprinting a large number of relatively inaccessible talks the volume contains the first printing of Some Fringe Benefits of Education; The British Scholar; and Admiration. Index.)

1974

Humanists Reply. *Humanist,* Vol. XXXIV, January–February, 1974, p. 9.
(A defense of the Humanist Manifesto as a reply to Jude P. Dougherty.)

A Reply to My Critics. *Idealistic Studies,* Vol. IV, May, 1974, pp. 107–130.
(The January, 1974 issue of this volume of *Idealistic Studies,* entitled Truth and Reason, contained essays written by Peter Caws, Donald W. Sherburne, Richard T. De George, Herbert M. Garelick, Milton Fisk, Alan Ross Anderson, and Charles Landesman to honor Blanshard on his eightieth birthday, August 27, 1972.)

Sidgwick the Man. *Monist,* Vol. LVIII, July, 1974, pp. 349–370.

Review of Anthony Kenny, J. R. Lucas, C. H. Waddington, and Christopher Longuet-Higgins's *The Nature of Mind.* In *The American Scientist,* Vol. LXII, July–August, 1974, p. 501. The Gifford Lectures, 1971–72.

Rationalism and Humanism. *Humanist,* Vol. XXXIV, November–December, 1974, pp. 24–27.

Rationalism in Ethics and Religion. In *Mid-Twentieth Century American Philosophy: Personal Statements,* edited by Peter A. Bertocci. New York: Humanities Press, 1974, pp. 20–46.

Rationalism. *Encyclopaedia Britannica.* 15th Edition. Chicago: Helen Hemingway Benton, Publisher, 1974, Vol. II, pp. 527–532.

Reason and Belief. London: George Allen & Unwin, Ltd., 1974; New Haven: Yale University Press, 1975. Pp. 620.
  (Second volume based on the Gifford Lectures delivered at St. Andrews in 1952 and 1953 and on the Noble Lectures delivered at Harvard University in 1948.)
  Contents: Preface—Part I, Reason and Faith—The Catholic View, Chapter I Catholic Teaching on Faith and Reason, Chapter II Reason and Revelation, Chapter III Catholic Teaching on Revelation and Natural Knowledge, Chapter IV Catholicism on the Marks of the Church; Part II, Reason and Faith—The Lutheran Succession, Chapter V Reason and Faith in Luther, Chapter VI Reason and Faith in Kierkegaard, Chapter VII Reason and Revelation for Emil Brunner, Chapter VIII Reason and Revelation for Karl Barth; Part III, Ethics and Belief, Chapter IX Rationalism and Christian Ethics (I), Chapter X Rationalism and Christian Ethics (II), Chapter XI The Ethics of Belief, Chapter XII Myth in Religion; Part IV, a Rationalist's Outlook, Chapter XIII Cosmology, Chapter XIV Human Nature and Its Values, Chapter XV Goodness and the Absolute, Chapter XVI Religion and Rationalism. Notes—Analytical Table of Contents—Index.

1975

For One Who Is Liberally Educated [On Being an Emeritus]. *Yale Alumni Magazine,* Vol. XXXIX, October, 1975, pp. 13–15.

George Van Santvoord: A Memoir. *American Oxonian,* Vol. LXII, October, 1975, pp. 26–28.

The Philosophic Enterprise. In *The Owl of Minerva: Philosophers on Philosophy,* edited by Charles J. Bontempo and S. Jack Odell. New York: McGraw-Hill, 1975, pp. 163–177.
  (A revised form of the Mahlon Powell Lecture at the University of Indiana, 1961, and its first printing.)

1976

Democracy and Distinction in American Education. In *On the Meaning of the University,* edited by Sterling M. McMurrin. Salt Lake City: University of Utah Press, 1976, pp. 29–49.
  (Address on the inauguration, November 19, 1973, of David Pierpont Gardner as President of the University of Utah.)

Practical Reason: Reason and Feeling in 20th-Century Ethics. In *The Abdication of Philosophy: Philosophy and the Public Good,* edited by Eugene Freeman. La Salle, Illinois: Open Court Publishing Company, 1976, pp. 49–65.
  (Blanshard wrote this essay in May, 1972.)

Necessity in Causation. In *The Nature of Causation,* edited and with an introduction by Myles Brand. Urbana, Chicago, London: University of Illinois Press, 1976, pp. 225–253.
  (Reprint of *Reason and Analysis,* pp. 444–471 under Section III. The Logical Entailment Theory.)

1978

Sidgwick, A Subtle Reasoner. Review of J. B. Schneewind's *Sidgwick's Ethics and Victorian Moral Philosophy.* In *Yale Review,* Vol. LXVII. Summer, 1978, pp. 585–588.

Pater's Inner Life. Review of Michael Levey's *The Case of Walter Pater.* In *Yale Review,* Vol. LXVIII, Winter, 1978, pp. 273–279.

1979

Einstein, Quakers, and Peace. *Friends Journal,* May 1, 1979, pp. 8–10.

Some Oxford Philosophers. *American Oxonian,* Vol. LXVI, No. 4, Fall, 1979, pp. 259–269.

1980

My Brother Paul. *Church & State,* Vol. XXXIII, No. 3, March, 1980, pp. 12–14.

Forthcoming

Introduction. In *Studies in Personalism: Selected Writings of Edgar Sheffield Brightman,* edited by Robert N. Beck and Warren E. Steinkraus. Hartford, Vermont: Claude Stark & Company.

INDEX

p